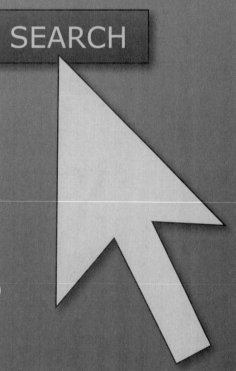

Hoover's Handbook of

Emerging Companies

2007

HOOVERS™

A D&B COMPANY

Austin, Texas

Hoover's Handbook of Emerging Companies 2007 is intended to provide readers with accurate and authoritative information about the enterprises covered in it. Hoover's asked all companies and organizations profiled to provide information. Many did so; a number did not. The information contained herein is as accurate as we could reasonably make it. In many cases we have relied on third-party material that we believe to be trustworthy, but were unable to independently verify. We do not warrant that the book is absolutely accurate or without error. Readers should not rely on any information contained herein in instances where such reliance might cause loss or damage. The publisher, the editors, and their data suppliers specifically disclaim all warranties, including the implied warranties of merchantability and fitness for a specific purpose. This book is sold with the understanding that neither the publisher, the editors, nor any content contributors are engaged in providing investment, financial, accounting, legal, or other professional advice.

The financial data (Historical Financials sections) in this book are from a variety of sources. EDGAR Online provided selected data for the Historical Financials sections of publicly traded companies. For private companies and for historical information on public companies prior to their becoming public, we obtained information directly from the companies or from trade sources deemed to be reliable. Hoover's, Inc., is solely responsible for the presentation of all data.

Many of the names of products and services mentioned in this book are the trademarks or service marks of the companies manufacturing or selling them and are subject to protection under US law. Space has not permitted us to indicate which names are subject to such protection, and readers are advised to consult with the owners of such marks regarding their use. Hoover's is a trademark of Hoover's, Inc.

10 9 8 7 6 5 4 3 2 1

Publishers Cataloging-in-Publication Data
Hoover's Handbook of Emerging Companies 2007

   Includes indexes.

   ISBN 978-1-57311-117-1

   ISSN 1069-7519

   1. Business enterprises — Directories. 2. Corporations — Directories.

HF3010 338.7

Hoover's Company Information is also available on the Internet at Hoover's Online (www.hoovers.com). A catalog of Hoover's products is available on the Internet at www.hooversbooks.com.

The Hoover's Handbook series is produced for Hoover's Business Press by:

Sycamore Productions, Inc.
5808 Balcones Drive, Suite 205
Austin, Texas 78731
info@sycamoreproductions.com

Cover design is by John Baker. Electronic prepress and printing are by Von Hoffman Corporation, Owensville, Missouri.

U.S. AND WORLD BOOK SALES

Hoover's, Inc.
5800 Airport Blvd.
Austin, TX 78752
Phone: 512-374-4500
Fax: 512-374-4538
e-mail: orders@hoovers.com
Web: www.hooversbooks.com

EUROPEAN BOOK SALES

William Snyder Publishing Associates
5 Five Mile Drive
Oxford OX2 8HT
England
Phone & fax: +44-186-551-3186
e-mail: snyderpub@aol.com

Hoover's, Inc.

Founder: Gary Hoover
Interim President: Paul Pellman
EVP Customer Experience and International: Russell Secker
EVP Product and Technology: Jeffrey (Jeff) Guillot
EVP US Sales: John Lysinger
VP Acquisition Marketing: Chris Warwick
VP Advertising: Paul Rostkowski
VP Finance: Charles (Chuck) Harvey
VP Marketing: Fred Howard
VP Subscription Sales: Mel Yarbrough

EDITORIAL

Managing Editor: Margaret C. Lynch
Senior Editors: Kathleen Kelly, Laurie Najjar, Barbara Redding, Dennis Sutton
Team Leads: Larry Bills, Zack Gonzales, Lisa Goodgame, Nancy Kay, Greg Perliski, Lee Simmons
Editors: Sally Alt, Adi Anand, Adam Anderson, Alex Biesada, Joe Bramhall, James Bryant, Ryan Caione, Jason Cella, Catherine Colbert, Elizabeth Cornell, Danny Cummings, Jeff Dorsch, Bobby Duncan, Jarrod Dunham, Lesley Epperson, Rachel Gallo, Stuart Hampton, Jim Harris, Chris Huston, Donna Iroabuchi, Jessica Jimenez, Kenny Jones, Linnea Anderson Kirgan, Julie Krippel, Anne Law, Josh Lower, John MacAyeal, Barbara Murray, Nell Newton, Kristi Park, Peter Partheymuller, David Ramirez, Melanie Robertson, Belen Rodriguez, Matt Saucedo, Amy Schein, Seth Shafer, Katherine Smith, Paula Smith, Anthony Staats, Betsy Staton, Diane Stimets, Barbara Strickland, Daysha Taylor, Vanita Trippe, Ryan Wade, Tim Walker, Kathi Whitley, Randy Williams, David Woodruff
QA Editors: Jason Cother, Carrie Geis, Rosie Hatch, Diane Lee, John Willis
Project Analyst: Tara LoPresti
Editorial Customer Advocate: Anna Porlas

HOOVER'S BUSINESS PRESS

Senior Director: Jim Currie
Distribution Manager: Rhonda Mitchell
Customer Support and Fulfillment Manager: Michael Febonio

ABOUT HOOVER'S, INC. – THE BUSINESS INFORMATION AUTHORITY™

Hoover's, a D&B company, gives its customers a competitive edge with insightful information about industries, companies, and key decision makers. Hoover's provides this updated information for sales, marketing, business development, and other professionals who need intelligence on U.S. and global companies, industries, and the people who lead them. This information, along with powerful tools to search, sort, download, and integrate the content, is available through Hoover's (www.hoovers.com), the company's premier online service. Hoover's business information is also available through corporate intranets and distribution agreements with licensees, as well as via Hoover's books. The company is headquartered in Austin, Texas.

Abbreviations

AFL-CIO – American Federation of Labor and Congress of Industrial Organizations
AMA – American Medical Association
AMEX – American Stock Exchange
ARM – adjustable-rate mortgage
ASP – application services provider
ATM – asynchronous transfer mode
ATM – automated teller machine
CAD/CAM – computer-aided design/computer-aided manufacturing
CD-ROM – compact disc – read-only memory
CD-R – CD-recordable
CEO – chief executive officer
CFO – chief financial officer
CMOS – complimentary metal oxide silicon
COO – chief operating officer
DAT – digital audiotape
DOD – Department of Defense
DOE – Department of Energy
DOS – disk operating system
DOT – Department of Transportation
DRAM – dynamic random-access memory
DSL – digital subscriber line
DVD – digital versatile disc/digital video disc
DVD-R – DVD-recordable
EPA – Environmental Protection Agency
EPROM – erasable programmable read-only memory
EPS – earnings per share
ESOP – employee stock ownership plan
EU – European Union
EVP – executive vice president
FCC – Federal Communications Commission
FDA – Food and Drug Administration

FDIC – Federal Deposit Insurance Corporation
FTC – Federal Trade Commission
FTP – file transfer protocol
GATT – General Agreement on Tariffs and Trade
GDP – gross domestic product
HMO – health maintenance organization
HR – human resources
HTML – hypertext markup language
ICC – Interstate Commerce Commission
IPO – initial public offering
IRS – Internal Revenue Service
ISP – Internet service provider
kWh – kilowatt-hour
LAN – local-area network
LBO – leveraged buyout
LCD – liquid crystal display
LNG – liquefied natural gas
LP – limited partnership
Ltd. – limited
mips – millions of instructions per second
MW – megawatt
NAFTA – North American Free Trade Agreement
NASA – National Aeronautics and Space Administration
Nasdaq – National Association of Securities Dealers Automated Quotations
NATO – North Atlantic Treaty Organization
NYSE – New York Stock Exchange
OCR – optical character recognition
OECD – Organization for Economic Cooperation and Development
OEM – original equipment manufacturer
OPEC – Organization of Petroleum Exporting Countries

OS – operating system
OSHA – Occupational Safety and Health Administration
OTC – over-the-counter
PBX – private branch exchange
PCMCIA – Personal Computer Memory Card International Association
P/E – price to earnings ratio
RAID – redundant array of independent disks
RAM – random-access memory
R&D – research and development
RBOC – regional Bell operating company
RISC – reduced instruction set computer
REIT – real estate investment trust
ROA – return on assets
ROE – return on equity
ROI – return on investment
ROM – read-only memory
S&L – savings and loan
SCSI – Small Computer System Interface
SEC – Securities and Exchange Commission
SEVP – senior executive vice president
SIC – Standard Industrial Classification
SOC – system on a chip
SVP – senior vice president
USB – universal serial bus
VAR – value-added reseller
VAT – value-added tax
VC – venture capitalist
VoIP – Voice over Internet Protocol
VP – vice president
WAN – wide-area network
WWW – World Wide Web

Contents

Companies Profiled

Companies Profiled (continued)

Companies Profiled (continued)

About Hoover's Handbook of Emerging Companies 2007

Hoover's Handbook of Emerging Companies enters its 14th year as one of America's premier sources of business information on young, growth-oriented enterprises. Given our current economic realities, finding value in the marketplace becomes ever more difficult, and so we are particularly pleased to present this 2007 edition — the result of a search of our extensive database of business information for companies with demonstrated growth and the potential for future gains.

The 600 companies in this book were chosen from the universe of public US companies with sales between $10 million and $1 billion. Their selection was based primarily on sales growth and profitability, although in a few cases we made some rather subjective decisions about which companies we chose to include. They all have reported at least three years of sales and have sustained annualized sales growth of at least 15% during that time. Also, they are profitable (through year-end September 2006).

HOOVER'S ONLINE FOR BUSINESS NEEDS

In addition to the 2,550 companies featured in our handbooks, comprehensive coverage of more than 40,000 business enterprises is available in electronic format on our Web site, Hoover's Online (www.hoovers.com). Our goal is to provide one site that offers authoritative, updated intelligence on US and global companies, industries, and the people who shape them. Hoover's has partnered with other prestigious business information and service providers to bring you all the right business information, services, and links in one place.

Hoover's Handbook of Emerging Companies is one of our four-title series of handbooks that covers, literally, the world of business. The series is available as an indexed set, and also includes *Hoover's Handbook of American Business*, *Hoover's Handbook of World Business*, and *Hoover's Handbook of Private Companies*. This series brings you information on the biggest, fastest-growing, and most influential enterprises in the world.

We believe that anyone who buys from, sells to, invests in, lends to, competes with, interviews with, or works for a company should know as much as possible about that enterprise. Taken together, *Hoover's Handbook of Emerging Companies 2007* and the other Hoover's products represent the most complete source of basic corporate information readily available to the general public.

HOW TO USE THIS BOOK

This book has four sections:

1. "Using Hoover's Handbooks" describes the contents of our profiles.

2. "A List-Lover's Compendium" contains lists of the fastest-growing and most profitable companies. The lists are based on the information in our profiles, or compiled from well-known sources.

3. The company profiles section makes up the largest and most important part of the book — 600 profiles arranged alphabetically. Each profile features an overview of the company; some larger and more visible companies have an additional History section. All companies have up to five years of financial information, product information where available, and a list of company executives and key competitors.

4. At the end of this volume are the combined indexes from our 2007 editions of all Hoover's Handbooks. The information is organized into three separate sections. The first sorts companies by industry groups, the second by headquarters location. The third index is a list of all the executives found in the Executives section of each company profile. For a more thorough description of our indexing style, see page xiv.

As always, we hope you find our books useful. We invite your comments via phone (512-374-4500), fax (512-374-4538), mail (5800 Airport Boulevard, Austin, Texas 78752), or e-mail (custsupport@hoovers.com).

The Editors
Austin, Texas
February 2007

Using Hoover's Handbooks

ORGANIZATION

The profiles in this volume are presented in alphabetical order. This alphabetization is generally word by word, which means that EV Energy Partners, L.P. precedes EVCI Career Colleges Holding Corp. You will find the commonly used name of the enterprise at the beginning of the profile; the full, legal name is found in the Locations section. If a company name is also a person's name, such as Perry Ellis International, Inc., it will be alphabetized under the first name; if the company name starts with initials, such as I.D. Systems or P.F. Chang's China Bistro, look for it under the combined initials (in the above example, ID and PF, respectively).

Basic financial data is listed under the heading Historical Financials; also included is the exchange on which the company's stock is traded, the ticker symbol used by the stock exchange, and the company's fiscal year-end. The annual financial information contained in the profiles is current through fiscal year-ends occurring as late as September 2006. We have included certain nonfinancial developments, such as officer changes, through January 2007.

OVERVIEW

In the first section of the profile, we have tried to give a thumbnail description of the company and what it does. The description will usually include information on the company's strategy, reputation, and ownership. We recommend that you read this section first.

HISTORY

This extended section, which is available for some of the larger and more well-known companies, reflects our belief that every enterprise is the sum of its history and that you have to know where you came from in order to know where you are going. While some companies have limited historical awareness and were unable to help us much and other companies are just plain boring, we think the vast majority of the enterprises in this book have colorful backgrounds. We have tried to focus on the people who made the enterprises what they are today. We have found these histories to be full of twists and ironies; they make fascinating reading.

EXECUTIVES

Here we list the names of the people who run the company, insofar as space allows. In the case of public companies, we have shown the ages and pay of key officers. The published data is for the previous fiscal year, although the company may have announced promotions or retirements since year-end. The pay represents cash compensation, including bonuses, but excludes stock option programs.

Although companies are free to structure their management titles any way they please, most modern corporations follow standard practices. The ultimate power in any corporation lies with the shareholders, who elect a board of directors, usually including officers or "insiders" as well as individuals from outside the company. The chief officer, the person on whose desk the buck stops, is usually called the chief executive officer (CEO). Often, he or she is also the chairman of the board.

As corporate management has become more complex, it is common for the CEO to have a "right-hand person" who oversees the day-to-day operations of the company, allowing the CEO plenty of time to focus on strategy and long-term issues. This right-hand person is usually designated the chief operating officer (COO) and is often the president of the company. In other cases one person is both chairman and president.

A multitude of other titles exists, including chief financial officer (CFO), chief administrative officer, and vice chairman. We have always tried to include the CFO, the chief legal officer, and the chief human resources or personnel officer. Our best advice is that officers' pay levels are clear indicators of who the board of directors thinks are the most important members of the management team.

The people named in the Executives section are indexed at the back of the book.

The Executives section also includes the name of the company's auditing (accounting) firm, where available.

LOCATIONS

Here we include the company's full legal name and its headquarters, street address, telephone and fax numbers, and Web site, as available. The back of the book includes an index of companies by headquarters locations.

In some cases we have also included information on the geographic distribution of the company's business, including sales and profit data. Note that these profit numbers, like those in the Products/Operations section below, are usually operating or pretax profits rather than net profits. Operating profits are generally those before financing costs (interest income and payments) and before taxes, which are considered costs attributable to the whole company rather than to one division or part of the world. For this reason the net income figures (in the Historical Financials section) are usually much lower, since they are after interest and taxes. Pretax profits are after interest but before taxes.

PRODUCTS/OPERATIONS

This section lists as many of the company's products, services, brand names, divisions, subsidiaries, and joint ventures as we could fit. We have tried to include all its major lines and all familiar brand names. The nature of this section varies by company and the amount of information available. If the company publishes sales and profit information by type of business, we have included it.

COMPETITORS

In this section we have listed companies that compete with the profiled company. This feature is included as a quick way to locate similar companies and compare them. The universe of competitors includes all public companies and all private companies with sales in excess of $500 million. In a few instances we have identified smaller private companies as key competitors.

HISTORICAL FINANCIALS

Here we have tried to present as much data about each enterprise's financial performance as we could compile in the allocated space. Although the information varies somewhat from industry to industry, the following is generally present.

A five-year table, with relevant annualized compound growth rates, covers:
- Sales — fiscal year sales (year-end assets for most financial companies)
- Net income — fiscal year net income (before accounting changes)
- Net profit margin — fiscal year net income as a percent of sales (as a percent of assets for most financial firms)

- Employees — fiscal year-end or average number of employees
- Stock price — the fiscal year closing price
- P/E — high and low price/earnings ratio
- Earnings per share — fiscal year earnings per share (EPS)
- Dividends per share — fiscal year dividends per share
- Book value per share — fiscal year-end book value (common shareholders' equity per share)

The information on the number of employees is intended to aid the reader interested in knowing whether a company has a long-term trend of increasing or decreasing employment. As far as we know, we are the only company that publishes this information in print format.

The numbers on the left in each row of the Historical Financials section give the month and the year in which the company's fiscal year actually ends. Thus, a company with a September 30, 2006, year-end is shown as 9/06. Note that numbers in this section are expressed in millions, rounded to the nearest whole number; therefore, you may see a "0" or "(0)."

In addition, we have provided in graph form a stock price history for each company. The graphs, covering up to five years, show the range of trading between the high and the low price, as well as the closing price for each fiscal year.

Key year-end statistics in this section generally show the financial strength of the enterprise, including:
- Debt ratio (long-term debt as a percent of shareholders' equity)
- Return on equity (net income divided by the average of beginning and ending common shareholders' equity)
- Cash and cash equivalents
- Current ratio (ratio of current assets to current liabilities)
- Total long-term debt (including capital lease obligations)
- Number of shares of common stock outstanding
- Dividend yield (fiscal year dividends per share divided by the fiscal year-end closing stock price)
- Dividend payout (fiscal year dividends divided by fiscal year EPS)
- Market value at fiscal year-end (fiscal year-end closing stock price multiplied by fiscal year-end number of shares outstanding)

Per share data has been adjusted for stock splits. The data for public companies has been provided to us by EDGAR Online. Other public company information was compiled by Hoover's, which takes full responsibility for the content of this section.

Using the Index to Hoover's Handbooks

PAGE NUMBERS

The letter preceding each page number of an index entry indicates the handbook volume that is being referenced:

A=American Business
E=Emerging Companies
P=Private Companies
W=World Business

(For convenience, this list of handbook titles and the corresponding letters are also included at the top of every index page.)

ALPHABETIZATION

English-language articles (a, an, the) are ignored when they appear at the beginning of a company name, but foreign articles are not ignored and are alphabetized as they appear. Ampersands are treated as though they are spelled out, as are the abbreviations Ft., Mt., and St.

If a company name is also a person's name, such as Edward J. DeBartolo or Mary Kay, it will be alphabetized under the first name; if the company name starts with initials, for example, L.L. Bean or S.C. Johnson, look for it under the combined initials (in the above examples, LL and SC, respectively).

Initials or words indicating limited liability appearing at the beginning of international company names (AB, A/S, NV, P.T., S.A., AS, Industrias, Gesellschaft, Koninklijke, Kongl, and Oy) are ignored and the company is sorted on the following word. Similarly, foreign-language words (Grupo, Gruppo, Compagnie, Sociedad, etc.) that begin foreign company names are ignored and the names are sorted by the key word that follows.

INDUSTRY INDEX

Companies are listed alphabetically within industry types. Similar types are grouped under industry categories. For example, Appliances and Housewares are found under the category Consumer Products Manufacturers, while Dairy Products and Fish & Seafood are found under the category Food. For your convenience, a listing of Hoover's industry categories and the pages on which each begins can be found on page 400.

Hoover's Handbook of

Emerging Companies

A List-Lover's Compendium

The Top 100 Companies in Five-Year Sales Growth
in *Hoover's Handbook of Emerging Companies 2007*

Rank	Company	Five-Year Annualized Sales Growth (%)	Rank	Company	Five-Year Annualized Sales Growth (%)	Rank	Company	Five-Year Annualized Sales Growth (%)
1	Darwin Professional Underwriters	367.2	36	DivX	107.0	71	Youbet.com	71.4
2	VeraSun Energy	331.4	37	NeuroMetrix	101.4	72	Ikanos Communications	71.3
3	Whittier Energy	305.0	38	Monolithic Power Systems	101.0	73	LECG	71.2
4	Pharmion	261.0	39	Align Technology	98.6	74	Tennessee Commerce Bancorp	70.5
5	HealthSpring	220.2	40	Rackable Systems	98.2	75	Martek Biosciences	70.5
6	Franklin Bank Corp.	215.2	41	Boardwalk Pipeline Partners	98.0	76	New Century Bancorp	70.3
7	NetLogic Microsystems	204.4	42	First Advantage	96.6	77	VNUS Medical Technologies	70.1
8	Complete Production Services	193.1	43	Cbeyond	96.4	78	ENGlobal	68.9
9	optionsXpress Holdings	180.0	44	Techwell	95.7	79	Natural Gas Services	67.9
10	POZEN	178.0	45	FreightCar America	94.8	80	VCG Holding	67.8
11	Bill Barrett	161.8	46	Home BancShares	90.1	81	Accredited Home Lenders	67.4
12	Affirmative Insurance	159.6	47	Capital Southwest	89.8	82	Travelzoo	67.1
13	Adams Respiratory Therapeutics	157.5	48	Ultra Petroleum	89.7	83	Cerus	66.6
14	InfraSource Services	150.4	49	NewAlliance Bancshares	87.4	84	Bare Escentuals	65.5
15	Pinnacle Financial Partners	143.8	50	Allis-Chalmers Energy	87.0	85	WebEx Communications	64.8
16	First Marblehead Corporation	141.9	51	Penn Virginia Resource Partners	85.7	86	Bank of Florida	63.8
17	Gladstone Capital	141.6	52	Psychiatric Solutions	85.6	87	Shutterfly	63.5
18	Marchex	139.2	53	International Assets Holding	85.3	88	ExlService Holdings	63.0
19	First Acceptance	137.4	54	PharmaNet Development	85.2	89	Allegiant Travel	62.8
20	Visicu	136.0	55	Sirona Dental Systems	84.4	90	Double Eagle Petroleum	62.7
21	ViroPharma	131.3	56	I.D. Systems	84.0	91	Covanta	62.6
22	VAALCO Energy	130.7	57	Bank Holdings	83.4	92	Newtek Business Services	61.9
23	Natural Resource Partners	125.4	58	EV Energy Partners	83.2	93	SiRF Technology Holdings	61.6
24	United Therapeutics	125.2	59	Synchronoss Technologies	81.2	94	Vineyard National Bancorp	61.4
25	salesforce.com	124.8	60	Netflix	80.2	95	Tower Group	60.8
26	True Religion Apparel	123.4	61	ACA Capital Holdings	79.8	96	Advanced Analogic Technologies	60.5
27	CapitalSource	123.3	62	Altiris	79.7	97	NutriSystem	60.1
28	Kyphon	118.8	63	Under Armour	78.4	98	j2 Global Communications	59.6
29	InnerWorkings	117.9	64	Bay National	76.5	99	GSI Commerce	59.4
30	DealerTrack Holdings	117.4	65	Collegiate Pacific	75.9	100	Prestige Brands	59.2
31	Cogent	113.6	66	ZipRealty	75.8			
32	iRobot	112.5	67	Argon ST	73.6			
33	Infocrossing	111.5	68	HealthExtras	73.5			
34	WSB Financial Group	110.9	69	Calamos Asset Management	72.4			
35	Atlas Pipeline Partners	108.2	70	LoopNet	71.8			

Note: These rates are compounded annualized increases in sales growth for the most current fiscal years and may have resulted from acquisitions or one-time gains. If the company has been public for less than six years, sales growth is for the years available.

SOURCE: HOOVER'S, INC., DATABASE, FEBRUARY 2007

The Top 100 Companies in One-Year Sales Growth
in *Hoover's Handbook of Emerging Companies 2007*

Rank	Company	One-Year Sales Growth (%)	Rank	Company	One-Year Sales Growth (%)	Rank	Company	One-Year Sales Growth (%)
1	Harris & Harris	2,533.3	36	Central Jersey Bancorp	114.5	71	LoopNet	82.4
2	Crocs	704.4	37	Boardwalk Pipeline Partners	112.6	72	Cogent	82.3
3	Sirona Dental Systems	641.6	38	Presstek	111.0	73	Charles & Colvard	82.0
4	ViroPharma	491.1	39	Collegiate Pacific	110.9	74	HouseValues	81.8
5	Penn Virginia Resource Partners	490.5	40	Union Drilling	108.8	75	Parlux Fragrances	81.5
6	NutriSystem	459.2	41	Monolithic Power Systems	108.2	76	Edge Petroleum	80.9
7	Capital Southwest	334.4	42	Techwell	108.1	77	Nextest Systems	80.8
8	Atlas Pipeline Partners	306.9	43	Tower Group	104.1	78	ValueClick	79.7
9	International Assets Holding	292.4	44	GAINSCO	103.7	79	Tennessee Commerce Bancorp	78.6
10	True Religion Apparel	270.4	45	DivX	101.2	80	Integrated BioPharma	76.8
11	Capital Lease Funding	248.1	46	Ultra Petroleum	100.2	81	Central Pacific Financial	76.5
12	Visicu	234.5	47	Synchronoss Technologies	99.3	82	FirstFed Financial	76.4
13	Natural Gas Services	208.1	48	InfoSonics	98.6	83	GeoPharma	76.2
14	Arena Resources	203.5	49	Commercial Vehicle Group	98.3	84	salesforce.com	75.7
15	Valero	198.7	50	InnerWorkings	97.7	85	Wireless Telecom	75.6
16	Penn Virginia	195.1	51	SEACOR Holdings	97.6	86	Cerus	75.5
17	Delta Financial	182.2	52	Intevac	97.1	87	WebSideStory	74.8
18	PharmaNet Development	169.2	53	Rackable Systems	96.0	88	Optelecom-NKF	74.7
19	Whittier Energy	166.3	54	WSB Financial Group	93.5	89	Beach First National Bancshares	74.6
20	U.S. Global Investors	163.5	55	Hansen Natural	93.5	90	Powerwave Technologies	74.1
21	Atlas America	162.3	56	FreightCar America	92.3	91	Corus Bankshares	73.6
22	UTEK Corporation	160.9	57	Tarragon	91.7	92	Bolt Technology	73.4
23	Schawk	157.9	58	NeuroMetrix	91.6	93	Jupitermedia	73.3
24	American Mortgage Acceptance	146.5	59	Micronetics	90.8	94	Superior Well Services	73.3
25	GMX Resources	146.2	60	Darwin Professional Underwriters	90.4	95	Benjamin Franklin Bancorp	72.9
26	First Advantage	141.6	61	Whiting Petroleum	88.3	96	Quicksilver Resources	72.8
27	Complete Production Services	136.2	62	Bank of Florida	88.2	97	Sun American Bancorp	72.7
28	Comstock Homebuilding	133.6	63	Gateway Financial Holdings	87.5	98	DealerTrack Holdings	71.7
29	Rocky Brands	123.7	64	Home BancShares	86.0	99	ACA Capital Holdings	71.3
30	Allis-Chalmers Energy	120.8	65	American Science and Engineering	85.3	100	American Railcar Industries	71.3
31	Home Solutions of America	119.0	66	First Regional Bancorp	85.2			
32	Alkermes	118.9	67	Cardinal Financial	84.4			
33	Astronics	117.0	68	Bare Escentuals	82.9			
34	Marchex	116.9	69	Hungarian Telephone and Cable	82.8			
35	Sepracor	115.5	70	VASCO Data Security	82.6			

Note: These rates are for sales growth for the most current fiscal year and may have resulted from acquisitions or one-time gains.

SOURCE: HOOVER'S, INC., DATABASE, FEBRUARY 2007

The Top 100 Companies in Five-Year Net Income Growth
in *Hoover's Handbook of Emerging Companies 2007*

Rank	Company	Five-Year Net Income Growth (%)	Rank	Company	Five-Year Net Income Growth (%)	Rank	Company	Five-Year Net Income Growth (%)
1	Symmetry Medical	441.8	36	Southcoast Financial	83.8	71	Temecula Valley Bancorp	60.6
2	First Advantage	356.7	37	Central European Distribution	82.6	72	Stratasys	60.3
3	Shutterfly	280.1	38	Pioneer Drilling	79.7	73	South Financial	58.4
4	LoopNet	233.4	39	A.S.V.	79.4	74	Martin Midstream Partners	58.3
5	InfraSource Services	224.6	40	First Community Bank Corporation	76.3	75	First Cash Financial Services	57.8
6	NYMEX Holdings	217.5	41	Beach First National Bancshares	76.2	76	Comstock Homebuilding	57.4
7	Cogent	205.1	42	First State Financial	75.6	77	Empire Resources	56.9
8	Tower Group	168.5	43	Accredited Home Lenders	75.4	78	Cognizant Technology Solutions	56.5
9	Rocky Brands	164.7	44	Argon ST	74.5	79	Ceradyne	55.8
10	Prestige Brands	157.3	45	Hansen Natural	74.3	80	Nexity Financial	55.4
11	First Marblehead Corporation	157.1	46	Sciele Pharma	73.4	81	InfoSonics	55.2
12	InnerWorkings	156.3	47	Home BancShares	73.2	82	RC2 Corporation	55.2
13	Natural Resource Partners	143.0	48	Portfolio Recovery Associates	71.2	83	First Security Group	54.6
14	EV Energy Partners	136.5	49	Hittite Microwave	71.2	84	Biosite	54.2
15	Covanta	126.3	50	FormFactor	70.4	85	Central Jersey Bancorp	54.0
16	Willow Financial Bancorp	123.3	51	Zumiez	69.3	86	Omni Financial Services	52.8
17	CapitalSource	121.8	52	Cutera	69.0	87	Advanced Analogic Technologies	52.8
18	Boardwalk Pipeline Partners	111.8	53	Multi-Fineline Electronix	68.6	88	NeuStar	51.9
19	American Science and Engineering	111.8	54	USANA Health Sciences	68.2	89	Amedisys	51.3
20	Travelzoo	111.5	55	Psychiatric Solutions	68.2	90	Tempur-Pedic International	51.1
21	Double Eagle Petroleum	109.1	56	Franklin Credit Management	67.5	91	Umpqua Holdings	50.9
22	NewAlliance Bancshares	108.5	57	Build-A-Bear Workshop	66.6	92	Panera Bread	50.3
23	WSB Financial Group	100.0	58	Tarragon	66.1	93	ResMed	50.0
24	Vineyard National Bancorp	99.4	59	Basic Energy Services	65.3	94	PrivateBancorp	50.0
25	Anika Therapeutics	96.8	60	Itron	65.1	95	HealthSpring	49.9
26	Under Armour	91.6	61	Copano Energy	65.0	96	Western Alliance Bancorporation	49.6
27	U.S. Shipping Partners	89.6	62	DCP Midstream Partners	64.7	97	PremierWest Bancorp	49.0
28	Republic Airways Holdings	89.3	63	Bolt Technology	64.4	98	GMX Resources	48.4
29	LHC Group	88.5	64	ENGlobal	64.4	99	Cohen & Steers	48.3
30	Providence Service	88.0	65	HouseValues	64.0	100	TALX Corporation	48.0
31	Emergent BioSolutions	87.4	66	Healthways	63.3			
32	Ultra Petroleum	87.3	67	Calamos Asset Management	62.4			
33	Drew Industries	86.2	68	First Acceptance	62.2			
34	Tennessee Commerce Bancorp	85.6	69	AngioDynamics	62.1			
35	Commonwealth Bankshares	85.6	70	First Regional Bancorp	61.7			

Note: These rates are compounded annualized increases in net income for the most current fiscal years and may have resulted from acquisitions or one-time gains. If the company has been public for less than six years, net income growth is for the years available.

SOURCE: HOOVER'S, INC., DATABASE, FEBRUARY 2007

The Top 100 Companies in One-Year Net Income Growth
in *Hoover's Handbook of Emerging Companies 2007*

Rank	Company	One-Year Net Income Growth (%)	Rank	Company	One-Year Net Income Growth (%)	Rank	Company	One-Year Net Income Growth (%)
1	Globalstar	4,575.0	36	Pioneer Drilling	368.5	71	Radiation Therapy Services	171.7
2	Darwin Professional Underwriters	3,600.0	37	Sirenza Microdevices	366.7	72	Partners Trust Financial Group	171.1
3	Aspect Medical Systems	2,733.3	38	Bank Holdings	366.7	73	American Science and Engineering	166.1
4	CommVault Systems	2,060.0	39	True Religion Apparel	364.3	74	IRIS International	165.2
5	NutriSystem	2,000.0	40	Cohen & Steers	337.0	75	Range Resources	163.0
6	Vital Images	1,833.3	41	United Therapeutics	322.1	76	NYMEX Holdings	159.5
7	Internet Commerce	1,400.0	42	Titanium Metals	290.7	77	InnerWorkings	155.6
8	Grey Wolf	1,388.9	43	salesforce.com	290.4	78	Gulfport Energy	153.5
9	iRobot	1,200.0	44	Complete Production Services	287.8	79	Barnwell Industries	143.3
10	NewAlliance Bancshares	1,182.9	45	Arena Resources	280.0	80	Beach First National Bancshares	142.9
11	Stratus Properties	1,114.3	46	Whittier Energy	278.6	81	Traffix, Inc.	140.0
12	U.S. Shipping Partners	1,106.7	47	Tejon Ranch	275.0	82	Willamette Valley Vineyards	140.0
13	HealthTronics	922.2	48	Dynamic Materials	271.4	83	First Regional Bancorp	138.7
14	Akamai Technologies	853.5	49	Charles & Colvard	268.8	84	Unit Corporation	135.2
15	Bucyrus International	778.7	50	Capital Lease Funding	264.3	85	Sonic Solutions	134.1
16	SEACOR Holdings	757.8	51	Cutera	263.2	86	ADA-ES	133.3
17	Allis-Chalmers Energy	700.0	52	Morningstar	253.4	87	VASCO Data Security	133.3
18	Shutterfly	681.1	53	Basic Energy Services	247.3	88	Tower Group	131.1
19	American Railcar Industries	678.9	54	Miller Industries	238.2	89	Mac-Gray	128.3
20	U.S. Global Investors	593.3	55	Bay National	237.5	90	Health Grades	127.8
21	Capital Southwest	577.5	56	Municipal Mortgage & Equity	223.7	91	EFJ	125.0
22	Pericom Semiconductor	566.7	57	NAVTEQ	215.7	92	I.D. Systems	125.0
23	ZipRealty	540.6	58	DATATRAK International	212.5	93	Komag	124.9
24	Chipotle Mexican Grill	518.0	59	Lufkin Industries	209.0	94	First Security Group	123.3
25	Advanced Environmental Recycling	500.0	60	Hansen Natural	207.8	95	Edge Petroleum	121.2
26	Kreisler Manufacturing	500.0	61	MOD-PAC	197.3	96	Team, Inc.	120.8
27	Bare Escentuals	497.5	62	Cardinal Financial	182.9	97	RightNow Technologies	120.0
28	California Coastal Communities	491.7	63	Bolt Technology	182.4	98	Cuisine Solutions	117.6
29	First Advantage	489.9	64	Commercial Vehicle Group	182.3	99	Central Jersey Bancorp	116.7
30	WebSideStory	438.9	65	Quicksilver Resources	179.2	100	TETRA Technologies	115.3
31	Mitcham Industries	419.0	66	Home Solutions of America	176.9			
32	GMX Resources	414.3	67	PeopleSupport	174.7			
33	LoopNet	410.8	68	W-H Energy Services	173.7			
34	Jupitermedia	399.4	69	CheckFree	172.0			
35	Exploration Company of Delaware	389.3	70	Symmetry Medical	171.8			

Note: These rates are for net income for the most current fiscal year and may have resulted from acquisitions or one-time gains.

SOURCE: HOOVER'S, INC., DATABASE, FEBRUARY 2007

The Top 100 Companies in Five-Year Employment Growth
in *Hoover's Handbook of Emerging Companies 2007*

Rank	Company	Five-Year Annualized Employment Growth (%)	Rank	Company	Five-Year Annualized Employment Growth (%)	Rank	Company	Five-Year Annualized Employment Growth (%)
1	Crocs	420.8	36	Bank of Florida	52.9	71	CompuCredit	40.0
2	First Acceptance	397.5	37	Monolithic Power Systems	51.9	72	Coinstar	40.0
3	Cathay General Bancorp	316.2	38	Under Armour	51.6	73	PharmaNet Development	39.8
4	Allis-Chalmers Energy	168.2	39	Cohen & Steers	50.0	74	Pioneer Drilling	39.2
5	Covanta	135.5	40	Atlas America	49.8	75	Unica Corporation	39.1
6	OMI Corporation	130.1	41	SI International	49.4	76	Netflix	39.0
7	Commercial Vehicle Group	113.6	42	Texas Capital Bancshares	48.8	77	EVCI Career Colleges	38.3
8	Psychiatric Solutions	99.3	43	ZipRealty	48.2	78	eCollege.com	38.3
9	Collegiate Pacific	98.1	44	Jacksonville Bancorp	48.0	79	NewAlliance Bancshares	38.1
10	Double Eagle Petroleum	93.4	45	ArthroCare	46.7	80	Traffix, Inc.	37.9
11	HouseValues	90.6	46	First Marblehead Corporation	46.6	81	EPIQ Systems	37.5
12	InnerWorkings	89.2	47	American Capital Strategies	45.9	82	HealthTronics	37.4
13	Home Solutions of America	86.4	48	Community Bancorp	45.6	83	Travelzoo	37.4
14	SigmaTel	82.7	49	Allegiant Travel	45.4	84	Pacific CMA	37.3
15	Rackable Systems	77.7	50	NGAS Resources	45.0	85	Gateway Financial Holdings	37.3
16	UTEK Corporation	76.8	51	Central European Distribution	45.0	86	LGL Group, Inc.	37.3
17	ValueClick	75.5	52	Merix Corporation	44.7	87	HealthExtras	36.4
18	salesforce.com	70.0	53	Prestige Brands	44.2	88	Cutera	36.0
19	Kentucky First Federal Bancorp	69.0	54	NutriSystem	44.0	89	WebSideStory	35.8
20	Valero	68.5	55	Omni Financial Services	44.0	90	WCA Waste	35.8
21	Phoenix Footwear	68.0	56	Guidance Software	43.3	91	Coldwater Creek	35.7
22	Whiting Petroleum	67.6	57	Team, Inc.	43.3	92	Natural Gas Services	35.5
23	ExlService Holdings	66.7	58	Martek Biosciences	43.2	93	Partners Trust Financial Group	35.5
24	SafeNet	65.5	59	WebEx Communications	43.2	94	Vineyard National Bancorp	35.5
25	First Advantage	64.8	60	Argon ST	43.0	95	Hansen Natural	35.4
26	Arena Resources	63.9	61	Perry Ellis International	42.8	96	Asta Funding	35.0
27	Varsity Group	62.3	62	Range Resources	42.3	97	Multi-Fineline Electronix	34.7
28	Providence Service	62.1	63	Amedisys	42.1	98	Buffalo Wild Wings	34.7
29	Copano Energy	60.5	64	Brooke	41.8	99	Simclar	34.5
30	Sonic Solutions	58.9	65	Ceradyne	41.1	100	LECG	33.8
31	Cognizant Technology Solutions	57.7	66	Infocrossing	40.8			
32	Newtek Business Services	56.5	67	Powerwave Technologies	40.4			
33	Perficient	56.4	68	Cardinal Financial	40.2			
34	Citi Trends	55.6	69	Kyphon	40.2			
35	International Assets Holding	55.0	70	NeuroMetrix	40.0			

Note: These rates are compounded annualized increases in employment growth for
the most current fiscal years and may have resulted from acquisitions or one-time gains.
If the company has been public for less than six years, employment growth is for the
years available.

SOURCE: HOOVER'S, INC., DATABASE, FEBRUARY 2007

The Top 40 Companies in Five-Year Stock Appreciation
in *Hoover's Handbook of Emerging Companies 2007*

Rank	Company	Five-Year Annualized Stock Appreciation (%)	Rank	Company	Five-Year Annualized Stock Appreciation (%)	Rank	Company	Five-Year Annualized Stock Appreciation (%)
1	InfoSonics	353.6	16	Immucor	121.6	31	Greenhill & Co	95.7
2	NutriSystem	218.5	17	Psychiatric Solutions	118.9	32	CAS Medical Systems	94.9
3	True Religion Apparel	214.2	18	LCA-Vision	112.0	33	Southwestern Energy	92.8
4	Health Grades	208.3	19	Cutera	110.9	34	Charles & Colvard	92.0
5	salesforce.com	199.6	20	EFJ	110.2	35	TGC Industries	89.7
6	Encore Capital Group	185.8	21	Radiation Therapy Services	107.7	36	Universal Security Instruments	87.8
7	USANA Health Sciences	179.3	22	TODCO	106.6	37	International Assets Holding	87.8
8	NetLogic Microsystems	172.4	23	j2 Global Communications	103.7	38	Empire Resources	86.5
9	Wireless Xcessories	149.5	24	Imperial Industries	103.1	39	NGAS Resources	86.3
10	Hansen Natural	148.1	25	LivePerson	103.1	40	Anika Therapeutics	84.9
11	Brooke	135.2	26	Integrated BioPharma	99.6			
12	SiRF Technology Holdings	134.3	27	Titanium Metals	99.4			
13	Palomar Medical Technologies	132.9	28	Komag	98.2			
14	NeuroMetrix	132.2	29	Sirona Dental Systems	97.8			
15	Atlas America	124.5	30	Dynamic Materials	97.3			

Note: These rates are compounded annualized increases based on fiscal year-end closing prices. If the company has been public for less than six years, stock appreciation is for the years available.

SOURCE: HOOVER'S, INC., DATABASE, FEBRUARY 2007

The Top 40 Companies in Market Value
in *Hoover's Handbook of Emerging Companies 2007*

Rank	Company	Market Value ($ mil.)	Rank	Company	Market Value ($ mil.)	Rank	Company	Market Value ($ mil.)
1	Celgene	11,086	16	Corporate Executive Board	3,542	31	Avid Technology	2,305
2	Ultra Petroleum	8,662	17	Range Resources	3,422	32	Hologic	2,287
3	Cognizant Technology Solutions	7,005	18	Cytyc	3,254	33	F5 Networks	2,191
4	Southwestern Energy	6,010	19	Eagle Materials	3,208	34	CNET Networks	2,184
5	Sepracor	5,371	20	Quicksilver Resources	3,196	35	FactSet Research Systems	2,156
6	Citrix Systems	5,074	21	CapitalSource	3,145	36	Cogent	2,132
7	Monster Worldwide	4,927	22	Affiliated Managers Group	3,132	37	Covanta	2,126
8	Red Hat	4,920	23	Akamai Technologies	3,048	38	CompuCredit	2,101
9	salesforce.com	4,537	24	Helix Energy Solutions	2,788	39	St. Mary Land & Exploration	2,089
10	CheckFree	4,503	25	Laureate Education	2,618	40	NeuStar	2,078
11	American Capital Strategies	4,306	26	Denbury Resources	2,613			
12	NAVTEQ	4,040	27	Cooper Companies	2,567			
13	Eaton Vance	3,915	28	Unit Corporation	2,541			
14	Intuitive Surgical	3,557	29	First Marblehead Corporation	2,393			
15	ResMed	3,553	30	TODCO	2,342			

Note: These values are based on the latest available fiscal year-end stock price and the number of shares outstanding.

SOURCE: HOOVER'S, INC., DATABASE, FEBRUARY 2007

The Top 40 Companies with the Highest Profit Margin
in *Hoover's Handbook of Emerging Companies 2007*

Rank	Company	Profit Margin (%)	Rank	Company	Profit Margin (%)	Rank	Company	Profit Margin (%)
1	MVC Capital	255.7	16	Evercore Partners	50.3	31	PeopleSupport	36.7
2	Akamai Technologies	115.9	17	InfoSpace	46.9	32	CREDO Petroleum	35.8
3	Petroleum & Resources	97.8	18	Asta Funding	44.9	33	j2 Global Communications	35.6
4	Capital Southwest	97.6	19	Ultra Petroleum	44.2	34	Shutterfly	34.4
5	RealNetworks	96.1	20	Harris & Harris	42.4	35	NAVTEQ	34.4
6	ViroPharma	85.9	21	OMI Corporation	42.2	36	VAALCO Energy	34.4
7	Gladstone Capital	74.2	22	First Marblehead Corporation	41.9	37	Toreador Resources	34.1
8	Dorchester Minerals	66.2	23	Cogent	40.8	38	Tessera Technologies	33.3
9	American Capital Strategies	65.8	24	OraSure Technologies	39.6	39	EV Energy Partners	32.6
10	Jupitermedia	62.9	25	Gulfport Energy	39.5	40	Ambassadors Group	32.3
11	LoopNet	61.0	26	American Mortgage Acceptance	38.8			
12	Natural Resource Partners	57.7	27	Somanetics	38.0			
13	United Therapeutics	56.1	28	optionsXpress Holdings	37.8			
14	Visicu	54.9	29	GMX Resources	37.5			
15	Cerus	53.7	30	Arena Resources	36.8			

Note: These values are based on the latest available fiscal year-end net income and sales.

SOURCE: HOOVER'S, INC., DATABASE, FEBRUARY 2007

The Top 40 Companies with the Highest Return on Equity
in *Hoover's Handbook of Emerging Companies 2007*

Rank	Company	Return on Equity (%)	Rank	Company	Return on Equity (%)	Rank	Company	Return on Equity (%)
1	Kenexa	1,297.9	16	NeuStar	71.8	31	Integrated BioPharma	50.2
2	Cbeyond	725.5	17	Cerus	69.4	32	Titanium Metals	49.0
3	InnerWorkings	685.0	18	U.S. Global Investors	68.3	33	Parker Drilling	48.4
4	Pinnacle Airlines	464.3	19	Hansen Natural	68.2	34	Advanced Environmental Recycling	47.5
5	Crocs	221.9	20	optionsXpress Holdings	64.3	35	First Marblehead Corporation	47.3
6	FreightCar America	165.9	21	Health Grades	62.1	36	NAVTEQ	47.3
7	United Industrial	143.6	22	American Railcar Industries	61.6	37	VAALCO Energy	46.4
8	Akamai Technologies	131.7	23	Allegiant Travel	60.6	38	NutriSystem	46.1
9	Evercore Partners	123.0	24	NYMEX Holdings	60.1	39	Greenhill & Co	45.9
10	PW Eagle	95.3	25	Ultra Petroleum	54.4	40	Mannatech	45.2
11	VeriFone Holdings	95.0	26	Jupitermedia	52.7			
12	Rackable Systems	91.9	27	Clayton Holdings	51.6			
13	True Religion Apparel	91.1	28	RealNetworks	51.1			
14	USANA Health Sciences	83.4	29	DivX	51.0			
15	ViroPharma	75.6	30	Metalico	50.3			

Note: These values are based on the latest available fiscal year-end net income and average total equity.

SOURCE: HOOVER'S, INC., DATABASE, FEBRUARY 2007

The Top 40 Companies with the Highest P/E Ratios
in *Hoover's Handbook of Emerging Companies 2007*

Rank	Company	P/E High	Rank	Company	P/E High	Rank	Company	P/E High
1	MarkWest Energy Partners	2,675	16	Altiris	322	31	ACE*COMM	185
2	Clayton Williams Energy	2,248	17	SafeNet	319	32	Celgene	182
3	Sepracor	2,218	18	NGAS Resources	317	33	salesforce.com	179
4	Tejon Ranch	697	19	Celebrate Express	311	34	DealerTrack Holdings	177
5	Alkermes	670	20	Advanced Analogic Technologies	310	35	PharmaNet Development	176
6	Marchex	660	21	I.D. Systems	266	36	Sirenza Microdevices	168
7	Pharmion	636	22	Repligen	254	37	Infocrossing	168
8	Align Technology	544	23	ADA-ES	241	38	Jones Soda	166
9	NeuroMetrix	535	24	Oplink Communications	228	39	POZEN	158
10	Rockwell Medical Technologies	530	25	Global Entertainment	225	40	Aptimus	154
11	Unica Corporation	504	26	Travelzoo	222			
12	EVCI Career Colleges	368	27	Shuffle Master	214			
13	Community Capital Bancshares	340	28	Sonus Networks	214			
14	iRobot	339	29	Merix Corporation	204			
15	LaserCard	325	30	FalconStor Software	195			

Note: These values are based on the latest available fiscal year earnings per share and the highest stock price for that fiscal year.

SOURCE: HOOVER'S, INC., DATABASE, FEBRUARY 2007

The Top 40 Companies with the Lowest P/E Ratios
in *Hoover's Handbook of Emerging Companies 2007*

Rank	Company	P/E Low	Rank	Company	P/E Low	Rank	Company	P/E Low
1	PW Eagle	1	16	MVC Capital	4	31	Mitcham Industries	5
2	ViroPharma	1	17	Home Solutions of America	4	32	Varsity Group	6
3	InfoSonics	3	18	Accredited Home Lenders	4	33	TGC Industries	6
4	RealNetworks	3	19	OMI Corporation	4	34	First Marblehead Corporation	6
5	U.S. Global Investors	3	20	Integrated BioPharma	5	35	PeopleSupport	6
6	MOD-PAC	3	21	Orleans Homebuilders	5	36	Lufkin Industries	6
7	Titanium Metals	3	22	BTU International	5	37	Jupitermedia	6
8	Parker Drilling	4	23	Universal Security Instruments	5	38	Universal Stainless & Alloy Products	6
9	Empire Resources	4	24	NutriSystem	5	39	EFJ	6
10	Pinnacle Airlines	4	25	InfoSpace	5	40	VAALCO Energy	6
11	Encore Wire	4	26	Komag	5			
12	Wireless Xcessories	4	27	Aldila	5			
13	Imperial Industries	4	28	Dynamic Materials	5			
14	Tarragon	4	29	Akamai Technologies	5			
15	FreightCar America	4	30	Cerus	5			

Note: These values are based on the latest available fiscal year earnings per share and the lowest stock price for that fiscal year.

SOURCE: HOOVER'S, INC., DATABASE, FEBRUARY 2007

BusinessWeek 100 Hot Growth Companies

Rank	Company	Three-Year Sales Increase (%)	Rank	Company	Three-Year Sales Increase (%)	Rank	Company	Three-Year Sales Increase (%)
1	VAALCO Energy	98.9	36	Cimarex Energy	81.2	71	Providence Service	52.8
2	Hansen Natural	56.7	37	Alliance Resource Partners	17.7	72	Miller Industries	19.6
3	Palomar Medical Technologies	44.8	38	VSE	30.7	73	Headwaters	99.8
4	W&T Offshore	42.5	39	Chico's FAS	38.3	74	Hydril	17.7
5	NAVTEQ	44.1	40	Build-A-Bear Workshop	30.0	75	aQuantive	24.5
6	Under Armour	78.3	41	St. Mary Land & Exploration	50.6	76	Commercial Vehicle Group	35.8
7	VASCO Data Security International	41.2	42	Hurco	22.2	77	Brigham Exploration	40.2
8	Programmer's Paradise	30.2	43	Unit	68.2	78	Guess?	17.4
9	LCA-Vision	47.0	44	Barrett Business Services	31.2	79	NETGEAR	24.2
10	Blue Nile	40.2	45	Encore Wire	40.2	80	Labor Ready	13.2
11	Volcom	41.7	46	Ansoft	16.9	81	Pharmaceutical Product Development	19.1
12	American Science & Engineering	32.2	47	Sonic Solutions	63.4	82	Korn/Ferry International	18.0
13	ASV	75.9	48	Reliv' International	22.2	83	DSW	21.1
14	PeopleSupport	46.6	49	Quality Systems	25.8	84	Rofin-Sinar Technologies	19.7
15	Imperial Industries	26.4	50	LoJack	17.7	85	ADTRAN	14.1
16	Cognizant Technology Solutions	57.2	51	Dynamic Materials	21.6	86	MSC Industrial Direct	11.6
17	Multi-Fineline Electronix	52.0	52	Diodes	24.1	87	MICROS Systems	18.0
18	Hittite Microwave	38.1	53	Leucadia National	78.0	88	Concur Technologies	14.9
19	OmniVision Technologies	57.4	54	Argon ST	107.1	89	Kforce	17.7
20	NutriSystem	94.4	55	ValueClick	70.7	90	Lamson & Sessions	15.9
21	Resources Connection	46.9	56	eCollege.com	69.7	91	Stratasys	28.7
22	EFJ	33.5	57	Ventiv Health	39.1	92	AngioDynamics	23.3
23	InfoSonics	42.5	58	Packeteer	27.1	93	AMCOL International	21.9
24	Amedisys	44.9	59	Digital River	42.6	94	Denbury Resources	24.3
25	LifeCell	41.1	60	TTM Technologies	38.6	95	Lufkin Industries	29.8
26	RPC	26.8	61	Sun Hydraulics	23.0	96	Lifetime Brands	31.3
27	PetMed Express	31.8	62	Coldwater Creek	18.1	97	II-VI	19.3
28	NeuStar	39.5	63	Parlux Fragrances	28.6	98	Digitas	20.9
29	Netflix	66.7	64	CNX Gas	61.9	99	Old Dominion Freight Line	23.3
30	Ceradyne	84.7	65	Altera	17.1	100	Brady	16.9
31	MEMC Electronic Materials	19.2	66	Ventana Medical Systems	23.8			
32	Empire Resources	29.5	67	Gen-Probe	25.8			
33	Gevity HR	19.4	68	Trimble Navigation	18.9			
34	Berry Petroleum	46.4	69	Radyne	18.8			
35	Endo Pharmaceuticals Holdings	24.5	70	Helix Energy Solutions	38.1			

Ranked by composite score based on sales and earnings growth and average return on capital over a three-year period.

SOURCE: *BUSINESSWEEK*, JUNE 5, 2006

FORTUNE 100 Fastest-Growing Companies

Rank	Company	Three-Year EPS Annual Growth Rate (%)	Rank	Company	Three-Year EPS Annual Growth Rate (%)	Rank	Company	Three-Year EPS Annual Growth Rate (%)
1	VAALCO Energy	147	36	Euronet Worldwide	57	71	Schnitzer Steel	98
2	Hansen Natural	177	37	Unit	98	72	Commercial Capital Bancorp	41
3	Armor Holdings	250	38	RPC	197	73	Dynamic Materials	42
4	Southern Copper	173	39	XTO Energy	67	74	OmniVision Technologies	74
5	LCA-Vision	154	40	Swift Energy	107	75	ConocoPhillips	107
6	Palomar Medical Technologies	122	41	Building Materials Holding	130	76	Rush Enterprises	71
7	Amedisys	121	42	LifeCell	77	77	Digital River	78
8	Edge Petroleum	139	43	Patterson-UTI Energy	270	78	Murphy Oil	77
9	Maverick Tube	350	44	United States Steel	182	79	Genentech	104
10	Nucor	172	45	PrimeEnergy	106	80	Greenbrier Cos.	86
11	Frontier Oil	678	46	Steel Dynamics	66	81	Chicago Mercantile Exchange Holdings	45
12	Jupitermedia	374	47	Children's Place Retail Stores	167	82	Diodes	68
13	Commercial Metals	163	48	Grant Prideco	196	83	Sonic Solutions	43
14	Holly	96	49	Penn Virginia	45	84	Quality Systems	47
15	inVentiv Health	98	50	Helix Energy Solutions Group	121	85	TETRA Technologies	64
16	Valero Energy	142	51	Reliance Steel & Aluminum	122	86	Headwaters	41
17	ASV	109	52	World Fuel Services	34	87	Epicor Software	155
18	Netflix	253	53	EOG Resources	93	88	St. Mary Land & Exploration	45
19	Yahoo	170	54	Lam Research	256	89	Pioneer Natural Resources	78
20	Leucadia National	110	55	Oneok	67	90	Corus Bankshares	46
21	Celgene	75	56	Gilead Sciences	84	91	Comtech Telecommunications	81
22	JLG Industries	85	57	American Capital Strategies	106	92	Cimarex Energy	42
23	Joy Global	245	58	TTM Technologies	143	93	National Oilwell Varco	34
24	Deckers Outdoor	99	59	Berry Petroleum	65	94	Quanex	52
25	Encore Wire	108	60	SanDisk	69	95	Oil States International	43
26	Tesoro	119	61	Resources Connection	81	96	SEACOR Holdings	67
27	Phelps Dodge	199	62	Autodesk	115	97	Energy Partners	71
28	Overseas Shipholding Group	134	63	Vineyard National Bancorp	46	98	Toll Brothers	57
29	Red Hat	143	64	Lufkin Industries	75	99	Meritage Homes	56
30	Chesapeake Energy	79	65	Sunoco	86	100	Chico's FAS	40
31	Cognizant Technology Solutions	63	66	YRC Worldwide	78			
32	ValueClick	105	67	Urban Outfitters	66			
33	CompuCredit	116	68	Range Resources	34			
34	Psychiatric Solutions	33	69	Gardner Denver	38			
35	Southwestern Energy	81	70	Wilshire Bancorp	45			

Ranked by composite score based on profit and sales growth and three-year total return.

SOURCE: *FORTUNE*, SEPTEMBER 18, 2006

Forbes 200 Best Small Companies

Rank	Company	Five-Year Average ROE (%)	Rank	Company	Five-Year Average ROE (%)	Rank	Company	Five-Year Average ROE (%)
1	NutriSystem	26	51	Corporate Executive Board	19	101	LKQ	8
2	Hansen Natural	31	52	OMI	24	102	Meridian Bioscience	13
3	optionsXpress Holdings	167	53	Vital Images	6	103	Conn's	20
4	PetMed Express	60	54	MTC Technologies	49	104	Sonic	21
5	Mannatech	23	55	Amedisys	18	105	Hydril	17
6	Travelzoo	46	56	Streamline Health Solutions	21	106	RPC	15
7	Citi Trends	33	57	Strayer Education	100	107	Techne	20
8	j2 Global Communications	22	58	K-Swiss	29	108	McGrath RentCorp	18
9	Middleby	47	59	Daktronics	18	109	Intersections	19
10	Ceradyne	17	60	Chattem	25	110	Bright Horizons Family Solutions	16
11	AngioDynamics	58	61	Range Resources	12	111	Sciele Pharma	7
12	USANA Health Sciences	57	62	Computer Programs & Systems	54	112	Micros Systems	13
13	Radiation Therapy Services	38	63	Ambassadors	34	113	Gymboree	11
14	Reliv' International	33	64	ITT Educational Services	46	114	First Cash Financial Services	15
15	GFI	27	65	FactSet Research Systems	29	115	Ventana Medical Systems	9
16	TradeStation	12	66	Resources Connection	17	116	Balchem	20
17	Providence Service	18	67	Natural Gas Services	11	117	Portec Rail Products	13
18	Blue Nile	26	68	Raven Industries	24	118	CNS	18
19	Avatar Holdings	8	69	Denbury Resources	18	119	Mikron Infrared	15
20	Berry Petroleum	24	70	FormFactor	9	120	Integra LifeSciences Holdings	13
21	LifeCell	15	71	Swift Energy	9	121	Forward Air	21
22	Comtech Telecommunications	14	72	Schawk	16	122	Genesee & Wyoming	12
23	ASV	11	73	Charles & Colvard	9	123	Heartland Express	18
24	Websense	15	74	CREDO Petroleum	17	124	Rocky Mountain Chocolate Factory	22
25	Abaxis	19	75	Lamson & Sessions	14	125	Supertex	6
26	Quality Systems	22	76	Cantel Medical	16	126	Core Molding Technologies	10
27	Jos. A. Bank Clothiers	21	77	Hibbett Sporting Goods	19	127	Lifeway Foods	13
28	Medifast	27	78	CRA International	12	128	Stratasys	11
29	Multi-Fineline Electronix	18	79	Advisory Board	44	129	United Surgical Partners	6
30	Panera Bread	16	80	Edge Petroleum	11	130	Cherokee	121
31	Sterling Construction	31	81	Amrep	11	131	Rofin-Sinar Technologies	11
32	Kanbay International	25	82	Ansoft	11	132	Bolt Technology	8
33	Dolby Laboratories	28	83	FLIR Systems	30	133	Badger Meter	15
34	United Industrial	53	84	inVentiv Health	9	134	Adtran	12
35	Micronetics	13	85	Pioneer Drilling	7	135	WD-40	29
36	Cytyc	16	86	ResMed	18	136	Amcol International	12
37	Diodes	15	87	Sun Hydraulics	11	137	PetroQuest Energy	12
38	Texas Roadhouse	42	88	FTI Consulting	14	138	Copart	15
39	Optelecom-NKF	25	89	GeoResources	11	139	Idexx Laboratories	16
40	TALX	11	90	Knight Transportation	16	140	Lufkin Industries	10
41	Dynamic Materials	23	91	Cascade	12	141	Marten Transport	11
42	American Vanguard	22	92	GMX Resources	6	142	Cavco Industries	9
43	Quicksilver Resources	16	93	Ennis	15	143	Hi-Shear Technology	12
44	Blackbaud	26	94	Gen-Probe	12	144	Franklin Electric	20
45	W&T Offshore	41	95	Bentley Pharmaceuticals	8	145	Tandy Leather Factory	19
46	Healthways	16	96	Yankee Candle	43	146	infoUSA	14
47	Deckers Outdoor	13	97	Monarch Casino & Resort	24	147	Medical Action Industries	19
48	PRA International	17	98	RC2	15	148	Progress Software	13
49	LoJack	20	99	Whiting Petroleum	17	149	U.S. Lime & Minerals	9
50	Encore Acquisition	16	100	Matthews International	21	150	Neogen	12

Ranked by composite score based on growth in sales, earnings, and ROE for the past five years and the latest 12 months.

SOURCE: *FORBES*, OCTOBER 12, 2006

Forbes 200 Best Small Companies (continued)

Rank	Company	Five-Year Average ROE (%)	Rank	Company	Five-Year Average ROE (%)	Rank	Company	Five-Year Average ROE (%)
151	Comstock Resources	15	171	QLogic	13	191	Tootsie Roll Industries	13
152	Speedway Motorsports	13	172	Benihana	11	192	Carbo Ceramics	17
153	Symbion	13	173	National Instruments	10	193	Jack Henry & Associates	16
154	Dril-Quip	7	174	Jackson Hewitt Tax Service	9	194	ATMI	3
155	Twin Disc	8	175	American Dental Partners	9	195	ViaSat	4
156	Universal Stainless & Alloy Products	9	176	Exponent	11	196	Aeroflex	5
157	Haemonetics	13	177	Universal Electronics	10	197	Willamette Valley Vineyards	5
158	Ezcorp	6	178	J&J Snack Foods	11	198	Standard Microsystems	3
159	Interactive Data	8	179	ADAM	18	199	MapInfo	2
160	Oakley	15	180	ICU Medical	12	200	Anaren	4
161	Marlin Business Services	14	181	Christopher & Banks	25			
162	Cash America International	9	182	Ladish	6			
163	NN	9	183	Boston Beer	15			
164	TETRA Technologies	11	184	Kaydon	11			
165	Steven Madden	13	185	Vital Signs	13			
166	Mobile Mini	11	186	Courier	17			
167	Monro Muffler Brake	12	187	Gorman-Rupp	9			
168	Buckle	14	188	Napco Security Systems	9			
169	Heico	8	189	Met-Pro	11			
170	Cass Information Systems	14	190	Microsemi	5			

Forbes Fastest-Growing Tech Companies

Rank	Company	Industry	Five-Year Annualized Sales Growth (%)
1	Illumina	Biotechnology equipment	250
2	Google	Online search engine	222
3	Growthforce.com	Growth management software	117
4	Monolithic Power Systems	Semiconductors	81
5	Altiris	Software	76
6	Martek Biosciences	Nutritional supplements	70
7	Euronet Worldwide	Banking software	69
8	Cephalon	Biotechnology	65
9	Sonic Solutions	Software for digital media	59
10	WebEx Communications	Internet videoconferencing	59
11	Websense	Web security software	51
12	Celgene	Biotechnology	47
13	Cognizant Technology Solutions	IT services	47
14	NAVTEQ	Digital maps	46
15	Digital River	E-commerce services	45
16	MTC Technologies	IT services	40
17	LifeCell	Biotechnology	40
18	NII Holdings	Wireless telecom services	35
19	Genentech	Biotechnology	34
20	DRS Technologies	Aerospace, defense	34
21	SRA International	Government IT services	32
22	Color Kinetics	LED lighting systems	32
23	Amgen	Biotechnology	31
24	Online Resources	IT services for finance cos.	28
25	Dolby Laboratories	Audio equipment, software	26

SOURCE: *FORBES*, JANUARY 26, 2007

Hoover's Handbook of

Emerging Companies

The Companies

II-VI Incorporated

II-VI maintains a laser-like focus on focusing lasers. The company (pronounced "two-six") makes lenses, mirrors, prisms, and other optical components used to manipulate laser beams. The company's 5,000-plus clients — drawn from the industrial, military, health care, and telecom equipment sectors — employ these components in lasers for precision manufacturing, fiber-optic transmission and reception, and other applications. Through its eV unit, II-VI makes X-ray and gamma-ray products for nuclear radiation detection; subsidiary VLOC makes laser and sensing system parts and materials. The company also offers specialized military infrared optics, commercial optics, and custom coatings.

II-VI has expanded its toolbox through both internal R&D and acquisitions.

The company gets about 40% of sales outside the US.

II-VI owns 36% of 5NPlus, a supplier of high-purity antimony, cadmium, selenium, tellurium, and zinc — all materials that go into II-VI products, among other elements.

Founder, chairman, and CEO Carl Johnson owns about 15% of II-VI. Lord, Abbett & Co. holds around 9% of the company. Babson Capital Management has an equity stake of nearly 7%.

HISTORY

Electrical engineer Carl Johnson, who had worked at Bell Labs (now part of Lucent), among other companies, founded II-VI in 1971 to produce infrared optical materials for the emerging laser market. These materials — including cadmium zinc telluride, zinc selenide, and zinc sulfide — gave the company its name; they are from the "two-six" family of materials. (Cadmium and zinc are from column two on the periodic table; tellurium and selenium are from column six.)

By the 1980s II-VI was the leading maker of optical components for carbon dioxide lasers. The company went public in 1987 and the next year added a factory in Singapore.

Decreased military spending during the early 1990s stifled II-VI's growth. To compensate, the company invested: it acquired eV PRODUCTS in 1992 and Sandoz Chemicals' Virgo Optics Division (now VLOC) in 1994. The company opened a factory in China in 1996.

In 1999 II-VI formed a new division, Electronic & Photonic Materials, to develop uses for silicon carbide and sapphire materials. That year II-VI acquired 15% of rival Laser Power.

II-VI completed its acquisition of Laser Power in 2001. That year it also purchased Silicon Carbide (SiC) Group from Litton Systems (now part of Northrop Grumman). In 2003 II-VI consolidated Laser Power's operations into other branches of the company.

In late 2004 the company bought Dallas-based Marlow Industries for around $31 million in cash. Marlow became an operating unit of II-VI's Compound Semiconductor Group.

In 2005 the company set plans to establish a silicon carbide semiconductor substrate manufacturing facility in Mississippi in cooperation with Mississippi State University and SemiSouth Laboratories. II-VI also made an equity investment in SemiSouth.

In mid-2005 the company acquired the 25% equity interest in II-VI Deutschland GmbH it didn't already own, buying the minority equity stake from L.O.T.-Oriel Laser Optik GmbH & Co. KG.

EXECUTIVES

Chairman and CEO: Carl J. Johnson, age 64, $851,000 pay
President, COO, and Director: Francis J. Kramer, age 57, $697,000 pay
CFO and Treasurer: Craig A. Creaturo, age 36, $375,000 pay
EVP, Infrared Optics: Herman E. Reedy, age 63, $443,000 pay
VP; General Manager, Compound Semiconductor Group: Vincent D. (Chuck) Mattera Jr., age 50, $412,000 pay
VP, Government and Military Businesses: James Martinelli, age 48, $269,000 pay
Secretary: Robert D. German
Auditors: Deloitte & Touche LLP

LOCATIONS

HQ: II-VI Incorporated
   375 Saxonburg Blvd., Saxonburg, PA 16056
Phone: 724-352-4455   **Fax:** 724-352-5284
Web: www.ii-vi.com

II-VI has manufacturing and office facilities in Belgium, China, Germany, Japan, Singapore, Switzerland, the UK, the US, and Vietnam.

2006 Sales

	$ mil.	% of total
US	156.2	67
Europe		
Germany	23.1	10
Switzerland	9.8	4
UK	9.5	4
Belgium	4.1	2
Asia/Pacific		
Japan	23.6	10
Singapore	6.1	3
China	0.1	—
Total	**232.5**	**100**

PRODUCTS/OPERATIONS

2006 Sales

	$ mil.	% of total
Infrared Optics	120.4	52
Compound Semiconductors	48.7	21
Near-Infrared Optics	34.0	14
Military-Infrared Optics	29.4	13
Total	**232.5**	**100**

Selected Products

Beam expanders
Beam splitters
Detectors
Etalons
Laser crystals
  Clear yttrium aluminum garnet (YAG) laser crystals
  Custom crystals and fluorides
  Machined and polished laser rods
  Monolithic crystal assemblies (MCA)
  Neodymium doped YAG
  Nonlinear crystals
  Oxide laser crystal products
  Ruby laser crystals

Laser gain materials
Lenses
Military infrared optics
Mirrors
Modulators
Optical assemblies
Optical coatings
Output windows
Partial reflectors
Phase retarders
Polarization devices
Prisms
Rhombs
Solid-state laser optics and optical cavities
Substrates
Wave plates

COMPETITORS

Coherent
Cymer
DRS Technologies
Ferrotec
Goodrich
Jenoptik
Laird Technologies
LightPath
Newport
Northrop Grumman
Orbotech
Raytheon
Rohm and Haas
Saint-Gobain
Spectra-Physics
Sumitomo
Zygo

HISTORICAL FINANCIALS

Company Type: Public

Income Statement

FYE: June 30

	REVENUE ($ mil.)	NET INCOME ($ mil.)	NET PROFIT MARGIN	EMPLOYEES
6/06	232.5	10.8	4.6%	1,690
6/05	194.0	24.8	12.8%	1,548
6/04	150.9	17.3	11.5%	1,242
6/03	128.2	11.6	9.0%	1,094
6/02	113.7	7.3	6.4%	976
Annual Growth	**19.6%**	**10.3%**	**—**	**14.7%**

2006 Year-End Financials

Debt ratio: 13.8%
Return on equity: 6.6%
Cash ($ mil.): 26.9
Current ratio: 2.83
Long-term debt ($ mil.): 23.6
No. of shares (mil.): 29.1

Dividends
  Yield: —
  Payout: —
Market value ($ mil.): 533.3
R&D as % of sales: —
Advertising as % of sales: —

Stock History

NASDAQ (GS): IIVI

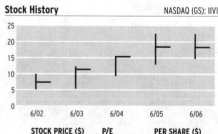

	STOCK PRICE ($) FY Close	P/E High/Low		PER SHARE ($) Earnings	Dividends	Book Value
6/06	18.30	62	41	0.36	—	5.85
6/05	18.39	27	16	0.83	—	5.44
6/04	15.33	26	16	0.59	—	9.12
6/03	11.37	30	14	0.41	—	7.85
6/02	7.39	38	21	0.25	—	6.96
Annual Growth	**25.4%**	**—**	**—**	**9.5%**	**—**	**(4.2%)**

ACA Capital Holdings

ACA Capital assures bonds won't be broken. ACA Capital provides financial guaranty insurance, primarily for municipal bonds. It receives premiums in exchange for providing protection against payment defaults. Partnering with investment banks, ACA Capital's structured finance segment originates collateralized debt obligations (CDOs) for which it charges risk premiums and asset management fees. The firm also offers quantitative risk assessment. ACA Capital targets sectors historically underserved by financial guaranty insurers, including smaller customers with lower financial ratings. Chairman David King is a stockholder through Bear Stearns Merchant Banking which holds nearly 35% of the company's stock.

EXECUTIVES

Chairman: David E. King, age 47
Deputy Chairman, President, and CEO:
 Alan S. Roseman, age 49, $1,900,000 pay
EVP, CFO, and Director: Edward U. (Ted) Gilpin,
 $940,000 pay
EVP, Credit: William T. (Bill) Tomljanovic, age 43,
 $1,050,000 pay
EVP, Municipal Finance: Ruben Selles, age 53
Senior Managing Director, CDO Asset Management:
 Laura Schwartz, age 43, $885,000 pay
Senior Managing Director, Structured Credit:
 James A. Rothman, age 42, $900,000 pay
Managing Director and Chief Accounting Officer:
 Lisa Mumford
Managing Director and General Counsel: Nora Dahlman
Director, Human Resources: Eileen Hatcher
Director, Marketing and Corporate Communications:
 Cathy Bailey
Auditors: Deloitte & Touche LLP

LOCATIONS

HQ: ACA Capital Holdings, Inc.
 140 Broadway, 47th Fl., New York, NY 10005
Phone: 212-375-2000   **Fax:** 212-375-2100
Web: www.aca.com

ACA Capital operates all across the US.

PRODUCTS/OPERATIONS

2005 Sales

	$ mil.	% of total
Net investment income	254.6	76
Premiums earned	60.6	18
Fee income	11.1	3
Derivative income	8.6	3
Net realized gains (losses) on investments	(2.8)	—
Net realized & unrealized gains (losses) on derivative instruments	(1.7)	—
Other income	.2	—
Total	**330.6**	**100**

COMPETITORS

Ambac
Clinton Group
CNA Surety
FGIC
Financial Security Assurance
GSC Group
MBIA
Radian Group
St. Paul Travelers Bond
TCW

HISTORICAL FINANCIALS

Company Type: Public

Income Statement

FYE: December 31

	ASSETS ($ mil.)	NET INCOME ($ mil.)	INCOME AS % OF ASSETS	EMPLOYEES
12/05	5,798.2	28.8	0.5%	86
12/04	5,692.0	(3.8)	—	86
12/03	3,468.4	17.2	0.5%	87
12/02	915.6	4.6	0.5%	88
12/01	299.1	2.6	0.9%	—
Annual Growth	**109.8%**	**82.4%**	**—**	**(0.8%)**

2005 Year-End Financials

Equity as % of assets: 6.6%
Return on assets: 0.5%
Return on equity: 7.7%
Long-term debt ($ mil.): 2,254.6
Sales ($ mil.): 330.6

Net Income History

NYSE: ACA

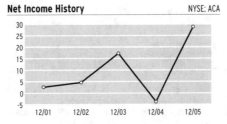

Accredited Home Lenders

Accredited Home Lenders is willing to give credit where it's due . . . or not. The mortgage banker originates, acquires, services, and sells subprime single-family mortgages for homebuyers who may not otherwise qualify, selling to customers throughout the US and in Canada. Accredited Home Lenders operates through a network of some 12,000 independent mortgage brokers. In addition to its wholesale operations, the firm's Home Funds Direct retail division has four regional offices and about 40 branch offices across the country (one-third of which are in California) responding to leads from the Internet, telemarketing, and direct marketing.

Accredited Home Lenders moved to boost its wholesale and retail operations in 2006 with the purchase of Aames Investment, which has about 75 retail branches and three regional wholesale offices. The company branched out internationally through the 2004 formation of a Canadian subsidiary. Some 90% of Accredited Home Lenders' mortgage loan originations are wholesale, conducted through mortgage brokers. It once operated retail branches under the name Axiom Financial Services, but merged its retail businesses under the Home Funds Direct name in 2004. Accredited Home Lenders originated more than $16 billion of mortgage loans in 2005. Chairman and CEO James Konrath owns about 9% of Accredited Home Lenders.

EXECUTIVES

Chairman and CEO: James A. Konrath, age 59,
 $925,673 pay
President, COO, and Director: Joseph J. Lydon, age 47,
 $925,673 pay
CFO: John S. Buchanan, age 50, $339,423 pay
CIO: Larry Murphy, age 64
EVP, Finance and Capital Markets:
 Stuart D. (Stu) Marvin, age 46, $1,082,168 pay (partial-
 year salary)
Director, Human Resources and Administration:
 Joseph F. (Joe) Weinbrecht, age 60
Director, Corporate Communications:
 Richard W. (Rick) Howe
Director, Marketing: Roxane W. Helstrom, age 49
Director, Operations: Jeffrey W. (Jeff) Crawford, age 51,
 $588,341 pay
General Counsel: David E. Hertzel, age 51
Auditors: Grant Thornton LLP

LOCATIONS

HQ: Accredited Home Lenders Holding Co.
 15090 Avenue of Science, Ste. 200,
 San Diego, CA 92128
Phone: 858-676-2100   **Fax:** 858-676-2170
Web: www.accredhome.com

Accredited Home Lenders operates more than 60 offices throughout the US and one in Canada.

PRODUCTS/OPERATIONS

2005 Sales

	$ mil.	% of total
Interest income	610.1	65
Gain on loan sales	313.1	33
Loan servicing income	10.7	1
Other	7.5	1
Total	**941.4**	**100**

COMPETITORS

ACC Capital Holdings
Bank of America
BNC Mortgage
Citigroup
Countrywide Financial
JPMorgan Chase
Long Beach Mortgage
New Century Financial

HISTORICAL FINANCIALS

Company Type: Public

Income Statement

FYE: December 31

	ASSETS ($ mil.)	NET INCOME ($ mil.)	INCOME AS % OF ASSETS	EMPLOYEES
12/05	9,853.3	155.4	1.6%	2,762
12/04	6,688.4	130.8	2.0%	2,694
12/03	3,501.4	100.0	2.9%	2,056
12/02	1,807.3	28.8	1.6%	1,294
Annual Growth	**76.0%**	**75.4%**	**—**	**28.8%**

2005 Year-End Financials

Equity as % of assets: 5.6%
Return on assets: 1.9%
Return on equity: 33.9%
Long-term debt ($ mil.): 9,045.9
No. of shares (mil.): 21.3
Market value ($ mil.): 1,056.7
Dividends
 Yield: —
 Payout: —
Sales ($ mil.): 941.4
R&D as % of sales: —
Advertising as % of sales: 2.0%

Stock History

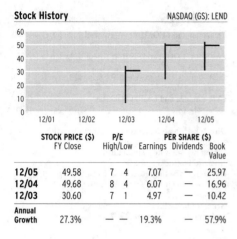

NASDAQ (GS): LEND

	STOCK PRICE ($) FY Close	P/E High/Low		PER SHARE ($) Earnings	Dividends	Book Value
12/05	49.58	7	4	7.07	—	25.97
12/04	49.68	8	4	6.07	—	16.96
12/03	30.60	7	1	4.97	—	10.42
Annual Growth	27.3%	—	—	19.3%	—	57.9%

ACE*COMM

ACE*COMM's got a whole lot of network data up its sleeve. The company provides data collection and analysis products for voice and data networks. ACE*COMM's products are used by telecommunications service providers to collect, manage, analyze, and distribute data collected from network elements. The company also offers products that enable enterprises (including corporations, government agencies, and educational institutions) to automate certain network operations, such as performance and fault management. Leading customers include Northrop Grumman.

In 2005 the company acquired Double Helix Solutions, known as 2helix, a supplier of network asset assurance, revenue optimization, and business intelligence software for telecommunications carriers. The purchase price was about $8 million.

ACE*COMM acquired the assets of i3 Mobile in 2003 and the assets of Intasys Billing Technologies in 2004, taking the company into the operations support systems (OSS) software market for telecom service providers.

EXECUTIVES

Chairman, CEO, and Treasurer: George T. Jimenez, age 70, $200,769 pay (prior to title change)
President: Jim Greenwell
SVP and CFO: Steven R. Delmar, age 50, $190,731 pay
SVP and Chief Marketing Officer:
  Christopher C. (Chris) Couch, age 36, $165,635 pay
Corporate Secretary and Director of Human Resources:
  Loretta L. Rivers, age 49
CTO: Jean-Francois Jodouin
Managing Director, European Business Development:
  Noga Confino
Media Relations: Marcie Weber
Auditors: Grant Thornton LLP

LOCATIONS

HQ: ACE*COMM Corporation
  704 Quince Orchard Rd., Ste. 100,
  Gaithersburg, MD 20878
Phone: 301-721-3000   **Fax:** 301-721-3001
Web: www.acecomm.com

2006 Sales

	$ mil.	% of total
North America		
US	11.4	43
Canada & Mexico	1.2	4
Europe	7.1	27
Africa & Middle East	3.5	13
Asia	3.1	12
South America	0.4	1
Total	**26.7**	**100**

PRODUCTS/OPERATIONS

2006 Sales by Customer

	$ mil.	% of total
Enterprise	10.2	38
Network service provider	10.1	38
Operations support systems	6.4	24
Total	**26.7**	**100**

Selected Products

Enterprise network management (NetPlus)
Network data collection and management (Convergent Mediation)

Selected Services

Consulting
Installation
Maintenance
Support
Systems integration
Training

COMPETITORS

Accenture
Amdocs
Boston Communications Group
CA
Comptel
Computer Sciences Corp.
Comverse
Convergys
EDS
Elron TeleSoft
Ericsson
Fujitsu Network Communications
Intec Telecom
MetaSolv
Narus
Paetec Communications
Telcordia
TeleSciences
Vallent
Veramark Technologies

HISTORICAL FINANCIALS

Company Type: Public

Income Statement

FYE: June 30

	REVENUE ($ mil.)	NET INCOME ($ mil.)	NET PROFIT MARGIN	EMPLOYEES
6/06	26.7	0.3	1.1%	128
6/05	20.0	(6.5)	—	146
6/04	13.7	(5.9)	—	142
6/03	13.8	(2.0)	—	97
6/02	18.1	(4.0)	—	113
Annual Growth	10.2%	—	—	3.2%

2006 Year-End Financials

Debt ratio: 0.3%
Return on equity: 5.2%
Cash ($ mil.): 0.9
Current ratio: 1.30
Long-term debt ($ mil.): 0.0
No. of shares (mil.): 17.8

Dividends
  Yield: —
  Payout: —
Market value ($ mil.): 48.6
R&D as % of sales: —
Advertising as % of sales: —

Stock History

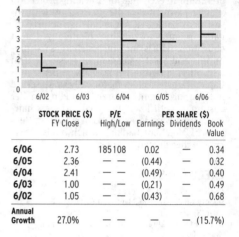

NASDAQ (GM): ACEC

	STOCK PRICE ($) FY Close	P/E High/Low		PER SHARE ($) Earnings	Dividends	Book Value
6/06	2.73	185	108	0.02	—	0.34
6/05	2.36	—	—	(0.44)	—	0.32
6/04	2.41	—	—	(0.49)	—	0.40
6/03	1.00	—	—	(0.21)	—	0.49
6/02	1.05	—	—	(0.43)	—	0.68
Annual Growth	27.0%	—	—	—	—	(15.7%)

ADA-ES

Coal: not just for the 19th century anymore. ADA-ES tries to make coal an economically and environmentally viable energy option once again. The company (which was spun off from Earth Sciences in 2003) makes environmental technology systems and specialty chemicals that reduce emissions at coal-burning power plants. It offers integrated mercury control systems, as well as flue gas conditioning and combustion aid chemicals. ADA-ES also provides consulting and testing services and mercury measurement equipment. In 2005 some 21% of the company's sales came from government contracts.

EXECUTIVES

President, CEO, and Director:
  Michael D. (Mike) Durham, age 56
SVP, CFO, Secretary, and Director: Mark H. McKinnies, age 54
COO: C. Jean Bustard, age 48
VP, Sales and Marketing: Jonathan S. (Jon) Barr, age 48
VP, Business Development, Utility Systems:
  Richard L. Miller, age 51
VP, Contract Research and Development:
  Richard J. Schlager, age 54
Human Resources and Office Manager:
  Beth Turner-Graziano

LOCATIONS

HQ: ADA-ES, Inc.
  8100 SouthPark Way, Unit B, Littleton, CO 80120
Phone: 303-734-1727   **Fax:** 303-734-0330
Web: www.adaes.com

PRODUCTS/OPERATIONS

2005 Sales

	$ mil.	% of total
Mercury emission control	8.8	80
Flue gas conditioning & consulting	1.9	17
Combustion aids & consulting	0.3	3
Total	**11.0**	**100**

COMPETITORS

Calgon Carbon	Thermatrix
Donaldson	Wahlco
Ebara	Wheelabrator
Marsulex	Woodward

HISTORICAL FINANCIALS

Company Type: Public

Income Statement

FYE: December 31

	REVENUE ($ mil.)	NET INCOME ($ mil.)	NET PROFIT MARGIN	EMPLOYEES
12/05	11.0	0.7	6.4%	32
12/04	8.4	0.3	3.6%	27
12/03	5.9	0.4	6.8%	21
12/02	5.7	0.5	8.8%	—
Annual Growth	**24.5%**	**11.9%**	**—**	**23.4%**

2005 Year-End Financials

Debt ratio: —
Return on equity: 3.7%
Cash ($ mil.): 16.5
Current ratio: 7.04
Long-term debt ($ mil.): —
No. of shares (mil.): 5.6

Dividends
Yield: —
Payout: —
Market value ($ mil.): 102.3
R&D as % of sales: 8.9%
Advertising as % of sales: —

Stock History

NASDAQ (CM): ADES

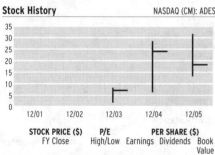

	STOCK PRICE ($) FY Close	P/E High/Low		Earnings	PER SHARE ($) Dividends	Book Value
12/05	18.24	241	104	0.13	—	4.61
12/04	24.01	353	83	0.08	—	2.50
12/03	7.10	67	17	0.12	—	0.83
Annual Growth	**60.3%**	**—**	**—**	**4.1%**	**—**	**135.8%**

Adams Respiratory Therapeutics

Adams Respiratory Therapeutics is responsible for more productive coughs. Formerly known as Adams Laboratories, the firm makes over-the-counter remedies for respiratory ailments. The drugmaker's best-selling Mucinex-branded products are expectorants that rely on guaifenesin to help move excess mucus out of the body. Its other products include Humibid (a maximum-strength expectorant) and Delsym (a time-released cough suppressant). Adams'

products are sold at food, drug, and mass retail stores in the US. Wholesale drug distribution accounts for about a quarter of Adams' sales.

Guaifenesin was a standard ingredient in cold and cough remedies for years, but Adams Respiratory managed to press it into a two-layered, time-released form, making it effective up to 12 hours. After the successful launch of its basic 600 mg Mucinex product, the company created other formulations with other ingredients including pseudoephedrine (decongestant) and dextromethorphan (cough suppressant), as well as a children's formula.

The company has approval to market similar, but stronger, products marketed under the name Humibid and styled more as a "professional" brand. However, its plan to sell Humibid products from behind the pharmacy counters, and market it through word of mouth and recommendations from pharmacists and pharmacy technicians did not meet expectations.

Adams and niche drug company Cornerstone Biopharma swapped brands in early 2005. Adams transferred its AlleRx brands (allergy, sinus, and cold remedies) to Cornerstone; in return, Cornerstone reassigned its Humibid brand to Adams. In 2006, Adams acquired the Delsym branded products from UCB and immediately integrated them into its portfolio.

One of the company's key business strategies is to shift its customer base from doctors to consumers, i.e., roll customers over to OTC products from prescriptive products. It also plans to continue in its brand-acquisitive phase.

Adams' products are manufactured by Cardinal Health. In 2006, however, Adams bought back its former plant in Fort Worth, Texas, with plans to resume some of its own manufacturing. Cardinal is also one of Adams' top customers, as are fellow wholesale giants AmerisourceBergen and McKesson. CVS, Wal-Mart, Walgreens, Albertsons, Safeway, Target, and Rite Aid are among the drugmaker's top retail customers.

EXECUTIVES

Chairman: Harold F. Oberkfell, age 60
President, CEO, and Director:
Michael J. (Mike) Valentino, age 52, $1,430,000 pay
EVP, CFO, and Treasurer: David (Dave) Becker, age 40, $546,250 pay
EVP, Chief Legal and Compliance Officer, and Secretary: Walter E. (Walt) Riehemann, age 40, $487,500 pay
COO: Robert (Bob) Casale, age 48, $546,250 pay
EVP, Sales and Business Development:
John S. Thievon, age 38, $482,500 pay
SVP and General Manager, Manufacturing and Operations: Thomas L. Long
SVP, Research and Development: Helmut H. Albrecht, age 50
VP, Investor and Public Relations: Janet M. Barth
EVP, Human Resources: Peter D. Wentworth, age 51
Auditors: Ernst & Young LLP

LOCATIONS

HQ: Adams Respiratory Therapeutics, Inc.
4 Mill Ridge Ln., Mill Ridge Farm, Chester, NJ 07930
Phone: 908-879-1400   **Fax:** 908-879-9191
Web: www.adamslaboratories.com

COMPETITORS

Bayer
Johnson & Johnson
McNeil
Novartis
Pfizer
Procter & Gamble
Schering-Plough
Wyeth
Wyeth Pharmaceuticals

HISTORICAL FINANCIALS

Company Type: Public

Income Statement

FYE: June 30

	REVENUE ($ mil.)	NET INCOME ($ mil.)	NET PROFIT MARGIN	EMPLOYEES
6/06	239.1	46.3	19.4%	209
6/05	160.2	27.0	16.9%	176
6/04	61.3	35.8	58.4%	—
6/03	14.0	(22.6)	—	—
Annual Growth	**157.5%**	**—**	**—**	**18.8%**

2006 Year-End Financials

Debt ratio: —
Return on equity: —
Cash ($ mil.): 57.0
Current ratio: 3.52
Long-term debt ($ mil.): —
No. of shares (mil.): 34.9

Dividends
Yield: —
Payout: —
Market value ($ mil.): 1,556.1
R&D as % of sales: —
Advertising as % of sales: —

Stock History

NASDAQ (GS): ARXT

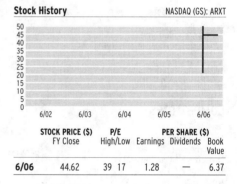

	STOCK PRICE ($) FY Close	P/E High/Low		Earnings	PER SHARE ($) Dividends	Book Value
6/06	44.62	39	17	1.28	—	6.37

Adeza Biomedical

Say what you want about early birds getting worms, Adeza Biomedical knows that early babies are something to be concerned about. The company develops and sells diagnostic testing products for women's health care, specifically pregnancy, infertility, and other reproductive disorders. Its FullTerm test checks levels of fetal fibronectin that breaks down as delivery approaches, allowing obstetricians to assess the risk of preterm labor and premature birth. Adeza Biomedical also offers the E-tegrity diagnostic test, which can indicate infertility and the likelihood of pregnancy. The firm is developing diagnostics for cancer and to predict the success of inducing labor and likelihood of full-term delivery.

The FullTerm tests are analyzed by the TLiIQ system, a compact unit that is available to hospitals. E-tegrity tests are administered by doctors and processed by the company's Adeza Diagnostic Services laboratory.

Adeza is hoping for FDA approval for Gestiva, a drug intended to prevent premature births. Clinical studies of the drug showed a statistically significant reduction in preterm births (less than 37 weeks of pregnancy) for the women who took it, but they also raised concerns about possible increased risk of miscarriage and stillbirth.

Chairman Andrew Senyei owns about 11% of the company; director Craig C. Taylor holds 5%.

EXECUTIVES

Chairman: Andrew E. (Drew) Senyei, age 56
President, CEO, and Director: Emory V. Anderson, age 52, $549,899 pay
SVP, Finance and Administration and CFO: Mark D. Fischer-Colbrie, age 50
SVP, Medical Affairs: Durlin E. Hickok, age 58
SVP, Sales and Marketing: Marian E. Sacco, age 52
VP, Research and Development: Robert O. Hussa, age 64, $238,733 pay
Human Resources Manager: Judy Wilson
Auditors: Ernst & Young LLP

LOCATIONS

HQ: Adeza Biomedical Corporation
1240 Elko Dr., Sunnyvale, CA 94089
Phone: 408-745-0975 **Fax:** 408-745-0968
Web: www.adeza.com

PRODUCTS/OPERATIONS

Selected Products

Approved
E-tegrity (infertility)
FullTerm (premature delivery)
In Development
Oncofetal fibronectin test (bladder cancer)
SalEst (preterm birth)

COMPETITORS

Beckman Coulter
Columbia Laboratories
Esoterix
Inverness Medical Innovations
LabCorp
Quest Diagnostics
Vysis

HISTORICAL FINANCIALS

Company Type: Public

Income Statement — FYE: December 31

	REVENUE ($ mil.)	NET INCOME ($ mil.)	NET PROFIT MARGIN	EMPLOYEES
12/05	43.6	12.3	28.2%	103
12/04	33.6	8.9	26.5%	83
12/03	26.5	3.2	12.1%	—
12/02	15.3	(0.3)	—	—
Annual Growth	41.8%	—	—	24.1%

2005 Year-End Financials

Debt ratio: —
Return on equity: 13.7%
Cash ($ mil.): 89.7
Current ratio: 12.74
Long-term debt ($ mil.): —
No. of shares (mil.): 17.4
Dividends
  Yield: —
  Payout: —
Market value ($ mil.): 366.9
R&D as % of sales: 11.7%
Advertising as % of sales: 3.1%

Stock History — NASDAQ (GS): ADZA

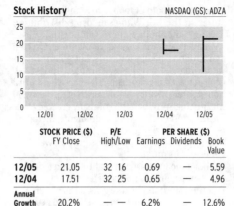

	STOCK PRICE ($) FY Close	P/E High/Low		PER SHARE ($) Earnings	Dividends	Book Value
12/05	21.05	32	16	0.69	—	5.59
12/04	17.51	32	25	0.65	—	4.96
Annual Growth	20.2%	—	—	6.2%	—	12.6%

Advanced Analogic Technologies

Advanced Analogic Technologies tries to take an advanced approach to analog chip technology. The company, known as AnalogicTech, provides specialized power management semiconductors for use in a variety of computing, communications, and consumer electronics applications. AnalogicTech's chips go into digital audio players, digital cameras, notebook and tablet computers, and wireless handsets. The company's investors include Samsung Electronics. Another Korean company, LG Electronics, accounts for 37% of sales. AnalogicTech gets most of its revenues from Asian customers.

Sales are about evenly divided between end users on one side and distributors, original design manufacturers, and contract electronics manufacturers on the other side.

AnalogicTech has acquired the power management analog business of IPCore Technologies, including IPCore's Analog Power Semiconductor (AP Semi) subsidiary, and related assets for about $22 million in cash. The Shanghai-based AP Semi develops components for mobile electronics.

FMR (Fidelity Investments) owns about 10% of AnalogicTech, while Battery Ventures holds more than 7% of the company. Investor Philippe Laffont has an equity stake of nearly 6% in AnalogicTech. CEO Richard Williams owns more than 5% of the company.

EXECUTIVES

Chairman: Samuel J. Anderson, age 49
President, CEO, CTO, and Director:
Richard K. Williams, age 47, $309,924 pay
VP, Worldwide Finance, CFO, and Secretary:
Brian R. McDonald, age 49, $319,000 pay
VP, Engineering: Kevin P. D'Angelo, age 46, $311,912 pay
VP, Marketing and Business Development:
Jan O. G. Nilsson, age 46, $312,680 pay
VP, Technology: Jun-Wei Chen, age 55
VP, Worldwide Operations: Allen K. Lam, age 42, $289,750 pay
VP, Worldwide Sales: Nicholas A. Aretakis, age 44
Auditors: Deloitte & Touche LLP

LOCATIONS

HQ: Advanced Analogic Technologies Incorporated
830 E. Arques Ave., Sunnyvale, CA 94085
Phone: 408-737-4600 **Fax:** 408-737-4611
Web: www.analogictech.com

Advanced Analogic Technologies has facilities in China, France, Hong Kong, Japan, South Korea, Sweden, Taiwan, the UK, and the US.

2005 Sales

	$ mil.	% of total
Asia		
South Korea	39.9	59
Taiwan	13.9	20
China	10.3	15
Japan	1.6	2
Europe	1.8	3
North America	0.8	1
Total	**68.3**	**100**

PRODUCTS/OPERATIONS

2005 Sales

	$ mil.	% of total
Power management ICs	50.8	74
Application-specific power MOSFETs	17.0	25
Other	0.5	1
Total	**68.3**	**100**

COMPETITORS

Analog Devices
International Rectifier
Linear Technology
Maxim Integrated Products
Microsemi
National Semiconductor
ON Semiconductor
Semtech
Siliconix
Texas Instruments
Vishay Intertechnology
Volterra

HISTORICAL FINANCIALS

Company Type: Public

Income Statement — FYE: December 31

	REVENUE ($ mil.)	NET INCOME ($ mil.)	NET PROFIT MARGIN	EMPLOYEES
12/05	68.3	2.1	3.1%	200
12/04	51.3	15.2	29.6%	183
12/03	26.5	0.9	3.4%	—
Annual Growth	60.5%	52.8%	—	9.3%

2005 Year-End Financials

Debt ratio: —
Return on equity: 2.3%
Cash ($ mil.): 124.4
Current ratio: 13.47
Long-term debt ($ mil.): —
No. of shares (mil.): 43.2
Dividends
  Yield: —
  Payout: —
Market value ($ mil.): 597.8
R&D as % of sales: 28.5%
Advertising as % of sales: 0.9%

Stock History — NASDAQ (GS): AATI

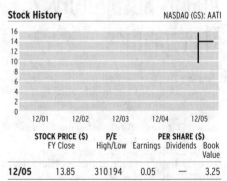

	STOCK PRICE ($) FY Close	P/E High/Low		PER SHARE ($) Earnings	Dividends	Book Value
12/05	13.85	310	194	0.05	—	3.25

Advanced Environmental Recycling

It may not turn straw into gold, but Advanced Environmental Recycling Technologies (AERT) does practice a kind of alchemy by turning recycled plastics and wood filler into building materials for windows, doors, floors, and decks. AERT recycles waste plastics and plastic byproducts of paper-recycling mills at plants in Louisiana and Arkansas. The recycled plastic then goes to AERT manufacturing plants in Arkansas and Texas, where it is combined with cedar or hardwood fiber to create composite building materials. AERT markets its products under the MoistureShield, ChoiceDek, CornerLoc, and LifeCycle names. Weyerhaeuser is AERT's largest customer (nearly 80% of sales). The founding Brooks family controls AERT.

EXECUTIVES

Chairman, President, and Co-CEO: Joe G. Brooks, age 50, $335,625 pay
Vice Chairman: Sal Miwa, age 49
Co-CEO and Director: Stephen W. Brooks, age 49, $151,423 pay
SVP and CFO: Robert A. Thayer, age 54, $217,500 pay
SVP, Logistics, Laboratories, and Plastic Operations: Alford Drinkwater, age 54, $107,000 pay
SVP, Raw Materials: J. Douglas Brooks, age 46, $117,500 pay
SVP, Sales and Marketing: James (Jim) Precht, age 60, $192,500 pay
Secretary, Treasurer, and Director: Marjorie S. Brooks, age 70
Director, Human Resources: Marcy Zahm
Auditors: Tullius Taylor Sartain & Sartain LLP

LOCATIONS

HQ: Advanced Environmental Recycling Technologies, Inc.
914 N. Jefferson St., Springdale, AR 72764
Phone: 479-756-7400 **Fax:** 479-756-7410
Web: www.aertinc.com

Advanced Environmental Recycling Technologies has manufacturing plants in Springdale, Lowell, and Tontitown, Arkansas; Junction, Texas; and Alexandria, Louisiana.

PRODUCTS/OPERATIONS

2005 Sales

	$ mil.	% of total
Commercial & residential decking surface components	73.4	84
Exterior door, window & housing trim components	13.9	16
Total	**87.3**	**100**

Selected Product Applications

Commercial and residential decking components
Exterior door components
Fencing
Industrial flooring
Ramps and handrails

COMPETITORS

CertainTeed	Plastic Lumber
ElkCorp	Trex Company
Louisiana-Pacific	Trimax
NEW Plastics	

HISTORICAL FINANCIALS

Company Type: Public

Income Statement — FYE: December 31

	REVENUE ($ mil.)	NET INCOME ($ mil.)	NET PROFIT MARGIN	EMPLOYEES
12/05	87.3	7.8	8.9%	670
12/04	63.6	1.3	2.0%	585
12/03	43.5	2.3	5.3%	388
12/02	41.4	1.2	2.9%	410
12/01	33.2	0.6	1.8%	382
Annual Growth	**27.3%**	**89.9%**	**—**	**15.1%**

2005 Year-End Financials

Debt ratio: 80.5%
Return on equity: 47.5%
Cash ($ mil.): 2.4
Current ratio: 0.96
Long-term debt ($ mil.): 17.0
No. of shares (mil.): 37.7
Dividends
Yield: —
Payout: —
Market value ($ mil.): 67.4
R&D as % of sales: 0.1%
Advertising as % of sales: 1.7%

Stock History — NASDAQ (CM): AERT

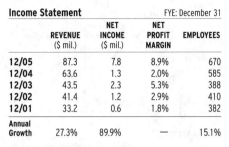

	STOCK PRICE ($) FY Close	P/E High/Low		PER SHARE ($) Earnings	Dividends	Book Value
12/05	1.79	10	6	0.19	—	0.56
12/04	1.27	57	33	0.03	—	0.37
12/03	1.57	26	14	0.07	—	0.31
12/02	1.20	137	55	0.02	—	0.20
12/01	1.15	160	71	0.01	—	0.15
Annual Growth	**11.7%**	**—**	**—**	**108.8%**	**—**	**38.0%**

Affiliated Managers Group

AMG knows a good asset when it sees one — and it knows how to make the most of the ones it finds. Affiliated Managers Group (AMG) is an asset management company that owns interests in more than 30 midsized investment management firms. The company typically acquires majority stakes of between 50% and 70% in its affiliates, firms that cater to institutional investors and wealthy individuals. AMG's structure lets affiliates retain partial ownership of their firms and operate with relative autonomy. The company usually contracts to allocate a percentage of revenues to affiliates for such operating expenses as salaries and bonuses.

Together, AMG's affiliates manage more than $180 billion in assets through some 300 invest-ment products, including more than 100 mutual funds. AMG's largest mutual fund families include Tweedy, Browne's Global Value and American Value funds, Brandywine funds, Third Avenue Value funds, and The Managers Fund.

In 2005 AMG purchased a family of mutual funds from the Fremont Group's Fremont Investment Advisors, which has been beleaguered by improper trading allegations. It further added to its affiliate ranks — and also boosted its presence outside the US — by acquiring First Asset Management, a holding company for six Canadian asset managers. The firms included in the deal collectively manage some $25 billion.

AMG's Managers Investment Group provides an avenue through which AMG affiliates can distribute mutual funds and other products through intermediaries such as banks or brokerage firms. Its DFD Select Group makes available alternative investments to international high-net-worth and institutional clients.

EXECUTIVES

Chairman: William J. (Bill) Nutt, age 61
CEO, President, and Director: Sean M. Healey, age 45
EVP and COO: Nathaniel Dalton, age 39
EVP, CFO, and Treasurer: Darrell W. Crate, age 39
SVP and General Counsel: John Kingston III
SVP and Director of Marketing, Managers Investment Group: Bill Fergusson
VP, Corporate Communications: Brett S. Perryman
VP, Finance and Accounting: Daniel J. Shea
Auditors: PricewaterhouseCoopers LLP

LOCATIONS

HQ: Affiliated Managers Group, Inc.
600 Hale St., Prides Crossing, MA 01965
Phone: 617-747-3300 **Fax:** 617-747-3380
Web: www.amg.com

PRODUCTS/OPERATIONS

2005 Sales

	$ mil.	% of total
Mutual fund	400.3	44
Institutional	384.5	42
High net worth	131.7	14
Total	**916.5**	**100**

COMPETITORS

AllianceBernstein	Neuberger Berman
Asset Alliance	Nuveen
Conning	Old Mutual (US)
Federated Investors	Phoenix Investment
FMR	Partners
GAMCO Investors	T. Rowe Price
Gundaker/Jordan American	UBS Financial Services
Investment Advisers	U.S. Trust
Merrill Lynch	The Vanguard Group
National Financial Partners	

HISTORICAL FINANCIALS

Company Type: Public

Income Statement — FYE: December 31

	ASSETS ($ mil.)	NET INCOME ($ mil.)	INCOME AS % OF ASSETS	EMPLOYEES
12/05	2,321.6	119.1	5.1%	1,270
12/04	1,933.4	77.2	4.0%	974
12/03	1,519.2	60.5	4.0%	822
12/02	1,243.0	55.9	4.5%	849
12/01	1,160.3	50.0	4.3%	795
Annual Growth	**18.9%**	**24.2%**	**—**	**12.4%**

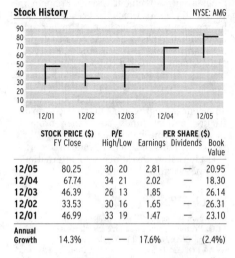

2005 Year-End Financials

Equity as % of assets: 35.2%
Return on assets: 5.6%
Return on equity: 15.6%
Long-term debt ($ mil.): 899.7
No. of shares (mil.): 39.0
Market value ($ mil.): 3,131.7

Dividends
Yield: —
Payout: —
Sales ($ mil.): 916.5
R&D as % of sales: —
Advertising as % of sales: —

Stock History

NYSE: AMG

	STOCK PRICE ($) FY Close	P/E High/Low		Earnings	PER SHARE ($) Dividends	Book Value
12/05	80.25	30	20	2.81	—	20.95
12/04	67.74	34	21	2.02	—	18.30
12/03	46.39	26	13	1.85	—	26.14
12/02	33.53	30	16	1.65	—	26.31
12/01	46.99	33	19	1.47	—	23.10
Annual Growth	14.3%	—	—	17.6%	—	(2.4%)

Affirmative Insurance

Affirmative Insurance Holdings insures the old, the bad, and the ugly drivers. The company sells non-standard auto insurance (coverage for individuals with bad driving records and/or limited financial resources) in about a dozen states, with its largest presence in California, Florida, Illinois, and Texas. Affirmative Insurance Holdings operates through its two subsidiaries, Affirmative Insurance and Insura Property and Casualty, and close to 225 owned or franchised retail store locations. Vesta Insurance Group, which held a 42% stake in the company in early 2005, sold a portion of its interest back to Affirmative Insurance Holdings and the rest to investment group New Affirmative LLC.

Affirmative Insurance Holdings acquired Michigan-based underwriting agency IPA, LLC, in 2005. The agency generates personal nonstandard auto insurance premiums of about $20 million annually.

EXECUTIVES

Chairman and CEO: Kevin R. Callahan, age 44
COO: Robert Bondi, age 44
EVP; President, Underwriting: M. Sean McPadden, age 40, $332,077 pay
EVP and CFO: Mark E. Pape, age 55, $35,712 pay (partial-year salary)
SVP and CIO: Emil G. Sommerlad, age 62
SVP and Chief Claims Officer: Wilson A. Wheeler, age 51
SVP Human Resources: Chad M. Emmerich, age 35
SVP, Chief Accounting Officer, and Treasurer: Scott K. Billings, age 43, $238,342 pay
SVP, Associate General Counsel, and Secretary: David B. Snyder, age 44
Chief Marketing Officer: Charlene Barnard, age 46
President, Retail: Alan T. Rasof, age 41
General Counsel: Joseph Fisher, age 36
Investor Relations: Stewart P. Yee
Auditors: KPMG LLP

LOCATIONS

HQ: Affirmative Insurance Holdings, Inc.
4450 Sojourn Dr., Ste. 500, Addison, TX 75001
Phone: 972-728-6300 **Fax:** 972-991-0882
Web: www.affirmativeholdings.com

COMPETITORS

AIG
Allstate
Auto-Owners Insurance
Bristol West
Direct General
Farmers Group
First Acceptance
GEICO
GMAC Insurance
The Hartford
Infinity Property
 & Casualty
Progressive Corporation
Safe Auto
State Farm

HISTORICAL FINANCIALS

Company Type: Public

Income Statement

FYE: December 31

	ASSETS ($ mil.)	NET INCOME ($ mil.)	INCOME AS % OF ASSETS	EMPLOYEES
12/05	544.1	18.3	3.4%	1,203
12/04	520.9	24.4	4.7%	1,218
12/03	314.6	19.1	6.1%	—
12/02	297.7	13.7	4.6%	—
Annual Growth	22.3%	—	—	(1.2%)

2005 Year-End Financials

Equity as % of assets: 36.8%
Return on assets: 3.4%
Return on equity: 9.0%
Long-term debt ($ mil.): 56.7
No. of shares (mil.): 15.4
Market value ($ mil.): 225.2

Dividends
Yield: 0.5%
Payout: 7.0%
Sales ($ mil.): 381.5
R&D as % of sales: —
Advertising as % of sales: —

Stock History

NASDAQ (GS): AFFM

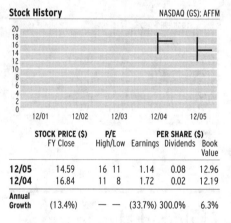

	STOCK PRICE ($) FY Close	P/E High/Low		Earnings	PER SHARE ($) Dividends	Book Value
12/05	14.59	16	11	1.14	0.08	12.96
12/04	16.84	11	8	1.72	0.02	12.19
Annual Growth	(13.4%)	—	—	(33.7%)	300.0%	6.3%

Akamai Technologies

Akamai Technologies wasn't content to confine itself to the delivery business. The company's EdgePlatform technology enables companies and government agencies to deliver Web content and applications, such as ads, video, and other high-bandwidth content. Through its network of some 15,000 servers in nearly 70 countries, Akamai's services analyze and manage Web traffic, transmitting content from the server geographically closest to the end user. The company serves more than 1,800 customers, including Airbus, Apple, Best Buy, FedEx, Microsoft, MTV Networks, Sony Ericsson Mobile

Communications, the US Department of Defense, the US Department of Labor, Victoria's Secret, and XM Satellite Radio.

The company also offers audio and video streaming services, business intelligence and content targeting applications, and pay-as-you-go extra capacity on demand to avoid network congestion during periodic spikes in traffic through a partnership with IBM. Akamai has begun offering its Web Application Accelerator service, which speeds up applications based on the Web and Internet protocol by compression, connection optimization, dynamic caching, and routing. The new service is tailored for such online applications as airline reservation systems, course planning tools, customer order processing, and human resources.

In 2005 Akamai acquired archrival Speedera Networks for approximately 12 million shares of Akamai common stock, valued at about $130 million. As part of the merger agreement, Akamai and Speedera agreed to dismiss all pending litigation between the two companies. Late in 2006 Akamai purchased Nine Systems, a provider of rich media production and publishing tools, for about $160 million.

A hot market for content delivery network (CDN) services and "new economy" fervor helped propel Akamai (Hawaiian for "clever, intelligent, or cool") to the forefront of runaway tech stocks in the late 1990s. Since then the CDN sector has cooled and many of the company's competitors have evaporated, while Akamai has been forced to slash jobs and reorganize to cut costs. In the process, the company terminated a joint venture with ES Ventures in Australia, and sold its stakes in Akamai Technologies Japan K.K. and Sockeye Networks.

Following the September 11th terrorist attacks, the company found a new way to bring in some extra revenue. Inspired by the denial-of-service attacks that brought down some of its clients' Web sites, Akamai started charging for its own kind of insurance policy. If hackers bring down a site, Akamai will step in and turn on its caching service to quickly reestablish traffic.

The company is the creation of Daniel Lewin, who won the 1998 MIT Entrepreneur's Competition. He died three years later as a passenger in one of the planes that hit the World Trade Center on September 11, 2001.

FMR (Fidelity Investments) owns about 10% of Akamai. Chief scientist Tom Leighton holds around 6% of the company.

EXECUTIVES

Chairman: George H. Conrades, age 67, $20,000 pay
President, CEO, and Director: Paul L. Sagan, age 47, $772,875 pay (prior to title change)
EVP, Global Sales, Services, and Marketing: Robert W. (Bob) Hughes, age 38, $803,422 pay
EVP, Technology, Networks, and Support: Chris Schoettle, age 42, $473,938 pay
SVP and CFO: J. Donald (J. D.) Sherman, age 40
VP, Public Sector: Betsy Appleby
VP and General Counsel: Melanie Haratunian, age 46, $306,193 pay
CTO: Michael M. (Mike) Afergan
Chief Human Resources Officer: Cathy Welsh, age 55
Chief Scientist and Director: F. Thomson (Tom) Leighton, age 49
Director, Investor Relations: Sandy Smith
Director, Corporate Communications: Jeff Young
Auditors: PricewaterhouseCoopers LLP

LOCATIONS

HQ: Akamai Technologies, Inc.
8 Cambridge Center, Cambridge, MA 02142
Phone: 617-444-3000   **Fax:** 617-444-3001
Web: www.akamai.com

Akamai Technologies has offices in Australia, China, France, Germany, India, Japan, Singapore, Spain, the UK, and the US.

2005 Sales

	% of total
US	79
Europe	16
Other regions	5
Total	**100**

PRODUCTS/OPERATIONS

2005 Sales

	$ mil.	% of total
Services	281.5	99
Software	1.6	1
Total	**283.1**	**100**

Selected Services

Business intelligence
Content and application delivery
Edge processing and content targeting
EdgeSuite content delivery network
Geolocation services
Internet traffic monitoring
Streaming media

COMPETITORS

Akimbo Systems
Anystream
Brilliant Digital Entertainment
Chyron
Globix
Google
Intraware
Kontiki
Mirror Image Internet
NetApp
On2 Technologies
Onstream Media
Propel Software
Radiance Technologies
RealNetworks
Resonate
SAVVIS
Sorenson Media
Teknowledge
Virage
Yahoo!

HISTORICAL FINANCIALS

Company Type: Public

Income Statement

FYE: December 31

	REVENUE ($ mil.)	NET INCOME ($ mil.)	NET PROFIT MARGIN	EMPLOYEES
12/05	283.1	328.0	115.9%	784
12/04	210.0	34.4	16.4%	605
12/03	161.3	(29.3)	—	535
12/02	145.0	(204.4)	—	567
12/01	163.2	(2,435.5)	—	841
Annual Growth	**14.8%**	**—**	**—**	**(1.7%)**

2005 Year-End Financials

Debt ratio: 32.0%
Return on equity: 131.7%
Cash ($ mil.): 292.4
Current ratio: 5.74
Long-term debt ($ mil.): 200.0
No. of shares (mil.): 152.9
Dividends
   Yield: —
   Payout: —
Market value ($ mil.): 3,047.7
R&D as % of sales: 6.4%
Advertising as % of sales: 0.3%

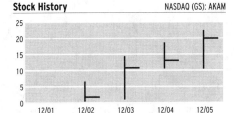

Stock History   NASDAQ (GS): AKAM

	STOCK PRICE ($) FY Close	P/E High/Low		PER SHARE ($) Earnings	Dividends	Book Value
12/05	19.93	11	5	2.11	—	4.08
12/04	13.03	74	43	0.25	—	(0.99)
12/03	10.76	—	—	(0.25)	—	(1.44)
12/02	1.73	—	—	(1.81)	—	(1.43)
Annual Growth	**125.9%**		**—**	**—**	**—**	**128.5%**

Aldila

The golf industry doesn't mind when Aldila gives it the shaft. Under the Aldila brand name, the company makes graphite golf club shafts for companies such as Callaway Golf, Ping, and Acushnet (which combine for more than 60% of sales). Other customers include custom club builders, distributors, pro shops, and repair centers. Aldila is protecting itself against any erratic swings in the industry by producing its own graphite and selling the excess to other sporting goods manufacturers. Carbon Fiber Technology, Aldila's joint venture with SGL Carbon, makes carbon products for recreational and industrial markets. Aldila makes its shafts in the US, Mexico, and China.

EXECUTIVES

Chairman, President, and CEO; President and COO, Aldila Golf: Peter R. Mathewson, age 55, $486,130 pay
VP Finance, Secretary, and Treasurer: Robert J. (Bob) Cierzan, age 59, $360,165 pay
VP and Controller, Aldila Golf: Scott Bier
VP Engineering, Aldila Golf: John E. Oldenburg
VP Manufacturing, Aldila Golf: David B. Lopez
VP Sales and Marketing, Aldila Golf: Michael J. (Mike) Rossi, age 52, $338,956 pay
Human Resources Manager: Maryann Jacoub
Investor Relations: Sylvia J. Castle
Auditors: Squar, Milner, Peterson, Miranda & Williamson, LLP

LOCATIONS

HQ: Aldila, Inc.
13450 Stowe Dr., Poway, CA 92064
Phone: 858-513-1801   **Fax:** 858-513-1870
Web: www.aldila.com

2005 Sales

	$ mil.	% of total
US	59.5	77
UK	7.5	10
China	6.9	9
Canada	1.0	1
Australia	0.8	1
Other foreign countries	1.3	2
Total	**77.0**	**100**

COMPETITORS

Carbite Golf	Toray
Graphite Design	True Temper Sports
Royal Precision	

HISTORICAL FINANCIALS

Company Type: Public

Income Statement

FYE: December 31

	REVENUE ($ mil.)	NET INCOME ($ mil.)	NET PROFIT MARGIN	EMPLOYEES
12/05	77.0	13.4	17.4%	1,274
12/04	52.8	9.3	17.6%	—
12/03	37.8	(1.7)	—	—
12/02	37.5	(2.8)	—	1,081
12/01	39.6	(51.4)	—	1,168
Annual Growth	**18.1%**	**—**	**—**	**2.2%**

2005 Year-End Financials

Debt ratio: —
Return on equity: 36.4%
Cash ($ mil.): 15.8
Current ratio: 4.03
Long-term debt ($ mil.): —
No. of shares (mil.): 5.4
Dividends
   Yield: 9.6%
   Payout: 99.6%
Market value ($ mil.): 137.2
R&D as % of sales: —
Advertising as % of sales: 1.6%

Stock History   NASDAQ (GM): ALDA

	STOCK PRICE ($) FY Close	P/E High/Low		PER SHARE ($) Earnings	Dividends	Book Value
12/05	25.43	12	5	2.46	2.45	7.14
12/04	15.25	10	2	1.77	0.15	6.84
12/03	3.56	—	—	(0.35)	—	5.04
12/02	1.52	—	—	(0.57)	—	5.33
12/01	3.15	—	—	(10.11)	—	1.97
Annual Growth	**68.6%**		**—**	**—1,533.3%**		**38.0%**

Align Technology

Brace-face begone! Align Technology produces and sells the Invisalign System, which corrects malocclusion, or crooked teeth. Instead of using metal or ceramic mounts cemented on the teeth that are connected by wires, the system involves using an array of clear and removable dental Aligners to move a patient's teeth into a desired tooth alignment. The company markets its products to orthodontists and dentists primarily in the US and Canada. Align also provides training for them to model treatment schemes using its Internet-based application called ClinCheck, which simulates tooth movement and suggests the appropriate Aligner.

Align Technology plans to improve its Invisalign System and develop new products. The company also intends to focus on educating dental students about Invisalign in more colleges and post-graduate programs.

EXECUTIVES

Chairman: C. Raymond Larkin Jr., age 56
President, CEO, and Director: Thomas M. Prescott, age 50, $768,670 pay
VP, Finance and CFO: Eldon M. Bullington, age 54, $357,294 pay
VP, Global Marketing and Chief Marketing Officer: Darrell Zoromski, age 41
VP, Human Resources: Sonia Clark
VP, Information Technology and CIO: Michael J. Henry, age 43
VP, Legal and Corporate Affairs, Corporate Secretary, and General Counsel: Roger E. George, age 40, $337,847 pay
VP, North American Sales: Dan S. Ellis, age 55
VP, Operations: Len W. Hedge, age 48, $346,280 pay
VP, Research and Development: Hossein Arjomand, age 45
Investor Relations: Barbara Domingo
Auditors: PricewaterhouseCoopers LLP

LOCATIONS

HQ: Align Technology, Inc.
    881 Martin Ave., Santa Clara, CA 95050
Phone: 408-470-1000   **Fax:** 408-470-1010
Web: www.aligntech.com

Align Technologies manufactures its products in California, Costa Rica, and Mexico.

PRODUCTS/OPERATIONS

2005 Sales

	$ mil.	% of total
Invisalign	197.7	95
Other	9.4	5
Total	**207.1**	**100**

COMPETITORS

3M
Ceradyne
Darby Group
DENTSPLY
Henry Schein
Patterson Companies
Sybron Dental

HISTORICAL FINANCIALS

Company Type: Public

Income Statement

FYE: December 31

	REVENUE ($ mil.)	NET INCOME ($ mil.)	NET PROFIT MARGIN	EMPLOYEES
12/05	207.1	1.4	0.7%	1,097
12/04	172.8	8.8	5.1%	969
12/03	122.7	(20.1)	—	741
12/02	69.7	(72.8)	—	608
12/01	46.4	(97.5)	—	1,093
Annual Growth	**45.4%**	**—**	**—**	**0.1%**

2005 Year-End Financials

Debt ratio: —
Return on equity: 1.6%
Cash ($ mil.): 74.4
Current ratio: 2.30
Long-term debt ($ mil.): —
No. of shares (mil.): 62.1
Dividends
  Yield: —
  Payout: —
Market value ($ mil.): 401.7
R&D as % of sales: 9.0%
Advertising as % of sales: 5.5%

Stock History

NASDAQ (GM): ALGN

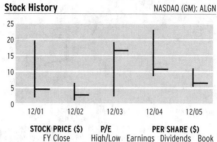

	STOCK PRICE ($) FY Close	P/E High/Low		PER SHARE ($) Earnings	Dividends	Book Value
12/05	6.47	544	282	0.02	—	1.51
12/04	10.75	163	63	0.14	—	1.41
12/03	16.51	—	—	(0.35)	—	1.07
12/02	2.76	—	—	(1.52)	—	1.12
12/01	4.50	—	—	(2.57)	—	2.08
Annual Growth	**9.5%**	**—**	**—**	**—**	**—**	**(7.8%)**

Alkermes

Alkermes, whose name is Arabic for "magic potion," is working some biotech alchemy. The company develops drug-delivery systems for fragile biotech compounds or drugs with molecular chemistry too large for traditional delivery methods. Products include ProLease (a sustained-release injection technology that enables a controlled release of drugs and longer intervals between doses than traditional injectable compounds) and AIR (an inhaler-based delivery system). The company works with Eli Lilly and others to develop delivery systems for their drugs, but it keeps the rights to the technology. Alkermes' own drug pipeline includes Vivitrol, a potential drug therapy for alcohol addiction.

The company began production in 2005 on a treatment for schizophrenia called Risperdal Consta through another partnership with Janssen, a division of Johnson & Johnson. Also that year Alkermes inked a deal with Cephalon to commercialize Vivitrol as a treatment for alcoholism.

The AIR inhaled insulin delivery system developed in partnership with Eli Lilly is continuing Phase III clinical trials begun in mid-2005. The two companies signed an agreement in early 2007 whereby Alkermes would be the exclusive manufacturer of the handheld inhaler and Lilly would construct and operate a second manufacturing line for Alkermes.

HISTORY

Floyd Bloom, Alexander Rich, Paul Schimmel, and Michael Wall founded Alkermes in 1987. The company targeted the development of diagnostic and therapeutic agents for central nervous system diseases. It went public in 1991.

The next year Alkermes created a separate partnership to fund development of Cereport technology, and in the mid-1990s it branched out into other types of delivery systems and forged alliances with major drug companies to adapt its technologies to their products.

In the late 1990s Alkermes began collaborations with Johnson & Johnson to develop erythropoietin blood booster Procrit with ProLease and with Genentech to develop Nutropin Depot, a sustained-release formulation of Genentech's human growth hormone. In 1999, Alkermes bought AIR (Advanced Inhalation Research), its pulmonary drug delivery unit.

In 2004 the company ceased making its first FDA-approved product, Nutropin Depot.

EXECUTIVES

Chairman: Michael A. Wall, age 77
CEO and Director: Richard F. Pops, age 45, $1,004,474 pay
President and COO: David A. Broecker, age 45, $619,377 pay
VP, CFO, and Treasurer: James M. (Jim) Frates, age 39, $559,436 pay
VP, General Counsel, and Secretary: Kathryn L. (Kathy) Biberstein, age 47, $441,724 pay
VP, Clinical Development: Bernard L. (Bernie) Silverman
VP, Corporate Development: Michael J. (Mike) Landine, age 52, $490,481 pay
VP, Corporate Communications: Rebecca Peterson
VP, Research and Development: Richard P. (Rick) Batycky
VP, Science and Development and Chief Medical Officer: Elliot W. Ehrich
Auditors: Deloitte & Touche LLP

LOCATIONS

HQ: Alkermes, Inc.
    88 Sidney St., Cambridge, MA 02139
Phone: 617-494-0171   **Fax:** 617-494-9263
Web: www.alkermes.com

Alkermes has facilities in Massachusetts and Ohio.

PRODUCTS/OPERATIONS

2006 Sales

	$ mil.	% of total
Research & development agreements	85.2	51
Manufacturing & royalties	81.4	49
Total	**166.6**	**100**

Selected Products

AIR (inhaler-based drug delivery)
ProLease (sustained release of fragile biotechnology drugs through injection)

Subsidiaries

Advanced Inhalation Research, Inc.
Alkermes Controlled Therapeutics, Inc.
Alkermes Controlled Therapeutics Inc. II
Alkermes Europe, Ltd. (UK)
Alkermes Investments, Inc.

COMPETITORS

ALZA
Amarin
Biovail
Bristol-Myers Squibb
DURECT
Emisphere
Forest Labs
Johnson & Johnson
K-V Pharmaceutical
Mallinckrodt
Nektar Therapeutics
Noven Pharmaceuticals
NPS Pharmaceuticals
Penwest Pharmaceuticals
Pfizer
SkyePharma
Watson Pharmaceuticals

HISTORICAL FINANCIALS

Company Type: Public

Income Statement

FYE: March 31

	REVENUE ($ mil.)	NET INCOME ($ mil.)	NET PROFIT MARGIN	EMPLOYEES
3/06	166.6	3.8	2.3%	760
3/05	76.1	(73.9)	—	528
3/04	39.0	(102.4)	—	490
3/03	47.3	(106.9)	—	436
3/02	54.1	(61.3)	—	520
Annual Growth	32.5%	—		10.0%

2006 Year-End Financials

Debt ratio: 841.4%
Return on equity: 20.4%
Cash ($ mil.): 298.0
Current ratio: 2.77
Long-term debt ($ mil.): 279.5
No. of shares (mil.): 91.7

Dividends
  Yield: —
  Payout: —
Market value ($ mil.): 2,023.0
R&D as % of sales: 53.5%
Advertising as % of sales: —

Stock History

NASDAQ (GS): ALKS

	STOCK PRICE ($) FY Close	P/E High/Low	PER SHARE ($) Earnings	Dividends	Book Value
3/06	22.05	670 242	0.04	—	0.36
3/05	10.38	— —	(0.82)	—	0.05
3/04	15.99	— —	(1.25)	—	0.85
3/03	9.07	— —	(1.66)	—	(0.08)
3/02	26.06	— —	(0.96)	—	1.55
Annual Growth	(4.1%)	— —	—	—	(30.5%)

Allegiant Travel

Allegiant Travel pledges to serve the vacation needs of residents of about 45 small US cities. Through Allegiant Air, the company provides nonstop service to Las Vegas, Tampa, and Orlando, Florida, from places such as Abilene, Texas; Fargo, North Dakota; and Toledo, Ohio. It maintains a fleet of about 20 MD80 series aircraft. Besides scheduled service, it offers charter flights for casino operator Harrah's and other customers. Subsidiary Allegiant Vacations works with partners to allow customers to book hotel rooms and rental cars with their airline tickets. CEO Maurice Gallagher controls about 25% of Allegiant Travel.

The company hopes to thrive by sticking to what it believes to be an underserved niche: Allegiant Air is the only provider of nonstop service to Las Vegas or Orlando in most of the markets where it operates. Allegiant Travel has identified more than 50 additional small cities in the US and Canada as candidates for its services. The company also is considering adding vacation spots elsewhere in the US and in Mexico and the Caribbean to its route map.

It plans to use the proceeds of its 2006 IPO to buy more aircraft in order to expand services on existing routes and add new markets. The company's chosen MD80 models, formerly an industry mainstay, are more expensive to operate than new planes but cheaper to obtain.

Just as the company's aircraft have been tested, so has Allegiant Travel's management team. This isn't the first go-round in the airline industry for Gallagher and director Robert Priddy, who helped found low-fare carrier ValuJet (now AirTran). Allegiant Travel's board also includes Declan Ryan, a co-founder and former CEO of European low-fare carrier Ryanair.

Investors in Allegiant Travel include private equity firm ComVest, which owns about 19% of the company and is represented on its board by directors Michael Falk and Priddy. Other shareholders include PAR Investment Partners, which owns about 9%, and Ryan, who owns about 6%.

Mitchell Allee, who owns 4% of Allegiant Travel, founded the original Allegiant Air in 1997 and served as its chairman and CEO. That company filed for Chapter 11 bankruptcy protection in 2000 and emerged from its reorganization in 2002 under new ownership and management, led by Gallagher. Allegiant Travel was formed in 2005 as a holding company for Allegiant Air.

EXECUTIVES

President, CEO, and Director:
  Maurice J. (Maury) Gallagher Jr., age 56
SVP, Operations: Michael P. Baxter, age 63, $190,000 pay
VP, Flight Operations: James R. Carr
Managing Director and CFO: Linda A. Marvin, age 44, $213,196 pay
Managing Director, Marketing and Sales:
  M. Ponder Harrison, age 44
Managing Director, Planning and Secretary:
  Andrew C. Levy, age 36, $245,650 pay
Director, Corporate Communications: Tyri Squyres
Director, Sales: Eric Woodson
Auditors: Ernst & Young LLP

LOCATIONS

HQ: Allegiant Travel Company, LLC
  3301 N. Buffalo Dr., Ste. B-9, Las Vegas, NV 89129
Phone: 702-851-7300 **Fax:** 702-256-7209
Web: www.allegiantair.com

PRODUCTS/OPERATIONS

2005 Sales

	$ mil.	% of total
Scheduled service	90.7	68
Charter service	30.6	23
Other	11.2	9
Total	132.5	100

COMPETITORS

AirTran Holdings
AMR Corp.
Continental Airlines
Delta Air
Frontier Airlines
JetBlue
Mesa Air
Midwest Air
Northwest Airlines
Southwest Airlines
UAL
US Airways

HISTORICAL FINANCIALS

Company Type: Public

Income Statement

FYE: December 31

	REVENUE ($ mil.)	NET INCOME ($ mil.)	NET PROFIT MARGIN	EMPLOYEES
12/05	132.5	7.3	5.5%	596
12/04	90.4	9.1	10.1%	391
12/03	50.0	4.3	8.6%	282
Annual Growth	62.8%	30.3%	—	45.4%

2005 Year-End Financials

Debt ratio: 336.2%
Return on equity: 60.6%
Cash ($ mil.): 56.9

Current ratio: 1.15
Long-term debt ($ mil.): 49.1

Net Income History

NASDAQ (GM): ALGT

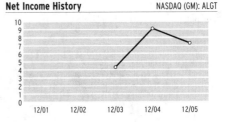

Allied Motion Technologies

Allied Motion Technologies has the drive to put you in control of your own motions. The company makes specialized motors, optical encoders, and frequency converters used in mechanical motion control applications. Its products are incorporated into a number of end products, including high-definition printers, robotic systems, and satellite tracking systems. Allied Motion targets applications in the aerospace and military, computer, industrial automation, medical equipment, and semiconductor manufacturing markets. The company operates through five subsidiaries.

The US accounts for more than three-quarters of sales.

In 2002 Allied Motion sold its power and process instrumentation business to Qualitrol Power, a subsidiary of Danaher. Allied Motion acquired Owosso's electric motor division for around $17 million in 2004.

Allied Motion acquired Netherlands-based Precision Motor Technology (Premotec; small electric motors) for about $5 million in 2004.

Including stock options, director and former chairman Eugene Prince owns about 13% of Allied Motion; CEO Richard Smith holds 11% of the company; and COO Richard Warzala has an equity stake of nearly 8%. Investor Peter H. Kamin owns nearly 9% of the company.

EXECUTIVES

Chairman: Delwin D. Hock, age 70
CEO, CFO, and Director: Richard D. (Dick) Smith, age 58, $248,333 pay
President, COO, and Director:
  Richard S. (Dick) Warzala, age 52
VP, Marketing: Kenneth R. Wyman, age 63, $129,333 pay
General Manager, Emoteq: Joseph (Joe) Ivey
Auditors: KPMG LLP

LOCATIONS

HQ: Allied Motion Technologies Inc.
23 Inverness Way E., Ste. 150,
Englewood, CO 80112
Phone: 303-799-8520   **Fax:** 303-799-8521
Web: www.alliedmotion.com

Allied Motion has facilities in the Netherlands and
the US.

2005 Sales

	$ mil.	% of total
US	54.2	73
Other countries	20.1	27
Total	**74.3**	**100**

PRODUCTS/OPERATIONS

Selected Subsidiaries

Computer Optical Products (optical encoders)
Emoteq Corporation (brushless motors, drives,
   frequency converters)
Motor Products Corporation (permanent magnet DC and
   brushless DC motors)
Owosso Corporation (fractional and integral horsepower
   motors, gear motors, and motor part sets)
Precision Motor Technology BV (Premotec; small
   electric motors)

COMPETITORS

ACS Motion Control	Danaher
Aeroflex	Dynamics Research
Applied Industrial	Newport
Technologies	TSI
Axsys	UQM Technologies
BEI Technologies	

HISTORICAL FINANCIALS

Company Type: Public

Income Statement

FYE: December 31

	REVENUE ($ mil.)	NET INCOME ($ mil.)	NET PROFIT MARGIN	EMPLOYEES
12/05	74.3	0.9	1.2%	515
12/04	62.7	2.3	3.7%	495
12/03	39.4	0.9	2.3%	343
12/02*	17.2	0.3	1.7%	341
6/02	42.1	(0.3)	—	331
Annual Growth	**15.3%**	—	—	**11.7%**

*Fiscal year change

2005 Year-End Financials

Debt ratio: 18.4%
Return on equity: 3.6%
Cash ($ mil.): 0.6
Current ratio: 1.20
Long-term debt ($ mil.): 4.8
No. of shares (mil.): 6.4

Dividends
   Yield: —
   Payout: —
Market value ($ mil.): 26.6
R&D as % of sales: —
Advertising as % of sales: —

Stock History

NASDAQ (CM): AMOT

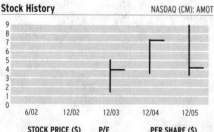

	STOCK PRICE ($) FY Close	P/E High/Low		Earnings	PER SHARE ($) Dividends	Book Value
12/05	4.17	68	26	0.13	—	4.05
12/04	7.22	20	10	0.36	—	4.01
12/03	3.93	26	8	0.19	—	3.20
Annual Growth	**3.0%**	—	—	**(17.3%)**	—	**12.6%**

Allis-Chalmers Energy

This company knows the drill. Allis-Chalmers
Energy provides drilling and oil field services to
oil and gas exploration companies operating primarily in the western US. It installs casing and
tubing and provides drilling and workover services. Its Strata Directional Technology subsidiary offers drilling services to clients in Texas
and Louisiana. Through its AirComp unit, Allis-
Chalmers operates a fleet of more than 130 compressors used for well production enhancement
and completion. Moving into the tool rental field,
the company acquired Safco-Oil Field Products
in 2004 and Delta Rental Service in 2005. In
2006 it acquired Oil & Gas Rental Services for
about $342 million in cash and stock.

Allis-Chalmers, through its AirComp subsidiary, has expanded its drilling technology
products business through the 2004 acquisition
of Diamond Air. The acquisition also included
Diamond Air's Marquis Bit subsidiary. It has also
acquired Texas-based oil and gas field services
provider Downhole Injection Systems for $1 mil-
lion. In 2005 the company acquired $15 million
in used casing and tubing installation equipment
from Patterson Services, Inc., a subsidiary of
RPC, Inc. It also acquired Target Energy Inc.,
the US measurement-while-drilling (MWD) operations of UK-based Target Energy Group. Continuing its acquisition streak into 2006,
Allis-Chalmers acquired Specialty Rental Tools
Inc. for about $90 million, and bought Rogers Oil
Tool Services for about $14 million. That year it
also acquired Petro Rentals for $29.78 million.

EXECUTIVES

Chairman and CEO: Munawar H. (Micki) Hidayatallah,
age 62
Vice Chairman: Leonard Toboroff, age 73
President, COO, and Vice Chairman: Burt A. Adams,
age 45
CFO: Victor M. Perez, age 53
President and CEO, AirComp LLC:
Terrence P. (Terry) Keane, age 54
President and CEO, Strata: David K. Bryan, age 49
VP and Corporate Controller: Bruce Sauers, age 42
General Counsel and Secretary: Theodore F. Pound III,
age 52
Auditors: UHY LLP

LOCATIONS

HQ: Allis-Chalmers Energy Inc.
   5075 Westheimer, Ste. 890, Houston, TX 77056
Phone: 713-369-0550   **Fax:** 713-369-0555

Allis-Chalmers provides services to customers operating
in the US (in the West and the Gulf of Mexico) and
Mexico.

2005 Sales

	$ mil.	% of total
US	98.5	94
Other countries	6.8	6
Total	**105.3**	**100**

PRODUCTS/OPERATIONS

2005 Sales

	$ mil.	% of total
Directional drilling services	43.9	42
Compressed air drilling services	25.7	24
Casing & tubing services	20.9	20
Production services	9.8	9
Rental tools	5.0	5
Total	**105.3**	**100**

Selected Subsidiaries

AirComp, LLC
Allis-Chalmers Production Services, Inc.
Allis-Chalmers Rental Tools, Inc.
Allis-Chalmers Tubular Services, Inc.
Mountain Compressed Air Inc.
OilQuip Rentals, Inc.
Strata Directional Technology, Inc.
Target Energy Inc.

COMPETITORS

Boots & Coots
Cudd Pressure Control
Eaton Oil Tools
GulfMark Offshore
Rogers Oil Tool Services
Trico Marine
Weatherford International

HISTORICAL FINANCIALS

Company Type: Public

Income Statement

FYE: December 31

	REVENUE ($ mil.)	NET INCOME ($ mil.)	NET PROFIT MARGIN	EMPLOYEES
12/05	105.3	7.2	6.8%	700
12/04	47.7	0.9	1.9%	261
12/03	32.7	2.9	8.9%	—
12/02	18.0	(4.0)	—	—
12/01	4.8	(4.6)	—	—
Annual Growth	**116.4%**	—	—	**168.2%**

2005 Year-End Financials

Debt ratio: 90.2%
Return on equity: 15.0%
Cash ($ mil.): 1.9
Current ratio: 1.73
Long-term debt ($ mil.): 54.9
No. of shares (mil.): 16.9

Dividends
   Yield: —
   Payout: —
Market value ($ mil.): 210.2
R&D as % of sales: —
Advertising as % of sales: —

Stock History

AMEX: ALY

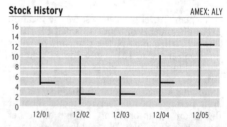

	STOCK PRICE ($) FY Close	P/E High/Low		Earnings	PER SHARE ($) Dividends	Book Value
12/05	12.47	33	8	0.44	—	3.61
12/04	4.90	114	11	0.09	—	2.53
12/03	2.60	—	—	(0.01)	—	0.23
12/02	2.55	—	—	(1.15)	—	0.05
12/01	4.75	—	—	(5.75)	—	0.11
Annual Growth	**27.3%**	—	—	—	—	**140.5%**

Altiris

Altiris wants to help companies keep their information technology (IT) assets up to snuff. The company provides IT asset management software that helps organizations manage their technology systems. Altiris' client, server, and asset management software handles IT deployment and migration, server provisioning and management, inventory and asset management, performance tracking, and help desk and problem resolution. The company offers consulting, implementation, and support services. Customers include Hewlett-Packard and Dell, both of which have technology partnerships with Altiris. In early 2007 the company agreed to be acquired by Symantec for about $830 million.

Altiris continues to use acquisitions to expand and enhance its offerings. The company bought Wise Solutions in late 2003, adding software installation and maintenance capabilities, and in 2004 it bought FSLogic, a provider of application management technologies; the same year it acquired BridgeWater Technologies, which provided network device discovery and provisioning technologies.

Early in 2005 Altiris extended its server management offerings with its purchase of Web application management company Tonic Software, and it bought privately held security vulnerability management software provider Pedestal Software for $65 million.

EXECUTIVES

Chairman, President, and CEO:
Gregory S. (Greg) Butterfield, age 46, $421,574 pay
VP and CFO: Stephen C. (Steve) Erickson, age 49, $273,980 pay
VP and Chief Technology Officer: Dwain A. Kinghorn, age 40, $269,117 pay
VP and General Counsel: Craig H. Christensen, age 48
VP, Business Development: Poul E. Nielsen, age 48, $209,222 pay
VP, Human Resources: Deanne Matheny
VP, Marketing: Carine Clark
VP, Operations: Chad S. Latimer, age 45
VP, Worldwide Sales: Michael R. (Mike) Samuelian, age 47, $252,750 pay
Public Relations: Rhett Glauser
Auditors: KPMG LLP

LOCATIONS

HQ: Altiris, Inc.
588 W. 400 South, Lindon, UT 84042
Phone: 801-805-2400   **Fax:** 801-226-8506
Web: www.altiris.com

Altiris has offices in Australia, Estonia, France, Germany, Japan, the Netherlands, Singapore, Sweden, the UK, and the US.

2005 Sales

	$ mil.	% of total
US	127.2	68
Europe		
UK	19.6	10
Other countries	31.4	17
Other regions	9.4	5
Total	**187.6**	**100**

PRODUCTS/OPERATIONS

2005 Sales

	$ mil.	% of total
Software	103.4	55
Services	84.2	45
Total	**187.6**	**100**

Selected Software

Deployment and migration management (PC Transplant Pro, RapiDeploy)
Help desk and problem management (Carbon Copy, Helpdesk Solution)
Inventory and asset management (Application Metering, UNIX Inventory Solution)
Software and operations management (Client Manager, Web Admin for SMS)

Selected Services

Consulting
Implementation
Support
Training

COMPETITORS

BMC Software
CA
Hewlett-Packard
LANDesk
McAfee
Microsoft
Novell
Symantec
Tivoli Software

HISTORICAL FINANCIALS

Company Type: Public

Income Statement

FYE: December 31

	REVENUE ($ mil.)	NET INCOME ($ mil.)	NET PROFIT MARGIN	EMPLOYEES
12/05	187.6	3.3	1.8%	878
12/04	166.6	16.7	10.0%	750
12/03	99.3	14.0	14.1%	600
12/02	62.9	(0.1)	—	424
12/01	34.5	(10.2)	—	295
Annual Growth	**52.7%**	**—**	**—**	**31.3%**

2005 Year-End Financials

Debt ratio: 0.7%
Return on equity: 1.5%
Cash ($ mil.): 146.9
Current ratio: 2.50
Long-term debt ($ mil.): 1.6
No. of shares (mil.): 28.9
Dividends
  Yield: —
  Payout: —
Market value ($ mil.): 488.0
R&D as % of sales: 21.0%
Advertising as % of sales: —

Stock History

NASDAQ (GS): ATRS

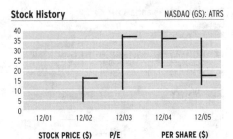

	STOCK PRICE ($) FY Close	P/E High/Low		PER SHARE ($) Earnings	Dividends	Book Value
12/05	16.89	322	114	0.11	—	7.76
12/04	35.43	64	35	0.61	—	7.38
12/03	36.48	64	18	0.58	—	6.35
12/02	15.92	—	—	(0.89)	—	3.26
Annual Growth	**2.0%**	**—**	**—**	**—**	**—**	**—**

Ambassadors Group

Why bother with pen pals when you can be an ambassador? Ambassadors Group's travel programs provide students and professionals with opportunities to travel to foreign lands. Most trips are organized through the student organization People to People, which was founded by Dwight D. Eisenhower. Specialized programs allow student athletes to join international sports travel programs. Professional Ambassador trips offer meetings and seminars involving participants and comparable professionals from other countries. Former parent Ambassador International spun off the company in 2002.

EXECUTIVES

Chairman: John A. Ueberroth, age 62, $100,000 pay
President, CEO, and Director: Jeffrey D. (Jeff) Thomas, age 39, $1,200,000 pay
CFO and Secretary: Chadwick J. Byrd, age 34, $94,577 pay (partial-year salary)
CFO, Ambassador Programs: Colleen K. McCann-Lillie, age 39, $183,167 pay
Investor Relations: Julie Strugar
Auditors: BDO Seidman, LLP

LOCATIONS

HQ: Ambassadors Group, Inc.
Dwight D. Eisenhower Bldg., 110 S. Ferrall St., Spokane, WA 99202
Phone: 509-534-6200   **Fax:** 509-534-5245
Web: www.ambassadorsgroup.com

2005 Sales

	% of total
Europe	46
South Pacific (primarily Australia & New Zealand)	30
US	12
Asia (primarily China)	11
Other	1
Total	**100**

COMPETITORS

American Express
BCD Travel
Carlson Wagonlit
Expedia
Orbitz
Travelocity
University of Pennsylvania

HISTORICAL FINANCIALS

Company Type: Public

Income Statement

FYE: December 31

	REVENUE ($ mil.)	NET INCOME ($ mil.)	NET PROFIT MARGIN	EMPLOYEES
12/05	69.3	22.4	32.3%	234
12/04	51.8	15.6	30.1%	183
12/03	37.7	10.1	26.8%	164
12/02	36.1	10.8	29.9%	153
12/01	43.4	9.5	21.9%	129
Annual Growth	**12.4%**	**23.9%**	**—**	**16.1%**

2005 Year-End Financials

Debt ratio: 0.6%
Return on equity: 38.6%
Cash ($ mil.): 116.6
Current ratio: 2.05
Long-term debt ($ mil.): 0.4
No. of shares (mil.): 20.7
Dividends
  Yield: 0.9%
  Payout: 21.0%
Market value ($ mil.): 472.8
R&D as % of sales: —
Advertising as % of sales: —

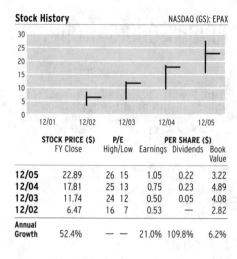

	STOCK PRICE ($) FY Close	P/E High/Low		PER SHARE ($) Earnings	Dividends	Book Value
12/05	22.89	26	15	1.05	0.22	3.22
12/04	17.81	25	13	0.75	0.23	4.89
12/03	11.74	24	12	0.50	0.05	4.08
12/02	6.47	16	7	0.53	—	2.82
Annual Growth	52.4%	—	—	21.0%	109.8%	6.2%

Ambassadors International

Ambassadors International could be an international ambassador for a diversified business. The company offers river and coastal cruises in North America; services for convention and trade shows, including incentive programs; hotel reservation, registration, and travel services for meetings, conventions, expositions, and trade shows; and event portfolio management software. It owns about 35% of a Japanese marine company, 20% of Grand Prix Tours (packaged tours to Formula One, Indy Car, and NASCAR races), a luxury marina in California, and reinsurance firm Cypress Re.

The company moved into water recreation in 2005 by purchasing BellPort's luxury waterfont facilities in the US and Mexico, as well as American West Steamboat Company, which operates cruises in the Pacific Northwest and Alaska. Ambassadors International also picked up an option to acquire about a third of BellPort's Japanese business.

Hoping to rock the boat a little in 2006, Ambassadors International bought Delta Queen Steamboat Company, the three-vessel cruise line owned by Delaware North Companies. The acquisition doubled Ambassadors' fleet of cruise vessels and added the Mississippi River region to its list of destinations. Later in the year, the company combined American West Steamboat Company and Delta Queen Steamboat Company under a new brand, the Majestic America Line. Ambassadors International subsequently acquired a seventh vessel, *Columbia Queen*, which will ply the Columbia and Snake rivers in the Northwest as part of the Majestic America Line.

In 2002 Ambassadors International spun off its successful education division Ambassadors Group, Inc., which helps students and professionals travel to foreign countries through not-for-profit People to People International.

Ambassadors International chairman, president, and CEO Joseph Ueberroth and his brother, company director and former Major League Baseball commissioner Peter Ueberroth, own about 10% of the company each. The brothers were co-chairmen before Peter stepped aside in August 2006.

EXECUTIVES

Chairman, President, and CEO:
Joseph J. (Joe) Ueberroth, age 37, $595,000 pay (prior to title change)
CFO and Secretary: Brian R. Schaefgen, age 36, $285,000 pay
VP and Controller: Laura L. Tuthill, age 29, $140,000 pay
VP Corporate Development: Joseph G. McCarthy
VP Human Resources: Tricia Mora
VP Information Technology: Brett Jones
President and COO, Ambassadors Cruise Group:
David A. Giersdorf, age 49
President and COO, Ambassadors: Jerry G. McGee, age 35, $387,500 pay
Director Human Resources: Cheryl Howard
Auditors: Ernst & Young LLP

LOCATIONS

HQ: Ambassadors International, Inc.
1071 Camelback St., Newport Beach, CA 92660
Phone: 949-759-5900   **Fax:** 949-759-5909
Web: www.ambassadors.com

Ambassadors International has operations in Atlanta; Chicago; Newport Beach, San Francisco, and San Diego, California.

COMPETITORS

American Express	Carnival
BCD Travel	Sekisui House
Carlson Wagonlit	Trump

HISTORICAL FINANCIALS

Company Type: Public

Income Statement

FYE: December 31

	REVENUE ($ mil.)	NET INCOME ($ mil.)	NET PROFIT MARGIN	EMPLOYEES
12/05	26.9	3.1	11.5%	157
12/04	18.7	(1.9)	—	132
12/03	13.7	(1.0)	—	121
12/02	14.7	1.6	10.9%	147
12/01	60.5	7.5	12.4%	279
Annual Growth	(18.3%)	(19.8%)	—	(13.4%)

2005 Year-End Financials

Debt ratio: —
Return on equity: 2.9%
Cash ($ mil.): 95.1
Current ratio: 4.67
Long-term debt ($ mil.): —
No. of shares (mil.): 10.5
Dividends
  Yield: 2.6%
  Payout: 133.3%
Market value ($ mil.): 163.0
R&D as % of sales: —
Advertising as % of sales: —

Stock History

NASDAQ (GM): AMIE

	STOCK PRICE ($) FY Close	P/E High/Low		PER SHARE ($) Earnings	Dividends	Book Value
12/05	15.50	55	40	0.30	0.40	10.39
12/04	15.73	—	—	(0.20)	0.40	10.51
12/03	12.55	—	—	(0.10)	0.20	11.30
12/02	8.99	68	52	0.15	—	11.60
12/01	9.22	16	8	0.75	0.53	12.86
Annual Growth	13.9%	—	—	(20.5%)	(6.8%)	(5.2%)

Amedisys

Because the last thing you want to do when you're sick is drive to a doctor's office, Amedisys has decided to bring health care to you. The company's home health care services include infusion therapy for administration of intravenous medications and nutrition; home health care nursing; physical, occupational, and speech therapy; social services; wound care management; and home health aides. Amedisys also provides terminal illness hospice care, disease management, and therapy staffing services. Amedisys operates through more than 200 offices located in nearly 20 southern and eastern states.

Looking to benefit from changes in Medicare reimbursement of home health services (more than 90% of its revenues), the firm has jettisoned its outpatient surgery and infusion therapy centers to focus on providing home health care.

Amedisys plans to grow via acquisitions and by providing its services in large metropolitan areas in its geographic market. In 2005, the company rapidly expanded by purchasing or opening over 100 home care and hospice offices.

EXECUTIVES

Chairman and CEO: William F. (Bill) Borne, age 48, $775,000 pay
President and COO: Larry R. Graham, age 40, $463,750 pay
CFO: John F. Giblin, age 49
SVP, Accounting and Corporate Controller:
Don Loverich
SVP, Business Development: William Mayes
SVP, Compliance and Corporate Counsel:
Jeffrey D. Jeter, age 33, $155,000 pay
SVP, Finance: Dorrie Rambo
SVP, Human Resources: Cindy L Phillips
SVP, Marketing: Patty Graham
CIO: Alice Ann Schwartz, age 39, $185,730 pay
Auditors: KPMG LLP

LOCATIONS

HQ: Amedisys, Inc.
11100 Mead Rd., Ste. 300, Baton Rouge, LA 70816
Phone: 225-292-2031   **Fax:** 225-295-9624
Web: www.amedisys.com

Amedisys operates in Alabama, Arkansas, Florida, Georgia, Indiana, Kentucky, Louisiana, Maryland, Mississippi, Missouri, North Carolina, Ohio, Oklahoma, South Carolina, Tennessee, Texas, Virginia, and West Virginia.

PRODUCTS/OPERATIONS

Selected Services
Home health aides
Infusion therapy
Occupation therapy
Pain management
Patient education
Physical therapy
Psychiatric services
Skilled nursing
Social services
Speech therapy
Wound management

COMPETITORS

Almost Family	National HealthCare
Apria Healthcare	Option Care
Coram Healthcare	Pediatric Services
Gentiva	Tender Loving Care
Home Health Corporation	VITAS Healthcare
Home Instead	

HISTORICAL FINANCIALS

Company Type: Public

Income Statement

FYE: December 31

	REVENUE ($ mil.)	NET INCOME ($ mil.)	NET PROFIT MARGIN	EMPLOYEES
12/05	381.6	30.1	7.9%	6,206
12/04	227.1	20.5	9.0%	3,594
12/03	142.5	8.4	5.9%	2,520
12/02	129.4	0.8	0.6%	2,237
12/01	110.2	5.4	4.9%	1,521
Annual Growth	36.4%	53.7%	—	42.1%

2005 Year-End Financials

Debt ratio: 22.4%
Return on equity: 17.7%
Cash ($ mil.): 17.2
Current ratio: 0.92
Long-term debt ($ mil.): 43.1
No. of shares (mil.): 15.9
Dividends
  Yield: —
  Payout: —
Market value ($ mil.): 503.0
R&D as % of sales: —
Advertising as % of sales: 1.0%

Stock History

NASDAQ (GS): AMED

	STOCK PRICE ($) FY Close	P/E High/Low		PER SHARE ($) Earnings	Dividends	Book Value
12/05	31.68	25	14	1.41	—	12.13
12/04	24.29	24	9	1.13	—	9.70
12/03	11.37	20	5	0.62	—	4.32
12/02	4.53	150	54	0.06	—	1.85
12/01	5.25	16	5	0.51	—	0.46
Annual Growth	56.7%	—	—	28.9%	—	126.5%

American Capital Strategies

Whether you make musical instruments or molded plastics, salon appliances or safes, this company has a strategy for you. American Capital Strategies invests in middle-market companies through ten offices in the US, France, and the UK. It typically invests up to $300 million, or provides loans from $5 million to $100 million, to fund management and employee buyouts, private equity firm buyouts, acquisitions, and restructurings. American Capital Strategies' portfolio consists of stakes in some 150 companies, with holdings in such sectors as automotive supplies, commercial services, consumer goods, construction, chemicals, food, electrical equipment, health care, packaging, and transportation.

One of the largest publicly traded US investment firms, American Capital Strategies has invested approximately $9 billion since its 1997 IPO. The company takes an active role in the management of its portfolio companies and has board seats on most of them.

EXECUTIVES

Chairman, President, and CEO: Malon Wilkus, age 54
EVP and COO: Ira J. Wagner, age 53
EVP and CFO: John R. Erickson, age 46
EVP, General Counsel, Chief Compliance Officer, and Secretary: Samuel A. Flax, age 49
SVP, Corporate Development: David Ehrenfest Steinglass
SVP, Human Resources: Lionel Ferguson
SVP and Managing Director, Operations Team: Gordon O'Brien, age 40
SVP, Business Development and Principal: Mark Opel
VP, Finance and Investor Relations: Thomas (Tom) McHale
Director, Corporate Communications: Brian Maney
Marketing Coordinator: Miriam Tejada
Auditors: Ernst & Young LLP

LOCATIONS

HQ: American Capital Strategies, Ltd.
  2 Bethesda Metro Center, 14th Fl.,
  Bethesda, MD 20814
Phone: 301-951-6122   **Fax:** 301-654-6714
Web: www.american-capital.com

American Capital Strategies has offices in Bethesda, Maryland; Chicago; Dallas; Los Angeles; New York; Palo Alto, California; San Francisco; and West Conshohocken (Philadelphia), Pennsylvania. It has international offices in London and Paris.

PRODUCTS/OPERATIONS

2005 Sales

	$ mil.	% of total
Control investments	263.2	48
Non-control, non-affiliate investments	222.8	40
Affiliate investments	68.5	12
Total	**554.5**	**100**

2005 Sales

	$ mil.	% of total
Interest & dividend income	425.9	77
Fee & other income	128.6	23
Total	**554.5**	**100**

COMPETITORS

Agility Capital
Allied Capital
Apax Partners
CapEx
Capital Across America
CapitalSource
Gladstone Capital
Harris & Harris
KBK Capital
MCG Capital
Sprout Group
Stonehenge Partners

HISTORICAL FINANCIALS

Company Type: Public

Income Statement

FYE: December 31

	REVENUE ($ mil.)	NET INCOME ($ mil.)	NET PROFIT MARGIN	EMPLOYEES
12/05	554.5	364.9	65.8%	308
12/04	435.3	281.4	64.6%	191
12/03	206.3	118.0	57.2%	132
12/02	147.0	20.1	13.7%	108
12/01	104.2	18.6	17.9%	68
Annual Growth	51.9%	110.5%	—	45.9%

2005 Year-End Financials

Debt ratio: 85.2%
Return on equity: 15.3%
Cash ($ mil.): 218.9
Current ratio: —
Long-term debt ($ mil.): 2,469.0
No. of shares (mil.): 118.9
Dividends
  Yield: 8.6%
  Payout: 86.4%
Market value ($ mil.): 4,305.8
R&D as % of sales: —
Advertising as % of sales: —

Stock History

NASDAQ (GS): ACAS

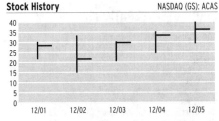

	STOCK PRICE ($) FY Close	P/E High/Low		PER SHARE ($) Earnings	Dividends	Book Value
12/05	36.21	11	8	3.60	3.11	24.37
12/04	33.35	10	7	3.63	2.91	21.11
12/03	29.73	14	10	2.15	2.79	17.83
12/02	21.59	66	30	0.50	2.57	15.82
12/01	28.35	52	38	0.58	2.30	16.84
Annual Growth	6.3%	—	—	57.8%	7.8%	9.7%

American Community Bancshares

American Community Bancshares is the holding company for American Community Bank, which serves individuals and small to midsized businesses through about a dozen branches in North and South Carolina. The bank offers standard products such as checking and savings, money market, and NOW accounts; certificates of deposit; and IRAs. Commercial mortgages and business loans make up the majority of the company's loan portfolio (more than 25% each). Construction loans, consumer loans, leases, and residential mortgages round out American Community Bancshares' lending activities.

The company entered South Carolina with the 2004 purchase of FNB Bancshares and its First National Bank of the Carolinas subsidiary, which was merged into American Community Bank the following year.

EXECUTIVES

Chairman, President, and CEO; President and CEO, American Community Bank: Randy P. Helton, age 50, $355,000 pay
SVP and COO: E. Michael Gudely, age 48, $143,500 pay
SVP, CFO, and Corporate Secretary: Dan R. Ellis Jr., age 50, $123,550 pay
SVP and Director; South Carolina Regional Executive, American Community Bank: V. Stephen Moss, age 56, $135,000 pay
Chief Credit Officer: Harry Parlier
SVP, Chief Administrative Officer, and Director of Corporate Communications, American Community Bank: Stephanie D. Helms, age 35
SVP and Mountain Island City Executive, American Community Bank: G. Michael Gray, age 55
SVP and Chief Credit Officer, American Community Bank: Douglas F. Sutherland, age 50, $115,000 pay
Commercial Lending: Robert Small
Auditors: Dixon Hughes PLLC

LOCATIONS

HQ: American Community Bancshares, Inc.
4500 Cameron Valley Pkwy., Ste. 150,
Charlotte, NC 28211
Phone: 704-225-8444　　**Fax:** 704-225-8445
Web: www.americancommunitybank.com

PRODUCTS/OPERATIONS

2005 Sales

	$ mil.	% of total
Interest		
Loans, including fees	23.1	80
Investment securities	2.2	8
Interest-earning deposits with banks	0.3	1
Noninterest		
Service charges on deposit accounts	2.3	8
Mortgage banking operations	0.4	1
Other	0.6	2
Total	**28.9**	**100**

COMPETITORS

Bank of America
BB&T
First Charter
First Citizens BancShares
First Trust Bank
M&F Bancorp
RBC Centura Banks
Southern Community Financial
Wachovia

HISTORICAL FINANCIALS

Company Type: Public

Income Statement

FYE: December 31

	ASSETS ($ mil.)	NET INCOME ($ mil.)	INCOME AS % OF ASSETS	EMPLOYEES
12/05	436.7	4.5	1.0%	109
12/04	399.5	2.7	0.7%	102
12/03	281.3	1.4	0.5%	80
12/02	215.1	1.3	0.6%	65
12/01	182.0	0.8	0.4%	60
Annual Growth	**24.5%**	**54.0%**	**—**	**16.1%**

2005 Year-End Financials

Equity as % of assets: 11.7%
Return on assets: 1.1%
Return on equity: 10.2%
Long-term debt ($ mil.): 26.7
No. of shares (mil.): 4.6
Market value ($ mil.): 57.1
Dividends
　Yield: 1.1%
　Payout: 29.5%
Sales ($ mil.): 28.9
R&D as % of sales: —
Advertising as % of sales: 0.9%

Stock History

NASDAQ (CM): ACBA

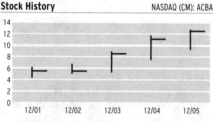

	STOCK PRICE ($) FY Close	P/E High/Low		PER SHARE ($) Earnings	Dividends	Book Value
12/05	12.49	29	21	0.44	0.13	11.14
12/04	11.09	23	15	0.50	0.07	10.60
12/03	8.51	28	17	0.32	0.05	8.56
12/02	5.48	20	15	0.34	—	8.17
12/01	5.49	22	16	0.28	—	8.27
Annual Growth	**22.8%**	**—**	**—**	**12.0%**	**61.2%**	**7.7%**

American Mortgage Acceptance

American Mortgage Acceptance Company is accepting a greater range of operations into its business. The firm was formed as a real estate investment trust (REIT) to invest in multi-family residential mortgages. It now originates and acquires Fannie Mae and other government-insured mortgages, uninsured mezzanine loans, construction loans, and bridge loans. The firm also offers Government National Mortgage Association (GNMA, or Ginnie Mae) certificates. AMI Associates, an affiliate of CharterMac, manages the REIT's operations. The company has announced plans to sell its interest in ARCap Investors, a company that invests in unrated and non-investment grade commercial mortgage-backed securities, to CharterMac.

More than 60% of American Mortgage's real estate assets are located in or secured by properties located in Texas. In 2003, five of the REIT's loans defaulted and the company took ownership of those properties; this raised American Mortgage's income from owned properties and decreased its interest revenue. The company has since sold most of those properties.

EXECUTIVES

Chairman: Marc D. Schnitzer, age 45
CEO: James L. Duggins
President: Daryl J. Carter, age 49
CFO: Robert L. (Rob) Levy
Controller: Gary Parkinson, age 56
Secretary: Theresa Wicelinski, age 39
Auditors: Ernst & Young Ltd.

LOCATIONS

HQ: American Mortgage Acceptance Company
625 Madison Ave., New York, NY 10022
Phone: 212-421-5333　　**Fax:** 212-751-3550
Web: www.americanmortgageco.com/default.cfm

PRODUCTS/OPERATIONS

2005 Sales

	$ mil.	% of total
Interest	20.6	53
Rental income	9.0	23
Equity in earnings of ARCap	2.9	7
Other	6.7	17
Total	**39.2**	**100**

COMPETITORS

Anthracite Capital
BRT Realty
Capital Lease Funding
CRIIMI MAE
Dynex Capital
iStar Financial Inc
MFA Mortgage Investments
Newcastle Investment
RAIT Financial Trust

HISTORICAL FINANCIALS

Company Type: Public

Income Statement

FYE: December 31

	REVENUE ($ mil.)	NET INCOME ($ mil.)	NET PROFIT MARGIN	EMPLOYEES
12/05	39.2	15.2	38.8%	—
12/04	15.9	11.3	71.1%	—
12/03	15.5	11.9	76.8%	—
12/02	10.5	9.7	92.4%	—
12/01	8.1	5.2	64.2%	—
Annual Growth	**48.3%**	**30.8%**	**—**	**—**

2005 Year-End Financials

Debt ratio: 222.2%
Return on equity: 13.0%
Cash ($ mil.): 11.2
Current ratio: —
Long-term debt ($ mil.): 253.7
No. of shares (mil.): 8.3
Dividends
　Yield: 13.0%
　Payout: 103.8%
Market value ($ mil.): 121.2
R&D as % of sales: —
Advertising as % of sales: —

Stock History

AMEX: AMC

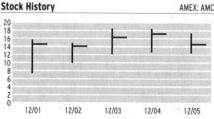

	STOCK PRICE ($) FY Close	P/E High/Low		PER SHARE ($) Earnings	Dividends	Book Value
12/05	14.60	9	7	1.83	1.90	13.75
12/04	17.20	14	9	1.35	1.60	15.15
12/03	16.30	12	8	1.52	1.60	14.50
12/02	14.09	9	6	1.61	1.51	14.82
12/01	14.55	11	6	1.35	1.45	14.40
Annual Growth	**0.1%**	**—**	**—**	**7.9%**	**7.0%**	**(1.1%)**

American Railcar Industries

American Railcar Industries doesn't make the little engine that could or the little red caboose — just the cars that go in between. The company is a leading manufacturer of covered hopper cars, used for dry bulk commodities, and tank cars, used for liquid and compressed bulk commodities. American Railcar Industries also makes railcar components and offers railcar maintenance and fleet management services. It operates two manufacturing facilities in Arkansas, and manufacturing operations account for more than 90% of the company's sales. The company's main customers are railcar leasing companies, rail shippers, and railroads. Financier Carl Icahn controls about a 53% stake in American Railcar Industries.

Icahn also controls railcar lessors ACF Industries and American Railcar Leasing, which together accounted for about 11% of American

Railcar Industries' sales in 2005. Lessor CIT Group, which accounted for about 20% of sales in 2005, has agreed to buy at least 9,000 railcars from the company by the end of 2008.

American Railcar Industries moved to expand in 2006 when it bought Custom Steel, a subsidiary of Steel Technologies. Custom Steel makes fabricated parts that are used in American Railcar Industries' railcar manufacturing operations.

EXECUTIVES

Chairman: Carl C. Icahn, age 70
President, CEO, and Director: James J. Unger, age 57, $350,000 pay
EVP and COO: James A. (Jim) Cowan, age 48, $22,727 pay
SVP and CFO: William P. Benac, age 59, $229,167 pay
SVP Sales, Marketing and Services: Alan C. Lullman, age 50, $158,333 pay
VP Engineering and Manufacturing: Michael R. Williams, age 44
Director Railcar Manufacturing: Jackie R. Pipkin, age 56
Auditors: Grant Thornton LLP

LOCATIONS

HQ: American Railcar Industries, Inc.
100 Clark St., St. Charles, MO 63301
Phone: 636-940-6000   **Fax:** 636-940-6030
Web: www.americanrailcar.com

PRODUCTS/OPERATIONS

2005 Sales

	$ mil.	% of total
Manufacturing operations	564.5	93
Railcar services	43.7	7
Total	**608.2**	**100**

COMPETITORS

Greenbrier
Meridian Rail Acquisition Corp
Millennium Rail
Miner Enterprises
Trinity Industries
Union Tank Car

HISTORICAL FINANCIALS

Company Type: Public

Income Statement				FYE: December 31
	REVENUE ($ mil.)	NET INCOME ($ mil.)	NET PROFIT MARGIN	EMPLOYEES
12/05	608.2	14.8	2.4%	2,425
12/04	355.1	1.9	0.5%	2,372
12/03	218.0	1.1	0.5%	—
12/02	168.8	(3.9)	—	—
Annual Growth	**53.3%**	**—**	**—**	**2.2%**

2005 Year-End Financials

Debt ratio: 28.7%
Return on equity: 61.6%
Cash ($ mil.): 28.7
Current ratio: 1.19
Long-term debt ($ mil.): 7.1

Net Income History

NASDAQ (GS): ARII

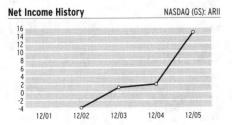

American River Bankshares

American River Bankshares' family is growing. Formerly American River Holdings, it's the parent of American River Bank, which has five branches in California's Sacramento and Placer counties. The bank, in turn, operates two banking divisions: North Coast Bank, which has three branches in Sonoma County; and Bank of Amador (acquired in late 2004), which operates three branches in Amador County, California. The banks offer local small to midsized businesses and individuals such traditional deposit options as checking and savings accounts and CDs. They also offer commercial and residential mortgages, as well as business, construction, and consumer loans.

American River Bankshares also provides lease financing for business equipment. The bank owns two inactive companies: ARBCO and American River Mortgage.

The only beneficial owner of American River Bankshares' stock is Keefe Managers, which controls nearly 6%. New York-based Keefe Managers is an investment firm that focuses entirely on bank holding companies, banks, and thrifts.

EXECUTIVES

Chairman, American River Bankshares, American River Bank, and First Source Capital: Charles D. Fite, age 48
President, CEO, and Director; CEO, American River Bank: David T. Taber, age 45, $370,946 pay
EVP and CFO; CFO, American River Bank, First Source Capital, and North Coast Bank: Mitchell A. (Mitch) Derenzo, age 44, $177,795 pay
EVP and CIO: Kevin B. Bender, age 42, $133,189 pay
EVP and Chief Credit Officer; SVP and Chief Credit Officer, American River Bank: Douglas E. (Doug) Tow, age 51, $172,587 pay
President, American River Bank: Gregory N. (Greg) Patton, age 47, $174,678 pay
President, Bank of Amador: Larry D. Standing, age 63, $150,000 pay
President and CEO, North Coast Bank: Raymond F. (Ray) Byrne, age 58, $156,532 pay
AVP, Human Resources: Anneliese Hein
Director, Corporate Communications: Diana Walery
Auditors: Perry-Smith & Co., LLP

LOCATIONS

HQ: American River Bankshares
3100 Zinfandel Dr., Ste. 450,
Rancho Cordova, CA 95670
Phone: 916-851-0123   **Fax:** 916-641-1262
Web: www.amrb.com

American River Bank operates offices in Fair Oaks, Roseville, and Sacramento, California. North Coast Bank, a division of American River Bank, operates offices in Healdsburg, Santa Rosa, and Windsor, California. American River Bank division, Bank of Amador, operates out of Ione, Jackson, and Pioneer, California.

PRODUCTS/OPERATIONS

2005 Sales

	$ mil.	% of total
Interest		
Loans	26.5	74
Securities	6.4	18
Other	0.3	1
Noninterest	2.3	7
Total	**35.5**	**100**

Subsidiaries and Divisions

American River Bank
  Bank of Amador
  North Coast Bank
American River Financial (inactive)

COMPETITORS

BancWest
Bank of America
Washington Mutual
Wells Fargo
Zions Bancorporation

HISTORICAL FINANCIALS

Company Type: Public

Income Statement				FYE: December 31
	ASSETS ($ mil.)	NET INCOME ($ mil.)	INCOME AS % OF ASSETS	EMPLOYEES
12/05	612.8	9.2	1.5%	122
12/04	586.7	5.8	1.0%	123
12/03	397.4	4.7	1.2%	101
12/02	342.6	4.5	1.3%	99
12/01	286.6	4.0	1.4%	100
Annual Growth	**20.9%**	**23.1%**	**—**	**5.1%**

2005 Year-End Financials

Equity as % of assets: 10.2%
Return on assets: 1.5%
Return on equity: 15.1%
Long-term debt ($ mil.): 4.3
No. of shares (mil.): 5.6
Market value ($ mil.): 117.3
Dividends
  Yield: 2.2%
  Payout: 30.9%
Sales ($ mil.): 35.5
R&D as % of sales: —
Advertising as % of sales: 0.9%

Stock History

NASDAQ (GS): AMRB

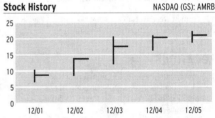

	STOCK PRICE ($)	P/E		PER SHARE ($)		
	FY Close	High/Low		Earnings	Dividends	Book Value
12/05	20.92	14	12	1.52	0.47	11.20
12/04	20.29	19	15	1.07	0.30	11.10
12/03	17.54	22	13	0.95	0.38	8.74
12/02	13.72	15	10	0.90	0.16	12.08
12/01	8.69	12	8	0.82	0.14	11.09
Annual Growth	**24.6%**	**—**	**—**	**16.7%**	**35.4%**	**0.2%**

American Science and Engineering

You can't hide from American Science and Engineering (AS&E). The company makes X-ray detection systems for inspection and security applications at airports, border control sites, shipping ports, and special events. Unlike ordinary X-rays, AS&E's backscatter technology detects organic materials such as illegal drugs, plastic explosives, and plastic weapons; its Z Backscatter Van features an X-ray system built into a delivery van. AS&E also makes scanning equipment for detecting contraband on persons

and in luggage and packages. Customers include the US Customs Service and Department of Homeland Security. About three-quarters of sales are to the US government and its contractors.

The US Department of Defense has ordered AS&E's MobileSearch X-ray inspection systems and Z Backscatter Vans with radioactive threat detection technology that will be deployed at domestic military bases to guard against the threat of nuclear devices and dirty bombs.

In 2005 AS&E sold its High Energy Systems division (linear accelerators) to Accuray for about $8 million in cash and notes.

Customers located in the US account for around 85% of sales, though the company also sells to foreign government entities, primarily in the Pacific Rim and Middle East regions.

FMR (Fidelity Investments) owns about 11% of American Science and Engineering. Pyramis Global Advisors and Thompson, Siegal & Walmsley each hold about 5% of the company.

EXECUTIVES

Chairman: William E. Odom, age 74
President, CEO, and Director: Anthony R. Fabiano, age 53, $1,086,000 pay
VP, Science and Technology: Joseph Callerame, age 56, $371,934 pay
CFO and Treasurer: Kenneth J. (Ken) Galaznik, age 55, $425,000 pay
VP, Operations: Kenneth A. Breur, age 51, $425,000 pay
VP, Worldwide Marketing and Sales: Robert G. (Bob) Postle, age 52, $460,000 pay
VP, General Counsel, and Clerk: William F. Grieco, age 52
VP, Human Resources: George M. Peterman, age 58
Auditors: Vitale, Caturano & Company, Ltd.

LOCATIONS

HQ: American Science and Engineering, Inc.
829 Middlesex Tpke., Billerica, MA 01821
Phone: 978-262-8700   **Fax:** 978-262-8804
Web: www.as-e.com

American Science and Engineering has facilities in Billerica, Massachusetts.

2006 Sales

	$ mil.	% of total
US	141.5	86
Other countries	22.1	14
Total	**163.6**	**100**

PRODUCTS/OPERATIONS

2006 Sales

	$ mil.	% of total
Product sales & contract revenue	128.1	78
Service revenue	35.5	22
Total	**163.6**	**100**

Selected Security Products

Backscatter-only Inspection Systems
Z Backscatter Portal (drive-through inspection system for scanning vehicles)
Z Backscatter Van (screening system built into commercial delivery van)
BodySearch (personnel screening system)

CargoSearch Series
MobileSearch (inspection of containers, vehicles, and other large items)
PalletSearch (cargo inspection on large, dense pallets)
Shaped Energy CargoSearch (vehicle inspection system)
Shaped Energy Gantry System (mobile sea container inspection system)
ParcelSearch Series
101GT (portable customs and mail inspection)
101VAN (vehicle-mounted inspection system)
101XL (pallet inspection system)
101Z Luggage and Parcel Inspection System
101ZZ (mobile inspection system for small cargo)
Model 66Zplus (compact system for briefcases, carry-on luggage, and mail)

COMPETITORS

Analogic
GE Infrastructure
ICTS International
Magal
OSI Systems
Smiths Detection
Thermo Fisher Scientific

HISTORICAL FINANCIALS

Company Type: Public

Income Statement
FYE: Friday nearest March 31

	REVENUE ($ mil.)	NET INCOME ($ mil.)	NET PROFIT MARGIN	EMPLOYEES
3/06	163.6	29.8	18.2%	288
3/05	88.3	11.2	12.7%	286
3/04	76.3	1.9	2.5%	324
3/03	62.0	(7.9)	—	304
3/02	65.4	(4.5)	—	373
Annual Growth	**25.8%**	**—**	**—**	**(6.3%)**

2006 Year-End Financials

Debt ratio: 7.4%
Return on equity: 31.1%
Cash ($ mil.): 93.9
Current ratio: 5.33
Long-term debt ($ mil.): 9.6
No. of shares (mil.): 9.1
Dividends
   Yield: —
   Payout: —
Market value ($ mil.): 847.2
R&D as % of sales: —
Advertising as % of sales: —

Stock History
NASDAQ (GM): ASEI

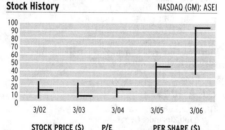

	STOCK PRICE ($) FY Close	P/E High/Low		PER SHARE ($) Earnings	Dividends	Book Value
3/06	93.40	29	11	3.27	—	14.35
3/05	44.71	38	10	1.31	—	7.38
3/04	16.50	65	28	0.26	—	5.18
3/03	8.00	—	—	(1.20)	—	4.71
3/02	15.14	—	—	(0.87)	—	4.17
Annual Growth	**57.6%**	**—**	**—**	**—**	**—**	**36.2%**

Analex

Analex brings together science and security. Formerly Hadron, the company provides a wide range of research, science, and technology services for homeland security and defense-related projects. Its systems engineering and homeland security units provide engineering, program management, and systems integration services to the US Department of Defense (about 70% of revenue), US intelligence agencies, NASA (nearly 30%), and aerospace contractors. In 2006 the company sold its SyCom Services subsidiary to Florida-based staffing firm Ameri-Force Craft Services. Analex is merging with QinetiQ North America, a subsidiary of British firm QinetiQ Group.

Upon completion of the merger, Analex will operate as a subsidiary of QinetiQ North America.

In 2004 the company acquired security support services provider Beta Analytics and sold Advanced Biosystems, a subsidiary that worked with defense and intelligence agencies to analyze the threat of biological weapons and bioterrorism. The following year Analex purchased software engineering and IT services firm ComGlobal Systems for about $47 million.

EXECUTIVES

Chairman and CEO: Sterling E. Phillips Jr., age 59, $513,337 pay
President and COO: Michael G. Stolarik, age 55, $383,367 pay
SVP, CFO, and Treasurer: C. Wayne Grubbs, age 38, $106,250 pay (partial-year salary)
SVP, Business Development: Stephen (Steve) Matthews
SVP, National Security Group: V. Joseph (Joe) Broadwater, age 50, $25,568 pay (partial-year salary)
VP and President, ComGlobal Systems: Frank F. Hewitt, age 60, $322,042 pay
VP, Human Resources: Elisa Rivera
Corporate Secretary: Catherine M. Clark
Director, Corporate Marketing: Stephanie Gilbert
Investor Relations: Amber Gordon
Auditors: Ernst & Young LLP

LOCATIONS

HQ: Analex Corporation
2677 Prosperity Ave., Ste. 400, Fairfax, VA 22031
Phone: 703-852-4000   **Fax:** 703-852-2200
Web: www.analex.com

PRODUCTS/OPERATIONS

2005 Sales

	$ mil.	% of total
Homeland Security Group	98.7	70
Systems Engineering Group	42.5	30
Total	**141.2**	**100**

2005 Sales

	% of total
Prime contract revenues	73
Subcontract revenues	27
Total	**100**

COMPETITORS

Boeing
Booz Allen
CACI International
Computer Sciences Corp.
Lockheed Martin
Northrop Grumman

HISTORICAL FINANCIALS
Company Type: Public

Income Statement				FYE: December 31
	REVENUE ($ mil.)	NET INCOME ($ mil.)	NET PROFIT MARGIN	EMPLOYEES
12/05	141.2	1.8	1.3%	1,100
12/04	94.4	(4.3)	—	920
12/03	66.1	2.8	4.2%	552
12/02	59.3	2.4	4.0%	534
12/01	21.9	0.2	0.9%	450
Annual Growth	59.3%	73.2%	—	25.0%

2005 Year-End Financials
Debt ratio: 87.6%
Return on equity: 5.0%
Cash ($ mil.): 3.5
Current ratio: 2.32
Long-term debt ($ mil.): 34.1
No. of shares (mil.): 16.3

Dividends
Yield: —
Payout: —
Market value ($ mil.): 47.6
R&D as % of sales: —
Advertising as % of sales: —

Stock History
AMEX: NLX

	STOCK PRICE ($) FY Close	P/E High/Low	PER SHARE ($) Earnings	Dividends	Book Value
12/05	2.91	— —	(0.42)	—	4.60
12/04	4.40	— —	(0.64)	—	3.17
12/03	3.65	31 14	0.14	—	2.26
12/02	2.35	22 11	0.14	—	0.96
12/01	1.75	268 45	0.02	—	0.78
Annual Growth	13.6%	— —	—	—	56.0%

AngioDynamics

AngioDynamics gets your blood flowing, and flowing cleaner if need be. The company makes medical devices for the treatment of peripheral vascular disease (PVD), end-stage renal disease, varicose veins, and other non-coronary vascular diseases. Millions of Americans suffer from PVD, a condition in which non-cardiac arteries become obstructed, narrowed, or ballooned. AngioDynamics' product line includes catheters for angiography, dialysis, and angioplasty, image-guided vascular access products, endovascular laser venous system products, and drainage products. AngioDynamics' direct sales force sells to doctors in the US; internationally, distributors sell the products in more than 30 countries.

AngioDynamics acquired oncology device maker RITA Medical Systems in early 2007 for $220 million.

While it manufactures most of its products, the company purchases some of its lines from Medcomp (dialysis catheters) and biolitec (laser fibers) and resells them under its own brands.

It has licensed the exclusive US distribution rights for Sotradecol, a drug to treat varicose veins, from Bioniche.

AngioDynamics' former parent company, E-Z-EM, distributed its 80% stake in the company to AngioDynamics shareholders as dividends in late 2004. After doing so, E-Z-EM ceased being the parent company. The companies agreed not to compete during AngioDynamics' first couple of years as a public company.

EXECUTIVES
Chairman: Paul S. Echenberg, age 62
President, CEO, and Director: Eamonn P. Hobbs, age 48, $393,618 pay
EVP and COO: Robert D. Mitchell, age 44
VP, CFO, and Treasurer: Joseph G. Gerardi, age 44
VP, Marketing: Robert M. Rossell, age 50, $224,505 pay
VP, Operations: Harold C. Mapes, age 46
VP, Product Development: Daniel K. Recinella, age 47
VP, Research: William M. Appling, age 43, $213,711 pay
VP, Sales: Paul J. Shea, age 53, $230,684 pay
Auditors: PricewaterhouseCoopers LLP

LOCATIONS
HQ: AngioDynamics, Inc.
603 Queensbury Ave., Queensbury, NY 12804
Phone: 518-798-1215   **Fax:** 518-798-3625
Web: www.angiodynamics.com

PRODUCTS/OPERATIONS

2006 Sales

	$ mil.	% of total
Angiographic products	21.4	27
Dialysis products	19.6	25
Vascular access products	12.2	16
Venous products	12.2	15
Thrombolytic products	4.5	6
PTA products	4.1	5
Drainage products	2.2	3
Other	2.2	3
Total	**78.4**	**100**

Selected Products
Angiographic products
  Accu-Vu
  Angioptic
  AQUALiner
  Mariner
  Soft-Vu
Dialysis products
  Dura-Flow
  Dynamic Flow
  EvenMore
  Schon
Drainage products
  Total Abscession
PTA products (percutaneous transluminal angioplasty)
  WorkHorse
Thrombolytic products
  Pulse*Spray
  Speedlyser
  Uni*Fuse
Vascular access products
  Morpheus
Venous products
  Sotradecol (under license)
  VenaCure

COMPETITORS
Arrow International
Boston Scientific
C. R. Bard
Cook Incorporated
Cordis
Diomed

Dornier
ev3
Smiths Group
Tyco
Vascular Solutions
VNUS Medical

HISTORICAL FINANCIALS
Company Type: Public

Income Statement				FYE: May 31
	REVENUE ($ mil.)	NET INCOME ($ mil.)	NET PROFIT MARGIN	EMPLOYEES
5/06	78.4	6.9	8.8%	306
5/05	60.3	4.6	7.6%	257
5/04	49.1	3.1	6.3%	217
5/03	38.4	1.2	3.1%	221
5/02	30.9	1.0	3.2%	—
Annual Growth	26.2%	62.1%	—	11.5%

2006 Year-End Financials
Debt ratio: 2.2%
Return on equity: 8.0%
Cash ($ mil.): 89.8
Current ratio: 11.30
Long-term debt ($ mil.): 2.8
No. of shares (mil.): 15.5

Dividends
Yield: —
Payout: —
Market value ($ mil.): 455.5
R&D as % of sales: 7.5%
Advertising as % of sales: —

Stock History
NASDAQ (GS): ANGO

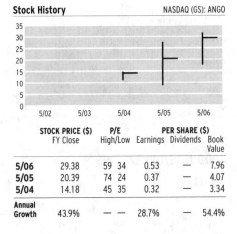

	STOCK PRICE ($) FY Close	P/E High/Low	PER SHARE ($) Earnings	Dividends	Book Value
5/06	29.38	59 34	0.53	—	7.96
5/05	20.39	74 24	0.37	—	4.07
5/04	14.18	45 35	0.32	—	3.34
Annual Growth	43.9%	— —	28.7%	—	54.4%

Anika Therapeutics

Anika Therapeutics is roosterrific. The firm uses hyaluronic acid, a natural polymer extracted from rooster combs and other sources, to make products that treat bone, cartilage, and soft tissue. Anika's OrthoVisc treats osteoarthritis of the knee and is available in the US and overseas. DePuy Mitek sells the product in the US and Mexico. A unit of Boehringer Ingelheim sells Anika's osteoarthritis treatment for racehorses, Hyvisc. Bausch & Lomb sells two of the firm's products that maintain eye shape and protect tissue during eye surgery. The company's products in development may prevent post-surgery tissue adhesions and help fill in scars, wrinkles, and lips.

OrthoVisc was approved for sale in the US by the FDA in 2004. The product has been available for several years in Canada, Turkey, and select other European and Middle Eastern countries.

Bausch & Lomb is the company's largest customer, accounting for about 46% of sales. Pharmaren, which distributes OrthoVisc in Turkey, accounts for about 23% of sales.

EXECUTIVES

President, CEO, and Director: Charles H. Sherwood, age 60, $561,923 pay

CFO: Kevin W. Quinlan, age 55, $124,808 pay (partial-year salary)

VP, Business Development and Marketing: Peter Litman, age 54

VP, Operations: Frank Luppino, age 37, $240,481 pay

VP, Regulatory and Clinical Affairs: Constance H. Garrison

VP, Research and Development: Carol Toth, age 50, $276,750 pay

Executive Director, Clinical and Regulatory Affairs: Julie Broderick

Executive Director, Human Resources: William Mrachek

Executive Director, Marketing and New Business Development: Edward (Ed) Gaj Jr., age 49

Investor Relations: Connie Andrews

Auditors: PricewaterhouseCoopers LLP

LOCATIONS

HQ: Anika Therapeutics, Inc.
160 New Boston St., Woburn, MA 01801
Phone: 781-932-6616   **Fax:** 781-935-4120
Web: www.anikatherapeutics.com

2005 Sales

	$ mil.	% of total
US	21.1	71
Turkey	4.7	16
Europe	3.2	11
Other countries	0.8	2
Total	**29.8**	**100**

PRODUCTS/OPERATIONS

2005 Sales

	$ mil.	% of total
Products		
Ophthalmic	10.5	35
OrthoVisc	7.9	27
Hyvisc	2.1	7
Licenses	9.3	31
Total	**29.8**	**100**

Selected Products

Approved
Amvisc (eye surgery product, sold by Bausch & Lomb)
Amvisc Plus (eye surgery product, sold by Bausch & Lomb)
Hyvisc (equine osteoarthritis treatment, distributed by Boehringer Ingelheim)
OrthoVisc (human osteoarthritis treatment, marketed by DePuy Mitek)
ShellGel (ophthalmic product, sold by Cytosol Ophthalmics)
STAARVISC II (ophthalmic product, sold by STAAR Surgical)
In Development
INCERT (post-surgical adhesion prevention product)
REDEFYNE (dermal filler for cosmetic tissue augmentation)

COMPETITORS

Artes Medical
BioMS Medical
Genzyme Biosurgery
Lifecore Biomedical
OrthoLogic

HISTORICAL FINANCIALS

Company Type: Public

Income Statement

FYE: December 31

	REVENUE ($ mil.)	NET INCOME ($ mil.)	NET PROFIT MARGIN	EMPLOYEES
12/05	29.8	5.9	19.8%	65
12/04	26.5	11.2	42.3%	61
12/03	15.4	0.8	5.2%	62
12/02	13.2	(3.0)	—	60
12/01	11.3	(6.8)	—	67
Annual Growth	**27.4%**	**—**		**(0.8%)**

2005 Year-End Financials

Debt ratio: —
Return on equity: 17.3%
Cash ($ mil.): 44.8
Current ratio: 8.99
Long-term debt ($ mil.): —
No. of shares (mil.): 10.5
Dividends
Yield: —
Payout: —
Market value ($ mil.): 122.7
R&D as % of sales: —
Advertising as % of sales: —

Stock History

NASDAQ (GS): ANIK

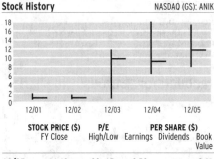

	STOCK PRICE ($) FY Close	P/E High/Low		PER SHARE ($) Earnings	Dividends	Book Value
12/05	11.69	33	15	0.52	—	3.61
12/04	9.15	18	7	0.98	—	2.96
12/03	9.74	146	12	0.08	—	1.80
12/02	0.99	—	—	(0.31)	—	1.72
12/01	1.00	—	—	(0.68)	—	2.02
Annual Growth	**84.9%**	—	—	—	—	**15.6%**

Applied Signal Technology

Eavesdropping is no accident at Applied Signal Technology. The company makes reconnaissance equipment — including receivers, processors, and software — that collects and processes telecommunications signals. Applied Signal's products scan and filter thousands of cell phone, ship-to-shore, microwave, and military transmissions and evaluate them for relevant information. The US government accounts for nearly all of the company's sales. Applied Signal is expanding into the electronics intelligence market, making equipment to collect and process radar signals from weapons systems.

The company also wants to diversify its product offerings with systems that detect chemicals, explosives, nuclear materials, and other hazardous items. To that end, it is developing neu-VISION, an imaging and identification system used to "see" through containers and walls. Additionally, it has purchased privately held Dynamics Technology, a maker of electronic sensors for such applications.

Applied Signal provides some products for commercial use, such as its DoubleTalk satellite compression system, which the company has licensed to a subsidiary of Comtech Telecommunications. After an attempt to expand its presence in the commercial market through two subsidiaries intended to develop Internet security products and services, the company dissolved those businesses and reintegrated their operations.

Applied Signal is focused on government clients, primarily intelligence agencies, but also military and law enforcement entities with signal reconnaissance needs.

HISTORY

James Collins (laboratory manager), John Treichler (chief technology officer), and Gary Yancey (chairman and CEO), all employees of reconnaissance systems maker ARGOSystems, co-founded Applied Signal Technology in 1984. Its early products were designed for the military, but with defense spending cuts in the early 1990s, the company began developing commercial products.

Applied Signal went public in 1993. Two years later it teamed up with semiconductor maker VLSI Technology (now part of Philips Electronics) to develop a chip for cable TV set-top boxes, and with Coral Systems to produce cellular call fraud-detection products. Ericsson tapped Applied Signal to develop modems for use with PCS digital wireless systems.

In 1997 Applied Signal won a subcontract from Lockheed Martin to participate in a joint services project to provide signal intelligence and geopositioning to airborne reconnaissance. It also grabbed a contract from Hughes Electronics for work on the Milsatcom network of military communications satellites. To expand its commercial customer segment, the company in 1998 sold 11 satellite monitoring systems to PanAmSat. The next year Applied Signal entered the digital radio market with a line of modem cards.

To further its quest for commercial customers, Applied Signal in 2000 formed two subsidiaries — eNetSecure (Internet security products) and Transcendent Technologies (network management and monitoring systems). The next year the company's sales slipped thanks to the unexpected loss of several key contracts; it responded by cutting staff by 30% and consolidating facilities. Applied Signal suffered a loss for fiscal 2001 and reintegrated the operations of its fledgling commercial subsidiaries.

EXECUTIVES

Chairman, President, and CEO: Gary L. Yancey, age 60, $552,858 pay

COO: Bani M. Scribner Jr., age 61, $411,319 pay

EVP, Communications Systems Group: Renato F. Roscher Jr., age 53

EVP, Sensor Signal Processing Group: William B. Van Vleet III, age 47

VP, Electronic Systems Division: Robert Blanchard, age 49
VP, Finance and CFO: James E. Doyle, age 50, $323,478 pay
VP, Multichannel Systems Division: Albert Ovadia, age 65, $330,352 pay
VP, National Security Systems Division: Robert T. Teague, age 57
VP, Ocean Systems Division: John F. Pesaturo, age 51
VP, Wireless Communication Systems Division: Joseph Leonelli, age 50
CTO and Director: John R. Treichler, age 58, $333,997 pay
Chief Marketing Officer: Michael J. Ready, age 52
Investor Relations: Alice Delgado
Auditors: Ernst & Young LLP

LOCATIONS

HQ: Applied Signal Technology, Inc.
400 W. California Ave., Sunnyvale, CA 94086
Phone: 408-749-1888   **Fax:** 408-738-1928
Web: www.appsig.com

Applied Signal Technology has facilities in California, Florida, Maryland, Oregon, Texas, Utah, and Virginia.

PRODUCTS/OPERATIONS

2006 Sales by Market

	% of total
Intelligence agencies	74
Military	23
Commercial	2
Foreign	1
Total	**100**

Selected Products and Systems

Broadband compression systems (DoubleTalk)
IF/RF processing equipment
  Frequency translators
Naval and coastal surveillance tools (COASTAL WATCH, REACT)
Neutron imaging and materials identification systems (neu-VISION)
Recorder/signal generation products
  Signal storage units
  Tape interface units
Software
  Bio-surveillance modeling and simulation
  Digital signal distribution
  Signals analysis (ELVIRA)
  Underground facilities modeling and simulation (DUGOUT)
Systems support products
  Multiplexers/demultiplexers
  Optical converters
  Splitters
  Switches
Underwater imaging systems
  Synthetic aperture sonar processors (PROSAS)
  Mine detection systems (MINE*SCOUT*)
Voice-grade channel processors
  Multichannel processors
  Raptor processing system
  Voice channel demodulators
Wideband digital signal processors
Wireless signal processing systems

COMPETITORS

Argon ST
BAE SYSTEMS
Boeing
DRS Technologies
EDO
General Dynamics
Harris Corp.
L-3 Communications
Lockheed Martin
Northrop Grumman
QinetiQ
Raytheon
Sierra Nevada Corp.
Spectrum Signal

HISTORICAL FINANCIALS

Company Type: Public

Income Statement

FYE: October 31

	REVENUE ($ mil.)	NET INCOME ($ mil.)	NET PROFIT MARGIN	EMPLOYEES
10/06	161.9	4.3	2.7%	647
10/05	156.1	9.2	5.9%	677
10/04	142.8	12.0	8.4%	498
10/03	95.4	8.7	9.1%	425
10/02	76.2	3.9	5.1%	357
Annual Growth	**20.7%**	**2.5%**	**—**	**16.0%**

2006 Year-End Financials

Debt ratio: 6.4%
Return on equity: 4.2%
Cash ($ mil.): 29.8
Current ratio: 4.02
Long-term debt ($ mil.): 6.8
No. of shares (mil.): 11.9
Dividends
  Yield: 1.7%
  Payout: 69.4%
Market value ($ mil.): 176.9
R&D as % of sales: —
Advertising as % of sales: —

Stock History

NASDAQ (GS): APSG

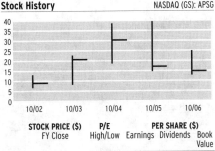

	STOCK PRICE ($) FY Close	P/E High/Low		PER SHARE ($) Earnings	Dividends	Book Value
10/06	14.84	68	37	0.36	0.25	8.86
10/05	17.16	50	19	0.79	0.50	8.49
10/04	30.29	37	18	1.03	0.19	7.97
10/03	20.70	28	11	0.80	—	7.08
10/02	9.01	33	18	0.39	—	6.46
Annual Growth	**13.3%**	**—**	**—**	**(2.0%)**	**14.7%**	**8.2%**

Aptimus

Aptimus thinks it's the most qualified to bring you online shopping deals. The company, whose name is derived from the Latin words *aptus* (unusually qualified) and *optimus* (most beneficial), operates an ad network that showcases free, trial, and promotional offers from a variety of corporate clients. Aptimus provides banner ads, hyperlinks, and pop-ups across its network of sites as part of its clients' marketing campaigns and coordinates mailings using its database of e-mail addresses of people who have opted to receive promotional offers. Clients have included Procter & Gamble, Advertising.com, and Quinstreet. Chairman Timothy Choate owns about 24% of the company.

Aptimus expanded in 2006 by buying online marketing firm High Voltage Interactive, which specializes in recruitment campaigns for education companies such as the University of Phoenix and ITT.

EXECUTIVES

Chairman: Timothy C. (Tim) Choate, age 40
President, CEO, and Director: Robert W. (Rob) Wrubel, age 45
SVP and COO, High Voltage Interactive: Paul Epstein
SVP Sales and Marketing: Dayton Keane
SVP Strategic Business Development, East Coast: Michael Mayor, age 44
SVP Strategic Business Development, West Coast: Brad Benz
VP Finance, CFO, and Chief Accounting Officer: John A. Wade, age 43
VP Technology: Lance J. Nelson, age 36
General Counsel and Secretary: David H. (Dave) Davis, age 47
Public Relations Contact: Holly Nuss
Auditors: Moss Adams, LLP

LOCATIONS

HQ: Aptimus, Inc.
100 Spear St., Ste. 1115, San Francisco, CA 94105
Phone: 415-896-2123   **Fax:** 415-896-2561
Web: www.aptimus.com

PRODUCTS/OPERATIONS

Selected Services

Co-Registration (registration on company Web sites that allow visitors to opt-in for promotional offers)
E-mail Direct Marketing
Pop-Up Ads

COMPETITORS

24/7 Real Media
Advertising.com
Claria
DoubleClick
E-centives
Google
Q Interactive
Traffix
ValueClick
Yahoo!

HISTORICAL FINANCIALS

Company Type: Public

Income Statement

FYE: December 31

	REVENUE ($ mil.)	NET INCOME ($ mil.)	NET PROFIT MARGIN	EMPLOYEES
12/05	15.9	1.4	8.8%	48
12/04	14.0	2.1	15.0%	34
12/03	4.6	(1.5)	—	25
12/02	2.9	(5.5)	—	21
12/01	1.9	(17.9)	—	28
Annual Growth	**70.1%**	**—**	**—**	**14.4%**

2005 Year-End Financials

Debt ratio: —
Return on equity: 15.8%
Cash ($ mil.): 10.4
Current ratio: 9.76
Long-term debt ($ mil.): —
No. of shares (mil.): 6.5
Dividends
  Yield: —
  Payout: —
Market value ($ mil.): 51.6
R&D as % of sales: 4.1%
Advertising as % of sales: 1.3%

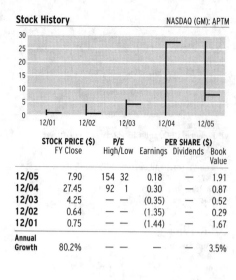

	STOCK PRICE ($) FY Close	P/E High/Low		PER SHARE ($) Earnings	Dividends	Book Value
12/05	7.90	154	32	0.18	—	1.91
12/04	27.45	92	1	0.30	—	0.87
12/03	4.25	—	—	(0.35)	—	0.52
12/02	0.64	—	—	(1.35)	—	0.29
12/01	0.75	—	—	(1.44)	—	1.67
Annual Growth	80.2%	—	—	—	—	3.5%

Arena Resources

Independent energy company Arena Resources battles with the big boys in the arena of oil and gas exploration and production. The company operates in Kansas, New Mexico, Oklahoma, and Texas, and has proved reserves of 30.2 million barrels of oil equivalent. Its assets in Oklahoma and Texas account for the bulk of the company's proved reserves. Arena Resources had an average daily production of 2,050 barrels of oil equivalent in 2004. Navajo Refining accounted for 72% of the company's revenues in 2005; Plains Marketing, 12%. President and CEO Lloyd Rochford holds a 9% stake in Arena Resources.

Arena Resources was founded in 2000. The exploration and production independent drilled its first successful well (in Oklahoma) in 2001. It expanded its operations that year by acquiring assets in Texas. In 2005 the company acquired the Parrish Lease located in Andrews County, Texas for a price of $1.2 million. The deal added 945,000 barrels of oil equivalent to Arena Resources' proved reserves.

EXECUTIVES

Chairman, Secretary, and Treasurer: Stanley M. McCabe, age 73
President, CEO, and Director: Lloyd T. (Tim) Rochford, age 59
VP and CFO: William Randall (Randy) Broaddrick, age 27, $55,667 pay
Auditors: Hansen, Barnett & Maxwell

LOCATIONS

HQ: Arena Resources, Inc.
4290 S. Lewis Ave., Ste. 107, Tulsa, OK 74105
Phone: 918-747-6060   **Fax:** 918-747-7620
Web: www.arenaresourcesinc.com

PRODUCTS/OPERATIONS

2005 Sales

	% of total
Navajo Refining	72
Plains Marketing	12
Other customers	16
Total	**100**

COMPETITORS

Anadarko Petroleum
Apache
Cabot Oil & Gas
Chesapeake Energy
Key Energy
Pioneer Natural Resources

HISTORICAL FINANCIALS
Company Type: Public

Income Statement   FYE: December 31

	REVENUE ($ mil.)	NET INCOME ($ mil.)	NET PROFIT MARGIN	EMPLOYEES
12/05	25.8	9.5	36.8%	22
12/04	8.5	2.5	29.4%	10
12/03	3.7	0.8	21.6%	7
12/02	1.7	0.4	23.5%	5
12/01	0.3	0.0	—	
Annual Growth	204.5%	—	—	63.9%

2005 Year-End Financials

Debt ratio: 0.7%
Return on equity: 23.9%
Cash ($ mil.): 4.3
Current ratio: 1.16
Long-term debt ($ mil.): 0.4
No. of shares (mil.): 13.1

Dividends
 Yield: —
 Payout: —
Market value ($ mil.): 361.6
R&D as % of sales: —
Advertising as % of sales: —

Stock History   NYSE: ARD

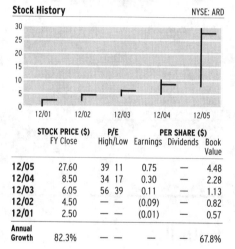

	STOCK PRICE ($) FY Close	P/E High/Low		PER SHARE ($) Earnings	Dividends	Book Value
12/05	27.60	39	11	0.75	—	4.48
12/04	8.50	34	17	0.30	—	2.28
12/03	6.05	56	39	0.11	—	1.13
12/02	4.50	—	—	(0.09)	—	0.82
12/01	2.50	—	—	(0.01)	—	0.57
Annual Growth	82.3%	—	—	—	—	67.8%

Argon ST

Argon ST makes electronic intelligence, communications, and imaging systems. Offerings include electronic intelligence systems that intercept, interpret, and track microwave signals from hostile radar and weapons; systems that intercept and locate the source of microwave communications; secure communications systems; and imaging systems used to survey geographic areas of interest. The US Navy accounts for nearly 60% of the company's sales; other US government entities account for another 31%. In 2005 Argon ST acquired Radix Technologies, a maker of signal processing equipment.

Argon ST was formed when defense communications specialist Argon Engineering Associates combined with Sensytech in a reverse acquisition in September 2004.

In 2006 Argon ST acquired wireless communications network provider San Diego Research Center Inc. for $41 million.

Chairman, president, and CEO Terry Collins owns about 12% of Argon ST, as does VP, CFO, and director Victor Sellier. VP and director Thomas Murdock owns about 11%.

EXECUTIVES

Chairman, President and CEO: Terry L. Collins, age 61, $420,244 pay
Vice Chairman and VP, Corporate Development: S. Kent Rockwell, age 62, $266,537 pay
COO: Kerry M. Rowe, age 47, $398,973 pay
VP, Information Dominance, Engineering: W. Joseph Carlin, age 43
VP, Business Operations, Treasurer, CFO, and Director: Victor (Vic) Sellier, age 57, $434,680 pay
VP, Strategic Program Development: Thomas E. (Tom) Murdock, age 64, $372,800 pay
VP, Technology and Strategic Development, Advanced Systems: Robert S. Tamaru, age 51
Investor Relations: Betty Wells
Human Resources Manager: Abbey Flowers
Auditors: Grant Thornton LLP

LOCATIONS

HQ: Argon ST, Inc.
12701 Fair Lakes Cir., Ste. 800, Fairfax, VA 22033
Phone: 703-322-0881   **Fax:** 703-322-0885
Web: www.argonst.com

Argon ST operates from facilities in California, Florida, Michigan, Pennsylvania, and Virginia.

COMPETITORS

Applied Signal
BAE SYSTEMS
Boeing
DRS Technologies
EDO
General Dynamics
Harris Corp.
L-3 Communications
Lockheed Martin
Northrop Grumman
Raytheon
Southwest Research Institute

HISTORICAL FINANCIALS
Company Type: Public

Income Statement   FYE: September 30

	REVENUE ($ mil.)	NET INCOME ($ mil.)	NET PROFIT MARGIN	EMPLOYEES
9/06	258.8	19.4	7.5%	840
9/05	271.8	21.8	8.0%	637
9/04	129.2	9.9	7.7%	601
9/03	53.2	4.1	7.7%	220
9/02	32.3	2.2	6.8%	201
Annual Growth	68.2%	72.3%	—	43.0%

2006 Year-End Financials

Debt ratio: 0.0%
Return on equity: 8.5%
Cash ($ mil.): 33.5
Current ratio: 3.08
Long-term debt ($ mil.): 0.1
No. of shares (mil.): 22.2

Dividends
 Yield: —
 Payout: —
Market value ($ mil.): 531.8
R&D as % of sales: —
Advertising as % of sales: —

Stock History

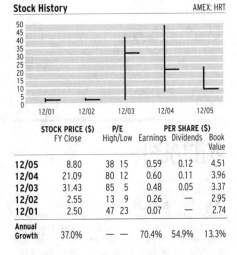

	STOCK PRICE ($) FY Close	P/E High/Low		PER SHARE ($) Earnings	Dividends	Book Value
9/06	23.97	41	24	0.87	—	11.98
9/05	29.34	36	21	1.06	—	9.59
9/04	28.10	40	16	0.74	—	8.27
9/03	15.84	31	11	0.65	—	—
9/02	9.01	20	10	0.52	—	—
Annual Growth	27.7%	—	—	13.7%	—	20.4%

Arrhythmia Research Technology

It's all about heart for Arrhythmia Research Technology (ART). The company offers signal-averaging electrocardiographic (SAECG) software that collects data and analyzes electrical impulses of the heart in an effort to detect potentially lethal heart arrhythmias. The company plans to sell the products through licensing agreements with equipment makers. Until it finds a marketing partner, however, ART is relying on sales from its Micron Products subsidiary, which makes snaps and sensors used in the manufacture and operation of disposable electrodes for electrocardiographic (ECG) equipment.

EXECUTIVES

Chairman: E. P. Marinos, age 64
President, CEO, and Director: James E. Rouse, age 51, $175,000 pay
EVP, Finance and CFO: David A. Garrison, age 38, $125,000 pay
Auditors: Carlin, Charron & Rosen LLP

LOCATIONS

HQ: Arrhythmia Research Technology, Inc.
25 Sawyer Passway, Fitchburg, MA 01420
Phone: 978-345-5000 **Fax:** 978-342-0168
Web: www.arthrt.com

2005 Sales

	% of total
Canada	38
US	34
Europe	23
Pacific Rim	3
Other regions	2
Total	**100**

COMPETITORS

Criticare
Merit Medical Systems
Spacelabs Medical

HISTORICAL FINANCIALS

Company Type: Public

Income Statement

FYE: December 31

	REVENUE ($ mil.)	NET INCOME ($ mil.)	NET PROFIT MARGIN	EMPLOYEES
12/05	12.9	1.6	12.4%	75
12/04	11.1	1.6	14.4%	63
12/03	7.7	1.3	16.9%	49
12/02	7.2	0.8	11.1%	46
12/01	7.2	0.2	2.8%	48
Annual Growth	15.7%	68.2%	—	11.8%

2005 Year-End Financials

Debt ratio: —
Return on equity: 14.2%
Cash ($ mil.): 2.3
Current ratio: 7.74
Long-term debt ($ mil.): —
No. of shares (mil.): 2.7

Dividends
　Yield: 1.4%
　Payout: 20.3%
Market value ($ mil.): 23.5
R&D as % of sales: 0.4%
Advertising as % of sales: —

Stock History

	STOCK PRICE ($) FY Close	P/E High/Low		PER SHARE ($) Earnings	Dividends	Book Value
12/05	8.80	38	15	0.59	0.12	4.51
12/04	21.09	80	12	0.60	0.11	3.96
12/03	31.43	85	5	0.48	0.05	3.37
12/02	2.55	13	9	0.26	—	2.95
12/01	2.50	47	23	0.07	—	2.74
Annual Growth	37.0%	—	—	70.4%	54.9%	13.3%

ARRIS Group

ARRIS brings the idea of broadband home. The company makes communications equipment and components used to enable voice and data transmission in high-speed networks and to build television broadcast networks. ARRIS' products include cable network headend gear, IP switching systems, modems and other consumer premises products, and associated software. The company also sells such related hardware as cable, connectors, and other supplies used for mounting and installation. ARRIS primarily serves cable operators; other clients include local and long distance carriers.

ARRIS's largest customers — Comcast, Cox Communications, Liberty Media, and Time Warner Cable — collectively account for more than 65% of the company's sales; Portuguese cable operator Cabovisao is also a customer.

HISTORY

Formed as a division of Anixter Bros. (now Anixter International) in 1969, ANTEC became a wholly owned subsidiary of that company in 1993 and went public later that year. The company made several strategic acquisitions in 1994, in-

cluding broadband consulting company Electronic System Products, broadband power supply manufacturer Power Guard, and telecommunications equipment maker Keptel.

In 1995 ANTEC and Northern Telecom (now Nortel Networks) created a joint venture called Arris Interactive to sell voice and Internet access equipment to cable operators. ANTEC also opened a research and development facility near Atlanta that year.

When cable giant — and major customer — TCI stopped its capital spending in 1996, ANTEC's sales and profits suffered into the next year. The company in 1997 acquired optical node and distribution amplifier maker TSX. The next year Anixter sold its stake in the company.

In 1999 Nortel's broadband operations (formerly LANcity) became part of Arris Interactive, reducing ANTEC's stake in the joint venture from 25% to 19%. That year the company moved its headquarters from Illinois to Georgia.

In early 2000 John Egan, who had joined ANTEC in 1973 and served as CEO since 1980, passed the torch on to president and COO Robert Stanzione; Egan remains chairman. Later that year the company laid off workers when AT&T Broadband, its largest customer, began canceling orders.

Amid continued slowing sales of telecom gear the company announced in 2001 that it would continue cutting staff. Also that year ANTEC increased its stake in Arris Interactive, from 19% to 51%. ANTEC effectively became a subsidiary of the combined company, which changed its name to ARRIS Group. The company bought privately held cable modem termination system maker Cadant in 2002, and network traffic flow specialist Atoga in 2003. The company also bought assets of cable modem termination systems maker Com21 and sold its engineering services product line in 2003.

EXECUTIVES

Chairman and CEO: Robert J. (Bob) Stanzione, age 58, $1,800,000 pay
EVP, CFO, and CIO: David B. (Dave) Potts, age 47, $509,500 pay
EVP, Strategic Planning and Administration, Chief Counsel, and Secretary: Lawrence A. (Larry) Margolis, age 57, $765,550 pay
SVP, Asia Sales: George Fletcher
SVP, Sales Engineering: Richard Rommes
VP and Treasurer: Marc S. Geraci, age 53
President, Broadband: James D. Lakin, age 62, $524,323 pay
President, New Business Ventures: Bryant K. Isaacs, age 46
President, TeleWire Supply: Robert (Bob) Puccini, age 44
President, Worldwide Sales: Ronald M. (Ron) Coppock, age 51, $449,050 pay
Investor Relations Contact: James A. Bauer
Auditors: Ernst & Young LLP

LOCATIONS

HQ: ARRIS Group, Inc.
3871 Lakefield Dr., Suwanee, GA 30024
Phone: 770-622-8400 **Fax:** 770-622-8770
Web: www.arrisi.com

2005 Sales

	$ mil.	% of total
North America		
US	495.8	73
Canada	41.1	6
Europe	67.4	10
Asia/Pacific	51.1	7
Latin America	25.0	4
Total	**680.4**	**100**

PRODUCTS/OPERATIONS

2005 Sales

	$ mil.	% of total
Customer premise equipment & supplies	365.3	54
Broadband	315.1	46
Total	**680.4**	**100**

Selected Products and Services

Broadband

Headend equipment
- Constant bit rate host digital terminals (Cornerstone Voice)
- Voice over IP and data cable modem termination systems (Cornerstone Cadant)

Subscriber premises
- Cable modems (Touchstone)
- Network interface units (Voice Port)
- Services (systems integration and operations center design, installation, activation, and traffic planning)

Optical transmission
- Amplifiers
- Block converters
- DWDM transport systems (Transplex)
- Element management software
- Receivers (Laser Link)
- Routers (Optical Application Routers)
- Transmitters (Laser Link)

Interconnectivity
- Connectors (Digicon)
- Demarcation housings
- Optical entrance enclosures
- Outside plant fiber optics
- Splice closures (LightGuard)
- Transmission equipment

Supplies
- Conduit
- Galvanized steel cables and strand
- Pedestals
- Power protection materials
- Test equipment
- Tools
- Underground vaults

COMPETITORS

ADC Telecommunications
Alcatel-Lucent
Aurora Networks
C-COR
Cisco Systems
CommScope
Fujitsu
Harmonic
JDS Uniphase
Juniper Networks
Motorola
Philips Electronics
Scientific-Atlanta
Siemens AG
Tellabs
Terayon Communication Systems
Vyyo

HISTORICAL FINANCIALS

Company Type: Public

Income Statement — FYE: December 31

	REVENUE ($ mil.)	NET INCOME ($ mil.)	NET PROFIT MARGIN	EMPLOYEES
12/05	680.4	51.5	7.6%	732
12/04	490.0	(28.4)	—	728
12/03	434.0	(47.3)	—	791
12/02	651.9	(191.2)	—	959
12/01	747.7	(167.7)	—	1,416
Annual Growth	**(2.3%)**	**—**	**—**	**(15.2%)**

2005 Year-End Financials

Debt ratio: —
Return on equity: 14.6%
Cash ($ mil.): 135.6
Current ratio: 4.08
Long-term debt ($ mil.): —
No. of shares (mil.): 105.6

Dividends
Yield: —
Payout: —
Market value ($ mil.): 1,000.0
R&D as % of sales: 8.8%
Advertising as % of sales: 0.0%

Stock History — NASDAQ (GS): ARRS

	STOCK PRICE ($) FY Close	P/E High/Low	Earnings	Dividends	Book Value
12/05	9.47	25 10	0.52	—	4.03
12/04	7.04	— —	(0.33)	—	3.21
12/03	7.24	— —	(0.62)	—	2.88
12/02	3.57	— —	(2.33)	—	4.29
12/01	9.76	— —	(3.13)	—	5.51
Annual Growth	**(0.8%)**	**— —**	**—**	**—**	**(7.5%)**

ArthroCare

With the wave of a wand, ArthroCare makes tissue disappear. The company's proprietary Coblation technology uses radio frequency energy to remove soft tissue from the body. Its Arthroscopic Surgery System lets surgeons use specialized wands to focus the energy and minimize damage to nearby healthy tissue, simultaneously sealing small, bleeding vessels. First used in arthroscopic procedures to repair joints, the electrosurgery system product line now includes equipment used in ear, nose, and throat procedures; cardiology and gynecology; spinal and neurological surgery; and cosmetic surgery.

ArthroCare plans to continue to expand its product line and develop strategic partnerships. The company also intends to focus on the sale of disposable devices.

EXECUTIVES

President, CEO, and Director: Michael A. Baker, age 47, $599,575 pay
SVP and CFO: Michael Gluk, age 48
SVP, Operations: Richard A. (Rich) Christensen, age 46, $319,293 pay
SVP, Strategic Business Units: John T. Raffle
SVP and President, Sports Medicine: John H. (Jack) Giroux, age 61, $346,353 pay
VP and General Manager, ArthroCare ENT and Visage: Ronald A. (Ron) Underwood, age 54
VP and General Manager, ArthroCare Europe: Sten I. Dahlborg, age 43
VP and General Manager, ArthroCare Spine: David B. Applegate, age 47
VP and General Manager, Coblation Technologies and Regulatory Affairs: Bruce C. Prothro, age 44
VP, Corporate Development and Medical Director: Norman R. (Norm) Sanders
VP, CTO, and Chief Scientific Officer: Jean A. Woloszko, age 48
VP, Sales: Ross Beam
Auditors: PricewaterhouseCoopers LLP

LOCATIONS

HQ: ArthroCare Corporation
111 Congress Ave., Ste. 510, Austin, TX 78701
Phone: 512-391-3900   **Fax:** 512-391-3901
Web: www.arthrocare.com

2005 Product Sales

	$ mil.	% of total
Americas	163.2	79
UK	11.7	6
Other countries	31.6	15
Total	**206.5**	**100**

PRODUCTS/OPERATIONS

2005 Sales

	$ mil.	% of total
Product sales	206.5	96
Royalties, fees & other	7.8	4
Total	**214.3**	**100**

COMPETITORS

Arthrex
C. R. Bard
Cardinal Health
Codman & Shurtleff
CONMED Corporation
Cook Incorporated
DePuy Spine
Edwards Lifesciences
Ethicon Endo-Surgery
Guidant
Gyrus
Johnson & Johnson
Karl Storz
Kyphon
Laserscope
Medtronic
Medtronic Sofamor Danek
Radionics
Smith & Nephew
St. Jude Medical
Stryker
Synthes
Trimedyne
United States Surgical
Urologix

HISTORICAL FINANCIALS

Company Type: Public

Income Statement — FYE: Saturday nearest December 31

	REVENUE ($ mil.)	NET INCOME ($ mil.)	NET PROFIT MARGIN	EMPLOYEES
12/05	214.3	23.5	11.0%	1,324
12/04	154.1	(26.2)	—	643
12/03	118.8	7.5	6.3%	565
12/02	88.8	1.1	1.2%	498
12/01	83.3	10.1	12.1%	286
Annual Growth	**26.6%**	**23.5%**	**—**	**46.7%**

2005 Year-End Financials

Debt ratio: —
Return on equity: 11.6%
Cash ($ mil.): 23.3
Current ratio: 3.91
Long-term debt ($ mil.): —
No. of shares (mil.): 25.3

Dividends
Yield: —
Payout: —
Market value ($ mil.): 1,064.2
R&D as % of sales: 9.8%
Advertising as % of sales: 1.8%

Stock History

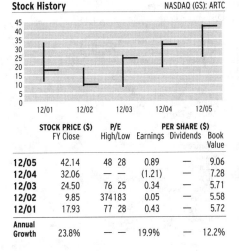

	STOCK PRICE ($) FY Close	P/E High/Low		PER SHARE ($) Earnings	Dividends	Book Value
12/05	42.14	48	28	0.89	—	9.06
12/04	32.06	—	—	(1.21)	—	7.28
12/03	24.50	76	25	0.34	—	5.71
12/02	9.85	374	183	0.05	—	5.58
12/01	17.93	77	28	0.43	—	5.72
Annual Growth	23.8%	—	—	19.9%	—	12.2%

Aspect Medical Systems

"Frère Jacques. Frère Jacques. Dormez-vous?" Aspect Medical Systems can give you the answer. The company makes the BIS System, which can assess consciousness levels during surgery. The system is based on its Bispectral Index technology, which measures the effects of anesthetics on the brain. The BIS is designed to prevent surgical awareness, wherein patients become conscious during surgery though they appear anesthetized and are unable to communicate. Aspect Medical Systems markets the product in the US and abroad through direct sales and distribution agreements.

Aspect Medical Systems generates most of its revenue through the sale of BIS monitors. The company plans to expand its operations in international markets.

EXECUTIVES

Chairman: J. Breckenridge Eagle, age 55
President, CEO, and Director: Nassib G. Chamoun, age 42, $453,156 pay
President, International Operations and Director: Boudewijn L.P.M. Bollen, age 58, $514,572 pay
VP, CFO, and Secretary: Michael Falvey, age 46
VP, Clinical, Regulatory, and Quality Assurance: Paul J. Manberg, age 50
VP, Corporate Communications: Emily Anderson
VP, Sales and Marketing: William H. Floyd, age 48, $355,252 pay
VP and Medical Director: Scott D. Kelley, age 46, $338,294 pay
Director, Human Resources: Margie Ahearn
Auditors: Ernst & Young LLP

LOCATIONS

HQ: Aspect Medical Systems, Inc.
141 Needham St., Newton, MA 02464
Phone: 617-559-7000   **Fax:** 617-559-7400
Web: www.aspectms.com

2005 Sales

	$ mil.	% of total
US	58.4	76
International	18.6	24
Total	**77.0**	**100**

PRODUCTS/OPERATIONS

2005 Sales

	$ mil.	% of total
Products	73.5	95
Strategic alliance	3.5	5
Total	**77.0**	**100**

Selected Products

A-2000 BIS Monitor
BIS Module Kit
BIS sensors
BIS XP System
Zipprep EEG Electrode

COMPETITORS

Bio-logic
Criticare
Invivo
Somanetics

HISTORICAL FINANCIALS

Company Type: Public

Income Statement

FYE: December 31

	REVENUE ($ mil.)	NET INCOME ($ mil.)	NET PROFIT MARGIN	EMPLOYEES
12/05	77.0	8.5	11.0%	258
12/04	55.6	0.3	0.5%	208
12/03	44.1	(6.5)	—	198
12/02	39.8	(15.3)	—	205
12/01	35.8	(17.7)	—	226
Annual Growth	21.1%	—	—	3.4%

2005 Year-End Financials

Debt ratio: —
Return on equity: 15.0%
Cash ($ mil.): 45.4
Current ratio: 4.05
Long-term debt ($ mil.): —
No. of shares (mil.): 22.3
Dividends
 Yield: —
 Payout: —
Market value ($ mil.): 765.4
R&D as % of sales: 13.6%
Advertising as % of sales: —

Stock History

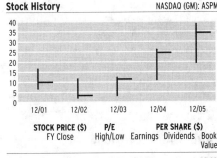

	STOCK PRICE ($) FY Close	P/E High/Low		PER SHARE ($) Earnings	Dividends	Book Value
12/05	34.35	111	56	0.35	—	3.03
12/04	24.46	2,596	1,110	0.01	—	2.19
12/03	11.43	—	—	(0.34)	—	1.59
12/02	3.39	—	—	(0.83)	—	1.90
12/01	10.00	—	—	(1.01)	—	2.70
Annual Growth	36.1%	—	—	—	—	2.9%

Asta Funding

If you can't make your car payment, Asta Funding hopes you'll pay your credit card bill instead. The company has exited the subprime auto lending business in favor of the purchase, sale, and service of unpaid credit card debts and consumer loans. Through auctions and brokers, or directly from the credit grantor, the company buys, at a discount, delinquent accounts that have been written off; these include primarily Visa, MasterCard, and private label credit card accounts; telecom wireless charge-offs; and other types of receivables. Chairman Arthur Stern, his son CEO Gary Stern, and other members of their family own nearly 30% of the company.

Asta Funding has also exited the factoring business, through which it provided accounts receivable financing to small companies. It boosted capabilities in its core business in 2002 through the purchase of a collection center. Asta Funding has also been pumping up its portfolio purchases, the latest being through its acquisition in 2005 of Denver-based consumer debt buyer and debt management company Option Card, LLC, which includes portfolios of distressed consumer receivable debt valued at nearly $200 million.

In early 2006 Asta Funding announced plans to acquire Sugar Land, Texas-based VATIV Recovery Solutions. Founded in 1989, VATIV provides bankruptcy and deceased account recovery services nationwide.

EXECUTIVES

Chairman and EVP: Arthur Stern, age 86, $401,923 pay
President, CEO, and Director: Gary Stern, age 54, $638,462 pay
CFO and Secretary: Mitchell M. Cohen, age 50, $276,923 pay
VP, Business Development: Rob Knight
VP, Operations: Mary Curtin
VP and National Sales Manager: Nan Beilinson
Director, Human Resources: Gihan Elsmira
Auditors: Eisner LLP

LOCATIONS

HQ: Asta Funding, Inc.
210 Sylvan Ave., Englewood Cliffs, NJ 07632
Phone: 201-567-5648   **Fax:** 201-569-4595
Web: www.astafunding.com

COMPETITORS

Aegis Consumer Funding
Applied Card Systems
Arrow Financial Services
Asset Acceptance
Encore Capital Group, Inc.
FirstCity Financial
Genesis Financial Solutions
NCO
Outsourcing Solutions
Performance Capital
Plaza Associates
Portfolio Recovery
Rampart Capital

HISTORICAL FINANCIALS

Company Type: Public

Income Statement

FYE: September 30

	REVENUE ($ mil.)	NET INCOME ($ mil.)	NET PROFIT MARGIN	EMPLOYEES
9/06	102.0	45.8	44.9%	166
9/05	69.5	31.0	44.6%	131
9/04	51.2	22.2	43.4%	66
9/03	34.9	11.6	33.2%	81
9/02	36.0	10.4	28.9%	50
Annual Growth	29.7%	44.9%	—	35.0%

2006 Year-End Financials

Debt ratio: 44.9%
Return on equity: 27.8%
Cash ($ mil.): 7.8
Current ratio: —
Long-term debt ($ mil.): 82.8
No. of shares (mil.): 13.8

Dividends
Yield: 1.5%
Payout: 17.9%
Market value ($ mil.): 515.7
R&D as % of sales: —
Advertising as % of sales: —

Stock History

NASDAQ (GS): ASFI

	STOCK PRICE ($) FY Close	P/E High/Low		PER SHARE ($) Earnings	Dividends	Book Value
9/06	37.49	14	7	3.13	0.56	13.40
9/05	30.36	15	7	2.15	0.14	10.68
9/04	16.19	13	8	1.57	0.12	8.52
9/03	12.99	13	4	1.13	0.03	13.84
9/02	5.45	9	3	1.19	—	8.24
Annual Growth	61.9%	—	—	27.4%	165.3%	12.9%

Astea International

Astea International aspires to serve a wide field of customers. The company's customer relationship management (CRM) software is used to automate sales and service processes, manage contracts and warranties, and distribute information to employees, customers, and suppliers. Astea's customers (primarily professional services firms or organizations that sell and service equipment) come from a variety of industries, including health care, medical devices, controls and instrumentation, information technology, facilities management, and telecommunications. The company also offers services such as consulting, implementation, and maintenance. Founder and CEO Zack Bergreen owns about 45% of Astea.

HISTORY

Zack Bergreen left computer maker Unisys and invested $25,000 to start Applied System Technologies in 1979. The company provided professional software consulting services until 1986 when it introduced its DISPATCH-1 software. By 1990 sales had reached $4.1 million as companies put more emphasis on service. In

1991 Bergreen bought the DATA Group, a provider of field service software for mainframe computers. The company changed its name to Astea International in 1992 and went public three years later.

In 1996, seeking to expand its service product offerings, Astea bought help desk software maker Bendata and Swedish sales and marketing software maker Abalon. It also expanded into the Pacific Rim. In 1997 Astea introduced Service-Alliance, customer service automation software for small and mid-sized companies. Hoping to take advantage of a growing trend of companies outsourcing their support, Astea also formed subsidiary Virtual Service in 1997, which offered Web access to DISPATCH-1.

Falling sales led Astea to trim expenses by selling Bendata to South Africa-based Ixchange Technology Holdings in 1998, and sold its Abalon unit in 1999. Bruce Rusch was named president and CEO that year; he resigned in 2000 and Bergreen resumed the CEO post.

In 2001 Astea redesigned its customer relationship software, signaling a move away from its legacy field service management products.

EXECUTIVES

Chairman and CEO: Zack B. Bergreen, age 60, $250,000 pay
President, General Counsel, and Secretary: John Tobin, age 41, $198,714 pay
CFO and Treasurer: Frederic (Rick) Etskovitz, age 51, $184,423 pay
VP, Client Services: Mark Solomon
VP, Marketing: Debbie Geiger
VP, Research and Development, and General Manager, Israel: Ariel Katz
VP, Sales: Kenneth (Ken) Roy, age 45
VP, Sales, Americas: Tim Irvine
Managing Director, Asia Pacific: Paul Buzby, $133,000 pay
Managing Director, EMEA: Mark L. Kent, $299,469 pay
Product Manager: Danny Klein
Auditors: BDO Seidman, LLP

LOCATIONS

HQ: Astea International Inc.
240 Gibraltar Rd., Ste. 300, Horsham, PA 19044
Phone: 215-682-2500   **Fax:** 215-682-2515
Web: www.astea.com

Astea International has offices in Australia, Israel, the Netherlands, the UK, and the US.

2005 Sales

	$ mil.	% of total
US	11.4	50
UK	7.5	33
Other countries	3.9	17
Total	**22.8**	**100**

PRODUCTS/OPERATIONS

2005 Sales

	$ mil.	% of total
Services & maintenance	14.5	64
Software license fees	8.3	36
Total	**22.8**	**100**

Selected Services

Consulting
Customization
Implementation
Project management
Support
Training

Selected Software

Customer relationship management (Astea Alliance)
Alliance 2-way Paging
Alliance BizTalk Connector
Alliance Consulting
Alliance Contact Center
Alliance Customer Support
Alliance Depot Repair
Alliance Education and Training
Alliance Field Service
Alliance Financial Link
Alliance Global Database
Alliance Knowledge Base
Alliance Links
Alliance Logistics
Alliance Marketing Campaigns
Alliance Notebook for Sales
Alliance Notebook for Service
Alliance PocketPC for Service
Alliance Order Processing
Alliance Professional Services
Alliance Sales
Alliance Studio
Analytics Framework

COMPETITORS

Amdocs
Chordiant Software
MDSI
Microsoft
Onyx Software
Oracle
Pivotal
SAP
Servigistics
ViryaNet

HISTORICAL FINANCIALS

Company Type: Public

Income Statement

FYE: December 31

	REVENUE ($ mil.)	NET INCOME ($ mil.)	NET PROFIT MARGIN	EMPLOYEES
12/05	22.8	1.8	7.9%	195
12/04	19.3	2.1	10.9%	139
12/03	12.8	(5.5)	—	136
12/02	16.8	(1.3)	—	137
12/01	17.1	(1.5)	—	140
Annual Growth	7.5%	—	—	8.6%

2005 Year-End Financials

Debt ratio: —
Return on equity: 20.1%
Cash ($ mil.): 9.7
Current ratio: 1.56
Long-term debt ($ mil.): —
No. of shares (mil.): 3.5

Dividends
Yield: —
Payout: —
Market value ($ mil.): 50.2
R&D as % of sales: 11.0%
Advertising as % of sales: 0.4%

Stock History

NASDAQ (CM): ATEA

	STOCK PRICE ($) FY Close	P/E High/Low		PER SHARE ($) Earnings	Dividends	Book Value
12/05	14.17	31	9	0.59	—	3.35
12/04	6.75	19	3	0.71	—	2.05
12/03	3.00	—	—	(1.89)	—	1.28
12/02	3.10	—	—	(0.45)	—	0.62
12/01	3.65	—	—	(0.50)	—	0.69
Annual Growth	40.4%	—	—	—	—	48.3%

Astronics

Lights in the sky that aren't UFOs or shooting stars may well be the work of Astronics. The company makes external and internal lighting systems, as well as power generation and distribution technology, for commercial, general aviation, and military aircraft. Products include cabin emergency lighting systems (floor and seat escape path markers, exit locators), cockpit lighting systems (avionics keyboards, ambient light sensors, annunciator panels, electronic dimmers), and formation lighting systems (external lights). Astronics' lighting systems are made by the company's Luminescent Systems unit.

In 2005 sales to commercial aviation customers (41% of sales) surpassed those to military customers (37%). The US government, once the company's largest customer, is becoming less critical to the company's success. Sales to the government accounted for about 10% of Astronics' revenue in 2005 compared to 19% in 2004, 26% in 2003, and 37% in 2002.

Astronics entered the market for electrical power generation, control, and distribution systems for aircraft in 2005 by buying the assets of Airborne Electronics Systems from a unit of General Dynamics. Astronics paid $13 million for Airborne Electronics Systems, which had revenue of about $25 million in 2004.

Chairman Kevin Keane controls a 6% equity stake and a 35% voting stake in Astronics.

HISTORY

Founded in 1968, Astronics was originally involved in electroluminescent products until it began to diversify into the packaging and printing industries. The company acquired MOD-PAC, a maker of paperboard packaging, in 1972, and Krepe-Kraft, a specialized printing company, in 1987.

In 1995 Astronics bought Loctite Luminescent Systems and integrated it with E-L FlexKey Technologies, which specialized in components used in the aerospace and military electronics industries. Later renamed Luminescent Systems, the division was awarded two high-dollar Canadian contracts the following year. One contract was for cockpit lighting systems for Bombardier's long-range business jets; the other was for ruggedized keyboards for the control room of a Canadian nuclear power plant.

The US Air Force awarded Astronics a contract to manufacture night-vision lighting for the F-16 aircraft in 1998. The next year the company was awarded an additional contract that almost doubled the number of units it would provide for F-16s. Astronics' aerospace and electronics segment doubled its manufacturing capabilities with the addition of two new facilities.

Astronics further enhanced its ability to fulfill its F-16 contract with the acquisition of Canada-based CRL Technologies (lighted keyboards) in 2000. Also that year the company acquired illuminated indicators for use in aircraft cockpits from Aerospace Avionics. In late 2001 the company was awarded a contract from the US government to provide lighted control panels for the Bradley M2A3 infantry fighting vehicle. The following year Astronics received a contract from the US Air Force valued at up to $30 million to develop spare parts for the F-16.

Astronics discontinued its electroluminescent lamp business in 2002 and spun off MOD-PAC in 2003.

EXECUTIVES

Chairman: Kevin T. Keane, age 73, $150,000 pay
President, CEO, and Director: Peter J. Gundermann, age 43, $285,000 pay
EVP, Astronics Advanced Electronics Systems: Mark Peabody
VP, CFO, Treasurer, and Secretary: David C. Burney, age 43, $182,000 pay
VP, Luminescent Systems, Inc.: Frank J. Johns III
VP, Luminescent Systems, Inc.: James S. (Jim) Kramer
VP, Luminescent Systems, Inc.: Richard C. (Rick) Miller
Manager, Human Resources: Jeanine Kusmierski
Auditors: Ernst & Young LLP

LOCATIONS

HQ: Astronics Corporation
130 Commerce Way, East Aurora, NY 14052
Phone: 716-805-1599   **Fax:** 716-805-1286
Web: www.astronics.com

Astronics has operations in Canada and the US.

2005 Sales

	$ mil.	% of total
North America	51.5	69
Asia	11.1	15
Europe	10.8	14
South America	0.9	1
Other regions	1.0	1
Total	**75.3**	**100**

PRODUCTS/OPERATIONS

2005 Sales by Customer

	% of total
Commercial transport	41
Military	37
Business jet	20
Other	2
Total	**100**

COMPETITORS

Ducommun	Key Tronic
Goodrich	Lumen Technologies
Honeywell Aerospace	Ultra Electronics
Indel	

HISTORICAL FINANCIALS

Company Type: Public

Income Statement

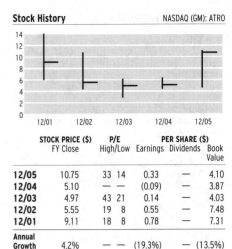

Stock History   NASDAQ (GM): ATRO

	STOCK PRICE ($) FY Close	P/E High/Low		PER SHARE ($) Earnings	Dividends	Book Value
12/05	10.75	33	14	0.33	—	4.10
12/04	5.10	—	—	(0.09)	—	3.87
12/03	4.97	43	21	0.14	—	4.03
12/02	5.55	19	8	0.55	—	7.48
12/01	9.11	18	8	0.78	—	7.31
Annual Growth	4.2%	—	—	(19.3%)	—	(13.5%)

FYE: December 31

	REVENUE ($ mil.)	NET INCOME ($ mil.)	NET PROFIT MARGIN	EMPLOYEES
12/05	75.3	2.7	3.6%	700
12/04	34.7	(0.7)	—	424
12/03	33.2	1.1	3.3%	369
12/02	42.9	4.6	10.7%	412
12/01	85.4	6.5	7.6%	700
Annual Growth	(3.1%)	(19.7%)	—	0.0%

2005 Year-End Financials

Debt ratio: 39.9%	Dividends
Return on equity: 11.1%	Yield: —
Cash ($ mil.): 4.5	Payout: —
Current ratio: 1.58	Market value ($ mil.): 67.7
Long-term debt ($ mil.): 10.3	R&D as % of sales: 11.8%
No. of shares (mil.): 6.3	Advertising as % of sales: —

A.S.V.

To everything there is a season, and A.S.V. has a vehicle for all seasons. The company uses rubber track suspension systems that make its vehicles operable in mud and snow and on slippery slopes and rough terrain. Its Posi-Track crawler/trailer models can be used instead of skid-steer vehicles and small dozers for construction needs, and in agricultural uses as small tractors. A.S.V. also makes loaders; its Loegering subsidiary makes bolt on/bolt off track systems that can convert most skid-steers from wheels to rubber tracks. A.S.V. markets its products in North America, Australia, New Zealand, and Portugal through independent dealers and Caterpillar's dealer network. Caterpillar owns about 23% of A.S.V.

Besides its 23% ownership of A.S.V., Caterpillar has options that, if exercised, would give it control of the company. It also generates nearly 40% of A.S.V.'s total sales.

The company announced plans in 2006 to expand its manufacturing plant in Grand Rapids, Minnesota, roughly doubling its machine production space by adding 120,000 sq. ft.

EXECUTIVES

Chairman and CEO: Richard A. (Dick) Benson, age 63
Vice Chairman: Jerome T. Miner, age 70
President: Mark S. Glasnapp, age 50
CFO: Thomas R. Karges, age 45, $175,000 pay
Investor Relations Manager: Lisa Walsh
Auditors: Grant Thornton LLP

LOCATIONS

HQ: A.S.V., Inc.
840 Lily Ln., Grand Rapids, MN 55744
Phone: 218-327-3434   **Fax:** 218-327-9122
Web: asvi.com

A.S.V. operates manufacturing and office facilities in Grand Rapids, Minnesota, and Casselton, North Dakota. It also has a manufacturing plant in Cohasset, Minnesota.

PRODUCTS/OPERATIONS

2005 Sales

	$ mil.	% of total
Trade	149.9	61
Caterpillar	95.2	39
Total	**245.1**	**100**

Selected Product Lines

Loegering (traction products and attachments for
wheeled skid-steers)
Multi-terrain loader undercarriages (sold to Caterpillar
for use on the company's line of skid-steer loaders)
R-Series Posi-Track line
  MD-70 (for specialty military use)
  RC-30 (31.5 hp engine)
  RC-50 (50 hp engine)
  RC-60 (turbo-charged 60 hp engine)
  RC-85 (85 hp naturally aspirated engine)
  RC-100 (99.5 hp engine)
  RCV (86 hp engine; RC-85/100 platform and vertical
    lift loader)
  SR-70 (71 hp engine)
  SR-80 (80.5 hp engine)

Selected Subsidiaries

A.S.V. Distribution, Inc.
Loegering Mfg. Inc.

COMPETITORS

Caterpillar
CNH Global
Deere
Gehl
Ingersoll-Rand
Toro

HISTORICAL FINANCIALS

Company Type: Public

Income Statement

FYE: December 31

	REVENUE ($ mil.)	NET INCOME ($ mil.)	NET PROFIT MARGIN	EMPLOYEES
12/05	245.1	27.9	11.4%	264
12/04	160.9	17.2	10.7%	224
12/03	96.4	8.7	9.0%	151
12/02	44.2	1.4	3.2%	112
12/01	50.1	0.8	1.6%	112
Annual Growth	**48.7%**	**143.0%**	**—**	**23.9%**

2005 Year-End Financials

Debt ratio: 0.1%
Return on equity: 19.6%
Cash ($ mil.): 36.7
Current ratio: 5.80
Long-term debt ($ mil.): 0.1
No. of shares (mil.): 27.0

Dividends
  Yield: —
  Payout: —
Market value ($ mil.): 674.2
R&D as % of sales: —
Advertising as % of sales: —

Stock History

NASDAQ (GS): ASVI

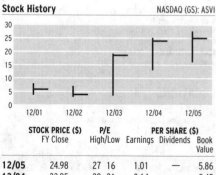

	STOCK PRICE ($) FY Close	P/E High/Low	PER SHARE ($) Earnings	Dividends	Book Value
12/05	24.98	27 16	1.01	—	5.86
12/04	23.95	39 21	0.64	—	9.45
12/03	18.63	49 10	0.39	—	6.54
12/02	3.92	105 50	0.06	—	5.01
12/01	5.83	221 114	0.04	—	4.96
Annual Growth	**43.9%**	**— —**	**124.2%**	**—**	**4.3%**

Atheros Communications

Atheros Communications builds high-speed connections right through the ether. Its radio-frequency transceiver chipsets combine features such as a radio, power amplifier, low-noise amplifier, and a media access control (MAC) processor onto just two or three chips, eliminating the need for bulkier components in wireless networking equipment. The company's top customers include networking device makers such as Alpha Networks (15% of sales), Hon Hai Precision Industry (also 15%), Cameo Communications (13%), and Askey Computer (10%). The fabless semiconductor company was started by faculty members from Stanford and Berkeley.

Nearly all sales are to customers in Asia, principally in Taiwan.

Atheros contracts out manufacturing of its chips to such silicon foundries as Taiwan Semiconductor Manufacturing, Semiconductor Manufacturing International, and Tower Semiconductor. Semiconductor packaging and testing chores are done for the company by Amkor Technology, ASAT, Siliconware Precision Industries, and STATS ChipPAC, among others.

The company has acquired ZyDAS Technology, a Taiwan-based designer of chips for wireless networks used in embedded, mobile, and PC applications. Atheros paid around $23 million in cash and stock for ZyDAS, and more than 70 employees of the privately held Taiwanese company joined Atheros following the acquisition.

Atheros has acquired Attansic Technology, a developer of networking semiconductors, for more than $71 million in cash and stock. Attansic was a subsidiary of Asustek Computer, the PC motherboard and modem manufacturer.

FMR (Fidelity Investments) owns nearly 13% of Atheros Communications. Capital Research & Management holds around 7% of the company. All officers and directors as a group own nearly 12% of Atheros.

EXECUTIVES

Chairman: John L. Hennessy, age 53
President, CEO, and Director: Craig H. Barratt, age 43, $452,360 pay
VP, CFO, and Secretary: Jack R. Lazar, age 41, $367,875 pay
VP and CTO: William J. (Bill) McFarland
VP and Chief Accounting Officer: Dave D. Torre
VP, General Counsel, and Assistant Secretary:
  Adam H. Tachner, age 40
VP, Engineering: Richard G. (Rick) Bahr, age 52, $386,942 pay
VP, Global Human Resources: Edward L. Martin
VP, Marketing: Todd D. Antes
Director, Corporate Marketing: Cheryl Patstone
Director, Human Resources: Sharon Thompson
Director, Sales, North America and Europe:
  Gary Lee McGarr
Senior Corporate Communications Manager:
  Dakota Lee
Auditors: Deloitte & Touche LLP

LOCATIONS

HQ: Atheros Communications, Inc.
  529 Almanor Ave., Sunnyvale, CA 94085
Phone: 408-773-5200   **Fax:** 408-773-9940
Web: www.atheros.com

Atheros Communications has operations in China, Hong Kong, India, Japan, Taiwan, and the US.

2005 Sales

	% of total
Taiwan	70
China	16
US	3
Other countries	11
Total	**100**

COMPETITORS

Agere Systems
Airgo Networks
Broadcom
Conexant Systems
Freescale Semiconductor
Intel
Intersil
Marvell Technology
Micro Linear
Motia
National Semiconductor
NXP
QUALCOMM
RF Micro Devices
Texas Instruments
Toshiba Semiconductor
WAV

HISTORICAL FINANCIALS

Company Type: Public

Income Statement

FYE: December 31

	REVENUE ($ mil.)	NET INCOME ($ mil.)	NET PROFIT MARGIN	EMPLOYEES
12/05	183.5	16.7	9.1%	327
12/04	169.6	10.8	6.4%	260
12/03	87.4	(13.2)	—	184
12/02	22.2	(22.4)	—	—
12/01	1.8	(30.6)	—	—
Annual Growth	**217.8%**	**—**		**33.3%**

2005 Year-End Financials

Debt ratio: —
Return on equity: 9.0%
Cash ($ mil.): 173.6
Current ratio: 5.62
Long-term debt ($ mil.): —
No. of shares (mil.): 49.8

Dividends
  Yield: —
  Payout: —
Market value ($ mil.): 647.3
R&D as % of sales: —
Advertising as % of sales: —

Stock History

NASDAQ (GS): ATHR

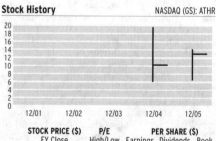

	STOCK PRICE ($) FY Close	P/E High/Low	PER SHARE ($) Earnings	Dividends	Book Value
12/05	13.00	45 21	0.31	—	3.96
12/04	10.25	93 30	0.21	—	3.61
Annual Growth	**26.8%**	**— —**	**47.6%**	**—**	**9.6%**

Atlas America

Atlas America's production map can be found on the page titled Appalachia. The independent energy company is engaged in the development, production, and transportation of natural gas (and some oil) in the Appalachian Basin. The company, which drills through partnerships, has proved reserves of 171.6 billion cu. ft. of natural gas equivalent. Atlas America has interests in 6,379 gross wells. Its natural gas transportation business is conducted through 15%-owned Atlas Pipeline Partners, which operates 3,800 miles of intrastate natural gas gathering systems in New York, Ohio, Oklahoma, Pennsylvania, and Texas. In 2006 Atlas America formed Atlas Energy Resources to own and operate its oil and gas business.

Resource America owned 80% of Atlas America before the spinoff, which took effect in June 2005. Resource America's stake was distributed to its shareholders.

In 2004, Atlas Pipeline Partners acquired Spectrum Field Services, Inc., for $142.4 million. The acquisition greatly increased Atlas Pipeline's size and expanded the natural gas supply basins in which it operates.

Atlas America announced in November 2005 that it was forming a subsidiary to hold its ownership stake in the general partner of Atlas Pipeline Partners; the company filed for an IPO of a minority stake in the new company (Atlas Pipeline Holdings, L.P.) in 2006.

EXECUTIVES

Chairman, CEO, and President: Edward E. Cohen, age 67, $1,346,154 pay
Vice Chairman: Jonathan Z. Cohen, age 35
CFO: Matthew A. Jones, age 44
EVP: Frank P. Carolas, age 46, $350,962 pay
EVP: Freddie M. Kotek, age 49, $603,846 pay
EVP: Jeffrey C. Simmons, age 47, $350,962 pay
SVP and Chief Accounting Officer: Nancy J. McGurk, age 50
SVP Direct Participation Programs: Jack L. Hollander
VP Investor Relations: Brian J. Begley
VP Marketing: Marci F. Bleichmar, age 33
VP Public Relations and Investors Relations Contact: Pamela Schreiber
Secretary and Chief Legal Officer: Lisa Washington, age 38
Auditors: Grant Thornton LLP

LOCATIONS

HQ: Atlas America, Inc.
311 Rouser Rd., Moon Township, PA 15108
Phone: 412-262-2830   **Fax:** 412-262-7430
Web: www.atlasamerica.com

PRODUCTS/OPERATIONS

2005 Sales

	$ mil.	% of total
Gathering, transmission & processing	266.8	56
Well drilling	134.3	28
Gas & oil production	63.5	14
Well services	9.6	2
Other	0.3	—
Total	**474.5**	**100**

COMPETITORS

Anadarko Petroleum
Belden & Blake
Cabot Oil & Gas
Dominion Resources
Petroleum Development
Range Resources

HISTORICAL FINANCIALS

Company Type: Public

Income Statement

FYE: December 31*

	REVENUE ($ mil.)	NET INCOME ($ mil.)	NET PROFIT MARGIN	EMPLOYEES
9/05	474.5	32.9	6.9%	340
9/04	180.9	21.2	11.7%	227
9/03	105.7	13.9	13.2%	—
9/02	99.3	7.2	7.3%	—
9/01	95.9	11.4	11.9%	—
Annual Growth	**49.1%**	**30.3%**	**—**	**49.8%**

*Fiscal year change

2005 Year-End Financials

Debt ratio: 159.2%
Return on equity: 31.1%
Cash ($ mil.): 18.3
Current ratio: 0.58
Long-term debt ($ mil.): 191.6
No. of shares (mil.): 13.3

Dividends
　Yield: —
　Payout: —
Market value ($ mil.): 434.3
R&D as % of sales: —
Advertising as % of sales: —

Stock History

NASDAQ (GS): ATLS

STOCK PRICE ($) FY Close	P/E High/Low		PER SHARE ($) Earnings	Dividends	Book Value
9/05	32.57	21	9	1.64	—	9.03
9/04	14.51	13	9	1.21	—	6.83
Annual Growth	124.5%	—	—	35.5%	—	32.2%

Atlas Pipeline Partners

Atlas Pipeline Partners shoulders the burden of getting natural gas from wellheads to major gas utilities such as Peoples Natural Gas, National Fuel Gas, and East Ohio Gas. Atlas Pipeline operates about 3,830 miles of natural gas gathering systems in Arkansas, southeastern Missouri, eastern Ohio, southern Oklahoma, western New York, western Pennsylvania, and northern Texas. The company was formed to buy the gas gathering systems of its former owners Atlas America and Resource Energy. In 2006 Atlas America filed an IPO for subsidiary Atlas Pipeline Holdings L.P. to hold its ownership stake in the general partner of Atlas Pipeline.

In 2004 Atlas Pipeline acquired Spectrum Field Services, which added more than 1,900 miles of natural gas pipelines and a gas processing facility to Atlas Pipeline's asset base, for about $142 million. In an effort to further expand its geographical reach, Atlas Pipeline planned to acquire SEMCO Energy's Alaska Pipeline subsidiary for $95 million. Alaska Pipeline owns a 354-mile natural gas transmission pipeline that delivers gas to customers in Anchorage. SEMCO Energy terminated the deal in 2004.

In 2005 Atlas Pipeline acquired the Oklahoma gathering, treating, and processing assets of Energy Transfer Partners for $192 million. It also bought OGE Energy's 75% stake in NOARK Pipeline System for $173 million.

EXECUTIVES

Vice Chairman: Jonathan Z. Cohen, age 35
SVP: Alan F. Feldman, age 42
SVP and CFO, Resource America, Inc: Steven J. Kessler, age 63
SVP Resource America, Inc: David E. Bloom, age 41
VP Investor Relations: Brian J. Begley
VP Resource America, Inc.: Thomas Elliott, age 32
Chief Accounting Officer and Treasurer: Nancy J. McGurk, age 50
Secretary: Michael S. Yecies, age 38
President and CEO, Atlas Pipeline Mid-Continent LLC: Robert R. Firth, age 51
Auditors: Grant Thornton LLP

LOCATIONS

HQ: Atlas Pipeline Partners, L.P.
311 Rouser Rd., Moon Township, PA 15108
Phone: 412-262-2830   **Fax:** 412-262-2820
Web: www.atlaspipelinepartners.com/home.html

2005 Sales

	$ mil.	% of total
Mid-Continent	346.7	93
Appalachia	24.8	7
Total	**371.5**	**100**

PRODUCTS/OPERATIONS

Selected Subsidiaries

Atlas Pipeline Mid-Continent LLC
Atlas Pipeline Ohio, LLC
Atlas Pipeline Operating Partnership, L.P.
Atlas Pipeline New York, LLC
Atlas Pipeline Pennsylvania, LLC
NOARK Energy Services, LLC
Ozark Gas Transmission, LLC

COMPETITORS

Belden & Blake
Cabot Oil & Gas
Dominion Resources
Duke Energy
Equitable Resources
MarkWest Hydrocarbon
ONEOK

HISTORICAL FINANCIALS

Company Type: Public

Income Statement

FYE: December 31

	REVENUE ($ mil.)	NET INCOME ($ mil.)	NET PROFIT MARGIN	EMPLOYEES
12/05	371.5	25.8	6.9%	210
12/04	91.3	18.3	20.0%	—
12/03	15.8	9.6	60.8%	—
12/02	10.7	5.4	50.5%	—
12/01	13.1	8.6	65.6%	—
Annual Growth	**130.8%**	**31.6%**	**—**	**—**

2005 Year-End Financials

Debt ratio: 97.0%
Return on equity: 11.1%
Cash ($ mil.): 45.6
Current ratio: 1.18
Long-term debt ($ mil.): 319.8
No. of shares (mil.): 12.5

Dividends
  Yield: 5.7%
  Payout: 126.6%
Market value ($ mil.): 509.5
R&D as % of sales: —
Advertising as % of sales: —

Stock History

NYSE: APL

	STOCK PRICE ($) FY Close	P/E High/Low		PER SHARE ($) Earnings	Dividends	Book Value
12/05	40.60	27	21	1.84	2.33	26.26
12/04	41.90	17	13	2.60	2.67	24.57
12/03	40.00	20	11	2.17	2.38	16.31
12/02	25.40	19	13	1.54	2.13	12.15
12/01	24.39	23	8	2.30	2.50	13.37
Annual Growth	13.6%	—	—	(5.4%)	(1.7%)	18.4%

ATMI

ATMI's original name — Advanced Technology Materials, Inc. — contains a pretty good summary of its business. The company furnishes semiconductor makers with ultrapure materials and related packaging and delivery systems used during chip production. ATMI has formed strategic alliances with the likes of IBM, Infineon, and Texas Instruments to develop new materials and processes. To address the burgeoning semiconductor market in China, ATMI has invested in Shanghai-based Anji Microelectronics, a developer of advanced, high-performance semiconductor materials, taking a 30% equity stake in the firm and signing a joint technology development with Anji.

In an effort to combat the wild up-and-down cycles of the chip equipment industry, ATMI put in motion its plan to exit most of the businesses — including electrochemical sensors, tool maintenance services, epitaxial deposition services, and the Emosyn smart card chip unit — associated with its former Technologies division.

As part of this divestment, ATMI sold its gallium nitride (GaN) materials business to Cree and its specialty silicon epitaxial unit to International Rectifier in 2004. It also sold its line of life safety sensors to a subsidiary of First Technology that same year.

ATMI sold 84% of Emosyn to Silicon Storage Technology (SST) in 2004; it sold the remaining 16% to SST in 2005.

In late 2004 ATMI sold the assets of its Treatment Systems Division to Applied Materials. The division provides point-of-use abatement systems to the semiconductor industry that treat gas emissions from process chambers before they are released into the environment. In mid-2005 the company sold its fab parts cleaning services business, known as fab services, to Materials Support Resources (Delaware).

In 2003 ATMI expanded its offerings with its purchase of ESC, Inc., a privately held maker of surface preparation tools used in chip fabrication. The move was part of the company's efforts to serve the semiconductor industry's transition from using aluminum in the interconnects of device structures to employing copper, which is more conductive than aluminum but presents some challenges in submicron manufacturing.

FMR (Fidelity Investments) owns nearly 9% of ATMI. Westfield Capital holds around 6% of the company, while Ziff Asset Management owns nearly 6%, as do Lord, Abbett & Co. and Kern Capital Management. Principled Capital Management holds more than 5% of ATMI. T. Rowe Price has an equity stake of about 5%.

EXECUTIVES

Chairman: Eugene G. (Gene) Banucci, age 62
President, CEO, and Director:
  Douglas A. (Doug) Neugold, age 48
SVP, Business Development: Tim Carlson
SVP; General Manager, Material Lifecycle Solutions:
  Tod Higinbotham
VP, CFO, and Treasurer: Daniel P. (Dan) Sharkey, age 49, $344,980 pay
VP and Chief Legal Officer: Cynthia L. Shereda, age 49
VP, Human Resources and Organizational Development: Tom McGowan
VP, Research and Development: Thomas (Tom) Baum
Director, Investor and Corporate Communications:
  Dean C. Hamilton
Auditors: Ernst & Young LLP

LOCATIONS

HQ: ATMI, Inc.
  7 Commerce Dr., Danbury, CT 06810
Phone: 203-794-1100   **Fax:** 203-792-8040
Web: www.atmi.com

ATMI has facilities in Belgium, China, Germany, Japan, Singapore, South Korea, Taiwan, the UK, and the US.

2005 Sales

	$ mil.	% of total
Asia/Pacific		
Taiwan	64.7	23
Japan	43.1	15
Other countries	52.2	19
US	92.8	33
Other regions	29.0	10
Total	**281.8**	**100**

PRODUCTS/OPERATIONS

Selected Products

Advanced packaging and dispensing systems (NOWPak container assemblies for semiconductor manufacturing chemicals)
Gas delivery systems (Safe Delivery System, or SDS)
Liquid delivery systems (continuous refill and delivery systems)
Liquid materials (chemical vapor deposition precursors, source reagents, and thin-film materials)

COMPETITORS

Air Products	Japan Pionics
AIXTRON	Mattson Technology
Cabot Microelectronics	Mitsubishi Corporation
Celerity	MKS Instruments
Clariant	Novellus
CVD Equipment	Praxair
DuPont	Rohm and Haas
Ebara	Semitool
FSI International	SEZ Group
FUJIFILM	Ultra Clean Technology
Hitachi Chemical	Wacker Chemie

HISTORICAL FINANCIALS

Company Type: Public

Income Statement

FYE: December 31

	REVENUE ($ mil.)	NET INCOME ($ mil.)	NET PROFIT MARGIN	EMPLOYEES
12/05	281.8	30.7	10.9%	711
12/04	246.3	31.5	12.8%	671
12/03	171.6	(9.9)	—	645
12/02	212.6	(30.7)	—	1,046
12/01	213.5	(9.7)	—	1,044
Annual Growth	7.2%	—	—	(9.2%)

2005 Year-End Financials

Debt ratio: —
Return on equity: 8.2%
Cash ($ mil.): 209.9
Current ratio: 7.21
Long-term debt ($ mil.): —
No. of shares (mil.): 37.4

Dividends
  Yield: —
  Payout: —
Market value ($ mil.): 1,047.4
R&D as % of sales: 7.9%
Advertising as % of sales: —

Stock History

NASDAQ (GS): ATMI

	STOCK PRICE ($) FY Close	P/E High/Low		PER SHARE ($) Earnings	Dividends	Book Value
12/05	27.97	40	24	0.85	—	12.08
12/04	22.53	30	17	1.00	—	9.45
12/03	23.21	—	—	(0.32)	—	8.21
12/02	18.52	—	—	(1.03)	—	8.36
12/01	23.85	—	—	(0.33)	—	9.21
Annual Growth	4.1%	—	—	—	—	7.0%

Avatar Holdings

Avatar aspires to be the embodiment of quality retirement living. The company develops residential communities in the popular retirement destinations of central Florida and Arizona; amenities include golf courses, restaurants, and fitness centers. Avatar's diverse activities include home building, property management, and running a water and wastewater utility serving its southern Arizona Rio Rico resort community. The company owns some 22,000 acres in Florida and Arizona that are in or are ready for development. Chairman Jack Nash owns about 26% of the company.

To focus on its core operations, Avatar Holdings has sold its cable television holdings in Poinciana, Florida, as well as its Harbor Island marina in Hollywood, Florida. The company also continues to purchase more land in Florida with an eye on future developments.

EXECUTIVES

Chairman: Joshua Nash, age 44
Vice Chairman, President, and CEO: Gerald D. Kelfer, age 60, $5,500,000 pay
EVP, CFO, and Treasurer: Charles L. McNairy, age 59, $285,000 pay

EVP and General Counsel: Dennis J. Getman, age 61,
$387,200 pay
VP and Secretary: Juanita I. Kerrigan, age 59
Controller and Chief Accounting Officer:
Michael P. Rama
President, Avatar Properties: Jonathan Fels, age 53,
$900,000 pay
Division President, Avatar Properties, South Florida
Homebuilding Operations: Steven Knot
EVP and COO, Avatar Properties: Michael Levy, age 47,
$900,000 pay
Auditors: Ernst & Young LLP

LOCATIONS

HQ: Avatar Holdings Inc.
201 Alhambra Cir., Coral Gables, FL 33134
Phone: 305-442-7000   **Fax:** 305-448-9927
Web: www.avatarhomes.com

PRODUCTS/OPERATIONS

Selected Subsidiaries

Avatar Properties, Inc.
Avatar Retirement Communities, Inc.
Avatar Utilities, Inc.
Brookman-Fels Communities, Inc.
Rio Rico Utilities, Inc.

COMPETITORS

ACTS	Ryland
John Wieland Homes	St. Joe Towns & Resorts
Lennar	Toll Brothers
Pulte Homes	WCI Communities

HISTORICAL FINANCIALS

Company Type: Public

Income Statement

	REVENUE ($ mil.)	NET INCOME ($ mil.)	NET PROFIT MARGIN	EMPLOYEES
12/05	516.8	63.1	12.2%	585
12/04	337.4	29.6	8.8%	483
12/03	253.0	18.5	7.3%	394
12/02	190.3	5.6	2.9%	351
12/01	163.0	3.0	1.8%	445
Annual Growth	**33.4%**	**114.2%**	**—**	**7.1%**

FYE: December 31

2005 Year-End Financials

Debt ratio: 51.9%
Return on equity: 22.6%
Cash ($ mil.): 44.5
Current ratio: 0.53
Long-term debt ($ mil.): 162.3
No. of shares (mil.): 8.2
Dividends
Yield: —
Payout: —
Market value ($ mil.): 449.2
R&D as % of sales: —
Advertising as % of sales: 0.7%

Stock History

NASDAQ (GS): AVTR

	STOCK PRICE ($) FY Close	P/E High/Low	PER SHARE ($) Earnings	Dividends	Book Value
12/05	54.92	9 7	6.28	—	38.25
12/04	48.10	16 12	3.10	—	30.56
12/03	36.93	18 10	2.11	—	28.08
12/02	23.00	45 32	0.64	—	26.07
12/01	23.56	82 55	0.36	—	24.56
Annual Growth	**23.6%**	**— —**	**104.4%**	**—**	**11.7%**

Avid Technology

Media professionals are keen on Avid Technology. The company is the leader in digital editing and professional audio systems used by the film, music, and television industries. Its products, including Film Composer, Symphony, and Avid Xpress, are used by music and film studios, post-production facilities, radio broadcasters, and television stations including the BBC, CBS, and NBC. Its Digidesign unit markets the ProTools line of sound editing systems. Avid also makes animation design software, newsroom automation systems, and digital storage systems. The company provides a line of video editing products for the consumer market through its Pinnacle Systems division.

Already the market leader in digital editing, Avid stands to gain business as the film and television industries continue to move toward digital film. About 60% of the company's sales come from customers outside the US.

Avid acquired digital video editing specialist Pinnacle Systems for approximately $435 million in cash and stock in 2005. Pinnacle now serves as Avid's consumer video division. The following year it acquired Sundance Digital, a developer of automation and control software used by TV broadcasters, for $12 million. Avid also acquired Sibelius Software in 2006.

FMR Corp. controls almost 13% of Avid.

HISTORY

William Warner founded Avid Technology in 1987 after quitting his job at Apollo Computers (now part of Hewlett-Packard) to develop a prototype digital editor based on Apollo workstation hardware. The new company captured the attention of Apple, and after switching to Macintosh hardware in 1989, Avid produced its first digital video-editing system. The company expanded into Europe in 1990, and Warner left the firm the following year to start Wildfire Communications. Avid went public in 1993, and the next year it expanded its presence in newsroom automation by acquiring SofTECH Systems and the newsroom systems division of Basys Automation Systems.

The CamCutter, unveiled by Avid in 1995, was the first machine to offer a disk-based recording and editing system. That year the company acquired Digidesign (digital audio production software and hardware), the Parallax Software Group (digital effects and animation software), and Elastic Reality (warping and morphing technology). It also formed an alliance with Silicon Graphics, a leading maker of high-end graphics systems, to develop disk-based production and delivery systems for broadcasters.

Avid bought special effects company Softimage from Microsoft for $285 million in 1998 (giving Microsoft a stake in Avid). It also formed an alliance with Tektronix to develop newsroom computer systems. Their 50-50 joint venture, AvStar Systems, launched the next year. Tektronix sold its interest in AvStar to Grass Valley Group in 1999.

In 2000 the company acquired The Motion Factory (3-D software technology). In 2001 Avid repurchased Grass Valley Group's stake in AvStar (now called iNews).

In December 2003, the company bought Bomb Factory Digital, a maker of real-time audio

effects plug-ins. The plug-ins are designed for Avid's Digidesign Pro Tools Platform.

In 2004, Avid bought Munich-based NXN, a provider of digital production management systems for entertainment and computer graphics industries. And in August 2004, Avid acquired Midiman, which does business as M-Audio and provides digital audio and MIDI solutions for electronic musicians and audio professionals. The deal cost Avid $80 million.

EXECUTIVES

Chairman: Nancy Hawthorne, age 54
President, CEO, and Director: David A. Krall, age 45,
$960,360 pay
Chief Marketing Officer: Greg Estes
VP, Business Development, Chief Legal Officer, and
Secretary: Ethan E. Jacks, age 51, $460,417 pay
VP and CFO: Paul J. Milbury, age 56, $464,768 pay
VP, Corporate Controller, and Principal Accounting
Officer: Joel Legon, age 55
VP and General Manager, Avid Video: Graham Sharp
VP; COO, Avid Video: Joseph (Joe) Bentivegna, age 44
VP; General Manager, Audio: David M. (Dave) Lebolt,
age 49, $464,768 pay
VP, Human Resources: Patricia A. (Trish) Baker, age 57
VP, Software Engineering and CTO:
Michael J. (Mike) Rockwell, age 39, $464,768 pay
Director, Corporate Communications: Carter Holland
Director, Investor Relations: Dean Ridlon
Auditors: Ernst & Young LLP

LOCATIONS

HQ: Avid Technology, Inc.
Avid Technology Park, 1 Park West,
Tewksbury, MA 01876
Phone: 978-640-6789   **Fax:** 978-640-1366
Web: www.avid.com

2005 Sales

	$ mil.	% of total
US	332.5	43
Other countries	442.9	57
Total	**775.4**	**100**

PRODUCTS/OPERATIONS

2005 Sales

	$ mil.	% of total
Professional film, video & broadcast	448.3	58
Audio	268.0	34
Consumer video	59.1	8
Total	**775.4**	**100**

Selected Products

Professional film, video, and broadcast
3D animation and digital asset management tools
Broadcast systems (newsroom, on-air graphics, play-to-air, production)
Finishing and compositing
Video and film editing and finishing tools
Storage systems
Audio
Digidesign (control surfaces, mixing consoles, Pro Tools)
M-Audio (audio interfaces, keyboards, microphones, speakers)
Consumer video (Pinnacle)
Digital media receivers
Tape-to-digital conversion
Video editing

Adaptec
Adobe
ADS Tech
AMS Neve
Apple
ATI Technologies
Autodesk
Bell Microproducts
Borland Software
Chyron
Ciprico
Creative Technology
EMC
Euphonix
Harris Corp.
Hauppauge Digital
Hewlett-Packard
IBM
Leitch Technology
LOUD Technologies
Mark of the Unicorn
Matsushita
Microsoft
Quantel
Roland
SeaChange
SGI
Sonic Solutions
Sony
TASCAM
Telex Communications
Ulead
Vizrt
Yamaha

HISTORICAL FINANCIALS

Company Type: Public

Income Statement

FYE: December 31

	REVENUE ($ mil.)	NET INCOME ($ mil.)	NET PROFIT MARGIN	EMPLOYEES
12/05	775.4	34.0	4.4%	2,613
12/04	589.6	71.7	12.2%	2,014
12/03	471.9	40.9	8.7%	1,582
12/02	418.7	3.0	0.7%	1,556
12/01	434.6	(38.2)	—	1,543
Annual Growth	15.6%	—	—	14.1%

2005 Year-End Financials

Debt ratio: —
Return on equity: 5.4%
Cash ($ mil.): 238.4
Current ratio: 2.35
Long-term debt ($ mil.): —
No. of shares (mil.): 42.1

Dividends
  Yield: —
  Payout: —
Market value ($ mil.): 2,305.1
R&D as % of sales: 14.4%
Advertising as % of sales: 1.6%

Stock History

NASDAQ (GS): AVID

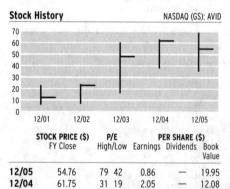

	STOCK PRICE ($) FY Close	P/E High/Low		PER SHARE ($) Earnings	Dividends	Book Value
12/05	54.76	79	42	0.86	—	19.95
12/04	61.75	31	19	2.05	—	12.08
12/03	48.00	48	13	1.25	—	7.31
12/02	22.95	213	66	0.11	—	4.53
12/01	12.15	—	—	(1.49)	—	4.02
Annual Growth	45.7%	—	—	—	—	49.3%

Ballantyne of Omaha

Ballantyne of Omaha projects a lot of images. The company is a leading supplier of motion picture theater equipment, such as film projectors and sound systems, used by major theater chains such as AMC Entertainment and Regal Entertainment. Ballantyne of Omaha's lighting division manufactures spotlights and searchlights used by movie and TV producers, hotels, sporting arenas, and amusement parks, including Walt Disney World and Universal Studios. While the company has phased out its food service equipment business, Ballantyne's restaurant segment continues to supply parts to its installed equipment customer base and distribute its seasonings, marinades, and barbeque sauces.

Ballantyne's commercial motion picture projection equipment is marketed under the Strong, Simplex, Century, Apogee, and Ballantyne brand names. Its spotlights include brands such as Strong, Xenotech, and Sky-Tracker. The company plans to introduce smaller, lower priced, more user-friendly spotlights under the Radiance and Canto brand names.

Ballantyne has entered the digital cinema marketplace as a distributor of digital equipment through an agreement with NEC Solutions. The company has expanded into the digital cinema arena with its acquisition of National Cinema Service Corp. (NCSC), a national provider of film and digital projector maintenance, repair, equipment installations, site surveys, and other theatre services.

The company's lighting products have been used at live performances such as Super Bowl half-time shows and the opening and closing ceremonies of the 2002 Winter Olympics. They also illuminate such venues as the Luxor Hotel and Casino and the Stratosphere Hotel and Casino in Las Vegas, Nevada.

HISTORY

Robert Ballantyne began supplying movie theater equipment in 1932, and after WWII his company, Ballantyne of Omaha, began making equipment for drive-in theaters. Ballantyne retired in 1960 and sold his firm to ABC Vending. Under its new parent, the company entered the food service business, making pressure fryers for theater snack stands. Light bulb maker Canrad-Hanovia bought Ballantyne in 1976, later merging it with its Strong Electric unit (spotlights and projector lamphouses). After Canrad acquired Simplex Projector in 1983, ARC International purchased Canrad in 1989 and merged Ballantyne, Strong, and Simplex. Ballantyne went public in 1995.

In 1996 the company was buoyed by the rapid growth of IMAX theaters and Iwerks motion simulator rides. Ballantyne acquired Xenotech and Sky-Tracker of America in 1997, makers of high-intensity searchlights. John Wilmers took over as CEO, and the following year Ballantyne acquired Design and Manufacturing (film platter systems), teamed with MegaSystems to develop a 3-D projection system, and increased its overseas sales force.

Ballantyne struck a $45 million agreement with Regal Cinemas (now part of Regal Entertainment Group) in 1999 to provide at least 2,000 projection systems over the next two years, marking the company's largest-ever purchase agreement. But a nationwide slowdown in theater construction hurt the company's bottom line in 2000, forcing it to lay off 18% of its employees. To add insult to injury, Ballantyne's stock was delisted from the New York Stock Exchange and its parent company, ARC International, went into receivership. ARC's stake in Ballantyne was acquired by Omaha merchant bank The McCarthy Group the next year. Also in 2001 the company was contracted to supply searchlights for the Kennedy Space Center in Florida.

EXECUTIVES

Chairman: William F. Welsh II, age 64
President, CEO, and Director: John P. Wilmers, age 61, $369,708 pay
CFO, Secretary, and Treasurer: Kevin Herrmann, age 41
EVP and COO: Daniel E. (Dan) Faltin, age 49, $310,266 pay
SVP: Ray F. Boegner, age 56, $263,892 pay
VP Cinema Products: Pat Moore
VP Latin American Sales: Daniel Benitez
VP Strong Digital: Larry Jacobson
VP Strong Digital Systems: John Wolski, age 50
President, National Cinema Service: Chris Pierce
Manager Customer Service: Rick Salts
Product Manager, LTI Xenon Lamps and ISCO Projection Systems: Ron Lutsock
Auditors: KPMG LLP

LOCATIONS

HQ: Ballantyne of Omaha, Inc.
  4350 McKinley St., Omaha, NE 68112
Phone: 402-453-4444   Fax: 402-453-7238
Web: www.ballantyne-omaha.com

Ballantyne of Omaha has operations in Florida, Illinois, Nebraska, and Hong Kong.

PRODUCTS/OPERATIONS

2005 Sales

	$ mil.	% of total
Theater	49.7	92
Lighting	3.4	6
Restaurant	0.8	2
Total	53.9	100

Selected Products

Lighting products
  4,000-watt spotlight (for large theaters, arenas, and stadiums)
  400-watt spotlights (for smaller venues)
  Computer-based lighting systems
  High-intensity searchlights
Movie theater equipment
  35mm and 70mm projectors
  Combination 35/70mm projectors
  Console systems
  Customized projectors and equipment
  Film handling equipment
  Replacement parts
  Sound systems
  Soundhead reproducers
  Xenon lamphouses and power supplies

Selected Product Brands

Lighting products
  SkyTracker
  Strong
  Xenotech
Movie theater equipment
  Ballantyne
  Century
  Simplex
  Strong
Restaurant products
  Chicken on the Run
  Flavor-Crisp
  Flavor-Pit

COMPETITORS

Barco
Christie Digital
Genlyte Thomas
Panavision
Production Resource Group

HISTORICAL FINANCIALS

Company Type: Public

Income Statement

FYE: December 31

	REVENUE ($ mil.)	NET INCOME ($ mil.)	NET PROFIT MARGIN	EMPLOYEES
12/05	53.9	4.3	8.0%	197
12/04	49.1	5.1	10.4%	207
12/03	37.4	0.6	1.6%	—
12/02	33.8	(3.6)	—	—
12/01	41.3	(4.1)	—	—
Annual Growth	6.9%	—	—	(4.8%)

2005 Year-End Financials

Debt ratio: 0.0%
Return on equity: 11.5%
Cash ($ mil.): 19.6
Current ratio: 6.07
Long-term debt ($ mil.): 0.0
No. of shares (mil.): 13.4

Dividends
  Yield: —
  Payout: —
Market value ($ mil.): 65.5
R&D as % of sales: 0.8%
Advertising as % of sales: —

Stock History

AMEX: BTN

	STOCK PRICE ($) FY Close	P/E High/Low		Earnings	PER SHARE ($) Dividends	Book Value
12/05	4.89	19	12	0.31	—	2.99
12/04	4.50	13	7	0.37	—	2.66
12/03	2.90	74	15	0.04	—	2.29
12/02	0.76	—	—	(0.29)	—	2.25
12/01	0.55	—	—	(0.32)	—	2.55
Annual Growth	72.7%	—	—	—	—	4.0%

BancTrust Financial

BancTrust Financial still makes its sweet home in Alabama, but also spends a little time in the Florida panhandle. It is the holding company of BankTrust (operating as Mobile Bank), BankTrust of Alabama (operating as Eufaula Bank), and BancTrust Company — all in southern Alabama; plus BankTrust (Florida) (operating as the Santa Rosa Beach Bank). Through approximately 30 branch offices, the banks offer such deposit products as CDs and checking, savings, and money market accounts. The company's loan portfolio is dominated by mortgages (more than 40%) and construction loans (about 35%); the portfolio also includes business and consumer loans.

The company is in the midst of a plan to consolidate many of its subsidiaries. It has also divested some operations, including its former subsidiary Sweet Water State Bank, which in 2005 was sold to Tombigbee Bancshares, a group primarily made up of Sweet Water State Bank directors and executive managers. In 2004 the company sold subsidiary BankTrust of Florida, which operated a savings bank with branches in Port St. Joe, St. Joe Beach, and Wewahitchka.

EXECUTIVES

Chairman: J. Stephen Nelson, age 68
President, CEO and Director; Chairman and CEO, Mobile Bank: W. Bibb Lamar Jr., age 62, $469,661 pay
EVP, CFO and Secretary, BancTrust Financial and Mobile Bank: F. Michael Johnson, age 60, $228,857 pay
EVP; President and CEO, Commercial Bank of Demopolis: J. Olen Kerby Jr., age 51
EVP; President and CEO, Santa Rosa Beach Bank and Eufala Bank: Caulie T. Knowles III, age 46, $224,893 pay
EVP; President and CEO, Florida Bank: Michael D. Fitzhugh, age 57, $236,947 pay
SVP and Senior Loan Officer; EVP, Mobile Bank: Bruce C. Finley Jr., age 57, $159,784 pay
VP, Marketing and Communications: Rebecca Minto
Human Resources Director: Diane Hollingsworth
Auditors: KPMG LLP

LOCATIONS

HQ: BancTrust Financial Group, Inc.
  100 St. Joseph St., Mobile, AL 36602
Phone: 251-431-7800   **Fax:** 251-431-7851
Web: www.banctrustfinancialgroupinc.com

BancTrust Financial Group operates in Autauga, Baldwin, Barbour, Escambia, Marengo, Mobile, Monroe, and Montgomery counties in Alabama and in Bay, Okaloosa, and Walton counties in Florida.

PRODUCTS/OPERATIONS

2005 Sales

	$ mil.	% of total
Interest		
Loans	66.7	79
Securities	5.7	7
Other	0.5	1
Service charges on deposit accounts	4.5	5
Trust revenue	1.7	2
Other	4.8	6
Total	83.9	100

COMPETITORS

Alabama National BanCorp
Ameris
Colonial BancGroup
Compass Bancshares
Regions Financial
SunTrust
Superior Bancorp
United Security Bancshares Inc.
Vision Bancshares
Wachovia
Whitney Holding

HISTORICAL FINANCIALS

Company Type: Public

Income Statement

FYE: December 31

	ASSETS ($ mil.)	NET INCOME ($ mil.)	INCOME AS % OF ASSETS	EMPLOYEES
12/05	1,305.5	15.1	1.2%	396
12/04	1,191.2	11.3	0.9%	380
12/03	1,076.9	6.3	0.6%	433
12/02	665.8	7.3	1.1%	299
12/01	592.4	6.2	1.0%	259
Annual Growth	21.8%	24.9%	—	11.2%

2005 Year-End Financials

Equity as % of assets: 10.0%
Return on assets: 1.2%
Return on equity: 11.9%
Long-term debt ($ mil.): 28.0
No. of shares (mil.): 11.1
Market value ($ mil.): 223.9

Dividends
  Yield: 2.6%
  Payout: 38.5%
Sales ($ mil.): 83.9
R&D as % of sales: —
Advertising as % of sales: 0.7%

Stock History

NASDAQ (GS): BTFG

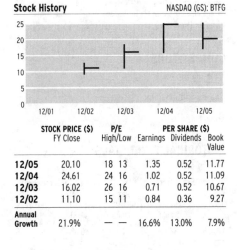

	STOCK PRICE ($) FY Close	P/E High/Low		Earnings	PER SHARE ($) Dividends	Book Value
12/05	20.10	18	13	1.35	0.52	11.77
12/04	24.61	24	16	1.02	0.52	11.09
12/03	16.02	26	16	0.71	0.52	10.67
12/02	11.10	15	11	0.84	0.36	9.27
Annual Growth	21.9%	—	—	16.6%	13.0%	7.9%

Bank Holdings

You can probably guess what The Bank Holdings does. Where they do it is out west. It is a holding company for Nevada Security Bank, which operates three branches in the northern portion of the state. Nevada Security Bank offers typical deposit products, such as checking and savings accounts, as well as CDs and IRAs.

Commercial real estate loans make up about 40% of the bank's loan portfolio, which also includes construction/development loans, consumer loans, residential mortgages, and business loans (including SBA loans). The Bank Holdings moved into California through its 2004 purchase of CNA Trust Corporation of Costa Mesa. The California branch (now located in Roseville) operates as Silverado Bank.

EXECUTIVES

Chairman and CEO: Harold G. (Hal) Giomi
President and Director: Joseph P. (Joe) Bourdeau
EVP and CFO: Jack B. Buchold
EVP and Chief Credit Officer: John N. Donovan
Director; President, Nevada Security Bank: David A. Funk
SVP, Bank Operations, Nevada Security Bank: Robin Orr
Auditors: Moss Adams, LLP

LOCATIONS

HQ: The Bank Holdings
  9990 Double R Blvd., Reno, NV 89521
Phone: 775-853-8600   **Fax:** 775-853-2068
Web: www.thebankholdings.com

The Bank Holdings has locations in Reno and Incline Village, Nevada, and in Roseville, California.

PRODUCTS/OPERATIONS

2005 Sales

	$ mil.	% of total
Interest		
Loans	14.5	81
Securities & other	2.7	15
Service charges & fees	0.4	2
Income on bank-owned life insurance	0.3	2
Total	**17.9**	**100**

COMPETITORS

Bank of America
Bank of the West
Charles Schwab Bank
U.S. Bancorp
Wells Fargo

HISTORICAL FINANCIALS

Company Type: Public

Income Statement

FYE: December 31

	ASSETS ($ mil.)	NET INCOME ($ mil.)	INCOME AS % OF ASSETS	EMPLOYEES
12/05	384.6	1.4	0.4%	59
12/04	246.8	0.3	0.1%	—
12/03	166.1	(0.6)	—	—
Annual Growth	**52.2%**	**—**	**—**	**—**

2005 Year-End Financials

Equity as % of assets: 7.5%	Dividends
Return on assets: 0.4%	Yield: —
Return on equity: 5.0%	Payout: —
Long-term debt ($ mil.): 15.5	Sales ($ mil.): 17.9
No. of shares (mil.): 3.1	R&D as % of sales: —
Market value ($ mil.): 58.9	Advertising as % of sales: —

Stock History

NASDAQ (CM): TBHS

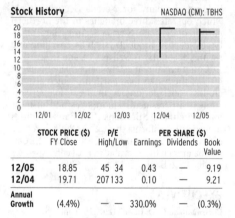

	STOCK PRICE ($) FY Close	P/E High/Low	PER SHARE ($) Earnings	Dividends	Book Value
12/05	18.85	45 34	0.43	—	9.19
12/04	19.71	207 133	0.10	—	9.21
Annual Growth	**(4.4%)**	**— —**	**330.0%**	**—**	**(0.3%)**

Bank of Florida

Bank of Florida (formerly Bancshares of Florida) is the holding company for its eponymous Bank of Florida subsidiary, which operates more than five branches on the state's southeastern, southwestern, and west-central coasts. Subsidiary Bank of Florida Trust offers trust, estate planning, and investment management services. The bank and the trust company cater to professionals, entrepreneurs, and small to midsized businesses, providing personalized deposit, lending, and investment services that larger superregional banks in their market often

do not. Bank of Florida plans to buy Old Florida Bancshares, which runs four branches in the southwestern part of the state.

Bank of Florida's loan portfolio is primarily composed of commercial real estate mortgages (more than 35% of all loans), followed by construction loans (almost 30%). Other loan offerings include residential mortgages, business loans, consumer loans, and lines of credit. The bank also offers deposit accounts, credit cards, and merchant services.

The company bought Bristol Bank, a single-branch institution in Dade County, in 2006.

EXECUTIVES

Chairman: Earl L. Frye, age 77
Vice Chairman; Chairman, Bank of Florida Trust Corporation: Joe B. Cox, age 66
President, CEO, and Director: Michael L. McMullan, age 51, $323,425 pay
SEVP and Director: John B. James, age 64, $202,863 pay (prior to promotion)
EVP and CFO: Tracy L. Keegan, age 40
EVP and Chief Risk Manager: Thomas M. (Tom) Whelan, age 53
President and CEO, Bank of Florida Southwest: James L. Goehler
Corporate Secretary: Arlette Yassa
Director; Chairman, Bank of Florida: Harry K. Moon, age 56
President and CEO, Bank of Florida, Fort Lauderdale: R. Mark Manitz
President and CEO, Bank of Florida Trust Company: Julie W. Husler, $202,964 pay
President, Southwest: Craig D. Sherman, age 48, $197,950 pay (prior to promotion)
Auditors: Hacker, Johnson & Smith PA

LOCATIONS

HQ: Bank of Florida Corporation
1185 Immokalee Rd., Naples, FL 34103
Phone: 239-254-2100   **Fax:** 239-254-2107
Web: www.bankoffloridaonline.com

Bancshares of Florida has branches in Boca Raton, Bonita Springs, Fort Lauderdale (2), Naples (2), and Tampa, Florida.

PRODUCTS/OPERATIONS

2005 Sales

	$ mil.	% of total
Interest		
Loans, including fees	26.4	83
Other	2.1	7
Noninterest		
Trust fees	1.6	5
Service charges & fees	1.4	4
Mortgage banking	0.3	1
Total	**31.8**	**100**

COMPETITORS

Bank of America
BankUnited
Colonial BancGroup
Fifth Third
First Citizens BancShares
F.N.B. (PA)
Northern Trust
Regions Financial
SunTrust
Wachovia

HISTORICAL FINANCIALS

Company Type: Public

Income Statement

FYE: December 31

	ASSETS ($ mil.)	NET INCOME ($ mil.)	INCOME AS % OF ASSETS	EMPLOYEES
12/05	569.8	4.9	0.9%	153
12/04	420.8	(2.9)	—	120
12/03	222.6	(2.7)	—	70
12/02	144.5	(2.6)	—	62
12/01	77.1	(0.6)	—	28
Annual Growth	**64.9%**	**—**	**—**	**52.9%**

2005 Year-End Financials

Equity as % of assets: 10.4%	Dividends
Return on assets: 1.0%	Yield: —
Return on equity: 10.1%	Payout: —
Long-term debt ($ mil.): 11.0	Sales ($ mil.): 31.8
No. of shares (mil.): 5.9	R&D as % of sales: —
Market value ($ mil.): 134.9	Advertising as % of sales: —

Stock History

NASDAQ (GM): BOFL

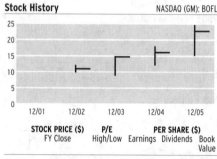

	STOCK PRICE ($) FY Close	P/E High/Low	PER SHARE ($) Earnings	Dividends	Book Value
12/05	22.70	31 19	0.79	—	9.94
12/04	16.11	— —	(0.81)	—	8.68
12/03	14.74	— —	(0.92)	—	6.89
12/02	11.00	— —	(1.48)	—	7.22
Annual Growth	**27.3%**	**— —**	**—**	**—**	**8.0%**

Bare Escentuals

When it comes to keeping its customers looking naturally pretty, Bare Escentuals has a mineral interest. The company, which rolled out its bareMinerals makeup brand in 1976 along with its first retail store, develops, markets, and sells natural cosmetics, skin care, and body care items. Brand names include RareMinerals, i.d. bareMinerals, md formulations, and its namesake line, among others. Formerly STB Beauty, Bare Escentuals sells its products through its 30 company-owned US boutiques, about 290 retailers, some 900 spas and salons, infomercials, and two Web sites. Berkshire Partners LLC and JH MDB Investors own a majority stake in the firm, which went public in September 2006.

The cosmetics firm raised $352 million in the 16 million share initial public offering. The company plans to use the net proceeds to repay a portion of its debt valued at more than $229 million and fund future growth initiatives. The company peddles products via its primary Web site, www.bareminerals.com. It operates a second Web site, www.mdformulations.com, through which it sells its professional skin care collection, md formulations, which was folded into its product portfolio in the early 2000s.

The face of Bare Escentuals and its operations are likely to morph as the company shifts to cater to its customers' changing needs. Customers typically choose its earthy and lightweight foundation as an alternative to liquid or cream makeup, which can be heavy. In 2005 Bare Escentuals earned the designation as a top seller at specialty retailers Sephora and Ulta. And its foundation products generated half of the cosmetic company's sales in 2005. Until other product categories drive the retailer and manufacturer's revenue, however, the fate of Bare Escentuals is tied to the trend of women shifting to a sheer, more natural foundation. Also, three customers, including Sephora, Ulta, and QVC, accounted for a substantial portion of the firm's sales in 2005 and into 2006.

Bare Escentuals attributes its 87% growth in net sales since 2001 to its marketing and distributing model that consists of an assortment of wholesaling and retailing ventures. At the wholesale level its strategy is to increase sales at specialty retailers, home shopping TV shows (such as QVC), and spas and salons. Boosting the number of company-owned boutiques is a key component of the company's retail strategy, as well as instituting more savvy media spending for infomercials.

The company, which changed its name from STB Beauty to Bare Escentuals in February 2006, is exploring an international expansion and pinpointing Japan, Germany, France, South Korea, and the UK as geographical areas of interest.

EXECUTIVES

Chairman: Ross M. Jones, age 41
CEO and Director: Leslie A. Blodgett, age 43
President: Diane M. Miles, age 51
SVP, CFO, COO, and Secretary: Myles B. McCormick, age 34
Auditors: Ernst & Young LLP

LOCATIONS

HQ: Bare Escentuals, Inc.
71 Stevenson St., 22nd Fl.,
San Francisco, CA 94105
Phone: 415-489-5000
Web: www.bareescentuals.com

2005 Sales

	$ mil.	% of total
North America	244.4	94
Other countries	14.9	6
Total	**259.3**	**100**

PRODUCTS/OPERATIONS

2005 Sales

	$ mil.	% of total
Retail	132.5	51
Wholesale	126.8	49
Total	**259.3**	**100**

2005 Retail Sales

	$ mil.	% of total
Infomercial	97.0	73
Boutiques	35.5	27
Total	**132.5**	**100**

2005 Wholesale Sales

	$ mil.	% of total
Premium wholesale	49.8	39
Home shopping TV	38.0	30
Spas & salons	24.1	19
International	14.9	12
Total	**126.8**	**100**

COMPETITORS

Avon	Guthy-Renker
BeautiControl	Ideal Shopping Direct
Beauty Brands	L'Oréal
BeneFit Cosmetics	Mary Kay
Borlind of Germany, Inc.	Nu Skin
CA Botana	Procter & Gamble
Canderm Pharma	PureBeauty
Clarins	Quixtar
Clinique Laboratories	QVC
CVS	Revlon
Del Labs	Rite Aid
drugstore.com	Sally Beauty
Elizabeth Arden Inc	Ulta
Estée Lauder Cosmetics	Vertical Branding
The Forever Group	Walgreen
Fresh	Whole Foods

HISTORICAL FINANCIALS

Company Type: Public

Income Statement

FYE: Sunday nearest December 31

	REVENUE ($ mil.)	NET INCOME ($ mil.)	NET PROFIT MARGIN	EMPLOYEES
12/05	259.3	23.9	9.2%	576
12/04	141.8	4.0	2.8%	—
12/03	94.7	11.8	12.5%	—
Annual Growth	**65.5%**	**42.3%**	**—**	**—**

2005 Year-End Financials

Debt ratio: —
Return on equity: —
Cash ($ mil.): 18.7
Current ratio: 1.82
Long-term debt ($ mil.): 377.2

Net Income History

NASDAQ (GS): BARE

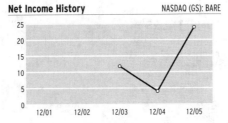

Barnwell Industries

Barnwell Industries has more than a barnful of assets. Its interests range from oil and gas production, contract well drilling operations, and Hawaiian property investments. Barnwell Industries explores for and produces oil and natural gas primarily in Alberta, Canada. It has proved reserves of 1.3 million barrels of oil and 24.8 billion cu. ft. of gas. Subsidiary Water Resources International drills water and geothermal wells and installs and repairs water pump systems in Hawaii. The company also owns a 78% interest in Kaupulehu Developments, which owns leasehold rights to more than 1,000 acres in Hawaii.

In 2006 Barnwell Industries' oil and natural gas segment generated 69% of its oil and natural gas revenues from four marketers: ProGas Limited (30%), Glencoe Resources Limited (15%), Plains Marketing Canada, L.P. (14%), and Seminole Canada Gas Company (10%).

EXECUTIVES

Chairman and CEO: Morton H. Kinzler, age 80, $1,070,000 pay
President, COO, General Counsel, and Director: Alexander C. Kinzler, age 47, $990,000 pay
EVP, CFO, Secretary, Treasurer, and Director: Russell M. Gifford, age 51, $693,750 pay
VP Canadian Operations: Warren D. Steckley, age 49, $243,504 pay
VP, Controller, and Assistant Secretary: Mark A. Murashige
Manager Information Services: Joseph R. Downs III
Auditors: KPMG LLP

LOCATIONS

HQ: Barnwell Industries, Inc.
1100 Alakea St., Ste. 2900, Honolulu, HI 96813
Phone: 808-531-8400   **Fax:** 808-531-7181
Web: www.brninc.com

Barnwell Industries operates in Hawaii, and in Alberta, British Columbia, and Saskatchewan.

2006 Sales

	$ mil.	% of total
Canada	38.5	68
US	18.4	32
Adjustments	1.1	—
Total	**58.0**	**100**

PRODUCTS/OPERATIONS

2006 Sales

	$ mil.	% of total
Oil & natural gas	37.9	67
Land investment	12.3	21
Contract drilling	5.9	10
Other	0.8	2
Adjustments	1.1	—
Total	**58.0**	**100**

Subsidiaries

Barnwell of Canada, Ltd. (oil and natural gas)
Kaupulehu Developments (78%, land investment)
Water Resources International, Inc. (contract drilling)

COMPETITORS

Alexander & Baldwin
BP
Canadian Natural
Castle & Cooke
D.R. Horton, Schuler
EnCana
Gentry Homes
Imperial Oil
Maui Land & Pineapple
Petrobank Energy and Resources
Petro-Canada
Roscoe Moss Hawaii
Royal Dutch Shell

HISTORICAL FINANCIALS

Company Type: Public

Income Statement

FYE: September 30

	REVENUE ($ mil.)	NET INCOME ($ mil.)	NET PROFIT MARGIN	EMPLOYEES
9/06	58.0	14.6	25.2%	55
9/05	44.2	6.0	13.6%	52
9/04	38.0	8.7	22.9%	52
9/03	23.7	2.3	9.7%	37
9/02	15.9	0.0	—	49
Annual Growth	**38.2%**	**—**	**—**	**2.9%**

2006 Year-End Financials

Debt ratio: 23.2%
Return on equity: 33.7%
Cash ($ mil.): 12.0
Current ratio: 1.15
Long-term debt ($ mil.): 11.7
No. of shares (mil.): 8.2

Dividends
Yield: 0.9%
Payout: 10.1%
Market value ($ mil.): 159.3
R&D as % of sales: —
Advertising as % of sales: —

Stock History

AMEX: BRN

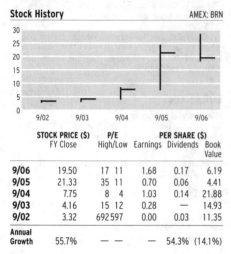

	STOCK PRICE ($) FY Close	P/E High/Low		Earnings	PER SHARE ($) Dividends	Book Value
9/06	19.50	17	11	1.68	0.17	6.19
9/05	21.33	35	11	0.70	0.06	4.41
9/04	7.75	8	4	1.03	0.14	21.88
9/03	4.16	15	12	0.28	—	14.93
9/02	3.32	692	597	0.00	0.03	11.35
Annual Growth	**55.7%**	—	—	—	**54.3%**	**(14.1%)**

Barrett Business Services

Barrett Business Services really puts people to work. The company offers both temporary and long-term staffing (almost 60% of sales) to some 2,000 small and midsized businesses. Its staffing services focus on light industrial businesses; clerical and technical staffing account for the rest. It also does business as a professional employment organization (PEO), providing outsourced human resource services, such as payroll management, benefits administration, recruiting, and placement for about 800 businesses. Barrett operates through 30 branch offices in eight states. It acquired Pro HR, a PEO with offices in Idaho and Colorado, in 2006. CEO William Sherertz and his family own about 40% of the company.

Barrett Business Services was established in Maryland in 1965. Nowadays, the company primarily serves customers residing in California (in 2005, 90% of the company's customer base was from the Golden State).

EXECUTIVES

Chairman, President, and CEO: William W. Sherertz, age 60, $331,825 pay
VP and COO: Michael L. Elich, age 40, $215,693 pay (partial-year salary)
VP Finance, CFO, Treasurer, and Secretary: Michael D. Mulholland, age 54, $265,469 pay
VP: Gregory R. Vaughn, age 50, $219,012 pay
Controller, Assistant Secretary, and Principal Accounting Officer: James D. Miller, age 42
Auditors: Moss Adams, LLP

LOCATIONS

HQ: Barrett Business Services, Inc.
8100 NE Parkway Dr., Ste. 200,
Vancouver, WA 98662
Phone: 360-828-0700 **Fax:** 360-828-0701
Web: www.barrettbusiness.com

Barrett Business Services has offices in Arizona, California, Delaware, Idaho, Maryland, North Carolina, Oregon, and Washington.

PRODUCTS/OPERATIONS

2005 Sales

	$ mil.	% of total
Staffing	130.1	56
PEO services	101.3	44
Total	**231.4**	**100**

Selected Services

PEO services
  Employee benefits
  Health insurance
  Human resource administration
    Drug testing
    Hiring
    Interviewing
    Placement
    Recruiting
    Regulatory compliance
  Payroll
  Workers' compensation coverage
  Workplace safety programs
Staffing services
  Contract
  Long-term
  Short-term

COMPETITORS

Adecco
Administaff
ADP TotalSource
Gevity HR
Kelly Services
Manpower
Paychex
Spherion
TeamStaff

HISTORICAL FINANCIALS

Company Type: Public

Income Statement

FYE: December 31

	REVENUE ($ mil.)	NET INCOME ($ mil.)	NET PROFIT MARGIN	EMPLOYEES
12/05	231.4	12.5	5.4%	27,400
12/04	195.0	7.4	3.8%	22,830
12/03	122.7	2.1	1.7%	17,000
12/02	109.3	(1.4)	—	8,380
12/01	216.7	(2.4)	—	10,425
Annual Growth	**1.7%**	—	—	**27.3%**

2005 Year-End Financials

Debt ratio: 1.3%
Return on equity: 20.1%
Cash ($ mil.): 64.9
Current ratio: 2.25
Long-term debt ($ mil.): 1.1
No. of shares (mil.): 11.0

Dividends
Yield: —
Payout: —
Market value ($ mil.): 276.1
R&D as % of sales: —
Advertising as % of sales: —

Stock History

NASDAQ (GS): BBSI

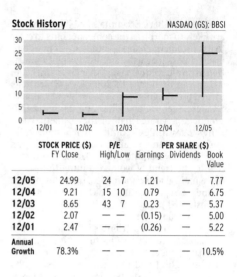

	STOCK PRICE ($) FY Close	P/E High/Low		Earnings	PER SHARE ($) Dividends	Book Value
12/05	24.99	24	7	1.21	—	7.77
12/04	9.21	15	10	0.79	—	6.75
12/03	8.65	43	7	0.23	—	5.37
12/02	2.07	—	—	(0.15)	—	5.00
12/01	2.47	—	—	(0.26)	—	5.22
Annual Growth	**78.3%**	—	—	—	—	**10.5%**

Basic Energy Services

Oil and gas producers turn to Basic Energy Services for the fundamentals. The company provides well site services with its fleet of well-servicing rigs (at more than 320, the third-largest in the US behind Key Energy Services and Nabors Industries), fluid service trucks, and related equipment. These services include acidizing, cementing, fluid handling, fracing, well construction, well maintenance, and workover. Basic Energy Services serves producers operating in Louisiana, New Mexico, Oklahoma, and Texas. It is a consolidator in the fragmented well services industry and has acquired more than 35 rivals since 1996. Investment firm DLJ Merchant Banking Partners III, L.P., controls the company.

Basic Energy Services has pursued a strategy of growth through acquisitions. In 2004 the company acquired underbalanced drilling services company Energy Air Drilling Service, and wireline firm AWS Wireline Services. In 2006 it acquired Globe Well Service and five other firms.

That year it also acquired Chaparral Services and Reddline Services for $20 million. In late 2006 the company agreed to buy two barge-mounted workover rigs and related equipment from Parker Drilling for $26 million.

Basic Energy Services agreed to acquire pressure pumping equipment operator JetStar Consolidated Holdings, Inc. in 2007 for $120 million.

EXECUTIVES

Chairman: Steven A. Webster, age 54
President, CEO, and Director: Kenneth V. (Ken) Huseman, age 54, $600,000 pay
EVP and Secretary: James J. (Jim) Carter, age 60, $230,000 pay
SVP, Finance and CFO: Alan Krenek, age 50, $358,269 pay
VP, Business Development: Mark D. Rankin, age 52
VP, Human Resources: James E. Tyner, age 55
Controller: David M. Dunn, age 61
Human Resources Manager: Vicki Burdette
Auditors: KPMG LLP

LOCATIONS

HQ: Basic Energy Services, Inc.
400 W. Illinios, Ste. 800, Midland, TX 79701
Phone: 432-620-5500   **Fax:** 432-570-0437
Web: www.basicenergyservices.com

Basic Energy Services operates in Louisiana, New Mexico, Oklahoma, Texas, and in the Rocky Mountains.

PRODUCTS/OPERATIONS

2005 Sales

	$ mil.	% of total
Well servicing	222.0	48
Fluid services	132.3	29
Drilling & completion services	59.8	13
Well site construction services	45.7	10
Total	**459.8**	**100**

COMPETITORS

BJ Services
Halliburton
Key Energy
Nabors Industries
Pride International
Schlumberger
Weatherford International

HISTORICAL FINANCIALS

Company Type: Public

Income Statement

FYE: December 31

	REVENUE ($ mil.)	NET INCOME ($ mil.)	NET PROFIT MARGIN	EMPLOYEES
12/05	459.8	44.8	9.7%	3,280
12/04	311.5	12.9	4.1%	—
12/03	180.9	2.8	1.5%	—
12/02	108.8	(1.3)	—	—
12/01	100.0	6.0	6.0%	1,200
Annual Growth	**46.4%**	**65.3%**	**—**	**28.6%**

2005 Year-End Financials

Debt ratio: 46.1%
Return on equity: 23.6%
Cash ($ mil.): 32.8
Current ratio: 2.10
Long-term debt ($ mil.): 119.2
No. of shares (mil.): 33.8
Dividends
  Yield: —
  Payout: —
Market value ($ mil.): 674.0
R&D as % of sales: —
Advertising as % of sales: —

Stock History

NYSE: BAS

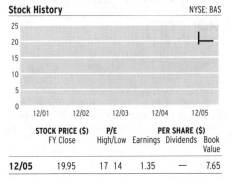

	STOCK PRICE ($) FY Close	P/E High/Low	PER SHARE ($) Earnings	Dividends	Book Value
12/05	19.95	17 14	1.35	—	7.65

Bay National

Bay National Corporation is staying afloat in the banking waters. The financial institution is a holding company for Bay National Bank, which operates two banking locations in Baltimore and Salisbury, Maryland. Targeting small to midsized businesses and individuals (primarily those associated with its business customers as well as professionals and high-net-worth individuals), Bay National Bank offers traditional banking products including checking and savings accounts, CDs, and loans. (Commercial loans and mortgages account for about three-fourths of its lending portfolio.) The company partners with other firms to provide its clients with investment advisory, risk management, and employee benefit services.

Bay National Bank's offices are organized in a nontraditional fashion, with customer transactions taking place at bank personnel desks rather than teller windows.

Directors and executives collectively own one-fifth of the company.

EXECUTIVES

Chairman, President, and CEO, Bay National and Bay National Bank: Hugh W. Mohler, age 60, $250,000 pay
EVP, CFO, Secretary, and Treasurer; EVP, CFO, Chief Compliance Officer, Secretary, and Treasurer, Bay National Bank: Mark A. Semanie, age 42, $205,000 pay
VP, Marketing and Investor Relations, Bay National Corporation and Bay National Bank: Lucy Mohler
EVP: Richard C. Springer
SVP and Regional Manager, Salisbury, Bay National Bank: Michael K. (Mike) Bloxham
SVP, Corporate Banking, Baltimore, Bay National Bank: Warren F. (Boot) Boutilier
Auditors: Stegman & Company

LOCATIONS

HQ: Bay National Corporation
2328 W. Joppa Rd., Lutherville, MD 21093
Phone: 410-494-2580   **Fax:** 410-494-2589
Web: www.baynational.com

PRODUCTS/OPERATIONS

2005 Sales

	$ mil.	% of total
Interest		
Loans, including fees	12.7	93
Federal funds sold & other	0.3	2
Noninterest		
Gain on sale of mortgages	0.5	4
Service charges on deposit accounts	0.2	1
Total	**13.7**	**100**

COMPETITORS

Bank of America
BCSB Bankcorp
Carrollton Bancorp
First Mariner Bancorp
M&T Bank
Mercantile Bankshares
Patapsco Bancorp
Provident Bankshares
SunTrust
Wachovia

HISTORICAL FINANCIALS

Company Type: Public

Income Statement

FYE: December 31

	ASSETS ($ mil.)	NET INCOME ($ mil.)	INCOME AS % OF ASSETS	EMPLOYEES
12/05	210.0	2.7	1.3%	56
12/04	170.8	0.8	0.5%	—
12/03	122.3	0.0	—	—
12/02	84.6	(1.0)	—	—
12/01	47.0	(1.6)	—	—
Annual Growth	**45.4%**	**—**	**—**	**—**

2005 Year-End Financials

Equity as % of assets: 7.7%
Return on assets: 1.4%
Return on equity: 18.2%
Long-term debt ($ mil.): 8.0
No. of shares (mil.): 1.9
Market value ($ mil.): 40.4
Dividends
  Yield: —
  Payout: —
Sales ($ mil.): 13.7
R&D as % of sales: —
Advertising as % of sales: —

Stock History

NASDAQ (GM): BAYN

	STOCK PRICE ($) FY Close	P/E High/Low	PER SHARE ($) Earnings	Dividends	Book Value
12/05	21.00	17 10	1.37	—	8.42
12/04	13.25	34 24	0.41	—	7.00
12/03	10.10	— —	—	—	6.48
12/02	8.10	— —	(0.80)	—	6.13
12/01	7.05	— —	(1.30)	—	6.92
Annual Growth	**31.4%**	**— —**	**—**	**—**	**5.0%**

BCB Bancorp

BCB Bancorp *be* the holding company for Bayonne Community Bank, a relative newcomer on the scene which opened its doors in late 2000. The independent bank serves Hudson County and the surrounding area from its offices in Bayonne, New Jersey. The bank offers traditional deposit products and services, including savings accounts, money market accounts, CDs, and IRAs. Funds from deposits are used to originate mortgages and loans, primarily commercial real estate and multi-family property loans (which together account for about two-thirds of the bank's loan portfolio).

EXECUTIVES

Chairman: Mark D. Hogan, age 40
President, CEO, and Director; President and CEO, Bayonne Community Bank: Donald Mindiak, age 47, $186,500 pay
COO, CFO, and Director; COO and CFO, Bayonne Community Bank: Thomas M. Coughlin, age 46, $149,000 pay
EVP Business Development, Bayonne Community Bank: Olivia M. Klim, age 60, $149,000 pay

VP Commercial Lending, Bayonne Community Bank:
Amer Saleem, age 51, $135,000 pay
Director; Senior Lending Officer, Bayonne Community Bank: James E. Collins, age 57, $149,000 pay
Auditors: Beard Miller Company LLP

LOCATIONS

HQ: BCB Bancorp, Inc.
104-110 Ave. C, Bayonne, NJ 07002
Phone: 201-823-0700 **Fax:** 201-339-5602

PRODUCTS/OPERATIONS

2005 Sales

	$ mil.	% of total
Interest		
Loans	18.8	72
Securities & other	6.4	25
Noninterest		
Fees & service charges	0.5	2
Loans originated for sale & other	0.3	1
Total	**26.0**	**100**

COMPETITORS

Bank of America
Hudson City Bancorp
Meridian Capital Group
New York Community Bancorp
Pamrapo Bancorp
PNC Financial
Provident New York Bancorp
Stewardship Financial
Wachovia
Washington Mutual

HISTORICAL FINANCIALS

Company Type: Public

Income Statement   FYE: December 31

	ASSETS ($ mil.)	NET INCOME ($ mil.)	INCOME AS % OF ASSETS	EMPLOYEES
12/05	466.2	4.7	1.0%	63
12/04	378.3	3.6	1.0%	—
12/03	300.7	2.4	0.8%	—
12/02	183.1	1.3	0.7%	—
12/01	113.2	(0.3)	—	—
Annual Growth	**42.5%**	**—**	**—**	**—**

2005 Year-End Financials

Equity as % of assets: 10.3%
Return on assets: 1.1%
Return on equity: 12.7%
Long-term debt ($ mil.): 54.1
No. of shares (mil.): 5.0
Market value ($ mil.): 78.0
Dividends
　Yield: —
　Payout: —
Sales ($ mil.): 26.0
R&D as % of sales: —
Advertising as % of sales: —

Stock History   NASDAQ (GM): BCBP

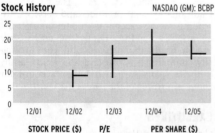

	STOCK PRICE ($) FY Close	P/E High/Low		PER SHARE ($) Earnings	Dividends	Book Value
12/05	15.60	16	12	1.20	—	9.57
12/04	15.32	25	12	0.94	—	8.70
12/03	14.08	28	13	0.65	—	9.22
12/02	8.73	24	12	0.43	—	9.89
Annual Growth	**21.3%**	**—**	**—**	**—**	**—**	**(0.4%)**

Beach First National Bancshares

Locals call the area The Grand Strand but it could also be called The Millions Strand. Beach First National Bancshares is the holding company for Beach First National Bank, a community bank serving South Carolina's Myrtle Beach and Hilton Head Island. Targeting commercial customers in the community, the bank's branches provide traditional deposit services, including checking and savings accounts, money markets, IRAs, and CDs. Real estate loans — mostly commercial — make up about 60% of the bank's loan portfolio. The bank also writes business loans and consumer loans. Beach First National Bank was established in 1996.

Executives and directors collectively own 31% of Beach First National Bancshares.

EXECUTIVES

Chairman, Beach First National Bancshares and Beach First National Bank: Raymond E. (Ray) Cleary III, age 57
President, CEO, and Director; President and CEO, Beach First National Bank:
Walter E. (Walt) Standish III, age 55, $409,021 pay
EVP, CFO, and Secretary, Beach First National Bancshares and Beach First National Bank:
Richard N. (Dick) Burch, age 47, $176,000 pay
Assistant Secretary; EVP and Chief Credit Officer, Beach First National Bank:
M. Katharine (Katie) Huntley, age 55, $183,000 pay
Assistant Secretary; EVP and Business Development Officer, Beach First National Bank: Julien E. Springs, age 49, $166,000 pay
VP and Marketing Director, Beach First National Bank: Barbara W. Marshall
VP, Human Resources, Beach First National Bank: Lorie Y. Runion
Auditors: Elliott Davis LLC

LOCATIONS

HQ: Beach First National Bancshares, Inc.
1550 Oak St., Myrtle Beach, SC 29577
Phone: 843-626-2265 **Fax:** 843-916-7818
Web: www.beachfirst.com

PRODUCTS/OPERATIONS

2005 Sales

	% of total
Interest	95
Noninterest	5
Total	**100**

COMPETITORS

Bank of America
BB&T
CNB Corp.
Coastal Financial
First Citizens BancShares
HCSB Financial
Nexity
RBC Centura Banks
South Financial
Wachovia

HISTORICAL FINANCIALS

Company Type: Public

Income Statement   FYE: December 31

	ASSETS ($ mil.)	NET INCOME ($ mil.)	INCOME AS % OF ASSETS	EMPLOYEES
12/05	397.4	3.4	0.9%	62
12/04	242.1	1.4	0.6%	—
12/03	165.1	1.0	0.6%	—
12/02	118.4	0.7	0.6%	—
12/01	80.8	0.5	0.6%	—
Annual Growth	**48.9%**	**61.5%**	**—**	**—**

2005 Year-End Financials

Equity as % of assets: 9.8%
Return on assets: 1.1%
Return on equity: 12.3%
Long-term debt ($ mil.): 11.8
No. of shares (mil.): 3.2
Market value ($ mil.): 77.7
Dividends
　Yield: —
　Payout: —
Sales ($ mil.): 22.0
R&D as % of sales: —
Advertising as % of sales: —

Stock History   NASDAQ (GM): BFNB

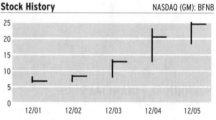

	STOCK PRICE ($) FY Close	P/E High/Low		PER SHARE ($) Earnings	Dividends	Book Value
12/05	24.50	20	15	1.23	—	12.34
12/04	20.50	33	19	0.69	—	8.11
12/03	12.85	27	16	0.50	—	11.13
12/02	8.30	24	19	0.35	—	10.57
12/01	6.73	26	21	0.31	—	9.97
Annual Growth	**38.1%**	**—**	**—**	**41.1%**	**—**	**5.5%**

Benjamin Franklin Bancorp

The Benjamin Franklin once said, "A penny saved is a penny earned," and *this* Benjamin Franklin wants to help you do both.

Benjamin Franklin Bancorp is the holding company for Benjamin Franklin Bank, which operates nine branches southwest of Boston in the Massachusetts towns of Bellingham, Foxboro, Franklin, Medfield, Milford, Newton, and Waltham. It offers individual and small to mid-sized business customers traditional deposit products. Its primary business (accounting for about 70% of its assets) is lending. Benjamin Franklin Bank (which dropped the word "Savings" from its name) acquired the three-branch Chart Bank in 2005.

Residential mortgage loans secured by one- to four-family residences make up the lion's share — more than 45% — of Benjamin Franklin's total loan portfolio. Commercial mortgage loans account for about 35%. The remainder of its portfolio consists of business, construction, consumer, and home equity lines of credit and loans.

EXECUTIVES

Chairman, Benjamin Franklin Bancorp and Benjamin Franklin Bank: Alfred H. Wahlers, age 72
President, CEO, and Director; President and CEO, Benjamin Franklin Bank: Thomas R. Venables, age 50, $440,000 pay
CFO and Treasurer; EVP and CFO, Benjamin Franklin Bank: Claire S. Bean, age 53, $270,000 pay
SVP Risk Management and Compliance, Benjamin Franklin Bank: Michael J. Piemonte, age 53
SVP and Senior Lending Officer, Benjamin Franklin Bank: Rose M. Buckley, age 38, $159,600 pay (prior to title change)
SVP Retail Banking, Benjamin Franklin Bank: Mariane E. Broadhurst, age 49, $134,400 pay
VP Human Resources, Benjamin Franklin Bank: Kathleen P. (Kathy) Sawyer, age 48
Secretary and Director: Anne M. King, age 76
Auditors: Wolf & Company, P.C.

LOCATIONS

HQ: Benjamin Franklin Bancorp, Inc.
58 Main St., Franklin, MA 02038
Phone: 508-528-7000   **Fax:** 508-520-8364
Web: www.benfranklinbank.com

PRODUCTS/OPERATIONS

2005 Sales

	$ mil.	% of total
Interest income		
Loans	30.4	77
Debt securities	3.8	10
Other	0.9	2
ATM servicing fees	1.6	4
Deposit service fees	1.2	3
Loan service fees	0.5	1
Other	1.2	3
Total	**39.6**	**100**

Subsidiaries

Benjamin Franklin Bank
 Benjamin Franklin Securities Corp.
Benjamin Franklin Bank Capital Trust I

COMPETITORS

Bank of America
Citigroup
Citizens Financial Group
Eastern Bank
JPMorgan Chase
Sovereign Bancorp
Wachovia

HISTORICAL FINANCIALS

Company Type: Public

Income Statement				FYE: December 31
	ASSETS ($ mil.)	NET INCOME ($ mil.)	INCOME AS % OF ASSETS	EMPLOYEES
12/05	867.1	0.4	0.0%	140
12/04	517.4	1.7	0.3%	133
12/03	458.8	1.7	0.4%	—
12/02	452.2	2.7	0.6%	—
Annual Growth	**24.2%**	**(47.1%)**	**—**	**5.3%**

2005 Year-End Financials

Equity as % of assets: 12.5%
Return on assets: 0.1%
Return on equity: 0.6%
Long-term debt ($ mil.): 140.3
No. of shares (mil.): 8.5
Market value ($ mil.): 119.4
Dividends
 Yield: 0.4%
 Payout: —
 Sales ($ mil.): 39.6
 R&D as % of sales: —
 Advertising as % of sales: —

Stock History

NASDAQ (GM): BFBC

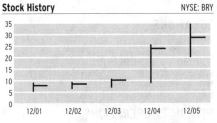

	STOCK PRICE ($) FY Close	P/E High/Low	PER SHARE ($) Earnings	Dividends	Book Value
12/05	14.07	— —	—	0.06	12.74

Berry Petroleum

It may be small fruit in the giant petroleum industry, but Berry Petroleum delivers the juice. The company buys properties with heavy crude oil reserves for exploitation and sale to refining companies. Berry Petroleum's core properties are in California's Kern, Los Angeles, and Ventura counties; it has proved reserves of 126 million barrels of oil equivalent. The company squeezes the most from its assets by using thermal recovery: Steam is injected into heavy crude oil reserves to reduce oil viscosity and allow it to flow to the surface. Berry Petroleum also owns three gas-fired cogeneration facilities. In 2005 the company acquired 130,000 acres of oil and gas assets in Colorado from J-W Operating Company.

In 2006 Berry Petroleum acquired a 50% stake in some natural gas assets in the Piceance Basin of western Colorado from a private concern for $150 million.

EXECUTIVES

Chairman: Martin H. Young Jr., age 53
President, CEO, and Director: Robert F. Heinemann, age 53
EVP and CFO: Ralph J. Goehring, age 48
EVP, Corporate Development: Michael Duginski, age 40
VP, Mountains and Mid-Continent Production: Dan Anderson
VP, California Production: George T. (Tim) Crawford, age 46
Corporate Secretary: Kenneth A. Olson, age 51
Investor Relations Specialist: Todd A. Crabtree
Treasurer: Shawn M. Canaday, age 30
Auditors: PricewaterhouseCoopers LLP

LOCATIONS

HQ: Berry Petroleum Company
 5201 Truxtun Ave., Ste. 300, Bakersfield, CA 93309
Phone: 661-616-3900   **Fax:** 661-616-3881
Web: www.bry.com

Berry Petroleum operates primarily in California. It also has oil assets in the Rocky Mountains.

PRODUCTS/OPERATIONS

2005 Sales

	$ mil.	% of total
Oil & gas	350	86
Electricity	55	14
Other	2	—
Total	**407**	**100**

COMPETITORS

Aera Energy
Chevron
Kestrel Energy
Petrohawk Energy
Royal Dutch Shell
Royale Energy
Vulcan Energy

HISTORICAL FINANCIALS

Company Type: Public

Income Statement			FYE: December 31
	REVENUE ($ mil.)	NET INCOME ($ mil.)	NET PROFIT MARGIN	EMPLOYEES
12/05	406.7	112.4	27.6%	209
12/04	275.0	69.2	25.2%	157
12/03	180.9	32.4	17.9%	129
12/02	132.5	30.0	22.6%	113
12/01	138.5	21.9	15.8%	110
Annual Growth	**30.9%**	**50.5%**	**—**	**17.4%**

2005 Year-End Financials

Debt ratio: 31.1%
Return on equity: 37.6%
Cash ($ mil.): 6.3
Current ratio: 0.58
Long-term debt ($ mil.): 103.8
No. of shares (mil.): 21.1
Dividends
 Yield: 1.0%
 Payout: 12.0%
 Market value ($ mil.): 603.5
 R&D as % of sales: —
 Advertising as % of sales: —

Stock History

NYSE: BRY

	STOCK PRICE ($) FY Close	P/E High/Low	PER SHARE ($) Earnings	Dividends	Book Value
12/05	28.60	14 8	2.50	0.30	15.84
12/04	23.85	16 6	1.54	0.26	12.49
12/03	10.13	13 9	0.78	0.22	9.44
12/02	8.52	13 10	0.69	0.20	8.25
12/01	7.85	18 11	0.50	0.20	7.35
Annual Growth	**38.2%**	**— —**	**49.5%**	**10.7%**	**21.2%**

Beverly Hills Bancorp

If Californy is the place you oughta be, load up your cash and deposit it in Beverly . . . Beverly Hills Bancorp, that is. Formerly Wilshire Financial Services Group, Beverly Hills Bancorp conducts business through its primary subsidiary, First Bank of Beverly Hills (FBBH), a state commercial bank serving individuals and businesses though two branches in Southern California. The bank's focus is the origination of real estate loans, especially for commercial (50% of the bank's loan portfolio) and multifamily (45%) uses. The company conducts mortgage investment operations through investment subsidiary WFC Inc.

Wilshire Financial moved its headquarters from Oregon to California in 2004 and changed its name soon thereafter to Beverly Hills Bancorp. Also that year it sold its Oregon-based mortgage servicing subsidiary, Wilshire Credit, to Merrill Lynch & Co. Director Howard Amster owns a 12% stake in Beverly Hills Bancorp. Director Robert Kanner owns nearly 9%, and director Stephen Glennon owns 5%.

EXECUTIVES

Chairman and CEO; President and CEO, First Bank of Beverly Hills: Larry B. Faigin, age 63, $91,667 pay (prior to title change)
CFO; SVP and CFO, First Bank of Beverly Hills: Takeo K. Sasaki, age 37, $228,667 pay
EVP and Chief Credit Officer, First Bank of Beverly Hills: Annette J. Vecchio, age 55, $217,000 pay (prior to promotion)
EVP and Chief Lending Officer, First Bank of Beverly Hills: Craig W. Kolasinski, age 43, $345,000 pay
SVP and Closing Manager, First Bank of Beverly Hills: Sheldon A. Eisenberg, age 56
SVP, Acquisitions, First Bank of Beverly Hills: Russell T. Campbell, age 40
SVP, Funding and Investments, First Bank of Beverly Hills: John A. Kardos, age 49
SVP Technology and Compliance, First Bank of Beverly Hills: Bryce W. Miller, age 44, $195,000 pay
Secretary: Carol Schardt
Human Resources: Susan Christian
Auditors: Deloitte & Touche LLP

LOCATIONS

HQ: Beverly Hills Bancorp Inc.
23901 Calabasas Rd., Ste. 1050,
Calabasas, CA 91302
Phone: 818-223-8084 **Fax:** 818-223-9742
Web: www.fbbh.com

PRODUCTS/OPERATIONS

2005 Sales

	$ mil.	% of total
Interest		
Loans	60.9	77
Mortgage-backed securities	14.8	19
Other	1.7	2
Noninterest	2.0	2
Total	**79.4**	**100**

COMPETITORS

Bank of America
Bank of the West
California National Bank
Countrywide Financial
Downey Financial
Ocwen Financial
UnionBanCal
Washington Mutual
Wells Fargo

HISTORICAL FINANCIALS

Company Type: Public

Income Statement

	ASSETS ($ mil.)	NET INCOME ($ mil.)	INCOME AS % OF ASSETS	FYE: December 31 EMPLOYEES
12/05	1,403.7	15.1	1.1%	52
12/04	1,338.9	25.6	1.9%	61
12/03	975.3	6.9	0.7%	455
12/02	843.0	2.0	0.2%	372
12/01	769.0	5.6	0.7%	318
Annual Growth	**16.2%**	**28.1%**	**—**	**(36.4%)**

2005 Year-End Financials

Equity as % of assets: 12.4% Dividends
Return on assets: 1.1% Yield: 4.8%
Return on equity: 8.8% Payout: 71.4%
Long-term debt ($ mil.): 20.6 Sales ($ mil.): 79.4
No. of shares (mil.): 21.3 R&D as % of sales: —
Market value ($ mil.): 221.2 Advertising as % of sales: —

Stock History

NASDAQ (GS): BHBC

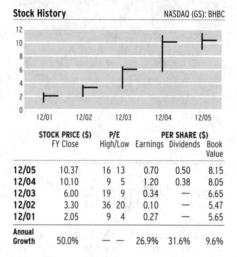

	STOCK PRICE ($) FY Close	P/E High/Low		PER SHARE ($) Earnings	Dividends	Book Value
12/05	10.37	16	13	0.70	0.50	8.15
12/04	10.10	9	5	1.20	0.38	8.05
12/03	6.00	19	9	0.34	—	6.65
12/02	3.30	36	20	0.10	—	5.47
12/01	2.05	9	4	0.27	—	5.65
Annual Growth	**50.0%**	**—**	**—**	**26.9%**	**31.6%**	**9.6%**

Big Dog Holdings

Beware of Big Dog Holdings. Best known for its T-shirts, sweatshirts, and boxer shorts for men, the apparel marketer is nipping at the heels of the industry's top dogs with its Saint Bernard logo and cheeky slogans. Big Dog also sells women's apparel, kids' clothing (Little Big Dog), big and tall apparel, and non-apparel items (golf bags, plush animals, watches, hot sauce, dog collars, and other accessories) with a dog theme. The company operates about 175 Big Dog and Little Big Dog retail stores, located mostly in US outlet malls but also in Puerto Rico, as well as 90-plus The Walking Company shoe stores. Chairman Fred Kayne owns about 60% of Big Dog.

In addition the company sells through its magalog (magazine/catalog combination) and Web site. Big Dog's catalog and Internet business accounts for about 6% of sales.

Shoppers who would hesitate to call themselves fashion hounds dig Big Dog Holdings' tags. Some of its wares espouse such doggerel as "If You Can't Run with the Big Dogs, Stay on the Porch" and "Unless You're the Lead Dog, the Scenery Never Changes." Nearly 95% of Big Dog's sales come from its retail stores. However, slumping sales at Big Dog stores have led to the shutdown of about two dozen underperforming locations in 2005 and early 2006.

To compensate for slowdown in sales at its main Big Dog chain, the company began sniffing out new territory: in 2004 Big Dog purchased bankrupt shoe retailer The Walking Company (TWC). Offering men and women's comfort footwear and related accessories, TWC has grown to 90-plus specialty stores across the US since the acquisition. TWC stores carry Birkenstock, ECCO, Dansko, Mephisto, and Merrell brand shoes. Further footwear purchases followed in 2005 (Footworks) and 2006 (Steve's Shoes). Most of those stores are being converted to the TWC banner.

Though a mere Chihuahua compared to casual top dog The Gap, Big Dog yawns at merchandising to the glitzy, youth-centric market in favor of catering to baby boomers with kids. The company takes special pains to appeal to large size customers and children; these pains are paying off with increased sales in these areas.

President and CEO Andrew Feshbach owns about 10% of the company.

HISTORY

Big Dog Holdings traces its roots to the mid-1980s and Sierra West Manufacturing, whose oversized shorts, dubbed "big puppies," were popular with outdoors enthusiasts. In 1992 apparel industry and investment veterans Fred Kayne and Andrew Feshbach, who had earlier co-founded Fortune Fashions, acquired the Big Dog brand and apparel line. There were five Big Dog retail stores in 1993; 35 stores were added the next year and 40 more in 1995.

That year the company sued basketball player Glenn Robinson, whose nickname is Big Dog, for signing a deal with sporting goods maker Roadmaster to market products using the Big Dog moniker. The company eventually prevailed. Big Dog went public in 1997 with more than 130 outlets.

In 1999 Big Dog signed an agreement to jointly promote with online pet care merchant PetSmart.com. Unhappy with its sagging stock price, in 2000 the company began a share buyback program.

In March 2004 Big Dog acquired bankrupt footwear retailer The Walking Company.

In May 2005 TWC acquired the assets of Footworks, a division of shoe retailer Bianca of Nevada, for $10 million. It followed that with the $35 million purchase of the bankrupt comfort shoe retailer Steve's Shoes in January 2006. Steve's Shoes added some 35 retail locations to TWC's operations. The company shuttered 15 underperforming Big Dog stores in 2005.

EXECUTIVES

Chairman: Fred Kayne, age 67
President, CEO, and Director: Andrew D. Feshbach, age 45, $545,071 pay
CFO, Treasurer, and Assistant Secretary: Roberta J. Morris, age 46, $269,769 pay
EVP, Merchandising Big Dog USA: Douglas N. Nilsen, age 57, $295,769 pay
EVP, Business Affairs, General Counsel, and Secretary: Anthony J. Wall, age 50, $348,069 pay
SVP, Merchandising, TWC: Michael Grenley, age 48, $294,833 pay
SVP, Retail Operations: Lee M. Cox, age 37, $287,538 pay
Director of Human Resources: Diana Lovan
Auditors: Singer Lewak Greenbaum & Goldstein LLP

LOCATIONS

HQ: Big Dog Holdings, Inc.
121 Gray Ave., Santa Barbara, CA 93101
Phone: 805-963-8727 **Fax:** 805-962-9460
Web: www.bigdogs.com

2005 Big Dog Stores

	No.
California	32
Florida	13
Texas	9
Pennsylvania	8
Missouri	7
Tennessee	7
Arizona	6
Georgia	6
Michigan	6
Colorado	5
Maryland	5
North Carolina	5
Oregon	5
South Carolina	5
Washington	5
Minnesota	4
New York	4
Ohio	4
Illinois	3
Indiana	3
Kansas	3
Massachusetts	3
Mississippi	3
Nevada	3
Wisconsin	3
Other states	19
Total	**176**

2005 TWC Stores

	No.
California	19
Florida	9
Nevada	6
Massachusetts	5
Washington	5
Illinois	4
Virginia	4
Georgia	3
Maryland	3
Michigan	3
North Carolina	3
Ohio	3
Oregon	3
Other states	22
Total	**92**

PRODUCTS/OPERATIONS

2005 Sales

	% of total
Adult apparel & accessories	55
Big-size apparel	26
Infants' & children's apparel & accessories	14
Non-apparel products	5
Total	**100**

2005 Sales

	$ mil.	% of total
Big Dog	92.1	51
TWC	87.0	49
Total	**179.1**	**100**

COMPETITORS

Abercrombie & Fitch
American Eagle Outfitters
Casual Male Retail Group
Cole Haan
Disney
Eddie Bauer Holdings
Federated
Gap
J. C. Penney
Nordstrom
OshKosh B'Gosh
Pacific Sunwear
Phoenix Footwear
Sears
Time Warner
Wal-Mart

HISTORICAL FINANCIALS

Company Type: Public

Income Statement
FYE: December 31

	REVENUE ($ mil.)	NET INCOME ($ mil.)	NET PROFIT MARGIN	EMPLOYEES
12/05	179.1	4.7	2.6%	2,100
12/04	161.4	3.7	2.3%	1,700
12/03	103.8	2.6	2.5%	1,400
12/02	108.8	3.8	3.5%	1,400
12/01	112.4	2.6	2.3%	1,300
Annual Growth	**12.4%**	**16.0%**	**—**	**12.7%**

2005 Year-End Financials

Debt ratio: 9.9%
Return on equity: 10.6%
Cash ($ mil.): 3.5
Current ratio: 2.58
Long-term debt ($ mil.): 4.6
No. of shares (mil.): 9.1

Dividends
  Yield: —
  Payout: —
Market value ($ mil.): 67.1
R&D as % of sales: —
Advertising as % of sales: 0.8%

Stock History
NASDAQ (GM): BDOG

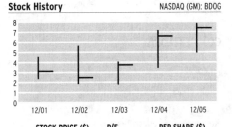

	STOCK PRICE ($) FY Close	P/E High/Low		PER SHARE ($) Earnings	Dividends	Book Value
12/05	7.39	16	10	0.49	—	5.12
12/04	6.58	18	9	0.40	—	4.63
12/03	3.73	13	6	0.32	—	4.15
12/02	2.46	12	4	0.45	—	3.81
12/01	3.12	15	8	0.31	—	3.36
Annual Growth	**24.1%**	**—**	**—**	**12.1%**	**—**	**11.1%**

Bill Barrett

Bill Barrett Corp. (named after a veteran oil industry wildcatter) is hoping for a Rocky Mountain high as it digs down deep for oil and gas. The company focuses its exploration and development activities in the Wind River, Uinta, Powder River, Williston, Denver-Julesburg, Big Horn, and Paradox Basins and the Montana and Utah Overthrusts. Bill Barrett holds more than 1 million net undeveloped leasehold acres. The oil and gas firm has 738 net producing wells. Bill Barrett has estimated net proved reserves of 341 billion cu. ft. of natural gas equivalent.

Bill Barrett was established in 2002 by former managers of Barrett Resources (which was acquired by The Williams Companies in 2001). The company went public in 2004. In 2006 Bill Barrett acquired CH4 Corp. for $82 million.

EXECUTIVES

Chairman and CEO: Fredrick J. (Fred) Barrett, age 45
President, COO, and Director: Joseph N. (Joe) Jaggers, age 53
SVP, Interim CFO, General Counsel, and Corporate Secretary: Francis B. Barron, age 44
SVP, Exploration, Northern Division: Terry R. Barrett, age 46
SVP, Exploration, Southern Division: Kurt M. Reinecke, age 47
SVP, Geophysics: Wilfred R. (Roy) Roux, age 48
SVP, Land: Huntington T. Walker, age 50
Auditors: Deloitte & Touche LLP

LOCATIONS

HQ: Bill Barrett Corporation
  1099 18th St., Ste. 2300, Denver, CO 80202
Phone: 303-293-9100   **Fax:** 303-291-0420
Web: www.billbarrettcorp.com

PRODUCTS/OPERATIONS

2005 Sales

	% of total
ONEOK	20
Xcel Energy	10
OGE Energy Resources	10
Other customers	60
Total	**100**

COMPETITORS

Abraxas Petroleum
Delta Petroleum
Double Eagle Petroleum

HISTORICAL FINANCIALS

Company Type: Public

Income Statement
FYE: December 31

	REVENUE ($ mil.)	NET INCOME ($ mil.)	NET PROFIT MARGIN	EMPLOYEES
12/05	288.8	23.8	8.2%	190
12/04	170.0	(5.3)	—	150
12/03	75.4	(4.0)	—	—
12/02	16.1	(5.0)	—	—
Annual Growth	**161.8%**	**—**		**26.7%**

2005 Year-End Financials

Debt ratio: 13.6%
Return on equity: 3.8%
Cash ($ mil.): 68.3
Current ratio: 1.06
Long-term debt ($ mil.): 86.0
No. of shares (mil.): 43.6

Dividends
  Yield: —
  Payout: —
Market value ($ mil.): 1,682.3
R&D as % of sales: —
Advertising as % of sales: —

Stock History
NYSE: BBG

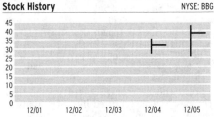

	STOCK PRICE ($) FY Close	P/E High/Low		PER SHARE ($) Earnings	Dividends	Book Value
12/05	38.61	77	47	0.55	—	14.48
12/04	31.99	—	—	(15.40)	—	14.30
Annual Growth	**20.7%**	**—**	**—**	**—**	**—**	**1.2%**

Bio-Reference Laboratories

Bio-Reference Laboratories has tested positive as the lab of choice for many in the Northeast. Through labs in New Jersey and New York, the company offers such routine clinical tests as Pap smears, pregnancy tests, cholesterol checks, and blood cell counts. It also performs some esoteric testing, including genetic, oncology, and toxicology tests. Its GenPath unit specializes in cancer pathology and molecular diagnostics. Its customers include hospitals, employers, and prisons in Connecticut, Pennsylvania, and the aforementioned states. CareEvolve, a joint venture with Roche, offers Web-based communication services for doctors, patients, and payers. Through PSIMedica, the firm sells informatics systems.

Bio-Reference expanded its genetic testing capabilities in 2006 with the acquisition of GeneDx, a Maryland-based laboratory that specializes in diagnosing rare genetic disorders.

The company maintains more than 50 patient service centers in New York City, where specimens are collected for testing at the firm's labs. Bio-Reference serves nearly 3 million patients. Routine testing accounts for nearly two-thirds of the company's bottom line; esoteric testing accounts for the remainder.

In addition to its joint venture with Roche, Bio-Reference has partnered with Visible Genetics to market its TRUGENE HIV-1 Genotyping Kit for AIDS patients.

CEO Marc Grodman owns 13% of the company.

HISTORY

Marc Grodman founded Med-Mobile in 1981, offering mobile medical examination services. In 1987 it opened a clinical laboratory in New Jersey. The purchase of Cytology and Pathology Associates, a small, specialized lab, followed in 1988. Demand for tests rose, leading the company to relocate all operations to a modern lab near New York City. It renamed itself Bio-Reference Laboratories in 1989 and went public in 1993.

The company moved into specialty testing to compensate for the industry-wide drop in reimbursement rates that hit its general labs, acquiring GenCare Biomedical Research (cancer testing, 1995), Oncodec Labs (gene mutations, 1995), and SmithKline Beecham's renal dialysis testing business (1996). Late in 1996 the firm sued SmithKline Beecham, accusing it of fraud regarding the purchase.

In 1997, the company sold part of its GenCare oncology laboratory services division to IMPATH. To build its regional presence, the company acquired Medilabs from Long Term Care in 1998. The next year it ventured into new frontiers, opening and acquiring Web sites for online ventures and buying the Right Body Foods health foods business. In 2000, Bio-Reference Laboratories expanded its Internet presence (including a business-to-business Web portal for health care professionals, CareEvolve.com) and re-entered the oncology market, resuming full service testing to physicians and institutions.

EXECUTIVES

Chairman, President, and CEO: Marc D. Grodman, age 55, $750,000 pay
EVP, COO, and Director: Howard Dubinett, age 55, $299,600 pay
SVP, Sales and Marketing: Charles T. Todd
VP, CFO, Chief Accounting Officer, and Director: Sam Singer, age 63, $299,600 pay
VP and General Manager: Warren Erdmann
VP and Director, Sales: John W. Littleton, age 40
Chief Medical Officer: James Weisberger
President, CareEvolve: Cory Fishkin
Director, Human Resources: Christopher Caruso
Director, Investor Relations: Kara Kelly
Auditors: Moore Stephens, P.C.

LOCATIONS

HQ: Bio-Reference Laboratories, Inc.
481 Edward H. Ross Dr., Elmwood Park, NJ 07407
Phone: 201-791-2600 **Fax:** 201-791-1941
Web: www.bioreference.com

Bio-Reference Laboratories operates facilities in New Jersey and New York.

COMPETITORS

American Bio Medica
AmeriPath
Avitar
Clinical Data
Covance
Esoterix
Kroll Laboratory Specialists
LabCorp
LabOne
Laboratory Sciences of Arizona
MEDTOX Laboratories
Medtox Scientific
PAREXEL
PharmChem
Psychemedics
Quest Diagnostics
Transgenomic

HISTORICAL FINANCIALS

Company Type: Public

Income Statement

FYE: October 31

	REVENUE ($ mil.)	NET INCOME ($ mil.)	NET PROFIT MARGIN	EMPLOYEES
10/06	193.1	11.3	5.9%	1,551
10/05	163.9	7.6	4.6%	1,276
10/04	136.2	8.5	6.2%	1,156
10/03	109.0	6.5	6.0%	1,022
10/02	96.6	4.9	5.1%	828
Annual Growth	18.9%	23.2%	—	17.0%

2006 Year-End Financials

Debt ratio: 10.3%
Return on equity: 18.9%
Cash ($ mil.): 8.9
Current ratio: 1.90
Long-term debt ($ mil.): 7.1
No. of shares (mil.): 13.6

Dividends
Yield: —
Payout: —
Market value ($ mil.): 320.3
R&D as % of sales: —
Advertising as % of sales: —

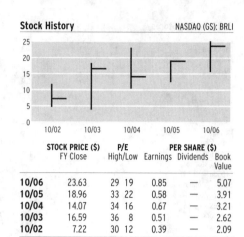

Stock History

NASDAQ (GS): BRLI

	STOCK PRICE ($) FY Close	P/E High/Low		Earnings	PER SHARE ($) Dividends	Book Value
10/06	23.63	29	19	0.85	—	5.07
10/05	18.96	33	22	0.58	—	3.91
10/04	14.07	34	16	0.67	—	3.21
10/03	16.59	36	8	0.51	—	2.62
10/02	7.22	30	12	0.39	—	2.09
Annual Growth	34.5%	—	—	21.5%	—	24.8%

Biosite

Biosite makes truth serum for specimen cups. The company's diagnostic products include its Triage Drugs of Abuse Panel and Triage TOX Drug Screen, single-sample urine tests that indicate illegal drug use, including amphetamines, cocaine, marijuana, and opiates. The firm's Triage C. difficile and Triage Parasite Panels detect intestinal parasites and other pathogens. The company's Triage BNP Test assists in diagnosing congestive heart failure. The Biosite Discovery program is a collaborative research effort to identify new protein markers for cardiovascular diseases, abdominal pain, kidney injuries, and sepsis. Biosite has collaboration agreements with companies including Eli Lilly, Amgen, and Lexicon Genetics.

Thermo Fisher, which distributes all of Biosite's products in the US, accounts for approximately 85% of company sales.

EXECUTIVES

Chairman and CEO: Kim D. Blickenstaff, age 53, $817,924 pay
President and Chief Scientific Officer: Kenneth F. (Ken) Buechler, age 52, $634,905 pay
SVP, Finance, CFO, and Secretary: Christopher J. (Chris) Twomey, age 46, $422,080 pay
SVP, Biosite Discovery: Gunars E. Valkirs, age 54
SVP, Corporate Development: Christopher R. Hibberd, age 40, $360,614 pay
SVP, Strategic and Global Product Marketing: Winton G. Gibbons, age 43
SVP, Worldwide Marketing and Sales: Robert B. Anacone, age 55
VP, Corporate and Investor Relations: Nadine E. Padilla, age 45
VP, Marketing: Bill Ferenczy
VP, Research and Development: Paul H. McPherson, age 47
Manager, Public Relations: Nicole Beckstrand
Auditors: Ernst & Young LLP

LOCATIONS

HQ: Biosite Incorporated
9975 Summers Ridge Rd., San Diego, CA 92121
Phone: 858-805-4808
Web: www.biosite.com

PRODUCTS/OPERATIONS

2005 Sales

	$ mil.	% of total
Products	282.8	98
Contract revenues	4.9	2
Total	**287.7**	**100**

Products

Triage BNP Test
Triage *C. difficile* Panel
Triage Cardiac Panel
Triage CardioProfilER Panel
Triage D-Timer Test
Triage Drugs of Abuse Panel (Triage DOA Panel)
Triage Parasite Panel
Triage Profiler Shortness of Breath Panel
Triage TOX Drug Screen
Triage Stroke Panel

COMPETITORS

Abbott Labs
American Bio Medica
Avitar
Beckman Coulter
Chiron
Dade Behring
Ivax Diagnostics
Johnson & Johnson
LipoScience
Meridian Bioscience
Psychemedics
Roche Diagnostics
Smart-tek Solutions
Spectral Diagnostics

HISTORICAL FINANCIALS

Company Type: Public

Income Statement				FYE: December 31
	REVENUE ($ mil.)	NET INCOME ($ mil.)	NET PROFIT MARGIN	EMPLOYEES
12/05	287.7	54.0	18.8%	1,003
12/04	244.9	41.5	16.9%	905
12/03	173.4	24.8	14.3%	817
12/02	105.2	13.4	12.7%	513
12/01	65.6	6.7	10.2%	351
Annual Growth	**44.7%**	**68.5%**	**—**	**30.0%**

2005 Year-End Financials

Debt ratio: 3.5%
Return on equity: 20.2%
Cash ($ mil.): 132.4
Current ratio: 5.24
Long-term debt ($ mil.): 11.0
No. of shares (mil.): 17.6
Dividends
  Yield: —
  Payout: —
Market value ($ mil.): 988.3
R&D as % of sales: 14.7%
Advertising as % of sales: —

Stock History

NASDAQ (GS): BSTE

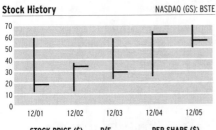

	STOCK PRICE ($) FY Close	P/E High/Low		PER SHARE ($) Earnings	Dividends	Book Value
12/05	56.29	24	17	2.92	—	17.96
12/04	61.54	26	11	2.42	—	13.12
12/03	28.95	38	16	1.50	—	9.79
12/02	34.02	42	15	0.86	—	7.25
12/01	18.37	133	28	0.44	—	6.21
Annual Growth	**32.3%**	**—**	**—**	**60.5%**	**—**	**30.4%**

Bitstream

Bitstream counts on its fonts to keep business flowing. The company develops software that creates and manages typefaces. It has a library of more than 500 fonts and develops technology for delivering typographic capabilities to hardware, software, and Web applications. Software products include its ThunderHawk browser, as well as text distribution applications (TrueDoc) and font managers (Font Reserve). Subsidiary Pageflex offers publishing software that designs and creates custom business documents based on customer profiles. Bitstream's MyFonts.com subsidiary offers a Web site for locating, testing, and purchasing different fonts.

The company licenses its products to original equipment manufacturers (OEMs) and software and technology vendors. Customers in the US account for about 80% of the company's sales.

EXECUTIVES

Chairman: Charles W. Ying, age 59
President, CEO, and Director: Anna M. Chagnon, age 39, $360,000 pay
VP and CFO: James P. (Jim) Dore, age 47, $210,000 pay
VP and CTO: John S. Collins, age 66, $182,000 pay
VP, Engineering: Costas Kitsos, age 45, $225,000 pay
VP, Research and Development: Sampo Kaasila, age 45, $210,000 pay
Director, Typographic Development: Jim Lyles
Director, Product Management: Bob Thomas
Director, Product Marketing: Alice Fackre
Marketing and Trade Show Coordinator: Paula Young
Auditors: PricewaterhouseCoopers LLP

LOCATIONS

HQ: Bitstream Inc.
  245 1st St., 17th Fl., Cambridge, MA 02142
Phone: 617-497-6222   **Fax:** 617-868-0784
Web: www.bitstream.com

2005 Sales

	$ mil.	% of total
US	12.6	80
UK	0.8	6
Canada	0.7	4
Japan	0.3	2
Other countries	1.2	8
Total	**15.6**	**100**

PRODUCTS/OPERATIONS

2005 Sales

	$ mil.	% of total
Software licenses	13.1	84
Services	2.5	16
Total	**15.6**	**100**

Selected Products

Developer products
  Font development for Linux and Unix (btX)
  Font rendering (TrueDoc Imaging System)
  Font subsystem (Font Fusion)
  Web browser for handheld devices and wireless networks (ThunderHawk)
  Web site to access fonts for Web pages (TrueDoc)
Typeface products
  Fonts (Cambridge collection, Express Yourself, Type Odyssey, and others)
  Font managers (Font Reserve)

Other
  Custom design services
  MyFonts.com (online font search engine and e-commerce site)
  Pageflex
    .EDIT (browser-based design and editing application)
    MPower (marketing documents software)
    Persona (Web-based marketing tool publishing software)

COMPETITORS

Adobe
Agfa
Apple Computer
Banta
Corel
Microsoft
Novarra
Opera Software
Quark

HISTORICAL FINANCIALS

Company Type: Public

Income Statement				FYE: December 31
	REVENUE ($ mil.)	NET INCOME ($ mil.)	NET PROFIT MARGIN	EMPLOYEES
12/05	15.6	1.0	6.4%	62
12/04	11.6	(0.6)	—	55
12/03	9.7	(1.2)	—	54
12/02	8.5	(1.0)	—	55
12/01	8.0	(3.5)	—	55
Annual Growth	**18.2%**	**—**	**—**	**3.0%**

2005 Year-End Financials

Debt ratio: —
Return on equity: 19.5%
Cash ($ mil.): 5.8
Current ratio: 2.54
Long-term debt ($ mil.): —
No. of shares (mil.): 8.7
Dividends
  Yield: —
  Payout: —
Market value ($ mil.): 32.7
R&D as % of sales: 25.2%
Advertising as % of sales: —

Stock History

NASDAQ (CM): BITS

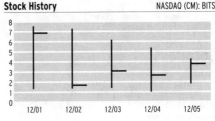

	STOCK PRICE ($) FY Close	P/E High/Low		PER SHARE ($) Earnings	Dividends	Book Value
12/05	3.76	38	17	0.11	—	0.66
12/04	2.65	—	—	(0.07)	—	0.52
12/03	3.07	—	—	(0.14)	—	0.58
12/02	1.68	—	—	(0.12)	—	0.71
12/01	6.86	—	—	(0.43)	—	0.83
Annual Growth	**(14.0%)**	**—**	**—**	**—**	**—**	**(5.7%)**

BJ's Restaurants

The Windy City inspires the food and drink at BJ's. BJ's Restaurants (formerly Chicago Pizza & Brewery) owns and operates about 50 restaurants in six western states (mostly in California) under the names BJ's Restaurant & Brewery, BJ's Pizza & Grill, and BJ's Restaurant & Brewhouse. The casual-dining eateries offer Chicago-style pizza, salad, sandwiches, pasta, and the company's own hand-crafted beers. Its 11 Restaurant & Brewery locations, which feature an onsite microbrewery, help supply beer to the rest of the chain. California food service distributor (and BJ's supplier) Jacmar owns about 20% of the company.

BJ's has been increasing the rate of its expansion the past few years, opening nine restaurants in 2005. It hopes to add about a dozen new locations during 2006.

Golden Resorts, a California-based real estate investment firm, owns 15% of the company.

EXECUTIVES

Co-Chairman: Jeremiah J. (Jerry) Hennessy, age 47, $300,000 pay (prior to title change)
Co-Chairman, VP, and Secretary: Paul A. Motenko, age 51, $300,000 pay
President, CEO, and Director:
  Gerald W. (Jerry) Deitchle, age 54, $423,000 pay
CFO: Gregory S. (Greg) Levin, age 38
SVP Brewing Operations: Alexander M. (Alex) Puchner, age 42
SVP Design and Marketing and Chief Design Officer: R. Dean Gerrie, age 54, $234,533 pay
SVP Restaurant Operations: Lon F. Ledwith, age 48, $239,313 pay
VP and Treasurer: Robert D. (Bob) Curran
VP Marketing and Communications:
  Robert (Rob) DeLiema
Chief Development Officer: Gregory S. (Greg) Lynds, age 44, $265,920 pay
Chief Human Resources Officer: Tom Norton
Auditors: Ernst & Young LLP

LOCATIONS

HQ: BJ's Restaurants, Inc.
  16162 Beach Blvd., Ste. 100,
  Huntington Beach, CA 92647
Phone: 714-848-3747   **Fax:** 714-848-8287
Web: www.bjsbrewhouse.com

2005 Locations

	No.
California	31
Texas	6
Arizona	3
Oregon	3
Colorado	1
Nevada	1
Total	**45**

PRODUCTS/OPERATIONS

2005 Locations

	No.
BJ's Restaurant & Brewhouse	27
BJ's Restaurant & Brewery	11
BJ's Pizza & Grill	7
Total	**45**

COMPETITORS

Applebee's	N.U. Pizza
Brinker	OSI Restaurant Partners
California Pizza Kitchen	Pizza Hut
Carlson Restaurants	Rock Bottom Restaurants
Darden	Round Table Pizza
Gordon Biersch	Shakey's
Metromedia Restaurant	Uno Restaurants

HISTORICAL FINANCIALS

Company Type: Public

Income Statement

FYE: Sunday nearest December 31

	REVENUE ($ mil.)	NET INCOME ($ mil.)	NET PROFIT MARGIN	EMPLOYEES
12/05	178.2	8.4	4.7%	5,341
12/04	129.1	6.3	4.9%	3,943
12/03	103.0	3.6	3.5%	3,352
12/02	75.7	1.7	2.2%	2,686
12/01	64.7	3.2	4.9%	2,567
Annual Growth	**28.8%**	**27.3%**	**—**	**20.1%**

2005 Year-End Financials

Debt ratio: —
Return on equity: 8.1%
Cash ($ mil.): 49.8
Current ratio: 2.21
Long-term debt ($ mil.): —
No. of shares (mil.): 22.9

Dividends
  Yield: —
  Payout: —
Market value ($ mil.): 523.7
R&D as % of sales: —
Advertising as % of sales: 0.6%

Stock History

NASDAQ (GS): BJRI

	STOCK PRICE ($) FY Close	P/E High/Low		PER SHARE ($) Earnings	Dividends	Book Value
12/05	22.86	69	36	0.36	—	5.67
12/04	14.00	59	38	0.30	—	3.98
12/03	14.92	86	29	0.18	—	3.62
12/02	6.90	116	53	0.09	—	3.45
12/01	5.19	19	6	0.30	—	2.39
Annual Growth	**44.9%**	**—**	**—**	**4.7%**	**—**	**24.1%**

Blue River Bancshares

Blue River Bancshares is the holding company for Shelby County Bank, which has four branches in Shelby County, Indiana, southwest of Indianapolis. It also owns Paramount Bank, which has an office in Lexington, Kentucky. The banks offer a variety of deposit products such as checking, savings, NOW, and money market accounts, certificates of deposit, and individual retirement accounts. With these funds, they primarily originate one- to four-family residential mortgage loans, commercial mortgages, home equity and other consumer loans, and business loans.

EXECUTIVES

Chairman, President, and CEO; Chairman, Paramount Bank: Russell Breeden III, age 55
Vice Chairman; Chairman and Chief Credit Officer, Shelby County Bank: Steven R. Abel, age 55
EVP and Secretary; President and CEO, Shelby County Bank: Randy J. Collier, age 44
President and CEO, Paramount Bank:
  Olin W. Bryant Jr.
EVP, COO, and Chief Lending Officer, Paramount Bank: Rodney L. Mitchell
EVP and CFO, Paramount Bank: Sarita S. Grace
VP and Controller; SVP and CFO, Shelby County Bank: Patrice M. Lima, age 50

LOCATIONS

HQ: Blue River Bancshares, Inc.
  29 E. Washington St., Shelbyville, IN 46176
Phone: 317-398-9721   **Fax:** 317-835-0306
Web: www.shelbycountybank.com

PRODUCTS/OPERATIONS

2005 Sales

	$ mil.	% of total
Interest		
Loans receivable	10.5	78
Taxable securities	1.2	9
Other	0.3	2
Noninterest		
Secondary market mortgage fees	0.6	5
Service charges & fees on deposit accounts	0.5	4
Other	0.3	2
Total	**13.4**	**100**

COMPETITORS

Fifth Third
First Financial (IN)
First Indiana
Irwin Financial
KeyCorp
National City

HISTORICAL FINANCIALS

Company Type: Public

Income Statement

FYE: December 31

	ASSETS ($ mil.)	NET INCOME ($ mil.)	INCOME AS % OF ASSETS	EMPLOYEES
12/05	221.2	1.6	0.7%	64
12/04	206.6	(0.3)	—	68
12/03	198.8	0.1	0.1%	63
12/02	95.1	(4.5)	—	43
12/01	125.8	(2.2)	—	48
Annual Growth	**15.2%**	**—**	**—**	**7.5%**

2005 Year-End Financials

Equity as % of assets: 7.9%
Return on assets: 0.7%
Return on equity: 9.6%
Long-term debt ($ mil.): 6.0
No. of shares (mil.): 3.5
Market value ($ mil.): 18.2

Dividends
  Yield: —
  Payout: —
Sales ($ mil.): 13.4
R&D as % of sales: —
Advertising as % of sales: —

Stock History

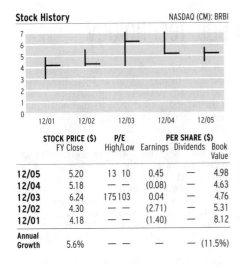

NASDAQ (CM): BRBI

	STOCK PRICE ($) FY Close	P/E High/Low		Earnings	PER SHARE ($) Dividends	Book Value
12/05	5.20	13	10	0.45	—	4.98
12/04	5.18	—	—	(0.08)	—	4.63
12/03	6.24	175	103	0.04	—	4.76
12/02	4.30	—	—	(2.71)	—	5.31
12/01	4.18	—	—	(1.40)	—	8.12
Annual Growth	**5.6%**	—	—	—	—	**(11.5%)**

BNC Bancorp

BNC Bancorp knows the ABCs of the financial world. The firm is the holding company for Bank of North Carolina, which has nine banking locations and loan offices in central and northeastern portions of the state. The bank offers community-oriented services to local business and retail customers, providing checking, savings, and other deposit accounts. Its loan portfolio is mainly composed of residential and commercial mortgages and business loans. Bank of North Carolina also offers mutual funds, annuities, and other investment products and services. BNC Bancorp acquired SterlingSouth Bank & Trust, a Greensboro banking company.

Company director Lenin Peters owns about 12% of BNC Bancorp; chairman W. Groome Fulton owns 6% and president W. Swope Montgomery 3%; as a group, executives and directors own nealy 30%.

EXECUTIVES

Chairman: W. Groome Fulton Jr., age 67
President, CEO, and Director; President and CEO, Bank of North Carolina: W. Swope Montgomery Jr., age 57, $309,000 pay
EVP, COO, and Director; EVP and COO, Bank of North Carolina: Richard D. Callicutt II, age 47, $227,000 pay
EVP, Secretary, and CFO; EVP and CFO, Bank of North Carolina: David B. Spencer, age 43, $222,500 pay
SVP and Regional Executive, Bank of North Carolina: H. Ed Campbell
SVP and Regional Executive, Bank of North Carolina: Mark N. Lewis
Secretary and Director: Richard F. Wood, age 60
Auditors: Cherry, Bekaert & Holland, LLP

LOCATIONS

HQ: BNC Bancorp
831 Julian Ave., Thomasville, NC 27360
Phone: 336-476-9200   **Fax:** 336-476-5818
Web: www.bankofnc.com

PRODUCTS/OPERATIONS

2005 Sales

	$ mil.	% of total
Interest		
Loans, including fees	31.3	86
State & municipal securities	1.7	5
Other	0.4	1
Noninterest		
Service charges	1.8	5
Mortgage fees	0.5	1
Cash surrender of life insurance	0.5	1
Other	0.2	1
Total	**36.4**	**100**

COMPETITORS

Bank of America
BB&T
First Bancorp (NC)
First Citizens BancShares
LSB Bancshares
RBC Centura Banks
Wachovia

HISTORICAL FINANCIALS

Company Type: Public

Income Statement

FYE: December 31

	ASSETS ($ mil.)	NET INCOME ($ mil.)	INCOME AS % OF ASSETS	EMPLOYEES
12/05	594.5	4.5	0.8%	142
12/04	497.5	3.8	0.8%	126
12/03	372.3	3.4	0.9%	106
12/02	306.6	2.6	0.8%	94
12/01	210.1	1.9	0.9%	63
Annual Growth	**29.7%**	**24.1%**	—	**22.5%**

2005 Year-End Financials

Equity as % of assets: 5.6%	Dividends
Return on assets: 0.8%	Yield: 0.7%
Return on equity: 14.5%	Payout: 13.6%
Long-term debt ($ mil.): 59.5	Sales ($ mil.): 36.4
No. of shares (mil.): 4.4	R&D as % of sales: —
Market value ($ mil.): 73.7	Advertising as % of sales: 1.2%

Stock History

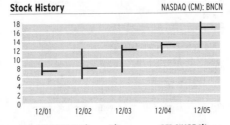

NASDAQ (CM): BNCN

	STOCK PRICE ($) FY Close	P/E High/Low		Earnings	PER SHARE ($) Dividends	Book Value
12/05	16.86	20	14	0.88	0.12	7.58
12/04	13.09	18	15	0.75	0.10	8.34
12/03	12.00	19	11	0.66	0.08	7.59
12/02	7.93	22	10	0.54	—	7.79
12/01	7.31	—	—	—	—	—
Annual Growth	**23.2%**	—	—	**17.7%**	**22.5%**	**(0.9%)**

Boardwalk Pipeline Partners

Boardwalk Pipeline Partners is in the business of interstate transportation, gathering, and storage of natural gas. The company operates through two subsidiaries — Texas Gas Transmission and Gulf South Pipeline Company — with a combined 13,470 miles of pipeline in 11 states. Texas Gas operates in Arkansas, Illinois, Indiana, Kentucky, Louisiana, Mississippi, Ohio, Tennessee, and Texas. Gulf South operates in Alabama, Florida, Louisiana, Mississippi, and Texas. Customers include local gas distribution companies, local governments, other interstate and intrastate pipeline companies, direct industrial users, and electric power generators. Boardwalk Pipeline Partners is owned by Loews Corporation.

Boardwalk Pipeline Partners has taken over the business formerly held by Loews unit Boardwalk Pipelines, LLC. In the reorganization, Loews retained an 83.5% stake in the new company. The remaining 2% stake belongs to Boardwalk GP, LLC, a Loews subsidiary and the managing general partner in Boardwalk Pipeline Partners.

EXECUTIVES

Chairman, Boardwalk GP, LLC: Arthur L. Rebell, age 64
Co-President and Director, Boardwalk GP, LLC: Rolf A. Gafvert, age 52
Co-President and Director, Boardwalk GP, LLC: H. Dean Jones II, age 53
CFO, Boardwalk GP, LLC: Jamie L. Buskill, age 41
Auditors: Deloitte & Touche LLP

LOCATIONS

HQ: Boardwalk Pipeline Partners, LP
3800 Frederica St., Owensboro, KY 42301
Phone: 270-926-8686   **Fax:** 270-688-5872
Web: www.boardwalkpipelines.com

PRODUCTS/OPERATIONS

2005 Sales

	$ mil.	% of total
Gas transportation	526.6	94
Gas storage	21.7	4
Other	12.2	2
Total	**560.5**	**100**

COMPETITORS

Columbia Gulf Transmission
El Paso
Florida Gas Transmission
Southwest Gas
TXU
Williams Gas Pipeline

HISTORICAL FINANCIALS

Company Type: Public

Income Statement

FYE: December 31

	REVENUE ($ mil.)	NET INCOME ($ mil.)	NET PROFIT MARGIN	EMPLOYEES
12/05	560.5	100.9	18.0%	1,100
12/04	263.6	48.8	18.5%	1,100
12/03	142.9	22.5	15.7%	—
Annual Growth	**98.0%**	**111.8%**	—	**0.0%**

2005 Year-End Financials

Debt ratio: 111.4%
Return on equity: 9.7%
Cash ($ mil.): 65.8
Current ratio: 1.02
Long-term debt ($ mil.): 1,101.3
No. of shares (mil.): 68.3
Dividends
Yield: —
Payout: —
Market value ($ mil.): 1,227.2
R&D as % of sales: —
Advertising as % of sales: —

Stock History

NYSE: BWP

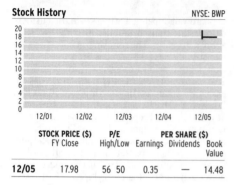

	STOCK PRICE ($) FY Close	P/E High/Low		PER SHARE ($) Earnings	Dividends	Book Value
12/05	17.98	56	50	0.35	—	14.48

BofI Holding

BofI wants you to leave the suckers behind in your bank's long drive-through window line and begin banking online. BofI Holding owns Bank of Internet USA, a nationwide savings bank operated online. The automated Internet-based banking platform allows Bank of Internet to keep customer fees fairly low and offer interest rates that are somewhat higher than average. The bank focuses on deposit products and multi-family real estate lending (some 75% of its loan portfolio, even though they are only offered in selected states). Residential mortgages make up more than 20% of the loan portfolio and are offered throughout the US. Bank of Internet USA targets such groups as students, senior citizens, and RV users.

The Chipman First Family Limited Partnership, managed by director Michael Chipman, owns more than 9% of BofI Holding. BofI chairman Jerry Englert owns more than 7% of the company; director J. Gary Burke and former director Robert Eprile each own more than 5%.

EXECUTIVES

Chairman: Jerry F. Englert, age 65
Vice Chairman: Theodore C. (Ted) Allrich, age 60
President and CEO, BofI Holding and Bank of Internet USA, and Director: Gary L. Evans, age 57, $221,506 pay
CFO; VP and CFO, Bank of Internet USA: Andrew J. Micheletti, age 47, $180,821 pay
VP and CTO, Bank of Internet USA: Michael J. (Mike) Berengolts, age 34, $137,532 pay
VP, Internet Development, Bank of Internet USA: Barbara Fronek
Multifamily Chief Credit Officer, Bank of Internet USA: Patrick A. Dunn, age 39, $426,242 pay (prior to title change)
Secretary and Director: Connie M. (Michelle) Paulus, age 46

LOCATIONS

HQ: BofI Holding, Inc.
12777 High Bluff Dr., Ste. 100,
San Diego, CA 92130
Phone: 858-350-6200 **Fax:** 858-350-0443
Web: www.bofiholding.com

PRODUCTS/OPERATIONS

2006 Sales

	% of total
Interest	
Loans	81
Investments	15
Noninterest	
Prepayment penalty fee income	2
Mortgage banking income	1
Banking service fees & other	1
Total	**100**

COMPETITORS

Bank of America
CalFirst
Citigroup
E*TRADE Bank
ebank
Emigrant Bank
FB BanCorp
First IB
ING Direct USA
interState Net Bank
NetBank
WebFinancial
Wells Fargo

HISTORICAL FINANCIALS

Company Type: Public

Income Statement

FYE: June 30

	ASSETS ($ mil.)	NET INCOME ($ mil.)	INCOME AS % OF ASSETS	EMPLOYEES
6/06	737.8	3.3	0.4%	26
6/05	609.5	2.9	0.5%	26
6/04	405.0	2.2	0.5%	—
6/03	273.5	1.7	0.6%	—
Annual Growth	**39.2%**	**34.8%**	**—**	**0.0%**

2006 Year-End Financials

Equity as % of assets: 8.8%
Return on assets: 0.5%
Return on equity: 5.2%
Long-term debt ($ mil.): 5.2
No. of shares (mil.): 8.4
Market value ($ mil.): 67.0
Dividends
Yield: —
Payout: —
Sales ($ mil.): 34.1
R&D as % of sales: —
Advertising as % of sales: —

Stock History

NASDAQ (GM): BOFI

	STOCK PRICE ($) FY Close	P/E High/Low		PER SHARE ($) Earnings	Dividends	Book Value
6/06	7.99	29	18	0.34	—	8.38
6/05	9.04	30	21	0.40	—	8.27
Annual Growth	**(11.6%)**	—	—	**(15.0%)**	—	**1.3%**

Bolt Technology

Bolt Technology's action is technology, the kind used to map out oil and gas discoveries. The company provides geophysical equipment to the oil and gas industry. Its marine air guns help produce 3-D seismic maps for oil and gas exploration by firing high-pressure air into the water, producing elastic waves that penetrate deep into the earth. These waves are then used to create a "map" of the subsurface geography. Through its Custom Products subsidiary, Bolt Technology makes miniature industrial clutches and brakes used in airplane video systems, hospital beds, barcode labelers, and banking machines. The company's customers in 2006 included WesternGeco (22% of sales) and CCG-Veritas (15%).

Bolt Technology was established in 1962. In 2004 the company completed development of stage one of its digital Seismic Source Monitoring System, designed to enhance the accuracy of its air gun seismic technology.

In 2006 the company was awarded a contract by BP Exploration (Caspian Sea) Limited for the supply of a portable Annular Port Air Gun source array.

EXECUTIVES

Chairman, President, and CEO: Raymond M. Soto, age 67, $694,400 pay
SVP Finance, CFO, and Director: Joseph Espeso, age 64, $312,000 pay
SVP Marketing, Secretary, and Director: Joseph (Joe) Mayerick Jr., age 64, $312,000 pay
Director; President and CEO, Custom Products: Gerald H. Shaff, age 73
Director Human Resources: Jolsen Stetso
Auditors: McGladrey & Pullen, LLP

LOCATIONS

HQ: Bolt Technology Corporation
4 Duke Place, Norwalk, CT 06854
Phone: 203-853-0700 **Fax:** 203-854-9601
Web: www.bolt-technology.com

Bolt Technology operates manufacturing facilities in Connecticut and Texas.

2006 Sales

	$ mil.	% of total
US	9.3	29
Norway	7.0	21
United Arab Emirates	6.1	19
Peoples Republic of China	2.5	8
France	2.1	6
India	1.8	5
Singapore	1.2	4
UK	0.7	2
Japan	0.6	2
Former Soviet Union	0.4	1
Canada	0.3	1
Germany	0.1	—
Other countries	0.5	2
Total	**32.6**	**100**

PRODUCTS/OPERATIONS

2006 Sales

	$ mil.	% of total
Geophysical equipment	29.4	90
Industrial products	3.2	10
Total	**32.6**	**100**

Selected Subsidiaries

A-G Geophysical Products, Inc. (underwater electrical connectors and cables, air gun hydrophones, and pressure transducers)

Custom Products Corporation (miniature industrial clutches, brakes, and sub-fractional horsepower electric motors)

COMPETITORS

Allegheny Technologies
CGGVeritas
Dawson Geophysical
Input/Output
OYO Geospace

HISTORICAL FINANCIALS

Company Type: Public

Income Statement

FYE: June 30

	REVENUE ($ mil.)	NET INCOME ($ mil.)	NET PROFIT MARGIN	EMPLOYEES
6/06	32.6	4.8	14.7%	100
6/05	18.8	1.7	9.0%	86
6/04	14.8	0.9	6.1%	86
6/03	10.8	(0.2)	—	83
6/02	18.0	1.9	10.6%	89
Annual Growth	**16.0%**	**26.1%**	**—**	**3.0%**

2006 Year-End Financials

Debt ratio: —
Return on equity: 18.7%
Cash ($ mil.): 4.6
Current ratio: 3.58
Long-term debt ($ mil.): —
No. of shares (mil.): 5.6
Dividends
 Yield: —
 Payout: —
Market value ($ mil.): 67.1
R&D as % of sales: —
Advertising as % of sales: —

Stock History

AMEX: BTJ

	STOCK PRICE ($) FY Close	P/E High/Low		PER SHARE ($) Earnings	Dividends	Book Value
6/06	12.07	23	7	0.86	—	5.09
6/05	6.40	23	9	0.30	—	4.26
6/04	4.50	29	20	0.16	—	3.95
6/03	3.45	—	—	(0.03)	—	3.79
6/02	4.05	17	11	0.35	—	3.82
Annual Growth	**31.4%**	**—**	**—**	**25.2%**	**—**	**7.4%**

Boston Private Financial Holdings

Boston Private — isn't that David Kelley's new TV series? Not exactly: The company is the parent of regional banks and financial companies serving primarily well-to-do and institutional clients on both coasts. Its subsidiaries' services and products include deposit accounts, investment management, and trust powers. Boston Private Bank & Trust operates seven New England branch locations; Borel Private Bank & Trust has three Northern California offices. The company serves Southern California through First State Bank of California (FSB), which it acquired in 2004 (it later bought Encino State Bank and merged it into FSB's operations).

Commercial loans account for nearly half of the company's loan portfolio. Boston Private also offers construction, residential construction, and home equity loans, among others.

In 2005 Boston Private moved into the fast-growing Florida market with the acquisition of Gibraltar Financial, which owns five Gibraltar Bank locations (primarily serving businesses and wealthy individuals). The next year it acquired the newly formed Anchor Holdings, consisting of the investment companies Anchor Capital and Anchor Russell.

EXECUTIVES

Chairman and CEO: Timothy L. Vaill, age 64, $1,445,538 pay
President and Director: Walter M. Pressey, age 61, $999,538 pay
President, Eastern Region: Joseph H. (Jay) Cromarty, age 49, $650,769 pay
President, Western Region: Jonathan H. Parker, age 60, $601,769 pay
EVP and CFO: Robert J. Whelan
EVP, General Counsel, and Secretary: Margaret W. (Megan) Chambers, age 46, $484,269 pay
SVP, Corporate Development: Kathryn A. Kearney
SVP, Human Resources: Gerald Raphel
VP, Investor Relations: Kathryn (Kate) Rajeck
Director; Chairman, Boston Private Bank & Trust: Eugene S. Colangelo, age 58
Chairman and CEO, RINET: Richard N. Thielen, age 63, $438,651 pay
Chairman and CEO, Westfield Capital: Arthur J. Bauernfeind, age 66
Chairman, Borel Private Bank & Trust: Sherie S. Dodsworth
Auditors: KPMG LLP

LOCATIONS

HQ: Boston Private Financial Holdings, Inc.
 10 Post Office Sq., Boston, MA 02109
Phone: 617-912-1900   **Fax:** 617-912-4550
Web: www.bostonprivate.com

PRODUCTS/OPERATIONS

2005 Sales

	$ mil.	% of total
Interest		
Loans	167.5	52
Securities	15.8	5
Other	6.6	2
Noninterest		
Investment management & trust fees	105.9	32
Wealth advisory fees	19.1	6
Other	9.7	3
Total	**324.6**	**100**

COMPETITORS

Bank of America	FMR
Brown Brothers Harriman	Merrill Lynch
Central Bancorp	Morgan Stanley
Century Bancorp (MA)	Sovereign Bancorp
Citigroup	TD Banknorth
Citizens Financial Group	

HISTORICAL FINANCIALS

Company Type: Public

Income Statement

FYE: December 31

	ASSETS ($ mil.)	NET INCOME ($ mil.)	INCOME AS % OF ASSETS	EMPLOYEES
12/05	5,134.1	46.3	0.9%	892
12/04	3,270.3	33.6	1.0%	592
12/03	2,196.3	21.8	1.0%	437
12/02	1,820.7	23.7	1.3%	391
12/01	1,509.5	11.6	0.8%	363
Annual Growth	**35.8%**	**41.3%**	**—**	**25.2%**

2005 Year-End Financials

Equity as % of assets: 10.4%
Return on assets: 1.1%
Return on equity: 10.8%
Long-term debt ($ mil.): 234.0
No. of shares (mil.): 34.8
Market value ($ mil.): 1,058.6
Dividends
 Yield: 0.9%
 Payout: 19.0%
Sales ($ mil.): 324.6
R&D as % of sales: —
Advertising as % of sales: —

Stock History

NASDAQ (GS): BPFH

	STOCK PRICE ($) FY Close	P/E High/Low		PER SHARE ($) Earnings	Dividends	Book Value
12/05	30.42	22	14	1.47	0.28	15.33
12/04	28.17	25	18	1.18	0.24	11.48
12/03	24.84	30	15	0.92	0.20	9.36
12/02	19.86	27	16	1.02	0.16	7.42
12/01	22.07	49	30	0.50	0.14	6.28
Annual Growth	**8.4%**	**—**	**—**	**30.9%**	**18.9%**	**25.0%**

Bradley Pharmaceuticals

Bradley Pharmaceuticals' ability to fix health problems isn't just skin-deep. Its Doak Dermatologics subsidiary markets the firm's dermatological products, including moisturizers and wart removers. Its Kenwood Laboratories division sells Brontex and Deconamine-brand respiratory products, as well as internal medicine brands, nutritional supplements, and personal hygiene items. All of the company's products are produced by third-party manufacturers. Chairman and CEO Daniel Glassman and his wife, company treasurer Iris Glassman, together own about 90% of the company.

Bradley Pharmaceuticals' strategy is to acquire the rights to over-the-counter and prescription health products that could use a marketing push. The company also seeks co-marketing and licensing agreements for drugs in its targeted therapeutic areas. In addition to acquisitions, the company is looking to expand its offerings by researching improvements and reformulations of existing drugs.

The company's biggest customers are major drug distributors; Cardinal Health accounts for 36% of Bradley Pharmaceuticals' sales. McKesson (25%), AmerisourceBergen (15%), and Quality King Distributors (11%) are the company's other major customers.

EXECUTIVES

Chairman: Leonard S. Jacob, age 57
President, CEO, and Director: Daniel Glassman, age 64
SVP, Sales and Marketing: Bradley Glassman, age 32, $291,730 pay
VP and CFO: R. Brent Lenczycki, age 34, $287,563 pay
VP and Chief Scientific Officer: Ralph Landau, age 45, $253,971 pay
VP, Business Development: Alton Delane
VP, Corporate Development: Alan Goldstein, age 46, $248,220 pay
VP, Investor Relations: Anthony Griffo, age 55
VP, Trade and Managed Care Relations: William Renzo, age 41, $11,519 pay (partial-year salary)
Director, Trade Relations: David Argento
Auditors: Grant Thornton LLP

LOCATIONS

HQ: Bradley Pharmaceuticals, Inc.
383 Rte. 46 West, Fairfield, NJ 07004
Phone: 973-882-1505   **Fax:** 973-575-5366
Web: www.bradpharm.com

2005 Sales

	$ mil.	% of total
US	130.1	97
Other countries	3.3	3
Total	**133.4**	**100**

PRODUCTS/OPERATIONS

2005 Sales

	$ mil.	% of total
Dermatology & podiatry	110.3	83
Gastrointestinal	17.0	13
Respiratory	4.1	3
Nutritional	1.7	1
Other	0.3	—
Total	**133.4**	**100**

Selected Products

Acidmantle/Lidamantle (skin acidifier/topical anesthetic)
Anamantle HC (topical hemorrhoid treatment)
Brontex (antitussive/expectorant)
Carmol (urea-based family of products for various dermatological conditions)
Deconamine (antihistamine/decongestant)
DPM Cream (dry feet)
Entsol (nasal wash)
Glutofac/ZX (vitamin and mineral supplements for various health conditions)
Pamine Tablets (anticholinergic/antispasmodic)
Rosula (rosacea, acne)
Tyzine Solution/Nasal Drops (nasal decongestant)
Zoderm (acne)

COMPETITORS

AstraZeneca
Axcan Pharma
Bristol-Myers Squibb
Chantal Pharmaceutical
Connetics
Dermik Laboratories
Ferndale Laboratories
Galderma Laboratories
GlaxoSmithKline
Medicis Pharmaceutical
Pfizer
Salix Pharmaceuticals
Sanofi-Aventis
Schering-Plough
Sciele Pharma
Upsher-Smith
Valeant
Warner Chilcott, Inc.

HISTORICAL FINANCIALS

Company Type: Public

Income Statement

FYE: December 31

	REVENUE ($ mil.)	NET INCOME ($ mil.)	NET PROFIT MARGIN	EMPLOYEES
12/05	133.4	8.0	6.0%	311
12/04	96.7	7.9	8.2%	300
12/03	74.7	16.8	22.5%	250
12/02	39.7	7.6	19.1%	181
12/01	25.7	3.6	14.0%	124
Annual Growth	**50.9%**	**22.1%**	**—**	**25.8%**

2005 Year-End Financials

Debt ratio: 40.0%
Return on equity: 4.8%
Cash ($ mil.): 19.8
Current ratio: 1.21
Long-term debt ($ mil.): 69.0
No. of shares (mil.): 15.9
Dividends
 Yield: —
 Payout: —
Market value ($ mil.): 151.5
R&D as % of sales: 1.1%
Advertising as % of sales: 12.4%

Stock History

NYSE: BDY

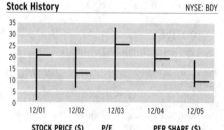

	STOCK PRICE ($) FY Close	P/E High/Low		PER SHARE ($) Earnings	Dividends	Book Value
12/05	9.50	38	15	0.49	—	10.82
12/04	19.40	61	29	0.49	—	9.74
12/03	25.43	24	7	1.35	—	10.25
12/02	13.03	36	10	0.67	—	3.80
12/01	20.75	63	4	0.37	—	3.03
Annual Growth	**(17.7%)**	**—**	**—**	**7.3%**	**—**	**37.4%**

Brigham Exploration

Still a young company, Brigham Exploration was one of the first small independent exploration and production firms to use 3-D seismic imaging. The company continues to rely on 3-D and other advanced technologies for onshore exploration. It explores mainly in the Anadarko Basin, the onshore Texas Gulf Coast, and West Texas. Since its founding by CEO Ben Brigham in 1990, it has drilled 688 wells. It has more than 190 potential exploration prospects and 151 potential development drilling locations. Brigham Exploration has net proved reserves of about 113.3 billion cu. ft. of natural gas and 3.3 million barrels of oil.

In 2006 the company announced that it had formed joint ventures with two operators in Southern Louisiana, expected to add nine potential exploration prospects and two potential development drilling locations.

EXECUTIVES

Chairman, President, and CEO: Ben M. (Bud) Brigham, age 46, $525,000 pay
EVP and CFO: Eugene B. Shepherd Jr., age 47, $370,907 pay
EVP Land and Administration and Director: David T. Brigham, age 45, $303,849 pay
EVP Operations: A. Lance Langford, age 43, $303,284 pay
EVP Exploration: Jeffery E. Larson, age 47, $284,845 pay
General Counsel and Corporate Secretary: Warren Ludlow
VP and Controller: Malcom Brown
Finance Manager: Rob Roosa
Auditors: KPMG LLP

LOCATIONS

HQ: Brigham Exploration Company
6300 Bridge Point Pkwy., Building 2, Ste. 500, Austin, TX 78730
Phone: 512-427-3300   **Fax:** 512-427-3400
Web: www.bexp3d.com

PRODUCTS/OPERATIONS

2005 Sales

	$ mil.	% of total
Oil & natural gas	96.8	100
Other	0.2	—
Total	**97.0**	**100**

Subsidiary

Brigham Oil & Gas, L.P.

COMPETITORS

Abraxas Petroleum
Anadarko Petroleum
Apache
BP
Cabot Oil & Gas
Carrizo Oil & Gas
Chesapeake Energy
Equitable Resources
Exxon Mobil
Forest Oil
McMoRan Exploration
Meridian Resource
Newfield Exploration
Noble Energy
Parallel Petroleum
Pioneer Natural Resources
Remington Oil and Gas
Royal Dutch Shell
Trek Resources
Unit Corporation
VAALCO

HISTORICAL FINANCIALS

Company Type: Public

Income Statement

FYE: December 31

	REVENUE ($ mil.)	NET INCOME ($ mil.)	NET PROFIT MARGIN	EMPLOYEES
12/05	97.0	27.4	28.2%	64
12/04	72.2	19.6	27.1%	57
12/03	51.7	18.3	35.4%	57
12/02	35.2	2.4	6.8%	52
12/01	32.5	11.7	36.0%	52
Annual Growth	**31.4%**	**23.7%**	**—**	**5.3%**

2005 Year-End Financials

Debt ratio: 26.1%
Return on equity: 12.9%
Cash ($ mil.): 4.2
Current ratio: 0.76
Long-term debt ($ mil.): 63.1
No. of shares (mil.): 44.9
Dividends
 Yield: —
 Payout: —
Market value ($ mil.): 532.7
R&D as % of sales: —
Advertising as % of sales: —

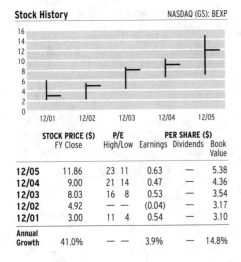

Stock History
NASDAQ (GS): BEXP

	STOCK PRICE ($) FY Close	P/E High/Low		Earnings	PER SHARE ($) Dividends	Book Value
12/05	11.86	23	11	0.63	—	5.38
12/04	9.00	21	14	0.47	—	4.36
12/03	8.03	16	8	0.53	—	3.54
12/02	4.92	—	—	(0.04)	—	3.17
12/01	3.00	11	4	0.54	—	3.10
Annual Growth	41.0%	—	—	—	3.9%	14.8%

Bristol West Holdings

Looking for auto coverage? Go West, young man. Bristol West Holdings sells non-standard private passenger insurance — that is, insurance for those who have trouble getting standard coverage because of bad driving records, age, limited financial resources, and the like. Most of Bristol West's policyholders purchase minimum liability coverage as required by the states they live in. The company operates in 21 states (it is licensed in 37 states and the District of Columbia), with about 75% of its gross written premiums coming from California, Florida, and Michigan. Affiliates of buy-out firm Kohlberg Kravis Roberts, which took the company public in 2004, own about 40% of Bristol West.

The company sells its products through more than 7,500 independent agents and brokers. It intends to grow the number of agents who sell its products and to diversify geographically, becoming less dependent on California customers, who produce 46% of its gross written premiums.

Though about 85% of Bristol West's customers buy minimum liability policies, the company also offers collision and comprehensive coverage, as well as medical payments coverage that pays for health care costs related to automobile accidents.

EXECUTIVES

Chairman: James R. Fisher, age 50
President, CEO, and Director: Jeffrey J. Dailey, age 49
COO: Simon J. Noonan, age 42
SVP and CFO: Craig E. Eisenacher, age 59, $338,303 pay
SVP and CFO: Robert D. Sadler, age 43
SVP and CIO: John L. Ondeck, age 46
SVP and General Counsel: Alexis S. Oster, age 37
SVP, Chief Legal Officer, and Corporate Secretary: George G. O'Brien, age 50
SVP Human Resources: Nila J. Harrison, age 42
Auditors: Deloitte & Touche LLP

LOCATIONS

HQ: Bristol West Holdings, Inc.
5701 Stirling Rd., Davie, FL 33314
Phone: 954-316-5200 **Fax:** 954-316-5275
Web: www.bristolwest.com

PRODUCTS/OPERATIONS

2005 Sales

	% of total
Net premiums earned	88
Policy service fees	9
Net investment income	3
Total	**100**

COMPETITORS

Affirmative Insurance
AIG
Allstate
Direct General
Farmers Group
GEICO
Infinity Property & Casualty
Mercury General
Nationwide
Progressive Corporation
Safeco
State Farm

HISTORICAL FINANCIALS
Company Type: Public

Income Statement
FYE: December 31

	ASSETS ($ mil.)	NET INCOME ($ mil.)	INCOME AS % OF ASSETS	EMPLOYEES
12/05	893.4	54.7	6.1%	1,205
12/04	1,040.9	61.1	5.9%	1,288
12/03	777.9	33.5	4.3%	1,285
12/02	633.1	11.5	1.8%	—
12/01	534.5	7.0	1.3%	—
Annual Growth	13.7%	67.2%	—	(3.2%)

2005 Year-End Financials

Equity as % of assets: 37.7%
Return on assets: 5.7%
Return on equity: 16.6%
Long-term debt ($ mil.): 66.0
No. of shares (mil.): 30.3
Market value ($ mil.): 576.0

Dividends
Yield: 1.4%
Payout: 15.3%
Sales ($ mil.): 677.5
R&D as % of sales: —
Advertising as % of sales: —

Stock History
NYSE: BRW

	STOCK PRICE ($) FY Close	P/E High/Low		Earnings	PER SHARE ($) Dividends	Book Value
12/05	19.03	13	9	1.70	0.26	11.13
12/04	20.00	12	8	1.89	0.15	10.11
Annual Growth	(4.8%)	—	—	(10.1%)	73.3%	10.1%

Brooke

Here comes the death of the (independent) insurance salesman: Brooke Corporation offers financial services and insurance policies, mainly property/casualty insurance, through its network of some 560 franchise locations in about 30 states. The company believes its franchise system (which includes selling insurance through local business owners) is more effective than regular independent agent models. Brooke also provides consulting, lending, and brokerage services through subsidiaries such as Brooke Credit Corporation and CJD and Associates. Brooke Holdings, which is controlled by brothers Robert Orr and Leland Orr (Brooke Corporation chairman and CEO, and CFO, respectively), owns 53% of Brooke Corporation.

Brooke Corporation subsidiary Brooke Franchise has been hard at work adding new and converted franchise locations to the company's portfolio. Since 2004 the company has gained more than 250 new locations, now totalling more than 560. It plans to acquire Generations Bank, a federal savings bank, from Kansas City Life Insurance for some $10.1 million. Through independent agents, the bank will offer Brooke Corporation's insurance products.

About 75% of the company's 2005 revenues were derived from personal (e.g., auto, homeowners') insurance. The remainder came from commercial (i.e., business owners') insurance products. Insurance commissions accounted for about 60% of 2005 revenues.

Texas accounted for about 20% of the company's franchise locations in 2005.

In 2006 Brooke Franchise acquired the property and casualty retail customer accounts from InsWeb Insurance Services. It also acquired a chain of savings banks called Generations Bank; the banks will be renamed Brooke Bank in 2007.

EXECUTIVES

Chairman and CEO: Robert D. Orr, age 52, $380,000 pay
President, COO, and Director: Anita F. Larson, age 44, $210,000 pay
CFO, Treasurer, Assistant Secretary, and Director: Leland G. Orr, age 43, $210,000 pay
SVP, Brooke Franchise: Kyle L. Garst, age 36
VP, Brooke Brokerage, and President, CJD & Associates: Michael S. Hess, age 50
President, Brooke Credit: Michael S. Lowry, age 30, $220,000 pay
Director; President, Brooke Franchise: Shawn T. Lowry, age 31
General Counsel and Secretary: James H. (Jim) Ingraham, age 52
Auditors: Summers, Spencer & Callison, CPAs, Chartered

LOCATIONS

HQ: Brooke Corporation
10950 Grandview Dr., Ste. 600, Overland Park, KS 66210
Phone: 913-661-0123 **Fax:** 913-451-3183
Web: www.brookecorp.com

COMPETITORS

AIG
Allstate
Aon
Arthur Gallagher

DCAP Group
Marsh & McLennan
Nationwide
State Farm

HISTORICAL FINANCIALS

Company Type: Public

Income Statement

FYE: December 31

	REVENUE ($ mil.)	NET INCOME ($ mil.)	NET PROFIT MARGIN	EMPLOYEES
12/05	145.4	9.7	6.7%	647
12/04	101.9	6.7	6.6%	600
12/03	66.0	4.2	6.4%	402
12/02	40.4	1.5	3.7%	227
12/01	27.5	0.9	3.3%	—
Annual Growth	51.6%	81.2%	—	41.8%

2005 Year-End Financials

Debt ratio: 84.3%
Return on equity: 43.3%
Cash ($ mil.): 58.1
Current ratio: 2.08
Long-term debt ($ mil.): 33.3
No. of shares (mil.): 12.4

Dividends
  Yield: 4.6%
  Payout: 74.4%
Market value ($ mil.): 174.8
R&D as % of sales: —
Advertising as % of sales: —

Stock History

NASDAQ (GM): BXXX

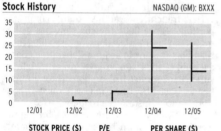

	STOCK PRICE ($) FY Close	P/E High/Low	PER SHARE ($) Earnings	Dividends	Book Value
12/05	14.05	31 11	0.86	0.64	3.33
12/04	24.16	48 8	0.65	0.55	0.78
12/03	5.05	13 3	0.40	0.14	1.24
12/02	1.08	19 7	0.13	—	3.98
Annual Growth	135.2%	— —	75.8%	113.8%	28.4%

BTU International

Things are heating up at BTU International. BTU makes, sells, and services thermal processing equipment and controls for the manufacture of printed circuit boards and for semiconductor packaging. The company supplies systems for solder reflow (for printed circuit boards), as well as technical ceramic sintering, electrical component brazing, and the deposition of film coatings. BTU equipment is also used to make photovoltaic solar cells and solid oxide fuel cells, and for sintering nuclear fuel. The company sells its products to manufacturers of computers, printed circuit board assemblies, and other consumer electronic devices throughout the world. Chairman Paul van der Wansem owns about 17% of BTU.

BTU International has customers that include Advanced Semiconductor Engineering, Celestica, Silicon Precision Industries, Motorola, IBM, Intel, and Solectron.

In 2006 the company selected Shanghai, China, as its Asia/Pacific headquarters. To enhance the energy generation and photovoltaic segments of its business, BTU acquired product lines, trademarks, and other assets of Radiant Technology Corporation for $500,000 in cash, up to 100,000 shares of BTU stock (30,000 of

which are dependent on satisfaction of certain non-financial performance criteria), and royalties on products made using Radiant technology over a four-year period.

Bjurman, Barry & Associates owns nearly 7% of BTU International.

EXECUTIVES

Chairman, President, and CEO:
  Paul J. van der Wansem, age 66, $535,125 pay
VP, Chief Accounting Officer, and Controller:
  Thomas P. Kealy, age 63, $179,942 pay
VP, Global Operations and Marketing:
  Thomas F. (Tom) Nash, age 52, $205,207 pay
VP, Global Sales and Service: James M. Griffin, age 48, $173,113 pay
Managing Director, Europe: Peter Franklin
Director, Information Technology: David J. Fancher
Director, Engineering: Stephen J. Parrott
Auditors: Vitale, Caturano and Company, P.C.

LOCATIONS

HQ: BTU International, Inc.
  23 Esquire Rd., North Billerica, MA 01862
Phone: 978-667-4111   **Fax:** 978-667-9068
Web: www.btu.com

BTU International has manufacturing operations in China and the US, with offices in China, France, Malaysia, the Philippines, Singapore, the UK, and the US.

2005 Sales

	$ mil.	% of total
Asia/Pacific	34.9	53
Americas		
US	10.9	16
Other countries	4.4	7
Europe & Middle East	16.2	24
Total	**66.4**	**100**

PRODUCTS/OPERATIONS

Selected Products

Continuous thermal processing systems
Dryers
Flip chip bump furnaces
Muffle furnaces
Ovens for solder reflow, adhesive curing, and conductive polymer processes
Transheat Controlled Atmosphere (TCA) furnaces
  TCA furnaces for solder
Walking beam furnaces

COMPETITORS

Axcelis Technologies
Bodycote Thermal Processing
Cookson Group
Dover
Eclipse
Furukawa Electric
Research, Incorporated
SPX
Vitronics

HISTORICAL FINANCIALS

Company Type: Public

Income Statement

FYE: December 31

	REVENUE ($ mil.)	NET INCOME ($ mil.)	NET PROFIT MARGIN	EMPLOYEES
12/05	66.4	4.6	6.9%	311
12/04	54.6	(4.2)	—	250
12/03	28.5	(6.8)	—	214
12/02	30.6	(7.1)	—	177
12/01	47.1	(3.8)	—	221
Annual Growth	9.0%	—	—	8.9%

2005 Year-End Financials

Debt ratio: 15.7%
Return on equity: 21.3%
Cash ($ mil.): 15.5
Current ratio: 4.21
Long-term debt ($ mil.): 5.1
No. of shares (mil.): 8.9

Dividends
  Yield: —
  Payout: —
Market value ($ mil.): 112.1
R&D as % of sales: —
Advertising as % of sales: —

Stock History

NASDAQ (GM): BTUI

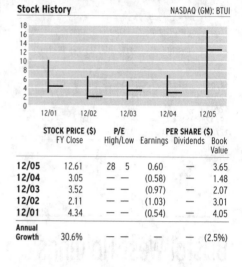

	STOCK PRICE ($) FY Close	P/E High/Low	PER SHARE ($) Earnings	Dividends	Book Value
12/05	12.61	28 5	0.60	—	3.65
12/04	3.05	— —	(0.58)	—	1.48
12/03	3.52	— —	(0.97)	—	2.07
12/02	2.11	— —	(1.03)	—	3.01
12/01	4.34	— —	(0.54)	—	4.05
Annual Growth	30.6%	— —	—	—	(2.5%)

Bucyrus International

Bucyrus International caters to those who mine their own business. The company (formerly Bucyrus-Erie Co.) provides replacement parts and services (almost 70% of sales) to the surface mining industry. Bucyrus also makes large excavation machinery used for surface mining. Its products, which include walking draglines, electric mining shovels, and blast-hole drills, are used for mining coal, gold, iron ore, and other minerals. Bucyrus' customers are primarily large companies and quasi-governmental agencies operating in South America and Australia, Canada, China, India, South Africa, and the US.

EXECUTIVES

Chairman: Theodore C. Rogers, age 71
President, CEO, and Director: Timothy W. Sullivan, age 52, $1,504,389 pay
CFO, Controller, and Secretary: Craig R. Mackus, age 53, $456,048 pay
SVP, Marketing and Sales: Marc L. Staff, age 59
VP, Human Resources: Frank P. Bruno, age 69, $273,939 pay
Chief Accounting Officer: Mark J. Knapp
Treasurer: John F. Bosbous, age 53, $252,623 pay
Auditors: Deloitte & Touche LLP

LOCATIONS

HQ: Bucyrus International, Inc.
  1100 Milwaukee Ave., South Milwaukee, WI 53172
Phone: 414-768-4000   **Fax:** 414-768-4474
Web: www.bucyrus.com

Bucyrus International sells its products through independent distributors, subsidiaries, and sales offices in Australia, Brazil, Canada, Chile, China, India, Peru, South Africa, the UK, and the US.

64

2005 Sales

	$ mil.	% of total
North America		
US	307.0	53
Canada	42.0	7
Australia	76.2	13
Chile	63.4	11
Africa	37.4	7
Other regions	49.0	9
Total	**575.0**	**100**

PRODUCTS/OPERATIONS

2005 Sales

	$ mil.	% of total
Parts & services	394.4	69
Machines	180.6	31
Total	**575.0**	**100**

COMPETITORS

Atlas Copco
Baker Hughes
Caterpillar
Charles Machine
CNH
Harnischfeger Corporation
Ingersoll-Rand Construction Technologies
Joy Global
Joy Mining Machinery
Komatsu
Sandvik
Terex

HISTORICAL FINANCIALS

Company Type: Public

Income Statement

FYE: December 31

	REVENUE ($ mil.)	NET INCOME ($ mil.)	NET PROFIT MARGIN	EMPLOYEES
12/05	575.0	53.6	9.3%	2,125
12/04	454.2	6.1	1.3%	1,725
12/03	337.7	(3.6)	—	—
12/02	289.6	(10.8)	—	—
Annual Growth	**25.7%**	**—**	**—**	**23.2%**

2005 Year-End Financials

Debt ratio: 30.3%
Return on equity: 27.6%
Cash ($ mil.): 12.4
Current ratio: 2.10
Long-term debt ($ mil.): 67.0
No. of shares (mil.): 21.0
Dividends
  Yield: 0.4%
  Payout: 8.8%
Market value ($ mil.): 739.0
R&D as % of sales: 1.3%
Advertising as % of sales: —

Stock History

NASDAQ (GS): BUCY

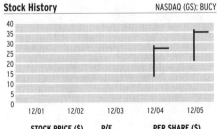

	STOCK PRICE ($) FY Close	P/E High/Low		PER SHARE ($) Earnings	Dividends	Book Value
12/05	35.13	21	12	1.71	0.15	10.50
12/04	27.09	111	53	0.25	0.04	8.34
Annual Growth	**29.7%**	**—**	**—**	**584.0%**	**275.0%**	**25.9%**

Buffalo Wild Wings

Hot sauce fuels the flight of this restaurateur. Buffalo Wild Wings (BWW) operates a chain of about 370 Buffalo Wild Wings Grill & Bar quick-casual dining spots in 35 states that specialize in Buffalo-style chicken wings. The eateries offer more than a dozen dipping sauces to go with their spicy wings, as well as a complement of other items such as chicken tenders and legs. BWW's menu also offers appetizers, burgers, tacos, salads, and desserts, along with beer, wine, and other beverages. The company owns and operates more than 120 of the restaurants, while the rest are operated by franchisees. Chairman Kenneth Dahlberg owns about 10% of BWW.

The company has been expanding rapidly since its 2003 IPO and plans to open about 70 new restaurants during 2006, of which 20 should be company-operated units. It has also inked a national marketing partnership with sports channel ESPN to raise its profile and brand image.

Jim Disbrow and Scott Lowery opened the first Buffalo Wild Wings restaurant on the campus of Ohio State University in Columbus in 1982. (Legend has it that they started the eatery because they craved the style of chicken wings they had eaten in Buffalo, New York.) Originally called Buffalo Wild Wings & Weck (a reference to the Kimmelweck brand rolls used for sandwiches), the chain became known as BW3 for short. Rapid expansion and financial mismanagement pushed Buffalo Wild Wings to the brink of bankruptcy by the mid-1990s. Sally Smith became CEO in 1996 and helped retool the chain's branding strategy to appeal more to families and non-students.

EXECUTIVES

Chairman: Kenneth H. Dahlberg, age 88
President, CEO, and Director: Sally J. Smith, age 48, $650,560 pay
EVP, CFO, and Treasurer: Mary J. Twinem, age 45, $406,600 pay
SVP Development and Franchising: Emil Lee Sanders, age 54, $305,346 pay
SVP Information Systems: Craig W. Donoghue, age 44
SVP Operations: Judith A. (Judy) Shoulak, age 46, $324,427 pay
SVP Marketing and Brand Development: Kathleen M. (Kathy) Benning, age 43
Auditors: KPMG LLP

LOCATIONS

HQ: Buffalo Wild Wings, Inc.
  1600 Utica Ave. South, Ste. 700,
  Minneapolis, MN 55416
Phone: 952-593-9943   **Fax:** 952-593-9787
Web: www.buffalowildwings.com

2005 Locations

	No.
Ohio	81
Texas	36
Indiana	28
Michigan	23
Illinois	19
Minnesota	18
Kentucky	13
Virginia	12
Florida	11
Missouri	11
North Carolina	11
Arizona	9
Tennessee	9
Wisconsin	9
Colorado	8
Georgia	7
Nebraska	7
Nevada	7
Alabama	6
Kansas	6
Other states	40
Total	**370**

PRODUCTS/OPERATIONS

2005 Sales

	$ mil.	% of total
Restaurants	185.8	89
Franchising	23.9	11
Total	**209.7**	**100**

2005 Locations

	No.
Franchised	248
Company-owned	122
Total	**370**

COMPETITORS

Applebee's
Brinker
Carlson Restaurants
Champps Entertainment
Damon's
Darden
Dave & Buster's
Family Sports Concepts
Fox & Hound Restaurant
Hooters
Houlihan's
JBC Entertainment
RAM International
Wing Zone
Wingstop
Zaxby's

HISTORICAL FINANCIALS

Company Type: Public

Income Statement

FYE: Last Sunday in December

	REVENUE ($ mil.)	NET INCOME ($ mil.)	NET PROFIT MARGIN	EMPLOYEES
12/05	209.7	8.9	4.2%	6,125
12/04	171.1	7.2	4.2%	4,532
12/03	126.5	3.6	2.8%	3,377
12/02	96.1	3.1	3.2%	—
12/01	74.6	2.7	3.6%	—
Annual Growth	**29.5%**	**34.7%**	**—**	**34.7%**

2005 Year-End Financials

Debt ratio: —
Return on equity: 9.8%
Cash ($ mil.): 52.4
Current ratio: 3.02
Long-term debt ($ mil.): —
No. of shares (mil.): 8.6
Dividends
  Yield: —
  Payout: —
Market value ($ mil.): 286.1
R&D as % of sales: —
Advertising as % of sales: 2.8%

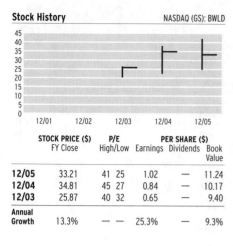

	STOCK PRICE ($) FY Close	P/E High/Low		PER SHARE ($) Earnings Dividends Book Value		
12/05	33.21	41	25	1.02	—	11.24
12/04	34.81	45	27	0.84	—	10.17
12/03	25.87	40	32	0.65	—	9.40
Annual Growth	13.3%	—	—	25.3%	—	9.3%

Build-A-Bear Workshop

The Build-A-Bear Workshop covers the "bear" necessities and much more. Located mainly in malls, the stores allow kids to design their own teddy bears and other stuffed animals complete with clothing (formalwear to western wear), shoes (including Skechers), and a barrage of accessories (eyewear, cell phones, sporting goods, and the like). Customers can also build bears online. Other offerings include the in-store Build-A-Party, online features such as e-cards and a book club, and bear fashions that match outfits sold at Limited Too clothing stores. The company, founded by CEO Maxine Clark in 1997, operates 200-plus stores in the US and Canada and franchised stores overseas; Clark owns about 17% of the company.

Exclusive franchise agreements with UK-based Amsbra Limited saw the opening of the first Build-A-Bear Workshop in the UK in November 2003, with other overseas stores following in Australia, Denmark, Japan, and South Korea. The company's international franchising plans include additional stores in Ireland and France, and expansion into India in 2006. Also that year the company's UK subsidiary, Build-A-Bear Workshop UK Holdings, acquired The Bear Factory, a U.K.-based stuffed animal retailer, for about $41 million. The transaction included the acquisition of Amsbra, its franchisee in the UK. Overall, the company operates 30 franchised stores overseas, including about a dozen in the UK.

In July 2005 the company opened its biggest store (22,000 square feet) to date at Fifth Avenue and 46th Street in Manhattan. In 2006 the first Build-A-Bear Workshop At The Zoo opened at the Saint Louis Zoo. The company also operates stores in three Major League Baseball ballparks with plans for two more in 2006.

A deal inked with toy maker Hasbro includes a specialty-sized line of stuffed animals, clothing, and accessories. Build-A-Bear has also introduced a line of dolls called Friends 2B Made that have their own range of clothing and accessories.

The company opened a new warehouse in Groveport, Ohio, near Columbus, in October 2006. The new 350,000-square-foot facility will serve as Build-A-Bear's primary distribution center for North America. (Previously, the company used three distribution centers operated by third-party providers.)

Directors Barney Ebsworth, Frank Vest, James Gould, and William Reisler collectively control about 60% of the company.

EXECUTIVES

Chairman and Chief Executive Bear: Maxine K. Clark, age 57, $676,251 pay
President and Chief Operating Bear: Robert (Scott) Seay, age 43
Chief Financial Bear, Treasurer, and Secretary: Tina Klocke, age 46, $257,139 pay
Chief Banker Bear: John Burtelow, age 57
Chief Marketing Bear: Teresa Kroll, age 51, $250,702 pay
Director, Investor Relations: Molly R. Salky, age 49
Director, Public Relations: Jill Saunders
Managing Director, Bear and Human Resources: Darlene Elder
Managing Director, Bear Stuff Development: Shari Stout
Managing Director, Inbearmation Technology: Jeff Fullmer
Managing Director, Strategic Bear Planning: Dorrie Krueger
Auditors: KPMG LLP

LOCATIONS

HQ: Build-A-Bear Workshop, Inc.
1954 Innerbelt Business Center Dr.,
St. Louis, MO 63114
Phone: 314-423-8000   **Fax:** 314-423-8188
Web: www.buildabear.com

2005 Franchised Stores

	No.
UK	11
Australia	5
Japan	5
Denmark	4
Other	5
Total	**30**

2005 Company-owned Stores

	No.
US	
California	16
Texas	15
New Jersey	12
New York	11
Ohio	10
Florida	8
Massachusetts	8
Pennsylvania	8
Illinois	7
North Carolina	7
Georgia	6
Indiana	6
Tennessee	6
Virginia	6
Colorado	5
Missouri	5
Arizona	4
Connecticut	4
Maryland	4
Other states	41
Canada	9
Total	**200**

PRODUCTS/OPERATIONS

Selected Products

Clothing
    Athletic uniforms (MLB, NBA, NHL)
    Casual sportswear
    Costumes
    Dress up
    Hibernities (sleepwear)
    Outerwear
    T-shirts
    UndiBears (underwear)

Accessories
    Backpacks
    Bear Care products
    Camping equipment
    Cell phones
    Comfy Stuff Fur-niture
    Glasses and sunglasses
    Handbags
    Hats
    Paw Wear (shoes and sandals)
    SKECHERS shoes (licensed)
    Slippers
    Socks
    Sports equipment
    Totes

COMPETITORS

Amazon.com
Boyds Collection
Dakin
Enesco Group
Gund
Hallmark
Hamleys
Hasbro
Kmart
Mattel
North American Bear
Russ Berrie
Sears
Target
Toys "R" Us
Vermont Teddy Bear
Wal-Mart

HISTORICAL FINANCIALS

Company Type: Public

Income Statement

FYE: Saturday nearest December 31

	REVENUE ($ mil.)	NET INCOME ($ mil.)	NET PROFIT MARGIN	EMPLOYEES
12/05	361.8	27.3	7.5%	6,350
12/04	301.7	20.0	6.6%	5,750
12/03	213.7	8.0	3.7%	4,460
12/02	169.1	5.9	3.5%	—
Annual Growth	**28.9%**	**66.6%**	**—**	**19.3%**

2005 Year-End Financials

Debt ratio: —   Dividends
Return on equity: 24.2%   Yield: —
Cash ($ mil.): 90.9   Payout: —
Current ratio: 1.82   Market value ($ mil.): 596.4
Long-term debt ($ mil.): —   R&D as % of sales: —
No. of shares (mil.): 20.1   Advertising as % of sales: —

Stock History

NYSE: BBW

	STOCK PRICE ($) FY Close	P/E High/Low		PER SHARE ($) Earnings Dividends Book Value		
12/05	29.64	27	14	1.35	—	6.48
12/04	35.15	33	22	1.07	—	4.88
Annual Growth	(15.7%)	—	—	26.2%	—	32.7%

Calamos Asset Management

Calamos Asset Management wants to make the most of your assets. Through its subsidiaries the company provides money management and investment advice to corporations, pension funds, endowments, and wealthy individual investors. The firm manages about a dozen open- and closed-end funds representing different investment strategies and risk levels; it also advises some 25,000 separately managed accounts. Calamos, which has more than $44 billion in its keep, was founded in 1977 and went public in 2004. Chairman and CEO John Calamos and his family control the company.

EXECUTIVES

Chairman, CEO, and Co-Chief Investment Officer:
John P. Calamos, age 65, $6,231,400 pay
SEVP, Co-Chief Investment Officer, and Director:
Nick P. Calamos, age 44, $4,171,800 pay
EVP, CFO, and Treasurer: Patrick H. Dudasik, age 50, $1,974,150 pay
EVP and Chief Administrative Officer:
Scott Craven Jones, age 44
EVP, General Counsel, and Secretary:
James S. Hamman Jr., age 36, $1,358,217 pay
SVP and CTO: Robert Kunimura, age 45
SVP and Director, Operations: Nimish S. Bhatt, age 42, $505,000 pay
SVP and Director, Human Resources: Bruce D. Innes, age 55
Director, Investor Relations: Maryellen T. Thielen
Auditors: KPMG LLP

LOCATIONS

HQ: Calamos Asset Management, Inc.
2020 Calamos Ct., Naperville, IL 60563
Phone: 630-245-7200 **Fax:** 630-245-6335
Web: www.calamos.com

PRODUCTS/OPERATIONS

2005 Sales

	$ mil.	% of total
Investment management fees	285.0	68
Distribution & underwriting fees	129.3	31
Other	3.3	1
Total	**417.6**	**100**

COMPETITORS

AIM Funds	Janus Capital
American Century	Nuveen
Bear Stearns	T. Rowe Price
Dodge & Cox	The Vanguard Group

HISTORICAL FINANCIALS

Company Type: Public

Income Statement

	ASSETS ($ mil.)	NET INCOME ($ mil.)	INCOME AS % OF ASSETS	EMPLOYEES	FYE: December 31
12/05	665.5	29.2	4.4%	331	
12/04	516.5	106.2	20.6%	264	
12/03	104.5	67.3	64.4%	—	
12/02	57.3	24.7	43.1%	—	
Annual Growth	**126.5%**	**62.4%**	**—**	**25.4%**	

2005 Year-End Financials

Equity as % of assets: 28.0%	Dividends
Return on assets: 4.9%	Yield: 0.9%
Return on equity: 16.9%	Payout: 22.2%
Long-term debt ($ mil.): 150.0	Sales ($ mil.): 417.6
No. of shares (mil.): 23.0	R&D as % of sales: —
Market value ($ mil.): 723.4	Advertising as % of sales: —

Stock History

NASDAQ (GS): CLMS

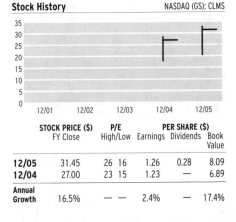

	STOCK PRICE ($) FY Close	P/E High/Low		PER SHARE ($) Earnings	Dividends	Book Value
12/05	31.45	26	16	1.26	0.28	8.09
12/04	27.00	23	15	1.23	—	6.89
Annual Growth	**16.5%**	**—**	**—**	**2.4%**	**—**	**17.4%**

California Coastal Communities

Long wrapped up in a battle over land development rights, California Coastal Communities can finally say the tides have turned. The company owns some 350 acres situated on important wetlands in Bolsa Chica (the last undeveloped strip of coastal property in Orange County), but environmental groups opposed the company's plans to build over them. Legal wrangling drove the firm into bankruptcy, from which it emerged in 1997, but the battle to develop residential lots continued. The company sold some 100 acres to California's Wildlife Conservation Board for $65 million on the condition that it get permission to develop some 350 homes on retained land; that approval was granted in 2005.

California Coastal Communities also owns Hearthside Homes, a homebuilder with developments in Chino and North Corona, California; it is looking to create residential sites near Oxnard.

Institutional investors including ING Capital Advisors, Mercury Real Estate Advisors, and Merrill Lynch, collectively own around 47% of California Coastal Communities.

EXECUTIVES

Chairman: Thomas W. Sabin Jr., age 48
President, CEO, and Director: Raymond J. Pacini, age 50, $639,600 pay
SVP, CFO, Secretary, and Treasurer: Sandra G. Sciutto, age 45, $341,600 pay
President, Hearthside Homes:
Michael J. (Mike) Rafferty, age 50, $815,400 pay
SVP, Finance, Hearthside Homes: John W. Marshall, $522,580 pay
SVP, Land Development, Hearthside Homes:
Ed Mountford, $1,365,350 pay
Auditors: Deloitte & Touche LLP

LOCATIONS

HQ: California Coastal Communities, Inc.
6 Executive Cir., Ste. 250, Irvine, CA 92614
Phone: 949-250-7700 **Fax:** 949-250-7705

PRODUCTS/OPERATIONS

2005 Sales

	$ mil.	% of total
Homebuilding	62.7	48
Nonresidential land	66.8	52
Total	**129.5**	**100**

COMPETITORS

Avatar
Castle & Cooke
C.J. Segerstrom & Sons
Corky McMillin
G & K Industries
Irvine Company
KB Home
MBK Real Estate
Newhall Land
Standard Pacific
Tejon Ranch

HISTORICAL FINANCIALS

Company Type: Public

Income Statement

	REVENUE ($ mil.)	NET INCOME ($ mil.)	NET PROFIT MARGIN	EMPLOYEES	FYE: December 31
12/05	129.5	28.4	21.9%	64	
12/04	76.0	4.8	6.3%	48	
12/03	55.8	2.9	5.2%	38	
12/02	32.8	1.7	5.2%	35	
12/01	39.0	11.1	28.5%	33	
Annual Growth	**35.0%**	**26.5%**	**—**	**18.0%**	

2005 Year-End Financials

Debt ratio: 23.5%	Dividends
Return on equity: 13.3%	Yield: —
Cash ($ mil.): 40.3	Payout: —
Current ratio: 18.93	Market value ($ mil.): 398.6
Long-term debt ($ mil.): 57.9	R&D as % of sales: —
No. of shares (mil.): 10.2	Advertising as % of sales: —

Stock History

NASDAQ (GM): CALC

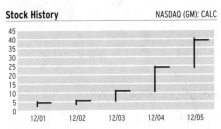

	STOCK PRICE ($) FY Close	P/E High/Low		PER SHARE ($) Earnings	Dividends	Book Value
12/05	39.23	15	9	2.70	—	24.30
12/04	24.05	56	24	0.44	—	17.66
12/03	10.92	41	19	0.27	—	16.34
12/02	5.53	36	22	0.16	—	15.90
12/01	4.50	5	2	1.10	—	15.81
Annual Growth	**71.8%**	**—**	**—**	**25.2%**	**—**	**11.3%**

Callon Petroleum

Callon Petroleum can call on new technologies to find old petroleum resources, employing computer-aided techniques such as 3-D surveys to explore and develop oil and gas properties. It also focuses on acquiring properties. Most of the firm's holdings are in federal waters in the Gulf of Mexico, although some are onshore in Alabama and Louisiana. Callon's estimated proved reserves stand at 188.6 billion cu. ft. of natural gas equivalent. The firm owns working and/or royalty interests in about 231 producing oil wells and 242 producing gas wells. Natural gas accounts for the bulk of its daily production. The company collaborates with Murphy Oil, BP, and others in its offshore exploration.

Callon was formed in 1994 through the consolidation of a publicly traded limited partnership, an independent energy company owned by some members of current Callon management, and a joint venture with a consortium of European entities.

EXECUTIVES

Chairman, President, and CEO, Callon Petroleum and Callon Petroleum Operating Company: Fred L. Callon, age 56
EVP, CFO, and Director: Bobby F. (Bob) Weatherly, age 62
VP Engineering and Operations, Callon Petroleum and Callon Petroleum Operating Company: Thomas E. Schwager, age 55, $252,463 pay
VP Exploration, Callon Petroleum and Callon Petroleum Operating Company: Stephen F. Woodcock, age 54, $263,555 pay
Corporate Information Officer: H. Clark Smith, age 53, $170,802 pay
Corporate Secretary, Callon Petroleum and Callon Petroleum Operating Company: Robert A. Mayfield, age 55
Treasurer and Controller, Callon Petroleum and Callon Petroleum Operating Company: Rodger W. Smith, age 56, $186,725 pay
Media Contact: Terry Trovato
Auditors: Ernst & Young LLP

LOCATIONS

HQ: Callon Petroleum Company
200 N. Canal St., Natchez, MS 39120
Phone: 601-442-1601   **Fax:** 601-446-1410
Web: www.callon.com

PRODUCTS/OPERATIONS

2005 Sales

	% of total
Shell Trading Company	34
Louis Dreyfus Energy Services	16
Plains Marketing, L.P.	16
Chevron Texaco Natural Gas	10
Other customers	24
Total	**100**

COMPETITORS

Apache	Meridian Resource
BP	Pioneer Natural Resources
Carrizo Oil & Gas	Range Resources
Chevron	Remington Oil and Gas
Devon Energy	Royal Dutch Shell
Exxon Mobil	TOTAL

HISTORICAL FINANCIALS

Company Type: Public

Income Statement

FYE: December 31

	REVENUE ($ mil.)	NET INCOME ($ mil.)	NET PROFIT MARGIN	EMPLOYEES
12/05	141.3	26.8	19.0%	87
12/04	119.8	21.5	17.9%	87
12/03	73.7	(18.0)	—	94
12/02	67.1	(1.7)	—	100
12/01	61.8	1.8	2.9%	103
Annual Growth	**23.0%**	**96.4%**	**—**	**(4.1%)**

2005 Year-End Financials

Debt ratio: 82.8%
Return on equity: 12.6%
Cash ($ mil.): 7.6
Current ratio: 1.10
Long-term debt ($ mil.): 188.8
No. of shares (mil.): 19.4
Dividends
  Yield: —
  Payout: —
Market value ($ mil.): 341.7
R&D as % of sales: —
Advertising as % of sales: —

Stock History

NYSE: CPE

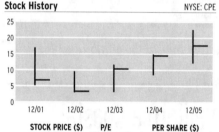

	STOCK PRICE ($) FY Close	P/E High/Low		PER SHARE ($) Earnings	Dividends	Book Value
12/05	17.65	17	10	1.28	—	11.78
12/04	14.46	12	7	1.22	—	11.26
12/03	10.37	—	—	(1.41)	—	9.56
12/02	3.35	—	—	(0.22)	—	10.14
12/01	6.85	417	134	0.04	—	10.99
Annual Growth	**26.7%**	**—**	**—**	**137.8%**	**—**	**1.8%**

Capital Lease Funding

Capital Lease Funding has an interest in business properties. The commercial mortgage lender finances and owns net-leased properties, including double-net, triple-net, and bond leases. The company focuses on financing and investing diversely within the capital structure. These practices include equity, debt, and mezzanine investments and the holding of the assets for the medium to long term. Capital Lease Funding's origination network encompasses more than 200 brokerages operating throughout the US. It also buys and sells commercial properties inhabited by investment-grade tenants. The firm's loans are funded through lines of credit provided by Bank of America and Wachovia Bank.

Founded it 1995, Capital Lease Funding has financed about $3 billion in credit tenant lease (CTL) loans covering in excess of 500 properties. CTL loans are generally considered only cost-effective for long-term leases; however, Capital Lease Funding has patented a short-term, 10-year CTL program designed to offer borrowers greater flexibility in obtaining CTL financing.

In addition to structuring, underwriting, and funding CTL loans, Capital Lease Funding also partners with developers of net leased properties and offers advisory services to individual borrowers, corporations, and net leased property investors.

In 2004 Aon Corporation, the REIT's largest tenant, accounted for more than 15% of revenues.

EXECUTIVES

Chairman: Lewis S. Ranieri, age 56
CEO and Director: Paul H. McDowell, age 45
President and Director: William R. (Bill) Pollert, age 59
EVP Program Development: Edwin J. Glickman, age 68
SVP, CFO, and Treasurer: Shawn P. Seale, age 41
SVP and Chief Accounting Officer: John E. Warch, age 49
SVP and Chief Investment Officer: Robert C. Blanz, age 46
SVP Marketing and Sales: Christopher Crovatto
VP, General Counsel, and Secretary: Paul C. Hughes, age 37
Auditors: McGladrey & Pullen, LLP

LOCATIONS

HQ: Capital Lease Funding, Inc.
1065 Avenue of the Americas, 19th Fl., New York, NY 10018
Phone: 212-217-6300   **Fax:** 212-217-6301
Web: www.caplease.com

PRODUCTS/OPERATIONS

2005 Sales

	$ mil.	% of total
Rental revenue	38.0	52
Interest income	27.9	38
Property expense recoveries	6.3	9
Gain on sale of mortgage loans & securities	0.4	—
Other	0.5	1
Total	**73.1**	**100**

COMPETITORS

AMAC
BRT Realty
CRIIMI MAE
Dynex Capital
Gramercy
iStar Financial Inc
Lexington Realty Trust
Redwood Trust
Transcontinental Realty
U.S. Bancorp

HISTORICAL FINANCIALS

Company Type: Public

Income Statement

FYE: December 31

	REVENUE ($ mil.)	NET INCOME ($ mil.)	NET PROFIT MARGIN	EMPLOYEES
12/05	73.1	5.1	7.0%	21
12/04	21.0	1.4	6.7%	23
12/03	19.1	6.6	34.6%	22
12/02	18.5	0.8	4.3%	—
12/01	31.2	4.1	13.1%	22
Annual Growth	**23.7%**	**5.6%**	**—**	**(1.2%)**

2005 Year-End Financials

Debt ratio: 360.0%
Return on equity: 2.1%
Cash ($ mil.): 19.3
Current ratio: —
Long-term debt ($ mil.): 850.9
No. of shares (mil.): 27.9
Dividends
  Yield: 7.0%
  Payout: 462.5%
Market value ($ mil.): 293.5
R&D as % of sales: —
Advertising as % of sales: —

Stock History

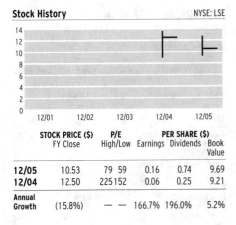

	STOCK PRICE ($) FY Close	P/E High/Low	PER SHARE ($) Earnings	Dividends	Book Value
12/05	10.53	79 59	0.16	0.74	9.69
12/04	12.50	225 152	0.06	0.25	9.21
Annual Growth	(15.8%)	— —	166.7%	196.0%	5.2%

Capital Southwest

Capital Southwest is one of a handful of publicly traded private equity firms in the US. The company owns significant stakes in nearly 20 companies, many of them in Texas, as well as small stakes in about a dozen public companies. The firm offers early-stage, mezzanine, and recapitalization financing, as well as funding for management buyouts to companies involved in a variety of industries. Its 12 largest holdings, including Alamo Group, Hologic, Palm Harbor Homes, and RectorSeal, account for nearly 90% of the value of the company's investment portfolio. Chairman and president William Thomas owns about a quarter of the company.

EXECUTIVES

Chairman and President: William R. Thomas, age 77, $260,417 pay
VP and Director: Gary L. Martin, age 59, $260,000 pay
Secretary and Treasurer: Susan K. Hodgson, age 44
Investment Associate: William R. Thomas III
Auditors: Grant Thornton LLP

LOCATIONS

HQ: Capital Southwest Corporation
12900 Preston Rd., Ste. 700, Dallas, TX 75230
Phone: 972-233-8242   **Fax:** 972-233-7362
Web: www.capitalsouthwest.com

PRODUCTS/OPERATIONS

Selected Holdings

Alamo Group, Inc. (26%, mowing, excavation, and street-sweeping equipment)
All Components, Inc. (57%, electronic contract manufacturing)
Balco, Inc. (89%, specialty architectural products)
Boxx Technologies, Inc. (15%, workstations for computer graphics imaging and design)
CMI Holding Company, Inc. (19%; devices to relieve congestive heart failure)
Comcast Corporation (less than 1%)

Dennis Tool Company (67%, diamond compacts used in oil field drill bits)
Discovery Holding Corporation (less than 1%)
Extreme International, Inc. (53%, radio and television commercial and corporate video production)
Heeling, Inc. (43%, skate shoes)
Lifemark Group (100%, cemeteries, mortuaries, and mausoleums in Northern California)
Media Recovery, Inc. (87%, computer and automation supplies)
Pallet One, Inc. (10%, wood pallet manufacturing)
Palm Harbor Homes, Inc. (31%, new home construction)
Pharmafab, Inc. (68%, branded and generic drugs)
The Rectorseal Corporation (100%, specialty chemicals)
Via Holdings, Inc. (29%, office seating)
Wellogix, Inc. (20%, software for the oil and gas industry)
The Whitmore Manufacturing Company (80%)

COMPETITORS

American Capital Strategies
Brantley Capital
Gladstone Capital
MACC Private Equities
MCG Capital

HISTORICAL FINANCIALS

Company Type: Public

Income Statement

FYE: March 31

	REVENUE ($ mil.)	NET INCOME ($ mil.)	NET PROFIT MARGIN	EMPLOYEES
3/06	98.6	96.2	97.6%	7
3/05	22.7	14.2	62.6%	—
3/04	4.7	85.5	1,819.1%	—
3/03	5.4	(41.7)	—	—
3/02	47.0	25.7	54.7%	—
Annual Growth	20.3%	39.1%	—	—

2006 Year-End Financials

Debt ratio: 2.0%
Return on equity: 27.5%
Cash ($ mil.): 11.5
Current ratio: —
Long-term debt ($ mil.): 8.0
No. of shares (mil.): 3.9

Dividends
  Yield: 0.6%
  Payout: —
Market value ($ mil.): 368.7
R&D as % of sales: —
Advertising as % of sales: —

Stock History

NASDAQ (GM): CSWC

	STOCK PRICE ($) FY Close	P/E High/Low	PER SHARE ($) Earnings	Dividends	Book Value
3/06	95.50	— —	—	0.60	102.74
3/05	79.10	— —	—	0.60	78.44
3/04	75.47	— —	—	0.60	75.35
3/03	48.15	— —	—	0.60	53.92
3/02	68.75	— —	—	0.60	65.42
Annual Growth	8.6%	— —	—	0.0%	11.9%

CapitalSource

If you're a small to midsized business owner in need of financing, CapitalSource wants to be your capital source. The company operates three distinct lending groups: Its corporate finance arm provides businesses with senior and mezzanine loans up to $100 million for such activities as leveraged buyouts, debt consolidation, and growth. Its health care and specialty finance group offers secured loans such as asset-based lines of credit and mortgages to health care businesses and other companies; and its structured finance group provides asset-backed lending to primarily finance and commercial real estate companies. CapitalSource has more than 600 clients in 44 states; Washington, DC; Canada; and the UK.

CapitalSource acquired CIG International LLC, a Washington, DC-based specialty lender, in mid-2004. The company provides subordinated debt financing to the residential real estate development market.

CapitalSource intends to convert to REIT status in 2006.

EXECUTIVES

Chairman and CEO: John K. Delaney, age 43, $400,000 pay
Vice Chairman and Chief Investment Officer: Jason M. Fish, age 48
President and COO: Dean C. Graham, age 40, $1,490,000 pay (prior to promotion)
Chief Credit Officer: Bryan M. Corsini, age 44
SVP and CFO: Thomas A. Fink, age 42, $1,202,818 pay
SVP, Chief Legal Officer, and Secretary: Steven A. Museles, age 42
VP Finance: Tony Skarupa
VP Investor Relations: Margaret (Meg) Nollen, age 43
President, Corporate Finance: Joseph A. Kenary Jr., age 41
Co-President, Healthcare and Specialty Finance: James J. (Jim) Pieczynski, age 43, $1,102,651 pay
Co-President, Healthcare and Specialty Finance: Keith D. Reuben, age 39
President, Structured Finance: Michael C. Szwajkowski, age 39, $1,240,000 pay
Chief Marketing Officer: Steven I. Silver
Auditors: Ernst & Young LLP

LOCATIONS

HQ: CapitalSource Inc.
4445 Willlard Ave., 12th Fl.,
Chevy Chase, MD 20815
Phone: 301-841-2700   **Fax:** 301-841-2340
Web: www.capitalsource.com

CapitalSource operates offices in California, Connecticut, Florida, Georgia, Illinois, Maryland, Massachusetts, Missouri, New York, Ohio, Pennsylvania, Tennessee, Texas, Utah, and the UK.

PRODUCTS/OPERATIONS

2005 Sales

	% of total
Interest income	77
Fee income	20
Other	3
Total	**100**

COMPETITORS

Capital Business Credit
CIT Commercial Finance
Citigroup
GECF
Rosenthal Group

HISTORICAL FINANCIALS

Company Type: Public

Income Statement

		ASSETS ($ mil.)	NET INCOME ($ mil.)	INCOME AS % OF ASSETS	EMPLOYEES
12/05		6,987.1	164.7	2.4%	520
12/04		4,736.8	124.8	2.6%	398
12/03		2,567.1	107.8	4.2%	285
12/02		1,160.6	41.6	3.6%	225
12/01		429.6	6.8	1.6%	—
Annual Growth		100.8%	121.8%		32.2%

2005 Year-End Financials

Equity as % of assets: 17.2%	Dividends
Return on assets: 2.8%	Yield: 11.2%
Return on equity: 15.3%	Payout: 188.0%
Long-term debt ($ mil.): 5,017.2	Sales ($ mil.): 666.7
No. of shares (mil.): 140.4	R&D as % of sales: —
Market value ($ mil.): 3,145.1	Advertising as % of sales: —

Stock History

NYSE: CSE

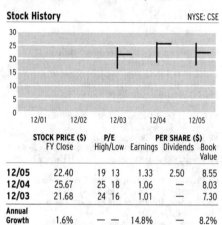

	STOCK PRICE ($) FY Close	P/E High/Low	PER SHARE ($) Earnings	Dividends	Book Value
12/05	22.40	19 13	1.33	2.50	8.55
12/04	25.67	25 18	1.06	—	8.03
12/03	21.68	24 16	1.01	—	7.30
Annual Growth	1.6%	—	14.8%	—	8.2%

CapitalSouth Bancorp

What a capital idea! CapitalSouth Bancorp (formerly Financial Investors of the South) is the holding company for CapitalSouth Bank (formerly Bank of Alabama), which serves metropolitan areas in northern and central Alabama and northern Florida. From about 10 branch locations, the commercial bank offers standard retail products and services, including checking and savings accounts, money market accounts, and CDs. The company focuses on real estate lending: Mortgages and construction loans account for nearly 85% of its loan portfolio. Targeting the Hispanic community, CapitalSouth Bank operates two offices under the name Banco Hispano; both are fully staffed with bilingual personnel.

CapitalSouth Bank's target market areas are Birmingham, Huntsville, and Montgomery, Alabama; and Jacksonville, Florida. It also has loan production offices in Atlanta, Tampa, and Fort Lauderdale, Florida, and owns 15% of Mississippi-based Consumer National Bank, which has offices in the Jackson area. Additionally, CapitalSouth Bank sells insurance through its CapitalSouth Insurance (CS Agency) division.

In 2006 CapitalSouth Bank merged banking subsidiary Capital Bank into its primary CapitalSouth Bank subsidiary.

EXECUTIVES

Chairman and CEO, CapitalSouth and CapitalSouth Bank: W. Dan Puckett, age 61
President and Director: W. Flake Oakley IV, age 52
SVP, Secretary, and CFO, CapitalSouth and CapitalSouth Bank: Carol W. Marsh, age 44, $166,000 pay (prior to title change)
EVP Lending, Chief Credit Officer, and Senior Lender, CapitalSouth Bank: James Cooper Jr., age 54, $178,108 pay
Birmingham City President, CapitalSouth Bank: William D. (Wil) Puckett II, age 36
President and COO, CapitalSouth Bank: John E. Bentley, age 46
SVP and Huntsville City President, CapitalSouth Bank: Richard T. Perdue, age 51, $154,749 pay
SVP and Jacksonville City President, CapitalSouth Bank: Fred Coble
Auditors: KPMG LLP

LOCATIONS

HQ: CapitalSouth Bancorp
2340 Woodcrest Place, Ste. 200,
Birmingham, AL 35209
Phone: 205-870-1939   **Fax:** 205-879-3885
Web: www.capitalsouthbank.com

CapitalSouth Bancorp subsidiary Capital Bank has two branches in Montgomery, Alabama. Subsidiary CapitalSouth Bank has offices in metropolitan Birmingham (5), Huntsville, and Montgomery, Alabama; it also has an office in Jacksonville, Florida.

PRODUCTS/OPERATIONS

2005 Sales

	$ mil.	% of total
Interest		
Loans	19.4	79
Securities	2.3	9
Other	0.2	1
Business Capital Group loan income	1.0	4
Service changes on deposits	1.0	4
Bank-owned life insurance	0.2	1
Net investment banking income	0.2	1
Other	0.2	1
Total	**24.5**	**100**

COMPETITORS

Alabama National BanCorp
BancorpSouth
Bank of America
Colonial BancGroup
Compass Bancshares
EverBank Financial
Regions Financial
SunTrust
Wachovia

HISTORICAL FINANCIALS

Company Type: Public

Income Statement

FYE: December 31

	ASSETS ($ mil.)	NET INCOME ($ mil.)	INCOME AS % OF ASSETS	EMPLOYEES
12/05	423.5	2.6	0.6%	124
12/04	337.7	1.9	0.6%	—
12/03	293.3	1.5	0.5%	—
Annual Growth	20.2%	31.7%	—	—

2005 Year-End Financials

Equity as % of assets: 8.7%	Dividends
Return on assets: 0.7%	Yield: 0.5%
Return on equity: 8.4%	Payout: 8.9%
Long-term debt ($ mil.): 13.7	Sales ($ mil.): 24.5
No. of shares (mil.): 2.9	R&D as % of sales: —
Market value ($ mil.): 52.2	Advertising as % of sales: 1.3%

Stock History

NASDAQ (GM): CAPB

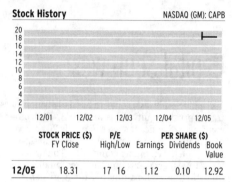

	STOCK PRICE ($) FY Close	P/E High/Low	PER SHARE ($) Earnings	Dividends	Book Value
12/05	18.31	17 16	1.12	0.10	12.92

Cardinal Financial

Cardinal Financial can help you keep out of the red. The holding company owns Cardinal Bank, which was founded in 1997 to provide a local alternative in the rapidly consolidating Virginia banking industry. The bank operates more than 20 branches in the Northern Virginia suburbs of Washington, DC. It offers commercial and retail checking, savings, and money market accounts; IRAs; and CDs. Commercial loans and mortgages make up nearly half of Cardinal Financial's loan portfolio, which also includes residential real estate, construction, home equity, and consumer loans. Subsidiary Cardinal Wealth Services provides brokerage and investment services in alliance with Raymond James Financial.

Other units include George Mason Mortgage, which originates residential mortgages for sale into the secondary market through nearly ten branches in Northern Virginia, and Wilson/Bennett Capital Management, an investment manager focusing on value-oriented investing and large-cap stocks. In 2006 Cardinal Bank acquired the trust business of FBR National Trust, a subsidiary of Friedman, Billings, Ramsey Group.

Directors and executive officers of Cardinal Financial collectively own more than 12% of the company.

EXECUTIVES

Chairman and CEO: Bernard H. Clineburg, age 57, $596,638 pay
Vice Chairman: John H. Rust Jr., age 58
President; SEVP, Cardinal Bank: Kendal E. Carson, age 49
EVP and COO, Cardinal Financial and Cardinal Bank: Kim C. Liddell, age 45, $151,912 pay (partial-year salary)
EVP and CFO, Cardinal Financial and Cardinal Bank: Robert A. Cern, age 54
EVP and Director, Marketing: Cynthia A. Cole, age 53
EVP and Senior Lending Officer; President, Cardinal Bank: F. Kevin Reynolds, age 46, $265,546 pay
EVP and Treasurer, Cardinal Financial and Cardinal Bank: Robert E. (Bob) Bradecamp, age 51
SVP, Controller, and Secretary; SVP and Controller, Cardinal Bank: Jennifer L. Deacon
President, Cardinal Bank: Christopher W. Bergstrom, age 46, $265,195 pay
President, George Mason Mortgage: H. Ed Dean, age 37
VP, Human Resources, Cardinal Bank: Janet L. Schuchmann
Auditors: KPMG LLP

LOCATIONS

HQ: Cardinal Financial Corporation
8270 Greensboro Dr., Ste. 500, McLean, VA 22102
Phone: 703-584-3400   **Fax:** 703-584-3410
Web: www.cardinalbank.com

PRODUCTS/OPERATIONS

2005 Sales

	$ mil.	% of total
Interest		
Loans receivable	35.4	39
Loans held for sale	19.4	21
Investment securities available for sale	6.2	7
Investment securities held to maturity	4.9	5
Federal funds sold	1.2	1
Other	0.3	—
Noninterest		
Net gain on sales of loans	16.0	17
Management fee income	3.0	3
Loan service charges	2.7	3
Investment fee income	1.4	2
Other	1.5	2
Total	**92.0**	**100**

COMPETITORS

Access National
Bank of America
BB&T
Chevy Chase Bank
Millennium Bankshares
SunTrust
United Bankshares
Virginia Commerce Bancorp
Wachovia

HISTORICAL FINANCIALS

Company Type: Public

Income Statement

FYE: December 31

	ASSETS ($ mil.)	NET INCOME ($ mil.)	INCOME AS % OF ASSETS	EMPLOYEES
12/05	1,452.3	9.9	0.7%	406
12/04	1,211.6	3.5	0.3%	385
12/03	636.3	6.2	1.0%	129
12/02	486.3	(0.5)	—	136
12/01	279.6	(12.7)	—	105
Annual Growth	**51.0%**	**—**		**40.2%**

2005 Year-End Financials

Equity as % of assets: 10.2%	**Dividends**
Return on assets: 0.7%	Yield: 0.1%
Return on equity: 8.1%	Payout: 2.3%
Long-term debt ($ mil.): 155.4	Sales ($ mil.): 92.0
No. of shares (mil.): 24.4	R&D as % of sales: —
Market value ($ mil.): 268.0	Advertising as % of sales: 2.2%

Stock History

NASDAQ (GS): CFNL

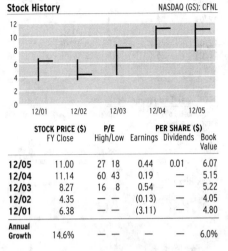

	STOCK PRICE ($) FY Close	P/E High/Low		PER SHARE ($) Earnings	Dividends	Book Value
12/05	11.00	27	18	0.44	0.01	6.07
12/04	11.14	60	43	0.19	—	5.15
12/03	8.27	16	8	0.54	—	5.22
12/02	4.35	—	—	(0.13)	—	4.05
12/01	6.38	—	—	(3.11)	—	4.80
Annual Growth	**14.6%**	**—**	**—**	**—**	**—**	**6.0%**

Carolina Bank Holdings

You'll have to ask James Taylor if he's going to Carolina Bank Holdings in his mind. The firm owns Carolina Bank, which targets individuals and small to midsized businesses for customers. The community-oriented financial institution offers such standard services as checking and savings accounts, money market and individual retirement accounts, CDs, ATM and debit cards, and online banking and bill payment. Its lending activities typically consist of commercial real estate loans, residential mortgages, construction and land development loans, and business loans.

Executive officers and directors collectively own more than 15% of Carolina Bank Holdings.

EXECUTIVES

Chairman: John D. (Jay) Cornet, age 59
Vice Chairman: Gary N. Brown, age 61
President, CEO, and Director; President and CEO, Carolina Bank: Robert T. Braswell, age 53, $291,147 pay
Treasurer and Secretary; EVP, CFO, and Secretary, Carolina Bank: T. Allen Liles, age 53, $160,078 pay
EVP and Senior Loan Officer, Carolina Bank: Gunnar N. R. Fromen, age 57, $167,466 pay
SVP and Chief Credit Officer, Carolina Bank: Daniel D. Hornfeck, age 38, $126,619 pay
SVP and Market Executive, Carolina Bank, Alamance County: W. Keith Strickland
Human Resource Officer, Carolina Bank: Angela J. Nowlin
Auditors: Cherry, Bekaert & Holland, LLP

LOCATIONS

HQ: Carolina Bank Holdings Inc.
2604 Lawndale Dr., Greensboro, NC 27408
Phone: 336-288-1898   **Fax:** 336-286-5553
Web: www.carolinabank.com

PRODUCTS/OPERATIONS

2005 Sales

	$ mil.	% of total
Interest		
Loans	16.4	82
Securities	2.2	11
Other	0.4	2
Noninterest		
Service charges	0.6	3
Mortgage banking income	0.3	1
Other	0.3	1
Total	**20.2**	**100**

COMPETITORS

BB&T
First Citizens BancShares
FNB Financial Services
FNB United
RBC Centura Banks
Wachovia

HISTORICAL FINANCIALS

Company Type: Public

Income Statement

FYE: December 31

	ASSETS ($ mil.)	NET INCOME ($ mil.)	INCOME AS % OF ASSETS	EMPLOYEES
12/05	365.2	2.0	0.5%	59
12/04	311.5	1.6	0.5%	51
12/03	226.9	1.1	0.5%	45
12/02	189.9	0.6	0.3%	38
12/01	151.5	0.4	0.3%	—
Annual Growth	**24.6%**	**49.5%**	**—**	**15.8%**

2005 Year-End Financials

Equity as % of assets: 6.2%	**Dividends**
Return on assets: 0.6%	Yield: —
Return on equity: 9.1%	Payout: —
Long-term debt ($ mil.): 10.3	Sales ($ mil.): 20.2
No. of shares (mil.): 2.7	R&D as % of sales: —
Market value ($ mil.): 30.6	Advertising as % of sales: —

Stock History

NASDAQ (CM): CLBH

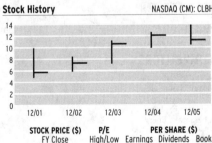

	STOCK PRICE ($) FY Close	P/E High/Low		PER SHARE ($) Earnings	Dividends	Book Value
12/05	11.26	19	14	0.73	—	8.38
12/04	12.08	21	17	0.59	—	9.38
12/03	10.63	26	17	0.42	—	10.44
12/02	7.33	22	16	0.38	—	9.93
12/01	5.73	36	18	0.27	—	9.29
Annual Growth	**18.4%**	**—**	**—**	**28.2%**	**—**	**(2.5%)**

Carrizo Oil & Gas

Carrizo Oil & Gas sees its future in 3-D. An independent exploration and production company that drills in proven onshore fields along the Gulf Coast of Texas and Louisiana, Carrizo aggressively acquires 3-D seismic data and arranges land lease options in conjunction with conducting seismic surveys. As part of a new strategy, the company is exploiting deeper, overpressured targets, which generally require higher cost. Carrizo has additional properties in North Texas, the Rockies, Alabama, Arkansas, Kentucky, New Mexico, and in the UK North Sea. Its total proved reserves stand at 150.6 billion cu. ft. of natural gas equivalent. Chairman Steven Webster owns about 11% of Carrizo.

The company has reported an exploratory drilling success rate in the onshore Gulf Coast area of 84%, and a 100% drilling success rate in the Barnett Shale area.

EXECUTIVES

Chairman: Steven A. Webster, age 55
President, CEO, and Director: S. P. Johnson IV, age 50, $490,889 pay
VP, CFO, Secretary, and Treasurer: Paul F. Boling, age 52, $281,339 pay
VP, Business Development: Andrew R. Agosto, age 39
VP, Operations: J. Bradley (Brad) Fisher, age 45, $397,455 pay
VP, Director Investor Relations: B. Allen Connell
VP, Land: Jack Bayless, age 51, $68,281 pay
Human Resources: Deborah Soho
Auditors: Pannell Kerr Forster of Texas, P.C.

LOCATIONS

HQ: Carrizo Oil & Gas, Inc.
1000 Louisiana St., Ste. 1500, Houston, TX 77002
Phone: 281-496-1352   **Fax:** 281-496-1251
Web: www.carrizo.cc

PRODUCTS/OPERATIONS

2005 Sales

	% of total
Chevron	12
Reichman Petroleum	11
Other customers	77
Total	**100**

COMPETITORS

Abraxas Petroleum
Adams Resources
BP
Brigham Exploration
Chesapeake Energy
Chevron
Clayton Williams Energy
Comstock Resources
Exxon Mobil
Forest Oil
National Onshore
Newfield Exploration
Pioneer Natural Resources
Remington Oil and Gas
Samson
Shell
TOTAL

HISTORICAL FINANCIALS

Company Type: Public

Income Statement

FYE: December 31

	REVENUE ($ mil.)	NET INCOME ($ mil.)	NET PROFIT MARGIN	EMPLOYEES
12/05	78.2	10.6	13.6%	50
12/04	52.4	11.1	21.2%	38
12/03	38.5	7.9	20.5%	38
12/02	26.8	4.8	17.9%	36
12/01	26.2	9.5	36.3%	36
Annual Growth	**31.4%**	**2.8%**	**—**	**8.6%**

2005 Year-End Financials

Debt ratio: 96.6%
Return on equity: 7.7%
Cash ($ mil.): 28.7
Current ratio: 1.21
Long-term debt ($ mil.): 150.1
No. of shares (mil.): 24.3
Dividends
  Yield: —
  Payout: —
Market value ($ mil.): 599.0
R&D as % of sales: —
Advertising as % of sales: —

Stock History

NASDAQ (GS): CRZO

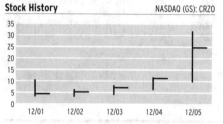

	STOCK PRICE ($) FY Close	P/E High/Low	Earnings	Dividends	Book Value
12/05	24.70	72 23	0.44	—	6.41
12/04	11.30	24 13	0.49	—	5.46
12/03	7.20	18 10	0.43	—	5.21
12/02	5.27	24 13	0.26	—	4.71
12/01	4.43	18 6	0.57	—	4.49
Annual Growth	**53.7%**	**—**	**(6.3%)**	**—**	**9.3%**

CAS Medical Systems

CAS Medical Systems makes blood pressure measurement devices, vital signs monitors, apnea monitors, and neonatal supplies. Major brands include the MAXNIBP blood pressure technology, the CAS 750 vital signs monitor, and the AMI and 511 cardio-respiratory monitoring system. The company sells its products in Europe, North America, Latin America, and the Pacific Rim to hospitals and other health care professionals. CAS Medical Systems is developing several other products to add to its product line. Customer Medtronic accounts for about 15% of sales.

CAS Medical Systems expanded its product offerings with the acquisition of Statcorp, which makes blood pressure cuffs, pressure infuser cuffs, and blood filter products.

Chairman, president, and CEO Louis Scheps owns approximately 10% of the company.

EXECUTIVES

Chairman, President, and CEO: Louis P. (Lou) Scheps, age 74, $317,088 pay
COO: Andrew E. Kersey, age 45, $183,973 pay
CFO and Secretary: Jeffery A. Baird, age 52, $160,820 pay
Auditors: UHY LLP

LOCATIONS

HQ: CAS Medical Systems, Inc.
44 E. Industrial Rd., Branford, CT 06405
Phone: 203-488-6056   **Fax:** 203-488-9438
Web: www.casmed.com

2005 Sales

	$ mil.	% of total
US	21.9	81
International	5.0	19
Total	**26.9**	**100**

COMPETITORS

Criticare
Invivo
Medwave
Somanetics
VSM MedTech

HISTORICAL FINANCIALS

Company Type: Public

Income Statement

FYE: December 31

	REVENUE ($ mil.)	NET INCOME ($ mil.)	NET PROFIT MARGIN	EMPLOYEES
12/05	26.9	1.8	6.7%	143
12/04	19.9	1.2	6.0%	—
12/03	16.9	0.7	4.1%	—
12/02	15.0	(0.3)	—	—
12/01	14.8	0.2	1.4%	—
Annual Growth	**16.1%**	**73.2%**	**—**	**—**

2005 Year-End Financials

Debt ratio: 48.5%
Return on equity: 22.1%
Cash ($ mil.): 1.9
Current ratio: 2.86
Long-term debt ($ mil.): 4.4
No. of shares (mil.): 9.9
Dividends
  Yield: —
  Payout: —
Market value ($ mil.): 86.0
R&D as % of sales: —
Advertising as % of sales: —

Stock History

NASDAQ (GM): CASM

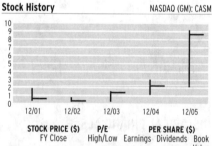

	STOCK PRICE ($) FY Close	P/E High/Low	Earnings	Dividends	Book Value
12/05	8.65	61 15	0.15	—	0.92
12/04	2.25	27 11	0.11	—	0.73
12/03	1.40	21 5	0.07	—	0.64
12/02	0.34	— —	(0.03)	—	0.57
12/01	0.60	91 20	0.02	—	0.60
Annual Growth	**94.9%**	**—**	**65.5%**	**—**	**11.2%**

Cascade Bancorp

Forget the dirty dishes. Cascade Bancorp wants to provide sparkling customer service. It's the holding company for Bank of the Cascades, which operates more than 30 branches in central, northwestern, and most recently, southern Oregon, as well as Idaho. Targeting individuals and small to midsized businesses, the bank offers checking, savings, and money market accounts, as well as CDs. Around two-thirds of its loan portfolio is composed of construction, mortgage, and commercial real estate loans; commercial loans make up about 30% of its loans. The bank also offers trust and investment services.

In January 2004 Cascade Bancorp acquired the $46 million Community Bank of Grants Pass, Oregon. The purchase marked the bank's expansion into southern Oregon. Also in 2004 it opened five new branches between its central and southern Oregon markets.

Cascade Bancorp acquired Boise, Idaho-based F&M Holding Company, parent to Farmers & Merchants State Bank, which operates 11 branches in Boise and surrounding markets. The acquisition provides a strategic expansion opportunity for Cascade, which is adding northwest growth markets to its franchise.

EXECUTIVES

EVP and COO; President and COO, Bank of the Cascades: Michael J. (Mike) Delvin, age 57, $420,000 pay

President, CEO, and Director; CEO, Bank of the Cascades: Patricia L. Moss, age 52, $678,524 pay

EVP, CFO, and Secretary: Gregory D. Newton, age 54, $306,000 pay

EVP, Human Resources: Peggy L. Biss, age 47, $275,400 pay

Chairman: Gary L. Hoffman, age 65

EVP, Mortgage Center: Frank I. Wheeler

Director and Assistant Secretary: James E. Petersen, age 66

EVP and Credit Administrator: Frank R. Weis, age 55, $275,400 pay

Auditors: Symonds, Evans & Larson, P.C.; Symonds, Evans & Company, P.C.

LOCATIONS

HQ: Cascade Bancorp
1100 NW Wall St., Bend, OR 97701
Phone: 541-385-6205   **Fax:** 541-382-8780
Web: www.botc.com

PRODUCTS/OPERATIONS

2005 Sales

	$ mil.	% of total
Interest income		
Interest & fees on loans	69.7	81
Securities	1.8	2
Other	1.3	1
Noninterest income		
Service charges on deposits	6.2	7
Mortgage banking income	2.3	3
Card and merchant fees	2.4	3
Other	2.2	3
Total	**85.9**	**100**

COMPETITORS

Bank of America
Columbia Bancorp (OR)
Sterling Financial (WA)
U.S. Bancorp
Washington Federal
Washington Mutual
Wells Fargo

HISTORICAL FINANCIALS

Company Type: Public

Income Statement

		NET	INCOME	
	ASSETS ($ mil.)	INCOME ($ mil.)	AS % OF ASSETS	EMPLOYEES
12/05	1,269.7	22.4	1.8%	336
12/04	1,004.8	16.0	1.6%	320
12/03	734.7	13.9	1.9%	283
12/02	578.4	11.7	2.0%	238
12/01	488.8	8.7	1.8%	207
Annual Growth	**27.0%**	**26.7%**	**—**	**12.9%**

FYE: December 31

2005 Year-End Financials

Equity as % of assets: 8.2%
Return on assets: 2.0%
Return on equity: 23.5%
Long-term debt ($ mil.): 85.0
No. of shares (mil.): 17.0
Market value ($ mil.): 312.1
Dividends
  Yield: 1.4%
  Payout: 25.2%
Sales ($ mil.): 85.9
R&D as % of sales: —
Advertising as % of sales: 0.8%

Stock History

NASDAQ (CM): CACB

	STOCK PRICE ($) FY Close	P/E High/Low	PER SHARE ($) Earnings	Dividends	Book Value
12/05	18.41	19 14	1.03	0.26	6.16
12/04	16.18	24 17	0.74	0.21	5.16
12/03	12.33	20 13	0.68	0.20	4.89
12/02	8.85	22 11	0.58	0.17	4.09
12/01	6.89	17 11	0.44	0.13	5.04
Annual Growth	**27.9%**	**— —**	**23.7%**	**18.9%**	**5.1%**

Cathay General Bancorp

Cathay General Bancorp (formerly known as plain ol' Cathay Bancorp) is a holding company for Cathay Bank, which caters to Chinese and Vietnamese individuals and businesses through about 20 branches in Southern California, nine in Northern California, three in New York, two in Massachusetts and Washington State, and one in Texas. It also has branches in Hong Kong and Shanghai. Real estate subsidiary Cathay Investment has an office in Taiwan.

Services include deposit accounts, online banking and stock trading, import/export financing, annuities, and mutual funds. Commercial mortgages account for slightly more than half of the bank's portfolio; business loans comprise nearly a quarter.

Cathay General Bancorp bought rival GBC Bancorp in 2003.

Two years later it announced an agreement with shareholders of Great Eastern Bank to purchase the privately held New York chartered bank, which operates five branches in the New York City area. It ended up in a bidding war with UCBH Holdings over the prize, but in 2006 Great Eastern voted in favor of Cathay General, calling its bid a "superior proposal." The deal closed that spring.

The bank is not resting on its laurels. Also in 2006 it bought a 20% stake in First Sino Bank of Shanghai for around $52.2 million. The deal gives it the the right to name two directors. The company also bought New Asia Bancorp for $23.5 million and United Heritage Bank for $9.4 million, which will give Cathay Bank its first branch in New Jersey.

EXECUTIVES

Chairman, President, and CEO, Cathay General Bancorp and Cathay Bank: Dunson K. Cheng, age 61, $1,782,000 pay

Executive Vice Chairman and COO, Cathay General Bancorp and Cathay Bank: Peter Wu, age 57, $818,625 pay

EVP and CFO, Cathay General Bancorp and Cathay Bank: Heng W. Chen, age 53, $501,800 pay

SVP and General Counsel, Cathay General Bancorp and Cathay Bank: Perry P. Oei, age 43

EVP and Director; SEVP and Chief Lending Officer, Cathay Bank: Anthony M. Tang, age 52, $532,730 pay

Secretary and Director, Cathay General Bancorp and Cathay Bank: Michael M. Y. Chang, age 69

EVP and Chief Credit Officer, Cathay Bank: Kim R. Bingham, age 49

EVP, Branch Administration, Cathay Bank: Irwin Wong, age 57, $410,134 pay

SVP and Director of Human Resources, Cathay Bank: Jennifer Laforcarde

Auditors: KPMG LLP

LOCATIONS

HQ: Cathay General Bancorp
777 N. Broadway, Los Angeles, CA 90012
Phone: 213-625-4700   **Fax:** 213-625-1368
Web: www.cathaybank.com

PRODUCTS/OPERATIONS

2005 Sales

	$ mil.	% of total
Interest & dividends		
Loans	285.1	76
Securities	63.5	17
Noninterest		
Service fees on deposits	5.6	2
Letters of credit commissions	4.2	1
Other interest & noninterest	14.7	4
Total	**373.1**	**100**

COMPETITORS

Bank of America
Citibank
East West Bancorp
Greater Bay
Hanmi Financial
Nara Bancorp
UCBH Holdings
U.S. Bancorp
Washington Mutual
Wells Fargo
Wilshire Bancorp

HISTORICAL FINANCIALS

Company Type: Public

Income Statement

FYE: December 31

		NET	INCOME	
	ASSETS ($ mil.)	INCOME ($ mil.)	AS % OF ASSETS	EMPLOYEES
12/05	6,397.5	104.1	1.6%	900
12/04	6,098.0	86.8	1.4%	7
12/03	5,541.9	55.6	1.0%	6
12/02	2,754.0	48.7	1.8%	5
12/01	2,453.1	42.6	1.7%	3
Annual Growth	**27.1%**	**25.0%**	**—**	**316.2%**

Equity as % of assets: 12.1% Dividends
Return on assets: 1.7%   Yield: 1.0%
Return on equity: 14.0%   Payout: 17.6%
Long-term debt ($ mil.): 94.5   Sales ($ mil.): 373.1
No. of shares (mil.): 50.2   R&D as % of sales: —
Market value ($ mil.): 1,803.9   Advertising as % of sales: —

Stock History

NASDAQ (GS): CATY

	STOCK PRICE ($) FY Close	P/E High/Low	PER SHARE ($) Earnings	Dividends	Book Value
12/05	35.94	19 14	2.05	0.36	15.41
12/04	37.50	23 16	1.72	0.30	14.12
12/03	28.00	20 12	1.42	0.28	24.97
12/02	19.00	18 11	1.35	0.20	16.00
12/01	16.01	14 9	1.17	0.25	27.40
Annual Growth	22.4%	— —	15.1%	9.5%	(13.4%)

Cavco Industries

Cavco's constructs keep kinfolk covered. Cavco Industries, former subsidiary of #1 US homebuilder Centex Corp., produces more than 4,000 manufactured residential homes a year at an average price of $48,500 per home, mainly for US markets in the Southwest and West. Its products include full-sized homes (ranging from about 500 sq. ft. to 3,000 sq. ft.); park model homes (less than 400 sq. ft.) for use as recreational and retirement units; camping cabins; and commercial structures for use as portable classrooms, showrooms, and offices. Cavco sells through 300 independent retail outlets in 14 states (mainly in Arizona, California, New Mexico, and Colorado) and eight company-owned outlets (mainly in Texas and Arizona).

Cavco focuses its marketing efforts on the sale of high-value homes to entry-level and move-up buyers — the mainstream market, and on specialty markets such as vacation homebuyers and developers of subdivisions and senior living communities. About 70% of the homes it produces are HUD code homes. These homes average about $48,000 wholesale, excluding delivery; retail prices of its HUD code homes, excluding land, range from about $32,000 to more than $100,000, depending upon factors such as size, floor plan, features, and options. About 80% of the homes the company sells are in transactions that cover both the home and the site on which it is placed.

The company disposed of seven of its company-owned sales retail outlets in fiscal 2005, and it expects to dispose of or close more than half of its remaining outlets during the next year to reduce its future operating losses from its retail operations and to generate cash through inventory liquidations.

Cavco has faced substantial operating losses in recent years, a time in which weak industry conditions have prevailed and adverse legislation enacted in Texas has impacted their operations. Although manufactured housing accounts for about 10% of the US market for new single-family housing, the troubled manufactured housing industry has forced Cavco to trim its manufacturing facilities down to three in the Phoenix area.

Because of its operational size, Cavco has flexible manufacturing options and strives to react more quickly to changes in the marketplace and to its retailers' and consumers' specific needs.

Gabelli Group Capital Partners owns 11% of the company; Chairman Joseph Stegmayer owns 7%.

HISTORY

Alfred Ghelfi and partner Bob Curtis began a part-time business in 1965 making pickup truck camper shells. The business, Roadrunner Manufacturing, became Cavalier Manufacturing in 1966, incorporated in 1968, and went public in 1969. The Cavalier name was already in use, so in 1974 the company's name was changed to Cavco. After the 1970s oil crisis nearly wiped out the firm, Ghelfi bought out Curtis' share and began making mobile homes. In time Cavco began leasing movable storage buildings, but the only successful part of that business was the security container segment (the rest was sold in 1994). A mid-1980s housing market crash in Arizona spurred Cavco to enter a totally new field — health care utilization management — in 1987.

In 1995 Cavco partnered with Japan's Auto Berg Enterprises to begin selling modular housing in Japan. The next year Cavco teamed up with Arizona Public Service to develop solar-powered manufactured housing, and it also sold its health care business. Centex acquired nearly 80% of Cavco for $75 million in 1997. The next year Cavco moved into Texas (one of the biggest markets for factory-built homes), acquiring Texas retailer Boerne Homes.

With demand shrinking and surplus inventory building up, the company closed its Belen, New Mexico, factory in 2000 and moved its production to plants in Phoenix and Seguin, Texas. That fall Centex tapped manufactured housing veteran Joseph Stegmayer as chairman of its manufactured housing segment.

In 2001 the company launched Factory Liquidators, a new retail concept focusing on repossessed homes.

Centex's board of directors approved the tax-free distribution to its shareholders of all of Cavco's outstanding common stock in 2003. The spin-off was completed in June of that year. Continued weakness within the industry forced Cavco to close eight of its company-owned retail outlets in fiscal 2004 and seven more in 2005.

EXECUTIVES

Chairman, President, and CEO:
  Joseph H. (Joe) Stegmayer, age 55, $1,602,673 pay
VP, CFO, and Treasurer: Daniel Urness, age 38, $172,269 pay (partial-year salary)
VP and General Manager (Litchfield):
  David L. (Dave) Blank, age 43, $573,951 pay
VP and General Manager, Durango: Paul A. Deroo
VP and General Manager, Specialty: Timothy M. Gage
VP Retail Operations: Daniel Blankenship
Director, IS: Robert Muralles
Director, Human Resources: Kirk Roles
General Counsel and Secretary: James P. Glew
Auditors: Ernst & Young LLP

LOCATIONS

HQ: Cavco Industries, Inc.
  1001 N. Central Ave., Ste. 800, Phoenix, AZ 85004
Phone: 602-256-6263   **Fax:** 602-256-6189
Web: www.cavco.com

Cavco Industries has three manufacturing facilities in the Phoenix metropolitan area and one in Seguin, Texas. It has a network of 311 independent retail outlets in 14 states.

PRODUCTS/OPERATIONS

2006 Homes Sold

	No. of homes
Multi-section	2,803
Single-section	1,448
Total	**4,251**

2006 Sales Channels

	No. of homes
Independent retail outlets	4,082
Company-owned retail centers	169
Total	**4,251**

Selected Operations

Camping cabins
Commercial structures
Manufactured homes
Manufactured-home subdivisions
Model homes and vacation homes
Park model homes

COMPETITORS

American Homestar
Cavalier Homes
Champion Enterprises
Clayton Homes
Coachmen
Fairmont Homes
Fleetwood Enterprises
Karsten Company
Liberty Homes
Mobile Mini
Nobility Homes
Palm Harbor Homes
Pulte Homes
Skyline
Sunshine Homes

HISTORICAL FINANCIALS

Company Type: Public

Income Statement

FYE: March 31

	REVENUE ($ mil.)	NET INCOME ($ mil.)	NET PROFIT MARGIN	EMPLOYEES
3/06	189.5	15.1	8.0%	1,320
3/05	157.4	10.1	6.4%	1,200
3/04	128.9	6.2	4.8%	1,200
3/03	110.0	(4.5)	—	1,105
3/02	224.3	—	—	1,000
Annual Growth	**(4.1%)**	**—**		**7.2%**

2006 Year-End Financials

Debt ratio: —   Dividends
Return on equity: 12.9%   Yield: —
Cash ($ mil.): 59.2   Payout: —
Current ratio: 2.73   Market value ($ mil.): 308.7
Long-term debt ($ mil.): —   R&D as % of sales: —
No. of shares (mil.): 6.4   Advertising as % of sales: —

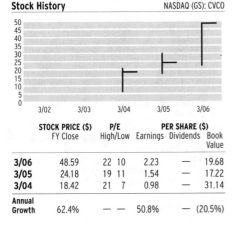

	STOCK PRICE ($)	P/E		PER SHARE ($)		
	FY Close	High/Low	Earnings	Dividends		Book Value
3/06	48.59	22	10	2.23	—	19.68
3/05	24.18	19	11	1.54	—	17.22
3/04	18.42	21	7	0.98	—	31.14
Annual Growth	62.4%	—	—	50.8%	—	(20.5%)

Cbeyond

Cbeyond isn't looking past the 25 million small businesses in the US to find customers for its broadband services. The facilities-based Voice over Internet Protocol (VoIP) carrier, formerly known as Cbeyond Communications, provides local and long-distance services and broadband Internet access over its own private IP network. The company hopes to side-step stiff competition from incumbent carriers by focusing on the traditionally underserved small-business market. Cbeyond offers services in the Atlanta, Dallas, Denver, Chicago, Houston, and Los Angeles metro areas and plans to expand services to additional markets.

In 2006 the company began offering mobile voice and data services as mobile virtual network operator (MVNO) CbeyondMobile.

Investors in Cbeyond include Madison Dearborn Partners (22%), Battery Ventures (13%), and VantagePoint Ventures Partners (13%). Cisco Systems, which supplies the company's VoIP technology, owns 7%.

EXECUTIVES

Chairman, President, and CEO: James F. (Jim) Geiger, age 47, $449,505 pay
COO: Richard J. Batelaan, age 40, $233,822 pay
EVP and CFO: J. Robert (Bob) Fugate, age 45, $319,000 pay
EVP Sales and Service: Robert R. (Bob) Morrice, age 57, $296,746 pay
VP and CTO: Christopher C. (Chris) Gatch, age 34, $233,822 pay
VP and CIO: Joseph A. (Joe) Oesterling, age 38, $233,822 pay
VP and Chief Marketing Officer: Brooks A. Robinson, age 34, $233,822 pay
VP Finance and Treasurer: Kurt J. Abkemeier, age 36
VP Human Resources: Joan L. Tolliver
VP Marketing: Mary N. Ford
Chief Accounting Officer: Henry C. Lyon, age 41, $233,822 pay
Auditors: Ernst & Young LLP

LOCATIONS

HQ: Cbeyond, Inc.
320 Interstate North Pkwy. SE, Ste. 300, Atlanta, GA 30339
Phone: 678-424-2400   **Fax:** 678-424-2500
Web: www.cbeyond.net

2005 Sales

	$ mil.	% of total
Atlanta	53.7	34
Denver	47.9	30
Dallas	42.3	27
Houston	13.1	8
Chicago	2.1	1
Total	**159.1**	**100**

PRODUCTS/OPERATIONS

2005 Sales

	$ mil.	% of total
Customer revenue	154.9	97
Terminating access revenue	4.2	3
Total	**159.1**	**100**

Selected Services

Broadband Internet access
Calling cards
Conference calling
E-mail
Local voice access
Long-distance voice
Toll-Free
Virtual private network (VPN)
Voicemail
Web hosting

COMPETITORS

8x8	ICG Communications
AT&T	ITC^DeltaCom
BellSouth	McLeodUSA
Birch	NuVox
Cablevision Systems	Qwest
Comcast	Time Warner Cable
Covad Communications	Time Warner Telecom
Cox Communications	US LEC
Deltathree	Verizon
DSL.net	Vonage
Eschelon	XO Holdings

HISTORICAL FINANCIALS

Company Type: Public

Income Statement

				FYE: December 31
	REVENUE ($ mil.)	NET INCOME ($ mil.)	NET PROFIT MARGIN	EMPLOYEES
12/05	159.1	3.7	2.3%	707
12/04	113.3	(11.5)	—	586
12/03	65.5	(29.5)	—	—
12/02	21.0	(47.2)	—	380
Annual Growth	96.4%	—	—	23.0%

2005 Year-End Financials

Debt ratio: —
Return on equity: 725.5%
Cash ($ mil.): 37.9
Current ratio: 1.33
Long-term debt ($ mil.): —
No. of shares (mil.): 26.7
Dividends
  Yield: —
  Payout: —
Market value ($ mil.): 274.7
R&D as % of sales: —
Advertising as % of sales: —

Stock History

NASDAQ (GM): CBEY

	STOCK PRICE ($)	P/E		PER SHARE ($)		
	FY Close	High/Low	Earnings	Dividends		Book Value
12/05	10.30	—	—	(1.16)	—	2.80

Celebrate Express

Celebrate Express provides everything for a birthday party except the suit. Operating as Birthday Express, the company offers more than 150 themed party packages through its catalog, Web site, and one retail store. Party packages include planning assistance (themes and activities) and supplies (paper products, balloons, favors). Celebrate Express also sells children's costumes (Costume Express). It produces much of its party merchandise (accounting for nearly 80% of sales), offering such private-label items as crepe paper and piñatas. Mike and Jan Jewell own about 15% of the firm, which they founded in 1994. Celebrate Express is exploring strategic options, including a possible sale of the company.

Newly elected board members Kenneth Shubin Stein and Stephen Roseman together hold a 15.4% stake in Celebrate Express. Their appointment, in August 2006, pacified a group of activist shareholders (including Spencer Capital Management) who were attempting to gain three board seats through a proxy solicitation that was subsequently dropped.

Celebrate Express shuttered its Storybook Heirloom (specialty outfits for girls) operations in mid-2006. The company cited years of losses as one reason why it exited the business.

EXECUTIVES

President, CEO, and Director: Kevin A. Green, age 48, $84,423 pay (partial-year salary)
VP, Finance and Secretary: Darin L. White, age 35, $212,184 pay
VP, Merchandising: Beth Sommers, age 45
VP, Operations: Dennis Everhart, age 58
VP, Information Technology: Lisa Tuttle, age 49
Director, Customer Service: Krys Richter
Director, Marketing: Katie Manning
Warehouse Supervisor: Greg Connor
Auditors: Grant Thornton LLP

LOCATIONS

HQ: Celebrate Express, Inc.
11220 120th Ave. NE, Kirkland, WA 98033
Phone: 425-250-1064   **Fax:** 425-828-6252
Web: www.birthdayexpress.com

PRODUCTS/OPERATIONS

2006 Sales

	$ mil.	% of total
Birthday Express	68.4	79
Costume Express	9.6	11
Storybook Heirlooms	9.0	10
Total	**87.0**	**100**

Online Services

Animated online invitations
Directory of party games and recipes
List of famous birthdays
Live Q&A help
Party-planning checklist
Party tips
Personalized birthday scrolls with history/events

Party Supplies
Balloons
Birthday scrolls
Cake decorating supplies
Crafts and activities
Crepe paper
Dress-up items and costumes
Favors and prizes
Gift wrap
Partyware (plates, cups, utensils, napkins, tablecloths)
Piñatas
Theme-related gifts
Toys
Wall decorations

Web Sites
Birthdayexpress.com (party supplies)
StorybookOnline.com (apparel and accessories for girls)

COMPETITORS
Ahold USA
CVS
Factory Card & Party Outlet
Garden Ridge
Hallmark
Hobby Lobby
iParty
Kmart
Kroger
Party America
Party City
Rite Aid
Safeway
Target
Walgreen
Wal-Mart

HISTORICAL FINANCIALS
Company Type: Public

Income Statement
FYE: May 31

	REVENUE ($ mil.)	NET INCOME ($ mil.)	NET PROFIT MARGIN	EMPLOYEES
5/06	87.0	0.4	0.5%	456
5/05	69.1	2.5	3.6%	345
5/04	51.9	9.5	18.3%	293
5/03	37.8	(1.6)	—	293
Annual Growth	32.0%	—	—	15.9%

2006 Year-End Financials
Debt ratio: —
Return on equity: 0.8%
Cash ($ mil.): 31.3
Current ratio: 6.25
Long-term debt ($ mil.): —
No. of shares (mil.): 7.8
Dividends
  Yield: —
  Payout: —
Market value ($ mil.): 99.1
R&D as % of sales: —
Advertising as % of sales: —

Stock History
NASDAQ (GM): BDAY

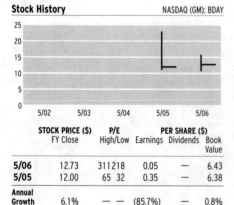

	STOCK PRICE ($) FY Close	P/E High/Low	PER SHARE ($) Earnings	Dividends	Book Value
5/06	12.73	31 12 18	0.05	—	6.43
5/05	12.00	65 32	0.35	—	6.38
Annual Growth	6.1%	— —	(85.7%)	—	0.8%

Celgene

A terror from the past has provided hope in the present. Celgene's flagship product THALOMID treats multiple myeloma (bone marrow cancer), as well as a type of leprosy; it is a form of thalidomide, a sedative and morning sickness therapy used in Europe in the late 1950s until it was linked to birth defects and pulled from the market in 1961. REVLIMID, which won FDA approval in late 2005, treats a malignant blood disease called MDS; it received approval for treating multiple myeloma the following year. The company develops drugs primarily to treat inflammatory diseases and cancer. Subsidiary Celgene Cellular Therapeutics researches stem cell therapies and provides placental stem cell banking.

Celgene sells ALKERAN, another multiple myeloma treatment, through a supply and distribution agreement with GlaxoSmithKline. It has licensed its internally developed FOCALIN, a relative of ADHD drug RITALIN, to Novartis.

Celgene's top customers are drug distributors Cardinal Health (which accounted for nearly 40% of sales), McKesson (27%), and Amerisource-Bergen (20%).

EXECUTIVES
Chairman and CEO: Sol J. Barer, age 60
President, COO, and Director: Robert J. Hugin, age 51
CFO: David W. Gryska, age 49
EVP, Pharmaceutical Research and Development; Chief Scientific Officer: David I. (Dave) Stirling
SVP, Sales and Marketing: Francis Brown
SVP, Regulatory Affairs, Pharmacovigilance, and Project Management: Graham Burton
SVP, Research and Development; SVP, Celgro: George W. J. Matcham
VP, Human Resources: Mary Weger
VP, Medical Affairs and Chief Medical Officer: Jerome B. (Jerry) Zeldis
Senior Director, Investor Relations and Public Relations: Brian P. Gill
Secretary: Robert C. Butler
Auditors: KPMG LLP

LOCATIONS
HQ: Celgene Corporation
  86 Morris Ave., Summit, NJ 07901
Phone: 908-673-9000   **Fax:** 908-673-9001
Web: www.celgene.com

Celgene has facilities in California, Louisiana, and New Jersey, as well as in Switzerland and the UK.

2005 Sales

	$ mil.	% of total
North America	518.4	97
Other regions	18.5	3
Total	**536.9**	**100**

PRODUCTS/OPERATIONS
2005 Sales

	$ mil.	% of total
Products		
THALOMID	387.8	72
ALKERAN	49.7	9
FOCALIN	4.2	1
REVLIMID	2.9	1
Other	1.0	—
Royalties	50.0	9
Collaborations & other	41.3	8
Total	**536.9**	**100**

Selected Products
Approved
  ALKERAN (multiple myeloma and ovarian cancer, licensed from GlaxoSmithKline)
  FOCALIN (attention deficit hyperactivity disorder, marketed by Novartis)
  LIFEBANK USA (stem cell banking kit)
  THALOMID (complications from leprosy, multiple myeloma)
  REVLIMID (multiple myeloma, myelodysplastic syndromes)
In Development
  CC-4047 (sickle cell anemia, myelofibrosis, and prostate cancer)
  CC-8490 (brain cancer)
  CC-10004 (chronic inflammatory diseases)
  CC-11006 (chronic inflammatory diseases)

COMPETITORS
Amgen	Merck
AstraZeneca	Millennium
Biogen Idec	Pharmaceuticals
Bristol-Myers Squibb	Novartis
Cell Therapeutics	Pfizer
Centocor	Pharmion
Eli Lilly	Sanofi-Aventis
EntreMed	Shire
Genentech	SuperGen
Hoffmann-La Roche	Vertex Pharmaceuticals

HISTORICAL FINANCIALS
Company Type: Public

Income Statement
FYE: December 31

	REVENUE ($ mil.)	NET INCOME ($ mil.)	NET PROFIT MARGIN	EMPLOYEES
12/05	536.9	63.7	11.9%	944
12/04	377.5	52.8	14.0%	766
12/03	271.5	13.5	5.0%	679
12/02	135.8	(100.0)	—	560
12/01	114.2	(1.9)	—	383
Annual Growth	47.3%	—	—	25.3%

2005 Year-End Financials
Debt ratio: 62.9%
Return on equity: 11.4%
Cash ($ mil.): 724.3
Current ratio: 7.17
Long-term debt ($ mil.): 400.0
No. of shares (mil.): 342.2
Dividends
  Yield: —
  Payout: —
Market value ($ mil.): 11,086.4
R&D as % of sales: 0.0%
Advertising as % of sales: —

Stock History
NASDAQ (GS): CELG

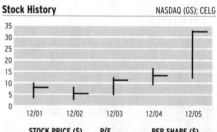

	STOCK PRICE ($) FY Close	P/E High/Low	PER SHARE ($) Earnings	Dividends	Book Value
12/05	32.40	182 69	0.18	—	1.86
12/04	13.26	105 60	0.16	—	2.89
12/03	11.22	306 126	0.04	—	3.81
12/02	5.37	— —	(0.32)	—	3.44
12/01	7.98	— —	(0.01)	—	4.11
Annual Growth	42.0%	— —	—	—	(18.0%)

Center Financial

Center Financial wants to be in the middle of your finances. Center Financial Corporation is the holding company for Center Bank, which has more than 15 branches in Southern California, Chicago, and Seattle, plus about ten additional loan production offices scattered across the US mainland and Hawaii in areas heavily concentrated with Korean-American businesses and individuals, Center Financial's target market. The bank focuses on commercial lending, including Small Business Administration loans and short-term trade finance for importers/exporters.

Commercial real estate loans comprise the largest portion of its loan book (more than 60%), followed by commercial operating loans (nearly 20%).

In 2004 Center Financial acquired its first out-of-state full service branch when it bought the Korea Exchange Bank's Chicago branch. The company also expanded its loan production office network in 2004, adding branches in Atlanta, Dallas, Honolulu, and Houston. It opened a location in the Seattle area the following year.

Fund manager FMR owns nearly 10% of Center Financial.

EXECUTIVES

Chairman: Peter Y. S. Kim, age 57
President and CEO, Center Financial Corporation and Center Bank: Jae Whan (J. W.) Yoo, age 57
EVP and Chief Credit Officer, Center Financial and Center Bank: James Hong, age 52, $175,226 pay
EVP and CFO: Patrick Hartman, age 56, $180,682 pay
EVP and CIO: Jong Ha Choi
SVP, Compliance: James Ryu
Chief Marketing Officer: Susanna H. Rivera
Secretary and General Counsel: Thomas Levine, age 53
Treasurer: James Park
Auditors: Grant Thornton LLP

LOCATIONS

HQ: Center Financial Corporation
3435 Wilshire Blvd., Ste. 700,
Los Angeles, CA 90010
Phone: 213-251-2222   **Fax:** 213-386-6774
Web: www.centerbank.com

Center Financial has bank branches in Artesia, Buena Park, Colton, Gardena, Garden Grove, Irvine, Los Angeles (6), Northridge, San Diego, and Torrance, California, as well as Chicago and Seattle. It has loan production offices in Atlanta, Dallas, Denver, Honolulu, Houston, Las Vegas, Phoenix, Seattle, and Washington, DC.

PRODUCTS/OPERATIONS

2005 Sales

	$ mil.	% of total
Interest		
Loans, including fees	85.1	75
Investment securities	6.4	6
Other	1.4	1
Noninterest		
Customer service fees	9.1	8
Fee income from trade finance transactions	3.5	3
Gain on sale of loans	2.5	2
Loan service fees	2.0	2
Other	3.4	3
Total	**113.4**	**100**

COMPETITORS

Bank of America	Nara Bancorp
City National	Washington Mutual
First Republic (CA)	Wells Fargo
Hanmi Financial	Wilshire Bancorp

HISTORICAL FINANCIALS
Company Type: Public

Income Statement				FYE: December 31
	ASSETS ($ mil.)	NET INCOME ($ mil.)	INCOME AS % OF ASSETS	EMPLOYEES
12/05	1,661.0	24.6	1.5%	327
12/04	1,338.1	14.2	1.1%	275
12/03	1,027.4	11.6	1.1%	250
12/02	818.6	9.4	1.1%	228
12/01	586.8	7.8	1.3%	—
Annual Growth	**29.7%**	**33.3%**	**—**	**12.8%**

2005 Year-End Financials

Equity as % of assets: 6.8%
Return on assets: 1.6%
Return on equity: 24.2%
Long-term debt ($ mil.): 47.2
No. of shares (mil.): 16.4
Market value ($ mil.): 413.6
Dividends
Yield: 0.6%
Payout: 10.8%
Sales ($ mil.): 113.4
R&D as % of sales: —
Advertising as % of sales: —

Stock History

NASDAQ (GS): CLFC

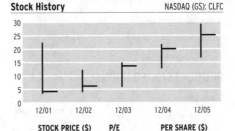

	STOCK PRICE ($) FY Close	P/E High/Low		PER SHARE ($)		
				Earnings	Dividends	Book Value
12/05	25.16	20	11	1.48	0.16	6.86
12/04	20.02	25	15	0.86	0.20	5.57
12/03	13.63	20	8	0.72	0.04	4.88
12/02	6.18	20	7	0.61	—	9.16
12/01	4.21	—	—	—	—	21.51
Annual Growth	**56.4%**			**34.4%**	**100.0%**	**(24.9%)**

Central European Distribution

Central European Distribution Corporation (CEDC) helped Poland toast its post-Communist economy in 1991 when co-founders William O. Carey and Jeffrey Peterson introduced Foster's lager to the country. CEDC imports and distributes nearly 700 brands of beer, spirits, and wines in Poland through more than 39,000 outlets. CEDC spirits include those made by Bacardi and Diageo. Other brands include Beck's Pilsner, Corona beers, Jim Beam bourbon, and E&J Gallo wines. It also distributes bottled water and cigars. The company operates 15 distribution centers throughout the country and offers next-day delivery of orders.

CEDC plans to grow through the addition of regional offices and brands throughout Poland.

To that end, the purchase of vodka maker Bols, Poland's third largest distiller, from Rémy Cointreau in 2005 not only added the vodka distillery but brought exclusive import deals covering Rémy Martin, Piper-Heidsieck, Cointreau, and Metaxa. CEDC also owns a majority stake in Polmos Bialystok, Poland's second largest vodka distiller and producer of the Absolwent and Zubrowka brands. Also fitting in with its growth strategy, the company owns Delikates, an alcohol distributor serving Central Poland. Poland is the fourth largest vodka market in the world. CEDC added the rights to popular Polish rum brand Rum Senorita, and acquired another Polish distributor (Classic) in 2006.

Company CEO William V. Carey, son of founder William O. Carey, owns about 17% of CEDC.

EXECUTIVES

Chairman, President, and CEO: William V. Carey, age 41, $367,000 pay
VP and COO: Evangelos Evangelou, age 38, $285,000 pay
VP and CFO: Christopher (Chris) Biedermann, age 38, $100,000 pay
VP and Director Investor Relations: James Archbold, age 45, $175,000 pay
VP and Export Director: Richard S. Roberts, age 57, $100,000 pay
Auditors: PricewaterhouseCoopers Sp. z o.o.

LOCATIONS

HQ: Central European Distribution Corporation
2 Bala Plaza, Ste. 300, Bala Cynwyd, PA 19004
Phone: 610-660-7817   **Fax:** 610-667-3308
Web: www.ced-c.com

Central European Distribution Corporation has 15 distribution centers and nearly 90 offices throughout Poland.

PRODUCTS/OPERATIONS

Select Subsidiaries

Agis
Astor
Carey Agri International Poland
Dako Galant
Damianex S.A.
Fine Wines & Spirits
Multi Trade Company
Onufry
Panta Hurt
Piwnica Wybornych Win
Polskie Hurtownie Alkoholi

Select Brands

Absolwent
Bols Excellent
Ludowa
Palace Vodka
Soplica
Zubrowka

COMPETITORS

Carlsberg
Diageo
Heineken
InBev
Nestlé
Pernod Ricard
Rémy Cointreau
SABMiller
Suntory Ltd.

HISTORICAL FINANCIALS

Company Type: Public

Income Statement

FYE: December 31

	REVENUE ($ mil.)	NET INCOME ($ mil.)	NET PROFIT MARGIN	EMPLOYEES
12/05	749.4	20.3	2.7%	2,917
12/04	580.7	21.8	3.8%	2,015
12/03	429.1	15.1	3.5%	1,905
12/02	294.0	8.3	2.8%	1,480
12/01	178.2	2.5	1.4%	660
Annual Growth	43.2%	68.8%	—	45.0%

2005 Year-End Financials

Debt ratio: 98.4%
Return on equity: 8.2%
Cash ($ mil.): 65.0
Current ratio: 1.32
Long-term debt ($ mil.): 369.0
No. of shares (mil.): 23.7

Dividends
  Yield: —
  Payout: —
Market value ($ mil.): 634.8
R&D as % of sales: —
Advertising as % of sales: —

Stock History

NASDAQ (GS): CEDC

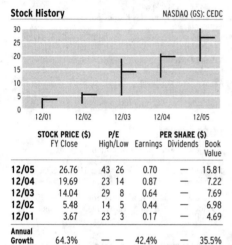

	STOCK PRICE ($) FY Close	P/E High/Low		Earnings	PER SHARE ($) Dividends	Book Value
12/05	26.76	43	26	0.70	—	15.81
12/04	19.69	23	14	0.87	—	7.22
12/03	14.04	29	8	0.64	—	7.69
12/02	5.48	14	5	0.44	—	6.98
12/01	3.67	23	3	0.17	—	4.69
Annual Growth	64.3%	—	—	42.4%	—	35.5%

Central Jersey Bancorp

Central Jersey Bancorp (formerly Monmouth Community Bancorp) is keeping the Garden State funded. The institution is the holding company for Central Jersey Bank, created by the merger of Monmouth Community Bank and Allaire Community Bank in 2005. Central Jersey Bank has about 15 branches in Monmouth and Ocean counties; they offer standard deposit products such as checking and savings accounts, CDs, and IRAs, as well as ancillary offerings like debit cards, wire transfers, and safe deposit boxes. Lending activities mainly consist of commercial real estate loans (some two-thirds of all loans), business and industrial loans, home equity loans, and second mortgages.

John Brockriede, a bank director since early 2005, owns 5% of Central Jersey Bancorp; collectively, bank executive officers and directors own a 28% stake.

EXECUTIVES

Chairman: George S. Callas, age 73
Vice Chairman: Carl F. Chirico, age 65
President, CEO, and Director; President and CEO, Central Jersey Bank: James S. Vaccaro, age 49, $257,500 pay
SEVP, COO, Secretary, and Director; SEVP, COO, and Secretary, Central Jersey Bank: Robert S. Vuono, age 56, $165,855 pay
EVP and Chief Lending Officer, Central Jersey Bancorp and Central Jersey Bank: Richard O. Lindsey, age 65, $147,500 pay
EVP and Senior Lending Officer, Central Jersey Bank: Kevin W. Hunt, $113,816 pay
EVP, CFO, Treasurer, and Assistant Secretary, Central Jersey Bancorp and Central Jersey Bank: Anthony Giordano III, age 40, $117,500 pay
SVP Branch Operations, Central Jersey Bank: Nancy L. Malinconico
SVP Business Development, Central Jersey Bank: David A. O'Connor
SVP Commercial Lending, Central Jersey Bank: Lisa A. Borghese
VP, Human Resources, Central Jersey Bank: Gail Corrigan
Auditors: KPMG LLP

LOCATIONS

HQ: Central Jersey Bancorp
  627 2nd Ave., Long Branch, NJ 07740
Phone: 732-571-1300   **Fax:** 732-571-1037
Web: www.mcbna.com

Central Jersey Bancorp has offices in Monmouth and Ocean counties.

PRODUCTS/OPERATIONS

2005 Sales

	$ mil.	% of total
Interest		
Loans, including fees	18.7	70
Interests on securities available for sale	4.9	19
Interests on securities held to maturity	1.1	4
Other	0.3	1
Service charges on deposit accounts & other	1.6	6
Total	**26.6**	**100**

COMPETITORS

Bank of New York
Commerce Bancorp
PNC Financial
Sovereign Bancorp
Sun Bancorp (NJ)
Wachovia

HISTORICAL FINANCIALS

Company Type: Public

Income Statement

FYE: December 31

	ASSETS ($ mil.)	NET INCOME ($ mil.)	INCOME AS % OF ASSETS	EMPLOYEES
12/05	514.6	2.6	0.5%	152
12/04	254.1	1.2	0.5%	166
12/03	222.6	0.5	0.2%	80
12/02	179.5	0.8	0.4%	76
12/01	118.0	0.5	0.4%	56
Annual Growth	44.5%	51.0%	—	28.4%

2005 Year-End Financials

Equity as % of assets: 12.0%
Return on assets: 0.7%
Return on equity: 6.7%
Long-term debt ($ mil.): 43.3
No. of shares (mil.): 7.8
Market value ($ mil.): 95.5

Dividends
  Yield: —
  Payout: —
Sales ($ mil.): 26.6
R&D as % of sales: —
Advertising as % of sales: —

Stock History

NASDAQ (CM): CJBK

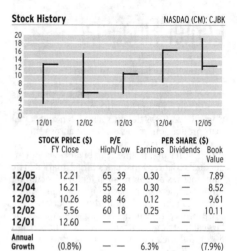

	STOCK PRICE ($) FY Close	P/E High/Low		Earnings	PER SHARE ($) Dividends	Book Value
12/05	12.21	65	39	0.30	—	7.89
12/04	16.21	55	28	0.30	—	8.52
12/03	10.26	88	46	0.12	—	9.61
12/02	5.56	60	18	0.25	—	10.11
12/01	12.60	—	—	—	—	—
Annual Growth	(0.8%)	—	—	6.3%	—	(7.9%)

Central Pacific Financial

When in the Central Pacific, do as the islanders do! This might include doing business with Central Pacific Financial, the holding company for Central Pacific Bank. The bank operates nearly 40 branch locations throughout the Hawaiian Islands. Targeting individuals and local businesses, the bank provides such standard retail banking products as checking and savings accounts, money market accounts, and CDs. Commercial real estate loans make up about 35% of the bank's loan portfolio, which also includes residential mortgages (more than 20%) and business, construction, and consumer loans. The company has real estate loan production offices in California, Hawaii, and Washington.

Central Pacific Financial acquired competitor CB Bancshares in 2004, then merged its City Bank branches into Central Pacific Bank. The following year it acquired Hawaii HomeLoans, which it renamed Central Pacific HomeLoans. The addition of Central Pacific HomeLoans expanded Central Pacific Financial's mortgage offerings, making it one of the largest mortgage writers in the state. In addition to traditional deposit products and loans, Central Pacific Bank provides business cash management services, equipment leasing, and trust and investment services. A subsidiary provides data-processing services to financial institutions in California and Hawaii.

Florida-based Private Capital Management controls nearly 10% of Central Pacific Financial's stock.

EXECUTIVES

Chairman, Central Pacific Financial and Central Pacific Bank: Ronald K. Migita, age 64
Vice Chairman, President, and CEO, Central Pacific Financial and Central Pacific Bank: Clinton L. (Clint) Arnoldus, age 59, $960,000 pay
EVP and CFO, Central Pacific Financial and Central Pacific Bank: Dean K. Hirata, age 49
EVP and Chief Credit Officer: Curtis W. Chinn
EVP, Operations and Services, Central Pacific Financial and Central Pacific Bank: Denis K. Isono, age 54, $274,431 pay

Vice Chairman, Hawaii Market, Central Pacific Bank:
  Blenn A. Fujimoto, age 47
SVP and Corporate Secretary: Glenn Ching
SVP, Manager, and Treasurer, Central Pacific Bank:
  David Morimoto
SVP and Director of Human Resources, Central Pacific
  Bank: Patty B. Martin
SVP and Public Relations and Communications
  Manager, Central Pacific Bank: Ann Takiguchi Marcos
Auditors: KPMG LLP

LOCATIONS

HQ: Central Pacific Financial Corp.
  220 S. King St., Honolulu, HI 96813
Phone: 808-544-0500   **Fax:** 808-531-2875
Web: www.cpbi.com

Central Pacific Financial operates branches on the
islands of Hawaii (2), Kauai, Maui (3), and Oahu (31).
The company also has four loan production offices in
California and two in Washington.

PRODUCTS/OPERATIONS

2005 Sales

	$ mil.	% of total
Interest		
Loans	222.8	73
Securities & other	40.4	13
Service charges on deposit accounts	11.8	4
Other service charges & fees	12.1	4
Gains on sales of loans	5.8	2
Income from fiduciary activities	2.4	1
Income from life insurance	2.2	1
Other	6.8	2
Total	**304.3**	**100**

COMPETITORS

American Savings Bank
BancWest
Bank of Hawaii
First Hawaiian Bank
Hawaiian Electric Industries
Mitsubishi UFJ Financial Group
Territorial Savings
Washington Mutual
Wells Fargo

HISTORICAL FINANCIALS

Company Type: Public

Income Statement

FYE: December 31

	ASSETS ($ mil.)	NET INCOME ($ mil.)	INCOME AS % OF ASSETS	EMPLOYEES
12/05	5,239.1	72.5	1.4%	904
12/04	4,651.9	37.4	0.8%	923
12/03	2,170.3	33.9	1.6%	506
12/02	2,028.2	33.3	1.6%	506
12/01	1,835.6	28.7	1.6%	531
Annual Growth	**30.0%**	**26.1%**	**—**	**14.2%**

2005 Year-End Financials

Equity as % of assets: 12.9%
Return on assets: 1.5%
Return on equity: 11.7%
Long-term debt ($ mil.): 749.3
No. of shares (mil.): 30.4
Market value ($ mil.): 1,093.3
Dividends
  Yield: 2.0%
  Payout: 30.7%
Sales ($ mil.): 304.3
R&D as % of sales: —
Advertising as % of sales: 0.8%

Stock History

NYSE: CPF

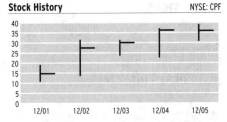

	STOCK PRICE ($) FY Close	P/E High/Low		PER SHARE ($) Earnings	Dividends	Book Value
12/05	35.92	16	13	2.38	0.73	22.22
12/04	36.17	20	12	1.87	0.64	20.09
12/03	30.04	15	12	2.07	0.64	12.11
12/02	27.45	15	7	2.04	—	10.86
12/01	14.70	11	6	1.72	—	18.54
Annual Growth	**25.0%**	**—**	**—**	**8.5%**	**6.8%**	**4.6%**

Ceradyne

A bull in a china shop wouldn't stand a chance
against Ceradyne's ceramics. The company's advanced ceramics products combine hardness
with light weight and the ability to withstand
high temperatures, resist corrosion, and insu-
late against electricity. Some uses of Ceradyne's
materials include armor for military helicopters, missile nose cones, body armor for sol-
diers, diesel engine components, ceramic
industrial products, and orthodontic brackets.
The company sells to contractors and OEMs.
Co-founder and chairman Joel Moskowitz owns
8% of the company. Ceradyne acquired raw materials supplier ESK Ceramics and injection
moldings firm Quest Technology in 2004.

In mid-2006 Ceradyne exercised its more recent diversification strategy with the purchase of
an 86,000 sq. ft. industrial facility in Quebec,
Canada and a boron carbide/aluminum product
line known as Boral. The company paid AAR
Corp. approximately $14.1 million for the facil-
ity, equipment, product line, and inventory, officially marking its entrance into the universe of
manufacturing and marketing structural neutron absorbing materials.

EXECUTIVES

Chairman, President, and CEO: Joel P. Moskowitz,
  age 66
CFO and Corporate Secretary:
  Jerrold J. (Jerry) Pellizzon, age 52
VP; President, ESK Ceramics: Peter Hartl, age 49
VP; President, Thermo Materials: Bruce R. Lockhart,
  age 43
**VP; President, North American Operations and
  Assistant Corporate Secretary:** David P. Reed, age 51
VP; President, Semicon Associates: Jeff Waldal, age 41
VP, Operations: Alvin Gerk, age 63
VP, Sales, Marketing, and Business Development:
  Michael A. Kraft, age 43
Chief Technology Officer: Thomas Juengling
Auditors: PricewaterhouseCoopers LLP

LOCATIONS

HQ: Ceradyne, Inc.
  3169 Red Hill Ave., Costa Mesa, CA 92626
Phone: 714-549-0421   **Fax:** 714-549-5787
Web: www.ceradyne.com

Ceradyne operates facilities in Costa Mesa and Irvine,
California; Lexington, Kentucky; and Scottdale and
Clarkston, Georgia.

2005 Sales

	% of total
US	74
Other countries	26
Total	**100**

PRODUCTS/OPERATIONS

2005 Sales

	$ mil.	% of total
Advanced Ceramics		
Armor	207.1	56
Automotive	16.0	4
Orthodontics	9.8	3
Semiconductors	1.0	1
Other	8.9	2
ESK Ceramics	105.8	29
Thermo Materials	12.2	3
Semicon Associates	7.5	2
Total	**368.3**	**100**

Selected Applications

Defense
  Military aircraft and vehicle armor
  Missile radomes
  Personnel (body) armor
Industrial
  Fused silica ceramic crucibles
  Industrial wear components
  Photovoltaic (solar cell) manufacturing
  Precision ceramics
  Samarium cobalt permanent magnets
  Semiconductor equipment components
Commercial
  Orthodontic brackets
Automotive
  Ceramic armor for armored civilian vehicles
  Diesel truck engine components

COMPETITORS

Align Technology
American Technical Ceramics
Armor Holdings
BAE Systems Land and Armaments
Cookson Group
CoorsTek
DHB Industries
GEA Group
Kyocera
Morgan Crucible
NGK INSULATORS
NP Aerospace
Saint-Gobain

HISTORICAL FINANCIALS

Company Type: Public

Income Statement

FYE: December 31

	REVENUE ($ mil.)	NET INCOME ($ mil.)	NET PROFIT MARGIN	EMPLOYEES
12/05	368.3	46.8	12.7%	1,835
12/04	215.6	27.6	12.8%	1,442
12/03	101.5	11.2	11.0%	500
12/02	61.2	2.7	4.4%	435
12/01	45.3	4.0	8.8%	463
Annual Growth	**68.9%**	**84.9%**	**—**	**41.1%**

2005 Year-End Financials

Debt ratio: 48.3%
Return on equity: 24.3%
Cash ($ mil.): 99.4
Current ratio: 5.95
Long-term debt ($ mil.): 121.0
No. of shares (mil.): 26.8

Dividends
  Yield: —
  Payout: —
Market value ($ mil.): 1,173.7
R&D as % of sales: 2.1%
Advertising as % of sales: —

Stock History

NASDAQ (GS): CRDN

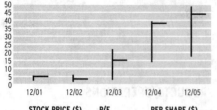

	STOCK PRICE ($) FY Close	P/E High/Low		PER SHARE ($) Earnings	Dividends	Book Value
12/05	43.80	26	10	1.86	—	9.35
12/04	38.14	35	13	1.12	—	5.52
12/03	15.14	42	7	0.51	—	8.17
12/02	3.47	41	15	0.14	—	5.06
12/01	5.01	25	14	0.20	—	4.72
Annual Growth	72.0%	—	—	74.6%	—	18.6%

Cerus

Cerus is keeping it pure for the world. The firm develops blood-pathogen inactivation systems intended to purify donated blood and improve the safety of blood transfusions. The company's Intercept blood systems use proprietary small-molecule compounds to prevent pathogens, including HIV, hepatitis B and C viruses, and other bacteria and viruses, from replicating in blood products. Cerus is also developing therapies for the treatment of cancer and infectious diseases using its Listeria vaccine and KBMA technology platforms. The firm has a marketing and development agreement with medical instrument maker Baxter International.

EXECUTIVES

Chairman: B. J. Cassin, age 72
President, CEO, and Director: Claes Glassell, $448,667 pay
President, Cerus Europe: William M. (Obi) Greenman
VP, Finance and CFO: William J. Dawson, age 52, $133,193 pay
VP, Administration and Corporate Secretary: Lori L. Roll
VP, Clinical Research and Medical Affairs: Joseph J. Eiden Jr., age 52
VP, Legal Affairs: Howard G. Ervin, age 57, $392,480 pay
VP, Medical Affairs, Chief Medical Officer, and Director: Laurence M. Corash, age 61, $490,963 pay
VP, Regulatory Affairs and Quality: Elizabeth M. Tillson
VP, Research and Development: David N. Cook, age 46, $404,387 pay
Corporate Communications and Investor Relations: Myesha Edwards
Auditors: Ernst & Young LLP

LOCATIONS

HQ: Cerus Corporation
  2411 Stanwell Dr., Concord, CA 94520
Phone: 925-288-6000   **Fax:** 925-288-6001
Web: www.cerus.com

COMPETITORS

Abbott Labs	Immucor
Biopure	Northfield Labs
Cypress Bioscience	Panacos

HISTORICAL FINANCIALS
Company Type: Public

Income Statement
FYE: December 31

	REVENUE ($ mil.)	NET INCOME ($ mil.)	NET PROFIT MARGIN	EMPLOYEES
12/05	24.4	13.1	53.7%	97
12/04	13.9	(31.1)	—	83
12/03	9.7	(58.3)	—	120
12/02	8.5	(57.2)	—	158
12/01	4.5	(49.4)	—	169
Annual Growth	52.6%	—	—	(13.0%)

2005 Year-End Financials

Debt ratio: 0.3%
Return on equity: 69.4%
Cash ($ mil.): 45.8
Current ratio: 2.19
Long-term debt ($ mil.): 0.1
No. of shares (mil.): 22.5

Dividends
  Yield: —
  Payout: —
Market value ($ mil.): 227.9
R&D as % of sales: 98.9%
Advertising as % of sales: —

Stock History

NASDAQ (GM): CERS

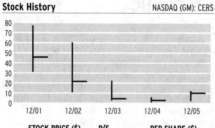

	STOCK PRICE ($) FY Close	P/E High/Low		PER SHARE ($) Earnings	Dividends	Book Value
12/05	10.15	21	5	0.55	—	1.57
12/04	2.95	—	—	(1.41)	—	0.97
12/03	4.54	—	—	(3.01)	—	2.38
12/02	21.50	—	—	(3.61)	—	3.52
12/01	45.75	—	—	(3.27)	—	6.78
Annual Growth	(31.4%)	—	—	—	—	(30.6%)

Charles & Colvard

Charles & Colvard hopes that it isn't just some shooting star. The company makes gemstones made from moissanite, a diamond substitute created in laboratories. Composed of silicon and carbon, moissanite (AKA silicon carbide or SiC) is typically found in meteorites. Charles & Colvard makes its gemstones from SiC crystals purchased primarily from Cree, Inc. (and, since 2005, from the Swedish Norstel and the US Intrinsic Semiconductor). Charles & Colvard markets its gemstones through two distributors (Stuller and Rio Grande) in North America and has agreements with some 40 distributors in Europe, Australia, and Asia. It also has supply agreements with jewelry manufacturers such as K&G Creations and Reeves Park.

In early 2006 the company announced that its products would be placed in Helzberg Diamonds stores and that Zale Corporation would be testing moissanite products in stores across the US and in Canada. Charles & Colvard nearly doubled its revenue figure in 2005.

The company established a wholly owned subsidiary in China in 2003 to enhance its operations in Asia. (It had already opened up shop in Hong Kong in 2000.) CEO Robert Thomas and former director Chester Paulson together own 16% of the company.

EXECUTIVES

Chairman, President, and CEO: Robert S. (Bob) Thomas, age 58
CFO, Secretary, and Treasurer: James R. (Jim) Braun, age 51
EVP, Sales and Chief Marketing Officer: Dennis M. Reed, age 38
SVP, Manufacturing: Earl R. Hines, age 69
Lead Director, Manufacturing: Steven L. Abate
Director, Manufacturing: Jeri Kemerait
Human Resources Specialist: Amy Wagner
Auditors: Deloitte & Touche LLP

LOCATIONS

HQ: Charles & Colvard, Ltd.
  300 Perimeter Park Dr., Ste. A,
  Morrisville, NC 27560
Phone: 919-468-0399   **Fax:** 919-468-0486
Web: www.moissanite.com

2005 Sales

	$ mil.	% of total
US	40.3	93
Other	3.2	7
Total	**43.5**	**100**

COMPETITORS

ALROSA
BHP Billiton
DTC
Lazare Kaplan
Sumitomo Chemical

HISTORICAL FINANCIALS
Company Type: Public

Income Statement
FYE: December 31

	REVENUE ($ mil.)	NET INCOME ($ mil.)	NET PROFIT MARGIN	EMPLOYEES
12/05	43.5	5.9	13.6%	60
12/04	23.9	1.6	6.7%	50
12/03	17.2	1.0	5.8%	52
12/02	16.5	9.4	57.0%	41
12/01	11.5	1.2	10.4%	32
Annual Growth	39.5%	48.9%	—	17.0%

2005 Year-End Financials

Debt ratio: —
Return on equity: 11.2%
Cash ($ mil.): 21.0
Current ratio: 10.65
Long-term debt ($ mil.): —
No. of shares (mil.): 18.3

Dividends
  Yield: —
  Payout: —
Market value ($ mil.): 295.7
R&D as % of sales: 0.5%
Advertising as % of sales: 22.5%

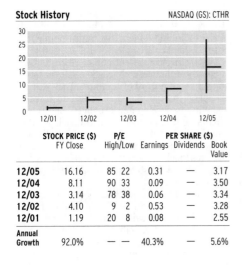

	STOCK PRICE ($) FY Close	P/E High/Low		PER SHARE ($) Earnings	Dividends	Book Value
12/05	16.16	85	22	0.31	—	3.17
12/04	8.11	90	33	0.09	—	3.50
12/03	3.14	78	38	0.06	—	3.34
12/02	4.10	9	2	0.53	—	3.28
12/01	1.19	20	8	0.08	—	2.55
Annual Growth	92.0%	—	—	40.3%	—	5.6%

Chart Industries

They're just chillin' at Chart Industries. The company (which was acquired by First Reserve Corp. in 2005) designs equipment for low-temperature uses, including cryogenic systems that can operate at temperatures near absolute zero. Chart's vessels are used to process, liquefy, store, and transport gases and are marketed to petrochemical and natural gas processors, producers of industrial gas, and satellite testing companies. The company also performs engineered bulk gas installations, and makes specialty liquid nitrogen end-use equipment used in the hydrocarbon processing and industrial gas industries.

To streamline operations, Chart Industries reorganized its subsidiaries into three business segments: distribution and storage, biomedical, and energy and chemicals. Chart Industries' products are sold worldwide; the US accounts for more than three-quarters of sales.

HISTORY

In 1986 Arthur Holmes teamed up with his brother Charles to purchase ALTEC International, a struggling maker of brazed aluminum heat exchangers that dated to 1949. The brothers turned ALTEC around and used it to acquire undervalued companies. From 1986 to 1991, they purchased storage and transportation equipment for liquefied gases and high-pressure cryogenic equipment, including Greenville Tube Corporation (stainless steel tubing, 1987); Process Engineering, Inc. (cryogenic tanks, 1990); and Process Systems International (cold boxes, 1991). The Holmes brothers finally established a public holding company in 1992, and named it Chart Industries (for CHarles and ARThur).

The company ran into trouble over the next few years trying to make its acquisitions profitable. Chart restructured its most troubled unit, Process Engineering, Inc., in 1994. It bought cryogenic vacuum pumps maker CVI to build systems for NASA. In 1995 the company began supplying vacuum equipment for the Laser Interferometer Gravitational-Wave Observatory project, a research program that searches for cosmic gravitational waves.

In 1997 Chart bought Cryenco Sciences, which makes cryogenic road trailers. The next year the company acquired the Industrial Heat Exchanger division of UK-based IMI Marston Limited. In a move intended to increase foreign sales, Chart in 1999 bought MVE Holding, a cryogenic storage and transportation company with facilities in the US and Europe, for $240 million in cash. The company also expanded its cryogenic equipment repair services across the US with the purchase of Northcoast Cryogenics.

Chart signed an agreement in 2000 to build and maintain a new liquid natural gas fueling station for Waste Management Corporation. The new refueling station will be the world's largest, capable of refueling 120 trucks per 4 hours. In March 2002 the company announced it would place surcharges on its bulk storage tanks to offset the tariffs set by the US government on imported steel products, which would increase manufacturing costs.

In 2003 the NYSE suspended trading of the company's shares after the company fell below continued listing standards and fell into bankruptcy protection. Later that year, Chart Industries came out of bankruptcy protection with a new board membership and senior management. Chairman Arthur Holmes also resigned his post in 2003, but continued as a board member until 2005.

Chart Industries filed for another IPO in 2006, applying to list on the Big Board once more.

EXECUTIVES

Chairman: Ben A. Guill, age 56
President, CEO, and Director: Samuel F. Thomas, age 54
EVP, CFO and Treasurer: Michael F. Biehl, age 50
VP, General Counsel and Secretary: Matthew J. Klaben, age 36
VP, Manufacturing: Charles R. (Chip) Lovett, age 61
VP, Human Resources and Secretary: Mark H. Ludwig
President, Energy and Chemicals Group: John T. Romain, age 42
President, Distribution and Storage Group: Thomas M. (Tom) Carey, age 48
President, Chart Asia: Eric Rottier
President, Biomedical Group: Steve T. Shaw, age 44
Chief Accounting Officer, Controller and Assistant Treasurer: James H. Hoppel Jr., age 42
Auditors: Ernst & Young LLP

LOCATIONS

HQ: Chart Industries, Inc.
　　1 Infinity Corporate Centre Dr., Ste. 300,
　　Garfield Heights, OH 44125
Phone: 440-753-1490　　　**Fax:** 440-753-1491
Web: www.chart-ind.com

Chart Industries has operations in eight states in the US and in Australia, China, the Czech Republic, Germany, and the UK.

2005 Sales

	$ mil.	% of total
US	309.3	77
Czech Republic	55.5	14
Other countries	38.3	9
Total	**403.1**	**100**

PRODUCTS/OPERATIONS

2005 Sales

	$ mil.	% of total
Distribution & storage	209.2	52
Energy & chemicals	121.0	30
Biomedical	72.9	18
Total	**403.1**	**100**

Selected Products

Cold boxes (reduce the temperature of gas mixtures to liquefy and separate them)
Cryogenic components (pumps, valves, vacuum-jacketed piping systems, and specialty components)
Cryogenic storage tanks (tanks, trailers, intermodal containers, and railcars)
Heat exchangers (facilitate cooling and liquefaction of air or hydrocarbons)
Space simulation systems (satellite and spacecraft testing)
Thermal vacuum systems (aerospace and research applications)

COMPETITORS

Air Products	L'Air Liquide
Chicago Bridge & Iron	Linde
Cobham	Nordon et Compagnie
Flowserve	Reliance Steel
Graham Corporation	Senior
Harsco	Sumitomo Metal Industries
Ingersoll-Rand	Technip
Intermagnetics General	Tyco
Kobe Steel	

HISTORICAL FINANCIALS

Company Type: Public

Income Statement

				FYE: December 31
	REVENUE ($ mil.)	NET INCOME ($ mil.)	NET PROFIT MARGIN	EMPLOYEES
12/05	403.1	8.4	2.1%	2,271
12/04	305.6	22.6	7.4%	1,770
12/03	265.6	(7.0)	—	1,524
12/02	296.3	(130.8)	—	2,022
Annual Growth	10.8%	—	—	3.9%

2005 Year-End Financials

Debt ratio: 296.6%　　　　Current ratio: 1.66
Return on equity: 7.2%　　Long-term debt ($ mil.): 345.0
Cash ($ mil.): 15.4

Net Income History　　　　　　NASDAQ (GM): GTLS

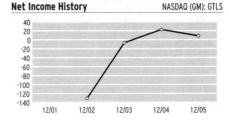

CharterMac

CharterMac helps keep the multifamily housing finance market liquid. Through subsidiaries, the firm invests in tax-exempt multifamily mortgage bonds and uses the proceeds to finance multifamily housing, particularly properties meeting low-income housing tax credit requirements. It holds investments in more than 300 bonds on housing located in metropolitan areas nationwide, about a quarter of which are located in Texas. The company also owns CharterMac Capital, which provides management and advisory services to CharterMac and its subsidiaries, as well as to publicly traded real estate investment trust (REIT) American Mortgage Acceptance.

EXECUTIVES

Chairman: Stephen M. Ross, age 64
President, CEO, and Managing Trustee; CEO, CharterMac Capital: Marc D. Schnitzer, age 45, $1,021,323 pay (prior to title change)
COO and Managing Trustee; President, Related Capital: Alan P. Hirmes, age 50
CFO: Robert L. (Rob) Levy
Chief Investment Officer: Donald J. (Don) Meyer
CEO, CharterMac Mortgage Capital: Daryl J. Carter, age 49
Corporate Managing Director, CharterMac Mortgage Capital: Neil P. Cullen
Corporate Managing Director, CharterMac Mortgage Capital: Patti Saylor
Corporate Managing Director, CharterMac Mortgage Capital: Katherine B. (Kelly) Schnur, age 41
Corporate Managing Director and National Sales Director, CharterMac Mortgage Capital: William T. Hyman, age 45
Auditors: Deloitte & Touche LLP

LOCATIONS

HQ: CharterMac
 625 Madison Ave., New York, NY 10022
Phone: 212-317-5700   **Fax:** 212-751-3550
Web: www.chartermac.com

PRODUCTS/OPERATIONS

2005 Sales

	$ mil.	% of total
Interest income		
Mortgage revenue bond interest income	146.0	50
Other interest income	16.1	5
Fee income	87.7	30
Revenues of consolidated partnerships	24.1	8
Other	21.1	7
Total	**295.0**	**100**

Selected Subsidiaries

CharterMac Corporation
 Centerbrook Holdings LLC
 CharterMac Capital Company, LLC
 CharterMac Mortgage Capital Corp.
 CharterMac Mortgage Partners Corp.
 CM Investor LLC

COMPETITORS

Fannie Mae
Freddie Mac
Long Beach Mortgage
MuniMae

HISTORICAL FINANCIALS

Company Type: Public

Income Statement

FYE: December 31

	ASSETS ($ mil.)	NET INCOME ($ mil.)	INCOME AS % OF ASSETS	EMPLOYEES
12/05	6,978.8	59.0	0.8%	400
12/04	5,757.4	65.4	1.1%	300
12/03	2,583.3	66.6	2.6%	250
12/02	1,852.9	60.8	3.3%	220
12/01	1,420.1	39.0	2.7%	145
Annual Growth	**48.9%**	**10.9%**	**—**	**28.9%**

2005 Year-End Financials

Equity as % of assets: 12.0%
Return on assets: 0.9%
Return on equity: 6.8%
Long-term debt ($ mil.): 3,635.6
No. of shares (mil.): 52.0
Market value ($ mil.): 1,101.8

Dividends
 Yield: 7.8%
 Payout: 168.4%
Sales ($ mil.): 295.0
R&D as % of sales: —
Advertising as % of sales: —

Stock History

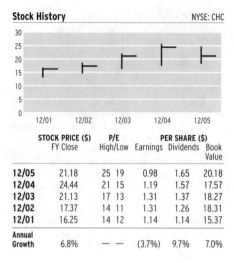

NYSE: CHC

	STOCK PRICE ($) FY Close	P/E High/Low	PER SHARE ($) Earnings	PER SHARE ($) Dividends	PER SHARE ($) Book Value
12/05	21.18	25 19	0.98	1.65	20.18
12/04	24.44	21 15	1.19	1.57	17.57
12/03	21.13	17 13	1.31	1.37	18.27
12/02	17.37	14 11	1.31	1.26	18.31
12/01	16.25	14 12	1.14	1.14	15.37
Annual Growth	**6.8%**	**— —**	**(3.7%)**	**9.7%**	**7.0%**

CheckFree

You've got bills! CheckFree provides electronic bill payment and presentment (EBPP) and other types of electronic commerce and payment services to consumers through numerous sources, including leading US banks, brokerage firms, Web sites, and personal financial management software. The company also offers portfolio management services to broker-dealers, money managers, and investment advisors, and produces financial application software used by large financial institutions and other corporate clients. CheckFree's electronic commerce services generate about three-quarters of the company's sales. The company has agreed to acquire Carreker, a financial services software developer, for a reported $206 million.

The company processes more than 1 billion transactions and some 185 million electronic bills (e-bills) per year.

CheckFree broadened its services with the 2004 purchase of American Payment Systems, which processes "walk-in" payments of utilities; CheckFree acquired the unit from UIL Holdings. It bolstered its pay-by-phone capabilities with its 2006 purchase of PhoneCharge, Inc. (now Check-Free PhonePay Services). Major stockholders include Microsoft, which controls nearly 10% of the company; CheckFree founder, chairman, and CEO Pete Kight owns around 7%. Institutional investors Waddell & Reed, American Century, and Capital Group also hold about 7% each.

HISTORY

In the early 1980s, health club manager Peter Kight sought a way for his customers to pay their annual fees other than in one lump sum. Backed by what is now BANK ONE, he devised a consumer bill payment system, and his first customer was an apartment complex. The service became viable, and in 1984 CompuServe began offering CheckFree's system to its subscribers.

During the 1980s and early 1990s CheckFree's growth was powered by consumer business. The company offered its software both as an independent package and as part of other financial packages, including Managing Your Money and Intuit's Quicken.

When CheckFree went public in 1995, it was modestly profitable, with Quicken sales accounting for about a third of revenues. That year the company sharply increased sales and research spending to develop new products and bring in clients, and it plunged into the red. In 1996 CheckFree targeted banks via several alliances and acquisitions; purchases included Servantis Systems (back-office software) and Security APL (whose PAWWS system offered securities portfolio accounting).

In the late 1990s CheckFree focused on its commercial clients (including BANK ONE and other regional banks). It sold its credit card and recovery management operations (1997) and the majority of its software business (1998). In 1999 CheckFree said it would expand its business-to-business (B2B) services by buying software firm BlueGill Technologies, which later became the core of CheckFree i-Solutions.

In 2000 the company bought Transpoint, its top competitor in the electronic bill payment business. (Transpoint's sponsors, Microsoft and First Data, became major CheckFree shareholders in the transaction.) That year the company signed a deal with Countrywide Credit, making CheckFree's services available to more than 2 million mortgage customers. Also, Bank of America sold its electronic billing assets to CheckFree in exchange for a stake in the company; CheckFree would handle Bank of America's electronic payment business. The company also changed its name from CheckFree Holdings Corporation to CheckFree Corporation.

In 2001 the company teamed with the US Postal Service on an electronic payment system for USPS-delivered packages.

EXECUTIVES

Chairman and CEO: Peter J. (Pete) Kight, age 50, $1,109,160 pay
Vice Chairman: Mark A. Johnson, age 53
COO: Stephen (Steve) Olsen, age 46, $603,043 pay (prior to title change)
EVP, CFO, and Chief Accounting Officer: David E. Mangum, age 40, $437,507 pay
EVP and General Counsel: Laura Binion, age 49
EVP and General Manager, CheckFree Investment Services Division: Michael Gianoni, age 45
EVP and General Manager, Electronic Commerce Division: Matthew S. (Matt) Lewis, age 41, $427,310 pay
EVP and General Manager, Investment Services Division: Alexander R. (Alex) Marasco, age 53, $400,513 pay
EVP, CTO, and General Manager, Software Division: Randal A. (Randy) McCoy, age 43, $444,905 pay
SVP, Corporate Marketing: Leigh Asher, age 44
SVP, Human Resources: Deborah N. Gable, age 51
Secretary: Curtis A. Loveland
Investor Relations Manager: Tina Moore
SVP, Controller, and Chief Accounting Officer: Samuel R. Schwartz, age 57
Auditors: Deloitte & Touche LLP

LOCATIONS

HQ: CheckFree Corporation
 4411 E. Jones Bridge Rd., Norcross, GA 30092
Phone: 678-375-3000   **Fax:** 678-375-1477
Web: www.checkfreecorp.com

PRODUCTS/OPERATIONS

2006 Sales

	$ mil.	% of total
Processing & servicing	754.1	86
Professional fees	47.9	5
Maintenance fees	42.2	5
License fees	35.2	4
Total	**879.4**	**100**

2006 Sales

	$ mil.	% of total
Electronic Commerce	662.7	75
Software	109.4	13
Investment Services	107.3	12
Total	**879.4**	**100**

COMPETITORS

Advent Software
Avolent
BISYS
Bottomline Technologies
DigiCash
DST
IBM
IDS Scheer
MasterCard
Metavante
MoneyGram International
Online Resources
PayPal
Sterling Commerce
SunGard
TSA
TSYS
Western Union

HISTORICAL FINANCIALS

Company Type: Public

Income Statement

FYE: June 30

	REVENUE ($ mil.)	NET INCOME ($ mil.)	NET PROFIT MARGIN	EMPLOYEES
6/06	879.4	127.3	14.5%	3,450
6/05	757.8	46.8	6.2%	3,050
6/04	606.5	10.5	1.7%	3,000
6/03	551.7	(52.2)	—	2,700
6/02	490.5	(441.0)	—	2,650
Annual Growth	**15.7%**	—	—	**6.8%**

2006 Year-End Financials

Debt ratio: 1.9%
Return on equity: 9.0%
Cash ($ mil.): 317.6
Current ratio: 2.62
Long-term debt ($ mil.): 28.4
No. of shares (mil.): 90.9
Dividends
  Yield: —
  Payout: —
Market value ($ mil.): 4,503.4
R&D as % of sales: —
Advertising as % of sales: —

Stock History

NASDAQ (GS): CKFR

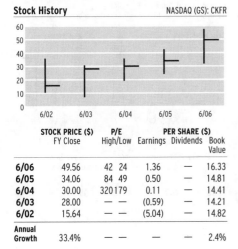

	STOCK PRICE ($) FY Close	P/E High/Low	PER SHARE ($) Earnings	Dividends	Book Value
6/06	49.56	42 24	1.36	—	16.33
6/05	34.06	84 49	0.50	—	14.81
6/04	30.00	320 179	0.11	—	14.41
6/03	28.00	— —	(0.59)	—	14.21
6/02	15.64	— —	(5.04)	—	14.82
Annual Growth	**33.4%**	— —	—	—	**2.4%**

Chemed

When it comes to fixing things, Chemed Corporation (formerly Roto-Rooter) plunges right in. Chemed is a diversified company that provides plumbing and drain-cleaning services for residential and commercial customers through its Roto-Rooter subsidiary. Roto-Rooter operates through company-owned, contractor-operated, and franchised locations, some 600 total. Additionally, Chemed offers care to terminally ill patients through VITAS Healthcare, which operates more than 35 hospice programs in 12 states.

In late 2004 the company sold its Service America subsidiary, a provider of air conditioner and appliance sales and repair to residential customers, primarily through service contracts.

EXECUTIVES

Chairman: Edward L. Hutton, age 86
President, CEO, and Director: Kevin J. McNamara, age 52, $1,590,000 pay
EVP; Chairman and CEO, Roto-Rooter Management: Spencer S. Lee, age 50, $455,802 pay
EVP and Director; CEO, VITAS Healthcare: Timothy S. (Tim) O'Toole, age 50, $730,000 pay
VP and CFO; SVP and CFO, Roto-Rooter Management: David P. Williams, age 45, $530,000 pay
VP and Secretary; SVP and General Counsel, VITAS Healthcare: Naomi C. Dallob, age 51
VP and Controller: Arthur V. Tucker Jr., age 56, $264,000 pay
VP Human Resources: Jim Taylor
President, VITAS Healthcare: David A. Wester, age 46
Investor Relations: Janelle Jessie
Auditors: PricewaterhouseCoopers LLP

LOCATIONS

HQ: Chemed Corporation
2600 Chemed Center, 255 E. 5th St.,
Cincinnati, OH 45202
Phone: 513-762-6900   **Fax:** 513-762-6919
Web: www.chemed.com

PRODUCTS/OPERATIONS

2005 Sales

	$ mil.	% of total
VITAS	629.2	68
Roto-Rooter	297.3	32
Total	**926.5**	**100**

Selected Services

Roto-Rooter
  Drain care products
  Plumbing services
  Septic tank pumping
  Sewer, drain, and pipe cleaning
  Water heaters
VITAS
  Home health care
  Hospice inpatient care
  Physician & nursing care
  Social services

COMPETITORS

ABM Industries
Dwyer Group
Ecolab
EMCOR
Golden Horizons
Home Depot
Lennox
Odyssey HealthCare
ServiceMaster
UNICCO Service

HISTORICAL FINANCIALS

Company Type: Public

Income Statement

FYE: December 31

	REVENUE ($ mil.)	NET INCOME ($ mil.)	NET PROFIT MARGIN	EMPLOYEES
12/05	926.5	35.8	3.9%	10,881
12/04	735.3	27.5	3.7%	9,822
12/03	308.9	(3.4)	—	3,357
12/02	314.2	(1.5)	—	3,335
12/01	477.1	(10.4)	—	7,595
Annual Growth	**18.0%**	—	—	**9.4%**

2005 Year-End Financials

Debt ratio: 60.9%
Return on equity: 10.0%
Cash ($ mil.): 57.1
Current ratio: 1.21
Long-term debt ($ mil.): 234.1
No. of shares (mil.): 26.0
Dividends
  Yield: 0.5%
  Payout: 17.6%
Market value ($ mil.): 1,290.7
R&D as % of sales: —
Advertising as % of sales: 2.3%

Stock History

NYSE: CHE

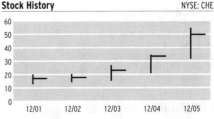

	STOCK PRICE ($) FY Close	P/E High/Low	PER SHARE ($) Earnings	Dividends	Book Value
12/05	49.68	40 24	1.36	0.24	14.79
12/04	33.56	31 19	1.12	0.18	26.26
12/03	23.05	— —	(0.17)	—	19.38
12/02	17.67	— —	(0.13)	—	20.21
12/01	16.95	— —	(0.54)	—	21.18
Annual Growth	**30.8%**	— —	—	**33.3%**	**(8.6%)**

Chipotle Mexican Grill

This company is spicing up the restaurant business. Chipotle Mexican Grill operates a chain of about 500 quick-casual Mexican eateries in more than 20 states. Customers can build a 1-1/4 pound burrito or taco from a lineup that includes chicken, steak, barbecue or free-range pork, as well as beans, rice, guacamole, and various other veggies and salsas. The company maintains that with extras its menu offers more than 65,000 choices. It also serves chips and salsa, beer, and margaritas. Just a handful of the restaurants are franchised, while the rest are company-owned.

The restaurant chain distinguishes itself from its competitors by offering "food with integrity" — that is, it uses pork from pigs and eggs from chickens that are naturally raised and antibiotic free. It also uses only fresh vegetables and beans (that are organic whenever possible) and made-on-site sauces. In addition Chipotle has no "corporate" look to its restaurants, preferring to design and build individual outlets that suit their space.

CEO Steve Ells, who trained at the Culinary Institute of America, was working in the kitchen of San Francisco's Stars restaurant when he decided to switch from gourmet food to burritos. His father loaned him the money to open his first store, and later invested $2 million in the growing operation. Chipotle had expanded to 14 locations when McDonald's acquired the business in 1998. After funding Chipotle's rapid expansion, the Golden Arches spun off a 35% stake in the business through an IPO in 2006 and later divested its remaining shares.

EXECUTIVES

Chairman and CEO: M. Steven (Steve) Ells, age 41, $870,602 pay
President, COO, Secretary, and Director: Montgomery F. (Monty) Moran, age 39
CFO and Chief Development Officer: John R. (Jack) Hartung, age 48, $544,187 pay
Chief Administrative Officer: Robert D. (Bob) Wilner, age 51, $431,817 pay
Executive Director, Human Resources: Ann Dowell
Director, IT: Joel Chrisman
Director, Marketing: Jim Adams
Director, Operations: Lisa Crosby
Director, Public Relations: Chris Arnold
Investor Relations: Brian Prenoveau
Auditors: Ernst & Young LLP

LOCATIONS

HQ: Chipotle Mexican Grill, Inc.
1543 Wazee St., Ste. 200, Denver, CO 80202
Phone: 303-595-4000   **Fax:** 303-222-2500
Web: www.chipotle.com

2005 Locations

	No.
California	67
Ohio	60
Texas	60
Colorado	55
Illinois	47
Minnesota	36
Arizona	21
Maryland	21
Virginia	20
Florida	14
New York	13
Kansas	12
Georgia	10
Missouri	8
Wisconsin	8
Other states	37
Total	**489**

PRODUCTS/OPERATIONS

2005 Sales

	$ mil.	% of total
Restaurant sales	625.1	99
Franchise royalties & fees	2.6	1
Total	**627.7**	**100**

2005 Locations

	No.
Company-owned	481
Franchised	8
Total	**489**

COMPETITORS

Del Taco	Qdoba
El Pollo Loco	Quiznos
Fresh Enterprises	Rubio's Restaurants
Moe's Southwest Grill	Subway
New World Restaurants	Taco Bell
Noodles & Company	Taco Del Mar
Panda Restaurant Group	Zaxby's
Panera Bread	

HISTORICAL FINANCIALS

Company Type: Public

Income Statement

FYE: December 31

	REVENUE ($ mil.)	NET INCOME ($ mil.)	NET PROFIT MARGIN	EMPLOYEES
12/05	627.7	37.7	6.0%	13,000
12/04	470.7	6.1	1.3%	—
12/03	315.5	(7.7)	—	—
12/02	204.6	(17.3)	—	—
Annual Growth	**45.3%**	**—**	**—**	**—**

2005 Year-End Financials

Debt ratio: 1.1%
Return on equity: 13.2%
Cash ($ mil.): 0.1
Current ratio: 0.42
Long-term debt ($ mil.): 3.5

Net Income History

NYSE: CMG

[Line chart of net income from 12/01 to 12/05, y-axis from -20 to 40. Values rise from about -15 in 12/02 to about -9 in 12/03, about 6 in 12/04, to about 38 in 12/05.]

Citi Trends

Citi Trends hopes to transport its customers to Trend City as quickly as possible. The urban fashion apparel and accessory chain operates about 275 stores in 16 US states that focus primarily on the African-American market. Its brand-name and private-label offerings, which include hip-hop jeans and oversized T-shirts; men's, women's, and children's clothing; shoes; housewares; and accessories, are sold at 20%-60% less than department and specialty stores' regular prices. Founded in 1946 as Allied Department Stores, the company was acquired by Hampshire Equity Partners and was renamed Citi Trends in 1999. The fast-growing company went public in 2005. Hampshire Equity Partners retained about 47% of the company.

Citi Trends opened 36 new stores last year and opened about 40 more in 2006.

Citi Trends purchased a new distribution center in South Carolina in late 2005, expecting the 286,500 sq. ft. property to be large enough to support an additional 250 to 300 stores; this would allow room for future company expansion.

EXECUTIVES

Chairman and CEO: R. Edward (Ed) Anderson, age 56
President and Chief Merchandising Officer: George A. Bellino, age 58, $489,519 pay
SVP, Store Operations: James A. Dunn, age 49, $254,077 pay
Interim Principal Financial and Accounting Officer; Director of Financial Reporting: Christopher Bergen, age 34
Auditors: KPMG LLP

LOCATIONS

HQ: Citi Trends, Inc.
102 Fahm St., Savannah, GA 31401
Phone: 912-236-1561   **Fax:** 912-443-3674
Web: www.cititrends.com

2006 Stores

	No.
Georgia	48
South Carolina	32
North Carolina	31
Louisiana	21
Alabama	19
Mississippi	19
Florida	16
Texas	16
Virginia	13
Tennessee	10
Arkansas	5
Maryland	3
Kentucky	1
Ohio	1
Total	**235**

PRODUCTS/OPERATIONS

2006 Sales

	% of total
Women's	38
Children's	25
Men's	22
Accessories	13
Home decor	2
Total	**100**

COMPETITORS

Burlington Coat Factory
Dollar General
DOTS
Family Dollar Stores
Kmart
Rainbow Apparel
Ross Stores
TJX Companies
Wal-Mart

HISTORICAL FINANCIALS

Company Type: Public

Income Statement

FYE: Saturday nearest January 31

	REVENUE ($ mil.)	NET INCOME ($ mil.)	NET PROFIT MARGIN	EMPLOYEES
1/06	289.8	14.2	4.9%	2,800
1/05	203.4	7.3	3.6%	1,800
1/04	157.2	5.9	3.8%	—
1/03	124.9	5.0	4.0%	—
Annual Growth	**32.4%**	**41.6%**	**—**	**55.6%**

2006 Year-End Financials

Debt ratio: 0.6%
Return on equity: 26.4%
Cash ($ mil.): 63.5
Current ratio: 2.05
Long-term debt ($ mil.): 0.5
No. of shares (mil.): 13.0
Dividends
 Yield: —
 Payout: —
Market value ($ mil.): 607.9
R&D as % of sales: —
Advertising as % of sales: 0.6%

Stock History

NASDAQ (GS): CTRN

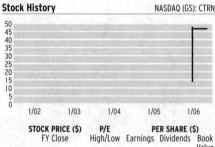

	STOCK PRICE ($) FY Close	P/E High/Low		PER SHARE ($) Earnings	Dividends	Book Value
1/06	46.71	44	13	1.08	—	6.44

Citrix Systems

Citrix Systems takes connectivity to the next level. The company provides access infrastructure products that enable PCs, IP phones, and other devices to remotely and securely access applications across wired and wireless networks. Its comprehensive Citrix Access Suite encompasses application virtualization software, VPN appliances, and password management tools, and it can be deployed in both Windows and UNIX-based computing environments. The company also offers consulting, support, and training services. Citrix has more than 160,000 customers worldwide, ranging from individual professionals to multinational corporations; it also serves the government and education markets.

The company continues to bolster its extensive roster of strategic partners, which include Microsoft, Dell, and EMC. Citrix has also expanded its offerings with acquisitions. Its 2004 purchases of ExpertCity and Net6 formed the company's Online and Gateway divisions, respectively. Citrix also acquired NetScaler, a developer of application acceleration appliances, for $300 million in cash and stock in 2005. The company agreed to acquire software provisioning specialist Ardence in late 2006.

HISTORY

Citrix Systems was founded in 1989 by a crew of former IBM engineers that included Edward Iacobucci. It was Iacobucci who, as a Big Blue designer in 1984 working alongside Bill Gates and a cadre of engineers from IBM and the fledgling Microsoft, led the team that developed the OS/2 operating system. Iacobucci quit IBM in 1989 and turned down a technology officer position at Microsoft to start his own business.

Iacobucci licensed Microsoft's OS/2 source code to start the Citrus Company, quickly changing the company name when one venture capitalist mistook it for a fruit concern. Waiting for investment funds, Iacobucci wrote an OS/2 programmer's guide (featuring a foreword by Gates) that significantly boosted his credibility among the software elite.

By 1991 Citrix had developed an OS/2-based program that let users on separate terminals run software off a larger computer. The week the product shipped, IBM and Microsoft called off their OS/2 development partnership. With business publications sounding the death of OS/2, Citrix in 1992 regrouped its network vision around Windows. The changes contributed to losses for 1992 and 1993.

Through a partnership with network software specialist Novell, in 1993 Citrix introduced WinView, which let non-Windows PC users tap into Microsoft programs on a network of disparate systems. Novell's clout boosted the company's distribution capabilities, and sales ballooned. Citrix went public in 1995.

Microsoft in 1997 made plans to incorporate some features offered by Citrix into Windows. Knowing his company's future was on the line, Iacobucci flew to Microsoft headquarters in the wake of a Citrix stock drop and shareholder lawsuits, rented an apartment, and spent 11 weeks negotiating. Microsoft signed a $175 million deal to continue licensing Citrix software.

In a burst of international expansion, Citrix in 1998 opened offices across Europe. It formed an e-business unit in 1999 to help application service providers host Web-based applications. In 2000 Citrix acquired Internet consultancy Innovex. Iacobucci resigned as chairman and chief technology officer that year.

In 2001 the company bought XML specialist Sequoia Software for about $185 million. President Mark Templeton was also appointed CEO.

EXECUTIVES

Chairman: Thomas F. (Tom) Bogan, age 54
President, CEO, and Director: Mark B. Templeton, age 53
SVP and CFO: David J. Henshall, age 38
SVP, Corporate Sales and Services: John C. Burris, age 51
VP and Chief of Staff: Mick Hollison
VP, General Counsel, and Secretary: David Friedman, age 45
VP, Business Development and Corporate Affairs: David A. G. Jones
VP, EMEA Sales, and General Manager: Stefan Sjostrom, age 52
VP, Finance and Controller: David D. Urbani
VP, Human Resources: Bruce Gant
VP, Marketing: Kate Hutchison
VP, Operations, Access Management Group: Jeffrey M. (Jeff) Russo
Group VP and General Manager, Access Management Group: Scott Herren
Group VP and General Manager, Application Networking Group: B. V. Jagadeesh
Group VP and General Manager, Gateways Group: Murli M. Thirumale
Group VP and General Manager, Online Group: Brett M. Caine, age 46
Director of Corporate Communications: Eric Armstrong
Auditors: Ernst & Young LLP

LOCATIONS

HQ: Citrix Systems, Inc.
851 W. Cypress Creek Rd.,
Fort Lauderdale, FL 33309
Phone: 954-267-3000   **Fax:** 954-267-9319
Web: www.citrix.com

2005 Sales

	$ mil.	% of total
Americas	397.2	44
Europe, Middle East & Africa	334.9	37
Asia/Pacific	77.5	8
Citrix Online division	99.1	11
Total	**908.7**	**100**

PRODUCTS/OPERATIONS

2005 Sales

	$ mil.	% of total
Product licenses	409.4	45
License updates	331.1	36
Online services	99.1	11
Technical services	69.1	8
Total	**908.7**	**100**

Selected Products and Services

Citrix Access Infrastructure
 Citrix Gateway
  Access Gateway
  Application Gateway
 Citrix MetaFrame
  Conferencing Manager
  Presentation Server for Windows
  Presentation Server for UNIX
  Password Manager
  Secure Access Manager
 Citrix Online
  GoToAssist
  GoToMeeting
  GoToMyPC
Citrix Services
 Consulting
 Product training and certification
 Technical Support

COMPETITORS

Adobe	Juniper Networks
Cisco Systems	Microsoft
EMC	Oracle
F5 Networks	Sun Microsystems
GraphOn	Tarantella
Hewlett-Packard	WebEx
IBM	

HISTORICAL FINANCIALS

Company Type: Public

Income Statement

FYE: December 31

	REVENUE ($ mil.)	NET INCOME ($ mil.)	NET PROFIT MARGIN	EMPLOYEES
12/05	908.7	166.3	18.3%	3,171
12/04	741.2	131.6	17.8%	2,656
12/03	588.6	126.9	21.6%	1,885
12/02	527.5	93.9	17.8%	1,670
12/01	591.6	105.3	17.8%	1,880
Annual Growth	11.3%	12.1%	—	14.0%

2005 Year-End Financials

Debt ratio: 2.6%
Return on equity: 15.6%
Cash ($ mil.): 502.9
Current ratio: 1.70
Long-term debt ($ mil.): 31.0
No. of shares (mil.): 176.6
Dividends
 Yield: —
 Payout: —
Market value ($ mil.): 5,073.9
R&D as % of sales: —
Advertising as % of sales: —

Stock History

NASDAQ (GS): CTXS

	STOCK PRICE ($) FY Close	P/E High/Low		PER SHARE ($) Earnings	Dividends	Book Value
12/05	28.73	32	22	0.93	—	6.81
12/04	24.46	35	20	0.75	—	5.43
12/03	21.16	38	14	0.74	—	4.30
12/02	12.32	48	9	0.52	—	3.66
12/01	22.66	69	31	0.54	—	3.50
Annual Growth	6.1%	—	—	14.6%	—	18.2%

Clayton Holdings

Clayton Holdings provides technology-based services to help lenders, investors, and other financial services firms manage their operations and risk. Clayton Holdings was formed in 2005 when TA Associates combined two of its portfolio companies, Clayton Fixed Income Services and Clayton Services, as subsidiaries operating under a single holding company.

Clayton Services offers operations support, loan and portfolio analysis, and consulting for lenders and capital markets firms, and it provides transaction management, compliance, and other

software. Clayton Fixed Income Services provides credit risk management services and risk-filtering technologies for the fixed-income securities market.

Clayton Services founder Steve Lamando and Clayton Fixed Income Services (formerly The Murrayhill Company) founder Sue Ellis own minority stakes in Clayton Holdings.

EXECUTIVES

Chairman and CEO: Frank P. Filipps, age 58
President and COO: D. Keith Johnson
CFO: Frederick C. (Rick) Herbst, age 48, $167,308 pay
Senior Managing Director, Consulting Services: Bruce Legan
SVP, General Counsel, and Secretary: Steven L. Cohen, age 42, $295,769 pay
SVP, Marketing and Communications: Jonathan T. (Jon) McGrain
CIO: John P. Courtney
President, Staffing Services: Robert F. Bladek
Head of Sales and Business Development: Corey Owens
Auditors: Grant Thornton LLP

LOCATIONS

HQ: Clayton Holdings, Inc.
2 Corporate Dr., Shelton, CT 06484
Phone: 203-926-5600 **Fax:** 203-926-5750
Web: www.clayton.com

Clayton Holdings has offices in California, Connecticut, Florida, Indiana, Massachusetts, Oklahoma, and Texas.

COMPETITORS

Fidelity National Title Insurance
Fiserv
Genalytics
Misys
Sigma Analytics & Consulting

HISTORICAL FINANCIALS

Company Type: Public

Income Statement

	REVENUE ($ mil.)	NET INCOME ($ mil.)	NET PROFIT MARGIN	EMPLOYEES
12/05	207.5	5.1	2.5%	2,354
12/04	156.1	16.7	10.7%	1,973
12/03	85.2	15.4	18.1%	—
12/02	52.1	10.1	19.4%	—
Annual Growth	58.5%	(20.4%)	—	19.3%

FYE: December 31

2005 Year-End Financials

Debt ratio: 1,186.4%   Current ratio: 2.84
Return on equity: 51.6%   Long-term debt ($ mil.): 148.8
Cash ($ mil.): 12.2

Net Income History NASDAQ (GM): CLAY

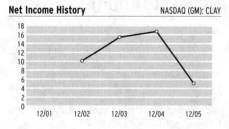

Clayton Williams Energy

Former Texas gubernatorial candidate Clayton Williams once devoted his energy to politics. Now he's devoted to the independent oil and gas firm that he founded. Clayton Williams Energy explores for oil and gas deposits in Louisiana, New Mexico, and Texas and exploits those resources. The company has proved reserves of 293.8 billion cu. ft. of natural gas equivalent. Most of those reserves are in the Permian Basin and in East Texas. It also operates 94 miles of gas pipeline and processing plants in Texas and Mississippi. Williams is CEO and controls the firm. In 2004 and 2005 Clayton Williams Energy boosted its reserves with the acquisition of Southwest Royalties and a property in Ward County.

Clayton Williams Energy has stakes in more than 6,600 gross (about 900 net) producing oil and gas wells. It also holds leasehold interests in approximately 1.2 million gross (788,000 net) undeveloped acres.

EXECUTIVES

Chairman, President, and CEO: Clayton W. Williams, age 74, $538,125 pay
EVP, COO, and Director: L. Paul Latham, age 54, $437,159 pay
SVP, Finance, CFO, Secretary, Treasurer, and Director: Mel G. Riggs, age 51, $393,267 pay
VP and General Counsel: T. Mark Tisdale, age 49, $144,208 pay
VP Accounting: Michael L. Pollard, age 56, $257,089 pay
VP Acquisitions and New Ventures: Patrick C. Reesby, age 53, $185,618 pay
VP Gas Gathering and Marketing: Robert C. Lyon, age 69
Director Investor Relations: Patti Hollums
Director Human Resources: LuAnn Bolding
Auditors: KPMG LLP

LOCATIONS

HQ: Clayton Williams Energy, Inc.
6 Desta Dr., Ste. 3000, Midland, TX 79705
Phone: 432-682-6324 **Fax:** 432-682-1452
Web: www.claytonwilliams.com

Clayton Williams Energy has oil and gas assets in Louisiana, Mississippi, New Mexico, and Texas.

PRODUCTS/OPERATIONS

2005 Sales

	$ mil.	% of total
Oil & gas	252.6	89
Gain on sales of property & equipment	18.9	7
Natural gas services	12.1	4
Total	**283.6**	**100**

COMPETITORS

Anadarko Petroleum
Chevron
EOG
Exxon Mobil
Pioneer Natural Resources
XTO Energy

HISTORICAL FINANCIALS

Company Type: Public

Income Statement

	REVENUE ($ mil.)	NET INCOME ($ mil.)	NET PROFIT MARGIN	EMPLOYEES
12/05	283.6	0.3	0.1%	174
12/04	206.3	(14.0)	—	173
12/03	172.0	22.9	13.3%	112
12/02	91.9	(4.0)	—	116
12/01	115.0	(5.3)	—	101
Annual Growth	25.3%	—	—	14.6%

FYE: December 31

2005 Year-End Financials

Debt ratio: 237.3%   Dividends
Return on equity: 0.3%   Yield: —
Cash ($ mil.): 6.1   Payout: —
Current ratio: 0.71   Market value ($ mil.): 451.4
Long-term debt ($ mil.): 285.4 R&D as % of sales: —
No. of shares (mil.): 10.8   Advertising as % of sales: —

Stock History NASDAQ (GM): CWEI

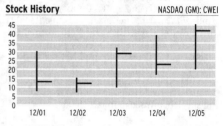

	STOCK PRICE ($) FY Close	P/E High/Low		PER SHARE ($) Earnings	Dividends	Book Value
12/05	41.74	2,248	1,031	0.02	—	11.12
12/04	22.90	—	—	(1.37)	—	10.90
12/03	28.93	13	4	2.40	—	10.76
12/02	12.14	—	—	(0.43)	—	7.41
12/01	13.10	—	—	(0.58)	—	8.90
Annual Growth	33.6%			—		5.7%

CNET Networks

Tune into this network and you can get the scoop on the latest and greatest technology and entertainment. CNET Networks provides information, product reviews, and price comparisons for the tech-savvy and not-so-tech-savvy through its flagship Web sites CNET.com and ZDnet. Its GameSpot site offers video game reviews and other game-related content, and it provides information on digital music through MP3.com. Other Web sites include Download.com (freeware and shareware software), News.com (technology and business news), and Webshots (online photo sharing). CNET also owns mySimon, a price comparison site for general consumer goods.

CNET gets most of its revenue through advertising sales on its Web sites, which draw in more than 100 million users each month. The company also licenses its product information content through its CNET Channel unit to such customers as Dow Jones, Microsoft's MSN, and The New York Times Company.

The company has been expanding its reach into new audience segments through its acquisitions of MP3.com (which it bought in 2003 from Vivendi's now-defunct VUNet USA unit) and

Webshots (acquired for $70 million in 2004). In 2005 it acquired TVTome (now TV.com), an audience-driven Web site featuring information about television shows, and Metacritic, which operates an entertainment review Web site. The following year, the company sold its *Computer Shopper* magazine and related Web site.

With renewed interest in online advertising, the company is hopeful that its online operations will begin to generate increasing amounts of revenue. It is also finding new markets for licensing its technology product information: In 2005 it inked a deal with sports Web site ESPN.com to provide information for its ESPN Tech Gear Guide. In addition, CNET is reaching into new geographic markets, such as China, through acquisitions and partnerships. (International business accounts for about 20% of the company's sales.)

CNET is expanding into television. The company has announced plans to begin offering original content adapted from its Web sites as video-on-demand programming through deals with companies such as Cox Communications, TiVo, and TVN Entertainment.

Former chairman and CEO Shelby Bonnie resigned in 2006 as a result of an internal probe that found deficiencies in the way company stock options were granted.

HISTORY

Halsey Minor, a veteran of executive search firm Russell Reynolds, launched CNET in 1992 with a goal of bringing technology information to the masses. After Microsoft co-founder Paul Allen chimed in with an $11 million investment, the company's first TV series, *CNET Central,* debuted in 1995. Its first Web site, CNET.com, premiered shortly thereafter.

The company went public in 1996, and by the end of that year, its portfolio had grown to include six Web sites and five television programs. CNET developed Internet portal Snap.com in 1997. Investors initially cast a skeptical eye, but when the company sold 60% of the portal to NBC the following year, Snap's cachet grew.

CNET unveiled Shopper.com, a comparison shopping service for technology products, in 1998. The following year, the company embarked on a series of acquisitions that further elevated its profile. CNET's purchases that year included NetVentures (operates the online store creator ShopBuilder), AuctionGate Interactive (online computer auction service), KillerApp (online comparison shopping service), and Nordby (financial information).

In the midst of its 1999 acquisition spree, the company inked a deal with America Online (now part of Time Warner) to become AOL's exclusive provider of computer buying guides. CNET and NBC also folded Snap.com into NBC's Web venture, NBC Internet (CNET later sold its 11% of the company to NBC). In an effort to make the CNET brand a household name, the company initiated a $100 million marketing campaign later that year, switching to a new set of ads mid-campaign when the first series (one ad featured a visit to a proctologist) proved a little *too* irreverent.

The company inked a deal with radio station owner AMFM (which later merged with Clear Channel) in 2000 and launched a high-technology radio format called CNET Radio. Allen sold his stake after buying rival computing

cable channel ZDTV. The company also changed its name to CNET Networks to reflect its growing number of non-technology related acquisitions. Minor handed off the mantle of CEO to Harvard graduate and CNET vice chairman Shelby Bonnie in early 2000. (Bonnie later replaced Minor as chairman of the company as well.) Later that year the company inked a $1.6 billion deal to purchase rival Ziff-Davis and its online tracking stock, ZDNet, a leading operator of Web sites about high technology.

In 2001 CNET relinquished about a dozen Web addresses for technology publications to Ziff Davis Media, a company that bought the magazine division of Ziff-Davis. The following year the company announced cost cutting plans (such as reducing its workforce and reorganizing its business categories) in an effort to become profitable. In 2003 CNET purchased MP3.com from Vivendi's VUNnet USA unit and the following year it acquired online photo sharing Web site Webshots for about $70 million.

Bonnie resigned in 2006 after the company found he had received improperly priced stock options. Neil Ashe was named CEO.

EXECUTIVES

Chairman: Jarl Mohn, age 54
CEO and Director: Neil M. Ashe, age 38
CFO: George E. Mazzotta, age 45, $410,307 pay (partial-year salary)
EVP and Chief Marketing Officer:
 Joseph (Joe) Gillespie, age 45, $613,000 pay
SVP, Finance and Chief Accounting Officer:
 David C. Bernstein, age 44
SVP, Business: Ted Smith
SVP, Community: Martin Green
SVP, Network: Sam Parker
SVP, Strategy and Development: Zander Lurie
VP, Corporate Communications: Martha Papalia
VP, International Advertising Sales: Michael C. Bird
President, CNET Channel: Greg Mason
President, International Media: Adam Power
SVP, CNET.com: Candice Meyers
SVP, Games & Entertainment: George V. (Vince) Broady
SVP, Shopping Services and Advice:
 Thomas (Tom) Jones
SVP, ZDNet.com: Dan Farber
SVP and Editor-in-Chief, News.com: Jai Singh
Director of Investor Relations: Cammeron McLaughlin
Auditors: KPMG LLP

LOCATIONS

HQ: CNET Networks, Inc.
 235 Second St., San Francisco, CA 94105
Phone: 415-344-2000   **Fax:** 415-395-9207
Web: www.cnetnetworks.com

2005 Sales

	$ mil.	% of total
US	287.2	81
International	65.8	19
Total	**353.0**	**100**

PRODUCTS/OPERATIONS

2005 Sales

	$ mil.	% of total
Interactive		
Marketing services	283.7	80
Licensing, fees & users	40.4	11
Publishing	28.9	9
Total	**353.0**	**100**

Selected Web Sites

BNET (executive business information)
Builder.com (Web site developers)
CNET (product reviews)
Download.com (software downloads)
GameSpot (video game reviews)
Metacritic (movie reviews)
MP3.com (music reviews and online music content)
mySimon (comparison shopping)
News.com (technology related news)
Release 1.0 (information technology industry news and information)
Search.com (metasearch engine)
TechRepublic (information technology professionals)
TV.com (television show information)
Webshots (online photo sharing)
ZDnet (business technology reviews)

Other Selected Operations

CNET Channel (product information distribution)

COMPETITORS

101communications	NYTimes.com
About	O'Reilly Media
Amazon.com	OSTG
AOL	PriceGrabber.com
BusinessWeek	Red Herring
CMP Media	Shopping.com
Dice	Shopzilla
eBay	TechTarget
Forbes	Time
Future Network USA	Tucows
Google	UGO Networks
IGN Entertainment	Wall Street Journal Online
International Data Group	Yahoo!
Jupitermedia	Ziff Davis Media
MSN	

HISTORICAL FINANCIALS

Company Type: Public

Income Statement

	REVENUE ($ mil.)	NET INCOME ($ mil.)	NET PROFIT MARGIN	EMPLOYEES
			FYE: December 31	
12/05	353.0	27.7	7.8%	2,340
12/04	291.2	11.7	4.0%	2,080
12/03	246.2	(26.3)	—	1,700
12/02	237.0	(360.6)	—	1,800
12/01	285.8	(1,989.5)	—	2,000
Annual Growth	**5.4%**	**—**	**—**	**4.0%**

2005 Year-End Financials

Debt ratio: 54.9%	Dividends
Return on equity: 12.4%	Yield: —
Cash ($ mil.): 97.5	Payout: —
Current ratio: 3.17	Market value ($ mil.): 2,206.4
Long-term debt ($ mil.): 139.1	R&D as % of sales: —
No. of shares (mil.): 150.2	Advertising as % of sales: 4.9%

Stock History

NASDAQ (GS): CNET

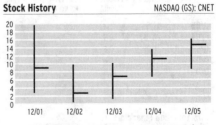

	STOCK PRICE ($) FY Close	P/E High/Low		Earnings	PER SHARE ($) Dividends	Book Value
12/05	14.69	89	49	0.18	—	1.69
12/04	11.23	168	86	0.08	—	1.34
12/03	6.82	—	—	(0.19)	—	1.20
12/02	2.71	—	—	(2.60)	—	1.34
12/01	8.97	—	—	(14.52)	—	3.92
Annual Growth	**13.1%**			**—**	**—**	**(19.0%)**

Coffee Holding Co.

Coffee Holding Co. has brewed up the idea of selling a wide spectrum of raw and roasted Arabica coffee beans to wholesalers like Green Mountain Roasters and private label coffees to supermarkets such as Nash Finch. Coffee Holding imports its beans from Indonesia, Mexico, and South America through several dealers. In addition to producing private-label coffees for stores, the company also sells name brands. Cafe Caribe, an espresso coffee, is targeted to the Hispanic market. The company has expanded operations in the western US through Premier Roasters. CEO Andrew Gordon, son of company founder Sterling Gordon, and the Gordon family own about 60% of the company.

EXECUTIVES

President, CEO, Treasurer, and Director:
Andrew Gordon, age 44, $290,172 pay
EVP, Operations, Secretary, and Director:
David Gordon, age 41, $284,073 pay
Director of Specialty Coffee: Karen Gordon
Auditors: Lazar Levine & Felix LLP

LOCATIONS

HQ: Coffee Holding Co., Inc.
4401 1st Ave., Ste. 1507, Brooklyn, NY 11232
Phone: 718-832-0800   **Fax:** 718-832-0892
Web: www.coffeeholding.com

PRODUCTS/OPERATIONS

Selected Brands
Cafe Caribe
Cafe Supremo
Don Manuel
Fifth Avenue
S&W (license)
Via Roma

COMPETITORS

Kraft Foods
Kroger
Procter & Gamble
Sara Lee Food & Beverage

HISTORICAL FINANCIALS

Company Type: Public

Income Statement

	REVENUE ($ mil.)	NET INCOME ($ mil.)	NET PROFIT MARGIN	EMPLOYEES
10/05	41.5	1.2	2.9%	74
10/04	28.0	0.9	3.2%	62
10/03	20.2	0.6	3.0%	—
10/02	17.4	0.8	4.6%	33
10/01	20.3	0.5	2.5%	27
Annual Growth	19.6%	24.5%	—	28.7%

2005 Year-End Financials

Debt ratio: —
Return on equity: 17.6%
Cash ($ mil.): 0.7
Current ratio: 2.45
Long-term debt ($ mil.): —
No. of shares (mil.): 5.5
Dividends
Yield: —
Payout: —
Market value ($ mil.): 35.9
R&D as % of sales: —
Advertising as % of sales: 0.4%

FYE: October 31

Stock History   AMEX: JVA

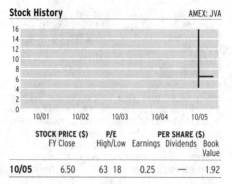

	STOCK PRICE ($) FY Close	P/E High/Low	PER SHARE ($) Earnings	Dividends	Book Value
10/05	6.50	63 18	0.25	—	1.92

Cogent

Cogent knows the power of good security. The company provides Automated Fingerprint Identification Systems that governments, law enforcement agencies, and other organizations use to capture, analyze, and compare fingerprints. Cogent's offerings include proprietary fingerprint biometrics software, hardware, and professional services such as consulting, implementation, and systems integration. The company's customers include the US Department of Homeland Security and the National Electoral Council of Venezuela, each of which accounts for more than 30% of sales. Chairman, president, and CEO Ming Hsieh controls 54% of the company, which was founded in 1990.

Cogent's contract for the Electoral Council of Venezuela includes capturing voters' fingerprints, creating a database, and matching the fingerprints to authenticate voters' identities and prevent duplicate registration for the country's state and county elections.

EXECUTIVES

Chairman, President, and CEO: Ming Hsieh, age 49, $317,718 pay
CFO: Paul Kim, age 39, $264,300 pay
EVP Federal and State Systems: James Jasinski, age 55, $241,325 pay
EVP Operations: Michael Hollowich, age 57, $230,536 pay
VP Commercial Systems: Bruno Lassus
VP International: Wally Briefs
VP Systems Integration: Jian (James) Xie, age 38
Auditors: Deloitte & Touche LLP

LOCATIONS

HQ: Cogent, Inc.
209 Fair Oaks Ave., South Pasadena, CA 91030
Phone: 626-799-8090   **Fax:** 626-799-8996
Web: www.cogentsystems.com

Cogent has offices in Austria, Taiwan, the UK, and the US.

2005 Sales

	$ mil.	% of total
Americas	149.7	93
Asia	4.2	3
Europe	3.5	2
Other regions	2.5	2
Total	**159.9**	**100**

PRODUCTS/OPERATIONS

2005 Sales

	$ mil.	% of total
Products	141.7	77
Maintenance & services	18.2	23
Total	**159.9**	**100**

COMPETITORS

Bioscrypt
L-1 Identity Solutions
NEC
Northrop Grumman
SAFRAN

HISTORICAL FINANCIALS

Company Type: Public

Income Statement

FYE: December 31

	REVENUE ($ mil.)	NET INCOME ($ mil.)	NET PROFIT MARGIN	EMPLOYEES
12/05	159.9	65.3	40.8%	164
12/04	87.7	42.6	48.6%	137
12/03	32.2	9.2	28.6%	—
12/02	16.4	2.3	14.0%	—
Annual Growth	113.6%	205.1%	—	19.7%

2005 Year-End Financials

Debt ratio: —
Return on equity: 19.2%
Cash ($ mil.): 301.2
Current ratio: 9.17
Long-term debt ($ mil.): —
No. of shares (mil.): 94.0
Dividends
Yield: —
Payout: —
Market value ($ mil.): 2,132.2
R&D as % of sales: 4.5%
Advertising as % of sales: —

Stock History   NASDAQ (GS): COGT

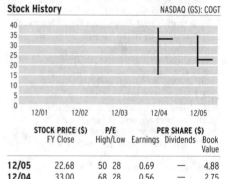

	STOCK PRICE ($) FY Close	P/E High/Low	PER SHARE ($) Earnings	Dividends	Book Value
12/05	22.68	50 28	0.69	—	4.88
12/04	33.00	68 28	0.56	—	2.75
Annual Growth	(31.3%)	— —	23.2%	—	77.5%

Cognex

Cognex machines see what mere mortals cannot. The company is one of the world's largest producers of systems that, linked to a video camera, serve as eyes where human vision is insufficient. Semiconductor, consumer goods, health care, and automotive companies, among others, use the company's machine vision systems to position and identify products, gauge sizes, and locate defects. Customers include manufacturers such as Ford Motor, Palomar Technologies, and Inex Vision Systems. Cognex also offers consulting and educational services, as well as technical support for its products. In 2005 Cognex bought DVT Corp. for $104 million in cash; DVT makes vision sensors used on factory floors.

Cognex sells primarily to semiconductor and electronics manufacturers in Europe, Japan, and North America. The company has reduced its dependence on the highly cyclical semiconductor and electronics industries, which now account for about 27% of sales, down from 61% in 2000. Sales to customers located outside the US account for more than 60% of sales. Cognex is expanding its presence in Asia by opening an office in China.

While original equipment manufacturers account for the majority of the company's sales, Cognex intends to attract more end-user customers by developing and acquiring products that meet their needs. Despite attempts to diversify beyond its chip maker base, the company has acquired the wafer identification business of Siemens Logistics and Assembly Systems (formerly Siemens Dematic), expanding its presence in Europe. However, Cognex has also acquired the industrial parts identification business of Gavitec AG, further expanding both its geographic and market reach.

Cognex has acquired AssistWare Technology, a developer of lane departure warning systems. AssistWare's SafeTRAC system combines a small video camera, a digital signal processor, and machine-vision software into a box about the size of a radar detector. SafeTRAC warns drivers when they are crossing into another lane on the roadway or drifting off the road.

Co-founder and CEO Robert Shillman owns about 8% of the company. Shillman, known as "Dr. Bob" to his employees (who are officially designated as "Cognoids"), is famous for wearing elaborate costumes to the company's annual Halloween celebration and even to meetings with customers and the board of directors. Shillman and other senior executives encourage Cognoids to incorporate fun into both the workday and their spare time by allowing them to play "Ultimate Frisbee" outside the corporate headquarters at lunchtime and by hosting family events, such as going to the circus and putting on a winter carnival for children.

Wellington Management owns more than 8% of Cognex. The Hartford Series Fund and Royce & Associates each hold about 5%.

HISTORY

Robert Shillman and two MIT colleagues, Marilyn Matz and William Silver, started Cognex (short for "cognition experts") in 1981 to create vision replacement machines for factories. Competition and inadequate technology forced the firm to reevaluate its distribution strategy in 1986. Cognex began supplying machine vision technology to original equipment manufacturers. The company introduced the first custom vision chip in 1988 and went public the next year.

Cognex found success where human vision fails — in the high-speed, detailed, repetitive processes required in making semiconductors. The company expanded by purchasing Acumen, a developer of machine vision systems for semiconductor wafer identification (1995); Isys Controls, a maker of quality control systems (1996); and Mayan Automation, a maker of surface inspection systems (1997).

Low demand for semiconductor and PC board manufacturing equipment in Asia hurt sales in 1998. (Semiconductor manufacturers account for most of Cognex's sales.) Nonetheless, the company boosted R&D by 10% and acquired some of Rockwell Automation's machine vision operations, also becoming the preferred global supplier

to Rockwell's plants. Orders picked up in early 1999 and Cognex invested $1 million in upstart Avalon Imaging (machine vision for the plastics industry), its first investment in such a company.

In 2000 Cognex acquired Komatsu Ltd.'s machine vision business. The Komatsu unit is one of the largest machine vision system suppliers in Japan. Also that year the company acquired additional machine vision products by purchasing UK-based Image Industries. In early 2002 Cognex won an appeal in its ongoing patent lawsuit with Lemelson Medical, Education & Research Foundation. (The company legally prevailed over the Lemelson trust again in 2005.) In 2004 the company reached a legal settlement and licensing agreement with rival Electro Scientific Industries (ESI), with ESI paying a license fee to Cognex.

Cognex celebrated its 25th anniversary in early 2006 with a gala celebration at its corporate headquarters and in downtown Boston.

EXECUTIVES

Chairman: William A. Krivsky, age 76
CEO and Director: Robert J. (Bob) Shillman, age 59
President and COO; President, Modular Vision Systems Division: James F. (Jim) Hoffmaster, age 54, $480,406 pay
SVP and Director: Patrick A. Alias, age 60
SVP, Finance and Administration, CFO, and Treasurer: Richard A. Morin, age 56, $294,099 pay
SVP and General Manager, Surface Inspection Systems Division: Markku Jaaskelainen, age 50
SVP, ID Products: Justin Testa, age 58
SVP, Research and Development: E. John McGarry, age 49
SVP, PC Vision: Marilyn Matz, age 51
SVP and Senior Fellow: William M. (Bill) Silver, age 51
SVP, Vision Sensors: Kris Nelson, age 58
President, International Operations: Eric Ceyrolle, age 51
President, Cognex K.K.: Akira Nakamura, age 61
Director of Investor Relations: Susan Conway
Secretary: Anthony J. Medaglia Jr.
Corporate Communications Manager: Robin Pratt
Public Relations Manager: John Lewis
Auditors: Ernst & Young LLP

LOCATIONS

HQ: Cognex Corporation
1 Vision Dr., Natick, MA 01760
Phone: 508-650-3000   **Fax:** 508-650-3344
Web: www.cognex.com

Cognex has offices located in California, Illinois, Massachusetts, Michigan, and Tennessee, and in China, France, Germany, Ireland, Italy, Japan, the Netherlands, Singapore, South Korea, Sweden, Taiwan, and the UK.

2005 Sales

	$ mil.	% of total
US	80.5	37
Europe	63.4	29
Japan	60.3	28
Other regions	12.7	6
Total	**216.9**	**100**

PRODUCTS/OPERATIONS

2005 Sales

	$ mil.	% of total
Modular Vision Systems		
Products	168.3	78
Services	14.2	6
Surface Inspection Systems		
Products	24.5	11
Services	9.9	5
Total	**216.9**	**100**

2005 Sales

	$ mil.	% of total
Products	192.8	89
Services	24.1	11
Total	**216.9**	**100**

Selected Products

Ball Grid Array Inspection Package (solder ball inspection)
Checkpoint (software vision system)
DisplayInspect (LCD inspection software)
Fiducial Finder II (circuit board alignment detection)
In-Sight 2000 (low-cost machine vision system)
iS High Performance Inspection Systems (large-scale defect detection)
MVS Series (programmable vision system)
SmartView Imaging Camera Network (surface inspection system)
SmartView Modular Camera Network (surface inspection system)
Surface Mount Device Placement Guidance Package (circuit board inspection)
Vision Software Library (image processing and analysis software)
Wafer ID (semiconductor wafer identification)

COMPETITORS

Adept Technology	Image Sensing Systems
August Technology	Integral Vision
Camtek	KLA-Tencor
CyberOptics	National Instruments
Elbit Vision	Orbotech
Electro Scientific Industries	Perceptron
	PPT VISION
ICOS Vision Systems	RoboGroup T.E.K.

HISTORICAL FINANCIALS

Company Type: Public

Income Statement

FYE: December 31

	REVENUE ($ mil.)	NET INCOME ($ mil.)	NET PROFIT MARGIN	EMPLOYEES
12/05	216.9	35.7	16.5%	740
12/04	202.0	37.7	18.7%	662
12/03	150.1	15.9	10.6%	634
12/02	114.1	(6.0)	—	622
12/01	140.7	(11.1)	—	697
Annual Growth	**11.4%**			**1.5%**

2005 Year-End Financials

Debt ratio: —
Return on equity: 7.4%
Cash ($ mil.): 242.0
Current ratio: 5.63
Long-term debt ($ mil.): —
No. of shares (mil.): 47.2

Dividends
Yield: 1.1%
Payout: 43.2%
Market value ($ mil.): 1,419.4
R&D as % of sales: —
Advertising as % of sales: —

Stock History

NASDAQ (GS): CGNX

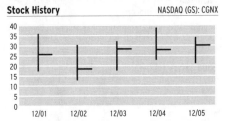

	STOCK PRICE ($) FY Close	P/E High/Low	PER SHARE ($) Earnings	Dividends	Book Value
12/05	30.09	46 29	0.74	0.32	10.74
12/04	27.90	48 29	0.80	0.28	10.03
12/03	28.29	88 50	0.36	0.12	8.76
12/02	18.43	— —	(0.14)	—	8.32
12/01	25.61	— —	(0.25)	—	8.61
Annual Growth	**4.1%**	**— —**	**—**	**63.3%**	**5.7%**

Cognizant Technology Solutions

Cognizant Technology Solutions (CTS) remains mindful of the state of your software. CTS provides application maintenance services, data warehousing, software development and integration, and reengineering services for legacy systems, primarily to medium-sized and large businesses. The majority of its sales are to customers in North America, including IMS Health, First Data, and ACNielsen. Most of the company's software development centers and employees are located in India, with others in the US. CTS serves clients in industries including financial services, health care, retail, and manufacturing.

Cognizant Technology Solutions began as an in-house technology center for Dun & Bradstreet in 1994 and was spun off from D&B in 1996. Cognizant gradually has decreased its dependence on D&B companies and affiliates.

The company has announced plans to expand through acquisitions. In 2006 it bought Massachusetts-based AimNet Solutions, a privately held provider of managed infrastructure and professional services. Its growth plans include further expansion in the US as well as in Europe and India.

EXECUTIVES

Chairman: John E. Klein, age 64
Vice Chairman: Lakshmi Narayanan, age 53
President, CEO, and Director: Francisco D'Souza, age 37
EVP, COO, CFO, Secretary, and Treasurer: Gordon J. Coburn, age 42
President and Managing Director, Global Delivery: Ramakrishnan (Chandra) Chandrasekaran, age 48
VP and Head, Onsite Insurance Practice: Michael E. Nemeth
VP, Business Technology Consulting Practice: Kaushik Bhaumik
VP, Corporate Development: John Raveret
VP, European Operations: Kim Rajah
VP, North American Sales and Business Development: Charles Keith Gallacher
Auditors: PricewaterhouseCoopers LLP

LOCATIONS

HQ: Cognizant Technology Solutions Corporation
500 Glenpointe Centre West, Teaneck, NJ 07666
Phone: 201-801-0233   **Fax:** 201-801-0243
Web: www.cognizant.com

Cognizant Technology Solutions has offices in Canada, China, Germany, India, Japan, Switzerland, the UK, and the US.

2005 Sales

	$ mil.	% of total
North America	772.8	87
Europe	103.7	12
Asia	9.3	1
Total	**885.8**	**100**

PRODUCTS/OPERATIONS

2005 Sales

	$ mil.	% of total
Financial services	441.0	50
Health care	176.1	20
Manufacturing, retail & logistics	152.5	17
Other	116.2	13
Total	**885.8**	**100**

Selected Services

Application development
Application management and maintenance
Reengineering
Systems integration

COMPETITORS

Accenture
Computer Sciences Corp.
EDS
IBM Global Services
Infosys
Perot Systems
Satyam
Tata Consultancy
Wipro

HISTORICAL FINANCIALS

Company Type: Public

Income Statement

FYE: December 31

	REVENUE ($ mil.)	NET INCOME ($ mil.)	NET PROFIT MARGIN	EMPLOYEES
12/05	885.8	166.3	18.8%	24,300
12/04	586.7	100.2	17.1%	15,300
12/03	368.2	57.4	15.6%	9,240
12/02	229.1	34.6	15.1%	6,165
12/01	177.8	22.2	12.5%	3,925
Annual Growth	**49.4%**	**65.4%**		**57.7%**

2005 Year-End Financials

Debt ratio: —
Return on equity: 28.5%
Cash ($ mil.): 424.0
Current ratio: 4.26
Long-term debt ($ mil.): —
No. of shares (mil.): 139.3

Dividends
  Yield: —
  Payout: —
Market value ($ mil.): 7,004.9
R&D as % of sales: —
Advertising as % of sales: —

Stock History

NASDAQ (GS): CTSH

	STOCK PRICE ($) FY Close	P/E High/Low		PER SHARE ($) Earnings	Dividends	Book Value
12/05	50.27	46	31	1.13	—	5.12
12/04	42.33	61	28	0.70	—	3.38
12/03	22.82	59	20	0.42	—	4.26
12/02	12.04	47	20	0.27	—	18.12
12/01	6.83	49	16	0.18	—	12.25
Annual Growth	**64.7%**	**—**	**—**	**58.3%**	**—**	**(19.6%)**

Cohen & Steers

Cohen & Steers wants to be in the REIT place at the REIT time. Cohen & Steers was formed to be the holding company for Cohen & Steers Capital Management, which focuses primarily on asset management and investment banking products and services relating to REITs (real estate investment trusts) and other real estate investments; it also invests in electric and gas utilities. Cohen & Steers has more than $20 billion in assets under management held in 17 real estate mutual funds, as well as in 46 separate accounts managed for institutional investors. Martin Cohen and Robert Steers founded the firm in 1986 and continue to share top billing; the two combined own about 70% of Cohen & Steers.

The company's investment banking services include mergers and acquisitions advisory; restructuring advisory; and capital raising. Investment banking customers are primarily businesses in the real estate industry or in other industries that are real estate-intensive, such as health care. Cohen & Steers broadened its geographic scope in 2004 with the acquisition of 50% of European real estate securities asset management firm Houlihan Rovers. The company also opened a Hong Kong office to research real estate investment securities in the Asia/Pacific region. It opened a London office in 2006. Founders Cohen and Steers cut their ownership stakes in the company from 50% each to around 35% each following the company's 2004 IPO.

EXECUTIVES

Co-Chairman and Co-CEO: Martin Cohen, age 57, $500,000 pay
Co-Chairman and Co-CEO: Robert H. Steers, age 53, $500,000 pay
President: Joseph M. Harvey, age 42, $1,165,000 pay
COO: Adam M. Derechin, age 41
EVP and CFO: Matthew S. (Matt) Stadler, age 51
EVP, Corporate Development: Douglas R. Bond, age 46
EVP and Chief Investment Officer: James S. Corl, age 39, $1,288,000 pay
EVP and Director of Marketing: John J. McCombe, age 45, $1,095,000 pay
EVP, General Counsel, and Secretary: Lawrence B. Stoller, age 42
SVP and Director of Institutional Marketing: Stephen (Steve) Dunn
SVP and Director, European Research: Leonard Geiger
VP, Finance and Chief Accounting Officer: Bernard M. Doucette, age 37
National Sales Manager: Kevin Crook
Auditors: Deloitte & Touche LLP

LOCATIONS

HQ: Cohen & Steers, Inc.
280 Park Ave., New York, NY 10017
Phone: 212-832-3232   **Fax:** 212-832-3622
Web: www.cohenandsteers.com

PRODUCTS/OPERATIONS

2005 Sales

	$ mil.	% of total
Investment & advisory fees		
Closed-end mutual funds	61.0	40
Open-end mutual funds	42.1	27
Institutional separate accounts	16.1	11
Distribution & service fee revenue	12.0	8
Investment banking fees	11.8	8
Portfolio consulting & other	3.2	4
Total	**146.2**	**100**

2005 Assets Under Management

	% of total
Closed-end mutual funds	47
Open-end mutual funds	27
Institutional separate accounts	26
Total	**100**

Selected Subsidiaries and Affiliates

Cohen & Steers Asia Limited
Cohen & Steers Capital Advisors, L.L.C.
Cohen & Steers Capital Management, Inc.
Cohen & Steers Securities, LLC

COMPETITORS

AllianceBernstein
Bear Stearns Asset Management
Greenhill
Janus Capital
John Hancock Financial Services
Ladenburg Thalmann
Mellon Financial
Merrill Lynch
MFS
Nuveen
Phoenix Companies
Principal Financial
Schonbraun McCann Group
State Street
T. Rowe Price
The Vanguard Group
Ziegler

HISTORICAL FINANCIALS

Company Type: Public

Income Statement

FYE: December 31

	ASSETS ($ mil.)	NET INCOME ($ mil.)	INCOME AS % OF ASSETS	EMPLOYEES
12/05	198.6	31.9	16.1%	117
12/04	160.3	7.3	4.6%	78
12/03	34.5	12.1	35.1%	—
12/02	24.4	8.4	34.4%	—
Annual Growth	101.2%	48.3%	—	50.0%

2005 Year-End Financials

Equity as % of assets: 82.9%
Return on assets: 17.8%
Return on equity: 20.6%
Long-term debt ($ mil.): —
No. of shares (mil.): 35.4
Market value ($ mil.): 660.0

Dividends
Yield: 2.3%
Payout: 53.2%
Sales ($ mil.): 146.2
R&D as % of sales: —
Advertising as % of sales: —

Stock History

NYSE: CNS

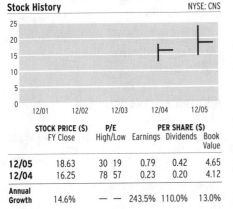

	STOCK PRICE ($) FY Close	P/E High/Low		PER SHARE ($) Earnings	Dividends	Book Value
12/05	18.63	30	19	0.79	0.42	4.65
12/04	16.25	78	57	0.23	0.20	4.12
Annual Growth	14.6%	—	—	243.5%	110.0%	13.0%

Cohu

Cohu tries to blend various technologies into one coherent business. Of the company's three segments, the largest is Delta Design, a top maker of the test handling equipment that protects semiconductors during testing procedures. The company's customers include chip giants Intel (43% of sales), Advanced Micro Devices (12%), and Texas Instruments (8%). Other operations include Cohu Electronics (closed-circuit television systems for surveillance, medical, and industrial applications) and Broadcast Microwave Services (microwave radios, antenna systems, and support equipment).

The company derives more than 70% of sales from customers outside the US.

Delta Design accounts for about four-fifths of Cohu's sales; the company's other operations help cushion its dependence on the notoriously volatile semiconductor industry. (Cohu nonetheless consolidated some facilities during the dismal chip industry slump of 2001-2003.)

Cohu has sold the assets of its Fisher Research Laboratory (metal and leak detectors for industry and hobbyists) subsidiary, also known as FRL, to First Texas Holdings for about $3 million in cash. The unprofitable business accounted for around 3% of Cohu's sales. First Texas Holdings is the parent firm of First Texas Products, which makes the Bounty Hunter line of metal detectors.

Nicholas Cedrone, former owner of Daymarc (which Cohu bought in 1994), owns nearly 6% of Cohu.

HISTORY

Kalbfell Laboratories was incorporated in 1947, an outgrowth of a research and development partnership founded in 1945. The company originally made electronic devices for government agencies. It shifted emphasis to power supply units in 1952 and a year later expanded into closed-circuit television (CCTV) equipment. The company was renamed Kay Lab in 1954 and Cohu Electronics (after chairman La Motte Cohu) in 1957. It became Cohu, Inc. in 1972.

During the 1980s, CEO James Barnes directed Cohu's entry into semiconductor test handling equipment. Cohu acquired microwave equipment maker Broadcast Microwave Services in 1984.

Chip handling gear became Cohu's primary business during the chip boom of the early 1990s. The company established its Singapore subsidiary in 1993. The next year it acquired Daymarc, a maker of gravity-feed semiconductor handling equipment, to complement its Delta Design pick-and-place machines.

Company insider Charles Schwan replaced the retiring Barnes in 1996. Sales fell in 1998, the result of a prolonged downturn in the semiconductor industry, but then surged in 1999 as the chip industry entered a record boom.

In early 2000 Cohu merged Delta Design and Daymarc to create its Delta Design test handler subsidiary. Later that spring Schwan announced that he would retire as CEO in June (he remains chairman); president and COO James Donahue became CEO.

In 2001 Cohu acquired the automated systems business of Schlumberger's Semiconductor Solutions division to shore up its own chip testing

capabilities. During a brutal chip industry slump that lasted from 2001 to 2003, Cohu consolidated some facilities to control its costs.

After consolidating facilities in the US, Delta Design in 2004 opened a facility for equipment assembly and spare-parts supply in the Philippines, near Manila.

In 2005 Delta Design received a supplier award from Intel, a rare distinction from the world's largest chip maker, which generally doesn't reveal its suppliers of semiconductor equipment and materials. It was the second time Delta Design has received Intel's highest award for suppliers.

EXECUTIVES

Chairman: Charles A. Schwan, age 66
President, CEO, and Director: James A. Donahue, age 57
VP, Finance, CFO, and Secretary: John H. Allen, age 54
President, Broadcast Microwave Services: Graham Bunney, age 50
President, Fisher Research Laboratory: John J. Chernekoff Jr., age 43
President, Cohu Electronics Division: Brian Leedy, age 41
Auditors: Ernst & Young LLP

LOCATIONS

HQ: Cohu, Inc.
   12367 Crosthwaite Cir., Poway, CA 92064
Phone: 858-848-8100   **Fax:** 858-848-8185
Web: www.cohu.com

Cohu has operations in the Philippines, Singapore, Taiwan, and the US.

2005 Sales

	$ mil.	% of total
US	58.8	25
Singapore	42.7	18
Malaysia	40.5	17
Philippines	26.9	11
Costa Rica	21.7	9
China	15.4	6
Other countries	32.9	14
Total	**238.9**	**100**

PRODUCTS/OPERATIONS

2005 Sales

	$ mil.	% of total
Semiconductor equipment	200.8	84
Television cameras	17.8	8
Microwave communications	12.8	5
Metal detection	7.5	3
Total	**238.9**	**100**

Operations and Selected Products

Delta Design (semiconductor test handling equipment)
   Automated test handlers
   Burn-in board loaders and unloaders
   Device kits
   Docking interfaces
   Environmental chambers
Cohu Electronics (closed-circuit television systems)
   Cameras
   Control systems
   Design services
   Software
Broadcast Microwave Services (microwave communications equipment)
   Antenna systems
   Microwave radio equipment

HISTORICAL FINANCIALS

Company Type: Public

Income Statement

FYE: December 31

	REVENUE ($ mil.)	NET INCOME ($ mil.)	NET PROFIT MARGIN	EMPLOYEES
12/05	238.9	34.0	14.2%	1,000
12/04	176.2	16.7	9.5%	900
12/03	138.6	(0.1)	—	800
12/02	134.7	(0.9)	—	840
12/01	126.6	(6.5)	—	930
Annual Growth	17.2%	—	—	1.8%

2005 Year-End Financials

Debt ratio: —
Return on equity: 14.8%
Cash ($ mil.): 138.9
Current ratio: 5.10
Long-term debt ($ mil.): —
No. of shares (mil.): 22.4

Dividends
  Yield: 1.0%
  Payout: 14.7%
Market value ($ mil.): 511.8
R&D as % of sales: 12.5%
Advertising as % of sales: —

Stock History

NASDAQ (GS): COHU

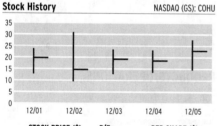

	STOCK PRICE ($) FY Close	P/E High/Low		PER SHARE ($) Earnings	Dividends	Book Value
12/05	22.87	18	10	1.50	0.22	11.18
12/04	18.56	30	18	0.76	0.20	9.63
12/03	19.19	—	—	—	0.20	8.99
12/02	14.70	—	—	(0.04)	0.20	9.11
12/01	19.75	—	—	(0.32)	0.20	9.27
Annual Growth	3.7%			—	2.4%	4.8%

Coinstar

Coinstar takes the contents of your penny jar and turns it into real money. The company owns and operates nearly 13,000 coin-counting machines in the US, Canada, and the UK, and 320,000 entertainment services (skill-crane, bulk vending, and kiddie ride) machines across the US and Mexico. Additionally, Coinstar utilizes more than 19,300 point-of-sale terminals and owns and operates approximately 360 stand-alone e-payment kiosks in the US and the UK. The coin-counting units are located primarily in supermarkets (such as Kroger and Albertsons); the entertainment services machines can be found in more than 33,000 retail locations including Wal-Mart and Kmart stores.

Coinstar's machines charge transaction fees (of which retail partners receive a portion) and transmit information to the company daily, reducing downtime by alerting field service staff when collection or maintenance is necessary. In 2005 consumers processed more than $2.3 billion worth of coins through the company's coin-counting machines.

Coinstar has transitioned from a one-product company — offering just coin-counting services — to a business with a variety of products and services through several key acquisitions. Its most recent service will allow customers to change their coins for retailer gift cards or eCertificates, a move that will cheer anyone who has ever stood in line behind someone counting out exact change. Its first partner is retailer Eddie Bauer.

In a move designed to provide greater access to drugstore customers, Coinstar bought Chicago-based CellCards of Illinois in May 2004. CellCards offers a set of prepaid products, including wireless, long-distance, and MasterCard cards, in addition to bill payment capabilities for public services such as utilities. Later that year Coinstar acquired ACMI Holdings and its two subsidiaries, American Coin Merchandising and Wellspring Capital Management, for $235 million in cash. ACMI Holdings, operating as SugarLoaf Creations, owns and operates coin-operated amusement vending equipment such as plush toy "grabbers," kiddie rides, and video games.

In March 2005 Coinstar acquired Mundo Communications Network (dba El Toro Prepaid), adding retail accounts and additional pay-as-you-go products to its e-payment services. Later in 2005 it acquired Amusement Factory. One of the largest operators of entertainment services in the US, Van Nuys, California-based Amusement Factory has skill crane machines, bulk vending, and kiddie rides in more than 14,000 mass merchants, supermarkets, restaurants, entertainment centers, and dollar stores across the nation.

In November it acquired a nearly 50% interest in McDonald's Corporation subsidiary Redbox Automated Retail, a leading renter of DVDs through self-service kiosks with about 800 locations in the US, including McDonald's restaurants. Additionally, the company made a strategic investment in Video Vending New York (dba DVDXpress) which is also in the self-service DVD kiosk business.

Continuing its investment streak, Coinstar bought Travelex Holdings' Travelex Money Transfer business for $27 million in cash (presumably not in change). Travelex Money Transfer operates in nearly 140 countries.

HISTORICAL FINANCIALS

Company Type: Public

Income Statement

FYE: December 31

	REVENUE ($ mil.)	NET INCOME ($ mil.)	NET PROFIT MARGIN	EMPLOYEES
12/05	459.7	22.3	4.9%	2,000
12/04	307.1	20.4	6.6%	1,694
12/03	176.1	19.6	11.1%	429
12/02	155.7	58.5	37.6%	557
12/01	129.4	(7.4)	—	521
Annual Growth	37.3%	—	—	40.0%

2005 Year-End Financials

Debt ratio: 70.3%
Return on equity: 8.6%
Cash ($ mil.): 175.3
Current ratio: 1.71
Long-term debt ($ mil.): 206.6
No. of shares (mil.): 27.8

Dividends
  Yield: —
  Payout: —
Market value ($ mil.): 634.1
R&D as % of sales: 1.2%
Advertising as % of sales: —

Stock History

NASDAQ (GS): CSTR

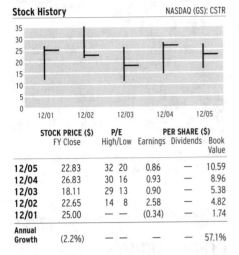

	STOCK PRICE ($) FY Close	P/E High/Low		PER SHARE ($) Earnings	Dividends	Book Value
12/05	22.83	32	20	0.86	—	10.59
12/04	26.83	30	16	0.93	—	8.96
12/03	18.11	29	13	0.90	—	5.38
12/02	22.65	14	8	2.58	—	4.82
12/01	25.00	—	—	(0.34)	—	1.74
Annual Growth	(2.2%)	—	—	—	—	57.1%

Coldwater Creek

Shoppers quench their thirst for classic, casual clothing from Coldwater Creek's stores and catalogs. The upscale multi-channel retailer sells mostly traditional apparel through several catalogs, a Web site, some 175 full-line retail stores, and about 20 outlets, targeting middle- and upper-income baby boomers. *Northcountry*, the company's main catalog, features women's apparel, jewelry, and art. *Spirit* offers more upscale women's apparel and jewelry, while its *Sport* catalog (introduced in 2004) features casual women's activewear; all apparel catalogs include plus-sizes. Co-founders Dennis and Ann Pence own about 35% of Coldwater Creek.

Almost 60% of sales now come from Coldwater Creek's nearly 200 retail stores. The company opened 60 stores in 2005 and planned to open another 65 in 2006. Ultimately, the company hopes to grow its store count to as many as 500 outlets.

The company is testing a new concept called Coldwater Creek — The Spa. The first spa location has opened and five more were planned for the first half of 2006. Averaging 5,000 sq. ft., the spas offer facials, massages, manicures, pedicures, and a line of women's clothing and personal care products.

Coldwater Creek mails more than 100 million catalogs a year. In early 2004 the company combined its two smaller catalogs, *Spirit* and *Elements*, and re-introduced the combined catalog under the *Spirit* title. A holiday catalog, *Gifts-to-Go*, comes out at the end-of-the year shopping season. The company phased out its *Home* catalog in 2002 and incorporated its housewares into other merchandise lines. All shipping is done through its Mineral Wells, West Virginia facility.

HISTORY

Dennis Pence, a marketing executive at Sony Corp. of America, and his wife, Ann, an advertising copy director for Macy's, fled big-city life in 1983, starting Coldwater Creek in their Sandpoint, Idaho apartment. The fledgling retailer sold Indian jewelry, binoculars, birdfeeders, and other items through flyers and ads in such magazines as *Smithsonian* and *Audubon*. The Pences mailed 55,000 copies of their first catalog, *Northcountry*, in 1985. Nearly broke, they gambled and mailed 90,000 the next year, banking on Christmas sales. The gamble paid off with $140,000 in orders. *Northcountry* remains the company's biggest-selling catalog.

Coldwater Creek began publishing its *Spirit of the West* catalog, featuring women's clothing and accessories, in 1993. In 1996 the company added *Milepost Four*, featuring men's clothing and accessories (it was sold in 1999). Also in 1996 Coldwater Creek began offering its own line of private-label apparel. The next year it went public and added its Bed & Bath catalog (renamed *Home* in 1999).

The company grew from less than 400,000 active customers in 1993 to more than 1.6 million (about 70% of whom lived in the eastern US) by 1998. To accommodate the growth, Coldwater Creek added a distribution center in Parkersburg, West Virginia in 1998 and opened two new full-line stores in Seattle and Kansas City in 1999.

In 2000 Dennis Pence stepped aside as CEO and promoted catalog and retail sales division president (and Spiegel catalog veteran) Georgia Shonk-Simmons to the top post. In March 2002 Coldwater Creek closed its Idaho distribution center and laid off 150 employees. In September Pence reassumed the CEO position and Shonk-Simmons was named chief merchandising officer.

In 2002 Coldwater Creek phased out its *Home* catalog. In 2004 it debuted the *Sport* catalog, as well as combining its two smaller catalogs, *Spirit* and *Elements*. The company re-introduced the combined catalog under the *Spirit* title.

Vice chairman and co-founder of the company, Ann Pence, resigned from the board in 2004 following her divorce from chairman and CEO Dennis in 2003.

Over the past several years the company has transformed itself from a direct marketer to a multi-channel retailer by opening retail stores, with nearly 200 stores contributing 58% of revenue in fiscal 2006.

EXECUTIVES

Chairman, CEO, and Secretary: Dennis C. Pence, age 56, $1,837,066 pay
President, Chief Merchandising Officer, and Director: Georgia Shonk-Simmons, age 54, $2,301,455 pay
EVP and CFO: Melvin (Mel) Dick, age 52, $649,997 pay
EVP, Sales and Marketing: Daniel (Dan) Griesemer, age 46, $1,037,096 pay
SVP and CIO: Dan Moen, age 34, $490,111 pay
SVP, Human Resources: Brett Avner, age 56
SVP, Operations: Gerard El Chaar, age 45
Director of Corporate Communications and Investor Relations: David Gunter
Auditors: Deloitte & Touche LLP

LOCATIONS

HQ: Coldwater Creek Inc.
  1 Coldwater Creek Dr., Sandpoint, ID 83864
Phone: 208-263-2266   **Fax:** 208-263-1582
Web: www.coldwater-creek.com

PRODUCTS/OPERATIONS

2006 Sales

	% of total
Retail	58
Internet	26
Catalog	16
Total	**100**

COMPETITORS

AnnTaylor	J. Jill Group
Blair	Kohl's
Bloomingdale's	Lands' End
Chico's FAS	L.L. Bean
Cornerstone Brands	Nordstrom
Dillard's	Norm Thompson
Eddie Bauer	Saks Inc.
Eddie Bauer Holdings	Talbots
Federated	Target
Hanover Direct	TravelSmith
J. C. Penney	United Retail
J. Crew	Williams-Sonoma

HISTORICAL FINANCIALS

Company Type: Public

Income Statement

FYE: Saturday nearest January 31

	REVENUE ($ mil.)	NET INCOME ($ mil.)	NET PROFIT MARGIN	EMPLOYEES
1/06	779.7	41.6	5.3%	8,170
1/05	590.3	29.1	4.9%	5,402
1/04	518.8	12.5	2.4%	3,433
1/03*	473.2	9.4	2.0%	2,680
2/02	464.0	1.8	0.4%	2,411
Annual Growth	13.9%	119.3%	—	35.7%

*Fiscal year change

2006 Year-End Financials

Debt ratio: —
Return on equity: 18.6%
Cash ($ mil.): 131.9
Current ratio: 1.97
Long-term debt ($ mil.): —
No. of shares (mil.): 92.0

Dividends
  Yield: —
  Payout: —
Market value ($ mil.): 1,910.4
R&D as % of sales: —
Advertising as % of sales: 1.6%

Stock History

NASDAQ (GM): CWTR

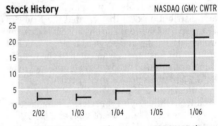

	STOCK PRICE ($) FY Close	P/E High/Low		PER SHARE ($) Earnings	Dividends	Book Value
1/06	20.76	52	24	0.44	—	2.70
1/05	12.15	44	13	0.32	—	3.27
1/04	4.32	30	11	0.15	—	5.00
1/03*	2.44	29	14	0.11	—	6.63
2/02	2.07	172	77	0.02	—	8.99
Annual Growth	78.0%	—	—	116.6%	—	(26.0%)

*Fiscal year change

Collegiate Pacific

Collegiate Pacific knows how to play the game. Primarily through its catalogs, the company markets about 23,000 sports equipment products to some 173,000 customers, including balls of all types, tennis court nets, soccer goals, weight-lifting equipment, and other sporting and recreational equipment. It also sells through telemarketing programs and the Internet. Collegiate Pacific sells mostly to institutional customers like youth sports programs, YMCAs, schools, and municipal recreation departments. In late 2006 Collegiate Pacific acquired the shares of Texas-based Sport Supply Group (SSG) that it didn't already own for about $24 million. The two companies plan to merge and adopt the SSG name.

Chairman and CEO Michael Blumenfeld and his son and president, Adam, own nearly 20% of Collegiate Pacific. Michael Blumenfeld announced in September 2006 that he planned to retire by 2007.

The company has been growing through acquisitions of sports equipment manufacturers and distributors. It bought a company owned by Blumenfeld, as well as a tennis court maintenance company, Equipmart. Collegiate Pacific purchased California-based Tomark, maker of baseball and other sports equipment; Kesslers Team Sports, a leading team sporting goods distributor based in Richmond, Indiana; and Richmond, Virginia-based team sports distributor Dixie Sporting Goods.

Tomark Sports became the exclusive supplier of Porter Athletic gymnasium equipment in Southern California, covering 10 counties. More recently, Collegiate Pacific signed a multi-year agreement to become the exclusive supplier of sports equipment to Varsity Group.

Collegiate Pacific acquired Florida-based sporting goods distributor Orlando Team Sports in January 2005. The company partnered with New Era Cap in mid-2006 in an exclusive marketing and distribution deal that created the New Era Team Sports Division. The division will be run by Collegiate Pacific and serve as a single point of contact for customers who cater to the institutional and sporting goods markets and want marketing and order processing expertise.

Collegiate Pacific makes about 11% of its products, while relying on external manufacturers for the rest. About 2% of sales are to US government agencies.

EXECUTIVES

Chairman: Michael J. Blumenfeld, age 60, $375,000 pay
CEO: Adam Blumenfeld, age 36, $375,000 pay
President: Terrence M. (Terry) Babilla
COO: Arthur J. Coerver, age 63
CFO, Secretary, and Treasurer: William R. Estill, age 57, $245,000 pay
EVP, Sales and Marketing: Kurt Hagan, age 37, $80,000 pay (partial-year salary)
EVP, US Operations: Tevis Martin, age 50, $175,000 pay
VP, Corporate Development: Chadd H. Edlein, age 33
VP, Marketing: Harvey Rothenberg, age 64
General Manager, Team Sports Division: Bob Dickman
Auditors: Grant Thornton LLP

LOCATIONS

HQ: Collegiate Pacific Inc.
13950 Senlac, Ste. 100, Dallas, TX 75234
Phone: 972-243-8100   **Fax:** 972-243-8424
Web: www.cpacsports.com

Collegiate Pacific has production and distribution facilities in California, Florida, Illinois, Indiana, Texas, and Virginia and manufacturing facilities in Alabama.

PRODUCTS/OPERATIONS

2006 Sales

	$ mil.	% of total
Sporting goods equipment	148.6	66
Athletic apparel & footwear	75.6	34
Total	**224.2**	**100**

Selected Products

Archery equipment
Baseball equipment
Basketball equipment
Boxing equipment
Camping equipment
Coaching equipment
Equipment carts
Field hockey
Floor covers
Football equipment
Goalpost pads
Goals and nets
Golf equipment
Inflatable balls
Lacrosse equipment
Protective equipment
Soccer equipment
Track and field equipment
Weight-lifting equipment

COMPETITORS

adidas
Amer Sports
NIKE
Rawlings
SAM'S CLUB

HISTORICAL FINANCIALS

Company Type: Public

Income Statement

FYE: June 30

	REVENUE ($ mil.)	NET INCOME ($ mil.)	NET PROFIT MARGIN	EMPLOYEES
6/06	224.2	1.9	0.8%	863
6/05	106.3	3.6	3.4%	570
6/04	39.6	1.9	4.8%	400
6/03	21.1	1.3	6.2%	66
6/02	16.9	0.8	4.7%	56
Annual Growth	**90.8%**	**24.1%**	**—**	**98.1%**

2006 Year-End Financials

Debt ratio: 131.9%
Return on equity: 4.1%
Cash ($ mil.): 4.1
Current ratio: 3.35
Long-term debt ($ mil.): 62.3
No. of shares (mil.): 10.2

Dividends
Yield: 0.9%
Payout: 55.6%
Market value ($ mil.): 110.0
R&D as % of sales: —
Advertising as % of sales: —

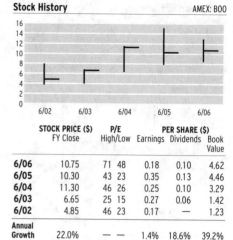

	STOCK PRICE ($) FY Close	P/E High/Low		Earnings	PER SHARE ($) Dividends	Book Value
6/06	10.75	71	48	0.18	0.10	4.62
6/05	10.30	43	23	0.35	0.13	4.46
6/04	11.30	46	26	0.25	0.10	3.29
6/03	6.65	25	15	0.27	0.06	1.42
6/02	4.85	46	23	0.17	—	1.23
Annual Growth	**22.0%**	**—**	**—**	**1.4%**	**18.6%**	**39.2%**

Color Kinetics

Color Kinetics (CK) can give a chameleon a run for its money. The company, founded in 1997, manufactures digital lighting products used in a variety of commercial and consumer applications. Its Chromacore products can generate virtually millions of colors and a variety of dynamic lighting effects by utilizing microprocessor-controlled light emitting diodes (LEDs). CK also manufactures the power supplies and controllers used in conjunction with its lighting products. Customers include members of the aerospace, architectural, entertainment, and vending and gaming industries. Co-founders George Mueller (director) and Ihor Lys (chief scientist) control about 7% and 8% of the company respectively.

CK sells lighting systems and OEM products through its direct sales force and manufacturers' representatives and distributors, which are located in Asia, Europe, Latin America, North America, and the Middle East.

EXECUTIVES

Chairperson: Elisabeth Allison, age 60
President, CEO, and Director: William J. (Bill) Sims, age 46, $504,000 pay
SVP and CFO: David K. Johnson, age 44, $263,681 pay
SVP and COO: Jeffrey A. (Jeff) Cassis, age 53
VP, APAC Lighting Systems Sales: Ray Letasi
VP, Marketing: Ellen Bossert
VP and General Counsel: Peter Karrol
VP, Human Resources: Paula LaPalme
Investor Relations: Justine Alonzo
Senior Corporate Communications Specialist: Felicia Spagnoli
Auditors: Deloitte & Touche LLP

LOCATIONS

HQ: Color Kinetics Incorporated
10 Milk St., Ste. 1100, Boston, MA 02108
Phone: 617-423-9999   **Fax:** 617-423-9998
Web: www.colorkinetics.com

Color Kinetics maintains facilities in China and the US.

2005 Sales

	$ mil.	% of total
US	33.5	63
Asia	10.8	21
Europe	3.9	7
Other regions	4.7	9
Total	**52.9**	**100**

PRODUCTS/OPERATIONS

2005 Sales

	$ mil.	% of total
Lighting systems	44.1	83
OEM & licensing	8.8	17
Total	**52.9**	**100**

Selected Products

Controllers
Data cables and adapters
Lights and fixtures (color-changing LED fixtures; low-voltage indoor, outdoor, and direct-view linear lights; and digital, single-color cove lights)
Power cables
Power and data supplies

COMPETITORS

Burelle	Morgan Crucible
Cooper Lighting	OSRAM SYLVANIA
GE	Philips Lighting
General Cable	Pirelli & C.
Genlyte Group	Richco
Intermatic	SL Industries
Juno Lighting	Technical Consumer
Matsushita Electric Works	Products

HISTORICAL FINANCIALS

Company Type: Public

Income Statement

FYE: December 31

	REVENUE ($ mil.)	NET INCOME ($ mil.)	NET PROFIT MARGIN	EMPLOYEES
12/05	52.9	4.3	8.1%	122
12/04	40.2	2.4	6.0%	87
12/03	28.9	(0.7)	—	76
12/02	20.2	(7.5)	—	—
Annual Growth	**37.8%**	**—**	**—**	**26.7%**

2005 Year-End Financials

Debt ratio: —
Return on equity: 6.5%
Cash ($ mil.): 57.3
Current ratio: 10.58
Long-term debt ($ mil.): —
No. of shares (mil.): 18.4

Dividends
  Yield: —
  Payout: —
Market value ($ mil.): 264.6
R&D as % of sales: 8.7%
Advertising as % of sales: 0.7%

Stock History

NASDAQ (GM): CLRK

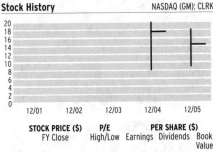

	STOCK PRICE ($) FY Close	P/E High/Low	PER SHARE ($) Earnings	Dividends	Book Value
12/05	14.39	82 41	0.22	—	3.78
12/04	17.58	141 58	0.14	—	3.50
Annual Growth	**(18.1%)**	**— —**	**57.1%**	**—**	**7.9%**

Commercial Vehicle Group

CB radio lingo might have gone the way of mood rings, but Commercial Vehicle Group (CVG) is still a trucker's good buddy. The company makes components for the cabs of heavy-duty trucks that help keep drivers comfortable and safe. Products include seats and suspension seat systems, interior trim (instrument panels, door panels, headliners), mirrors, wiper systems, and controls. The company's customers include heavy-duty truck manufacturers such as Navistar's International Truck (19% of sales), PACCAR (17%), and DaimlerChrysler's Freightliner subsidiary (16%). CVG expanded in 2005 by buying a truck cab manufacturer. That year it also purchased plastic molded parts maker Cabarrus Plastics.

In 2005 CVG paid $107.5 million for the assets of Mayflower Vehicle Systems North American Commercial Vehicle Operations, a maker of truck cab frames and assemblies, sleeper boxes, and other components. (The Mayflower Vehicle Systems unit posted revenue of about $207 million in 2004.) CVG also purchased Monona Corporation and its Monona Wire Corporation subsidiary for $55 million, adding eight manufacturing facilities in the US (in Illinois, Iowa, and Wisconsin) and Mexico. Monona makes electronic wire harnesses and instrument panel assemblies and assembles cabs for Caterpillar, Oshkosh Truck, Deere, and other construction equipment companies.

Besides truck manufacturers, CVG sells its products to the fleet maintenance aftermarket and to manufacturers of construction equipment and buses.

The addition of Mayflower's operations contributed significantly to CVG's 2005 revenue. In fact cab structures surpassed seating systems as the company's top-earning product segment.

In late 2006 CVG bought commercial truck and bus seat manufacturer C.I.E.B. Kahovec spol. of the Czech Republic. The move gives CVG a foothold in the European market upon which it hopes to build in the future.

Investment firm Onex Corporation, which formerly controlled CVG sold the last of its stake in the company in 2005.

EXECUTIVES

Chairman: Scott D. Rued, age 49
President, CEO, and Director: Mervin Dunn, age 52, $909,105 pay
VP Finance and CFO: Chad M. Utrup, age 32, $407,094 pay
VP Human Resources: James F. Williams, age 58, $315,688 pay
President, CVG Americas; President, Mayflower Vehicle Systems: Gerald L. (Jerry) Armstrong, age 43, $399,257 pay
President, CVG International: William Gordon Boyd, $613,068 pay
General Manager, Trim Systems: Robert E. Averitt, age 43
President, CVG, Europe and Asia: Donald P. Lorraine, age 51, $573,285 pay
Auditors: Deloitte & Touche LLP

LOCATIONS

HQ: Commercial Vehicle Group, Inc.
6530 W. Campus Way, New Albany, OH 43054
Phone: 614-289-5360   **Fax:** 614-289-5367
Web: www.cvgrp.com

Commercial Vehicle Group operates manufacturing facilities in Australia, Belgium, China, Mexico, Sweden, the UK, and the US.

2005 Sales

	$ mil.	% of total
North America	636.5	84
Other regions	118.0	16
Total	**754.5**	**100**

PRODUCTS/OPERATIONS

2005 Sales

	$ mil.	% of total
Cab structures, sleeper boxes, body panels & structural components	252.1	33
Seats & seating systems	237.9	32
Trim systems & components	133.6	18
Mirrors, wipers & controls	75.9	10
Electronic wire harnesses & panel assemblies	55.0	7
Total	**754.5**	**100**

2005 Sales by Customer

	% of total
International	19
PACCAR	17
Freightliner	16
Volvo/Mack	14
Caterpillar	7
Komatsu	2
Deer & Co.	2
Oshkosh Truck	2
Other	21
Total	**100**

COMPETITORS

Accuride
Johnson Electric
Tomkins
Valeo

HISTORICAL FINANCIALS

Company Type: Public

Income Statement

FYE: December 31

	REVENUE ($ mil.)	NET INCOME ($ mil.)	NET PROFIT MARGIN	EMPLOYEES
12/05	754.5	49.4	6.5%	5,339
12/04	380.4	17.5	4.6%	2,500
12/03	287.6	4.0	1.4%	—
12/02	298.7	(45.5)	—	—
Annual Growth	**36.2%**	**—**	**—**	**113.6%**

2005 Year-End Financials

Debt ratio: 91.9%
Return on equity: 31.6%
Cash ($ mil.): 40.6
Current ratio: 1.98
Long-term debt ($ mil.): 185.7
No. of shares (mil.): 21.1

Dividends
  Yield: —
  Payout: —
Market value ($ mil.): 397.1
R&D as % of sales: —
Advertising as % of sales: —

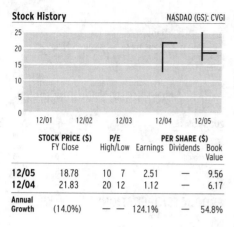

	STOCK PRICE ($) FY Close	P/E High/Low		PER SHARE ($) Earnings	Dividends	Book Value
12/05	18.78	10	7	2.51	—	9.56
12/04	21.83	20	12	1.12	—	6.17
Annual Growth	(14.0%)	—	—	124.1%	—	54.8%

Commonwealth Bankshares

Commonwealth Bankshares is the holding company for the Bank of the Commonwealth, which has about 10 branches in the southeastern corner of Virginia. The commercial bank attracts deposits from individuals and small to midsized businesses in the communities of Chesapeake, Norfolk, Portsmouth, and Virginia Beach by offering checking and savings accounts, IRAs, and CDs. Commercial mortgages represent more than half of the company's loan portfolio. The bank also originates residential mortgages, business loans, construction and development loans, and consumer installment loans.

Collectively, directors and executive officers of Commonwealth Bankshares own more than 20% of the company, led by directors Laurence Fentriss and Richard Tavss, who each have approximately 5% stakes.

EXECUTIVES

Chairman, President, and CEO, Commonwealth Bankshares and Bank of the Commonwealth: Edward J. Woodard Jr., age 63, $428,300 pay
EVP, CFO, and Secretary, Commonwealth Bankshares and Bank of the Commonwealth: Cynthia A. Sabol, age 43, $193,815 pay
EVP and Chief Lending Officer, Bank of the Commonwealth: Simon Hounslow, age 41, $176,462 pay
EVP and Commercial Loan Officer, Bank of the Commonwealth: R. Craig Baker
EVP and Commercial Loan Officer, Bank of the Commonwealth: Stephen G. Fields, age 42, $156,538 pay
EVP and Commercial Loan Officer, Bank of the Commonwealth: Donald F. Price
SVP and Chief Information Officer, Bank of the Commonwealth: Deborah B. Coon
SVP and Senior Trust Officer, Bank of the Commonwealth: Richard Early
SVP and Commercial Loan Officer, Bank of the Commonwealth: Robert L. White
VP and Human Resources Officer, Bank of the Commonwealth: Linda W. Greenough
Auditors: PKF Witt Mares, PLC

LOCATIONS

HQ: Commonwealth Bankshares, Inc.
403 Boush St., Norfolk, VA 23510
Phone: 757-446-6900   **Fax:** 757-446-6929
Web: www.bankofthecommonwealth.com

PRODUCTS/OPERATIONS

2005 Sales

	$ mil.	% of total
Interest		
Loans, including fees	33.7	88
Investment securities	0.3	1
Other	0.3	1
Noninterest		
Mortgage brokerage income	1.6	4
Service charges on deposit accounts	1.2	3
Other service charges & fees	0.5	1
Other	0.6	2
Total	**38.2**	**100**

COMPETITORS

Bank of America
BB&T
Hampton Roads Bankshares
Heritage Bankshares
Monarch Financial Holdings inc
RBC Centura Banks
SunTrust
Wachovia

HISTORICAL FINANCIALS

Company Type: Public

Income Statement

	ASSETS ($ mil.)	NET INCOME ($ mil.)	INCOME AS % OF ASSETS	EMPLOYEES
12/05	549.5	6.6	1.2%	142
12/04	374.1	3.1	0.8%	112
12/03	318.3	2.5	0.8%	91
12/02	256.5	1.7	0.7%	84
12/01	230.6	0.6	0.3%	93
Annual Growth	**24.2%**	**82.1%**	**—**	**11.2%**

FYE: December 31

2005 Year-End Financials

Equity as % of assets: 11.4%
Return on assets: 1.4%
Return on equity: 13.2%
Long-term debt ($ mil.): 30.9
No. of shares (mil.): 4.1
Market value ($ mil.): 92.2

Dividends
  Yield: 0.8%
  Payout: 12.5%
Sales ($ mil.): 38.2
R&D as % of sales: —
Advertising as % of sales: 2.2%

Stock History   NASDAQ (GM): CWBS

	STOCK PRICE ($) FY Close	P/E High/Low		PER SHARE ($) Earnings	Dividends	Book Value
12/05	22.65	17	11	1.36	0.17	15.40
12/04	15.58	17	13	0.96	0.12	12.40
12/03	15.70	20	11	0.85	0.13	10.16
12/02	9.28	14	7	0.73	0.06	8.97
12/01	5.78	24	16	0.26	0.09	7.97
Annual Growth	**40.7%**	**—**	**—**	**51.2%**	**17.2%**	**17.9%**

Community Bancorp

Las Vegas = Lost Wages? Not if Community Bank of Nevada has something to say about it. The subsidiary of holding company Community Bancorp (not to be confused with firms of the same name in Vermont and California) operates nine branches in and around Sin City. The bank offers thrifty residents standard deposit products, such as checking and savings accounts, NOW and money market accounts, CDs, and IRAs. It has played a part in Las Vegas' rapid growth by lending to area businesses, with commercial mortgages, construction loans, land acquisition and development loans, and Small Business Administration (SBA) loans comprising most of its portfolio. Community Bancorp bought rival Valley Bancorp in 2006.

Community Bancorp in 2006 also acquired Cactus Commerce Bank, a financial institution formed in 2003 to serve neighborhoods in the greater Phoenix metropolitan area. Community Bancorp acquired another Las Vegas-area competitor, Bank of Commerce, in 2005. The acquisition boosted Community Bank of Nevada's branch count by three locations in Las Vegas and Henderson, Nevada; it also made Community Bancorp the largest community-based bank focusing on the Las Vegas market. Community Bank of Nevada intends to build upon its "winning streak" by continuing to add new locations, either through acquisition or establishment. In addition to its banking offices, Community Bank of Nevada has loan production offices in Phoenix and San Diego.

EXECUTIVES

Chairman, President, and CEO; CEO, Community Bank of Nevada: Edward M. (Ed) Jamison, age 58
EVP, COO, and Director; President and COO, Community Bank of Nevada: Lawrence K. Scott, age 46
EVP, CFO, and Secretary: Cathy Robinson, age 46, $320,000 pay
EVP and Chief Operations Officer: Cassandra L. (Cassi) Eisinger, age 44
EVP and Chief Credit Officer: Bruce Ford, age 41, $348,827 pay
EVP and Chief Risk Manager, Community Bank of Nevada: Thomas P. (Tom) McGrath, age 61
EVP and Chief Credit Administration Officer: Don F. Bigger, age 54, $212,017 pay
SVP and CIO: Charles (Chuck) McCluer
VP and Investor Relations Officer: Judith A. (Judi) Lindsay
Public Relations: Jessie Lansing
Auditors: McGladrey & Pullen, LLP

LOCATIONS

HQ: Community Bancorp
400 S. 4th St., Ste. 215, Las Vegas, NV 89101
Phone: 702-878-0700   **Fax:** 702-947-3502
Web: www.communitybanknv.com

PRODUCTS/OPERATIONS

2005 Sales

	$ mil.	% of total
Interest		
Loans	40.9	84
Securities	5.4	11
Service charges	1.6	3
Other	0.7	2
Total	**48.6**	**100**

COMPETITORS

Bank of America	U.S. Bancorp
Business Bank (NV)	Washington Mutual
Citibank	Wells Fargo
Nevada State Bank	Western Alliance
Silver State Bancorp	

HISTORICAL FINANCIALS

Company Type: Public

Income Statement

FYE: December 31

	ASSETS ($ mil.)	NET INCOME ($ mil.)	INCOME AS % OF ASSETS	EMPLOYEES
12/05	892.7	10.1	1.1%	166
12/04	574.0	5.4	0.9%	114
12/03	463.4	5.2	1.1%	—
12/02	400.6	4.7	1.2%	—
Annual Growth	30.6%	33.3%	—	45.6%

2005 Year-End Financials

Equity as % of assets: 12.0%
Return on assets: 1.4%
Return on equity: 11.0%
Long-term debt ($ mil.): 39.6
No. of shares (mil.): 7.4
Market value ($ mil.): 233.1

Dividends
  Yield: —
  Payout: —
Sales ($ mil.): 48.6
R&D as % of sales: —
Advertising as % of sales: 1.9%

Stock History

NASDAQ (GM): CBON

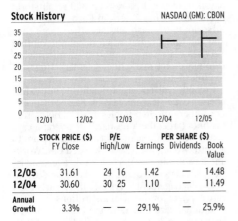

	STOCK PRICE ($) FY Close	P/E High/Low		PER SHARE ($) Earnings	Dividends	Book Value
12/05	31.61	24	16	1.42	—	14.48
12/04	30.60	30	25	1.10	—	11.49
Annual Growth	3.3%	—	—	29.1%	—	25.9%

Community Capital Bancshares

Thumbing its nose at the "bigger is better" trend in the banking industry, Community Capital Bancshares opened Albany Bank & Trust, a community bank serving southwestern Georgia, in 1999. It then made its first acquisition in 2003, buying First Bank of Dothan in Alabama, which is now AB&T National Bank. Through about five offices, the banks offer standard deposit products and services including checking and savings accounts, money market accounts, CDs, and IRAs. The company mainly uses these deposits to fund residential and commercial construction loans and mortgages, as well as business and consumer loans.

Community Capital Bancshares expanded into South Carolina with the opening of a loan production office in Charleston in 2005.

Directors and executive officers collectively own more than a quarter of the company.

EXECUTIVES

Chairman and CEO; Chairman, Albany Bank & Trust: Charles M. Jones III, age 55, $24,450 pay
Interim President, EVP, and Chief Credit Officer; Chief Credit Officer, Albany Bank & Trust: Paul E. Joiner Jr., $139,541 pay (prior to promotion)
CFO, Community Capital and Albany Bank & Trust; VP, AB&T National Bank: David J. Baranko, age 49, $108,164 pay
EVP and Senior Lending Officer, Albany Bank & Trust: David C. Guillebeau, age 44, $127,755 pay
Director, Human Resources, Albany Bank & Trust: Misty Bruce
General Auditor, Albany Bank & Trust: Stan W. Edmonds
Auditors: Mauldin & Jenkins, LLC

LOCATIONS

HQ: Community Capital Bancshares, Inc.
  2815 Meredyth Dr., Albany, GA 31707
Phone: 229-446-2265   **Fax:** 229-446-7030
Web: www.albanybankandtrust.com

PRODUCTS/OPERATIONS

2005 Sales

	$ mil.	% of total
Interest		
Loans	13.0	80
Securities	1.7	10
Other	0.2	1
Noninterest		
Service charges on deposit accounts	1.0	6
Other	1.2	3
Total	**17.1**	**100**

COMPETITORS

Ameris
Bank of America
Colony Bankcorp
Regions Financial
Southwest Georgia Financial
SunTrust
Synovus

HISTORICAL FINANCIALS

Company Type: Public

Income Statement

FYE: December 31

	ASSETS ($ mil.)	NET INCOME ($ mil.)	INCOME AS % OF ASSETS	EMPLOYEES
12/05	309.5	0.1	0.0%	81
12/04	195.3	0.9	0.5%	84
12/03	158.7	0.6	0.4%	65
12/02	109.2	0.6	0.5%	39
12/01	88.7	0.6	0.7%	30
Annual Growth	36.7%	(36.1%)	—	28.2%

2005 Year-End Financials

Equity as % of assets: 8.2%
Return on assets: 0.0%
Return on equity: 0.4%
Long-term debt ($ mil.): 24.1
No. of shares (mil.): 3.0
Market value ($ mil.): 32.4

Dividends
  Yield: 0.7%
  Payout: 200.0%
Sales ($ mil.): 17.1
R&D as % of sales: —
Advertising as % of sales: —

Stock History

NASDAQ (CM): ALBY

	STOCK PRICE ($) FY Close	P/E High/Low		PER SHARE ($) Earnings	Dividends	Book Value
12/05	10.90	340	253	0.04	0.08	8.54
12/04	11.62	38	26	0.38	0.10	8.77
12/03	12.00	38	26	0.39	0.06	7.64
12/02	11.10	29	17	0.38	—	6.81
12/01	8.05	21	14	0.44	—	6.13
Annual Growth	7.9%	—	—	(45.1%)	15.5%	8.6%

CommVault Systems

CommVault Systems doesn't want your data locked away in an inaccessible vault. The company provides storage and data management software that customers use to manage and store enterprise data. CommVault's products are used for tasks such as data migration, backup, archiving, data replication, and disaster recovery. The company's customers come from industries such as manufacturing, financial services, health care, and transportation, as well as from the public sector. CommVault's strategic partners include systems integrators and professional services firms, distributors and resellers, and technology providers.

The company was founded as an independent segment of Bell Laboratories in 1988; senior management (backed in part by funding from Sprout Group) purchased the company's assets from Lucent Technologies in 1996.

EXECUTIVES

Chairman, President, and CEO: N. Robert (Bob) Hammer, age 64, $599,712 pay
EVP and COO: Alan G. (Al) Bunte, age 53, $387,546 pay
VP and CFO: Louis F. (Lou) Miceli, age 57, $380,631 pay
VP and General Counsel: Warren H. Mondschein
VP, Europe, Middle East, and Africa: Steven Rose, age 48
VP, Human Resources: William (Bill) Beattie
VP, Marketing and Business Development: David (Dave) West, age 41, $284,154 pay
VP, Operations: Allen Shoemaker
VP, Product Development: Anand Prahlad, age 38
VP, Sales, Americas: Ron Miiller, age 39, $397,512 pay
VP, Sales Operations: Brian D. McAteer
Auditors: Ernst & Young LLP

LOCATIONS

HQ: CommVault Systems, Inc.
  2 Crescent Place, Oceanport, NJ 07757
Phone: 732-870-4000   **Fax:** 732-870-4525
Web: www.commvault.com

PRODUCTS/OPERATIONS

Selected Products

Data backup and recovery (Galaxy Backup & Recovery, QiNetix Quick Recovery)
Data migration (QiNetix DataMigrator)

COMPETITORS

CA
EMC
Hewlett-Packard
IBM Software
Symantec

HISTORICAL FINANCIALS

Company Type: Public

Income Statement

FYE: March 31

	REVENUE ($ mil.)	NET INCOME ($ mil.)	NET PROFIT MARGIN	EMPLOYEES
3/06	109.5	10.8	9.9%	642
3/05	82.6	0.5	0.6%	575
3/04	61.2	(11.7)	—	—
3/03	44.4	(16.4)	—	325
3/02	30.0	(29.9)	—	300
Annual Growth	38.2%			20.9%

2006 Year-End Financials

Debt ratio: —
Return on equity: —
Cash ($ mil.): 48.0

Current ratio: 1.55
Long-term debt ($ mil.): —

Net Income History

NASDAQ (GM): CVLT

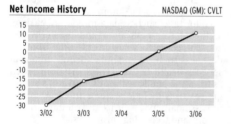

Complete Production Services

In order to compete (with the big boys) Complete Production Services has merged three companies to set itself up as a major provider of specialized services and products that help oil and gas companies develop reserves, enhance production, and reduce costs. Focusing on hydrocarbon-rich basins in North America that have long-term growth potential, the company offers a range of oil field services, including drilling, completion and production services (intervention, downhole and wellsite services, and fluid handling), and product sales. Complete Production Services is banking on the growing demand for natural gas exploration to drive demand for its products and services. The company is 69%-owned by SCF Partners.

Complete Production Services was formed through the 2005 combination of oilfield services and production support companies (Complete Energy Services, I.E. Miller Services, and Integrated Production Services).

EXECUTIVES

Chairman: Andrew L. Waite, age 45
President, CEO, and Director: Joseph C. Winkler, age 54, $532,750 pay
VP Accounting and Controller: Robert L. Weisgarber, age 54, $401,465 pay
VP Corporate Development: Jose A. Bayardo
SVP and CFO: J. Michael Mayer, age 49, $529,714 pay
VP Corporate Development: Thomas Burke
VP Human Resources and Administration: Kenneth L. Nibling, age 55, $89,582 pay
VP, Secretary, and General Counsel: James F. Maroney III, age 55, $98,322 pay
Auditors: Grant Thornton LLP

LOCATIONS

HQ: Complete Production Services, Inc.
11700 Old Katy Rd., Ste. 300, Houston, TX 77079
Phone: 281-372-2300   **Fax:** 281-582-9689
Web: www.completeprodsvcs.com

Complete Production Services operates regional field service facilities in the Rocky Mountain region, as well as in Louisiana, Oklahoma, Texas, and western Canada and Mexico.

COMPETITORS

Baker Hughes
Basic Energy Services
BJ Services
Grey Wolf
Halliburton
Helmerich & Payne
Nabors Industries
National Oilwell Varco
Patterson-UTI Energy
Schlumberger
Smith International
Superior Energy
Technip
TETRA Technologies
Unit Corporation
Weatherford International

HISTORICAL FINANCIALS

Company Type: Public

Income Statement

FYE: December 31

	REVENUE ($ mil.)	NET INCOME ($ mil.)	NET PROFIT MARGIN	EMPLOYEES
12/05	757.7	53.9	7.1%	4,485
12/04	320.8	13.9	4.3%	—
12/03	103.3	1.6	1.5%	—
12/02	30.1	(0.6)	—	—
Annual Growth	193.1%			

2005 Year-End Financials

Debt ratio: 203.4%
Return on equity: 25.5%
Cash ($ mil.): 11.4

Current ratio: 2.06
Long-term debt ($ mil.): 510.0

Net Income History

NYSE: CPX

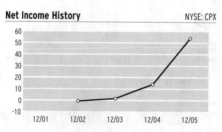

CompuCredit

Recovering from a fiscal near-death experience? CompuCredit might take a chance on you. The company uses a proprietary computer-scoring program to target borrowers who may be acceptable credit risks and reaches out to them via direct mail, telemarketing, and the Internet. CompuCredit doesn't issue or process its unsecured Aspire Visa, Emerge MasterCard, and Purpose Advantage Discover cards, instead relying on subsidiaries of Synovus Financial to perform these functions.

The company also offers life, credit, disability, and unemployment insurance; club memberships; and travel service programs. Subsidiary Jefferson Capital Systems acquires and sells previously charged-off credit card receivables.

Chairman David Hanna and his brother Frank, a director, own more than half of the company.

In 2004 CompuCredit entered the micro-lending business (sometimes called payday lending), which involves the marketing, originating, and servicing of small, short-term loans (generally less than $500 in value for fewer than 30 days). It acquired more than 300 retail stores operating as First American Cash Advance and First Southern Cash Advance, then more than 160 additional stores when it bought Venture Services of Kentucky. It also offers micro loans through direct marketing, telemarketing, and the Internet.

CompuCredit added auto lending to its product offerings when it acquired Wells Fargo Financial's Consumer Auto Receivables in 2005. Both product lines target the "unbanked" demographic.

Also in 2005 CompuCredit announced plans to acquire Woodbury, New York-based CardWorks and its subsidiaries Merrick Bank, a leading issuer of MasterCard and Visa cards, and Cardholder Management Services, a third-party bank card servicer for financial institutions and non-traditional card issuers in the US and Canada. However the deal has been stalled by the FDIC, which has placed a moratorium on the sale of industrial loan corporations (ILCs) such as Merrick Bank.

EXECUTIVES

Chairman and CEO: David G. Hanna, age 41, $50,000 pay
Vice Chairman and COO: Richard W. (Rick) Gilbert, age 52, $175,000 pay
President and Director: Richard R. House Jr., age 42, $583,333 pay
CFO: J. Paul Whitehead III, age 44, $340,000 pay
EVP and Chief Credit Officer: Krishnakumar (K. K.) Srinivasan, age 46, $400,000 pay
Secretary and General Counsel: Rohit H. Kirpalani
Treasurer: William R. (Bill) McCamey
Employee Benefits: Cindy Robinson
Investor Relations: Jay Putnam
Auditors: BDO Seidman, LLP

LOCATIONS

HQ: CompuCredit Corporation
245 Perimeter Center Pkwy., Ste. 600,
Atlanta, GA 30346
Phone: 770-206-6200   **Fax:** 678-259-8181
Web: www.compucredit.com

CompuCredit has offices in Atlanta; North Wilkesboro, North Carolina; St. Cloud, Minnesota; and Salt Lake City. Its Investments in Previously Charged-Off Receivables segment operates out of St. Cloud, Minnesota; the Retail Micro-Loans segment is headquartered in Peachtree City, Georgia; the Auto Finance segment principally operates out of Lake Mary, Florida, with additional operation centers in Nevada, North Carolina, and Texas.

COMPETITORS

Advance America
American Express
Bank of America
Capital One
Check Into Cash
Citigroup
CNG Financial
Credit Acceptance
Discover
HSBC Finance
JPMorgan Chase
Providian Corporation

HISTORICAL FINANCIALS

Company Type: Public

Income Statement

FYE: December 31

	ASSETS ($ mil.)	NET INCOME ($ mil.)	INCOME AS % OF ASSETS	EMPLOYEES
12/05	1,821.2	171.4	9.4%	3,400
12/04	1,003.5	100.7	10.0%	2,755
12/03	761.4	121.7	16.0%	1,750
12/02	518.9	5.9	1.1%	1,650
12/01	536.5	2.9	0.5%	885
Annual Growth	**35.7%**	**177.3%**	**—**	**40.0%**

2005 Year-End Financials

Equity as % of assets: 42.1%
Return on assets: 12.1%
Return on equity: 23.6%
Long-term debt ($ mil.): 715.2
No. of shares (mil.): 54.6
Market value ($ mil.): 2,101.0
Dividends
   Yield: —
   Payout: —
Sales ($ mil.): 948.6
R&D as % of sales: —
Advertising as % of sales: —

Stock History

NASDAQ (GS): CCRT

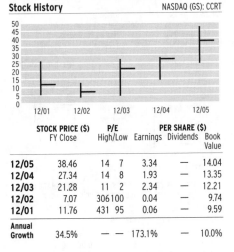

	STOCK PRICE ($) FY Close	P/E High/Low		PER SHARE ($) Earnings	Dividends	Book Value
12/05	38.46	14	7	3.34	—	14.04
12/04	27.34	14	8	1.93	—	13.35
12/03	21.28	11	2	2.34	—	12.21
12/02	7.07	306	100	0.04	—	9.74
12/01	11.76	431	95	0.06	—	9.59
Annual Growth	**34.5%**	**—**	**—**	**173.1%**	**—**	**10.0%**

Comstock Homebuilding

Comstock Homebuilding Companies develops land and builds single-family homes, townhomes, and mid-rise and high-rise condominium units for first-time, early move-up, secondary move-up, empty nester move-down, and active-adult homebuyers in the metropolitan Washington, DC, area (including parts of northern Virginia, Maryland, and eastern West Virginia) and in Raleigh, North Carolina. The company annually delivers some 260 homes with an average price of more than $350,000. Chairman and CEO Christopher Clemente started the enterprise in 1985; he controls more than 40% of the company, as does president and COO Gregory Benson.

Comstock controls more than 4,200 building lots, about half of which it owns, and it also converts existing rental apartment properties to for-sale condominium projects.

Comstock typically acts as the general contractor in building its communities. Its single-family homes range in size from roughly 2,000 sq. ft. to more than 6,000 sq. ft. and in price from the $200,000s to the $900,000s; its townhomes range in size from 1,200 sq. ft. to 4,500 sq. ft. and in price from the $200,000s to the $600,000s. Its condominiums range from about 400 sq. ft. to more than 2,400 sq. ft. in size and from the $100,000s to the $800,000s in price.

In 2006 Comstock extended its geographic reach and added about 1,600 lots to its land bank by acquiring Parker Chandler Homes for an undisclosed amount. The homebuilder mainly constructs single-family detached homes in Atlanta; Charlotte, North Carolina; and Myrtle Beach, South Carolina. Its homes range in price from about $200,000 to $500,000.

The company plans to continue to expand its operations in the eastern US through start-up operations and by acquiring other homebuilders. Comstock is also counting on the baby boom generation to fuel its growth in the mixed-use and active-adult market.

EXECUTIVES

Chairman and CEO: Christopher (Chris) Clemente, age 46, $1,250,000 pay
President, COO, and Director: Gregory V. Benson, age 51, $1,050,000 pay
CFO: Bruce J. Labovitz, age 37, $876,912 pay
Chief Accounting Officer: Jason Parikh, age 34, $273,167 pay
SVP, Business Development: William P. Bensten, age 58, $376,918 pay
VP, Construction: Dale Spradlin
General Counsel and Secretary: Jubal R. Thompson, age 36
Executive Administrator: Lyn Browne
Auditors: PricewaterhouseCoopers LLP

LOCATIONS

HQ: Comstock Homebuilding Companies, Inc.
11465 Sunset Hills Rd., Ste. 510, Reston, VA 20190
Phone: 703-883-1700   **Fax:** 703-760-1520
Web: www.comstockhomebuilding.com

PRODUCTS/OPERATIONS

2005 Sales

	$ mil.	% of total
Sale of real estate — homes	216.3	96
Other	8.0	4
Total	**224.3**	**100**

COMPETITORS

Centex
Lennar
Pulte Homes

HISTORICAL FINANCIALS

Company Type: Public

Income Statement

FYE: December 31

	REVENUE ($ mil.)	NET INCOME ($ mil.)	NET PROFIT MARGIN	EMPLOYEES
12/05	224.3	27.6	12.3%	130
12/04	96.0	14.3	14.9%	102
12/03	55.5	5.9	10.6%	121
12/02	34.8	3.6	10.3%	—
12/01	50.9	4.5	8.8%	—
Annual Growth	**44.9%**	**57.4%**	**—**	**3.7%**

2005 Year-End Financials

Debt ratio: 156.2%
Return on equity: 26.6%
Cash ($ mil.): 53.0
Current ratio: 2.57
Long-term debt ($ mil.): 226.7
No. of shares (mil.): 11.5
Dividends
   Yield: —
   Payout: —
Market value ($ mil.): 162.7
R&D as % of sales: —
Advertising as % of sales: 0.7%

Stock History

NASDAQ (GM): CHCI

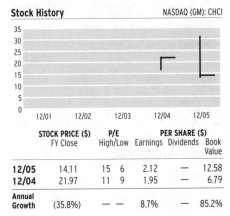

	STOCK PRICE ($) FY Close	P/E High/Low		PER SHARE ($) Earnings	Dividends	Book Value
12/05	14.11	15	6	2.12	—	12.58
12/04	21.97	11	9	1.95	—	6.79
Annual Growth	**(35.8%)**	**—**	**—**	**8.7%**	**—**	**85.2%**

Comtech Telecommunications

Comtech means contact. Through its subsidiaries, Comtech Telecommunications operates in three divisions: telecommunications transmission, mobile data communications, and RF microwave amplifiers. The company makes equipment used by satellite systems integrators, communications service providers, defense contractors, and oil companies. Its transmission equipment includes modems, frequency converters, high-power amplifiers, very-small-aperture terminal (VSAT) satellite transceivers and antennas, and microwave radios. Comtech

makes radio-frequency signal amplifiers that are used for wireless instrumentation and medical and defense systems.

The company also provides satellite-based messaging services and location tracking. Customers include Hughes Network Systems, Northrop Grumman, Raytheon, and the US Army.

EXECUTIVES

Chairman, President, and CEO: Fred V. Kornberg, age 70, $3,172,219 pay
EVP and COO: Robert G. (Rob) Rouse, age 42, $1,453,094 pay
SVP and CFO: Michael D. Porcelain, age 37, $390,000 pay (prior to promotion)
SVP; President, Comtech EF Data: Robert L. McCollum, age 57, $1,090,000 pay
SVP; President, Comtech Systems: Richard L. Burt, age 65, $605,000 pay
SVP, Strategy and Business Development: Jerome V. Kapelus
President, Comtech AHA Corporation: William Thomson
President, Comtech Antenna Systems: Thomas C. Christy
President, Comtech Mobile Datacom: Daniel S. Wood, age 48, $540,000 pay
Auditors: KPMG LLP

LOCATIONS

HQ: Comtech Telecommunications Corp.
68 S. Service Rd., Ste. 230, Melville, NY 11747
Phone: 631-962-7000   **Fax:** 631-962-7001
Web: www.comtechtel.com

Comtech Telecommunications has US offices in Arizona, California, Florida, Idaho, Maryland, Massachusetts, New York, Pennsylvania, and Washington. It has international operations in Africa, Asia, and Europe.

2006 Sales

	% of total
US	
Government	47
Commercial	17
North Africa	10
Other countries	26
Total	**100**

PRODUCTS/OPERATIONS

2006 Sales

	$ mil.	% of total
Telecommunications transmission	197.9	51
Mobile data communications	149.5	38
RF microwave amplifiers	44.1	11
Total	**391.5**	**100**

Selected Products

Telecommunications transmission equipment
  Error-correction and compression chips
  Over-the-horizon microwave communications products
  Satellite earth station equipment (modems, frequency converters, amplifiers, transceivers)
Mobile data communications services
  Location tracking
  Two-way messaging
Radio-frequency microwave amplifiers

COMPETITORS

DRS Technologies	Northrop Grumman
EMS Technologies	QUALCOMM
Filtronic	Radyne Corp.
Gilat Satellite	Raytheon
Harris Corp.	Rockwell Collins
Herley Industries	TCI International
iDirect Technologies	Thales
Lockheed Martin	Varian
Norsat	ViaSat

HISTORICAL FINANCIALS

Company Type: Public

Income Statement

FYE: July 31

	REVENUE ($ mil.)	NET INCOME ($ mil.)	NET PROFIT MARGIN	EMPLOYEES
7/06	391.5	45.3	11.6%	1,228
7/05	307.9	36.7	11.9%	1,090
7/04	223.4	21.8	9.8%	842
7/03	174.0	9.7	5.6%	689
7/02	119.4	1.1	0.9%	626
Annual Growth	**34.6%**	**153.3%**	**—**	**18.3%**

2006 Year-End Financials

Debt ratio: 41.4%	Dividends
Return on equity: 20.1%	Yield: —
Cash ($ mil.): 252.6	Payout: —
Current ratio: 4.45	Market value ($ mil.): 634.1
Long-term debt ($ mil.): 105.2	R&D as % of sales: 6.6%
No. of shares (mil.): 22.8	Advertising as % of sales: —

Stock History

NASDAQ (GS): CMTL

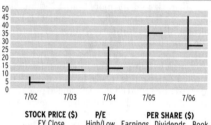

	STOCK PRICE ($) FY Close	P/E High/Low		PER SHARE ($) Earnings	Dividends	Book Value
7/06	27.76	27	15	1.72	—	11.13
7/05	35.35	28	8	1.42	—	8.71
7/04	13.27	28	10	0.95	—	10.01
7/03	12.05	30	5	0.53	—	8.47
7/02	4.15	110	42	0.07	—	8.96
Annual Growth	**60.8%**	**—**	**—**	**122.6%**	**—**	**5.6%**

Consumer Portfolio Services

Consumer Portfolio Services (CPS) buys, sells, and services auto loans made to consumers who probably don't have portfolios — in other words, subprime borrowers who can't get traditional financing due to poor or limited credit. CPS purchases contracts from more than 7,000 dealers in 47 states, more than 90% of which are franchised new car dealers. The remaining are independent used car dealers, and more than 80% of the contracts CPS acquires finance used vehicles. Investment firm Levine Leichtman Capital Partners owns more than a quarter of the company.

EXECUTIVES

Chairman, President, and CEO: Charles E. Bradley Jr., age 46, $1,735,000 pay
Vice Chairman: John G. Poole, age 63
Principal Financial Officer: Jeffrey P. (Jeff) Fritz, age 46, $437,000 pay
Chief Investment Officer: Robert E. Riedl, age 42, $464,000 pay (prior to title change)

SVP, Asset Recovery: Christopher (Chris) Terry, age 38, $394,000 pay
SVP, Collections: Nicholas P. Brockman, age 60, $411,000 pay
SVP, Contract Origination and Marketing: Curtis K. Powell, age 49, $478,000 pay
SVP, General Counsel, and Secretary: Mark A. Creatura, age 45, $326,000 pay
VP, Human Resources: Dottie Warren
Auditors: McGladrey & Pullen, LLP

LOCATIONS

HQ: Consumer Portfolio Services, Inc.
16355 Laguna Canyon Rd., Irvine, CA 92618
Phone: 949-753-6800   **Fax:** 949-753-6805
Web: www.consumerportfolio.com

PRODUCTS/OPERATIONS

2005 Sales

	$ mil.	% of total
Interest	171.8	89
Servicing fees	6.7	3
Other	15.2	8
Total	**193.7**	**100**

COMPETITORS

Aegis Consumer Funding	Ford Motor Credit
AmeriCredit	GMAC
Credit Acceptance	Nissan
DaimlerChrysler	Toyota Motor Credit
First Investors Financial	Union Acceptance
FirstCity Financial	

HISTORICAL FINANCIALS

Company Type: Public

Income Statement

FYE: December 31

	ASSETS ($ mil.)	NET INCOME ($ mil.)	INCOME AS % OF ASSETS	EMPLOYEES
12/05	1,155.1	3.4	0.3%	749
12/04	766.6	(15.9)	—	772
12/03	492.5	0.4	0.1%	692
12/02	285.5	20.4	7.1%	643
12/01	151.2	0.3	0.2%	491
Annual Growth	**66.3%**	**83.5%**	**—**	**11.1%**

2005 Year-End Financials

Equity as % of assets: 6.4%	Dividends
Return on assets: 0.4%	Yield: —
Return on equity: 4.7%	Payout: —
Long-term debt ($ mil.): 1,062.0	Sales ($ mil.): 193.7
No. of shares (mil.): 21.9	R&D as % of sales: —
Market value ($ mil.): 125.6	Advertising as % of sales: —

Stock History

NASDAQ (GM): CPSS

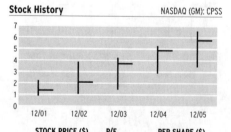

	STOCK PRICE ($) FY Close	P/E High/Low		PER SHARE ($) Earnings	Dividends	Book Value
12/05	5.75	46	25	0.14	—	3.37
12/04	4.87	—	—	(0.75)	—	3.24
12/03	3.72	209	75	0.02	—	3.99
12/02	2.09	4	1	0.97	—	4.08
12/01	1.37			—	—	3.19
Annual Growth	**43.1%**	**—**	**—**	**(47.5%)**	**—**	**1.3%**

Cooper Companies

The Cooper Companies makes specialty medical devices in two niche markets: vision care and gynecology. Its CooperVision subsidiary makes specialty contact lenses, including toric lenses for astigmatism and cosmetic lenses; through the 2005 acquisition of Ocular Sciences, the company also offers lenses for more common vision problems such as myopia. Subsidiary CooperSurgical specializes in the women's health care market; its wide range of products include bone densitometers (for diagnosing osteoporosis), hysteroscopes, and fetal monitors. The company markets its products through its own sales representatives in North America and through a mix of direct sales and distributors elsewhere.

The CooperVision subsidiary nearly doubled its revenue with the acquisition of Ocular Sciences. The purchase strengthened its presence in the spheric (non-specialty) lens market; it also opened up new geographic markets particularly in Germany and Japan. The unit accounts for around 85% of sales.

For years the younger sibling to CooperVision, CooperSurgical has been trying to balance out the relationship between the two subsidiaries. It has been adding product lines to its portfolio through acquisitions of smaller niche companies. In 2005, for example, it purchased NeoSurg Technologies and Inlet Medical, both of which make devices used in laparoscopic surgeries.

HISTORY

Cooper Labs (medical devices, dissolved 1985) created CooperVision as a subsidiary in 1980. CooperVision diversified into diagnostic equipment and drugs; by 1987 (when it was renamed The Cooper Companies), debt had increased sixfold and creditors came knocking.

Two scandal-tainted families (the Sturmans and the Singers — fraud/organized crime and Medicaid fraud, respectively) then bought their way onto the board. Proxy fights, cronyism, nepotism, indictments, and lawsuits ensued. Meanwhile, cash-strapped Cooper sold most of its international and part of its US contact lens business, as well as its ophthalmic surgical products and medical diagnostics businesses. Co-chairman Gary Singer took a leave of absence after being indicted in 1992.

Cooper bought Hospital Group of America and its hospitals that year. Singer resigned shortly before being convicted on 21 counts, including racketeering, mail and wire fraud, and money laundering in 1994.

Cooper rebuilt its contact business and turned to the women's health field in the early 1990s. In 1996 it bought a line of disposable gynecological products and worked to boost lens-making capacity. The next year it bought a line of colored contact lenses, a minimally invasive gynecological surgical and disposable products company, and a UK lens maker.

In 1998 The Cooper Companies discontinued its Hospital Group of America operations. It sold the group's hospitals, treatment centers, and clinics to Universal Health Services in 1999. In 2000 the company made three acquisitions, including two makers of gynecological instruments. In 2002

The Cooper Companies bought Biocompatibles Eye Care, one of the world's largest contact lens manufacturers. The company's acquisitions in 2003 included Avalon Medical Corporation (distributor of female sterilization system) and Prism Enterprises (manufacturer of medical devices for the women's health care markets). The Cooper Companies acquired gynecology products manufacturer Milex Products in 2004, and leading contact lens company Ocular Sciences in 2005.

EXECUTIVES

Chairman, President, and CEO: A. Thomas Bender, age 67, $699,000 pay
Vice Chairman: Allan E. Rubenstein, age 61
EVP, COO, and Director: Robert S. Weiss, age 59, $460,000 pay
SVP, Legal Affairs, Secretary, and Chief Administrative Officer: Carol R. Kaufman, age 56, $356,265 pay
VP and CFO: Steven M. (Steve) Neil, age 54
VP, Investor Relations and Communications: B. Norris Battin, age 69
VP, Taxes: Eugene J. (Gene) Midlock, age 61
VP and Treasurer: Albert G. White
President and COO, CooperSurgical: Paul L. Remmell, age 48
President and COO, CooperVision: Gregory A. Fryling, age 51, $448,080 pay
CEO, CooperSurgical: Nicholas J. Pichotta, age 61, $392,000 pay
President, Asian Operations, CooperVision: James M. Welch, age 45
President, European Operations, CooperVision: Andrew Sedgwick, age 40
President, U.S. Operations, CooperVision: Jeffrey A. McLean, age 52
Human Resources Director: Ruby Varner
Auditors: KPMG LLP

LOCATIONS

HQ: The Cooper Companies, Inc.
21062 Bake Pkwy., Ste. 200, Lake Forest, CA 92630
Phone: 949-597-4700   **Fax:** 949-768-3688
Web: www.coopercos.com

The Cooper Companies has offices in North America, Europe, and Australia.

2006 Sales

	$ mil.	% of total
US	427.6	50
Europe	269.5	31
Other regions	161.9	19
Total	**859.0**	**100**

PRODUCTS/OPERATIONS

2006 Sales

	$ mil.	% of total
CooperVision	734.2	85
CooperSurgical	124.8	15
Total	**859.0**	**100**

COMPETITORS

Bausch & Lomb
Boston Scientific
CIBA Vision
Essilor International
Ethicon
GE Healthcare Lunar
Hologic
SonoSite
United States Surgical
Vistakon

HISTORICAL FINANCIALS

Company Type: Public

Income Statement

FYE: October 31

	REVENUE ($ mil.)	NET INCOME ($ mil.)	NET PROFIT MARGIN	EMPLOYEES
10/06	859.0	66.2	7.7%	7,500
10/05	806.6	91.7	11.4%	7,034
10/04	490.2	92.8	18.9%	4,100
10/03	411.8	68.8	16.7%	3,700
10/02	315.3	48.9	15.5%	3,500
Annual Growth	**28.5%**	**7.9%**	**—**	**21.0%**

2006 Year-End Financials

Debt ratio: 49.4%
Return on equity: 5.0%
Cash ($ mil.): 8.2
Current ratio: 1.65
Long-term debt ($ mil.): 681.3
No. of shares (mil.): 44.5
Dividends
　Yield: 0.1%
　Payout: 4.2%
Market value ($ mil.): 2,567.3
R&D as % of sales: 4.0%
Advertising as % of sales: —

Stock History

NYSE: COO

	STOCK PRICE ($) FY Close	P/E High/Low	Earnings	Dividends	Book Value
10/06	57.63	52 29	1.44	0.06	30.94
10/05	68.84	42 28	2.04	0.06	28.66
10/04	70.35	28 16	2.59	0.06	16.62
10/03	43.45	21 11	2.13	0.06	13.15
10/02	26.50	18 12	1.57	0.05	10.09
Annual Growth	**21.4%**	**— —**	**(2.1%)**	**4.7%**	**32.3%**

Copano Energy

Copano Energy hopes its business goes down the tubes. The natural gas pipeline and processing company operates and maintains a network of natural gas gathering and intrastate pipelines (totaling more than 4,700 miles) in Texas' Gulf Coast region and in Oklahoma. This includes 144 miles of pipelines owned by Webb/Duval Gatherers, an unconsolidated general partnership 62.5%-owned by Copano Energy.

The company also provides natural gas processing operations through its Houston Central Processing plant and Sheridan NGL pipeline.

Copano Energy went public in late 2004. Chairman and CEO John Eckel holds an 11% stake in the company.

In 2005 the company acquired Tulsa-based ScissorTail Energy, LLC for $500 million. ScissorTail's assets include 3,200 miles of gas gathering pipelines and three processing plants.

EXECUTIVES

Chairman and CEO: John R. Eckel Jr., age 54, $512,213 pay
President and COO: R. Bruce Northcutt, age 46, $478,200 pay
SVP and CFO: Matthew J. (Matt) Assiff, age 39, $270,833 pay
SVP, Transportation and Supply: Brian D. Eckhart, age 50, $237,592 pay
SVP, Corporate Development: Ronald W. Bopp, age 59, $309,732 pay
VP and Controller: Lari Paradee, age 43
VP, Government and Regulatory Affairs: Kathryn S. De Young, age 45
VP, Operations: J. Terrell White, age 42
VP, Processing: James J. (Jim) Gibson III, age 60
VP, General Counsel, and Secretary: Douglas L. Lawing, age 45
Director Accounting: Carolyn Kroll
Director Energy Services: Louis Cox
Director Tax and Personnel: Jeff Casey
Auditors: Deloitte & Touche LLP

LOCATIONS

HQ: Copano Energy, L.L.C.
2727 Allen Pkwy., Ste. 1200, Houston, TX 77019
Phone: 713-621-9547 **Fax:** 713-621-9545
Web: www.copanoenergy.com

Copano Energy operates pipelines and processing plants located in the Gulf Coast region of Texas, and in Oklahoma.

PRODUCTS/OPERATIONS

2005 Sales

	$ mil.	% of total
Natural gas	496.9	66
Natural gas liquids	224.7	30
Transportation, compression & processing fees	15.1	2
Other	11.0	2
Total	**747.7**	**100**

Selected Operations

Texas Gulf Coast Pipelines
Texas Gulf Coast Processing
  Houston Central Processing plant
  Sheridan NGL pipeline

COMPETITORS

CenterPoint Energy
Crosstex Energy, Inc.
Southwestern Energy

HISTORICAL FINANCIALS

Company Type: Public

Income Statement

FYE: December 31

	REVENUE ($ mil.)	NET INCOME ($ mil.)	NET PROFIT MARGIN	EMPLOYEES
12/05	747.7	30.4	4.1%	206
12/04	437.7	(0.9)	—	85
12/03	384.6	(4.7)	—	80
12/02	224.9	(1.6)	—	—
12/01	160.4	4.1	2.6%	—
Annual Growth	**46.9%**	**65.0%**	**—**	**60.5%**

2005 Year-End Financials

Debt ratio: 141.2%
Return on equity: 16.7%
Cash ($ mil.): 25.3
Current ratio: 1.12
Long-term debt ($ mil.): 398.0
No. of shares (mil.): 14.1
Dividends
Yield: 4.0%
Payout: 68.6%
Market value ($ mil.): 550.6
R&D as % of sales: —
Advertising as % of sales: —

Stock History

NASDAQ (GS): CPNO

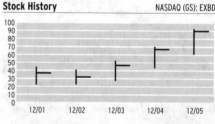

	STOCK PRICE ($) FY Close	P/E High/Low		PER SHARE ($) Earnings	Dividends	Book Value
12/05	39.05	19	11	2.29	1.57	19.99
12/04	28.50	—	—	(0.35)	—	11.67
Annual Growth	**37.0%**	**—**	**—**	**—**	**—**	**71.2%**

Corporate Executive Board

Don't fear the competition; learn from them. So says The Corporate Executive Board Company (CEB), a provider of business research and analysis services to more than 2,800 companies worldwide. Its 35-plus program areas cover "best practices" in such areas as finance, human resources, information technology, operations, and sales and marketing. Unlike consulting firms, which engage with one client at a time, CEB operates on a membership-based business model. Members subscribe to one or more of the company's programs and participate in the research and analysis. Besides reports on best practices, CEB offers seminars, customized research briefs, and decision-support tools.

The annual cost of a CEB membership averages about $35,000. The company has enjoyed a 90% membership renewal rate.

About 25% of CEB's members are based outside the US, mainly in Europe. The company's sole overseas office is in London.

The company's plans for growth rely on adding more clients to its network, persuading existing clients to subscribe to more research programs, and expanding its list of program areas.

CEB was spun off in 1999 from The Advisory Board Company, which offers similar research and analysis services for clients in the health care industry. A noncompete agreement that prevented CEB from seeking health care clients and kept The Advisory Board from operating outside that industry expired in January 2007.

EXECUTIVES

Chairman: James J. (Jay) McGonigle, age 43
CEO and Director: Thomas L. Monahan III, age 39
CFO: Timothy R. (Tim) Yost, age 35
CIO: Jonathan N. Dyke
President, Marketing and International: Michael A. (Mike) Archer, age 42
General Manager: Peter Freire
Chief Administrative Officer: Pete Buer
Chief Human Resources Officer: Melody L. Jones
Chief Research Officer: Derek C. M. van Bever, age 48
Controller, Treasurer, and Secretary: James Edgemond
Investor Relations: Lisa Herold
Media and Public Relations: Christina Borg
Auditors: Ernst & Young LLP

LOCATIONS

HQ: The Corporate Executive Board Company
2000 Pennsylvania Ave. NW, Ste. 6000, Washington, DC 20006
Phone: 202-777-5000 **Fax:** 202-777-5100
Web: www.executiveboard.com

PRODUCTS/OPERATIONS

Selected Program Areas

Communications
Corporate finance
Financial services
General management
Human resources
Information technology
Legal and compliance
Operations and procurement
Sales and marketing
Strategy and research and development

COMPETITORS

Accenture
BearingPoint
Booz Allen
Boston Consulting
The Concours Group
Conference Board
George S. May
GP Strategies
International Profit Associates
Kurt Salmon Associates
Linkage
McKinsey & Company
Thomas Group

HISTORICAL FINANCIALS

Company Type: Public

Income Statement

FYE: December 31

	REVENUE ($ mil.)	NET INCOME ($ mil.)	NET PROFIT MARGIN	EMPLOYEES
12/05	362.2	75.1	20.7%	1,865
12/04	280.7	53.7	19.1%	1,448
12/03	210.2	35.7	17.0%	1,222
12/02	162.4	29.6	18.2%	997
12/01	128.1	21.6	16.9%	818
Annual Growth	**29.7%**	**36.6%**	**—**	**22.9%**

2005 Year-End Financials

Debt ratio: —
Return on equity: 21.1%
Cash ($ mil.): 426.5
Current ratio: 1.74
Long-term debt ($ mil.): —
No. of shares (mil.): 39.5
Dividends
Yield: 0.4%
Payout: 21.9%
Market value ($ mil.): 3,541.6
R&D as % of sales: —
Advertising as % of sales: —

Stock History

NASDAQ (GS): EXBD

	STOCK PRICE ($) FY Close	P/E High/Low		PER SHARE ($) Earnings	Dividends	Book Value
12/05	89.70	50	34	1.83	0.40	9.76
12/04	66.94	52	33	1.34	0.38	8.41
12/03	46.67	56	30	0.93	—	6.49
12/02	31.92	51	30	0.79	—	5.74
12/01	36.70	74	39	0.59	—	4.12
Annual Growth	**25.0%**	**—**	**—**	**32.7%**	**5.3%**	**24.0%**

Corus Bankshares

Money is at the heart of the matter for Corus Bankshares, the holding company for Corus Bank, which operates about a dozen branches in the Chicago metropolitan area. The bank offers such deposit products as checking and savings accounts, as well as NOW and money market accounts. Its primary emphasis is on commercial real estate loans, which make up around 98% of its loan portfolio. Corus Bank also provides trust services, retirement products, and Internet banking. In Chicago and Milwaukee, the bank provides clearing, depository, and credit services to more than 50 check cashing businesses. Chairman Joseph Glickman and his family together own 42% of the company.

Corus Bank lends nationwide, helping to diversify its commercial real estate-heavy loan portfolio. In fact, more than 90% of its loan commitments are secured by properties outside of its home state of Illinois.

EXECUTIVES

Chairman: Joseph C. Glickman, age 90
President, CEO, and Director: Robert J. Glickman, age 59, $1,000,000 pay
EVP, CFO, and Secretary: Timothy H. (Tim) Taylor, age 41, $636,000 pay
EVP Commercial Lending: Michael G. Stein, age 45, $2,430,664 pay
EVP Retail Banking: Randy P. Curtis, $535,000 pay
SVP and Chief Accounting Officer: Michael E. Dulberg, age 40
SVP Commercial Lending: John M. Barkidjija
SVP Commercial Lending: Brian J. Brodeur
SVP Commercial Lending: Terence W. Keenan, age 60, $355,587 pay
SVP Commercial Lending: John R. Markowicz
SVP Commercial Lending: Joel C. Solomon, age 51
SVP Finance: Richard J. Koretz, age 42, $395,000 pay
VP Human Resources: Jennifer Haughey, age 33
Auditors: Ernst & Young LLP

LOCATIONS

HQ: Corus Bankshares, Inc.
3959 N. Lincoln Ave., Chicago, IL 60613
Phone: 773-832-3088   **Fax:** 773-832-3460
Web: www.corusbank.com

PRODUCTS/OPERATIONS

2005 Sales

	$ mil.	% of total
Interest		
Interest & fees on loans	346.7	73
Securities	78.3	16
Federal funds sold	21.9	5
Noninterest		
Securities gains	12.7	3
Service charges on deposit accounts	11.6	2
Other	3.7	1
Total	**474.9**	**100**

COMPETITORS

ABN AMRO	LaSalle Bank
Bank of America	MAF Bancorp
Citigroup	MB Financial
Citizens Republic Bancorp	National City
Fifth Third	Wells Fargo
First Midwest Bancorp	Wintrust Financial
Harris Bankcorp	

HISTORICAL FINANCIALS

Company Type: Public

Income Statement

FYE: December 31

	ASSETS ($ mil.)	NET INCOME ($ mil.)	INCOME AS % OF ASSETS	EMPLOYEES
12/05	8,458.7	137.2	1.6%	519
12/04	5,017.8	97.9	2.0%	471
12/03	3,643.8	58.4	1.6%	468
12/02	2,617.1	49.3	1.9%	475
12/01	2,659.3	54.2	2.0%	506
Annual Growth	**33.5%**	**26.1%**	**—**	**0.6%**

2005 Year-End Financials

Equity as % of assets: 8.2%
Return on assets: 2.0%
Return on equity: 21.3%
Long-term debt ($ mil.): 379.9
No. of shares (mil.): 27.9
Market value ($ mil.): 785.7
Dividends
　Yield: 2.5%
　Payout: 29.4%
Sales ($ mil.): 474.9
R&D as % of sales: —
Advertising as % of sales: —

Stock History

NASDAQ (GS): CORS

	STOCK PRICE ($) FY Close	P/E High/Low		PER SHARE ($) Earnings	Dividends	Book Value
12/05	28.14	14	9	2.38	0.70	24.70
12/04	24.00	15	9	1.70	0.63	21.57
12/03	15.51	16	10	1.02	0.41	19.48
12/02	10.91	16	11	0.86	0.16	34.14
Annual Growth	**37.1%**	**—**	**—**	**25.8%**	**47.0%**	**(6.2%)**

Covanta

Covanta Holding (formerly Danielson Holding) has seen the light: There's more money in energy than insurance. Through the strategic acquisitions of Covanta Energy and ARC Holdings, the former insurance-focused company has made itself a leader in the waste and energy services markets. It also provides contract construction, maintenance, and operation services for water and wastewater systems in the US. The purchase of Covana Energy's energy and water business in 2004 broadened the company's interests and gave it a new direction and name. Through its subsidiary National American Insurance Company of California (NAICC) Covanta Holding writes policies for automobile drivers.

Covanta acquired American Ref-Fuel Holdings, a waste-to-energy business, for $740 million in cash and the assumption of $1.2 billion in debt.

Chairman and former CEO Samuel Zell owns about 16% of the company through his investment company SZ Investments.

EXECUTIVES

Chairman: Samuel (Sam) Zell, age 64
President, CEO, and Director: Anthony J. Orlando, age 46, $931,000 pay
SVP and CFO: Mark A. Pytosh, age 42
SVP, General Counsel, and Secretary: Timothy J. Simpson, age 47, $455,000 pay
SVP Operations, Covanta Energy: John M. Klett, age 59, $522,391 pay
VP and Chief Accounting Officer: Thomas E. Bucks, age 49, $166,923 pay (partial-year salary)
Auditors: Ernst & Young LLP

LOCATIONS

HQ: Covanta Holding Corporation
40 Lane Rd., Fairfield, NJ 07004
Phone: 973-882-9000   **Fax:** 973-882-7076
Web: www.danielsonholding.com

PRODUCTS/OPERATIONS

2005 Sales

	$ mil.	% of total
Waste & service	638.5	65
Electricity & steam	322.8	33
Other	17.5	2
Total	**978.8**	**100**

COMPETITORS

Crowley Maritime	Midland Company
Environmental Power	Omni Insurance
GEICO	PAULA Financial
Kirby	Safeway Insurance
Mercury General	U.S. Energy Systems

HISTORICAL FINANCIALS

Company Type: Public

Income Statement

FYE: December 31

	REVENUE ($ mil.)	NET INCOME ($ mil.)	NET PROFIT MARGIN	EMPLOYEES
12/05	978.8	59.3	6.1%	3,600
12/04	578.6	34.1	5.9%	1,837
12/03	42.6	(69.2)	—	64
12/02	531.5	(33.0)	—	4,030
12/01	94.1	(14.3)	—	117
Annual Growth	**79.6%**	**—**	**—**	**135.5%**

2005 Year-End Financials

Debt ratio: 448.0%
Return on equity: 16.2%
Cash ($ mil.): 335.0
Current ratio: 1.51
Long-term debt ($ mil.): 2,684.7
No. of shares (mil.): 141.2
Dividends
　Yield: —
　Payout: —
Market value ($ mil.): 2,126.0
R&D as % of sales: —
Advertising as % of sales: —

Stock History

NYSE: CVA

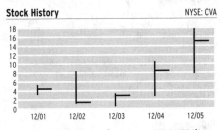

	STOCK PRICE ($) FY Close	P/E High/Low		PER SHARE ($) Earnings	Dividends	Book Value
12/05	15.06	38	17	0.46	—	4.24
12/04	8.45	20	6	0.52	—	—
12/03	2.91	—	—	(2.25)	—	—
12/02	1.40	—	—	(1.26)	—	—
12/01	4.44	—	—	(0.74)	—	—
Annual Growth	**35.7%**	**—**	**—**	**—**	**—**	**—**

CPI International

CPI International makes broadcast and wireless components, such as satellite communications transmitters, amplifiers, sensors, X-ray equipment, power supplies, transmitters, and microwave components. Its radio-frequency (RF) and microwave components go into a great deal of military hardware (governments account for about half of sales), including Aegis-class cruisers and destroyers, electronic warfare decoys, Patriot missile systems, and fighter aircraft. The company's products also go into civilian communications equipment, industrial gear, medical systems, and scientific instruments. The Cypress Group, a private equity firm, owns about 55% of CPI International.

Providing replacement parts, spares, repairs, and upgrades to its installed equipment generates around half of CPI's sales.

The company sells in more than 85 countries, with Europe making up one-quarter of sales.

CPI was once part of the Electron Devices group at the old Varian Associates; it was spun off from Varian in 1995. Varian engineers invented the klystron in 1937, which played an important role in the development of radar during WWII and is still used in high-power microwave equipment. CPI International was formerly known as Communications & Power Industries, which remains the name of the company's main operating subsidiary.

In 2004 the company acquired ECONCO Broadcast Service, a provider of rebuilding services for vacuum electron devices, for about $18 million in cash.

CEO O. Joe Caldarelli owns nearly 5% of CPI International, including stock options.

EXECUTIVES

Chairman: Michael B. (Mickey) Targoff, age 62
CEO and Director: O. Joe Caldarelli, age 56, $2,316,948 pay
President, COO, and Director: Robert A. (Bob) Fickett, age 46, $1,278,033 pay
CFO, Treasurer, and Secretary: Joel A. Littman, age 53, $806,171 pay
VP and Assistant Secretary: John R. Beighley, age 54, $378,876 pay
VP; President, Beverly Microwave: Don C. Coleman, age 52, $527,730 pay
VP; President, Satcom: Andrew E. Tafler, age 51
Auditors: KPMG LLP

LOCATIONS

HQ: CPI International, Inc.
811 Hansen Way, Palo Alto, CA 94303
Phone: 650-846-2900   **Fax:** 650-846-3391
Web: www.cpii.com

CPI International has assembly, manufacturing, and warehouse facilities in California and Massachusetts, and also in Ontario, Canada. The company has sales and service offices across the US and in more than a dozen countries overseas.

2006 Sales

	$ mil.	% of total
US	214.6	63
Other countries	125.1	37
Total	**339.7**	**100**

PRODUCTS/OPERATIONS

2006 Sales

	$ mil.	% of total
Vacuum electron devices	275.2	81
Satcom equipment	64.5	19
Total	**339.7**	**100**

2006 Sales by Market

	$ mil.	% of total
Radar	119.9	35
Communications	106.7	31
Medical	57.6	17
Electronic warfare	26.8	8
Industrial	22.1	7
Scientific	6.6	2
Total	**339.7**	**100**

Selected Products

Beverly Microwave
  Magnetrons
  Switches
  Traveling wave tubes (TWTs)
Communications and Medical Products
  DC power supplies
  Medium-power klystrons
  X-ray generators
Microwave Power Products
  Coupled cavity TWTs
  Gyrotrons
  Helix TWTs
  Klystrode inductive output tubes
  Power grid tubes
  Transmitter subsystems
Satellite Communications (Satcom)
  Klystron amplifiers
  TWT amplifiers

COMPETITORS

e2v
Intelek
L-3 Communications
Radyne Corp.
STC Microwave Systems
Thales
Wi-Tron

HISTORICAL FINANCIALS

Company Type: Public

Income Statement

FYE: Friday nearest September 30

	REVENUE ($ mil.)	NET INCOME ($ mil.)	NET PROFIT MARGIN	EMPLOYEES
9/06	339.7	17.2	5.1%	1,610
9/05	320.7	13.7	4.3%	1,700
9/04	202.3	2.7	1.3%	1,510
9/03	265.4	16.5	6.2%	1,490
9/02	251.2	—	—	1,480
Annual Growth	**7.8%**	**1.4%**	**—**	**2.1%**

2006 Year-End Financials

Debt ratio: 245.9%
Return on equity: 22.6%
Cash ($ mil.): 31.9
Current ratio: 2.15
Long-term debt ($ mil.): 245.1
No. of shares (mil.): 16.0
Dividends
  Yield: —
  Payout: —
Market value ($ mil.): 211.4
R&D as % of sales: 2.5%
Advertising as % of sales: —

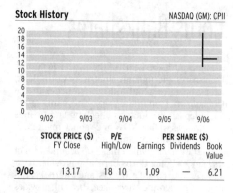

STOCK PRICE ($) FY Close	P/E High/Low	PER SHARE ($) Earnings	Dividends	Book Value
9/06 13.17	18 10	1.09	—	6.21

CRA International

CRA International (formerly Charles River Associates) acts as a Dear Abby for its clients, dispensing advice to law firms, corporations, utilities, and other entities. The company's more than 650 consultants offer economic and business counsel from more than 20 offices worldwide. Its legal and regulatory services cover antitrust litigation, mergers and acquisitions, intellectual property, and environmental disputes, for companies that need independent and expert analysis. CRA's business consulting services include business strategy, market analysis, and technology management.

CRA International has expanded its consulting services operations through a series of acquisitions. In May 2006 the company bought the assets of Washington, DC-based consulting firm Ballentine Barbera Group, a specialist in transfer pricing services. In 2005 CRA International acquired two London-based firms: Lexecon Ltd (now Economics of Competition and Litigation Limited), a specialist in competitive economics consulting and commercial litigation, and Lee & Allen Consulting Limited, which offers dispute resolution and forensic accounting services.

Consulting services account for nearly all of CRA International's revenue. It also has a minority stake in NeuCo, which provides neural network software to electric and gas companies.

In 2006 NeuCo acquired Pegasus Technologies, a unit of Rio Tinto Energy America Services that provides software for power companies, in a stock swap. The deal settled a patent infringement lawsuit that Pegasus had brought against NeuCo. As a result of the transaction, CRA International's stake in NeuCo fell to about 36%. Other NeuCo shareholders include utility operator NSTAR and company employees.

EXECUTIVES

Chairman: Rowland T. (Row) Moriarty, age 59
Vice Chairman: Franklin M. (Frank) Fisher, age 71
President, CEO, and Director: James C. Burrows, age 62, $1,050,000 pay
EVP; Head, Economic Litigation Group and Competition Practices: Robert J. Larner, age 64, $485,000 pay
EVP and Director Research: C. Christopher Maxwell, age 51, $400,000 pay
EVP and Chief Corporate Development Officer: Fred Baird
EVP and Chief Strategy Officer: Arnie Lowenstein
EVP and Platform Leader, Finance: Paul Maleh

EVP and Platform Leader, Strategy and Business Consulting: Greg Bell
EVP and Platform Leader, Litigation and Applied Economics: Monica Noether
VP, CFO, and Treasurer: Wayne D. Mackie, age 57, $92,668 pay
VP and General Counsel: Jonathan D. Yellin
Secretary: Peter M. Rosenblum
Director, Human Resources: Cynthia Butler
Auditors: KPMG LLP

LOCATIONS

HQ: CRA International, Inc.
200 Clarendon St., Ste. T-33, Boston, MA 02116
Phone: 617-425-3000 **Fax:** 617-425-3132
Web: www.crai.com

CRA International has offices in Boston and Cambridge, Massachusetts; Chicago; College Station, Dallas, and Houston, Texas; New York City; Oakland, Palo Alto, and Pasadena, California; Philadelphia; Salt Lake City; and Washington, DC. Outside the US, it has offices in Australia, Bahrain, Belgium, Canada, China, Mexico, New Zealand, and the UK.

2005 Sales

	% of total
US	81
UK	12
Australia	5
Other countries	2
Total	**100**

PRODUCTS/OPERATIONS

Selected Practice Areas

Business consulting
Business strategy
Finance
Intellectual property and technology strategy
Market analysis
Legal and regulatory consulting
Antitrust
Commercial damages
Environmental
Forensic accounting
Intellectual property
International trade
Mergers and acquisitions

COMPETITORS

Accenture
Bain & Company
BearingPoint
Booz Allen
Boston Consulting
Cornerstone Research
Economics Research Associates
Exponent
FTI Consulting
Huron Consulting
International Profit Associates
LECG
McKinsey & Company
Navigant Consulting
UHY Advisors

HISTORICAL FINANCIALS

Company Type: Public

Income Statement

FYE: Last Saturday in November

	REVENUE ($ mil.)	NET INCOME ($ mil.)	NET PROFIT MARGIN	EMPLOYEES
11/05	295.5	24.6	8.3%	906
11/04	216.7	16.3	7.5%	765
11/03	163.5	11.4	7.0%	486
11/02	130.7	8.4	6.4%	490
11/01	109.8	7.4	6.7%	293
Annual Growth	**28.1%**	**35.0%**	**—**	**32.6%**

2005 Year-End Financials

Debt ratio: 44.1%
Return on equity: 14.8%
Cash ($ mil.): 115.2
Current ratio: 2.89
Long-term debt ($ mil.): 90.2
No. of shares (mil.): 11.2
Dividends
Yield: —
Payout: —
Market value ($ mil.): 514.6
R&D as % of sales: —
Advertising as % of sales: —

Stock History

NASDAQ (GS): CRAI

	STOCK PRICE ($) FY Close	P/E High/Low		PER SHARE ($) Earnings	Dividends	Book Value
11/05	45.77	27	19	2.13	—	18.20
11/04	43.18	28	18	1.55	—	12.80
11/03	32.75	31	11	1.16	—	11.60
11/02	15.68	24	12	0.91	—	8.70
11/01	19.59	25	9	0.81	—	7.69
Annual Growth	**23.6%**	**—**	**—**	**27.3%**	**—**	**24.0%**

CREDO Petroleum

CREDO Petroleum believes strongly in fossil fuels: It explores for, produces, and markets natural gas and crude oil in the US Gulf Coast, Mid-continent, and Rocky Mountain regions. The company has traditionally concentrated on shallow and medium-depth properties (7,000-9,000 feet), but in 2005 it launched new projects in Kansas and South Texas (where it is drilling to well depths ranging from 10,000 to 15,500 feet). The company has estimated proved reserves of 16.6 billion cu. ft. of gas and 422,000 barrels of oil. Subsidiary United Oil operates the company's properties in Oklahoma, and CREDO Petroleum's other subsidiary, SECO Energy, owns royalty interests in the Rocky Mountains.

Established in 1978, CREDO Petroleum is also focusing on developing fluid lift technology (Calliope) to extend well life, and on buying oil and gas properties.

EXECUTIVES

Chairman, President, CEO, and COO: James T. Huffman, age 58, $200,000 pay
CFO: David E. Dennis
Manager, Regulatory Compliance: Alford B. Neely
Manager Operations: Jeffrey E. Carlson
Manager, Petroleum Engineering: Kenneth J. DeFehr, age 56
Manager, Geology and Exploration: Torie A. Vandeven, age 51

LOCATIONS

HQ: CREDO Petroleum Corporation
1801 Broadway, Ste. 900, Denver, CO 80202
Phone: 303-297-2200 **Fax:** 303-297-2204
Web: www.credopetroleum.com

PRODUCTS/OPERATIONS

2006 Sales

	% of total
Duke Energy	39
Enogex	8
Other customers	53
Total	**100**

Subsidiaries

SECO Energy Corp.
United Oil Corp.

COMPETITORS

Apache
BP
Cabot Oil & Gas
Chesapeake Energy
Delta Petroleum
Devon Energy
Exxon Mobil
Hunt Consolidated
Noble Energy
Royal Dutch Shell
Swift Energy
XTO Energy

HISTORICAL FINANCIALS

Company Type: Public

Income Statement

FYE: October 31

	REVENUE ($ mil.)	NET INCOME ($ mil.)	NET PROFIT MARGIN	EMPLOYEES
10/06	16.5	5.9	35.8%	12
10/05	14.0	5.2	37.1%	12
10/04	10.3	3.7	35.9%	10
10/03	8.5	3.1	36.5%	10
10/02	5.4	1.3	24.1%	10
Annual Growth	**32.2%**	**46.0%**	**—**	**4.7%**

2006 Year-End Financials

Debt ratio: —
Return on equity: 19.1%
Cash ($ mil.): 11.1
Current ratio: 3.62
Long-term debt ($ mil.): —
No. of shares (mil.): 9.5
Dividends
Yield: —
Payout: —
Market value ($ mil.): 123.8
R&D as % of sales: —
Advertising as % of sales: —

Stock History

NASDAQ (CM): CRED

	STOCK PRICE ($) FY Close	P/E High/Low		PER SHARE ($) Earnings	Dividends	Book Value
10/06	13.02	51	20	0.62	—	3.66
10/05	17.47	35	15	0.56	—	2.83
10/04	9.17	33	18	0.39	—	3.47
10/03	7.67	23	8	0.35	—	4.46
10/02	2.96	25	13	0.14	—	4.36
Annual Growth	**44.8%**	**—**	**—**	**45.1%**	**—**	**(4.3%)**

Crescent Banking

This crescent gives a whole new meaning to "dough boy." Crescent Banking Company is the holding company of Crescent Bank & Trust, which serves north-central Georgia from about 10 branches and four loan offices. The bank offers standard retail and commercial banking services, including checking and savings accounts, money market accounts, and IRAs. The company uses funds from deposits to mainly originate loans secured by real estate in its market area, such as real estate mortgages and construction and land development loans, which account for more than 90% of its loan portfolio. Other offerings include business loans and consumer installment loans.

Crescent Banking Company bought Alpharetta, Georgia-based bank Futurus Financial Services in 2005.

Director Michael Lowe owns more than 20% of Crescent Banking Company. Including his stake, directors and executive officers own more than 40% of the company.

EXECUTIVES

Chairman: John S. Dean Sr., age 66
President, CEO, and Director, Crescent Banking Company and Crescent Bank & Trust; Secretary, Crescent Mortgage Services: J. Donald Boggus Jr., age 42, $350,000 pay
SVP and CFO, Crescent Banking Company and Crescent Bank & Trust: Leland W. Brantley Jr., age 34, $245,000 pay
EVP and Chief of Loan Administration, Crescent Bank & Trust: A. Bradley Rutledge Sr., age 42, $293,282 pay
EVP and Chief of Loan Production, Crescent Bank & Trust: Anthony N. (Tony) Stancil, age 42, $300,000 pay
EVP and Internal Auditor, Crescent Bank & Trust: Bonnie Boling, age 51, $154,894 pay
Banking Officer and Human Resources Manager, Crescent Bank & Trust: Eva Howell
Auditors: Dixon Hughes PLLC

LOCATIONS

HQ: Crescent Banking Company
7 Caring Way, Jasper, GA 30143
Phone: 678-454-2266   **Fax:** 678-454-2282
Web: www.crescentbank.com

Crescent Banking Company has bank branches in Adairsville, Alpharetta (2), Canton, Cartersville (2), Cumming, Jasper, Marble Hill, and Woodstock, Georgia. It has additional lending centers in Canton, Cartersville, Loganville, and Marietta, Georgia.

PRODUCTS/OPERATIONS

2005 Sales

	$ mil.	% of total
Interest		
Loans, including fees	36.8	85
Other	1.8	4
Noninterest		
Service charges on deposit accounts	0.9	2
Gains on sales of Small Business Administration loans	0.9	2
Other	2.8	7
Total	**43.2**	**100**

COMPETITORS

Bank of America	Habersham Bancorp
BB&T	Regions Financial
Chestatee Bancshares	Wachovia
GB&T Bancshares	

HISTORICAL FINANCIALS

Company Type: Public

Income Statement

FYE: December 31

	ASSETS ($ mil.)	NET INCOME ($ mil.)	INCOME AS % OF ASSETS	EMPLOYEES
12/05	704.1	4.1	0.6%	196
12/04	513.4	(0.8)	—	144
12/03	366.4	17.3	4.7%	115
12/02	559.4	11.5	2.1%	230
12/01	484.5	7.0	1.4%	207
Annual Growth	**9.8%**	**(12.5%)**	**—**	**(1.4%)**

2005 Year-End Financials

Equity as % of assets: 7.8%	Dividends
Return on assets: 0.7%	Yield: 1.0%
Return on equity: 7.8%	Payout: 22.0%
Long-term debt ($ mil.): 44.8	Sales ($ mil.): 43.2
No. of shares (mil.): 2.6	R&D as % of sales: —
Market value ($ mil.): 91.8	Advertising as % of sales: —

Stock History

NASDAQ (CM): CSNT

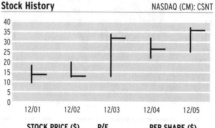

	STOCK PRICE ($) FY Close	P/E High/Low	PER SHARE ($) Earnings	Dividends	Book Value
12/05	35.80	23 16	1.59	0.35	21.52
12/04	26.40	— —	(0.33)	0.32	20.19
12/03	31.78	5 2	6.74	0.31	21.02
12/02	12.91	4 2	5.04	0.31	14.38
12/01	13.65	5 3	3.73	0.31	8.86
Annual Growth	**27.3%**	**— —**	**(19.2%)**	**3.1%**	**24.9%**

Crescent Financial

This Crescent can help you wrench the most bang from your buck. Crescent Financial is the holding company for Crescent State Bank, which operates branches in the Raleigh, North Carolina area. The community bank offers standard products and services, including checking and savings accounts, NOW and sweep accounts, lines of credit, and cash management services. Commercial mortgages make up about half of its loan portfolio; construction loans make up about 15%. The company also writes industrial loans, home equity loans, and residential mortgages.

Crescent Financial bought local rival Centennial Bank in 2003, and Port City Capital Bank, which will keep its name, in 2006.

Executive officers and directors collectively own nearly 20% of the company.

EXECUTIVES

Chairman: Bruce I. Howell, age 63
President, CEO, and Director, Crescent Financial and Crescent State Bank: Michael G. Carlton, age 44, $282,218 pay
VP and Secretary; SVP and CFO, Crescent State Bank: Bruce W. Elder, age 43, $167,473 pay
President and CEO, Port City Capital Bank: W. Keith Betts
EVP and CFO, Port City Capital Bank: Lawrence S. Brobst
EVP and Senior Lending Officer, Port City Capital Bank: John M. Franck
SVP and COO, Cresent State Bank: Ray D. Vaughn, age 53
SVP and Senior Credit Officer, Crescent State Bank: Thomas E. Holder Jr., age 46, $161,165 pay
Auditors: Dixon Hughes PLLC

LOCATIONS

HQ: Crescent Financial Corporation
1005 High House Rd., Cary, NC 27513
Phone: 919-460-7770   **Fax:** 919-460-2512
Web: www.crescentstatebank.com

Crescent Financial has branches in Apex, Cary (2), Clayton, Garner, Holly Springs, Raleigh, Pinehurst, Sanford, and Southern Pines, North Carolina.

PRODUCTS/OPERATIONS

2005 Sales

	$ mil.	% of total
Interest		
Loans, including fees	20.4	81
Securities & other	2.4	10
Noninterest		
Service charges & fees on deposit accounts	1.0	4
Mortgage loan origination fees	0.8	3
Other	0.6	2
Total	**25.2**	**100**

COMPETITORS

Bank of America
BB&T
KS Bancorp
RBC Centura Banks
Wachovia

HISTORICAL FINANCIALS

Company Type: Public

Income Statement

FYE: December 31

	ASSETS ($ mil.)	NET INCOME ($ mil.)	INCOME AS % OF ASSETS	EMPLOYEES
12/05	410.8	3.1	0.8%	99
12/04	331.2	2.3	0.7%	83
12/03	273.7	1.6	0.6%	70
12/02	182.0	1.2	0.7%	41
12/01	129.2	0.3	0.2%	34
Annual Growth	**33.5%**	**79.3%**	**—**	**30.6%**

2005 Year-End Financials

Equity as % of assets: 10.1%	Dividends
Return on assets: 0.8%	Yield: —
Return on equity: 9.1%	Payout: —
Long-term debt ($ mil.): 30.3	Sales ($ mil.): 25.2
No. of shares (mil.): 5.0	R&D as % of sales: —
Market value ($ mil.): 66.4	Advertising as % of sales: 1.6%

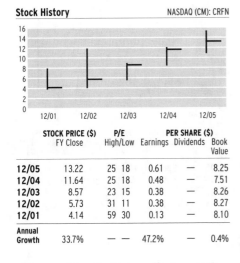

	STOCK PRICE ($) FY Close	P/E High/Low	PER SHARE ($) Earnings	Dividends	Book Value
12/05	13.22	25 18	0.61	—	8.25
12/04	11.64	25 18	0.48	—	7.51
12/03	8.57	23 15	0.38	—	8.26
12/02	5.73	31 11	0.38	—	8.27
12/01	4.14	59 30	0.13	—	8.10
Annual Growth	33.7%	— —	47.2%	—	0.4%

Crocs

Although they don't promise protection if you encounter the real thing, Crocs and its trademark colorful slip-on shoes are quickly gaining popularity in the watersports arena and in mainstream fashion. The shoes, sold under the Crocs brand name, are made of proprietary closed-cell resin and are known for their comfort. The firm operates manufacturing facilities in China and Mexico — as well as Italy and Canada — and distributes through retailers, including Dillard's, Nordstrom, REI, and The Sports Authority. Crocs' shoes, designed for men, women, and children, feature a rear handle and are sold in nearly 20 different colors. The company is aggressively expanding on both domestic and international fronts.

To that end, the firm acquired family-run Jibbitz LLC, which makes accessories to decorate Crocs clogs, for about $10 million in late 2006. Also in the second half of 2006, Crocs announced that it had acquired EXO Italia, maker of ethylene vinyl acetate-based finished products. The deal allows Crocs to diversify into new product areas. To compete in the sports arena, Crocs in early 2007 acquired Fury, which specializes in manufacturing sports-protection items — such as sticks, gloves, pants, and shin and elbow pads — using its Croslite antimicrobial material. Also Crocs expanded its agreements with the NFL and NHL to give it rights to use all NFL and NHL team logos, as well as those for the football league, the Super Bowl, and Pro Bowl.

The shoes sell in 6,500 US shops, such as Nordstrom and specialty stores, and in 40 countries. Crocs gets most of its revenue from sales to customers younger than 18 years old and older than 30.

To attract its younger customer, Crocs in August 2006 announced an agreement with Disney to make a limited edition line of Crocs footwear named Disney by Crocs. A soft product launch was planned for the 2006 holiday season and the balance of the line bows in spring 2007.

Volleyball fans in Southern California are snapping up the shoes. In 2006 Crocs became the primary sponsor of the Los Angeles-based AVP Pro Beach Volleyball tour.

EXECUTIVES

Chairman: Richard L. Sharp, age 59
President, CEO, and Director: Ronald R. (Ron) Snyder, age 49, $640,000 pay
SVP, Finance, CFO, and Treasurer: Peter S. Case, age 45
SVP, Global Operations: John P. McCarvel, age 50
VP, Finance: Caryn D. Ellison, age 53
VP, Customer Relations: Lyndon V. (Duke) Hanson III
VP, Sales and Marketing: Michael C. Margolis, age 55, $443,131 pay
Auditors: Deloitte & Touche LLP

LOCATIONS

HQ: Crocs, Inc.
6273 Monarch Park Place, Niwot, CO 80503
Phone: 303-468-4260   **Fax:** 303-468-4266
Web: www.crocs.com

COMPETITORS

adidas
Birkenstock Distribution USA
Columbia Sportswear
Deckers Outdoor
L.L. Bean
NIKE
R. Griggs
Skechers U.S.A.
Timberland
Wolverine World Wide

HISTORICAL FINANCIALS

Company Type: Public

Income Statement				FYE: December 31
	REVENUE ($ mil.)	NET INCOME ($ mil.)	NET PROFIT MARGIN	EMPLOYEES
12/05	108.6	17.0	15.7%	1,130
12/04	13.5	(1.5)	—	260
12/03	1.2	(1.2)	—	—
12/02	0.0	(0.4)	—	8
Annual Growth	—	—	—	420.8%

2005 Year-End Financials

Debt ratio: 17.0%   Current ratio: 1.22
Return on equity: 221.9%   Long-term debt ($ mil.): 3.2
Cash ($ mil.): 4.8

Net Income History   NASDAQ (GS): CROX

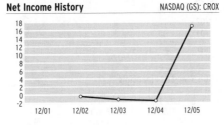

Cuisine Solutions

Whether you're traveling for pleasure or to serve your country, this company tries to make sure you get a good meal. Cuisine Solutions is a leading supplier of prepared meals for a variety of customers, including travel and transportation providers, the military, retail stores, and foodservice operators. Through its production facilities in the US and France, the company makes fully cooked and frozen meals, including chicken, seafood, and beef items, along with pasta and sauces, and distributes those meals throughout the US and in Europe. The family of chairman Jean-Louis Vilgrain owns about 60% of the company.

Supplying military customers has been a rapidly growing part of Cuisine Solutions' business as more and more personnel are being deployed around the world. It currently accounts for more than 20% of sales. Cuisine Solutions gets almost 30% of its revenue from customers in the travel industry, which include airlines, cruise ship operators, and rail lines. Supplying prepared foods for supermarkets and other retail customers accounts for about a quarter of its business.

In addition to its manufacturing facilities in the US and France, Cuisine Solutions has a 10% stake in a production facility in Chile.

EXECUTIVES

Chairman: Jean-Louis Vilgrain, age 70
CEO and Director: Stanislas Vilgrain, age 47, $463,338 pay
President and Director: Thomas L. Gregg, age 42, $328,310 pay
COO: Felipe Hasselmann, age 37, $249,104 pay
CFO, Treasurer, and Corporate Secretary: Yuyun Tristan Kuo, age 52, $246,000 pay
VP, Product Development: Marc Brennet
VP, Sales and Corporate Chef: Gerard Bertholon, age 46, $145,000 pay
Controller: Ronnie Lai
Manager, Military Accounts: Elizabeth Lauer
Manager, Corporate Communications: Lillian Liu
Auditors: BDO Seidman, LLP

LOCATIONS

HQ: Cuisine Solutions, Inc.
85 S. Bragg St., Ste. 600, Alexandria, VA 22312
Phone: 703-270-2900   **Fax:** 703-750-1158
Web: www.cuisinesolutions.com

2006 Sales

	$ mil.	% of total
US	44.5	69
France	19.6	31
Total	**64.1**	**100**

PRODUCTS/OPERATIONS

2006 Sales

	$ mil.	% of total
On Board Services	17.5	27
Retail	15.9	25
Military	13.9	22
Foodservice	13.2	20
Restaurant chains	3.6	6
Total	**64.1**	**100**

Selected Operations

On Board Services (transportation and tourism meal
  services)
Retail (in-store meal services and frozen packaged foods)
Military (on-site meal services for military personnel)
Foodservice (catering and event foodservices)
Restaurant chains (foodservice supply for restaurant
  operators)

COMPETITORS

Alpha Airports
ARAMARK
Armanino Foods of Distinction
Campbell Soup
ConAgra
Delaware North
Gate Gourmet
LSG Sky Chefs
Overhill Farms
Performance Food
Sanderson Farms
SYSCO
Tyson Foods
U.S. Foodservice

HISTORICAL FINANCIALS

Company Type: Public

Income Statement			FYE: Last Saturday in June	
	REVENUE ($ mil.)	NET INCOME ($ mil.)	NET PROFIT MARGIN	EMPLOYEES
6/06	64.1	3.7	5.8%	302
6/05	46.3	1.7	3.7%	263
6/04	36.7	(1.0)	—	230
6/03	27.8	(4.1)	—	180
6/02	28.6	(6.0)	—	210
Annual Growth	22.4%	—	—	9.5%

2006 Year-End Financials

Debt ratio: 25.0%
Return on equity: 33.8%
Cash ($ mil.): 2.2
Current ratio: 1.84
Long-term debt ($ mil.): 3.3
No. of shares (mil.): 16.4
Dividends
  Yield: —
  Payout: —
Market value ($ mil.): 83.0
R&D as % of sales: 0.8%
Advertising as % of sales: —

Stock History

AMEX: FZN

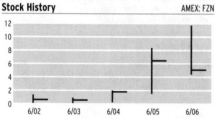

	STOCK PRICE ($) FY Close	P/E High/Low		PER SHARE ($) Earnings	Dividends	Book Value
6/06	5.05	58	22	0.20	—	0.81
6/05	6.45	82	16	0.10	—	0.54
6/04	1.80	—	—	(0.06)	—	0.41
6/03	0.56	—	—	(0.26)	—	0.47
6/02	0.60	—	—	(0.38)	—	0.71
Annual Growth	70.3%	—		—	—	3.4%

Cutera

Cutera has a handle on hairy situations. The
firm makes CoolGlide, which uses lasers to remove hair. The FDA-approved CoolGlide consists of a control console and the accompanying
ClearView handpiece. Its Xeo products can be
used for permanent hair reductions and boast an
array of skin-treatment options for pigmented lesions, wrinkles, and veins. In addition, its Solera
products can be used for dermal heating to treat
wrinkles. The company markets its products
through a direct sales force in the US and relies
on a small sales group and distributors in about
30 other countries. Director Annette Campbell-
White controls about 21% of the company.

Cutera plans to expand its international operations. The company also intends to develop
new products for additional treatments.

EXECUTIVES

President, CEO, and Director: Kevin P. Connors, age 43,
$332,893 pay
VP, Finance and Administration and CFO:
  Ronald J. Santilli, age 45, $189,276 pay
VP, Research and Development and Director:
  David A. Gollnick, age 41, $192,151 pay
VP, Clinical Development: Michael J. Levernier, age 43,
$156,908 pay
VP, Human Resources: Stacie Rodgers
VP, International: Tom J. Liolios
VP, North American Sales: John J. Connors
Auditors: PricewaterhouseCoopers LLP

LOCATIONS

HQ: Cutera, Inc.
  3240 Bayshore Blvd., Brisbane, CA 94005
Phone: 415-657-5500   **Fax:** 415-330-2444
Web: www.cutera.com

COMPETITORS

Candela Corporation
Cynosure
IRIDEX
Laserscope
Lumenis
Palomar Medical
Syneron

HISTORICAL FINANCIALS

Company Type: Public

Income Statement			FYE: December 31	
	REVENUE ($ mil.)	NET INCOME ($ mil.)	NET PROFIT MARGIN	EMPLOYEES
12/05	75.6	13.8	18.3%	195
12/04	52.6	3.8	7.2%	140
12/03	39.1	3.1	7.9%	—
12/02	28.3	0.7	2.5%	—
12/01	19.3	2.3	11.9%	57
Annual Growth	40.7%	56.5%	—	36.0%

2005 Year-End Financials

Debt ratio: —
Return on equity: 16.7%
Cash ($ mil.): 92.0
Current ratio: 9.08
Long-term debt ($ mil.): —
No. of shares (mil.): 12.2
Dividends
  Yield: —
  Payout: —
Market value ($ mil.): 321.9
R&D as % of sales: 6.7%
Advertising as % of sales: 1.6%

Stock History

NASDAQ (GS): CUTR

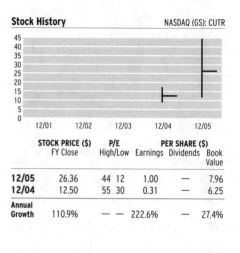

	STOCK PRICE ($) FY Close	P/E High/Low		PER SHARE ($) Earnings	Dividends	Book Value
12/05	26.36	44	12	1.00	—	7.96
12/04	12.50	55	30	0.31	—	6.25
Annual Growth	110.9%	—	—	222.6%	—	27.4%

CyberSource

Cyber security has to start somewhere.
CyberSource provides software and services that
help ensure that e-commerce and other
Internet-based transactions are processed securely. Companies use its software to process
credit card payments and electronic checks, as
well as to screen for payment fraud. Other applications manage gift certificate programs and verify personal information. The company's
software can be integrated with other enterprise
applications from vendors such as Microsoft, Oracle, and SAP. In addition to its software,
CyberSource offers outsourced payment processing and fraud detection services.

The company processes some 200 million
transactions per year for its customers including British Airways, H&R Block, Overstock.com,
and Starbucks.

EXECUTIVES

Chairman and CEO: William S. (Bill) McKiernan, age 49
President, COO, and Director: Scott R. Cruickshank,
  age 43
EVP, Product Development and CTO: Robert J. Ford,
  age 56
VP, Finance and CFO: Steven D. Pellizzer, age 36
VP, Customer Support: Patricia A. (Trish) Martin, age 44
VP, Engineering: Jay Martin
VP, Marketing: Perry Dembner, age 45
VP, Worldwide Sales: Michael Walsh, age 37
VP and General Counsel: David J. Kim, age 38
**Director, Corporate Communications and Investor
  Relations:** Bruce Frymire
Auditors: Ernst & Young LLP

LOCATIONS

HQ: CyberSource Corporation
  1295 Charleston Rd., Mountain View, CA 94043
Phone: 650-965-6000   **Fax:** 650-625-9145
Web: www.cybersource.com

CyberSource has offices in Japan, the UK, and the US.

PRODUCTS/OPERATIONS

Transaction Services and Software

Address information standardization and validation
Credit card authorization
Electronic payment
Export control
Fraud prediction and detection

Gift certificate and promotional coupon issuance and
  redemption
Payment services implementation and integration
Payment systems management (CyberSource Payment
  Manager)
Reporting systems development and integration
Risk management operation assessment
Sales and use tax calculation

Professional Services
Business process analyses
Capacity planning and security
Commerce infrastructure integration
Custom reporting
Database sizing
Disaster recovery
Finance and administrative process/systems impact
Installation and integration
Maintenance
Sales and customer service process/systems impact
System optimization
Technology selection
Transaction cost analyses

COMPETITORS

Bottomline Technologies	Microsoft
CheckFree	Retail Decisions
ClearCommerce	SAS Institute
Fair Isaac	SPSS
First Data	Sterling Commerce
IBM	Trintech
InfoSpace	VeriSign

HISTORICAL FINANCIALS
Company Type: Public

Income Statement   FYE: December 31

	REVENUE ($ mil.)	NET INCOME ($ mil.)	NET PROFIT MARGIN	EMPLOYEES
12/05	50.5	9.3	18.4%	185
12/04	36.7	4.5	12.3%	168
12/03	27.5	(5.4)	—	154
12/02	28.0	(12.5)	—	163
12/01	30.8	(185.1)	—	178
Annual Growth	13.2%	—	—	1.0%

2005 Year-End Financials
Debt ratio: —
Return on equity: 17.8%
Cash ($ mil.): 47.0
Current ratio: 7.35
Long-term debt ($ mil.): —
No. of shares (mil.): 33.9
Dividends
  Yield: —
  Payout: —
Market value ($ mil.): 224.0
R&D as % of sales: 15.8%
Advertising as % of sales: 0.0%

Stock History   NASDAQ (GM): CYBS

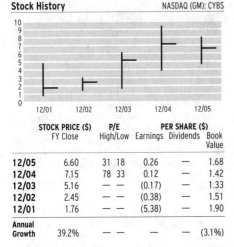

	STOCK PRICE ($) FY Close	P/E High/Low		PER SHARE ($) Earnings	Dividends	Book Value
12/05	6.60	31	18	0.26	—	1.68
12/04	7.15	78	33	0.12	—	1.42
12/03	5.16	—	—	(0.17)	—	1.33
12/02	2.45	—	—	(0.38)	—	1.51
12/01	1.76	—	—	(5.38)	—	1.90
Annual Growth	39.2%			—	—	(3.1%)

Cynosure

Beauty may be skin deep, but that's just deep enough for Cynosure to help. The company makes laser and pulsed-light devices used to perform non-invasive procedures to remove hair, treat varicose veins, and reduce the appearance of birthmarks, freckles, and cellulite. Cynosure's 15 different systems are marketed under such names as Apogee, Cynergy, and PhotoSilk. The company, along with its six subsidiaries, sells its systems to doctors, health spas, and veterinarians in nearly 50 countries from sales offices located in more than 30 countries. Italian laser maker El. En. controls 35% of the company's voting shares and manufactures many of the company's products.

EXECUTIVES

Chairman, President, and CEO: Michael R. Davin, age 48, $562,298 pay
EVP, CFO, and Treasurer: Timothy W. Baker, age 45, $301,938 pay
EVP, Sales: Douglas J. Delaney, age 39, $353,240 pay
SVP, Global Marketing: Stephen May, age 44
SVP, International Sales: Kenji Shimizu, age 53
VP, Marketing: Marina Kamenakis, age 47
VP, Operations: David Mackie, age 44
VP, Strategic Planning: John A. Theroux, age 53
CTO: Rafael Sierra, age 56
Auditors: Ernst & Young LLP

LOCATIONS

HQ: Cynosure, Inc.
  5 Carlisle Rd., Westford, MA 01886
Phone: 978-256-4200   **Fax:** 978-256-6556
Web: www.cynosurelaser.com

2005 Sales

	% of total
North America	59
Europe	23
Asia/Pacific	12
Other regions	6
Total	**100**

PRODUCTS/OPERATIONS

Selected Products
Apogee Elite (hair removal)
Cynergy (treatment of vascular lesions)
PhotoSilk Plus (treatment of shallow vascular lesions
  and pigmented lesions)
TriActive Laser Dermology (temporary cellulite
  appearance reduction)

COMPETITORS

Candela Corporation	Palomar Medical
Cutera	PhotoMedex
Laserscope	Syneron
Lumenis	Thermage

HISTORICAL FINANCIALS
Company Type: Public

Income Statement   FYE: December 31

	REVENUE ($ mil.)	NET INCOME ($ mil.)	NET PROFIT MARGIN	EMPLOYEES
12/05	56.3	4.2	7.5%	184
12/04	41.6	5.3	12.7%	—
12/03	27.1	(0.5)	—	—
12/02	23.0	(1.9)	—	138
Annual Growth	34.8%	—	—	10.1%

2005 Year-End Financials
Debt ratio: 1.0%
Return on equity: 8.6%
Cash ($ mil.): 64.7
Current ratio: 6.04
Long-term debt ($ mil.): 0.8
No. of shares (mil.): 5.9
Dividends
  Yield: —
  Payout: —
Market value ($ mil.): 122.8
R&D as % of sales: —
Advertising as % of sales: —

Stock History   NASDAQ (GM): CYNO

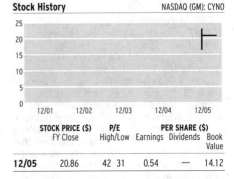

	STOCK PRICE ($) FY Close	P/E High/Low		PER SHARE ($) Earnings	Dividends	Book Value
12/05	20.86	42	31	0.54	—	14.12

Cytyc

Cytyc knows the business of detecting cancer backward and forward. The palindromically-named company makes sample-preparation systems used in medical testing. Its ThinPrep System stores patients' samples in liquid and incorporates an automated slide-preparation process that results in clearer samples for clinical diagnosis. The system is used as a replacement for the conventional Pap smear to detect the human papillomavirus, a cause of cervical cancer. The ThinPrep System can also be used to perform cancer analysis on tissues from the breast, liver, lung, thyroid, or other organs.

Despite the tests' advantages, the company has had to convince some physicians, insurers, and labs that ThinPrep tests are worth the additional costs ($20-$30 more than traditional Pap smears). The company has also received FDA approval for its ThinPrep Imaging System, a computer imaging technology used with the ThinPrep System to screen for cervical cancer. Cytyc plans to offer a ThinPrep Breast Test to scan for breast cancer, which it gained through its acquisition of Pro Duct Health.

Cytyc in 2006 entered a bidding war with Ventana Medical and industrial conglomerate Danaher to acquire Australia-based Vision Systems, which makes tissue and slide preparations systems. Cytyc raised its original offer to about $518 million after Ventana Medical bought up about 10% of Vision Systems' shares. However, Danaher has entered the fray with a higher $520 million offer.

The company acquired women's health medical device company Novacept in March 2004 to strengthen its focus on women's health. Novacept's NovaSure system treats menorrhagia, or excessive menstrual bleeding. In addition, Cytyc has also developed FirstCyte, a test for breast cancer.

It also purchased cancer treatment delivery system developer Proxima Therapeutics for $160 million in March 2005. That purchase

brought the MammoSite Radiation Therapy System and GliaSite Radiation Therapy System into the company's product lines.

Quest Diagnostics accounts for 11% of Cytyc's sales.

HISTORY

Entrepreneur Stanley Lapidus founded Cytyc in 1987 to develop an improved alternative to conventional Pap smears. Developed by Dr. George Papanicolaou as a test for cervical cancer in the late 1940s, Pap smears led to a more than 70% decrease in mortality from cervical cancer. But despite this success, the test was inaccurate, leading to a substantial number of false negative diagnoses. Cytyc began working on a system for automated computer image analysis of Pap smears. When it became apparent that the main obstacle to computer imaging was the poor quality of Pap smears, Cytyc's staff began to focus on developing a better way to prepare slides for cervical screening. In 1991 the company started selling its ThinPrep Processor to cytology labs across the US for use in non-gynecological testing. Cytyc completed clinical trials of the ThinPrep System for gynecological testing in 1995 — using the ThinPrep 2000 (an upgrade of the original processor) plus related disposable reagents, filters, and other supplies.

In 1996 the FDA approved the ThinPrep Pap System as a replacement for the conventional Pap smear for cervical cancer screening. Cytyc went public that year.

The next year the company enlisted Mead Johnson to co-promote ThinPrep across the US and also began marketing the product in Europe. In 1998 Cytyc signed up laboratory services provider DIANON Systems to market ThinPrep to its client base of more than 50,000 physicians nationwide.

In 1999 — the same year Cytyc broke into profitability for the first time — the company sued rival AutoCyte (now TriPath Imaging) over its sample-preserving solution; the battle continued in 2000, when TriPath Imaging countersued, alleging anticompetitive conduct by Cytyc. The companies settled their differences in early 2001. Also in 2001 the company bought Pro Duct Health and gained a ductal lavage device to aid in breast cancer tests. The following year, Cytyc made plans to buy Digene, but the acquisition was scuttled after the FTC protested. In 2005 Cytyc acquired cancer treatment delivery system developer Proxima Therapeutics for $160 million.

EXECUTIVES

Chairman, President, and CEO: Patrick J. Sullivan, age 54, $1,312,693 pay
Vice Chairman: C. William McDaniel, age 65
EVP, Chief Commercial Officer, and Director: Daniel J. (Dan) Levangie, age 56, $847,116 pay
SVP and Chief Medical Officer: James M. Linder, age 52, $525,000 pay
SVP; President, Cytyc International: David P. Harding, age 41
SVP; President, Cytyc Diagnostic Products Division: Stuart A. Kingsley
SVP, Secretary, and General Counsel: A. Suzanne Meszner-Eltrich, age 53
SVP, Development and Operations: John P. McDonough, age 46, $549,423 pay

VP, CFO, and Treasurer: Timothy M. (Tim) Adams, age 47, $550,000 pay
VP and Controller: Leslie Teso-Lichtman, age 47
VP, Commercial Operations: Christopher A. Bleck, age 49, $625,000 pay
VP, Organizational Effectiveness and Human Resources: John M. Melo
VP, Technical Operations: Peter D'Errico, age 48
Auditors: Deloitte & Touche LLP

LOCATIONS

HQ: Cytyc Corporation
250 Campus Dr., Marlborough, MA 01752
Phone: 508-263-2900   **Fax:** 508-229-2795
Web: www.cytyc.com

Cytyc has facilities in Boxborough, Massachusetts and Londonderry, New Hampshire.

2005 Sales

	$ mil.	% of total
Domestic Diagnostic Products	311.3	61
Domestic Surgical Products	143.9	28
International	53.1	11
Total	**508.3**	**100**

PRODUCTS/OPERATIONS

Selected Subsidiaries

Cruiser, Inc.
Cytyc (Australia) PTY LTD
Cytyc Canada, Limited
Cytyc Europe, S.A. (Switzerland)
  Cytyc SARL
    Cytyc Italia s.r.l.
    Cytyc France s.a.r.l.
Cytyc Healthcare Ventures, LLC
Cytyc Iberia S.L. (Spain)
Cytyc Interim, Inc.
Cytyc International, Inc.
Cytyc Securities Corporation
Cytyc Surgical Products
Cytyc (UK) Limited

COMPETITORS

Boston Scientific
Clarient
Digene
Hemagen Diagnostics
Johnson & Johnson
Molecular Diagnostics
Neoprobe
TriPath Imaging

HISTORICAL FINANCIALS

Company Type: Public

Income Statement

FYE: December 31

	REVENUE ($ mil.)	NET INCOME ($ mil.)	NET PROFIT MARGIN	EMPLOYEES
12/05	508.3	113.5	22.3%	1,331
12/04	393.6	73.6	18.7%	1,118
12/03	303.1	76.2	25.1%	723
12/02	236.5	47.9	20.3%	626
12/01	221.0	12.6	5.7%	554
Annual Growth	**23.1%**	**73.2%**	**—**	**24.5%**

2005 Year-End Financials

Debt ratio: 40.1%
Return on equity: 20.3%
Cash ($ mil.): 220.6
Current ratio: 3.78
Long-term debt ($ mil.): 252.2
No. of shares (mil.): 115.3

Dividends
  Yield: —
  Payout: —
Market value ($ mil.): 3,254.2
R&D as % of sales: 6.4%
Advertising as % of sales: —

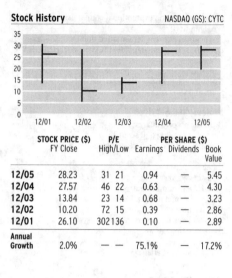

Stock History   NASDAQ (GS): CYTC

	STOCK PRICE ($) FY Close	P/E High/Low	PER SHARE ($) Earnings	Dividends	Book Value
12/05	28.23	31 21	0.94	—	5.45
12/04	27.57	46 22	0.63	—	4.30
12/03	13.84	23 14	0.68	—	3.23
12/02	10.20	72 15	0.39	—	2.86
12/01	26.10	302 136	0.10	—	2.89
Annual Growth	**2.0%**	**— —**	**75.1%**	**—**	**17.2%**

Daktronics

Daktronics always knows the score. The company designs and manufactures electronic display systems. Its products include scoreboards, game timers, shot clocks, and animation displays for sports facilities; advertising and information displays for businesses; and electronic messaging displays used by transportation departments for motorist alerts. Other applications include airport information, securities trading, and outdoor advertising signs. Daktronics has converted many of its products to LED technology. The company's high-profile installations include two of the biggest scoreboards in the world, for the football stadiums of the Miami Dolphins and the University of Texas Longhorns.

Daktronics' programmable signs display everything from a pitcher's statistics to road conditions to the time and temperature. Its products also tally votes in legislative chambers and tout beer in Times Square. With its 2004 acquisition of UK-based European Timing Systems, Daktronics' signs also keep cricket and rugby scores in the UK. Nearly 90 percent of the company's sales come from the US.

Because its product is becoming more affordable, Daktronics is selling more to midsized universities and the minor leagues. The company is also seeing an increase in sales to commercial customers, due in part to Daktronics' increased use of LED; the technology has become more popular since the mid-1990s, because of its visual clarity and cost efficiency.

Co-founder Aelred Kurtenbach (chairman) and his brother Frank (VP) together own about 10% of Daktronics. Independence Investments has an equity stake of 6%. The company's 401(k) plan holds around 4% of the equity.

HISTORY

Daktronics was founded in a garage in 1968 by engineering professors Aelred Kurtenbach and Duane Sander (who later became dean of engineering at South Dakota State University). The company name comes from combining "Dakota"

with "electronics." Two years later the company delivered its first product, a voting display system for the Utah legislature. Scoreboards were added to the product line in 1971; commercial displays in 1973. It introduced computerized controllers in the late 1970s.

The 1980 Winter Olympics in Lake Placid, New York, marked the first time the company provided scoreboards to the Olympic games. During the 1980s Daktronics began installing displays in major-league sports stadiums. In 1988 it bought auto-racing timing equipment maker Chondek. Daktronics continued to advance sign technology during the 1990s, acquiring technology for light-emitting diode (LED) displays. It went public in 1994.

The company supplied five displays and 24 digital clocks to Times Square locations in 1995. Daktronics also provided scoreboards to the 1996 Atlanta Summer Olympics. That year the blue LED, a tiny bulb used with green and red LEDs to produce color on large TV-like screens, was introduced. This allowed the company to add video to its scoreboards. In 1998 Daktronics installed systems in the Indianapolis Motor Speedway, and sports venues in Cleveland, Seattle, and Phoenix.

The company's displays were featured at the 2000 Olympics in Sydney. In 2001 Daktronics bought 80% of Servtrotech (a Canadian electronic display system maker) and Sportslink, Ltd. (a large screen video rental display company). James Morgan became CEO in 2001; Kurtenbach remained chairman.

In July 2003 the company won a contract to provide digital advertising and information displays at the Hubert H. Humphrey Metrodome in Minneapolis. The following year Daktronics expanded its product line and geographic reach with the acquisition of UK-based European Timing Systems (scoreboards and timing systems for cricket, aquatics, and rugby).

Also in late 2004 the company acquired the assets of Dodge Electronics, doing business as Dodge Systems, a supplier of audio systems for sports facilities.

Daktronics expanded its manufacturing facilities in 2006, adding 110,000 sq. ft. of space to its main manufacturing facility in Brookings, South Dakota, and leasing a vacant plant in Sioux Falls with 120,000 sq. ft. of manufacturing space.

The company also agreed to acquire an existing plant in Redwood Falls, Minnesota, from Emerson Electric. Daktronics will use the facility to manufacture its Galaxy line of electronic message displays. The transaction is expected to close in early 2007, with production of Galaxy displays commencing by spring. Moving Galaxy production to Minnesota will free up manufacturing space at the company's plant in Brookings.

EXECUTIVES

Chairman: Aelred J. (Al) Kurtenbach, age 72, $187,550 pay
President, CEO, and Director: James B. (Jim) Morgan, age 60, $348,369 pay
CFO and Treasurer: William R. (Bill) Retterath, age 45, $199,085 pay
VP, Sales and Director: Frank J. Kurtenbach, age 68
VP, Commercial and Transportation Markets:
Bradley T. (Brad) Wiemann, age 43, $167,618 pay
VP, Sports Systems: Seth T. Hansen, age 42
VP, Video Systems: Reece A. Kurtenbach, age 41, $172,661 pay
Personnel Manager and Corporate Secretary:
Carla S. Gatzke, age 44
Large Sports System Sales Manager: Kirk Simet
Auditors: Ernst & Young LLP

LOCATIONS

HQ: Daktronics, Inc.
331 32nd Ave., Brookings, SD 57006
Phone: 605-697-4000   **Fax:** 605-697-4700
Web: www.daktronics.com

Daktronics has manufacturing facilities in Europe and North America, with offices in Canada, China, Germany, the UK, and the US.

2006 Sales

	$ mil.	% of total
US	278.2	90
Other countries	31.2	10
Total	**309.4**	**100**

PRODUCTS/OPERATIONS

Selected Applications and Brands

Business (text-based message displays)
 DataMaster
 DataTime
 DataTrac
 InfoNet
 Galaxy
Sports (indoor and outdoor scoreboards)
 All Sport
 DakStats
 OmniSport
Transportation (traffic direction and motorist information)
 Vanguard
Video (displays combining video, graphics, animation, and text)
 ProAd
 ProStar

COMPETITORS

Advanced Optics Electronics
Aristocrat Leisure
AutoComm
Colorado Time Systems
Digital Recorders
LSI Industries
Mitsubishi Electric
Onscreen Technologies
Panasonic Corporation of North America
PolyVision
Screen Technology
Sony
Trans-Industries
Trans-Lux

HISTORICAL FINANCIALS

Company Type: Public

Income Statement

FYE: Saturday nearest April 30

	REVENUE ($ mil.)	NET INCOME ($ mil.)	NET PROFIT MARGIN	EMPLOYEES
4/06	309.4	21.0	6.8%	2,100
4/05	230.4	15.7	6.8%	1,630
4/04	209.9	17.7	8.4%	1,442
4/03	177.8	12.5	7.0%	1,238
4/02	148.8	4.9	3.3%	1,138
Annual Growth	**20.1%**	**43.9%**	**—**	**16.6%**

2006 Year-End Financials

Debt ratio: 3.6%	Dividends
Return on equity: 18.3%	Yield: 0.3%
Cash ($ mil.): 35.5	Payout: 9.6%
Current ratio: 2.11	Market value ($ mil.): 763.1
Long-term debt ($ mil.): 4.6	R&D as % of sales: 3.6%
No. of shares (mil.): 38.9	Advertising as % of sales: 0.5%

Stock History

NASDAQ (GS): DAKT

	STOCK PRICE ($) FY Close	P/E High/Low		PER SHARE ($) Earnings	Dividends	Book Value
4/06	19.61	41	18	0.52	0.05	3.22
4/05	10.18	38	25	0.39	—	5.43
4/04	10.61	31	16	0.44	—	4.57
4/03	7.34	27	11	0.32	—	3.52
4/02	4.63	69	24	0.13	—	2.82
Annual Growth	**43.5%**	**—**	**—**	**41.4%**	**—**	**3.4%**

Darwin Professional Underwriters

The professionals at Darwin Professional Underwriters know all about the evolution of specialty liability insurance underwriting. The company provides directors and officers (D&O) liability insurance and errors and omissions (E&O) liability insurance for health care professionals and non-medical professionals. The company also writes medical malpractice insurance for the health care industry, as well as commercial risk management and loss control services for large private companies and public corporations.

Alleghany Corporation owns 55% of Darwin Professional Underwriters, which operates under the Alleghany Insurance Holdings umbrella. Members of Darwin management own about 10% of the company, which was founded in 2003 by CEO Stephen Sills. The company went public in 2006.

Darwin Professional Underwriters specializes in difficult-to-place professional liability clients. It targets small legal firms (with fewer than 50 attorneys) and offers medical malpractice coverage for hospitals, health care facilities, and physician and medical groups.

EXECUTIVES

Chairman, President, and CEO: Stephen J. Sills, age 57, $726,900 pay
SVP, CFO, and Director: John L. (Jack) Sennott Jr., age 40, $382,520 pay
SVP and CIO: Robert J. (Bob) Asensio, age 49
SVP and General Counsel: Mark I. Rosen, age 54, $484,590 pay
Secretary and Director: Christopher K. Dalrymple, age 38
Senior Risk Management Officer: Susan R. Chmieleski
Senior Risk Management Officer: Laura P. Martinez
Auditors: KPMG LLP

LOCATIONS

HQ: Darwin Professional Underwriters, Inc.
9 Farm Springs Rd., Farmington, CT 06032
Phone: 860-284-1300   **Fax:** 860-284-1301
Web: www.darwinpro.com

PRODUCTS/OPERATIONS

2005 Sales

	$ mil.	% of total
Net premiums earned	84.7	95
Net investment income	4.9	5
Other income	0.1	—
Net realized investment losses	(0.2)	—
Total	**89.5**	**100**

2005 Gross Premiums Written

	% of total
Medical malpractice liability	45
Errors & omissions	35
Directors & officers	20
Total	**100**

COMPETITORS

ACE Limited	CNA Financial
AIG	RSUI Group
Chubb Corp	Zurich Financial

HISTORICAL FINANCIALS

Company Type: Public

Income Statement

FYE: December 31

	REVENUE ($ mil.)	NET INCOME ($ mil.)	NET PROFIT MARGIN	EMPLOYEES
12/05	89.5	3.7	4.1%	—
12/04	47.0	0.1	0.2%	—
12/03	4.1	(2.3)	—	—
Annual Growth	**367.2%**	**—**	**—**	**—**

2005 Year-End Financials

Debt ratio: —
Return on equity: 3.2%
Cash ($ mil.): —
Current ratio: —
Long-term debt ($ mil.): —

Net Income History

NYSE Arca: DR

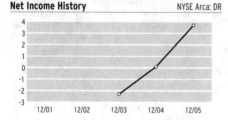

DATATRAK International

Researchers rely on DATATRAK to keep track of their clinical data. The company develops online, hosted electronic data capture (EDC) software for the biotechnology, medical device, contract research, and pharmaceutical industries. The company' software speeds up the process of gathering data during clinical trials by collecting and electronically transmitting trial data from remote research sites to sponsors. DATATRAK also offers project management, site assessment, training, and hosting services.

DATATRAK has an alliance with SAS Institute to offer a joint clinical trial data analysis product, combining SAS's drug development applications with DATATRAK software.

EXECUTIVES

President, CEO, and Director: Jeffrey A. (Jeff) Green, age 50, $209,230 pay
VP, Finance, CFO, Treasurer, and Assistant Secretary: Terry C. Black, age 48, $148,830 pay
VP, eClinical Development: Bob Ward, age 45
VP, Product Strategy: Marc J. Shlaes, age 51, $151,040 pay
VP, Strategic Business Relationships: Wolfgang Summa, age 41
Secretary: Thomas F. McKee, age 57
Director, Product Development: Jochen van Berkel
Database Administrator: Jeffrey Cowen
Auditors: Ernst & Young LLP

LOCATIONS

HQ: DATATRAK International, Inc.
6150 Parkland Blvd., Ste. 100,
Mayfield Heights, OH 44124
Phone: 440-443-0082   **Fax:** 440-442-3482
Web: www.datatraknet.com

DATATRAK International has offices in Germany and the US.

PRODUCTS/OPERATIONS

Software

DATATRAK EDC (electronic data capture application)
  DATATRAK DATALOADER (automated data loading)
  DATATRAK Design (electronic case form design)
  DATATRAK Entry (for data entry over the Web)
  DATATRAK Export (for data transfer)
  DATATRAK Report (report creation for online viewing and printing)
  DATATRAK Review (for review of cross patient information)

Selected Services

Application and data hosting
Project management
Technical support
Training
Web-based site assessment

COMPETITORS

AMICAS
Bio-Imaging Technologies
Cerner
Emdeon
Encorium Group
eResearchTechnology
McKesson
MDS
Oracle
Orchard Software
PAREXEL
Pharmaceutical Product Development
Phase Forward
PRA International

HISTORICAL FINANCIALS

Company Type: Public

Income Statement

FYE: December 31

	REVENUE ($ mil.)	NET INCOME ($ mil.)	NET PROFIT MARGIN	EMPLOYEES
12/05	15.7	2.5	15.9%	110
12/04	11.3	0.8	7.1%	75
12/03	7.1	(1.0)	—	65
12/02	4.7	(6.4)	—	55
12/01	2.3	(7.3)	—	80
Annual Growth	**61.6%**	**—**	**—**	**8.3%**

2005 Year-End Financials

Debt ratio: —
Return on equity: 21.0%
Cash ($ mil.): 9.4
Current ratio: 5.48
Long-term debt ($ mil.): —
No. of shares (mil.): 10.3
Dividends
  Yield: —
  Payout: —
Market value ($ mil.): 103.0
R&D as % of sales: 10.2%
Advertising as % of sales: 1.0%

Stock History

NASDAQ (CM): DATA

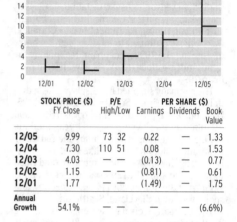

	STOCK PRICE ($) FY Close	P/E High/Low		PER SHARE ($) Earnings	Dividends	Book Value
12/05	9.99	73	32	0.22	—	1.33
12/04	7.30	110	51	0.08	—	1.53
12/03	4.03	—	—	(0.13)	—	0.77
12/02	1.15	—	—	(0.81)	—	0.61
12/01	1.77	—	—	(1.49)	—	1.75
Annual Growth	**54.1%**	**—**	**—**	**—**	**—**	**(6.6%)**

Dawson Geophysical

The oil industry can be shaky at times, but Dawson Geophysical always looks for good vibrations. The company, founded in 1952, provides data acquisition and data processing services including the analysis of 2-D, 3-D, and 4-D seismic data to assess potential underground oil and gas deposits. Dawson Geophysical's customers, both major and independent oil and gas operators, use the data in exploration and development activities. The company's 12 3-D seismic data acquisition crews work in the lower 48 states of the US; data processing is performed by geophysicists at the firm's computer center in Midland, Texas.

A rebound in the oil industry has enabled Dawson Geophysical to put more crews back to work, although competition has driven down the prices. The company has expanded the number of data acquisition crews it has working in the field and has upgraded its data processing center. 3-D seismic services account for the majority of the company's total sales. Beddow Capital Management owns 6.4% of the company. Founder and chairman Decker Dawson owns 5.4% of the company.

HISTORY

Geophysicist Decker Dawson started Dawson Geophysical in 1952 as a sole proprietorship, with one crew. At the time, seismic surveying consisted of setting off dynamite charges and recording tremors on a 24-channel recorder. In the 1950s and 1960s the company upgraded its services as technologies improved.

When the 1973 OPEC oil embargo fueled a major US oil exploration drive, Dawson Geophysical brought on line the nation's first 120-channel land-based system and the country's second 1,000-channel system. Anticipating demand for 3-D seismic data, the firm went public

in 1981 to raise capital to develop the technology. In 1988 it became one of the first companies to employ 3-D seismic surveying in West Texas. Demand for Dawson Geophysical's services increased during the 1990s.

In 1995 a work-related vehicle crash killed four Dawson employees and opened the company up to yet-to-be adjudicated lawsuits. The company raised about $21 million in a public stock offering in 1997 to fund expansion and reduce its debt. It bought $6 million worth of new equipment that year.

El Niño storms in 1998 disrupted work and crimped Dawson Geophysical's earnings. Worse, world oil prices softened, suggesting that oil companies would stop drilling. A backlog of orders, however, helped Dawson withstand market conditions for a while, but by early 1999 the firm was operating only one crew. In 1999 the industry as a whole began to rebound, and Dawson put five of its six crews back in operation in 2000.

In 2003 Dawson completed the opening of an office in Oklahoma City in an effort to better serve the US Midcontinent region.

EXECUTIVES

Chairman: L. Decker Dawson, age 85
President, CEO, and Director: Stephen C. Jumper, age 44
EVP, CFO, Secretary, and Treasurer: Christina W. Hagan, age 50, $145,243 pay
EVP: Howell W. Pardue, age 69
COO: C. Ray Tobias, age 48
SVP: Edward L. Huff, age 68, $136,357 pay
Human Resources: Olga Seay
Auditors: KPMG LLP

LOCATIONS

HQ: Dawson Geophysical Company
508 W. Wall, Ste. 800, Midland, TX 79701
Phone: 432-684-3000   **Fax:** 432-684-3030
Web: www.dawson3d.com

Dawson Geophysical operates throughout the lower 48 states in the US through offices in Denver; Houston and Midland, Texas; and Oklahoma City.

PRODUCTS/OPERATIONS

Services

Data processing and analysis
Seismic data acquisition services

COMPETITORS

CGGVeritas	Seitel
Input/Output	TGC Industries
OYO Geospace	TGS-NOPEC
Paradigm Ltd.	WesternGeco
Petroleum Geo-Services	

HISTORICAL FINANCIALS

Company Type: Public

Income Statement				FYE: September 30
	REVENUE ($ mil.)	NET INCOME ($ mil.)	NET PROFIT MARGIN	EMPLOYEES
9/06	168.6	15.9	9.4%	1,023
9/05	116.7	10.0	8.6%	803
9/04	69.3	8.6	12.4%	567
9/03	51.6	(0.9)	—	448
9/02	36.1	(2.3)	—	375
Annual Growth	47.0%	—		28.5%

2006 Year-End Financials

Debt ratio: —
Return on equity: 14.4%
Cash ($ mil.): 14.5
Current ratio: 2.70
Long-term debt ($ mil.): —
No. of shares (mil.): 7.5

Dividends
Yield: —
Payout: —
Market value ($ mil.): 224.2
R&D as % of sales: —
Advertising as % of sales: —

Stock History

NASDAQ (GM): DWSN

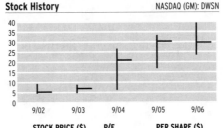

	STOCK PRICE ($) FY Close	P/E High/Low		PER SHARE ($) Earnings	Dividends	Book Value
9/06	29.70	19	11	2.09	—	15.79
9/05	30.25	22	12	1.48	—	13.62
9/04	20.92	17	4	1.53	—	8.92
9/03	6.89	—	—	(0.16)	—	7.41
9/02	5.24	—	—	(0.42)	—	7.61
Annual Growth	54.3%	—	—	—	—	20.0%

DCP Midstream Partners

The D in DCP Midstream Partners (formerly Duke Energy Field Services) is for Duke Energy; the CP, ConocoPhillips. These two energy majors formed DCP Midstream Partners in 2005. It is engaged in natural gas gathering, compressing, treating, processing, transporting, and selling. DCP Midstream Partners also transports and sells natural gas liquids (NGLs). The company operates in 16 US states, gathers raw natural gas through 56,000 miles of gathering pipe and processes it through 53 plants. DCP Midstream Partners operates 10 fractionating plants. Following the spin off of Spectra Energy from Duke Energy, Spectra Energy assumed Duke Energy's 50% holding.

DCP Midstream Partners is one of the largest natural gas gatherers in North America. It is also the largest producer and one of the largest marketers of NGLs.

EXECUTIVES

Chairman, DCP Midstream GP: Jim W. Mogg, age 57
President, CEO and Director, DCP Midstream GP: Mark A. Borer, age 51
VP and CFO, DCP Midstream GP: Thomas E. Long, age 49
VP and Controller, DCP Midstream GP: Patrick J. Welch
VP, General Counsel, and Secretary, DCP Midstream GP: Michael S. Richards, age 46
VP, Business Development, DCP Midstream GP: Greg K. Smith, age 39
Auditors: Deloitte & Touche LLP

LOCATIONS

HQ: DCP Midstream Partners, LP
370 17th St., Ste. 2775, Denver, CO 80202
Phone: 303-633-2900   **Fax:** 303-605-2225
Web: www.dcppartners.com

COMPETITORS

Dynegy
El Paso
Enterprise Products
SandRidge Energy
Williams Companies
XTO Energy

HISTORICAL FINANCIALS

Company Type: Public

Income Statement				FYE: December 31
	REVENUE ($ mil.)	NET INCOME ($ mil.)	NET PROFIT MARGIN	EMPLOYEES
12/05	784.5	38.0	4.8%	64
12/04	509.5	20.4	4.0%	65
12/03	475.1	10.0	2.1%	—
12/02	297.2	8.5	2.9%	—
Annual Growth	38.2%	64.7%	—	(1.5%)

2005 Year-End Financials

Debt ratio: 210.7%
Return on equity: 25.4%
Cash ($ mil.): 42.3
Current ratio: 1.33
Long-term debt ($ mil.): 212.6
No. of shares (mil.): 10.4

Dividends
Yield: —
Payout: —
Market value ($ mil.): 253.7
R&D as % of sales: —
Advertising as % of sales: —

Stock History

NYSE: DPM

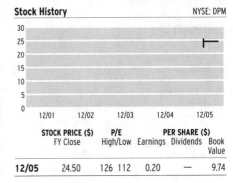

	STOCK PRICE ($) FY Close	P/E High/Low		PER SHARE ($) Earnings	Dividends	Book Value
12/05	24.50	126	112	0.20	—	9.74

DealerTrack Holdings

DealerTrack Holdings helps car dealers play their cards right in the financing game. The company provides Web-based software that links automotive dealerships with banks, finance companies, credit unions, credit reporting agencies, and other players in the car sales and financing process. Through its software, DealerTrack connects clients to its network of auto dealers, financing sources, and other service and information providers. The company, which generates revenues through subscriptions and transaction-based fees, also offers tools that automate credit application processing, ensure document legal compliance, and execute electronic financing contracts.

DealerTrack has also been using acquisitions to build its business. In 2005 the company bought the assets of Automotive Lease Guide (a provider of lease residual value data for automobiles), North American Advanced Technology (tools for automating after-market product administration), and Chrome Systems (data collection and enhancement tools for vertical industries).

First Advantage and JPMorgan each own about 15% of the company.

EXECUTIVES

Chairman, President, and CEO: Mark F. O'Neil, age 47, $1,076,000 pay
SVP, CFO, and Treasurer: Robert J. Cox III, age 40
SVP, General Counsel, and Secretary: Eric D. Jacobs, age 39, $430,000 pay
SVP and Head of Dealer Solutions: Raj Sundaram, age 39
SVP and Head of Network Solutions: David P. Trinder, age 47
SVP, Strategy and Development: Richard McLeer, age 41
VP, Marketing: Alexi Venneri
President, DealerTrack Data Services: John A. Blair, age 45, $418,995 pay (partial-year salary)
VP, Human Resources, DealerTrack, Inc.: Ana M. Herrera, age 49
Senior Lender Sales Manager: Frank Noto
Auditors: PricewaterhouseCoopers LLP

LOCATIONS

HQ: DealerTrack Holdings, Inc.
1111 Marcus Ave., Ste. M04,
Lake Success, NY 11042
Phone: 516-734-3600 **Fax:** 516-734-3809
Web: www.dealertrack.com

COMPETITORS

ADP
Auto Data Network
Microsoft Business Solutions
NSB Retail Systems
Reynolds and Reynolds
RouteOne
TSA

HISTORICAL FINANCIALS
Company Type: Public

Income Statement
FYE: December 31

	REVENUE ($ mil.)	NET INCOME ($ mil.)	NET PROFIT MARGIN	EMPLOYEES
12/05	120.2	4.5	3.7%	539
12/04	70.0	11.3	16.1%	499
12/03	38.7	(3.3)	—	—
12/02	11.7	(16.8)	—	—
Annual Growth	117.4%	—	—	8.0%

2005 Year-End Financials

Debt ratio: 0.0%
Return on equity: 5.4%
Cash ($ mil.): 103.3
Current ratio: 4.94
Long-term debt ($ mil.): 0.0
No. of shares (mil.): 35.4
Dividends
  Yield: —
  Payout: —
Market value ($ mil.): 742.3
R&D as % of sales: 4.6%
Advertising as % of sales: 0.6%

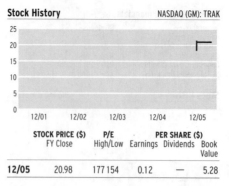
Dearborn Bancorp

Frankly, my Dearborn, they do give a damn. Dearborn Bancorp is the holding company for Community Bank of Dearborn, founded in 1994, and Fidelity Bank, acquired in early 2007. The banks use community involvement and telemarketing campaigns to market their products to local citizens and small businesses. They have about 20 locations in suburban Detroit and points west, offering checking and savings accounts, money market accounts, and CDs. Lending activities include commercial mortgages (slightly more than half of the company's loan portfolio), as well as residential, business, consumer, and construction loans. Subsidiaries provide insurance, mortgage, and auditing services.

In 2004 Dearborn Bancorp bought Bank of Washtenaw, which operated three branches in Ann Arbor and Saline, Michigan, from Pavillion Bancorp. The company finalized its purchase of Fidelity Financial Corporation of Michigan, the holding company for Fidelity Bank, for some $70 million in 2007. Fidelity Bank, which operates seven branches in southeastern Michigan, retained its name after the merger.

Directors and executive officers of Dearborn Bancorp own about a quarter of the company; institutional investor Wellington Management holds around 10%.

EXECUTIVES

Chairman, Dearborn Bancorp and Community Bank of Dearborn: John E. Demmer, age 82
President, CEO, and Director, Dearborn Bancorp and Community Bank of Dearborn: Michael J. Ross, age 55, $424,039 pay
VP, Treasurer, and Secretary; SVP, CFO, and Secretary, Community Bank of Dearborn: Jeffrey L. Karafa, age 41, $195,885 pay
Northeast Regional President, Community Bank of Dearborn: Stephen C. Tarczy, age 56, $219,039 pay
Oakland Regional President, Community Bank of Dearborn: John Lindsey
Washtenaw Regional President, Community Bank of Dearborn: Walter G. Byers, age 56
SVP and Head of Lending, Community Bank of Dearborn: Warren R. Musson, age 49, $219,039 pay
SVP, Branch Operations, Community Bank of Dearborn: Jeffrey J. Wolber, age 50, $161,808 pay
Human Resources Officer, Community Bank of Dearborn: Elizabeth A. Pizzo

LOCATIONS

HQ: Dearborn Bancorp, Inc.
1360 Porter St., Dearborn, MI 48124
Phone: 313-565-5700 **Fax:** 313-561-2291
Web: www.cbdear.com

Dearborn Bancorp has offices in the Michigan communities of Allen Park, Ann Arbor (2), Auburn Hills, Canton, Clinton Township (2), Dearborn (2), Dearborn Heights, Plymouth, Saline, and Southgate.

PRODUCTS/OPERATIONS

2005 Sales

	$ mil.	% of total
Interest income		
Interest on loans	42.9	95
Other interest income	0.9	2
Noninterest income	1.5	3
Total	**45.3**	**100**

Selected Subsidiaries

Community Bank of Dearborn
  Community Bank Audit Services, Inc.
  Community Bank Insurance Agency, Inc.
  Community Bank Mortgage, Inc.

COMPETITORS

Comerica
Fifth Third
Flagstar Bancorp
Huntington Bancshares
LaSalle Bank
National City

HISTORICAL FINANCIALS
Company Type: Public

Income Statement
FYE: December 31

	ASSETS ($ mil.)	NET INCOME ($ mil.)	INCOME AS % OF ASSETS	EMPLOYEES
12/05	706.5	7.5	1.1%	151
12/04	652.7	5.5	0.8%	153
12/03	446.1	3.5	0.8%	125
12/02	325.1	2.7	0.8%	112
12/01	226.9	1.5	0.7%	70
Annual Growth	32.8%	49.5%	—	21.2%

2005 Year-End Financials

Equity as % of assets: 11.9%
Return on assets: 1.1%
Return on equity: 9.4%
Long-term debt ($ mil.): 10.0
No. of shares (mil.): 5.4
Market value ($ mil.): 121.8
Dividends
  Yield: —
  Payout: —
Sales ($ mil.): 45.3
R&D as % of sales: —
Advertising as % of sales: —

Stock History NASDAQ (GM): DEAR

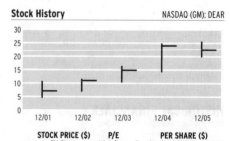

	STOCK PRICE ($) FY Close	P/E High/Low	PER SHARE ($) Earnings	Dividends	Book Value
12/05	22.45	21 17	1.20	—	15.53
12/04	23.99	23 14	1.05	—	15.56
12/03	14.84	20 13	0.83	—	11.76
12/02	10.97	17 11	0.66	—	11.74
12/01	7.09	28 12	0.38	—	11.85
Annual Growth	33.4%	— —	33.3%	—	7.0%

Deckers Outdoor

There's no business like shoe business for Deckers Outdoor. The company designs and markets Teva sports sandals, a cross between a hiking boot and a flip-flop, which are used for walking, hiking, and rafting, among other pursuits. While imitations flood the market, the company distinguishes Teva from its numerous competitors by avoiding distribution in off-price outlets, creating a superior brand image for the sandals. Other product lines include Simple (casual footwear) and UGG (sheepskin boots/shoes). Deckers Outdoor's products are made by independent contractors in Asia, Australia, and New Zealand. Chairman Douglas Otto owns about 13% of the company.

Deckers Outdoor sells through independent distributors, catalogs, the Internet, and two company owned retail outlets.

The company intends to continue its growth by expanding internationally (currently less than 15% of sales) and acquiring or developing new brands. International growth will be supported through adding offices in Europe and Asia to support advertising, distribution, marketing, and sales initiatives there.

Deckers has also made a gesture catering to UGG (short for "ugly" in its original down-underese) loyals: in 2004 it signed licensing deals for the manufacture of handbags and outerwear, as well as cold-weather accessories including gloves, hats, and scarves, that match the hideous boots.

The surge of UGG sales has led to a debate over whether the name is generic or a trademark that could possibly be defended over international boundaries. Australian makers of the sheepskin boots, traditionally called uggs, contend that the name is generic, akin to trying to protect the name "sneaker" as a trademark. However, the trend has reached its height, and suddenly American consumers are looking beyond Deckers for ugg sources, which has loosened Deckers' grip on the brand name. As the word "ugg" is not as widespread stateside, Deckers contends that the trademark is therefore regional, and that the company has a right to ask Aussie producers of uggs to cease and desist.

HISTORY

Douglas Otto and his former partner, Karl Lopker, founded Styled Steers in 1973. But the small, obscure maker of leather sandals gained prominence with a line of multicolored rubber sandals. Surfers in Hawaii called them "deckers," and the company soon adopted the name. In 1985 Deckers Outdoor licensed Teva from river guide Mark Thatcher, who invented the Teva strapping system for rafters to ensure sandals remained attached in turbulent waters. Teva sport sandals became a popular form of casual footwear, largely through word of mouth. The company is the exclusive licensee of Teva shoes, the design of which Thatcher has defended repeatedly against would-be copycats.

In 1994 Deckers Outdoor expanded the Teva line to include closed footwear. With the popularity of Teva sandals seemingly on the wane, the next year it diversified, acquiring rival shoe companies Alp Sport Sandals and UGG Holdings and expanding into the women's and children's markets. A glut of sports sandals depressed sales the following year, but with new products and new marketing, Teva sales increased in 1997.

That year, targeting international expansion, the company acquired German distribution rights to Simple shoes from Vision Warenhandels. Also in 1997 Deckers Outdoor sold its interest in Trukke Winter Sports Products to focus on its core lines.

Thatcher settled with Wal-Mart Stores in 1998 after suing the company over patent and copyright infringement. The firm exited the manufacturing business that year and turned production over to suppliers, mainly in China. In mid-1999 Deckers Outdoor renewed its license with Thatcher through 2011. Continuing to divest noncore operations, in 2000 the company sold its 50% interest in Heirlooms, the makers of the Picante line. The company also hired an ex-adidas exec to help increase Teva's global business (26% in 1999).

In 2000 Otto gave up the president in his title to Peter Benjamin, who was charged with rejuvenating and giving each brand more individualized marketing. In 2001 sales slumped nearly 20% due in part to the weak economy and a bankruptcy filing by one of Deckers Outdoor's largest customers, Track n' Trail. In late 2002, Peter Benjamin resigned as president so that he could return to focusing on sales to Asia.

The company purchased Teva's total assets from its inventor and trademarks and patents holder, Mark Thatcher, in November 2002.

In the second half of 2003 the UGG brand enjoyed unusually rapid growth in demand, helping to send Deckers Outdoor's sales up 22% for the year. In 2004 Deckers inked licensing agreements for the manufacture of UGG handbags and outerwear, as well as gloves, hats, and scarves. The same year the company signed a separate licensing deal with RMP Athletic Locker for the manufacture of Teva sportswear.

In April 2005 Angel Martinez, a former Reebok executive, became president and CEO of the company. Doug Otto retains his position as chairman of the board.

EXECUTIVES

Chairman: Douglas B. Otto, age 54, $401,000 pay (prior to title change)
President, CEO, and Director: Angel R. Martinez, age 50
CFO, EVP, Finance and Administration, and Assistant Secretary: Zohar Ziv, age 53
SVP, Global Sourcing, Production and Development: Patrick C. Devaney, age 51, $279,000 pay
SVP, International Business: Colin G. Clark, age 43
VP, Operations: Janice M. Howell, age 56
President, Teva Brand: Peter (Pete) Worley, age 45
President, Ugg and Simple Divisions: Constance X. (Connie) Rishwain, age 48, $371,000 pay
Human Resources Coordinator: Jennifer Toth
Auditors: KPMG LLP

LOCATIONS

HQ: Deckers Outdoor Corporation
495-A S. Fairview Ave., Goleta, CA 93117
Phone: 805-967-7611   **Fax:** 805-967-7862
Web: www.deckers.com

Deckers Outdoor operates retail outlets in Camarillo and Ventura, California.

2005 Sales

	$ mil.	% of total
US	229.5	87
Other countries	35.3	13
Total	**264.8**	**100**

PRODUCTS/OPERATIONS

2005 Sales

	$ mil.	% of total
UGG wholesale	150.3	57
Teva wholesale	80.4	30
Consumer direct	27.1	10
Simple wholesale	7.0	3
Total	**264.8**	**100**

Selected Products

Teva sports sandals and footwear (casual and sport sandals and shoes)
  Hydro
  Kids and infants
  Nomadic
  Sun and Moon
  Terrain
UGG Footwear (sheepskin boots and shoes)
  Casual collection
  Classic collection
  Cold weather collection
  Driving collection
  Fluff momma collection
  Slipper collection
  Ultra collection
Simple Casual Footwear (casual shoes)
  "9 to 5" Casuals
  Clogs
  Green Toe
  Sandals
  Sneakers

COMPETITORS

adidas
Birkenstock Distribution USA
Columbia Sportswear
Converse
Crocs
Diesel
Fila USA
Guess
Jimlar
Kenneth Cole
K-Swiss
L.L. Bean
NIKE
Phoenix Footwear
PUMA
R. Griggs
Reebok
Rocky Brands
Skechers U.S.A.
Steven Madden
Timberland
Vans
Wolverine World Wide

HISTORICAL FINANCIALS

Company Type: Public

Income Statement

	REVENUE ($ mil.)	NET INCOME ($ mil.)	NET PROFIT MARGIN	EMPLOYEES
12/05	264.8	31.8	12.0%	225
12/04	214.8	25.5	11.9%	187
12/03	121.1	9.1	7.5%	163
12/02	99.1	(7.3)	—	162
12/01	91.5	1.6	1.7%	130
Annual Growth	**30.4%**	**111.1%**	**—**	**14.7%**

FYE: December 31

2005 Year-End Financials

Debt ratio: —	Dividends
Return on equity: 20.0%	Yield: —
Cash ($ mil.): 53.3	Payout: —
Current ratio: 4.86	Market value ($ mil.): 343.4
Long-term debt ($ mil.): —	R&D as % of sales: 0.7%
No. of shares (mil.): 12.4	Advertising as % of sales: —

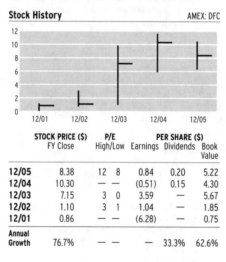

	STOCK PRICE ($) FY Close	P/E High/Low		PER SHARE ($) Earnings	Dividends	Book Value
12/05	27.62	19	7	2.48	—	14.28
12/04	46.99	23	8	2.10	—	11.57
12/03	20.50	29	4	0.77	—	7.25
12/02	3.34	—	—	(0.75)	—	6.89
12/01	4.25	30	19	0.17	—	7.14
Annual Growth	59.7%	—	—	95.4%	—	18.9%

Delta Financial

Delta Financial specializes in originating non-conforming mortgage loans usually secured by first liens on one- to four-family residential properties (i.e. home equity loans). Wholesale subsidiary Delta Funding operates through a network of some 3,000 independent brokers in more than 30 states. Its Fidelity Mortgage unit comprises the retail segment and has about a dozen offices that lend directly to borrowers across the US. The company securitizes and sells a majority of its loans. Delta Financial's customers, who typically don't meet conventional guidelines, typically use loans for debt consolidation, refinancing, education, and home improvement.

EXECUTIVES

Chairman: Sidney A. Miller, age 71
President, CEO, and Director: Hugh I. Miller, age 42, $1,700,000 pay
EVP, CFO, and Director: Richard Blass, age 42, $950,000 pay
EVP, Chief Credit Officer, and Treasurer: Lee Miller, age 36, $625,000 pay
EVP, Sales and Marketing: Randall F. Michaels, age 46, $906,284 pay
SVP and Assistant CFO: William A. (Bill) Walter
SVP, General Counsel, and Secretary: Marc E. Miller, age 39, $500,000 pay
VP, Corporate Tax: Richard F. Schneider
VP, Human Resources: Louise Juliano
Director, Corporate Communications: Drew Biondo
Director, Investor Relations: Jayne L. Cavuoto-Krafchik
Auditors: BDO Seidman, LLP

LOCATIONS

HQ: Delta Financial Corporation
1000 Woodbury Rd., Ste. 200, Woodbury, NY 11797
Phone: 516-364-8500   **Fax:** 516-364-9459
Web: www.deltafinancial.com

PRODUCTS/OPERATIONS

2005 Sales

	$ mil.	% of total
Interest income	290.8	88
Net gain on sale of mortgage loans	27.2	8
Other	14.7	4
Total	**332.7**	**100**

COMPETITORS

1st Franklin Financial
ACC Capital Holdings
Accredited Home Lenders
AmeriCredit
CitiFinancial
Green Tree Servicing
HSBC Finance
Impac Mortgage Holdings
New Century Mortgage
Quicken Loans

HISTORICAL FINANCIALS

Company Type: Public

Income Statement

FYE: December 31

	ASSETS ($ mil.)	NET INCOME ($ mil.)	INCOME AS % OF ASSETS	EMPLOYEES
12/05	4,819.6	18.0	0.4%	1,327
12/04	2,490.8	(9.4)	—	1,123
12/03	257.0	67.4	26.2%	912
12/02	73.5	17.6	23.9%	693
12/01	132.4	(99.8)	—	609
Annual Growth	145.6%	—	—	21.5%

2005 Year-End Financials

Equity as % of assets: 2.2%
Return on assets: 0.5%
Return on equity: 18.6%
Long-term debt ($ mil.): 4,666.5
No. of shares (mil.): 20.5
Market value ($ mil.): 171.5

Dividends
  Yield: 2.4%
  Payout: 23.8%
Sales ($ mil.): 332.7
R&D as % of sales: —
Advertising as % of sales: —

Stock History

AMEX: DFC

	STOCK PRICE ($) FY Close	P/E High/Low		PER SHARE ($) Earnings	Dividends	Book Value
12/05	8.38	12	8	0.84	0.20	5.22
12/04	10.30	—	—	(0.51)	0.15	4.30
12/03	7.15	3	0	3.59	—	5.67
12/02	1.10	3	1	1.04	—	1.85
12/01	0.86	—	—	(6.28)	—	0.75
Annual Growth	76.7%	—	—	—	33.3%	62.6%

Denbury Resources

Denbury Resources has long since capped its oil and gas operations in its native Canada to try its luck in the Deep South. The independent exploration and production company has estimated proved reserves of 152.6 million barrels of oil equivalent and working interests in wells across Louisiana, Mississippi, Texas, and in the Gulf of Mexico. In Mississippi it also owns wells that produce carbon dioxide (CO_2), which it uses to force oil out of the ground at nearby abandoned wells. In 2002 Denbury Resources bought Genesis Energy LLC, the general partner of Gulf Coast crude oil marketer Genesis Energy, L.P., and the Gulf Coast properties of Coho Energy.

EXECUTIVES

Chairman: Ronald G. Greene, age 57
President, CEO, and Director: Gareth Roberts, age 53, $538,337 pay
SVP, CFO, Secretary, and Treasurer: Phil Rykhoek, age 49, $384,526 pay
SVP Operations: Robert Cornelius, age 51
SVP Reservoir Engineering: Ronald T. (Tracy) Evans, age 43, $384,526 pay
VP and Chief Accounting Officer: Mark C. Allen, age 38, $271,515 pay
VP Exploration: James H. Sinclair, age 43
VP Land: Ray Dubuisson, age 55
VP Marketing: Dan Cole
Director, Investor Relations: Laurie Burkes
Auditors: PricewaterhouseCoopers LLP

LOCATIONS

HQ: Denbury Resources Inc.
5100 Tennyson Pkwy., Ste. 1200, Plano, TX 75024
Phone: 972-673-2000   **Fax:** 972-673-2150
Web: www.denbury.com

Denbury Resources operates in Louisiana, Mississippi, Texas, and the Gulf of Mexico.

PRODUCTS/OPERATIONS

2005 Sales

	$ mil.	% of total
Oil, natural gas & related products	549.1	98
CO2 sales and transportation fees	8.1	1
Other	3.2	1
Total	**560.4**	**100**

Selected Subsidiaries

Denbury Energy Services, Inc.
Denbury Marine, L.L.C.
Genesis Energy LLC (general partner of Genesis Energy, L.P.)

COMPETITORS

Abraxas Petroleum
Apache
BP
Chevron
Delta Petroleum
Exxon Mobil
Forest Oil
McMoRan Exploration
Meridian Resource
Murphy Oil
Newfield Exploration
Remington Oil and Gas
Royal Dutch Shell
Swift Energy

HISTORICAL FINANCIALS

Company Type: Public

Income Statement

FYE: December 31

	REVENUE ($ mil.)	NET INCOME ($ mil.)	NET PROFIT MARGIN	EMPLOYEES
12/05	560.4	166.5	29.7%	460
12/04	383.0	82.4	21.5%	380
12/03	333.0	56.5	17.0%	374
12/02	285.1	46.8	16.4%	356
12/01	285.1	56.5	19.8%	320
Annual Growth	18.4%	31.0%	—	9.5%

2005 Year-End Financials

Debt ratio: 52.6%
Return on equity: 26.1%
Cash ($ mil.): 165.1
Current ratio: 1.94
Long-term debt ($ mil.): 386.1
No. of shares (mil.): 114.7

Dividends
  Yield: —
  Payout: —
Market value ($ mil.): 2,612.8
R&D as % of sales: —
Advertising as % of sales: —

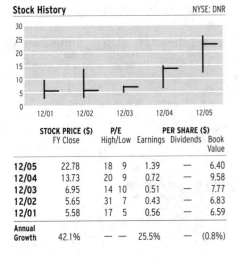

	STOCK PRICE ($) FY Close	P/E High/Low		PER SHARE ($) Earnings	Dividends	Book Value
12/05	22.78	18	9	1.39	—	6.40
12/04	13.73	20	9	0.72	—	9.58
12/03	6.95	14	10	0.51	—	7.77
12/02	5.65	31	7	0.43	—	6.83
12/01	5.58	17	5	0.56	—	6.59
Annual Growth	42.1%	—	—	25.5%	—	(0.8%)

Digene

Digene checks to see if women's genes fit a dangerous profile. The company is focused on developing DNA and RNA tests that screen for infectious diseases and cancers afflicting women. Using its Hybrid Capture technology, Digene has developed tests for the detection of human papillomavirus (linked to cervical cancer) and sexually transmitted diseases including chlamydia, gonorrhea, and hepatitis B. Its HPV diagnostic is the only test of its kind to be approved by the FDA. The company currently markets the test worldwide, directly in the US and through subsidiaries and distribution agreements abroad.

The company is looking to expand its offerings of gene-based diagnostic tests through acquisitions and in-licensing. To that end it has bought marketing and distribution rights to Asuragen's cystic fibrosis screening products. It has also licensed access to Luminex's xMAP technology, which can analyze a variety of bioassays quickly, to develop new women's health diagnostics.

Chairman Evan Jones and former executive Charles Fleischman jointly own about 6% of Digene through Armonk Partners.

EXECUTIVES

Chairman: Evan Jones, age 49, $954,833 pay
President, CEO, and Director: Daryl J. Faulkner, age 57
SVP and CFO: Joseph P. Slattery, age 41
SVP, Science and Technology and Chief Scientific Officer: Attila T. Lörincz, age 51, $506,475 pay
SVP, Global Sales and Marketing: Robert McG. Lilley, age 61
SVP, Manufacturing Operations: Belinda O. Patrick, age 50
SVP, Research and Development: James H. Godsey, age 55
SVP, Sales and Marketing, Americas and Asia Pacific: C. Douglas White, age 44, $418,883 pay
SVP, General Counsel, and Secretary: Vincent J. Napoleon, age 46
VP, Corporate Communications: Pamela (Pam) Rasmussen
VP, Human Resources: Larry Wellman
Investor Relations: Albert Fleury
Auditors: Ernst & Young LLP

LOCATIONS

HQ: Digene Corporation
1201 Clopper Rd., Gaithersburg, MD 20878
Phone: 301-944-7000   **Fax:** 240-632-7121
Web: www.digene.com

2006 Sales

	$ mil.	% of total
North America	123.1	80
Europe	19.4	13
Pacific Rim	5.7	4
Latin America	4.7	3
Total	**152.9**	**100**

PRODUCTS/OPERATIONS

2006 Sales

	$ mil.	% of total
Product sales	150.8	99
Other	2.1	1
Total	**152.9**	**100**

COMPETITORS

Abbott Labs	Orgenics
Bayer	Quidel
Chiron	Roche Diagnostics
Cytyc	Third Wave Technologies
Gen-Probe	TriPath Imaging
Healthcare Technologies	Ventana Medical
Meridian Bioscience	

HISTORICAL FINANCIALS

Company Type: Public

Income Statement

FYE: June 30

	REVENUE ($ mil.)	NET INCOME ($ mil.)	NET PROFIT MARGIN	EMPLOYEES
6/06	152.9	8.4	5.5%	490
6/05	115.1	(8.2)	—	401
6/04	90.2	21.5	23.8%	359
6/03	63.1	(4.3)	—	297
6/02	48.8	(9.4)	—	243
Annual Growth	33.0%	—	—	19.2%

2006 Year-End Financials

Debt ratio: 11.2%
Return on equity: 6.6%
Cash ($ mil.): 139.3
Current ratio: 5.27
Long-term debt ($ mil.): 19.8
No. of shares (mil.): 23.2
Dividends
  Yield: —
  Payout: —
Market value ($ mil.): 900.5
R&D as % of sales: —
Advertising as % of sales: —

Stock History

NASDAQ (GS): DIGE

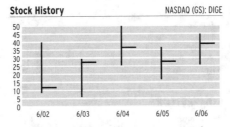

	STOCK PRICE ($) FY Close	P/E High/Low		PER SHARE ($) Earnings	Dividends	Book Value
6/06	38.74	117	68	0.38	—	7.62
6/05	27.68	—	—	(0.41)	—	3.96
6/04	36.53	48	25	1.04	—	4.33
6/03	27.34	—	—	(0.24)	—	2.35
6/02	11.76	—	—	(0.54)	—	2.21
Annual Growth	34.7%	—	—	—	—	36.3%

Digital River

Digital River helps keep the e-commerce flowing. The company provides technology and services that enable its clients to sell their products on the Web without building an e-commerce platform from the ground up. Using its own proprietary server technology, Digital River offers Web development and hosting, transaction processing, fulfillment, and fraud screening services to more than 40,000 customers operating online retail and distribution businesses. It also provides its customers with Web traffic data that allows them to better market their online presence. The company boasts such clients as Autodesk, eBay, Symantec, and Trend Micro. Digital River acquired software maker Commerce5 in late 2005.

Already owning a catalog of 100,000 products, the company expects the Commerce5 acquisition and eventual integration to more than double the number of products in its e-commerce portfolio.

Most of Digital River's business comes from software publishers and online software retailers (security software maker Symantec alone accounts for nearly 30% of sales), but it is also trying to build up more business with manufacturers and distributors of physical goods.

On the expansion front, Digital River's tributaries are branching out internationally. The company bought software distributor element 5 GmbH for $120 million in 2004, expanding its presence in Europe; element 5 changed its name to Digital River GmbH in 2006. Further extending its reach in Europe, the company launched two subsidiaries in Ireland and Luxembourg in mid-2006.

Digital River was established in 1994 and began offering online stores for its clients in 1996.

EXECUTIVES

Chairman and CEO: Joel A. Ronning, age 49, $1,250,000 pay
CFO: Thomas M. (Tom) Donnelly, age 41, $293,558 pay (partial-year salary)
VP Investor Relations: Bob Kleiber
President and CEO, Direct Response Technologies: Jason Wolfe
Associate Director Public Relations: Gerri Dyrek
Senior Public Relations Specialist: Kristin Mattson
Auditors: Ernst & Young LLP

LOCATIONS

HQ: Digital River, Inc.
9625 W. 76th St., Ste. 150, Eden Prairie, MN 55344
Phone: 952-253-1234   **Fax:** 952-253-8497
Web: www.digitalriver.com

Digital River has offices throughout the US, as well as in Germany, Ireland, Japan, Luxembourg, Taiwan, and the UK.

2005 Sales

	% of total
US	61
Europe	27
Other regions	12
Total	**100**

PRODUCTS/OPERATIONS

Selected Services

Customer service
Digital and physical fulfillment
Fraud detection
Merchandising and marketing
Transaction processing
Web commerce hosting

COMPETITORS

Accenture
Amazon.com
aQuantive
Ariba
Art Technology Group
BEA Systems
BroadVision
CyberSource
DoubleClick
EDS
GSI Commerce
IBM
Intershop
Microsoft
NaviSite
Oracle
SAP
Sterling Commerce
USinternetworking
ValueClick
Vignette

HISTORICAL FINANCIALS

Company Type: Public

Income Statement

FYE: December 31

	REVENUE ($ mil.)	NET INCOME ($ mil.)	NET PROFIT MARGIN	EMPLOYEES
12/05	220.4	54.3	24.6%	948
12/04	154.1	35.3	22.9%	727
12/03	101.2	17.1	16.9%	503
12/02	77.8	(0.5)	—	481
12/01	57.8	(19.2)	—	573
Annual Growth	39.7%	—	—	13.4%

2005 Year-End Financials

Debt ratio: 63.9%
Return on equity: 21.8%
Cash ($ mil.): 352.3
Current ratio: 2.45
Long-term debt ($ mil.): 195.0
No. of shares (mil.): 35.0
Dividends
  Yield: —
  Payout: —
Market value ($ mil.): 1,041.9
R&D as % of sales: 9.3%
Advertising as % of sales: 0.0%

Stock History

NASDAQ (GS): DRIV

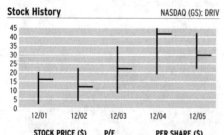

	STOCK PRICE ($) FY Close	P/E High/Low		PER SHARE ($) Earnings	Dividends	Book Value
12/05	29.74	31	16	1.36	—	8.71
12/04	41.61	46	20	0.96	—	5.73
12/03	22.10	66	17	0.52	—	4.19
12/02	11.95	—	—	(0.02)	—	2.08
12/01	15.92	—	—	(0.79)	—	1.91
Annual Growth	16.9%	—	—	—	—	46.2%

Direct General

It's an Adair family affair. Founded in 1991 by chairman and CEO William Adair, Direct General offers non-standard personal automobile coverage, life insurance, hospital indemnity insurance, and travel protection plans. The company also operates a premium financing subsidiary (where the insurer makes a loan to the customer that is backed by the unearned portion of the insurance premiums being financed). Direct General sells its products through more than 300 neighborhood sales offices, primarily in the southeastern part of the US. Before its IPO in 2003, the Adair family owned some 60% of the company; it still controls about 30%.

Florida accounted for about 50% of written premiums in 2005. The company expanded into Missouri in 2004 and began operating in Virginia and Texas in 2005.

EXECUTIVES

Chairman and CEO: William C. Adair Jr., age 64, $800,000 pay
President: Tammy R. Adair, age 42, $307,000 pay (prior to promotion)
EVP, COO, and Director: Jacqueline C. (Jackie) Adair, age 47, $307,000 pay
SVP and CFO: J. Todd Hagely, age 42, $207,341 pay
SVP, Corporate Development, Banking, and Finance: William J. (Bill) Harter, age 49
President, Direct General Financial Services and Direct General Premium Finance: Brian G. Moore, age 53
General Counsel and Secretary: Ronald F. Wilson, age 60, $155,769 pay
Auditors: Ernst & Young LLP

LOCATIONS

HQ: Direct General Corporation
  1281 Murfreesboro Rd., Nashville, TN 37217
Phone: 615-399-0600 **Fax:** 800-541-0856
Web: www.direct-general.com

Direct General operates in Arkansas, Florida, Georgia, Kentucky, Louisiana, Mississippi, Missouri, North Carolina, South Carolina, Tennessee, Texas, and Virginia.

PRODUCTS/OPERATIONS

2005 Sales

	% of total
Premiums	
Property & liability insurance	76
Life insurance	4
Commission & service fees	9
Finance income	9
Investment income	2
Total	**100**

COMPETITORS

21st Century
Allstate
Arrowhead Insurance
Auto-Owners Insurance
Bristol West
Farmers Group
GEICO
Infinity Property & Casualty
Progressive Corporation
Safe Auto
State Farm

HISTORICAL FINANCIALS

Company Type: Public

Income Statement

FYE: December 31

	ASSETS ($ mil.)	NET INCOME ($ mil.)	INCOME AS % OF ASSETS	EMPLOYEES
12/05	841.0	39.0	4.6%	2,453
12/04	787.5	54.0	6.9%	2,265
12/03	751.2	43.1	5.7%	2,000
12/02	569.1	31.0	5.4%	1,530
12/01	433.0	0.4	0.1%	—
Annual Growth	18.1%	214.2%	—	17.0%

2005 Year-End Financials

Equity as % of assets: 28.2%
Return on assets: 4.8%
Return on equity: 16.2%
Long-term debt ($ mil.): 200.1
No. of shares (mil.): 20.3
Market value ($ mil.): 343.7
Dividends
  Yield: 0.9%
  Payout: 8.8%
Sales ($ mil.): 510.0
R&D as % of sales: —
Advertising as % of sales: 2.6%

Stock History

NASDAQ (GS): DRCT

	STOCK PRICE ($) FY Close	P/E High/Low		PER SHARE ($) Earnings	Dividends	Book Value
12/05	16.90	18	8	1.82	0.16	11.68
12/04	32.10	16	12	2.38	0.16	10.96
12/03	33.10	15	10	2.20	0.04	8.31
Annual Growth	(28.5%)	—	—	(9.0%)	100.0%	18.6%

DivX

FX from DVDs benefit from DivX. The technology is a digital media format. DivX, the company, first introduced a library of video compression-decompression (or codec) software that has been downloaded more than 250 million times. It has built on the success of this technology by distributing the DivX software through its own Web site and through licenses with consumer video hardware manufacturers, including Samsung and Philips. The company also has begun working with video content developers to integrate DivX technology into the creation process.

CEO Jordan Greenhall and executives Darrius Thompson, Joe Bezdek, Tay Nguyen, and Gej Vashisht-Rota founded DivX in 2000.

Once known as DivXNetworks, the company began as Project Mayo, a collection of underground video "experts" (replace with "hackers" if desired) who developed the technology to pirate DVD video based on the MPEG-4 video format.

In 2006 the company acquired online community platform developer Corporate Green in a cash-and-stock transaction.

Leading investors in the company include Los Angeles-based Zone Venture Fund (35%), WI Harper Group of San Francisco (17%), and New York-based Insight Holdings (11%). CEO Greenhall owns 12%.

EXECUTIVES

Chairman and CEO: R. Jordan Greenhall, age 34, $153,375 pay
CFO, Finance and Administration: John A. Tanner, age 47, $230,063 pay
Chief DivX Officer, Community and Internet: Darrius Thompson, age 33
Chief DivX Officer, Partners and Licensing: Kevin Hell, age 42, $219,995 pay (prior to title change)
CTO, Strategy and Technology: Chris Russell, age 39, $159,039 pay
General Counsel, Legal and Corporate Development: David J. Richter, age 38, $217,563 pay
Director, Corporate Communications: Tom Huntington
Auditors: Ernst & Young LLP

LOCATIONS

HQ: DivX, Inc.
4780 Eastgate Mall, San Diego, CA 92121
Phone: 858-882-0600   **Fax:** 858-882-0601
Web: www.divx.com

PRODUCTS/OPERATIONS

2005 Sales

	$ mil.	% of total
Technology licensing		
Consumer hardware devices	23.4	71
Software	3.5	10
Advertising & third-party product distribution	4.9	15
Digital media distribution & services	1.2	4
Total	**33.0**	**100**

COMPETITORS

Adobe
Amazon.com
Apple
CinemaNow
ContentGuard
Google
InterTrust Technologies
Microsoft
Movielink
NDS Group
Netflix
News Corp.
RealNetworks
Sony
Yahoo!

HISTORICAL FINANCIALS

Company Type: Public

Income Statement				FYE: December 31
	REVENUE ($ mil.)	NET INCOME ($ mil.)	NET PROFIT MARGIN	EMPLOYEES
12/05	33.0	2.3	7.0%	189
12/04	16.4	(4.3)	—	—
12/03	7.7	(3.9)	—	—
Annual Growth	107.0%	—	—	—

2005 Year-End Financials

Debt ratio: 8.1%   Current ratio: 3.82
Return on equity: 51.0%   Long-term debt ($ mil.): 0.5
Cash ($ mil.): 25.3

Net Income History   NASDAQ (GM): DIVX

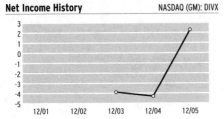

Dorchester Minerals

The stakeholders of Dorchester Minerals are enjoying the benefits of three natural resource exploitation enterprises which came together as one. The oil and gas exploration company was formed by the 2003 merger of oil trust Dorchester Hugoton with Republic Royalty and Spinnaker Royalty. Dorchester Mineral's holdings include 74,632 net acres in Oklahoma and 7,055 net acres in Kansas. The company holds assets (producing and nonproducing mineral, royalty, overriding royalty, net profits, and leasehold interests) in properties in 573 counties in 25 states. It has proved reserves of 66.3 billion cu. ft. of natural gas and 4 million barrels of oil.

EXECUTIVES

CEO; Manager, Dorchester Minerals Management; CEO, Dorchester Minerals Operating GP LLC: William Casey McManemin, age 45, $96,000 pay
COO; Manager, Dorchester Minerals Management GP LLC; COO, Dorchester Minerals Operating GP LLC: James E. Raley, age 66, $96,000 pay
CFO; Manager, Dorchester Minerals Management GP LLC; CFO, Dorchester Minerals Operating GP LLC: H. C. Allen Jr., age 66, $96,000 pay
Auditors: Grant Thornton LLP

LOCATIONS

HQ: Dorchester Minerals, L.P.
3838 Oak Lawn Ave., Ste. 300, Dallas, TX 75219
Phone: 214-559-0300   **Fax:** 214-559-0301

2005 Net Acreage

	% of total
Oklahoma	87
Kansas	8
Other states	5
Total	**100**

COMPETITORS

Anadarko Petroleum
BP
Cabot Oil & Gas
Chesapeake Energy
Devon Energy
Exxon Mobil
GMX Resources
Noble Energy
Occidental Petroleum
Pioneer Natural Resources
Royal Dutch Shell
Southwestern Energy
Unit Corporation
XTO Energy

HISTORICAL FINANCIALS

Company Type: Public

Income Statement				FYE: December 31
	REVENUE ($ mil.)	NET INCOME ($ mil.)	NET PROFIT MARGIN	EMPLOYEES
12/05	79.8	52.8	66.2%	26
12/04	56.8	30.1	53.0%	25
12/03	49.2	(26.8)	—	24
Annual Growth	27.4%	—	—	4.1%

2005 Year-End Financials

Debt ratio: —   Dividends
Return on equity: 26.1%   Yield: 7.8%
Cash ($ mil.): 23.4   Payout: 109.9%
Current ratio: 61.40   Market value ($ mil.): 719.3
Long-term debt ($ mil.): —   R&D as % of sales: —
No. of shares (mil.): 28.2   Advertising as % of sales: —

Stock History   NASDAQ (GM): DMLP

	STOCK PRICE ($) FY Close	P/E High/Low		PER SHARE ($) Earnings	Dividends	Book Value
12/05	25.47	17	12	1.82	2.00	7.08
12/04	23.92	23	16	1.07	1.70	7.26
12/03	19.41	—	—	(1.02)	1.09	7.34
Annual Growth	14.6%	—	—	—	35.5%	(1.8%)

Double Eagle Petroleum

It's double or nothing for Double Eagle Petroleum (formerly Double Eagle Petroleum and Mining) which gambles on hitting pay dirt as it explores for and produces oil and gas in the Rocky Mountains of Utah and Wyoming. Double Eagle Petroleum owns interests in 626 producing wells, and natural gas accounts for 96% of the oil and gas independent's production. The company has proved reserves of more than 329,000 barrels of oil and 49.2 billion cu. ft. of natural gas, and leases acreage in seven states. Double Eagle Petroleum sells its oil and gas on the spot market. CEO Stephen Hollis owns 8.3% of the company.

Double Eagle Petroleum has working interests in 504,899 gross developed and undeveloped acres.

EXECUTIVES

Chairman, President, and CEO: Stephen H. Hollis, age 55, $215,000 pay
CFO: Lonnie R. Brock
VP Land: D. Steven Degenfelder, $145,000 pay
VP Engineering and Production: C. K. (Keith) Adams, age 64, $186,667 pay
Corporate Secretary and Office Manager: Carol A. Osborne, age 54

LOCATIONS

HQ: Double Eagle Petroleum Co.
777 Overland Trail, Ste. 206, Casper, WY 82602
Phone: 307-237-9330   **Fax:** 307-266-1823
Web: www.dble.us

Double Eagle Petroleum explores for oil and gas in the Christmas Meadows area in northeastern Utah, the Green River Basin in southwestern Wyoming, the Powder River Basin in northeastern Wyoming, the Washakie Basin in south central Wyoming, and the Wind River Basin in central Wyoming.

COMPETITORS

Abraxas Petroleum
BP
Delta Petroleum
Devon Energy
Exxon Mobil
Kestrel Energy
Noble Energy
Stone Energy
Swift Energy

HISTORICAL FINANCIALS

Company Type: Public

Income Statement

FYE: December 31

	REVENUE ($ mil.)	NET INCOME ($ mil.)	NET PROFIT MARGIN	EMPLOYEES
12/05	20.5	4.0	19.5%	14
12/04	13.3	4.0	30.1%	1
12/03*	6.1	1.0	16.4%	1
8/02	2.3	(2.8)	—	1
8/01	2.6	0.3	11.5%	1
Annual Growth	67.6%	91.1%	—	93.4%

*Fiscal year change

2005 Year-End Financials

Debt ratio: 10.1%
Return on equity: 14.6%
Cash ($ mil.): 1.4
Current ratio: 0.68
Long-term debt ($ mil.): 3.0
No. of shares (mil.): 8.6
Dividends
  Yield: —
  Payout: —
Market value ($ mil.): 175.2
R&D as % of sales: —
Advertising as % of sales: —

Stock History

NASDAQ (GS): DBLE

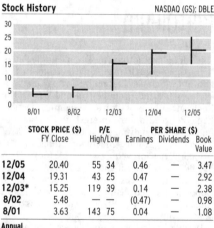

	STOCK PRICE ($) FY Close	P/E High/Low	PER SHARE ($) Earnings	Dividends	Book Value
12/05	20.40	55 34	0.46	—	3.47
12/04	19.31	43 25	0.47	—	2.92
12/03*	15.25	119 39	0.14	—	2.38
8/02	5.48	— —	(0.47)	—	0.98
8/01	3.63	143 75	0.04	—	1.08
Annual Growth	54.0%	— —	84.2%	—	33.7%

*Fiscal year change

Drew Industries

Drew Industries knows that when one door closes, another one opens — and that goes for windows too. The company supplies aluminum and vinyl windows and doors for recreational vehicles (67% of sales) and manufactured homes (33%) through nearly 50 factories in the US. Windows produced by the company's Kinro subsidiary include storm and insulated windows and horizontal and vertical sliders. Its Lippert Components subsidiary makes axles and chassis parts used to transport manufactured homes. Other products include galvanized roofing. Customers include Clayton Homes, Cavalier Homes, and

Champion Enterprises (manufactured homes) and makers of RVs such as Fleetwood Enterprises and Thor Industries.

The hurricane extravaganza of 2005 was good to Drew Industries. Although not a FEMA supplier, the company estimated a 5% increase in sales of both RVs and manufactured homes as dealers sold off inventory to meet demand. The increase offset to a certain extent slowing sales of RVs due to high gas prices.

Chairman Edward Rose III and director L. Douglas Lippert own 7% and 6% of Drew, respectively.

HISTORY

Drew Industries was founded as Drew National Corp. in 1962. Drew purchased Kinro, a maker of aluminum primary and storm windows for the manufactured-housing industry, in 1980. The company reincorporated as Drew Industries in 1984. Under the leadership of Kinro president David Webster, investor (and chairman) Edward Rose, and CEO Leigh Abrams (who all took up their leadership positions in 1984), Drew pursued a strategy of diversifying within its niche market of supplying components to the RV and manufactured-home industries. Kinro subsequently acquired makers of aluminum windows for manufactured homes and manufacturers of doors and windows for recreational vehicles, and in 1993 it began production of vinyl windows in addition to aluminum windows.

In 1996 Drew acquired Shoals, a maker of axles and a distributor of refurbished axles and new and refurbished tires for manufactured homes. The next year Drew purchased Lippert, which makes chassis and chassis parts and galvanized roofing for manufactured homes. Lippert CEO Douglas Lippert gained about a 19% stake in Drew as part of the deal. Drew bought Coil Clip (specialty steel parts supplier) in 1998. The company added five plants in 2000 to accommodate its booming RV chassis business.

In April 2001 the company gave a boost to its MH sales by acquiring rival Kevco's Better Bath division (bath fixtures). The next year Drew gained higher quarter sales numbers due to its implementation of cost-cutting measures and lower-than-normal product inventories.

Drew's Lippert Tire & Axle subsidiary sold its one remaining operation which engaged in refurbishing used axles and distributing used tires for manufactured homes in January 2003. Mid-year Drew expanded its RV segment through the purchase of LTM Manufacturing; later in the year Drew boosted its chassis manufacturing business into specialty chassis when subsidiary Lippert Components paid $3.6 million to acquire certain business and assets of specialty chassis manufacturer ET&T Frames, Inc. of Elkhart, Indiana.

Also in 2003 Drew transferred its stock listing to the New York Stock Exchange from the American Stock Exchange and began trading on the NYSE under the ticker DW in December of that year.

In 2004 the company's Better Bath division, a part of its Kinro subsidiary, entered into an equipment lease and license agreement with the buyer of certain of its intellectual property rights related to a process used in manufacturing a new composite material for use in fiberglass bathtubs. The $4 million sale included a five-year payoff period. Drew also acquired privately held Zieman Manufacturing Company, a Whittier, California-based manufacturer of trailers for equipment hauling, boats, personal watercrafts, and snowmobiles; chassis and chassis parts for

manufactured homes and RVs (mainly travel and fifth-wheel trailers); and specialty chassis for modular offices. Zieman became a part of Drew's Lippert Components business.

Lippert Components acquired the Venture Welding division of Banks Corporation for about $19 million in May 2005. Venture Welding manufactures chassis and chassis parts in Elkhart, Indiana.

In 2004 and into 2005, a California state court rendered a verdict in favor of a former employee of Drew's Lippert Components subsidiary in connection with a workplace injury. The former employee was awarded $4 million in punitive damages and compensatory damages of $464,000.

In 2006 Lippert acquired recreational vehicle and manufactured home chassis supplier SteelCo, Inc. for $4.5 million, and Happijac, which supplies bed-lift systems for RVs, for $29.5 million.

EXECUTIVES

Chairman: Edward W. (Rusty) Rose III, age 65
President, CEO, and Director: Leigh J. Abrams, age 63, $1,337,288 pay
EVP and CFO: Fredric M. (Fred) Zinn, age 55, $509,600 pay
VP and Chief Legal Officer: Harvey F. Milman, age 64
Corporate Controller and Treasurer: Joseph S. Giordano III, age 37
Secretary and Director, Taxation and Internal Audit: John F. Cupak, age 56
Director; Chairman, President, and CEO, Kinro, Inc.: David L. Webster, age 70, $1,482,000 pay
Director; Chairman, Lippert Components, Inc.: L. Douglas (Doug) Lippert, age 58
President and CEO, Lippert Components, Inc.: Jason D. Lippert, age 33, $1,061,760 pay
EVP and COO, Lippert Components: Scott T. Mereness, age 34, $909,160 pay
EVP and CFO, Kinro: Domenic D. Gattuso, age 65
Auditors: KPMG LLP

LOCATIONS

HQ: Drew Industries Incorporated
  200 Mamaroneck Ave., White Plains, NY 10601
Phone: 914-428-9098   **Fax:** 914-428-4581
Web: www.drewindustries.com

Drew Industries operates approximately 50 plants in the US and a factory in Canada.

PRODUCTS/OPERATIONS

2005 Sales

	$ mil.	% of total
Recreational vehicles	447.9	67
Manufactured housing	221.3	33
Total	**669.2**	**100**

Selected Products

Aluminum doors
Aluminum windows
Axels
Coil steel
Galvanized roofing
Screens
Sheet steel
Steel chassis
Steel chassis parts
Tires
Trailers (travel trailers and fifth-wheel trailers)
Vinyl windows

Selected Subsidiaries

Kinro, Inc.
Lippert Components, Inc.

Atrium
Featherlite
Fleetwood Folding Trailers
International Aluminum
JELD-WEN
Masonite Canada
NTK Holdings
Quality Trailer Products
Royal Group Technologies
Ryerson
Utility Trailer
Wozniak Industries

HISTORICAL FINANCIALS
Company Type: Public

Income Statement
FYE: December 31

	REVENUE ($ mil.)	NET INCOME ($ mil.)	NET PROFIT MARGIN	EMPLOYEES
12/05	669.2	33.6	5.0%	4,541
12/04	530.9	25.1	4.7%	3,670
12/03	353.1	19.4	5.5%	2,900
12/02	325.4	(14.6)	—	2,800
12/01	269.5	8.9	3.3%	2,379
Annual Growth	25.5%	39.4%	—	17.5%

2005 Year-End Financials
Debt ratio: 37.0%
Return on equity: 23.2%
Cash ($ mil.): 5.1
Current ratio: 2.02
Long-term debt ($ mil.): 62.1
No. of shares (mil.): 21.5
Dividends
  Yield: —
  Payout: —
Market value ($ mil.): 605.4
R&D as % of sales: —
Advertising as % of sales: —

Stock History
NYSE: DW

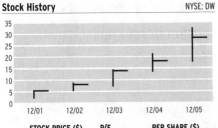

	STOCK PRICE ($) FY Close	P/E High/Low		PER SHARE ($) Earnings	Dividends	Book Value
12/05	28.19	21	11	1.56	—	7.81
12/04	18.08	18	11	1.18	—	11.84
12/03	13.90	15	8	0.94	—	9.18
12/02	8.02	—	—	(0.73)	—	7.06
12/01	5.38	12	5	0.46	—	8.40
Annual Growth	51.3%	—	—	35.7%	—	(1.8%)

Dynamic Materials

Dynamic Materials Corporation (DMC) has an explosive personality when it comes to working with metal. The company (formerly Explosive Fabricators) uses explosives to metallurgically bond, or "clad," metal plates (usually joining a corrosion-resistant alloy and carbon steel). Clad metal is used to make heavy-duty industrial pressure vessels and heat exchangers. The company also produces components using more traditional metalworking techniques such as machining, rolling, and hydraulic expansion. DMC's AMK Welding subsidiary machines and welds

parts primarily for the commercial aircraft and aerospace industries.

Geographically, the US accounts for 40% of sales. The company has stretched its global sales and marketing efforts to serve Australia, Europe, East Asia, and Latin America. DMC has also fortified its presence in Europe by purchasing Nobelclad Europe.

EXECUTIVES
Chairman: Dean K. Allen, age 70
VP, CFO, and Secretary: Richard A. (Rick) Santa, age 53, $362,900 pay
VP, Marketing and Sales, Clad Metal Products Division: John G. Banker, age 57, $370,000 pay
President and General Manager AMK Welding Division: Harold Wiegard, age 44
President and General Manager, Spin Forge Division: Chester Crone
Managing Director, DMC Nitro Metall: Seth Dalkarls
Department Managing Director and Manager Sales, DMC Nitro Metall: Matz Jonson
Director Sales; Customer Service and Purchasing, DMC Clad Metal USA: John Knoll
Director Finance and Human Resources, DMC Nobelclad: Philippe Roquette
Director Marketing, DMC Clad Metal Group: George Young
Director Sales, DMC Nobelclad: Cladue Fernandez
Manager Human Resources: Christy Cope
Auditors: Ernst & Young LLP

LOCATIONS
HQ: Dynamic Materials Corporation
  5405 Spine Rd., Boulder, CO 80301
Phone: 303-665-5700   **Fax:** 303-604-1897
Web: www.dynamicmaterials.com

Dynamic Materials Corporation has plants and other assets in Colorado, Connecticut, and Pennsylvania, in the US, and in France and Sweden.

2005 Sales

	$ mil.	% of total
US	32.1	41
South Korea	7.8	10
Canada	7.5	10
Spain	5.4	7
Malaysia	5.1	6
China	3.4	4
The Netherlands	2.7	3
Belgium	2.5	3
France	2.4	3
Italy	2.2	3
Australia	1.9	2
Germany	1.0	1
Russia	1.0	1
Mexico	0.6	1
Other countries	3.7	5
Total	**79.3**	**100**

PRODUCTS/OPERATIONS

2005 Sales

	$ mil.	% of total
Explosive Metalworking	75.6	95
AMK Welding	3.7	5
Total	**79.3**	**100**

COMPETITORS

Alliant Techsystems
AMETEK
Asahi Kasei
Eagle-Picher
HITCO
Japan Steel Works
Kaiser Aluminum

HISTORICAL FINANCIALS
Company Type: Public

Income Statement
FYE: December 31

	REVENUE ($ mil.)	NET INCOME ($ mil.)	NET PROFIT MARGIN	EMPLOYEES
12/05	79.3	10.4	13.1%	181
12/04	54.2	2.8	5.2%	163
12/03	40.3	(0.7)	—	190
12/02	45.7	0.2	0.4%	234
12/01	42.5	2.8	6.6%	230
Annual Growth	16.9%	38.8%	—	(5.8%)

2005 Year-End Financials
Debt ratio: 6.4%
Return on equity: 37.8%
Cash ($ mil.): 7.7
Current ratio: 2.46
Long-term debt ($ mil.): 2.2
No. of shares (mil.): 11.8
Dividends
  Yield: 0.3%
  Payout: 11.6%
Market value ($ mil.): 353.0
R&D as % of sales: —
Advertising as % of sales: —

Stock History
NASDAQ (GS): BOOM

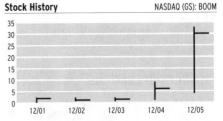

	STOCK PRICE ($) FY Close	P/E High/Low		PER SHARE ($) Earnings	Dividends	Book Value
12/05	30.02	38	5	0.86	0.10	2.97
12/04	6.07	33	5	0.26	—	3.77
12/03	1.50	—	—	(0.07)	—	3.06
12/02	1.19	138	67	0.01	—	3.07
12/01	1.98	8	2	0.28	—	2.91
Annual Growth	97.3%	—	—	32.4%	—	0.5%

Eagle Bancorp

For those nest eggs that need a little help hatching, holding company Eagle Bancorp would recommend its community-oriented EagleBank subsidiary. The bank serves businesses and individuals through nearly 10 branches in Washington, DC, and its Maryland suburbs. Deposit products include checking, savings, and money market accounts; certificates of deposit; and IRAs. Commercial real estate loans make up more than half of the bank's loan portfolio, which also includes business (almost one-quarter of the portfolio), consumer, home equity, and construction loans.

The bank sells virtually all of the residential mortgages that it originates into the secondary market. Eagle Land Title, a bank subsidiary established in 2005, offers title insurance and other real estate services.

EXECUTIVES

Chairman: Leonard L. Abel, age 79
Vice Chairman, President, and Treasurer; Chairman, EagleBank: Ronald D. (Ron) Paul, age 50, $140,000 pay
EVP and COO, EagleBank; President, EagleBank (Washington, DC): Michael T. (Mike) Flynn, age 58, $274,492 pay (prior to promotion)
EVP and COO, EagleBank; President-EagleBank (Montgomery County Operations): Thomas D. Murphy, age 58, $240,137 pay
EVP and CFO, Eaglebank: James H. Langmead, age 57
EVP and Chief Lending Officer, EagleBank: Martha Foulon-Tonat, age 50, $222,211 pay
EVP and Chief Administrative Officer, EagleBank: Susan G. Riel, age 56, $222,118 pay
VP Marketing and Advertising Manager, EagleBank: Janette S. Shaw
VP and Business Development Officer: Jackie Starr
VP and Team Leader, Commercial Lending, EagleBank: John A. Beck Jr.
Auditors: Stegman & Company

LOCATIONS

HQ: Eagle Bancorp, Inc.
7815 Woodmont Ave., Bethesda, MD 20814
Phone: 301-986-1800   **Fax:** 301-986-8529
Web: www.eaglebankmd.com

PRODUCTS/OPERATIONS

2005 Sales

	$ mil.	% of total
Interest		
Loans, including fees	33.5	82
Investment securities	2.4	6
Other	0.8	2
Noninterest		
Gain on sale of loans	1.2	3
Service charges on deposits	1.2	3
Other	1.6	4
Total	**40.7**	**100**

COMPETITORS

Bank of America
BB&T
Chevy Chase Bank
Provident Bankshares
SunTrust
Wachovia

HISTORICAL FINANCIALS

Company Type: Public

Income Statement
FYE: December 31

	ASSETS ($ mil.)	NET INCOME ($ mil.)	INCOME AS % OF ASSETS	EMPLOYEES
12/05	672.3	7.5	1.1%	145
12/04	553.5	5.1	0.9%	124
12/03	443.0	3.2	0.7%	104
12/02	347.8	2.7	0.8%	81
12/01	236.8	1.8	0.8%	62
Annual Growth	**29.8%**	**42.9%**	**—**	**23.7%**

2005 Year-End Financials

Equity as % of assets: 9.7%
Return on assets: 1.2%
Return on equity: 12.1%
Long-term debt ($ mil.): —
No. of shares (mil.): 7.2
Market value ($ mil.): 127.9
Dividends
Yield: 0.9%
Payout: 20.8%
Sales ($ mil.): 40.7
R&D as % of sales: —
Advertising as % of sales: —

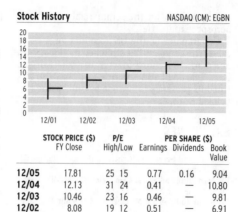

Stock History
NASDAQ (CM): EGBN

	STOCK PRICE ($) FY Close	P/E High/Low		PER SHARE ($) Earnings	Dividends	Book Value
12/05	17.81	25	15	0.77	0.16	9.04
12/04	12.13	31	24	0.41	—	10.80
12/03	10.46	23	16	0.46	—	9.81
12/02	8.08	19	12	0.51	—	6.91
12/01	6.01	24	10	0.34	—	5.92
Annual Growth	**31.2%**	**—**	**—**	**22.7%**	**—**	**11.2%**

Eagle Materials

Eagle Materials is perched near the top of the building materials business. The company produces and distributes gypsum wallboard (48% of sales), cement (almost 30% of sales), ready-mix concrete, recycled paperboard, and aggregates. Eagle Materials sells primarily to residential, commercial, and industrial construction customers located near its plants in the western and southwestern US. The company's cement operations include a joint venture with Lehigh Cement. Eagle Materials is a spinoff of megahomebuilder Centex Corporation, which founded the company in 1963.

The company owns and operates four gypsum wallboard manufacturing plants in Albuquerque and Bernalillo, New Mexico; Duke, Oklahoma; and Gypsum, Colorado. It has four cement plants in Buda, Texas; LaSalle, Illinois; Fernley, Nevada; and Laramie, Wyoming. The Texas plant is managed through its Texas Lehigh Cement Company LP joint venture. There is also a gypsum recycled paperboard plant in Lawton, Oklahoma; and eight concrete batching plants and aggregates facilities in Northern California (sand and gravel) and Texas (limestone).

Eagle Materials' plan for growth includes expanding its core wallboard and cement business in key geographic areas. As part of this strategy, the company is building a gypsum wallboard plant in Georgetown, South Carolina, which it expects to be completed by the middle of 2007. The plant will increase its annual wallboard capacity by 25%.

The company is spending $65 million to expand its cement operations in Illinois, with completion expected by early 2007. It also plans to modernize its Nevada cement plant by 2008. Additionally, Eagle Materials continues to seek opportunities to expand its northern California aggregates business to the Bay area.

EXECUTIVES

Chairman: Laurence E. (Larry) Hirsch
President, CEO, and Director: Steven R. (Steve) Rowley, age 53, $1,787,548 pay
EVP, Gypsum; President, American Gypsum Company: David B. (Dave) Powers, age 56, $1,084,080 pay
EVP, General Counsel, and Secretary: James H. (Jim) Graass, age 49, $682,242 pay
EVP, Cement/Concrete and Aggregates: Gerald J. (Gerry) Essl, age 57, $607,692 pay
SVP Finance, Treasurer, and CFO: Arthur R. (Art) Zunker Jr., age 63, $791,620 pay
VP and Controller: William R. Devlin, age 40
VP: Rodney E. Cummickel
EVP, Strategy and Development, American Gypsum Company: William C. (Bill) Boor, age 49
VP, Gypsum Manufacturing; SVP, Manufacturing, American Gypsum Company: Kerry Gannaway, age 47
SVP and Deputy General Counsel: David A. Greenblatt
VP, Investor Relations and Corporate Development: D. Craig Kesler, age 30
Auditors: Ernst & Young LLP

LOCATIONS

HQ: Eagle Materials Inc.
3811 Turtle Creek Blvd., Ste. 1100,
Dallas, TX 75219
Phone: 214-432-2000   **Fax:** 214-432-2100
Web: www.eaglematerials.com

Eagle Materials has manufacturing operations in California, Colorado, Illinois, Nevada, New Mexico, Oklahoma, Texas, and Wyoming.

PRODUCTS/OPERATIONS

2006 Sales

	$ mil.	% of total
Gypsum wallboard	479.1	48
Cement	285.3	29
Paperboard	133.5	13
Concrete & aggregates	89.8	9
Other	2.3	1
Adjustments	(130.3)	—
Total	**859.7**	**100**

Selected Operations

Cement plants (Illinois, Nevada, Texas, and Wyoming)
Concrete and aggregate plants (California and Texas)
Gypsum wallboard factories (Colorado, New Mexico, and Oklahoma)
Paperboard (Oklahoma)
Ready-mix concrete plants (California and Texas)

COMPETITORS

Boral	Martin Marietta Materials
BPB	New NGC
Caraustar	Temple-Inland
CEMEX	TXI
Georgia-Pacific	U.S. Concrete
Hanson Building Products	USG
Holcim (US)	Vulcan Materials
Koch	Weyerhaeuser
Lafarge North America	

HISTORICAL FINANCIALS

Company Type: Public

Income Statement
FYE: March 31

	REVENUE ($ mil.)	NET INCOME ($ mil.)	NET PROFIT MARGIN	EMPLOYEES
3/06	859.7	161.0	18.7%	1,600
3/05	616.5	106.7	17.3%	1,557
3/04	502.6	66.9	13.3%	1,529
3/03	429.2	57.6	13.4%	1,529
3/02	508.6	39.7	7.8%	1,552
Annual Growth	**14.0%**	**41.9%**	**—**	**0.8%**

2006 Year-End Financials

Debt ratio: 43.0%
Return on equity: 33.9%
Cash ($ mil.): 54.8
Current ratio: 2.07
Long-term debt ($ mil.): 200.0
No. of shares (mil.): 50.3

Dividends
  Yield: 0.7%
  Payout: 15.6%
Market value ($ mil.): 3,208.3
R&D as % of sales: —
Advertising as % of sales: —

Stock History

NYSE: EXP

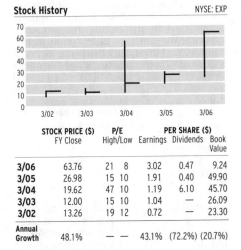

	STOCK PRICE ($) FY Close	P/E High/Low		PER SHARE ($) Earnings	Dividends	Book Value
3/06	63.76	21	8	3.02	0.47	9.24
3/05	26.98	15	10	1.91	0.40	49.90
3/04	19.62	47	10	1.19	6.10	45.70
3/03	12.00	15	10	1.04	—	26.09
3/02	13.26	19	12	0.72	—	23.30
Annual Growth	48.1%	—	—	43.1%	(72.2%)	(20.7%)

East West Bancorp

Getting directions to this bank may be tricky. East West Bancorp operates as the holding company for East West Bank, which has more than 60 branches in and around Los Angeles and the San Francisco Bay area, plus one each in Houston and Beijing. The bank offers individual and business loans; checking, savings, money market, and NOW accounts; CDs; IRAs; insurance; and credit card merchant services. It primarily serves the Chinese-American community; most customers are engaged in business in the Asia/Pacific Rim region. It offers multilingual service in English, Cantonese, Mandarin, Vietnamese, and Spanish.

Commercial and industrial real estate loans constitute the largest segment of East West's lending activities, accounting for nearly half of its loan portfolio. The company also writes multifamily real estate, residential mortgage, construction, business, and consumer loans.

East West Bancorp has been making about one acquisition per year since 1999: In 2005 it acquired United National Bank, which had 11 branches in California and Houston. The following year the company bought Los Angeles-area rival Standard Bank for more than $200 million in a move to expand its Chinese-American customer base.

EXECUTIVES

Chairman, President, and CEO, East West Bancorp and East West Bank: Dominic Ng, age 47, $2,190,000 pay
EVP, CFO, and Director; EVP and CFO, East West Bank: Julia S. Gouw, age 46, $458,338 pay
EVP and CIO, East West Bank: Robert L. Dingle Jr., age 54
EVP, General Counsel, and Secretary, East West Bancorp and East West Bank: Douglas P. Krause, age 49, $348,338 pay
EVP and Chief Credit Officer, East West Bank: William J. Lewis, age 63, $347,504 pay
EVP and Chief Strategic Officer, East West Bank: David L. Spigner, age 45
EVP and Director of Commercial Lending, East West Bank: Donald S. Chow, age 54
EVP and Director of Corporate Banking, East West Bank: Wellington Chen, age 46, $316,670 pay
Auditors: Deloitte & Touche LLP

LOCATIONS

HQ: East West Bancorp, Inc.
  135 N. Los Robles Ave., Pasadena, CA 91101
Phone: 626-768-6000   **Fax:** 626-799-3167
Web: www.eastwestbank.com

PRODUCTS/OPERATIONS

2005 Sales

	$ mil.	% of total
Interest		
Loans receivable, including fees	381.3	86
Investment securities available for sale	25.9	6
Other	4.2	1
Noninterest		
Letters of credit fees & commissions	8.6	2
Branch fees	7.4	2
Other	13.6	3
Total	**441.0**	**100**

COMPETITORS

Bank of America
Bank of East Asia
Cathay General Bancorp
Citibank
City National
Nara Bancorp
UCBH Holdings
Washington Mutual

HISTORICAL FINANCIALS

Company Type: Public

Income Statement

FYE: December 31

	ASSETS ($ mil.)	NET INCOME ($ mil.)	INCOME AS % OF ASSETS	EMPLOYEES
12/05	8,278.3	108.4	1.3%	1,078
12/04	6,028.9	78.0	1.3%	913
12/03	4,055.4	59.0	1.5%	692
12/02	3,321.5	49.5	1.5%	581
12/01	2,825.3	38.8	1.4%	531
Annual Growth	30.8%	29.3%	—	19.4%

2005 Year-End Financials

Equity as % of assets: 8.9%
Return on assets: 1.5%
Return on equity: 17.4%
Long-term debt ($ mil.): 161.9
No. of shares (mil.): 56.7
Market value ($ mil.): 2,068.0

Dividends
  Yield: 0.5%
  Payout: 10.2%
Sales ($ mil.): 441.0
R&D as % of sales: —
Advertising as % of sales: —

Stock History

NASDAQ (GS): EWBC

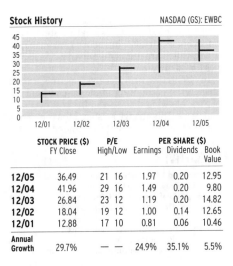

	STOCK PRICE ($) FY Close	P/E High/Low		PER SHARE ($) Earnings	Dividends	Book Value
12/05	36.49	21	16	1.97	0.20	12.95
12/04	41.96	29	16	1.49	0.20	9.80
12/03	26.84	23	12	1.19	0.20	14.82
12/02	18.04	19	12	1.00	0.14	12.65
12/01	12.88	17	10	0.81	0.06	10.46
Annual Growth	29.7%	—	—	24.9%	35.1%	5.5%

Eaton Vance

A veritable supermarket of investing, Eaton Vance offers more than 70 mutual funds and manages investments for institutional as well as wealthy individual clients. Its signature investment products include tax-managed funds, municipal bond funds, floating-rate bank-loan funds, and closed-end funds. The company also offers equity and money market funds. Its Eaton Vance Distributors unit markets and sells its funds via a network of independent brokers, banks, and insurance firms. Chairman Jim Hawkes owns about 25% of the firm; he and 10 other owners control Eaton Vance through a voting trust.

The firm bought Weston Asset Management in mid-2005 and Voyageur Asset Management later that year. The acquisitions are just the latest in a series of deals that Eaton Vance has made in recent years. Others include Atlanta Capital Management (equity value investing), Fox Asset Management (growth-oriented investments), and Parametric Portfolio Associates (tax-managed separate accounts).

Altogether Eaton Vance has about $110 billion in assets under management. It employs sales associates in the US, Europe, and Latin America.

HISTORY

In 1924 Harvard graduate Charles F. Eaton Jr. founded the investment firm Eaton & Howard, which created and managed investment funds throughout the next several decades. The company went public in 1978; the next year it was purchased by Vance Sanders & Company and did business under the moniker Eaton & Howard, Vance Sanders. By 1983 the company had $2.3 billion under management.

After 1987's stock market dive, the company's tax-free, low-interest bond funds made it an industry leader. Early in the 1990s it began to market its funds through more than 60 banks; the company also partnered with Lloyd George Management, a move that allowed its mutual funds to be sold internationally.

Eaton Vance weathered storms in the 1990s (including a failed restructuring and battles with the IRS) and became a sometime-darling of the

business press. With the flush economy of the late 1990s, Eaton Vance tried its hand investing in unrated bonds. It also introduced tax-managed funds, which are geared to minimize tax liabilities for its investors.

In 1999 the firm received permission to change the accounting of closed-end fund expenses, allowing it to spread the cost over several years. This change bolstered the company's bottom line and earned it fans among analysts.

EXECUTIVES

Chairman and CEO: James B. (Jim) Hawkes, age 64, $5,115,000 pay (prior to title change)
President, Chief Investment Officer, and Director: Thomas E. (Tom) Faust Jr., age 48, $4,274,500 pay (prior to title change)
EVP and Chief Equity Investment Officer: Duncan W. Richardson, age 48
Director, Product Management and Client Service: Susan Brengle
VP and Chief Accounting Officer: Laurie G. Hylton, age 40
VP and Chief Administrative Officer: Jeffrey P. Beale, age 50
VP, CFO, and Treasurer: William M. (Bill) Steul, age 64, $1,122,000 pay
VP, Chief Legal Officer, and Secretary: Alan R. Dynner, age 66, $1,397,000 pay
VP and Chief Sales and Marketing Officer; President, Eaton Vance Distributors: Wharton P. Whitaker, age 61, $2,338,482 pay
VP and Director of Business Analysis & Development, Eaton Vance Management: Clifford H. (Cliff) Krauss
VP, Financial Planning and Analysis: Daniel C. (Dan) Cataldo
VP, Institutional Business Development: Daniel J. McCarthy
VP and Senior Relationship Manager: M. Katharine (Kathy) Kasper
VP and Portfolio Manager, Eaton Vance Special Equities Fund, Eaton Vance Small-Cap Growth Fund, and Eaton Vance Tax-Managed Small-Cap Growth Fund: Nancy B. Tooke
CEO and Chief Investment Officer, Fox Asset Management: William E. (Bill) Dodge
President and CEO, Eaton Vance Investment Counsel: G. West (Westy) Saltonstall
Director, Human Resources: Mark Burkhard
Auditors: Deloitte & Touche LLP

LOCATIONS

HQ: Eaton Vance Corp.
The Eaton Vance Bldg., 255 State St., Boston, MA 02109
Phone: 617-482-8260   **Fax:** 617-482-2396
Web: www.eatonvance.com

Eaton Vance has US offices in Atlanta; Boston; Red Bank, New Jersey; and Seattle. The company also has a London office.

PRODUCTS/OPERATIONS

2006 Sales

	$ mil.	% of total
Investment adviser & administration fees	594.7	69
Distribution & underwriter fees	140.3	16
Service fees	122.8	14
Other	4.4	1
Total	**862.2**	**100**

Selected Subsidiaries and Affiliates

Eaton Vance Acquisitions
  Atlanta Capital Management Company, LLC (70%)
  Fox Asset Management LLC (80%)
  Parametric Portfolio Associates LLC (80%)
Eaton Vance Management
  Boston Management and Research
  Eaton Vance Distributors, Inc.
  Eaton Vance Investment Counsel
  Eaton Vance Management (International) Limited (UK)

COMPETITORS

A.G. Edwards	Nuveen
AllianceBernstein	Old Mutual (US)
AMVESCAP	PIMCO
BISYS	Pioneer Investment
Charles Schwab	Putnam
Detwiler, Mitchell	SEI
FMR	T. Rowe Price
Franklin Resources	UBS Financial Services
Janus Capital	Van Kampen Investments
Mackenzie Financial	The Vanguard Group
Merrill Lynch	Waddell & Reed
Morgan Keegan	Wells Fargo
Neuberger Berman	

HISTORICAL FINANCIALS

Company Type: Public

Income Statement

FYE: October 31

	ASSETS ($ mil.)	NET INCOME ($ mil.)	INCOME AS % OF ASSETS	EMPLOYEES
10/06	668.2	159.4	23.9%	—
10/05	702.5	159.9	22.8%	757
10/04	743.6	138.9	18.7%	686
10/03	658.7	106.1	16.1%	616
10/02	616.6	121.1	19.6%	575
Annual Growth	**2.0%**	**7.1%**	**—**	**9.6%**

2006 Year-End Financials

Equity as % of assets: 74.3%
Return on assets: 23.3%
Return on equity: 33.5%
Long-term debt ($ mil.): —
No. of shares (mil.): 126.1
Market value ($ mil.): 3,914.9
Dividends
  Yield: 1.3%
  Payout: 34.2%
Sales ($ mil.): 862.2
R&D as % of sales: —
Advertising as % of sales: —

Stock History

NYSE: EV

	STOCK PRICE ($) FY Close	P/E High/Low	PER SHARE ($) Earnings	Dividends	Book Value
10/06	31.04	27 20	1.17	0.40	3.94
10/05	24.89	24 19	1.13	0.24	3.52
10/04	21.81	22 16	1.00	0.28	6.75
10/03	17.44	24 15	0.75	0.20	6.10
10/02	14.35	24 13	0.85	0.15	5.39
Annual Growth	**21.3%**	**— —**	**8.3%**	**27.8%**	**(7.5%)**

Ebix

Ebix (formerly Delphi Information Systems) sells insurance industry software products and professional services to property/casualty insurers, brokerages, and individuals in Asia, Australia, Europe, and North America. The company's Ebix.com Web site acts as an online auction house where buyers and carriers can exchange bids for auto, home, health, life, and other types of insurance, while paying Ebix a fee on each transaction. Its Ebix.one and e.global agency management software build upon its legacy products with added workflow and customer relationship management capabilities. UK insurer BRiT Insurance Holdings owns 34% of the firm.

Ebix makes nearly all of its revenues through its consulting, training, software development, and project management services. International sales account for about one-third of the company's business.

In 2006 Ebix acquired insurance software developer and supplier Infinity Systems Consulting.

International revenue accounted for 37% of total revenue in 2005. Professional and support services accounted for 95% of revenue in the same period.

CEO Robin Raina owns 16% of Ebix; European investment group Rennes Foundation owns 13% of the company.

EXECUTIVES

Chairman, President, and CEO: Robin Raina, age 38, $600,000 pay
SVP and CFO: Carl Serger
Auditors: BDO Seidman, LLP

LOCATIONS

HQ: Ebix, Inc.
  5 Concourse Pkwy., Ste. 3200, Atlanta, GA 30328
Phone: 678-281-2020   **Fax:** 678-281-2019
Web: www.ebix.com

Ebix has offices in Australia, Canada, India, New Zealand, Singapore, and the US.

PRODUCTS/OPERATIONS

2005 Sales

	$ mil.	% of total
Software	1.2	5
Services & other	22.9	95
Total	**24.1**	**100**

Selected Subsidiaries

Canadian Insurance Computer Systems, Inc.
Complete Broking Systems Australia PTY, Ltd.
Delphi Information Systems International, Inc.
Delphi Information Systems, (NZ) Ltd.
Ebix Australia (Vic) Pty Ltd.
Ebix Insurance Agency, Inc.
ebix Software India, Private Limited
Ebix Singapore Pte Ltd.

COMPETITORS

Answer Financial	Healthaxis
Applied Systems	Insure.com
CCC Information	InsWeb
Computer Sciences Corp.	Intuit
Cover-All	SunGard
Crawford & Company	SunGard Sherwood
E*TRADE Bank	

HISTORICAL FINANCIALS

Company Type: Public

Income Statement

FYE: December 31

	REVENUE ($ mil.)	NET INCOME ($ mil.)	NET PROFIT MARGIN	EMPLOYEES
12/05	24.1	4.3	17.8%	95
12/04	20.0	2.2	11.0%	239
12/03	14.4	1.7	11.8%	211
12/02	12.6	0.5	4.0%	165
12/01	12.9	0.1	0.8%	84
Annual Growth	16.9%	156.1%	—	3.1%

2005 Year-End Financials

Debt ratio: 10.5%
Return on equity: 27.7%
Cash ($ mil.): 6.7
Current ratio: 1.49
Long-term debt ($ mil.): 1.8
No. of shares (mil.): 2.7
Dividends
 Yield: —
 Payout: —
Market value ($ mil.): 54.2
R&D as % of sales: 13.5%
Advertising as % of sales: 1.3%

Stock History

NASDAQ (GM): EBIX

	STOCK PRICE ($) FY Close	P/E High/Low		PER SHARE ($) Earnings	Dividends	Book Value
12/05	19.76	16	7	1.38	—	6.39
12/04	15.00	24	15	0.72	—	4.64
12/03	12.26	19	4	0.71	—	2.89
12/02	2.60	38	11	0.22	—	2.06
Annual Growth	96.6%	—	—	103.8%	—	134.0%

eCollege.com

You don't have to eat dorm food if you go to college online. eCollege.com is propelling higher education into cyberspace by creating online campuses for universities and high schools. The company sets up online academic communities replete with computer-based courses, testing, online registration, and other student services. Customers include career colleges, community colleges, school districts, and universities. eCollege.com also has corporate clients who use its services to build online training courses for employees.

EXECUTIVES

Chairman and CEO: Oakleigh Thorne, age 48, $502,300 pay
President, COO, and Director:
 Douglas H. (Doug) Kelsall, age 52, $399,459 pay
CFO: Reid E. Simpson, age 49, $317,024 pay
SVP and General Counsel:
 Marguerite M. (Margee) Elias, age 51
CTO: Vance Allen
CEO, Datamark: Thomas L. (Tom) Dearden, age 49, $310,878 pay
COO, Datamark: Don Bailey
President, eLearning Division: Matthew T. Schnittman, age 34, $256,897 pay

Director Human Resources: David Smith
Manager Public Relations: Kristi Emerson
Auditors: Grant Thornton LLP

LOCATIONS

HQ: eCollege.com
 1 N. LaSalle St., Ste. 1800, Chicago, IL 60602
Phone: 312-706-1710 **Fax:** 312-706-1703
Web: www.ecollege.com

eCollege.com has offices in Colorado, Illinois, Kansas, Missouri, Utah, and Washington.

PRODUCTS/OPERATIONS

2005 Sales

	$ mil.	% of total
Enrollment division	61.4	60
eLearning division	41.5	40
Total	**102.9**	**100**

2005 Sales

	$ mil.	% of total
Direct mail enrollment marketing	37.6	37
Student fees	36.8	36
Interactive enrollment marketing	17.0	16
Other	11.5	11
Total	**102.9**	**100**

Selected Products and Services

Enrollment products and services (Datamark)
 Direct mail
 eMax (interactive marketing)
 eOpt (media buying)
 Mediamax (media placement)
 Path Finder (student retention)
eLearning products (eCollege System)
 CampusPortal (total campus environment)
 Content Manager
 eCompanion (interactive course component)
 eCourse (course management)
 Gateway Campus (online campus environment)
Other services
 Competitive analysis
 Course design
 Help desk
 Hosting
 Instructional design consulting and training
 Instructor training
 Internet connectivity
 Media buying
 Online campus design and management
 Product advancement
 Search engine optimization
 Software customization
 Technical consulting

COMPETITORS

Arel Communications and Software
Blackboard
SkillSoft
VCampus

HISTORICAL FINANCIALS

Company Type: Public

Income Statement

FYE: December 31

	REVENUE ($ mil.)	NET INCOME ($ mil.)	NET PROFIT MARGIN	EMPLOYEES
12/05	102.9	5.9	5.7%	519
12/04	89.3	19.4	21.7%	443
12/03	36.9	0.6	1.6%	412
12/02	23.7	(4.9)	—	210
12/01	19.9	(12.3)	—	142
Annual Growth	50.8%	—	—	38.3%

2005 Year-End Financials

Debt ratio: 21.5%
Return on equity: 6.8%
Cash ($ mil.): 23.0
Current ratio: 2.19
Long-term debt ($ mil.): 20.3
No. of shares (mil.): 22.2
Dividends
 Yield: —
 Payout: —
Market value ($ mil.): 400.5
R&D as % of sales: 7.0%
Advertising as % of sales: 0.2%

Stock History

NASDAQ (GM): ECLG

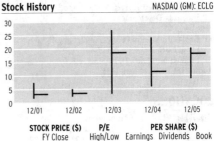

	STOCK PRICE ($) FY Close	P/E High/Low		PER SHARE ($) Earnings	Dividends	Book Value
12/05	18.03	77	35	0.26	—	4.25
12/04	11.36	27	7	0.88	—	3.59
12/03	18.46	890	115	0.03	—	2.50
12/02	3.45	—	—	(0.30)	—	0.63
12/01	3.17	—	—	(0.76)	—	0.92
Annual Growth	54.4%	—	—	—	—	46.7%

Edge Petroleum

Edge Petroleum goes high-tech to gain an edge over its rivals in the oil and gas exploration and production business. The company relies on visualization software and a 3-D seismic database to find natural gas and oil prospects onshore along the Gulf of Mexico region. Edge Petroleum has proved reserves of 102.7 billion cu. ft. of natural gas equivalent, of which 80% is natural gas and natural gas liquids. Although its primary operations are in Texas, where most of its net developed acreage is located, the company also has major developed holdings in Alabama, Louisiana, Mississippi, and New Mexico. In 2004 the company acquired Contango Oil & Gas' south Texas natural gas and oil interests for about $50 million.

In 2006 it announced plans to boost its stake in the Chapman Ranch Field in south Texas by buying the interests of Anadarko Petroleum for $26 million.

Edge Petroleum was founded in 1983 and went public in 1997 through an initial public offering. Following a management shake up in 1998, the company has followed a business plan that integrates technology-driven drilling activities with a disciplined portfolio mix of high-risk and low/moderate-risk drilling and a geographic focus.

EXECUTIVES

Chairman, President, and CEO: John W. Elias, age 65, $540,000 pay
EVP and COO: John O. Tugwell, age 41, $304,500 pay
EVP and CFO: Michael G. Long, age 52, $289,625 pay
VP, General Counsel, and Corporate Secretary: Robert C. Thomas, age 77
VP and Controller: Kirsten A. Hink, age 38
VP Business Development and Planning: C.W. MacLeod, age 54
VP Exploration: John O. Hastings Jr., age 45
VP Land: Mark J. Gabrisch, age 44
VP Production: James D. Keisling, age 57
Auditors: BDO Seidman, LLP

LOCATIONS

HQ: Edge Petroleum Corporation
  1301 Travis, Ste. 2000, Houston, TX 77002
Phone: 713-654-8960   **Fax:** 713-654-7722
Web: www.edgepet.com

Edge Petroleum operates primarily in Alabama, Louisiana, Mississippi, New Mexico, and Texas.

PRODUCTS/OPERATIONS

2005 Sales

	$ mil.	% of total
Natural gas	100.4	81
Oil & condensate	17.3	14
Natural gas liquids	5.7	5
Adjustments	(2.3)	—
Total	**121.2**	**100**

Subsidiaries

Edge Petroleum Exploration Company
Edge Petroleum Operating Company, Inc.
Miller Exploration Company
Miller Oil Corporation

COMPETITORS

Abraxas Petroleum
Apache
BP
Brigham Exploration
Chesapeake Energy
Chevron
Exxon Mobil
Forest Oil
Houston Exploration
Meridian Resource
National Onshore
Parallel Petroleum
Pogo Producing
Remington Oil and Gas
Royal Dutch Shell
Tesoro
TOTAL

HISTORICAL FINANCIALS

Company Type: Public

Income Statement

FYE: December 31

	REVENUE ($ mil.)	NET INCOME ($ mil.)	NET PROFIT MARGIN	EMPLOYEES
12/05	121.2	33.4	27.6%	67
12/04	67.0	15.1	22.5%	53
12/03	33.9	4.3	12.7%	35
12/02	20.9	0.8	3.8%	33
12/01	29.8	8.1	27.2%	31
Annual Growth	**42.0%**	**42.5%**	**—**	**21.2%**

2005 Year-End Financials

Debt ratio: 44.3%
Return on equity: 19.5%
Cash ($ mil.): 0.7
Current ratio: 1.40
Long-term debt ($ mil.): 85.0
No. of shares (mil.): 17.2
Dividends
  Yield: —
  Payout: —
Market value ($ mil.): 428.9
R&D as % of sales: —
Advertising as % of sales: —

Stock History   NASDAQ (GS): EPEX

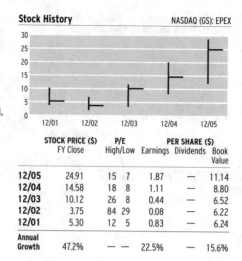

	STOCK PRICE ($) FY Close	P/E High/Low		PER SHARE ($) Earnings	Dividends	Book Value
12/05	24.91	15	7	1.87	—	11.14
12/04	14.58	18	8	1.11	—	8.80
12/03	10.12	26	8	0.44	—	6.52
12/02	3.75	84	29	0.08	—	6.22
12/01	5.30	12	5	0.83	—	6.24
Annual Growth	**47.2%**	**—**	**—**	**22.5%**	**—**	**15.6%**

Edgewater Technology

Edgewater Technology is on the cutting edge of technology management consulting. Among other things, Edgewater helps businesses improve call center operations, design customized software applications, and build integrated systems. Its managed services division allows clients to outsource management and maintenance of information technology (IT) facilities. The company has expertise in such industries as financial services, health care, insurance, and higher education. It targets middle-market clients and offers specialized services to divisions of large (Global 2000) firms. Its clients include American Express, Merrill, and MIT.

Subsidiary Ranzal & Associates, acquired in 2004, helps companies develop business intelligence systems, based primarily on Hyperion software applications.

In 2006 Edgewater acquired Connecticut-based consulting firm National Decision Systems, which specializes in strategic business process consulting. The acquired company brings expertise in such industry verticals as hospitality consumer goods, and financial services; it also adds merger and acquisition consulting and research advisory services to Edgewater's service offering.

Formerly known as StaffMark, the company sold its staffing business units in 2000 to focus on providing IT consulting services.

EXECUTIVES

Chairman, President, and CEO: Shirley Singleton, age 54, $481,250 pay
COO: David J. Gallo, age 44, $378,625 pay
CFO, Secretary, and Treasurer: Kevin R. Rhodes, age 37, $220,313 pay
EVP and CTO: David Clancey, age 50, $423,500 pay
VP Business Development: Betsy Norris
VP Corporate Communications: Barbara Warren-Sica
VP Delivery Management and Methodology: Eva Vinson
VP Human Resources: Kristin Zaepfel, age 42, $151,731 pay
VP Insurance Practice: Lawrence (Larry) Fortin
VP Operations: Veda Gagliardi
VP Technology: Joseph Navetta
President, Ranzal & Associates: Robin Ranzal
Auditors: Deloitte & Touche LLP

LOCATIONS

HQ: Edgewater Technology, Inc.
  20 Harvard Mill Sq., Wakefield, MA 01880
Phone: 781-246-3343   **Fax:** 781-246-5903
Web: www.edgewater.com

Edgewater Technology operates through four offices in Arkansas, Connecticut, Massachusetts, New Hampshire, and Virginia. Subsidiary Ranzal & Associates has offices in Florida, Georgia, Massachusetts, Michigan, New York, South Carolina, and Virginia.

PRODUCTS/OPERATIONS

2005 Sales

	$ mil.	% of total
Services	39.8	93
Software	1.5	3
Other revenues	1.8	4
Total	**43.1**	**100**

Selected Services

Application server development and administration
Architecture design and development
Data analysis and visualization
Data integration, analytics, and warehousing
Database design and development
Web and portal development

COMPETITORS

Accenture
Answerthink
Bain & Company
Booz Allen
Boston Consulting
Cognizant Tech Solutions
Diamond
EDS
Greenbrier and Russel
Hewlett-Packard
IBM
IBM Global Services
INDUS Corp.
Informatica
Inforte
Infosys
Keane
Knightsbridge Solutions
LogicaCMG
Longview Solutions
McKinsey & Company
MicroStrategy
Oracle
Perficient
SAP
Sapient
Satyam
Tata Consultancy
Wipro

HISTORICAL FINANCIALS

Company Type: Public

Income Statement

FYE: December 31

	REVENUE ($ mil.)	NET INCOME ($ mil.)	NET PROFIT MARGIN	EMPLOYEES
12/05	43.1	1.6	3.7%	282
12/04	25.3	(0.6)	—	205
12/03	25.0	1.0	4.0%	191
12/02	18.7	(23.5)	—	152
12/01	26.6	1.9	7.1%	200
Annual Growth	**12.8%**	**(4.2%)**	**—**	**9.0%**

2005 Year-End Financials

Debt ratio: —
Return on equity: 2.1%
Cash ($ mil.): 33.4
Current ratio: 7.07
Long-term debt ($ mil.): —
No. of shares (mil.): 10.7
Dividends
  Yield: —
  Payout: —
Market value ($ mil.): 63.0
R&D as % of sales: —
Advertising as % of sales: —

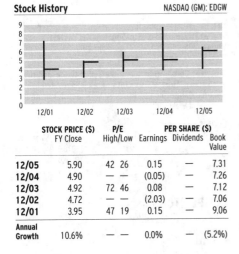

	STOCK PRICE ($) FY Close	P/E High/Low		PER SHARE ($) Earnings	Dividends	Book Value
12/05	5.90	42	26	0.15	—	7.31
12/04	4.90	—	—	(0.05)	—	7.26
12/03	4.92	72	46	0.08	—	7.12
12/02	4.72	—	—	(2.03)	—	7.06
12/01	3.95	47	19	0.15	—	9.06
Annual Growth	10.6%	—	—	0.0%	—	(5.2%)

EFJ

EFJ makes sure certain communications remain on the QT. Through its E.F. Johnson division, the company makes radio and radio-security systems for police departments, government agencies, the military, and cellular service providers. Its primary products are handheld and mobile radios, base stations, and signal repeaters. EFJ's Transcrypt International subsidiary makes security modules that encrypt and decode radio and wireless phone signals to prevent eavesdropping. Customers include state, local, and foreign governments as well as other equipment makers.

EFJ, which licenses core technology from Motorola, is incorporating encryption functionality into some of its wireless products to diversify its product offerings. The Department of Defense is responsible for about 30% of sales.

Boston-based Wellington Management owns a 12% stake in the company.

HISTORY

Transcrypt was started in 1978 to make embedded voice privacy and specialized signaling add-on devices for land mobile radios (LMRs). In 1991 a group led by John Connor (former chairman) acquired the company and began diversifying its product lines. By 1993 Transcrypt was developing digital products.

The 1995 Oklahoma City bombing caused a major shift in the LMR industry, as agencies responding to the tragedy had difficulty communicating because their various two-way radios were not standardized. After the bombing, the Federal Trade Commission ordered new communications compatibility among law enforcement agencies. Manufacturers soon adopted the APCO 25 standard for LMRs. Transcrypt launched its APCO 25 line in 1996.

In 1997 Transcrypt bought E.F. Johnson, a struggling two-way radio maker three times its size. The purchase added significant manufacturing capacity, an established distribution system, and a well-known brand name to Transcrypt's competitive arsenal. It also resulted in red ink for the year.

E.F. Johnson enabled Transcrypt to bid on larger contracts. Demand for its technology by other communications equipment manufacturers grew. But in 1998 Transcrypt was forced to restate 1997 and 1996 financial results, prompting an SEC investigation and shareholder lawsuits (the company agreed to settle in 1999). Telemetry executive Michael Jalbert took over as chairman and CEO in 1999, and Transcrypt closed its Hong Kong office. The next year Motorola licensed radio technology from E.F. Johnson, and BearCom agreed to distribute Transcrypt's products.

In 2001, in an effort to return to profitability, Transcrypt discontinued lower margin commercial products to focus on equipment for the public safety market. The company also used other cost cutting measures, including layoffs, to bring down expenses that year. In 2002, Transcrypt International changed its name to EFJ, Inc.

EXECUTIVES

Chairman, President, and CEO: Michael E. Jalbert, age 61, $740,000 pay
EVP, Operations and Engineering: Kenneth M. Wasko, age 47
SVP and CFO: Jana Ahlfinger Bell, age 41, $261,962 pay (partial-year salary)
SVP, General Counsel, and Secretary: Robert C. (Bob) Donohoo, age 43
VP Administration: Michael Gamble, $189,000 pay
VP Investor Relations: Jim Stark
President and COO, EFJohnson: Ellen O. O'Hara, $333,600 pay (partial-year salary)
President and COO, Secured Communications Division: Massoud Safavi, age 51
Controller: Terry A. Watkins, age 53
Auditors: Grant Thornton LLP

LOCATIONS

HQ: EFJ, Inc.
1440 Corporate Dr., Irving, TX 75038
Phone: 972-819-0700   **Fax:** 972-819-0639
Web: www.efji.com

PRODUCTS/OPERATIONS

2005 Sales

	$ mil.	% of total
Private wireless communication	64.6	68
Secured communications	30.0	32
Total	**94.6**	**100**

Selected Products

Private wireless communications
 Mobile and portable digital and analog radios
 Radio base stations and repeaters
Secured communications
 Radio security modules
 Wireless phone security modules

Selected Subsidiaries

E.F. Johnson Company (wireless radio and communications infrastructure and systems)
Transcrypt International, Inc. (secured communications encryption technologies)

COMPETITORS

Ericsson
Harris Corp.
Hitachi
Kenwood
Motorola
Nokia
RELM Wireless
Thales
Tyco
Uniden

HISTORICAL FINANCIALS

Company Type: Public

Income Statement

	REVENUE ($ mil.)	NET INCOME ($ mil.)	NET PROFIT MARGIN	EMPLOYEES	FYE: December 31
12/05	94.6	22.5	23.8%	272	
12/04	80.9	10.0	12.4%	260	
12/03	56.2	4.0	7.1%	216	
12/02	40.8	1.4	3.4%	206	
12/01	44.2	0.5	1.1%	215	
Annual Growth	21.0%	159.0%	—	6.1%	

2005 Year-End Financials

Debt ratio: 0.0%
Return on equity: 25.9%
Cash ($ mil.): 39.1
Current ratio: 7.46
Long-term debt ($ mil.): 0.0
No. of shares (mil.): 26.0
Dividends
 Yield: —
 Payout: —
Market value ($ mil.): 263.5
R&D as % of sales: 14.5%
Advertising as % of sales: —

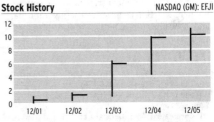

	STOCK PRICE ($) FY Close	P/E High/Low		PER SHARE ($) Earnings	Dividends	Book Value
12/05	10.15	10	6	1.06	—	4.66
12/04	9.75	19	8	0.53	—	2.90
12/03	5.90	30	5	0.21	—	2.33
12/02	1.25	19	6	0.08	—	1.87
12/01	0.52	33	4	0.03	—	1.74
Annual Growth	110.2%	—	—	143.8%	—	27.9%

Emergent BioSolutions

Emergent BioSolutions protects your thorax against anthrax. Emergent BioSolutions develops and produces, for the US government and commercial markets, drugs that treat and/or protect against infectious diseases and bioagents. The company supplies BioThrax (the US's only FDA-approved anthrax vaccine) primarily to the departments of Defense and Health and Human Services; it has combined contracts worth $243 million with HHS. The firm's biodefense unit is also developing a post-exposure treatment for anthrax. For commercial markets, Emergent is working on therapies and vaccines for typhoid, Group B strep, and hepatitis B, among other things. Chairman and CEO Fuad El-Hibri controls about 80% of the company.

In 2003 the company bought the assets of vaccine-developer Antex Biologics to expand its pipeline. To expand into Europe, the vaccine maker in 2005 bought British infectious disease vaccine start-up Microscience. Emergent BioSolutions renamed its purchase Emergent Europe. A year later, it purchased Germany-based biotech company Vivacs GmbH in a move to fortify its German presence.

The Microscience deal greatly expands Emergent's pipeline of vaccines, including five targeting infectious diseases, and decreases its reliance on its anthrax vaccine.

The anthrax vaccine's efficacy and possible side effects led to immediate scrutiny and lawsuits. A federal judge halted its use in late 2003, months after the FDA's initial approval. The FDA's 2005 decision, ruling the drug safe and effective for all methods of delivery, caused the ban to be lifted.

More than 8 million troops have been inoculated against anthrax in the past five years. Emergent BioSolutions' contract with the Department of Defense expired in September 2006, but earlier in the year it negotiated a contract for an additional 11 million doses of the BioThrax over the next five years. Emergent is also pushing to have BioThrax added to the US government's plans to protect the populace from a possible bioterrorist attack.

The company's 2006 initial public offering raised funds for clinical trials and the construction of production facilities in Michigan and Maryland, as well as for general corporate purposes.

EXECUTIVES

Chairman, President, and CEO; Chairman, BioPort: Fuad El-Hibri, age 48, $490,818 pay
EVP and COO: Edward J. (Ed) Arcuri, age 55, $280,192 pay
SVP Corporate Affairs, General Counsel, and Secretary: Daniel J. Abdun-Nabi, age 52, $272,631 pay
SVP Marketing and Communications: Kyle W. Keese, age 44
VP Finance, CFO, and Treasurer: R. Don Elsey, age 53
VP Corporate Planning and Business Development: Mauro Gibellini
Chief Scientific Officer and President, Emergent Product Development UK Limited: Steven Chatfield, age 49, $225,162 pay
President, Product Development: Michael J. Langford
President and CEO, BioPort: Robert G. Kramer Sr., age 49, $371,192 pay
Director Communications and Government Affairs, BioPort: Kimberly Brennen (Kim) Root
Auditors: Ernst & Young LLP

LOCATIONS

HQ: Emergent BioSolutions Inc.
2273 Research Blvd., Ste. 400, Rockville, MD 20850
Phone: 301-795-1800   **Fax:** 301-795-1899
Web: www.emergentbiosolutions.com

COMPETITORS

Abbott Labs
Acambis
AVANT Immunotherapeutics
Avecia
Bayer
bioMérieux
Bristol-Myers Squibb
Cangene
Chiron
Gilead Sciences
GlaxoSmithKline
Human Genome Sciences
Merck
Novartis
Novo Nordisk
Pfizer
Sanofi-Aventis
VaxGen
Wyeth

HISTORICAL FINANCIALS

Company Type: Public

Income Statement

	REVENUE ($ mil.)	NET INCOME ($ mil.)	NET PROFIT MARGIN	EMPLOYEES
12/05	130.7	15.8	12.1%	469
12/04	83.5	11.5	13.8%	—
12/03	55.8	4.5	8.1%	400
Annual Growth	53.0%	87.4%	—	8.3%

FYE: December 31

2005 Year-End Financials

Debt ratio: 17.6%
Return on equity: 38.2%
Cash ($ mil.): 36.3
Current ratio: 1.96
Long-term debt ($ mil.): 10.5

Net Income History   NYSE: EBS

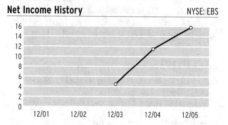

Emeritus

The Emeritus Corporation honors the retirement set. The company runs assisted-living homes for people who may need some help with daily activities but don't need skilled nursing care (offered at a few of its properties). Emeritus Corporation owns or manages about 200 communities in 35 states. The company's services are divided into three major categories: basic services, assisted-living services, and services for residents with Alzheimer's disease. Chairman and CEO Daniel Baty owns about 48% of Emeritus; New York investment firm Saratoga Partners owns about 34%.

Emeritus Corporation plans to expand by acquisitions and by targeting wealthier seniors in suburban communities. It has formed a joint venture with Blackstone Real Estate Partners (a subsidiary of The Blackstone Group) as a means to acquiring 25 senior care facilities. Emeritus will own about 20% of the venture and will manage the properties for a fee of 5% of revenue.

The company generates about 90% of its revenue from private-pay sources.

EXECUTIVES

Chairman and CEO: Daniel R. Baty, age 62, $287,500 pay
SVP, Operations: Gary S. Becker, age 58, $265,000 pay
VP, Finance, CFO, Secretary, and Director: Raymond R. Brandstrom, age 53, $265,000 pay
VP, Administration: Frank A. Ruffo Jr., age 63
VP, Financial Planning: Martin D. Roffe, age 58
VP, Operations, Central Division: Christopher M. Belford, age 44
VP, Operations, Eastern Division: Suzette P. McCanless, age 57, $242,600 pay
VP, Operations, Western Division: P. Kacy Kang, age 38, $210,000 pay
Auditors: KPMG LLP

LOCATIONS

HQ: Emeritus Corporation
3131 Elliott Ave., Ste. 500, Seattle, WA 98121
Phone: 206-298-2909   **Fax:** 206-301-4500
Web: www.emeritus.com

Emeritus Corporation operates assisted-living facilities in 35 states. Most of its facilities are concentrated in Arizona, California, Florida, New York, South Carolina, Texas, and Washington.

2005 Sales

	$ mil.	% of total
Community	378.9	98
Other	8.8	2
Total	**387.7**	**100**

COMPETITORS

Atria Senior Living Group
Balanced Care
CabelTel
Capital Senior Living
Golden Horizons
Regent Assisted Living
Sunrise Senior Living

HISTORICAL FINANCIALS

Company Type: Public

Income Statement

	REVENUE ($ mil.)	NET INCOME ($ mil.)	NET PROFIT MARGIN	EMPLOYEES
12/05	387.7	12.3	3.2%	8,548
12/04	317.9	(40.5)	—	8,541
12/03	206.7	(8.1)	—	7,500
12/02	153.1	(6.2)	—	7,950
12/01	140.6	(4.2)	—	6,005
Annual Growth	28.9%	—	—	9.2%

FYE: December 31

2005 Year-End Financials

Debt ratio: —
Return on equity: —
Cash ($ mil.): 64.9
Current ratio: 0.75
Long-term debt ($ mil.): 712.0
No. of shares (mil.): 16.5
Dividends
  Yield: —
  Payout: —
Market value ($ mil.): 345.4
R&D as % of sales: —
Advertising as % of sales: —

Stock History   AMEX: ESC

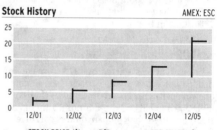

	STOCK PRICE ($) FY Close	P/E High/Low		PER SHARE ($) Earnings	Dividends	Book Value
12/05	20.95	32	14	0.69	—	(6.86)
12/04	12.90	—	—	(4.17)	—	(11.87)
12/03	8.21	435	166	0.02	—	(8.44)
12/02	5.39	—	—	(1.33)	—	(8.30)
12/01	2.11	—	—	(1.04)	—	(7.27)
Annual Growth	77.5%	—	—	—	—	—

Empire Resources

When it comes to aluminum, Empire Resources is especially resourceful. The company distributes semifinished aluminum products, including sheet, foil, wire, plate, and coil. Products are sold primarily to manufacturers of appliances, automobiles, packaging, and housing materials. Empire Resources provides a variety of related services, including sourcing of aluminum products, storage and delivery, and handling foreign exchange transactions. Company president and CEO Nathan Kahn and CFO Sandra Kahn, who are husband and wife, own 54% of Empire Resources.

Empire Resources relies on a single supplier, Hulett Aluminium, for more than half of its products. However, Empire Resources has begun to make its own aluminum extrusions. As for customers, Ryerson is the company's largest, accounting for nearly 15% of sales.

EXECUTIVES

Chairman: William Spier, age 71
President, CEO, and Director: Nathan Kahn, age 51
VP, CFO, Secretary, Treasurer, and Director:
 Sandra R. Kahn, age 48
VP, Sales and Director: Harvey Wrubel, age 52
Customer Service Manager: Ginette Raymond
Sales Manager: Jeff Lowy
Sales Manager: Alan Papier
General Manager, Empire Resources Extrusions LLC:
 Joe Wolf
Director; Managing Director, Empire-Pacific:
 Peter G. Howard, age 70
Human Resources: Deborah Waltuch
Auditors: Eisner LLP

LOCATIONS

HQ: Empire Resources, Inc.
 1 Parker Plaza, Fort Lee, NJ 07024
Phone: 201-944-2200   **Fax:** 201-944-2226
Web: www.empireresources.com

Empire Resources operates from offices in Maryland and New Jersey and sells its products throughout North America and in Australia, Europe, and New Zealand.

2005 Sales

	$ mil.	% of total
US	299.9	84
Canada & Pacific Rim	58.6	16
Total	**358.5**	**100**

PRODUCTS/OPERATIONS

Selected Aluminum Products

Circles
Coil/sheet
Foil
Plate
Profiles/extruded products
Treadplate

COMPETITORS

Alcan
Alcoa
Commercial Metals

HISTORICAL FINANCIALS
Company Type: Public

Income Statement — FYE: December 31

	REVENUE ($ mil.)	NET INCOME ($ mil.)	NET PROFIT MARGIN	EMPLOYEES
12/05	358.5	9.5	2.6%	50
12/04	212.6	4.8	2.3%	30
12/03	184.4	3.5	1.9%	30
12/02	158.7	2.4	1.5%	21
12/01	143.2	1.3	0.9%	30
Annual Growth	**25.8%**	**64.4%**	**—**	**13.6%**

2005 Year-End Financials

Debt ratio: 9.5%
Return on equity: 45.0%
Cash ($ mil.): 6.6
Current ratio: 1.15
Long-term debt ($ mil.): 2.3
No. of shares (mil.): 9.7

Dividends
 Yield: 3.2%
 Payout: 36.5%
Market value ($ mil.): 106.1
R&D as % of sales: —
Advertising as % of sales: —

Stock History — AMEX: ERS

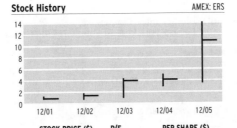

	STOCK PRICE ($) FY Close	P/E High/Low		PER SHARE ($) Earnings	Dividends	Book Value
12/05	10.89	15	4	0.96	0.35	2.49
12/04	4.12	10	6	0.49	0.22	1.87
12/03	3.95	11	3	0.37	0.16	1.59
12/02	1.40	7	3	0.23	—	1.37
12/01	0.90	10	7	0.12	—	1.13
Annual Growth	**86.5%**	**—**	**—**	**68.2%**	**47.9%**	**21.8%**

Emrise

The sun doesn't set on EMRISE. Through its worldwide subsidiaries, the company makes electronic components and communications equipment for customers in the aerospace, defense, and telecom industries. Its CXR Larus units produce network transmission and access equipment and a range of testing gear. EMRISE's XET Corporation subsidiary manufactures power converters, digital and rotary switches, and subsystem assemblies. The company counts BAE SYSTEMS, Essential Components, Raytheon, Rockwell Collins (about 10% of sales), and Thales Defense among its top clients.

EMRISE acquired Larus Corporation, a maker of network synchronization and timing products, along with its engineering subsidiary Vista Labs for nearly $6 million in 2004. EMRISE has combined its CXR Telcom subsidiary with Larus as part of a cost reduction effort and has announced plans to use Larus' sales and marketing staff to support the network access products of CXR Anderson Jacobson, an EMRISE subsidiary based in France.

In 2005 EMRISE acquired Pascall Electronics, a UK supplier of radio-frequency (RF) components and subsystems, as a way to broaden the company's power systems line. EMRISE paid around $6 million in cash and extended a loan of about $3 million to Pascall to pay off a corporate obligation to Intelek, Pascall's former parent company.

AWM Investment owns nearly 11% of EMRISE. Jon B. Gruber and related investors hold about 6% of the company.

EXECUTIVES

Chairman, President, CEO, and Interim CFO:
 Carmine T. Oliva, age 63
EVP and COO: Graham Jefferies, age 48
President, CXR Telecom: Kevin Haug
President, CXR S.A.: Jacques Moisset
President, CXR Larus Corporation: Larry Taillie
Secretary and Director: Robert B. Runyon, age 80
Director, Human Resources: Gale Belger
Director, Sales and Marketing, CXR Anderson Jacobson: Eric Piaget

LOCATIONS

HQ: Emrise Corporation
 9485 Haven Ave., Ste. 100,
 Rancho Cucamonga, CA 91730
Phone: 909-987-9220   **Fax:** 909-987-9228
Web: www.emrise.com

EMRISE and its subsidiaries have offices in France, Japan, the UK, and the US.

2005 Sales

	% of total
UK	42
US	39
France	16
Japan	3
Total	**100**

PRODUCTS/OPERATIONS

2005 Sales

	% of total
Electronic components	63
Communications equipment	37
Total	**100**

2005 Sales

	% of total
Electronic components	
Electronic power supplies	34
Digital & rotary switches	16
Radio-frequency (RF) components	8
Other products & services	5
Communications equipment	
Network access & transmission products	21
Communications test instruments	7
Satellite communication timing & synchronization products	6
Other products & services	3
Total	**100**

Selected Products

Electronic components
  Digital and rotary switches
  Electronic power supplies
  Subsystem assemblies (input and display devices)
Telecommunications
  Network access and transmission products
  Test instruments

COMPETITORS

3Com	Oscilloquartz SA
ADC Telecommunications	Panasonic Mobile
ADTRAN	Communications
Agilent Technologies	Power-One
Alcatel-Lucent	Powerstax plc
Catapult Communications	RADCOM
Cisco Systems	Spirent
Comtech	Sunrise Telecom
Telecommunications	Symmetricom
Dynatec International	Tekelec
Esterline	Tektronix
Fluke Networks	Teradyne
Ixia	Tollgrade
Nortel Networks	Zhone Technologies
OMRON	

HISTORICAL FINANCIALS

Company Type: Public

Income Statement

FYE: December 31

	REVENUE ($ mil.)	NET INCOME ($ mil.)	NET PROFIT MARGIN	EMPLOYEES
12/05	41.3	1.4	3.4%	329
12/04	29.9	1.5	5.0%	—
12/03	25.5	1.2	4.7%	—
12/02	22.7	(0.6)	—	—
12/01	27.4	0.3	1.1%	—
Annual Growth	10.8%	47.0%	—	—

2005 Year-End Financials

Debt ratio: 9.2%
Return on equity: 7.4%
Cash ($ mil.): 4.4

Current ratio: 2.00
Long-term debt ($ mil.): 2.5

Net Income History

NYSE Arca: ERI

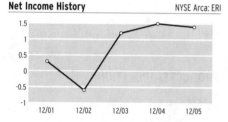

Encore Acquisition

"Drill it again, and buy some more oil and gas properties" appear to be operating guidelines for Encore Acquisition, an independent oil and natural gas company engaged in the acquisition, development, and exploitation of reserves in several basins. Operations include drilling in the Williston Basin of Montana and North Dakota, the Permian Basin of Texas and New Mexico, and the Anadarko Basin of Oklahoma. Its proved reserves of 195.7 million barrels of oil equivalent are primarily from its Cedar Creek Anticline asset (in Montana and North Dakota). Encore Acquisition was formed in 1998 by J.P. Morgan Partners, Warburg Pincus & Co., and Natural Gas Partners.

In 2004 the company acquired Cortez Oil & Gas. In 2005 Encore Acquisition bought oil and gas properties in Oklahoma, Montana, and North Dakota, from some private companies for about $123 million. It also purchased oil and gas properties in the Permian Basin in West Texas and the

Anadarko Basin in Oklahoma from Kerr-McGee for $104 million.

In early 2007 the company agreed to buy assets in the Elk Basin and Gooseberry oil fields in Wyoming from Anadarko Petroleum for $400 million.

EXECUTIVES

Chairman: I. Jon Brumley, age 67, $1,187,500 pay
President, CEO, and Director: Jon S. (Jonny) Brumley, age 35
SVP and COO: L. Ben Nivens, age 46
SVP, Administration: Robert S. Jacobs, age 44
SVP, North Region and Drilling: Donald P. Gann Jr., age 44, $346,667 pay
SVP, CFO, Treasurer, Principal Accounting Officer, and Corporate Secretary: Robert C. Reeves, age 37
VP, Business Development: John W. Arms, age 38
Media Contact: William J. Van Wyk
Auditors: Ernst & Young LLP

LOCATIONS

HQ: Encore Acquisition Company
777 Main St., Ste. 1400, Fort Worth, TX 76102
Phone: 817-877-9955   **Fax:** 817-877-1655
Web: www.encoreacq.com

Encore Acquisition has operations in Louisiana, Montana, New Mexico, North Dakota, Oklahoma, and Texas.

2005 Proved Reserves

	% of total
Cedar Creek Anticline (Williston Basin)	60
Permian Basin	18
Mid-Continent	17
Rockies	5
Total	**100**

PRODUCTS/OPERATIONS

2005 Sales

	$ mil.	% of total
Oil	307.9	67
Natural gas	149.4	33
Total	**457.3**	**100**

COMPETITORS

Abraxas Petroleum
Anadarko Petroleum
Apache
BP
Exxon Mobil
Pioneer Natural Resources
Royal Dutch Shell

HISTORICAL FINANCIALS

Company Type: Public

Income Statement

FYE: December 31

	REVENUE ($ mil.)	NET INCOME ($ mil.)	NET PROFIT MARGIN	EMPLOYEES
12/05	457.3	103.4	22.6%	205
12/04	298.5	82.2	27.5%	164
12/03	220.1	63.6	28.9%	119
12/02	160.7	37.7	23.5%	108
12/01	135.9	16.2	11.9%	92
Annual Growth	35.4%	58.9%	—	22.2%

2005 Year-End Financials

Debt ratio: 133.8%
Return on equity: 20.3%
Cash ($ mil.): 10.5
Current ratio: 0.70
Long-term debt ($ mil.): 731.7
No. of shares (mil.): 49.4

Dividends
Yield: —
Payout: —
Market value ($ mil.): 1,581.8
R&D as % of sales: —
Advertising as % of sales: —

Stock History

NYSE: EAC

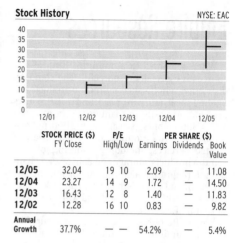

	STOCK PRICE ($) FY Close	P/E High/Low		PER SHARE ($) Earnings	Dividends	Book Value
12/05	32.04	19	10	2.09	—	11.08
12/04	23.27	14	9	1.72	—	14.50
12/03	16.43	12	8	1.40	—	11.83
12/02	12.28	16	10	0.83	—	9.82
Annual Growth	37.7%	—	—	54.2%	—	5.4%

Encore Capital Group

Credit junkies, beware: Encore Capital Group has your number. Through subsidiary Midland Credit Management, the firm (formerly MCM Capital Group) buys at a discount charged-off receivables that credit card issuers have given up on, then does its best to collect the money. The company says it applies a "friendly, but firm approach" and concentrates on getting the balance owed over time. Encore Capital's account managers evaluate customers' ability to pay, then develop tailored payment programs; the company also uses skip-tracers to track down stubborn debtors.

In 2005 Encore Capital acquired Ascension Capital Group, an Arlington, Texas firm that negotiates and monitors consumers' bankruptcy plans. The acquisition is in line with Encore's strategy to diversify into complementary businesses operating within the consumer debt recovery industry.

Consolidated Press International Holdings owns more than 15% of Encore Capital; activist director Nelson Peltz owns nearly 9%.

EXECUTIVES

Chairman: Richard A. Mandell, age 63
Vice Chairman: Carl C. Gregory III, age 61, $777,395 pay (prior to title change)
President, CEO, and Director: J. Brandon Black, age 38, $765,310 pay (prior to promotion)
EVP, CFO, and Treasurer: Paul J. Grinberg, age 45, $550,000 pay
EVP and General Manager, Consumer Debt: Ron Eckhardt, age 62, $181,731 pay (partial-year salary)
SVP and CIO: John R. Treiman, age 43
SVP, Business Development and Portfolio Acquisitions: Anthony Riggio
SVP, Collection Operations: Anna Hansen
SVP, General Counsel, and Secretary: Robin R. Pruitt, age 48, $309,734 pay
SVP, Human Resources: Alison James, age 39
VP and Controller: George R. Brooker, age 41, $235,659 pay
Auditors: BDO Seidman, LLP

LOCATIONS

HQ: Encore Capital Group, Inc.
8875 Aero Dr., Ste. 200, San Diego, CA 92123
Phone: 858-560-2600 **Fax:** 858-309-6978
Web: www.mcmcg.com

Encore Capital operates offices in Arlington, Texas; Phoenix; St. Cloud, Minnesota; and San Diego.

PRODUCTS/OPERATIONS

2005 Sales

	$ mil.	% of total
Receivable portfolios	215.9	97
Servicing fees & other	5.9	3
Total	**221.8**	**100**

COMPETITORS

Asset Acceptance
Asta Funding
FirstCity Financial
NCO
Outsourcing Solutions
Portfolio Recovery

HISTORICAL FINANCIALS

Company Type: Public

Income Statement

FYE: December 31

	REVENUE ($ mil.)	NET INCOME ($ mil.)	NET PROFIT MARGIN	EMPLOYEES
12/05	221.8	31.1	14.0%	905
12/04	178.5	23.2	13.0%	705
12/03	117.5	18.4	15.7%	716
12/02	90.4	13.8	15.3%	628
12/01	47.8	(10.9)	—	596
Annual Growth	**46.8%**	**—**	**—**	**11.0%**

2005 Year-End Financials

Debt ratio: 168.9%
Return on equity: 29.0%
Cash ($ mil.): 11.2
Current ratio: —
Long-term debt ($ mil.): 199.9
No. of shares (mil.): 22.7

Dividends
  Yield: —
  Payout: —
Market value ($ mil.): 393.0
R&D as % of sales: —
Advertising as % of sales: —

Stock History

NASDAQ (GS): ECPG

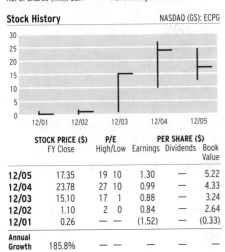

	STOCK PRICE ($) FY Close	P/E High/Low		PER SHARE ($) Earnings	Dividends	Book Value
12/05	17.35	19	10	1.30	—	5.22
12/04	23.78	27	10	0.99	—	4.33
12/03	15.10	17	1	0.88	—	3.24
12/02	1.10	2	0	0.84	—	2.64
12/01	0.26	—	—	(1.52)	—	(0.33)
Annual Growth	**185.8%**	**—**	**—**	**—**	**—**	**—**

Encore Wire

Encore Wire likes to leave its customers applauding and calling for more — more wire, that is. A manufacturer of copper electrical building wire and cable, Encore produces THWN-2 cable (feeder, circuit, and branch wiring for commercial and industrial buildings) and NM cable (sheathed cable used to wire homes, apartments, and manufactured housing). It also produces UF cable, an underground feeder cable for outside lighting and other remote uses in residential buildings. The company sells primarily to wholesale electrical distributors across the US and to some retail home-improvement centers.

Encore emphasizes low-cost production to remain competitive. Its manufacturing operations are highly automated and Encore maintains a small workforce; hourly employees receive incentive-based pay to further improve productivity. Public venture capital firm Capital Southwest Corporation owns about 18% of the company.

HISTORY

Industry veterans Vincent Rego and Donald Spurgin founded Encore Wire in 1989 to make wire for residential use after their previous company, Capital Wire, was bought out by Penn Central in 1988. Encore rolled through the home-building recession of the early 1990s, gathering market share along the way. The company went public in 1992. Proceeds from the offering bought additional manufacturing equipment and paid off debt.

The firm began manufacturing commercial wire in 1994, following completion of a major plant expansion. A strong housing market helped charge the company's sales in 1996, prompting it to build a fabrication and reprocessing plant for copper rod (completed in 1998). Encore started to manufacture polyvinyl chloride (used in wire sheaths) in 1999. The company also restructured that year, transferring its operations to Encore Wire Limited, a limited partnership.

In 2000 Encore Wire introduced NONLEDEX, a proprietary lead-free building wire. In 2002 the firm built an $18 million manufacturing facility adjacent to its McKinney, Texas, headquarters.

EXECUTIVES

Chairman Emeritus: Vincent A. Rego, age 82
President, CEO, and Director: Daniel L. Jones, age 42
VP, Finance, CFO, Treasurer, and Secretary:
  Frank J. Bilban, age 49, $280,000 pay
VP, Operations: David K. Smith, age 44
Director, Human Resources: Brad Rattan
Auditors: Ernst & Young LLP

LOCATIONS

HQ: Encore Wire Corporation
1410 Millwood Rd., McKinney, TX 75069
Phone: 972-562-9473 **Fax:** 972-562-4744
Web: www.encorewire.com

Encore Wire has a plant in McKinney, Texas, and distribution operations in California, Kentucky, Michigan, New Jersey, North Carolina, Ohio, Pennsylvania, and Tennessee.

PRODUCTS/OPERATIONS

Selected Products

NM Cable (non-metallic sheathed cable is used primarily as interior wiring in homes, apartments, and manufactured housing)
THWN-2 Cable (single conductor, either stranded or solid, and insulated with PVC, which is further coated with nylon, used primarily as feeder, circuit, and branch wiring in commercial and industrial buildings)
UF Cable (underground feeder cable is used to conduct power underground to outside lighting and other applications remote from residential buildings)

COMPETITORS

AFC Cable
Alpine Group
Belden CDT
Cerro Wire & Cable
General Cable
Genesis Cable
International Wire
Legrand
Madeco
Phelps Dodge
Pirelli & C.
Southwire
Superior Essex
Thomas & Betts
Volex

HISTORICAL FINANCIALS

Company Type: Public

Income Statement

FYE: December 31

	REVENUE ($ mil.)	NET INCOME ($ mil.)	NET PROFIT MARGIN	EMPLOYEES
12/05	758.1	50.1	6.6%	686
12/04	603.2	33.4	5.5%	643
12/03	384.8	14.4	3.7%	714
12/02	285.2	6.0	2.1%	617
12/01	281.0	9.1	3.2%	599
Annual Growth	**28.2%**	**53.2%**	**—**	**3.4%**

2005 Year-End Financials

Debt ratio: 33.5%
Return on equity: 27.1%
Cash ($ mil.): 2.6
Current ratio: 4.55
Long-term debt ($ mil.): 70.4
No. of shares (mil.): 25.9

Dividends
  Yield: —
  Payout: —
Market value ($ mil.): 590.4
R&D as % of sales: —
Advertising as % of sales: —

Stock History

NASDAQ (GS): WIRE

	STOCK PRICE ($) FY Close	P/E High/Low		PER SHARE ($) Earnings	Dividends	Book Value
12/05	22.76	12	4	2.13	—	8.12
12/04	13.33	20	8	1.42	—	6.17
12/03	11.90	20	9	0.63	—	8.05
12/02	6.03	45	19	0.26	—	7.05
12/01	8.07	25	9	0.40	—	6.75
Annual Growth	**29.6%**	**—**	**—**	**51.9%**	**—**	**4.7%**

Energy Partners

It pays for Energy Partners to have friends in the oil and gas business. The independent explorer and producer focuses on the deep and shallow waters of the Gulf of Mexico and the Gulf Coast. It partners with big oil companies to explore for reserves on properties the majors have left behind; Energy Partners earns an interest in the new reserves and production. The company has interests in 384 productive wells, and has proved reserves of 59.3 million barrels of oil equivalent. Energy Partners has grown through acquisitions. In 2006 Energy Partners bid $1.4 billion for Stone Energy, besting an offer from Plains Exploration and Production, but later terminated the offer.

Energy Partners has begun to expand its 308,000 gross oil and gas acreage position in the Gulf of Mexico with an additional 85,000 acres. It is also expanding its onshore acreage.

EXECUTIVES

Chairman and CEO: Richard A. Bachmann, age 61, $1,330,000 pay
President, COO, and Director: Phillip A. Gobe, age 53, $499,000 pay
EVP and CFO: Timothy Woodall
EVP, General Counsel, and Corporate Secretary: John H. Peper, age 53, $356,970 pay
SVP, Drilling and Engineering: Javan D. (Jay) Ottoson, age 48
SVP, Production: T. Rodney Dykes, age 49, $326,600 pay
Treasurer: Joseph H. LeBlanc Jr., age 45
Controller and Principal Accounting Officer: Dina Bracci Riviere
Director Investor Relations: T.J. Thom
Auditors: KPMG LLP

LOCATIONS

HQ: Energy Partners, Ltd.
201 St. Charles Ave., Ste. 3400,
New Orleans, LA 70170
Phone: 504-569-1875 **Fax:** 504-569-1874
Web: www.eplweb.com

Energy Partners operates in the Gulf of Mexico and on the Gulf Coast.

PRODUCTS/OPERATIONS

2005 Sales

	$ mil.	% of total
Natural gas	266.7	66
Oil	135.3	34
Adjustments	1.0	—
Total	**403.0**	**100**

COMPETITORS

BP
Chevron
El Paso
Exxon Mobil
Forest Oil
Houston Exploration
Marathon Oil
Murphy Oil
Newfield Exploration
Pioneer Natural Resources
Stone Energy

HISTORICAL FINANCIALS

Company Type: Public

Income Statement

FYE: December 31

	REVENUE ($ mil.)	NET INCOME ($ mil.)	NET PROFIT MARGIN	EMPLOYEES
12/05	403.0	73.1	18.1%	170
12/04	295.2	46.4	15.7%	151
12/03	230.2	33.3	14.5%	142
12/02	134.0	(8.8)	—	132
12/01	145.9	12.0	8.2%	124
Annual Growth	**28.9%**	**57.1%**	**—**	**8.2%**

2005 Year-End Financials

Debt ratio: 59.6%
Return on equity: 21.6%
Cash ($ mil.): 6.8
Current ratio: 0.97
Long-term debt ($ mil.): 235.0
No. of shares (mil.): 41.5
Dividends
  Yield: —
  Payout: —
Market value ($ mil.): 903.6
R&D as % of sales: —
Advertising as % of sales: —

Stock History

NYSE: EPL

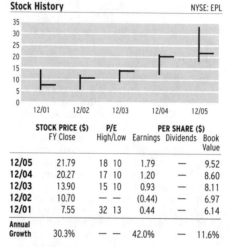

	STOCK PRICE ($) FY Close	P/E High/Low		PER SHARE ($) Earnings	Dividends	Book Value
12/05	21.79	18	10	1.79	—	9.52
12/04	20.27	17	10	1.20	—	8.60
12/03	13.90	15	10	0.93	—	8.11
12/02	10.70	—	—	(0.44)	—	6.97
12/01	7.55	32	13	0.44	—	6.14
Annual Growth	**30.3%**	**—**	**—**	**42.0%**	**—**	**11.6%**

ENGlobal

ENGlobal hopes to engineer its way into the hearts of energy companies throughout the world. The company provides engineering and systems services, procurement, construction management, inspection, and control system automation services to the pipeline and process divisions of major oil and gas companies. It also designs and installs control and instrumentation systems for energy companies. Subsidiary WRC Corporation provides land management, environmental compliance, and other services. Founder and president William Coskey controls around 33% of the firm; activist investor Jeffrey Gendell of Tontine Partners owns nearly 10%.

ENGlobal bought WRC in a cash and stock deal in 2006.

The company focuses on growing its engineering services division through geographical expansion and acquisitions. To that end, the company purchased its much-larger rival Petrocon, and other acquisitions which included selected assets of Petro-Chem Engineering, Engineering Design Group, AmTech Inspection, and Cleveland Inspection Services. The company also seeks strategic acquisitions in such areas as technical outsourcing, government

compliance, technological obsolescence, and energy-related projects.

The firm changed its name from Industrial Data Systems to ENGlobal Corporation in 2001. The group sold its manufacturing subsidiary, Thermaire, which did business as Thermal Corp., and restructured to unify its units under the ENGlobal name.

In 2005 ENGlobal formed its ENGlobal Automation Group, Inc. (EAG) subsidiary to build up its automation operations throughout the Gulf Coast region and in Canada. The unit was awarded control system automation contracts valued at about $13 million by year end.

The company also formed an Analyzer Technology division. In 2006 the company expanded its capabilities in process analyzers through subsidiary ENGlobal Systems, Inc.'s acquisition of certain assets of Houston-based Analyzer Technology International, Inc. (ATI), a provider of online process analyzer systems. ATI was selected to supply analyzer systems for a major Middle Eastern petrochemical plant.

EXECUTIVES

Chairman: William A. (Bill) Coskey, age 53, $435,000 pay
President, CEO, and Director:
  Michael L. (Mike) Burrow, age 58, $570,000 pay
CFO and Treasurer: Robert W. (Bob) Raiford, age 60, $435,000 pay
CIO and Corporate Strategist: Abraham Madha
SVP Business Development: Michael M. Patton, age 53, $239,922 pay
President, ENGlobal Automation Group:
  Shelly D. Leedy
President, ENGlobal Construction Resources and Corporate General Manager of Construction:
  Ronald W. Winthrop
President, ENGlobal Engineering — Eastern Division:
  David W. Smith
President, ENGlobal Engineering — Western Division:
  R. David Kelley
President, ENGlobal Systems: Myron C. Glidewell
President and COO, WRC Corporation: Michael H. Lee
Corporate Human Resources Manager:
  Robert J. Church
Investor Relations Officer, Chief Governance Officer, and Corporate Secretary: Natalie S. Hairston

LOCATIONS

HQ: ENGlobal Corporation
  654 N. Sam Houston Pkwy. East, Ste. 400,
  Houston, TX 77060
Phone: 281-878-1000 **Fax:** 281-878-1010
Web: www.englobal.com

ENGlobal has offices in Baton Rouge and Lake Charles, Louisiana; Blackwell, Cleveland, and Tulsa, Oklahoma; Houston, Beaumont, Freeport, Midland, and Dallas, Texas; and Calgary, Alberta, Canada.

PRODUCTS/OPERATIONS

2005 Sales

	$ mil.	% of total
Engineering	215.7	92
Systems	17.9	8
Total	**233.6**	**100**

COMPETITORS

Austin Industries
CDI
Eagleton Engineering
Jacobs Engineering
Matrix Service
Mustang Engineering
SNC-Lavalin
TAG International

Income Statement
FYE: December 31

	REVENUE ($ mil.)	NET INCOME ($ mil.)	NET PROFIT MARGIN	EMPLOYEES
12/05	233.6	4.8	2.1%	1,724
12/04	148.9	2.4	1.6%	1,329
12/03	123.7	2.2	1.8%	1,023
12/02	91.6	1.8	2.0%	910
12/01	22.0	1.0	4.5%	875
Annual Growth	80.5%	48.0%	—	18.5%

2005 Year-End Financials
Debt ratio: 13.1%
Return on equity: 16.0%
Cash ($ mil.): 0.2
Current ratio: 1.71
Long-term debt ($ mil.): 5.2
No. of shares (mil.): 26.3

Dividends
Yield: —
Payout: —
Market value ($ mil.): 220.8
R&D as % of sales: —
Advertising as % of sales: —

Stock History
AMEX: ENG

	STOCK PRICE ($) FY Close	P/E High/Low	PER SHARE ($) Earnings	Dividends	Book Value
12/05	8.40	58 10	0.19	—	1.52
12/04	3.10	34 11	0.10	—	0.85
12/03	1.97	42 11	0.09	—	0.76
12/02	1.19	22 9	0.07	—	0.59
12/01	0.72	18 7	0.07	—	0.63
Annual Growth	84.8%	— —	28.4%	—	24.7%

Ennis

Ennis (formerly Ennis Business Forms) is in the forms and fashion business. It makes a variety of custom business forms and promotional products (Post-it Notes, presentation products, advertising specialty items). It also sells printed bank forms, secure and negotiable documents, and apparel. Most of its sales, however, come from custom items. The firm sells throughout the US — to end users and forms distributors and resellers. It operates more than 35 manufacturing plants in 16 states, as well as in Mexico and Canada. Ennis runs a dozen other units, including Adams McClure (retail promotions), Northstar Computer Forms (bank forms), Connolly Tool and Machine (tools, dies, machinery), and Alstyle Apparel.

Ennis is continuing to grow through acquisitions. Most recently it agreed to acquire Block Graphics for an undisclosed amount. The purchase will add envelopes and additional short-run print products like continuous and cut-sheet forms to Ennis' offerings. Previously the company expanded its business forms and labels segment through purchases of Crabar/GBF and Royal Business Forms. Ennis' Alstyle Apparel (promotional apparel) buy helped the firm expand into T-shirt and activewear manufacturing and distribution.

John McLinden and Arthur Slaven each own about 9% of the company's stock through Centrum Properties.

EXECUTIVES

Chairman, President, and CEO: Keith S. Walters, age 56, $1,387,692 pay
EVP and Treasurer: Michael D. Magill, age 58, $542,269 pay (prior to promotion)
VP, Administration and Director: Ronald M. Graham, age 58, $282,115 pay
VP, Apparel Division; President, Alstyle Apparel: Todd Scarborough, age 38, $465,768 pay
VP, Finance, CFO, and Secretary: Richard L. Travis Jr., age 50, $104,038 pay (partial-year salary)
Director, Human Resources: Richard Maresh
Director, Marketing: Steven Osterloh
Auditors: Grant Thornton LLP

LOCATIONS

HQ: Ennis, Inc.
2441 Presidential Pkwy., Midlothian, TX 76065
Phone: 972-775-9801   **Fax:** 972-775-9820
Web: www.ennis.com

Ennis has manufacturing plants in California, Illinois, Iowa, Georgia, Kansas, Massachusetts, Missouri, New Jersey, Oregon, Pennsylvania, Tennessee, Texas, Virginia, and Wisconsin.

PRODUCTS/OPERATIONS

2006 Sales

	$ mil.	% of total
Apparel Solutions	238.0	43
Forms Solutions	188.6	34
Promotionals Solutions	85.6	15
Financial Solutions	47.2	8
Total	559.4	100

Selected Segments and Products
Forms Solutions Group
  Business forms
  Other printed business products
Promotional Solutions Group
  Advertising specialties
  Flexographic printing
  Post-it Notes
  Presentation products
  Printed and electronic media
Financial Solutions Group
  Internal bank forms
  Secure and negotiable documents
  Other custom products
Apparel Solutions Group
  Activewear

Selected Subsidiaries
Adams McClure, LP
Admore, Inc.
Alstyle Apparel, LLC
American Forms I, LP
Calibrated Forms Co., Inc.
Connolly Tool and Machine Company
General Financial Supply, Inc.
Northstar Computer Forms, Inc.
PFC Products, Inc.
Texas EBF, LP

COMPETITORS

Avery Dennison	Liberty Enterprises
Cenveo	New England Business
Delta Apparel	Service
Gildan Activewear	R.R. Donnelley
Hanes Companies	Russell
John Harland	Standard Register

Income Statement
FYE: February 28

	REVENUE ($ mil.)	NET INCOME ($ mil.)	NET PROFIT MARGIN	EMPLOYEES
2/06	559.4	40.5	7.2%	5,950
2/05	365.4	23.0	6.3%	6,200
2/04	259.4	18.0	6.9%	2,200
2/03	240.8	15.3	6.4%	2,298
2/02	236.9	15.0	6.3%	2,144
Annual Growth	24.0%	28.2%	—	29.1%

2006 Year-End Financials
Debt ratio: 34.6%
Return on equity: 14.2%
Cash ($ mil.): 13.9
Current ratio: 2.48
Long-term debt ($ mil.): 102.9
No. of shares (mil.): 25.5

Dividends
Yield: 3.1%
Payout: 39.2%
Market value ($ mil.): 502.4
R&D as % of sales: —
Advertising as % of sales: 0.3%

Stock History
NYSE: EBF

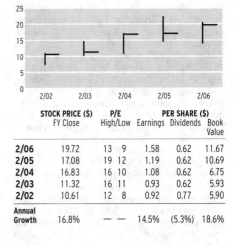

	STOCK PRICE ($) FY Close	P/E High/Low	PER SHARE ($) Earnings	Dividends	Book Value
2/06	19.72	13 9	1.58	0.62	11.67
2/05	17.08	19 12	1.19	0.62	10.69
2/04	16.83	16 10	1.08	0.62	6.75
2/03	11.32	16 11	0.93	0.62	5.93
2/02	10.61	12 8	0.92	0.77	5.90
Annual Growth	16.8%	— —	14.5%	(5.3%)	18.6%

Epicor Software

Epicor Software hopes the middle of the road proves paved with gold. The company provides enterprise resource planning software for midsized businesses. Epicor's software integrates back-office applications for manufacturing, distribution, and accounting with customer relationship management functions, including sales, marketing, and customer support. The company's software also includes collaborative applications that link employees, distributors, and suppliers, encompassing operations such as supply chain management, sourcing, and procurement.

Epicor primarily targets midsized companies with sales between $10 million and $500 million. The company's more than 20,000 clients come from industries such as manufacturing, distribution, financial services, and hospitality.

Epicor's products can be implemented across local area networks (LANs), wide area networks (WANs), and the Internet. The company continues to leverage its products to the Web, and has expanded its offering to include business intelligence and collaborative applications. Epicor has also expanded its roster of strategic partners, which include Hewlett-Packard, Microsoft, and IBM.

HISTORY

Platinum Holdings was founded in 1984 by Gerald Blackie, former CEO of bankrupt software maker Heritage Computing, and former Heritage programmers Timothy McMullen and Kevin Riegelsberger. They introduced the Platinum line of financial accounting software in 1985. Platinum expanded by signing marketing agreements with Arthur Andersen in 1987 and IBM in 1989. In 1992 the company went public and changed its name to Platinum Software.

Two years later Platinum revealed that it had misstated its earnings by booking some sales before they had closed. The company paid $17 million to settle a class-action lawsuit and reorganized. (Blackie and two other ex-execs were later forced to repay hundreds of thousands of dollars in gains and bonuses.)

George Klaus was recruited as CEO in 1996 after twice turning down Platinum's board. The company quickly expanded into enterprise resource planning applications through acquisitions. The next year it bought customer relationship management software developer Clientele Software and manufacturing and distribution software provider FocusSoft. The moves helped Platinum to a profitable fiscal 1998, its first in six years. In late 1998 it bought larger rival DataWorks, cut 15% of its workforce, and changed its fiscal year to December.

The next year the company settled a trademark lawsuit, filed in 1997, with PLATINUM Technology, and Platinum changed its name to Epicor Software in 1999.

Amid declining sales in 2001 the company restructured, cutting jobs and selling its Impresa and Platinum for Windows product lines.

Epicor boosted its procurement and supply chain management offerings by acquiring certain assets of Clarus in 2002. In 2004 the company purchased Scala Business Solutions for about $45 million, as well as buying the assets of Platsoft and Strongline.

EXECUTIVES

Chairman and CEO: L. George Klaus, age 65, $1,417,576 pay
President and COO: Mark Duffell, age 44, $650,723 pay
EVP and CFO: Michael A. Piraino, age 52, $451,592 pay
EVP, Worldwide Sales: Lauri Klaus
SVP and Chief Marketing Officer: John Hiraoka
SVP and General Counsel: John D. Ireland
SVP, Worldwide Support: Daniel (Dan) Whelan, age 40
VP and General Manager, CRS Retail Systems: Kathy Frommer
VP, Sales, Asia: Bryan Tan
VP, Worldwide Research and Development: Paul Farrell
Senior Director, Investor Relations: Damon S. Wright
Director, Public Relations and Analyst Relations: Lisa A. Preuss
Auditors: McGladrey & Pullen, LLP

LOCATIONS

HQ: Epicor Software Corporation
18200 Von Karman Ave., Ste. 1000,
Irvine, CA 92612
Phone: 949-585-4000   **Fax:** 949-585-4091
Web: www.epicor.com

PRODUCTS/OPERATIONS

2005 Sales

	$ mil.	% of total
Maintenance	134.5	46
License fees	77.1	27
Consulting & other	77.8	27
Total	**289.4**	**100**

Selected Software

Customer relationship management (Clientele)
Manufacturing and supply chain management (Avanté, Vantage, Vista)
Web-based enterprise resource management (e by Epicor suite)

Selected Services

Consulting
Custom software development
Technical support
Training

COMPETITORS

Intentia
Lawson Software
Microsoft
Oracle
Pivotal
QAD
SAP

HISTORICAL FINANCIALS

Company Type: Public

Income Statement

FYE: December 31

	REVENUE ($ mil.)	NET INCOME ($ mil.)	NET PROFIT MARGIN	EMPLOYEES
12/05	289.4	52.0	18.0%	1,887
12/04	226.2	25.3	11.2%	1,409
12/03	155.4	9.3	6.0%	886
12/02	143.5	(7.3)	—	799
12/01	171.0	(28.7)	—	973
Annual Growth	**14.1%**	**—**	**—**	**18.0%**

2005 Year-End Financials

Debt ratio: 73.1%
Return on equity: 38.8%
Cash ($ mil.): 53.0
Current ratio: 1.19
Long-term debt ($ mil.): 124.6
No. of shares (mil.): 55.7
Dividends
  Yield: —
  Payout: —
Market value ($ mil.): 787.5
R&D as % of sales: 9.8%
Advertising as % of sales: 0.4%

Stock History

NASDAQ (GS): EPIC

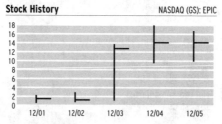

	STOCK PRICE ($) FY Close	P/E High/Low		PER SHARE ($) Earnings	Dividends	Book Value
12/05	14.13	18	11	0.92	—	3.06
12/04	14.09	38	21	0.47	—	1.90
12/03	12.76	76	7	0.18	—	0.64
12/02	1.25	—	—	(0.17)	—	0.09
12/01	1.49	—	—	—	—	0.16
Annual Growth	**75.5%**			**—**	**—**	**108.3%**

EPIQ Systems

EPIQ Systems wants to make bankruptcy quick and painless. The company provides case and document management software for bankruptcy, class action, mass tort, and other legal proceedings. Its software automates tasks including legal notice and claims management, funds distribution, and government reporting. EPIQ's software line includes products for Chapter 7 liquidations, Chapter 13 individual debt reorganizations, and Chapter 11 reorganizations. The company, which caters primarily to bankruptcy trustees as opposed to debtors and creditors, also offers Chapter 11 case management services. Through subsidiary Poorman-Douglas, EPIQ provides software for class action, mass tort, and bankruptcy case administration.

Because most bankruptcies fall under the Chapter 7 or Chapter 13 models — which together account for 99% of all bankruptcy filings — EPIQ has focused primarily on its products for these types of filings. Looking to cover the bankruptcy spectrum by moving into the Chapter 11 market, EPIQ acquired Chapter 11 case management service provider Bankruptcy Services LLC in 2003. The company beefed up its liquidation software offerings with its 2002 purchase of CPT Group's Chapter 7 business.

In 2004 the company expanded beyond the bankruptcy market with its $116 million purchase of Poorman-Douglas, a provider of software and technology-based services for class action, mass tort, and bankruptcy case administration. EPIQ has sold its infrastructure software business, including its DataExpress data file transmission software product line.

EPIQ has an agreement with Bank of America whereby the two companies jointly market EPIQ's software and Bank of America's services to Chapter 7 trustees.

In November 2005 EPIQ acquired nMatrix, a provider of case and document management products for electronic discovery and litigation support, for approximately $125 million.

CEO Tom Olofson owns 15% of EPIQ; president Christopher Olofson owns 5%.

EXECUTIVES

Chairman and CEO: Tom W. Olofson, age 64, $1,275,000 pay
President, COO, and Director: Christopher E. Olofson, age 36, $1,275,000 pay
EVP, CFO, and Corporate Secretary: Elizabeth M. (Betsy) Braham, age 47, $925,000 pay
CEO, Poorman-Douglas: Jeffrey B. Baker, age 52, $350,000 pay
President, Bankruptcy Services: Ron L. Jacobs, age 49, $878,000 pay
SVP, Bankruptcy Services: Kathleen S. Gerber
Investor Relations: Mary Ellen Berthold
Auditors: Deloitte & Touche LLP

LOCATIONS

HQ: EPIQ Systems, Inc.
501 Kansas Ave., Kansas City, KS 66105
Phone: 913-621-9500   **Fax:** 913-321-1243
Web: www.epiqsystems.com

EPIQ Systems has offices in California, Florida, Kansas, New York, and Oregon.

PRODUCTS/OPERATIONS

Software and Services

Bankruptcy Services (Chapter 11 case management services and technology)

CasePower (trustee case management software for Chapter 13 filings)

Class action, mass tort, and bankruptcy case administration software (Poorman-Douglas)

CPT (trustee case management software for Chapter 7 filings)

DCI (trustee case management software for Chapter 7 filings)

Eagle Trust (trustee case management software for Chapter 7 filings)

TCMS (trustee case management system for Chapter 7 filings)

TSI (trustee case management software for Chapter 13 filings)

COMPETITORS

Fiserv
JPMorgan Chase
Misys
SunGard
Thomson Elite

HISTORICAL FINANCIALS

Company Type: Public

Income Statement

	REVENUE ($ mil.)	NET INCOME ($ mil.)	NET PROFIT MARGIN	EMPLOYEES
12/05	130.8	10.9	8.3%	500
12/04	125.4	9.7	7.7%	400
12/03	67.9	8.7	12.8%	180
12/02	38.3	8.2	21.4%	170
12/01	30.1	4.9	16.3%	140
Annual Growth	44.4%	22.1%	—	37.5%

FYE: December 31

2005 Year-End Financials

Debt ratio: 82.6%
Return on equity: 6.9%
Cash ($ mil.): 13.6
Current ratio: 1.24
Long-term debt ($ mil.): 145.9
No. of shares (mil.): 19.3

Dividends
  Yield: —
  Payout: —
Market value ($ mil.): 357.0
R&D as % of sales: —
Advertising as % of sales: —

Stock History

NASDAQ (GS): EPIQ

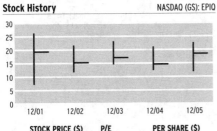

	STOCK PRICE ($) FY Close	P/E High/Low	PER SHARE ($) Earnings	Dividends	Book Value
12/05	18.54	40 22	0.56	—	9.17
12/04	14.64	40 24	0.52	—	7.82
12/03	17.12	48 31	0.48	—	7.27
12/02	15.27	40 22	0.54	—	6.19
12/01	19.35	74 21	0.35	—	4.52
Annual Growth	(1.1%)	— —	12.5%	—	19.3%

Esterline Technologies

Esterline Technologies has a trio of aerospace and defense business segments: Avionics & Controls, Sensors & Systems, and Advanced Materials. The Avionics & Controls unit makes interface systems — switches, indicators, keyboards, displays — for aircraft and military vehicles, communications systems, and medical equipment. Sensors & Systems operations include temperature and pressure sensors as well as fluid and motion control products. The Advanced Materials segment makes elastomer products and ordnance and military countermeasures (Esterline Defense Group, formerly Armtec).

Esterline's strategy has been to expand its product offerings through acquisitions. In December 2005 the company paid about $120 million for UK-based Darchem, a maker of thermally engineered components such as insulation for jet exhaust ducting, nacelle and thrust reverser units, as well as environmental control ducting and heat shields. Darchem, which has annual sales of about $70 million, operates as part of Esterline's Advanced Materials segment.

Esterline bought another UK company, Wallop Defence Systems, for about $59 million in March 2006. Wallop, a maker of military countermeasure flares, operates as part of Esterline Defense Group.

In 2006, about 43% of Esterline's sales were from the commercial aerospace market, 38% were aerospace customers, and 19% were from the general industrial market.

HISTORY

Esterline Technologies Corporation was formed in 1967 as Boyar-Schultz. The company adopted its current name later that year after it merged with Esterline Angus Instrument. Esterline went public in 1968.

Esterline soon began a major period of expansion through acquisitions, including Federal Products (industrial automation, 1969), Auxitrol (precision measuring devices, 1972), and Excellon Automation (drilling systems, 1977). By the end of 1986, Esterline had acquired some 20 companies.

In 1987 Esterline turned over its operations to a management team from aerospace company Criton Technologies (the two shared a major investor, Dyson-Kissner-Moran, or DKM). The new management moved Esterline's headquarters from Darien, Connecticut, to Bellevue, Washington. Esterline bought back DKM's shares in its business in 1989. That year Wendell Hurlbut was named president and CEO.

Esterline encompassed 22 subsidiaries in six countries by 1990. Following a 1993 restructuring, the company began selling its smaller businesses, including Republic Electronics. It sold its Angus Electronics subsidiary to Thermo Instruments in 1997, and later that year it made three strategic acquisitions, including hydraulic controls manufacturer Fluid Regulators, to bolster its aircraft offerings.

The company continued to expand through acquisitions in 1998. Among its seven purchases made that year were Kirkhill Rubber (aerospace components), Memtron Technologies (membrane switches used in instrumentation), and Korry Electronics (lighted switches and panels for the aerospace market).

Robert Cremin, a 22-year Esterline veteran, succeeded Hurlbut as CEO in 1999; Hurlbut remained chairman. That year the company opened an office in Hong Kong to boost sales in Asia. Esterline sold its Federal Products (automotive metrology technology) subsidiary, and later in 1999 it acquired privately held Advanced Input Devices (custom keyboards and multifunction data-input subsystems) and UK-based Muirhead (motion control devices, UK).

In 2001 Esterline received a contract potentially worth $40 million to produce combustible cases for US Army 155mm artillery rounds. The next year the company paid about $68 million for BAE SYSTEMS' Electronic Warfare Passive Expendables Division, a maker of defensive countermeasures such as chaff, which confuses radar, and flares, which draw off heat-seeking weapons. In 2003 Esterline acquired Weston Group (speed, temperature, and rotational sensors) and BVR Aero Precision Corporation (gears data concentrators).

Esterline in 2004 acquired Leach Holding Company, a maker of relays, power distribution assemblies, and switching devices, in a deal worth about $145 million. Acquisitions continued in 2005 with the addition of secure military communication product manufacturer Palomar Products, Inc., which enhanced the company's Avionics & Controls segment.

EXECUTIVES

Chairman, President, and CEO: Robert W. Cremin, age 65, $2,783,135 pay
VP, CFO, Secretary, and Treasurer: Robert D. George, age 49, $1,060,057 pay
Group VP: Richard Wood, age 52, $720,024 pay
VP, Human Resources: Marcia J. M. Greenberg, age 53
VP, Strategy and Technology: Stephen R. Larson, age 61, $923,135 pay
Corporate Controller and Chief Accounting Officer: Gary Posner
Director, Corporate Communications: Brian D. Keogh
Auditors: Ernst & Young LLP

LOCATIONS

HQ: Esterline Technologies Corporation
500 108th Ave. NE, Bellevue, WA 98004
Phone: 425-453-9400   Fax: 425-453-2916
Web: www.esterline.com

Esterline Technologies operates manufacturing plants in France, the UK, and the US.

2006 Sales

	$ mil.	% of total
US	667.5	66
UK	177.1	18
France	136.4	13
Other countries	34.8	3
Adjustments	(43.5)	—
Total	**972.3**	**100**

PRODUCTS/OPERATIONS

2006 Sales

	$ mil.	% of total
Advanced Materials	356.0	37
Sensors & Systems	333.3	34
Avionics & Controls	283.0	29
Total	**972.3**	**100**

Selected Products

Advanced Materials
- Chaff
- Combustible ammunition components
- Elastomer products
- Flares
- Igniter tubes
- Molded fiber cartridge cases (120mm tank rounds and 60mm, 81mm, and 120mm mortar rounds)
- Mortar increments
- Thermal insulation

Sensors and Systems
- Temperature sensing devices
- Pressure sensing devices
- Micro-motors
- Motion control sensors

Avionics and Controls
- Active-matrix liquid-crystal displays
- Control grips
- Control sticks
- Control wheels
- Motion-control sensors
- Switching systems

COMPETITORS

AMETEK
BNS
Chemring
Doncasters
Ducommun
Eaton
Electro Scientific Industries
Emerson Electric
Giddings & Lewis
Goodrich
GSI
Hitachi
InPlay Technologies
Intermec Inc.
Israel Aircraft Industries
L. S. Starrett
Labfacility
Meggitt
Milacron
Parker Hannifin
PLURITEC
Renishaw
Schlumberger
Sypris Solutions
TRUMPF
Tyco
Ultra Electronics
Williams Controls
Yokogawa Electric

HISTORICAL FINANCIALS
Company Type: Public

Income Statement
FYE: October 31

	REVENUE ($ mil.)	NET INCOME ($ mil.)	NET PROFIT MARGIN	EMPLOYEES
10/06	972.3	55.6	5.7%	8,150
10/05	835.4	58.0	6.9%	6,700
10/04	628.2	39.6	6.3%	6,100
10/03	562.5	23.9	4.2%	4,700
10/02	434.8	(1.3)	—	4,200
Annual Growth	22.3%	—	—	18.0%

2006 Year-End Financials

Debt ratio: 39.9%
Return on equity: 8.4%
Cash ($ mil.): 47.0
Current ratio: 2.33
Long-term debt ($ mil.): 282.3
No. of shares (mil.): 25.5
Dividends
  Yield: —
  Payout: —
Market value ($ mil.): 955.9
R&D as % of sales: —
Advertising as % of sales: —

Stock History
NYSE: ESL

	STOCK PRICE ($) FY Close	P/E High/Low		PER SHARE ($) Earnings	Dividends	Book Value
10/06	37.50	22	14	2.15	—	27.78
10/05	36.93	19	13	2.29	—	24.49
10/04	31.60	19	12	1.84	—	21.62
10/03	22.15	20	13	1.13	—	18.70
10/02	17.98	—	—	(0.06)	—	17.05
Annual Growth	20.2%	—	—	—	—	13.0%

EuroBancshares

Far, far away from the old country is Puerto Rico-based EuroBancshares, which is the holding company for Eurobank. Through nearly 25 branches around the island, Eurobank targets small and midsized businesses, owners and employees of such firms, and professionals. Bank business focuses on four areas — commercial banking, leasing, mortgage banking, and trust and wealth management. The company's lending activities are concentrated on products related to real estate development, particularly of single-family homes and townhouses. Nonbank subsidiary EuroSeguros offers property/casualty insurance. Vice chairman Pedro Feliciano Benítez owns more than 25% of the company.

In 2004 EuroBancshares acquired The Bank & Trust of Puerto Rico. The company plans to open or acquire additional new banking offices to reach its goal of having a EuroBank branch within a short drive of more than 80% of Puerto Rico's population.

EXECUTIVES

Chairman, President, and CEO, EuroBancshares and EuroBank: Rafael Arrillaga-Torréns Jr., age 57, $720,200 pay
Vice Chairman, EuroBancshares and EuroBank: Pedro Feliciano Benítez, age 63
EVP, CFO, and Corporate Secretary, EuroBancshares and EuroBank: Yadira R. Mercado Piñiero, age 46, $370,200 pay
EVP and Chief Lending Officer: Luis J. Berrios
EVP, Operations, EuroBank: Felix M. León León, age 63, $170,200 pay
SVP and Treasurer, EuroBancshares and EuroBank: Jorge E. Sepúlveda-Estrada, age 51
SVP, EuroLease, EuroBank: Jaime Noble Fernández, age 55, $280,000 pay
SVP, EuroMortgage, Eurobank: José M. Del Río Jiménez, age 47
SVP, San Juan-Metropolitan Area, EuroBank: Luis S. Suau Hernández, age 55
Assistant VP, Human Resources, EuroBank: Eva Cordero
Auditors: KPMG LLP

LOCATIONS

HQ: EuroBancshares, Inc.
  270 Muñoz Rivera Ave., San Juan, PR 00918
Phone: 787-751-7340   **Fax:** 787-758-5611
Web: www.eurobankpr.com

PRODUCTS/OPERATIONS

2005 Sales

	$ mil.	% of total
Interest		
Loans	108.0	75
Securities	25.3	18
Service charges & fees	9.1	6
Gain on sale of loans	0.9	1
Total	**143.3**	**100**

COMPETITORS

Addison Avenue FCU
American Airlines FCU
BBVA
Citigroup
Doral Financial
First BanCorp (Puerto Rico)
Oriental Financial
Popular
R&G Financial
RBC Financial Group
Santander BanCorp
W Holding

HISTORICAL FINANCIALS
Company Type: Public

Income Statement
FYE: December 31

	ASSETS ($ mil.)	NET INCOME ($ mil.)	INCOME AS % OF ASSETS	EMPLOYEES
12/05	2,391.3	16.5	0.7%	477
12/04	2,102.8	22.7	1.1%	—
12/03	1,320.9	9.9	0.7%	—
12/02	1,035.3	6.9	0.7%	—
Annual Growth	32.2%	29.9%	—	—

2005 Year-End Financials

Equity as % of assets: 6.9%
Return on assets: 0.7%
Return on equity: 10.2%
Long-term debt ($ mil.): 47.1
No. of shares (mil.): 19.4
Market value ($ mil.): 274.9
Dividends
  Yield: —
  Payout: —
Sales ($ mil.): 143.3
R&D as % of sales: —
Advertising as % of sales: —

Stock History
NASDAQ (GS): EUBK

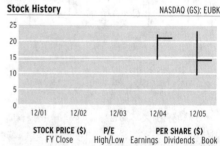

	STOCK PRICE ($) FY Close	P/E High/Low		PER SHARE ($) Earnings	Dividends	Book Value
12/05	14.17	29	12	0.78	—	8.50
12/04	21.00	17	11	1.30	—	8.09
Annual Growth	(32.5%)	—	—	(40.0%)	—	5.1%

Euronet Worldwide

Euronet Worldwide might soon have the whole world in its net — thanks to its network of automatic teller machines (ATMs) and other electronic financial services. Banks, card issuers, and other institutions pay Euronet fees for managing transactions at more than 7,200 ATMs and some 260,000 point-of-sale terminals in 80 countries across Africa, Europe, India, and the Middle East. It also offers related EFT (electronic funds transfer) services. Euronet Worldwide's software division offers banking products, including ATM management, credit and debit card systems, and Internet and wireless banking. The company also provides terminals that let mobile phone users recharge their pre-paid airtime plans.

Euronet has shifted from operating company-owned ATMs to managing outsourced ATMs for banks. In 2002 the company sold all of its ATM operations in France because of new stringent and costly safety requirements. In January 2003, Euronet sold its UK ATM network and simultaneously signed an ATM outsourcing agreement with the buyer. It made a similar arrangement in Hungary just months later.

The company has also been making acquisitions in the growing prepaid transactions arena over the past several years. Deals include the acquisition of US and European companies, including its 2006 acquisition of Ria Envia for around $490 million. In 2007 it agreed to acquire Envios de Valores La Nacional Corp., a US-based money transfer firm. About half of La Nacional's business is transferring funds to the Dominican Republic.

The company entered China in 2006 with its 75%-owned joint venture with Ray Holdings.

Chairman and CEO Michael Brown owns 7% of the company.

EXECUTIVES

Chairman, President, and CEO:
Michael J. (Mike) Brown, age 49
EVP and CFO: Rick L. Weller, age 48, $451,100 pay
EVP and COO, Prepaid Processing: Miro I. Bergman, age 43, $443,333 pay
EVP and Managing Director, Europe, Middle East, and Africa: John Romney, age 39
EVP and Director; EVP and Co-Managing Director, e-pay: Paul S. Althasen, age 41
EVP, General Counsel, and Secretary:
Jeffrey B. (Jeff) Newman, age 51, $422,057 pay
President, PaySpot: Tom Cregan
SVP and Managing Director, Asia Pacific Region:
Anthony Grandidge
SVP and Managing Director, Western Europe:
Roger Heinz, age 41
SVP, Human Resources: Karyn Clewes Zaborny
Marketing Communications Manager: Shruthi Dyapaiah
Auditors: KPMG LLP; KPMG Polska Sp. z o.o.

LOCATIONS

HQ: Euronet Worldwide, Inc.
4601 College Blvd., Ste. 300, Leawood, KS 66211
Phone: 913-327-4200   **Fax:** 913-327-1921
Web: www.euronetworldwide.com

Euronet operates principal offices in the US in Kansas and Arkansas, as well as in Australia, Croatia, the Czech Republic, Egypt, Germany, Greece, Indonesia, New Zealand, Poland, Romania, and Slovakia. It operates processing centers in Kansas, as well as in Germany, Hungary, India, Spain, and the UK.

PRODUCTS/OPERATIONS

2005 Sales

	$ mil.	% of total
Prepaid processing	411.3	77
EFT processing	105.6	20
Software & related	14.3	3
Total	**531.2**	**100**

Selected Subsidiaries

Bankomat 24/Euronet Sp. z o.o. (Poland)
Call Processing Inc. (US)
Delta Euronet GmbH (Germany)
EFT Services Hellas EPE (Greece)
EFT Services Holding B.V. (Netherlands)
EFT-Usluge d o.o. (Croatia)
e-pay Australia Holdings Pty Ltd (Australia)
e-pay Australia Pty Ltd (Australia)
e-pay Holdings Limited (UK)
e-pay Limited (UK)
e-pay New Zealand Pty Ltd
Euronet Adminisztracios Szolgaltato Kft (Hungary)
Euronet Asia Holdings Limited (Hong Kong)
Euronet Banktechnikai Szolgaltato Kft. (Hungary)
Euronet Corporate Services Beograd d.o.o. (Serbia-Montenegro)
Euronet e-pay (Spain) S.L. (Spain)
Euronet Payments and Remittance Inc. (US)
Euronet Services (Slovakia) spol. s r.o.
Euronet Services GmbH (Germany)
Euronet Services Private Limited (India)
Euronet Services spol. s.r.o. (Czech Republic)
Euronet Services SRL (Romania)
Euronet Telerecarga. S.L. (Spain)
Euronet USA Inc. (US)
Europlanet a.d. (Federal Republic of Serbia)
EWI Foreign Holdings Limited (Cyprus)
Instreamline S.A. (Greece)
PaySpot Inc. (US)
Transact Elektronische Zahlungssysteme GmbH (Germany)

COMPETITORS

American Express
Barclays
EDS
Equant
First Data
Global Payments
Hypercom
Magyar Telekom
MasterCard
Telefónica O2 Czech Republic
Telekom Austria
TeliaSonera
TRM

HISTORICAL FINANCIALS
Company Type: Public

Income Statement
FYE: December 31

	REVENUE ($ mil.)	NET INCOME ($ mil.)	NET PROFIT MARGIN	EMPLOYEES
12/05	531.2	27.4	5.2%	926
12/04	381.1	18.4	4.8%	651
12/03	204.4	11.8	5.8%	548
12/02	71.1	(6.5)	—	385
12/01	64.2	0.7	1.1%	478
Annual Growth	**69.6%**	**150.1%**	**—**	**18.0%**

2005 Year-End Financials

Debt ratio: 158.6%
Return on equity: 15.7%
Cash ($ mil.): 293.9
Current ratio: 1.55
Long-term debt ($ mil.): 327.2
No. of shares (mil.): 35.8
Dividends
  Yield: —
  Payout: —
Market value ($ mil.): 994.6
R&D as % of sales: —
Advertising as % of sales: —

Stock History
NASDAQ (GS): EEFT

	STOCK PRICE ($) FY Close	P/E High	P/E Low	PER SHARE ($) Earnings	PER SHARE ($) Dividends	PER SHARE ($) Book Value
12/05	27.80	43	31	0.74	—	5.77
12/04	26.02	49	28	0.55	—	4.28
12/03	18.04	45	15	0.41	—	2.77
12/02	7.51	—	—	(0.28)	—	0.26
12/01	18.10	625	135	0.03	—	(0.35)
Annual Growth	**11.3%**	**—**	**—**	**122.9%**	**—**	**—**

EV Energy Partners

EV Energy is a natural gas and oil production company. The company operates gas wells in the Appalachian Basin, primarily in West Virginia and Ohio, as well as in northern Louisiana. EV Energy has proved reserves of about 45 billion cu. ft. equivalent of natural gas and a million barrels of oil. Its base in the Appalachian Basin puts EV Energy in close proximity to the nation's major consuming markets, allowing for stronger pricing power. The company was formed in 2006 by Canadian energy industry investment group EnerVest; with its affiliates, EnerVest owns 49% of EV Energy and owns 71% of EV Energy's general partner.

EXECUTIVES

Chairman and CEO: John B. Walker, age 60
President, COO, and Director, EV Management; EVP and COO, EnerVest: Mark A. Houser, age 45
SVP and CFO: Michael E. (Mike) Mercer, age 48
SVP Acquisitions and Divestitures:
Kathryn S. MacAskie, age 50
Auditors: Deloitte & Touche LLP

LOCATIONS

HQ: EV Energy Partners, L.P.
1001 Fannin St., Ste. 800, Houston, TX 77002
Phone: 713-659-3500   **Fax:** 713-659-3556
Web: www.evenergypartners.com

EV Energy Partners operates properties in Louisiana, Ohio, and West Virginia.

PRODUCTS/OPERATIONS

2005 Sales

	$ mil.	% of total
Natural gas & oil	45.1	84
Transportation & marketing	8.4	16
Loss on natural gas swaps	(7.2)	—
Total	**46.3**	**100**

COMPETITORS

Atlas America
Chesapeake Energy
Energy Corporation of America

HISTORICAL FINANCIALS

Company Type: Public

Income Statement

FYE: December 31

	REVENUE ($ mil.)	NET INCOME ($ mil.)	NET PROFIT MARGIN	EMPLOYEES
12/05	46.3	15.1	32.6%	332
12/04	30.1	8.4	27.9%	—
12/03	13.8	2.7	19.6%	—
Annual Growth	83.2%	136.5%	—	—

2005 Year-End Financials

Debt ratio: 25.7%
Return on equity: 36.8%
Cash ($ mil.): 7.2
Current ratio: 0.97
Long-term debt ($ mil.): 10.5

Net Income History NASDAQ (GS): EVEP

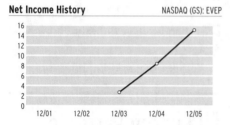

EVCI Career Colleges

EVCI graduates want a second opportunity for a cap and gown. The company provides on-campus college education through the Interboro Institute, which offers associate degrees to students who have GEDs or did not graduate from high school. Students earn an associate of occupational studies degree in areas such as accounting, medical assistant, executive assistant, paralegal studies, ophthalmic dispensing, and security services. Interboro has four locations in New York and provides day and evening classes year-round to some 3,700 full-time students.

In 2005 EVCI purchased Pennsylvania School of Business, located in Allentown, Pennsylvania. Later that year EVCI acquired Technical Career Institutes, expanding its student population in New York.

EXECUTIVES

Chairman; Chairman and Chancellor, Interboro: Arol I. Buntzman, age 62, $655,620 pay
President, CEO, and Director; CEO, Interboro: John J. McGrath, age 52, $486,654 pay
CFO: Joseph J. Looney, age 48
VP Corporate Affairs, General Counsel, Secretary, and Director: Joseph D. Alperin, age 62, $219,985 pay
President, Interboro Institute: Stephen Adolphus
CFO, Interboro and Director: Richard Goldenberg, age 59, $219,100 pay (prior to title change)
General Counsel: Michael J. O'Brien
Auditors: Goldstein Golub Kessler LLP

LOCATIONS

HQ: EVCI Career Colleges Holding Corp.
1 Van Der Donck St., 2nd Fl., Yonkers, NY 10701
Phone: 914-623-0700 **Fax:** 914-395-3498
Web: www.evcinc.com

PRODUCTS/OPERATIONS

Selected Course Categories

Business administration
  Accounting
  Management
Computer technology
  Networking
Office technologies
  Executive assistant
  Medical office assistant
Ophthalmic dispensing
Paralegal studies
Security services and management

COMPETITORS

Apollo Group
Argosy Education Group
Career Education
Corinthian Colleges
DeVry
Strayer Education

HISTORICAL FINANCIALS

Company Type: Public

Income Statement

FYE: December 31

	REVENUE ($ mil.)	NET INCOME ($ mil.)	NET PROFIT MARGIN	EMPLOYEES
12/05	50.7	0.4	0.8%	849
12/04	33.1	6.3	19.0%	531
12/03	20.2	3.4	16.8%	303
12/02	15.4	(2.0)	—	237
12/01	14.7	(8.8)	—	232
Annual Growth	36.3%	—	—	38.3%

2005 Year-End Financials

Debt ratio: 42.7%
Return on equity: 1.6%
Cash ($ mil.): 9.3
Current ratio: 1.28
Long-term debt ($ mil.): 10.8
No. of shares (mil.): 12.4
Dividends
  Yield: —
  Payout: —
Market value ($ mil.): 19.9
R&D as % of sales: —
Advertising as % of sales: 10.1%

Stock History NASDAQ (CM): EVCI

	STOCK PRICE ($) FY Close	P/E High/Low		PER SHARE ($) Earnings	Dividends	Book Value
12/05	1.60	368	50	0.03	—	2.04
12/04	9.60	30	10	0.50	—	1.94
12/03	5.39	20	1	0.31	—	0.64
12/02	0.65	—	—	(0.65)	—	0.47
12/01	1.90	—	—	(2.23)	—	0.82
Annual Growth	(4.2%)	—	—	—	—	25.6%

Evercore Partners

Ever looking to the core of a business to find untapped potential, Evercore Partners provides financial, corporate restructuring, and mergers and acquisitions advisory services. The company also manages more than $1 billion in private equity investments on behalf of institutional and high-net-worth clients, including holdings in American Media, publisher of *National Enquirer* and *Star* magazines, Fidelity National Information Services, and advertising firm Vertis. Evercore was launched in 1996 by Roger Altman, who formerly led investment banking and merger advisory practices at Lehman Brothers and The Blackstone Group.

Evercore has been an advisor on several high-profile transactions: In early 2005 it helped then SBC Corporation hammer out its bid for AT&T, then advised the new AT&T on its acquisition of BellSouth a year later. It also assisted General Motors on the sale of a majority interest in the carmaker's GMAC unit.

In early 2006 Evercore formed Evercore Asset Management, which focuses on small- and mid-cap equities. The company also acquired Protego, a boutique investment bank founded by Pedro Aspe, Mexico's former Minister of Finance. In addition to corporate advisory services, Protego specializes in financing municipal infrastructure and energy projects in Mexico.

Evercore hopes to utilize funds from its 2006 IPO to start another private equity fund and to expand in Japan, where it has a joint venture with Mizuho Securities and The Bridgeford Group.

The company acquired UK investment firm Braveheart Financial Services in a stock-only deal in 2006.

EXECUTIVES

Co-Chairman and co-CEO: Roger C. Altman, age 60
Co-Chairman and Senior Managing Director; Chairman and CEO, Protego: Pedro Aspe
Co-Vice Chairman: Eduardo G. Mestre, age 57
Co-Vice Chairman and Senior Managing Director: Bernard Taylor, age 48
President, Co-CEO, Chief Investment Officer, and Director: Austin M. Beutner, age 46
CFO: David E. Wezdenko, age 42
Controller: Thomas J. Gavenda, age 37
CEO and Director, Protego Asset Management Business: Sergio Sanchez, age 47
Senior Managing Director and Vice Chairman, Investment Management Business: John T. Dillon, age 67
Senior Managing Director and Head of Sales and Marketing, Investment Management Business: Gail Landis, age 53
Senior Managing Director and General Counsel: Adam B. Frankel, age 38
Auditors: Deloitte & Touche LLP

LOCATIONS

HQ: Evercore Partners Inc.
55 E. 52nd St., 43rd Fl., New York, NY 10055
Phone: 212-857-3100 **Fax:** 212-857-3101
Web: www.evercore.com

PRODUCTS/OPERATIONS

2005 Sales

	$ mil.	% of total
Advisory revenue	110.8	88
Investment management revenue	14.6	12
Interest & other	0.2	—
Total	**125.6**	**100**

Selected Investments

American Media, Inc. (publishing)
Continental Energy Services, Inc. (non-utility electric generation)
Davis Petroleum Corp. (oil and gas production)
Energy Partners, Ltd. (oil and gas exploration)
Fidelity National Information Services, Inc. (data processing)
Michigan Electric Transmission Company, LLC
Resources Connection, Inc. (outsourced staffing services)
Specialty Products & Insulation Co.
Telenet Group Holding N.V. (telecom provider, Belgium)
Test Equity, LLC (testing and diagnostic equipment)
Vertis, Inc. (advertising and marketing)

COMPETITORS

Allen & Company	Lazard
Apollo Advisors	Lehman Brothers
Blackstone Group	Merrill Lynch
Citigroup Global Markets	Morgan Stanley
Credit Suisse	Sequoia Capital
Gleacher Partners	Thomas H. Lee Partners
Goldman Sachs	UBS Investment Bank
Greenhill	

HISTORICAL FINANCIALS

Company Type: Public

Income Statement				FYE: December 31
	REVENUE ($ mil.)	NET INCOME ($ mil.)	NET PROFIT MARGIN	EMPLOYEES
12/05	125.6	63.2	50.3%	120
12/04	86.3	49.8	57.7%	—
12/03	60.1	34.3	57.1%	—
Annual Growth	44.6%	35.7%	—	—

2005 Year-End Financials

Debt ratio: 0.5%
Return on equity: 123.0%
Cash ($ mil.): 37.9
Current ratio: 1.93
Long-term debt ($ mil.): 0.2

Net Income History   NYSE: EVR

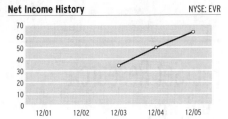

ExlService Holdings

Have an extra-large task you'd rather not take on? Outsource it to ExlService Holdings. The company, known as EXL, offers business process outsourcing (BPO), research and analytics, and consulting services, mainly to companies in the banking, financial services, and insurance industries. Its BPO offerings include claims processing, collections, customer support, and finance and accounting. The company's three top customers — UK insurer Norwich Union, American Express, and Dell — account for more than 60% of sales. Affiliates of Texas investment firm Oak Hill Capital Partners control a 38% stake in EXL.

EXL markets and sells its services through offices in the US, the UK, and Singapore and operates from facilities in India.

The company expanded in 2006 by acquiring Inductis, a provider of consulting and data analysis services for companies in the financial services, insurance, and information services industries. Inductis, which posted sales of about $21 million in 2005, continues to operate under its own brand.

EXECUTIVES

Chairman: Steven B. Gruber, age 48
Vice Chairman and CEO: Vikram Talwar, age 55
President, CFO, and Director: Rohit Kapoor, age 40
VP and General Counsel, EXL Inc.: Amit Shashank, age 34
VP and Business Leader Insurance Operations, EXL India: Lalit Vij, age 40
VP Finance, EXL India: Vinay Mittal, age 42
VP Human Resources, EXL India: Deepak Dhawan, age 52
VP Quality and Process Excellence, EXL India: Vikas Bhalla, age 33
VP Marketing, EXL Service: Alka Misra
Chief Sales and Marketing Officer, EXL: Shiv Kumar, age 37
Head of Investor Relations and Corporate Development: Jarrod Yahes
Auditors: Ernst & Young LLP

LOCATIONS

HQ: ExlService Holdings, Inc.
350 Park Ave., 10th Fl., New York, NY 10022
Phone: 212-277-7100   **Fax:** 212-277-7111
Web: www.exlservice.com

COMPETITORS

Accenture
Affiliated Computer Services
Capita
EDS
IBM Global Services
Infosys
Liberata
Tata Consultancy
Wipro
WNS (Holdings)
xchanging

HISTORICAL FINANCIALS

Company Type: Public

Income Statement				FYE: December 31
	REVENUE ($ mil.)	NET INCOME ($ mil.)	NET PROFIT MARGIN	EMPLOYEES
12/05	73.9	7.1	9.6%	7,300
12/04	60.5	5.4	8.9%	—
12/03	27.8	(0.5)	—	2,626
Annual Growth	63.0%	—	—	66.7%

2005 Year-End Financials

Debt ratio: 18.9%
Return on equity: 25.5%
Cash ($ mil.): 24.7
Current ratio: 2.18
Long-term debt ($ mil.): 5.8

Net Income History   NASDAQ (GM): EXLS

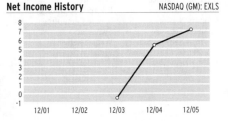

Exploration Company of Delaware

The Exploration Company of Delaware isn't looking to go where no one has gone before — only where no other drillers have gone. Through its direct efforts and joint ventures with other oil and gas firms, the company explores for oil and natural gas in the Dakotas, Montana, and South Texas. It has proved reserves of 9.7 billion cu. ft. of natural gas and 5 million barrels of oil. The Exploration Company sells its oil and gas wholesale through independent marketers. To support its core operations in the Maverick Basin in South Texas, in 2002 the company acquired a 69-mile-long pipeline gathering system. By the end of 2004 The Exploration Company was operating 90 miles of gas gathering pipeline.

During 2004 The Exploration Company participated in drilling 60 gross wells and nine re-entries. Of these, 44 were completed and 16 remained in progress at year-end. No dry holes were reported. In 2005 the company sold some interests in its 670,000-acre Maverick Basin holding in Southwest Texas to EnCana Oil & Gas (USA) Inc. for $80 million.

EXECUTIVES

Chairman, President and CEO: James E. (Jim) Sigmon, age 58
VP Finance, CFO and Treasurer: P. Mark Stark, age 51, $174,000 pay
VP and COO: James J. (Jeff) Bookout, age 44, $160,850 pay
VP and General Counsel: M. Frank Russell, age 57
VP, Capital Markets; Corporate Secretary: Roberto R. (Bob) Thomae, age 55, $177,500 pay
Chief Geologist: Robert J. Scott
Controller: Richard A. Sartor, age 53, $116,155 pay
Media Relations: Paul Hart
Land Manager: Robert E. Lee Jr.
Auditors: Akin, Doherty, Klein & Feuge, P.C.

LOCATIONS

HQ: The Exploration Company of Delaware, Inc.
500 N. Loop 1604 East, Ste. 250,
San Antonio, TX 78232
Phone: 210-496-5300   **Fax:** 210-496-3232
Web: www.txco.com

The Exploration Company explores for oil and natural gas in Montana, North Dakota, South Dakota, and Texas.

PRODUCTS/OPERATIONS

2005 Sales

	$ mil.	% of total
Oil & gas	38.5	57
Gas gathering	28.5	43
Total	**67.0**	**100**

COMPETITORS

Anadarko Petroleum
Clayton Williams Energy
Comstock Resources
ConocoPhillips
Devon Energy
Edge Petroleum
El Paso
Exxon Mobil
Noble Energy
Royal Dutch Shell
Swift Energy

HISTORICAL FINANCIALS
Company Type: Public

Income Statement
FYE: December 31

	REVENUE ($ mil.)	NET INCOME ($ mil.)	NET PROFIT MARGIN	EMPLOYEES
12/05	67.0	13.7	20.4%	49
12/04	57.7	2.8	4.9%	47
12/03	39.5	0.0	—	45
12/02	19.0	(0.3)	—	35
12/01	14.5	(0.1)	—	21
Annual Growth	46.6%	—	—	23.6%

2005 Year-End Financials
Debt ratio: 0.0%
Return on equity: 18.4%
Cash ($ mil.): 6.1
Current ratio: 0.70
Long-term debt ($ mil.): 0.0
No. of shares (mil.): 29.8
Dividends
  Yield: —
  Payout: —
Market value ($ mil.): 192.7
R&D as % of sales: —
Advertising as % of sales: —

Stock History
NASDAQ (GS): TXCO

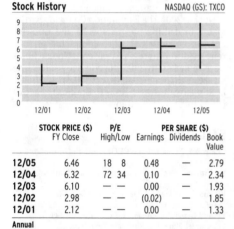

		STOCK PRICE ($) FY Close	P/E High/Low		PER SHARE ($) Earnings	Dividends	Book Value
12/05		6.46	18	8	0.48	—	2.79
12/04		6.32	72	34	0.10	—	2.34
12/03		6.10	—	—	0.00	—	1.93
12/02		2.98	—	—	(0.02)	—	1.85
12/01		2.12	—	—	0.00	—	1.33
Annual Growth		32.1%	—	—	—	—	20.5%

F5 Networks

F5 Networks wants to help your network take a load off. The company's products include server appliances and IP application switches that are used to manage and route network traffic. Companies including Microsoft and The Motley Fool use F5's products for tasks such as load balancing, availability assurance, and security assessment. Customers come from a variety of industries, including telecommunication, financial services, manufacturing, and e-commerce. The company also offers services such as network monitoring, performance analysis, and training.

F5 sells primarily though distributors, systems integrators, and resellers, but it also maintains a direct sales force. Distributing giant Ingram Micro accounted for about 14% of the company's sales in fiscal 2006.

F5 acquired rival Swan Labs, a supplier of wide area network optimization and application acceleration tools, for $43 million in cash in 2005. In 2004 F5 acquired MagniFire WebSystems as part of a push to expand its application security product line.

F5's offerings can be incorporated into a variety of enterprise software and systems, including databases, CRM software, ERP applications, and Web services.

FMR (Fidelity Investments) owns about 11% of F5 Networks. Franklin Resources holds nearly 5% of the company.

EXECUTIVES
President, CEO, and Director: John McAdam, age 54, $912,830 pay
SVP and CFO: Andy Reinland
SVP and Chief Accounting Officer: John Rodriguez
SVP of Business Operations and Global Services: Edward J. Eames, age 46, $444,824 pay
SVP of Marketing: Dan Matte, age 38
SVP of Product Development and CTO: Karl D. Triebes, age 37, $495,544 pay
SVP of Worldwide Sales: M. Thomas (Tom) Hull, age 45, $458,159 pay
VP, General Counsel, and Secretary: Joann M. Reiter, age 47
VP of Product Management and Marketing: Erik Giesa
Auditors: PricewaterhouseCoopers LLP

LOCATIONS
HQ: F5 Networks, Inc.
  401 Elliott Ave. West, Seattle, WA 98119
Phone: 206-272-5555   **Fax:** 206-272-5556
Web: www.f5.com

2006 Sales
	$ mil.	% of total
Americas	226.2	57
Europe, Middle East & Africa	70.7	18
Asia/Pacific		
Japan	51.6	13
Other countries	45.5	12
Total	**394.0**	**100**

PRODUCTS/OPERATIONS

2006 Sales
	$ mil.	% of total
Products	304.9	77
Services	89.1	23
Total	**394.0**	**100**

Selected Products
Network management software
Server appliances and IP application switches

Selected Services
Installation
Network management
Performance analysis
Technical support
Training

COMPETITORS
2Wire	nCipher
Aventail	Nokia
Check Point Software	Nortel Networks
Cisco Systems	Opsware
Citrix Systems	Packeteer
Coyote Point	Radware
Extreme Networks	Resonate
Fortinet	Riverbed Technology
Foundry Networks	Secure Computing
GoAhead Software	Symantec
Internap Network Services	Vernier Networks
Internet Security Systems	Visual Networks
Juniper Networks	

HISTORICAL FINANCIALS
Company Type: Public

Income Statement
FYE: September 30

	REVENUE ($ mil.)	NET INCOME ($ mil.)	NET PROFIT MARGIN	EMPLOYEES
9/06	394.0	66.0	16.8%	1,068
9/05	281.4	46.9	16.7%	792
9/04	171.2	33.0	19.3%	613
9/03	115.9	4.1	3.5%	507
9/02	108.3	(8.6)	—	467
Annual Growth	38.1%	—	—	23.0%

2006 Year-End Financials
Debt ratio: —
Return on equity: 12.3%
Cash ($ mil.): 374.2
Current ratio: 4.65
Long-term debt ($ mil.): —
No. of shares (mil.): 40.8
Dividends
  Yield: —
  Payout: —
Market value ($ mil.): 2,190.6
R&D as % of sales: —
Advertising as % of sales: —

Stock History
NASDAQ (GS): FFIV

		STOCK PRICE ($) FY Close	P/E High/Low		PER SHARE ($) Earnings	Dividends	Book Value
9/06		53.72	47	25	1.59	—	15.12
9/05		43.47	49	25	1.21	—	11.92
9/04		30.46	43	21	0.92	—	8.85
9/03		19.24	156	46	0.14	—	4.01
9/02		7.55	—	—	(0.34)	—	3.64
Annual Growth		63.3%	—	—	—	—	42.7%

FactSet Research Systems

Analysts, portfolio managers, and investment bankers know FactSet Research Systems has the scoop. The company offers financial information from more than 200 databases focusing on areas such as broker research data, financial information, and newswires. FactSet complements its databases with a variety of software for use in downloading and manipulating the data. Among the company's applications are tools for presentations, data warehousing, economic analysis, portfolio analysis, and report writing. Revenues are derived from month-to-month subscriptions to services, databases, and financial applications. About 75% of revenue comes from investment managers; investment banking clients account for the rest.

FactSet has expanded its product offerings with a string of acquisitions. Recent purchases include Derivative Solutions (DSI), which offers fixed income analytics, portfolio management, and risk management services to financial institutions, and AlphaMetrics, which provides institutional clients with software for capturing, measuring,

and ranking financial information. The company next purchased europrospectus.com, now known as FactSet Global Filings Limited, a provider of equity, fixed income, and derivatives prospectuses.

Vice chairman Charles Snyder owns about 8% of FactSet.

HISTORY

Howard Wille and Charles Snyder founded FactSet in 1978. Both had previously worked for Wall Street investment firm Faulkner Dawkins & Sullivan (acquired by Shearson Hayden Stone in 1977). The company spent the 1980s building its client base and developing software that allowed clients to manipulate data on their own PCs.

FactSet opened an office in London in 1993 and one in Tokyo the next year. In 1994 the company added Morgan Stanley Capital International and EDGAR SEC filings to its database offerings. It added World Bank subsidiary International Finance Corp. in 1995 and the Russell U.S. Equity Profile report and Toyo Keizai, a Japanese company database, the next year. FactSet went public in 1996. Market Guide's information on US firms and ADRs (American depositary receipts) as well as the economic and financial databases of DRI/McGraw-Hill were added in 1997.

Snyder retired in 1999 but remained vice chairman. The following year Wille retired and Philip Hadley became chairman and CEO. The company made its first acquisition in 2000 when it bought Innovative Systems Techniques (Insyte), a maker of database management and decision support systems.

The company then began acquiring several content businesses. Its 2003 purchase of Mergerstat gave the company a database of global merger and acquisition and related information. In 2004 the company purchased JCF Group, a provider of broker estimates and other financial data to institutional investors, and CallStreet, a provider of quarterly earnings call transcripts to the investment community. The following year the company purchased TrueCourse, a provider of corporate competitive intelligence.

EXECUTIVES

Chairman and CEO: Philip A. Hadley, age 44, $799,615 pay
Vice Chairman: Charles J. Snyder, age 64
President, COO, and Director: Michael F. DiChristina, age 44, $799,615 pay
SVP, CFO, and Treasurer: Peter G. Walsh, age 41, $569,615 pay
SVP and CTO: Jeff Young
SVP and Chief Content Officer: Townsend Thomas, age 43, $349,615 pay
SVP and Director International Operations: Scott L. Beyer
SVP and Director Investment Banking and Brokerage Services: Kieran M. Kennedy
SVP and Director Investment Management Services: Michael D. Frankenfield, age 41, $629,038 pay
SVP and Director Software Engineering: Mark J. Hale
SVP and Director Portfolio Analytics: Christopher (Chris) Ellis
SVP and Director Global Investment Management and Product Development: Laura C. Ruhe
CEO, Derivative Solutions: Douglas Wheeler
Auditors: PricewaterhouseCoopers LLP

LOCATIONS

HQ: FactSet Research Systems Inc.
601 Merritt 7, Norwalk, CT 06851
Phone: 203-810-1000   **Fax:** 203-810-1001
Web: www.factset.com

FactSet has operations in Australia, France, Germany, Hong Kong, Italy, Japan, Singapore, the UK, and the US.

2006 Sales

	$ mil.	% of total
US	277.2	72
Europe	90.2	23
Asia/Pacific	20.0	5
Total	**387.4**	**100**

PRODUCTS/OPERATIONS

Selected Applications

Company Analysis
Data Warehousing
Economic Analysis
Fixed Income Analysis
Pitchbook Building
Portfolio Analysis
Quantitative Analysis
Real-time Market Data

COMPETITORS

Bloomberg	McGraw-Hill
Data Transmission Network	OneSource
Dow Jones	Pearson
Hoover's	Reuters
IDD Information Services	Thomson Corporation
INVESTools	Track Data
LexisNexis	

HISTORICAL FINANCIALS

Company Type: Public

Income Statement

FYE: August 31

	REVENUE ($ mil.)	NET INCOME ($ mil.)	NET PROFIT MARGIN	EMPLOYEES
8/06	387.4	82.9	21.4%	1,431
8/05	312.6	71.8	23.0%	1,226
8/04	251.9	58.0	23.0%	1,000
8/03	222.3	51.4	23.1%	793
8/02	205.9	40.8	19.8%	700
Annual Growth	**17.1%**	**19.4%**	**—**	**19.6%**

2006 Year-End Financials

Debt ratio: —
Return on equity: 26.5%
Cash ($ mil.): 143.2
Current ratio: 2.61
Long-term debt ($ mil.): —
No. of shares (mil.): 48.9
Dividends
  Yield: 0.5%
  Payout: 13.4%
Market value ($ mil.): 2,156.0
R&D as % of sales: —
Advertising as % of sales: —

Stock History

NYSE: FDS

	STOCK PRICE ($) FY Close	P/E High/Low	PER SHARE ($) Earnings	Dividends	Book Value
8/06	44.10	29 19	1.64	0.22	7.34
8/05	35.00	28 19	1.43	0.20	5.55
8/04	29.69	31 20	1.15	0.17	5.28
8/03	32.37	33 15	0.99	0.15	6.31
8/02	16.53	35 15	0.78	0.12	5.24
Annual Growth	**27.8%**	**— —**	**20.4%**	**16.4%**	**8.8%**

FalconStor Software

FalconStor Software watches data like a hawk. The company provides network storage management software and related services. Its IPStor software is used to manage storage provisioning, data availability, replication, and disaster recovery functions. FalconStor also offers consulting, engineering, implementation, and maintenance services. The company's customers come from fields such as health care, financial services, education, and information technology. FalconStor's clients have included Southern Pacific Mortgages, A&I Systems, and The American Museum of Natural History. Chairman and CEO ReiJane Huai owns about 22% of the company.

FalconStor has continued to bolster its roster of strategic partners, including companies such as Hitachi Data Systems and NetGear.

EXECUTIVES

Chairman and CEO: ReiJane Huai, age 47, $322,545 pay
VP, CFO, and Treasurer: James Weber, age 35, $180,000 pay
VP: Wayne Lam, age 42, $180,000 pay
VP and Chief Technologist: Jimmy (Jimmy) Wu
VP and General Manager, Asia Pacific Operations: Eric Chen
VP and General Manager, EMEA Operations: Guillaume Imberti
VP, Business Development: Bernard (Bernie) Wu, age 48, $180,000 pay
VP, Engineering and CTO: Wai Lam
VP, General Counsel, and Secretary: Seth Horowitz
VP, North American Sales: Wendy Petty
VP, Sales and Marketing, Asia/Pacific: Alex Jiang
Media Relations: Herman Chin
Auditors: KPMG

LOCATIONS

HQ: FalconStor Software, Inc.
2 Huntington Quadrangle, Ste. 2S01, Melville, NY 11747
Phone: 631-777-5188   **Fax:** 631-501-7633
Web: www.falconstor.com

2005 Sales

	$ mil.	% of total
US	28.3	69
Asia	6.6	16
Other regions	6.1	15
Total	**41.0**	**100**

PRODUCTS/OPERATIONS

2005 Sales

	$ mil.	% of total
Software licenses	29.6	72
Maintenance	7.6	19
Software services & other	3.8	9
Total	**41.0**	**100**

COMPETITORS

CA
DataCore
EMC
Hewlett-Packard
NuView
Softek
Symantec
Tivoli Software

HISTORICAL FINANCIALS

Company Type: Public

Income Statement FYE: December 31

	REVENUE ($ mil.)	NET INCOME ($ mil.)	NET PROFIT MARGIN	EMPLOYEES
12/05	41.0	2.3	5.6%	279
12/04	28.7	(5.9)	—	217
12/03	16.9	(7.4)	—	178
12/02	10.6	(11.5)	—	138
12/01	5.6	(10.1)	—	113
Annual Growth	64.5%	—	—	25.4%

2005 Year-End Financials

Debt ratio: —	Dividends
Return on equity: 4.8%	Yield: —
Cash ($ mil.): 36.6	Payout: —
Current ratio: 4.03	Market value ($ mil.): 353.9
Long-term debt ($ mil.): —	R&D as % of sales: 29.4%
No. of shares (mil.): 47.9	Advertising as % of sales: —

Stock History NASDAQ (GM): FALC

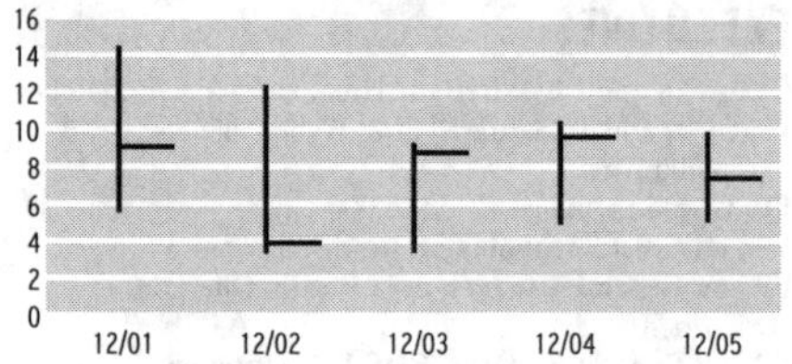

	STOCK PRICE ($) FY Close	P/E High/Low	PER SHARE ($) Earnings	Dividends	Book Value
12/05	7.39	195 103	0.05	—	1.02
12/04	9.57	— —	(0.13)	—	0.98
12/03	8.74	— —	(0.16)	—	1.09
12/02	3.88	— —	(0.26)	—	1.23
12/01	9.06	— —	(0.40)	—	1.40
Annual Growth	(5.0%)	— —	—	—	(7.8%)

FARO Technologies

FARO Technologies is putting the Arm on companies around the world — and they like it. With the touch of its mechanical arm, FARO's Control Station measuring system can facilitate reverse engineering of an undocumented part or a competitor's product. The FARO Arm is a portable, jointed device that simulates the human arm's movement and works with FARO's CAM2 3-D measurement software to take measurements, perform reverse engineering, and inspect parts by comparing them to digital designs. Aerospace, automotive, consumer goods, and heavy equipment companies such as Boeing, Caterpillar, General Motors, and Siemens use FARO Arm units in their factories. The company has nearly 5,000 customers worldwide.

Customers located outside the Americas account for more than half of sales. The company has grown internationally by opening sales offices in Asia and Europe.

FARO has expanded its product lines through internal development, as well as the 2002 acquisition of SpatialMetrix, a maker of laser trackers and metrology software.

FMR (Fidelity Investments) owns nearly 15% of FARO Technologies. Downtown Associates holds nearly 10% of the company. Co-founder and chairman Simon Raab has an equity stake of nearly 9%. Franklin Advisors owns about 8%. Lazard Asset Management holds nearly 6%. Principled Asset Management and Sovereign Asset Management count FARO equity stakes of around 5% among their assets.

EXECUTIVES

President, CEO, and Director: Jay W. Freeland, age 35
SVP and CFO: Keith S. Bair
EVP and Director: Gregory A. Fraser, age 51
SVP and Managing Director, Asia/Pacific: Robert P. Large, age 56
VP of Product Development, Laser: Jim West
VP and CTO: Allen S. Sajedi, age 46
Director, Sales and Marketing: David Morse
Managing Director of FARO Europe: Siegfried K. Buss, age 40
Software Product Development Manager: Ken Steffey
Global Public Relations Officer: Darin Sahler
Auditors: Grant Thornton LLP

LOCATIONS

HQ: FARO Technologies, Inc.
125 Technology Park, Lake Mary, FL 32746
Phone: 407-333-9911 **Fax:** 407-333-4181
Web: www.faro.com

FARO Technologies has facilities in Brazil, Canada, China, France, Germany, India, Italy, Japan, the Netherlands, Poland, Singapore, South Korea, Spain, Switzerland, the UK, and the US.

2005 Sales

	$ mil.	% of total
Americas	55.9	44
Europe/Africa	44.9	36
Asia/Pacific	24.8	20
Total	**125.6**	**100**

PRODUCTS/OPERATIONS

Products

- 3-D measurement system (Control Station; includes FAROarm articulated arm, SoftCheck Tool custom software, and a touch-screen computer)
- Laser tracker (portable 3-D measurement device)
- Measurement and statistical process control software (CAM2)
  - Automotive design (CAM2 Automotive)
  - Computer-assisted design (CAM2 CAD Analyzer)
  - Measurement (CAM2 Measure)
  - Process control and measurement (CAM2 SPC Process)

COMPETITORS

ANSYS
Autodesk
Braintech
Cimatron
Dassault
Delcam
Hexagon
Leica Geosystems
Parametric Technology
Perceptron
Renishaw
Veri-Tek

HISTORICAL FINANCIALS

Company Type: Public

Income Statement FYE: December 31

	REVENUE ($ mil.)	NET INCOME ($ mil.)	NET PROFIT MARGIN	EMPLOYEES
12/05	125.6	8.2	6.5%	657
12/04	97.0	14.9	15.4%	453
12/03	71.8	8.3	11.6%	341
12/02	46.3	(2.0)	—	291
12/01	35.1	(2.8)	—	235
Annual Growth	37.5%	—	—	29.3%

2005 Year-End Financials

Debt ratio: 0.2%	Dividends
Return on equity: 8.7%	Yield: —
Cash ($ mil.): 25.8	Payout: —
Current ratio: 3.83	Market value ($ mil.): 285.8
Long-term debt ($ mil.): 0.2	R&D as % of sales: 5.1%
No. of shares (mil.): 14.3	Advertising as % of sales: —

Stock History NASDAQ (GM): FARO

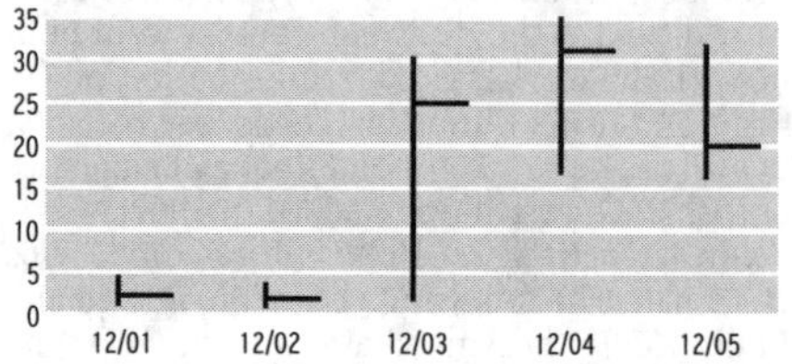

	STOCK PRICE ($) FY Close	P/E High/Low	PER SHARE ($) Earnings	Dividends	Book Value
12/05	20.00	56 29	0.57	—	6.92
12/04	31.18	33 16	1.06	—	6.38
12/03	24.98	47 3	0.64	—	5.11
12/02	1.89	— —	(0.17)	—	2.81
12/01	2.24	— —	(0.26)	—	2.93
Annual Growth	72.9%	— —	—	—	24.0%

First Acceptance

First Acceptance (formerly Liberté Investors) would not accept defeat. After emerging from bankruptcy, Liberté Investors discontinued its mortgage-lending operation with plans to create or buy a new business. In 2004 it bought auto insurance firm USAuto Holdings and changed its name to First Acceptance. The firm operates more than 350 retail insurance offices in about a dozen eastern states; it is licensed in 24 states and has been expanding operations since it entered the insurance field. First Acceptance specializes in providing non-standard coverage, or insurance for customers who have difficulty obtaining coverage otherwise. Chairman Gerald Ford owns 33% of the company.

In 2006, First Acceptance acquired the assets (but not in-force policies) of about 75 retail stores in and around Chicago for some $30 million. The stores will remain operating under the same names, Insurance Plus and Yale Insurance.

CEO Stephen Harrison owns 15% of First Acceptance; his brother and company secretary Thomas Harrison also owns 15%. Director Donald Edwards owns 8%. Executive officers and directors collectively own 68% of the company.

EXECUTIVES

Chairman: Gerald J. Ford, age 62
President, CEO, and Director:
  Stephen J. (Steve) Harrison, age 54, $725,000 pay
CFO: Edward L. Pierce, age 49
EVP, Secretary, and Director: Thomas J. Harrison Jr.,
  age 56, $400,000 pay
CIO: William R. Pentecost, age 47, $221,650 pay
SVP, Sales and Marketing: Randy L. Reed, age 50,
  $215,000 pay
VP, Chief Accounting Officer, and Corporate Controller:
  Kevin P. Cohn, age 35
Auditors: Ernst & Young LLP

LOCATIONS

HQ: First Acceptance Corporation
  3813 Green Hills Village Dr., Nashville, TN 37215
Phone: 615-844-2800   **Fax:** 615-844-2835
Web: www.firstacceptancecorp.com

First Acceptance has offices in Alabama, Florida,
Georgia, Illinois, Indiana, Mississippi, Missouri, Ohio,
Pennsylvania, South Carolina, Tennessee, and Texas.

PRODUCTS/OPERATIONS

Selected Subsidiaries

Acceptance Insurance Agency, Inc.
LNC Holdings, Inc.
USAuto Holdings, Inc.
USAuto Insurance Company, Inc.
USAuto Services, Inc.
Village Auto Insurance Company, Inc.

COMPETITORS

GEICO
Kemper Auto and Home
Progressive Corporation
Safe Auto
State Farm

HISTORICAL FINANCIALS

Company Type: Public

Income Statement

FYE: June 30

	REVENUE ($ mil.)	NET INCOME ($ mil.)	NET PROFIT MARGIN	EMPLOYEES
6/06	249.0	28.1	11.3%	1,225
6/05	166.8	26.2	15.7%	725
6/04	23.1	(3.8)	—	475
6/03	1.3	(1.9)	—	5
6/02	1.5	0.5	33.3%	2
Annual Growth	258.9%	173.8%	—	397.5%

2006 Year-End Financials

Debt ratio: 9.5%
Return on equity: 11.7%
Cash ($ mil.): 32.1
Current ratio: —
Long-term debt ($ mil.): 24.0
No. of shares (mil.): 47.5
Dividends
  Yield: —
  Payout: —
Market value ($ mil.): 560.0
R&D as % of sales: —
Advertising as % of sales: —

Stock History
NYSE: FAC

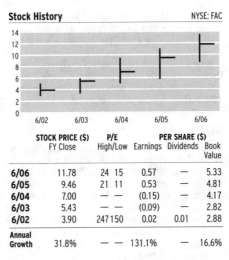

	STOCK PRICE ($) FY Close	P/E High/Low	PER SHARE ($) Earnings	Dividends	Book Value
6/06	11.78	24 15	0.57	—	5.33
6/05	9.46	21 11	0.53	—	4.81
6/04	7.00	— —	(0.15)	—	4.17
6/03	5.43	— —	(0.09)	—	2.82
6/02	3.90	247 150	0.02	0.01	2.88
Annual Growth	31.8%	— —	131.1%	—	16.6%

First Advantage

I screen, you screen, we all screen with First
Advantage. Created after The First American Corporation acquired US Search.com and merged it
with its Screening Technology (FAST) Division,
First Advantage provides such risk management
services as employment background screening,
occupational health (especially drug testing), tenant screening (credit history, eviction actions,
and rental payment history), and motor vehicle
reports. Its First Advantage Investigative Services
subsidiary provides investigative services for detecting insurance fraud. Individual locater services are also available. First American owns 80%
of First Advantage.

First Advantage has an apparent shopping
habit, too. In 2005 it acquired First American's
Credit Information Group (CIG), which included
that company's mortgage, automotive, consumer, and subprime credit businesses. In exchange, First American's ownership of First
Advantage increased from 67% to 80%; the all-
stock transaction was valued at an estimated
$570 million.

The company also acquired Quest Research, a
leading employment screening services provider
in India and East Asia. In addition to its customers in its home base, the subsidiary provides
outsourced services for other screening companies in the US and Europe. Now dubbed First Advantage Quest Research, the company has offices
India, Asia, and Australia. The company's Asian
coverage expanded in 2006 when First Advantage
bought Tokyo-based Brooke Consulting.

Further adding to its investigative capabilities, First Advantage acquired majority ownership of PrideRock, a company which digitizes
and transmits fingerprints to law enforcement
agencies for employee background checks. Other
acquisitions include ITax, a provider of tax credit
services; and Data Recovery Services, providing
restored digital data for attorneys and companies. First Advantage has agreed to acquire
EvidentData, a computer forensics and electronic discovery consulting firm.

Experian owns 6% of the company.

EXECUTIVES

Chairman: Parker S. Kennedy, age 58
CEO and Director: John Long, age 49
President: Anand K. Nallathambi
EVP and COO: Akshaya Mehta, age 45, $238,864 pay
EVP and CFO: John Lamson, age 54, $405,570 pay
EVP International Sales: Chuck Papageorgiou
SVP and Chief Marketing Officer: Rick Mansfield,
  age 41
VP, Human Resources: Anita Tefft
President, Background Verifications Group:
  David V. Kennedy
President, First Advantage Tax Consulting Division:
  Beth Henricks, age 45
President, Enterprise Screening Services Division:
  Bart K. Valdez, age 42
President, Occupational Health Services Group:
  Steven Flack
President, Residential Screening Services Division:
  Evan Barnett, age 57, $431,686 pay
President, Transportation Services Division: Billie Lee
Corporate Secretary and Regulatory Counsel:
  Ken J. Chin
Auditors: PricewaterhouseCoopers LLP

LOCATIONS

HQ: First Advantage Corporation
  100 Carillon Pkwy., St. Petersburg, FL 33716
Phone: 727-214-3411   **Fax:** 727-214-3410
Web: www.fadv.com

First Advantage has more than 42 US offices in Arizona,
California, Colorado, Delaware, Florida, Maryland, New
York, and Wisconsin, as well as an office in Canada and a
service center in India.

PRODUCTS/OPERATIONS

2005 Sales by Services

	% of total
Lender	26
Employer	24
Data	20
Dealer (auto)	15
Multifamily	10
Investigative and litigation support	5
Total	**100**

Selected Subsidiaries

American Driving Records, Inc.
BackTrack Reports, Inc.
CIC Enterprises, LLC
Employee Health Programs, Inc.
First Advantage Enterprise Screening Corporation
First American Indian Holdings LLC
Hirecheck, Inc.
Multifamily Community Insurance Agency, Inc.
Omega Insurance Services, Inc.
Proudfoot Reports Incorporated
Quantitative Risk Solutions LLC
SafeRent, Inc.
Seconda LLC (d/b/a Continental Compliance)
US SEARCH.com Inc.
ZapApp India Private Limited

COMPETITORS

ADP Screening and Selection
ChoicePoint
Deloitte
Ernst & Young
Guardsmark
KPMG
Kroll
LabCorp
PricewaterhouseCoopers
USIS

HISTORICAL FINANCIALS

Company Type: Public

Income Statement

FYE: December 31

	REVENUE ($ mil.)	NET INCOME ($ mil.)	NET PROFIT MARGIN	EMPLOYEES
12/05	643.8	58.4	9.1%	3,800
12/04	266.5	9.9	3.7%	1,700
12/03	166.5	2.8	1.7%	1,400
Annual Growth	96.6%	356.7%	—	64.8%

2005 Year-End Financials

Debt ratio: 31.2%
Return on equity: 13.4%
Cash ($ mil.): 28.4
Current ratio: 1.10
Long-term debt ($ mil.): 182.1
No. of shares (mil.): 9.8

Dividends
  Yield: —
  Payout: —
  Market value ($ mil.): 261.5
  R&D as % of sales: —
  Advertising as % of sales: —

Stock History

NASDAQ (GS): FADV

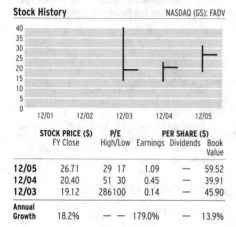

	STOCK PRICE ($) FY Close	P/E High/Low	PER SHARE ($) Earnings	Dividends	Book Value
12/05	26.71	29 17	1.09	—	59.52
12/04	20.40	51 30	0.45	—	39.91
12/03	19.12	286 100	0.14	—	45.90
Annual Growth	18.2%	— —	179.0%	—	13.9%

First Cash Financial Services

Texas isn't just oil, land, and cattle. Since the 1980s, a new industry has discovered a home on the range: pawnshops. First Cash Financial Services operates more than 220 pawnshops in Texas and in five other states, the District of Columbia, and Mexico, mostly under the First Cash or Famous Pawn names.

The company lends money secured by such personal property as jewelry, electronic equipment, tools, firearms (no handguns), sporting goods, and musical equipment. First Cash also offers check cashing, cash advances, money orders and transfers, and bill payment services through more than 100 additional stores; and is half-owner of Cash & Go, a partnership which operates about 40 check-cashing kiosks inside convenience stores.

First Cash's sales are about evenly divided between retail sales of merchandise and interest earned from the loans it makes. The company charges its pawn customers annual interest rates of up to 240%.

The firm combats the industry's traditional image problem by offering large, clean, and well-lit stores. It has expanded its offerings to include

such products as short-term payday loans. It also added auto loans to its menu by purchasing dealer and lender Auto Master, which has about 10 locations.

Board members and executive officers collectively own nearly a quarter of First Cash Financial, led by director Richard Burke's approximately 12% stake.

HISTORY

First Cash grew from a single pawnshop in Dallas. John Payne traded some land in Colorado for the store after selling his Dallas bank in 1979. He and his wife ran the shop until 1985, when they sold it and built a new shop in the suburbs, aiming to achieve the ambience of a video store.

It was an opportune moment: The Texas economy, particularly the banking industry, was just beginning its slide. Payne (who later left the company) incorporated First Cash in 1988 and brought in professional management under former banker Rick Powell in 1990.

Eight-store First Cash went public in 1991. Acquisitions and expansions included the 1994 purchase of a Baltimore/Washington, DC, area chain. The next year First Cash upgraded its computers to improve inventory control and loan valuations, and became the first major pawn chain to stop selling or making loans on handguns.

In 1996 and 1997 First Cash added stores in Maryland and Texas. The next year it bought 10-store chain JB Pawn (from a brother of First Cash director Richard Burke) and about 20 individual shops. First Cash also moved into check-cashing, buying 11-store Miraglia.

To reflect the diversification, the company changed its name to First Cash Financial Services in early 1999. That year First Cash joined other pawnbrokers and short-term lenders in moving into Mexico. In 2000 First Cash partnered with Pawnbroker.com to provide online financial and support services to pawn shops.

EXECUTIVES

Chairman: Phillip E. (Rick) Powell, age 55, $775,000 pay
CEO: Rick L. Wessel, age 48, $851,000 pay
  (prior to promotion)
EVP, CFO, Secretary, and Treasurer:
  R. Douglas (Doug) Orr, age 45, $345,000 pay
  (prior to title change)
SVP and Director, Information Technology:
  John C. Powell, age 51, $225,000 pay
VP, Human Resources and Administration: Jan Hartz

LOCATIONS

HQ: First Cash Financial Services, Inc.
  690 E. Lamar Blvd., Ste. 400, Arlington, TX 76011
Phone: 817-460-3947   **Fax:** 817-461-7019
Web: www.firstcash.com

2005 Pawn Shops

	No.
Mexico	130
Texas	58
Maryland	21
South Carolina	7
Missouri	3
Oklahoma	3
Virginia	2
Washington, DC	2
Total	**226**

2005 Payday Advance Stores

	No.
Texas	60
California	15
Illinois	10
Oregon	7
Washington, DC	7
Washington	3
Total	**102**

PRODUCTS/OPERATIONS

2005 Sales

	$ mil.	% of total
Merchandise sales	102.2	49
Short-term advance & credit services fees	60.9	29
Pawn service fees	40.8	20
Check cashing fees	2.9	2
Other	1.0	—
Total	**207.8**	**100**

Selected Subsidiaries

American Loan and Jewelry, Inc.
American Loan Employee Services, S.A. de C.V. (Mexico)
Capital Pawnbrokers, Inc.
Cash & Go, Inc.
Cash & Go, Ltd.
Cash & Go Management, LLC
Elegant Floors, Inc.
Famous Pawn, Inc.
First Cash Corp.
First Cash, Inc.
First Cash, Ltd.
First Cash Management, LLC
First Cash, S.A. de C.V. (Mexico)
JB Pawn, Inc.
One Iron Ventures, Inc.
Silver Hill Pawn, Inc.
WR Financial, Inc.

COMPETITORS

Ace Cash Express
Cash America
Check Into Cash
EZCORP
World Acceptance
Xponential

HISTORICAL FINANCIALS

Company Type: Public

Income Statement

FYE: December 31

	ASSETS ($ mil.)	NET INCOME ($ mil.)	INCOME AS % OF ASSETS	EMPLOYEES
12/05	185.9	25.4	13.7%	2,314
12/04	160.9	20.7	12.9%	1,822
12/03	140.1	15.0	10.7%	1,531
12/02	131.0	10.9	8.3%	1,257
12/01	122.8	7.9	6.4%	1,026
Annual Growth	10.9%	33.9%	—	22.5%

2005 Year-End Financials

Equity as % of assets: 87.5%
Return on assets: 14.6%
Return on equity: 16.6%
Long-term debt ($ mil.): —
No. of shares (mil.): 15.8
Market value ($ mil.): 229.7

Dividends
  Yield: —
  Payout: —
  Sales ($ mil.): 207.8
  R&D as % of sales: —
  Advertising as % of sales: 0.9%

	STOCK PRICE ($) FY Close	P/E High/Low		PER SHARE ($) Earnings	Dividends	Book Value
12/05	14.58	39	22	0.38	—	10.33
12/04	13.35	23	14	0.61	—	9.01
12/03	8.55	19	6	0.48	—	11.59
12/02	3.40	10	6	0.38	—	9.75
12/01	2.27	11	3	0.28	—	8.46
Annual Growth	59.2%	—	—	7.9%	—	5.1%

First Community Bank Corporation

Although not the first community bank *in* America, First Community Bank Corporation of America *is* the holding company for First Community Bank of America, which has about 10 branches in the Sunshine State's Tampa Bay area, with more planned to open. The thrift concentrates on real estate lending, with commercial mortgages and residential mortgages representing the bulk of its activities. It also makes business and consumer installment loans.

Chairman Robert M. Menke owns 37% of First Community Bank Corporation of America; company officers and directors collectively own about 49%.

EXECUTIVES

Chairman: Robert M. Menke, age 72
President, CEO, and Director; CEO, First Community Bank: Kenneth P. Cherven, age 46, $290,348 pay
EVP and COO: Sue A. Gilman
CFO: Stan B. McClelland, age 55
Regional President, Charlotte County, First Community Bank: Michael J. Bullerdick, age 52, $154,404 pay
Regional President, Hillsborough County, First Community Bank: S. T. (Sie) Kamide, age 49, $132,000 pay
Regional President, Pinellas County, First Community Bank: Scott C. Boyle, age 51, $215,261 pay
EVP and COO, First Community Bank: Gilbert K. Grass
EVP and Senior Credit Officer, First Community Bank: Thomas P. Croom
VP, Human Resources, First Community Bank: Patricia TC Daerda
Auditors: Hacker, Johnson & Smith PA

LOCATIONS

HQ: First Community Bank Corporation of America
9001 Belcher Rd., Pinellas Park, FL 33782
Phone: 727-520-0987   **Fax:** 727-471-0010
Web: www.efirstcommbank.com

PRODUCTS/OPERATIONS

2005 Sales

	$ mil.	% of total
Interest		
Loans	16.1	90
Securities	0.5	3
Other	0.2	1
Noninterest		
Service charges on deposit accounts	0.5	3
Other	0.6	3
Total	**17.9**	**100**

COMPETITORS

Bank of America
BankAtlantic
Colonial BancGroup
F.N.B. (PA)
South Financial
SunTrust
Valrico Bancorp, Inc.
Wachovia
Whitney Holding

HISTORICAL FINANCIALS

Company Type: Public

Income Statement				FYE: December 31
	ASSETS ($ mil.)	NET INCOME ($ mil.)	INCOME AS % OF ASSETS	EMPLOYEES
12/05	324.8	2.9	0.9%	74
12/04	241.8	2.0	0.8%	60
12/03	180.4	1.5	0.8%	52
12/02	147.3	0.8	0.5%	49
12/01	107.6	0.3	0.3%	—
Annual Growth	31.8%	76.3%	—	14.7%

2005 Year-End Financials

Equity as % of assets: 9.0%
Return on assets: 1.0%
Return on equity: 11.0%
Long-term debt ($ mil.): 13.7
No. of shares (mil.): 3.8
Market value ($ mil.): 67.9

Dividends
Yield: —
Payout: —
Sales ($ mil.): 17.9
R&D as % of sales: —
Advertising as % of sales: 0.2%

Stock History   NASDAQ (CM): FCFL

	STOCK PRICE ($) FY Close	P/E High/Low		PER SHARE ($) Earnings	Dividends	Book Value
12/05	17.89	25	20	0.78	—	7.68
12/04	18.41	35	16	0.56	—	11.17
12/03	9.71	21	14	0.51	—	10.12
Annual Growth	35.7%	—	—	23.7%	—	(12.9%)

First Community Corporation

Putting first things first, First Community is the holding company for First Community Bank, which serves individuals and smaller businesses in central South Carolina's Lexington, Richland, and Newberry counties. Through about a dozen offices, the bank offers such products and services as checking and savings accounts, money market accounts, CDs, IRAs, credit cards, insurance, and investment services. Commercial mortgages make up about 50% of First Community Bank's loan portfolio, which also includes residential mortgages and business, consumer, and construction loans. The company bought DutchFork Bancshares in 2004 and DeKalb Bankshares (parent of The Bank of Camden) in 2006.

EXECUTIVES

Chairman, First Community Corporation and First Community Bank: James C. (Jim) Leventis, age 68
Vice Chairman; Vice Chairman and EVP, First Community Bank: J. Thomas (Tommy) Johnson, age 59, $198,412 pay
President, CEO, and Director, First Community Corporation and First Community Bank: Michael C. (Mike) Crapps, age 47, $226,002 pay
SVP and CFO, First Community Corporation and First Community Bank: Joseph G. Sawyer, age 55, $133,542 pay
SVP and Chief Credit Officer, First Community Corporation and First Community Bank: David K. Proctor, age 49, $123,095 pay
SVP, Human Resources and Marketing, First Community Bank: Robin D. Brown
VP and Commercial Lender, First Community Bank: Harry Deith
Auditors: Elliott Davis LLC

LOCATIONS

HQ: First Community Corporation
5455 Sunset Blvd., Lexington, SC 29072
Phone: 803-951-2265   **Fax:** 803-951-1722
Web: www.firstcommunitysc.com

PRODUCTS/OPERATIONS

2005 Sales

	$ mil.	% of total
Interest & dividends		
Loans	13.6	55
Investment securities	7.4	30
Other	0.3	1
Deposit service charges	1.5	6
Mortgage origination fees	0.4	2
Other	1.4	6
Total	**24.6**	**100**

COMPETITORS

Bank of America
BB&T
First Citizens Bancorporation
Regions Financial
Security Federal
South Financial
Synovus
Wachovia

HISTORICAL FINANCIALS

Company Type: Public

Income Statement

FYE: December 31

	ASSETS ($ mil.)	NET INCOME ($ mil.)	INCOME AS % OF ASSETS	EMPLOYEES
12/05	467.5	3.1	0.7%	123
12/04	455.7	2.2	0.5%	—
12/03	215.0	1.8	0.8%	—
12/02	195.2	1.5	0.8%	—
12/01	156.6	1.1	0.7%	—
Annual Growth	31.4%	29.6%	—	—

2005 Year-End Financials

Equity as % of assets: 10.9%
Return on assets: 0.7%
Return on equity: 6.1%
Long-term debt ($ mil.): 48.7
No. of shares (mil.): 2.8
Market value ($ mil.): 52.7

Dividends
  Yield: 1.1%
  Payout: 19.2%
Sales ($ mil.): 24.6
R&D as % of sales: —
Advertising as % of sales: —

Stock History

NASDAQ (CM): FCCO

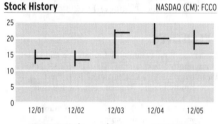

	STOCK PRICE ($) FY Close	P/E High/Low		PER SHARE ($) Earnings	Dividends	Book Value
12/05	18.50	22	16	1.04	0.20	17.82
12/04	19.97	22	17	1.09	0.20	18.09
12/03	21.75	21	13	1.08	0.19	12.21
12/02	13.30	18	13	0.90	0.12	11.61
12/01	13.70	24	18	0.68	—	13.21
Annual Growth	7.8%	—	—	11.2%	18.6%	7.8%

First Marblehead Corporation

With a Harvard education costing six figures, that government student loan just isn't going to cut it anymore. Enter First Marblehead. The company creates programs and provides services for lenders who offer private (non-government secured) student loans. First Marblehead provides marketing, servicing, processing, securitization, and guarantee services. The company bought the loan processing business of The Education Resources Institute (TERI) in 1991, more than doubling its size. Houston Rockets owner Leslie Alexander owns more than a quarter of the company. Insurance heavy William Berkley (of W. R. Berkley) owns about 20% independently and through Interlaken Investment Partners.

First Marblehead has filed the necessary paperwork to become a bank with the intention of acquiring Union Bank's Union Federal Savings Bank in North Providence, Rhode Island.

Former chairman and CEO Daniel Maxwell Meyers controls more than 11% of the company, while vice chairman Stephen Anbinder owns nearly 6%.

EXECUTIVES

Chairman and General Counsel: Peter B. Tarr, age 54, $2,381,317 pay (partial-year salary)
Vice Chairman: Stephen E. Anbinder, age 68, $1,222,298 pay
President, CEO, COO, and Director: Jack L. Kopnisky, age 50, $2,257,215 pay (prior to title change)
SEVP and CFO: John A. Hupalo, age 46, $1,170,833 pay (prior to promotion)
EVP and Chief Administrative Officer: Anne P. Bowen, age 54, $841,666 pay
EVP Strategic Alliances: Larry A. Lutz, age 49
EVP and CIO: Richard E. (Dick) Ross
EVP Business Development: Sandra M. (Sandy) Stark
EVP Client Services: Andrew J. (Andy) Hawley, age 42
SVP Finance, Treasurer, and Chief Accounting Officer: Kenneth Klipper, age 47
VP Corporate Communications: Larry Marchese
Chief Marketing Officer: Greg D. Johnson
Auditors: KPMG LLP

LOCATIONS

HQ: The First Marblehead Corporation
  The Prudential Tower, 800 Boylston St., 34th Fl., Boston, MA 02199
Phone: 617-638-2000   **Fax:** 617-638-2100
Web: www.firstmarblehead.com

PRODUCTS/OPERATIONS

2006 Sales

	% of total
Structural advisory fees	43
Residuals	36
Processing fees from TERI	19
Administrative & other	2
Total	**100**

COMPETITORS

Access Group
American Student Assistance
Bank of America
Campus Door
Citigroup
Education Lending Group
Educational Funding of The South
KeyCorp
Sallie Mae
Sallie Mae Servicing
Wells Fargo

HISTORICAL FINANCIALS

Company Type: Public

Income Statement

FYE: June 30

	ASSETS ($ mil.)	NET INCOME ($ mil.)	INCOME AS % OF ASSETS	EMPLOYEES
6/06	770.3	236.0	30.6%	932
6/05	558.2	159.7	28.6%	842
6/04	360.1	75.3	20.9%	710
6/03	87.1	31.5	36.2%	296
6/02	39.0	12.2	31.3%	—
Annual Growth	110.8%	109.7%	—	46.6%

2006 Year-End Financials

Equity as % of assets: 74.8%
Return on assets: 35.5%
Return on equity: 47.3%
Long-term debt ($ mil.): 13.3
No. of shares (mil.): 63.0
Market value ($ mil.): 2,393.1

Dividends
  Yield: 0.8%
  Payout: 13.1%
Sales ($ mil.): 563.6
R&D as % of sales: —
Advertising as % of sales: —

Stock History

NYSE: FMD

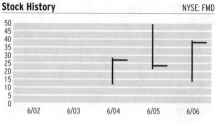

	STOCK PRICE ($) FY Close	P/E High/Low		PER SHARE ($) Earnings	Dividends	Book Value
6/06	37.96	16	6	2.45	0.32	9.14
6/05	23.37	31	14	1.59	—	6.50
6/04	26.84	35	15	0.79	—	4.35
Annual Growth	18.9%	—	—	76.1%	—	45.0%

First Mercury Financial

First Mercury Financial Corporation (FMFC) would like to take after its namesake, the Roman god of commerce and profit, by capitalizing on its expertise in niche insurance markets. Through its CoverX wholesale brokerage, the company underwrites general liability policies for businesses, with a special focus on the security industry — private investigators, security guards, armored car units, and the like. It has also formed a special general liability unit that insures small to midsized builders, oil and gas contractors, and apartment complexes, among others. Founder and director Jerome Shaw owns about 22% of First Mercury.

FMFC provides insurance nationwide on a non-admitted basis, meaning it generally is not licensed in the states where it operates.

In addition to CoverX, FMFC has three other operating subsidiaries: First Mercury Insurance (which writes policies for CoverX); All Nation Insurance (which reinsures CoverX business), and American Risk Pooling Consultants (a third-party administrator for public entity risk sharing pools).

The company is using the funds from its 2006 IPO to pay down debt; it has also bought back a majority of shares held by Glencoe Capital, a Chicago-based private equity firm that previously held a majority stake. Following the offering, Glencoe owns 11% of First Mercury.

To facilitate the rapid growth of its CoverX subsidiary, First Mercury Financial has opened regional offices in Boston; Chicago; Dallas; and Naples, Florida.

EXECUTIVES

President, CEO, and Director: Richard H. Smith, age 55, $1,050,000 pay
SVP, Treasurer, and CFO: William S. Weaver, age 63, $475,000 pay
SVP, ARPCO: John Brockschmidt, age 50
VP, Administration: Marcia Paulsen, age 51
VP, Corporate Development: William A. Kindorf, age 28
VP, Finance: James M. Thomas, age 59
VP, Operations: Thomas Dulapa, age 45
Chief Claims Officer: Joseph Knox, age 59
Chief Underwriting Officer, Specialty Casualty: Joseph J. George, age 51
Auditors: BDO Seidman, LLP

LOCATIONS

HQ: First Mercury Financial Corporation
29621 Northwestern Hwy., Southfield, MI 48034
Phone: 800-762-6837
Web: www.firstmercury.com

First Mercury Financial Corporation has offices in
Florida, Illinois, Massachusetts, and Texas.

PRODUCTS/OPERATIONS

2005 Sales

	$ mil.	% of total
Premiums	97.7	75
Commissions & fees	26.1	20
Investment income	6.8	5
Other	0.2	—
Total	**130.8**	**100**

COMPETITORS

21st Century Holding
Acadia Insurance
ACE Limited
Admiral Insurance
All Risks
American Country Insurance
Argonaut Group
CNA Financial
GE Insurance Solutions
The Hartford
IFG
Lexington Insurance
OneBeacon
RLI

HISTORICAL FINANCIALS

Company Type: Public

Income Statement

				FYE: December 31
	REVENUE ($ mil.)	NET INCOME ($ mil.)	NET PROFIT MARGIN	EMPLOYEES
12/05	130.8	22.8	17.4%	136
12/04	99.5	17.7	17.8%	—
12/03	78.6	11.0	14.0%	—
Annual Growth	29.0%	44.0%	—	—

2005 Year-End Financials

Debt ratio: 133.1%
Return on equity: 29.2%
Cash ($ mil.): —
Current ratio: —
Long-term debt ($ mil.): 85.6

Net Income History

NYSE: FMR

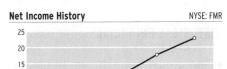

First National Bancshares

The first thing you should know about First National Bancshares is that it is the holding company for First National Bank of the South, which is also known as First National Bank of Spartanburg, serving the Spartanburg, South Carolina area. The bank, which has about five branches (one serving Charleston) and three loan production offices, opened for business in 2000 and the holding company began trading on Nasdaq in 2005. First National Bancshares also operates a trust company, as well as small business lending division First National Business Capital.

The bank in 2006 announced it would convert its loan production office in Greenville into a full-service banking branch. Commercial real estate loans represent the largest portion of the company's lending portfolio (about 60%), followed by residential mortgages (nearly 30%).

EXECUTIVES

Chairman: Norman F. Pulliam, age 63
President, CEO, and Director; President and CEO, First National Bank of the South: Jerry L. Calvert, age 56, $272,351 pay
EVP and CFO, First National Bancshares and First National Bank of the South: Kitty B. Payne, age 35, $167,592 pay
EVP, Chief Lending Officer, and Community Reinvestment Act Officer, First National Bank of the South: David H. Zabriskie, age 44, $178,039 pay
EVP and Retail Banking Manager, First National Bank of the South: Robert W. (Bob) Murdoch Jr., age 61, $151,322 pay
SVP, Commercial Lending and Business Development, First National Bank of the South: Louie Blanton
SVP, Risk Management, First National Bank of the South: Fred Moore
Market President, Mt. Pleasant, First National Bank of the South: Rudy Gill
VP and City Executive Officer, First National Bank of the South: Mary Jane Davidson
VP and Human Resource Manager, First National Bank of the South: Van Clark
Auditors: Elliott Davis LLC

LOCATIONS

HQ: First National Bancshares, Inc.
215 N. Pine St., Spartanburg, SC 29302
Phone: 864-948-9001   **Fax:** 864-948-0001
Web: www.firstnational-online.com

PRODUCTS/OPERATIONS

2005 Sales

	$ mil.	% of total
Interest		
Loans	15.5	81
Securities	1.6	8
Federal funds sold & other	0.3	1
Service charges & fees on deposit accounts	0.9	5
Gain on sale of loans	0.4	2
Loan service charges & fees	0.2	1
Mortgage loan fees from correspondent bank	0.1	1
Other	0.2	1
Total	**19.2**	**100**

COMPETITORS

Bank of America
Bank of South Carolina
BB&T
First Citizens
South Financial
SunTrust
Synovus
Wachovia

HISTORICAL FINANCIALS

Company Type: Public

Income Statement

				FYE: December 31
	ASSETS ($ mil.)	NET INCOME ($ mil.)	INCOME AS % OF ASSETS	EMPLOYEES
12/05	328.7	2.8	0.9%	77
12/04	236.3	1.8	0.8%	—
12/03	180.6	0.9	0.5%	—
12/02	139.2	0.6	0.4%	—
12/01	82.3	(0.2)	—	—
Annual Growth	41.4%	—	—	—

2005 Year-End Financials

Equity as % of assets: 6.7%
Return on assets: 1.0%
Return on equity: 15.6%
Long-term debt ($ mil.): 6.2
No. of shares (mil.): 3.1
Market value ($ mil.): 59.0
Dividends
   Yield: —
   Payout: —
Sales ($ mil.): 19.2
R&D as % of sales: —
Advertising as % of sales: —

Stock History

NASDAQ (GM): FNSC

	STOCK PRICE ($) FY Close	P/E High/Low		PER SHARE ($) Earnings	Dividends	Book Value
12/05	18.83	26	15	0.78	—	7.04
12/04	16.67	46	15	0.52	—	7.72
12/03	7.86	28	21	0.28	—	6.78
12/02	6.29	34	23	0.19	—	9.60
12/01	4.53	—	—	(0.07)	—	8.97
Annual Growth	42.8%	—	—	—	—	(5.9%)

First National Lincoln

First National Lincoln is the holding company for The First, a regional bank serving coastal Maine from about 15 branches. Tracing its roots to 1852, the bank offers traditional retail products and services, including checking and savings accounts, CDs, IRAs, and loans. Residential mortgages make up more than half of the company's loan portfolio; business loans account for about 30%. Bank division First Advisors offers private banking and investment management services. First National Lincoln acquired competitor FNB Bankshares and its First National Bank of Bar Harbor, in early 2005.

First National Bank was subsequently merged into First National Lincoln subsidiary The First National Bank of Damariscotta, which was renamed The First.

EXECUTIVES

Chairman, First National Lincoln and The First National Bank: Robert B. Gregory, age 52
President, CEO, and Director, First National Lincoln and The First National Bank: Daniel R. Daigneault, age 53, $333,500 pay
EVP, COO, and Director; EVP and COO, The First National Bank: Tony C. McKim, age 38, $180,581 pay
EVP and Clerk; EVP Banking Services and Senior Loan Officer, The First National Bank: Charles A. Wootton, age 49, $149,500 pay (prior to title change)
EVP, CFO, and Treasurer, First National Lincoln and The First National Bank: F. Stephen Ward, age 52, $166,750 pay (prior to title change)
SVP Human Resources and Compliance: Susan A. Norton, age 45
Managing Principal and Chief Investment Officer, First Advisors: William M. Hunter II, age 54
Senior Managing Principal and Senior Trust Officer, First Advisors: Daniel M. Lay, age 44, $112,922 pay
SVP and Senior Operations Officer, The First National Bank: Walter F. Vietze, age 63, $110,168 pay
Assistant VP and Director of Human Resources, The First National Bank: Joyce P. Dexter
Auditors: Berry, Dunn, McNeil & Parker

LOCATIONS

HQ: First National Lincoln Corporation
223 Main St., Damariscotta, ME 04543
Phone: 207-563-3195 **Fax:** 207-563-3225
Web: www.the1st.com

PRODUCTS/OPERATIONS

2005 Sales

	$ mil.	% of total
Interest		
Loans, including fees	42.6	72
Investments & other	7.8	13
Noninterest		
Service charges on deposit accounts	2.5	4
Fiduciary & investment management income	1.7	3
Mortgage origination & servicing income	0.6	1
Other	4.3	7
Total	**59.5**	**100**

COMPETITORS

Camden National
KeyCorp
Northeast Bancorp
TD Banknorth

HISTORICAL FINANCIALS

Company Type: Public

Income Statement

FYE: December 31

	ASSETS ($ mil.)	NET INCOME ($ mil.)	INCOME AS % OF ASSETS	EMPLOYEES
12/05	1,042.2	12.8	1.2%	216
12/04	634.2	8.5	1.3%	137
12/03	568.8	7.4	1.3%	134
12/02	494.1	6.5	1.3%	134
12/01	434.5	5.5	1.3%	129
Annual Growth	**24.4%**	**23.5%**	**—**	**13.8%**

2005 Year-End Financials

Equity as % of assets: 9.9%
Return on assets: 1.5%
Return on equity: 16.4%
Long-term debt ($ mil.): 34.5
No. of shares (mil.): 9.8
Market value ($ mil.): 172.9
Dividends
  Yield: 2.9%
  Payout: 39.2%
  Sales ($ mil.): 59.5
  R&D as % of sales: —
  Advertising as % of sales: —

Stock History

NASDAQ (GS): FNLC

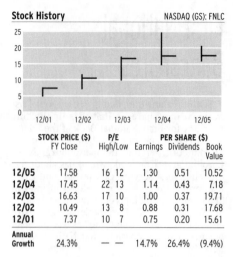

	STOCK PRICE ($) FY Close	P/E High/Low	PER SHARE ($) Earnings	PER SHARE ($) Dividends	PER SHARE ($) Book Value
12/05	17.58	16 12	1.30	0.51	10.52
12/04	17.45	22 13	1.14	0.43	7.18
12/03	16.63	17 10	1.00	0.37	19.71
12/02	10.49	13 8	0.88	0.31	17.68
12/01	7.37	10 7	0.75	0.20	15.61
Annual Growth	**24.3%**	**— —**	**14.7%**	**26.4%**	**(9.4%)**

First Niagara Financial Group

A lot of water and a few barrels have gone over Niagara Falls since First Niagara Bank was founded. Tracing its roots to 1870, the flagship subsidiary of acquisitive First Niagara Financial Group operates more than 115 offices in western and central New York, offering deposit and loan products, brokerage services, insurance, and asset management. Residential mortgages comprise more than 40% of the company's loan portfolio; commercial real estate loans are more than 30%. The bank also writes business, construction, home equity, and consumer loans. First Niagara bought Troy Financial in 2004 and Hudson River Bancorp the following year.

First Niagara Financial has more than doubled in size with its recent acquisition activity: It had fewer than 50 branches operating under its banner at the end of 2003. That year, First Niagara Financial acquired Finger Lakes Bancorp.

In 2005 First Niagara Financial acquired employee benefits administration and consulting firm Burke Group, which the company renamed First Niagara Benefits Consulting.

Also in 2005, First Niagara Risk Management acquired and absorbed Hatch Leonard Naples, one of the region's largest insurance agencies. It arranged to buy another Buffalo-area insurance agency, Gernold Agency, in 2006.

EXECUTIVES

Chairman: Robert G. Weber, age 68
Acting CEO, President, and COO: John R. Koelmel, age 54, $772,583 pay (prior to title change)
CFO: Michael W. Harrington
EVP and Chief Lending Officer: G. Gary Berner, age 58, $698,908 pay
EVP and Chief Administrative Officer; EVP, Human Resources and Administration, First Niagara Bank: Kathleen P. Monti, age 55, $265,384 pay
EVP, Consumer Banking: Michael R. Giaquinto, age 41, $617,863 pay
EVP, Consumer Banking and Central New York Regional Executive: David J. Nasca, age 46, $246,574 pay

SVP and CIO: Frank J. Polino, age 44
VP, Marketing and Public Relations: Charles D. Clark
Assistant VP and Investor Relations Contact: Christopher J. Thome
Regional President, Central New York: Greg Gilroy
Regional President, Eastern New York: Carl A. Florio, age 57, $1,694,377 pay
Corporate Secretary: Robert N. Murphy
Auditors: KPMG LLP

LOCATIONS

HQ: First Niagara Financial Group, Inc.
6950 S. Transit Rd., Lockport, NY 14095
Phone: 716-625-7500 **Fax:** 716-625-8405
Web: www.fnfg.com

PRODUCTS/OPERATIONS

2005 Sales

	$ mil.	% of total
Interest		
Loans & leases	313.8	67
Securities available for sale	58.4	13
Money market & other investments	3.0	1
Noninterest		
Banking services	37.3	8
Risk management services	32.6	7
Other	20.8	4
Total	**465.9**	**100**

Selected Subsidiaries

Burke Group, Inc. (employee benefits administration and consulting)
First Niagara Bank
  First Niagara Capital, Inc. (small business loans and equity investments)
  First Niagara Commercial Bank
  First Niagara Funding, Inc. (real estate investment trust)
  First Niagara Leasing, Inc. (equipment lease financing)
  First Niagara Portfolio Management, Inc. (investment in US Treasury obligations)
  First Niagara Realty, Inc. (real estate investment)
  First Niagara Risk Management, Inc. (insurance agency)
  First Niagara Securities, Inc.

COMPETITORS

Alliance Financial	KeyCorp
Citigroup	M&T Bank
Citizens Financial Group	NBT Bancorp
Community Bank System	Tompkins Trustco
HSBC USA	TrustCo Bank Corp NY
JPMorgan Chase	

HISTORICAL FINANCIALS

Company Type: Public

Income Statement

FYE: December 31

	ASSETS ($ mil.)	NET INCOME ($ mil.)	INCOME AS % OF ASSETS	EMPLOYEES
12/05	8,064.8	92.9	1.2%	1,984
12/04	5,078.4	51.8	1.0%	1,200
12/03	3,589.5	36.1	1.0%	944
12/02	2,934.8	30.8	1.0%	945
12/01	2,857.9	21.2	0.7%	919
Annual Growth	**29.6%**	**44.7%**	**—**	**21.2%**

2005 Year-End Financials

Equity as % of assets: 17.0%
Return on assets: 1.4%
Return on equity: 8.1%
Long-term debt ($ mil.): 655.7
No. of shares (mil.): 112.8
Market value ($ mil.): 1,632.3
Dividends
  Yield: 2.6%
  Payout: 45.2%
  Sales ($ mil.): 465.9
  R&D as % of sales: —
  Advertising as % of sales: 1.5%

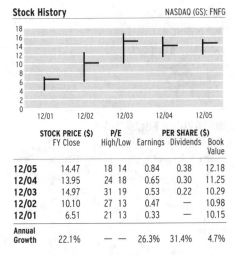

	STOCK PRICE ($) FY Close	P/E High/Low		PER SHARE ($) Earnings	Dividends	Book Value
12/05	14.47	18	14	0.84	0.38	12.18
12/04	13.95	24	18	0.65	0.30	11.25
12/03	14.97	31	19	0.53	0.22	10.29
12/02	10.10	27	13	0.47	—	10.98
12/01	6.51	21	13	0.33	—	10.15
Annual Growth	22.1%	—	—	26.3%	31.4%	4.7%

First Place Financial

First Place Financial is the holding company for First Place Bank, which serves businesses and consumers through more than 30 branch offices in northeastern Ohio and southeastern Michigan; it also has about 15 loan production offices. Franklin Bank, acquired in 2004 when the company bought Franklin Bancorp, has six branches near Detroit and operates as a division of First Place Bank. The company also owns a real estate brokerage; a general insurance agency that sells life, health, and property/casualty coverage; a title insurance agency; and two employee benefits consulting firms.

One- to four-family residential real estate loans make up almost half of First Place Financial's loan portfolio; commercial loans make up more than 35%.

In 2006 the company acquired Northern Savings and Loan, a northern Ohio thrift with seven branches and a loan production office. Later that year, it planned to expand its market area by arranging to purchase seven branches in Flint, Michigan from Republic Bancorp.

EXECUTIVES

Chairman, First Place Financial and First Place Bank: Samuel A. (Sam) Roth, age 63
President, CEO, and Director; CEO and Director, First Place Bank: Steven R. Lewis, age 48, $505,758 pay
CFO; EVP, CFO, and Treasurer, First Place Bank: Paul S. Musgrove, age 44, $241,791 pay
EVP, General Counsel, and Secretary: J. Craig Carr, age 58
EVP, Retail Banking, First Place Bank: Dominique K. Stoeber, age 42
EVP, Human Resources: Robert J. Kowalski, age 41
President and COO, First Place Bank: Albert P. Blank, age 44, $359,967 pay
Corporate EVP and CIO: Brian E. Hoopes, age 49
Corporate EVP and Chief Credit Officer, First Place Bank: Timothy A. (Tim) Beaumont, age 48

SVP and Chief Lending Officer, First Place Bank: Darlene A. Nowak-Baker
Corporate EVP, Retail Lending, First Place Bank: R. Bruce Wenmoth, age 51, $181,214 pay
Regional President and Corporate Director, Business Financial Services, First Place Bank: Kenton A. Thompson, age 50, $296,226 pay
Michigan Regional President and Corporate Director, Commercial Real Estate, First Place Bank: Craig L. Johnson, age 47, $296,092 pay
VP, Marketing, First Place Bank: Joseph M. Noss
Controller, First Place Bank: Peggy R. DeBartolo
Auditors: Crowe Chizek and Company LLC

LOCATIONS

HQ: First Place Financial Corp.
185 E. Market St., Warren, OH 44481
Phone: 330-373-1221   **Fax:** 330-393-5578
Web: www.firstplacebank.net

PRODUCTS/OPERATIONS

2006 Sales

	$ mil.	% of total
Interest		
Loans, including fees	134.9	75
Securities	14.1	8
Noninterest		
Nonbank subsidiaries	8.0	5
Net gains on sales of loans	5.9	3
Service charges & fees on deposit accounts	5.5	3
Other	10.6	6
Total	**179.0**	**100**

Selected Subsidiaries

First Place Bank
First Place Holdings, Inc.
  American Pension Benefits, Inc. (employee benefits consulting)
  APB Financial Group, Ltd. (wealth management)
  Coldwell Banker First Place Real Estate, Ltd. (real estate brokerage)
  First Place Insurance Agency, Ltd. (life, health & property/casualty)
  TitleWorks, LLC (75%, title insurance)

COMPETITORS

National City
Park National
Sky Financial
United Community Financial
U.S. Bancorp

HISTORICAL FINANCIALS

Company Type: Public

Income Statement

	ASSETS ($ mil.)	NET INCOME ($ mil.)	INCOME AS % OF ASSETS	EMPLOYEES
6/06	3,113.2	23.0	0.7%	868
6/05	2,498.9	18.9	0.8%	780
6/04	2,247.1	14.1	0.6%	607
6/03	1,558.6	16.7	1.1%	445
6/02	1,590.9	16.2	1.0%	445
Annual Growth	18.3%	9.2%	—	18.2%

FYE: June 30

2006 Year-End Financials

Equity as % of assets: 10.0%
Return on assets: 0.8%
Return on equity: 8.4%
Long-term debt ($ mil.): 665.8
No. of shares (mil.): 17.4
Market value ($ mil.): 401.1
Dividends
  Yield: 2.4%
  Payout: 36.1%
Sales ($ mil.): 179.0
R&D as % of sales: —
Advertising as % of sales: —

	STOCK PRICE ($) FY Close	P/E High/Low		PER SHARE ($) Earnings	Dividends	Book Value
6/06	23.01	17	12	1.55	0.56	17.87
6/05	20.09	18	13	1.30	0.70	15.75
6/04	18.59	18	15	1.09	0.56	14.74
6/03	16.89	15	10	1.29	0.50	13.73
6/02	19.91	17	11	1.16	0.50	13.18
Annual Growth	3.7%	—	—	7.5%	2.9%	7.9%

First Regional Bancorp

Wholesale banking company First Regional Bancorp caters to Southern California businesses through subsidiary First Regional Bank. Through about 10 locations, the bank mainly offers real estate loans (accounting for the majority of its portfolio), as well as commercial and construction loans. It specializes in equipment financing and mid-sized residential and commercial projects. The bank admits it has fewer customer deposit accounts than its competitors, but its accounts typically have higher balances. First Regional Bancorp also offers merchant credit card clearing and trust services, and administrative services for self-directed retirement plans. Chairman and CEO Jack Sweeney owns some 30% of the company.

EXECUTIVES

Chairman and CEO, First Regional Bancorp and First Regional Bank: Jack A. Sweeney, age 76, $1,224,535 pay
Vice Chairman: Lawrence J. Sherman, age 82
President and Director, First Regional Bancorp and First Regional Bank: H. Anthony Gartshore, age 62, $744,097 pay
CFO, First Regional Bancorp; SVP and CFO, First Regional Bank: Elizabeth Thompson, age 45, $139,601 pay
Secretary and Director; EVP, COO, and Secretary, First Regional Bank: Thomas E. McCullough, age 53, $571,096 pay
General Counsel; EVP, General Counsel, and Director, First Regional Bank: Steven J. Sweeney, age 41, $216,409 pay
President and CEO, Trust Administration Services: James Wagner
SVP and Human Resources Manager, First Regional Bank: Kim Meyer
Auditors: Deloitte & Touche LLP

LOCATIONS

HQ: First Regional Bancorp
  1801 Century Park East, Ste. 800,
  Los Angeles, CA 90067
Phone: 310-552-1776   **Fax:** 310-552-1772
Web: www.firstregional.com

First Regional Bancorp operates offices in Agoura Hills, Carlsbad, Encino, Glendale, Hollywood, Irvine, Los Angeles, Santa Monica, Torrance, and Westlake Village, California.

PRODUCTS/OPERATIONS

2005 Sales

	$ mil.	% of total
Interest		
Loans, including fees	105.7	94
Other	0.5	—
Noninterest		
Customer service fees	5.6	5
Other	0.8	1
Total	**112.6**	**100**

COMPETITORS

American Business Bank
California National Bank
Citigroup
City National
Comerica
East West Bancorp
First Republic (CA)
National Mercantile
UnionBanCal
U.S. Bancorp
Wells Fargo

HISTORICAL FINANCIALS

Company Type: Public

Income Statement

	ASSETS ($ mil.)	NET INCOME ($ mil.)	INCOME AS % OF ASSETS	EMPLOYEES	FYE: December 31
12/05	1,811.7	26.5	1.5%	224	
12/04	1,306.1	11.1	0.8%	187	
12/03	775.3	4.6	0.6%	159	
12/02	467.3	3.0	0.6%	132	
12/01	347.0	2.4	0.7%	110	
Annual Growth	**51.2%**	**82.3%**	**—**	**19.5%**	

2005 Year-End Financials

Equity as % of assets: 5.9%
Return on assets: 1.7%
Return on equity: 28.9%
Long-term debt ($ mil.): 272.3
No. of shares (mil.): 4.1
Market value ($ mil.): 91.9
Dividends
  Yield: —
  Payout: —
Sales ($ mil.): 112.6
R&D as % of sales: —
Advertising as % of sales: —

Stock History

NASDAQ (GM): FRGB

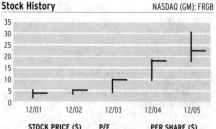

	STOCK PRICE ($) FY Close	P/E High/Low		PER SHARE ($) Earnings	Dividends	Book Value
12/05	22.52	15	9	2.06	—	25.99
12/04	18.00	20	10	0.95	—	19.40
12/03	9.77	19	8	0.53	—	12.28
12/02	5.21	14	9	0.38	—	10.57
12/01	3.83	17	7	0.30	—	9.44
Annual Growth	**55.7%**	**—**	**—**	**61.9%**	**—**	**28.8%**

First Security Group

Pardon me boy, as Glenn Miller would say, but if you've got your fare and a trifle to spare, you might want to turn to First Security Group. The holding company for FSGBank operates nearly 40 branches in eastern and middle Tennessee (including Chattanooga) and northern Georgia; in addition to the FSGBank brand, the company also operates certain locations under the Catoosa Community Bank, Dalton Whitfield Bank, Jackson Bank, and Primer Banco Seguro names. The banks offer standard deposit and lending services, including checking and savings accounts and CDs. Real estate mortgages make up about 50% of First Security's loan portfolio, which also includes construction, business, and consumer loans.

First Security Group also has two leasing subsidiaries and a wealth management division, which offers financial planning, trust management, and other services. Its Primer Banco Seguro branches were opened in 2004 to target northern Georgia's Latino community. In 2005, First Security Group acquired Gainesboro, Tennessee-based Jackson Bank, increasing the company's branch count by five and enabling First Security Group to build its presence along the Interstate 40 corridor stretching from Nashville to Knoxville, Tennessee. The purchase also is in line with the company's plan to grow both through acquisitions and by opening new branches (seven were added during 2005). A portion of the proceeds from First Security Group's 2005 initial public offering were used to finance the Jackson Bank deal.

EXECUTIVES

Chairman, President, and CEO, First Security Group and FSGBank: Rodger B. Holley, age 58, $358,680 pay
EVP and COO, First Security Group and FSGBank: Lloyd L. (Monty) Montgomery III, age 52, $234,860 pay
EVP, CFO, and Secretary, First Security Group and FSGBank: William L. (Chip) Lusk Jr., age 37, $199,180 pay
VP, Controller, and Principal Accounting Officer: John R. Haddock, age 28
Regional President, Chattanooga, FSGBank: R. Ryan Murphy III
Regional President, Sweetwater, FSGBank: Larry R. Belk
Regional President, Dalton Whitfield Bank: J. Alan Wells
Auditors: Joseph Decosimo and Company, LLP

LOCATIONS

HQ: First Security Group, Inc.
  817 Broad St., Chattanooga, TN 37402
Phone: 423-266-2000   **Fax:** 423-267-3383
Web: www.fsgbank.com

PRODUCTS/OPERATIONS

2005 Sales

	$ mil.	% of total
Interest income		
Loans	50.8	78
Securities	5.0	8
Other	0.6	1
Service charges on deposit accounts	4.2	6
Other	4.7	7
Total	**65.3**	**100**

COMPETITORS

Bank of America
BB&T
Cornerstone Bancshares
First Horizon
Regions Financial
SunTrust
Wachovia

HISTORICAL FINANCIALS

Company Type: Public

Income Statement

	ASSETS ($ mil.)	NET INCOME ($ mil.)	INCOME AS % OF ASSETS	EMPLOYEES	FYE: December 31
12/05	1,040.7	9.6	0.9%	366	
12/04	766.7	4.3	0.6%	—	
12/03	644.8	2.5	0.4%	—	
Annual Growth	**27.0%**	**96.0%**	**—**	**—**	

2005 Year-End Financials

Equity as % of assets: 13.3%
Return on assets: 1.1%
Return on equity: 8.5%
Long-term debt ($ mil.): 10.1
No. of shares (mil.): 17.7
Market value ($ mil.): 171.9
Dividends
  Yield: 0.3%
  Payout: 4.7%
Sales ($ mil.): 65.3
R&D as % of sales: —
Advertising as % of sales: —

Stock History

NASDAQ (GS): FSGI

	STOCK PRICE ($) FY Close	P/E High/Low		PER SHARE ($) Earnings	Dividends	Book Value
12/05	9.74	16	14	0.64	0.03	7.84

First State Financial

Florida certainly wasn't the first state, but First State Financial is the holding company for First State Bank, which serves west-central Florida's Sarasota and Pinellas counties through six branch locations. The bank offers standard deposit services such as checking and savings accounts, money market and retirement accounts, and certificates of deposit. It focuses on real estate and business lending, with commercial mortgages making up the largest portion of its loan portfolio (about 55%). Several members of First State Financial's board of directors also have seats on the board of Pittsburgh-based Portec Rail Products.

First State Financial is looking to grow through acquisition, seeking opportunities in both of its existing markets and looking to expand into new geographical markets.

EXECUTIVES

President, CEO, and Director, First State Financial and First State Bank: Corey J. Coughlin, age 58, $285,000 pay
EVP and Senior Lending Officer, First State Bank: Michael K. Worthington, age 49, $95,401 pay
SVP and CFO, First State Bank: Dennis Grinsteiner, age 61, $107,448 pay
Chairman: Neal W. Scaggs, age 70

LOCATIONS

HQ: First State Financial Corporation
22 S. Links Ave., Sarasota, FL 34236
Phone: 941-929-9000   **Fax:** 941-951-6189
Web: www.firststatefl.com

PRODUCTS/OPERATIONS

2005 Sales

	$ mil.	% of total
Interest		
Loans	19.8	86
Securities	0.7	3
Federal funds sold & other	0.3	1
Mortgage banking fees	1.2	5
Service charges & fees	1.0	5
Total	**23.0**	**100**

COMPETITORS

Bank of America
BB&T
Coast Financial
RBC Centura Banks
SunTrust
Wachovia

HISTORICAL FINANCIALS

Company Type: Public

Income Statement

	ASSETS ($ mil.)	NET INCOME ($ mil.)	INCOME AS % OF ASSETS	EMPLOYEES
			FYE: December 31	
12/05	372.7	3.8	1.0%	93
12/04	274.0	2.1	0.8%	79
12/03	212.3	0.8	0.4%	73
12/02	153.5	0.4	0.3%	—
Annual Growth	**34.4%**	**75.6%**	**—**	**12.9%**

2005 Year-End Financials

Equity as % of assets: 11.9%
Return on assets: 1.2%
Return on equity: 8.8%
Long-term debt ($ mil.): —
No. of shares (mil.): 5.9
Market value ($ mil.): 89.5

Dividends
Yield: 1.3%
Payout: 30.8%
Sales ($ mil.): 23.0
R&D as % of sales: —
Advertising as % of sales: 1.1%

Stock History

NASDAQ (GM): FSTF

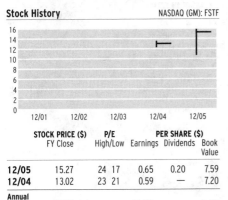

	STOCK PRICE ($) FY Close	P/E High/Low		PER SHARE ($) Earnings	Dividends	Book Value
12/05	15.27	24	17	0.65	0.20	7.59
12/04	13.02	23	21	0.59	—	7.20
Annual Growth	**17.3%**	**—**	**—**	**10.2%**	**—**	**5.4%**

FirstFed Financial

Southern Californians are on a first come, FirstFed basis. FirstFed Financial is the savings and loan holding company for First Federal Bank of California. Founded in 1929, First Federal serves consumers and businesses through some 30 branches and six lending offices. The bank uses funds from deposits mainly to finance single-family residential real estate mortgages, which account for 70% of FirstFed's total loans, and mortgages for multifamily units, which comprise another 21%. It also writes business and consumer loans. Subsidiary Oceanside Insurance Agency sells annuities. The company received regulatory approval to commence trust operations in 2004.

Buoyed by Southern California's robust housing market, FirstFed had been able to maintain a squeaky clean loan portfolio; it made no provisions for bad loans from 1998 through 2003 (it recorded a $3 million provision for loan losses in 2004), and nonperforming assets account for a miniscule 0.07% of its balance sheet. That all changed drastically in 2005; that year the company made a $19.8 million provision for loan losses; nonperforming assets fell to 0.05%.

Investment management companies own nearly one-third of FirstFed.

EXECUTIVES

President, COO, and Director: James P. Giraldin, age 53, $751,700 pay
EVP and Chief Credit Officer: David W. Anderson, age 37, $251,505 pay
EVP and CFO: Douglas J. Goddard, age 53, $294,216 pay
EVP and Chief Residential Lending Officer: Shannon Millard, age 43, $530,000 pay
EVP, Community Banking: Brad McCoy, age 36, $442,236 pay
SVP, General Counsel, and Corporate Secretary: Ann E. Lederer
SVP and Controller: Brenda J. Battey
Chairman and CEO, FirstFed Financial and First Federal Bank of California: Babette E. Heimbuch, age 58, $975,560 pay
SVP, Human Resources, First Federal Bank of California: Caroline Galbraith
Auditors: Grant Thornton LLP

LOCATIONS

HQ: FirstFed Financial Corp.
401 Wilshire Blvd., Santa Monica, CA 90401
Phone: 310-319-6000   **Fax:** 310-319-5899
Web: www.firstfedca.com

PRODUCTS/OPERATIONS

2005 Sales

	$ mil.	% of total
Interest		
Loans	450.3	90
Interest & dividends on investments & mortgage-backed securities	19.4	4
Noninterest		
Loan servicing & other fees	22.8	5
Banking service fees	5.8	1
Real estate operations	2.0	—
Other	0.6	—
Total	**500.9**	**100**

COMPETITORS

Bank of America   Washington Mutual
City National   Wells Fargo
UnionBanCal

HISTORICAL FINANCIALS

Company Type: Public

Income Statement

	ASSETS ($ mil.)	NET INCOME ($ mil.)	INCOME AS % OF ASSETS	EMPLOYEES
			FYE: December 31	
12/05	10,457.0	91.7	0.9%	629
12/04	7,469.0	65.8	0.9%	604
12/03	4,825.0	64.5	1.3%	574
12/02	4,253.7	55.2	1.3%	497
12/01	4,726.3	50.3	1.1%	508
Annual Growth	**22.0%**	**16.2%**	**—**	**5.5%**

2005 Year-End Financials

Equity as % of assets: 5.5%
Return on assets: 1.0%
Return on equity: 17.5%
Long-term debt ($ mil.): 100.0
No. of shares (mil.): 16.6
Market value ($ mil.): 903.2

Dividends
Yield: —
Payout: —
Sales ($ mil.): 500.9
R&D as % of sales: —
Advertising as % of sales: —

Stock History

NYSE: FED

	STOCK PRICE ($) FY Close	P/E High/Low		PER SHARE ($) Earnings	Dividends	Book Value
12/05	54.52	12	9	5.43	—	34.46
12/04	51.87	14	10	3.85	—	28.94
12/03	43.50	13	7	3.70	—	25.61
12/02	28.95	10	7	3.15	—	21.95
12/01	25.63	13	8	2.85	—	18.88
Annual Growth	**20.8%**	**—**	**—**	**17.5%**	**—**	**16.2%**

FLIR Systems

FLIR Systems can see through smoke screens. The company's thermal imaging and obscurant-proof camera systems detect heat and radiation, thus allowing operators to see objects through fog, darkness, or smoke. FLIR's imaging products enhance vision for military and commercial applications such as search and rescue, drug interdiction, border patrol, surveillance, navigation, and newsgathering. Industrial customers use FLIR's thermography products, which employ infrared cameras to measure temperatures from a distance for equipment monitoring, process control, product development, and other applications. US government agencies collectively account for about 33% of FLIR's sales.

In 2004 FLIR acquired Indigo Systems, a privately held maker of thermal imaging and camera systems, in a deal worth about $190 million. The next year FLIR formed a product development alliance with Pelco, a leading manufacturer of video surveillance equipment.

Also in 2005 FLIR acquired Scientific Materials, a supplier of laser assemblies, laser components, and materials, for $13 million.

FLIR is enjoying record sales and profits, largely because of the introduction of new products and the highly successful integration of recent acquisitions such as Indigo Systems. To stay on top of its market FLIR is investing $62 million in R&D ($51 million in company funds and $11 million in government-funded R&D projects), and watching for more acquisitions that make a good strategic fit.

EXECUTIVES

Chairman, President, and CEO: Earl R. Lewis, age 62, $1,294,231 pay
EVP; President, Thermography Business: Arne Almerfors, age 60, $617,397 pay
SVP Finance and CFO: Stephen M. Bailey, age 57, $481,135 pay
SVP Business Development: Denis A. Helm, age 67
SVP Corporate Operations and Law: James A. Fitzhenry, age 50, $204,089 pay
SVP Corporate Strategy and Development: Anthony L. Trunzo, age 42
SVP Human Resources: Detlev H. Suderow, age 59
Co-President, Imaging Division: Andrew C. Teich, age 45, $425,096 pay
SVP and General Manager, Boston Operations: Daniel L. Manitakos, age 48
Co-President, Imaging Division: William A. Sundermeier, age 42, $422,154 pay
Auditors: KPMG LLP

LOCATIONS

HQ: FLIR Systems, Inc.
  27700A SW Parkway Avenue, Wilsonville, OR 97070
Phone: 503-498-3547   **Fax:** 503-498-3904
Web: www.flir.com

FLIR Systems operates from facilities in Belgium, Brazil, Canada, China, France, Germany, Italy, Sweden, the UK, and the US.

2005 Sales

	$ mil.	% of total
US	286.9	57
Europe	133.9	26
Other regions	87.8	17
Total	**508.6**	**100**

PRODUCTS/OPERATIONS

2005 Sales

	$ mil.	% of total
Imaging	325.0	64
Thermography	183.6	36
Total	**508.6**	**100**

Selected Products

Imaging
  Camera systems for broadcast news and surveillance (UltraMedia lines)
  Driver's vision enhancement devices for emergency and military vehicles (ThermoVision PathfindIR)
  Ground-based thermal imaging systems (ThermoVision 2000/3000 and ThermoVision Sentry lines)
  Handheld infrared imaging systems (MilCAM)
  Marine infrared imaging systems (SeaFLIR)
  Maritime navigation and security device (ThermoVision Mariner)
  Search and rescue thermal imaging systems (Star SAFIRE lines)
Thermography
  Industrial handheld and fixed thermal imaging systems (ThermaCAM lines)
  Uncooled thermography cameras for process control (ThermoVision lines)

COMPETITORS

BAE SYSTEMS	Lockheed Martin
Boeing	Mikron Infrared
CIC International	NEC
DRS Technologies	Raytheon
Fluke	SAFRAN
Kollsman	Thales
L-3 Communications	WESCAM

HISTORICAL FINANCIALS
Company Type: Public

Income Statement

FYE: December 31

	REVENUE ($ mil.)	NET INCOME ($ mil.)	NET PROFIT MARGIN	EMPLOYEES
12/05	508.6	90.8	17.9%	1,320
12/04	482.6	71.5	14.8%	1,204
12/03	312.0	44.7	14.3%	885
12/02	261.1	41.6	15.9%	838
12/01	214.4	25.9	12.1%	798
Annual Growth	**24.1%**	**36.8%**	**—**	**13.4%**

2005 Year-End Financials

Debt ratio: 55.9%
Return on equity: 26.6%
Cash ($ mil.): 107.1
Current ratio: 4.50
Long-term debt ($ mil.): 206.2
No. of shares (mil.): 69.2

Dividends
  Yield: —
  Payout: —
Market value ($ mil.): 1,545.6
R&D as % of sales: —
Advertising as % of sales: —

Stock History

NASDAQ (GS): FLIR

	STOCK PRICE ($) FY Close	P/E High/Low		PER SHARE ($) Earnings	Dividends	Book Value
12/05	22.33	31	18	1.16	—	5.33
12/04	31.90	35	19	0.94	—	4.53
12/03	18.25	29	16	0.63	—	5.02
12/02	12.20	26	12	0.58	—	9.96
12/01	9.48	31	3	0.41	—	6.33
Annual Growth	**23.9%**	**—**	**—**	**29.7%**	**—**	**(4.2%)**

FormFactor

Good evening, and welcome to FormFactor! On tonight's show, our contestants will dive off a high platform, retrieve a silicon wafer at the bottom of the water tank, and then run tests on the semiconductors! Using an interconnect technology it calls MicroSpring, FormFactor makes wafer probe cards that test semiconductor circuits (especially memory chips) while they are still part of semiconductor wafers — before the wafers are cut into individual chips. FormFactor touts the process for its cost-effectiveness, since it allows testing of many chips at once across a range of scales and temperatures. The company has also licensed MicroSpring technology for other applications in chip packaging.

The company's top customers include Asian distributor Spirox (23% of sales) and big chip

makers Elpida (also 23%), Samsung Electronics (15%), Intel (12%), and Infineon. Spirox's sales on behalf of FormFactor were chiefly from Taiwan, where FormFactor has now set up a direct sales force. Spirox continues to represent FormFactor in other Asia/Pacific markets.

FormFactor has been involved in patent litigation against rival Phicom Corp. in South Korea since early 2004. The long-running litigation is in the discovery process.

FMR (Fidelity Investments) owns about 13% of FormFactor. Franklin Resources holds nearly 8% of the company. CEO Igor Khandros has an equity stake of nearly 6%.

EXECUTIVES

Chairperson: James A. (Jim) Prestridge, age 74
President, CEO and Director: Igor Y. Khandros, age 51, $788,847 pay (prior to title change)
SVP, Operations: Richard M. Freeman, age 56
CFO: Ronald C. (Ron) Foster, age 56, $275,289 pay
SVP, Development and CTO: Benjamin N. (Ben) Eldridge, age 45, $424,130 pay
SVP, General Counsel, and Secretary: Stuart L. Merkadeau, age 44, $383,992 pay
SVP, Asia/Pacific Operations; President, FormFactor K.K.: Yoshikazu Hatsukano, age 65, $428,535 pay
SVP, Worldwide Sales: Peter B. Mathews, age 43, $297,407 pay
VP, Human Resources: Hank Feir
Auditors: PricewaterhouseCoopers LLP

LOCATIONS

HQ: FormFactor, Inc.
  7005 Southfront Rd., Livermore, CA 94551
Phone: 925-290-4000   **Fax:** 925-290-4010
Web: www.formfactor.com

FormFactor has offices in Germany, Italy, Japan, South Korea, Taiwan, and the US.

2005 Sales

	$ mil.	% of total
Asia/Pacific		
Japan	62.2	26
Other countries	71.4	30
North America	81.2	34
Europe	22.7	10
Total	**237.5**	**100**

PRODUCTS/OPERATIONS

Selected Products

MicroSpring interconnects (T1, T2 type contacts; BladeRunner contacts)
Probe cards
Probe heads (PH50, PH75, PH100, PH150 models)

COMPETITORS

Advantest
ASE Test Limited
Cadence Design
Cascade Microtech
Dover Technologies
Electroglas
Everett Charles Technologies
Interconnect Devices
LogicVision
LTX
Mentor Graphics
Mitsubishi Materials
PDF Solutions
Synopsys
Teradyne
Tokyo Electron

HISTORICAL FINANCIALS

Company Type: Public

Income Statement
FYE: Last Saturday in December

	REVENUE ($ mil.)	NET INCOME ($ mil.)	NET PROFIT MARGIN	EMPLOYEES
12/05	237.5	30.2	12.7%	653
12/04	177.8	25.2	14.2%	485
12/03	98.3	7.5	7.6%	341
12/02	78.7	10.4	13.2%	299
12/01	73.4	0.3	0.4%	—
Annual Growth	34.1%	216.8%	—	29.7%

2005 Year-End Financials

Debt ratio: —
Return on equity: 10.4%
Cash ($ mil.): 211.6
Current ratio: 4.84
Long-term debt ($ mil.): —
No. of shares (mil.): 40.2

Dividends
  Yield: —
  Payout: —
Market value ($ mil.): 983.0
R&D as % of sales: —
Advertising as % of sales: —

Stock History
NASDAQ (GS): FORM

	STOCK PRICE ($) FY Close	P/E High/Low	PER SHARE ($) Earnings	Dividends	Book Value
12/05	24.43	41 27	0.73	—	7.90
12/04	27.14	46 25	0.63	—	6.82
12/03	19.80	146 85	0.19	—	5.84
Annual Growth	11.1%	— —	96.0%	—	16.3%

Franklin Bank Corp.

A bubble in the housing market doesn't rankle Franklin Bank Corp. The company is the parent of Franklin Bank, a thrift with about 30 branches in the Austin, Tyler, and Kingsland areas of central and east Texas. In addition to these locations, the company has more than 50 offices in some 20 states from which it originates residential mortgages and residential construction loans. It also purchases mortgages on the secondary market and provides financing to small and midsized mortgage banking companies. Franklin was founded in 2001 by executives of the former Bank United Corp. The institution is acquiring the First National Bank of Bryan.

Franklin is eyeing growth by opening branches or buying banks in Austin and other parts of Texas. Its 2005 purchase of First National Bank of Athens gave the bank four additional branches. That same year it acquired Elgin Bank of Texas (with three locations), and the Texas-based Washington Mutual (not to be confused with publicly traded Seattle, Washington-based Washington Mutual, Inc.).

EXECUTIVES

Chairman: Lewis S. Ranieri, age 60
President, CEO, and Director; Chairman, President, and CEO, Franklin Bank: Anthony J. Nocella, age 64, $400,000 pay
EVP, CFO, and Treasurer; CFO, Franklin Bank: Russell McCann, age 49, $220,665 pay
EVP and Chief Credit Officer, Franklin Bank: Max Epperson, age 63
EVP and Managing Director, Central Texas Banking, Franklin Bank: Andy Black, age 53
EVP and Managing Director, Commercial Lending, Franklin Bank: Michael Davitt, age 56, $208,052 pay
EVP and Managing Director, Mortgage Banking, Franklin Bank: Daniel E. Cooper, age 48
President, Elgin Bank; Market Manager, Bastrop County: Jeff Carter
VP and Company Secretary: Diane Tregre
Investor Relations: Kris Dillon
Auditors: Deloitte & Touche LLP

LOCATIONS

HQ: Franklin Bank Corp.
  9800 Richmond Ave., Ste. 680, Houston, TX 77042
Phone: 713-339-8900   **Fax:** 713-343-8122
Web: www.bankfranklin.com

PRODUCTS/OPERATIONS

2005 Sales

	$ mil.	% of total
Interest		
Loans	185.0	86
Cash equivalents & short-term investments	7.7	2
Mortgage-backed securities	4.5	
Noninterest		
Loan fee income	6.9	3
Deposit fees	4.9	2
Gain on sale of single family loans	4.2	2
Gain on sale of securities	1.0	—
Other	1.8	1
Total	**216.0**	**100**

COMPETITORS

Bank of America
Colonial BancGroup
Compass Bancshares
Cullen/Frost Bankers
First State Bank Central Texas
Henderson Citizens Bancshares
Lone Star Bank
PlainsCapital
Southside Bancshares
Washington Mutual
Wells Fargo

HISTORICAL FINANCIALS

Company Type: Public

Income Statement
FYE: December 31

	ASSETS ($ mil.)	NET INCOME ($ mil.)	INCOME AS % OF ASSETS	EMPLOYEES
12/05	4,471.3	26.3	0.6%	710
12/04	3,479.7	23.1	0.7%	548
12/03	2,251.3	3.2	0.1%	399
12/02	365.7	(0.7)	—	—
Annual Growth	130.4%	—	—	33.4%

2005 Year-End Financials

Equity as % of assets: 7.4%
Return on assets: 0.7%
Return on equity: 8.6%
Long-term debt ($ mil.): 108.0
No. of shares (mil.): 23.4
Market value ($ mil.): 420.5

Dividends
  Yield: —
  Payout: —
Sales ($ mil.): 216.0
R&D as % of sales: —
Advertising as % of sales: —

Stock History
NASDAQ (GS): FBTX

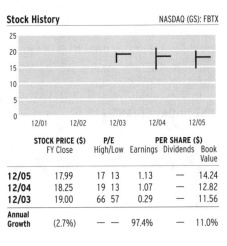

	STOCK PRICE ($) FY Close	P/E High/Low	PER SHARE ($) Earnings	Dividends	Book Value
12/05	17.99	17 13	1.13	—	14.24
12/04	18.25	19 13	1.07	—	12.82
12/03	19.00	66 57	0.29	—	11.56
Annual Growth	(2.7%)	— —	97.4%	—	11.0%

Franklin Credit Management

Franklin Credit Management ends up with a lot of the mortgage loans other companies don't want, but gets them without spending a lot of Benjamins. Franklin Credit buys primarily discounted subprime mortgage assets (sometimes referred to as "scratch and dent" loans), then services or resells them. The company focuses on obtaining primarily higher coupon non-investment grade performing loans in order to increase its amount of acquisitions. Subsidiary Tribeca Lending offers subprime residential mortgage loans (loans to borrowers with poor or limited credit histories). Chairman and president Thomas Axon owns more than 40% of the firm.

Franklin Credit acquires scratch and dent loans through negotiated sales, ongoing purchase agreements, joint bids with other institutions, and auctions. Sellers include mortgage bankers, commercial banks and thrifts, and other financial institutions.

EXECUTIVES

Chairman and President: Thomas J. (Tom) Axon, age 54, $300,000 pay (prior to title change)
CEO and Director: Alexander Gordon Jardin, age 53
COO and Director: William F. Sullivan, age 57
EVP and CFO: Paul D. Colasono, age 59, $365,096 pay
EVP, Loan Servicing and Secretary; President, Tribeca Lending: Joseph (Joe) Caiazzo, age 48, $349,466 pay
VP, Credit/Acquisitions: John Devine, age 37, $250,000 pay
VP, Finance, Treasurer, and Controller: Kimberly Shaw, age 44
General Counsel: John M. Collins
Auditors: Deloitte & Touche LLP

LOCATIONS

HQ: Franklin Credit Management Corporation
  101 Hudson St., New Jersey, NJ 07302
Phone: 201-604-4402   **Fax:** 201-604-4400
Web: www.franklincredit.com

COMPETITORS

Bank of America	JPMorgan Chase
Bear Stearns & Co.	Residential Funding
Citigroup	Washington Mutual
Countrywide Financial	Wells Fargo
Goldman Sachs	

HISTORICAL FINANCIALS

Company Type: Public

Income Statement

FYE: December 31

	ASSETS ($ mil.)	NET INCOME ($ mil.)	INCOME AS % OF ASSETS	EMPLOYEES
12/05	1,328.2	7.9	0.6%	216
12/04	891.5	9.5	1.1%	—
12/03	476.7	6.7	1.4%	—
12/02	424.4	6.7	1.6%	—
12/01	334.2	2.9	0.9%	—
Annual Growth	**41.2%**	**28.5%**	**—**	**—**

2005 Year-End Financials

Equity as % of assets: 3.6%	Dividends
Return on assets: 0.7%	Yield: —
Return on equity: 20.5%	Payout: —
Long-term debt ($ mil.): 1,261.2	Sales ($ mil.): 121.4
No. of shares (mil.): 7.5	R&D as % of sales: —
Market value ($ mil.): 59.6	Advertising as % of sales: —

Stock History

NASDAQ (GM): FCMC

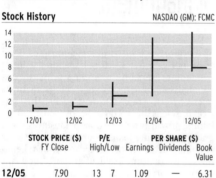

	STOCK PRICE ($) FY Close	P/E High/Low		PER SHARE ($) Earnings Dividends Book Value		
12/05	7.90	13	7	1.09	—	6.31
12/04	9.20	9	2	1.43	—	4.88
12/03	2.97	5	1	1.02	—	3.33
12/02	1.07	2	1	1.07	—	2.20
12/01	0.70	3	1	0.49	—	1.07
Annual Growth	**83.3%**	**—**	**—**	**22.1%**	**—**	**55.9%**

FreightCar America

Coal keeps FreightCar America in the black. The company designs and makes railroad freight cars, more than 90% of which are aluminum-bodied coal-carrying cars. FreightCar America claims leadership in the North American market for coal-carrying cars. Other products include coil steel cars, flatcars, intermodal cars, mill gondola cars, and motor vehicle carriers. The company maintains manufacturing facilities in Illinois, Pennsylvania, and Virginia. FreightCar America also refurbishes and rebuilds railcars and supplies parts for railcars made by other companies. Customers include leasing companies, railroads, and utilities.

What is now FreightCar America was owned by Bethlehem Steel from 1923 to 1991, when Transportation Technologies Industries (TTI) acquired it. TTI sold the company to an investor group in 1999. FreightCar America went public in 2005.

EXECUTIVES

Chairman: Camillo M. Santomero III, age 48
President, CEO, and Director: John E. Carroll Jr., age 64
COO: Christian B. (Chris) Ragot, age 48
SVP, Marketing and Sales: Edward J. Whalen, age 57
VP, Finance, CFO, Treasurer, and Secretary: Kevin P. Bagby, age 54
Managing Director International: Charles Magolske
Manager, Customer Service: Kevin Knarr
Auditors: Deloitte & Touche LLP

LOCATIONS

HQ: FreightCar America, Inc.
2 N. Riverside Plaza, Ste. 1250, Chicago, IL 60606
Phone: 312-928-0850
Web: www.freightcaramerica.com

PRODUCTS/OPERATIONS

2005 Sales

	$ mil.	% of total
New railcar sales	911.1	98
Used railcar sales	6.9	1
Leasing	0.1	—
Other	9.1	1
Total	**927.2**	**100**

COMPETITORS

ACF	Greenbrier
American Railcar	Trinity Industries
CAF	Union Tank Car

HISTORICAL FINANCIALS

Company Type: Public

Income Statement

FYE: December 31

	REVENUE ($ mil.)	NET INCOME ($ mil.)	NET PROFIT MARGIN	EMPLOYEES
12/05	927.2	45.7	4.9%	1,289
12/04	482.2	(24.9)	—	—
12/03	244.4	(7.4)	—	—
Annual Growth	**94.8%**	**—**	**—**	**—**

2005 Year-End Financials

Debt ratio: 0.2%	Dividends
Return on equity: 165.9%	Yield: 0.1%
Cash ($ mil.): 61.7	Payout: 1.5%
Current ratio: 1.56	Market value ($ mil.): 604.4
Long-term debt ($ mil.): 0.2	R&D as % of sales: —
No. of shares (mil.): 12.6	Advertising as % of sales: —

Stock History

NASDAQ (GS): RAIL

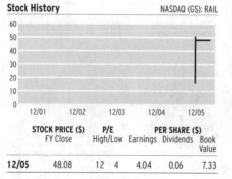

	STOCK PRICE ($) FY Close	P/E High/Low		PER SHARE ($) Earnings Dividends Book Value		
12/05	48.08	12	4	4.04	0.06	7.33

GAINSCO

Although at times it might be more appropriate, you wouldn't call an insurance company LOSSCO, would you? GAINSCO's subsidiaries General Agents Insurance Company of America and MGA Insurance sell personal nonstandard auto insurance in over 40 states. Restructuring its operations, GAINSCO exited all of its commercial lines of business, including auto, garage, liability, property, and specialty lines such as lawyers and educators insurance. The company does most of its business in Florida but has laid the groundwork for sales growth in Arizona, California, Nevada, and Texas. GAINSCO executives and directors collectively own 71% of the company.

Chairman Robert Stallings controls 22% of GAINSCO; EVP James Reis controls 11% through First Western Capital, and director John Goff controls 35% through Goff Moore Strategic Partners.

EXECUTIVES

Chairman and Chief Strategic Officer:
Robert W. Stallings, age 56, $546,719 pay
Vice Chairman: Joel C. Puckett, age 62
President, CEO, and Director: Glenn W. Anderson, age 53, $772,229 pay
EVP and Chief Risk Management Officer:
James R. Reis, age 48, $317,159 pay
SVP, Corporate Affairs and Human Resources:
Richard M. Buxton, age 57, $205,000 pay
SVP, CFO, and Chief Accounting Officer:
Daniel J. Coots, age 54
President, South Central Region: Stephen W. Mudd
SVP and Chief Investment Officer: Terence J. Lynch
President, Southwest Region: Brian L. Kirkham
President, Southeast Region: Michael S. Johnston, age 45, $248,000 pay
General Counsel and Secretary: John S. Daniels
Assistant VP, Investor Relations: Scott A. Marek
Auditors: KPMG LLP

LOCATIONS

HQ: GAINSCO, INC.
3333 Lee Pkwy., Ste. 1200, Dallas, TX 75219
Phone: 214-647-0415   **Fax:** 214-647-0430
Web: www.gainsco.com

PRODUCTS/OPERATIONS

2005 Sales

	$ mil.	% of total
Net premiums earned	85.8	86
Agency revenues	9.5	10
Net investment income	3.7	4
Other	0.6	—
Total	**99.6**	**100**

Selected Subsidiaries

Agents Processing Systems, Inc.
DLT Insurance Adjusters, Inc.
GAINSCO Service Corp.
General Agents Insurance Company of America, Inc.
  MGA Insurance Company, Inc.
    MGA Agency, Inc.
General Agents Premium Finance Company
Lalande Financial Group, Inc.
MGA Premium Finance Company
National Specialty Lines, Inc.
Risk Retention Administrators, Inc.

COMPETITORS

Allstate
Farmers Group
GEICO
Progressive Corporation
State Farm

HISTORICAL FINANCIALS
Company Type: Public

Income Statement

FYE: December 31

	ASSETS ($ mil.)	NET INCOME ($ mil.)	INCOME AS % OF ASSETS	EMPLOYEES
12/05	212.2	8.9	4.2%	295
12/04	164.6	5.5	3.3%	—
12/03	185.7	3.4	1.8%	—
12/02	214.4	(8.8)	—	—
12/01	379.2	(75.6)	—	227
Annual Growth	(13.5%)	—	—	6.8%

2005 Year-End Financials

Equity as % of assets: 26.7%	Dividends
Return on assets: 4.7%	Yield: —
Return on equity: 25.6%	Payout: —
Long-term debt ($ mil.): 0.5	Sales ($ mil.): 99.6
No. of shares (mil.): 20.2	R&D as % of sales: —
Market value ($ mil.): 153.5	Advertising as % of sales: —

Stock History

AMEX: GAN

	STOCK PRICE ($) FY Close	P/E High/Low		PER SHARE ($) Earnings	Dividends	Book Value
12/05	7.59	26	16	0.33	—	2.80
12/04	5.96	38	5	0.16	—	0.21
12/03	0.90	—	—	(0.08)	—	0.63
12/02	0.34	—	—	(2.28)	—	0.67
12/01	6.40	—	—	(14.72)	—	1.30
Annual Growth	4.4%	—	—	—	—	21.1%

Gaming Partners International

Thousands of gamblers crap out every day on Gaming Partners International Corporation (GPIC) tables with GPIC dice. The company (formerly Paul-Son Gaming) manufactures and supplies a myriad of table-game casino products, including chips and playing cards, dice, dealing shoes, roulette wheels, and table furniture and layouts for blackjack, poker, baccarat, craps, and other casino games. GPIC peddles its wares (consisting of such brand names as Paulson, Bud Jones, and T-K) wherever gambling is legal in the world. The company established an international presence through its purchase of French table-game equipment manufacturer Bourgogne et Grasset. Director Elisabeth Carretté owns 49% of GPIC.

GPIC hopes to tap foreign markets as legalized casinos and gaming become more prevalent in other countries, particularly in China's Macao. In addition, expansion of US-based companies into new overseas markets also shows promise for GPIC.

The company offers chips embedded with radio frequency ID (RFID) devices and readers to help casinos ensure the validity of chips in play and discourage counterfeiting. GPIC can build other security features into most of its products and custom designs graphics and other product features.

HISTORY

Paul Endy Sr. distributed cards to legal gaming establishments in California in the 1940s and 1950s. His son, Paul Jr., struck out on his own in 1963 when he bought a bankrupt dice factory in Las Vegas. Over time the company's offerings expanded, and Paul-Son (the name originally differentiated Paul Jr.'s business from his father's) became the big fish in its small market. The business received a big boost when New Jersey legalized gambling (other states soon followed suit), and when Native Americans entered the business to boost tribal income and employment. Paul-Son was able to solidify its hold on the market. Paul Jr.'s son Eric, an audiologist by training, joined the company in 1983.

Paul-Son went public in 1994, but took a beating the next year when gambling operations that bought equipment from the company on credit folded. With DeBartolo Entertainment the company formed Brand One Marketing in 1997 to market Paul-Son collectible and commemorative chips and playing cards. It bought out DeBartolo's share in 1998. Founder Paul Endy Jr. died the following year, and his son Eric took over the business.

In 2000 Paul-Son won major accounts to provide playing cards to Harrah's Louisiana casino and gambling chips to Trump Casinos-Atlantic City. The following year the company filed a letter of intent to acquire US competitor Bud Jones Co. and its French parent Bourgogne et Grasset (B&G), manufacturers and suppliers of gaming equipment. When the deadline passed, Paul-Son demanded a $1 million termination fee. Arbitration had begun before both companies agreed to reenter talks.

In 2002 Paul-Son and B&G reached a definitive agreement to combine the companies whereby B&G and Bud Jones became wholly owned subsidiaries of Paul-Son. As a result of the combination, Endy stepped down as chairman and CEO and became EVP. B&G director Francois Carretté became chairman, and Gerard Charlier assumed the roles of president and CEO. The following year Paul-Son merged Bud Jones with Paul-Son Gaming Supplies, consolidating the two gaming supply manufacturing units into a single facility.

In 2004 Paul-Son changed its name to Gaming Partners International Corporation to reflect the significant changes the company had undergone since merging with B&G.

EXECUTIVES

President, CEO, and Director: Gérard P. Charlier, age 67
CFO: David W. Grimes, age 48
VP Authentic Products: William B. McCoy
Chief Legal and Gaming Compliance Officer: Laura McAllister Cox, age 46, $192,743 pay
Corporate Secretary: Gay A. Nordfelt
Manager Human Resources: Jennifer Jones

LOCATIONS

HQ: Gaming Partners International Corporation
    1700 S. Industrial Rd., Las Vegas, NV 89102
Phone: 702-384-2425   **Fax:** 702-384-1965
Web: www.gpigaming.com

Gaming Partners International has manufacturing facilities in San Luis Rio Colorado, Mexico; Las Vegas; and Beaune, France; and operates sales and administrative offices in Beaune, France; Atlantic City, New Jersey; Gulfport, Mississippi; and Las Vegas.

2005 Sales

	$ mil.	% of total
US	28.7	50
Asia	20.5	36
Europe	4.8	9
Other	3.1	5
Total	**57.1**	**100**

PRODUCTS/OPERATIONS

2005 Sales

	$ mil.	% of total
Casino chips	37.9	66
Table layouts	5.0	9
Playing cards	3.9	7
Dice	2.7	5
Gaming furniture	2.6	4
Table accessories and other products	5.0	9
Total	**57.1**	**100**

Selected Products

Casino chips
Chip trays
Commemorative chips
Dealing shoes
Dice
Drop boxes
Gaming furniture
Playing cards
Roulette wheels
Table layouts and accessories

COMPETITORS

CHIPCO
Gemaco
Jarden
Lucky Gaming
Midwest Game Supply
Shuffle Master
USPCC

HISTORICAL FINANCIALS
Company Type: Public

Income Statement

FYE: December 31

	REVENUE ($ mil.)	NET INCOME ($ mil.)	NET PROFIT MARGIN	EMPLOYEES
12/05	57.1	4.3	7.5%	870
12/04	44.6	2.6	5.8%	650
12/03	36.2	1.2	3.3%	540
12/02*	21.9	(2.2)	—	480
5/02	16.6	(1.8)	—	425
Annual Growth	36.2%	—	—	19.6%

*Fiscal year change

2005 Year-End Financials

Debt ratio: 7.3%
Return on equity: 18.1%
Cash ($ mil.): 13.6
Current ratio: 1.46
Long-term debt ($ mil.): 1.9
No. of shares (mil.): 7.9

Dividends
  Yield: 0.9%
  Payout: 18.9%
Market value ($ mil.): 88.3
R&D as % of sales: —
Advertising as % of sales: —

Stock History

NASDAQ (GM): GPIC

	STOCK PRICE ($) FY Close	P/E High/Low		PER SHARE ($) Earnings	Dividends	Book Value
12/05	11.18	48	19	0.53	0.10	3.29
12/04	20.63	76	10	0.34	—	2.80
12/03	5.75	39	20	0.16	—	2.34
12/02	4.24	—	—	(0.42)	—	2.05
Annual Growth	38.2%	—	—	—	—	2.4%

Gateway Financial Holdings

Gateway Financial Holdings wants to be the portal to all things financial in northeastern North Carolina and Virginia's Tidewater region. Subsidiary Gateway Bank & Trust is a full-service bank with some 20 branches offering products including checking and savings accounts, CDs, IRAs, and merchant services. It primarily uses funds from deposits to write real estate loans: Construction loans, commercial mortgages, and commercial loans account for more than 60% of its loan portfolio. It also offers business, consumer, and home equity loans. Subsidiaries Gateway Insurance Services and Gateway Investment Services offer insurance and investment products and services.

Already growing in Virginia as evidenced by the acquisition of C.D. West & Company insurance agency and the announced purchase of The Bank of Richmond, Gateway Financial plans to expand its operations in the Raleigh, North Carolina area. It expects to open about five branches in the region by 2008. The company is converting some of its loan production offices into full-service banking offices, and continues to seek other markets for expansion.

EXECUTIVES

Chairman, President, and CEO; President and CEO, Gateway Bank & Trust: Daniel B. (Ben) Berry, age 51, $425,000 pay
President and COO: David R. Twiddy, age 48, $250,000 pay
SEVP and Chief Administrative Officer, Gateway Bank & Trust: Donna C. Kitchen
SEVP and Chief Credit Officer, Gateway Bank & Trust: J. Daniel Fisher
SEVP and CFO: Theodore L. (Teddy) Salter

VP and Controller: Mark A. Jeffries
President and CEO, Gateway Insurance Services, Inc.: Brian J. Hellenga
Auditors: Dixon Hughes PLLC

LOCATIONS

HQ: Gateway Financial Holdings, Inc.
  1145 N. Road St., Elizabeth City, NC 27909
Phone: 252-334-1511   **Fax:** 252-334-1743
Web: www.trustgateway.com

PRODUCTS/OPERATIONS

2005 Sales

	$ mil.	% of total
Interest		
Loans, including fees	36.4	76
Investment securities	2.7	6
Other	0.6	1
Noninterest		
Insurance operations	2.4	5
Service charges on deposit accounts	2.3	5
Mortgage operations	0.8	2
Brokerage operations	0.7	1
Other	1.9	4
Total	**47.8**	**100**

COMPETITORS

BB&T
First Citizens BancShares
Hampton Roads
  Bankshares
Old Point Financial
Provident Bankshares
RBC Centura Banks
SunTrust
Wachovia

HISTORICAL FINANCIALS

Company Type: Public

Income Statement

FYE: December 31

	ASSETS ($ mil.)	NET INCOME ($ mil.)	INCOME AS % OF ASSETS	EMPLOYEES
12/05	882.4	3.9	0.4%	245
12/04	535.7	2.0	0.4%	191
12/03	314.8	1.2	0.4%	123
12/02	231.1	0.6	0.3%	96
12/01	160.8	0.6	0.4%	69
Annual Growth	53.1%	59.7%	—	37.3%

2005 Year-End Financials

Equity as % of assets: 11.2%
Return on assets: 0.6%
Return on equity: 4.8%
Long-term debt ($ mil.): 72.7
No. of shares (mil.): 9.5
Market value ($ mil.): 142.8

Dividends
  Yield: 0.5%
  Payout: 17.4%
Sales ($ mil.): 47.8
R&D as % of sales: —
Advertising as % of sales: —

Stock History

NASDAQ (GM): GBTS

	STOCK PRICE ($) FY Close	P/E High/Low		PER SHARE ($) Earnings	Dividends	Book Value
12/05	15.05	37	28	0.46	0.08	10.40
12/04	13.26	40	27	0.34	—	9.66
12/03	9.48	33	20	0.29	—	7.88
12/02	6.03	50	33	0.16	—	7.97
12/01	5.89	48	32	0.17	—	8.42
Annual Growth	26.4%	—	—	28.3%	—	5.4%

GB&T Bancshares

Could GB&T stand for Grab 'em, Bag 'em, and Tag 'em? Ever-acquisitive GB&T Bancshares is the multibank holding company for Gainesville Bank & Trust (and its Bank of Athens, Lumpkin County Bank, and Southern Heritage Bank divisions), United Bank & Trust, Community Trust Bank, HomeTown Bank of Villa Rica, First National Bank of the South, First National Bank of Gwinnet, and Mountain State Bank (acquired in 2006). The community banks together serve individuals and local businesses through about 30 branches near Atlanta, Georgia. Lending activity includes real estate mortgages (about half of the company's loan portfolio) and construction, commercial, and consumer loans.

GB&T Bancshares also runs Community Loan Company, which provides consumer financing.

GB&T Bancshares acquired Lumpkin County Bank and Southern Heritage Bank in 2004; those banks now operate as divisions of Gainesville Bank & Trust, the holding company's lead bank. The following year it acquired hometown competitor FNBG Bancshares and its First National Bank of Gwinnett subsidiary.

Eager to keep growing, GB&T Bancshares in 2006 bought Georgia's Mountain Bancshares, parent of Mountain State Bank, which has branches in Georgia's Dawson and Forsyth counties, among the fastest-growing counties in the state and the nation.

EXECUTIVES

Chairman: Philip A. Wilheit, age 61
Vice Chairman: Samuel L. (Sam) Oliver, age 63
EVP and CFO, GB&T Bancshares and Gainesville Bank & Trust: Gregory L. Hamby, age 51, $253,918 pay
President and CEO, Community Trust Bank: Randy Taylor
President and CEO, HomeTown Bank of Villa Rica: S. Pope Cleghorn Jr.
President, CEO, and Director; CEO, Gainesville Bank & Trust: Richard A. Hunt Jr., age 62, $492,900 pay
President and CEO, United Bank & Trust: David T. Sawyer
President and COO, Gainesville Bank & Trust: J. Michael (Mike) Whitmire
EVP and Chief Credit Officer: Sid J. Sims
EVP, Real Estate Lending Services, Gainesville Bank & Trust: John B. Stump
SVP, Marketing, Gainesville Bank & Trust: W. Michael Banks
Secretary and Director: Alan A. Wayne, age 63
Auditors: Mauldin & Jenkins, LLC

LOCATIONS

HQ: GB&T Bancshares, Inc.
  500 Jesse Jewell Pkwy. SE, Gainesville, GA 30501
Phone: 770-532-1212   **Fax:** 770-531-7368
Web: www.gbt.com

PRODUCTS/OPERATIONS

2005 Sales

	$ mil.	% of total
Interest		
Loans, including fees	82.5	81
Securities	7.9	8
Other	0.4	—
Noninterest		
Service charges on deposit accounts	6.4	6
Mortgage origination fees	2.3	2
Other service charges & fees	1.1	1
Other	1.8	2
Total	**102.4**	**100**

COMPETITORS

Bank of America
BB&T
Colonial BancGroup
Crescent Banking
Fidelity Southern

Habersham Bancorp
Regions Financial
SunTrust
Wachovia

HISTORICAL FINANCIALS

Company Type: Public

Income Statement

FYE: December 31

	ASSETS ($ mil.)	NET INCOME ($ mil.)	INCOME AS % OF ASSETS	EMPLOYEES
12/05	1,584.1	12.0	0.8%	452
12/04	1,274.1	9.8	0.8%	453
12/03	944.3	7.7	0.8%	380
12/02	742.0	6.5	0.9%	312
12/01	547.6	4.0	0.7%	233
Annual Growth	30.4%	31.6%	—	18.0%

2005 Year-End Financials

Equity as % of assets: 12.5%
Return on assets: 0.8%
Return on equity: 6.4%
Long-term debt ($ mil.): 128.2
No. of shares (mil.): 12.8
Market value ($ mil.): 273.7
Dividends
  Yield: 1.5%
  Payout: 35.5%
Sales ($ mil.): 102.4
R&D as % of sales: —
Advertising as % of sales: —

Stock History

NASDAQ (GS): GBTB

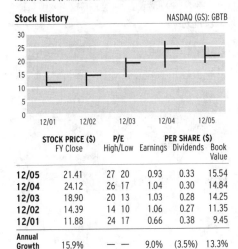

	STOCK PRICE ($) FY Close	P/E High/Low		PER SHARE ($) Earnings	Dividends	Book Value
12/05	21.41	27	20	0.93	0.33	15.54
12/04	24.12	26	17	1.04	0.30	14.84
12/03	18.90	20	13	1.03	0.28	14.25
12/02	14.39	14	10	1.06	0.27	11.35
12/01	11.88	24	17	0.66	0.38	9.45
Annual Growth	15.9%	—	—	9.0%	(3.5%)	13.3%

Gehl Company

Gehl Company asks the question, "Can you dig it?" The company makes light-construction and agricultural equipment primarily used by building contractors and dairy and livestock farmers. Construction equipment includes Gehl and Mustang mini-excavators, mini-loaders, and skid steer loaders for material handling; Dynalift telescopic loaders; and Power Box asphalt pavers for building sidewalks, parking lots, trails, and driveways. The company's agricultural equipment is used for haymaking, forage harvesting, manure spreading (the Scavenger), and feedmaking (Gehl Mix-All grinder mixers).

EXECUTIVES

Chairman and CEO: William D. (Bill) Gehl, age 59, $826,073 pay
President and COO: Malcolm F. (Mac) Moore, age 55, $587,143 pay
VP, Secretary, and General Counsel: Michael J. Mulcahy, age 59, $191,366 pay
VP and CFO: Thomas M. Rettler, age 45, $380,880 pay
VP, Human Resources: Kenneth H. Feucht, age 57
VP, Manufacturing Operations: Daniel L. (Dan) Miller, age 47, $216,117 pay
VP, Sales and Marketing: Daniel M. (Dan) Keyes, age 37, $260,423 pay
Marketing Coordinator: Lori A. Heidecker
Treasurer: James J. Monnat, age 50
Auditors: PricewaterhouseCoopers LLP

LOCATIONS

HQ: Gehl Company
    143 Water St., West Bend, WI 53095
Phone: 262-334-9461   **Fax:** 262-338-7517
Web: www.gehl.com

Gehl Company has manufacturing plants in Minnesota, South Dakota, and Wisconsin, and dealers and distributors throughout Europe, Latin and North America, the Middle East, and the Pacific Rim.

PRODUCTS/OPERATIONS

2005 Sales

	$ mil.	% of total
Construction equipment	344.0	72
Agricultural equipment	134.2	28
Total	478.2	100

Selected Products and Brand Names

Construction Equipment
  Asphalt pavers (Gehl Power Box)
  Compact excavators (Gehl and Mustang)
  Compact-loaders (Gehl Advantage)
  Skid steer loaders (Gehl and Mustang)
  Telescopic handlers (Dynalift)
Agriculture Equipment
  Balers (Gehl)
  Disc mowers (Gehl)
  Forage harvesters (Gehl)
  Grinder mixers (Gehl Mix-All)
  Hay rakes (Gehl)
  Manure spreaders (Scavenger)
  Mixer feeders (Gehl)
  Skid steer loaders (Gehl and Mustang)

COMPETITORS

AGCO
Art's-Way
A.S.V.
Caterpillar
CNH
Deere
Gencor Industries

Jungheinrich
Manitou
NACCO Industries
Wacker Construction
  Equipment
Woods Equipment

HISTORICAL FINANCIALS

Company Type: Public

Income Statement

FYE: December 31

	REVENUE ($ mil.)	NET INCOME ($ mil.)	NET PROFIT MARGIN	EMPLOYEES
12/05	478.2	21.8	4.6%	982
12/04	361.6	13.4	3.7%	908
12/03	244.4	2.6	1.1%	796
12/02	232.6	1.0	0.4%	716
12/01	251.6	2.3	0.9%	987
Annual Growth	17.4%	75.5%	—	(0.1%)

2005 Year-End Financials

Debt ratio: 25.0%
Return on equity: 12.6%
Cash ($ mil.): 4.8
Current ratio: 3.69
Long-term debt ($ mil.): 52.1
No. of shares (mil.): 12.0
Dividends
  Yield: —
  Payout: —
Market value ($ mil.): 315.2
R&D as % of sales: —
Advertising as % of sales: —

Stock History

NASDAQ (GS): GEHL

	STOCK PRICE ($) FY Close	P/E High/Low		PER SHARE ($) Earnings	Dividends	Book Value
12/05	26.25	18	7	1.97	—	17.36
12/04	15.57	13	6	1.47	—	20.55
12/03	9.43	33	15	0.33	—	18.37
12/02	5.81	87	43	0.13	—	17.89
12/01	9.93	45	24	0.28	—	18.66
Annual Growth	27.5%	—	—	62.9%	—	(1.8%)

GeoPharma

GeoPharma makes OTC drugs, vitamins, and health and beauty care products, primarily as a contract manufacturer through subsidiaries Innovative Health Products and Belcher Pharmaceutical. The company also makes proprietary products, including Nutrisure (meal replacement powder), Arth-Aid (arthritis cream), and the Physician's Pharmaceuticals brand of dietary supplements. Subsidiary Breakthrough Engineered Nutrition markets the Lean Protein line of high-protein snacks and OxyFirm, a supplement that purportedly improves oxygen and nutrient delivery in the body. Pharmacy benefit management services are offered by subsidiary Go2PBM Services. The Taneja family owns about a quarter of the company.

In 2005 the company acquired Consolidated Pharmaceutical Group, an antibiotic maker, and created American Antibiotics to oversee the newly acquired operations. Consolidated Pharmaceuticals makes several penicillin-based antibiotics, including Amoxicillin.

In 2006 GeoPharma formed a new subsidiary, Libi Labs, to create nutraceutical and cosmeceutical products.

Former director Joseph Zappala owns about 8% of the company.

EXECUTIVES

Chairman: Jugal K. Taneja, age 62
CEO, Secretary, and Director: Mihir K. Taneja, age 31, $266,425 pay
President and Director: Kotha S. Sekharam, age 55, $214,076 pay
VP, CFO, and Director: Carol Dore-Falcone, age 41, $201,053 pay
President, Belcher Pharmaceuticals:
  Joseph Mastronardy
President, Innovative Health Products:
  Robert A. Herrmann Jr., age 57
Auditors: Brimmer, Burek & Keelan LLP

LOCATIONS

HQ: GeoPharma, Inc.
    6950 Bryan Dairy Rd., Largo, FL 33777
Phone: 727-544-8866   **Fax:** 727-544-4386
Web: www.onlineihp.com

PRODUCTS/OPERATIONS

2006 Sales

	$ mil.	% of total
Manufacturing	17.9	36
PBM	16.6	33
Distribution	14.7	30
Pharmaceuticals	0.5	1
Total	**49.7**	**100**

Selected Branded Products

Arth-Aid (arthritis cream and roll-on)
Lean Protein (line of high protein/low carbohydrate snacks)
Nutri-Sure (meal replacement powder mix)
Physicians' Pharmaceuticals (dietary supplement product line)

COMPETITORS

Bactolac Pharmaceutical	NBTY
BJ's Wholesale Club	Nutraceutical
Costco Wholesale	Reliv'
CVS	Shaklee
Enzymatic Therapy, Inc.	Unicity
Express Scripts	USANA Health Sciences
Natural Alternatives	Walgreen
Nature's Sunshine	

HISTORICAL FINANCIALS

Company Type: Public

Income Statement   FYE: March 31

	REVENUE ($ mil.)	NET INCOME ($ mil.)	NET PROFIT MARGIN	EMPLOYEES
3/06	49.7	1.8	3.6%	150
3/05	28.2	(0.9)	—	—
3/04	23.0	1.1	4.8%	83
3/03	14.7	1.1	7.5%	68
3/02	9.0	(1.1)	—	67
Annual Growth	**53.3%**	**—**	**—**	**22.3%**

2006 Year-End Financials

Debt ratio: 7.8%
Return on equity: 9.7%
Cash ($ mil.): 1.6
Current ratio: 1.87
Long-term debt ($ mil.): 1.7
No. of shares (mil.): 10.1
Dividends
  Yield: —
  Payout: —
Market value ($ mil.): 43.7
R&D as % of sales: 1.0%
Advertising as % of sales: 3.2%

Stock History   NASDAQ (CM): GORX

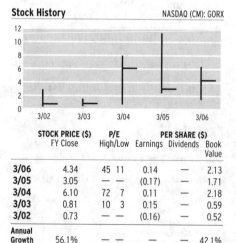

	STOCK PRICE ($) FY Close	P/E High/Low	PER SHARE ($) Earnings	Dividends	Book Value
3/06	4.34	45 11	0.14	—	2.13
3/05	3.05	— —	(0.17)	—	1.71
3/04	6.10	72 7	0.11	—	2.18
3/03	0.81	10 3	0.15	—	0.59
3/02	0.73	— —	(0.16)	—	0.52
Annual Growth	**56.1%**	**— —**	**—**	**—**	**42.1%**

GFI Group

A financial matchmaker, GFI Group makes sure the party of the first part gets together with the party of the second part. The company is an inter-dealer brokerage that acts as an intermediary for institutional clients such as banks, brokers, insurance companies, hedge funds, and utilities. The firm trades primarily in derivatives, and also offers data and analytical tools for market analysis: its FENIC software is used for the foreign exchange market and its MarketHub tool is designed for cross-asset analysis. Jersey Partners, which is controlled by chairman and CEO Michael Gooch, owns about 49% of GFI.

GFI made headlines in August 2005 when it acquired leading oil products broker Starsupply Petroleum LLC. GFI embarked on a joint venture with London-based shipbroker ACM Shipping in 2002; together the companies launched FreightMatch, a screen-based trading service, in 2005.

EXECUTIVES

Chairman and CEO: Michael Gooch, age 47, $1,150,000 pay
President and Director: Colin Heffron, age 43, $1,600,000 pay
COO: Ron Levi, age 44
CFO: James A. Peers, age 55, $550,000 pay
EVP, Corporate Development: J. Christopher Giancarlo, age 46
Global Head of Product Marketing: Michel Everaert, age 37
Senior Managing Director and Head of Asia: Jurgen Breuer, age 40, $952,159 pay
Senior Managing Director, Head of Europe: Stephen (Steve) McMillan, age 43, $1,587,193 pay
Senior Managing Director, Head of North America: Donald P. (Don) Fewer, age 41, $7,350,000 pay
Global Human Resources Director: Sheena Griffiths, age 40
Auditors: Deloitte & Touche LLP

LOCATIONS

HQ: GFI Group Inc.
    100 Wall St., New York, NY 10005
Phone: 212-968-4100   **Fax:** 212-968-4124
Web: www.gfigroup.com

GFI has offices in New York City, as well as in Hong Kong, London, Paris, Singapore, Sydney, and Tokyo.

2005 Sales

	% of total
North America	51
Europe	42
Asia-Pacific	7
Total	**100**

PRODUCTS/OPERATIONS

2005 Sales

	$ mil.	% of total
Brokerage		
Agency commissions	391.6	73
Principal transactions	114.4	21
Analytics and market data	17.4	4
Interest	4.6	1
Other	5.6	1
Total	**533.6**	**100**

COMPETITORS

Cantor Fitzgerald
ICAP
Interactive Brokers
Maxcor
Susquehanna International Group, LLP
VIEL

HISTORICAL FINANCIALS

Company Type: Public

Income Statement   FYE: December 31

	REVENUE ($ mil.)	NET INCOME ($ mil.)	NET PROFIT MARGIN	EMPLOYEES
12/05	533.6	48.1	9.0%	1,151
12/04	385.0	23.1	6.0%	868
12/03	265.8	14.5	5.5%	668
12/02	275.2	12.3	4.5%	655
12/01	220.4	(31.8)	—	572
Annual Growth	**24.7%**	**—**	**—**	**19.1%**

2005 Year-End Financials

Debt ratio: 13.1%
Return on equity: 36.6%
Cash ($ mil.): 152.0
Current ratio: —
Long-term debt ($ mil.): 31.3
No. of shares (mil.): 27.9
Dividends
  Yield: —
  Payout: —
Market value ($ mil.): 1,323.5
R&D as % of sales: —
Advertising as % of sales: —

Stock History   NASDAQ (GS): GFIG

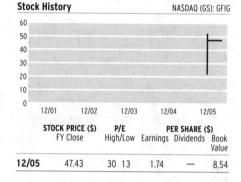

	STOCK PRICE ($) FY Close	P/E High/Low	PER SHARE ($) Earnings	Dividends	Book Value
12/05	47.43	30 13	1.74	—	8.54

Gladstone Capital

If your fledgling company shows promise, Gladstone Capital might be glad to provide some capital. The business development company (BDC) provides loans ($5 million–$15 million) to small and medium-sized family-owned companies or firms backed by leveraged buyout funds or venture capital outfits. Gladstone Capital particularly targets firms undergoing ownership transitions. The firm hopes to shepherd its portfolio companies through a merger, acquisition, or initial public offering to receive a return on its investment. Affiliated company Gladstone Management Corporation provides management services to the firm's portfolio companies. Subsidiary Gladstone Business Loan holds the firm's loan investment portfolio.

Gladstone typically does not invest in technology, financial services, real estate, or oil and gas concerns. The company also does not usually back turnaround situations.

EXECUTIVES

Chairman and CEO: David Gladstone, age 63
Vice Chairman and COO: Terry Lee Brubaker, age 62
President, Chief Investment Officer, and Director:
George (Chip) Stelljes III, age 44
CFO and Treasurer: Harry Brill, age 59
Investor Relations Manager: Kelly Sargent
Compliance Officer: Allyson K. Williams
Controller: Donya Kolcio
Human Resources and Chief Compliance Officer:
Paula Novara
Auditors: PricewaterhouseCoopers LLP

LOCATIONS

HQ: Gladstone Capital Corporation
1521 Westbranch Dr., Ste. 200, McLean, VA 22102
Phone: 703-287-5800   **Fax:** 703-287-5801
Web: www.gladstonecapital.com

PRODUCTS/OPERATIONS

2006 Sales

	% of total
Interest income	97
Prepayment fees & other	3
Total	**100**

Selected Investments

Advanced Homecare Management (home health care services)
Allied Extruders Inc. (polyethylene film manufacturing)
Alstyle Apparel (active wear manufacturer and distributor)
America's Water Heater Rentals
Badanco Enterprises (luggage manufacturing)
Bear Creek Corporation (fresh fruit and gourmet foods production and marketing)
Benetech (dust management systems for the coal and electric utility industries)
Burt's Bees Wax (lip, hair, and oral care products)
Choice Cable TV (cable television and broadband Internet provider)
Consolidated Bedding (mattress manufacturing)
Coyne Textile Services (industrial laundry operations)
Environmental Reclamation Services, Inc. (printer and wireless communications aftermarket products and services)
Express Courier, Inc (ground delivery and logistics services)
Finn Corporation (landscape and erosion-control equipment)
Gammill Quilting Systems (quilting machines and accessories)
Global Material Technologies, Inc. (steel wool and metal fiber products manufacturer)
Home Care Supply (home health care equipment distributor)
INCA Metal Products (material-handling products manufacturer)
It's Just Lunch Holdings, LLC (matchmaking service franchisor)
John Henry Company (printing and packaging)
Local Tel Yellow Pages, Inc (directory publisher)
Maidenform (intimate apparel)
Marietta Corporation (personal care products manufacturer and supplier)
MD Beauty (cosmetics and skin care)
MedAssets (group purchasing organization)
Mistras/Conam (non-destructive testing)
Network Solutions, LLC (Internet domain-name registration and services)
NextiraOne (integrated enterprise network software and services)

Penn Engineering (specialty fasteners and fractional horsepower motor manufacturer)
Polar Corporation (trailers, trailer parts, repair, and services)
Quiznos Subs (sandwich store franchisor)
Santana Plastic Products (plastic partitions, dividers, and similar products)
Sea Con Phoenix, Inc. (underwater and harsh-environment components manufacturer)
Specialty Coating Systems (parylene coatings)
Survey Sampling International (online and telephone samples and research)
Tech Lighting, LLC (low-voltage lighting)
Thibaut (wallpaper and décor fabric)
Visual Edge Technology (copier and printer distribution, sales, and service)
Westlake Hardware, Inc. (home hardware retailer)
Winchester Electronics (specialty connectors and cables)
Wing Stop (restaurant franchisor)
Woven Electronics Corporation (electrical cable assemblies, harnessing, and electronic interconnections)
Xspedius Communications (CLEC, or competitive local exchange carrier)

COMPETITORS

Allied Capital
American Capital Strategies
MCG Capital
MVC Capital

HISTORICAL FINANCIALS

Company Type: Public

Income Statement

FYE: September 30

	REVENUE ($ mil.)	NET INCOME ($ mil.)	NET PROFIT MARGIN	EMPLOYEES
9/06	32.9	24.4	74.2%	—
9/05	24.0	15.5	64.6%	—
9/04	20.4	10.6	52.0%	—
9/03	15.1	11.1	73.5%	15
9/02	10.5	7.6	72.4%	13
Annual Growth	**33.0%**	**33.9%**	**—**	**—**

2006 Year-End Financials

Debt ratio: 29.1%
Return on equity: 15.1%
Cash ($ mil.): 0.7
Current ratio: —
Long-term debt ($ mil.): 50.2
No. of shares (mil.): 12.3
Dividends
  Yield: 2.5%
  Payout: 26.2%
Market value ($ mil.): 270.8
R&D as % of sales: —
Advertising as % of sales: —

Stock History

NASDAQ (GS): GLAD

	STOCK PRICE ($) FY Close	P/E High	P/E Low	PER SHARE ($) Earnings	PER SHARE ($) Dividends	PER SHARE ($) Book Value
9/06	22.01	11	9	2.10	0.55	14.02
9/05	22.55	20	15	1.33	0.50	13.41
9/04	22.71	23	19	1.02	0.46	13.50
9/03	19.45	19	13	1.09	1.10	12.97
9/02	16.88	26	21	0.75	0.81	12.97
Annual Growth	**6.9%**	**—**	**—**	**29.4%**	**(9.2%)**	**2.0%**

Global Entertainment

Global Entertainment Corporation is helping to bring sports to the hinterlands. The company, through its subsidiaries, offers project management services to small communities looking to develop event centers and sports facilities. It also offers facilities management services, as well as sponsorship and marketing consulting. Through its WPHL subsidiary, Global Entertainment manages Central Hockey League, a development league affiliated with the National Hockey League. In addition, the company's Cragar Industries unit licenses the Cragar brand to automobile aftermarket manufacturers. WPHL Holdings, a group that includes chairman James Treliving and his son Brad Treliving, controls more than 40% of the company.

Having built up its portfolio of subsidiaries, the company has been focused on growing its business units by coordinating their activities together, creating a one-stop-shop for communities looking to develop and operate sports arenas. Its International Coliseums project management subsidiary for instance, opened three new facilities in 2006 in time for the new CHL season, which has expanded to 18 teams.

EXECUTIVES

Chairman: James Treliving, age 64
President, CEO, and Director; Chairman and President, WPHL: Richard (Rich) Kozuback, age 52, $200,000 pay
EVP; President, Central Hockey League:
Bradford (Brad) Treliving, age 36, $145,500 pay
SVP and CFO: J. Craig Johnson, age 43, $145,500 pay
President, Global Entertainment Marketing Systems:
Wayne H. Davis, age 46
President, International Coliseums Company:
Daniel Vaillant
President, Facility Management Company: Tom Sadler
President, Global Properties: Steven J. Bielewicz
VP Operations, Facility Management Company:
Roger J. Swanson
Secretary and Director: George Melville, age 61
Auditors: Semple & Cooper, LLP

LOCATIONS

HQ: Global Entertainment Corporation
4909 E. McDowell Rd., Ste. 104, Phoenix, AZ 85008
Phone: 480-994-0772   **Fax:** 480-994-0759
Web: www.globalentertainment2000.com

PRODUCTS/OPERATIONS

2006 Sales

	$ mil.	% of total
Project management fees	7.7	54
Licensing & advertising	2.7	19
Ticket service fees	1.9	13
Facility management fees	1.8	12
Franchise fees	0.1	1
Other	0.1	1
Total	**14.3**	**100**

Selected Subsidiaries

Cragar International (automobile aftermarket product licensing)
Encore Facility Management (facility management services)
Global Entertainment Marketing Systems (GEMS, arena marketing and event promotion)
Global Entertainment Ticketing (GetTix.com, online ticket sales)
International Coliseums Company (event arena development and management)
Western Professional Hockey League (WPHL, management and operation of Central Hockey League)

COMPETITORS

AFL	NAPBL
American Eagle Wheel	NASCAR
American Racing	NBA
Equipment	NFL
Anschutz Entertainment	NHL
Comcast Spectacor	SMG Management
Front Row Marketing	Superior Industries
Hayes Lemmerz	Ticketmaster
Major League Baseball	Tickets.com
Major League Soccer	Titan International
MISL	World Wrestling

HISTORICAL FINANCIALS

Company Type: Public

Income Statement

FYE: May 31

	REVENUE ($ mil.)	NET INCOME ($ mil.)	NET PROFIT MARGIN	EMPLOYEES
5/06	14.3	0.3	2.1%	453
5/05	13.5	0.4	3.0%	110
5/04	5.3	0.9	17.0%	—
5/03	3.8	0.6	15.8%	—
Annual Growth	55.5%	(20.6%)	—	311.8%

2006 Year-End Financials

Debt ratio: —
Return on equity: 3.7%
Cash ($ mil.): 5.4
Current ratio: 2.26
Long-term debt ($ mil.): —
No. of shares (mil.): 6.5

Dividends
Yield: —
Payout: —
Market value ($ mil.): 44.8
R&D as % of sales: —
Advertising as % of sales: —

Stock History

AMEX: GEE

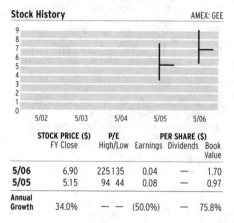

	STOCK PRICE ($) FY Close	P/E High/Low	PER SHARE ($) Earnings	Dividends	Book Value
5/06	6.90	225 135	0.04	—	1.70
5/05	5.15	94 44	0.08	—	0.97
Annual Growth	34.0%	— —	(50.0%)	—	75.8%

Globalstar

Is the success of another mobile phone network written in the stars? Globalstar hopes so. The satellite communications company bets on simplicity with a "bent pipe" design: Because its earthbound gateways connect to terrestrial phone networks, the system avoids complex in-orbit switching and satellite-to-satellite transmissions envisioned for other networks. It serves up voice and data using digital CDMA (code division multiple access) technology developed by Globalstar co-founder QUALCOMM. The firm's satellites bounce calls from special mobile phones back to ground-based gateways connected to traditional phone networks. Private equity firm Thermo Capital Partners owns 63% of Globalstar; QUALCOMM owns 7%.

Globalstar's star shone bright during recent natural disasters. In the wake of hurricanes Katrina and Rita, which devastated the US Gulf Coast, and the disastrous tsunami that caused massive loss of life and property in Asia, Globalstar's network provided reliable communications services, and its customer base rose to more than 200,000.

The company's history, however, provides another example of how tough it is to get a satellite phone service off the ground and keep it there. Having emerged in 2004 after two years of financial restructuring under bankruptcy protection, it has fared better than would-be rivals Iridium Satellite (formerly known as Iridium before its spectacular flameout in 2000) and New ICO (previously ICO Global Communications).

Globalstar, which has provided uninterrupted service throughout its financing woes, has shifted its focus away from terrestrial cellular markets toward remote areas where cell phone service is not a viable option. Target industries include oil, gas, and maritime. It also provides asset tracking and monitoring services.

The company, which relies on such traditional cellular partners as Vodafone and China Mobile (Hong Kong) to provide retail service, acts as a wholesale supplier of network capacity.

What's the catch? Globalstar's service is more expensive than conventional cellular; its handsets are bulkier and more costly. And the company has discovered that while the competition to provide telephone service is sparse in the world's most remote regions, so are the customers.

HISTORY

Ford Aerospace, a subsidiary of Ford Motor Company, had the concept of developing mobile communications for automobiles in 1986, but the idea was soon abandoned. In 1990 Ford Aerospace was acquired by Loral Corp. and the satellite manufacturing unit, based in Palo Alto, California, was renamed Space Systems/Loral (SS/Loral).

A year later Loral and QUALCOMM announced Globalstar, an $850 million, 48-satellite system designed to compete with Motorola's Iridium project (which shut down in 2000 but reemerged as Iridium Satellite, snatched from bankruptcy by a defense contract).

Incorporated in 1994, the venture went public the next year as Globalstar Telecommunications (a holding company and general partner of operating unit Globalstar, L.P.). Loral and Lockheed Martin merged in 1996, giving Lockheed Martin a 20% stake in Globalstar. Loral's space and communications interests, including Globalstar, transferred to Loral Space & Communications.

In early 1998 Globalstar launched its first four satellites; days later, QUALCOMM chairman Irwin Jacobs placed a call to Globalstar CEO Bernard Schwartz. The San Diego-to-New York phone call validated the use of QUALCOMM's code division multiple access (CDMA) technology. Three more launches of four satellites each quickly followed. However, a rocket malfunction on another launch cost the company 12 satellites.

Globalstar began 1999 with two successful launches of four satellites each, and completed the launch of the satellite constellation in 2000. That year it commenced commercial operations in several countries. The company raised hackles among doubters, however, when it drew down a $250 million bank line of credit, then immediately defaulted — leaving such partners as QUALCOMM and Lockheed Martin (who had guaranteed the loan) to repay.

In 2001 Globalstar suspended payments on its debt to conserve cash for operations. Schwartz stepped down as chairman and CEO that year, and Inmarsat veteran Olof Lundberg took over.

The company cut its workforce by more than 70% in order to maintain enough cash to continue operations, and in 2001 it began negotiating with creditors on a restructuring plan. In 2002 Globalstar, L.P. filed for Chapter 11 bankruptcy protection under the shadow of $3.3 billion in debt.

The next year Thermo Capital agreed to pay $43 million for a controlling stake in the company (with the remaining equity distributed among creditors) and Globalstar came out of bankruptcy in 2004 with no debt and about 100,000 subscribers. That same year Jay Monroe was elected chairman; he became CEO in 2005.

EXECUTIVES

Chairman and CEO: James (Jay) Monroe III, age 51
President, Global Operations:
Anthony J. (Tony) Navarra, age 58
SVP, Engineering and Ground Operations:
Robert D. (Bob) Miller, age 42
SVP, International Sales, Marketing and Customer Care; General Manager, Globalstar Canada:
Steven F. Bell, age 42
SVP, Sales and Marketing: Dennis C. Allen, age 55
SVP, Strategic Initiatives and Space Operations:
Megan L. Fitzgerald, age 46
VP and CFO: Fuad Ahmad, age 36
VP, Engineering and Product Development:
Paul A. Monte, age 47
VP, Legal and Regulatory Affairs: William F. (Bill) Adler, age 60
Secretary and Director: Richard S. Roberts, age 60
Media Contact: Dean Hirasawa
Human Resources Specialist: Carla Filipe
Auditors: GHP Horwath, PC; Crowe Chizek and Company LLP

LOCATIONS

HQ: Globalstar, Inc.
461 S. Milpitas Blvd., Milpitas, CA 95035
Phone: 408-933-4000   **Fax:** 408-933-4100
Web: www.globalstar.com

2005 Sales

	$ mil.	% of total
Service		
US	37.3	29
Canada	32.8	.26
Europe	5.7	4
Central & South America	3.2	3
Other regions	2.5	2
Subscriber equipment		
US	24.7	19
Canada	12.7	10
Europe	4.4	4
Central & South America	1.4	1
Other regions	2.5	2
Total	**127.2**	**100**

PRODUCTS/OPERATIONS

2005 Sales

	$ mil.	% of total
Services		
Voice & Data		
Mobile	60.1	47
Fixed	6.6	5
Independent gateway operators	9.1	7
Satellite data modems	1.2	1
Asset tracking & monitoring	0.9	1
Other	3.5	3
Subscriber equipment sales		
Mobile equipment	23.7	19
Fixed equipment	5.3	4
Data equipment	1.1	1
Accessories & other	15.7	12
Total	**127.2**	**100**

Selected Partners

AXONN, LLC
Guardian Mobility Corporation
QUALCOMM
Space Systems/Loral, Inc.
Spatial Data, Inc.
WaveCall Communications, Inc.

COMPETITORS

ICO Global Communications
Inmarsat
Iridium Satellite
Mobile Satellite Ventures
Optus

HISTORICAL FINANCIALS

Company Type: Public

Income Statement

FYE: December 31

	REVENUE ($ mil.)	NET INCOME ($ mil.)	NET PROFIT MARGIN	EMPLOYEES
12/05	127.2	18.7	14.7%	316
12/04	84.4	0.4	0.5%	—
12/03	60.2	(266.4)	—	—
12/02	0.0	(55.2)	—	148
12/01	0.0	(142.3)	—	124
Annual Growth	—	—	—	26.3%

2005 Year-End Financials

Debt ratio: 0.9%
Return on equity: 33.4%
Cash ($ mil.): 20.3
Current ratio: 2.50
Long-term debt ($ mil.): 0.6

Net Income History

NASDAQ (GM): GSAT

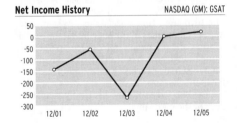

GMX Resources

The natural resources in productive, hydrocarbon-rich geological basins are the target for GMX Resources. The Oklahoma-based independent oil and natural gas company explores on more than 17,160 combined net acres located in the Sabine Uplift in Texas and Louisiana, and the Tatum basin in New Mexico. With 60 net producing wells, GMX Resources has proved reserves of 162 billion cu. ft. of natural gas equivalent. It has a large inventory of drilling and recompletion projects with an estimated 115.9 billion cu. ft. of natural gas equivalent of proved undeveloped reserves. Ken L. Kenworthy Jr. and Ken L. Kenworthy Sr. own 14% and 8% of the company, respectively.

President and petroleum geologist Ken Kenworthy Jr. and his father Ken L. Kenworthy Sr. founded GMX Resources in 1998. The company is pursuing a strategy of developing its proved undeveloped properties in East Texas.

EXECUTIVES

President, CEO, and Director: Ken L. Kenworthy Jr., age 49, $225,000 pay
EVP, CFO, Secretary, Treasurer, and Director: Ken L. Kenworthy Sr., age 70, $225,000 pay
VP Land: Kyle Kenworthy
Operations Manager: Rick Hart Jr.
Assistant Production and Engineering Operations: Monnie Dehart
VP Gas Marketing: Keith Leffel
Land Division Order Analyst: Debra Barker
Production Analyst: Diane Newman
Geology Technician and Webmaster: Marilyn Leonard
Office Manager and Administrator, Public Relations and Payroll: Amber Croisant
Controller: James Merrill
Auditors: KPMG LLP

LOCATIONS

HQ: GMX Resources Inc.
9400 N. Broadway, Ste. 600,
Oklahoma City, OK 73114
Phone: 405-600-0711   **Fax:** 405-600-0600
Web: www.gmxresources.com

2005 Net Acreage

	% of total
East Texas/Louisiana	98
Southeast New Mexico	2
Total	**100**

PRODUCTS/OPERATIONS

2005 Proved Reserves

	% of total
Natural gas	93
Crude oil	7
Total	**100**

COMPETITORS

BP
Cabot Oil & Gas
Chevron
Devon Energy
Exxon Mobil
Frontier Oil
Pogo Producing
Royal Dutch Shell
Southwestern Energy

HISTORICAL FINANCIALS

Company Type: Public

Income Statement

FYE: December 31

	REVENUE ($ mil.)	NET INCOME ($ mil.)	NET PROFIT MARGIN	EMPLOYEES
12/05	19.2	7.2	37.5%	16
12/04	7.8	1.4	17.9%	18
12/03	5.4	0.5	9.3%	8
12/02	6.0	(0.4)	—	16
12/01	6.4	1.1	17.2%	18
Annual Growth	31.6%	60.0%	—	(2.9%)

2005 Year-End Financials

Debt ratio: 2.3%
Return on equity: 15.4%
Cash ($ mil.): 2.4
Current ratio: 0.49
Long-term debt ($ mil.): 1.4
No. of shares (mil.): 10.0
Dividends
 Yield: —
 Payout: —
Market value ($ mil.): 359.1
R&D as % of sales: —
Advertising as % of sales: —

Stock History

NASDAQ (GM): GMXR

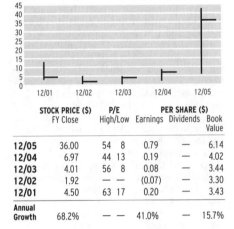

	STOCK PRICE ($) FY Close	P/E High/Low		Earnings	Dividends	Book Value
12/05	36.00	54	8	0.79	—	6.14
12/04	6.97	44	13	0.19	—	4.02
12/03	4.01	56	8	0.08	—	3.44
12/02	1.92	—	—	(0.07)	—	3.30
12/01	4.50	63	17	0.20	—	3.43
Annual Growth	68.2%	—	—	41.0%	—	15.7%

Green Mountain Coffee Roasters

Green Mountain Coffee Roasters' business amounts to more than a hill of beans. The company roasts about 100 varieties of Arabica coffee, which it sells to more than 8,000 wholesale customers including supermarkets, convenience stores, resorts, and office delivery services. Among its customers are more than 1,000 convenience stores operated by ExxonMobil. Green Mountain coffee is sold under the Newman's Own Organics brand, as well as the Green Mountain Coffee label. The company also markets its coffees and related accessories via catalogs and the Internet. Chairman and CEO Robert Stiller owns about 32% of Green Mountain.

Supermarket and convenience store sales account for about 55% of the company's coffee sales. In the early 2000s the company began shipments to Wild Oats Markets and Costco Wholesale. Green Mountain's flagship customers, such as Amtrak and Sodexho, have improved the company's visibility and aided its expansion across the US from its roots on the East Coast. The company currently ships about

45% of its coffee to customers in New England. Green Mountain Coffee has also increased its visibility through a partnership with Ben & Jerry's Homemade with a roll out of co-branded ice cream shop-coffee houses. Green Mountain is pinning growth hopes to the trend of "single-cup" brewers. The company had been a minority owner of single-cup brewing-system manufacturer Keurig since 2002. In 2006 Green Mountain acquired the remaining 65% of Keurig that it did not already own for $104 million. That year it also announced that in conjunction with International Paper, it created an environmentally friendly coffee cup made of corn, natural paper, and water, which, unlike traditional paper cups, will breakdown into organic matter after use. Green Mountain plans to use the new cup in all of its US outlets.

HISTORY

In 1981 Robert Stiller had his first cup of Green Mountain coffee at a small Vermont coffee shop. He was so impressed, he bought the one-store company (using proceeds from the sale of E-Z Wider, the marijuana-rolling-paper-business he co-founded in 1971). Stiller sought a wider market, and in 1984 he began generating word-of-mouth business by donating coffee to charities and civic groups and placing mail-order ads. By 1985 Green Mountain Coffee had four stores and was turning a profit.

Using direct-mail sales as a vanguard, Green Mountain continued its efforts to build a multi-channel distribution network. It was successful: Supermarkets began selling Green Mountain coffees, and institutions such as the Harvard Club began serving them. The company added retail locations in the late 1980s and early 1990s and went public in 1993. It had 12 stores by 1994, but earnings suffered as Green Mountain's expansion outpaced its sales growth.

The company began selling its products online in 1995, and Business Express Airlines began serving Green Mountain coffee on its flights in the US and Canada. Delta Air Lines' shuttle service followed suit the next year. Green Mountain signed a five-year agreement with Mobil Oil (later, ExxonMobil) in 1997 to provide coffee at its On The Run convenience stores.

Green Mountain inked a deal in 1998 with American Skiing Company to supply its nine US ski resorts, including Vermont's Killington and Sugarbush resorts. Also that year it expanded its organic coffee line, revamped its Web site, and began closing or selling its retail operations to concentrate on its wholesale business; all stores were closed by August 1999. Also in 1999 Green Mountain partnered with Keurig to offer one-cup brewing varieties of its coffees.

In 2000 the company agreed to supply coffee to more than 900 (up from nearly 500) ExxonMobil corporately owned convenience stores; as part of the deal, Green Mountain also became the recommended coffee to about 13,000 ExxonMobil dealer and franchise store locations. In mid-2001 Green Mountain purchased the Frontier Organic Coffee brand from Frontier Natural Products Co-op for about $2.4 million.

Green Mountain began selling coffee under the Newman's Own name in 2003. That same year, the company signed an agreement with Hain Celestial Group to sell a line of teas.

In 2004 the company expanded its Vermont manufacturing and distribution facility with a 52,000-sq.-ft. warehouse and packaging plant.

The added space boosted Green Mountain annual production capacity from 17 million pounds of coffee to 50 million pounds. Also in 2004, the company announced plans to sell Heifer Hope Blend, an organic coffee that generates income for Heifer Project International. The organization provides support and training for coffee farmers in Guatemala.

EXECUTIVES

Chairman, President, and CEO: Robert P. (Bob) Stiller, age 62, $353,846 pay
COO: Richard Scott McCreary, age 46, $240,000 pay
VP, CFO, Treasurer, and Director: Frances G. Rathke, age 48, $206,000 pay
VP and CIO: James K. Prevo, age 52, $175,819 pay
VP, Development: Stephen J. (Steve) Sabol, age 44, $170,717 pay
VP, Finance; Secretary; and Treasurer: Robert D. (Bob) Britt, age 46, $175,134 pay
VP, Human Resources and Organizational Development: Kathryn S. Brooks, age 50
VP, Sales: James (Jim) Travis
VP, Marketing: T. J. Whalen
VP, Operations: Jonathan C. Wettstein, age 56, $170,000 pay
Director, Sustainable Coffee: Liam Brody
Manager, Corporate Quality: Don Holly
Investor Services Coordinator: Maureen Martin
Auditors: PricewaterhouseCoopers LLP

LOCATIONS

HQ: Green Mountain Coffee Roasters, Inc.
33 Coffee Ln., Waterbury, VT 05676
Phone: 802-244-5621 **Fax:** 802-244-5436
Web: www.greenmountaincoffee.com

Green Mountain Coffee has operations in Connecticut, Maine, Massachusetts, New York, and Vermont.

PRODUCTS/OPERATIONS

2006 Coffee Shipped

	% of total
Supermarkets	26
Office coffee service	26
Convenience stores	24
Food service	20
Consumer direct	4
Total	**100**

COMPETITORS

Bucks County Nut and Coffee	Kraft Foods
	Mars
Cafe Britt Coffee	Nestlé
Caribou Coffee	Peet's
Community Coffee	Procter & Gamble
Diedrich Coffee	Sara Lee Food & Beverage
Dunkin	Starbucks
Farmer Bros.	Van Houtte
Hawaii Coffee	

HISTORICAL FINANCIALS

Company Type: Public

Income Statement

FYE: Last Saturday in September

	REVENUE ($ mil.)	NET INCOME ($ mil.)	NET PROFIT MARGIN	EMPLOYEES
9/06	225.3	8.4	3.7%	849
9/05	161.5	9.0	5.6%	676
9/04	137.4	7.8	5.7%	608
9/03	116.7	6.3	5.4%	573
9/02	100.0	6.0	6.0%	529
Annual Growth	**22.5%**	**8.8%**	**—**	**12.6%**

2006 Year-End Financials

Debt ratio: 137.3%	Dividends
Return on equity: 12.4%	Yield: —
Cash ($ mil.): 1.3	Payout: —
Current ratio: 1.75	Market value ($ mil.): 280.7
Long-term debt ($ mil.): 102.9	R&D as % of sales: —
No. of shares (mil.): 7.6	Advertising as % of sales: —

Stock History

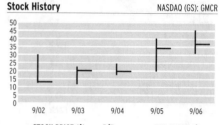

NASDAQ (GS): GMCR

	STOCK PRICE ($) FY Close	P/E High/Low		Earnings	PER SHARE ($) Dividends	Book Value
9/06	36.80	42	29	1.07	—	9.82
9/05	34.16	34	17	1.17	—	8.06
9/04	19.76	23	17	1.06	—	6.23
9/03	20.12	26	14	0.86	—	5.01
9/02	13.05	36	16	0.82	—	3.95
Annual Growth	**29.6%**	**—**	**—**	**6.9%**	**—**	**25.6%**

Greenhill & Co

It's no secret what the favorite color is around the offices of Greenhill & Co. The investment bank specializes in mergers and acquisitions, corporate restructurings, and merchant banking for clients worldwide. Merchant banking activities are conducted through the firm's Greenhill Capital Partners unit, which makes private equity investments typically in the $10 million to $75 million range. Greenhill was founded in 1996 by former Morgan Stanley president Robert Greenhill. The company left the ever-shrinking ranks of independent, privately owned investment banks in May 2004 when it completed its first public stock offering.

In 2005 Greenhill closed its second private equity fund, which raised some $875 million. The firm used the proceeds to invest in mid-market companies in the energy, telecommunications, and financial services sectors. Portfolio companies from Greenhill's first fund include Global Signal, Everlast Energy, and Heartland Payment Systems.

CEO Bob Greenhill and his family own about 20% of the company.

EXECUTIVES

Chairman and CEO: Robert F. (Bob) Greenhill, age 70, $4,464,838 pay
Vice Chairman: Lord James Blyth of Rowington, age 66
Vice Chairman: Harvey R. Miller, age 73
US President and Director: Scott L. Bok, age 46, $3,060,734 pay
Non-US President and Director: Simon A. Borrows, age 47, $4,364,601 pay
CFO: John D. Liu, age 38, $1,525,477 pay
Chairman, Greenhill Capital Partners: Robert H. (Bob) Niehaus, age 50, $1,487,556 pay
Managing Director, Finance, Regulation, and Operations and Chief Compliance Officer: Harold (Hal) Rodriguez Jr., age 50
Auditors: Ernst & Young LLP

LOCATIONS

HQ: Greenhill & Co, Inc.
    300 Park Ave., 23rd Fl., New York, NY 10022
Phone: 212-389-1500   **Fax:** 212-389-1700
Web: www.greenhill-co.com

Greenhill & Co. has offices in Dallas, Frankfurt, London, and New York.

2005 Sales

	$ mil.	% of total
US	142.4	64
Europe	78.7	36
Total	**221.1**	**100**

PRODUCTS/OPERATIONS

2005 Sales

	$ mil.	% of total
Financial advisory services	142.0	64
Merchant banking fund management & other	79.1	36
Total	**221.1**	**100**

COMPETITORS

Blackstone Group
Citigroup Global Markets
Credit Suisse (USA)
Goldman Sachs
Houlihan Lokey
Jefferies Group
JPMorgan Chase
Lazard
Lehman Brothers
Merrill Lynch
Morgan Stanley
Stephens
Thomas Weisel Partners
UBS Investment Bank
Unterberg, Towbin

HISTORICAL FINANCIALS

Company Type: Public

Income Statement

FYE: December 31

	REVENUE ($ mil.)	NET INCOME ($ mil.)	NET PROFIT MARGIN	EMPLOYEES
12/05	221.1	55.5	25.1%	151
12/04	151.9	38.3	25.2%	127
12/03	126.7	45.4	35.8%	107
12/02	112.6	57.8	51.3%	—
12/01	100.0	35.0	35.0%	—
Annual Growth	**21.9%**	**12.2%**	**—**	**18.8%**

2005 Year-End Financials

Debt ratio: —
Return on equity: 45.9%
Cash ($ mil.): 83.2
Current ratio: —
Long-term debt ($ mil.): —
No. of shares (mil.): 30.9
Dividends
    Yield: 0.8%
    Payout: 24.3%
Market value ($ mil.): 1,734.2
R&D as % of sales: —
Advertising as % of sales: —

Stock History

NYSE: GHL

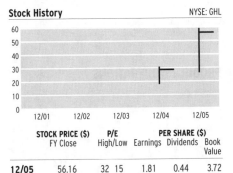

	STOCK PRICE ($) FY Close	P/E High/Low	Earnings	PER SHARE ($) Dividends	Book Value
12/05	56.16	32 15	1.81	0.44	3.72
12/04	28.70	23 14	1.33	0.16	4.14
Annual Growth	**95.7%**	**—**	**36.1%**	**175.0%**	**(10.2%)**

Greenville First Bancshares

Greenville First Bancshares is the holding company for Greenville First Bank, which operates three branches in and near Greenville, South Carolina. The young bank (opened in 2000) targets individuals and small to midsized businesses, selling itself as a local alternative to larger institutions. It offers traditional deposit services and products including checking accounts, savings accounts, and CDs. The bank uses funds from deposits to write mortgages and other real estate loans (more than 80% of its loan book), business loans, and consumer loans. Directors and executive officers collectively own almost a quarter of Greenville First Bancshares.

EXECUTIVES

Chairman: James B. Orders III, age 53
CEO and Director, Greenville First Bancshares and Greenville First Bank: R. Arthur (Art) Seaver Jr., age 42, $280,910 pay (prior to title change)
President, Greenville First Bancshares and Greenville First Bank: F. Justin Strickland
EVP, CFO, and Director, Greenville First Bancshares and Greenville First Bank: James M. (Jim) Austin III, age 49, $196,010 pay
SVP, Secretary, and Director, Greenville First Bancshares and Greenville First Bank: Frederick (Fred) Gilmer Jr., age 70
Director; EVP and Senior Lending Officer, Greenville First Bank: Frederick (Fred) Gilmer III, age 41, $211,535 pay
Director; EVP, Greenville First Bank: J. Edward (Eddie) Terrell, age 43, $169,235 pay
Auditors: Elliott Davis LLC

LOCATIONS

HQ: Greenville First Bancshares, Inc.
    112 Haywood Rd., Greenville, SC 29607
Phone: 864-679-9000   **Fax:** 864-679-9099
Web: www.greenvillefirst.com

PRODUCTS/OPERATIONS

2005 Sales

		$ mil.	% of total
Interest			
	Loans	19.9	89
	Investment securities	1.6	7
	Federal funds sold	0.1	—
Noninterest			
	Service fees on deposit accounts	0.3	1
	Loan fee income	0.2	1
	Other	0.4	2
Total		**22.5**	**100**

COMPETITORS

Bank of America
BB&T
First Citizens Bancorporation
Regions Financial
South Financial
Wachovia

HISTORICAL FINANCIALS

Company Type: Public

Income Statement

FYE: December 31

	ASSETS ($ mil.)	NET INCOME ($ mil.)	INCOME AS % OF ASSETS	EMPLOYEES
12/05	405.3	2.5	0.6%	55
12/04	315.8	2.0	0.6%	—
12/03	230.7	1.0	0.4%	—
12/02	170.4	0.8	0.5%	—
12/01	118.6	(0.1)	—	—
Annual Growth	**36.0%**	**—**	**—**	**—**

2005 Year-End Financials

Equity as % of assets: 7.5%
Return on assets: 0.7%
Return on equity: 8.5%
Long-term debt ($ mil.): 13.4
No. of shares (mil.): 2.7
Market value ($ mil.): 59.8
Dividends
    Yield: —
    Payout: —
Sales ($ mil.): 22.5
R&D as % of sales: —
Advertising as % of sales: —

Stock History

NASDAQ (GM): GVBK

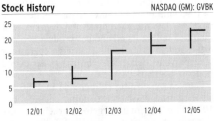

	STOCK PRICE ($) FY Close	P/E High/Low	Earnings	PER SHARE ($) Dividends	Book Value
12/05	22.50	29 22	0.78	—	11.46
12/04	17.83	27 19	0.82	—	10.60
12/03	16.36	34 16	0.48	—	6.49
12/02	7.79	30 16	0.39	—	8.90
12/01	6.88	— —	(0.06)	—	8.23
Annual Growth	**34.5%**	**—**	**—**	**—**	**8.6%**

Grey Wolf

Grey Wolf makes its living hunting down onshore oil and gas drilling contracts. The company performs onshore contract drilling, primarily for natural gas, using a US-based fleet of 111 marketed rigs that can reach depths of up to 40,000 feet. Grey Wolf's operations are focused on six regions: South Texas; West Texas; the Gulf Coast (Texas and Louisiana); Ark-La-Tex (northeastern Texas, northern Louisiana, and southern Arkansas); southern Mississippi and Alabama; and the Rocky Mountains. The company provides rigs, related equipment, and field personnel to customers on a turnkey, footage, or day-work basis.

Grey Wolf, which has survived difficult market conditions for the deep-drilling segment of the industry by selling off noncore assets and cutting personnel and wages, is slowly recovering. It has closed its operations in Venezuela to focus more on the producing regions of the US. Buoyed by rising oil prices, the company has moved into a new drilling market, the Rocky Mountains. It has also expanded its West Texas operations by increasing the number of rigs in this region. Through more

investment in turnkey operations (drilling contracts that pay on completion of the well), Grey Wolf hopes to stabilize revenue growth.

In 2004 the company acquired New Patriot Drilling for $51 million.

HISTORY

Grey Wolf began as an oil and gas exploration and production company, DI Industries, in 1980. In 1985 DI formed subsidiary Drillers, Inc., which specialized in oil and gas contract drilling, because of a sharp increase in demand for drilling rigs. The next year the price of oil collapsed, along with the US market for drilling rigs. DI turned to opportunities in Central and South America and began conducting drilling operations in Argentina, El Salvador, Guatemala, Mexico, and Venezuela.

Increased competition, slack demand, and heavy debt caused the company to struggle in the 1990s, racking up a string of unprofitable years. In 1995 founding CEO Max Dillard resigned. The next year DI embarked on a total overhaul that included selling its oil and gas producing properties and shutting in all its foreign operations (except Venezuela). The company also exited noncore US markets.

Buoyed by surging rig demand in 1996, DI also began aggressively expanding, adding about 100 drilling rigs in its targeted markets. In 1997 the company purchased Grey Wolf Drilling Company, a leading drilling contractor in the Texas and Louisiana Gulf Coast area with 18 rigs, and adopted the corporate name as its own.

In 1998 Grey Wolf bought Murco Drilling Corporation, a Louisiana-based company with 10 rigs operating in the Ark-La-Tex and Mississippi/Alabama markets. Low oil prices suppressed demand for land rigs in 1998, and Grey Wolf cut personnel and sold more noncore assets. It also suspended its drilling activities in Venezuela, the last of its international operations (and subsequently exited the business in 2001).

Lifted by rising oil prices, the company moved into a new drilling market, the Rocky Mountains, through a two-year contract with Burlington Resources. Later that year, Grey Wolf began operations in West Texas and Southeast New Mexico.

EXECUTIVES

Chairman, President, and CEO:
Thomas P. (Tom) Richards, age 62, $1,025,000 pay
EVP, CFO, and Secretary: David W. Wehlmann, age 47, $489,600 pay
SVP Operations: Edward S. Jacob III, age 53, $341,700 pay
VP and Controller: Kent D. Cauley, age 35
VP and Treasurer: Donald J. Guedry Jr., age 49
VP Arkansas, Louisiana, Texas Division:
Forrest M. Conley Jr.
VP Gulf Coast Division: Dale Love
VP Human Resources: Robert J. Proffit, age 50, $194,100 pay
VP Rocky Mountain Division: J.D. Ricks
Operations Manager, South Texas Division:
David Webber
District Manager, West Texas Division:
Oscar L. Bradley Jr.
Auditors: KPMG LLP

LOCATIONS

HQ: Grey Wolf, Inc.
10370 Richmond Ave., Ste. 600, Houston, TX 77042
Phone: 713-435-6100   **Fax:** 713-435-6170
Web: www.gwdrilling.com

Grey Wolf operates in Alabama, Arkansas, Louisiana, Mississippi, Texas, and in the Rocky Mountains.

PRODUCTS/OPERATIONS

2005 Sales

	$ mil.	% of total
Daywork operations	538.3	77
Turnkey operations	158.7	23
Total	**697.0**	**100**

Contract Services

Daywork (drill rigs, related equipment, and personnel only, on a fixed per-day rate)
Footage (fixed amount of payment for each foot drilled)
Turnkey (drill rig, related equipment, personnel, and engineering services, on a fixed price rate)

COMPETITORS

Baker Hughes
Diamond Offshore
ENSCO
GlobalSantaFe
Helmerich & Payne
Nabors Industries
Noble
Parker Drilling
Patterson-UTI Energy
Pioneer Drilling
Precision Drilling
Pride International
Schlumberger
Transocean
Unit Corporation

HISTORICAL FINANCIALS

Company Type: Public

Income Statement

FYE: December 31

	REVENUE ($ mil.)	NET INCOME ($ mil.)	NET PROFIT MARGIN	EMPLOYEES
12/05	697.0	120.6	17.3%	3,200
12/04	424.6	8.1	1.9%	2,900
12/03	286.0	(30.2)	—	1,750
12/02	250.3	(21.5)	—	1,750
12/01	421.5	68.4	16.2%	1,700
Annual Growth	**13.4%**	**15.2%**	**—**	**17.1%**

2005 Year-End Financials

Debt ratio: 74.5%
Return on equity: 39.8%
Cash ($ mil.): 173.9
Current ratio: 3.63
Long-term debt ($ mil.): 275.0
No. of shares (mil.): 192.6
Dividends
  Yield: —
  Payout: —
Market value ($ mil.): 1,489.0
R&D as % of sales: —
Advertising as % of sales: —

Stock History

AMEX: GW

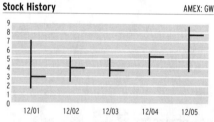

	STOCK PRICE ($) FY Close	P/E High/Low		PER SHARE ($) Earnings	Dividends	Book Value
12/05	7.73	16	7	0.54	—	1.92
12/04	5.27	140	83	0.04	—	1.25
12/03	3.74	—	—	(0.17)	—	1.08
12/02	3.99	—	—	(0.12)	—	1.24
12/01	2.97	18	5	0.38	—	1.36
Annual Growth	**27.0%**	**—**	**—**	**9.2%**	**—**	**9.0%**

GSI Commerce

GSI Commerce is a big dog in online retail. The company creates and operates e-commerce Web sites for about 50 retailers and consumer goods manufacturers in addition to its own fogdog.com sporting goods retail operation. It offers Web site design and hosting services as well as merchandising for such clients as palmOne, Polo Ralph Lauren, Reebok, and Sport Chalet. GSI also offers outsourced order fulfillment and customer service operations. In addition to retailers and manufacturers, the company serves media outlets such as Comedy Central, HBO, and FOX Sports, as well as professional sports teams.

More than 80% of the company's revenue comes from the sale of products for its customers through its two fulfillment centers in Louisville and Shepherdsville, Kentucky. The sale of sporting goods alone accounts for more than half of GSI's business. About 19% of its revenue comes from fees related to its Web site design and maintenance operations.

Founder and CEO Michael Rubin started his career distributing off-price sporting goods through KPR Sports International. His company eventually developed its own brand of footwear (Yukon) and later acquired the RYKA footwear brand.

Changing its name to Global Sports, the company acquired online sports retailer Fogdog in 2000 and Ashford.com, a retailer of luxury goods, in 2002. Also in 2002, it changed its name to GSI Commerce and, later that year, sold Ashford.com.

Rubin owns nearly 20% of the company, along with SOFTBANK (21%) and QVC (20%).

EXECUTIVES

Chairman, President, and CEO: Michael G. Rubin, age 33
EVP Global Operations: Robert (Bob) Wuesthoff
EVP Merchandising: Robert W. (Bob) Liewald, age 56
EVP Strategic Development: Jordan M. Copland, age 44
EVP and CIO: Stephen J. Gold, age 45, $621,020 pay (partial-year salary)
EVP, Secretary, and General Counsel: Arthur H. Miller, age 51, $440,988 pay
EVP Sales; President and COO, GSI Commerce West: Damon Mintzer, age 39, $354,000 pay
SVP and CFO: Michael R. Conn, age 35
SVP Human Resources: James (Jim) Flanagan, age 43
SVP Partner Services: Steven C. Davis, age 32
Director Corporate Communications: Greg Ryan
Auditors: Deloitte & Touche LLP

LOCATIONS

HQ: GSI Commerce, Inc.
935 1st Ave., King of Prussia, PA 19406
Phone: 610-491-7000   **Fax:** 610-491-7366
Web: www.gsicommerce.com

GSI Commerce has offices and operations in King of Prussia, Pennsylvania; Louisville and Shepherdsville, Kentucky; and Melbourne, Florida.

PRODUCTS/OPERATIONS

2005 Sales

	$ mil.	% of total
Products		
Sporting goods	213.0	49
Other	142.4	32
E-commerce services	85.0	19
Total	**440.4**	**100**

COMPETITORS

Accretive Commerce
Amazon.com
Ariba
Art Technology Group
BEA Systems
BroadVision
ClientLogic
commerce5
CyberSource
Digital River
EDS
Foot Locker
IBM
Intershop
Microsoft
NaviSite
Oracle
SAP
StarTek
Sterling Commerce
USinternetworking
ValueVision Media
Vignette

HISTORICAL FINANCIALS

Company Type: Public

Income Statement

	REVENUE ($ mil.)	NET INCOME ($ mil.)	NET PROFIT MARGIN	EMPLOYEES
12/05	440.4	2.7	0.6%	1,729
12/04	335.1	(0.3)	—	1,337
12/03	241.9	(12.1)	—	1,074
12/02	172.6	(33.8)	—	731
12/01	102.6	(30.6)	—	627
Annual Growth	43.9%	—	—	28.9%

FYE: December 31

2005 Year-End Financials

Debt ratio: 46.1%
Return on equity: 2.0%
Cash ($ mil.): 156.7
Current ratio: 2.01
Long-term debt ($ mil.): 70.6
No. of shares (mil.): 44.7
Dividends
  Yield: —
  Payout: —
Market value ($ mil.): 674.1
R&D as % of sales: 6.5%
Advertising as % of sales: 2.4%

Stock History

NASDAQ (GS): GSIC

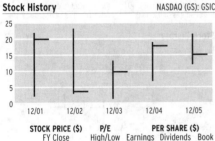

	STOCK PRICE ($) FY Close	P/E High/Low	Earnings	Dividends	Book Value
12/05	15.09	— —	(0.30)	—	3.43
12/04	17.78	— —	(0.01)	—	2.84
12/03	9.75	— —	(0.30)	—	2.71
12/02	3.65	— —	(0.88)	—	3.10
12/01	19.95	— —	(0.90)	—	3.88
Annual Growth	(6.7%)	— —	—	—	(3.1%)

Guaranty Federal Bancshares

Like the Simpsons, Guaranty Bank calls Springfield home. The flagship subsidiary of Guaranty Federal Bancshares serves the Springfield, Missouri, metropolitan area through seven locations, including one branch located inside a Wal-Mart in nearby Nixa. The bank offers CDs and checking, savings, NOW, and money market accounts, mainly using deposit funds to originate real estate loans such as one- to four-family residential mortgages (more than 20% of its loan portfolio), commercial mortgages (28%), multi-family residential loans, and construction loans. Guaranty Bank also writes business and consumer loans. Employees own 9% of the company.

EXECUTIVES

Chairman: Don M. Gibson, age 61
Vice Chairman: Jack L. Barham, age 71
President, CEO, and Director, Guaranty Federal Bancshares and Guaranty Bank: Shaun A. Burke, age 41
EVP and COO, Guaranty Federal Bancshares and Guaranty Bank: Carter M. Peters, age 35
SVP and CFO, Guaranty Federal Bancshares and Guaranty Bank: Bruce Winston, age 56
Director of Corporate Services: Dana Montgomery
Auditors: BKD, LLP

LOCATIONS

HQ: Guaranty Federal Bancshares, Inc.
1341 W. Battlefield, Springfield, MO 65807
Phone: 417-520-4333   **Fax:** 417-520-3607
Web: www.gfed.com

Guaranty Federal Savings Bank has branches in Nixa and Springfield, Missouri.

PRODUCTS/OPERATIONS

2005 Sales

	$ mil.	% of total
Interest		
Loans	26.6	86
Investment securities	0.4	1
Other	0.3	1
Noninterest		
Service charges	1.6	5
Gain on sale of investment securities	0.7	3
Other	1.3	4
Total	**30.9**	**100**

COMPETITORS

Bank of America
Commerce Bancshares
Great Southern Bancorp
NASB Financial
UMB Financial
U.S. Bancorp

HISTORICAL FINANCIALS

Company Type: Public

Income Statement

	ASSETS ($ mil.)	NET INCOME ($ mil.)	INCOME AS % OF ASSETS	EMPLOYEES
12/05	481.0	5.9	1.2%	105
12/04	440.6	4.3	1.0%	130
12/03*	386.8	1.5	0.4%	138
6/03	390.1	3.6	0.9%	138
6/02	376.9	3.6	1.0%	143
Annual Growth	6.3%	13.1%	—	(7.4%)

FYE: December 31
*Fiscal year change

2005 Year-End Financials

Equity as % of assets: 8.8%
Return on assets: 1.3%
Return on equity: 14.2%
Long-term debt ($ mil.): 15.5
No. of shares (mil.): 2.9
Market value ($ mil.): 81.8
Dividends
  Yield: 2.3%
  Payout: 31.5%
Sales ($ mil.): 30.9
R&D as % of sales: —
Advertising as % of sales: —

Stock History

NASDAQ (GM): GFED

	STOCK PRICE ($) FY Close	P/E High/Low	Earnings	Dividends	Book Value
12/05	27.90	14 11	2.03	0.64	14.36
12/04	24.06	16 13	1.47	0.63	13.59
12/03*	19.25	38 28	0.52	0.61	12.69
6/03	24.06	19 15	1.26	—	12.19
6/02	15.66	16 13	1.00	0.50	11.68
Annual Growth	15.5%	— —	19.4%	6.4%	5.3%

*Fiscal year change

Guess?

Guess? wants you to get in its pants. Founded as a designer jeans maker, it now designs and markets trendy, upscale apparel and accessories for men, women, and children. Its trademark sexy ads, which have featured the likes of Claudia Schiffer and Drew Barrymore, are designed in-house. Guess? sells its lines through about 315 retail and outlet stores, to department stores, through some 300 licensee stores in about 50 countries, and on its Web site. Guess? also licenses its name for a wide line of accessories including eyewear, footwear, jewelry, and watches. Maurice and Paul Marciano, brothers of founder Georges Marciano, control about 55% of the company.

Guess? has cut back on some of its licensing by bringing children's apparel in-house. It is also sniffing out business opportunities in perfume, having signed an agreement with Parlux Fragrances to develop and distribute fragrances under the Guess? trademark.

In 2004 Guess? spent the year exploring other markets — the upscale and accessories business. The company reached for a more upscale

customer by rebranding its Guess? Collection as MARCIANO in late 2004 and rolling it out with namesake MARCIANO-exclusive stores. The line is sold at 110 of the company's retail locations in the US and Canada. It has about 15 MARCIANO stores, ranging in size from 2,000 to 4,000 sq. ft.

In early 2005 Guess? licensed its name to Marc Fisher LLC in an exclusive 10-year agreement to develop, make, and distribute athletic and fashion footwear for sale in the US and a few other countries. The new lines debuted later that year. On the heels of its footwear license, Guess? in late 2005 inked another 10-year deal — this time with Timex Corporation unit Callanen International to make and distribute Guess? watches.

HISTORY

Guess? grew out of a jeans boutique owned by Georges Marciano in St. Tropez, France during the 1970s. After moving to Los Angeles with brothers Maurice and Armand, he launched the new company in 1981. A fourth brother, Paul, joined the firm that year and started the lush marketing campaign, which eventually featured supermodels Claudia Schiffer and Naomi Campbell. The trademark sexy style catapulted the company's jeans into major brand status.

In 1983 the company sold 50% of Guess? to the Nakash brothers, who owned Jordache. The following year the Marcianos sued the Nakashes, claiming they had stolen Guess? designs. After more than five years of wrangling, the parties settled out of court and the Marcianos resumed ownership of the business.

The company began licensing the Guess? name in 1990 when it allowed Revlon to use it for a perfume. Licenses for other products, including eyewear and footwear, soon followed. In 1993, when the Marciano brothers disagreed on the company's future (Georges wanted to target the mass market, but the others wanted to remain upscale), Georges left Guess?, selling his 40% stake to his brothers (he went on to own rival jeans company Yes Clothing).

Guess? went public in 1996. A fizzled expansion effort overseas and competition from hot brands like Tommy Hilfiger hurt earnings in 1997 and 1998. To correct the decline, Guess? began streamlining operations, revamping stores and product lines, and bringing apparel licenses in-house in 1999. In 2001 Guess? launched a higher-end line of clothing in 2001 under the G Brand label; G Brand denim is priced between $88 and $148 compared to the Guess? collection range of $48 and $98. It sells exclusively in New York City.

Alleging that Guess? misrepresented the security of its Web site, the Federal Trade Commission made a settlement in 2003 with the company that includes a requirement to improve the Web site's security. The settlement also prohibits Guess? from misrepresenting the security of consumer information on its Web site.

European expansion was brought back to the table in 2004, thanks to a revamped license agreement. Guess? got back a Florence-based jeanswear licensee that could add an extra $100 million in wholesale revenue to the company's European business.

In January 2007 Paul Marciano was named vice chairman and CEO of the company while his brother Maurice was named chairman.

EXECUTIVES

Chairman: Maurice Marciano, age 57
Vice Chairman and CEO: Paul Marciano, age 53
President, COO, Interim CFO, and Director:
 Carlos E. Alberini, age 50
EVP and Chief Supply Chain Officer:
 Stephen L. Pearson, age 51
Head, Guess? Business Development, Asia:
 Terrence W. Tsang, age 41
SVP and CFO: Dennis R. Secor, age 43
SVP, Information Technology and CIO:
 Michael (Mike) Relich, age 45, $438,800 pay
VP, International Licensing Business Development:
 Giuliano Sartori
President, Guess? Canada: Laurent Marchal
President, Wholesale: Nancy Shachtman, age 49,
 $499,200 pay
SVP, General Merchandise: Wendy Klarik
SVP and General Merchandise Manager, Retail Division:
 Harriet Sustarsic
SVP, Licensing Products, Guess? Europe:
 Stephane Labelle
Director, Human Resources: Susan Tenney
Integrated Corporate Relations: Joseph Teklits
Designer: Jason Ferro
Auditors: KPMG LLP

LOCATIONS

HQ: Guess?, Inc.
 1444 S. Alameda St., Los Angeles, CA 90021
Phone: 213-765-3100 **Fax:** 213-744-7838
Web: www.guess.com

2005 Sales

	$ mil.	% of total
US	640.6	69
Europe		
Italy	153.8	16
Other European countries	4.4	1
Canada	112.3	12
Asia	18.8	2
South America	2.8	—
Middle East	2.0	—
Other regions	1.3	—
Total	**936.1**	**100**

PRODUCTS/OPERATIONS

2005 Sales

	$ mil.	% of total
Products		
Retail	612.9	66
Wholesale	121.1	13
European operations	153.8	16
Licensing	48.3	5
Total	**936.1**	**100**

Selected Products

Blouses
Dresses
GUESS? Collection (women's apparel)
Jackets
Jeans
Knitwear
Overalls
Pants
Shirts
Shorts
Skirts

Licensed GUESS? Products

Eyewear
Fashion accessories
Footwear
Handbags
Jewelry
Leather apparel
Watches

COMPETITORS

Abercrombie & Fitch
American Eagle Outfitters
Buckle
Calvin Klein
Diesel
Donna Karan
Esprit Holdings
Express
Fossil
French Connection
Fruit of the Loom
Gap
J. Crew
Jordache Enterprises
Levi Strauss
Limited Brands
Liz Claiborne
Mossimo
Phillips-Van Heusen
Polo Ralph Lauren
Tommy Hilfiger
Urban Outfitters
VF
Warnaco Group
Wet Seal

HISTORICAL FINANCIALS

Company Type: Public

Income Statement

FYE: Saturday nearest January 31*

	REVENUE ($ mil.)	NET INCOME ($ mil.)	NET PROFIT MARGIN	EMPLOYEES
12/05	936.1	58.8	6.3%	7,300
12/04	729.3	29.6	4.1%	6,800
12/03	636.6	7.3	1.1%	4,800
12/02	583.1	(11.3)	—	4,900
12/01	677.6	6.2	0.9%	4,400
Annual Growth	**8.4%**	**75.5%**		**13.5%**

*Fiscal year change

2005 Year-End Financials

Debt ratio: 13.9%
Return on equity: 23.1%
Cash ($ mil.): 174.3
Current ratio: 1.89
Long-term debt ($ mil.): 40.0
No. of shares (mil.): 45.0
Dividends
 Yield: —
 Payout: —
Market value ($ mil.): 1,600.9
R&D as % of sales: —
Advertising as % of sales: 2.1%

Stock History

NYSE: GES

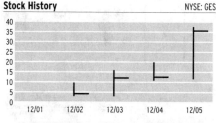

	STOCK PRICE ($) FY Close	P/E High/Low		PER SHARE ($) Earnings	Dividends	Book Value
12/05	35.60	28	9	1.31	—	6.41
12/04	12.55	30	17	0.66	—	4.99
12/03	12.07	92	19	0.17	—	4.19
12/02	4.19	—	—	(0.26)	—	3.86
Annual Growth	**104.1%**	—	—	**74.9%**	—	**11.8%**

Guidance Software

Guidance Software leads investigators down the right path. The company provides applications that government authorities, police agencies, and corporate investigators use for functions such as digital forensic investigations, information auditing, and information technology threat assessment and response. The company's software is a forensics platform that helps organizations respond quickly to threats and analyze information, including court-validated forensics tools for government and corporate investigations. Chairman and CTO Shawn McCreight owns about 56% of the company.

About 25% of the company's sales come from clients outside the US.

The company plans to use its IPO proceeds to pay a final distribution to its existing pre-IPO stockholders, as well as for general corporate expenses and potential acquisitions.

Vice chairman John Patzakis owns about 17% of the company, while EVP Bob Sheldon holds a 12% stake.

EXECUTIVES

Chairman and CTO: Shawn McCreight, age 40, $250,000 pay
Vice Chairman and Chief Legal Officer: John M. Patzakis, age 38, $251,041 pay
CEO and Director: John Colbert, age 41, $223,958 pay
President and Secretary: Victor Limongelli, age 40, $218,125 pay
CFO: Frank J. Sansone, age 35, $190,460 pay
SEVP: Larry Stinson
EVP, Training: Bob Sheldon
VP, Corporate Development and Marketing: Tim Leehealey, age 32
VP, Worldwide Sales: Sheldon Feinland, age 44
General Counsel: Mark Harrington, age 39
VP, Human Resources: Sandy Gyenes
Director, Professional Sales, Legal Markets: Alex Lubarsky
Public Relations: Cassondra Todd
Auditors: Deloitte & Touche LLP

LOCATIONS

HQ: Guidance Software, Inc.
215 N. Marengo Ave., 2nd Fl., Pasadena, CA 91101
Phone: 626-229-9191   **Fax:** 626-229-9199
Web: www.guidancesoftware.com

Guidance Software has offices and training facilities in California, New York, and Texas, as well as in the UK.

2005 Sales

	% of total
US	75
Other countries	25
Total	**100**

PRODUCTS/OPERATIONS

2005 Sales

	$ mil.	% of total
Products	23.1	59
Services & maintenance	16.4	41
Total	**39.5**	**100**

COMPETITORS

ABM	PricewaterhouseCoopers
Deloitte	SunGard
EMC	Symantec
Ernst & Young	Tyler
IBM	USTI
Kroll Ontrack	

HISTORICAL FINANCIALS

Company Type: Public

Income Statement

FYE: December 31

	REVENUE ($ mil.)	NET INCOME ($ mil.)	NET PROFIT MARGIN	EMPLOYEES
12/05	39.5	1.6	4.1%	308
12/04	27.6	(0.8)	—	—
12/03	17.7	(1.7)	—	150
Annual Growth	**49.4%**	**—**	**—**	**43.3%**

2005 Year-End Financials

Debt ratio: —
Return on equity: —
Cash ($ mil.): 7.6
Current ratio: 0.93
Long-term debt ($ mil.): 0.3

Net Income History

NASDAQ (GM): GUID

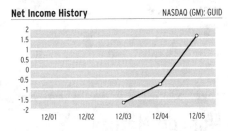

Gulfport Energy

Gulfport Energy puts most of its eggs into just a couple of baskets. The exploration and production company sells 99% of its oil to Shell and 88% of its gas to Chevron. It operates off the Gulf Coast of Louisiana, with a heavy concentration on two fields: West Cote Blanche Bay and Hackberry Fields. Gulfport operates about 70 producing wells and has proved reserves of nearly 25 million barrels of oil equivalent. The company emerged from the ashes of WRT Energy, which filed for bankruptcy in 1996 amid allegations of fraud. Gulfport emerged from Chapter 11 bankruptcy protection in 1997.

EXECUTIVES

Chairman: Mike Liddell, age 53
CEO and Director: James D. (Jim) Palm
VP and CFO: Michael G. (Mike) Moore
VP, General Counsel, and Secretary: Joel H. McNatt
Auditors: Grant Thornton LLP

LOCATIONS

HQ: Gulfport Energy Corporation
14313 N. May Ave., Ste. 100, Oklahoma City, OK 73134
Phone: 405-848-8807   **Fax:** 405-848-8816
Web: www.gulfportenergy.com

COMPETITORS

Abraxas Petroleum
Apache
Exxon Mobil

HISTORICAL FINANCIALS

Company Type: Public

Income Statement

FYE: December 31

	REVENUE ($ mil.)	NET INCOME ($ mil.)	NET PROFIT MARGIN	EMPLOYEES
12/05	27.6	10.9	39.5%	63
12/04	23.2	4.3	18.5%	—
12/03	15.9	0.6	3.8%	—
12/02	12.1	0.4	3.3%	—
12/01	15.7	5.4	34.4%	—
Annual Growth	**15.1%**	**19.2%**	**—**	**—**

2005 Year-End Financials

Debt ratio: 11.7%
Return on equity: 16.3%
Cash ($ mil.): 2.7
Current ratio: 1.29
Long-term debt ($ mil.): 9.8
No. of shares (mil.): 32.2

Dividends
Yield: —
Payout: —
Market value ($ mil.): 387.6
R&D as % of sales: —
Advertising as % of sales: —

Stock History

NASDAQ (GS): GPOR

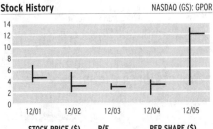

	STOCK PRICE ($) FY Close	P/E High/Low		PER SHARE ($) Earnings	Dividends	Book Value
12/05	12.05	38	10	0.34	—	2.62
12/04	3.30	14	6	0.28	—	1.53
12/03	2.90	—	—	(0.02)	—	3.27
12/02	3.05	—	—	(0.06)	—	3.29
12/01	4.55	13	7	0.52	—	3.35
Annual Growth	**27.6%**	**—**	**—**	**(10.1%)**	**—**	**(5.9%)**

Hanmi Financial

No hand-me-down operation, Hanmi Financial is headquartered in a penthouse suite along Los Angeles' Wilshire Boulevard. It's the holding company for Hanmi Bank, which serves California's Korean-American communities in Los Angeles, Orange, San Diego, San Francisco, and Santa Clara counties. Through more than 20 branches, the bank offers standard deposit products like checking, savings, and money market accounts, as well as CDs. Commercial and industrial loans, including Small Business Administration and international loans, account for more than 55% of Hanmi Financial's loan portfolio. Commercial real estate loans account for nearly 30%.

The bank also offers residential mortgages, consumer loans, and construction loans.

Hanmi Financial bought rival Pacific Union Bank in 2004. The following year Hanmi Bank expanded beyond California by opening loan production offices in Annandale, Virginia and Chicago to go with an existing office in Seattle.

EXECUTIVES

Chairman: Joon Hyung Lee, age 60
President, CEO, and Director, Hanmi Financial and Hanmi Bank: Sung Won Sohn, age 61, $1,171,500 pay
EVP and Chief Credit Officer, Hanmi Financial and Hanmi Bank: Kurt M. Wegleitner, age 54, $176,667 pay
SVP and CFO, Hanmi Financial and Hanmi Bank: Michael J. Winiarski, age 49, $237,084 pay
SVP and Regional Executive Officer: Suki H. Murayama, age 54, $196,198 pay
SVP and Manager, Capital Markets Group: Dong Wook Kim
SVP, Hanmi Bank: Eunice U. Lim, age 50, $159,278 pay (prior to title change)
Chief Planning and Marketing Officer: J. Han Park
Chief of Banking Services: Steve Choe
Chief of Operations: Greg Kim
Human Resources Manager: Miung Kim
Investor Relations: Stephanie Yoon
Auditors: KPMG LLP

LOCATIONS

HQ: Hanmi Financial Corporation
3660 Wilshire Blvd., Penthouse Ste. A,
Los Angeles, CA 90010
Phone: 213-382-2200 **Fax:** 213-384-0990
Web: www.hanmifinancial.com

PRODUCTS/OPERATIONS

2005 Sales

	$ mil.	% of total
Interest		
Loans, including fees	179.0	77
Investments	18.5	8
Federal funds sold	1.6	1
Noninterest		
Service charges on deposit accounts	15.8	7
Other service charges & fees	8.9	4
Other	7.5	3
Total	**231.3**	**100**

COMPETITORS

Bank of America
Cathay General Bancorp
Center Financial
East West Bancorp
Nara Bancorp
UCBH Holdings
Washington Mutual
Wells Fargo
Wilshire Bancorp

HISTORICAL FINANCIALS

Company Type: Public

Income Statement

FYE: December 31

	ASSETS ($ mil.)	NET INCOME ($ mil.)	INCOME AS % OF ASSETS	EMPLOYEES
12/05	3,414.3	58.2	1.7%	552
12/04	3,104.2	36.7	1.2%	533
12/03	1,785.8	19.2	1.1%	372
12/02	1,456.3	17.0	1.2%	356
12/01	1,158.8	16.8	1.4%	324
Annual Growth	**31.0%**	**36.4%**	**—**	**14.2%**

2005 Year-End Financials

Equity as % of assets: 12.5%
Return on assets: 1.8%
Return on equity: 14.1%
Long-term debt (mil.): 128.7
No. of shares (mil.): 48.7
Market value ($ mil.): 869.0
Dividends
Yield: 1.1%
Payout: 17.1%
Sales ($ mil.): 231.3
R&D as % of sales: —
Advertising as % of sales: —

Stock History

NASDAQ (GS): HAFC

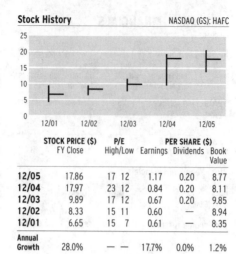

	STOCK PRICE ($) FY Close	P/E High/Low	PER SHARE ($) Earnings	Dividends	Book Value
12/05	17.86	17 12	1.17	0.20	8.77
12/04	17.97	23 12	0.84	0.20	8.11
12/03	9.89	17 12	0.67	0.20	9.85
12/02	8.33	15 11	0.60	—	8.94
12/01	6.65	15 7	0.61	—	8.35
Annual Growth	**28.0%**	**— —**	**17.7%**	**0.0%**	**1.2%**

Hansen Natural

No matter the weather, Hansen Natural always has the energy to reach for the blue sky. The company has expanded its stable of "alternative" sodas, juices, and teas to include a wide variety of energy drinks, such as the popular Monster brand. Other products made by Hansen include fruit juice, smoothies, lemonade, iced tea, and spring water — most of which are sold under the Hansen's brand name. Hansen also is branching out with soy drinks and juices aimed at toddlers. The company sells its products to grocery chains, wholesale clubs, and distributors, primarily in the western US. CEO Rodney Sacks and vice chairman Hilton Schlosberg each own about 20% of Hansen.

The $18 billion "alternative" beverage industry has grown increasingly crowded with bottled water and juices from beverage giants Coca-Cola and PepsiCo. Hansen's product line includes "functional" drinks made by adding Echinacea, ginseng, guarana, and other supplements to food and drinks.

Hansen produces numerous lines of energy drinks (most with a mixture of caffeine, sugar, and vitamins), and the segment now pulls in more than 75% of the company's sales. Hansen's Lost Energy is a joint marketing initiative with surf board designer Lost International. Its Rumba Energy Juice is an all-juice product designed to replace both morning coffee and juice. In 2006 the company struck a distribution deal with Anheuser-Busch for its energy drinks. It also signed an agreement with Cadbury Bebidas for the distribution of its Monster energy drinks in Mexico. In order to concentrate on its liquid offerings, Hansen has discontinued its line of nutrition bars and cereals.

While speaking at a conference in 2006, Sacks said that if the offer was good, he would consider selling the company.

EXECUTIVES

Chairman and CEO: Rodney C. Sacks, age 56, $382,250 pay
Vice Chairman, COO, CFO, President, and Secretary: Hilton H. Schlosberg, age 53, $382,250 pay
SVP, National Sales, Monster Beverage Division: Michael B. Schott, age 57, $230,000 pay
VP, Finance; Secretary, Hansen Beverage Company: Thomas J. Kelly, age 51, $190,000 pay
President, Monster Beverage Division: Mark J. Hall, age 50, $400,000 pay
Assistant Secretary and Director: Benjamin M. Polk, age 55
Director, Human Resources: Linda Lopez
Auditors: Deloitte & Touche LLP

LOCATIONS

HQ: Hansen Natural Corporation
1010 Railroad St., Corona, CA 92882
Phone: 951-739-6200 **Fax:** 951-739-6220
Web: www.hansens.com

PRODUCTS/OPERATIONS

2005 Sales

	$ mil.	% of total
Energy drinks	270.0	77
Non-carbonated beverages	51.5	15
Carbonated beverages	27.4	8
Total	**348.9**	**100**

Select Brands

Blue Sky (energy drinks, natural sodas, seltzer water)
Fizzit (powdered vitamin and mineral drink mixes)
Hansen's (energy drinks, fruit juices, iced tea, cider, smoothies)
Joker Mad Energy
Junior Juice (toddler fruit juice)
Lost Energy
Monster Energy
Rumba

COMPETITORS

Cadbury Schweppes
Chiquita Brands
Clearly Canadian
Coca-Cola
Cool Mountain Beverages
Cott
Ferolito, Vultaggio
Fuze Beverage
Global Beverage
Goya
Hobarama
Impulse Energy USA
IZZE
Jones Soda
Met-Rx Engineered Nutrition
Naked Juice
National Grape Cooperative
Nestlé
Northland Cranberries
Ocean Spray
Odwalla
PepsiCo
Red Bull
Reed's
Smucker
Snapple
South Beach Beverage
Tree Top
Tropicana
Unilever
Veryfine
Welch's
Wet Planet Beverages

HISTORICAL FINANCIALS

Company Type: Public

Income Statement

FYE: December 31

	REVENUE ($ mil.)	NET INCOME ($ mil.)	NET PROFIT MARGIN	EMPLOYEES
12/05	348.9	62.8	18.0%	363
12/04	180.3	20.4	11.3%	293
12/03	110.3	5.9	5.3%	173
12/02	92.1	3.0	3.3%	111
12/01	92.3	3.0	3.3%	108
Annual Growth	39.4%	113.9%	—	35.4%

2005 Year-End Financials

Debt ratio: 0.0%
Return on equity: 68.2%
Cash ($ mil.): 73.5
Current ratio: 4.26
Long-term debt ($ mil.): 0.0
No. of shares (mil.): 22.2
Dividends
  Yield: —
  Payout: —
Market value ($ mil.): 437.3
R&D as % of sales: —
Advertising as % of sales: —

Stock History

NASDAQ (CM): HANS

	STOCK PRICE ($) FY Close	P/E High/Low		PER SHARE ($) Earnings	Dividends	Book Value
12/05	19.70	34	6	0.65	—	5.66
12/04	4.55	21	4	0.22	—	5.36
12/03	1.05	17	6	0.07	—	3.36
12/02	0.53	16	10	0.04	—	2.82
12/01	0.52	15	9	0.04	—	2.52
Annual Growth	148.1%	—	—	100.8%	—	22.4%

Harris & Harris

Harris & Harris Group likes to think small. The business development company (BDC) invests mostly in startup firms developing so-called "tiny technology" — microsystems, microelectromechanical systems, biotechnology, and nanotechnology. The company identifies small, thinly capitalized firms lacking operating history or experienced management. It invests in those firms and provides assistance such as management and product development. The company's investment portfolio consists of about 20 companies, including several nanotechnology ventures, such as Nanomix, NanoOpto, and Nanosys.

EXECUTIVES

Chairman, CEO, and Managing Director:
  Charles E. Harris, age 63, $1,342,697 pay
President, COO, and CFO: Douglas W. Jamison, age 36, $415,308 pay
EVP and Managing Director: Alexei A. Andreev, age 33, $294,270 pay
EVP and Managing Director: Daniel V. Leff, age 37, $403,514 pay
VP and Controller: Thomas M. McCarthy, age 32
VP: Daniel B. Wolfe, age 30

Secretary: Susan T. Harris, age 57, $17,000 pay
General Counsel, Chief Compliance Officer, and Head of Human Resources: Sandra Matrick Forman, age 39, $237,685 pay
Auditors: PricewaterhouseCoopers LLP

LOCATIONS

HQ: Harris & Harris Group, Inc.
  111 W. 57th St., Ste. 1100, New York, NY 10019
Phone: 212-582-0900   **Fax:** 212-582-9563
Web: www.tinytechvc.com

PRODUCTS/OPERATIONS

2005 Sales

	$ mil.	% of total
Net realized income from investments	14.2	90
Interest from fixed-income securities	1.4	9
Other	0.2	1
Total	15.8	100

Selected Portfolio Companies

BridgeLux, Inc. (high-power iridium-gallium nitrate light-emitting diodes)
Cambrios Technologies Corp. (nanostructures)
Chlorogen, Inc (plant-derived drugs and vaccines)
Crystal IS (semiconductor substrates)
CSwitch, Inc. (systems-on-a-chip for communications applications)
D-Wave Systems, Inc. (quantum computing systems)
Evolved Nanomaterial Sciences, Inc.
Innovalight, Inc. (renewable energy products based on silicon nanotechnology)
Kereos, Inc. (molecular imaging and targeted therapeutics for cancer and cardiovascular disease)
Kovio, Inc. (semiconductors)
Mersana Therapeutics, Inc. (biodegradable nanoscopic drug delivery vehicles)
Metabolon, Inc. (products to measure metabolic pathways)
Molecular Imprints, Inc. (nano-lithography systems)
NanoGram Corporation (nanomaterial research and development)
Nanomix, Inc. (nanoelectric sensors)
NanoOpto Corporation (optical components for consumer electronics)
Nanosys, Inc. (nanotechnology-enabled computer systems)
Nantero, Inc. (high-density nonvolatile random access memory (NRAM) chips)
NeoPhotonics Corp. (planar optical devices)
Nextreme Thermal Solutions, Inc. (thermoelectrics)
Polatis, Inc. (optical networking components)
Questech Corporation (decorative metal products)
Solazyme, Inc. (photosynthetic microbial bioproduction)
Starfire Systems (polymers for ceramic materials applications)

COMPETITORS

Accel Partners
Applied Technology
Benchmark Capital
Capital Southwest
Draper Fisher Jurvetson
Norwest Venture Partners

HISTORICAL FINANCIALS

Company Type: Public

Income Statement

FYE: December 31

	REVENUE ($ mil.)	NET INCOME ($ mil.)	NET PROFIT MARGIN	EMPLOYEES
12/05	15.8	6.7	42.4%	11
12/04	0.6	(2.1)	—	—
12/03	0.5	(3.2)	—	—
12/02	3.5	(2.7)	—	—
12/01	1.9	(6.9)	—	—
Annual Growth	69.8%	—	—	—

2005 Year-End Financials

Debt ratio: —
Return on equity: 7.0%
Cash ($ mil.): 1.2
Current ratio: —
Long-term debt ($ mil.): —
No. of shares (mil.): 20.8
Dividends
  Yield: —
  Payout: —
Market value ($ mil.): 288.5
R&D as % of sales: —
Advertising as % of sales: —

Stock History

NASDAQ (GM): TINY

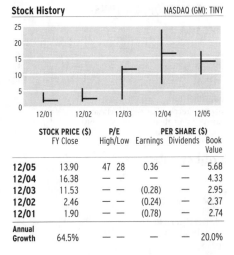

	STOCK PRICE ($) FY Close	P/E High/Low		PER SHARE ($) Earnings	Dividends	Book Value
12/05	13.90	47	28	0.36	—	5.68
12/04	16.38	—	—	—	—	4.33
12/03	11.53	—	—	(0.28)	—	2.95
12/02	2.46	—	—	(0.24)	—	2.37
12/01	1.90	—	—	(0.78)	—	2.74
Annual Growth	64.5%	—	—	—	—	20.0%

Harvest Natural Resources

Harvest Natural Resources is keen to harvest the natural resources of oil and gas. The independent's main exploration and production work takes place in Venezuela, where it has proved reserves of 36 million barrels of oil equivalent. It operates through its 80%-owned Venezuelan subsidiary, Harvest Vinccler C.A., which operates the South Monagas Unit in Venezuela. Founded in 1989, the company sold its stakes in Siberian ventures Arctic Gas and Geoilbent to Yukos in 2002 and 2003, although the company is still keen on developing Russian oil and assets. It also has interests in China.

In 2005 Harvest Natural Resource temporarily suspended its Venezuelan operations because of delays in receiving government permits for drilling additional wells. In 2006 the company agreed to form a Venezuelan joint venture with PDVSA (Petrodelta and Corporacion Venezolana del Petroleo S.A., 40%-owned by Harvest Vinccler).

EXECUTIVES

Chairman: H. H. (Will) Hardee, age 51
President, CEO, and Director: James A. Edminston, age 46, $467,500 pay (prior to promotion)
SVP Corporate Development: Byron A. Dunn, age 47
SVP Finance, CFO, and Treasurer: Steven W. Tholen, age 55, $340,000 pay
SVP, General Counsel, and Corporate Secretary:
  Kerry R. Brittain, age 59, $345,000 pay
VP, Controller, and Chief Accounting Officer:
  Kurt A. Nelson, age 53, $230,000 pay
VP Engineering and Business Development:
  Karl L. Nesselrode, age 48, $220,000 pay
VP and General Manager, Harvest-Vinccler:
  Jean-Michel Bonnet
Auditors: PricewaterhouseCoopers LLP

LOCATIONS

HQ: Harvest Natural Resources, Inc.
  1177 Enclave Pkwy., Ste. 300, Houston, TX 77077
Phone: 281-899-5700   **Fax:** 281-899-5702
Web: www.harvestnr.com

PRODUCTS/OPERATIONS

2005 Sales

	$ mil.	% of total
Oil	210.5	89
Gas	26.4	11
Total	**236.9**	**100**

Subsidiaries

Benton-Vinccler, C.A. (80%, Venezuela)
Energy International Financial Institution, Ltd. (80%, Cayman Islands)

COMPETITORS

BP
Exxon Mobil
Occidental Petroleum
PDVSA
Pioneer Natural Resources
Royal Dutch Shell
TOTAL

HISTORICAL FINANCIALS

Company Type: Public

Income Statement

FYE: December 31

	REVENUE ($ mil.)	NET INCOME ($ mil.)	NET PROFIT MARGIN	EMPLOYEES
12/05	236.9	50.8	21.4%	252
12/04	186.1	34.4	18.5%	221
12/03	106.1	27.3	25.7%	221
12/02	126.7	100.4	79.2%	902
12/01	122.4	43.2	35.3%	1,054
Annual Growth	17.9%	4.1%	—	(30.1%)

2005 Year-End Financials

Debt ratio: —
Return on equity: 18.8%
Cash ($ mil.): 163.0
Current ratio: 3.88
Long-term debt ($ mil.): —
No. of shares (mil.): 37.0
Dividends
  Yield: —
  Payout: —
Market value ($ mil.): 328.4
R&D as % of sales: —
Advertising as % of sales: —

Stock History

NYSE: HNR

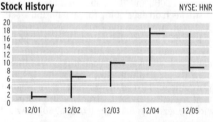

	STOCK PRICE ($) FY Close	P/E High/Low		PER SHARE ($) Earnings	Dividends	Book Value
12/05	8.88	13	6	1.32	—	8.04
12/04	17.27	21	10	0.90	—	6.61
12/03	9.95	14	6	0.74	—	5.60
12/02	6.45	3	0	2.78	—	4.86
12/01	1.44	2	1	1.27	—	1.97
Annual Growth	57.6%	—	—	1.0%	—	42.1%

Hauppauge Digital

Wanna watch TV at work? Hauppauge Digital's WinTV analog and digital video boards let viewers videoconference, watch TV, and view input from VCRs and camcorders in a resizable window on a PC monitor. Hauppauge (pronounced "HAW-pog") also offers boards that accommodate radio and Internet broadcasts, and makes a line of PC video editing boards. The company outsources its manufacturing to companies in Europe and Asia. Hauppauge primarily distributes its products through retailers such as CompUSA, as well as distributors including Ingram Micro and D&H Distributing.

While about three-quarters of sales come from the retail market, the company also sells its products to manufacturers and has partnered with companies such as Intel and Microsoft. Hauppauge is expanding international sales distribution; customers outside the US make up more than half of sales.

Co-founder, chairman, and CEO Kenneth Plotkin and his wife own about 14% of Hauppauge. Laura Aupperle, the widow of Kenneth Aupperle (former president), holds nearly 10% of the company.

HISTORY

Kenneth Plotkin and Kenneth Aupperle, former Intel employees, co-founded Hauppauge Digital in 1982. The business originally manufactured PC hardware and software used to accelerate scientific and mathematical calculations. By 1985 Hauppauge Digital was marketing 12 software products to universities and research labs; that year it started exporting to Europe.

When Intel began making math coprocessors, Hauppauge got into developing motherboards — until Intel moved into that market, too. In 1991 Hauppauge introduced the PC/TV video board, underpricing rivals IBM and Apple. Since 1992 it has focused almost exclusively on digital video products. The company went public in 1995 and introduced several new products, including a low-priced video board aimed at the consumer market. The following year Hauppauge Digital teamed with Intel to develop boards that enable PCs to receive Internet broadcasts.

In 1997 Hauppauge Digital's products were tapped for incorporation into electronics made by Compaq (acquired in 2002 by Hewlett-Packard) and U.S. Robotics (subsequently part of 3Com, which later sold most of its stake to Accton Technology and NatSteel). Sales jumped 50% in fiscal 1998, the result of growth in the company's distribution channels. That year Hauppauge began developing digital TV reception cards for PC makers. In 2000 the company bought video interface specialist Eskape Labs. (Eskape Labs' co-founder and EVP Christopher Knight is a former child actor who played middle son Peter on *The Brady Bunch*.)

In 2001 Aupperle died; Plotkin took on the additional title and duties of president. The next year former Priority Call executive Dean Cirielli joined the company as president. Cirielli resigned in 2004, and Plotkin reassumed the title of president.

EXECUTIVES

Chairman, President, CEO, COO, and VP of Marketing: Kenneth H. (Ken) Plotkin, age 55
CFO, Treasurer, and Secretary: Gerald (Jerry) Tucciarone, age 50
VP of Technology: John Casey, age 50
Corporate Counsel: Benjamin Tan
Manager of Human Resources: Cheryl Willins
Auditors: BDO Seidman, LLP

LOCATIONS

HQ: Hauppauge Digital, Inc.
  91 Cabot Ct., Hauppauge, NY 11788
Phone: 631-434-1600   **Fax:** 631-434-3198
Web: www.hauppauge.com

Hauppauge Digital has offices in France, Germany, Ireland, Italy, Luxembourg, the Netherlands, Singapore, Spain, Sweden, Taiwan, the UK, and the US.

2006 Sales

	% of total
US	46
Germany	22
UK	9
Ireland	5
France	4
Scandinavia	4
Asia	3
Spain & Portugal	3
Netherlands	2
Italy	1
Other countries	1
Total	**100**

PRODUCTS/OPERATIONS

2006 Sales

	$ mil.	% of total
Analog TV receivers	62.8	64
Digital TV receivers	33.1	34
Non-TV tuner products	1.8	2
Total	**97.7**	**100**

Selected Products

DV-Wizard-PRO (PC desktop video editing)
EsKape Labs line (video for the Macintosh)
ImpactVCB boards (video capture, integrated into other manufacturers' products)
WinTV board line (video access from PC screens)
  WinTV-D (allows user to watch analog and digital TV on PC)
  WinTV-DVB-s (for viewing digital satellite broadcasts)
  WinTV-HD (allows user to watch analog and digital TV in high-definition video quality)
  WinTV-Go (low-cost WinTV for the mass consumer market)
  WinTV-PCI (single-slot internal board for TV and data broadcasts on PCs)
  WinTV-PVR (WinTV personal video recorder products)
  WinTV-Theater (WinTV with Dolby surround sound)
  WinTV-USB (connects via USB ports on desktops and laptops)

COMPETITORS

Apple
ATI Technologies
Avid Technology
Cisco Systems
Creative Technology
FOCUS Enhancements
Matrox Electronic Systems
Matsushita
NVIDIA
Philips Electronics
Pinnacle Systems
RealNetworks
Sony
Toshiba

HISTORICAL FINANCIALS

Company Type: Public

Income Statement

FYE: September 30

	REVENUE ($ mil.)	NET INCOME ($ mil.)	NET PROFIT MARGIN	EMPLOYEES
9/06	97.7	2.4	2.5%	141
9/05	78.5	1.4	1.8%	138
9/04	65.3	1.8	2.8%	135
9/03	51.0	(0.8)	—	113
9/02	42.8	0.3	0.7%	107
Annual Growth	22.9%	68.2%	—	7.1%

2006 Year-End Financials

Debt ratio: —
Return on equity: 14.2%
Cash ($ mil.): 9.0
Current ratio: 1.91
Long-term debt ($ mil.): —
No. of shares (mil.): 9.7

Dividends
  Yield: —
  Payout: —
Market value ($ mil.): 52.0
R&D as % of sales: —
Advertising as % of sales: —

Stock History

NASDAQ (GM): HAUP

	STOCK PRICE ($) FY Close	P/E High/Low		PER SHARE ($) Earnings	Dividends	Book Value
9/06	5.39	30	13	0.24	—	1.84
9/05	3.39	48	22	0.14	—	1.68
9/04	3.25	53	12	0.19	—	1.56
9/03	2.71	—	—	(0.09)	—	1.29
9/02	1.24	85	26	0.04	—	1.35
Annual Growth	44.4%	—	—	56.5%	—	8.0%

Health Grades

Health Grades takes the health care industry to school. Through its Web site, the company offers report cards on hospitals, physicians, nursing homes, home health agencies, hospice programs, and other health care providers. Basic profiles on the site are free; the company charges fees for more comprehensive reports. Customers include consumers, health plans and employers, doctors, and liability insurance companies. Health Grades also offers marketing help to hospitals who receive high ratings, helping them capitalize on their high quality of service, and it provides quality improvement consulting to those with low scores.

EXECUTIVES

Chairman, President, and CEO: Kerry R. Hicks, age 46, $390,542 pay
Vice Chairman: J.D. Kleinke, age 44
EVP: Steve Wood
EVP: David G. Hicks, age 48, $240,407 pay
SVP, Finance, CFO, Secretary, and Treasurer:
 Allen Dodge, age 38, $190,340 pay
SVP, Provider Sales: Michael D. (Mike) Phillips, $274,293 pay

VP, Corporate Communications and Marketing:
 Scott Shapiro
Director, Human Resources: Carloyne Petty
Auditors: Grant Thornton LLP

LOCATIONS

HQ: Health Grades, Inc.
 500 Golden Ridge Rd., Golden, CO 80401
Phone: 303-716-0041 **Fax:** 303-716-1298
Web: www.healthgrades.com

PRODUCTS/OPERATIONS

2005 Sales

	% of total
Marketing services to hospitals	59
Quality improvement services to hospitals	28
Quality information sales to employers, consumers & others	12
Other	1
Total	**100**

COMPETITORS

GE Healthcare
Solucient
WebMD Health

HISTORICAL FINANCIALS

Company Type: Public

Income Statement

FYE: December 31

	REVENUE ($ mil.)	NET INCOME ($ mil.)	NET PROFIT MARGIN	EMPLOYEES
12/05	20.8	4.1	19.7%	106
12/04	14.5	1.8	12.4%	—
12/03	8.8	(1.3)	—	—
12/02	5.3	(1.6)	—	—
12/01	3.6	(7.4)	—	—
Annual Growth	55.0%	—	—	—

2005 Year-End Financials

Debt ratio: 0.1%
Return on equity: 62.1%
Cash ($ mil.): 11.7
Current ratio: 1.36
Long-term debt ($ mil.): 0.0
No. of shares (mil.): 28.3

Dividends
  Yield: —
  Payout: —
Market value ($ mil.): 179.0
R&D as % of sales: —
Advertising as % of sales: —

Stock History

NASDAQ (CM): HGRD

	STOCK PRICE ($) FY Close	P/E High/Low		PER SHARE ($) Earnings	Dividends	Book Value
12/05	6.32	54	23	0.12	—	0.34
12/04	2.90	65	11	0.05	—	0.14
12/03	0.60	—	—	(0.05)	—	0.06
12/02	0.03	—	—	(0.05)	—	0.13
12/01	0.07	—	—	(0.30)	—	0.13
Annual Growth	208.3%	—	—	—	—	27.4%

HealthExtras

Extra, extra! Read all about it: HealthExtras provides pharmacy benefit management (PBM) services to managed care organizations, self-insured employers, and third-party administrators. Its PBM segment, known as Catalyst Rx, helps clients design drug benefit plans that encourage the use of preferred prescriptions bought from one of 55,000 pharmacies (including mail order pharmacies) in the company's nationwide network. It also provides customized reporting and data analysis services. The State of Louisiana is its largest customer, accounting for 20% of sales. In addition to its main PBM business, HealthExtras markets customizable supplemental health and disability insurance programs.

HealthExtras targets employer groups and managed care organizations large enough to need a PBM service, but not so large that they are more likely to use one of the major PBM players (Caremark or Medco, for example). It also is looking to increase sales to third-party administrators (TPAs); to that end, the company acquired midwestern firm EBRx, which caters to TPAs, in late 2005.

Negotiating drug discounts with its network pharmacies is key to the company's success. It works to keep costs under control through a number of other strategies as well, including using data analysis and regionalized networks to identify regional trends in drug usage. It also designs benefit programs and chronic disease management programs to encourage cost-effective drug use.

The company looks for acquisitions to complement and grow its existing PBM business; it has bought about a half dozen companies since 2000, including RXx Pharmacy Solutions from HMA in 2006.

Principal Financial Group owns 16% of HealthExtras; founder and director Thomas Blair owns 11%.

EXECUTIVES

Chairman: Edward S. (Ed) Civera, age 55
CEO and Director: David T. Blair, age 35, $700,000 pay
CFO: Richard W. Hunt, age 50
EVP, Corporate Development:
 Michael P. (Mike) Donovan, age 46
EVP and COO: Nick J. Grujich, age 43
EVP; President, Catalyst Rx: Kevin C. Hooks, age 43, $400,000 pay
General Counsel and Secretary:
 Thomas M. (Tom) Farah, age 51, $290,000 pay
Director, Human Resources: Monica Wolfe
Auditors: PricewaterhouseCoopers LLP

LOCATIONS

HQ: HealthExtras, Inc.
 800 King Farm Blvd., Rockville, MD 20850
Phone: 301-548-2900 **Fax:** 301-548-2991
Web: www.healthextras.com

PRODUCTS/OPERATIONS

2005 Sales

	$ mil.	% of total
Pharmacy benefit management services	650.9	94
Supplemental benefits	43.6	6
Total	**694.5**	**100**

COMPETITORS

Aetna	CVS
Aflac	Express Scripts
American Fidelity	Medco Health Solutions
Assurance	PacifiCare
BioScrip	PharmaCare
Caremark	Rite Aid
CIGNA	UnitedHealth Group
Colonial Life & Accident	Walgreen
Conseco	WellPoint

HISTORICAL FINANCIALS

Company Type: Public

Income Statement

FYE: December 31

	REVENUE ($ mil.)	NET INCOME ($ mil.)	NET PROFIT MARGIN	EMPLOYEES
12/05	694.5	23.0	3.3%	284
12/04	521.3	16.4	3.1%	227
12/03	384.1	10.3	2.7%	150
12/02	248.4	13.5	5.4%	105
12/01	124.3	(6.8)	—	82
Annual Growth	**53.7%**	**—**	**—**	**36.4%**

2005 Year-End Financials

Debt ratio: 4.0%
Return on equity: 13.8%
Cash ($ mil.): 55.6
Current ratio: 1.74
Long-term debt ($ mil.): 7.5
No. of shares (mil.): 39.8

Dividends
Yield: —
Payout: —
Market value ($ mil.): 999.7
R&D as % of sales: —
Advertising as % of sales: —

Stock History

NASDAQ (GS): HLEX

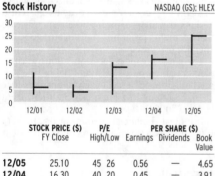

	STOCK PRICE ($) FY Close	P/E High/Low		PER SHARE ($) Earnings	Dividends	Book Value
12/05	25.10	45	26	0.56	—	4.65
12/04	16.30	40	20	0.45	—	3.91
12/03	13.40	50	11	0.30	—	2.18
12/02	4.05	16	5	0.42	—	1.84
12/01	5.71	—	—	(0.23)	—	1.42
Annual Growth	**44.8%**			**—**	**—**	**34.5%**

HealthSpring

HealthSpring wants to give Medicare enrollees an extra advantage. The company is a managed care organization that focuses on providing supplemental Medicare plans to more than 101,200 members in Alabama, Illinois, Mississippi, Tennessee, and Texas. Its Medicare Advantage plans offer the support of Medicare with additional benefits such as generic prescription drug coverage, discounts on brand-name drugs, vision and hearing benefits, and transportation programs. HealthSpring also provides HMO, PPO, and other commercial health plans. In addition,

the company offers management services to independent physician associations. Director Joseph Nolan is part of an investment group which owns 24% of HealthSpring.

The company issued its initial public offering in early 2006. Chairman, president, and CEO Herbert Fritch owns about 10% of the company.

EXECUTIVES

Chairman, President, and CEO:
Herbert A. (Herb) Fritch, age 55, $1,050,000 pay
EVP and COO: Jeffrey L. (Jeff) Rothenberger, age 46, $800,000 pay
EVP and Interim COO: Gerald V. (Jerry) Coil, age 54
EVP, CFO, and Treasurer: Kevin M. McNamara, age 50, $565,385 pay (partial-year salary)
SVP, Corporate General Counsel, and Secretary:
J. Gentry Barden, age 44
SVP and Chief Actuary: David L. Terry Jr., age 54
President and CEO, Healthspring of Alabama:
W. Bradley Green
President, HealthSpring of Illinois: Randy K. Fike
Chief Marketing Officer: Craig Schub
Auditors: KPMG LLP

LOCATIONS

HQ: HealthSpring, Inc.
44 Vantage Way, Ste. 300, Nashville, TN 37228
Phone: 615-291-7000   **Fax:** 615-401-4566
Web: www.myhealthspring.com

PRODUCTS/OPERATIONS

2005 Sales

	$ mil.	% of total
Medicare premiums	705.7	82
Commercial premiums	126.9	15
Other	24.2	3
Total	**856.8**	**100**

COMPETITORS

Aetna
Blue Cross
Cariten
Humana
Tenet Healthcare
United Healthcare Insurance
Universal American Financial

HISTORICAL FINANCIALS

Company Type: Public

Income Statement

FYE: December 31

	REVENUE ($ mil.)	NET INCOME ($ mil.)	NET PROFIT MARGIN	EMPLOYEES
12/05	856.8	29.3	3.4%	900
12/04	599.4	23.7	4.0%	780
12/03	372.7	22.9	6.1%	—
12/02	26.1	8.7	33.3%	—
Annual Growth	**220.2%**	**49.9%**	**—**	**15.4%**

2005 Year-End Financials

Debt ratio: 66.0%
Return on equity: 18.4%
Cash ($ mil.): 133.0

Current ratio: 1.27
Long-term debt ($ mil.): 172.0

Net Income History

NYSE: HS

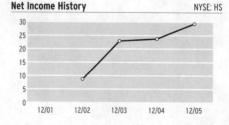

HealthTronics

HealthTronics is sending shock waves through urology patients across the nation . . . literally. The company makes and sells lithotripters, which use extracorporeal shock waves to break up kidney and gall-bladder stones, and it supplies clinical technicians to help physicians run the equipment. It also offers other urology-related services, including treatments for enlarged prostate and prostate cancer, as well as equipment such as patient tables and X-ray imaging systems. HealthTronics has added urological laboratory testing to its service offering, opening its ClariPath pathology lab in 2006. HealthTronics has sold its AK Specialty Vehicles division to Oshkosh Truck for $140 million.

The divestiture of the unit — which made trucks and trailers used to transport medical devices, broadcasting equipment, and mobile command and control centers — was part of the company's strategy to focus exclusively on health services and medical technology.

HealthTronics was known as HealthTronics Surgical Services before merging with Prime Medical Services in late 2004.

Prides Capital Partners (director Kevin Richardson is a partner) owns about 15% of the company; director and former chairman Argil Wheelock owns 5%.

EXECUTIVES

Chairman: R. Steven Hicks, age 55
President, CEO, and Director: Sam B. Humphries, age 64
CFO and SVP: Ross A. Goolsby, age 38
SVP, Development, President, Specialty Vehicle Manufacturing, Secretary, and General Counsel:
James S. B. Whittenburg, age 34
VP and Controller: Richard A. Rusk, age 43, $245,000 pay
President, Medical Device Sales and Services and COO, Urology Division: Christopher B. Schneider, age 38, $271,200 pay
COO, Lithotripsy: W. Price Dunaway, age 52
Auditors: KPMG LLP

LOCATIONS

HQ: HealthTronics, Inc.
1301 Capital of Texas Hwy., Ste. 200B, Austin, TX 78746
Phone: 512-328-2892   **Fax:** 512-328-8510
Web: www.healthtronics.com

COMPETITORS

Boston Scientific	Endocare
C. R. Bard	InSight Health Corp.
Celsion	Medtronic
Dornier	Siemens AG
EDAP TMS	

HISTORICAL FINANCIALS

Company Type: Public

Income Statement

FYE: December 31

	REVENUE ($ mil.)	NET INCOME ($ mil.)	NET PROFIT MARGIN	EMPLOYEES
12/05	267.7	9.2	3.4%	930
12/04	193.1	0.9	0.5%	928
12/03	88.4	5.3	6.0%	321
12/02	87.2	8.5	9.7%	312
12/01	43.9	3.1	7.1%	261
Annual Growth	**57.1%**	**31.3%**	**—**	**37.4%**

2005 Year-End Financials

Debt ratio: 53.5%
Return on equity: 4.0%
Cash ($ mil.): 25.7
Current ratio: 2.43
Long-term debt ($ mil.): 129.2
No. of shares (mil.): 34.9

Dividends
Yield: —
Payout: —
Market value ($ mil.): 266.7
R&D as % of sales: —
Advertising as % of sales: —

Stock History

NASDAQ (GS): HTRN

	STOCK PRICE ($) FY Close	P/E High/Low		PER SHARE ($) Earnings	Dividends	Book Value
12/05	7.65	55	24	0.26	—	6.93
12/04	10.63	273	133	0.04	—	6.54
12/03	6.30	26	11	0.45	—	3.49
12/02	8.01	24	8	0.73	—	2.91
12/01	9.00	49	16	0.28	—	1.98
Annual Growth	(4.0%)	—	—	(1.8%)	—	36.8%

Healthways

Healthways (formerly American Healthways) paves the way for disease management. The company provides disease and care management, as well as wellness programs, for health plans, hospitals, and self-insured employers nationwide. Its services help plan members with diabetes, chronic respiratory diseases, cancer, and other chronic and serious diseases to coordinate their health care, keep up with treatment plans, and maintain healthy behaviors. The company also has screening and prevention programs to find people at risk for various diseases and to promote healthy living. In 2006 the firm acquired preventive health services provider AXIA Health Management for $450 million.

Healthways provides services to some 2.5 million people in all 50 states, Puerto Rico, and Guam.

In 2006 the company announced plans to acquire disease management company LifeMasters Supported Selfcare for $307 million, but the agreement was later terminated.

FMR owns nearly 15% of the company. Wasatch Advisors owns nearly 10% of Healthways.

HISTORY

In 1981 Thomas Cigarran and Henry Herr (alumni of a company that's now part of HCA) joined with venture capitalist Martin Koldyke to found American Healthcorp to buy hospitals. The company diversified, entering the diabetes market in 1984 and arthritis care in 1987.

With profitability lagging, the company sold its hospitals to focus on niche care. In the same spirit, it de-emphasized arthritis care in 1990. The company went public in 1991.

After a brief foray into obesity treatment, the company in 1994 invested in AmSurg, a manager of ambulatory surgery centers. (AmSurg was spun off in 1997.)

By the late 1990s the company increasingly targeted HMOs. It signed its first contract with Principal Health Care (1996, ended in 1998 after Coventry Health Care bought the HMO). Contracts with such HMOs as John Deere Health Care and Health Options of Blue Cross & Blue Shield of Florida followed in 1998.

To standardize income, the company in 1998 converted all of its contracts from shared savings arrangements (in which the company's earnings were based on the payers' savings) to fee-based arrangements. In 1999 American Healthcorp began offering a cardiac health management program to its hospital and HMO clients; that year it changed its name to American Healthways to reflect its expanded product line.

American Healthways in 2000 signed a deal with Agilent Technologies to offer that company's home heart monitoring systems to its patients. It also launched MYHEALTHWAYS, a Web-based application, which offers disease-prevention plans to health plan members.

In 2001 American Healthways launched Comprehensive Care Enhancement Programs, under which all health plan members are screened and provided with any needed health care programs.

In 2003 the company acquired Company StatusOne Health Systems in order to expand its health management service offerings for high-risk populations. American Healthways changed its name to Healthways in early 2006.

EXECUTIVES

Chairman: Thomas G. Cigarran, age 65, $250,000 pay
President, CEO, and Director: Ben R. Leedle Jr., age 45, $916,800 pay
EVP, Alliances: Donald B. Taylor, age 48, $523,500 pay
EVP and COO: James E. Pope, age 53
EVP and Chief Strategy Officer: Robert E. Stone, age 60, $460,680 pay
EVP: Mary D. Hunter, age 61
EVP, International Business: Matthew E. Kelliher, age 51, $460,680 pay
SVP and CIO: Robert L. Chaput, age 56
SVP, Chief Accounting Officer, and Corporate Controller: Alfred Lumsdaine, age 41
SVP and Chief Communications Officer: Nicholas E. Dantona
SVP, Business Development: Michael H. King
SVP, Government Relations: Michael F. Montijo
SVP, Human Resources: Rita R. Sailer
SVP, IT: C. Don McConnell
SVP, Outcomes Improvement and Chief Medical Officer: Dexter Shurney
SVP, Strategic Alliances: William R. (Bill) Gold
Auditors: Ernst & Young LLP

LOCATIONS

HQ: Healthways, Inc.
3841 Green Hills Village Dr., Nashville, TN 37215
Phone: 615-665-1122 **Fax:** 615-665-7697
Web: www.healthways.com

COMPETITORS

AvMed Health Plans
CareGuide
Critical Care Systems International
Express Scripts
ivpcare
Landacorp
Matria Healthcare
PharMetrics, Inc.
SHPS

HISTORICAL FINANCIALS
Company Type: Public

Income Statement

FYE: August 31

	REVENUE ($ mil.)	NET INCOME ($ mil.)	NET PROFIT MARGIN	EMPLOYEES
8/06	412.3	37.2	9.0%	2,855
8/05	312.5	33.1	10.6%	2,231
8/04	245.4	26.1	10.6%	1,875
8/03	165.5	18.5	11.2%	1,511
8/02	122.8	10.4	8.5%	1,017
Annual Growth	35.4%	37.5%	—	29.4%

2006 Year-End Financials

Debt ratio: 0.1%
Return on equity: 15.4%
Cash ($ mil.): 154.8
Current ratio: 2.29
Long-term debt ($ mil.): 0.2
No. of shares (mil.): 34.6

Dividends
Yield: —
Payout: —
Market value ($ mil.): 1,785.9
R&D as % of sales: —
Advertising as % of sales: —

Stock History

NASDAQ (GS): HWAY

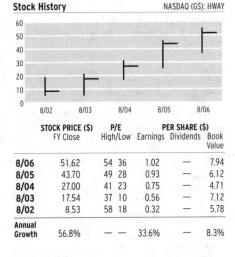

	STOCK PRICE ($) FY Close	P/E High/Low		PER SHARE ($) Earnings	Dividends	Book Value
8/06	51.62	54	36	1.02	—	7.94
8/05	43.70	49	28	0.93	—	6.12
8/04	27.00	41	23	0.75	—	4.71
8/03	17.54	37	10	0.56	—	7.12
8/02	8.53	58	18	0.32	—	5.78
Annual Growth	56.8%	—	—	33.6%	—	8.3%

Heartland Payment Systems

If you're using your credit card to charge throughout the heartland, or just about anywhere else across the US, Heartland Payment Systems (HPS) makes sure the transactions don't get lost along the way. The company provides credit card, debit card, and payroll processing services to more than 110,000 small and midsized retailers, hotels, and restaurants. (The latter account for about a third of HPS' customer base and about 40% of its processing volume.) HPS also processes merchant-issued gift cards and sells and rents point-of-sale card processing equipment. CEO Robert Carr owns about 30% of HPS; affiliates of Greenhill & Co. control another 34%.

Helping its growth along are key acquisitions, such as that of Chattanooga, Tennessee-based Debitek, which the company bought in 2006. Debitek offers prepaid and stored-value products and

services to universities, businesses, and government agencies across the country, including the University of Florida, Northwestern University, BMW, Coca-Cola, Morgan Stanley, and the federal penitentiary system. Debitek was previously owned by France-based payment terminal manufacturer Ingenico.

EXECUTIVES

Chairman and CEO: Robert O. (Bob) Carr, age 60, $448,665 pay
CFO and Secretary: Robert H. B. (Bob) Baldwin Jr., age 51, $320,475 pay
Chief Services Officer: David L. Morris, age 59
CTO: Brooks L. Terrell, age 42, $275,609 pay
Media Relations: Mikel Anderson
Chief Portfolio Officer: Thomas M. Sheridan, age 60, $256,350 pay
Chief Sales Officer: Sanford C. Brown, age 34, $329,276 pay

LOCATIONS

HQ: Heartland Payment Systems, Inc.
90 Nassau St., Princeton, NJ 08542
Phone: 609-683-3831 **Fax:** 609-683-3815
Web: www.heartlandpaymentsystems.com

In addition to its Princeton, New Jersey corporate office, Heartland Payment Systems has offices in Cleveland; Frisco, Texas; Jeffersonville, Indiana; and Scottsdale, Arizona.

PRODUCTS/OPERATIONS

2005 Sales

	$ mil.	% of total
Card services	830.3	99
Payroll services	4.3	1
Total	**834.6**	**100**

2005 Processing Volume

	% of total
Restaurants	40
Retail	23
Convenience & liquor stores	9
Automotive	9
Lodging	5
Professional services	4
Other	10
Total	**100**

COMPETITORS

BA Merchant Services
Chase Paymentech Solutions
Fifth Third
First Data Commercial Services
Global Payments
iPayment
NOVA
Retail Decisions
TSYS

HISTORICAL FINANCIALS

Company Type: Public

Income Statement

FYE: December 31

	REVENUE ($ mil.)	NET INCOME ($ mil.)	NET PROFIT MARGIN	EMPLOYEES
12/05	834.6	19.1	2.3%	1,616
12/04	602.8	8.9	1.5%	1,336
12/03	422.2	20.1	4.8%	—
12/02	280.0	(7.9)	—	850
12/01	189.5	(28.2)	—	636
Annual Growth	**44.9%**	**—**	**—**	**26.3%**

2005 Year-End Financials

Debt ratio: 0.2%
Return on equity: 44.3%
Cash ($ mil.): 19.9
Current ratio: 1.41
Long-term debt ($ mil.): 0.2
No. of shares (mil.): 34.2
Dividends
 Yield: —
 Payout: —
Market value ($ mil.): 740.8
R&D as % of sales: —
Advertising as % of sales: —

Stock History

NYSE: HPY

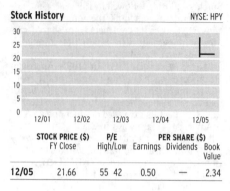

	STOCK PRICE ($) FY Close	P/E High/Low	PER SHARE ($) Earnings	Dividends	Book Value
12/05	21.66	55 42	0.50	—	2.34

HEICO

Here's a HEICO haiku: HEICO companies/ Providing for jet engines/ In flight or on land. Through the subsidiaries that make up the company's Flight Support Group, HEICO manufactures parts for jet engines that can be substituted for original parts. Products include combustion chambers and compressor blades. Flight Support operations, which include repair and overhaul services, account for about 70% of HEICO's sales. Subsidiaries in HEICO's Electronic Technologies Group make a variety of electro-optical, electronic, and microwave products, primarily for defense applications.

HEICO has benefited by diversifying its product line. Customers outside the commercial aviation industry, such as electronics, industrial, medical, and telecommunications companies, account for a significant portion of the company's sales.

In November 2005 HEICO moved to expand its flight support business by buying a 51% stake in Seal Dynamics, a designer and distributor of hydraulic, pneumatic, mechanical, and electro-mechanical components for the commercial, regional, and general aviation markets. The following year HEICO's Flight Support Group acquired Arger Enterprises, a subsidiary of Melrose PLC. Arger makes and distributes aircraft parts, mainly for the commercial aviation market. Also in 2006, HEICO bought a controlling stake in Prime Air Parts, which deals in spare parts for aircraft.

Chairman and CEO Laurans Mendelson and his family own about 22% of HEICO; Florida investor Herbert Wertheim owns about 11%.

HISTORY

Founded in 1957 as Heinicke Instruments to make laboratory products, the company moved into jet engine parts in 1974 with the acquisition of Jet Avion. The company changed its name to HEICO (a shortened version of its previous name) in 1985. After a faulty combustion chamber erupted in flames that year, the FAA ordered all combustion chambers on US jets to be inspected and, if necessary, replaced. HEICO's sales skyrocketed, but descended back to earth after airlines found they had overstocked.

By the early 1990s defense cutbacks and declining aircraft orders reduced business, and HEICO began to diversify. In 1991 it formed MediTek to acquire medical imaging facilities but then sold the company to U.S. Diagnostic for $24 million five years later. Lufthansa Technik AG, the service subsidiary of Deutsche Lufthansa, paid HEICO $26 million for a 20% stake in HEICO's flight support operations in 1997.

HEICO acquired jet engine parts companies McClain International and Rogers-Dierks in 1998. The next year the company added Radiant Power (back-up power supplies and battery packs for aerospace applications), Turbine Kinetics and AeroKinetics (replacement parts for aircraft engines), Santa Barbara Infrared (infrared and ground support equipment), and Thermal Structures (insulation products).

HEICO sold its Trilectron Industries ground support equipment subsidiary to Illinois Tool Works in 2000 in a deal worth about $64 million. The following year the company formed a joint venture with AMR (parent of American Airlines) to accelerate development of FAA-approved replacement parts. Also in 2001, HEICO bought Inertial Airline Services, Avitech Engineering Corp., and Aviation Facilities, Inc. In 2003 HEICO acquired Niacc Technology, an aircraft component repair and overhaul company.

The company added to its aerospace electronics operations with the acquisition of Connectronics, a maker of high-voltage wire and interconnection devices, in 2004.

EXECUTIVES

Chairman, President, and CEO: Laurans A. Mendelson, age 67, $1,441,836 pay
EVP and CFO: Thomas S. Irwin, age 59, $737,890 pay
President, Flight Support Group, and Director; President and CEO, HEICO Aerospace: Eric A. Mendelson, age 40, $737,890 pay
President, Electronic Technologies Group and Director, General Counsel, and Director; President and CEO HEICO Electronics Technologies: Victor H. Mendelson, age 38, $737,890 pay
EVP, HEICO Aerospace: James L. Reum, age 74, $39,520 pay
President, Inertial Aerospace Services and Inertial Airline Services: Surin M. Malhotra
Auditors: Deloitte & Touche LLP

LOCATIONS

HQ: HEICO Corporation
3000 Taft St., Hollywood, FL 33021
Phone: 954-987-4000 **Fax:** 954-987-8228
Web: www.heico.com

HEICO maintains engineering and manfacturing facilities in the US (California, Connecticut, Florida, Georgia, Illinois, Massachusetts, New Mexico, Ohio, Oregon, Tennessee, Texas, and Washington) and the UK.

2006 Sales

	$ mil.	% of total
US	284.0	72
Other countries	108.2	28
Total	**392.2**	**100**

PRODUCTS/OPERATIONS

2006 Sales

	$ mil.	% of total
Flight Support Group	277.3	71
Electronic Technologies Group	115.0	29
Adjustments	(0.1)	—
Total	**392.2**	**100**

Selected Subsidiaries and Affiliates

Flight Support
  HEICO Aerospace Holdings Corp. (HEICO Aerospace, 80%)
    Aircraft Technology, Inc.
    Aviation Facilities, Inc.
    Future Aviation, Inc.
    HEICO Aerospace Corporation
    HEICO Aerospace Parts Corp.
    Jet Avion Corporation
    Jetseal, Inc.
    LPI Industries Corporation
    McClain International, Inc.
    Niacc-Avitech Technologies Inc.
    Northwings Accessories Corporation
    Rogers-Dierks, Inc.
    Seal Dynamics LLC (51%)
    Thermal Structures, Inc.
    Turbine Kinetics, Inc.
  Electronic Technologies
    HEICO Electronic Technologies Corp.
      Analog Modules, Inc.
      Connectronics Corporation
      Engineering Design Team, Inc.
      HVT Group, Inc.
      Leader Tech, Inc.
      Lumina Power, Inc.
      Radiant Power Corp.
      Santa Barbara Infrared, Inc.
      Sierra Microwave Technology, LLC

COMPETITORS

AAR
Barnes Group
BBA Aviation
CIC International
DeCrane
Doncasters
GE Aircraft Engines
Goodrich
Kellstrom Aerospace
Ladish Co.
Pratt & Whitney
Rolls-Royce
SIFCO
TIMCO Aviation
Triumph Group
United Technologies
Wyman-Gordon

HISTORICAL FINANCIALS

Company Type: Public

Income Statement

FYE: October 31

	REVENUE ($ mil.)	NET INCOME ($ mil.)	NET PROFIT MARGIN	EMPLOYEES
10/06	392.2	31.9	8.1%	1,843
10/05	269.6	22.8	8.5%	1,556
10/04	215.7	20.6	9.6%	1,263
10/03	176.4	12.2	6.9%	1,011
10/02	172.1	15.2	8.8%	953
Annual Growth	**22.9%**	**20.4%**	**—**	**17.9%**

2006 Year-End Financials

Debt ratio: 17.3%
Return on equity: 10.8%
Cash ($ mil.): 5.0
Current ratio: 2.75
Long-term debt ($ mil.): 55.0
No. of shares (mil.): 10.3
Dividends
  Yield: 0.2%
  Payout: 6.7%
Market value ($ mil.): 374.1
R&D as % of sales: —
Advertising as % of sales: —

Stock History

NYSE: HEI

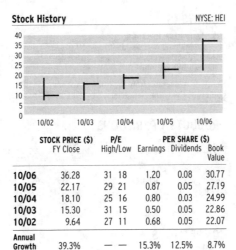

	STOCK PRICE ($) FY Close	P/E High/Low		PER SHARE ($) Earnings	Dividends	Book Value
10/06	36.28	31	18	1.20	0.08	30.77
10/05	22.17	29	21	0.87	0.05	27.19
10/04	18.10	25	16	0.80	0.03	24.99
10/03	15.30	31	15	0.50	0.05	22.86
10/02	9.64	27	11	0.68	0.05	22.07
Annual Growth	**39.3%**	**—**	**—**	**15.3%**	**12.5%**	**8.7%**

Helix Energy Solutions

Helix Energy Solutions is in the energy services mix as a top marine contractor and operator of offshore oil and gas properties and production facilities. Its Deepwater Contracting unit works in water depths greater than 1,000 feet, using dynamically positioned and remotely operated vehicles that offer a range of engineering, repair, maintenance, and pipe and cable burial services in global offshore markets. Subsidiary Energy Resource Technology buys and operates mature fields in the Gulf of Mexico, controlling estimated proved reserves of 144 billion cu. ft. of natural gas equivalent. In 2006 the company agreed to spin off its Outer Continental Shelf shallow water contracting business (Cal Dive International).

In 2005 the company acquired some oil and natural gas properties on the continental shelf of the Gulf of Mexico from Murphy Oil. That year the company acquired assets from bankrupt Torch Offshore.

In 2006 Helix Energy Solutions bought oil and gas explorer Remington Oil and Gas for $1.4 billion.

EXECUTIVES

Chairman: Owen E. Kratz, age 51
Vice Chairman: John V. Lovoi, age 45
CEO, President, and Director: Martin R. Ferron, age 49
EVP and COO: Bart H. Heijermans
SVP, CFO, and Treasurer: A. Wade Pursell, age 40
SVP, General Counsel, and Corporate Secretary:
  Alisa B. Johnson
SVP International: Michael V. Ambrose
President, CDI/Aquatica: Steve Brazda
President, Energy Resource Technology:
  Johnny E. Edwards, age 50
Co-President and COO, Canyon Offshore:
  John S. Edwards
Co-President and CFO, Canyon Offshore:
  Martin O'Carroll
VP, Corporate Controller, and Chief Accounting Officer:
  Lloyd A. Hajdik, age 39
VP Finance and Audit: G. Kregg Lunsford, age 37
Auditors: Ernst & Young LLP

LOCATIONS

HQ: Helix Energy Solutions Group, Inc.
  400 N. Sam Houston Pkwy. East, Ste. 400,
  Houston, TX 77060
Phone: 281-618-0400   **Fax:** 281-618-0501
Web: www.helixesg.com

Helix Energy Solutions has an operations center in Morgan City, Louisiana, and sales offices in Lafayette and New Orleans, Louisiana, and Houston, and in Singapore and the UK. The company provides its underwater services in the Gulf of Mexico, the North Sea, and in the Asia/Pacific region.

PRODUCTS/OPERATIONS

2005 Sales

	$ mil.	% of total
Deepwater contracting	328.3	40
Oil & gas production	275.8	33
Shelf contracting	223.2	27
Adjustments	(27.8)	—
Total	**799.5**	**100**

Major Operations

Cal Dive International
Canyon
Deepwater Contracting
Energy Resource Technology
Helix Energy Solutions Group, Inc.
Production Facilities
Well Ops

COMPETITORS

Acergy
Global Industries
Halliburton
McDermott
Oceaneering International
Parker Drilling
Pride International
Saipem
Subsea 7
Technip
TETRA Technologies
Tidewater

HISTORICAL FINANCIALS

Company Type: Public

Income Statement

FYE: December 31

	REVENUE ($ mil.)	NET INCOME ($ mil.)	NET PROFIT MARGIN	EMPLOYEES
12/05	799.5	152.6	19.1%	1,800
12/04	543.4	82.7	15.2%	900
12/03	396.3	34.2	8.6%	1,114
12/02	302.7	12.4	4.1%	1,184
12/01	227.1	28.9	12.7%	835
Annual Growth	**37.0%**	**51.6%**	**—**	**21.2%**

2005 Year-End Financials

Debt ratio: 70.0%
Return on equity: 27.4%
Cash ($ mil.): 91.1
Current ratio: 1.48
Long-term debt ($ mil.): 440.7
No. of shares (mil.): 77.7
Dividends
  Yield: —
  Payout: —
Market value ($ mil.): 2,788.4
R&D as % of sales: —
Advertising as % of sales: —

Stock History

NYSE: HLX

	STOCK PRICE ($) FY Close	P/E High/Low	PER SHARE ($) Earnings	Dividends	Book Value
12/05	35.89	22 10	1.86	—	8.10
12/04	20.38	21 11	1.03	—	12.63
12/03	12.06	29 18	0.44	—	10.07
12/02	11.75	80 44	0.17	—	9.01
12/01	12.34	36 18	0.44	—	6.97
Annual Growth	30.6%	— —	43.4%	—	3.8%

Henry Bros. Electronics

Security systems integrator Henry Bros. Electronics (formerly Diversified Security Solutions) designs, installs, and maintains closed-circuit television (CCTV) and access control systems. The company also installs system components such as CCTVs, intercoms, alarm monitors, video recorders, and card access controls. Henry Bros. Electronics markets its services to large and medium-sized businesses and to government agencies. Operations in Southern California and the New York metropolitan area together account for about three-fourths of the company's sales.

Installation of security systems accounts for most of the company's revenue; it also sells specialized wireless communications equipment used in mobile security applications.

Henry Bros. Electronics expanded in 2005 by buying Colorado-based security systems integrator Securus. It picked up Southwest Securityscan in Texas, and CIS Security Systems in the Washington, DC area in 2006.

The company, which was founded in 1952 as Henry Bros. Electronics but later sold, changed its name from Diversified Security Solutions to Henry Bros. Electronics in 2005.

Chairman and CEO James Henry and president and director Irvin Witcosky each own about 24% of the company.

EXECUTIVES

Chairman, CEO, and Treasurer: James E. (Jim) Henry, age 52, $130,680 pay
Vice Chairman, COO, and Secretary: Brian L. Reach, age 51
President and Director: Irvin F. (Irv) Witcosky, age 67
CFO: John P. Hopkins
VP Business Development: David Fitzgerald, age 50
VP; VP Sales, HBE California: Alex Pavlis
VP: Theodore (Ted) Gjini
CTO: Emil J. Marone
President, Airorlite Communications: Lee Masoian
General Manager, HBE Arizona: Michael Tiffin
VP Operations, HBE Texas: Jane McCallum
Corporate Controller: Philip A. Timpanaro, age 58
Manager Field Service: Gerard Romolo
Auditors: Demetrius & Company, L.L.C.

LOCATIONS

HQ: Henry Bros. Electronics, Inc.
280 Midland Ave., Saddle Brook, NJ 07663
Phone: 201-794-6500   **Fax:** 201-794-8341
Web: www.hbe-inc.com

Henry Bros. operates from facilities in Arizona, California, Colorado, New Jersey, New York, and Texas.

PRODUCTS/OPERATIONS

2005 Sales

	$ mil.	% of total
Total integration	38.8	91
Specialty products & services	3.9	9
Adjustments	(0.5)	0
Total	**42.2**	**100**

COMPETITORS

ADT Security
Bosch
Checkpoint Systems
Extreme CCTV
GE Security
Honeywell International
MDI
Sentry Technology
Vicon Industries

HISTORICAL FINANCIALS

Company Type: Public

Income Statement

FYE: December 31

	REVENUE ($ mil.)	NET INCOME ($ mil.)	NET PROFIT MARGIN	EMPLOYEES
12/05	42.2	1.1	2.6%	172
12/04	29.7	0.0	—	148
12/03	18.3	(3.0)	—	101
12/02	18.8	0.3	1.6%	116
12/01	11.9	0.3	2.5%	73
Annual Growth	37.2%	38.4%	—	23.9%

2005 Year-End Financials

Debt ratio: 4.6%
Return on equity: 7.1%
Cash ($ mil.): 2.2
Current ratio: 2.34
Long-term debt ($ mil.): 0.7
No. of shares (mil.): 5.9
Dividends
 Yield: —
 Payout: —
Market value ($ mil.): 26.4
R&D as % of sales: —
Advertising as % of sales: 0.1%

Stock History

AMEX: HBE

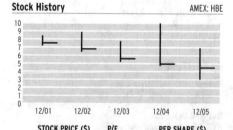

	STOCK PRICE ($) FY Close	P/E High/Low	PER SHARE ($) Earnings	Dividends	Book Value
12/05	4.48	36 16	0.19	—	2.72
12/04	4.95	990 481	0.01	—	2.57
12/03	5.60	— —	(0.58)	—	2.17
12/02	6.79	147 108	0.06	—	2.80
12/01	7.50	93 81	0.09	—	2.35
Annual Growth	(12.1%)	— —	20.5%	—	3.8%

Heritage Oaks Bancorp

Stash your acorns at Heritage Oaks Bancorp. It's the holding company for Heritage Oaks Bank, which serves primarily retail customers, farmers, and small to midsized businesses in California's San Luis Obispo and northern Santa Barbara counties through about 12 offices. The bank offers standard deposit products such as checking, savings, and money market accounts, and loan products including agricultural, commercial, consumer, real estate, and SBA loans. Real estate mortgages account for more than 60% of its loan portfolio; construction loans make up another 20%. Through bank division Heritage Oaks Financial Services, the company provides investment and financial planning.

Chairman B. R. Bryant owns nearly 8% of Heritage Oaks Bancorp; director Ole Viborg owns nearly 7%; and president, CEO, and director Lawrence Ward and director Merle Miller each own about 6%.

EXECUTIVES

Chairman, Heritage Oaks Bancorp and Heritage Oaks Bank: B. R. Bryant, age 73
Vice Chairman, Heritage Oaks Bancorp and Heritage Oaks Bank: Donald H. Campbell, age 64
President, CEO, and Director, Heritage Oaks Bancorp and Heritage Oaks Bank: Lawrence P. Ward, age 54, $423,223 pay
EVP and CFO, Heritage Oaks Bancorp and Heritage Oaks Bank: Margaret A. Torres, age 55, $227,904 pay
President and COO, Hacienda Bank: David A. Duarte, age 54, $109,173 pay
Secretary; EVP, Secretary, and Chief Administrative Officer, Heritage Oaks Bank: Gwen R. Pelfrey, age 54, $200,028 pay
EVP and Chief Lending Officer, Heritage Oaks Bank: Paul Tognazzini, age 56, $220,634 pay
EVP Client Services, Heritage Oaks Bank: Craig Heyl
EVP Human Resources, Heritage Oaks Bank: Joni Watson
Investor Relations: Tana L. Eade-Davis
Auditors: Vavrinek, Trine, Day & Co., LLP

LOCATIONS

HQ: Heritage Oaks Bancorp
545 12th St., Paso Robles, CA 93446
Phone: 805-239-5200   **Fax:** 805-238-6257
Web: www.heritageoaksbank.com

COMPETITORS

Bank of America
Bank of the West
Mid-State Bancshares
North Bay Bancorp
Washington Mutual
Wells Fargo

HISTORICAL FINANCIALS

Company Type: Public

Income Statement

FYE: December 31

	ASSETS ($ mil.)	NET INCOME ($ mil.)	INCOME AS % OF ASSETS	EMPLOYEES
12/05	488.5	6.6	1.4%	190
12/04	448.0	4.6	1.0%	170
12/03	442.0	3.6	0.8%	164
12/02	337.3	2.7	0.8%	118
12/01	214.9	2.3	1.1%	106
Annual Growth	22.8%	30.2%	—	15.7%

Equity as % of assets: 9.2%
Return on assets: 1.4%
Return on equity: 16.1%
Long-term debt ($ mil.): 8.3
No. of shares (mil.): 6.2
Market value ($ mil.): 127.8

Dividends
  Yield: —
  Payout: —
Sales ($ mil.): 35.2
R&D as % of sales: —
Advertising as % of sales: 1.7%

Stock History   NASDAQ (CM): HEOP

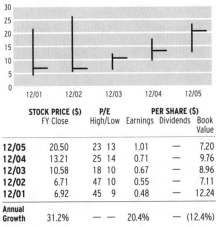

	STOCK PRICE ($) FY Close	P/E High/Low		PER SHARE ($) Earnings	Dividends	Book Value
12/05	20.50	23	13	1.01	—	7.20
12/04	13.21	25	14	0.71	—	9.76
12/03	10.58	18	10	0.67	—	8.96
12/02	6.71	47	10	0.55	—	7.11
12/01	6.92	45	9	0.48	—	12.24
Annual Growth	31.2%	—	—	20.4%	—	(12.4%)

Herley Industries

Herley Industries makes microwave products for aerospace, defense, and commercial customers. Defense and aerospace offerings include flight instruments such as transponders and flight telemetry systems, navigation system components, missile guidance systems, unmanned vehicle command-and-control systems, and flight-termination receivers (used to trigger explosives to destroy a craft if something goes wrong). The company sells its products to US and overseas military organizations and defense contractors. Herley's commercial products include amplifiers for nuclear magnetic resonance systems (used by researchers and scientists) and amplifiers and components used in medical magnetic resonance imaging (MRI) systems.

The US government accounts for about 25% of Herley's sales. Other customers include defense contractors Northrop Grumman, Boeing, Lockheed Martin, and Raytheon.

Initially, Herley primarily provided microwave components, but it has grown to provide complete microwave communications systems. The company has expanded steadily via acquisitions. In 2005 Herley bought Micro Systems, a maker of command and control systems for operation and tracking of unmanned targets and missiles, and Innovative Concepts, Inc. (ICI), which makes wireless communications software and systems for defense applications.

Herley intends to continue to work to integrate its product offerings and to look for complementary companies to buy.

Founder Lee Blatt and chairman and CEO Myron Levy each own about 10% of Herley.

In 2006 Herley and Blatt were indicted on charges alleging Herley plotted to overcharge the US military. Blatt is accused of doctoring bids to hide overcharging for F-16 fighter jet oscillators and a surge protector for the E-2C Hawkeye aircraft.

The company has since announced it will not likely receive any more business from the US Navy unless there is no other competitor that can provide the necessary products or services.

HISTORY

In 1965 Herman Kagan and Lee Blatt (the "Her" and "Lee" in "Herley") founded the company to make microwave products. Herley focused on making microwave components for tactical military equipment until 1986, when it expanded into flight instrumentation in anticipation of cutbacks in military budgets. The new business had an attractive component — an entry into commercial operations such as the tracking of commercial rockets carrying satellites into orbit.

Herley bought microwave subsystem maker Micro-Dynamics in 1992, and it added archrival Vega Precision Laboratories the next year. In 1995 Herley bought high-frequency communications products maker Stewart Warner Electronics. However, the company's sales dipped about 20% due to a drop in foreign orders that fiscal year. Herley also settled a 1992 theft-of-trade-secrets suit (for $4 million) brought by Litton Systems, which also contributed to its fiscal 1995 losses.

In 1997 Herley gained the facilities to offer complete airborne telemetry systems when it acquired Metraplex, a maker of airborne telemetry and data acquisition systems. The company signed a multiyear licensing and royalty agreement with Motorola Space and Systems in 1998 to assume Motorola's flight instrument contracts. To boost its offerings in military and commercial microwave products, Herley bought General Microwave in 1999 and Robinson Laboratories and American Microwave Technology in 2000.

Late in 2002 Herley acquired EW Simulation Technology Limited (EWST), a UK-based maker of warfare simulator systems. Two years later, the company acquired command and control communications systems maker Communications Techniques, Inc. (CTI), and secure-satellite communications specialist Reliable System Services Corporation (RSS).

EXECUTIVES

Chairman and CEO: Myron Levy, age 66, $1,163,132 pay (prior to title change)
Vice Chairman: Edward K. Walker Jr., age 73
President: John M. Kelley, age 53, $275,016 pay
VP and CFO: Kevin J. Purcell, age 48, $29,616 pay
VP, Finance: Anello C. (Neil) Garefino, age 59
VP and CTO: Andy Feldstein, age 55
VP, Strategic Initiatives: Rozalie Schachter, age 60
VP and COO: William R. Wilson, age 57, $240,011 pay
VP; President, Herley New England: Richard Poirier, age 41
VP, Human Resources: John A. Carroll, age 55
Secretary and Director: John A. Thonet, age 56
Director, Administration and Governance: Charles L. Pouciau Jr., age 58
Director, Engineering, Herley Lancaster: Sridhar Kanamaluru
General Manager, Micro Systems: Wayne Armstrong
Investor Relations: Peg Guzzetti
Chief Scientist: Vernon M. Moore
Auditors: Marcum & Kliegman LLP

LOCATIONS

HQ: Herley Industries, Inc.
  101 N. Pointe Blvd., Lancaster, PA 17601
Phone: 717-735-8117   **Fax:** 717-397-9503
Web: www.herley.com

Herley Industries operates from facilities in the US (Florida, Illinois, Massachusetts, New Jersey, New York, Pennsylvania, and Virginia), and in Israel and the UK.

2006 Sales

	$ mil.	% of total
US	155.1	88
Israel	14.0	8
UK	7.2	4
Total	**176.3**	**100**

PRODUCTS/OPERATIONS

Selected Products

Amplifiers (for medical and scientific equipment)
Command-and-control systems (used to control unmanned aircraft)
Flight-termination receivers (used to destroy errant unmanned aircraft or rockets)
Microwave devices (air and ship navigation, missile guidance systems)
Telemetry systems (data transmission between ground and vehicle)
Transponders (command-and-control components, identification of friend or foe, range safety, scoring systems)

COMPETITORS

C4 Systems
CMC Electronics
L-3 Communications
Lockheed Martin
Northrop Grumman
Raytheon
Thales

HISTORICAL FINANCIALS

Company Type: Public

Income Statement				FYE: Sunday nearest July 31
	REVENUE ($ mil.)	NET INCOME ($ mil.)	NET PROFIT MARGIN	EMPLOYEES
7/06	176.3	10.4	5.9%	1,014
7/05	151.4	10.8	7.1%	1,026
7/04	122.2	13.7	11.2%	832
7/03	110.2	13.9	12.6%	707
7/02	92.9	5.2	5.6%	618
Annual Growth	17.4%	18.9%	—	13.2%

2006 Year-End Financials

Debt ratio: 2.9%
Return on equity: 5.2%
Cash ($ mil.): 22.3
Current ratio: 3.76
Long-term debt ($ mil.): 5.9
No. of shares (mil.): 13.9

Dividends
  Yield: —
  Payout: —
Market value ($ mil.): 150.7
R&D as % of sales: —
Advertising as % of sales: —

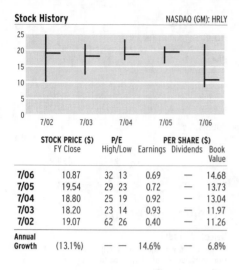

	STOCK PRICE ($) FY Close	P/E High/Low		PER SHARE ($) Earnings	Dividends	Book Value
7/06	10.87	32	13	0.69	—	14.68
7/05	19.54	29	23	0.72	—	13.73
7/04	18.80	25	19	0.92	—	13.04
7/03	18.20	23	14	0.93	—	11.97
7/02	19.07	62	26	0.40	—	11.26
Annual Growth	(13.1%)	—	—	14.6%	—	6.8%

Hittite Microwave

And lo, the Hittites did rise up out of their land, and they sacked Babylon. Actually, these Hittites rise up out of the Commonwealth of Massachusetts, and they're out to sell semiconductors. Hittite Microwave designs and develops microwave, millimeter-wave, and radio-frequency (RF) chips for aerospace, broadband, cellular, and military applications. In addition to amplifiers, frequency multipliers, mixers, modulators, switches, and other components, the company provides custom RF integrated circuits (ICs). Boeing (16% of sales) and Motorola are among the largest of Hittite's more than 2,300 customers. Chairman emeritus and founder Yalcin Ayasli controls nearly 56% of Hittite Microwave.

Hittite Microwave is a fabless semiconductor company, which means that it contracts out the production of its chips to other companies, known as silicon foundries. Hittite's principal foundry contractors are Atmel, Global Communication Semiconductors (GCS), IBM Microelectronics, M/A-Com, TriQuint Semiconductor, United Monolithic Semiconductors (UMS), and WIN Semiconductors. Hittite also competes with some of those companies with its microwave and RF ICs.

In 2005 Hittite acquired the assets of Q-DOT, a government R&D contractor, from Simtek for $2.2 million in cash.

Hittite does a lot of its own semiconductor assembly and testing at its facilities in Massachusetts. In 2005 the company established its first remote design center, in Istanbul, Turkey.

Ayasli Children LLC owns about 16% of Hittite Microwave; Dr. Ayasli is the sole manager for the LLC.

EXECUTIVES

Chairman Emeritus: Yalcin Ayasli, age 60
Chairman, President, and CEO: Stephen G. Daly, age 40, $240,000 pay
EVP, Engineering: Michael J. Koechlin, age 46, $196,500 pay
VP, Operations: Brian J. Jablonski, age 46
VP, CFO, and Treasurer: William W. Boecke, age 54, $205,833 pay

VP, Sales and Marketing: Norman G. Hildreth Jr., age 43, $190,000 pay
Public Relations: Beth McGreevy
Auditors: PricewaterhouseCoopers LLP

LOCATIONS

HQ: Hittite Microwave Corporation
20 Alpha Rd., Chelmsford, MA 01824
Phone: 978-250-3343 **Fax:** 978-250-3373
Web: www.hittite.com

Hittite Microwave has facilities in Canada, China, Germany, South Korea, Turkey, the UK, and the US.

2005 Sales

	$ mil.	% of total
US	43.3	54
Other countries	37.4	46
Total	**80.7**	**100**

PRODUCTS/OPERATIONS

Selected Products

Amplifiers
Attenuators
Frequency dividers and detectors
Frequency multipliers
Mixers and converters
Modulators
Oscillators
Sensors
Switches

COMPETITORS

ANADIGICS
Analog Devices
Avago Technologies
Endwave
Eudyna Devices
L-3 Communications
Linear Technology
M/A-Com
Merrimac Industries
NEC Electronics
Peregrine Semi
Powerwave Technologies
RF Magic
RF Micro Devices
RF Monolithics
Sirenza Microdevices
SiRF Technology
Skyworks
TriQuint
WJ Communications

HISTORICAL FINANCIALS

Company Type: Public

Income Statement

FYE: December 31

	REVENUE ($ mil.)	NET INCOME ($ mil.)	NET PROFIT MARGIN	EMPLOYEES
12/05	80.7	21.1	26.1%	220
12/04	61.7	13.4	21.7%	—
12/03	42.0	7.2	17.1%	—
Annual Growth	38.6%	71.2%	—	—

2005 Year-End Financials

Debt ratio: 0.3%
Return on equity: 39.4%
Cash ($ mil.): 62.6
Current ratio: 8.31
Long-term debt ($ mil.): 0.2
No. of shares (mil.): 28.7

Dividends
 Yield: —
 Payout: —
Market value ($ mil.): 663.7
R&D as % of sales: —
Advertising as % of sales: —

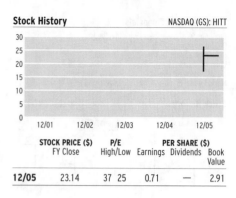

	STOCK PRICE ($) FY Close	P/E High/Low		PER SHARE ($) Earnings	Dividends	Book Value
12/05	23.14	37	25	0.71	—	2.91

Hologic

Hologic puts the squeeze on women to help save their lives. The company makes mammography and breast biopsy systems. Its mammography products include both film-based and digital systems, sold under the Lorad brand, as well as the workstations and computer-aided detection (CAD) systems to help with interpreting images. Hologic's additional products include X-ray and ultrasound bone densitometers, which measure bone density to diagnose and monitor metabolic bone diseases such as osteoporosis. The company markets its products to hospitals, radiologists, and drug firms worldwide through distributors and through a direct sales force.

Its Suros division produces breast biopsy collection systems under the ATEC brand of products.

Hologic also manufactures and sells photoconductor materials used in electrophotographic devices and small fluoroscopic imaging systems used by orthopedic surgeons on extremities such as hands, feet, and knees. The company is also the US distributor of Esaote's MRI systems designed for use on extremities.

Hologic has grown steadily and expanded its business in the areas of bone densitometry and mammography through acquisitions.

HISTORY

In 1981 S. David Ellenbogen and Jay Stein founded Diagnostic Technology (DTI) and developed a digital angiography product. A Squibb subsidiary bought DTI in 1982, and in 1985 Ellenbogen and Stein founded Hologic.

The firm shipped its first bone scanner in 1987 and went public in 1990. Increased global focus on women's health fueled Hologic's growth in 1994. That year it penetrated the Latin American and Japanese markets, and Medicare patients started receiving reimbursement for bone density examinations. Also in 1994 Hologic partnered with Serex to develop a test to monitor biochemical indicators of bone loss (Ostex International joined the effort in 1996).

Targeting private practices requiring less-expensive equipment, Hologic bought Walker Magnetic Group's ultrasound bone analyzer business and that of European rival Sophia Medical Systems in 1995. That year it purchased FluoroScan Imaging Systems, a maker of X-ray equipment.

In 1998 the company introduced its Sahara Clinical Bone Sonometer in the US. In 1999 Hologic acquired Direct Radiography, another X-ray equipment maker. That year Fleet Business Credit, which had an agreement with Hologic through which it purchased bone densitometers and then leased them to physicians, pulled out of the partnership; sales sank, and Hologic filed a lawsuit against Fleet to recoup losses. Also in 1999 Hologic sold its Medical Data Management division to focus on core operations.

In 2000 the company bought the US operations of medical imaging company Trex Medical Corporation. This acquisition added the Lorad-brand line of mammography and breast biopsy systems, to Hologic's operations. The acquisition was costly, and, to recover, Hologic implemented a restructuring plan in 2001 that led to a reduction of the workforce, a reduction of operating expenses, and phasing out unprofitable units. The company closed its conventional X-ray equipment manufacturing facility in Littleton, Massachusetts and relocated some of the product lines and personnel to Bedford, Massachusetts.

With a renewed appetite for growth, in 2005 Hologic resumed its acquisition strategy, starting with the purchase of Fischer Imaging's SenoScan digital mammography and MammoTest stereotactic breast biopsy systems for $32 million. The following year it acquired R2 Technology for $220 million to gain that company's computer-aided detection (CAD) technology. Also in 2006 it acquired breast biopsy and tissue excision device producer Suros Surgical Systems for $240 million. Suros' ATEC (automated tissue excision and collection) system provides minimally invasive breast biopsies.

EXECUTIVES

Chairman Emeritus and CTO: Jay A. Stein, age 64, $417,914 pay
Chairman and CEO: John W. (Jack) Cumming, age 61, $1,261,348 pay
President and COO: Robert A. Cascella, age 52, $867,580 pay
EVP, Finance and Administration, CFO, Treasurer, and Director: Glenn P. Muir, age 47, $730,033 pay
SVP, International Sales: Mark A. Duerst
SVP, Sales and Strategic Accounts: John Pekarsky, age 53, $521,756 pay
SVP and Chief Accounting Officer: Robert H. Lavallee
VP, Human Resources: David J. Brady
VP and Head, Digital Detector: Peter Soltani
VP, Clinical and Product Management: Georgia Hitzke
VP, Skeletal Health Imaging: Brad Herrington
Director, Tomosynthesis Programs: Loren T. Niklason
VP, Information Systems and CIO: David M. Rudzinsky
SVP, Business Development: Thomas Umbel
Director, Investor Relations: Frances Crecco
Auditors: Ernst & Young LLP

LOCATIONS

HQ: Hologic, Inc.
35 Crosby Dr., Bedford, MA 01730
Phone: 781-999-7300   **Fax:** 781-280-0669
Web: www.hologic.com

Hologic has offices in Belgium and the US. Its manufacturing facilities are in Bedford, Massachusetts; Danbury, Connecticut; and Newark, Delaware in the US. It also operates manufacturing facilities in China and Germany.

PRODUCTS/OPERATIONS

2006 Sales

	$ mil.	% of total
Products	388.1	84
Services & other	74.6	16
Total	**462.7**	**100**

Selected Products

ATEC (Automated Tissue Excision and Collection, breast biopsy system)
InSight fluoroscan imaging system (mini c-arm X-ray imaging devices)
Lorad Affinity (mammography system)
Lorad Selenia (mammography system)
QDR series bone densitometer
Sahara Bone Sonometer (ultrasound-based densitometer)
StereoLoc (stereotactic breast biopsy systems)

Selected Subsidiaries

AEG Elektrofotografie GmbH
R2 Technology, Inc.
Suros Surgical Systems, Inc.

COMPETITORS

Agfa	Intact Medical Corporation
C. R. Bard	Kodak Health Group
Cedara Software	Philips Electronics
Ethicon	Sectra
FUJIFILM	SenoRx
GE Healthcare	Siemens Medical
GE OEC Medical Systems	Toshiba
iCAD	

HISTORICAL FINANCIALS

Company Type: Public

Income Statement

FYE: Last Saturday in September

	REVENUE ($ mil.)	NET INCOME ($ mil.)	NET PROFIT MARGIN	EMPLOYEES
9/06	462.7	27.4	5.9%	1,617
9/05	287.7	28.3	9.8%	870
9/04	228.7	12.2	5.3%	761
9/03	204.0	2.9	1.4%	722
9/02	190.2	0.2	0.1%	729
Annual Growth	**24.9%**	**242.1%**	**—**	**22.0%**

2006 Year-End Financials

Debt ratio: 1.0%
Return on equity: 6.7%
Cash ($ mil.): 29.9
Current ratio: 1.66
Long-term debt ($ mil.): 6.2
No. of shares (mil.): 52.6
Dividends
  Yield: —
  Payout: —
Market value ($ mil.): 2,287.2
R&D as % of sales: —
Advertising as % of sales: —

Stock History

NASDAQ (GS): HOLX

	STOCK PRICE ($) FY Close	P/E High/Low	PER SHARE ($) Earnings	Dividends	Book Value
9/06	43.52	101 44	0.56	—	11.53
9/05	26.88	44 14	0.63	—	4.93
9/04	9.53	42 22	0.28	—	8.10
9/03	6.81	120 51	0.07	—	7.48
9/02	4.93	1,805 472	0.00	—	7.33
Annual Growth	**72.4%**	**— —**	**—**	**—**	**12.0%**

Home BancShares

At this Home, you don't have to stash your cash under the mattress. Instead, you can choose from five bank subsidiaries in Arkansas and Florida. Home BancShares serves businesses, real estate developers, investors, individuals, and municipalities in central and north central Arkansas through subsidiaries Bank of Mountain View, Community Bank, First State Bank, and Twin City Bank. It serves the Florida Keys and southwestern Florida through Marine Bank. With a combined network of some 50 branches, the banks offer checking, savings, NOW, and money market accounts, and CDs. Real estate loans account for 80% of the total portfolio, but the banks also make agricultural, business, and consumer loans.

Non-bank subsidiaries provide bank customers with trust and title services and insurance products.

"The Year of the Acquisition" was 2005 for Home BancShares. It purchased the remaining 68% of TCBancorp that it didn't previously own. TCBancorp owned Twin City Bank, with branches in the Little Rock metropolitan area. Additionally, it acquired 20% of the common stock of White River Bancshares of Fayetteville, Arkansas, parent company for Signature Bank of Arkansas; Marine Bancorp, a Florida holding company that owned Marine Bank of the Florida Keys; and finally, Mountain View Bancshares, an Arkansas bank holding company for Bank of Mountain View.

Home BancShares will continue to look toward Arkansas and southwestern Florida for potential acquisitions. The company also plans to add up to 10 *de novo* branches in the coming year in Arkansas, the Florida Keys, and along the southwestern coast of Florida.

Prior to Home Bancshares' 2006 IPO, chairman John Allison and his family controlled about 20% of the company. Vice chairman Richard Ashley controlled 8%; Robert Adcock (a business associate of Allison's through Allison, Adcock, Rankin, LLC) owned 7%; and director Frank Hickingbotham, 5%.

EXECUTIVES

Chairman and CEO; Chairman, First State Bank: John W. Allison, age 59
Vice Chairman: Richard H. Ashley, age 50
President, COO, and Director: Ron W. Strother, age 57, $300,000 pay
CFO and Treasurer: Randy E. Mayor, age 41
CEO, Bank of Mountain View: M. L. Mickey Waddington
President and CEO, Twin City Bank: Robert F. Birch Jr., age 55, $256,500 pay
President and CEO, Community Bank: Tracey M. French, age 44, $269,336 pay
President and CEO, Marine Bank: Robert Hunter Padgett, age 47
President and CEO, Bank of Mountain View: James Ronnie Sims, age 59
Secretary and Director; President and CEO, First State Bank: C. Randall Sims, age 51, $270,750 pay
Auditors: BKD, LLP

LOCATIONS

HQ: Home BancShares, Inc.
719 Harkrider, Conway, AR 72032
Phone: 501-328-4757 **Fax:** 501-329-9139
Web: www.homebancshares.com

Home BancShares operates offices in the Arkansas communities of Beebe, Cabot, Conway, Greenbrier, Jacksonville, Little Rock, Lonoke, Maumelle, Mayflower, Mountain View, North Little Rock, Searcy, Sherwood, Vilonia, and Ward; and in the Florida communities of Charlotte Harbor, Islamorada, Key Largo, Key West, Marathon, Marco Island, and Summerland Key.

PRODUCTS/OPERATIONS

2005 Sales

	% of total
Interest	
Loans	64
Securities	20
Noninterest	
Service charges on deposit accounts	8
Other service charges & fees	2
Mortgage banking	2
Other	4
Total	**100**

Selected Subsidiaries and Affiliates

Bank of Mountain View
Community Bank
Community Financial Statutory Trust I
Community Insurance Agency, Inc.
First Data Solutions, Inc.
First State Bank
FirsTrust Financial Services, Inc.
Grand Prairie Title Co., Inc.
Home BancShares Statutory Trust I
Home BancShares Statutory Trust II
Insurance Mart First State Insurance Agency, Inc.
Marine Bank
Marine (FL) Statutory Trust I
Mountain Lodge, L.P.
Sylamore Properties, Inc.
Twin City Bank

COMPETITORS

Bank of America
Bank of the Ozarks
BB&T
First Federal Bancshares
of Arkansas

First State Financial
Regions Financial
U.S. Bancorp

HISTORICAL FINANCIALS

Company Type: Public

Income Statement

	REVENUE ($ mil.)	NET INCOME ($ mil.)	NET PROFIT MARGIN	EMPLOYEES
12/05	102.3	11.4	11.1%	544
12/04	55.0	9.2	16.7%	—
12/03	28.3	3.8	13.4%	—
Annual Growth	**90.1%**	**73.2%**	**—**	**—**

FYE: December 31

2005 Year-End Financials

Debt ratio: —
Return on equity: 8.4%
Cash ($ mil.): —

Current ratio: —
Long-term debt ($ mil.): 44.8

Net Income History

NASDAQ (GM): HOMB

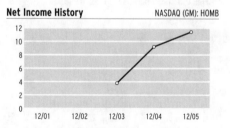

Home Solutions of America

Home Solutions of America can't solve the problems of hurricanes and flooding in coastal areas, but the company *can* do something about the aftermath. It provides specialty interior services through a number of subsidiaries. Home Solutions Restoration of Louisiana and PW Stephens provide recovery services (debris removal, dehumidification); the latter firm, along with Fiber Seal Systems, also provides such restoration services as air decontamination and removal of mold and asbestos. The company's rebuilding and remodeling operations include kitchen cabinet and counter construction and installation performed by subsidiaries Southern Exposure, SouthernStone Cabinets, and Cornerstone Building and Remodeling.

The company has agreements for manufacture and installation of cabinet and countertops with such clients as Centex, The Home Depot, and Lowe's in selected markets. Home Solutions of America, as part of its growth-by-acquisition strategy, is aggressively seeking out and acquiring complementary specialty residential services businesses. In 2005, it acquired the assets of Florida Environmental Remediation Services. The purchase of the restoration company expanded Home Solutions of America's presence in Florida and opens markets in Louisiana and Mississippi. The next year the company acquired Fireline Restoration, a home recovery and restoration provider, for $11.5 million. Fireline Restoration also operates in Florida, Louisiana, and Mississippi. CEO Frank Fradella owns about 6% of Home Solutions of America; Anthony Leeber Jr. (president of subsidiary Cornerstone Building & Remodeling) owns about 7%.

EXECUTIVES

Chairman and CEO: Frank Fradella, age 49, $409,000 pay
President and COO: Rick J. O'Brien, age 40, $150,000 pay
CFO: Jeffrey M. Mattich
VP; President, Southern Exposure Holdings, Southern Exposure Unlimited of Florida, and S.E. Tops of Florida: Dale W. Mars, age 57
Auditors: Corbin & Company, LLP

LOCATIONS

HQ: Home Solutions of America, Inc.
5565 Red Bird Center Dr., Ste. 150,
Dallas, TX 75237
Phone: 214-623-8446 **Fax:** 214-333-9435
Web: www.hsoacorp.com

Home Solutions of America has operations in Alabama, California, Florida, Georgia, Louisiana, Mississippi, South Carolina, and Texas.

PRODUCTS/OPERATIONS

2005 Sales By Segment

	$ mil.	% of total
Recovery/Restoration Services	37.1	54
Rebuilding/Remodeling	31.0	46
Total	**68.1**	**100**

Selected Subsidiaries

Cornerstone Building and Remodeling
Fiber Seal Systems, L.P.
Home Solutions Restoration of Lousiana, Inc.
PW Stephens, Inc.
Southern Exposure Unlimited of Florida, Inc.
SouthernStone Cabinets, Inc. (50%)

COMPETITORS

The BMS Enterprises
InStar Services
Masco
PDG Environmental
ServiceMaster
Servpro Industries
WaterMasters Restoration

HISTORICAL FINANCIALS

Company Type: Public

Income Statement

	REVENUE ($ mil.)	NET INCOME ($ mil.)	NET PROFIT MARGIN	EMPLOYEES
12/05	68.1	7.2	10.6%	483
12/04	31.1	2.6	8.4%	186
12/03	14.0	(0.7)	—	195
12/02	2.6	(0.5)	—	166
12/01	4.4	(2.5)	—	40
Annual Growth	**98.3%**	**—**	**—**	**86.4%**

FYE: December 31

2005 Year-End Financials

Debt ratio: 2.0%
Return on equity: 14.9%
Cash ($ mil.): 8.2
Current ratio: 3.00
Long-term debt ($ mil.): 1.5
No. of shares (mil.): 35.5

Dividends
 Yield: —
 Payout: —
Market value ($ mil.): 159.1
R&D as % of sales: —
Advertising as % of sales: —

Stock History

AMEX: HOM

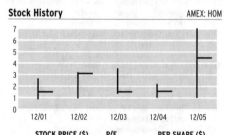

	STOCK PRICE ($) FY Close	P/E High/Low	PER SHARE ($) Earnings	Dividends	Book Value
12/05	4.48	28 4	0.25	—	2.13
12/04	1.57	22 11	0.10	—	1.26
12/03	1.52	— —	(0.06)	—	1.04
12/02	3.10	— —	(0.05)	—	0.42
12/01	1.50	— —	(0.25)	—	0.44
Annual Growth	**31.5%**	**— —**	**—**	**—**	**48.5%**

Hornbeck Offshore Services

At the beck and call of oil companies, Hornbeck Offshore Services provides marine transportation of oil field equipment and supplies and petroleum products. The company operates offshore supply vessels (OSVs) that support offshore oil and gas drilling and production in the deepwater regions of the Gulf of Mexico. The company's fleet of about 25 OSVs transports cargo such as pipe and drilling mud, as well as rig crew members. In addition, Hornbeck Offshore operates about a dozen oceangoing tug and tank barge units that transport crude and refined petroleum products in the northeastern US and in Puerto Rico.

The company's OSVs, which were built beginning in 1997, were designed specifically to take advantage of the trend toward deepwater exploration in the Gulf of Mexico. Operations in US waters account for most of Hornbeck's sales, but the company also undertakes work in international offshore oil production areas.

Although Hurricane Katrina temporarily halted some offshore oil production in 2005, demand for Hornbeck's services remained strong, and in September 2005 the company announced plans to expand both its OSV fleet and its tug and tank barge fleet.

Houston-based investor L. E. Simmons controls a 6% stake in Hornbeck Offshore.

EXECUTIVES

Chairman, President, CEO, and Secretary:
Todd M. Hornbeck, age 37, $900,000 pay
EVP and COO: Carl G. Annessa, age 49, $600,000 pay
EVP and CFO: James O. Harp Jr., age 45, $537,500 pay
SVP and General Counsel: Samuel A. Giberga, age 43, $346,875 pay
Treasurer: Paul M. Ordogne, age 52, $136,000 pay
Corporate Controller: Timothy P. McCarthy, age 38, $232,800 pay
Business Development, Offshore Supply Vessels:
Cleve Ammons
Sales Manager, Tugs and Tank Barges: Paul Cooke
Director of Quality, Health, Safety, and Environment:
Andrew Bruzdzinski
Director Human Resources: Louis Buisson
Auditors: Ernst & Young LLP

LOCATIONS

HQ: Hornbeck Offshore Services, Inc.
103 Northpark Blvd., Ste. 300, Covington, LA 70433
Phone: 985-727-2000   **Fax:** 985-727-2006
Web: www.hornbeckoffshore.com

2005 Sales

	$ mil.	% of total
US	146.2	80
Other countries	36.4	20
Total	**182.6**	**100**

PRODUCTS/OPERATIONS

2005 Sales

	$ mil.	% of total
Offshore supply vessels	117.4	64
Tugs & tank barges	65.2	36
Total	**182.6**	**100**

COMPETITORS

Apex Oil
Chemoil
Crowley Maritime
GulfMark Offshore
K-Sea Transportation
Seabulk
SEACOR
Siem Offshore
Tidewater
Trico Marine
U.S. Shipping

HISTORICAL FINANCIALS

Company Type: Public

Income Statement

FYE: December 31

	REVENUE ($ mil.)	NET INCOME ($ mil.)	NET PROFIT MARGIN	EMPLOYEES
12/05	182.6	37.4	20.5%	657
12/04	132.3	(2.5)	—	601
12/03	110.8	11.2	10.1%	—
12/02	92.6	11.6	12.5%	—
12/01	68.8	10.0	14.5%	—
Annual Growth	**27.6%**	**39.1%**	**—**	**9.3%**

2005 Year-End Financials

Debt ratio: 69.7%
Return on equity: 12.2%
Cash ($ mil.): 271.7
Current ratio: 12.46
Long-term debt ($ mil.): 299.5
No. of shares (mil.): 27.2
Dividends
  Yield: —
  Payout: —
Market value ($ mil.): 887.8
R&D as % of sales: —
Advertising as % of sales: —

Stock History

NYSE: HOS

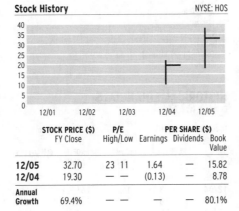

40						
35						
30						
25						
20						
15						
10						
5						
0						
	12/01	12/02	12/03	12/04	12/05	

	STOCK PRICE ($) FY Close	P/E High/Low		PER SHARE ($) Earnings	Dividends	Book Value
12/05	32.70	23	11	1.64	—	15.82
12/04	19.30	—	—	(0.13)	—	8.78
Annual Growth	**69.4%**	**—**	**—**	**—**	**—**	**80.1%**

HouseValues

HouseValues doesn't give your residence a lesson in ethics, but the company can assess your home's market value. The company offers a bevy of services to aid real estate agents, home buyers, and home sellers. Its HouseValues.com targets home sellers; the site assigns a suggested listing price to a house based on property information and connects local real estate agents with buyers and sellers. The company's JustListed.com site targets home buyers by e-mailing listings to them based on personalized requests. HouseValues also provides real estate agents with an online prospect management system called Market Leader. Private equity firm William Blair Capital owns 26% of the company.

In 2005 HouseValues purchased The Loan Page, which generates and markets mortgage leads to mortgage lenders, for about $5.2 million in cash and $1.6 million in debt. Also that year the company launched HomePages, a Web site that combines aerial maps, neighborhood information, and nationwide home listings in one integrated site.

Chairman Mark S. Powell owns 11% of HouseValues. Directors Nicolas J. Hanauer and Frank M. "Pete" Higgins own 6% and 5%, respectively. Investment firm Gilder, Gagnon, Howe & Co. owns nearly 6%.

EXECUTIVES

Chairman: Mark S. Powell, age 47
CEO and Director: Ian Morris, age 37, $412,708 pay
EVP Operations and CFO: R. Barry Allen, age 54
VP Finance: Jacqueline L. (Jackie) Davidson, age 45
VP Customer Success: Scott Smith
VP Human Resources: Jill M. Maguire-Ward
VP Mortgage; President and CEO, The Loan Page:
Kevin Akeroyd
VP Product Strategy and Business Development:
Nikesh S. (Niki) Parekh
VP Sales: Ken Hansen, age 35, $243,928 pay
VP Technology: Mark Jancola
General Counsel and Secretary: Gregg I. Eskenazi, age 45, $273,750 pay
Director Investor Relations: Mark Lamb
Director Marketing: Matt Heinz
Auditors: KPMG LLP

LOCATIONS

HQ: HouseValues, Inc.
11332 NE 122nd Way, Kirkland, WA 98034
Phone: 425-952-5500   **Fax:** 425-952-5809
Web: www.housevalues.com

COMPETITORS

HomeGain.com
LendingTree
Move
Realigent
RE/MAX
ServiceMagic
Zillow

HISTORICAL FINANCIALS

Company Type: Public

Income Statement

FYE: December 31

	REVENUE ($ mil.)	NET INCOME ($ mil.)	NET PROFIT MARGIN	EMPLOYEES
12/05	86.7	15.0	17.3%	507
12/04	47.7	7.5	15.7%	266
12/03	25.1	3.8	15.1%	—
12/02	21.8	3.4	15.6%	—
Annual Growth	**58.4%**	**64.0%**	**—**	**90.6%**

2005 Year-End Financials

Debt ratio: 1.7%
Return on equity: 17.8%
Cash ($ mil.): 84.9
Current ratio: 6.46
Long-term debt ($ mil.): 1.6
No. of shares (mil.): 25.8
Dividends
  Yield: —
  Payout: —
Market value ($ mil.): 336.2
R&D as % of sales: —
Advertising as % of sales: 19.9%

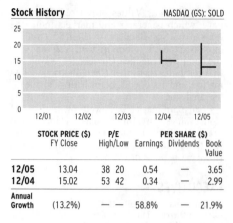

	STOCK PRICE ($) FY Close	P/E High/Low		PER SHARE ($) Earnings	Dividends	Book Value
12/05	13.04	38	20	0.54	—	3.65
12/04	15.02	53	42	0.34	—	2.99
Annual Growth	(13.2%)	—	—	58.8%	—	21.9%

Hungarian Telephone and Cable

Hungarian Telephone and Cable (HTCC) has stretched across the Atlantic to provide fixed-line local phone service in three regions of Hungary. Created in 1992 on the heels of the privatization of Hungarian telecom monopoly Magyar Telekom, HTCC consolidated its operations under one subsidiary, Hungarotel Tavkozlesi. It maintains about 160,000 access lines and offers Internet and long-distance services, as well as Voice over Internet Protocol (VoIP). The company acquired alternative telecom carrier PanTel, which provides voice and data services to businesses throughout Hungary and into other European countries, and agreed to acquire Invitel in 2007. Denmark's TDC owns about 65% of HTCC.

Invitel is Hungary's second largest fixed-line telecommunications service provider. Its acquisition will create a telecommunications company with greater market share and make it a more formidable competitor for the privatized Magyar Telekom.

TDC gained its controlling interest in the company by purchasing shares held by Ashmore Investment Management, which previously acquired the roughly 19% stake held by US-based Citizens Communications. Hungary's Postabank sold its 20% stake to institutional investors.

EXECUTIVES

Chairman: Jesper T. Eriksen, age 38
Vice Chairman: Carsten D. Revsbech, age 37
President and CEO: Torben V. Holm, age 54, $148,600 pay
Interim CFO: Steve Fast, age 46
General Counsel and Secretary: Peter T. Noone, $236,061 pay
Chief Commercial Officer: Tamas Vagany, $129,373 pay (partial-year salary)
Head of Corporate Business Development: Alex Wurtz, $96,300 pay
Auditors: KPMG Hungaria Kft.

LOCATIONS

HQ: Hungarian Telephone and Cable Corp.
1201 Third Ave., Ste. 3400, Seattle, WA 98101
Phone: 206-654-0204   **Fax:** 206-652-2911
Web: www.htcc.hu

Hungarian Telephone and Cable Corp. operates in more than 260 Hungarian municipalities in areas bordering Austria, Romania, Slovakia, and Slovenia. PanTel's network covers all of Hungary and extends into Austria, Bulgaria, Croatia, the Czech Republic, Romania, Serbia, Slovakia, Slovenia, and Ukraine.

PRODUCTS/OPERATIONS

2005 Sales

	$ mil.	% of total
Telephone services	61.8	56
Network services	39.7	36
Other service & product revenues	8.7	8
Total	**110.2**	**100**

Selected Services

Audio text services
Data transmission
Internet access
Internet service provider (Globonet)
Local exchange access
Long-distance (domestic and international)
Toll-free calling
Voice mail
Voice over Internet Protocol (VoIP)

COMPETITORS

BT
Deutsche Telekom AG
Magyar Telekom
Swisscom
Tele2
TeliaSonera
T-Mobile International
Vodafone

HISTORICAL FINANCIALS

Company Type: Public

Income Statement

FYE: December 31

	REVENUE ($ mil.)	NET INCOME ($ mil.)	NET PROFIT MARGIN	EMPLOYEES
12/05	110.2	2.9	2.6%	700
12/04	60.3	16.2	26.9%	900
12/03	59.6	12.5	21.0%	600
12/02	52.2	27.3	52.3%	603
12/01	45.2	11.1	24.6%	630
Annual Growth	25.0%	(28.5%)	—	2.7%

2005 Year-End Financials

Debt ratio: 224.3%
Return on equity: 3.8%
Cash ($ mil.): 25.7
Current ratio: 1.05
Long-term debt ($ mil.): 159.0
No. of shares (mil.): 12.8
Dividends
  Yield: —
  Payout: —
Market value ($ mil.): 199.0
R&D as % of sales: —
Advertising as % of sales: —

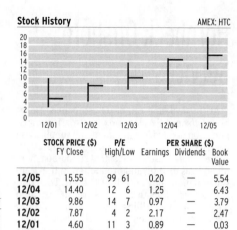

	STOCK PRICE ($) FY Close	P/E High/Low		PER SHARE ($) Earnings	Dividends	Book Value
12/05	15.55	99	61	0.20	—	5.54
12/04	14.40	12	6	1.25	—	6.43
12/03	9.86	14	7	0.97	—	3.79
12/02	7.87	4	2	2.17	—	2.47
12/01	4.60	11	3	0.89	—	0.03
Annual Growth	35.6%	—	—	(31.1%)	—	266.9%

Hurco Companies

Hurco produces PC-based computer control systems and software and computerized machining tools designed to increase efficiencies in metal component production for the metalworking industry. Its products include computerized machine tools with integrated software and computer control systems that allow production floor operators to create programs for making new parts from a blueprint or electronic design in order to begin production quickly. Products include vertical machining and turning centers for metal-cutting and metal-forming applications. Europe is Hurco's largest market, generating about 60% of sales.

Hurco outsources manufacturing of all its machine systems and some of its computer controls. The company has distribution facilities in Los Angeles and in Venlo, the Netherlands. Hurco sells to customers in the aerospace, energy, defense, medical equipment, and transportation industries in about 50 countries throughout North America, Europe, and Asia.

The company's brands include Ultimax and MAX software and computer control systems, VM and VMX vertical machining centers, Autobend computer control systems, and Advanced Velocity Control and Adaptive Surface Finish machining software.

Director Richard Niner controls 11% of Hurco.

EXECUTIVES

Chairman and CEO: Michael Doar, age 50, $571,154 pay
President and COO: James D. Fabris, age 54, $523,077 pay
CFO: John Oblazney
VP, Technology: David E. Platts, age 53, $162,885 pay
President, Hurco North America: Bernard C. Faulkner, age 50
Controller and Assistant Secretary: Sonja K. McClelland, age 34, $139,352 pay
Director, Human Resources: Judy Summers
Investor Relations Contact: Janie Robinson

LOCATIONS

HQ: Hurco Companies, Inc.
1 Technology Way, Indianapolis, IN 46268
Phone: 317-293-5309   **Fax:** 317-328-2811
Web: www.hurco.com

Hurco has operations in China, France, Germany, Italy, Singapore, Taiwan, the UK, and the US.

2006 Sales

	$ mil.	% of total
Europe		
Germany	54.6	37
UK	17.8	12
Other countries	15.4	10
US	50.5	34
Asia & other regions	10.2	7
Total	**148.5**	**100**

PRODUCTS/OPERATIONS

2006 Sales

	$ mil.	% of total
Computerized machine tools	128.9	87
Service parts & fees	14.9	10
Computer control systems & software	4.7	3
Total	**148.5**	**100**

Selected Products

Computerized Machine Tools
  Machining centers
  Metal-forming systems
  Milling machines
Other
  Control upgrades
  Hardware accessories
  Replacement parts
  Retrofit systems for metal-cutting and metal-forming
    machine applications
  Software

COMPETITORS

Doosan Infracore
Fanuc
Genesis Worldwide
Giddings & Lewis
GILDEMEISTER
Gleason
Haas Automation
Hardinge
Intermec Inc.
Mazak
Milacron
Mitsubishi International
Nicolás Correa
Okuma
Precision Twist Drill
Siemens AG
Thermwood
TRUMPF

HISTORICAL FINANCIALS

Company Type: Public

Income Statement   FYE: October 31

	REVENUE ($ mil.)	NET INCOME ($ mil.)	NET PROFIT MARGIN	EMPLOYEES
10/06	148.5	15.5	10.4%	320
10/05	125.5	16.4	13.1%	284
10/04	99.6	6.3	6.3%	250
10/03	75.5	0.5	0.7%	232
10/02	70.5	(8.3)	—	240
Annual Growth	**20.5%**	**—**	**—**	**7.5%**

2006 Year-End Financials

Debt ratio: 5.1%	Dividends
Return on equity: 23.1%	Yield: —
Cash ($ mil.): 29.9	Payout: —
Current ratio: 2.28	Market value ($ mil.): 165.4
Long-term debt ($ mil.): 3.9	R&D as % of sales: —
No. of shares (mil.): 6.3	Advertising as % of sales: —

Stock History   NASDAQ (GS): HURC

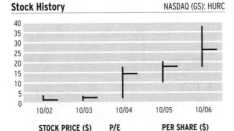

	STOCK PRICE ($) FY Close	P/E High	P/E Low	PER SHARE ($) Earnings	PER SHARE ($) Dividends	PER SHARE ($) Book Value
10/06	26.06	15	7	2.42	—	11.88
10/05	17.83	8	4	2.60	—	9.48
10/04	14.33	17	2	1.04	—	6.39
10/03	2.57	39	16	0.08	—	5.15
10/02	1.55	—	—	(1.48)	—	5.02
Annual Growth	**102.5%**	**—**	**—**	**—**	**—**	**24.0%**

Huron Consulting

Huron Consulting Group dredges through financial statements when businesses fail to stay afloat. The firm provides a variety of financial and legal consulting services to corporate clients that are in financial distress or involved in other legal and regulatory disputes. Its consultants offer forensic accounting and economic analysis expertise and often serve as expert witnesses. Huron Consulting also provides a range of management consulting services to help keep companies out of dire financial straits. The business was started in 2002 by a group of former Arthur Andersen partners, including Huron Consulting chairman, president, and CEO Gary Holdren.

Huron Consulting expanded in 2006 by buying the assets of Galt & Company, an advisory firm that specializes in corporate revitalizations. Huron Consulting paid about $20 million for Galt, which posted revenue of some $17 million in 2005. The company's operational consulting segment gains Galt's management team and about two dozen other staffers. Also that year, Huron Consulting bought three companies that specialize in litigation-related services: Aaxis Technologies, Document Review Consulting Services, and FAB Advisory Services.

The acquisitions continued in 2007 when Huron Consulting acquired Wellspring Partners, a management consulting firm specializing in hospitals and health systems, for $65 million. It also agreed to acquire turnaround specialist Glass & Associates for $30 million.

Since its founding, Huron Consulting has tripled the number of consultants it employs, partly through acquisitions but largely via organic growth, as it has benefited from SEC scrutiny of accounting practices, a lawsuit-happy populace in the US, Sarbanes-Oxley legislation, and an improving economy that has driven mergers and acquisitions.

Better economic conditions cut two ways for the company's business, however. With fewer companies in financial distress, Huron Consulting has seen slowing demand for turnaround, restructuring, and bankruptcy services.

Investment firm Lake Capital Management, which has backed the company since its founding, controls a 9% stake in Huron Consulting. Holdren owns about 5%.

EXECUTIVES

Chairman, President, and CEO: Gary E. Holdren, age 55
Vice Chairman: George E. Massaro, age 58
VP Operations and Assistant Secretary:
Daniel P. (Dan) Broadhurst, age 47
VP, CFO, and Treasurer: Gary L. Burge, age 52
VP, General Counsel and Corporate Secretary:
Natalia Delgado, age 52
VP Human Resources: Mary M. Sawall, age 50
VP Strategy and Business Development:
Stanley N. Logan
Managing Director and Controller: Wayne Lipski, age 50
Corporate Communications: Jennifer Frost Hennagir
Auditors: PricewaterhouseCoopers LLP

LOCATIONS

HQ: Huron Consulting Group Inc.
550 W. Van Buren St., Chicago, IL 60607
Phone: 312-583-8700   **Fax:** 312-583-8701
Web: www.huronconsultinggroup.com

Huron Consulting Group has offices in Boston; Charlotte, North Carolina; Chicago; Houston; Los Angeles; New York City; San Francisco; and Washington, DC.

PRODUCTS/OPERATIONS

2005 Sales

	$ mil.	% of total
Financial consulting	118.2	52
Operational consulting	89.0	40
Reimbursable expenses	18.8	8
Total	**226.0**	**100**

Selected Practice Areas and Services

Financial consulting
  Corporate advisory services
  Disputes and investigations
  Interim management and focused consulting
  Valuation
Operational consulting
  Health care
  Higher education
  Legal business consulting
  Performance improvement
  Strategic sourcing

COMPETITORS

Accenture
Alvarez & Marsal
Bain & Company
BearingPoint
Booz Allen
Boston Consulting
CRA International
Deloitte
Ernst & Young
FTI Consulting
KPMG
LECG
McKinsey & Company
Navigant Consulting
PricewaterhouseCoopers

HISTORICAL FINANCIALS

Company Type: Public

Income Statement

FYE: December 31

	REVENUE ($ mil.)	NET INCOME ($ mil.)	NET PROFIT MARGIN	EMPLOYEES
12/05	226.0	17.8	7.9%	773
12/04	173.9	10.9	6.3%	612
12/03	110.3	(1.1)	—	—
Annual Growth	43.1%	—	—	26.3%

2005 Year-End Financials

Debt ratio: 2.8%
Return on equity: 28.5%
Cash ($ mil.): 31.8
Current ratio: 2.15
Long-term debt ($ mil.): 2.1
No. of shares (mil.): 17.2

Dividends
 Yield: —
 Payout: —
Market value ($ mil.): 413.8
R&D as % of sales: —
Advertising as % of sales: 0.5%

Stock History

NASDAQ (GS): HURN

	STOCK PRICE ($) FY Close	P/E High/Low	PER SHARE ($) Earnings	Dividends	Book Value
12/05	23.99	28 18	1.05	—	4.38
12/04	22.20	34 25	0.72	—	3.01
Annual Growth	8.1%	— —	45.8%	—	45.6%

Hutchinson Technology

Suspensions at Hutchinson Technology have nothing to do with getting kicked out of school. The company is a top global maker of disk drive suspension assemblies. These support the read-write head above the spinning magnetic disk in hard drives, typically at a height of about a millionth of an inch — 3,000 times thinner than a piece of paper. The company's products include conventional assemblies, trace suspension assemblies, and accessories such as base plates and flexures. Hutchinson supplies a select number of large disk drive makers; its top five customers (TDK, Alps Electric, Western Digital, Innovex, and Seagate) account for more than 85% of sales.

The company's trace suspension assemblies, which have the added feature of pre-installed copper leads, make up more than 90% of sales. Customers in Asia account for nearly 95% of sales.

Hutchinson is using its technical expertise to expand into the medical sensing device market. The company has received approval from the FDA to market its tissue spectrometer (the InSpectra StO2 System) that measures oxygen saturation in muscle tissue. The InSpectra instrument was officially launched in late 2006.

No stranger to the volatility of the computer hardware industry, Hutchinson experienced a demand lull in the early 21st century that went beyond market fluctuations. Ever-improving storage density of hard disks has allowed drive makers to cut down on the number of components they employ, including suspension assemblies. In an effort to stem the flow of red ink on its balance sheets, Hutchinson cut jobs and consolidated operations.

OppenheimerFunds owns nearly 14% of Hutchinson Technology. Van Den Berg Management holds around 13% of the company. Wellington Management has an equity stake of about 10%. Goldman Sachs Asset Management owns approximately 9% of Hutchinson. Galleon Management holds around 5% of the company.

HISTORY

Jeffrey Green (chairman) and Jon Geiss founded Hutchinson Industrial in 1965 in Geiss' hometown of Hutchinson, Minnesota. The company set up shop in a converted chicken coop and began providing photoetching services. Its first big contract was to provide circuit boards for mainframe computer maker Sperry (now Unisys). Geiss left the company in 1982, the year it changed its name to Hutchinson Technology. During the early 1980s the company expanded operations to produce disk drive products.

Hutchinson Technology's continuing development of suspension assemblies for ever-smaller read-write heads, which increased disk drive performance, led to a shift to nano head assemblies (a billionth-of-an-inch measurement). In 1995 it began making assemblies for pico heads, measuring a trillionth of an inch.

The company opened new production facilities in 1996, but pricing pressures caused income to dip. Also that year longtime president Wayne Fortun was named CEO. Fiscal 1998 turned out to be an unhealthy year for the company as softness in the disk drive market mixed with a technology transition led to a loss. Hutchinson responded to continuing weak demand in 1999 by consolidating production operations and cutting staff; the company returned to profitability that year.

Hutchinson's stint in the black proved short-lived. Slumping demand for suspension assemblies, due in part to improvements in hard disk technology, led to more layoffs and consolidation in 2000 and 2001. In 2001 the company licensed its trace suspension assembly technology to rivals Magnecomp and NHK.

In early 2002 Hutchinson won FDA clearance to sell a fiber-optic medical device used to measure oxygenated blood in tissue.

The company returned to profitability in 2002. In 2003 Hutchinson signed long-term contracts with certain disk-drive manufacturers.

The following year, the company inked joint development and supply agreements with two leading customers.

Richard Penn, the company's VP of operations since 2003, was promoted to SVP and named president of the Disk Drive Components division, Hutchinson's main line of business, in late 2005.

EXECUTIVES

Chairman: Jeffrey W. (Jeff) Green, age 66
President, CEO, and Director: Wayne M. Fortun, age 57, $776,461 pay
SVP and CFO: John A. Ingleman, age 60, $335,595 pay
SVP; President, Disk Drive Components:
 Richard J. (Rick) Penn, age 50, $379,630 pay

VP, Corporate Finance: David P. (Dave) Radloff
VP and CTO: R. Scott Schaefer, age 53, $352,467 pay
VP, Business Development: Beatrice A. (Bea) Graczyk, age 58, $387,814 pay
VP, Human Resources: Rebecca A. (Becky) Albrecht, age 53
VP, Quality: Kevin D. Bjork, age 47
VP, Sales and Marketing, Disk Drive Components:
 Kathleen S. Skarvan, age 50
VP; President, BioMeasurement Division:
 Christina M. (Chris) Temperante, age 54
VP, Engineering, Disk Drive Components Division:
 Richard G. Fiedler
VP, Operations, Disk Drive Components Division:
 Peter J. (Pete) Ollmann
Secretary: Peggy Steif Abram
Treasurer: Ruth N. Bauer
Manager, Investor Relations: Chuck Ives
Auditors: Deloitte & Touche LLP

LOCATIONS

HQ: Hutchinson Technology Incorporated
 40 W. Highland Park Dr. NE,
 Hutchinson, MN 55350
Phone: 320-587-3797 **Fax:** 320-587-1645
Web: www.htch.com

Hutchinson Technology has manufacturing operations in Minnesota, South Dakota, and Wisconsin; it has international offices in China, Japan, the Netherlands, Singapore, South Korea, and Thailand.

2006 Sales

	$ mil.	% of total
Thailand	264.7	37
Hong Kong	200.3	28
Japan	187.1	26
US	52.7	7
China	16.4	2
Other countries	0.3	—
Total	**721.5**	**100**

PRODUCTS/OPERATIONS

2006 Sales

	$ mil.	% of total
Disk Drive Components		
Suspension assemblies	682.2	95
Other products	38.9	5
BioMeasurement	0.4	—
Total	**721.5**	**100**

2006 Sales by Customer

	% of total
SAE Magnetics/TDK	28
Alps Electric	20
Western Digital	15
Seagate Technology	15
Innovex	8
Others	14
Total	**100**

Products

Disk Drive Components Division
 Trace suspension assemblies (TSA)
 Conventional disk drive suspension assemblies
 Other components
  Base plates and flexures
BioMeasurement Division
 Tissue spectrometer

COMPETITORS

Brilliant Manufacturing Limited
CAS
Fujitsu
Hamamatsu Photonics
Innovex
Magnecomp International
Multek Flexible Circuits
Nippon Hatsujo Kogyo
Nitto Denko
Somanetics

HISTORICAL FINANCIALS

Company Type: Public

Income Statement

FYE: Last Sunday in September

	REVENUE ($ mil.)	NET INCOME ($ mil.)	NET PROFIT MARGIN	EMPLOYEES
9/06	721.5	20.5	2.8%	5,433
9/05	631.6	54.9	8.7%	5,310
9/04	469.7	73.1	15.6%	3,850
9/03	499.0	64.5	12.9%	3,656
9/02	390.7	15.0	3.8%	3,336
Annual Growth	16.6%	8.1%	—	13.0%

2006 Year-End Financials

Debt ratio: 65.7%
Return on equity: 3.6%
Cash ($ mil.): 290.4
Current ratio: 6.02
Long-term debt ($ mil.): 380.3
No. of shares (mil.): 25.6

Dividends
  Yield: —
  Payout: —
Market value ($ mil.): 554.8
R&D as % of sales: —
Advertising as % of sales: —

Stock History

NASDAQ (GS): HTCH

	STOCK PRICE ($) FY Close	P/E High/Low	PER SHARE ($) Earnings	Dividends	Book Value
9/06	21.64	41 22	0.77	—	22.57
9/05	26.49	23 13	1.88	—	21.71
9/04	26.15	16 9	2.42	—	19.41
9/03	32.78	17 7	2.21	—	16.64
9/02	16.54	46 22	0.59	—	14.08
Annual Growth	6.9%	— —	6.9%	—	12.5%

Hydril

The Hydril Company's connections help oil and gas companies pump out profits instead of leaking losses. The company makes connections and pressure-control products used to drill and produce oil and gas in deepwater, deep-formation, and horizontal well-drilling environments. Its tubular products include tubing, casings, and drill pipe connections; pressure-control products include blowout preventers, diverters, subsea control systems, and pulsation dampeners. Hydril has 25 sales and service offices worldwide. Chairman emeritus Richard Seaver, nephew of Hydril's founder, and The Seaver Institute (a charitable organization created by the late founder Frank Seaver) own about 42% of the company.

Hydril was established in 1933. Its pioneering innovations in the 1930s included the first hydraulically operated blowout preventer and the annular blowout preventer.

Richard Seaver retired as chairman in late 2006; president and CEO Christopher Seaver added the chairman's title at that time.

EXECUTIVES

Chairman, President, and CEO: Christopher T. Seaver, age 57
Chairman Emeritus: Richard C. Seaver, age 83
Vice Chairman: Patrick T. Seaver, age 55
VP, Human Resources: Michael D. (Mike) Danford
CFO and Secretary: Chris D. North, age 49, $319,240 pay
EVP and COO: Charles E. Jones, age 45, $522,744 pay
SVP Business Development and Premium Connections: Neil G. Russell, age 59, $246,626 pay
VP Pressure Control: E. Charles (Chuck) Chauviere III, age 40, $319,240 pay
Investor Relations: Sue Nutt
Auditors: Deloitte & Touche LLP

LOCATIONS

HQ: Hydril Company
3300 N. Sam Houston Pkwy. East,
Houston, TX 77032
Phone: 281-449-2000   **Fax:** 281-985-3376
Web: www.hydril.com

Hydril has manufacturing facilities in Houston; Bakersfield, California; and Westwego, Louisiana, as well as in Canada, India, Indonesia, Mexico, Nigeria, and the UK. Its domestic sales and service offices are located in Alaska, California, Louisiana, Texas, and Wyoming; international offices are located in Canada, Indonesia, Mexico, Malaysia, Nigeria, Singapore, the UK, and Venezuela.

2005 Sales

	$ mil.	% of total
Western hemisphere		
US	186.0	50
Other countries	73.0	19
Eastern hemisphere	117.7	31
Total	**376.7**	**100**

PRODUCTS/OPERATIONS

2005 Sales

	$ mil.	% of total
Premium connections	246.5	65
Pressure control	130.2	35
Total	**376.7**	**100**

Selected Products

Premium Connections
  Casings
  Drill pipe
  Tubing
Pressure Control Products
  Blowout preventers
  Diverters
  Drill stem valves
  Gas handlers
  Production chokes
  Pulsation dampeners
  Subsea control systems

COMPETITORS

CE Franklin
Grant Prideco
Hunting
Lone Star Technologies
Maverick Tube
RPC
Tenaris
Vallourec

HISTORICAL FINANCIALS

Company Type: Public

Income Statement

FYE: December 31

	REVENUE ($ mil.)	NET INCOME ($ mil.)	NET PROFIT MARGIN	EMPLOYEES
12/05	376.7	73.2	19.4%	1,700
12/04	285.4	46.5	16.3%	1,400
12/03	212.0	25.6	12.1%	1,300
12/02	241.5	26.5	11.0%	1,400
12/01	239.6	25.6	10.7%	1,500
Annual Growth	12.0%	30.0%	—	3.2%

2005 Year-End Financials

Debt ratio: —
Return on equity: 23.0%
Cash ($ mil.): 173.2
Current ratio: 5.11
Long-term debt ($ mil.): —
No. of shares (mil.): 20.2

Dividends
  Yield: —
  Payout: —
Market value ($ mil.): 1,263.4
R&D as % of sales: —
Advertising as % of sales: —

Stock History

NASDAQ (GS): HYDL

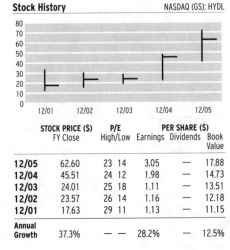

	STOCK PRICE ($) FY Close	P/E High/Low	PER SHARE ($) Earnings	Dividends	Book Value
12/05	62.60	23 14	3.05	—	17.88
12/04	45.51	24 12	1.98	—	14.73
12/03	24.01	25 18	1.11	—	13.51
12/02	23.57	26 14	1.16	—	12.18
12/01	17.63	29 11	1.13	—	11.15
Annual Growth	37.3%	— —	28.2%	—	12.5%

I.D. Systems

I.D. Systems is trying to get its tracking business on the road. The company's wireless systems track, analyze, and control the movements of objects such as packages and vehicles. Its systems use radio-frequency (RF) technology and tiny computers attached to the object to be monitored, and users can access tracking data via the Internet. The company is focused on vehicle management, rental car, package tracking, and airport ground security applications. Customers include 3M, DaimlerChrysler, the FAA, Ford (about 18% of sales), Hallmark Cards, Target, and the US Postal Service (45%).

I.D. Systems outsources manufacturing to such contractors as Flextronics International and Jabil Circuit.

Artis Capital Management owns about 10% of I.D. Systems. Co-founder and COO Ken Ehrman holds nearly 6% of the company. CEO Jeffrey Jagid owns about 5%, as does Oberweis Asset Management. EVP Michael Ehrman has an equity stake of about 4%.

EXECUTIVES

Chairman, CEO, and General Counsel: Jeffrey M. Jagid, age 36, $294,450 pay
President, COO, and Director:
Kenneth S. (Ken) Ehrman, age 36, $260,000 pay
CFO, Secretary, and Treasurer: Ned Mavrommatis, age 35, $235,300 pay
EVP of Sales and Marketing: Frederick F. (Rick) Muntz, age 52, $260,000 pay
EVP of Engineering: Michael L. Ehrman, age 33
Auditors: Eisner LLP

LOCATIONS

HQ: I.D. Systems, Inc.
1 University Plaza, 6th Fl., Hackensack, NJ 07601
Phone: 201-996-9000   **Fax:** 201-996-9144
Web: www.id-systems.com

PRODUCTS/OPERATIONS

Selected Markets

Airport security (airport ground service vehicle access control and remote deactivation)
Car rental companies (automated car rental and return)
Corporate fleets and construction vehicles (tracking vehicle use and location)
Railcar and transportation companies (railcar environment monitoring, tracking of railcar use)
Shipping and delivery companies (location of misrouted packages, package handling operations analysis)

COMPETITORS

AccuCode
Applied Digital
Axcess
Eid Passport
HID
International Electronics
Kasten Chase
Media Recovery
Motorola
Raytheon
Savi Technology
Symbol Technologies
Texas Instruments
Viscount Systems
WhereNet

HISTORICAL FINANCIALS

Company Type: Public

Income Statement

	REVENUE ($ mil.)	NET INCOME ($ mil.)	NET PROFIT MARGIN	EMPLOYEES
12/05	19.0	0.9	4.7%	61
12/04	13.7	0.4	2.9%	55
12/03	8.0	(1.2)	—	37
12/02	5.5	(1.4)	—	35
12/01	0.9	(3.9)	—	31
Annual Growth	114.4%	—	—	18.4%

2005 Year-End Financials

Debt ratio: 1.6%
Return on equity: 6.3%
Cash ($ mil.): 7.6
Current ratio: 4.27
Long-term debt ($ mil.): 0.2
No. of shares (mil.): 7.9
Dividends
  Yield: —
  Payout: —
Market value ($ mil.): 187.2
R&D as % of sales: 8.6%
Advertising as % of sales: 0.8%

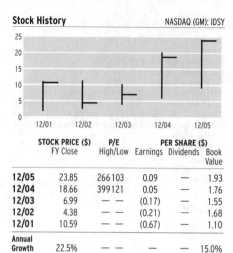

Stock History   NASDAQ (GM): IDSY

	STOCK PRICE ($) FY Close	P/E High/Low	PER SHARE ($) Earnings	Dividends	Book Value
12/05	23.85	266 103	0.09	—	1.93
12/04	18.66	399 121	0.05	—	1.76
12/03	6.99	— —	(0.17)	—	1.55
12/02	4.38	— —	(0.21)	—	1.68
12/01	10.59	— —	(0.67)	—	1.10
Annual Growth	22.5%	— —	—	—	15.0%

Ikanos Communications

Ikanos Communications hopes to become an icon in the field of networking semiconductors. The fabless company designs high-speed programmable single- and multi-port chipsets that allow networks to achieve broadband transmission speeds over existing copper wires. Its SmartLeap and CleverConnect chipsets enable such high speeds over a few thousand feet of wire; this allows network access equipment makers to join multitenant units to the edge of fiber-optic networks, and enables broadband connections between neighboring buildings. Ikanos derives about 44% of sales from NEC.

Other leading OEM customers include Sumitomo Electric Industries, which represents about 28% of sales, along with Millinet and Dasan Networks (12%).

Ikanos has acquired the network processor product line of Analog Devices for about $31 million in cash. Ikanos picked up ADI's FUSIV processor and asymmetrical digital subscriber line (ADSL) line of application-specific integrated circuits in the interest of enhancing its offerings in video services, especially in supplying video to homes. Ikanos will gain an engineering team related to the acquisition, some of which are based in India.

The company outsources fabrication of its of semiconductors to Taiwan Semiconductor Manufacturing Co. (TSMC) and austriamicrosystems. The chips are packaged and tested by Advanced Semiconductor Engineering (ASE) and STATS ChipPAC, among other contractors.

Ikanos raised more than $100 million in private equity funding before going public in September 2005.

Sequoia Capital owns nearly 12% of Ikanos Communications. Walden International holds nearly 7%. Greylock Management has an equity stake of nearly 6%. Telesoft Partners owns around 5%.

EXECUTIVES

Interim CEO: Daniel K. (Dan) Atler, age 46
Interim CFO: Cory Sindelar
VP of Business Development: Rakinder Grover
VP of Human Resources: Chris Smith
VP of Operations: Yehoshua (Joshua) Rom, age 52, $193,518 pay
VP of Worldwide Sales: Nick N. Shamlou
VP of Systems Engineering: Rouben Toumani, age 61, $209,037 pay
General Manager: Dean J. Westman, age 49
Managing Director, Japanese Operations:
Carlton Aihara, age 45
Auditors: PricewaterhouseCoopers LLP

LOCATIONS

HQ: Ikanos Communications, Inc.
47669 Fremont Blvd., Fremont, CA 94538
Phone: 510-979-0400   **Fax:** 510-979-0500
Web: www.ikanos.com

Ikanos Communications has offices in Canada, France, India, Japan, South Korea, Taiwan, and the US.

2005 Sales

	% of total
Japan	72
South Korea	24
Other countries	4
Total	**100**

PRODUCTS/OPERATIONS

Selected Semiconductor Products

Eight-port chipsets for network access concentrators (SmartLeap line)
Single-port chipsets for customer premise equipment (CleverConnect 150)

COMPETITORS

Analog Devices
Broadcom
Centillium Communications
Conexant Systems
Freescale Semiconductor
Infineon Technologies
Intel
Marvell Technology
Metalink
PMC-Sierra
STMicroelectronics
Texas Instruments

HISTORICAL FINANCIALS

Company Type: Public

Income Statement

	REVENUE ($ mil.)	NET INCOME ($ mil.)	NET PROFIT MARGIN	EMPLOYEES
12/05	85.1	2.7	3.2%	178
12/04	66.7	(8.5)	—	154
12/03	29.0	(29.9)	—	—
Annual Growth	71.3%	—	—	15.6%

2005 Year-End Financials

Debt ratio: 0.9%
Return on equity: 19.8%
Cash ($ mil.): 93.9
Current ratio: 5.63
Long-term debt ($ mil.): 0.9
No. of shares (mil.): 23.7
Dividends
  Yield: —
  Payout: —
Market value ($ mil.): 349.6
R&D as % of sales: 33.4%
Advertising as % of sales: —

	STOCK PRICE ($)	P/E		PER SHARE ($)	
	FY Close	High/Low	Earnings	Dividends	Book Value
12/05	14.74	126 72	0.13	—	4.38

Immucor

Immucor makes sure you can be positive when getting your blood type. The company develops, makes, and sells blood test reagents and automated and semi-automated analysis systems that are used by blood banks, hospitals, and clinical laboratories in North America, Europe, and Asia. Immucor's products identify human blood properties for blood typing; they also detect foreign antibodies. Immucor markets directly and through distribution agreements. The company has consolidated its distribution operations and standardized its pricing mechanisms to become more competitive.

The company made a step toward increasing its foothold in Japan, which has the third-largest market behind Europe and the US for transfusion diagnostics, through the creation of a joint venture with its former Japanese distributor, Kainos. The new company, Immucor-Kainos, is 51% owned by Immucor; Immucor plans to purchase Kainos' 49% stake.

EXECUTIVES

Chairman: Joseph E. Rosen, age 63
President, CEO, and Director:
Gioacchino (Nino) De Chirico, age 53
SVP, Chief Scientific Officer, and Director:
Ralph A. Eatz, age 62
SVP, Sales: Michael C. (Mike) Poynter
VP, CFO, and Secretary; President, Dominion Biologicals: Patrick D. Waddy
Director, European Operations: Didier L. Lanson, age 56
Auditors: Grant Thornton LLP

LOCATIONS

HQ: Immucor, Inc.
    3130 Gateway Dr., Norcross, GA 30091
Phone: 770-441-2051   **Fax:** 770-441-3807
Web: www.immucor.com

2005 Sales

	$ mil.	% of total
US	141.6	71
Germany	17.8	9
Italy	13.3	6
Canada	9.8	5
Japan	7.4	4
Other countries	10.3	5
Adjustments	(16.7)	—
Total	**183.5**	**100**

PRODUCTS/OPERATIONS

Selected Products

ABO Blood Grouping (blood group classification test)
ABS2000 (fully automated blood bank system)
Antibody Potentiators (increase the sensitivity of antigen-antibody tests)
Anti-human Globulin Serums (crossmatching and antibody detection)
Capture -P, -R, -CMV, -S, -R Select (detection of various antibodies)
Capture Workstation (semi-automated components)
Fetal Bleed Screen Kit (detects excessive fetal-maternal hemorrhage)
GALILEO (second generation blood bank system)
Monoclonal (Hybridoma) Antibody-based Reagents (detects and identifies ABO and other antigens)
Quality Control Systems (daily evaluation of the reactivity of blood testing reagents)
Rare Serums (detects rare antigens)
Reagent Red Blood Cells (detect and identify antibodies in blood)
Rh Blood Typing (detect Rh antigens)
ROSYS Plato (microplate liquid handler and sample processor)
Technical Proficiency Systems (reagent tests used to determine technical proficiency and provide continuing education for technical staff)

COMPETITORS

Abaxis	MEDION
Beckman Coulter	Olympus
Biotest	Ortho-Clinical Diagnostics
Clarient	Serologicals
Grifols, Inc.	TECHNE
Hemagen Diagnostics	

HISTORICAL FINANCIALS

Company Type: Public

Income Statement   FYE: May 31

	REVENUE ($ mil.)	NET INCOME ($ mil.)	NET PROFIT MARGIN	EMPLOYEES
5/06	183.5	39.8	21.7%	563
5/05	144.8	23.9	16.5%	526
5/04	112.6	12.5	11.1%	531
5/03	98.3	14.4	14.6%	521
5/02	84.1	8.8	10.5%	481
Annual Growth	21.5%	45.8%	—	4.0%

2006 Year-End Financials

Debt ratio: —
Return on equity: 30.5%
Cash ($ mil.): 55.7
Current ratio: 4.33
Long-term debt ($ mil.): —
No. of shares (mil.): 67.9
Dividends
  Yield: —
  Payout: —
Market value ($ mil.): 1,234.9
R&D as % of sales: —
Advertising as % of sales: —

	STOCK PRICE ($)	P/E		PER SHARE ($)	
	FY Close	High/Low	Earnings	Dividends	Book Value
5/06	18.18	43 26	0.56	—	2.12
5/05	22.34	70 23	0.33	—	2.58
5/04	9.24	52 21	0.18	—	1.35
5/03	4.23	24 10	0.21	—	5.73
5/02	2.56	17 2	0.15	—	5.71
Annual Growth	63.2%	— —	39.0%	—	(21.9%)

Imperial Industries

Imperial Industries manufactures and distributes building materials to building materials dealers, real estate developers, and contractors primarily in the southeastern US. The company's Premix-Marbletite Manufacturing subsidiary manufactures roof tile mortar, stucco and plaster, adhesive, and pool finish products. Imperial Industries' Just-Rite Supply subsidiary distributes the company's products and such products as gypsum, roofing, insulation, and masonry materials made by other companies; it brings in two-thirds of Imperial Industries' sales. Just-Rite operates about a dozen distribution centers in Alabama, Florida, Georgia, and Mississippi.

In 2005 the company completed a roughly $1.5 million modernization project of its Premix manufacturing facility in Winter Springs, Florida. With the modernization complete, Imperial Industries is considering further expanding the plant's manufacturing capabilities.

As part of a strategic alliance with Degussa, Imperial's DFH (formerly Acrocrete) subsidiary shuttered its acrylic stucco production and sold the Acrocrete brand name and certain assets to Degussa Construction Chemicals' Degussa Wall Systems, Inc., for $1.1 million in 2005. The alliance stipulated that Imperial's Just-Rite Supply subsidiary will sell Acrocrete products made by Degussa for a three-year term.

In 2004 much of the company's sales were generated from areas impacted by the four hurricanes that struck the Southeast that year. Imperial Industries' facilities did not suffer, but initially the company lost sales and its production was lower due to delays in construction activity tied to storm contingency planning, storm damage, and lost power.

Director (and former VP of Premix-Marbletite Manufacturing and Acrocrete) Lisa Brock owns about 4% of the company; chairman S. Daniel Ponce owns about 3%.

EXECUTIVES

Chairman: S. Daniel Ponce, age 57
CFO: Steven M. Healy, age 43
President, Just-Rite Supply; VP, Sales and Marketing, Premix and Acrocrete: Stephen C. Brown, age 58, $225,000 pay
VP, Manufacturing, Premix-Marbletite Manufacturing Co. and Acrocrete, Inc.: Martin R. McDonald
Assistant VP and Assistant Secretary; Chief Accounting Officer, Premix-Marbletite Manufacturing: Betty J. Murchison, age 65
Auditors: PricewaterhouseCoopers LLP

LOCATIONS

HQ: Imperial Industries, Inc.
    1259 NW 21st St., Pompano Beach, FL 33069
Phone: 954-917-7665   **Fax:** 954-917-2775
Web: www.imperialindustries.com

Imperial Industries operates manufacturing plants in Pompano Beach and Winter Springs, Florida. Its Just-Rite Supply subsidiary operates distribution facilities in Alabama, Florida, Georgia, and Mississippi.

PRODUCTS/OPERATIONS

2005 Sales

	% of total
Just-Rite Supply	66
Premix-Marbletite	21
DFH (formerly Acrocrete)	13
Total	**100**

Selected Subsidiaries

Just-Rite Supply, Inc.
Premix-Marbletite Manufacturing Co.

COMPETITORS

CEMEX	Holcim (US)
CRH	Lafarge
HeidelbergCement	Stock Building Supply

HISTORICAL FINANCIALS

Company Type: Public

Income Statement

FYE: December 31

	REVENUE ($ mil.)	NET INCOME ($ mil.)	NET PROFIT MARGIN	EMPLOYEES
12/05	72.3	3.4	4.7%	148
12/04	55.3	2.5	4.5%	—
12/03	41.1	0.6	1.5%	—
12/02	36.5	(0.9)	—	—
12/01	39.5	(0.2)	—	—
Annual Growth	16.3%	—	—	—

2005 Year-End Financials

Debt ratio: 34.2%
Return on equity: 41.2%
Cash ($ mil.): 2.1
Current ratio: 1.68
Long-term debt ($ mil.): 3.5
No. of shares (mil.): 2.5

Dividends
  Yield: —
  Payout: —
Market value ($ mil.): 31.9
R&D as % of sales: —
Advertising as % of sales: —

Stock History

NASDAQ (CM): IPII

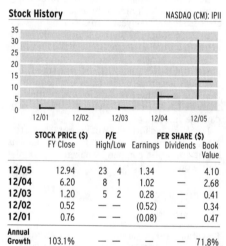

	STOCK PRICE ($) FY Close	P/E High/Low	PER SHARE ($) Earnings	Dividends	Book Value
12/05	12.94	23 4	1.34	—	4.10
12/04	6.20	8 1	1.02	—	2.68
12/03	1.20	5 2	0.28	—	0.41
12/02	0.52	— —	(0.52)	—	0.34
12/01	0.76	— —	(0.08)	—	0.47
Annual Growth	103.1%	— —	—	—	71.8%

Infocrossing

Infocrossing dots the i's and crosses the t's when it comes to managing your information technology (IT) services. The company provides a variety of outsourced IT services for customers, including ADT Security Services, Alicomp, IBM, and Elementis. Strategic partners include CA, Cisco, and Sun Microsystems. Infocrossing's services include computer facilities management, application development, remote monitoring, data center and data processing outsourcing, and network management. The company also offers infrastructure management consulting, mainframe and open system outsourcing, managed hosting, and disaster recovery services.

Expanding operations through acquisitions, the company bought messaging management firm IntelliReach in mid-2006. In late 2005 the company bought (i)Structure, the IT infrastructure management subsidiary formerly owned by Level 3 Communications, for about $82 million.

In early 2004, the company bought data center outsourcing company ITO Acquisition for $35 million. ITO does business as Systems Management Specialists. Infocrossing then acquired a part of Verizon Information Technologies' health care claims processing service for $43.5 million.

HISTORY

Zach Lonstein founded Transportation Computing Services in 1970 to offer batch processing services to the apparel industry. The company was acquired in 1981 by Informatics General (computer software and services, now Sterling Federal Systems), and Lonstein became VP of its commercial online division. He bought the division in 1984 to start Commercial On-Line Systems (COLS). COLS grew steadily throughout the 1980s and early 1990s, offering both online and batch processing services such as accounting, payroll, data entry, order entry, and production control.

COLS went public in 1993 as Computer Outsourcing Services, Inc. (COSI) and soon embarked on a series of acquisitions. Among its purchases were ESM Computer Service (1993), payroll outsourcing companies New England Data Services (1993) and Daton Data Processing (1994), marketing information processor Tru-Check Computer Systems (1994), and banking and transportation information technology outsourcing specialist MCC (1995).

Acquisition-related expenses led to a loss for fiscal 1995, but COSI returned to profitability the following year. In 1997 the company sold its unprofitable payroll processing business to Zurich Payroll Solutions. It bought infrastructure management consulting firm Enterprise Technology Group (now ETG) in 1998.

Branching into Internet services, COSI formed subsidiary Infocrossing the next year and opened its first Internet data center in early 2000. That year the company changed its name to Infocrossing. In 2002 the company acquired AmQUEST, the outsourced services subsidiary of American Software.

EXECUTIVES

Chairman and CEO: Zach Lonstein, age 62, $765,315 pay
Vice Chairman, President, and COO: Robert B. Wallach, age 67, $765,315 pay
EVP Marketing and Business Development: Lee C. Fields, age 47
SVP Finance, CFO, and Treasurer: William J. McHale Jr., age 50, $260,000 pay
SVP, General Counsel, and Secretary: Nicholas J. Letizia, age 54, $268,193 pay
SVP Client Services: Vincent Deluca, age 41
SVP Corporate Development: Michael Wilczak, age 35
SVP Enterprise Engineering: Thomas Laudati, age 47
SVP Research and Development: Garry Lazarewicz, age 56
SVP Sales; President, AmQUEST: Roger A. Barrios, age 53
President, Enterprise Application Services: Richard Giordanella, age 57
President, Infocrossing Healthcare Services: Michael J. (Mike) Luebke, age 54, $250,000 pay
President, Infrastructure Technology Outsourcing: Michael D. (Mike) Jones, age 48
Auditors: Ernst & Young LLP

LOCATIONS

HQ: Infocrossing, Inc.
2 Christie Heights St., Leonia, NJ 07605
Phone: 201-840-4700   **Fax:** 201-840-7100
Web: www.infocrossing.com

PRODUCTS/OPERATIONS

Selected Services

Business process outsourcing
Communication and network management
Custom application development
Data center outsourcing
Data conversion
Data processing
Disaster recovery
Electronic data interchange
Information systems processing
Infrastructure management consulting
Internet and intranet development
IT consulting
Legacy system processing and maintenance
Mainframe outsourcing
Migration support
PC and LAN support
Systems management outsourcing and hosting

COMPETITORS

Affiliated Computer	EDS
Capgemini	Hewlett-Packard
Computer Generated Solutions	IBM
	Perot Systems
Computer Sciences Corp.	SunGard

HISTORICAL FINANCIALS

Company Type: Public

Income Statement

FYE: December 31

	REVENUE ($ mil.)	NET INCOME ($ mil.)	NET PROFIT MARGIN	EMPLOYEES
12/05	148.0	2.6	1.8%	838
12/04	104.9	20.0	19.1%	553
12/03	55.2	1.4	2.5%	257
12/02	50.8	1.1	2.2%	236
12/01	27.0	(36.5)	—	213
Annual Growth	53.0%	—	—	40.8%

2005 Year-End Financials

Debt ratio: 115.9%
Return on equity: 2.6%
Cash ($ mil.): 16.9
Current ratio: 1.12
Long-term debt ($ mil.): 124.1
No. of shares (mil.): 20.5

Dividends
  Yield: —
  Payout: —
Market value ($ mil.): 176.9
R&D as % of sales: —
Advertising as % of sales: —

Stock History

NASDAQ (GS): IFOX

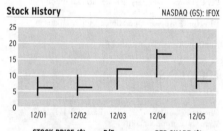

	STOCK PRICE ($) FY Close	P/E High/Low	PER SHARE ($) Earnings	Dividends	Book Value
12/05	8.61	168 53	0.12	—	5.21
12/04	16.93	19 10	0.95	—	4.61
12/03	12.13	— —	(0.76)	—	2.02
12/02	6.30	— —	(1.52)	—	(2.27)
12/01	6.08	— —	(7.77)	—	(1.13)
Annual Growth	9.1%	— —	—	—	—

InfoSonics

InfoSonics answers the call for phone fulfillment. The company distributes wireless handsets and accessories from manufacturers such as Motorola, Nokia, and Samsung. It supplies retailers, wireless carriers, and distributors in Central America and the US from distribution centers in San Diego and Miami. InfoSonics' services include programming, software loading, and light assembly. It plans to expand its logistics business to include outsourced supply-chain services such as inventory management and customized packaging. CEO Joseph Ram owns almost 40% of the company.

In 2004 InfoSonics sold off or closed its retail operations to focus on its core distribution business. Subsidiary Axcess Mobile had operated the retail segment, which consisted of 10 San Diego-area mall kiosks.

EXECUTIVES

President, CEO, and Director: Joseph Ram, age 43, $425,000 pay
EVP and Director: Abraham Rosler, age 45, $195,000 pay
CFO: Jeffrey (Jeff) Klausner, age 34, $225,000 pay
President, Latin America Division: John Althoff
VP, Sales and Marketing: Joseph (Joe) Murgo, age 38, $154,231 pay
VP, North America: Timmy Monico
VP, Finance and Operations: Josh Haims
Auditors: Singer Lewak Greenbaum & Goldstein LLP

LOCATIONS

HQ: InfoSonics Corporation
    5880 Pacific Center Blvd., San Diego, CA 92121
Phone: 858-373-1600   **Fax:** 858-373-1505
Web: www.infosonics.com

2005 Sales

	$ mil.	% of total
Latin America		
Argentina	72.3	50
Other countries	27.9	19
North America	45.6	31
Total	**145.8**	**100**

COMPETITORS

Aftermarket Technology
Brightpoint Inc.
Brightstar Corp.
CellStar
SED International
TESSCO
UPS Logistics Technologies

HISTORICAL FINANCIALS

Company Type: Public

Income Statement

FYE: December 31

	REVENUE ($ mil.)	NET INCOME ($ mil.)	NET PROFIT MARGIN	EMPLOYEES
12/05	145.8	2.7	1.9%	28
12/04	73.4	0.0	—	40
12/03	65.1	1.1	1.7%	88
12/02	46.7	0.4	0.9%	—
12/01	34.2	(0.1)	—	—
Annual Growth	**43.7%**	**—**	**—**	**(43.6%)**

2005 Year-End Financials

Debt ratio: —	Dividends
Return on equity: 17.7%	Yield: —
Cash ($ mil.): 7.7	Payout: —
Current ratio: 1.90	Market value ($ mil.): 45.7
Long-term debt ($ mil.): —	R&D as % of sales: —
No. of shares (mil.): 5.6	Advertising as % of sales: 0.0%

Stock History

NASDAQ (GM): IFON

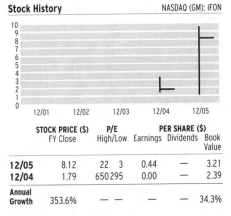

	STOCK PRICE ($) FY Close	P/E High/Low	PER SHARE ($) Earnings	Dividends	Book Value
12/05	8.12	22 3	0.44	—	3.21
12/04	1.79	650 295	0.00	—	2.39
Annual Growth	**353.6%**	**— —**	**—**	**—**	**34.3%**

InfoSpace

Why crawl the Web when others have done it for you? InfoSpace operates a portfolio of online search services that rely on metasearch technology. Its sites, including Dogpile.com, MetaCrawler.com, and WebCrawler.com, query such leading search engines as Ask.com and Google and then collate and rank those search results. Its metasearch technology also powers third-party search services, such as WhenU.com and WebSearch.com. In addition to search, the company provides online directory and yellow page services primarily through its Switchboard subsidiary. InfoSpace is also becoming a leading provider of interactive content and services for such mobile operators as AT&T Mobility and Verizon Wireless.

The company has been growing its mobile content offerings, which now account for about 45% of sales. In addition to games, graphics, and ringtones, InfoSpace provides services that allow mobile operators and other companies to easily offer content to their subscribers. InfoSpace has also partnered with Fuse Networks to develop an e-commerce center where the online entertainment company can offer ringtones and games to its mobile users.

The company's search and directory offerings primarily generate revenue through paid search results and other online advertising. It has renewed distribution and partnership agreements with search giants Google and Yahoo!, ensuring access to search results for several years.

In 2006 InfoSpace announced a restructuring plan as a response to revenue losses. The plan includes 250 job cuts and the closing of its Hamburg, Germany facility.

HISTORY

Indian immigrant Naveen Jain, a veteran of Microsoft's online services unit, set out to create an interactive "people and business finder" in 1996. Eschewing funding from venture capitalists (disdainfully calling them "vulture capitalists"), the

---

outspoken Jain launched his new enterprise, dubbed InfoSpace, with $250,000 of his own money. Its online phone directory service debuted in May, and a few months later it unveiled an online e-mail directory. Unlike most Internet players, InfoSpace wasn't looking to lure users to its own Web site (though it did have one). Instead, the company focused on supplying information to other sites.

By the beginning of 1997 InfoSpace had added industry stalwarts Lycos (now owned by South Korea's Daum Communications) and Microsoft to its customer list. That year it signed up Home Network, Playboy, Dow Jones' Wall Street Journal Online, and Go2Net. The company's content also found its way to cable TV that year by way of InfoSpace's alliance with Source Media's Interactive Channel. InfoSpace continued expanding beyond traditional Internet customers, inking deals to feed its content to Motorola and SkyTel pagers, the 3Com PalmPilot, and the AT&T PocketNet service.

The company secured two vital customers in 1998, signing America Online (AOL) and Netscape (later acquired by AOL) to content distribution deals. To get the agreements, however, InfoSpace had to pay AOL and Netscape to carry its content. Also in 1998 the company set up shop in the UK through a joint venture with Thomson Directories Limited. It went public later that year as InfoSpace.com.

After going public, the company entered into e-commerce agreements with Cyberian Outpost and Multiple Zones (now known as just Zones). In 1999 it joined with Quote.com to create a financial content package. It later established a venture capital fund, launched its comparison shopping application ActiveShopper, and expanded into Canada and India. InfoSpace bolstered its wireless operations in 2000 through acquisitions of Saraide and Millet Software and signed agreements with GTE Wireless (now Cingular) and VeriSign. The company later dropped the ".com" from its name and Jain handed the CEO title to Arun Sarin.

In October 2000 InfoSpace expanded its infrastructure services and content offerings when it acquired online content company Go2Net for about $1.5 billion. The company's stock sank into the single digits, however, and a management shakeup led to the departures of its COO and CFO. Jain took back the CEO title from Sarin (who briefly served as vice chairman before resigning from the board) and realigned the company's focus on its core distribution products. The company later acquired Locus Dialogue, a developer of speech recognition technologies. In late 2002 one of the company's directors, Jim Voelker, replaced Jain as chairman and CEO.

InfoSpace cut about 115 jobs and sold its Silicon Investor site in 2003. It also purchased mobile media company Moviso from the now defunct Vivendi Universal Net USA Group. Later that year, Jain resigned from the board of directors after the company filed a lawsuit against him claiming his new company, Intelius, violated non-compete clauses. (The suit was dismissed the following year.) InfoSpace sold its payment solutions business to Lightbridge in 2004 for $82 million and boosted its local directory offerings with the acquisition of Switchboard for $160 million. It also acquired mobile game creators Atlas Mobile and IOMO Limited.

EXECUTIVES

Chairman, President, and CEO: James F. (Jim) Voelker, age 55, $570,000 pay
CFO: Allen M. Hsieh, age 45
EVP Online Business: Brian T. McManus, age 48
EVP Mobile Business: Steven L. (Steve) Elfman, age 50
SVP and General Counsel: Bruce Easter
SVP, General Counsel, and Secretary: John M. Hall
VP Content: Kieve Huffman
VP Marketing: Russell Arons
VP Product Management: Brian Bowman
VP Sales: Daniel Russell
VP Technology and Research and Development: Reed Thorkildsen
President and CEO, Switchboard: Dean Polnerow, age 48
President, Mobile and Online Media: Stephen J. Davis, age 44
VP European Operations, InfoSpace Mobile: John Chasey
VP European Sales and Marketing, InfoSpace Mobile: George Fraser
VP New Product Development and Business Development, InfoSpace Mobile: Frank Barbieri
VP Product Management and Marketing, Europe: Alan Welsman
Chief Administrative Officer and Director: Edmund O. Belsheim Jr., age 53, $329,687 pay
Director of Marketing, Dogpile.com: Jon Nolz
Corporate Communications: Jeff Hasen
Investor Relations: Stacy Ybarra
Auditors: Deloitte & Touche LLP

LOCATIONS

HQ: InfoSpace, Inc.
601 108th Ave. NE, Ste. 1200, Bellevue, WA 98004
Phone: 425-201-6100   **Fax:** 425-201-6150
Web: www.infospaceinc.com

InfoSpace has operations in the Netherlands, the UK, and the US.

PRODUCTS/OPERATIONS

2005 Sales

	$ mil.	% of total
Search & directory	182.6	54
Mobile	157.4	46
Total	**340.0**	**100**

Selected Products and Services

Mobile content and services
- Games
- Graphics
- Music
- Ringtones

Search and directories
- E-mail search
- Maps and directions
- Public records
- Reverse phone number lookup
- Web search
- White pages
- Yellow pages

Selected Web Sites

Metasearch sites
- Dogpile.com
- InfoSpace.com
- MetaCrawler.com
- WebCrawler.com

Switchboard.com (online phone directory)

COMPETITORS

AG Interactive	MapQuest
AOL	MIVA
Citysearch	MSN
Daum Communications	VeriSign
Google	Verizon Information
IAC Search & Media	Services
LookSmart	Yahoo!
MapInfo	Yellow Book USA

HISTORICAL FINANCIALS

Company Type: Public

Income Statement

FYE: December 31

	REVENUE ($ mil.)	NET INCOME ($ mil.)	NET PROFIT MARGIN	EMPLOYEES
12/05	340.0	159.4	46.9%	620
12/04	249.4	82.4	33.0%	515
12/03	160.1	(6.3)	—	466
12/02	136.1	(345.3)	—	596
12/01	161.9	(502.1)	—	741
Annual Growth	**20.4%**	**—**	**—**	**(4.4%)**

2005 Year-End Financials

Debt ratio: —
Return on equity: 26.0%
Cash ($ mil.): 375.4
Current ratio: 7.03
Long-term debt ($ mil.): —
No. of shares (mil.): 31.0
Dividends
  Yield: —
  Payout: —
Market value ($ mil.): 800.9
R&D as % of sales: —
Advertising as % of sales: 2.2%

Stock History

NASDAQ (GS): INSP

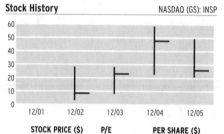

	STOCK PRICE ($) FY Close	P/E High/Low		PER SHARE ($) Earnings	Dividends	Book Value
12/05	25.82	11	5	4.47	—	21.44
12/04	47.55	26	10	2.26	—	17.10
12/03	23.05	—	—	(0.20)	—	14.19
12/02	8.45	—	—	(11.26)	—	14.39
Annual Growth	**45.1%**			**—**	**—**	**70.4%**

InfraSource Services

InfraSource Services is a source of infrastructure services for electric and gas utilities throughout the US. The company designs, builds, and maintains utilities' transmission and distribution systems. InfraSource Services also works on telecommunications infrastructure projects. More than half of the company's business comes from electric power infrastructure. In 2003 former parent Exelon sold InfraSource Services to funds managed by investment firms GFI Energy Ventures and Oaktree Capital Management; the firms took InfraSource Services public in 2004. GFI and Oaktree together own nearly one-third of the specialty contractor. Exelon, a utility holding company, remains a major InfraSource Services customer.

In 2004 InfraSource Services expanded by buying three utility construction businesses: EnStructure, a unit of SEMCO Energy; Utili-Trax, a unit of Connexus Energy; and Maslonka & Associates. The following year, InfraSource Services acquired EHV Power of Canada, which specializes in splicing underground high-voltage cables.

EXECUTIVES

Interim Chairman: Ian A. Schapiro, age 49
Chairman, President, and CEO: David R. (Dave) Helwig, age 55, $823,324 pay (prior to promotion)
SVP, CFO, and Secretary: Terence R. (Terry) Montgomery, age 42, $445,995 pay
SVP and General Counsel: Deborah C. Lofton, age 36
SVP, Business Development: Doug Link
SVP, Human Resources: James P. (Jim) Urbas
VP and General Counsel: James Leyden
VP, Corporate Controller, and Chief Accounting Officer: R. Barry Sauder, age 45
VP, Human Resources: William A. (Bill) Schwartz
President, Blair Park Services and Sunesys, Inc.: Lawrence P. (Larry) Coleman, age 48, $345,097 pay
President and CEO, InfraSource Underground Services: Paul M. Daily, age 49, $315,927 pay
President and COO, MJ Electric: Stephen J. (Steve) Reiten, age 56, $549,098 pay
Auditors: PricewaterhouseCoopers LLP

LOCATIONS

HQ: InfraSource Services, Inc.
100 W. 6th St., Ste. 300, Media, PA 19063
Phone: 610-480-8000   **Fax:** 610-480-8096
Web: www.infosourceinc.com

PRODUCTS/OPERATIONS

2005 Sales

	$ mil.	% of total
Infrastructure construction services	821.8	95
Telecommunication services	40.5	5
Corporate & eliminations	3.2	—
Total	**865.5**	**100**

COMPETITORS

Dycom
E-J Electric Installation Co.
EMCOR
Henkels & McCoy
InfrastruX
Integrated Electrical Services
MasTec
MYR Group
Pike Electric Corporation
Quanta Services
Siemens Industrial Solutions
SM&P Utility Resources
Utility Services
Xcelecom

HISTORICAL FINANCIALS

Company Type: Public

Income Statement

FYE: December 31

	REVENUE ($ mil.)	NET INCOME ($ mil.)	NET PROFIT MARGIN	EMPLOYEES
12/05	865.5	13.7	1.6%	3,920
12/04	651.0	9.6	1.5%	4,200
12/03	138.0	1.3	0.9%	2,900
Annual Growth	**150.4%**	**224.6%**	**—**	**16.3%**

2005 Year-End Financials

Debt ratio: 27.5%
Return on equity: 4.7%
Cash ($ mil.): 24.3
Current ratio: 1.78
Long-term debt ($ mil.): 83.0
No. of shares (mil.): 39.4
Dividends
  Yield: —
  Payout: —
Market value ($ mil.): 515.3
R&D as % of sales: —
Advertising as % of sales: —

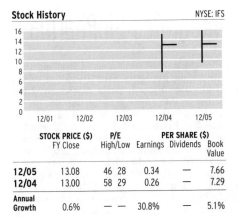

	STOCK PRICE ($) FY Close	P/E High/Low	PER SHARE ($) Earnings	Dividends	Book Value
12/05	13.08	46 28	0.34	—	7.66
12/04	13.00	58 29	0.26	—	7.29
Annual Growth	0.6%	— —	30.8%	—	5.1%

InnerWorkings

Printing procurement firm InnerWorkings has inserted itself into the process by which corporate customers get print jobs done. The company's proprietary software, PPM4, matches customers' jobs with printing companies' equipment and capacity. The InnerWorkings system submits a job to multiple printers, who then bid for the business. More than 2,700 printers participate in the company's network. InnerWorkings' customers include companies in the advertising, consumer products, publishing, and retail industries. InCorp, a company controlled by the families of two of InnerWorkings' founders, owns 34% of InnerWorkings, which was formed in 2001.

Most of InnerWorkings' business comes from enterprise customers, for whom the company handles print jobs on a recurring basis. InnerWorkings also takes work from customers on a transactional basis, one order at a time.

The company hopes to grow by converting transactional customers to enterprise customers. InnerWorkings also hopes to attract more business from outside its home state of Illinois, where about two-thirds of its clients are located.

Proceeds from the company's IPO are to be used to expand InnerWorkings' sales force in target markets such as Boston, Los Angeles, Minneapolis, New York, and San Francisco, as well as for acquisitions. In October 2006 the company bought Applied Graphics, a provider of print management and print-on-demand services that has sales offices in California and Hawaii. Applied Graphics posted sales of about $29 million in 2005.

In conjunction with InnerWorkings' May 2006 IPO filing, founders Richard Heise and Eric Lefkofsky left the company's board, but they retain interests through investment vehicle InCorp. Heise controls 46% of InCorp; Lefkofsky's wife, Elizabeth Kramer Lefkofsky, owns 43%.

Affiliates of venture capital firm New Enterprise Associates, represented on InnerWorkings' board by Peter Barris, own 19% of the company.

EXECUTIVES

Chairman: John R. Walter, age 59
President, CEO, and Director:
 Steven E. (Steve) Zuccarini, age 49, $425,000 pay
COO: Eric D. Belcher, age 37
CFO and Secretary: Nicholas J. (Nick) Galassi, age 33, $165,152 pay
EVP, Sales: Scott A. Frisoni, age 35, $177,573 pay
Chief Marketing Officer: Mark D. Desky, age 39
CTO: Neil P. Graver, age 35
Auditors: Ernst & Young LLP

LOCATIONS

HQ: InnerWorkings, Inc.
 600 W. Chicago Ave., Ste. 850, Chicago, IL 60610
Phone: 312-642-3700   **Fax:** 312-642-3704
Web: www.iwprint.com

PRODUCTS/OPERATIONS

2005 Sales

	% of total
Enterprise clients	69
Transactional clients	31
Total	**100**

COMPETITORS

Banta
Cirqit
Newline
Quad/Graphics
Quebecor World
R.R. Donnelley
Workflow Management

HISTORICAL FINANCIALS

Company Type: Public

Income Statement				FYE: December 31
	REVENUE ($ mil.)	NET INCOME ($ mil.)	NET PROFIT MARGIN	EMPLOYEES
12/05	76.9	4.6	6.0%	154
12/04	38.9	1.8	4.6%	85
12/03	16.2	0.7	4.3%	43
Annual Growth	117.9%	156.3%	—	89.2%

2005 Year-End Financials

Debt ratio: 22.7%   Current ratio: 1.18
Return on equity: 685.0%   Long-term debt ($ mil.): 0.3
Cash ($ mil.): 3.0

Net Income History   NASDAQ (GM): INWK

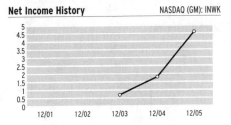

Input/Output

There's a whole lotta shakin' goin' on at Input/Output (I/O). The seismic data-acquisition imaging and software systems company helps worldwide petroleum exploration contractors identify and measure subsurface geological structures that could contain oil and gas. I/O's data acquisition products are capable of processing 3-D, 4-D, and multi-component 3-C seismic data. Its systems include modules for land, marine, and transition areas (such as swamps, shoreline, marsh, and jungle). China National Petroleum's BGP subsidiary accounted for 9% of I/O's revenues in 2005. That year, the impact of Hurricane Katrina forced the company to temporarily close its New Orleans office.

I/O also makes other products such as geophysical software, helicopter transportable enclosures, seismic sensors, specialty cables and connectors, and radio telemetry systems. Its marine positioning systems enable the company to map the geography of the ocean's floor. The company has sold its Applied MEMS subsidiary to Swiss MEMS (micro-electro mechanical systems) firm Colibrys.

I/O is turning to new technologies to help boost the demand for its seismic services. While 3-D seismic data acquisition has become a more common offering provided by oil and gas service companies, the company plans to further enhance the quality of survey results in an effort to better compete against other providers. It has acquired AXIS Geophysics, a specialized seismic data processing firm, and has combined it with its Green Mountain Geophysics subsidiary. I/O has also acquired seismic data software provider Concept Systems for about $36 million, as well as GX Technology for about $130 million.

HISTORY

Input/Output (I/O) was founded in 1968 by petroleum industry retiree Aubry Tilley, who pioneered a system for capturing shock waves that was used with existing seismic systems. Tilley sold I/O in 1980 to Walter Kidde & Co., which sold it to Triton Industries in 1986. After a six-year, $25 million research and development project, the company launched its I/O System for landbased seismic data acquisition in 1988.

I/O went public in 1991. The company bought the Exploration Products Group of Western Geophysical (the seismic exploration business of Western Atlas) in 1995. In 1997 I/O bought Green Mountain Geophysics (seismic software), but increased competition and costs related to the Western Geophysical purchase dampened the company's profits that year.

In 1998 I/O acquired CompuSeis (land seismic data-acquisition systems) and DigiCourse (marine positioning equipment). The company's sales and profits plummeted under pressures of an extended industry downturn in 1999 and 2000. I/O's 1999 sales dipped 51% below the previous year's record, and its stock fell to an all-time low. Several executives left the company. James Lapeyre, who had become a company shareholder when DigiCourse was acquired, was named chairman.

After losing money in 2000, sales picked up in 2001 and the company returned to profitability. A decrease in demand for seismic services put the company back in the red in 2002. Also that year, in an effort to boost its technology, I/O acquired AXIS Geophysics and combined it with its Green Mountain Geophysics subsidiary. In 2004 I/O continued to build up its seismic technology services by acquiring Scotland-based Concept Systems for $36 million. It also completed its acquisition of GX Technology for about $130 million. Later that year, I/O sold its Applied MEMS subsidiary to private Swiss firm Colibrys.

EXECUTIVES

Chairman: James M. (Jay) Lapeyre Jr., age 53
President, CEO, and Director; President, Imaging Systems: Robert P. (Bob) Peebler, age 58, $658,692 pay
EVP and CFO: R. Brian Hanson, age 41
EVP and COO, I/O Solutions Division: James (Jim) Hollis, age 42
VP, Commercial Development: Christopher M. (Chris) Friedemann, age 41, $293,028 pay
VP, Human Resources: Laura D. Guthrie, age 45
Managing Director, Concept Systems: Alistair Hay
Director, Accounting and Controller: Michael L. Morrison, age 35
Director, Corporate Marketing and Communications: Pam Griffin
Director, Manufacturing: Ken Maxwell
Chief Representative, China: David Meng
VP, General Counsel, and Corporate Secretary: David L. Roland, age 44, $250,715 pay
Auditors: Ernst & Young LLP

LOCATIONS

HQ: Input/Output, Inc.
12300 Parc Crest Dr., Stafford, TX 77477
Phone: 281-933-3339   **Fax:** 281-879-3626
Web: www.i-o.com

Input/Output has manufacturing facilities in the US in Stafford and Alvin, Texas, and in New Orleans. It operates international manufacturing facilities in Voorschoten, the Netherlands, and in Norwich, UK.

2005 Sales

	$ mil.	% of total
North America	113.7	31
Europe	91.7	25
Asia/Pacific	47.3	13
Middle East	38.3	11
Latin America	12.9	4
Commonwealth of Independent States	12.6	3
Africa & other regions	46.2	13
Total	**362.7**	**100**

PRODUCTS/OPERATIONS

2005 Sales

	$ mil.	% of total
Land imaging	155.2	43
Seismic imaging	121.9	34
Marine imaging	69.6	19
Data management	16.0	4
Total	**362.7**	**100**

Selected Products and Services

Land Imaging Systems Products
  Accessories
    Cables and connectors
    Helicopter transportable enclosures
  Applications software (geophysical software)
  Central electronics units
  Geophones (seismic sensors and acoustical receivers)
  Radio telemetry systems
  Recording systems
  Remote ground equipment
    Multiple remote and line taps
  Reservoir products
  Transition systems

Seismic Imaging Solutions Products and Services
  Processing and imaging for marine environments
  Processing and imaging for land environments (for marsh, jungle, mountainous areas)
  Vibrators
Marine Imaging Systems Products
  Airguns
  Hydrophones (seismic sensors devices)
  Marine energy sources
  Marine positioning systems (DigiCOURSE)
    Acoustical devices
    Compasses
    Velocimeters
  Ocean bottom systems
  Peripherals
  Seismic and data telemetry quality control systems
  Shipboard recording electronics
  Software (Green Mountain Geophysics)
  Streamer systems
    Electronic modules and cabling
Data Management Solutions Products and Services
  Marine imaging systems
  Seabed imaging systems

COMPETITORS

Bolt Technology
CGG
Dawson Geophysical
OYO Geospace
Schlumberger
TGC Industries
TGS-NOPEC
Veritas DGC
WesternGeco

HISTORICAL FINANCIALS

Company Type: Public

Income Statement

FYE: December 31

	REVENUE ($ mil.)	NET INCOME ($ mil.)	NET PROFIT MARGIN	EMPLOYEES
12/05	362.7	18.8	5.2%	804
12/04	247.3	(3.0)	—	743
12/03	150.0	(23.1)	—	479
12/02	118.6	(119.9)	—	704
12/01	212.1	9.3	4.4%	799
Annual Growth	**14.4%**	**19.2%**		**0.2%**

2005 Year-End Financials

Debt ratio: 21.8%
Return on equity: 5.9%
Cash ($ mil.): 17.4
Current ratio: 2.53
Long-term debt ($ mil.): 71.5
No. of shares (mil.): 79.8
Dividends
  Yield: —
  Payout: —
Market value ($ mil.): 560.7
R&D as % of sales: 5.6%
Advertising as % of sales: —

Stock History

NYSE: IO

	STOCK PRICE ($) FY Close	P/E High/Low		PER SHARE ($) Earnings	Dividends	Book Value
12/05	7.03	42	25	0.21	—	4.11
12/04	8.84	—	—	(0.05)	—	4.00
12/03	4.51	—	—	(0.45)	—	2.60
12/02	4.25	—	—	(2.37)	—	2.96
12/01	8.21	204	101	0.07	—	6.51
Annual Growth	**(3.8%)**	—	—	**31.6%**	—	**(10.9%)**

Integrated BioPharma

Integrated BioPharma is getting it all together. The company operates Manhattan Drug, which makes vitamins, nutritional supplements, and herbal products for sale to distributors, multi-level marketers, and specialized health care providers. Integrated BioPharma supplies nutritional and dietary supplements to companies such as Herbalife International. It also sells its products under the Vitamin Factory brand through the mail and on the Internet and provides raw material sourcing through its IHT Health Products subsidiary. Its pharmaceuticals unit makes Paclitaxel, a chemotherapy agent used to treat breast cancer. Chairman and CEO E. Gerald Kay and members of the Kay family own about 40% of the firm.

In addition to its nutritionals and pharmaceuticals operations, Integrated BioPharma is developing plant-based vaccines and other therapies through its InB:Biotechnologies subsidiary.

Herbalife, Costco, and Sam's Club are the company's principal customers; together, they account for about 85% of sales.

EXECUTIVES

Chairman and CEO: E. Gerald Kay, age 70, $127,875 pay
SVP, CFO, and Secretary: Dina L. Masi, age 45, $111,528 pay
EVP: Christina M. Kay, age 36, $115,414 pay
EVP: Riva Kay Sheppard, age 39, $115,414 pay
VP, Marketing, AgroLabs: Cheryl Richitt
VP, Production, AgroLabs: Monty C. Lloyd
VP, Operations and General Manager, InB:Hauser Pharmaceuticals and Paxis Pharmaceuticals: Rodney B. (Rod) McKeever
COO, Agrolabs: Kurt Cahill
Director; Chairman, President and CEO, Paxis Pharmaceuticals: Robert B. Kay, age 66, $25,096 pay
Director, Business Development, InB:Hauser Pharmaceuticals: Michaele Johnson
Director, Compliance, InB:Hauser Pharmaceuticals and Paxis Pharmaceuticals: Dan W. Childers
Auditors: Amper, Politziner & Mattia, P.C.

LOCATIONS

HQ: Integrated BioPharma, Inc.
225 Long Ave., Hillside, NJ 07205
Phone: 973-926-0816   **Fax:** 973-926-1735
Web: www.ibiopharma.com

Integrated BioPharma has facilities in Colorado, Delaware, New Jersey, and Texas.

2006 Sales

	$ mil.	% of total
US	47.9	83
Other countries	9.9	17
Total	**57.8**	**100**

PRODUCTS/OPERATIONS

2006 Sales

	% of total
Nutraceutical	96
Pharmaceutical	4
Total	**100**

Selected Subsidiaries

AgroLabs, Inc.
IHT Health Products, Inc.
IHT Properties, Inc.
InB: Manhattan Drug Company, Inc.
InB: Biotechnologies, Inc.
InB: Paxis Pharmaceuticals, Inc.
Vitamin Factory, Inc.

HISTORICAL FINANCIALS

Company Type: Public

Income Statement

FYE: June 30

	REVENUE ($ mil.)	NET INCOME ($ mil.)	NET PROFIT MARGIN	EMPLOYEES
6/06	57.8	8.4	14.5%	156
6/05	32.7	(8.6)	—	157
6/04	25.3	(5.3)	—	120
6/03	22.2	0.9	4.1%	90
6/02	23.5	1.4	6.0%	94
Annual Growth	25.2%	56.5%	—	13.5%

2006 Year-End Financials

Debt ratio: —
Return on equity: 50.2%
Cash ($ mil.): 5.8
Current ratio: 2.27
Long-term debt ($ mil.): —
No. of shares (mil.): 13.2

Dividends
 Yield: —
 Payout: —
Market value ($ mil.): 116.8
R&D as % of sales: —
Advertising as % of sales: —

Stock History

NASDAQ (GM): INBP

	STOCK PRICE ($) FY Close	P/E High/Low		PER SHARE ($) Earnings	Dividends	Book Value
6/06	8.87	28	5	0.34	—	1.57
6/05	3.79	—	—	(0.90)	—	1.01
6/04	8.16	—	—	(0.58)	—	1.91
6/03	7.48	83	3	0.09	—	1.78
6/02	0.42	4	0	0.20	—	1.22
Annual Growth	114.4%	—	—	14.2%	—	6.5%

Inter Parfums

Would a perfumer by any other name smell as sweet? Inter Parfums certainly hopes not. Most of the firm's sales come from prestige fragrances, including Burberry, Celine, Christian Lacroix, Lanvin, Diane von Furstenberg, Paul Smith, and S.T. Dupont. It also sells moderately priced perfumes and low-priced imitations of high-end perfumes. In addition Inter Parfums sells personal care products and cosmetics, including Aziza eye makeup (under license from Unilever) and has a majority stake in men's skincare company Nickel. Customers include department stores, mass merchandisers (Wal-Mart Stores), and drugstore chains. Founders Jean Madar (CEO) and Philippe Benacin (vice chairman) jointly own about 60% of the firm.

Inter Parfums plans to focus on its prestige division (89% of sales) by expanding existing product lines and licensing or acquiring new fragrances. The company's Burberry line accounts for about 60% of sales.

In April 2004 Inter Parfums acquired a 67.5% interest in Nickel S.A., a men's skincare company with 1,700 outlets in France, Western Europe, and the US, as well as men's spas in Paris and New York. The acquisition cost Inter Parfums approximately $8.3 million in cash.

In June 2004 Inter Parfums and Lanvin entered into a 15-year global licensing agreement whereby Inter Parfums will make and distribute fragrance lines under the Lanvin label. Another licensing agreement was reached by Inter Parfum's Paris-based subsidiary, Inter Parfums S.A., and Burberry in October 2004. As a result, Inter Parfums opened a Burberry Fragrances operating unit to focus on product development, marketing, and distribution.

In July 2005 Inter Parfums signed an exclusive agreement with Gap Inc. to design and manufacture personal care products under the Gap and Banana Republic brands. Inter Parfums is responsible for product development, production, packaging, and manufacturing while Gap handles marketing and sales of the products. The deal marked Inter Parfums' entry into the specialty retail market.

Still smelling sweet success in licensing, Inter Parfums inked an exclusive worldwide licensing deal in 2006 with sports manufacturer and retailer Quiksilver for a namesake and Roxy line of personal care products. As part of the deal Inter Parfums will develop and distribute a Roxy fragrance, suncare, skincare, and related items, and Quiksilver suncare and other products through 2017. The first two product categories expected to roll out from the agreement will be a Roxy scent and a Quiksilver suncare line. Inter Parfums is particularly interested in Quiksilver's outdoor, 15-year-old target audience. Quiksilver's strong presence in the US and its inroads into Western Europe and Australia bodes well for Inter Parfums, as well. Also in 2006 Inter Parfums replaced YSL Beaute as the licensing contractor for Van Cleef & Arpels. Inter Parfums was interested in inking the deal to add a jewelry brand to its portfolio.

Luxury goods maker LVMH licenses the Celine and Christian Lacroix lines to Inter Parfums.

HISTORY

Jean Madar and Philippe Benacin founded Jean Philippe Fragrances in 1985 to make knockoff fragrances in the US and took it public three years later. Jean Philippe bought fragrance and cosmetics rights from Jordache Enterprises in 1990. The next year it bought Inter Parfums S.A., a French affiliate Madar and Benacin founded in 1983. Jean Philippe took that subsidiary public in 1995.

The company has aggressively expanded its markets and product line. In 1994 Inter Parfums S.A. acquired trademarks for a variety of fragrances from Parfums Molyneux and Parfums Weil, and Jean Philippe bought the worldwide trademark for Intimate and Chaz from Revlon. From Chesebrough-Pond's, Jean Philippe acquired rights that year to Cutex nail enamel and lipsticks (later relinquished) and Aziza eye makeup, which brought it greater access to mass-merchandise channels such as Wal-Mart.

A year later Jean Philippe launched Romantic Illusions, a collection of eight perfumes packed in cartons designed to look like romance novels. Sales declined in 1996 and 1997, partly due to increased US competition, economic turmoil in Russia, and lagging sales in Brazil. (The company closed its Brazilian subsidiary in 1998.) Also in 1998 Jean Philippe developed a line of medium-priced fragrances (not knockoffs).

In 1999 Jean Philippe decided to take the name of its primary sales vehicle, subsidiary Inter Parfums S.A., adding an Americanized "Inc." to the end. France's LVMH, which bottles Christian Dior and Givenchy perfumes, upped its stake in Inter Parfums to 20%.

In 2000 the company launched its Paul Smith line of fragrances and announced plans for a new bath products line under the Burberry name. In 2002 Inter Parfums purchased certain mass-market fragrances and inventories of bankrupt and now defunct rival Tristar Corporation, and also signed a license agreement with Diane Von Furstenberg to market her fragrance and beauty products.

In the spring of 2004 Inter Parfums acquired a two-thirds interest in men's skincare company Nickel S.A.

EXECUTIVES

Chairman and CEO; Director General, Inter Parfums, S.A.: Jean Madar, age 45, $400,000 pay
Vice Chairman and President; President, Inter Parfums, S.A.: Philippe Benacin, age 47, $370,503 pay
EVP, CFO, and Director: Russell Greenberg, age 49, $375,000 pay
VP, Distribution and Warehousing: Alex Canavan
VP, Nickel and COO, Specialty Stores: Andy Clarke
VP, Management Information Systems: Kiet T. Huynh
VP, Marketing and Product Development, Specialty Stores: Sioux Saunders
VP, Marketing and Product Development, Specialty Stores: Renee Ordino
VP, Purchasing and Packaging: Jerry McKenna
VP, Retail Sales: Stuart Fishel
President, Parfums Burberry: Hugues de La Chevasnerie
President, Luxury and Fashion, Inter Parfums, S.A.: Frederic Garcia-Pelayo, age 47, $370,503 pay
Corporate Controller and Human Resources: Michelle Habert
Mexico/Texas Border Sales Manager: Eduardo Hermosilla
Senior Director, Packaging and Purchasing, Specialty Stores: Andrew Hoskins
Director, Marketing, Nickel; Brand Manager, Specialty Stores: Gaelle Loiseau
Director; EVP and Director of Finance, Inter Parfums S.A.: Philippe Santi, age 44
National Account Sales Manager: William Dachille
Auditors: Mazars LLP

LOCATIONS

HQ: Inter Parfums, Inc.
 551 5th Ave., Ste. 1500, New York, NY 10176
Phone: 212-983-2640   **Fax:** 212-983-4197
Web: www.interparfumsinc.com

Inter Parfums' products are sold in more than 120 countries worldwide.

2005 Sales

	$ mil.	% of total
Europe	241.7	88
US	34.3	12
Adjustments	(2.5)	—
Total	273.5	100

PRODUCTS/OPERATIONS

Selected Brand Name and Licensed Fragrances and Cosmetics
Burberry
Celine
Christian Lacroix
Diane Von Furstenberg
Lanvin
Molyneux
Nickel
Paul Smith
S.T. Dupont

Selected Products
Body sprays
Deodorants
Eye makeup
Fragrances
Lipsticks
Nail polish
Skin creams

COMPETITORS

Avon	L'Oréal USA
Body Shop	Mary Kay
Borghese	Parlux Fragrances
Clarins	Procter & Gamble
Coty Inc.	Revlon
Dana Classic Fragrances	Shiseido
Elizabeth Arden Inc	Unilever
Estée Lauder	Wella
L'Oréal	

HISTORICAL FINANCIALS
Company Type: Public

Income Statement
FYE: December 31

	REVENUE ($ mil.)	NET INCOME ($ mil.)	NET PROFIT MARGIN	EMPLOYEES
12/05	273.5	15.3	5.6%	201
12/04	236.1	15.7	6.6%	144
12/03	185.6	13.8	7.4%	117
12/02	130.4	9.4	7.2%	103
12/01	112.2	8.1	7.2%	99
Annual Growth	25.0%	17.2%	—	19.4%

2005 Year-End Financials
Debt ratio: 7.4%
Return on equity: 12.0%
Cash ($ mil.): 59.5
Current ratio: 2.91
Long-term debt ($ mil.): 9.4
No. of shares (mil.): 20.3
Dividends
  Yield: 0.9%
  Payout: 21.3%
Market value ($ mil.): 363.7
R&D as % of sales: —
Advertising as % of sales: 14.9%

Stock History
NASDAQ (GS): IPAR

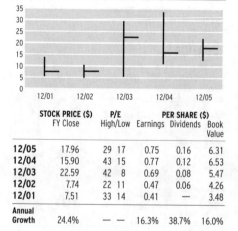

	STOCK PRICE ($) FY Close	P/E High/Low		PER SHARE ($) Earnings Dividends Book Value		
12/05	17.96	29	17	0.75	0.16	6.31
12/04	15.90	43	15	0.77	0.12	6.53
12/03	22.59	42	8	0.69	0.08	5.47
12/02	7.74	22	11	0.47	0.06	4.26
12/01	7.51	33	14	0.41	—	3.48
Annual Growth	24.4%	—	—	16.3%	38.7%	16.0%

Intercontinental-Exchange

If there was money to be made in ice futures, IntercontinentalExchange (ICE) would probably trade that as well. The company is a leading on-line marketplace for global commodity trading, primarily of electricity, natural gas, crude oil, refined petroleum products, precious metals, and weather and emission credits. It also owns the ICE Futures, a leading European energy futures and options platform. ICE's 10x Group unit provides real-time market data reports, and the company's eConfirm platform provides electronic trade confirmations. ICE offers real-time OTC clearing and credit and risk management services.

IntercontinentalExchange was formed by a group of top financial and energy firms in 2000. ICE is based in Atlanta, and has regional offices in Calgary, Chicago, Houston, New York, and Singapore. In 2007 the company acquired the New York Board of Trade for $1 billion.

EXECUTIVES

Chairman and CEO: Jeffrey C. Sprecher, age 51, $1,035,431 pay
President and COO: Charles A. (Chuck) Vice, age 42, $651,000 pay (prior to promotion)
SVP and CFO: Richard V. Spencer, age 51
SVP and CTO: Edwin Marcial, age 37, $600,250 pay
SVP Business Development and Sales: David S. Goone, age 44, $400,000 pay
SVP, General Counsel, and Secretary: Jonathan H. Short, age 39
SVP North American Sales: John Hill
Managing Director Oil Marketing, Europe, and Asia: Jason Gard
Auditors: Ernst & Young LLP

LOCATIONS

HQ: IntercontinentalExchange, Inc.
   2100 RiverEdge Pkwy., Ste. 500, Atlanta, GA 30328
Phone: 770-857-4700   **Fax:** 770-951-1307
Web: www.theice.com

PRODUCTS/OPERATIONS

2005 Sales

	$ mil.	% of total
OTC	79.8	51
Futures	57.2	37
Market data fees	11.6	7
Other	7.3	5
Total	**155.9**	**100**

Founding Partners
BP p.l.c.
Deutsche Bank AG
The Goldman Sachs Group, Inc.
Morgan Stanley Dean Witter & Co.
Royal Dutch Shell plc
Société Générale
TOTAL S.A.

Other Partners
American Electric Power Company, Inc.
Duke Energy Corporation
El Paso Energy Partners
Mirant

COMPETITORS
APX
Bloomberg
CHOICE! Energy
Enporion
ICAP
NYMEX Holdings
Prebon Yamane
Reuters
Unitil

HISTORICAL FINANCIALS
Company Type: Public

Income Statement
FYE: December 31

	REVENUE ($ mil.)	NET INCOME ($ mil.)	NET PROFIT MARGIN	EMPLOYEES
12/05	155.9	40.4	25.9%	203
12/04	108.4	22.0	20.3%	—
12/03	93.8	13.4	14.3%	—
12/02	125.5	34.7	27.6%	204
Annual Growth	7.5%	5.2%	—	(0.2%)

2005 Year-End Financials
Debt ratio: —
Return on equity: 22.2%
Cash ($ mil.): 143.8
Current ratio: 6.22
Long-term debt ($ mil.): —
No. of shares (mil.): 18.4
Dividends
  Yield: —
  Payout: —
Market value ($ mil.): 668.8
R&D as % of sales: —
Advertising as % of sales: 1.1%

Stock History
NYSE: ICE

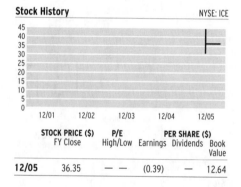

	STOCK PRICE ($) FY Close	P/E High/Low		PER SHARE ($) Earnings Dividends Book Value		
12/05	36.35	—	—	(0.39)	—	12.64

International Assets Holding Corporation

Going global is the name of the game for securities broker International Assets Holding and its subsidiaries. The company specializes in niche international markets, offering expertise in securities, foreign exchange, and commodities trading. Its primary subsidiary, INTL Trading, is a market-maker for foreign securities, bonds, and fixed income securities; INTL Consilium, a joint venture with Consilium Investment Capital, provides asset management services. International Assets Holding serves financial institutions, corporations, and other institutional investors in the US and abroad.

The company deals in the shares of more than 8,000 companies in some 20 countries, the debt of some 500 public and private entities in 30

countries, and more than 100 different currencies, as well as precious metals and derivatives.

Leucadia National Corporation holds more than 15% of International Assets Holding's stock; CEO Sean O'Connor owns slightly less than 15%.

EXECUTIVES

Chairman: Diego J. Veitia, age 62, $218,400 pay
CEO and Director: Sean M. O'Connor, age 43, $469,000 pay
President and Director: Scott J. Branch, age 44, $469,000 pay
VP and Corporate Secretary; Chief Compliance Officer, INTL Trading: Nancey M. McMurtry
CFO and Treasurer: Brian T. Sephton, age 48, $177,500 pay
Group Controller: Jonathan C. (John) Hinz, age 44, $180,000 pay
MIS Manager: William Cruz
Auditors: Rothstein, Kass & Company, P.C.

LOCATIONS

HQ: International Assets Holding Corporation, Inc.
220 E. Central Pkwy., Ste. 2060,
Altamonte Springs, FL 32701
Phone: 407-741-5300   **Fax:** 407-740-0808
Web: www.intlassets.com

In addition to its Altamonte Springs, Florida, headquarters, International Assets Holding has offices in Miami and New York. Other locations include Fort Lauderdale, Florida, as well as Dubai and London.

PRODUCTS/OPERATIONS

2006 Sales

	$ mil.	% of total
Sale of physical commodities	66.2	65
Net dealer inventory & investment gains	34.3	33
Other	2.3	2
Total	**102.8**	**100**

COMPETITORS

AIG Financial Products
Bear Stearns
CAPIS
Citigroup Global Markets
Credit Suisse (USA)
Fimat
Goldman Sachs
Interactive Brokers
Lehman Brothers
Morgan Stanley
Susquehanna International Group, LLP
Van der Moolen

HISTORICAL FINANCIALS

Company Type: Public

Income Statement

FYE: September 30

	REVENUE ($ mil.)	NET INCOME ($ mil.)	NET PROFIT MARGIN	EMPLOYEES
9/06	102.8	3.5	3.4%	—
9/05	26.2	2.6	9.9%	67
9/04	22.0	(0.1)	—	51
9/03	10.9	1.3	11.9%	28
9/02	5.4	(0.3)	—	18
Annual Growth	**108.9%**	**—**	**—**	**55.0%**

2006 Year-End Financials

Debt ratio: 98.4%
Return on equity: 11.3%
Cash ($ mil.): 38.0
Current ratio: —
Long-term debt ($ mil.): 33.4
No. of shares (mil.): 7.8

Dividends
  Yield: —
  Payout: —
Market value ($ mil.): 183.1
R&D as % of sales: —
Advertising as % of sales: —

Stock History

NASDAQ (CM): IAAC

	STOCK PRICE ($) FY Close	P/E High/Low		PER SHARE ($) Earnings	Dividends	Book Value
9/06	23.35	70	17	0.41	—	4.33
9/05	8.20	30	18	0.33	—	3.78
9/04	8.00	—	—	(0.02)	—	3.48
9/03	2.78	12	2	0.33	—	1.98
9/02	0.61	—	—	(0.11)	—	1.79
Annual Growth	**148.7%**	**—**	**—**	**—**	**—**	**24.7%**

Internet Commerce

Content equals commerce for ICC. Internet Commerce Corporation (ICC) operates an on-line value-added network (VAN) used by companies to exchange documents with their trading partners, including invoices, purchase orders, and shipping notices. By utilizing the Internet, customers can save the expense of setting up and maintaining private data networks for their business-to-business transactions. Its ICC.NET services also include online product catalogs and data translation services so that trading partners with incompatible information systems can still exchange documents. In addition, ICC offers outsourced document processing through its service bureau and services such as consulting and training.

Nearly all of ICC's revenues come from the US, with a small portion from Canada, China, and the UK.

A small player in the electronic data interchange (EDI) market, ICC competes with larger rivals such as Sterling Commerce and Global eXchange Services. ICC cites its early adoption of Internet-based systems instead of more costly private EDI networks as a competitive advantage. The company continues to add new features for data handling (such as XML capabilities) to its package of services.

In 2005 ICC acquired the Managed EC business of Inovis, adding some 1,500 customers to its clientele base. It also acquired The Kodiak Group, a supplier of e-commerce and data synchronization services, widening its portfolio of professional services. ICC acquired Enable, a provider of electronic marketplace software and services, in 2006.

More than 3,500 companies use ICC's ICC.NET service, including GlaxoSmithKline and Revlon.

HISTORY

Internet Commerce Corporation (ICC) traces its roots to Infosafe, a firm started in 1991 by Thomas Lipscomb, a veteran of the publishing industry and co-founder of data security innovator Wave Systems. Lipscomb teamed with computer scientist and brain researcher Robert Nagel to develop a system to provide digital information, while keeping track of the content used, without going through a commercial online service. Initial customers included the American Trucking Association, which wanted one of the company's systems to sell training and regulatory information to its members, and International Typeface Corporation, which used the system to license its fonts.

Infosafe went public in 1995. That year it introduced the Design Palette desktop system (a pay-per-use graphics library). In 1996 Arthur Medici succeeded Lipscomb as CEO. The firm's strategy shifted to focus more on Internet technology, and in 1997 Infosafe scrapped its Design Palette and Mark III hardware, deeming its technology dated due to the rapid development of the Internet. It acquired Internet Commerce Corporation, a developer of products for the e-commerce market, and took that company's name in 1998. Medici remained as president, but financier Richard Berman was brought in as CEO.

ICC worked to develop a commercial electronic data interchange (EDI) system for the secure delivery of electronic documents in support of online transactions. It signed its first contract with New York's Board of Education in 1999. Geoffrey Carroll became CEO later that year.

As interest in online commerce heated up, so did investor interest. UK-based Cable and Wireless took a stake in ICC and agreed to market its services to international customers. (Cable and Wireless sold most or all of its ICC stock in 2005.) Service agreements with blue-chip customers such as Barnes & Noble, OfficeMax, and Revlon came in 2000, and ICC began acquiring other EDI technology startups to grow its business. The company's stock took off like a rocket and peaked at $90 per share when the dot-com bubble burst.

ICC continued to sign up new customers for its services, but with the dot-conomy meltdown came new business realities. A reorganization to focus the business on achieving profitability brought Michael Cassidy as CEO in 2001. The Department of Defense signed on as a client, and the business continued to grow its top line despite continued losses.

ICC's lower costs and growing popularity with customers began to threaten rival EDI providers such as GE Global Exchange (now Global eXchange Services) and Sterling Commerce, both of which had cut the company off from exchanging data with their EDI systems by 2002.

In 2004 COO Thomas Stallings was elevated to CEO. Arthur Medici, who left ICC in 1999, returned to the company as COO.

Also in 2004 ICC acquired Electronic Commerce Systems (ECS) of Norcross, Georgia, adding some 600 clients to its portfolio. Following the ECS acquisition, ICC relocated its corporate headquarters to Atlanta from New York City. The company maintains an office on Long Island.

EXECUTIVES

CEO and Director: Thomas J. Stallings, age 59, $283,749 pay
COO and Director: Arthur R. (Art) Medici, age 57, $219,297 pay
CFO and Secretary: Glen E. Shipley, age 56, $181,771 pay
Chief Marketing Officer: Teresa A. Deuel, age 45, $157,031 pay
Chief Sales Officer: James J. Walsh III, age 42

SVP, Electronic Commerce Network Services and Sales Support: Anthony J. D'Angelo, age 44
Product Executive: David C. (Dave) Hubbard, age 50, $165,468 pay
Director, Business Development: G. Michael (Mike) Cassidy, age 54
Controller: Stephanie Kangdry
Auditors: Tauber & Balser, P.C.

LOCATIONS

HQ: Internet Commerce Corporation
6025 The Corners Pkwy., Ste. 100,
Norcross, GA 30092
Phone: 678-533-8000 **Fax:** 770-246-4697
Web: www.icc.net

PRODUCTS/OPERATIONS

2006 Sales

	$ mil.	% of total
ICC.NET	12.8	65
EC Service Bureau	7.0	35
Total	**19.8**	**100**

Selected Operations

ICC.NET
Data mapping
Document management
Electronic data interchange (EDI)
ICC.CATALOG (electronic vendor product catalogs)
Point of sale (POS) data exchange
Value added network

Selected Services

Professional services
  Consulting
  Custom programming
  Training
Service bureau services
  Product code maintenance
  Purchase order and invoice processing
  Shipping operations software
    EZ-EDI
    ScanPak Professional
    UPC Manager

COMPETITORS

Cyclone Commerce
EasyLink Services
GXS
IBM Global Services
Inovis
IntraLinks

Onvia
Open EC
Silanis Technologies
SPS Commerce
Sterling Commerce
Synchris

HISTORICAL FINANCIALS

Company Type: Public

Income Statement

FYE: July 31

	REVENUE ($ mil.)	NET INCOME ($ mil.)	NET PROFIT MARGIN	EMPLOYEES
7/06	19.8	3.0	15.2%	134
7/05	16.7	0.2	1.2%	108
7/04	11.7	(4.1)	—	91
7/03	12.1	(6.0)	—	90
7/02	14.2	(6.6)	—	115
Annual Growth	8.7%	—	—	3.9%

2006 Year-End Financials

Debt ratio: 4.7%
Return on equity: 19.4%
Cash ($ mil.): 7.0
Current ratio: 5.28
Long-term debt ($ mil.): 1.0
No. of shares (mil.): 22.7
Dividends
  Yield: —
  Payout: —
Market value ($ mil.): 81.1
R&D as % of sales: —
Advertising as % of sales: —

Stock History

NASDAQ (CM): ICCA

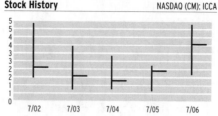

	STOCK PRICE ($) FY Close	P/E High/Low		Earnings	PER SHARE ($) Dividends	Book Value
7/06	3.57	43	16	0.11	—	0.91
7/05	1.90	—	—	(0.01)	—	0.53
7/04	1.29	—	—	(0.30)	—	0.49
7/03	1.58	—	—	(0.53)	—	0.42
7/02	2.10	—	—	(0.68)	—	0.80
Annual Growth	14.2%	—	—	—	—	3.1%

Intervest Bancshares

Intervest Bancshares is the holding company for Intervest National Bank, the rather grandly named bank that operates one branch in New York City and five other branches in Pinellas County, Florida. Most of the company's lending activities are real estate-related: Commercial mortgages make up more than half of its loan portfolio, while multifamily residential mortgages account for about 40%. A portion of the company's lending is originated through subsidiary Intervest Mortgage Corporation, which invests primarily in mortgages for commercial offices and apartment buildings in New York City. Subsidiary Intervest Securities Corporation brokers securities.

Chairman and CEO Lowell Dansker, his father Jerome, sister Helene Bergman, and brother-in-law Lawrence Bergman (another company executive) control the firm.

EXECUTIVES

Chairman, President, and CEO: Lowell S. Dansker, age 55, $777,317 pay (prior to title change)
CFO; SVP, CFO, and Secretary, Intervest National Bank: John J. Arvonio, age 43, $174,375 pay
VP and Secretary, Intervest Bancshares, Intervest Mortgage, and Intervest Securities: Lawrence G. Bergman, age 61, $471,426 pay
VP and Controller, Intervest Mortgage: John H. Hoffmann, age 54
President, Intervest National Bank: Raymond C. Sullivan, age 58
President, Florida Division, Intervest National Bank: Keith A. Olsen, age 51, $205,712 pay
Auditors: Hacker, Johnson & Smith PA

LOCATIONS

HQ: Intervest Bancshares Corporation
1 Rockefeller Plaza, Ste. 400, New York, NY 10020
Phone: 212-218-2800 **Fax:** 212-218-8390
Web: www.intervestnatbank.com

PRODUCTS/OPERATIONS

2005 Sales

	$ mil.	% of total
Interest		
Loans	89.6	86
Securities	7.2	7
Other	1.1	1
Noninterest		
Early repayment of mortgages	5.0	5
Mortgage lending	1.1	1
Service fees & other	0.5	—
Total	**104.5**	**100**

COMPETITORS

Bank of America
BB&T
Regions Financial
SunTrust
Wachovia

HISTORICAL FINANCIALS

Company Type: Public

Income Statement

FYE: December 31

	ASSETS ($ mil.)	NET INCOME ($ mil.)	INCOME AS % OF ASSETS	EMPLOYEES
12/05	1,706.4	18.2	1.1%	69
12/04	1,316.8	11.4	0.9%	64
12/03	910.6	9.1	1.0%	61
12/02	686.0	6.9	1.0%	57
12/01	512.6	3.8	0.7%	53
Annual Growth	35.1%	47.9%	—	6.8%

2005 Year-End Financials

Equity as % of assets: 8.0%
Return on assets: 1.2%
Return on equity: 16.1%
Long-term debt ($ mil.): 169.8
No. of shares (mil.): 7.4
Market value ($ mil.): 184.1
Dividends
  Yield: —
  Payout: —
Sales ($ mil.): 104.5
R&D as % of sales: —
Advertising as % of sales: 0.2%

Stock History

NASDAQ (GS): IBCA

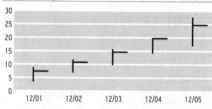

	STOCK PRICE ($) FY Close	P/E High/Low		Earnings	PER SHARE ($) Dividends	Book Value
12/05	24.75	11	7	2.47	—	18.31
12/04	19.74	12	8	1.71	—	15.30
12/03	14.65	10	7	1.53	—	13.45
12/02	10.80	8	5	1.37	—	12.22
12/01	7.40	9	4	0.97	—	11.40
Annual Growth	35.2%	—	—	26.3%	—	12.6%

Intevac

Intevac's sputtering doesn't stem from a speech impediment. The company's Equipment division manufactures sputtering systems that deposit alloy films onto hard disk drives; the films magnetize the drives and thus enable them to record information. The Equipment division also makes sputterers used to make flat-panel displays. Intevac's Imaging division develops sensitive electro-optical devices used in high-performance digital cameras and military targeting equipment. Leading customers include Hitachi Global Storage Technologies and Seagate. Intevac was spun out of the old Varian Associates (later split into Varian, Varian Medical, and Varian Semiconductor) in a 1991 leveraged buyout.

Intevac's Equipment division (more than 90% of sales) provides services such as applications support, installation, training, and repair services, as well as spare parts and consumables, for its sputtering systems. The company's Imaging business includes its Photonics division, which collaborates with research firms including Stanford University and The Charles Stark Draper Laboratory to perform research for the US government, as well as its Commercial Imaging division, formed in 2002 to develop products based on its photonics technology for commercial markets, including night vision and long-range video cameras for security applications. The company suspended its development of photodiodes for high-speed fiber optic systems due to weakness in the telecommunications market at the time; the product has been repositioned for applications in target identification and other military uses.

T. Rowe Price holds nearly 10% of the company. Cross Link Capital has an equity stake of nearly 7%. Redemco owns about 6% of Intevac. Chairman Norman Pond holds around 4%.

EXECUTIVES
Chairman: Norman H. Pond, age 67, $136,166 pay
President, CEO, and Director: Kevin Fairbairn, age 52, $361,316 pay
COO: Luke Marusiak, age 43, $189,155 pay
VP, Finance and Administration, CFO, Secretary, and Treasurer: Charles B. Eddy III, age 55, $216,002 pay
VP, New Product Development: Christopher Lane, age 39
VP and General Manager, Imaging: Joseph Pietras
VP, Business Development: Ralph Kerns, age 59
VP, Customer Support: James (Jim) Birt, age 40
VP, Engineering: Patrick (Pat) Leahey, age 44
VP, Chief Technical Officer: Michael Barnes, age 47
VP, Technology: Terry Bluck, age 46
President, Photonics Technology Division:
Verle W. Aebi, age 51, $199,106 pay
Director, Human Resources: Kimberly Burk, age 40
Auditors: Grant Thornton LLP

LOCATIONS
HQ: Intevac, Inc.
3560 Bassett St., Santa Clara, CA 95054
Phone: 408-986-9888 **Fax:** 408-727-5739
Web: www.intevac.com

Intevac has operations in China, Malaysia, Singapore, and the US.

2005 Sales

	$ mil.	% of total
Asia	96.7	70
US	39.7	29
Europe	0.8	1
Total	**137.2**	**100**

PRODUCTS/OPERATIONS

2005 Sales

	$ mil.	% of total
Equipment	129.3	94
Imaging	7.9	6
Total	**137.2**	**100**

2005 Sales

	$ mil.	% of total
Systems & components	130.2	95
Technology development	7.0	5
Total	**137.2**	**100**

Selected Products
Equipment
Disk lubrication equipment
Disk sputtering equipment (MDP-250 series)
Flat-panel display sputtering systems (D-Star series)
Commercial Imaging
Laser-illuminated viewing and ranging (LIVAR) systems
Low-cost, low-light-level cameras (NightVista)
Negative-electron-affinity (NEA) electron sources

COMPETITORS

Aviza Technology	Northrop Grumman
CIC International	Oerlikon Corporation
CMC Electronics	Raytheon
DRS Technologies	Sumitomo Heavy
e2v	Industries
FLIR	Texas Instruments
Hamamatsu Corp.	Thales
ITT Corporation	ULVAC
Mitsui	

HISTORICAL FINANCIALS
Company Type: Public

Income Statement
FYE: December 31

	REVENUE ($ mil.)	NET INCOME ($ mil.)	NET PROFIT MARGIN	EMPLOYEES
12/05	137.2	16.1	11.7%	362
12/04	69.6	(4.3)	—	191
12/03	36.3	(12.3)	—	180
12/02	33.8	8.8	26.0%	136
12/01	51.5	(16.9)	—	183
Annual Growth	**27.8%**	**—**		**18.6%**

2005 Year-End Financials
Debt ratio: —
Return on equity: 20.5%
Cash ($ mil.): 49.7
Current ratio: 2.85
Long-term debt ($ mil.): —
No. of shares (mil.): 20.7
Dividends
Yield: —
Payout: —
Market value ($ mil.): 272.8
R&D as % of sales: 10.5%
Advertising as % of sales: —

Stock History
NASDAQ (GM): IVAC

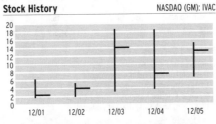

	STOCK PRICE ($) FY Close	P/E High/Low	PER SHARE ($) Earnings	Dividends	Book Value
12/05	13.20	20 9	0.76	—	4.25
12/04	7.56	— —	(0.22)	—	3.44
12/03	14.10	— —	(0.95)	—	1.82
12/02	3.99	8 3	0.66	—	0.87
12/01	2.38	— —	(1.42)	—	0.12
Annual Growth	**53.5%**		**—**	**—**	**145.3%**

Intuitive Surgical

Intuitive Surgical is haptic to meet you. Employing haptics (the science of computer-aided touch sensitivity), the firm has developed the da Vinci Surgical System of software, hardware, and optics to allow doctors to perform robotically aided surgery from a remote console. The company also makes EndoWrist surgical instruments for use with its system. The da Vinci system faithfully reproduces the doctor's hand movements in real time, with surgery performed by tiny electromechanical arms and instruments inserted in the patient's body through small openings. Intuitive sells its products in Asia, Australia, Europe, and North America through both a direct sales force and independent distributors.

Intuitive Surgical is focusing its marketing efforts within specialties including general, cardiothoracic, urologic, and gynecologic surgery. The company also plans to develop strategic alliances with medical device businesses. Intuitive Surgical currently has alliances with Medtronic, Olympus Corporation, and Ethicon Endo-Surgery.

EXECUTIVES
Chairman, President, and CEO: Lonnie M. Smith, age 61, $406,750 pay
EVP and COO: Gary S. Guthart, age 40, $263,000 pay (prior to title change)
SVP and CFO: Marshall L. Mohr, age 50
SVP and General Counsel: John F. (Rick) Runkel, age 50
SVP, Marketing: Eric C. Miller, age 46, $245,000 pay
SVP, Worldwide Sales: Jerome J. (Jerry) McNamara, age 47, $389,861 pay
VP, Business Development and Strategic Planning: Aleks Cukic
VP, Customer Service: Colin Morales
VP, Engineering: Sal Brogna
VP, Finance and Treasurer: Benjamin B. (Ben) Gong
VP, Human Resources: Heather Hand
Auditors: Ernst & Young LLP

LOCATIONS
HQ: Intuitive Surgical, Inc.
950 Kifer Rd., Sunnyvale, CA 94086
Phone: 408-523-2100 **Fax:** 408-523-1390
Web: www.intuitivesurgical.com

2005 Sales

	$ mil.	% of total
US	188.8	83
International	38.5	17
Total	**227.3**	**100**

PRODUCTS/OPERATIONS

2005 Sales

	$ mil.	% of total
Systems	124.6	55
Instruments & accessories	67.8	30
Services & training	34.9	15
Total	**227.3**	**100**

Selected Products
da Vinci Surgical System (surgeon's console, patient-side cart, and InSite 3-D visualization system)
EndoWrist surgical instruments

COMPETITORS

Armstrong Healthcare	Johnson & Johnson
Boston Scientific	Maquet
C. R. Bard	Medtronic
Guidant	MicroDexterity
Hitachi	Terumo Medical
Integrated Surgical	Toshiba
Systems	United States Surgical

HISTORICAL FINANCIALS
Company Type: Public

Income Statement
FYE: December 31

	REVENUE ($ mil.)	NET INCOME ($ mil.)	NET PROFIT MARGIN	EMPLOYEES
12/05	227.3	94.1	41.4%	419
12/04	138.8	23.5	16.9%	321
12/03	91.7	(9.6)	—	325
12/02	72.0	(18.4)	—	290
12/01	51.7	(16.7)	—	241
Annual Growth	44.8%	—	—	14.8%

2005 Year-End Financials

Debt ratio: —
Return on equity: 24.8%
Cash ($ mil.): 129.5
Current ratio: 3.60
Long-term debt ($ mil.): —
No. of shares (mil.): 36.2

Dividends
Yield: —
Payout: —
Market value ($ mil.): 4,243.8
R&D as % of sales: 7.6%
Advertising as % of sales: 0.6%

Stock History
NASDAQ (GS): ISRG

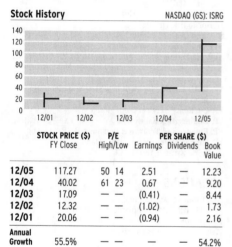

	STOCK PRICE ($) FY Close	P/E High/Low	PER SHARE ($) Earnings	Dividends	Book Value
12/05	117.27	50 14	2.51	—	12.23
12/04	40.02	61 23	0.67	—	9.20
12/03	17.09	— —	(0.41)	—	8.44
12/02	12.32	— —	(1.02)	—	1.73
12/01	20.06	— —	(0.94)	—	2.16
Annual Growth	55.5%	—	—	—	54.2%

inVentiv Health

To sell a new drug, it may be time to get inVentiv. A spinoff of global marketer Snyder Communications, inVentiv Health provides commercial and clinical services for the life sciences and pharmaceutical industries. The company's commercial services unit provides outsourced sales and marketing services, market research, data collection and management, recruitment, and training. The clinical services unit provides clinical staffing, clinical research and statistical analysis, and executive placement. Clients have included Bayer Corporation, Bristol-Myers Squibb, and Noven Pharmaceuticals. In late 2005 inVentiv acquired health care communications agency inChord Communications for $185 million.

The addition of new business lines necessitated changes in 2006; the company restructured along three service lines: Commercial Services, Clinical Services, and Communications. The Commercial Services segment (by far its most lucrative segment, representing more than 70% of sales) includes Health Products Research and Total Data Solutions while its Clinical Services segment consists of Smith Hanley, MedFocus, and HHI Statistical Services.

In 2006, inVentiv piled on the acquisitions, including those of Adheris, Synergos, and Jeffrey Simbrow Associates. The Adheris and Jeffrey Simbrow Associates acquisitions add heft to inVentiv's growing marketing communications operations. Synergos adds clinical trial management services to the company's operations.

inVentive expanded its commercial services operations in 2006 by acquiring two training companies, American Speakers Education Research Training (ASERT) and DialogCoach, along with online events producer Maxwell Group, which operates under the MedConference.

EXECUTIVES

Chairman Emeritus: Daniel M. Snyder, age 41
Chairman and CEO: Eran Broshy, age 47
CFO and Secretary: John R. Emery, age 49, $586,772 pay
Diversity Committee Chairman: Eric Manson
CEO, Smith Hanley Holding Company: Thomas A. (Tom) Hanley Jr.
President and CEO, Adheris: Daniel E. Rubin
President, inVentiv Clinical: Michael L. Hlinak
Director; President and CEO, inVentiv Commercial Services: Terrell G. (Terry) Herring, age 42, $690,000 pay
President and CEO, GSW Worldwide: Phil Deschamps
SVP, Ventiv Sales and Marketing Teams: Tom Sottile
Director; President and CEO, inVentiv Communications: R. Blane Walter, age 35, $118,757 pay
Media Contact: Felicia Vonella
Auditors: Deloitte & Touche LLP

LOCATIONS

HQ: inVentiv Health, Inc.
  Vantage Ct. North, 200 Cottontail Ln., Somerset, NJ 08873
Phone: 732-748-4666   **Fax:** 732-537-4912
Web: www.ventiv.com

PRODUCTS/OPERATIONS

2005 Sales

	$ mil.	% of total
inVentiv Commercial	393.9	71
inVentiv Clinical	113.7	20
inVentiv Communications	48.7	9
Total	**556.3**	**100**

Selected Services

Commercial Services
  Data collection and management
  Drug sample compliance
  Medical science liaisons/Clinical educator teams
  Planning, analytics, market research
  Recruitment
Clinical Services
  Clinical research and statistical analysis
  Clinical staffing
  Executive placement
Communications Services
  Advertising
  Contract marketing
  Interactive medical education
  Patient adherence services

COMPETITORS

Access Worldwide	Medical Staffing Network
ATC Healthcare	Nelson Communications
Cross Country Healthcare	Ogilvy Healthworld
Heidrick & Struggles	PAREXEL
IMS Health	PDI
InteliStaf Healthcare	Quintiles Transnational
Kforce	Topin
Korn/Ferry	Verispan

HISTORICAL FINANCIALS
Company Type: Public

Income Statement
FYE: December 31

	REVENUE ($ mil.)	NET INCOME ($ mil.)	NET PROFIT MARGIN	EMPLOYEES
12/05	556.3	43.9	7.9%	4,200
12/04	352.2	31.1	8.8%	4,000
12/03	224.4	5.8	2.6%	2,400
12/02	215.4	7.9	3.7%	1,800
12/01	398.5	(58.5)	—	4,500
Annual Growth	8.7%	—	—	(1.7%)

2005 Year-End Financials

Debt ratio: 75.2%
Return on equity: 20.6%
Cash ($ mil.): 77.0
Current ratio: 1.89
Long-term debt ($ mil.): 190.5
No. of shares (mil.): 27.9

Dividends
Yield: —
Payout: —
Market value ($ mil.): 658.1
R&D as % of sales: —
Advertising as % of sales: —

Stock History
NASDAQ (GS): VTIV

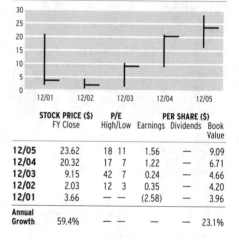

	STOCK PRICE ($) FY Close	P/E High/Low	PER SHARE ($) Earnings	Dividends	Book Value
12/05	23.62	18 11	1.56	—	9.09
12/04	20.32	17 7	1.22	—	6.71
12/03	9.15	42 7	0.24	—	4.66
12/02	2.03	12 3	0.35	—	4.20
12/01	3.66	— —	(2.58)	—	3.96
Annual Growth	59.4%	—	—	—	23.1%

IRIS International

IRIS International provides urinalysis technology to medical institutions around the globe. The company's iQ200 product line automates the steps of routine urinalysis. IRIS International's three divisions include Iris Diagnostics, which develops imaging systems used in urinalysis and microscopic analysis, and Iris Sample Processing, which makes a variety of other small instruments and laboratory supplies. Its Advanced Digitial Imaging Research subsidiary performs research for government and corporate clients. IRIS International has facilities in the US and Europe.

IRIS International plans to grow through acquisitions and by increasing its international marketing efforts. The company generated 30% of its revenue through international sales in 2005.

EXECUTIVES

Chairman: Richard H. Williams, age 68
President, CEO, and Director: Cesar M. Garcia, age 52, $375,143 pay
CTO and Director: Thomas H. Adams, age 64
Interim CFO: Veronica O. Tarrant, age 44
Corporate VP, Operations: John Yi
Corporate VP and President, Specimen Processing Business Unit: Robert A. Mello, age 51, $232,078 pay (prior to title change)
VP, Business Development: Yvonne Briggs
VP, Diagnostics Product Development: Dale Capewell
VP, Global Marketing and Clinical Affairs, Iris Diagnostics Division: Robert D. O'Malley
President, Advanced Digital Imaging Research: Kenneth R. Castleman, age 63, $200,962 pay
Auditors: BDO Seidman, LLP

LOCATIONS

HQ: IRIS International, Inc.
9172 Eton Ave., Chatsworth, CA 91311
Phone: 818-709-1244 **Fax:** 818-700-9661
Web: www.proiris.com

PRODUCTS/OPERATIONS

2005 Sales

	$ mil.	% of total
IVD instruments	27.6	44
IVD consumables & service	25.7	41
Sample processing instruments & supplies	9.5	15
Total	**62.8**	**100**

COMPETITORS

Applied Imaging
Bayer Corp.
Beckman Coulter
Biomerica
Clarient
Dade Behring
Hycor Biomedical
Roche Diagnostics
Siemens Medical Solutions Diagnostics
SYSMEX
Vysis

HISTORICAL FINANCIALS

Company Type: Public

Income Statement				FYE: December 31
	REVENUE ($ mil.)	NET INCOME ($ mil.)	NET PROFIT MARGIN	EMPLOYEES
12/05	62.8	6.1	9.7%	236
12/04	43.7	2.3	5.3%	182
12/03	31.3	(0.5)	—	156
12/02	28.2	0.9	3.2%	151
12/01	28.6	1.5	5.2%	137
Annual Growth	**21.7%**	**42.0%**	**—**	**14.6%**

2005 Year-End Financials

Debt ratio: —
Return on equity: 13.1%
Cash ($ mil.): 20.6
Current ratio: 4.35
Long-term debt ($ mil.): —
No. of shares (mil.): 17.5

Dividends
 Yield: —
 Payout: —
Market value ($ mil.): 381.6
R&D as % of sales: 8.0%
Advertising as % of sales: —

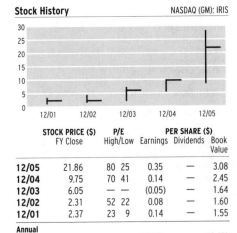

Stock History NASDAQ (GM): IRIS

	STOCK PRICE ($) FY Close	P/E High/Low		PER SHARE ($) Earnings	Dividends	Book Value
12/05	21.86	80	25	0.35	—	3.08
12/04	9.75	70	41	0.14	—	2.45
12/03	6.05	—	—	(0.05)	—	1.64
12/02	2.31	52	22	0.08	—	1.60
12/01	2.37	23	9	0.14	—	1.55
Annual Growth	**74.3%**	—	—	**25.7%**	—	**18.6%**

iRobot

If you're a Jetsons fan, you'll likely appreciate iRobot Corporation. The company makes robots for all sorts of applications, from government and military to toys and appliances. Its Roomba FloorVac, launched in 2002, is the first vacuum that automatically cleans floors. iRobot also makes the PackBot, which performs battlefield reconnaissance and bomb disposal for the US Army, and is developing the R-Gator, another unmanned ground vehicle model, with Deere & Company. The firm has offices in California, Massachusetts, Virginia, and Hong Kong and sells through more than 7,000 retail outlets globally. iRobot was founded in 1990 by robot engineers who performed research at the Massachusetts Institute of Technology.

The company hopes to expand its territory to include hard floors with its floor-washing robot, called Scooba. Initially the products were available in specialty stores such as Sharper Image.

Gregory White, president of the company's Home Robots division, announced in September 2006 that he would retire in 2007 to become an educator. iRobot plans to fill the position with an executive with experience taking similar products to a global level.

EXECUTIVES

Chairman: Helen Greiner, age 38, $384,934 pay
CEO and Director: Colin Angle, age 39, $384,934 pay
SVP, CFO, and Treasurer: Geoffrey P. (Geoff) Clear, age 56, $301,317 pay
SVP, Research and Development: Indrajit Purkayastha
SVP, Secretary, and General Counsel: Glen D. Weinstein, age 35
VP and Controller: Gerald C. Kent Jr., age 41
CTO and Director: Rodney A. Brooks, age 51
President, Government and Industrial Robots: Joseph W. (Joe) Dyer, age 59
Corporate Communications: Nancy Dussault
Auditors: PricewaterhouseCoopers LLP

LOCATIONS

HQ: iRobot Corporation
63 South Ave., Burlington, MA 01803
Phone: 781-345-0200 **Fax:** 781-345-0201
Web: www.irobot.com

PRODUCTS/OPERATIONS

2005 Sales

	$ mil.	% of total
Consumer	94.0	66
Government & Industrial	48.0	34
Total	**142.0**	**100**

COMPETITORS

Allen-Vanguard
BAE SYSTEMS
BISSELL
Electrolux
GE Consumer & Industrial

General Dynamics
Lockheed Martin
QinetiQ
REMOTEC UK
Samsung Electronics

HISTORICAL FINANCIALS

Company Type: Public

Income Statement				FYE: December 31
	REVENUE ($ mil.)	NET INCOME ($ mil.)	NET PROFIT MARGIN	EMPLOYEES
12/05	142.0	2.6	1.8%	276
12/04	95.0	0.2	0.2%	214
12/03	54.3	(7.4)	—	—
12/02	14.8	(10.8)	—	—
Annual Growth	**112.5%**	**—**		**29.0%**

2005 Year-End Financials

Debt ratio: —
Return on equity: 8.2%
Cash ($ mil.): 76.1
Current ratio: 3.16
Long-term debt ($ mil.): —
No. of shares (mil.): 23.4

Dividends
 Yield: —
 Payout: —
Market value ($ mil.): 780.1
R&D as % of sales: 8.1%
Advertising as % of sales: 7.4%

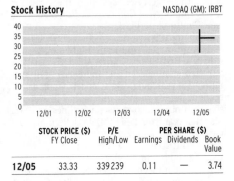

Stock History NASDAQ (GM): IRBT

	STOCK PRICE ($) FY Close	P/E High/Low		PER SHARE ($) Earnings	Dividends	Book Value
12/05	33.33	339	239	0.11	—	3.74

Itron

Itron aims to make meter reading a desk job. The company is a global supplier of wireless data acquisition and communication products for electric, gas, and water utilities. Itron makes radio- and telephone-based automatic meter reading (AMR) systems, handheld meter reading computers, and meter data acquisition and analysis software. Its systems are installed at more than 2,000 utilities worldwide — many using more than one Itron product. The company also provides consulting, project management, and outsourcing services. Customers include BC Hydro, Old Dominion Electric Cooperative, Ford, and Electrabel.

A major restructuring — including the replacement of top executives, the layoff of 15% of

its workforce, and the spinoff of its manufacturing operations as Servatron — has repositioned Itron to take advantage of new technologies and industry deregulation. The company targets the electric utility, water and public power, and natural gas markets. Customers in the US and Canada account for most of sales.

In 2004 Itron reorganized its market segments from five business units to two main segments: hardware and software. Within the hardware segment, the business is broken down into two lines of business, meter data collection and electricity metering.

The company is expanding into South America's biggest market with the acquisition of ELO Sistemas e Tecnologia, a Brazilian firm that has been distributing Itron products since late 2004 and manufacturing Itron's CENTRON meters since mid-2005. ELO Tecnologia has offices and a manufacturing assembly facility in Campinas and São Paulo, Brazil, and in Chile, employing about 80 people. Itron paid about $2 million in cash for the Brazilian firm.

Barclays Global Investors owns 6% of Itron. FMR (Fidelity Investments) holds nearly 6% of the company. Turner Investment Partners has an equity stake of about 5%.

HISTORY

Itron was formed by a group of engineers in 1977 with financial backing from utility Washington Water Power (now Avista). In 1992 Itron acquired EnScan, a maker of mobile automatic meter reading (AMR) systems. The company went public in 1993. During 1994 and 1995 it installed the largest AMR system in the world, for the Public Service Company of Colorado (now New Century Energies).

Itron in 1996 won a major contract from Pittsburgh-based Duquesne Light Co., a subsidiary of DQE. Itron acquired Utility Translation Services (commercial and industrial AMR systems) that year and Design Concepts (outage detection, quality monitoring, and AMR systems that communicate over telephone lines) in 1997. Also that year Itron and UK Data Collections Services (meter reading services) formed joint venture STAR Data Services to provide meter reading and billing services.

Restructuring charges related to cost-cutting efforts contributed to a loss in 1998. The next year Itron won an 11-year pact to provide meter reading services for Southern California Edison's 350,000 customers — a deal worth at least $20 million. During mid-1999 new CEO Michael Chesser led another restructuring — including layoffs and factory closures. Charges led to a loss for the year.

In 2000 Itron spun off part of its manufacturing operations as contract manufacturer Servatron. That year COO LeRoy Nosbaum replaced Chesser as CEO, and was later named chairman.

In 2002 Itron bolstered its energy consulting and software business through the acquisition of several privately held companies: LineSoft (consulting and software for utility transmission and distribution systems) for about $42 million; Regional Economic Research (energy consulting and software) for $14 million; and eMobile Data Corporation (wireless utility workforce management software) for about $6 million. The following year Itron acquired Silicon Energy (enterprise energy management software) for about $71 million.

In 2004 Itron acquired the Electricity Metering business unit of Schlumberger for nearly $250 million.

EXECUTIVES

Chairman and CEO: LeRoy D. Nosbaum, age 59, $853,560 pay
SVP and CFO: Steven M. (Steve) Helmbrecht, age 43, $404,576 pay
SVP and General Counsel:
Russell N. (Russ) Fairbanks Jr., age 62
SVP, Hardware Solutions: Malcolm Unsworth, age 56, $429,138 pay
SVP, Software Solutions: Philip C. Mezey, age 46, $443,705 pay
VP, Competitive Resources: Jared P. Serff, age 37
VP, Hardware Sales: Russell E. (Russ) Vanos
VP, Information Technology: Chuck McAtee
VP, Marketing: Kim Pearman-Gillman
VP, Investor Relations and Corporate Communications: Deloris Duquette
VP and General Manager, International Market Group: Douglas L. (Doug) Staker, age 46
Auditors: Deloitte & Touche LLP

LOCATIONS

HQ: Itron, Inc.
2818 N. Sullivan Rd., Spokane, WA 99216
Phone: 509-924-9900   **Fax:** 509-891-3355
Web: www.itron.com

Itron has facilities in California, Minnesota, North Carolina, South Carolina, and Washington, and sales offices in Australia, Canada, France, Mexico, the Netherlands, Qatar, Taiwan, the UK, and the US.

PRODUCTS/OPERATIONS

2005 Sales

	$ mil.	% of total
Hardware Solutions		
Meter data collection	262.0	48
Electricity metering	239.8	43
Software Solutions	50.9	9
Total	**552.7**	**100**

2005 Sales

	$ mil.	% of total
Sales	503.3	91
Service	49.4	9
Total	**552.7**	**100**

Selected Products

Automatic meter reading (AMR) systems and products
  Meter modules (utility meter attachments that transmit data to remote receivers)
  Mobile AMR (transportable systems for mounting on vehicles)
  Network AMR (utility-automated meter readers)
  Off-site meter reading units (remote reading of radio-equipped meters)
  Telephone-based technology (programmable modules for data collection over telephone lines)
Commercial and industrial meters
Forecasting, research, and analysis software
Handheld systems and products (electronic meter reading — EMR — handheld systems)
Surveying software
Workforce automation software (Service-Link)

Selected Services

Engineering consulting
Forecasting services
Installation
Outsourcing
Project management
System design and installation
Training

COMPETITORS

ABB
Accenture
Badger Meter
Bentley Systems
Capgemini
Comverge
ConneXt
Echelon
Electric & Gas Technology
eMeter
Equitrac
ESCO Technologies
GE
Honeywell International
IBM
Indus International
Intelligent Controls
Invensys
Landis & Gyr
LogicaCMG
MDSI
Metretek Technologies
Pointer Telocation
Power Measurement
Roper Industries
SAP
Siemens AG
Utility Partners

HISTORICAL FINANCIALS

Company Type: Public

Income Statement

FYE: December 31

	REVENUE ($ mil.)	NET INCOME ($ mil.)	NET PROFIT MARGIN	EMPLOYEES
12/05	552.7	33.1	6.0%	2,000
12/04	399.2	(5.3)	—	2,100
12/03	317.0	10.5	3.3%	1,500
12/02	284.8	8.7	3.1%	1,434
12/01	225.6	13.4	5.9%	1,092
Annual Growth	**25.1%**	**25.4%**	**—**	**16.3%**

2005 Year-End Financials

Debt ratio: 53.2%
Return on equity: 13.2%
Cash ($ mil.): 33.6
Current ratio: 2.10
Long-term debt ($ mil.): 169.0
No. of shares (mil.): 24.9

Dividends
  Yield: —
  Payout: —
Market value ($ mil.): 995.8
R&D as % of sales: —
Advertising as % of sales: 0.3%

Stock History

NASDAQ (GS): ITRI

	STOCK PRICE ($) FY Close	P/E High/Low		PER SHARE ($) Earnings	Dividends	Book Value
12/05	40.04	41	16	1.33	—	12.77
12/04	23.91	—	—	(0.25)	—	8.65
12/03	18.36	50	27	0.48	—	8.62
12/02	19.17	89	31	0.41	—	8.00
12/01	30.30	—	—	—	—	4.69
Annual Growth	**7.2%**	**—**	**—**	**48.0%**	**—**	**28.5%**

200

Ixia

Ixia nixes network glitches with its interface cards that transmit and analyze signals over fiber-optic and copper-line networks. Its equipment evaluates the quantity and speed of transmission of data packets, how many packets are lost during transmission, and whether the packets are received intact and in order. Ixia also designs chassis to hold the interface cards, and software to operate them. The company primarily serves network equipment manufacturers, service providers, and communications chip makers. Customers include AT&T, Cisco (around 35% of sales), and Intel. Luxembourg-based Technology Capital Group owns 36% of Ixia.

In 2006 Ixia acquired the video telephony test products of Dilithium Networks for around $5 million in cash. With the acquisition, the company introduced a product based on the Dilithium Network Analyzer (DNA). The IxMobile Video Telephony test tools are focused on mobile wireless conformance, interoperability, capacity, and performance testing.

In 2005 the company acquired Communication Machinery Corp. (CMC), a developer of Wi-Fi network testing tools. The purchase was for $4 million in cash.

In 2003 Ixia acquired G3 Nova Technology, a developer of VoIP test tools for enterprise call centers, communications networks, and network devices. Including earnout payments, the consideration paid was $8 million in cash, and 307,020 shares of common stock, valued at the time at around $3.8 million.

FMR (Fidelity Investments) has an equity stake of nearly 11% of the company. CEO Errol Ginsberg owns about 7% of Ixia, including options and shares held in a family trust owned by Ginsberg and his wife, Annette R. Michelson. All officers and directors of Ixia as a group hold nearly 10% of the company.

EXECUTIVES

Chairman: Jean-Claude Asscher, age 78
President, CEO, and Director: Errol Ginsberg, age 49
CFO: Thomas B. (Tom) Miller, age 49
EVP, Operations and Director: Robert W. (Sam) Bass, age 59
SVP, Worldwide Sales and Business Development Operations: David Anderson, age 49
VP, Acquisitions and Strategy: Cliff Hannel, age 43
VP, Asia Pacific Region: Joseph A. Noble, age 53
VP, EMEA: Mike McHale
VP, Software Development: Mark A. MacWhirter, age 45
Editorial Contact: Lori Choi
Auditors: PricewaterhouseCoopers LLP

LOCATIONS

HQ: Ixia
   26601 W. Agoura Rd., Calabasas, CA 91302
Phone: 818-871-1800   **Fax:** 818-871-1805
Web: www.ixiacom.com

Ixia has facilities in China, India, Japan, Romania, the UK, and the US.

2005 Sales

	$ mil.	% of total
US	116.1	73
Other countries	43.2	27
Total	**159.3**	**100**

PRODUCTS/OPERATIONS

2005 Sales

	$ mil.	% of total
Ethernet	105.0	66
SONET	8.3	5
Software	26.1	16
Chassis & other	19.9	13
Total	**159.3**	**100**

Selected Products

Electrical and optical interface cards
Multi-slot chassis (metal cases that contain a computer, a power supply, and interconnect components; used to house interface cards)
Software
   Application-specific test suites
   System management applications

COMPETITORS

Agilent Technologies
Anritsu
Digital Lightwave
Emrise
EXFO
RADCOM
Spirent
Tektronix
Teradyne
Tollgrade

HISTORICAL FINANCIALS

Company Type: Public

Income Statement

	REVENUE ($ mil.)	NET INCOME ($ mil.)	NET PROFIT MARGIN	EMPLOYEES
12/05	159.3	33.7	21.2%	640
12/04	117.0	18.9	16.2%	403
12/03	83.5	8.7	10.4%	287
12/02	67.6	3.4	5.0%	233
12/01	77.2	9.8	12.7%	204
Annual Growth	**19.9%**	**36.2%**	**—**	**33.1%**

FYE: December 31

2005 Year-End Financials

Debt ratio: —
Return on equity: 13.8%
Cash ($ mil.): 176.3
Current ratio: 8.13
Long-term debt ($ mil.): —
No. of shares (mil.): 66.6
Dividends
   Yield: —
   Payout: —
Market value ($ mil.): 985.4
R&D as % of sales: 20.3%
Advertising as % of sales: 0.9%

Stock History

NASDAQ (GS): XXIA

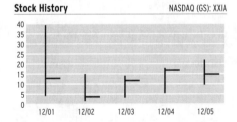

	STOCK PRICE ($) FY Close	P/E High/Low		PER SHARE ($) Earnings	Dividends	Book Value
12/05	14.80	44	20	0.49	—	4.24
12/04	16.81	61	20	0.29	—	3.31
12/03	11.70	98	25	0.14	—	2.80
12/02	3.65	243	31	0.06	—	2.59
12/01	12.85	244	28	0.16	—	2.47
Annual Growth	**3.6%**	**—**	**—**	**32.3%**	**—**	**14.4%**

j2 Global Communications

Checked your messages? Customers of j2 Global Communications can retrieve e-mail, faxes, and voice mail from a single phone line. Customers receive a private phone number that can handle unlimited incoming messages. The company, formerly known as JFAX.COM, operates primarily under the eFax, JFAX, and jConnect brands and claims more than 11 million phone numbers for customers located in 26 countries worldwide, including major US cities and international business centers such as Frankfurt, London, and Tokyo. The company counts more than 740,000 paid subscribers with the balance of phone lines going to advertising-supported free subscribers.

The company operates a global network based on both traditional phone infrastructure and Internet Protocol (IP) technology. The network is leased from telecom carriers and from colocation providers in the US and around the globe.

Chairman Richard Ressler owns about 5% of the company.

HISTORY

What do rock music, East Berlin, and the dot-com crowds have in common? The answer is Jaye Muller. Born in the former East Germany, Muller moved to Paris at 17 to pursue a rap music career. During a 1994 UK concert tour, he became frustrated at missing too many faxes and phone messages. Conveniently enough, Muller had attended tech school and invented a virtual fax machine. He moved to New York to work on music, but it was the siren song of a universal inbox that haunted him. Finding software programmers in Australia to help develop a system, he launched the company in 1995 as JFAX Communications.

JFAX began offering voice and fax messages via e-mail in 1996 in Atlanta, London, and New York. The service soon caught on, and by the end of the year the company had phone numbers available in 15 cities. Muller snagged professional talent, hiring Motorola's Hemi Zucker as COO.

In 1997 the company introduced its outbound faxing service, and Muller brought in big investors, including Richard Ressler, who left his job at IT firm MAI Systems to become CEO. Shifting coasts, JFAX left New York for Los Angeles. The company penned a deal with QUALCOMM to offer JFAX through its Eudora e-mail client, and closed out the year serving 45 cities.

JFAX came of age in 1998 when it embarked on a three-year marketing agreement with America Online, which promoted JFAX as its exclusive unified messaging service, while e-mail provider Critical Path, Internet portal Yahoo!, and ISP Prodigy became strategic partners. Anxious to get back to his music, at least part time, Muller hired former AT&T executive Gary Hickox as president.

The company went public in 1999 and changed its name to JFAX.COM, launching free service in hopes of attracting customers who would upgrade to fee-based plans.

In 2000 JFAX.COM acquired Internet-based messaging provider SureTalk.Com for $9 million. SureTalk's Steven Hamerslag became president (Hickox left the company) and CEO (Ressler became chairman). Later the company

changed its name again, this time to j2 Global Communications, and expanded by purchasing rival message services provider eFax.com. When Hamerslag resigned at year's end, the board replaced him with a management team made up of the company's top executives.

The next year j2 Global was granted a US patent for its core technology. Also in 2001 the company announced a planned expansion of its network into Argentina, Chile, Colombia, and Mexico.

Expansion has remained a big part of j2 Global Communications' scheme. The company increased its customer base with the acquisitions of rival messaging services providers SureTalk.com and eFax.com in 2002, and in 2004 it acquired British Columbia-based outsourced e-mail and messaging services provider The Electric Mail Company. That year the company also acquired the unified communications assets, branded Onebox, from Call Sciences.

Its expansion plans in Europe got a boost with the acquisition in 2005 of UK-based messaging services provider Puma United Communications.

EXECUTIVES

Chairman: Richard S. Ressler, age 47
Co-President and COO: Nehemia (Hemi) Zucker, age 49
Co-President and CFO: R. Scott Turicchi, age 42
EVP Corporate Strategy: Zohar Loshitzer, age 48
VP and Chief Accounting Officer:
 Greggory (Gregg) Kalvin, age 46, $157,703 pay
VP, General Counsel, and Secretary:
 Jeffrey D. (Jeff) Adelman, age 39
VP, Engineering: Doug Chey
VP, Finance: Nik Hallberg
VP, Human Resources: Patty Brunton
VP, Marketing Services and Support: Ken Ford
VP, Network Operations: John Bell
VP, Product Development: Ken Truesdale
VP, Sales: Thomas (Tom) Dolan
VP, Marketing: Mike Pugh
Auditors: Deloitte & Touche LLP

LOCATIONS

HQ: j2 Global Communications, Inc.
 6922 Hollywood Blvd., Ste. 500,
 Hollywood, CA 90028
Phone: 323-860-9200   **Fax:** 323-464-1446
Web: www.j2global.com

PRODUCTS/OPERATIONS

2005 Sales

	$ mil.	% of total
Subscriber revenues	139.7	97
Other revenues	4.2	3
Total	**143.9**	**100**

Selected Products

eFax Broadcast (high-volume faxing service)
eFax Corporate (similar to eFax Plus and jConnect Premier but focused on enterprise users)
eFax Plus (unique phone number allows subscribers to receive inbound fax messages in their e-mail inbox and to send documents to any fax number directly from the subscriber's desktop)
eFaxFree (free, advertising-supported service similar to eFax Plus)
jBlast (high-volume faxing service)
jConnect Free (free, advertising-supported service similar to jConnect Premier)
jConnect Premier (unique phone number allows subscribers to receive inbound fax and voicemail messages in their e-mail inbox and to send documents to any fax number directly from the subscriber's desktop)

M4 Internet (outsourced service allows the subscriber to create and execute e-mail campaigns from their desktop)
Messenger Plus (desktop software program allows subscribers to view faxes and listen to voicemail messages received through j2 Global Communications' services)
Onebox (unified communications services suite)
PaperMaster Pro (application allows subscribers to automate the organization, archiving, and retrieving of digital versions of documents and other file types)

Selected Subsidiaries

Call Sciences, Inc.
Call Science Limited (UK)
Data On Call, Inc.
Electric Mail (International) L.P. (Canada)
j2 Global Holdings Limited (UK)
j2 Global Ireland Limited (UK)
j2 Global UK Limited
Puma Unified Communications Limited (UK)
SureTalk.com, Inc. (Fax4Free.com)
The Electric Mail Company (Canada)

COMPETITORS

Active Voice
Auriga Laboratories
CallWave
Captaris
CommTouch Software
Critical Path
Deltathree
EasyLink Services
Notify Technology
PPOL
Premiere Global Services

HISTORICAL FINANCIALS

Company Type: Public

Income Statement				FYE: December 31
	REVENUE ($ mil.)	NET INCOME ($ mil.)	NET PROFIT MARGIN	EMPLOYEES
12/05	143.9	51.3	35.6%	288
12/04	106.3	31.6	29.7%	202
12/03	71.6	35.8	50.0%	175
12/02	48.2	14.3	29.7%	156
12/01	33.3	(7.8)	—	134
Annual Growth	**44.2%**	**—**	**—**	**21.1%**

2005 Year-End Financials

Debt ratio: 0.1%
Return on equity: 29.8%
Cash ($ mil.): 112.8
Current ratio: 7.00
Long-term debt ($ mil.): 0.2
No. of shares (mil.): 24.8

Dividends
 Yield: —
 Payout: —
Market value ($ mil.): 529.2
R&D as % of sales: 4.8%
Advertising as % of sales: —

Stock History

NASDAQ (GS): JCOM

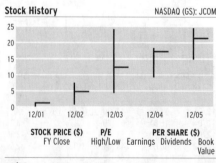

	STOCK PRICE ($) FY Close	P/E High/Low		PER SHARE ($) Earnings	Dividends	Book Value
12/05	21.37	24	15	1.00	—	8.23
12/04	17.25	29	15	0.63	—	5.93
12/03	12.40	34	6	0.71	—	4.46
12/02	4.76	24	3	0.30	—	5.13
12/01	1.24	—	—	(0.17)	—	3.83
Annual Growth	**103.7%**			**—**	**—**	**21.0%**

Jacksonville Bancorp

Jacksonville Bancorp is the holding company for The Jacksonville Bank, which operates about five branches in Jacksonville, Florida. The community bank, which opened in 1999, offers consumers and commercial customers standard deposit products including checking and savings accounts, money market accounts, CDs, and IRAs. The bank's lending activities primarily consist of commercial real estate loans, which make up more than half of its loan portfolio. Residential real estate loans make up almost another 25%; the bank also offers business, construction, and consumer loans. Jacksonville Bancorp is unrelated to the Illinois corporation of the same name.

Bank subsidiary Fountain Financial is an insurance agency.

Board members and executive officers collectively own more than a third of the company.

EXECUTIVES

Chairman: Donald E. Roller, age 68
President, CEO, and Director; President and CEO, The Jacksonville Bank: Gilbert J. Pomar III, age 45, $245,000 pay
EVP and CFO, Jacksonville Bancorp and The Jacksonville Bank: Valerie A. Kendall, age 53, $170,000 pay
EVP and Senior Loan Officer, The Jacksonville Bank: Scott M. Hall, age 41, $190,000 pay
SVP and Operations Manager, The Jacksonville Bank: Donna M. Donovan
Downtown Jacksonville Headquarters Manager, The Jacksonville Bank: John Hulsey
Mandarin Branch Manager, The Jacksonville Bank: Kimberly M. Delong
Queen's Harbour Branch Office Manager, The Jacksonville Bank: Lou Vaccaro

LOCATIONS

HQ: Jacksonville Bancorp, Inc.
 100 N. Laura St., Ste. 1000, Jacksonville, FL 32202
Phone: 904-421-3040   **Fax:** 904-421-3050
Web: www.jaxbank.com

PRODUCTS/OPERATIONS

2005 Sales

	$ mil.	% of total
Interest		
Loans, including fees	14.7	88
Securities	1.0	6
Federal funds sold & other	0.1	—
Noninterest		
Service charges on deposit accounts	0.6	4
Other	0.3	2
Total	**16.7**	**100**

COMPETITORS

Alabama National BanCorp
Bank of America
Compass Bancshares
Regions Financial
SunTrust
Wachovia

Income Statement

FYE: December 31

	ASSETS ($ mil.)	NET INCOME ($ mil.)	INCOME AS % OF ASSETS	EMPLOYEES
12/05	273.0	2.2	0.8%	120
12/04	223.7	1.3	0.6%	43
12/03	176.9	1.0	0.6%	34
12/02	130.8	0.6	0.5%	28
12/01	86.5	(0.2)	—	25
Annual Growth	33.3%	—	—	48.0%

2005 Year-End Financials

Equity as % of assets: 7.3%
Return on assets: 0.9%
Return on equity: 11.7%
Long-term debt ($ mil.): 4.0
No. of shares (mil.): 1.7
Market value ($ mil.): 56.8
Dividends
Yield: —
Payout: —
Sales ($ mil.): 16.7
R&D as % of sales: —
Advertising as % of sales: —

Stock History

NASDAQ (CM): JAXB

	STOCK PRICE ($) FY Close	P/E High/Low		PER SHARE ($) Earnings	Dividends	Book Value
12/05	33.15	28	21	1.21	—	11.58
12/04	26.95	35	20	0.79	—	10.42
12/03	16.40	26	18	0.67	—	9.14
12/02	11.93	28	20	0.44	—	8.57
12/01	9.60	—	—	(0.19)	—	7.18
Annual Growth	36.3%	—	—	—	—	12.7%

JAKKS Pacific

JAKKS Pacific is ready to rumble. JAKKS, one of the US's top toy companies, makes and sells action figures (including an exclusive license for World Wrestling Entertainment figures), activity sets (Flying Colors), die-cast and plastic cars (Road Champs, Remco), preschool toys (Child Guidance), pens and markers (Pentech), and fashion dolls. Its inexpensive toys are sold to US retailers such as Target, Toys "R" Us, and Wal-Mart (which together account for some 60% of company sales); hobby stores; and other retailers. JAKKS was founded in 1995 by chairman and CEO Jack Friedman and president Stephen Berman.

Part of JAKKS' growth strategy involves growing its product lines through licensing agreements and acquisitions. To that end, JAKKS has partnered with Jelly Belly Candy Co. to create a line of art activities and stationery based on Jelly Belly brand jelly beans. The Jelly Belly line is slated to debut in Spring 2007. Previously, in mid-2005, JAKKS acquired a collection of pet products, comprising licensed and non-licensed pet toys, from Pet Pal. In mid-2004 the company acquired Play Along, maker of plush toys, action figures, dolls, and preschool toys. Play Along holds several licenses such as Care Bears, Teletubbies, and Cabbage Patch Kids.

The company has also introduced pet toys and accessories ranging from Bratz-inspired clothes (for the fashion-conscious dog) to Batman hermit crab shells. A licensing agreement with Meow Mix will expand JAKKS' pet line for cats and kittens.

Early 2006 saw JAKKS further diversify its offerings with the purchase of Creative Designs International, a manufacturer of girls' dress-up and role-playing toys, for some $116 million.

EXECUTIVES

Chairman and CEO: Jack Friedman, age 67, $4,060,000 pay
President, COO, Secretary, and Director: Stephen G. Berman, age 41, $4,060,000 pay
EVP and CFO: Joel M. Bennett, age 43, $680,000 pay
SVP, International Sales: Carmine Russo
SVP, Licensing and Media: Jennifer Richmond
SVP, Marketing: Michael Bernstein
SVP, Operations: Jack McGrath
SVP, Sales: Bruce Katz
SVP, Sales: Ken Price
VP, Corporate Communications: Genna Goldberg
Senior Director, Human Resources: Tom Gerner
Auditors: PKF

LOCATIONS

HQ: JAKKS Pacific, Inc.
22619 Pacific Coast Hwy., Malibu, CA 90265
Phone: 310-456-7799   **Fax:** 310-317-8527
Web: www.jakkspacific.com

JAKKS Pacific sells its products globally and has offices in New York and Hong Kong.

2005 Sales

	$ mil.	% of total
US	562.4	85
Europe	38.6	6
Hong Kong	24.4	4
Canada	20.6	3
Other	15.5	2
Total	**661.5**	**100**

PRODUCTS/OPERATIONS

2005 Sales

	$ mil.	% of total
Traditional toys	569.9	86
Craft/activities/writing products	62.0	9
Seasonal products	19.8	3
Pet products	9.8	2
Total	**661.5**	**100**

Selected Products

Action figures and accessories
Crafts and activities
  Activity sets (jewelry-making sets, art studio sets, stamp sets)
  Clay compounds and sets
  Girls' accessories kits
  Lunch boxes
  Markers
  Notebooks
  Pens and pencils
  Stationery
Die-cast collectible and toy vehicles (cars, trucks, emergency vehicles, motorcycles, buses, aircraft, extreme sports vehicles)
Electronic products
  Karaoke machines
  Laser games
  NRG paintball
  RC and infrared vehicles
  TV games
Fashion dolls and accessories
Foam puzzle mats and blocks
Kites
Musical toys
Pet products
  Beds
  Clothing
  Toys
  Treats
Plastic vehicles
Plush toys
Role-playing sets (construction, fishing, police, fire, space, wrestling)
Sports activity toys
Slumber bags
Video games
Water toys

COMPETITORS

Activision
Binney & Smith
Corgi International
Dixon Ticonderoga
Electronic Arts
Grand Toys
Hasbro
Maisto
Marvel Entertainment
Mattel
Motorsports Authentics
Namco Bandai
Ohio Art
Radica Games
RC2
RoseArt
Small World Kids
SMOBY
Spin Master
Toy Quest

HISTORICAL FINANCIALS

Company Type: Public

Income Statement

FYE: December 31

	REVENUE ($ mil.)	NET INCOME ($ mil.)	NET PROFIT MARGIN	EMPLOYEES
12/05	661.5	63.5	9.6%	624
12/04	574.3	43.6	7.6%	419
12/03	315.8	15.9	5.0%	316
12/02	310.0	31.3	10.1%	284
12/01	284.3	28.2	9.9%	310
Annual Growth	23.5%	22.5%	—	19.1%

2005 Year-End Financials

Debt ratio: 18.7%
Return on equity: 13.0%
Cash ($ mil.): 240.2
Current ratio: 3.43
Long-term debt ($ mil.): 98.0
No. of shares (mil.): 26.9
Dividends
Yield: —
Payout: —
Market value ($ mil.): 564.2
R&D as % of sales: —
Advertising as % of sales: 5.9%

Stock History

NASDAQ (GS): JAKK

	STOCK PRICE ($) FY Close	P/E High/Low		PER SHARE ($) Earnings	Dividends	Book Value
12/05	20.94	12	7	2.06	—	19.47
12/04	22.11	17	9	1.49	—	17.21
12/03	13.15	23	15	0.64	—	15.20
12/02	13.47	17	7	1.37	—	15.69
12/01	18.95	18	6	1.45	—	12.98
Annual Growth	2.5%	—	—	9.2%	—	10.7%

Jones Soda

There's nothing average about Jones Soda. The company bottles and distributes brightly colored sodas with wacky flavors like Twisted Lime and Fufu Berry. Seasonal offerings include Turkey and Gravy for Thanksgiving and Chocolate Fudge for Valentine's Day. The company also regularly discontinues flavors. Jones, which distributes its drinks through retailers, including Barnes & Noble cafés, Panera Bread Company, Starbucks, and Target stores, also customizes its beverage labels with photos submitted by customers. The company sells a line of noncarbonated beverages (Jones Naturals), with added ginseng, zinc, or other ingredients, and citrus-flavored energy drinks under the Jones Energy and WhoopAss labels.

The company's practice or retiring flavors is designed to keep its line of sodas at about 12 flavors. In addition to carbonated drinks, Jones also offers organic tea and juice drinks.

Jones licenses its name, and sells its syrups, to grocer Kroger for a line of Jones Frozen Soda Pops. It also has a licensing agreement with Big Sky Brands for a line of Jones Soda Flavor Booster hard candy.

The company's additional products include lip balm in its soda flavors, apparel and accessories, and music sharing site MyJonesMusic.com. The company, which started out pushing its sodas from coolers placed in skate parks and tattoo parlors, fuels its alternative image by sponsoring extreme sport (BMX, skate boarding, surfing) athletes and inviting fans to submit flavor suggestions, quotes, and photos for labels on Jones' Web site.

Its products are available in the US and Canada and are distributed through a network of independent distributors. In 2006 the company announced that it would begin selling its soda in Kmart stores, boosting its presence in the US.

In 2006 the company acquired vitamin drink mix 24C in 2006 from mindful Inc. and has plans to use the drink formula to create a vitamin-enhanced bottled water. Jones has started selling a soda made with pure cane sugar, targeting consumers who want a more "natural" alternative to sodas made with high fructose corn syrup.

Founder, chairman, CEO, and president Peter van Stolk owns some 10% of the company.

EXECUTIVES

Chairman, President, and CEO: Peter M. van Stolk, age 42, $172,619 pay
CFO: Hassan N. Natha, age 46
EVP Sales: Lars P. Nilsen, age 44
VP Operations: Eric Chastain
VP Sales East, Carbonated Soft Drinks: Jeff Spector
VP Sales East, Direct Store Distribution: Jeff Hartwell
VP Sales Midwest, Direct Store Distribution: Chad Kennedy
VP Sales West, Direct Store Distribution: Paul Weinstein
Customer Service Manager: Laura Blazyk
Human Resources Manager: Nancy Bucher
Marketing Manager: Seth T. Godwin
Auditors: KPMG LLP

LOCATIONS

HQ: Jones Soda Co.
234 9th Ave. North, Seattle, WA 98109
Phone: 206-624-3357   **Fax:** 206-624-6857
Web: www.jonessoda.com

2005 Sales

	% of total
US	88
Canada	11
Other foreign	1
Total	**100**

Select Products

Jones Energy
Jones Organics
Jones Naturals
Jones Soda
  Mid calorie (reduced sugar, carbohydrates, and calories)
  Premium
  Sugar free

COMPETITORS

Big Red	Ocean Spray
Cadbury Schweppes	Odwalla
Coca-Cola	Old Orchard
Cool Mountain Beverages	PepsiCo
Ferolito, Vultaggio	Polar Beverages
Fuze Beverage	Red Bull
Hansen Natural	Reed's
Impulse Energy USA	Snapple
IZZE	South Beach Beverage
Mott's	Sunny Delight
Naked Juice	Tropicana
National Beverage	Welch's
National Grape Cooperative	Wet Planet Beverages
New Attitude Beverage	

HISTORICAL FINANCIALS

Company Type: Public

Income Statement

FYE: December 31

	REVENUE ($ mil.)	NET INCOME ($ mil.)	NET PROFIT MARGIN	EMPLOYEES
12/05	34.2	1.3	3.8%	52
12/04	27.5	1.3	4.7%	51
12/03	20.1	0.3	1.5%	38
12/02	18.6	(1.2)	—	34
12/01	23.6	(1.7)	—	36
Annual Growth	**9.7%**	**—**		**9.6%**

2005 Year-End Financials

Debt ratio: 1.4%
Return on equity: 24.3%
Cash ($ mil.): 1.2
Current ratio: 2.42
Long-term debt ($ mil.): 0.1
No. of shares (mil.): 21.6

Dividends
  Yield: —
  Payout: —
Market value ($ mil.): 116.7
R&D as % of sales: —
Advertising as % of sales: —

Stock History

NASDAQ (CM): JSDA

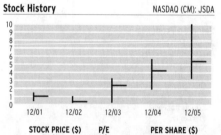

	STOCK PRICE ($) FY Close	P/E High/Low		PER SHARE ($) Earnings	Dividends	Book Value
12/05	5.40	166	55	0.06	—	0.29
12/04	4.23	93	33	0.06	—	0.21
12/03	2.40	160	17	0.02	—	0.12
12/02	0.37	—	—	(0.06)	—	0.09
12/01	1.03	—	—	(0.09)	—	0.16
Annual Growth	**51.3%**	—	—	—	—	**16.8%**

Jupitermedia

Owner of Internet.com, Jupitermedia isn't the homepage for the entire Web, but it does put lots of information within reach of your mouse. Targeting IT professionals, the company's JupiterWeb unit publishes industry news and information on more than 150 Web sites in its online network of information channels, and sends out nearly 150 e-newsletters. Jupitermedia provides online images through JupiterImages. It discontinued JupiterEvents (conferences and trade shows) in 2005 and sold off its JupiterResearch division in 2006. The company is primarily focused on its rapidly growing digital asset collections. Chairman and CEO Alan Meckler owns 35% of the company.

Previously named INT Media Group, the company became Jupitermedia after purchasing assets from Jupiter Media Metrix in 2002.

The firm's JupiterImages has more than 7 million images online with brands like Comstock Images, Creatas Images, PictureQuest, Liquid Library, Thinkstock Images, Thinkstock Footage, Photos.com, Ablestock.com, PhotoObjects.net, Clipart.com, IFA Bilderteam, and Animations.com.

Jupitermedia's JupiterWeb division operates four distinct online networks: Internet.com and EarthWeb.com for IT and business professionals; DevX.com for developers; and Graphics.com, for creative professionals.

In 2005 the acquisitive company purchased several image businesses, including Creatas for about $60 million; French image firm Goodshoot for nearly $10 million; image assets and distribution firm PictureArts for some $63 million; BananaStock, a UK-based provider of royalties-free digital images, for about $19 million; and graphics company Animation Factory for more than $9 million.

Also that year Jupitermedia sold its Search Engine Strategies trade show and its ClickZ.com Network of Web sites to Incisive Media for $43 million.

In 2006 the company added royalty-free music tracks to its content offerings through its purchase of Crank City Music.

EXECUTIVES

Chairman and CEO: Alan M. Meckler, age 60, $294,490 pay
President, COO, Interim CFO, and Director: Christopher S. Cardell, age 46
SVP and General Counsel: Mitchell S. (Mitch) Eisenberg
VP and CTO: Mark Labbe
VP Business Development and Licensing: David M. Arganbright
VP North American Sales, Jupiterimages: Rick Thompson
SVP and General Manager, Image Operations and Marketing, Jupiterimages: Edward Grossman
SVP and General Manager, Jupiter Web: Christopher (Chris) Elwell
Marketing and Public Relations Associate: Lisa DiGiacomo
Auditors: Deloitte & Touche LLP

LOCATIONS

HQ: Jupitermedia Corporation
23 Old Kings Hwy. South, Darien, CT 06820
Phone: 203-662-2800   **Fax:** 203-655-4686
Web: www.jupitermedia.com

Jupitermedia Corporation has offices in Australia, Canada, France, Germany, the UK, and the US.

PRODUCTS/OPERATIONS

2005 Sales

	$ mil.	% of total
Online images	80.7	65
Online media	33.1	27
Research	10.8	9
Total	**124.6**	**100**

Selected Products and Operations

JupiterImages (digital images for graphics professionals)
  AbleStock.com
  Animations.com
  BananaStock
  Clipart.com
  Comstock Images
  Creatas Images
  Goodshoot.com
  IFA Bilderteam
  Liquid Library
  Photos.com
  PhotoObjects.net
  PictureArts
  PictureQuest
  Thinkstock Footage
  Thinkstock Images
JupiterWeb
  DevX.com (content for developers)
  EarthWeb.com (content for IT professionals)
  Graphics.com (news and resources for creative
    professionals)
  Internet.com (content for IT and Internet
    professionals)

COMPETITORS

CMP Media
CNET Networks
Corbis
Forrester Research
Gartner
Getty Images
International Data Group
OSTG
TechTarget
Ziff Davis Media

HISTORICAL FINANCIALS

Company Type: Public

Income Statement

FYE: December 31

	REVENUE ($ mil.)	NET INCOME ($ mil.)	NET PROFIT MARGIN	EMPLOYEES
12/05	124.6	78.4	62.9%	639
12/04	71.9	15.7	21.8%	339
12/03	47.0	1.4	3.0%	279
12/02	40.7	(0.5)	—	265
12/01	44.0	(102.2)	—	223
Annual Growth	**29.7%**	**—**	**—**	**30.1%**

2005 Year-End Financials

Debt ratio: 22.5%
Return on equity: 52.7%
Cash ($ mil.): 18.5
Current ratio: 0.87
Long-term debt ($ mil.): 46.2
No. of shares (mil.): 34.9
Dividends
  Yield: —
  Payout: —
Market value ($ mil.): 515.4
R&D as % of sales: —
Advertising as % of sales: —

Stock History

NASDAQ (GS): JUPM

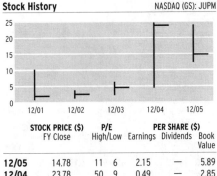

	STOCK PRICE ($) FY Close	P/E High/Low		PER SHARE ($) Earnings	Dividends	Book Value
12/05	14.78	11	6	2.15	—	5.89
12/04	23.78	50	9	0.49	—	2.85
12/03	4.55	122	47	0.05	—	1.48
12/02	2.49	—	—	(0.02)	—	1.38
12/01	1.90	—	—	(4.03)	—	1.40
Annual Growth	**67.0%**	**—**	**—**	**—**	**—**	**43.3%**

Kenexa

Kenexa wants to streamline your HR processes. The company markets Web-based applications that automate human resources activities, such as recruitment, skills testing, and tracking of employee development. Kenexa also offers outsourcing options to clients, taking over part or all of the recruitment and hiring process. The company sells its services and software products mostly on a subscription basis to more than 2,100 large and medium-sized corporations. In an expansion push, the company has acquired recruiting software providers BrassRing and Webhire, consultant Knowledge Workers, and survey firm Gantz Wiley Research in 2006. Kenexa was founded in 1987.

After launching an IPO in mid-2005, the company used the leftover proceeds to acquire Webhire in January 2006.

Kenexa hopes to expand into markets in Europe, the Middle East, and the Asia/Pacific region. (In 2005, only 10% of the company's sales came from outside the US.) To help achieve these goals, the company acquired Psychometric Services, a London-based diagnostic test provider, in late 2006 for $7.6 million.

Parthenon Investment Partners owns about 13% of Kenexa.

EXECUTIVES

Chairman and CEO: Nooruddin S. (Rudy) Karsan, age 48, $841,138 pay
COO, Secretary, and Director: Elliot H. Clark, age 44, $530,082 pay
CFO: Donald F. (Don) Volk, age 56, $538,000 pay
EVP: Bill L. Erickson, age 57
EVP: P. Grant Parker, age 48
SVP Talent Acquisition Services: Kevin T. Hudson, age 51
SVP Global Development Center: Raghuveer Sakuru, age 39
VP Business Development: Archie L. Jones Jr., age 34
President, Human Capital Management and Director: Troy A. Kanter, age 38
President, Kenexa Government Solutions: William Sebra
CTO: Ramarao V. Velpuri, age 42, $320,182 pay
Chief Marketing Officer: Sarah M. Teten, age 32
Auditors: BDO Seidman, LLP

LOCATIONS

HQ: Kenexa Corporation
  650 E. Swedesford Rd., 2nd Fl., Wayne, PA 19087
Phone: 610-971-9171   **Fax:** 610-971-9181
Web: www.kenexa.com

Kenexa Corporation has offices in England, India, Malaysia, and the US.

2005 Sales

	% of total
US	90
Europe, Middle East & Africa	6
Canada	3
Asia/Pacific & other	1
Total	**100**

PRODUCTS/OPERATIONS

2005 Sales

	$ mil.	% of total
Subscription	50.9	78
Other	14.7	22
Total	**65.6**	**100**

COMPETITORS

Authoria
Deploy Solutions
Gallup
iCIMS
Integrated Performance Systems
ISGN
Lawson Software
Oracle
Peopleclick
Pilat Technologies International
PreVisor
SAP
SHL Group
Spring Group
Taleo
Vurv
Workstream

HISTORICAL FINANCIALS

Company Type: Public

Income Statement

FYE: December 31

	REVENUE ($ mil.)	NET INCOME ($ mil.)	NET PROFIT MARGIN	EMPLOYEES
12/05	65.6	6.1	9.3%	693
12/04	46.3	(4.1)	—	—
12/03	34.0	(12.2)	—	—
Annual Growth	**38.9%**	**—**	**—**	**—**

2005 Year-End Financials

Debt ratio: 0.6%
Return on equity: 1,297.9%
Cash ($ mil.): 43.5
Current ratio: 2.58
Long-term debt ($ mil.): 0.3
No. of shares (mil.): 17.5
Dividends
  Yield: —
  Payout: —
Market value ($ mil.): 368.4
R&D as % of sales: —
Advertising as % of sales: —

Stock History

NASDAQ (GM): KNXA

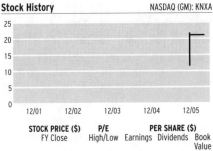

	STOCK PRICE ($) FY Close	P/E High/Low		PER SHARE ($) Earnings	Dividends	Book Value
12/05	21.10	—	—	(3.06)	—	2.91

Kentucky First Federal Bancorp

Kentucky First Federal wants to be second to none for banking in the Bluegrass State. Through subsidiaries First Federal Savings and Loan of Hazard and First Federal Savings Bank of Frankfort, the company operates three branches in the state's capital and one in the town of Hazard. The banks offer traditional deposit products, such as checking, savings, NOW and retirement accounts, as well as CDs. Lending is focused on residential mortgages, but the banks also offer other property loans, as well as consumer and construction loans. Kentucky First Federal acquired Frankfort First Bancorp in 2005. First Federal MHC, a mutual holding company, owns 55% of Kentucky First Federal.

EXECUTIVES

Chairman and CEO: Tony D. Whitaker, age 59, $175,050 pay
President, COO, and Director: Don D. Jennings, age 40
VP, CFO, and Treasurer; VP and Treasurer, First Federal of Frankfort: R. Clay Hulette, age 43
Auditors: Grant Thornton LLP

LOCATIONS

HQ: Kentucky First Federal Bancorp
479 Main St., Hazard, KY 41702
Phone: 502-223-1638

COMPETITORS

Community Trust
Fifth Third
Huntington Bancshares
National City
Old National Bancorp
Republic Bancorp

HISTORICAL FINANCIALS

Company Type: Public

Income Statement

FYE: June 30

	ASSETS ($ mil.)	NET INCOME ($ mil.)	INCOME AS % OF ASSETS	EMPLOYEES
6/06	261.9	1.6	0.6%	40
6/05	273.9	1.6	0.6%	40
6/04	138.1	0.9	0.7%	14
6/03	138.3	1.3	0.9%	—
Annual Growth	23.7%	5.3%	—	69.0%

2006 Year-End Financials

Equity as % of assets: 24.4%
Return on assets: 0.6%
Return on equity: 2.5%
Long-term debt ($ mil.): —
No. of shares (mil.): 8.6
Market value ($ mil.): 90.0
Dividends
  Yield: 3.8%
  Payout: 210.5%
  Sales ($ mil.): 12.9
R&D as % of sales: —
Advertising as % of sales: —

Kforce

Kforce is a corporate matchmaker, placing highly skilled workers with the companies that need them. The specialty staffing firm provides primarily temporary staffing services (and to a lesser extent permanent placement) in such areas as information technology, accounting, health care, and clinical research. Kforce operates about 70 field offices across the US and serves *FORTUNE* 1000 corporations, as well as small and midsized firms in all 50 states. The company also offers Web-based services such as online resumes, job postings, career management information, and interactive interviews.

More than 90% of Kforce's revenues come from the provision of temporary staffing services. Direct-hire placements account for the remainder of sales, with fees coming from a percentage of the hired employee's first-year salary.

Kforce operates in three segments: technology; accounting and finance; and health care and life sciences. Its IT segment (its biggest moneymaker) recruits programmers, systems analysts, and networking technicians. The unit has grown through a number of acquisitions, including the 2004 purchase of Hall, Kinion & Associates, a provider of contract and permanent IT professionals to the government services, finance, medical technology, real estate, and energy services sectors. Kforce also acquired tech staffing firm VistaRMS in 2005 and Pennsylvania-based Pinkerton Computer Consultants in 2006.

The company's health and life sciences unit recruits nurses and other health care workers, clinical research personnel for pharmaceutical companies, and scientific professionals.

The company expanded its accounting and finance segment in 2006 by buying Virginia-based Bradson, which primarily serves government agencies.

CEO David Dunkel owns 11% of Kforce.

EXECUTIVES

Chairman and CEO: David L. Dunkel, age 52, $1,265,000 pay
Vice Chairman and VP Mergers and Acquisitions: Howard W. Sutter, age 57
President and Secretary: William L. (Bill) Sanders, age 59, $997,150 pay

SVP and CFO: Joseph J. (Joe) Liberatore, age 43, $700,000 pay
SVP and Chief Services Officer: Michael L. (Mike) Ettore, age 49, $446,875 pay
SVP Investor Relations: Michael R. Blackman
SVP National Accounts: Kim Henderson
SVP National Champions and Product Management: Andy Thomas
VP and Chief Accounting Officer: Anthony B. Petitt, age 35
Chief Sales Officer: Stephen J. (Steve) McMahan, age 51
Auditors: Deloitte & Touche LLP

LOCATIONS

HQ: Kforce Inc.
1001 E. Palm Ave., Tampa, FL 33605
Phone: 813-552-5000   **Fax:** 813-552-2493
Web: www.kforce.com

PRODUCTS/OPERATIONS

2005 Sales

	$ mil.	% of total
Technology	370.8	46
Finance & accounting	243.7	30
Health & life sciences	187.8	24
Total	**802.3**	**100**

COMPETITORS

Ablest
Acsys
Adecco
AMN Healthcare
Butler International
CDI
CIBER
COMFORCE
Cross Country Healthcare
General Employment Enterprises
Jefferson Wells International
Judge Group
Kelly Services
Manpower
Medical Staffing Network
Monster
Monster Worldwide
MPS
On Assignment
Robert Half
Spherion
TAC Worldwide

HISTORICAL FINANCIALS

Company Type: Public

Income Statement

FYE: December 31

	REVENUE ($ mil.)	NET INCOME ($ mil.)	NET PROFIT MARGIN	EMPLOYEES
12/05	802.3	22.3	2.8%	11,193
12/04	661.5	25.0	3.8%	11,867
12/03	495.6	5.1	1.0%	7,659
12/02	513.5	(47.0)	—	7,200
12/01	646.0	(12.1)	—	8,700
Annual Growth	5.6%	—	—	6.5%

2005 Year-End Financials

Debt ratio: 18.1%
Return on equity: 11.7%
Cash ($ mil.): 37.1
Current ratio: 2.47
Long-term debt ($ mil.): 38.2
No. of shares (mil.): 38.7
Dividends
  Yield: —
  Payout: —
Market value ($ mil.): 431.4
R&D as % of sales: —
Advertising as % of sales: —

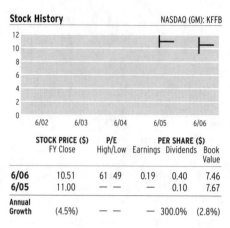

Stock History   NASDAQ (GM): KFFB

	STOCK PRICE ($) FY Close	P/E High/Low	Earnings	Dividends	Book Value
6/06	10.51	61 49	0.19	0.40	7.46
6/05	11.00	— —		0.10	7.67
Annual Growth	(4.5%)	— —	—	300.0%	(2.8%)

PER SHARE ($)

Stock History

Stock History NASDAQ (GS): KFRC

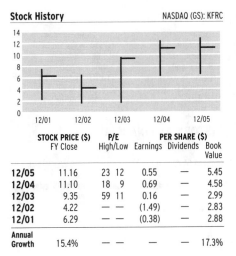

	12/01	12/02	12/03	12/04	12/05

	STOCK PRICE ($) FY Close	P/E High/Low		PER SHARE ($) Earnings	Dividends	Book Value
12/05	11.16	23	12	0.55	—	5.45
12/04	11.10	18	9	0.69	—	4.58
12/03	9.35	59	11	0.16	—	2.99
12/02	4.22	—	—	(1.49)	—	2.83
12/01	6.29	—	—	(0.38)	—	2.88
Annual Growth	**15.4%**	—	—	—	—	**17.3%**

KMG Chemicals

KMG Chemicals saves dead trees and kills weeds. The company makes and distributes wood preservatives and agricultural chemicals. Its wood preservatives are pentachlorophenol (penta), sodium penta, and creosote. KMG sells penta and creosote in the US, primarily to the railroad, construction, and utility industries. Sodium penta is sold in Latin America. The company makes herbicides used to protect cotton from weeds (Bueno) and to kill weeds along highways (Ansar), and its Rabon and Ravap pesticide lines keep pests from livestock and poultry. KMG also sells hydrochloric acid, a by-product of penta manufacturing, to the oil and steel industries. Chairman David Hatcher owns more than 60% of KMG.

The most common chemicals for wood preservation are chromated copper arsenate (CCA), creosote, and penta. CCA accounts for about 80% of the sales for wood preservation chemicals but is not produced by KMG.

In December 2002 KMG bought an insecticide product line that sells tetrachlorvinphos under the Rabon brand name. It is used to protect livestock and poultry from flies and other pests. It bought an additional line of insecticides in 2004, called Ravap.

In 2005 the company acquired the penta assets of Occidental Chemical; OxyChem gained the assets as part of its acquisition of Vulcan Chemicals earlier that year. This acquisition made KMG the sole distributor of penta for wood treatment purposes in the US.

KMG's largest customer (as well as a large supplier) is Koppers, which accounts for just under 10% of KMG's sales. Director Fred Leonard, through Valves Incorporated of Texas, owns approximately 12% of the company.

EXECUTIVES

CEO and Chairman: David L. Hatcher, age 63, $459,752 pay
COO and President: J. Neal Butler, age 54, $295,909 pay
CFO and VP: John V. Sobchak, age 46, $199,577 pay
VP, Sales, KMB-Bernuth, Inc.:
  Thomas H. (Tom) Mitchell, age 61, $189,513 pay
VP, General Counsel and Secretary: Roger C. Jackson, age 54, $170,983 pay
Auditors: UHY LLP

LOCATIONS

HQ: KMG Chemicals, Inc.
  10611 Harwin Dr., Ste. 402, Houston, TX 77036
Phone: 713-988-9252   **Fax:** 713-988-9298
Web: www.kmgb.com

KMG Chemicals has facilities in Alabama, Kansas, Texas, and Mexico.

2006 Sales

	% of total
US	97
Other	3
Total	**100**

PRODUCTS/OPERATIONS

2006 Sales

	$ mil.	% of total
Wood treatment		
Creosote	30.7	43
Penta	27.9	39
Animal health	8.6	12
Agricultural chemicals	3.8	6
Total	**71.0**	**100**

Selected Products

Creosote (wood preservative)
Hydrochloric acid (for use in the steel and oil well service industries)
Monosodium and disodium methanearsonic acids (MSMA; herbicide)
Pentachlorophenol (also known as "penta"; wood preservative)
Sodium pentachlorophenol (also known as "sodium penta"; wood preservative)
Tetrachlorvinphos (insecticide)

COMPETITORS

Arch Chemicals	Monsanto
Delta and Pine Land	Osmose
Eden Bioscience	Perstorp
Koppers Holdings	Pioneer Companies
Merichem	Rasa

HISTORICAL FINANCIALS

Company Type: Public

Income Statement				FYE: July 31
	REVENUE ($ mil.)	NET INCOME ($ mil.)	NET PROFIT MARGIN	EMPLOYEES
7/06	71.0	3.8	5.4%	110
7/05	59.2	3.0	5.1%	93
7/04	43.6	1.8	4.1%	90
7/03	35.5	1.9	5.4%	75
7/02	34.4	2.7	7.8%	67
Annual Growth	**19.9%**	**8.9%**	—	**13.2%**

2006 Year-End Financials

Debt ratio: 29.8%	Dividends
Return on equity: 9.5%	Yield: 0.9%
Cash ($ mil.): 11.2	Payout: 20.0%
Current ratio: 2.72	Market value ($ mil.): 84.3
Long-term debt ($ mil.): 14.0	R&D as % of sales: 1.7%
No. of shares (mil.): 10.5	Advertising as % of sales: —

Stock History NASDAQ (GM): KMGB

	7/02	7/03	7/04	7/05	7/06

	STOCK PRICE ($) FY Close	P/E High/Low		PER SHARE ($) Earnings	Dividends	Book Value
7/06	8.00	25	16	0.40	0.08	4.45
7/05	8.63	28	8	0.37	0.07	3.74
7/04	3.15	23	12	0.23	0.06	3.26
7/03	3.10	17	8	0.25	0.05	3.07
7/02	3.00	11	4	0.36	0.04	2.86
Annual Growth	**27.8%**	—	—	**2.7%**	**18.9%**	**11.7%**

KNBT Bancorp

KNBT holds the key to Keystone Nazareth Bank & Trust, which was formed when the company combined Keystone Bank & Trust with Nazareth Bank (acquired when KNBT bought First Colonial Group in 2003). Keystone Nazareth operates about 60 branches in eastern Pennsylvania, offering such services as checking and savings accounts, CDs, and insurance and investment products. It concentrates on real estate lending, particularly residential mortgages and home construction loans, but the company plans to place greater emphasis on loans to small and midsized businesses within its market area. KNBT acquired Northeast Pennsylvania Financial and its First Federal Bank subsidiary in 2005.

In 2004, KNBT Bancorp bought Oakwood Financial, a brokerage firm based in Allentown, Pennsylvania. Oakwood (under its same leadership) took the name KNBT Securities. The following year it acquired Caruso Benefits Group, a provider of group benefits management. In 2006 the company acquired Paragon Group, the holding company of the Trust Company of Lehigh Valley.

EXECUTIVES

Chairman: Jeffrey P. (Jeff) Feather, age 61
President, CEO, and Director, KNBT Bancorp. and Keystone Nazareth Bank: Scott V. Fainor, age 42
SEVP, CFO, and Treasurer, KNBT Bancorp and Keystone Nazareth Bank: Eugene T. (Gene) Sobol, age 59
EVP and Credit Risk Officer: Sandra L. Bodnyk
SVP, Branch Administration, Keystone Nazareth Bank: William L. Vitalos, age 39
SVP, Corporate and Private Banking, Keystone Nazareth Bank: David B. Kennedy, age 42
SVP, Marketing, Keystone Nazareth Bank: David W. Hughes, age 56
SVP, Retail/Mortgage Lending, Keystone Nazareth Bank: Karen Whitehill, age 51
President, KNBT Securities: Gerard (Gerry) Hallman
Corporate Secretary: Michele A. Linsky
Director, Marketing and Public Relations, Keystone Nazareth Bank: Mark Reimer
Auditors: Grant Thornton LLP

LOCATIONS

HQ: KNBT Bancorp, Inc.
90 Highland Ave., Bethlehem, PA 18017
Phone: 610-861-5000   **Fax:** 610-861-5727
Web: www.knbt.com

Keystone Nazareth Bank & Trust operates branches in Pennsylvania's Northampton (20), Lehigh (15), Luzerne (8), Monroe (6), Schuylkill (4), Carbon (3), and Columbia (2) counties.

PRODUCTS/OPERATIONS

2005 Sales

	$ mil.	% of total
Interest income		
Loans	77.5	49
Investment securities	52.3	33
Other	2.4	1
Deposit service charges	5.4	3
Benefit services revenue	4.1	3
Bank-owned life insurance	2.9	2
Check card/ATM fees	2.8	2
Brokerage services revenue	2.6	2
Trust revenue	2.1	1
Insurance services revenue	1.7	1
Lending fees	1.1	1
Other	3.7	2
Total	**158.6**	**100**

COMPETITORS

Bank of America
Fulton Financial
M&T Bank
PNC Financial
Sovereign Bancorp
Wachovia

HISTORICAL FINANCIALS

Company Type: Public

Income Statement

FYE: December 31

	ASSETS ($ mil.)	NET INCOME ($ mil.)	INCOME AS % OF ASSETS	EMPLOYEES
12/05	3,081.8	20.8	0.7%	838
12/04	2,415.1	17.6	0.7%	633
12/03	1,940.8	(5.8)	—	649
Annual Growth	**26.0%**	**—**	**—**	**13.6%**

2005 Year-End Financials

Equity as % of assets: 12.2%
Return on assets: 0.8%
Return on equity: 5.5%
Long-term debt ($ mil.): 38.9
No. of shares (mil.): 30.1
Market value ($ mil.): 489.8
Dividends
 Yield: 1.5%
 Payout: 33.8%
Sales ($ mil.): 158.6
R&D as % of sales: —
Advertising as % of sales: 0.9%

Stock History

NASDAQ (GM): KNBT

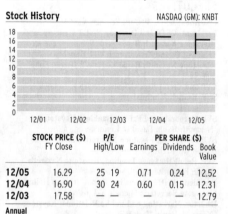

	STOCK PRICE ($) FY Close	P/E High/Low	PER SHARE ($) Earnings	Dividends	Book Value
12/05	16.29	25 19	0.71	0.24	12.52
12/04	16.90	30 24	0.60	0.15	12.31
12/03	17.58	— —	—	—	12.79
Annual Growth	**(3.7%)**	**— —**	**18.3%**	**60.0%**	**(1.0%)**

Knight Transportation

Knight Transportation drivers don't drive long hours into the night. The truckload carrier instead focuses on short- to medium-haul trips, averaging about 580 miles. From more than two dozen regional operations centers, located primarily in the southern, midwestern, and western US, Knight Transportation carries consumer goods, food and beverages, paper products, and other commodities. Its fleet consists of about 3,300 tractors and 7,900 trailers, including some 400 refrigerated trailers. The company's services include dedicated contract carriage, in which drivers and equipment are assigned to a customer long-term, and freight brokerage. Four members of the Knight family collectively own 34% of the company.

The company concentrates its sales and marketing efforts within a 750-mile radius of each of its operating centers. Knight Transportation believes its regional structure helps the company control costs. The regional system also serves as an aid in recruiting drivers, because it gives them more time at home.

In 2004 the company founded subsidiary Knight Refrigerated to handle temperature-controlled cargo; the unit was expanded in 2005 when Knight Transportation bought Idaho-based refrigerated carrier Edwards Bros.

Knight Transportation began offering freight brokerage services in 2005.

Knight Transportation has grown by opening new regional operating centers, and the company has signaled that it intends to pursue further expansion. Along these lines, it acquired Roads West Transportation, a refrigerated truckload carrier owning 133 tractors and 280 trailers, for about $16 million in late 2006.

EXECUTIVES

Chairman and CEO: Kevin P. Knight, age 49, $811,492 pay
Vice Chairman: Gary J. Knight, age 54, $269,530 pay
President and Secretary: Timothy M. Kohl, age 58
CFO: David A. Jackson, age 30
Interim Chief Accounting Officer: Wayne Yu
EVP: Keith T. Knight, age 51, $361,269 pay
EVP, Sales: Casey Comen, age 52, $264,469 pay
Auditors: Deloitte & Touche LLP

LOCATIONS

HQ: Knight Transportation, Inc.
5601 W. Buckeye Rd., Phoenix, AZ 85043
Phone: 602-269-2000   **Fax:** 602-269-8409
Web: www.knighttrans.com

Selected Regional Operating Locations

Atlanta
Boise, ID
Carlisle, PA
Charlotte, NC
Chicago
Gulfport, MS
Denver
El Paso, TX
Green Bay, WI
Idaho Falls, ID
Indianapolis
Kansas City, KS
Katy, TX
Lakeland, FL
Las Vegas
Memphis
Minneapolis
Phoenix
Portland, OR
Reno, NV
Salt Lake City
Seattle
Tulare, CA
Tulsa, OK

COMPETITORS

Celadon
C.H. Robinson Worldwide
Covenant Transport
C.R. England
Frozen Food Express
Greatwide Logistics
Heartland Express
J. B. Hunt
Landstar System
Prime
Schneider National
Swift Transportation
U.S. Xpress
Werner Enterprises

HISTORICAL FINANCIALS

Company Type: Public

Income Statement

FYE: December 31

	REVENUE ($ mil.)	NET INCOME ($ mil.)	NET PROFIT MARGIN	EMPLOYEES
12/05	566.8	61.7	10.9%	3,531
12/04	442.3	47.9	10.8%	3,465
12/03	340.1	35.5	10.4%	3,005
12/02	285.8	27.9	9.8%	2,772
12/01	250.8	19.0	7.6%	2,432
Annual Growth	**22.6%**	**34.2%**	**—**	**9.8%**

2005 Year-End Financials

Debt ratio: —
Return on equity: 19.2%
Cash ($ mil.): 21.3
Current ratio: 2.22
Long-term debt ($ mil.): —
No. of shares (mil.): 85.7
Dividends
 Yield: 0.2%
 Payout: 5.6%
Market value ($ mil.): 1,775.9
R&D as % of sales: —
Advertising as % of sales: —

Stock History

NYSE: KNX

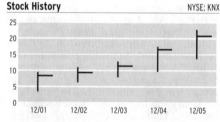

	STOCK PRICE ($) FY Close	P/E High/Low	PER SHARE ($) Earnings	Dividends	Book Value
12/05	20.73	32 19	0.71	0.04	4.12
12/04	16.53	31 18	0.55	0.01	5.14
12/03	11.40	30 20	0.41	—	6.40
12/02	9.33	33 20	0.32	—	5.38
12/01	8.35	38 15	0.24	—	4.55
Annual Growth	**25.5%**	**— —**	**31.1%**	**300.0%**	**(2.5%)**

Komag

Komag puts the disk in disk drives — literally. The company is among the leading independent makers of thin-film disks. The disks, which spin at up to 15,000 rpm, are made by depositing thin layers of metallic film on aluminum platters. The company's products are scanned by magnetic heads to record or retrieve information for desktop computers, network file servers, and other computer systems. Leading disk drive makers Hitachi Global Storage Technologies (HGST), Maxtor, Seagate Technology, and Western Digital account for about 90% of Komag's sales.

Maxtor, which is merging with rival Seagate, is Komag's leading customer, accounting for 32% of sales. Seagate is behind 16% of sales. Western Digital accounts for 24% of sales, while HGST represents 21%.

Mounting debt forced Komag to file for Chapter 11 protection from creditors in 2001. It also moved all of its high-volume production to more cost-effective Malaysian operations that year. The company's San Jose site now focuses exclusively on research and development. Since emerging from bankruptcy protection in 2002, Komag has introduced 80-gigabyte disks and added HGST to its customer base.

Mazama Capital Management owns about 9% of Komag. Barclays Global Investors and Federated Investors each hold around 7% of the company. Citadel LP has an equity stake of nearly 6%.

HISTORY

Tu Chen (former chairman), Scott Chen (no relation), and Stephen Johnson (former president and CEO) founded Komag in 1983. Four years later the company formed Asahi Komag Co., Ltd. (AKCL), its joint venture with Japanese firms Vacuum Metallurgical and Asahi Glass, to build and sell thin-film media products in Japan and to supply them to Komag for resale. Komag went public that year. It joined with Kobe Steel in 1988 to manufacture the aluminum substrates for recording disks, forming joint venture Komag Material Technology. In 1991 Komag acquired Dastek, a maker of the inductive thin-film heads that scan disks.

Besides joint ventures, Komag benefited from alliances designed to share research and development costs. In 1994 AKCL formed Headway Technologies with Hewlett-Packard to develop magnetoresistive heads. The next year Komag signed an agreement with Read-Rite to develop better disk-to-head interfaces.

As demand for its products slowed in 1997, Komag closed two plants in California (costing about 350 jobs) and moved production to Malaysia. That year the company sold its stake in Headway. Amid a slump in the disk drive market, Komag suffered increased research and development expenses (including the opening of a new facility), higher materials costs, reduced manufacturing yields, and inventory write-downs. These combined to cause a loss for the year.

The disk drive slump continued in 1998, and Komag laid off 10% of its US and Malaysian workforce. By the end of 1998 the company had phased out its inductive products. That year magnetoresistive products accounted for 97% of sales. Komag suffered record losses and its first-ever annual drop in sales.

The shakeout in the disk drive market persisted in 1999. That year Komag bought rival (and primary client) Western Digital's disk media business for $73 million. Scrambling to cut costs following the acquisition, Komag again made major workforce reductions, affecting management and engineering staffs. Johnson and Chen retired that year. SVP Thian Hoo Tan was named president and CEO.

At the close of 2000 the company acquired rival disk maker HMT Technology in a deal valued at about $125 million. The following year CTO Michael Russak added president to his title; Tan remained CEO. Komag later in 2001 announced it would reorganize under Chapter 11 bankruptcy protection; it emerged from Chapter 11 the following year.

Komag sold its facilities in Fremont, California, picked up in the HMT acquisition, in 2003. Later that same year, the company signed a five-year supply agreement with Maxtor, a longstanding customer.

In early 2004 Komag acquired a disk substrate plant in Malaysia from Trace Storage Technology Corp., paying about $10 million for the facility.

In 2006 CEO T. H. Tan retired after six years as chief executive; former COO Tim Harris replaced him.

EXECUTIVES

Chairman: Richard A. Kashnow, age 64
CEO and Director: Timothy D. (Tim) Harris, age 51
EVP and CTO: Tsutomu T. Yamashita, age 50
EVP, Customer Sales and Service: Ray L. Martin, age 62, $699,750 pay
EVP, Strategic Business Development: Peter S. Norris, age 54, $424,406 pay
SVP, CFO, and Secretary: Kathleen A. Bayless, age 49, $567,343 pay
SVP, Human Resources: William G. (Bill) Hammack, age 56
VP and COO: Edward Casey, age 51
VP, Corporate Controller, and Chief Accounting Officer: Paul G. Judy, age 43
VP and Managing Director, Malaysian Substrate Operations: ChunHong Tan
VP and Managing Director, Media Operations, Komag USA (Malaysia): Kheng Huat Oung, age 45
Treasurer: Jan Schwartz
Auditors: KPMG LLP

LOCATIONS

HQ: Komag, Incorporated
1710 Automation Pkwy., San Jose, CA 95131
Phone: 408-576-2000   **Fax:** 408-944-9255
Web: www.komag.com

Komag has offices in the US, with manufacturing operations in Malaysia and a sales office in Singapore.

2005 Sales

	$ mil.	% of total
Asia		
Taiwan	272.4	40
Singapore	201.0	29
Malaysia	78.1	11
China	65.3	10
Taiwan	32.9	5
Japan	1.0	—
US	33.7	5
Europe	1.6	—
Total	**686.0**	**100**

COMPETITORS

Fuji Electric
Hitachi Global Storage
IBM
Maxtor
Mitsubishi Corporation
Seagate Technology
Showa Denko

HISTORICAL FINANCIALS

Company Type: Public

Income Statement   FYE: Sunday nearest December 31

	REVENUE ($ mil.)	NET INCOME ($ mil.)	NET PROFIT MARGIN	EMPLOYEES
12/05	686.0	115.6	16.9%	7,121
12/04	458.4	51.4	11.2%	5,308
12/03	438.3	36.0	8.2%	4,743
12/02	286.7	270.5	94.3%	4,353
12/01	282.6	(296.4)	—	3,789
Annual Growth	**24.8%**	**—**		**17.1%**

2005 Year-End Financials

Debt ratio: 19.2%
Return on equity: 32.7%
Cash ($ mil.): 205.0
Current ratio: 1.64
Long-term debt ($ mil.): 80.5
No. of shares (mil.): 30.1
Dividends
  Yield: —
  Payout: —
Market value ($ mil.): 1,043.0
R&D as % of sales: —
Advertising as % of sales: —

Stock History   NASDAQ (GS): KOMG

	STOCK PRICE ($) FY Close	P/E High/Low		PER SHARE ($) Earnings	Dividends	Book Value
12/05	34.66	11	5	3.55	—	13.92
12/04	18.78	14	6	1.71	—	10.25
12/03	14.61	14	2	1.47	—	7.01
12/02	4.33	—	—	(1.84)	—	5.52
Annual Growth	**100.0%**	**—**	**—**	**—**	**—**	**36.1%**

Korn/Ferry International

High-level executives can jump ship via Korn/Ferry International. The world's largest executive recruitment firm, Korn/Ferry has 70 offices in more than 35 countries. The company's some 400 consultants help prominent public and private companies, as well as government and not-for-profit organizations, find qualified job applicants for openings in a variety of executive level positions (including CEOs, CFOs, and other senior-level jobs). Through Futurestep, job seekers can use the Internet and videotaped job interviews to find mid-level management positions. In addition, the company provides management assessment as well as coaching and executive development services. Korn/Ferry was founded in 1969.

Over the years, the company has been expanding beyond its traditional executive recruitment services (by beefing up its management assessment business, among others). In 2006, primarily focusing on its information technology products portfolio, Korn/Ferry launched its K/F One software platform. The product is designed to aggregate Microsoft Outlook, the Internet, and other Korn/Ferry proprietary software products. Keeping this focus on technology, the company acquired Lominger Limited, a provider of leadership development software, for $24 million later in the year.

Korn/Ferry relies heavily on customer loyalty, with more than 80% of work coming from previous clients.

Credit Suisse First Boston owns 12% of the company; Barclays Global Investors, about 10%.

HISTORY

Korn/Ferry was founded in 1969 by Lester Korn and Richard Ferry. A year later the firm debuted its first specialty division, a unit serving the national real estate industry. Its specialization approach was a unique (and successful) slant on the practice of headhunting, and the company soon added more specialties. Korn/Ferry went public in 1972; it also expanded overseas with offices in Brussels and London that year, and in Tokyo a year later. Volatile stock prices became a distraction to the two founders, so in 1974 they took the company private by repurchasing all its stock. Korn/Ferry moved into Latin America in 1977 by acquiring 49% of Hazzard & Associates.

By 1980 steady growth had made Korn/Ferry one of the top headhunting firms in the country. A decade later the firm established a foothold in central Europe by opening an office in Budapest, Hungary; it further strengthened its old-country presence by acquiring European search firm Carre/Orban (at the time it was the largest merger in search firm history). Traditionally a search firm for high-level executives, Korn/Ferry pushed into the middle management arena in 1998 with its Internet-based Futurestep service. Also that year former COO Windle Priem took over the company from Michael Boxberger, who left after 19 months.

Korn/Ferry went public again in 1999. The following year it acquired online college recruitment service JobDirect. In 2001 Priem stepped down as president and CEO and was replaced by Paul Reilly, former CEO of KPMG International. Also that year, in an effort to strengthen its Web offerings, the company cobranded its Futurestep site with online giant Yahoo!. Later in 2001 Korn/Ferry cut 500 jobs, or 20% of its workforce, and reduced salaries. It also reorganized management and closed JobDirect. In 2002 and 2003 the company continued reducing its workforce and streamlining its operations.

EXECUTIVES

Chairman and CEO: Paul C. Reilly, age 52, $2,100,000 pay
EVP, COO, and CFO: Gary D. Burnison, age 44, $1,075,000 pay
EVP; CEO, Futurestep: Robert H. (Bob) McNabb, age 58, $850,000 pay
EVP; President, Global Leadership Development: Gary C. Hourihan, age 56, $850,000 pay
SVP, Global Marketing and Communications and Chief Marketing Officer: Don Spetner
SVP and CIO: Dan Demeter
VP and Director; Regional Managing Director, Japan: Sakie T. Fukushima, age 57
VP, Global Marketing: Michael Distefano
VP, Human Resources: Janet Clardy
President, Asia/Pacific: Charles Tseng
President, Europe: Chris van Someren
President, North America: Robert A. Damon
Senior Client Partner; Co-Head, Legal Specialty Practice: Julie Goldberg
Senior Client Partner; Head, Financial Officer Specialty Practice: Charles B. (Chuck) Eldridge
Senior Client Partner; Global Managing Director, Technology Market: Richard Spitz
Senior Client Partner; Head, Healthcare Services Specialty Practice: Thomas J. Giella
Senior Client Partner; Head, Information Technology Specialty Consulting, Europe: Simon Wiggins
Senior Client Partner; Head, Information Technology Specialty Practice, North America: Mark Polansky
Senior Client Parter, Global Financial Services Market: Richard Stein
Auditors: Ernst & Young

LOCATIONS

HQ: Korn/Ferry International
 1900 Avenue of the Stars, Ste. 2600,
 Los Angeles, CA 90067
Phone: 310-552-1834 **Fax:** 310-553-6452
Web: www.kornferry.com

2006 Sales

	$ mil.	% of total
Executive recruitment		
North America	259.1	47
Europe	120.1	22
Asia/Pacific	57.9	10
South America	15.7	3
Futurestep	70.1	13
Other	28.9	5
Total	**551.8**	**100**

PRODUCTS/OPERATIONS

Selected Services

Executive coaching
Executive recruitment
Management assessment
Middle-management recruitment (Futurestep)

COMPETITORS

A.T. Kearney	J.C. Wilson Associates
Christian & Timbers	Michael Page
Diversified Search	Russell Reynolds
Egon Zehnder	Solomon-Page Group
Heidrick & Struggles	Spencer Stuart

HISTORICAL FINANCIALS

Company Type: Public

Income Statement

FYE: April 30

	REVENUE ($ mil.)	NET INCOME ($ mil.)	NET PROFIT MARGIN	EMPLOYEES
4/06	551.8	59.4	10.8%	1,841
4/05	476.4	38.6	8.1%	1,575
4/04	350.7	5.4	1.5%	1,425
4/03	338.5	(22.9)	—	1,550
4/02	393.9	(98.3)	—	1,495
Annual Growth	**8.8%**	**—**	**—**	**5.3%**

2006 Year-End Financials

Debt ratio: 13.9%
Return on equity: 20.6%
Cash ($ mil.): 278.2
Current ratio: 2.24
Long-term debt ($ mil.): 45.2
No. of shares (mil.): 41.2
Dividends
 Yield: —
 Payout: —
Market value ($ mil.): 865.2
R&D as % of sales: —
Advertising as % of sales: —

Stock History

NYSE: KFY

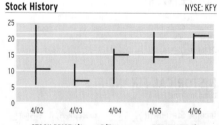

	STOCK PRICE ($) FY Close	P/E High/Low	PER SHARE ($) Earnings	Dividends	Book Value
4/06	21.00	16 11	1.32	—	7.86
4/05	14.40	24 14	0.90	—	6.34
4/04	14.98	128 48	0.13	—	4.74
4/03	6.88	— —	(0.63)	—	4.43
4/02	10.50	— —	(2.62)	—	4.73
Annual Growth	**18.9%**	**— —**	**—**	**—**	**13.5%**

Kreisler Manufacturing

Your Chrysler might have a hemi under the hood, but this Kreisler focuses on bigger engines. Kreisler Manufacturing, through subsidiary Kreisler Industrial, makes precision metal components for commercial and military aircraft engines and industrial gas turbines. Tube assemblies — used to transfer fuel for combustion, hydraulic fluid for thrust reversers, and oil for lubrication — account for most of the company's sales. A second subsidiary, Kreisler Polska, supplies machined components to Kreisler Industrial from a manufacturing plant in Krakow, Poland. Chairman Wallace Kelly controls a 38% stake in Kreisler Manufacturing.

Three industrial customers and the US government account for more than 80% of Kreisler Manufacturing's sales. The company has benefited from increased demand for the engines used to power two US military aircraft: the F/A-22 Raptor and the F-35 Joint Strike Fighter (officially named the Lightning II).

EXECUTIVES

Chairman: Wallace N. Kelly, age 66
Co-President, CEO, and Director; Co-President and CEO, Kreisler Industrial; President, Kreisler Polska: Michael D. Stern, age 40, $193,423 pay
Co-President, CFO, Secretary, Treasurer, and VP, Kreisler Polska: Edward A. Stern, age 45, $193,423 pay
Human Resources Manager: Lisa Sibrel
Auditors: Rothstein, Kass & Company, P.C.

LOCATIONS

HQ: Kreisler Manufacturing Corporation
 180 Van Riper Ave., Elmwood Park, NJ 07407
Phone: 201-791-0700 **Fax:** 201-791-8015
Web: www.kreisler-ind.com

PRODUCTS/OPERATIONS

2006 Sales

	$ mil.	% of total
Military aircraft engine components	9.2	47
Commercial aircraft engine components	8.1	41
Industrial gas turbine components	2.4	12
Total	**19.7**	**100**

COMPETITORS

Argo-Tech
Ducommun
Héroux-Devtek
Howmet Castings
Magellan Aerospace
Pacific Aerospace
Triumph Group

HISTORICAL FINANCIALS

Company Type: Public

Income Statement

FYE: July 30*

	REVENUE ($ mil.)	NET INCOME ($ mil.)	NET PROFIT MARGIN	EMPLOYEES
6/06	19.7	1.2	6.1%	155
6/05	14.4	0.2	1.4%	124
6/04	12.3	(0.7)	—	102
6/03	12.5	(0.7)	—	120
6/02	18.3	1.1	6.0%	133
Annual Growth	**1.9%**	**2.2%**	**—**	**3.9%**

*Fiscal year change

2006 Year-End Financials

Debt ratio: 3.4%
Return on equity: 11.8%
Cash ($ mil.): 3.3
Current ratio: 7.36
Long-term debt ($ mil.): 0.4
No. of shares (mil.): 1.8
Dividends
Yield: —
Payout: —
Market value ($ mil.): 24.5
R&D as % of sales: —
Advertising as % of sales: —

Stock History
NASDAQ (CM): KRSL

	STOCK PRICE ($) FY Close	P/E High/Low		PER SHARE ($) Earnings	Dividends	Book Value
6/06	13.37	26	8	0.63	—	5.86
6/05	5.30	101	46	0.10	—	5.23
6/04	7.20	—	—	(0.37)	—	5.23
6/03	4.80	—	—	(0.36)	—	5.61
6/02	8.84	20	9	0.53	—	5.83
Annual Growth	10.9%	—	—	4.4%	—	0.1%

K-Sea Transportation Partners

If you're transporting refined petroleum products, it's OK to go by K-Sea. K-Sea Tranportation operates a fleet of more than 100 vessels, consisting mainly of tank barges and the tugboats that propel them. Double-hulled vessels provide two-thirds of the company's 3.4-million-barrel carrying capacity. K-Sea serves major oil companies, refiners, and oil traders, primarily along the coast of the northeastern US. About 80% of its business comes from long-term contracts. Major customers include BP, Chevron, Exxon Mobil, and Rio Energy. Investment funds managed by Jefferies Capital Partners, an affiliate of Jefferies & Company, own a controlling stake in K-Sea.

The company has expanded its fleet both by contracting to have new vessels built and by acquisitions, and it hopes to continue to pursue both strategies. It bought Seattle-based Sea Coast Transportation from Marine Resources Group for about $81 million in October 2005. The Sea Coast deal gave K-Sea another 15 tank barges and 15 tugboats, representing about 694,000 barrels of capacity. K-Sea acquired 10 barges and seven tugboats from Bay Gulf Trading for $21 million in December 2004. The new vessels added some 255,000 barrels of capacity to the K-Sea fleet.

While expanding its fleet, K-Sea hopes to maintain a mix of business tilted in favor of long-term contracts, or time charters, rather than voyage-by-voyage charters. Time charters tend to provide a more stable revenue stream.

Nearly all of K-Sea's vessels operate under the Jones Act, which restricts marine shipping between US ports to vessels built in the US and owned and operated by US companies.

EXECUTIVES

Chairman: James J. Dowling, age 60
President, CEO, and Director: Timothy J. Casey, age 45, $239,038 pay
CFO: John J. Nicola, age 52, $180,192 pay
VP, Administration and Secretary: Richard P. Falcinelli, age 45, $180,192 pay
VP, Business Development: Carl Eklof Jr.
VP, Corporate Development: Charles Kauffman, age 55
VP, Operations: Thomas M. Sullivan, age 47, $180,192 pay
VP, Sales: Gregory Haslinsky, age 43, $134,808 pay
Controller: Terrence Gill
Director, Human Resources: Dennis Luba
Auditors: PricewaterhouseCoopers LLP

LOCATIONS

HQ: K-Sea Transportation Partners L.P.
1 Tower Center Blvd., 17th Fl.,
East Brunswick, NJ 10303
Phone: 732-339-6100   **Fax:** 732-339-6140
Web: www.k-sea.com

COMPETITORS

Apex Oil
Chemoil
Colonial Pipeline
Crowley Maritime
Hornbeck Offshore
Overseas Shipholding Group
Plantation Pipe Line
Seabulk
U.S. Shipping

HISTORICAL FINANCIALS
Company Type: Public

Income Statement
FYE: June 30

	REVENUE ($ mil.)	NET INCOME ($ mil.)	NET PROFIT MARGIN	EMPLOYEES
6/06	182.8	5.9	3.2%	690
6/05	121.4	8.1	6.7%	490
6/04	95.8	21.2	22.1%	419
Annual Growth	38.1%	(47.2%)	—	28.3%

2006 Year-End Financials

Debt ratio: 113.2%
Return on equity: 3.9%
Cash ($ mil.): 0.8
Current ratio: 0.98
Long-term debt ($ mil.): 185.6
No. of shares (mil.): 5.8
Dividends
Yield: 7.2%
Payout: 386.7%
Market value ($ mil.): 185.0
R&D as % of sales: —
Advertising as % of sales: —

Stock History
NYSE: KSP

	STOCK PRICE ($) FY Close	P/E High/Low		PER SHARE ($) Earnings	Dividends	Book Value
6/06	32.15	67	52	0.60	2.32	28.49
6/05	34.25	40	27	0.95	2.14	30.41
6/04	25.87	13	11	2.25	0.43	32.58
Annual Growth	11.5%	—	—	(48.4%)	132.3%	(6.5%)

Kyphon

No, the orthopedic surgeon won't make you a balloon animal when she's finished, but at least your spine fracture will be on the mend. Kyphon's KyphX system uses inflation devices to repair fractures involving crushed or collapsed bones. Its KyphX Inflatable Bone Tamp inflates to create space in a fractured bone, which a surgeon then fills with bone filler. The firm's minimally invasive products are sold in the US and some European and Asia/Pacific countries. KyphX is FDA-approved to repair fractures in the spine, hand, leg, arm, and heel. Kyphon in 2007 acquired St. Francis Medical Technologies, which makes a minimally invasive device that treats lumbar spinal stenosis, a degenerative spinal disease.

EXECUTIVES

Chairman: James T. Treace, age 60
President, CEO, and Director: Richard W. Mott, age 47, $829,953 pay
EVP, Chief Science Officer, and Director: Karen D. Talmadge, age 53
VP, CFO, and Treasurer: Maureen L. Lamb, age 45
VP and COO: Arthur T. Taylor, age 49
VP and Chief Compliance Officer: Robert E. Johnson
President, International: Robert A. (Bert) Vandervelde, age 43
VP, US Sales: Bradley W. Paddock, age 32, $348,760 pay
VP, Legal Affairs, General Counsel, and Secretary: David M. Shaw, age 39, $423,885 pay
VP, Research and Development: Alexandre M. (Alex) DiNello
VP, Strategy and Business Development: Frank P. Grillo
VP, Human Resources: Stephen C. (Steve) Hams, age 55
VP, Investor Relations and Corporate Marketing: Julie D. Tracy, age 44
Auditors: PricewaterhouseCoopers LLP

LOCATIONS

HQ: Kyphon Inc.
1221 Crossman Ave., Sunnyvale, CA 94089
Phone: 408-548-6500   **Fax:** 408-548-6501
Web: www.kyphon.com

COMPETITORS

Aventis Pharmaceuticals
Biomet
DePuy
Eli Lilly
Medtronic Sofamor Danek
Merck
Novartis
Procter & Gamble
Stryker
United States Surgical
Wyeth Pharmaceuticals

HISTORICAL FINANCIALS
Company Type: Public

Income Statement
FYE: December 31

	REVENUE ($ mil.)	NET INCOME ($ mil.)	NET PROFIT MARGIN	EMPLOYEES
12/05	306.1	29.8	9.7%	885
12/04	213.4	21.7	10.2%	706
12/03	131.0	27.3	20.8%	441
12/02	76.3	(15.3)	—	305
12/01	36.1	(17.8)	—	229
Annual Growth	70.6%	—	—	40.2%

2005 Year-End Financials

Debt ratio: —
Return on equity: 13.9%
Cash ($ mil.): 194.5
Current ratio: 4.66
Long-term debt ($ mil.): —
No. of shares (mil.): 43.8

Dividends
  Yield: —
  Payout: —
Market value ($ mil.): 1,788.9
R&D as % of sales: 15.2%
Advertising as % of sales: 1.6%

Stock History

NASDAQ (GS): KYPH

	STOCK PRICE ($) FY Close	P/E High/Low		PER SHARE ($) Earnings	Dividends	Book Value
12/05	40.83	71	36	0.66	—	5.71
12/04	25.76	62	41	0.50	—	4.35
12/03	24.83	46	11	0.65	—	3.40
12/02	8.54	—	—	(0.63)	—	2.45
Annual Growth	68.5%			—	—	—

LaBarge

Despite its name, LaBarge is more spacecraft than boat. As a contract manufacturer, LaBarge makes complex electronics and interconnect systems that are able to withstand the physical extremes of combat, space, sea, and inner earth. The company's printed circuit boards, cables, electronic assemblies, and other products are used in demanding applications such as military communication systems, commercial aircraft, satellites, and oil drilling equipment. LaBarge's customers include Northrop Grumman (12% of sales), Owens-Illinois (also 12%), Schlumberger (11%), and Lockheed Martin. The LaBarge family owns about 22% of the company.

About 40% of the company's business comes from customers working on subcontracts with US government contractors.

Investor Sanfurd G. Bluestein owns more than 9% of LaBarge.

HISTORY

LaBarge Pipe and Steel was founded in 1953 by Pierre LaBarge. In 1968 LaBarge merged with Dorsett Electronics, an Oklahoma-based manufacturer of electronics for the aerospace, communications, and medical industries, to form LaBarge, Inc. By 1992 defense contracts accounted for nearly three-fourths of the company's sales. With the end of the Cold War, cuts in military spending and large defense-contractor mergers forced LaBarge to seek new markets for its products.

In 1996 LaBarge acquired SOREP Technology, a specialist in oil exploration and development products, and formed a joint venture (LaBarge Clayco Wireless) with Clayco Construction, a Houston-based manufacturer of telecommunications electronics. In 1998 LaBarge bought 10% of telecommunications company Open Cellular Systems (network systems that monitor remote industrial equipment) and formed NotiCom with

Global Research Systems to make devices that give notice of approaching vehicles such as school buses. The same year LaBarge sued Transmedica for allegedly giving the Laser Lancet technology to a third company.

Poor oilfield equipment sales and a slump in the defense market prompted LaBarge to acquire the rest of Open Cellular Systems and expand its network technologies business in 1999. The following year LaBarge began to trim its operations, selling LaBarge Clayco Wireless (telecommunications services) and ending its involvement in Noticom, a joint venture with Global Research Systems. LaBarge secured a $3.2 million deal in 2002 with Raytheon Electronic Systems to provide fiber optic components for the F-22 Raptor, a new stealth fighter plane.

In 2002 and 2003 LaBarge sold separate parts of its Network Technologies Group (communication systems used to control remote industrial equipment for the railroad industry) in order to concentrate on its contract design and manufacturing units and to reduce debt, exiting the network equipment market.

In 2004 LaBarge expanded its non-military customer base through the acquisition of Pinnacle Electronics, a privately held contract manufacturer, for about $43 million.

EXECUTIVES

President, CEO, and Director: Craig E. LaBarge, age 55, $469,508 pay
VP and COO: Randy L. Buschling, age 46, $316,706 pay
VP, Finance, CFO, and Secretary:
  Donald H. Nonnenkamp, age 54, $270,010 pay
VP, Operations: Vernon R. Anderson, age 59, $222,118 pay
VP, Operations, Pittsburgh: Teresa K. Huber, age 43
VP, Sales and Marketing: John R. (Rick) Parmley, age 52, $222,131 pay
Corporate Controller: Rue L. Pugh
General Manager, Joplin, Missouri: Terry Geisz
General Manager, Houston, Texas: Weems D. Turner
Director, Corporate Communications:
  Colleen P. Clements
Director, Information Systems: George Hayward
Director, Supply Chain Management: Jim Key
Director, Human Resources: Robert Mihalco
Director, Operations: Tim Matthews
Auditors: KPMG LLP

LOCATIONS

HQ: LaBarge, Inc.
  9900-A Clayton Rd., St. Louis, MO 63124
Phone: 314-997-0800   **Fax:** 314-812-9438
Web: www.labarge.com

LaBarge has manufacturing facilities in Arkansas, Missouri, Oklahoma, Pennsylvania, and Texas.

PRODUCTS/OPERATIONS

2006 Sales

	% of total
Defense	40
Natural resource	20
Industrial	18
Government systems	10
Other	12
Total	**100**

Selected Markets and Products

Aerospace and Defense
  Equipment modules for space launch vehicles (Atlas/Centaur rockets)
  High-reliability electronic assemblies and systems (for the US Navy's AEGIS weapon system)
  High-temperature cable assemblies
  Ruggedized portable computer workstations

Natural Resource
  High-power drive controls and enclosures
  High-voltage controllers
Government Systems
  Airport baggage inspection equipment
  Postal sorting equipment

Selected Services

Cable assemblies (jacketing, looming and weaving, winding)
Coating (conformal and parylene)
Electromechanical assemblies
Hot stamp marking
Hot and cold molding
Laser marking
Multi-chip modules
Printed circuit board assembly (surface mount, through-hole, mixed technology)
Test and repair
Thermoplastic injection molding
Welding and brazing
Wirebonding

COMPETITORS

Aeroflex	Pirelli & C.
Amphenol	Plexus
Benchmark Electronics	Sandston
Celestica	Sanmina-SCI
Flextronics	Siegel-Robert
General Cable	Solectron
Jabil	SYNNEX
Merix	Sypris Solutions
Moog	Tyco
Parlex	

HISTORICAL FINANCIALS

Company Type: Public

Income Statement

FYE: Sunday nearest June 30

	REVENUE ($ mil.)	NET INCOME ($ mil.)	NET PROFIT MARGIN	EMPLOYEES
6/06	190.1	9.7	5.1%	1,200
6/05	182.3	10.9	6.0%	1,050
6/04	131.5	6.9	5.2%	980
6/03	102.9	2.3	2.2%	840
6/02	120.1	3.9	3.2%	850
Annual Growth	12.2%	25.6%	—	9.0%

2006 Year-End Financials

Debt ratio: 25.3%
Return on equity: 16.3%
Cash ($ mil.): 0.9
Current ratio: 1.56
Long-term debt ($ mil.): 16.4
No. of shares (mil.): 15.2

Dividends
  Yield: —
  Payout: —
Market value ($ mil.): 201.3
R&D as % of sales: —
Advertising as % of sales: —

Stock History

AMEX: LB

	STOCK PRICE ($) FY Close	P/E High/Low		PER SHARE ($) Earnings	Dividends	Book Value
6/06	13.27	37	18	0.60	—	4.27
6/05	18.00	27	10	0.68	—	3.58
6/04	7.28	21	8	0.44	—	2.85
6/03	3.60	27	15	0.15	—	2.40
6/02	3.95	22	10	0.26	—	2.25
Annual Growth	35.4%	—	—	23.3%	—	17.5%

LaserCard

Green cards are no longer green, but they are high-tech thanks to LaserCard. The company makes wallet-sized, recordable optical data cards that permanently store electronic text, graphics, photos, and security marks such as fingerprints and holograms. The tamper-resistant cards store data and can be read to display information on a computer screen. It also offers optical card drives and card system software. LaserCard's products are used by the US Immigration and Naturalization Service for immigrant identification; other applications include health record storage, security access, and e-commerce transactions. A program with the Italian government accounts for almost 20% of sales.

In 2004 LaserCard acquired two German companies, cards & more and Challenge Card Design Plastikkarten, to widen its international base and to increase manufacturing capacity. The company merged the two subsidiaries in 2006.

EXECUTIVES

Chairman: Donald E. Mattson, age 73
President, CEO, and Director: Richard M. Haddock, age 54, $574,403 pay
COO and Director: Christopher J. Dyball, age 55, $506,739 pay
VP, Finance, Treasurer, and Assistant Secretary: Steven G. Larson, age 56, $394,440 pay
VP, Business Development: Stephen D. Price-Francis, age 59, $260,683 pay
Secretary: Stephen M. Wurzburg
Auditors: Odenberg Ullakko Muranishi & Co., LLP

LOCATIONS

HQ: LaserCard Corporation
1875 N. Shoreline Blvd., Mountain View, CA 94043
Phone: 650-969-4428   **Fax:** 650-969-3140
Web: www.lasercard.com

LaserCard has facilities in Germany and the US.

2006 Sales

	$ mil.	% of total
Europe		
Italy	12.6	31
Germany	5.1	13
Other countries	4.6	12
North America		
US	11.0	28
Canada	2.1	5
Middle East & Africa	3.5	9
Asia	0.4	1
Other regions	0.6	1
Total	**39.9**	**100**

PRODUCTS/OPERATIONS

2006 Sales

	$ mil.	% of total
Optical memory cards	28.2	71
Specialty cards & card printers	10.7	27
Optical card drives	1.0	2
Total	**39.9**	**100**

COMPETITORS

ActivIdentity	Hypercom
ATSI Holdings	Ingenico
Canon	Ingenico Corp.
Dai Nippon Printing	Litronic
Datatrac	Oberthur Card Systems
De La Rue	Olympus
Diebold	SCM Microsystems
Fargo Electronics	Sharp
Gemalto	STMicroelectronics
Giesecke & Devrient	

HISTORICAL FINANCIALS

Company Type: Public

Income Statement

FYE: March 31

	REVENUE ($ mil.)	NET INCOME ($ mil.)	NET PROFIT MARGIN	EMPLOYEES
3/06	39.9	0.8	2.0%	261
3/05	28.5	(8.9)	—	198
3/04	17.0	(12.4)	—	128
3/03	26.3	2.3	8.7%	122
3/02	20.7	5.2	25.1%	117
Annual Growth	**17.8%**	**(37.4%)**	**—**	**22.2%**

2006 Year-End Financials

Debt ratio: —	Dividends
Return on equity: 2.7%	Yield: —
Cash ($ mil.): 23.5	Payout: —
Current ratio: 4.29	Market value ($ mil.): 264.0
Long-term debt ($ mil.): —	R&D as % of sales: 5.9%
No. of shares (mil.): 11.7	Advertising as % of sales: 0.5%

Stock History

NASDAQ (GM): LCRD

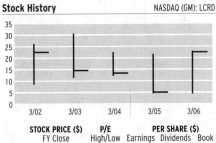

	STOCK PRICE ($) FY Close	P/E High/Low		PER SHARE ($) Earnings	Dividends	Book Value
3/06	22.50	325	65	0.07	—	2.73
3/05	4.98	—	—	(0.78)	—	2.33
3/04	13.32	—	—	(1.15)	—	3.13
3/03	14.50	144	55	0.21	—	3.53
3/02	22.49	52	18	0.50	—	3.16
Annual Growth	**0.0%**	**—**	**—**	**(38.8%)**	**—**	**(3.6%)**

Laureate Education

If higher education is a matter of degrees, Laureate must be hot. Laureate Education, formerly Sylvan Learning Systems, provides adult career education through online and campus-based programs in the Americas and Europe. Laureate's educational institutions offer bachelor's, master's, and doctoral degrees to a combined enrollment of more than 217,000. Students can earn degrees in areas such as business, education, hospitality management, law, and medicine. Its online courses are geared to working adults in the US, while its campuses are centered in Europe and Latin America. Laureate's

Canter unit provides professional development and training programs for teachers.

In 2003 Laureate (then Sylvan) sold its K-12 education units to Educate in order to focus on postsecondary education. The company also dissolved Sylvan Ventures, which invested in firms focused on emerging education and training technologies. Laureate is establishing a collection of private universities around the world.

Strong profits have allowed the company to expand its operations aggressively. In 2004 Laureate added two new college campuses in Mexico, and acquired majority stakes in a Peruvian college and in the French engineering school Ecole Centrale d'Electronique. The company also expanded its Switzerland-based Les Roches hospitality school to the US, licensing Chicago-area school Kendall College to offer the program.

Further acquisitions came in 2005, including a 51% interest in ISCP — Sociedade Educacional S.A., which owns and manages Universidade Anhembi Morumbi.

In 2006 Laureate agreed to purchase a 20% interest in its Chilean partner, Indeco, for an estimated $161 million. The deal included an Ecuadorean subsidiary.

HISTORY

W. Berry Fowler opened the first Sylvan Learning Center in 1979. By 1985 his burgeoning tutoring service had expanded to hundreds of franchises, and Fowler sold it to KinderCare Learning Systems the same year. Financially troubled, KinderCare entered into a joint venture with Douglas Becker and R. Christopher Hoehn-Saric in 1990 through which the two college dropouts acquired 50% of Sylvan. Three years later Becker and Hoehn-Saric (entrepreneurs who had launched several small businesses) bought the other half of Sylvan and took it public.

Sylvan's (now Laureate Education) 1995 acquisition of Drake Prometric (combined with a 1991 deal making Sylvan the exclusive commercial testing partner for Educational Testing Services) helped make testing services Sylvan's key moneymaker. The company expanded its adult education activities in 1996 by buying the Wall Street Institute (English language instruction) and forming a joint venture (Caliber) with MCI Communications (now MCI WorldCom) to provide professional education. Caliber went public in 1998, and Sylvan retained a 9% stake (Caliber went bankrupt and was liquidated in 2001).

Sylvan extended its reach with a string of 1998 acquisitions, including Aspect International Language Schools and Canter Group (training and staff development for educators). Its 1998 acquisition of Schülerhilfe brought 900 international learning centers in Austria, Germany, and Italy under the Sylvan umbrella.

Sylvan acquired 54% of the Universidad Europea de Madrid, a private, for-profit university in Spain, in 1999. Later that year the company abandoned plans to spin off at least a 20% stake in Prometric, opting instead to sell it to Canada's The Thompson Corporation for about $775 million (it completed the sale in 2000).

In 2000 Sylvan announced it would launch an Internet investment company with several partners. It also joined a consortium and created a new company, MindSurf, which provided elementary and high schools with mobile computing infrastructures.

In late 2000 the company added three global universities to its network: Universidad del Valle

de Mexico, Universidad de las Americas (60%, Chile), and Gesthotel SA Hotel Management School, also known as "Les Roches" (Switzerland). Sylvan sold its Aspect International Language Schools the same year. In 2002 the company bought National Technological University and hotel management school Glion Group and also sold MindSurf.

Sylvan sold its Sylvan Learning Centers to Educate in 2003 in order to expand its focus on the postsecondary education market. The company changed its name to Laureate Education in May 2004.

EXECUTIVES

Chairman and CEO: Douglas L. (Doug) Becker, age 41, $1,450,000 pay
President: Raph Appadoo, age 56, $1,216,000 pay
EVP and CFO: Rosemarie Mecca, age 50, $106,452 pay (partial-year salary)
EVP Corporate Operations: Daniel M. Nickel, age 53, $360,000 pay
SVP: Joseph D. Duffey, age 73
SVP, Secretary, and General Counsel: Robert W. (Bob) Zentz, age 52
President, Latin America Operations: William C. (Bill) Dennis Jr., age 62, $1,216,000 pay
President, Laureate Online Education: Paula R. Singer, age 52, $660,750 pay
Director Investor Relations and Corporate Communications: Christopher (Chris) Symanoskie
Auditors: Ernst & Young LLP

LOCATIONS

HQ: Laureate Education, Inc.
1001 Fleet St., Baltimore, MD 21202
Phone: 410-843-6100   **Fax:** 410-843-2123
Web: www.laureate-inc.com

Laureate Education has campuses in Chile, Costa Rica, Ecuador, France, Mexico, Panama, Peru, Spain, and Switzerland.

2005 Sales by Region

	$ mil.	% of total
Mexico	240.1	27
Chile	193.5	22
US	172.3	20
Spain	94.5	11
Other foreign countries	175.0	20
Total	**875.4**	**100**

PRODUCTS/OPERATIONS

2005 Sales

	$ mil.	% of total
Latin America	507.3	58
Europe	183.8	21
Online	184.3	21
Total	**875.4**	**100**

Selected Operations

Online
  Canter & Associates
  National Technological University (NTU)
  Walden University
Campus-based
  Academia de Idiomas y Estudios Profesionales (Chile)
  École Supérieure du Commerce Extérieur (France)
  Glion Hotel School (Switzerland)
  Les Roches (Spain and Switzerland)
  Universidad Andrés Bello (Chile)
  Universidad de las Américas (Chile)
  Universidad del Valle de México
  Universidad Europea de Madrid
  Universidad Interamericana (Costa Rica and Panama)
  Universidad Peruana de Ciencias Aplicadas (Peru)
  Wall Street Institute (English language instruction)

COMPETITORS

Apollo Group	ITT Educational
Berlitz	Mounte LLC
Corinthian Colleges	PLATO Learning
DeVry	Strayer Education

HISTORICAL FINANCIALS

Company Type: Public

Income Statement

FYE: December 31

	REVENUE ($ mil.)	NET INCOME ($ mil.)	NET PROFIT MARGIN	EMPLOYEES
12/05	875.4	75.2	8.6%	22,800
12/04	648.0	63.0	9.7%	17,534
12/03	472.8	46.1	9.8%	13,374
12/02	604.0	(95.9)	—	16,200
12/01	484.8	(17.5)	—	13,300
Annual Growth	**15.9%**	**—**	**—**	**14.4%**

2005 Year-End Financials

Debt ratio: 10.2%
Return on equity: 8.1%
Cash ($ mil.): 109.9
Current ratio: 0.73
Long-term debt ($ mil.): 100.0
No. of shares (mil.): 49.9
Dividends
  Yield: —
  Payout: —
Market value ($ mil.): 2,618.2
R&D as % of sales: —
Advertising as % of sales: 6.5%

Stock History

NASDAQ (GS): LAUR

	STOCK PRICE ($) FY Close	P/E High/Low	PER SHARE ($) Earnings	Dividends	Book Value
12/05	52.51	38 28	1.45	—	19.63
12/04	44.09	35 22	1.29	—	18.00
12/03	28.79	31 11	1.05	—	14.88
12/02	16.40	— —	(2.40)	—	12.05
12/01	22.07	— —	(0.46)	—	14.09
Annual Growth	**24.2%**	**— —**	**—**	**—**	**8.6%**

Layne Christensen

Layne Christensen cuts its way through the upper crust. The company offers a variety of drilling and related services to the water resources, mineral exploration, geotechnical construction, and energy services and production markets. The company provides water well drilling services for environmental consulting and engineering firms, industrial clients, and municipalities; mineral exploration and geological assessment drilling for gold and copper producers; and maintenance services for existing wells and pumps. The group has moved into coalbed methane production and is broadening its water resources services. Layne Christensen has drilling operations worldwide.

In 2005 the company purchased privately held Reynolds, a designer and builder of water and wastewater treatment plants, for $60 million and 2.2 million shares of stock. The deal added

waste treatment and sewer rehabilitation capabilities to Layne Christensen's offerings. The following year, the company reshuffled its divisional organization, placing its Water Resources and Geoconstruction operations under the Reynolds umbrella as a new Water and Wastewater Infrastructure division.

Layne Christensen plans to leverage the Reynolds acquisition to expand its water and wastewater business; a key element in this growth will be the addition of Reynolds' pipeline construction and sewer rehabilitation services. The company has expanded these operations with its acquisition of the Underground Infrastructure Group of American Water. The group provides cured-in-place pipe (CIPP) services for sewer line rehabilitation.

Layne Christensen is also looking for growth in its other divisions, including aggressively expanding its gas drilling operations. Layne Christensen's Water Resources group provides water-related services and products, including hydrological studies, engineering, water well design, well construction, and pump sales, installation, repair, and maintenance. The group also provides design and construction of water treatment facilities and the manufacture and sale of water treatment products. Local governmental entities account for about 66% of the division's sales; industrial businesses bring in another 12%.

The company's Geoconstruction division targets heavy civil construction contractors, governmental agencies, and mining and industrial companies that need to improve soil stability. The services include jet grouting, chemical grouting, vibratory ground improvement, drain hole drilling, and installation of anchors and tiebacks. The division also manufactures high-pressure pumping equipment and geotechnical drilling rigs.

Layne Christensen's Mineral Exploration division provides aboveground and underground drilling services, mainly for mining companies' exploration and development activities. Its services include core drilling, diamond, reverse circulation, dual tube, hammer, and rotary air-blast methods.

The company's Energy unit focuses mainly on coalbed methane development projects in the midwestern US through working interests in developed and undeveloped Cherokee Basin properties in Kansas and Oklahoma.

Director Warren Lichtenstein controls 9% of Layne Christensen through his partnership with Steel Partners II, L.P.

HISTORY

Layne Christensen was formed in 1882 as Layne Inc., a water well drilling equipment maker, by Mahlon Layne, a Kansas homesteader who had experimented with drilling techniques on his own land. During the early 20th century, Layne & Sons drilled water wells for individuals and small cities throughout Kansas. After WWII the company became a regional player. Reflecting its expansion into western states, Layne Inc. changed its name to Layne-Western in the 1960s.

In 1968 the company was acquired by Marley Holdings. Under new management, Layne-Western became an acquisition vehicle. Its most significant purchase in the 1970s was Singer, a major well-drilling and pump-repair business with operations across the western US. In 1991 Layne-Western began providing drilling services for mineral exploration in Mexico.

The next year Marley spun off the company as Layne, Inc. It expanded internationally, opening offices in Mexico and Thailand in 1995 and operating in Argentina, Bolivia, Canada, Chile, and Peru. Also that year Layne acquired Christensen Boyles, a top provider of drilling services for mining concerns. The firm changed its name to Layne Christensen in 1996.

Continuing its acquisition strategy, in 1997 the company acquired Stanley Mining Services, a top Australian and African mining concern, and in 1998 bought two African drilling firms, Drillinti Africa and Afridrill. A year later it acquired Italian pump manufacturer Tecniwell and two Louisiana-based oil and gas service companies, Vibration Technologies and Toledo Oil and Gas Services.

The company created Layne Financial in 2000 to provide funding options for water supply and treatment system upgrade and development. In 2001 Layne Christensen sold manufacturing unit Christensen Products to Swedish industrial equipment maker Atlas Copco. Also that year Layne Water Development and Storage was created to provide risk-management and financial services for water resources and development companies.

In 2002 the group restructured its operations along its primary product lines. To enhance its position in the coalbed methane industry, Layne Christensen acquired oil and gas engineering and geological firm Mohajir Engineering in 2003.

The company sold two of its energy segment subsidiaries in 2004 — Toledo Oil and Gas Services and Layne Christensen Canada Limited. That year Layne Christensen strengthened its water resources presence on the West Coast by acquiring Beylik Drilling and Pump Service, a water drilling company in California, for about $14.7 million.

EXECUTIVES

Chairman: David A. B. Brown, age 62
President, CEO, and Director: Andrew B. Schmitt, age 57, $628,900 pay
EVP, Water and Wastewater Infrastructure Group; Director: Jeffrey J. (Jeff) Reynolds, age 39, $224,397 pay (prior to promotion)
SVP and Division President, Water Resources: Gregory F. (Greg) Aluce, age 50
SVP and Division President, Mineral Exploration: Eric R. Despain, age 57, $267,220 pay
SVP, General Counsel, and Secretary: Steven F. Crooke, age 49, $258,411 pay
VP, Finance, and Treasurer: Jerry W. Fanska, age 57, $290,463 pay
VP, Human Resources: John Wright
Division President, Geoconstruction: Pier L. Iovino, age 60
Division President, Energy: Colin B. Kinley, age 46, $349,904 pay
Manager, Information Technology: Glenn Johnson
Supervisor, Human Resources: Lindsey A. Rupp
Auditors: Deloitte & Touche LLP

LOCATIONS

HQ: Layne Christensen Company
1900 Shawnee Mission Pkwy.,
Mission Woods, KS 66205
Phone: 913-362-0510   **Fax:** 913-362-0133
Web: www.laynechristensen.com

Layne Christensen has about 90 offices, operating in most regions of the US and in Africa, Australia, Italy, and Mexico. It also works through foreign affiliates in Mexico and South America.

2006 Sales

	$ mil.	% of total
US	357.0	77
Africa/Australia	71.6	15
Mexico	22.3	5
Other regions	12.1	3
Total	**463.0**	**100**

PRODUCTS/OPERATIONS

2006 Sales

	$ mil.	% of total
Water Resources	283.3	61
Mineral Exploration	124.2	27
Geoconstruction	37.7	8
Energy	12.5	3
Other	5.3	1
Total	**463.0**	**100**

COMPETITORS

Baker Hughes
Barnwell Industries
GeoTek Engineering & Testing Services
Major Drilling Group
STS Consultants
Water Development Corporation

HISTORICAL FINANCIALS

Company Type: Public

Income Statement

FYE: January 31

	REVENUE ($ mil.)	NET INCOME ($ mil.)	NET PROFIT MARGIN	EMPLOYEES
1/06	463.0	14.7	3.2%	3,551
1/05	343.5	9.8	2.9%	2,577
1/04	272.0	2.7	1.0%	2,331
1/03	269.9	(13.5)	—	2,414
1/02	308.4	1.1	0.4%	2,734
Annual Growth	**10.7%**	**91.2%**	**—**	**6.8%**

2006 Year-End Financials

Debt ratio: 75.1%
Return on equity: 10.6%
Cash ($ mil.): 18.0
Current ratio: 1.63
Long-term debt ($ mil.): 128.9
No. of shares (mil.): 15.2
Dividends
  Yield: —
  Payout: —
Market value ($ mil.): 459.3
R&D as % of sales: —
Advertising as % of sales: —

Stock History

NASDAQ (GS): LAYN

	STOCK PRICE ($) FY Close	P/E High/Low	PER SHARE ($) Earnings	Dividends	Book Value
1/06	30.15	29 14	1.05	—	11.27
1/05	18.50	27 17	0.75	—	8.30
1/04	12.51	63 33	0.21	—	7.47
1/03	8.55	— —	(1.11)	—	7.03
1/02	7.50	99 44	0.09	—	8.19
Annual Growth	**41.6%**	**— —**	**84.8%**	**—**	**8.3%**

Lazare Kaplan International

Sometimes plain old diamonds just aren't good enough. Lazare Kaplan International specializes in premium-priced diamonds and diamond jewelry. The company buys rough diamonds (primarily from De Beers), cuts and polishes the gems for maximum sparkle, and laser-inscribes the branded Lazare Diamonds with the firm's logo and an ID number. Plants in South Africa, Namibia, Puerto Rico, and Russia handle the processing. Lazare sells to wholesalers, manufacturers, and jewelry retailers worldwide. Chairman Maurice Tempelsman (longtime companion of Jackie Onassis), his son (vice chairman and president Leon), and their family own almost 90% of Lazare.

The company's subsidiary, Pegasus Overseas Ltd. (POL), works with General Electric to sell the Bellataire, a natural diamond that is color-enhanced by a high-pressure, high-temperature (HPHT) GE process.

Lazare has sales offices in the Americas, Asia, and Europe and has been expanding its network into China and the Middle East.

EXECUTIVES

Chairman: Maurice Tempelsman, age 77, $412,333 pay
Vice Chairman and President: Leon Tempelsman, age 50, $597,667 pay
VP and CFO: William H. Moryto, age 48, $404,167 pay
VP, Marketing: Marcee M. Feinberg
Auditors: BDO Seidman, LLP

LOCATIONS

HQ: Lazare Kaplan International Inc.
19 W. 44th St., New York, NY 10036
Phone: 212-972-9700   **Fax:** 212-972-8561
Web: www.lazarekaplan.com

2006 Sales

	% of total
Europe	80
North America	13
Asia	7
Total	**100**

COMPETITORS

Beauty Gems Holdings Co., Ltd.
Blue Nile
Charles & Colvard
Fabrikant
LJ International

HISTORICAL FINANCIALS

Company Type: Public

Income Statement

FYE: May 31

	REVENUE ($ mil.)	NET INCOME ($ mil.)	NET PROFIT MARGIN	EMPLOYEES
5/06	528.0	1.5	0.3%	223
5/05	421.4	5.2	1.2%	214
5/04	235.8	2.4	1.0%	199
5/03	203.2	1.1	0.5%	183
5/02	189.6	(1.2)	—	187
Annual Growth	**29.2%**	**—**	**—**	**4.5%**

2006 Year-End Financials

Debt ratio: 67.0%
Return on equity: 1.6%
Cash ($ mil.): 8.2
Current ratio: 2.39
Long-term debt ($ mil.): 64.2
No. of shares (mil.): 8.2

Dividends
Yield: —
Payout: —
Market value ($ mil.): 69.5
R&D as % of sales: —
Advertising as % of sales: 0.5%

Stock History
AMEX: LKI

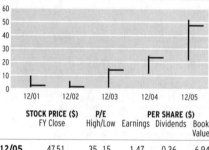

	STOCK PRICE ($) FY Close	P/E High/Low		PER SHARE ($) Earnings	Dividends	Book Value
5/06	8.48	65	41	0.18	—	11.69
5/05	8.62	21	12	0.60	—	11.47
5/04	8.80	33	20	0.28	—	10.87
5/03	5.65	59	34	0.13	—	10.58
5/02	7.75	—	—	(0.16)	—	11.98
Annual Growth	2.3%	—	—	—	—	(0.6%)

LCA-Vision

LCA-Vision thinks its services are a sight better than glasses. The company provides laser vision correction procedures at about 50 Lasik*Plus* free-standing facilities. LCA-Vision's facilities treat nearsightedness, farsightedness, and astigmatism primarily using laser-in-situkeratomileusis (LASIK), which reshapes the cornea with a computer-guided excimer laser. In addition, the company's centers offer photorefractive keratectomy (PRK), another corrective procedure. LCA-Vision operates through centers in major cities across 25 states and Canada.

LCA-Vision's strategy for growth is to offset the high cost of laser vision correction with customer financing plans, as well as to open new laser vision correction centers.

EXECUTIVES

Chairman: E. Anthony (Tony) Woods, age 64
CEO and Director: Steven C. Straus, age 50
COO, General Counsel, and Secretary: Craig P.R. Joffe, age 33
EVP, Finance, and CFO: Alan H. Buckey, age 46, $285,000 pay
VP, Investor Relations: Patricia Forsythe
Director, Human Resources: Karen Leisring
Director, Management Information Systems: Mark Good
Auditors: Ernst & Young LLP

LOCATIONS

HQ: LCA-Vision Inc.
7840 Montgomery Rd., Cincinnati, OH 45236
Phone: 513-792-9292   **Fax:** 513-792-5620
Web: www.lca-vision.com

PRODUCTS/OPERATIONS

Selected Subsidiaries

Lasik Insurance Company Ltd.
LCA-Vision (Canada) Inc. and Subsidiaries
The Baltimore Laser Sight Center, Ltd.

COMPETITORS

Emerging Vision
LaserSight

NovaMed
TLC Vision

HISTORICAL FINANCIALS

Company Type: Public

Income Statement
FYE: December 31

	REVENUE ($ mil.)	NET INCOME ($ mil.)	NET PROFIT MARGIN	EMPLOYEES
12/05	192.4	31.6	16.4%	574
12/04	127.1	32.0	25.2%	364
12/03	81.4	7.3	9.0%	274
12/02	61.8	(3.8)	—	233
12/01	68.1	(23.4)	—	241
Annual Growth	29.6%	—	—	24.2%

2005 Year-End Financials

Debt ratio: 1.0%
Return on equity: 24.7%
Cash ($ mil.): 111.0
Current ratio: 9.12
Long-term debt ($ mil.): 1.4
No. of shares (mil.): 20.8

Dividends
Yield: 0.8%
Payout: 24.5%
Market value ($ mil.): 986.7
R&D as % of sales: —
Advertising as % of sales: —

Stock History
NASDAQ (GS): LCAV

	STOCK PRICE ($) FY Close	P/E High/Low		PER SHARE ($) Earnings	Dividends	Book Value
12/05	47.51	35	15	1.47	0.36	6.94
12/04	23.39	16	8	1.54	0.05	5.53
12/03	14.11	34	3	0.44	—	5.94
12/02	1.52	—	—	(0.23)	—	2.99
12/01	2.35	—	—	(1.33)	—	0.83
Annual Growth	112.0%	—	—	—	620.0%	70.1%

LECG

You ask, "Can I get a witness?" and LECG answers, "Yes!" The firm provides expert testimony and consulting services to a wide range of corporate clients and government agencies on issues such as competition and antitrust, intellectual property, labor and employment, and property insurance claims. In addition, LECG offers in-depth studies and advisory services. Clients typically come from industries such as energy, financial services, health care and pharmaceuticals, and telecommunications and have included Dow Chemical and New England Power. LECG operates primarily in the US; the firm also has offices elsewhere in the Americas and in Europe and the Asia/Pacific region.

Founded in 1988 as The Law and Economics Consulting Group, LECG was acquired by The Metzler Group (now Navigant Consulting) in 1998. In 2000 a management group led a $44 million buyout of the company with the backing of Thoma Cressey Equity Partners. LECG went public in 2003.

Since the IPO, acquisitions have been a key component of the company's growth strategy.

Chairman David Teece owns about 7% of LECG.

EXECUTIVES

Chairman: David J. Teece, age 57
COO and Director: Michael J. Jeffery, age 59
CFO: John C. (Jack) Burke, age 67
VP, General Counsel, and Secretary: Marvin A. Tenenbaum, age 54
Chief Accounting Officer: Gary S. Yellin, age 54
Director Administration: Tina M. Bussone, age 33
Director Client Services (Los Angeles): Bryan Vitner
Director Finance and Assistant Secretary: J. Geoffrey Colton, age 58
Director Marketing: Darcy Arnold Smoll
Director Investor Relations: Erin Glenn
Vice Chairman, LECG Europe: David S. Evans
EVP and Managing Director, Chicago: Craig Elson
Senior Managing Director, Intellectual Property Practice; Office Director, Washington, D.C.: Robert N. Yerman
Auditors: Deloitte & Touche LLP

LOCATIONS

HQ: LECG Corporation
2000 Powell St., Ste. 600, Emeryville, CA 94608
Phone: 510-985-6700   **Fax:** 510-653-9898
Web: www.lecg.com

2005 Sales

	$ mil.	% of total
US	245.2	86
Other countries	41.5	14
Total	**286.7**	**100**

PRODUCTS/OPERATIONS

Selected Practice Areas

Antitrust/competition
Bankruptcy
Claims services
Electronic discovery
Finance and damages
Forensic accounting
Intellectual property
International arbitration
Labor and employment
Mergers and acquisitions
Property insurance claims
Public policy
Strategy and performance improvement
Transfer pricing

COMPETITORS

Accenture
Bain & Company
BearingPoint
Booz Allen
Boston Consulting
Capgemini
Cornerstone Research
CRA International
Deloitte Consulting

Economics Research Associates
FTI Consulting
Huron Consulting
McKinsey & Company
Mercer
Navigant Consulting
PA Consulting
UHY Advisors

HISTORICAL FINANCIALS

Company Type: Public

Income Statement

	REVENUE ($ mil.)	NET INCOME ($ mil.)	NET PROFIT MARGIN	EMPLOYEES
			FYE: December 31	
12/05	286.7	22.4	7.8%	1,151
12/04	216.6	17.1	7.9%	875
12/03	165.6	26.7	16.1%	643
12/02	133.7	(12.1)	—	—
12/01	100.7	(8.4)	—	—
Annual Growth	29.9%	—	—	33.8%

2005 Year-End Financials

Debt ratio: —
Return on equity: 12.8%
Cash ($ mil.): 35.7
Current ratio: 2.36
Long-term debt ($ mil.): —
No. of shares (mil.): 24.2

Dividends
  Yield: —
  Payout: —
Market value ($ mil.): 421.4
R&D as % of sales: —
Advertising as % of sales: —

Stock History

NASDAQ (GS): XPRT

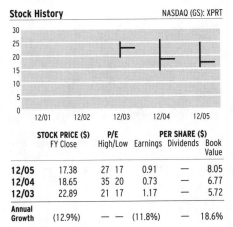

	STOCK PRICE ($) FY Close	P/E High/Low		Earnings	Dividends	Book Value
12/05	17.38	27	17	0.91	—	8.05
12/04	18.65	35	20	0.73	—	6.77
12/03	22.89	21	17	1.17	—	5.72
Annual Growth	(12.9%)	—	—	(11.8%)	—	18.6%

Levitt Corporation

Levitt Corporation has roots in early suburbia. Its operations include Levitt and Sons, a home developer best known for building pioneering Levittown suburbs in New York, New Jersey, and Pennsylvania; Core Communities, a developer of master-planned communities; Bowden Homes, a residential developer in Tennessee and northern Mississippi; and commercial real estate developer Levitt Commercial. The company also has title insurance and mortgage operations and holds a 31% stake in resort and golf community developer Bluegreen Corporation. Levitt was spun off by BankAtlantic Bancorp in early 2004; holding company BFC Financial, which controls BankAtlantic, also controls Levitt.

Active mainly in Florida, Georgia, South Carolina, and Tennessee, the company courts families and active adults over the age of 55 (read: "retiring baby boomers"). Its homes generally sell for between $100,000 and $500,000.

EXECUTIVES

Chairman and CEO: Alan B. Levan, age 61, $800,000 pay
Vice Chairman: John E. (Jack) Abdo, age 63, $1,523,437 pay
President; COO, Levitt and Sons, LLC: Seth M. Wise, age 36
EVP and CFO: George P. Scanlon, age 48
SVP: John Laguardia, age 67
SVP, Investor Relations: Leo Hinkley
Assistant VP, Investor Relations and Corporate Communications: Adrienne Zvi
President, Core Communities: Paul A. (Pete) Hegener, age 65, $2,186,592 pay
President, Levitt and Sons, LLC: Elliott M. Wiener, age 71, $1,670,984 pay
Regional President, South Florida, Levitt and Sons, LLC: Jeffrey Hoyos, age 50, $675,072 pay
Corporate Communications Director: Camille Lepre
Auditors: PricewaterhouseCoopers LLP

LOCATIONS

HQ: Levitt Corporation
2100 W. Cypress Creek Rd.,
Fort Lauderdale, FL 33309
Phone: 954-940-4950   **Fax:** 954-940-4960
Web: www.levittcorporation.com

Levitt Corporation's primary markets are Florida, Georgia, South Carolina, and Tennessee.

PRODUCTS/OPERATIONS

2005 Sales

	$ mil.	% of total
Sales of real estate	558.1	99
Title & mortgage operations	3.8	1
Total	**561.9**	**100**

COMPETITORS

A.G. Spanos
Caribe Homes
D.R. Horton
EastGroup Properties
KB Home
Lennar
Opus Corp.
Oriole Homes
Pulte Homes
St. Joe
Technical Olympic USA
WCI Communities

HISTORICAL FINANCIALS

Company Type: Public

Income Statement

	REVENUE ($ mil.)	NET INCOME ($ mil.)	NET PROFIT MARGIN	EMPLOYEES
			FYE: December 31	
12/05	561.9	54.9	9.8%	668
12/04	554.5	57.4	10.4%	559
12/03	285.5	26.8	9.4%	387
12/02	209.4	19.5	9.3%	—
Annual Growth	39.0%	41.2%	—	31.4%

2005 Year-End Financials

Debt ratio: 116.6%
Return on equity: 17.0%
Cash ($ mil.): 115.4
Current ratio: 5.55
Long-term debt ($ mil.): 408.0
No. of shares (mil.): 18.6

Dividends
  Yield: 0.4%
  Payout: 2.9%
Market value ($ mil.): 423.1
R&D as % of sales: —
Advertising as % of sales: —

Stock History

NYSE: LEV

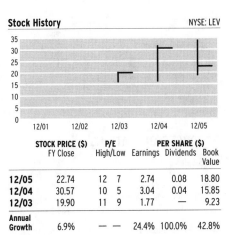

	STOCK PRICE ($) FY Close	P/E High/Low		Earnings	Dividends	Book Value
12/05	22.74	12	7	2.74	0.08	18.80
12/04	30.57	10	5	3.04	0.04	15.85
12/03	19.90	11	9	1.77	—	9.23
Annual Growth	6.9%	—	—	24.4%	100.0%	42.8%

LGL Group, Inc.

LGL, group of two, your business is waiting. The LGL Group (formerly known as Lynch Corporation) is made up of two separate businesses. The company's MtronPTI subsidiary makes frequency control devices, such as crystals and oscillators, used primarily in communications equipment. MtronPTI was formed in the 2004 merger of M-tron Industries and Piezo Technology, Inc. The LGL Group's Lynch Systems unit makes glass-forming equipment. Chairman Marc Gabelli and former vice chairman Mario Gabelli respectively own about 24% and 17% of The LGL Group.

The LGL Group changed its name from Lynch Corporation in mid-2006. The rationale was that there continued to be confusion among investors about the company and its relationship to Lynch Interactive, which was spun off by Lynch in 1999. The company had been known as Lynch Corporation since 1928.

While the holding company got most of its sales from Spinnaker Industries, which made adhesive-backed label stock, the financially troubled unit was a major drain on the company's resources. The LGL Group sold its controlling stake in Spinnaker in 2002 (the main reason for the considerable drop in revenue compared with 2001).

EXECUTIVES

Chairman: Marc J. Gabelli, age 38
President, CEO, and Director: John C. Ferrara, age 54, $350,000 pay
CFO: Jeremiah M. Healy, age 64
Auditors: Ernst & Young LLP

LOCATIONS

HQ: The LGL Group, Inc.
140 Greenwich Ave., 4th Fl., Greenwich, CT 06830
Phone: 203-622-1150   **Fax:** 203-622-1360
Web: www.lynchcorp.com

The LGL Group has facilities in Hong Kong, India, and the US.

2005 Sales

	$ mil.	% of total
Frequency control devices		
US	19.1	41
Other countries	16.0	35
Glass manufacturing equipment		
US	2.0	4
Other countries	9.1	20
Total	**46.2**	**100**

PRODUCTS/OPERATIONS

2005 Sales

	$ mil.	% of total
Frequency control devices	35.1	76
Glass manufacturing equipment	11.1	24
Total	**46.2**	**100**

Selected Subsidiaries

M-tron Industries, Inc. (frequency-control devices)
  M-tron Industries, Ltd.
  Piezo Technology, Inc.
    Piezo Technology India Private Ltd. (99.9%)
Lynch Systems, Inc. (glass-forming equipment)

COMPETITORS

BEI Technologies
CTS
Dover
Pericom Semiconductor
Symmetricom
Valpey-Fisher

HISTORICAL FINANCIALS

Company Type: Public

Income Statement				FYE: December 31
	REVENUE ($ mil.)	NET INCOME ($ mil.)	NET PROFIT MARGIN	EMPLOYEES
12/05	46.2	1.2	2.6%	355
12/04	33.8	(3.3)	—	355
12/03	28.0	0.1	0.4%	70
12/02	26.4	18.0	68.2%	70
12/01	141.1	(22.9)	—	100
Annual Growth	**(24.4%)**	**—**	**—**	**37.3%**

2005 Year-End Financials

Debt ratio: 34.2%
Return on equity: 9.7%
Cash ($ mil.): 8.9
Current ratio: 1.92
Long-term debt ($ mil.): 5.0
No. of shares (mil.): 2.2

Dividends
  Yield: —
  Payout: —
Market value ($ mil.): 17.8
R&D as % of sales: 5.4%
Advertising as % of sales: 0.4%

Stock History

AMEX: LGL

	STOCK PRICE ($) FY Close	P/E High/Low		PER SHARE ($) Earnings	Dividends	Book Value
12/05	8.25	21	10	0.73	—	6.82
12/04	14.50	—	—	(2.18)	—	6.12
12/03	10.45	186	90	0.07	—	7.36
12/02	7.75	2	0	11.99	—	7.30
12/01	18.00	—	—	(15.24)	—	(5.03)
Annual Growth	**(17.7%)**	**—**	**—**	**—**	**—**	**—**

LHC Group

LHC operates care facilities and provides home health care services to rural markets in the southern US. The company's more than 80 home nursing agencies provide post-acute care to Medicare beneficiaries with such services as private duty nursing, physical therapy, and medically-oriented social services while its four hospices provide palliative care for terminal patients. Its four acute-care hospitals are based inside host hospitals and serve patients who no longer need intensive care, but still require complex care in a hospital setting. The company also owns two outpatient rehabilitation clinics and provides rehabilitation services to third parties. Chairman and CEO Keith Myers owns 24% of the company.

Regulatory changes have made it less attractive to operate acute-care hospitals within host hospitals and the company is shifting away from such facility-based services. Instead the company sees it future lies with acquisitions of additional home health care businesses in new geographic markets. In mid-2006 LHC acquired the Kentucky and Florida-based operations of Lifeline Home Health Care.

EXECUTIVES

Chairman, President, and CEO: Keith G. Myers, age 46, $393,483 pay
SVP and CFO: Barry E. Stewart, age 51
SVP, Acquisitions and Market Development: Daryl J. Doise, age 48, $242,157 pay
SVP, Operations: Donald D. Stelly
EVP, COO, Secretary, and Director: John L. Indest, age 54, $341,993 pay
VP, Government Affairs: Harold Taylor
VP, Sales and Marketing: James Pittman III
Director, Clinical Operations, Facilities Based Division: Margaret Blansett
Director, Education and Clinical Program Development: Heidi Landry
Manager, Human Resources: Lolanda Butler
Auditors: Ernst & Young LLP

LOCATIONS

HQ: LHC Group, Inc.
  420 W. Pinhook Rd., Ste. A, Lafayette, LA 70503
Phone: 337-233-1307   **Fax:** 337-235-8037
Web: www.lhcgroup.com

LHC Group has facilities located in Alabama, Arkansas, Florida, Kentucky, Louisiana, Mississippi, Texas, and West Virginia.

PRODUCTS/OPERATIONS

2005 Sales

	$ mil.	% of total
Home-based services	107.4	66
Facility-based services	55.2	34
Total	**162.6**	**100**

COMPETITORS

Almost Family
Health First
Kindred Healthcare
NeighborCare
Personal-Touch Home Care
Texas Home Health

HISTORICAL FINANCIALS

Company Type: Public

Income Statement				FYE: December 31
	REVENUE ($ mil.)	NET INCOME ($ mil.)	NET PROFIT MARGIN	EMPLOYEES
12/05	162.6	10.1	6.2%	3,415
12/04	123.0	9.3	7.6%	—
12/03	72.4	2.8	3.9%	—
12/02	53.8	2.8	5.2%	—
12/01	28.9	0.8	2.8%	—
Annual Growth	**54.0%**	**88.5%**	**—**	**—**

2005 Year-End Financials

Debt ratio: 4.6%
Return on equity: 21.3%
Cash ($ mil.): 17.4
Current ratio: 3.81
Long-term debt ($ mil.): 3.6
No. of shares (mil.): 16.6

Dividends
  Yield: —
  Payout: —
Market value ($ mil.): 288.6
R&D as % of sales: —
Advertising as % of sales: —

Stock History

NASDAQ (GM): LHCG

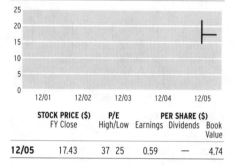

	STOCK PRICE ($) FY Close	P/E High/Low		PER SHARE ($) Earnings	Dividends	Book Value
12/05	17.43	37	25	0.59	—	4.74

LifeCell Corporation

LifeCell puts new life into the tissue graft market. The company makes skin graft materials processed from cadaver skin. Its products, which have been used in more than 800,000 procedures, include AlloDerm, used in reconstructive plastic, dental, and burn surgeries; Cymetra, marketed to dermatologists and plastic surgeons; and Repliform, used in urologic and gynecological procedures. These products are sold in the US and abroad through a direct sales force and distributors such as Boston Scientific (8% of LifeCell's sales). The company is developing other biomedical products for use in cardiovascular and orthopedic, as well as reconstructive, applications.

LifeCell found itself pulling some of its products off the market in late 2005. AlloDerm, Repliform, and GraftJacket were voluntarily recalled when the company's internal quality control processes found some discrepancies in donor information received from Biomedical Tissue Services, one of 40 tissue recovery organizations used by LifeCell.

EXECUTIVES

Chairman, President, and CEO: Paul G. Thomas, age 50, $784,592 pay
SVP, Commercial Operations: Lisa N. Colleran, age 48, $378,479 pay
SVP, Development, Regulatory Affairs, and Quality: Bruce Lamb, age 50, $268,887 pay (partial-year salary)
VP, Finance and Administration and CFO: Steven T. Sobieski, age 49, $336,748 pay
VP, Manufacturing Operations: Young C. McGuinn, age 46, $298,629 pay
Auditors: PricewaterhouseCoopers LLP

LOCATIONS

HQ: LifeCell Corporation
1 Millennium Way, Branchburg, NJ 08876
Phone: 908-947-1100   **Fax:** 908-947-1200
Web: www.lifecell.com

PRODUCTS/OPERATIONS

2005 Sales

	$ mil.	% of total
Products	93.3	99
Research grants	1.1	1
Total	**94.4**	**100**

Selected Products

AlloDerm (skin-graft tissue for the reconstructive plastic, burn and dental markets)
Cymetra (skin-graft tissue for the reconstructive plastic and dermatology markets)
Repliform (skin graft tissue for the urology and gynecology markets)

COMPETITORS

C. R. Bard
Cook Incorporated
CryoLife
Integra LifeSciences
IsoTis
Johnson & Johnson
Mentor Corporation
Organogenesis
Ortec
Osteotech
Regeneration Technologies
Synthes
Tissue Science Labs
Tutogen Medical
W.L. Gore
Wright Medical Group

HISTORICAL FINANCIALS

Company Type: Public

Income Statement

FYE: December 31

	REVENUE ($ mil.)	NET INCOME ($ mil.)	NET PROFIT MARGIN	EMPLOYEES
12/05	94.4	12.0	12.7%	269
12/04	61.1	7.2	11.8%	196
12/03	40.3	18.7	46.4%	173
12/02	34.4	1.4	4.1%	168
12/01	27.8	(2.1)	—	138
Annual Growth	**35.7%**	**—**	**—**	**18.2%**

2005 Year-End Financials

Debt ratio: —
Return on equity: 15.4%
Cash ($ mil.): 48.1
Current ratio: 5.97
Long-term debt ($ mil.): —
No. of shares (mil.): 32.8
Dividends
  Yield: —
  Payout: —
Market value ($ mil.): 625.3
R&D as % of sales: 11.0%
Advertising as % of sales: —

Stock History

NASDAQ (GS): LIFC

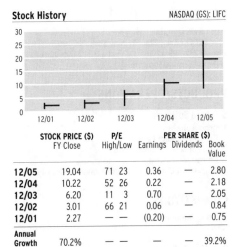

	STOCK PRICE ($) FY Close	P/E High/Low		PER SHARE ($) Earnings	Dividends	Book Value
12/05	19.04	71	23	0.36	—	2.80
12/04	10.22	52	26	0.22	—	2.18
12/03	6.20	11	3	0.70	—	2.05
12/02	3.01	66	21	0.06	—	0.84
12/01	2.27	—	—	(0.20)	—	0.75
Annual Growth	**70.2%**	**—**	**—**	**—**	**—**	**39.2%**

Lifetime Brands

Take-out meals and frozen dinners? Not in this lifetime. Lifetime Brands (formerly Lifetime Hoan) designs and distributes cutlery, cutting boards, bakeware, and kitchen widgets under the Baker's Advantage, Cuisinart, Farberware, Gemco, Hoffritz, Kamenstein, Hoan, and Roshco names, among others. The company also offers items under licensed brands and sells its varied lines in the US and Europe through high-end retailers, supermarkets, and discount stores. The company operates about 120 Farberware and Pfaltzgraff outlet stores in 38 states. Founder Milton Cohen and his family own 25% of the firm; his late partners' descendants, CEO Jeffrey Siegel and VP Craig Phillips, own 22%.

The majority of Lifetime's products are sourced from some 140 suppliers in China. To keep its cookware from going stale, the company developed or redesigned over 700 products in 2005, and did the same to some 1,400 products in 2006.

As the company's largest customer, Wal-Mart accounts for some 20% of annual sales.

In the last couple of years, Lifetime Brands' strategy has entailed growth through acquisition and licensing. In October 2003 the company acquired :USE Tools, a bathware products company, and that December it bought glassware maker Gemco Ware. Lifetime's decision (in 2004) to add Excel Importing to its lineup gives the firm a presence in cookware. In addition the company gained brands DBK-Daniel Boulud Kitchen, Farberware (for dinnerware and glassware), Joseph Abboud, and Sabatier. July 2005 saw Lifetime acquire dinnerware manufacturer The Pfaltzgraff Co.

In 2006 the company purchased Syratech. The deal added a large portfolio of flatware to Lifetime Brand's tabletop business, which the company entered with its acquisition of certain assets from Salton in 2005. Syratech also brought new product categories, such as picture frames and photo albums. Lifetime Brands tried but failed to acquire the WearEver cookware and bakeware unit of Global Home Products at auction in August 2006.

EXECUTIVES

Chairman, President, and CEO: Jeffrey (Jeff) Siegel, age 64, $1,663,677 pay
Vice Chairman and COO: Ronald Shiftan, age 61, $954,167 pay
VP Finance, CFO, and Treasurer: Robert McNally, age 59, $247,000 pay
EVP and President, Sales: Evan Miller, age 41, $677,727 pay
EVP; President, Cutlery and Cutting Boards, Bakeware, and At-Home Entertaining Divisions: Robert (Bob) Reichenbach, age 56, $525,000 pay
SVP Distribution, Secretary, and Director: Craig Phillips, age 56
President, Excel Tabletop Division: Steven Lizak
VP; President, Kitchenware Division: Larry Sklute, age 61, $450,000 pay
SVP and Chief Marketing Officer, Cutlery and Cutting Boards Division: Howard Ammerman
VP and Chief Marketing Officer, Kitchenware Division: Enrico Simpatico
Director of Human Resources: Sally Mogavero
Investor Relations: Harriet Fried
Auditors: Ernst & Young LLP

LOCATIONS

HQ: Lifetime Brands, Inc.
1000 Stewart Ave., Garden City, NY 11530
Phone: 516-683-6000   **Fax:** 516-683-6116
Web: www.lifetimebrands.com

Lifetime Brands operates distribution centers in Winchendon, Massachusetts; Robbinsville, New Jersey; and York, Pennsylvania.

PRODUCTS/OPERATIONS

2005 Sales

	$ mil.	% of total
Wholesale	241.6	78
Direct-to-customer	66.3	22
Total	**307.9**	**100**

Selected Products

Bakeware
Barbecue accessories
Barware
Cutlery
Cutting boards
Home Furnishings
Kitchenware
Pepper grinders
Scissors

COMPETITORS

Anchor Hocking
ARC International
Barbeques Galore
Guy Degrenne
Newell Rubbermaid
Pampered Chef
Tupperware
Wilton Industries
WKI Holding

HISTORICAL FINANCIALS

Company Type: Public

Income Statement

FYE: December 31

	REVENUE ($ mil.)	NET INCOME ($ mil.)	NET PROFIT MARGIN	EMPLOYEES
12/05	307.9	14.1	4.6%	1,686
12/04	189.5	8.5	4.5%	751
12/03	160.4	8.4	5.2%	731
12/02	131.2	2.2	1.7%	657
12/01	143.5	2.9	2.0%	685
Annual Growth	**21.0%**	**48.5%**	**—**	**25.3%**

2005 Year-End Financials

Debt ratio: 3.6%
Return on equity: 12.1%
Cash ($ mil.): 0.8
Current ratio: 2.23
Long-term debt ($ mil.): 5.0
No. of shares (mil.): 12.9

Dividends
  Yield: 0.9%
  Payout: 15.4%
Market value ($ mil.): 267.1
R&D as % of sales: —
Advertising as % of sales: —

Stock History
NASDAQ (GS): LCUT

	STOCK PRICE ($) FY Close	P/E High/Low		PER SHARE ($) Earnings	Dividends	Book Value
12/05	20.67	22	12	1.23	0.19	10.87
12/04	15.90	32	13	0.75	—	8.41
12/03	16.90	22	6	0.78	—	7.94
12/02	4.77	34	20	0.21	—	7.42
12/01	6.00	27	14	0.28	—	7.44
Annual Growth	36.2%	—	—	44.8%	—	9.9%

LivePerson

LivePerson wants to inject some life into your customer service operations. The company provides online, hosted software applications that enable retailers and other companies selling goods online to communicate with customers. LivePerson's Timpani software enables communications through multiple channels, including text-based chat, e-mail, and customer self-service tools. Clients install an icon on their Web sites that, when clicked, opens a dialogue window with customer service representatives. As part of its services, LivePerson also maintains transcripts of customer interactions and offers the option of conducting user exit surveys.

LivePerson provides its services via the application service provider (ASP) model, hosting all of the required software on its servers. In addition to its click-to-chat services, the company also offers tools to manage online sales as well as FAQ, e-mail, and document management services.

The company's clients come from fields such as retail, computer software and hardware, telecommunications, and financial services; customers include Microsoft, Neiman Marcus, and EarthLink.

Founder and CEO Robert LoCascio owns about 13% of LivePerson.

EXECUTIVES

Chairman and CEO: Robert P. LoCascio, age 37
President, CFO, Secretary, and Director: Timothy E. (Tim) Bixby, age 41
EVP, Marketing: Kevin Kohn
SVP, Professional Services and Customer Care: Tony Pante
SVP, Sales: Jim Dicso
Co-CTO: Tal Goldberg
Co-CTO: Eyal Halahmi
General Manager, Tel Aviv Office: Eitan Ron
Auditors: BDO Seidman, LLP

LOCATIONS

HQ: LivePerson, Inc.
  462 7th Ave., 21st Fl., New York, NY 10018
Phone: 212-609-4200   **Fax:** 212-609-4201
Web: www.liveperson.com

PRODUCTS/OPERATIONS

Selected Software

Timpani suite
  Timpani Contact Center
  Timpani Sales and Marketing
  Timpani SB Chat (for small businesses)
  Timpani SB Contact Center (for small businesses)

COMPETITORS

eGain Communications
KANA
Oracle
RightNow Technologies

HISTORICAL FINANCIALS

Company Type: Public

Income Statement
FYE: December 31

	REVENUE ($ mil.)	NET INCOME ($ mil.)	NET PROFIT MARGIN	EMPLOYEES
12/05	22.3	2.5	11.2%	111
12/04	17.4	2.1	12.1%	70
12/03	12.0	(0.8)	—	58
12/02	8.2	(6.8)	—	64
12/01	7.8	(27.3)	—	66
Annual Growth	30.0%	—	—	13.9%

2005 Year-End Financials

Debt ratio: —
Return on equity: 16.3%
Cash ($ mil.): 17.1
Current ratio: 5.16
Long-term debt ($ mil.): —
No. of shares (mil.): 38.0

Dividends
  Yield: —
  Payout: —
Market value ($ mil.): 213.1
R&D as % of sales: —
Advertising as % of sales: 5.5%

Stock History
NASDAQ (CM): LPSN

	STOCK PRICE ($) FY Close	P/E High/Low		PER SHARE ($) Earnings	Dividends	Book Value
12/05	5.61	95	37	0.06	—	0.45
12/04	3.15	125	37	0.05	—	0.36
12/03	5.00	—	—	(0.02)	—	0.25
12/02	0.94	—	—	(0.20)	—	0.23
12/01	0.33	—	—	(0.80)	—	0.42
Annual Growth	103.1%	—	—	—	—	1.9%

LKQ Corporation

Ever wonder what happens to a car once the insurance company declares it "totaled?" Enter LKQ. A nationwide recycler of damaged cars, LKQ buys wrecked cars at auction and distributes the reusable parts to collision repair and mechanical repair shops. LKQ buys popular models such as the Honda Accord, Toyota Camry, and Ford Explorer, from which it salvages reusable parts including engines, front end assemblies, doors, and fenders. The company sells mechanical parts that can't be reused as-is to parts reconditioners; items such as fluids, batteries, and tires are sold to other recyclers. LKQ operates from more than 100 facilities throughout the US.

The parts recycling business accounts for about 75% of LKQ's sales. In addition, the company distributes aftermarket collision repair parts, mainly in the eastern half of the US, and operates "you-pull-it" parts yards.

LKQ expanded in December 2005 by buying A-Reliable Auto Parts, an operator of three parts recycling facilities in the Chicago area, and Fit-Rite Body Parts, an operator of seven replacement parts warehouses in the northeastern US. In February 2006 the company acquired Transwheel, a refurbisher and distributor of aluminum alloy wheels. Later that year LKQ bought an aftermarket business, operating under the name Global Automotive Parts, with warehouses in California, Oregon, and Washington. LKQ also acquired three parts recycling facilities in Michigan around the same time.

Because insurance companies and extended warranty providers influence decisions about which replacement parts are used, LKQ leverages its national distribution system to build relationships with those companies, some of which maintain networks of repair facilities.

Chairman Donald Flynn owns about 7% of LKQ; SVP Leonard Damron owns a 6% stake.

EXECUTIVES

Chairman: Donald F. Flynn, age 66
President, CEO, and Director: Joseph M. Holsten, age 53, $1,125,000 pay
EVP and CFO: Mark T. Spears, age 48, $640,000 pay
SVP, Development and Associate General Counsel: Walter P. Hanley, age 39
VP, Finance and Controller: Frank P. Erlain, age 50
VP, General Counsel, and Secretary: Victor M. Casini, age 43
VP, Midwest Region: H. Bradley Willen, age 46, $330,000 pay
VP, West and Central Regions and Core Operations: Steven H. Jones, age 46
Auditors: Deloitte & Touche LLP

LOCATIONS

HQ: LKQ Corporation
  120 N. LaSalle St., Ste. 3300, Chicago, IL 60602
Phone: 312-621-1950   **Fax:** 312-621-1969
Web: www.lkqcorp.com

COMPETITORS

ArvinMeritor
Dana
Delphi
Federal-Mogul
Keystone Automotive
Siemens VDO Automotive
Valeo

HISTORICAL FINANCIALS

Company Type: Public

Income Statement

FYE: December 31

	REVENUE ($ mil.)	NET INCOME ($ mil.)	NET PROFIT MARGIN	EMPLOYEES
12/05	547.4	30.9	5.6%	3,370
12/04	424.8	20.6	4.8%	2,800
12/03	328.0	14.6	4.5%	1,900
12/02	287.1	(38.9)	—	—
12/01	250.5	4.2	1.7%	—
Annual Growth	21.6%	64.7%	—	33.2%

2005 Year-End Financials

Debt ratio: 13.5%
Return on equity: 11.3%
Cash ($ mil.): 3.6
Current ratio: 3.18
Long-term debt ($ mil.): 46.0
No. of shares (mil.): 51.4

Dividends
Yield: —
Payout: —
Market value ($ mil.): 890.0
R&D as % of sales: —
Advertising as % of sales: —

Stock History

NASDAQ (GS): LKQX

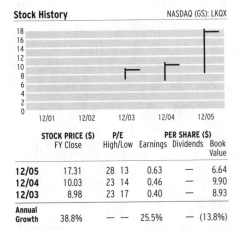

	STOCK PRICE ($) FY Close	P/E High/Low	PER SHARE ($) Earnings	Dividends	Book Value
12/05	17.31	28 13	0.63	—	6.64
12/04	10.03	23 14	0.46	—	9.90
12/03	8.98	23 17	0.40	—	8.93
Annual Growth	38.8%	— —	25.5%	—	(13.8%)

Logility

Logility brings logic and agility to the task of managing global supply chains. The company's Voyager software helps large corporations to manage relationships with raw materials suppliers, distributors, partners, and customers. Compatible with various enterprise resource planning software, including offerings from IBM and SSA Global Technologies, Logility's products address specific supply chain needs, such as boosting inventory in response to promotions, or collaborating online with partners and suppliers. Customers include Haverty's Furniture, Mercury Marine, and Pfizer. The company sells its products both directly and through American Software, which owns an 88% stake in Logility.

Logility is trying to expand its international business. To that end, the company acquired Demand Management (also known as Demand Solutions) in September 2004 for $9.5 million in cash. Demand Management's value-added reseller network extends to more than 70 countries around the world.

HISTORY

Logility was originally the Supply Chain Planning division of American Software. James Edenfield and Thomas Newberry started American Computer Systems in 1970 after leaving top jobs at a software development company. They developed a sales forecasting program for textile maker West Point-Pepperell (now West Point-Stevens), modified it for sale to other textile producers, and then adapted and sold the software to companies outside the textile industry. In 1978 American Computer Systems merged with American Software & Computer (founded 1971) and adopted the name American Software.

In 1997 American Software formed Logility and combined it with another subsidiary, Distribution Sciences, an operation that became Logility's transportation management and planning unit. Logility went public in that year. Later it introduced a software suite designed for the pharmaceutical industry. In 1998 Logility expanded its reach through distribution agreements with vendors in Mexico and Brazil.

Logility, staking a claim online, introduced a suite of Web-based business-to-business software products and application hosting services in 1999.

In 2004 Logility formed a business alliance with Adjoined Consulting, which provides management and technology consulting services.

EXECUTIVES

Chairman: James C. Edenfield, age 71
President, CEO, and Director:
  J. Michael (Mike) Edenfield, age 48, $765,000 pay
CFO: Vincent C. (Vince) Klinges, age 43, $212,000 pay
EVP, Worldwide Sales and Marketing: H. Allan Dow, age 42, $465,686 pay
VP, Customer Service: Donald L. Thomas, age 59, $224,201 pay
Controller and Principal Accounting Officer:
  Herman Moncrief, age 33
Investor Relations: Pat McManus
Media Relations: Michelle Duke
Auditors: KPMG LLP

LOCATIONS

HQ: Logility, Inc.
  470 E. Paces Ferry Rd. NE, Atlanta, GA 30305
Phone: 404-261-9777   **Fax:** 404-264-5206
Web: www.logility.com

Logility has offices in Spain, the UK, and the US.

2006 Sales

	% of total
US	86
Other countries	14
Total	**100**

PRODUCTS/OPERATIONS

2006 Sales

	$ mil.	% of total
Maintenance	17.6	47
License fees	13.9	37
Services & other	5.8	16
Total	**37.3**	**100**

Selected Products

Voyager Collaborate (supply chain planning tool)
Voyager Demand Planning (demand chain forecast and planning)
Voyager Fulfill (warehouse and transportation planning)
Voyager Global Sourcing (request for information and request for proposal management)
Voyager Inventory Planning (time-phased view of inventory)

Voyager Manufacturing Planning (capacity and scheduling planning)
Voyager Production Visibility (collaborative time and action calendars)
Voyager Replenishment Planning (replenishment support)
Voyager Supplier Logistics (packaging compliance and shipping coordination)
Voyager Supply Planning (sourcing process management)
Voyager Transportation Planning and Management (freight rating and routing database)
Voyager Value Chain Designer (distribution optimization)
Voyager WarehousePRO (management of pick, pack and ship activities)

Selected Services

ExpressROI (rapid implementation process)
General Training Services (integration assistance)
Support (maintenance and updates)

COMPETITORS

Adexa	JPMorgan Chase Vastera
Agile Software	Kewill Systems
AspenTech	Lawson Software
CarParts Technologies	Manhattan Associates
Catalyst International	Microsoft
ClearOrbit	NextLinx
Datasweep	Oracle
Descartes Systems	QAD
EDS	RedPrairie
Entomo	SAP
i2 Technologies	SupplyChainge
Industri-Matematik	Transentric
Infor global	Verticalnet
JDA Software	Viewlocity

HISTORICAL FINANCIALS

Company Type: Public

Income Statement

FYE: April 30

	REVENUE ($ mil.)	NET INCOME ($ mil.)	NET PROFIT MARGIN	EMPLOYEES
4/06	37.3	8.0	21.4%	139
4/05	24.9	(0.6)	—	141
4/04	22.8	1.7	7.5%	115
4/03	24.8	2.3	9.3%	132
4/02	29.4	2.1	7.1%	150
Annual Growth	6.1%	39.7%	—	(1.9%)

2006 Year-End Financials

Debt ratio: —
Return on equity: 24.7%
Cash ($ mil.): 26.5
Current ratio: 2.18
Long-term debt ($ mil.): —
No. of shares (mil.): 12.9

Dividends
Yield: —
Payout: —
Market value ($ mil.): 125.0
R&D as % of sales: 12.7%
Advertising as % of sales: —

Stock History

NASDAQ (GM): LGTY

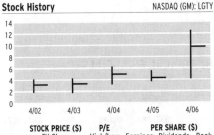

	STOCK PRICE ($) FY Close	P/E High/Low	PER SHARE ($) Earnings	Dividends	Book Value
4/06	9.70	21 7	0.60	—	2.63
4/05	4.30	— —	(0.05)	—	2.39
4/04	4.94	47 25	0.13	—	2.46
4/03	3.30	24 11	0.17	—	2.34
4/02	3.16	25 12	0.16	—	2.18
Annual Growth	32.4%	— —	39.2%	—	4.8%

LoopNet

Feeling out of the loop when it comes to commercial real estate? LoopNet provides information services to the commercial real estate market through its namesake Web site, LoopNet.com, an online marketplace that includes approximately 335,000 property listings worth more than $268 billion. The company offers a free basic membership, as well as a subscription-based premium membership, which accounts for about 80% of sales. LoopNet has more than 1 million registered members and some 57,000 premium members. The company also offers LoopLink, which helps real estate brokers integrate LoopNet listings into their own Web sites, and BizBuySell, an online marketplace for operating businesses for sale.

EXECUTIVES

Chairman, President, and CEO:
Richard J. (Rich) Boyle Jr., age 40, $362,500 pay (prior to promotion)
SVP Finance and Administration and CFO:
Brent Stumme, age 43, $270,000 pay (prior to promotion)
SVP Information Technology and CTO:
Wayne Warthen, age 42, $237,500 pay (prior to promotion)
SVP Business and Product Development and Chief Product Officer: Jason Greenman, age 38, $250,000 pay (prior to promotion)
SVP Marketing and Sales and Chief Marketing Officer:
Thomas Byrne, age 39, $280,000 pay (prior to promotion)
Public Relations: Cary Brazeman
Auditors: Ernst & Young LLP

LOCATIONS

HQ: LoopNet, Inc.
185 Berry St., Ste. 4000, San Francisco, CA 94107
Phone: 415-243-4200   **Fax:** 415-764-1622
Web: www.loopnet.com

PRODUCTS/OPERATIONS

Selected Offerings

BizBuySell (businesses for sale listings)
LoopLink (listing integration service)
LoopLender (financing service)
LoopNet.com (commercial real estate listings)

COMPETITORS

Cityfeet
CoStar Group
First American RES
Realigent
Stewart Transaction Solutions

HISTORICAL FINANCIALS
Company Type: Public

Income Statement
FYE: December 31

	REVENUE ($ mil.)	NET INCOME ($ mil.)	NET PROFIT MARGIN	EMPLOYEES
12/05	31.0	18.9	61.0%	138
12/04	17.0	3.7	21.8%	—
12/03	10.5	1.7	16.2%	—
Annual Growth	71.8%	233.4%	—	—

2005 Year-End Financials

Debt ratio: —	Current ratio: 3.57
Return on equity: —	Long-term debt ($ mil.): —
Cash ($ mil.): 21.9	

Net Income History NASDAQ (GM): LOOP

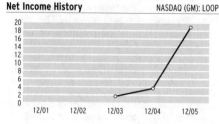

Lufkin Industries

Lufkin Industries is all geared up to help pump oil. Through its Oil Field division the company manufactures and services pumping units, automation equipment, and foundry castings. It also provides computer control equipment and analytical services used to maximize well efficiency. Through its Power Transmission unit, Lufkin manufactures and services gearboxes used in large-scale industrial applications. The company also makes and services highway trailers. Lufkin has expanded its product offerings through the acquisition of Basin Technical Services. It has strengthened its presence in Canada through the acquisition of D&R Oilfield Services.

EXECUTIVES

Chairman, President, and CEO: Douglas V. Smith, age 63, $1,000,000 pay
EVP, COO, and Director: Larry M. Hoes, age 59
VP, CFO, and Treasurer: R. D. Leslie, age 59, $298,858 pay
VP, General Counsel, and Secretary: Paul G. Perez, age 60
VP Power Transmission: John F. Glick, age 53, $314,618 pay
VP Trailer: Scott H. Semlinger, age 52, $250,077 pay
Auditors: Deloitte & Touche LLP

LOCATIONS

HQ: Lufkin Industries, Inc.
601 S. Raguet, Lufkin, TX 75904
Phone: 936-634-2211   **Fax:** 936-637-5272
Web: www.lufkin.com

Lufkin Industries operates manufacturing facilities in Lufkin, Texas, as well as in Argentina, Canada, and France.

2005 Sales

	$ mil.	% of total
US	355.6	72
Latin America	51.4	10
Canada	34.1	7
Europe	28.6	6
Other regions	22.5	5
Total	**492.2**	**100**

PRODUCTS/OPERATIONS

2005 Sales

	$ mil.	% of total
Oil field	307.1	62
Power transmission	106.6	22
Trailer	78.5	16
Total	**492.2**	**100**

COMPETITORS

CE Franklin	Twin Disc
Citation	Utility Trailer
Fontaine Trailer	Wabash National
Great Dane	Weatherford International
INTERMET	Wells Cargo

HISTORICAL FINANCIALS
Company Type: Public

Income Statement
FYE: December 31

	REVENUE ($ mil.)	NET INCOME ($ mil.)	NET PROFIT MARGIN	EMPLOYEES
12/05	492.2	44.5	9.0%	2,700
12/04	356.3	14.4	4.0%	2,300
12/03	262.3	9.7	3.7%	1,900
12/02	228.7	8.5	3.7%	1,800
12/01	278.9	19.5	7.0%	1,900
Annual Growth	15.3%	22.9%	—	9.2%

2005 Year-End Financials

Debt ratio: —	Dividends
Return on equity: 18.9%	Yield: 0.8%
Cash ($ mil.): 25.8	Payout: 12.5%
Current ratio: 3.37	Market value ($ mil.): 754.3
Long-term debt ($ mil.): —	R&D as % of sales: —
No. of shares (mil.): 15.1	Advertising as % of sales: —

Stock History NASDAQ (GS): LUFK

	STOCK PRICE ($) FY Close	P/E High/Low		PER SHARE ($) Earnings	Dividends	Book Value
12/05	49.87	19	6	3.03	0.38	17.26
12/04	19.82	20	13	1.03	0.36	29.89
12/03	14.38	20	13	0.73	0.36	28.56
12/02	11.73	24	17	0.63	0.36	27.41
12/01	13.40	10	5	1.51	0.36	26.76
Annual Growth	38.9%	—	—	19.0%	1.4%	(10.4%)

Macatawa Bank

Macatawa Bank Corporation is the holding company for Macatawa Bank. Since its 1997 founding, the company has grown into a network of more than 20 branches serving western Michigan's Allegan, Kent, and Ottawa counties. The bank offers a range of services, including checking and savings accounts, NOW accounts, certificates of deposit, safe deposit boxes, and debit cards. It also provides trust, financial planning, and brokerage services. With deposit funds, the bank primarily originates commercial mortgages and business loans, each accounting for approximately 50% and almost 25% of its loan book, respectively. The bank also writes residential real estate and consumer loans and invests in US government securities.

EXECUTIVES

Chairman and CEO; Chairman, Macatawa Bank:
Benjamin A. (Ben) Smith III, age 62, $200,000 pay
President, Secretary, Treasurer, and Director; President and CEO, Macatawa Bank: Philip J. Koning, age 51, $396,947 pay
EVP, Macatawa Bank: Ronald L. (Ron) Haan, age 52, $133,846 pay (partial-year salary)
SVP and CFO, Macatawa Bank Corporation and Macatawa Bank: Jon W. Swets, age 40, $221,322 pay
SVP and Senior Retail Banking Officer, Macatawa Bank: Jill A. Walcott
SVP, Commercial Loans, Macatawa Bank:
Richard D. Wieringa
SVP, Loan Administration, Macatawa Bank:
Ray D. Tooker, age 62, $187,565 pay
SVP and Director, Trust Services, Macatawa Bank:
Thomas R. Hilliker
SVP and Director, Retail Lending, Macatawa Bank:
Vicki K. DenBoer
VP, Marketing, Macatawa Bank: Christine M. Bart
VP and Director, Human Resources: Amy Ziel
President, Macatawa Investment Services, Inc.:
Melissa Secor

LOCATIONS

HQ: Macatawa Bank Corporation
10753 Macatawa Dr., Holland, MI 49424
Phone: 616-820-1444   **Fax:** 616-494-7644
Web: www.macatawabank.com

PRODUCTS/OPERATIONS

2005 Sales

	$ mil.	% of total
Interest		
Loans, including fees	98.0	83
Securities	6.5	5
Other	0.9	1
Noninterest		
Service charges & fees	4.3	4
Trust fees	2.9	2
Gain on sales of loans	2.3	2
Other	3.5	3
Total	**118.4**	**100**

Selected Subsidiaries

Macatawa Bank
  Macatawa Bank Mortgage Company
Macatawa Investment Services, Inc.

COMPETITORS

Capitol Bancorp
Comerica
Fifth Third
Flagstar Bancorp
Huntington Bancshares
National City

HISTORICAL FINANCIALS

Company Type: Public

Income Statement

FYE: December 31

	ASSETS ($ mil.)	NET INCOME ($ mil.)	INCOME AS % OF ASSETS	EMPLOYEES
12/05	1,870.0	20.9	1.1%	448
12/04	1,672.6	12.8	0.8%	407
12/03	1,401.1	11.8	0.8%	382
12/02	1,176.6	9.5	0.8%	317
12/01	670.2	5.1	0.8%	229
Annual Growth	**29.2%**	**42.3%**	**—**	**18.3%**

2005 Year-End Financials

Equity as % of assets: 7.6%	**Dividends**
Return on assets: 1.2%	Yield: 1.7%
Return on equity: 15.4%	Payout: 30.7%
Long-term debt ($ mil.): 41.2	Sales ($ mil.): 118.4
No. of shares (mil.): 10.2	R&D as % of sales: —
Market value ($ mil.): 236.2	Advertising as % of sales: —

Stock History

NASDAQ (GS): MCBC

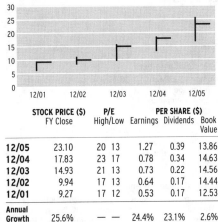

	STOCK PRICE ($) FY Close	P/E High/Low	Earnings	Dividends	Book Value
12/05	23.10	20 13	1.27	0.39	13.86
12/04	17.83	23 17	0.78	0.34	14.63
12/03	14.93	21 13	0.73	0.22	14.56
12/02	9.94	17 13	0.64	0.17	14.44
12/01	9.27	17 12	0.53	0.17	12.53
Annual Growth	**25.6%**	**— —**	**24.4%**	**23.1%**	**2.6%**

Mac-Gray

No change for laundry or copies? Mac-Gray operates debit card- and coin-operated washers and dryers in about 45,000 apartment buildings, dorms, and other housing complexes in 40 states and the District of Columbia. It also supplies card- and coin-operated copiers for college and public libraries, as well as MicroFridge units (combo refrigerator, freezer, and microwave) for academic, military, and other housing facilities. In addition, Mac-Gray distributes equipment to laundromats, hotels, hospitals, and restaurants. Laundry facilities account for most of the company's earnings. Chairman and CEO Stewart MacDonald and his family own nearly 60% of the firm, which was founded in 1927.

In early 2005 Mac-Gray Corporation expanded its portfolio by purchasing the laundry facilities management business of Web Service Company in more than a dozen Western and Southern states. Web Service Company retained ownership of its operations in California, Hawaii, and Nevada. The transaction, at a cost of about $110 million, included contracts, related equipment, service fleets, and other assets. Mac-Gray anticipates a 35% increase in revenue based on the acquisition.

It repeated the act in early 2006, buying the assets of Massachusetts-based multi-housing laundry provider Lundermac for about $11.5 million. Later that year, Mac-Gray turned down a merger offer from its #1 rival, Coinmach.

EXECUTIVES

Chairman and CEO: Stewart Gray MacDonald Jr., age 56, $680,755 pay
EVP and COO: Neil F. MacLellan III, age 46, $397,878 pay
EVP, CFO, Secretary, and Treasurer: Michael J. Shea, age 56, $397,878 pay
EVP, Operations: Todd Burger

VP, Academic Division: Michael Calderaro
VP, Field Technology: Robert J. (Bob) Tuttle
VP, Human Resources: Gail Wagner
VP, National Accounts: Phillip E. Bogucki
VP, Sales: Kevin Fahey
President, MicroFridge: Philip Emma
Auditors: PricewaterhouseCoopers LLP

LOCATIONS

HQ: Mac-Gray Corporation
22 Water St., Cambridge, MA 02141
Phone: 617-492-4040   **Fax:** 617-492-5386
Web: www.mac-gray.com

PRODUCTS/OPERATIONS

2005 Sales

	$ mil.	% of total
Laundry facilities management	211.9	81
MicroFridge sales & rental	30.5	12
Laundry equipment sales	15.3	6
Reprographics facilities management	2.9	1
Total	**260.6**	**100**

COMPETITORS

Absocold	Kinko's
Clean Rite Centers	Kwik Wash
Coinmach	SANYO
DRYCLEAN USA	SpinCycle
GE	Wal-Mart

HISTORICAL FINANCIALS

Company Type: Public

Income Statement

FYE: December 31

	REVENUE ($ mil.)	NET INCOME ($ mil.)	NET PROFIT MARGIN	EMPLOYEES
12/05	260.6	12.1	4.6%	743
12/04	182.7	5.3	2.9%	720
12/03	149.7	4.1	2.7%	539
12/02	150.4	2.9	1.9%	475
12/01	152.1	2.5	1.6%	515
Annual Growth	**14.4%**	**48.3%**	**—**	**9.6%**

2005 Year-End Financials

Debt ratio: 186.8%	**Dividends**
Return on equity: 14.7%	Yield: —
Cash ($ mil.): 11.1	Payout: —
Current ratio: 0.94	Market value ($ mil.): 150.6
Long-term debt ($ mil.): 165.5	R&D as % of sales: —
No. of shares (mil.): 12.9	Advertising as % of sales: 0.5%

Stock History

NYSE: TUC

	STOCK PRICE ($) FY Close	P/E High/Low	Earnings	Dividends	Book Value
12/05	11.65	15 8	0.91	—	6.86
12/04	8.09	20 13	0.40	—	5.94
12/03	5.40	17 9	0.32	—	5.46
12/02	3.29	18 11	0.23	—	5.03
12/01	2.81	21 14	0.20	—	4.79
Annual Growth	**42.7%**	**— —**	**46.1%**	**—**	**9.4%**

Macrovision

Even eggheads in Coke-bottle glasses get scrambled by Macrovision. The company develops copyright protection and video scrambling technologies for commercial videocassette duplicators, music labels, software companies, set-top decoder manufacturers, and the major motion picture studios. Macrovision's Entertainment Technologies Group offers digital content management products that prevent unauthorized copying and viewing of video, music, and other content, as well as unauthorized broadcasts on pay-per-view cable and satellite networks. The company's Software Technologies Group provides electronic licensing technology to software and hardware vendors.

Macrovision counts some high-profile media companies among its customers, including Universal Studios Home Entertainment, HBO, and Paramount Pictures in the video market; pay-per-view and video-on-demand system operators British Sky Broadcasting and DIRECTV; and music labels Universal Music Group and Sony BMG. Macrovision has expanded beyond its traditional focus on video into recorded music protection services, responding to the problems of Internet piracy that record labels have been battling.

Macrovision in 2004 acquired InstallShield Software, a developer of applications for installing and monitoring software on computers and networks.

In 2005 Macrovision acquired Zero G Software, a provider of multi-platform software deployment and delivery tools. Also that year the company acquired privately held Trymedia Systems, a provider of secure digital distribution software for the video gaming industry, for $34 million. The next year Macrovision bought eMeta for $35 million in cash.

In early 2007 the company purchased Mediabolic, a provider of software used to connect consumer electronics.

PRIMECAP Management Company owns about 12% of the company.

EXECUTIVES

Chairman: John O. Ryan, age 60
President, CEO, and Director: Alfred J. (Fred) Amoroso, age 56, $492,948 pay
CIO: John Adams
EVP and CFO: James W. Budge, age 39
EVP Corporate Development: Jim Wicket, age 55, $321,563 pay
EVP and Chief Marketing Officer: Greg Jorgensen, age 49
EVP Global Sales and Services: Mark C. Bishof, age 46
EVP Emerging Business and General Counsel: Loren E. Hillberg, age 47, $239,166 pay
EVP Products: Buff Jones, age 49
SVP Global Human Resources: Laura Owen
SVP and Managing Director, Japan and Asia K.K.: David Rowley, age 43, $254,833 pay
Public Relations: Julie Davey
Auditors: KPMG LLP

LOCATIONS

HQ: Macrovision Corporation
2830 De La Cruz Blvd., Santa Clara, CA 95050
Phone: 408-562-8400   **Fax:** 408-567-1800
Web: www.macrovision.com

PRODUCTS/OPERATIONS

2005 Sales

	$ mil.	% of total
Entertainment Technologies	102.7	59
Software Technologies	100.5	49
Total	**203.2**	**100**

2005 Sales

	$ mil.	% of total
Licenses	166.3	82
Services	36.9	18
Total	**203.2**	**100**

Selected Customers

Computer software, CD-ROM, and games publishers
  Activision
  Apple Computer
  Eidos
  Electronic Arts
  Hasbro
  Havas
  Infogrames Entertainment
  Mattel
  Microsoft
  Ubisoft Entertainment
Motion pictures studios and home video suppliers
  Buena Vista Home Entertainment (Walt Disney)
  Columbia TriStar Home Entertainment (Sony Pictures Entertainment)
  Home Box Office (Time Warner)
  Lionsgate
  New Line Cinema (Time Warner)
  Paramount Pictures (CBS Corporation)
  Twentieth Century Fox (Fox Entertainment Group)
Pay-per-view, satellite, and digital set-top box operators and manufacturers
  Acer
  Comcast
  British Sky Broadcasting
  Daewoo
  DIRECTV
  EchoStar Communications
  Panasonic
  Philips Electronics
  Pioneer Electronics
  Scientific-Atlanta
  Singapore Telecommunications
  Sony
  TiVo

COMPETITORS

Aladdin Knowledge Systems
ContentGuard
Hitachi
IBM
InterTrust Technologies
Intraware
Microsoft
NEC
Pioneer
RealNetworks
Sony

HISTORICAL FINANCIALS

Company Type: Public

Income Statement

FYE: December 31

	REVENUE ($ mil.)	NET INCOME ($ mil.)	NET PROFIT MARGIN	EMPLOYEES
12/05	203.2	22.1	10.9%	692
12/04	182.1	36.7	20.2%	606
12/03	128.4	26.9	21.0%	349
12/02	102.3	12.1	11.8%	283
12/01	98.8	19.2	19.4%	245
Annual Growth	**19.8%**	**3.6%**		**29.6%**

2005 Year-End Financials

Debt ratio: —
Return on equity: 5.3%
Cash ($ mil.): 246.7
Current ratio: 4.35
Long-term debt ($ mil.): —
No. of shares (mil.): 51.4
Dividends
  Yield: —
  Payout: —
Market value ($ mil.): 859.4
R&D as % of sales: 16.9%
Advertising as % of sales: —

Stock History

NASDAQ (GS): MVSN

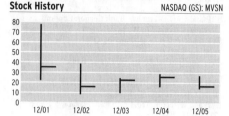

	STOCK PRICE ($) FY Close	P/E High/Low	PER SHARE ($) Earnings	Dividends	Book Value
12/05	16.73	62 35	0.43	—	8.33
12/04	25.72	39 23	0.73	—	7.94
12/03	22.59	44 19	0.54	—	6.95
12/02	16.04	158 37	0.24	—	6.13
12/01	35.22	208 61	0.37	—	6.26
Annual Growth	**(17.0%)**	**— —**	**3.8%**	**—**	**7.4%**

Mannatech

Who knew that manna was primarily carbohydrates? Well, at least if it comes from Mannatech. The multi-level marketing nutritional supplement company (one of the largest after Alticor's Amway and Herbalife) develops and sells vitamins, weight management products, and personal care items through a network of more than 500,000 independent salespeople. Many of its products, all made by third-party manufacturers, include Ambrotose, a proprietary carbohydrate made from natural sources that is claimed to promote cell-to-cell communication. The company's skin care products include the emu-oil lotion AmbroDerm.

While the US is still its largest market, Mannatech is expanding internationally and sells in Australia, Canada, Denmark, Japan, New Zealand, South Korea, Taiwan, and the UK.

Mannatech is facing the scrutiny of investigators after some of its more zealous sales associates made unsubstantiated claims that its products can cure cancer, attention-deficit disorder, and other ailments.

Chairman and CEO Samuel Caster owns 20% of Mannatech. Director J. Stanley Fredrick owns 12%, and director and co-founder Marlin Robbins owns 7.5%.

EXECUTIVES

Chairman and CEO: Samuel L. Caster, age 55, $765,000 pay
President, COO, and Director: Terry L. Persinger, age 71, $455,175 pay
SVP, Accounting and CFO: Stephen D. Fenstermacher, age 53, $324,104 pay
SVP and CIO: Cynthia L. (Cindy) Tysinger, age 48, $269,500 pay
SVP, Research and Development Administration: Eileen Vennum

SVP, General Counsel, and Secretary: B. Keith Clark, age 43
VP, Global Human Resources: Robert (Bob) Panico
VP, Global Marketing: Linda L. Padilla
VP, Research and Development and Chief Science Officer: Robert A. Sinnott, age 41
VP, Treasury and Investor Relations: Gary M. Spinell
President, International Operations: John W. Price, age 62
Senior Medical Director: Stephen Boyd, age 65
Media Relations: Kevin Young
Auditors: Grant Thornton LLP

LOCATIONS

HQ: Mannatech, Incorporated
600 S. Royal Ln., Ste. 200, Coppell, TX 75019
Phone: 972-471-7400   Fax: 972-471-8135
Web: www.mannatech.com

2005 Sales

	$ mil.	% of total
US	259.4	67
Australia	35.7	9
Japan	35.4	9
Canada	28.0	7
New Zealand	14.6	4
UK	8.9	2
South Korea	4.6	1
Taiwan	2.3	1
Denmark	0.5	—
Total	**389.4**	**100**

PRODUCTS/OPERATIONS

2005 Sales

	$ mil.	% of total
Product sales	284.8	73
Pack sales	87.8	23
Other, including freight	16.8	4
Total	**389.4**	**100**

Selected Products

AmbroDerm (skin care)
Ambrotose AO (vitamin supplements)
CardioBalance (dietary supplements)
Catalyst (vitamin supplement)
Emprizone (skin care)
Firm (skin care)
GI-Pro (digestive supplements)
Glycentials (vitamin supplements)
Glyco-Bears (children's vitamin supplements)
GlycoLEAN (weight management)
ImmunoSTART (dietary supplements)
MannaBears (children's nutrional supplements)
Manna-CLEANSE (dietary supplements)
Mannatonin (dietary supplements)
PhytAloe (vitamin supplements)
Phyto-Bears (children's nutritional supplements)
PhytoMatrix (vitamin supplements)
Plus (nutritional supplements)
Sport (sports nutrition)

COMPETITORS

Alticor
AMS Health Sciences
Bactolac Pharmaceutical
Forever Living
GNC
Herbalife Ltd.
Market America
Mary Kay
Nature's Sunshine
Nu Skin
Reliv'
The Right Solution
Schiff Nutrition International
Shaklee
Solgar Vitamin and Herb
Sunrider
Unicity
USANA Health Sciences

HISTORICAL FINANCIALS

Company Type: Public

Income Statement

FYE: December 31

	REVENUE ($ mil.)	NET INCOME ($ mil.)	NET PROFIT MARGIN	EMPLOYEES
12/05	389.4	28.6	7.3%	485
12/04	294.5	19.5	6.6%	388
12/03	191.0	8.8	4.6%	324
12/02	140.9	1.9	1.3%	312
12/01	128.7	(3.7)	—	240
Annual Growth	**31.9%**	**—**	**—**	**19.2%**

2005 Year-End Financials

Debt ratio: —
Return on equity: 45.2%
Cash ($ mil.): 61.0
Current ratio: 1.80
Long-term debt ($ mil.): —
No. of shares (mil.): 26.7
Dividends
Yield: 2.1%
Payout: 28.2%
Market value ($ mil.): 369.3
R&D as % of sales: 1.3%
Advertising as % of sales: 2.2%

Stock History

NASDAQ (GS): MTEX

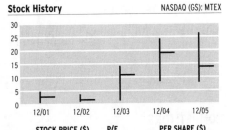

	STOCK PRICE ($) FY Close	P/E High/Low		Earnings	PER SHARE ($) Dividends	Book Value
12/05	13.81	25	8	1.03	0.29	2.63
12/04	19.04	34	12	0.71	0.27	2.08
12/03	10.89	41	4	0.34	—	1.25
12/02	1.62	49	16	0.07	—	0.72
12/01	2.82	—	—	(0.15)	—	0.64
Annual Growth	**48.8%**	**—**	**—**	**—**	**7.4%**	**42.4%**

Marchex

In its quest for a piece of the Internet search market pie, one company marches on. Marchex has joined the ranks of Yahoo!, Google, and other search firms to provide performance-based advertising and search marketing services that help companies advertise online. Marchex operates through its TrafficLeader, Enhance Interactive, and goClick businesses. TrafficLeader's paid search inclusion service delivers advertiser listings to search engines; Enhance Interactive and goClick offer performance-based pay-per-click services that let advertisers pay for keywords used by Web surfers that trigger the placement of listings. Marchex bought Name Development in 2005. Chairman and CEO Russell Horowitz owns 27% of the firm.

Marchex entered the direct navigation market in 2005 with the acquisition of Name Development, which owns some 200,000 Web sites. Direct navigation occurs when a Web user accesses a site without visiting a search engine. For example, when consumers type www.lasvegasvacations.com directly into the address or URL box of a Web browser they will arrive at the site and find relevant product listings and information. When the user clicks on

a particular listing, Name Development receives a pay-per-click fee.

Other recent acquisitions include Pike Street, an online yellow pages and lead generation provider for local merchants; contextual advertising firm IndustryBrains; and the assets of Open List, a content aggregation and search technology firm. Yahoo! is Marchex's largest distribution partner, accounting for about 11% of the company's 2005 revenue.

EXECUTIVES

Chairman, CEO, and Treasurer: Russell C. Horowitz, age 39, $120,000 pay
President, COO, and Director: John Keister, age 39
CFO: Michael A. Arends, age 35, $135,000 pay
SVP Advertising Services: Scott Greenberg
VP Investor Relations and Strategic Initiatives: Trevor Caldwell
VP Public Relations: Mark S. Peterson
VP Technology Operations: Dennis Lee
CTO: Cameron Ferroni, age 36
Chief Administrative Officer, General Counsel, and Secretary: Ethan A. Caldwell, age 37
Chief Strategy Officer: Peter Christothoulou, age 34
Auditors: KPMG LLP

LOCATIONS

HQ: Marchex, Inc.
413 Pine St., Ste. 500, Seattle, WA 98101
Phone: 206-331-3300   Fax: 206-331-3695
Web: www.marchex.com

PRODUCTS/OPERATIONS

Selected Operations

Enhance Interactive (pay-per-click listings)
goClick (pay-per-click listings)
IndustryBrains (contextual advertising)
Name Development (direct navigation)
Pike Street (online yellow pages and lead generation)
TrafficLeader (paid search inclusion)

COMPETITORS

AOL
Decide Interactive
DoubleClick
Google
IAC Search & Media
LookSmart
Microsoft
MIVA
ValueClick
Yahoo!

HISTORICAL FINANCIALS

Company Type: Public

Income Statement

FYE: December 31

	REVENUE ($ mil.)	NET INCOME ($ mil.)	NET PROFIT MARGIN	EMPLOYEES
12/05	95.0	3.9	4.1%	70
12/04	43.8	(0.7)	—	211
12/03	23.0	(1.8)	—	—
12/02	10.1	(0.1)	—	166
12/01	2.9	(1.3)	—	—
Annual Growth	**139.2%**	**—**	**—**	**(25.0%)**

2005 Year-End Financials

Debt ratio: —
Return on equity: 2.4%
Cash ($ mil.): 63.1
Current ratio: 6.28
Long-term debt ($ mil.): —
No. of shares (mil.): 25.5
Dividends
Yield: —
Payout: —
Market value ($ mil.): 573.1
R&D as % of sales: 4.7%
Advertising as % of sales: 10.5%

Stock History

NASDAQ (GM): MCHX

	STOCK PRICE ($) FY Close	P/E High/Low	PER SHARE ($) Earnings	Dividends	Book Value
12/05	22.49	660 329	0.04	—	12.58
12/04	21.00	— —	(0.05)	—	4.12
Annual Growth	7.1%	— —	—	—	205.3%

MarkWest Energy Partners

MarkWest Energy Partners marks its territory as the energy markets of America. A spinoff from oil and gas company MarkWest Hydrocarbon, MarkWest Energy Partners was created in 2002 to hold the natural gas gathering and processing assets of its parent. MarkWest Energy Partners has natural gas and natural gas liquids pipelines, storage terminals, and gathering and processing pipelines and fractionation plants in the Appalachian Basin, Michigan, and the Southwest. MarkWest Hydrocarbon retains a 24% stake in the partnership and controls its general partner. In 2005 the company acquired the Javelina gas processing and fractionation facility in South Texas for $156 million.

MarkWest Energy Partners has implemented a growth strategy associated with the expansion of its current pipeline system. The company has acquired Pinnacle Natural Gas, the owner of three natural gas pipelines in Texas. It has also acquired Hobbs Lateral pipeline, a connector to the Northern Natural Gas interstate pipeline and power generation stations in New Mexico, from Energy Spectrum.

MarkWest Energy Partners has expanded its gathering system capabilities through the acquisition of American Central East Texas Gas' gathering system and natural gas processing operations for about $240 million.

EXECUTIVES

Chairman: John M. Fox, age 66
President and CEO: Frank M. Semple, age 55, $428,462 pay
SVP and CFO: Nancy K. Masten-Buese, age 36
SVP and COO: John C. Mollenkopf, age 45
SVP and Chief Commercial Officer: Randy S. Nickerson, age 45
SVP Northeast Business Unit: David L. Young, age 46, $253,462 pay
VP and Chief Accounting Officer: Ted S. Smith, age 54
VP Finance and Treasurer: Andrew L. (Andy) Schroeder, age 47
VP Compliance: Richard Ostberg
VP NGL Marketing: Kim Marle
Manager Natural Gas Marketing: Jim Simpson
Manager Propane Marketing Services: Martha Card
Auditors: Deloitte & Touche LLP

LOCATIONS

HQ: MarkWest Energy Partners, L.P.
155 Inverness Dr. West, Ste. 200, Englewood, CO 80112
Phone: 303-290-8700   **Fax:** 303-290-8769
Web: www.markwest.com

MarkWest operates pipelines and facilities in Michigan, as well as in the Appalachian, Southwest, and Gulf Coast regions of the US.

2005 Sales

	$ mil.	% of total
Southwest		
Oklahoma	213.9	43
East Texas	86.2	17
Other regions	106.7	21
Appalachia	66.7	13
Gulf Coast	13.8	3
Michigan	12.5	3
Adjustments	(0.7)	—
Total	**499.1**	**100**

PRODUCTS/OPERATIONS

2005 Sales

	$ mil.	% of total
Unaffiliated parties	436.0	87
Affiliates	64.9	13
Adjustments	(1.8)	—
Total	**499.1**	**100**

COMPETITORS

DCP Midstream Partners	Kinder Morgan
Dynegy	Energy Partners
Enterprise Products	Williams Companies

HISTORICAL FINANCIALS

Company Type: Public

Income Statement

FYE: December 31

	REVENUE ($ mil.)	NET INCOME ($ mil.)	NET PROFIT MARGIN	EMPLOYEES
12/05	499.1	2.4	0.5%	0
12/04	301.3	10.0	3.3%	0
12/03	117.5	5.8	4.9%	0
12/02	70.3	21.8	31.0%	0
12/01	93.7	2.6	2.8%	0
Annual Growth	51.9%	(2.0%)	—	—

2005 Year-End Financials

Debt ratio: 195.7%
Return on equity: 0.9%
Cash ($ mil.): 20.1
Current ratio: 1.09
Long-term debt ($ mil.): 601.3
No. of shares (mil.): 11.1
Dividends
  Yield: 6.9%
  Payout: 16,000.0%
Market value ($ mil.): 514.1
R&D as % of sales: —
Advertising as % of sales: —

Stock History

AMEX: MWE

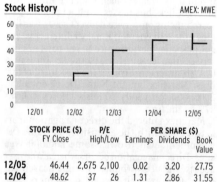

	STOCK PRICE ($) FY Close	P/E High/Low	PER SHARE ($) Earnings	Dividends	Book Value
12/05	46.44	2,675 2,100	0.02	3.20	27.75
12/04	48.62	37 26	1.31	2.86	31.55
12/03	40.70	43 24	0.96	2.32	16.27
12/02	23.29	5 4	4.83	0.71	25.20
Annual Growth	25.9%	—	(83.9%)	65.2%	3.3%

Martek Biosciences

Martek Biosciences' nutritional and pharmaceutical products may popularize lowly pond scum. The firm has developed nutritional oils from microalgae and fungi for use in baby formula (the oils provide fatty acids naturally present in human milk). The company licenses the oils to several manufacturers of formula and nutritional products for infants. Martek also sells its oils for use in dietary supplements, nutritional drinks, and fluorescent dyes used in diagnostic kits. Martek Biosciences uses its database of more than 3,500 species of microalgae for drug discovery and molecular research.

Martek's major customers include Mead Johnson (a Bristol-Myers Squibb subsidiary which accounts for 49% of sales), Wyeth (11%), and Abbott Laboratories (17%). In all, Martek has agreements with more than 20 infant formula manufacturers to supply its oils.

EXECUTIVES

Chairman: Henry (Pete) Linsert Jr., age 65
CEO: Steve Dubin, age 51
President: David M. Abramson, age 52
CFO, EVP Finance and Administration, and Treasurer: Peter L. Buzy, age 46
EVP and COO: Peter A. Nitze, age 47
SVP, Manufacturing: Barney Easterling, age 59
SVP, Research and Development: James Flatt, age 46
VP, Administration and Human Resources: Pat Francis
VP, Sales and Marketing: Joseph M. Buron
Deputy General Counsel: David M. Feitel
Auditors: Ernst & Young LLP

LOCATIONS

HQ: Martek Biosciences Corporation
6480 Dobbin Rd., Columbia, MD 21045
Phone: 410-740-0081   **Fax:** 410-740-2985
Web: www.martekbio.com

Martek Biosciences has facilities in Boulder, Colorado; Columbia, Maryland; Kingstree, South Carolina; and Winchester, Kentucky.

COMPETITORS

Abbott Labs
BASF AG
Cyanotech
GE Healthcare Bio-Sciences
Hoffmann-La Roche
Numico

HISTORICAL FINANCIALS

Company Type: Public

Income Statement

FYE: October 31

	REVENUE ($ mil.)	NET INCOME ($ mil.)	NET PROFIT MARGIN	EMPLOYEES
10/06	270.6	17.8	6.6%	—
10/05	217.9	15.3	7.0%	582
10/04	184.5	47.0	25.5%	541
10/03	114.7	16.0	13.9%	384
10/02	46.1	(24.2)	—	198
Annual Growth	55.7%	—	—	43.2%

2006 Year-End Financials

Debt ratio: 9.3%
Return on equity: 3.7%
Cash ($ mil.): 26.8
Current ratio: 3.41
Long-term debt ($ mil.): 46.3
No. of shares (mil.): 32.2
Dividends
  Yield: —
  Payout: —
Market value ($ mil.): 762.7
R&D as % of sales: —
Advertising as % of sales: —

	STOCK PRICE ($) FY Close	P/E High/Low		PER SHARE ($) Earnings	Dividends	Book Value
10/06	23.72	68	37	0.55	—	15.41
10/05	30.87	147	59	0.48	—	14.65
10/04	47.06	47	28	1.55	—	11.73
10/03	48.41	101	27	0.58	—	8.66
10/02	15.72	—	—	(1.10)	—	4.54
Annual Growth	10.8%	—	—	—	—	35.7%

Martin Midstream Partners

Martin Midstream Partners moves petroleum products. The company gets most of its sales from the distribution of liquefied petroleum gases (LPGs). Martin Midstream buys the LPGs from natural gas processors and oil refiners and sells them to propane retailers and industrial customers. Martin Midstream also manufactures fertilizer and provides marine transportation and storage of liquid hydrocarbons. The company, which operates primarily in the Gulf Coast region of the US, has acquired the bulk of Tesoro's Marine Services assets. Martin Resource Management controls a 50.2% stake in Martin Midstream and owns its general partner. In 2005 the company acquired CF Martin Sulphur, L.P. for $18.1 million.

The limited partnership was formed in 2002 by privately held Martin Resource Management. The parent company has operated an LPG distribution business since the 1950s. It moved into marine transportation operations in the late 1980s, and into fertilizer and terminalling businesses in the early 1990s.

In 2005 Martin Midstream acquired A & A Fertilizer for $6 million.

EXECUTIVES

President, CEO, and Director: Ruben S. Martin III, age 54, $118,434 pay
EVP and COO: Donald R. (Don) Neumeyer, age 58, $91,401 pay
EVP and CFO: Robert D. Bondurant, age 47, $87,492 pay
EVP, Chief Administrative Officer, and Controller: Wesley M. Skelton, age 58, $81,910 pay
EVP and Director; General Manager, Marine Operations: Scott D. Martin, age 40
VP LPG Sales, Martin Gas Sales: Tom Redd
General Manager, CF Martin Sulphur: Dick Wilkinson
Marketing Distribution Manager, CF Martin Sulphur: Darla Martin
General Manager, Martin Resources: Ron Garner
Auditors: KPMG LLP

LOCATIONS

HQ: Martin Midstream Partners L.P.
4200 Stone Rd., Kilgore, TX 75662
Phone: 903-983-6200 **Fax:** 903-983-6262
Web: www.martinmidstream.com

Martin Midstream Partners operates six LPG facilities in Louisiana, Mississippi, and Texas. It also owns seven fertilizer plants in Arizona, Illinois, Texas, and Utah.

PRODUCTS/OPERATIONS

2005 Sales

	$ mil.	% of total
Natural gas/LPG services	301.7	69
Sulfur	36.8	8
Marine transportation	35.4	8
Terminalling & storage	32.9	8
Fertilizer	31.6	7
Total	**438.4**	**100**

COMPETITORS

George Warren
Penn Octane
SandRidge Energy
TEPPCO Partners
Williams Companies

HISTORICAL FINANCIALS

Company Type: Public

Income Statement

	REVENUE ($ mil.)	NET INCOME ($ mil.)	NET PROFIT MARGIN	FYE: December 31 EMPLOYEES
12/05	438.4	13.9	3.2%	—
12/04	294.1	12.3	4.2%	—
12/03	192.7	12.0	6.2%	—
12/02	149.9	6.2	4.1%	—
12/01	162.8	5.2	3.2%	0
Annual Growth	28.1%	27.9%	—	—

2005 Year-End Financials

Debt ratio: 202.9%
Return on equity: 16.2%
Cash ($ mil.): 6.5
Current ratio: 1.18
Long-term debt ($ mil.): 193.9
No. of shares (mil.): 5.8

Dividends
Yield: 7.4%
Payout: 138.6%
Market value ($ mil.): 173.1
R&D as % of sales: —
Advertising as % of sales: —

Stock History

NASDAQ (GS): MMLP

	STOCK PRICE ($) FY Close	P/E High/Low		PER SHARE ($) Earnings	Dividends	Book Value
12/05	29.70	22	18	1.58	2.19	16.39
12/04	29.93	21	16	1.45	2.10	17.89
12/03	30.53	19	11	1.64	1.81	15.82
12/02	17.75	47	41	0.40	—	16.24
Annual Growth	18.7%	—	—	58.1%	10.0%	0.3%

Matrixx Initiatives

Matrixx Initiatives offers several ways to get its medicine up your nose without a rubber hose. The company makes oral and nasally-delivered over-the-counter cold, flu, and allergy remedies marketed under the Zicam name. Zicam products come in a variety of delivery methods, including nasal swabs, cough lozenges, chewable tablets, and nasal and oral sprays. Matrixx claims its Zicam Cold Remedy, a nasal gel spray with zinc, reduces the duration of the common cold. The company also produces Nasal Comfort saline nasal spray. Its major customers include retailing powerhouses Wal-Mart and Target, and large pharmacy chains, including Walgreens and CVS.

Third-party manufacturers produce all of the company's products. It acquired a company in 2005 to gain access to its swab technology. Over-the-counter is where it's at for Matrixx and it has its sights on developing new products such as antacids and analgesics.

Matrixx began life as Gum Tech, and manufactured nutritional and health care-related gums. It sold its chewing gum business to Wm. Wrigley Jr. in 2001 to focus on its Zicam products.

Next Century Growth Investors holds an 11% stake in the company.

EXECUTIVES

Chairman: Edward E. (Ed) Faber, age 73
President, CEO, and Director: Carl J. Johnson, age 57, $850,000 pay
EVP, Operations, CFO, and Treasurer: William J. Hemelt, age 52, $395,000 pay
VP, Administration and Secretary: Lynn Romero, age 41
VP, Research and Development: Timothy L. Clarot, age 51, $315,000 pay
VP, Sales: James A. Marini, age 44, $445,000 pay
Director, Research and Development: Regina Miskewitz
Director, Investor Relations: Bill Barba
Auditors: Mayer Hoffman McCann P.C.

LOCATIONS

HQ: Matrixx Initiatives, Inc.
4742 N. 24th St., Ste. 455, Phoenix, AZ 85016
Phone: 602-385-8888 **Fax:** 602-387-4112
Web: www.matrixxinc.com

PRODUCTS/OPERATIONS

2005 Sales

	$ mil.	% of total
Cold remedy	55.3	61
Allergy/sinus	16.0	18
Flu	8.5	9
Cough	6.5	7
Nasal comfort	4.2	5
Total	**90.5**	**100**

COMPETITORS

Boiron
CNS
K-V Pharmaceutical
NutraMax
Perrigo
Quigley
Schering-Plough

HISTORICAL FINANCIALS

Company Type: Public

Income Statement

FYE: December 31

	REVENUE ($ mil.)	NET INCOME ($ mil.)	NET PROFIT MARGIN	EMPLOYEES
12/05	90.5	3.1	3.4%	26
12/04	60.2	5.0	8.3%	18
12/03	43.5	3.3	7.6%	15
12/02	23.5	4.8	20.4%	14
12/01	16.1	12.6	78.3%	18
Annual Growth	54.0%	(29.6%)	—	9.6%

2005 Year-End Financials

Debt ratio: —
Return on equity: 6.7%
Cash ($ mil.): 12.3
Current ratio: 1.74
Long-term debt ($ mil.): —
No. of shares (mil.): 9.8

Dividends
 Yield: —
 Payout: —
Market value ($ mil.): 206.1
R&D as % of sales: —
Advertising as % of sales: —

Stock History

NASDAQ (GS): MTXX

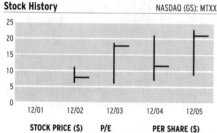

	STOCK PRICE ($) FY Close	P/E High/Low		PER SHARE ($) Earnings	Dividends	Book Value
12/05	21.00	71	28	0.32	—	4.90
12/04	11.56	40	14	0.52	—	4.64
12/03	17.74	53	18	0.35	—	4.09
12/02	7.95	22	13	0.50	—	3.72
Annual Growth	38.2%	—	—	(30.4%)	—	17.4%

McGrath RentCorp

In many cases, the little red schoolhouse of yore has become the modular building of present reality. Not real nostalgia, but it works for McGrath RentCorp. McGrath has three divisions: Mobile Modular Management Corporation (MMMC) rents and sells modular buildings — used as classrooms, on-site construction offices, and sales offices primarily in California, Florida, and Texas, but also serving the hurricane-ravaged states of Alabama, Louisiana, and Mississippi; TRS-RenTelco rents and sells communications, fiber-optics, and general purpose electronic test equipment; and Enviroplex, its 81%-owned subsidiary, makes portable classrooms that the company sells to California school districts.

McGrath's movable modules are available as single units or combined as multi-modular structures. Rental periods range from one month to 10 years; most contracts average about a year and a half. Rentals and related services account for about two-thirds of McGrath's revenues. More than one-third of McGrath's total revenues come from sales and rentals to public schools.

Although modules account for most of its business, McGrath also rents and sells test and measurement equipment under the trade name

TRS-RenTelco. Generally made by Agilent (a Hewlett-Packard spinoff) and Tektronix, the TRS-RenTelco equipment is provided to communications, computer, aerospace, and other high-tech firms nationwide. McGrath specializes in fiber-optic test equipment used for designing and installing voice and data networks.

Founder and chairman Robert McGrath and his wife, Joan (a company director), own about 8% of McGrath.

HISTORY

In 1977 entrepreneur Robert McGrath sold his electronic equipment rental company, Leasametric, and soon found himself at loose ends and bored, but only semiretired. While he was doing research as a part-time business consultant, he found the modular rental industry intriguing. When his client, Trans Union, declined to enter the modular business, McGrath decided to do it himself and organized McGrath RentCorp in 1979.

His timing was propitious. The mobile modular business hit a 20-25% annual growth spurt between 1982 and 1986. McGrath RentCorp was strong enough to go public in 1984. It also landed contracts to house CNN and ABC employees at the Democratic National Convention in San Francisco that year. In 1985 McGrath took a cue from his former business and added the rental of electronic testing and measurement equipment to his company's product line; the modular business still produced about 90% of revenues. McGrath introduced an employee stock ownership plan in 1985.

During McGrath's mid-1980s expansion, its rental fleet grew by 36% in 1985, and in 1986 it bought Space-Co, one of its California-based modular rental competitors. The next year McGrath discovered that an employee had embezzled $1.4 million, but it was still able to report a profit.

McGrath moved further into the test and measurement industry in 1991, buying telecommunications equipment specialist RenTelco from GE Capital affiliate ELLCO Leasing. It also increased its modular building business by funding startup Enviroplex, which produced portable classrooms for the California market. The Enviroplex investment proved to be a wise move for McGrath.

In 1996 the State of California gave schools an incentive to reduce the size of early elementary classrooms to 20 students, from an average of 30. Demand for portable classrooms shot up, and Enviroplex rose to meet it. In 1997 McGrath constructed a new 35,000-sq.-ft. headquarters at Livermore, California, completely from modular units.

After a period of bounding sales and income, McGrath suddenly hit the doldrums in 1999. The following year the company was named in a lawsuit alleging it failed to adequately warn people of potentially dangerous chemicals used in the building materials of its modular units. As part of the settlement reached in 2001, McGrath agreed to use alternative building materials and provide sub-roof ventilation for its modular buildings.

McGrath relocated RenTelco's facilities to a larger location in 2000; because of increased demand for its electronic test instruments, McGrath focused on expanding the division the next year. In late 2001 McGrath agreed to be acquired by a subsidiary of Tyco International for $482 million in cash and stock. The next year, however, when Tyco's problems with operations and management were reported, McGrath decided to terminate its

agreement. Founder Robert McGrath handed his CEO moniker to company president Dennis Kakures in 2003; McGrath retained the chairman title. In 2004 McGrath acquired the Dallas-based communication test equipment rental company Technology Rentals & Services, a division of CIT Group, for a reported $116 million; following that deal, McGrath's electronics test instrument business was renamed TRS-RenTelco.

EXECUTIVES

Chairman: Robert P. McGrath, age 72
President, CEO, and Director: Dennis C. Kakures, age 47, $660,978 pay
CFO: Keith E. Pratt, age 43
SVP, Operations: Joseph F. Hanna, age 42, $353,241 pay
VP, Principal Accounting Officer, and Controller: David M. Whitney, age 41
VP, Administration and Secretary: Randle F. Rose, age 46, $271,229 pay
VP and Division Manager, Mobile Modular: Richard G. Brown, age 35, $271,229 pay
VP and Division Manager, TRS-RenTelco: Susan P. Boutwell, age 50
Auditors: Grant Thornton LLP

LOCATIONS

HQ: McGrath RentCorp
 5700 Las Positas Rd., Livermore, CA 94551
Phone: 925-606-9200   **Fax:** 925-453-3202
Web: www.mgrc.com

McGrath RentCorp has operations in Livermore and Mira Loma, California; Celebration, Florida; and Grapevine, Pasadena, and Plano, Texas; as well as in Montreal. Enviroplex has a manufacturing plant in Stockton, California.

PRODUCTS/OPERATIONS

2005 Sales

	$ mil.	% of total
Rental business		
Rentals	152.3	56
Related services	26.5	10
Sales	93.4	34
Total	**272.2**	**100**

2005 Sales By Segment

	$ mil.	% of total
Modulars	156.0	57
Electronics	105.6	39
Enviroplex	10.6	4
Total	**272.2**	**100**

Selected Test and Measurement Equipment Products

General Purpose
 Amplifiers
 Calibration/detectors/bridges
 CATV test
 Component measurement
 Generators/signal source
 Industrial test
 Microprocessor development
 Oscilloscopes
 Power supplies
 Spectrum analyzers
Telecommunications
 CATV/broadcast test
 Fiber-optic test
 Microwave test
 Network and cable test
 Outside plant
 SONET test
 T-carrier test
 Test accessories
 Test sets

COMPETITORS

Butler Manufacturing	Modtech
Continental Resources	Sunrise Telecom
Electro Rent	Thermo Electron
GE Equipment Services	Trek Equipment
Miller Building Systems	Williams Scotsman
Mobile Mini	

HISTORICAL FINANCIALS

Company Type: Public

Income Statement

FYE: December 31

	REVENUE ($ mil.)	NET INCOME ($ mil.)	NET PROFIT MARGIN	EMPLOYEES
12/05	272.2	40.8	15.0%	610
12/04	202.5	30.0	14.8%	611
12/03	131.0	22.7	17.3%	475
12/02	145.1	12.6	8.7%	436
12/01	159.4	26.7	16.8%	418
Annual Growth	14.3%	11.2%	—	9.9%

2005 Year-End Financials

Debt ratio: 82.2%	Dividends
Return on equity: 22.3%	Yield: 1.9%
Cash ($ mil.): 0.3	Payout: 32.9%
Current ratio: 1.24	Market value ($ mil.): 690.3
Long-term debt ($ mil.): 163.2	R&D as % of sales: —
No. of shares (mil.): 24.8	Advertising as % of sales: —

Stock History

NASDAQ (GS): MGRC

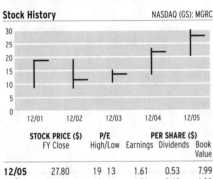

	STOCK PRICE ($) FY Close	P/E High/Low		PER SHARE ($) Earnings	Dividends	Book Value
12/05	27.80	19	13	1.61	0.53	7.99
12/04	21.81	19	11	1.21	0.43	6.80
12/03	13.63	16	12	0.93	0.39	11.88
12/02	11.58	38	17	0.50	0.34	11.13
12/01	18.76	18	8	1.07	0.31	10.67
Annual Growth	10.3%	—	—	10.8%	14.3%	(7.0%)

MEDecision

MEDecision helps clear the paperwork and leave doctors and other caregivers with only health care to worry about. MEDecision provides a variety of health care management software and services to physicians and managed care organizations. The company's products enable the health care providers on a patient's care team to share information about a patient's status and history. Among the company's clients are Blue Cross and Blue Shield, Liberty Mutual, and PacifiCare Health Systems. MEDecision was founded in 1988. Founder, chairman, and CEO David St. Clair owns about 17% of the company.

The company's Integrated Medical Management software allows health care payers to identify active care management opportunities and automated intervention practices based on shared best practices standards. Its Collaborative Data Exchange software provides a standardized platform enabling customers to retain patient information in one format. Services are provided on an annual subscription, limited term licenses, or one-off transactions.

MEDecision has nearly 60 regional and national managed care organizations.

The company plans to raise funds to increase its technological capabilities, as well as possibly to enter an acquisitive phase.

Directors Frank Adams and Charles Cullen each own more than 25% of the company through Grotech Capital.

MEDecision in 2005 founded CollaboraCare Consortium, a group of vendors with the mission to provide a national health information exchange. Together, members of the consortium will develop software that will be mutually compatible. Members besides MEDecision include CapMed, Covising, DiagnosisOne, DrFirst, Extended Care Network, Gold Standard, HealthTrio, HxTechnologies, iMetrikus, Intellicare, Medem, RPR Solutions, SureScripts, and Wellogic.

EXECUTIVES

Chairman and CEO: David St. Clair, age 53
President, COO, and Director: John H. Capobianco, age 54
EVP and CFO: Carl Smith, age 58
EVP and CIO: Ronald D. (Ron) Nall, age 59
EVP and Chief Medical Officer: Henry A. DePhillips III, age 46
EVP, Client Solutions: Danielle Russella Bantivoglio, age 39
SVP, Client Operations: Mary Jo Timlin-Hoag, age 48
SVP, Product Marketing: Kristel L. Schimmoller, age 43
VP, Corporate Marketing: Tracey Kohler Costello
VP, Finance: Dennis Johnson
VP, Sales: Terry Beck
Auditors: Grant Thornton LLP

LOCATIONS

HQ: MEDecision, Inc.
601 Lee Rd., Chesterbrook Corporate Center, Wayne, PA 19087
Phone: 610-540-0202   **Fax:** 610-540-0270
Web: www.medecision.com

COMPETITORS

Health Management Systems
IMS Health
Landacorp
McKesson Medical-Surgical
Microsoft
Microsoft Business Solutions
QuadraMed
SoftMed

HISTORICAL FINANCIALS

Company Type: Public

Income Statement

FYE: December 31

	REVENUE ($ mil.)	NET INCOME ($ mil.)	NET PROFIT MARGIN	EMPLOYEES
12/05	38.6	5.1	13.2%	207
12/04	28.0	(1.3)	—	—
12/03	20.5	(0.5)	—	—
Annual Growth	37.2%	—	—	—

2005 Year-End Financials

Debt ratio: —	Current ratio: 0.72
Return on equity: —	Long-term debt ($ mil.): 2.5
Cash ($ mil.): 2.5	

Net Income History

NASDAQ (GM): MEDE

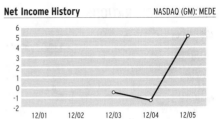

Mercantile Bank

Mercantile Bank Corporation is the holding company for Mercantile Bank of Michigan (formerly Mercantile Bank of West Michigan), which operates about a half-dozen branches in and around Grand Rapids. In 2005 it opened branches in the college towns of Ann Arbor and East Lansing, the community bank's first foray outside the western part of Michigan, prompting the name change. The bank targets local consumers and businesses, offering standard retail banking services such as checking and savings accounts, NOW and money market accounts, and CDs. Commercial and nonresidential real estate loans make up approximately three-quarters of its loan portfolio.

Mercantile Bank also offers financial planning services via an agreement with Raymond James Financial.

Subsidiary Mercantile Bank Mortgage originates home loans while another unit, Mercantile Insurance Center sells insurance products. Mercantile Bank dissolved its Mercantile BIDCO subsidiary, which provided specialized commercial financing, in 2005.

EXECUTIVES

Chairman and CEO; Chairman, Mercantile Bank: Gerald R. Johnson Jr., age 59, $675,000 pay
President, COO, and Director; President and CEO, Mercantile Bank: Michael H. Price, age 49, $582,500 pay
EVP and Secretary; EVP, COO, Secretary, and Community Relations Act Officer, Mercantile Bank: Robert B. Kaminski Jr., age 44, $336,750 pay
SVP, CFO, and Treasurer; SVP and CFO, Mercantile Bank: Charles E. (Chuck) Christmas, age 40, $281,000 pay
President, Mercantile Bank, Lansing: Howard Haas
President, Mercantile Bank, Ann Arbor: Walter (Walt) Byers
SVP, Commercial Loans, Mercantile Bank: Mark S. Augustyn
SVP and Director, Retail Loans Department, Mercantile Bank: Brian A. Chisholm
SVP, Business Development, Mercantile Bank: Harold L. Drenten
SVP, Business Development and Marketing Officer, Mercantile Bank: Deborah A. (Deb) Rogers
SVP and Human Resources Director, Mercantile Bank: Lonna Wiersma
Auditors: BDO Seidman, LLP

LOCATIONS

HQ: Mercantile Bank Corporation
310 Leonard St. NW, Grand Rapids, MI 49504
Phone: 616-406-3000
Web: www.mercbank.com

PRODUCTS/OPERATIONS

2005 Sales

	$ mil.	% of total
Interest		
Loans & leases, including fees	93.6	87
Securities	8.2	8
Other	0.3	—
Noninterest		
Service charges on accounts	1.4	1
Increase in cash surrender value		
of bank-owned life insurance policies	1.0	1
Other	3.3	3
Total	**107.8**	**100**

Selected Subsidiaries

MBWM Capital Trust I
Mercantile Bank of Michigan
  Mercantile Bank Mortgage Company,LLC
  Mercantile Bank Real Estate Co., LLC
  Mercantile Insurance Center, Inc.

COMPETITORS

Chemical Financial
Comerica
Fifth Third
Flagstar Bancorp
Huntington Bancshares
Independent Bank (MI)
LaSalle Bank
Macatawa Bank
National City

HISTORICAL FINANCIALS

Company Type: Public

Income Statement

FYE: December 31

	ASSETS ($ mil.)	NET INCOME ($ mil.)	INCOME AS % OF ASSETS	EMPLOYEES
12/05	1,838.2	17.9	1.0%	304
12/04	1,536.1	13.7	0.9%	209
12/03	1,202.8	10.0	0.8%	179
12/02	921.9	7.8	0.8%	134
12/01	698.7	4.5	0.6%	106
Annual Growth	**27.4%**	**41.2%**	**—**	**30.1%**

2005 Year-End Financials

Equity as % of assets: 8.4%
Return on assets: 1.1%
Return on equity: 12.1%
Long-term debt ($ mil.): 35.3
No. of shares (mil.): 7.6
Market value ($ mil.): 278.3
Dividends
  Yield: 1.1%
  Payout: 18.2%
Sales ($ mil.): 107.8
R&D as % of sales: —
Advertising as % of sales: 0.5%

Stock History

NASDAQ (GS): MBWM

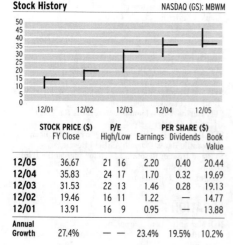

	STOCK PRICE ($) FY Close	P/E High/Low	Earnings	Dividends	Book Value
12/05	36.67	21 16	2.20	0.40	20.44
12/04	35.83	24 17	1.70	0.32	19.69
12/03	31.53	22 13	1.46	0.28	19.13
12/02	19.46	16 11	1.22	—	14.77
12/01	13.91	16 9	0.95	—	13.88
Annual Growth	**27.4%**	**— —**	**23.4%**	**19.5%**	**10.2%**

Mercer Insurance Group

Dating back to 1844, Mercer Insurance Group offers a range of property/casualty insurance policies through subsidiaries such as Mercer Mutual Insurance, Mercer Insurance Company of New Jersey, and Franklin Insurance. The company focuses on commercial coverage for small to midsized businesses and personal homeowners (the majority of personal lines) and automobile insurance. Mercer Insurance Group markets its products through independent agents in New Jersey and Pennsylvania. The company further expanded its reach through the 2005 acquisition of California-based Financial Pacific Insurance Group.

Financial Pacific provides specialty commercial coverage in four western states.

SVP H. Thomas Davis Jr. owns 6% of Mercer Insurance Group; directors and executive officers collectively control 13% of the company.

In 2005 almost 55% of all of the company's business was done in New Jersey.

EXECUTIVES

Chairman: Richard G. Van Noy, age 64
President, CEO, and Director: Andrew R. Speaker, age 43, $571,150 pay
SVP and CFO: David B. Merclean, age 55, $321,077 pay
SVP and Director: H. Thomas Davis Jr., age 57, $174,026 pay
SVP and Secretary: Paul D. Ehrhardt, age 48, $367,355 pay
Treasurer: Gordon A. Coleman, age 48, $136,118 pay
SVP; President, Financial Pacific Insurance Company: Robert T. Kingsley, age 40
Human Resources: Debbie Johnstone
Auditors: KPMG LLP

LOCATIONS

HQ: Mercer Insurance Group, Inc.
  10 N. Hwy. 31, Pennington, NJ 08534
Phone: 609-737-0426   **Fax:** 609-737-8719
Web: www.franklininsurance.com

PRODUCTS/OPERATIONS

2005 Premiums Written

	$ mil.	% of total
Commercial lines	52.3	64
Personal lines	29.0	36
Total	**81.3**	**100**

Selected Subsidiaries

Franklin Insurance Company
Mercer Insurance Company
Mercer Insurance Company of New Jersey
Mercer Mutual Insurance Company

COMPETITORS

ACE Limited	The Hartford
AIG	Liberty Mutual
Allstate	MetLife
American Financial	Progressive Corporation
Chubb Corp	Prudential
CNA Financial	Safeco
Farmers Group	St. Paul Travelers
GEICO	State Farm

HISTORICAL FINANCIALS

Company Type: Public

Income Statement

FYE: December 31

	ASSETS ($ mil.)	NET INCOME ($ mil.)	INCOME AS % OF ASSETS	EMPLOYEES
12/05	446.7	7.0	1.6%	193
12/04	180.4	3.3	1.8%	97
12/03	175.9	0.6	0.3%	91
12/02	105.8	2.2	2.1%	86
12/01	97.1	3.3	3.4%	70
Annual Growth	**46.5%**	**20.7%**	**—**	**28.9%**

2005 Year-End Financials

Equity as % of assets: 23.1%
Return on assets: 2.2%
Return on equity: 6.9%
Long-term debt ($ mil.): 18.5
No. of shares (mil.): 6.5
Market value ($ mil.): 97.0
Dividends
  Yield: —
  Payout: —
Sales ($ mil.): 81.3
R&D as % of sales: —
Advertising as % of sales: —

Stock History

NASDAQ (GM): MIGP

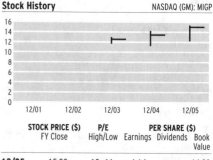

	STOCK PRICE ($) FY Close	P/E High/Low	Earnings	Dividends	Book Value
12/05	15.00	13 11	1.14	—	16.00
12/04	13.43	28 22	0.51	—	15.30
12/03	12.55	— —	—	—	15.65
Annual Growth	**9.3%**	**— —**	**123.5%**	**—**	**1.1%**

Meridian Bioscience

Detection is the name of Meridian Bioscience's game. The company makes diagnostic test kits and transport media for reference laboratories, hospitals, and doctors' offices. The company's tests analyze blood, urine, and other bodily fluids to diagnose such maladies as respiratory illness (pneumonia, influenza), gastrointestinal disease (ulcers), viruses (mononucleosis, chicken pox), and parasites. The company's Life Science division makes and sells antigens, antibodies, and reagents for use by researchers and other diagnostics firms; it also provides contract manufacturing of proteins and other biologics.

The company's Life Science division was built through a number of acquisitions, including Gull Laboratories (1999), Viral Antigens (2000), and OEM Concepts (2005). The company intends to grow the division by expanding its existing technologies into new product areas and by acquiring or licensing new biologics technologies.

HISTORY

Microbiology and diagnostics specialists William Motto and Jerry Ruyan launched Meridian Diagnostics in 1977, naming it for their desire to reach the highest point in diagnostic technology. The company began as a research

and development lab, but soon developed a variety of commercial products, including test kits for pneumocystis carinii pneumonia (a leading cause of death in AIDS patients) and mycoplasmal (or "walking") pneumonia.

In the 1990s Meridian made key acquisitions to further its offerings, including the Immuno*Card* rapid-response systems from Disease Detection International and the MonoSpot and Monolert mononucleosis diagnostics technologies from Johnson & Johnson. Other acquisitions include tests for Lyme disease and the viruses that cause pediatric diarrhea.

As a result of its entry into the life sciences market (spurred by its acquisition of antigens and test kits maker Viral Antigens), Meridian Diagnostics changed its name to Meridian Bioscience in 2001.

EXECUTIVES

Chairman and CEO: William J. Motto, age 65, $947,030 pay
President, COO, and Director: John A. Kraeutler, age 58, $749,073 pay
EVP; President, Meridian Life Science: Richard L. Eberly, age 45, $318,098 pay
EVP, Operations and Information Systems: Lawrence J. Baldini, age 47, $419,635 pay
VP, CFO, and Secretary: Melissa A. Lueke, age 43
VP, Regulatory Affairs and Quality Systems: Susan A. Rolih, age 57
VP, Research and Development: Kenneth J. Kozak, age 52
VP, Sales and Marketing: Todd W. Motto, age 40
SVP; President, Managing Director, Meridian Bioscience Europe: Antonio A. Interno, age 55, $598,940 pay
Auditors: Grant Thornton LLP

LOCATIONS

HQ: Meridian Bioscience, Inc.
3471 River Hills Dr., Cincinnati, OH 45244
Phone: 513-271-3700   **Fax:** 513-271-3762
Web: www.meridianbioscience.com

Meridian Bioscience has manufacturing operations in Boca Raton, Florida; Cincinnati; Memphis; and Saco, Maine. It has international sales, administration, and distribution facilities in Belgium, France, and Italy.

PRODUCTS/OPERATIONS

2006 Sales

	$ mil.	% of total
Diagnostics		
US	65.7	61
European	19.8	18
Life Science	22.9	21
Total	**108.4**	**100**

Selected Products and Brands

Diagnostics
Enzyme Immunoassay (EIA)/Rapid tests
Immuno*Card*
MONOLERT
Premier
Immunofluorescence
MERIFLUOR
Particle Agglutination
Meritec
MonoSpot
Other
Macro-CON
Para-Pak
Spin-Con

Life Science
BIODESIGN (monoclonal and polyclongal antibodies and assay reagents)
cGMP (contract biologics development and manufacturing)
OEM Concepts (contract ascites and antibody production)
Viral Antigens (viral proteins)

COMPETITORS

Abbott Labs
BD
Biomerica
bioMérieux
Dade Behring
Diagnostic Hybrids
Hemagen Diagnostics
Inverness Medical Innovations
Johnson & Johnson
Neogen
OraSure
Orgenics
Quidel
Roche Diagnostics
Siemens Medical Solutions Diagnostics
Trinity Biotech

HISTORICAL FINANCIALS

Company Type: Public

Income Statement

FYE: September 30

	REVENUE ($ mil.)	NET INCOME ($ mil.)	NET PROFIT MARGIN	EMPLOYEES
9/06	108.4	18.3	16.9%	402
9/05	93.0	12.6	13.5%	390
9/04	79.6	9.2	11.6%	363
9/03	65.9	7.0	10.6%	356
9/02	59.1	5.0	8.5%	350
Annual Growth	**16.4%**	**38.3%**	**—**	**3.5%**

2006 Year-End Financials

Debt ratio: —
Return on equity: 20.5%
Cash ($ mil.): 40.3
Current ratio: 3.94
Long-term debt ($ mil.): —
No. of shares (mil.): 26.2
Dividends
　Yield: 1.8%
　Payout: 63.2%
Market value ($ mil.): 615.0
R&D as % of sales: —
Advertising as % of sales: —

Stock History

NASDAQ (GS): VIVO

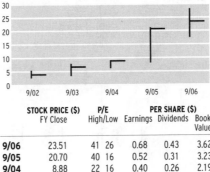

	STOCK PRICE ($) FY Close	P/E High	P/E Low	PER SHARE ($) Earnings	PER SHARE ($) Dividends	PER SHARE ($) Book Value
9/06	23.51	41	26	0.68	0.43	3.62
9/05	20.70	40	16	0.52	0.31	3.23
9/04	8.88	22	16	0.40	0.26	2.19
9/03	6.69	24	12	0.31	0.23	1.87
9/02	3.88	23	13	0.23	0.18	1.67
Annual Growth	**56.9%**	**—**	**—**	**31.1%**	**24.3%**	**21.4%**

Merix Corporation

Merix finds merit in the circuit board business. The company is a leading manufacturer of advanced multilayer printed circuit boards (PCBs), complex interconnection platforms used within electronic equipment to link components, such as integrated circuits. Merix also provides product design, engineering, and quick-turn prototyping services. The company's top customers include Cisco Systems (20% of sales), Juniper Networks, Motorola, Nokia, Nortel Networks, Robert Bosch, TRW Automotive, and Visteon. Leading contract electronics manufacturers, such as Solectron, also use Merix's products.

In 2005 Merix acquired Eastern Pacific Circuits (EPC), a Chinese producer of PCBs, for $115 million in cash. The acquisition of Eastern Pacific Circuits gives Merix more of an international manufacturing base, adding four plants in southern China and one in Hong Kong. The company previously had manufacturing plants at two locations in Oregon and one in California. EPC was a low-cost, mid- to high-volume supplier of printed circuit boards to a global customer base in the high-end computer, communications, consumer, industrial, and automotive end markets. The Hong Kong-based company, now called Merix Asia, has sales offices in Asia, Europe, and North America.

While more than half of sales comes from the communications market, Merix also sells PCBs to the high-end computing and test and measurement instrument markets. Customers located in the US account for nearly three-quarters of the company's business.

The company has continued to add to its customer roster, and to focus on garnering high-margin projects that rely on producing prototypes and volume orders with quick turnaround times.

Merix identified material weaknesses in the company's internal controls over financial reporting and took a number of steps in 2006 to remedy the problems, including the appointment of a new CFO and hiring more accounting staff.

FMR (Fidelity Investments) owns 10% of Merix. Security Management Co. holds around 7% of the company. Royce & Associates has an equity stake of nearly 6%. Dimensional Fund Advisors owns about 5%.

HISTORY

Merix began in 1959 as the Circuit Board Division of Tektronix. In 1983 the division was moved to a separate facility in Forest Grove, Oregon. By the mid-1980s its productivity was attracting customers such as IBM, NCR, and Rockwell. By the early 1990s, the division had an international customer base. In 1992 former Apple Computer VP and CFO Deborah Coleman joined Tektronix as VP of materials operations. The division was spun off as Merix and went public in 1994, with Coleman serving as chairman and CEO.

In 1995 Merix signed a supply agreement with Teradyne. The company also acquired certain assets of Hewlett-Packard's printed circuit board (PCB) unit, located in Loveland, Colorado. In 1996 Merix acquired Rogers Corporation's Soladyne division, which manufactured PCBs with microwave and radio-frequency applications. A downturn in the electronics industry, primarily the result of the Asian financial crisis and an

oversupply of electronic components, hammered Merix's profits in 1997 and again in 1998. In response, Merix implemented a restructuring plan in 1998 that included layoffs and the closure of the Loveland plant.

In 1999 Merix sold Soladyne to Tyco International. The company also completed an expansion of its Oregon manufacturing facility. Later that year Coleman relinquished her CEO title to president and COO Mark Hollinger.

The company broke ground on a new plant in Oregon in 2000. Coleman stepped down from Merix's board in 2001; Hollinger succeeded her as chairman.

In 2004 Merix bought Data Circuit Systems, a quick-turn multilayer PCB maker, for $43 million. The California-based business was renamed Merix San Jose. Also that year the company opened its new plant in Wood Village, Oregon, supplementing production at its facilities in Forest Grove, where Merix makes its headquarters.

Matsushita Electronic Materials, a supplier of laminate and prepeg material to Merix and its customers, closed its US facility in 2005. Merix turned to its other materials supplier, Isola, for help with its supply-chain needs.

Mark Hollinger resigned as chairman and CEO in early 2007. William McCormick, the lead director of the board, was named chairman and interim CEO to succeed him.

EXECUTIVES

Chairman and Interim President and CEO: William C. McCormick, age 72
VP, Finance and CFO: Kelly E. Lang, age 44
VP, Merix North American Operations; President, Merix San Jose: Steve Robinson, age 49, $275,000 pay
VP, Sales and Marketing: Thomas R. (Tom) Ingham, age 50, $253,846 pay
VP, General Counsel, and Secretary: Stephen M. Going, $114,923 pay
VP and Treasurer: Lynda C. Ramsey
VP, Sales Eastern Region: Roger Michalowski
SVP and CEO, Asian Operations: Daniel T. Olson, age 51, $278,182 pay
Director, Customer Service: Laura Woods
Director, RF and Microwave Products: Gary Pollard
Sales Director, China Sales: Jane Xu
Sales Director, European Sales: Ian Jones
Sales Director, Northwest Region: John Cavanaugh
Quick-Turn Program Manager: Dottie Fast
Auditors: PricewaterhouseCoopers LLP

LOCATIONS

HQ: Merix Corporation
1521 Poplar Ln., Forest Grove, OR 97116
Phone: 503-359-9300   **Fax:** 503-357-9755
Web: www.merix.com

Merix has manufacturing facilities in China, Hong Kong, and the US.

2006 Sales

	$ mil.	% of total
Merix Oregon	193.3	63
Merix Asia	83.5	27
Merix San Jose	32.2	10
Total	**309.0**	**100**

PRODUCTS/OPERATIONS

2006 Sales

	% of total
Communications	52
Automotive	13
High-end computing & storage	9
Test & measurement	6
Aerospace & defense	2
Medical, industrial & other	18
Total	**100**

Products

Backplanes and backplane assemblies
Multilayer printed circuit boards

Services

Design assistance
Engineering
Preproduction
Prototyping
Volume production

COMPETITORS

Benchmark Electronics
Celestica
DDi Corp.
Flash Electronics
Flextronics
Honeywell International
IEC Electronics
Jabil
Kingboard
LaBarge
LG Electronics
Park Electrochemical
Photocircuits
Plexus
Reptron Electronics
Sanmina-SCI
Solectron
Suntron
TTM Technologies
Tyco
Viasystems

HISTORICAL FINANCIALS

Company Type: Public

Income Statement

FYE: Last Saturday in May

	REVENUE ($ mil.)	NET INCOME ($ mil.)	NET PROFIT MARGIN	EMPLOYEES
5/06	309.0	1.4	0.5%	4,225
5/05	187.0	(2.6)	—	1,533
5/04	156.4	0.0	—	1,407
5/03	94.6	(30.1)	—	915
5/02	86.5	(9.6)	—	963
Annual Growth	**37.5%**	**—**		**44.7%**

2006 Year-End Financials

Debt ratio: 45.1%
Return on equity: 0.7%
Cash ($ mil.): 31.1
Current ratio: 1.74
Long-term debt ($ mil.): 91.1
No. of shares (mil.): 19.8
Dividends
  Yield: —
  Payout: —
Market value ($ mil.): 194.7
R&D as % of sales: —
Advertising as % of sales: —

Stock History

NASDAQ (GM): MERX

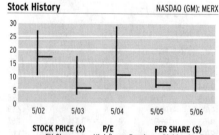

	STOCK PRICE ($) FY Close	P/E High/Low		Earnings	PER SHARE ($) Dividends	Book Value
5/06	9.83	204	72	0.07	—	10.20
5/05	7.06	—	—	(0.14)	—	10.24
5/04	10.70	—	—	—	—	10.41
5/03	5.75	—	—	(2.07)	—	7.13
5/02	17.30	—	—	(0.68)	—	9.22
Annual Growth	**(13.2%)**	—	—	—	—	**2.6%**

Metalico

No, dude, it's not a heavy metal band, but Metalico *is* into metal — specifically, scrap metal recycling and lead fabrication. The company collects ferrous and nonferrous metal at six facilities in western New York and recycles it into usable scrap. Recycled ferrous metal (iron and steel) is sold mainly to steelmakers, particularly to operators of electric arc furnace minimills. Metalico's nonferrous scrap includes aluminum, which is sold to makers of aluminum products; the company operates its own secondary aluminum smelter. Metalico engages in lead fabrication and recycling at six US facilities and operates a secondary lead smelter. Its lead products include sheet (for roofing) and shot (for reloading).

In 2006 Metalico agreed to buy Niles Iron & Metal Company, a leading northeastern Ohio-based scrap metal recycling business.

EXECUTIVES

Chairman, President, and CEO: Carlos E. Agüero, age 53, $857,403 pay
SVP and CFO: Eric W. Finlayson, age 46, $162,590 pay
EVP and Director: Michael J. Drury, age 49, $255,324 pay
EVP, General Counsel, and Secretary: Arnold S. Graber, age 51, $227,000 pay
Corporate Controller: Kevin R. Whalen
Manager, Investor Relations, Operations, and Business Development: David J. DelBianco
Operations Specialist: James S. Gill
Auditors: McGladrey & Pullen, LLP

LOCATIONS

HQ: Metalico, Inc.
186 North Ave. East, Cranford, NJ 07016
Phone: 908-497-9610   **Fax:** 908-497-1097
Web: www.metalico.com

Selected Operating Locations

Scrap metal recycling
  Buffalo, NY
  Lackawanna, NY
  Niagara Falls, NY
  Rochester, NY

Lead fabrication and recycling
  Birmingham, AL
  Carson City, NV
  Granite City, IL
  Healdsburg, CA
  Ontario, CA
  Tampa, FL

PRODUCTS/OPERATIONS

2005 Sales

	$ mil.	% of total
Scrap metal recycling		
Nonferrous metals	53.0	32
Ferrous metals	35.0	21
Lead fabrication & recycling		
Fabricating	67.2	41
Smelting	5.3	3
Tolling	3.8	3
Total	**164.3**	**100**

COMPETITORS

David J. Joseph
Doe Run
Joseph Behr and Sons
Metal Management
OmniSource
Philip Services
Sanders Lead

HISTORICAL FINANCIALS

Company Type: Public

Income Statement

FYE: December 31

	REVENUE ($ mil.)	NET INCOME ($ mil.)	NET PROFIT MARGIN	EMPLOYEES
12/05	164.3	5.6	3.4%	457
12/04	115.4	6.7	5.8%	—
12/03	61.3	2.0	3.3%	—
12/02	59.3	2.8	4.7%	—
Annual Growth	40.5%	26.0%	—	—

2005 Year-End Financials

Debt ratio: 115.2%
Return on equity: 50.3%
Cash ($ mil.): 1.9
Current ratio: 1.69
Long-term debt ($ mil.): 18.3
No. of shares (mil.): 8.0

Dividends
  Yield: —
  Payout: —
Market value ($ mil.): 24.2
R&D as % of sales: —
Advertising as % of sales: —

Stock History

AMEX: MEA

	STOCK PRICE ($) FY Close	P/E High/Low	PER SHARE ($) Earnings	Dividends	Book Value
12/05	3.03	27 12	0.23	—	6.90
12/04	5.50	21 10	0.29	—	5.71
Annual Growth	(44.9%)	— —	(20.7%)	—	20.8%

Micronetics

Micronetics fights noise with noise. The company designs radio-frequency (RF) components and test equipment that help keep signals clear in cellular, wireless cable, satellite, and radar systems worldwide. Products include RF controls for military radar and communications systems, noise source components that test reception and transmission quality, and other noise generators and frequency emulators. The company sells primarily to military contractors like Northrop Grumman and Raytheon; its commercial customers include Motorola and NEC. Contract electronics manufacturer Solectron accounts for about 22% of sales; Aerosat Avionics is another leading customer, responsible for more than 11% of sales.

Micronetics has been active in acquisitions, buying Stealth Microwave in 2005 and Microwave Concepts (Micro-Con) in 2003. Micronetics' Enon Microwave unit (acquired in 2002) makes switches, phase shifters, filters, control devices, and assemblies.

Stealth Microwave's acquisition greatly helped Micronetics nearly double its sales.

Noelle Kalin, the widow of former CEO Richard Kalin (who was killed in a 2003 auto accident), owns about 13% of Micronetics. Bjurman, Barry & Associates has an equity stake of around 7%.

EXECUTIVES

Chairman: David Siegel, age 80
President, CEO, and Director: David Robbins, age 41, $304,272 pay
CFO: Diane L. Bourque, age 52
VP, Business Development: Kevin Beals
VP, VCO Products: Stuart Bernstein, age 48, $125,637 pay
VP, Finance: Dennis Dow, age 56
VP; General Manager, Microwave Concepts: Anthony Pospishil, age 48, $254,388 pay
President, Microwave and Video Systems: Floyd S. Parin, age 62, $145,769 pay
President, Stealth Microwave and Director: Stephen N. Barthelmes Jr., age 39, $520,756 pay
Secretary and Treasurer: Donna Hillsgrove, age 57
Auditors: Grant Thornton LLP

LOCATIONS

HQ: Micronetics, Inc.
  26 Hampshire Dr., Hudson, NH 03051
Phone: 603-883-2900   Fax: 603-882-8987
Web: www.mwireless.com

Micronetics has offices and manufacturing operations in Connecticut, Massachusetts, New Hampshire, and New Jersey.

2006 Sales

	$ mil.	% of total
North America	18.2	68
Europe	8.2	30
Asia & other regions	0.5	2
Total	**26.9**	**100**

PRODUCTS/OPERATIONS

Selected Products

Control components and integrated subassemblies
  Attenuators
  Linearized power amplifiers
  Microwave integrated modules
  Phase shifters
  Switch filter assemblies
  Switches
Noise-based test equipment
  Carrier-to-noise instruments
  Handheld power meters
  Multipath fading emulators
  Noise generators
Voltage-controlled oscillators

COMPETITORS

Agilent Technologies
Crane Aerospace & Electronics
Filtronic
Herley Farmingdale
M/A-Com
Merrimac Industries
Mini-Circuits
Modco
NCT Group
ORBIT/FR
Sirenza Microdevices
Spirent
STC Microwave Systems
Synergy Microwave
Wireless Telecom

HISTORICAL FINANCIALS

Company Type: Public

Income Statement

FYE: March 31

	REVENUE ($ mil.)	NET INCOME ($ mil.)	NET PROFIT MARGIN	EMPLOYEES
3/06	26.9	2.5	9.3%	125
3/05	14.1	1.3	9.2%	87
3/04	13.8	1.5	10.9%	95
3/03	10.7	1.2	11.2%	91
3/02	7.6	0.4	5.3%	73
Annual Growth	37.2%	58.1%	—	14.4%

2006 Year-End Financials

Debt ratio: 33.6%
Return on equity: 18.1%
Cash ($ mil.): 5.8
Current ratio: 2.85
Long-term debt ($ mil.): 5.3
No. of shares (mil.): 5.0

Dividends
  Yield: —
  Payout: —
Market value ($ mil.): 109.6
R&D as % of sales: —
Advertising as % of sales: —

Stock History

NASDAQ (CM): NOIZ

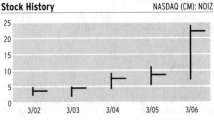

	STOCK PRICE ($) FY Close	P/E High/Low	PER SHARE ($) Earnings	Dividends	Book Value
3/06	22.12	44 13	0.54	—	3.20
3/05	8.63	38 19	0.29	—	2.68
3/04	7.44	26 13	0.34	—	2.31
3/03	4.50	18 8	0.27	—	2.05
3/02	3.65	47 24	0.10	—	1.79
Annual Growth	56.9%	— —	52.4%	—	15.7%

Microsemi

Microsemi is on a power trip. The company makes power management semiconductors that regulate and condition electricity to make it more usable by electrical and electronic systems. The company's products include discrete components such as diodes and rectifiers, along with integrated circuits, such as amplifiers and voltage regulators. It also makes devices for pacemakers, computer systems, and cellular phones. Microsemi's high-performance products go into missile systems, jet engines, and oil-field equipment. Top customers include BAE SYSTEMS, Boeing, Guidant, Medtronic, and Seagate Technology. The company has acquired PowerDsine for about $245 million in cash and stock.

PowerDsine specializes in chips for transmitting electrical power over Ethernet local-area networks. The Israeli-American firm will complement Microsemi's analog and mixed-signal semiconductor design expertise.

In 2006 Microsemi acquired Advanced Power Technology (APT) for about $130 million in cash and stock. APT became a wholly owned subsidiary of Microsemi, functioning as the company's Power Products Group.

Integrating two big acquisitions back to back will be a challenge for Microsemi.

While maintaining its traditional strongholds in businesses such as military and aerospace equipment (about 30% of sales are to businesses that have the US government as their main customer), Microsemi is targeting niche commercial markets for growth. Some of the markets identified by the company include the automotive, digital media, medical, and wireless communications industries. The US accounts for nearly 90% of the company's sales.

The company has retooled its operations during and after the deep semiconductor industry slump of the early 21st century. It closed some non-US facilities, consolidated operations in the US, and announced a shift to a fabless model — in which products are manufactured for the company by foundries — in order to reach profitability. Headcount has been reduced by nearly half.

Franklin Resources owns more than 12% of Microsemi. Wells Fargo holds nearly 7% of the company. AXA has an equity stake of almost 6%. Delaware Management Business Trust owns about 5%.

HISTORY

Microsemiconductor Corporation started in 1960 as a maker of power conditioning equipment. Early acquisitions included two lines of semiconductors from Globe Union. Philip Frey joined the company as CEO and president in 1971. It went public in 1981 and changed its name to Microsemi in 1982.

Throughout the mid-1980s and early 1990s, military business accounted for up to 75% of sales. By means of acquisitions Microsemi consolidated its clout as a military contractor and diversified its customer base. In 1992 it bought a semiconductor manufacturing division of Unitrode — a purchase that also increased its presence in Europe and Asia. Other acquisitions included units from Raytheon (1995), SGS-Thomson (now STMicroelectronics) and National Semiconductor (1996), PPC Products (1997), and BKC Semiconductors and Semicon (1998).

Microsemi sold its low-growth contract circuit board assembly operations in 1998. It formed a development pact with Advanced Power Technology that year to expand in the medical market. In 1999 Microsemi acquired SymmetriCom's Linfinity Microelectronics subsidiary (power management products for consumer electronics) and Narda Microwave's semiconductor operations.

In 2000 former Linfinity president James Peterson replaced Frey as CEO (Frey remained chairman until 2002). The following year saw Microsemi acquire Compensated Devices and New England Semiconductor, both makers of electronic components primarily used by aerospace customers.

In 2002 Microsemi launched a restructuring effort that included closing plants and relocating operations. The company also sold its Carlsbad design center to AMI Semiconductor, as well as its India-based Semcon Electronics subsidiary.

Nick Yocca, who had served as the company's chairman since 2002, retired from the board in mid-2004. Dennis Leibel succeeded him as chairman. Later that year, Microsemi sued rival

Monolithic Power Systems, alleging patent infringement involving certain products. In late 2004 the company licensed packaging technology from Diodes, Inc.

Microsemi initiated further consolidation in 2005, shutting its wafer fab in Broomfield, Colorado and closing its plant in Ireland. Work done in those two facilities was reassigned to other Microsemi facilities.

EXECUTIVES

Chairman: Dennis R. Leibel, age 62
President, CEO, and Director: James J. (Jim) Peterson, age 51, $973,320 pay
EVP, CFO, Treasurer, and Secretary:
David R. (Dave) Sonksen, age 61, $518,508 pay
EVP and COO: Ralph Brandi, age 62, $603,312 pay
EVP and Group President, High Performance Analog Mixed Signal: Steven G. Litchfield
SVP; General Manager, Integrated Products:
Paul R. Bibeau, age 49
SVP, Human Resources: John M. Holtrust, age 56
SVP, Worldwide Sales: James H. (Jim) Gentile, age 50, $380,490 pay
VP; General Manager, Microsemi Broomfield:
Sven Nelson
VP, Finance and Treasurer: John W. Hohener, age 51
VP, Hi-Rel Sales: John Costello
VP, Marketing, Integrated Products: Paul Pickle
VP, Distribution Sales: Michael G. (Mike) Sivetts III
General Manager, Ireland: Richard Finn
Director, Commercial Sales: Mark Russell
Corporate Communications Manager: Cliff Silver
Auditors: PricewaterhouseCoopers LLP

LOCATIONS

HQ: Microsemi Corporation
2381 Morse Ave., Irvine, CA 92614
Phone: 949-221-7100 **Fax:** 949-756-0308
Web: www.microsemi.com

Microsemi has operations in China, France, Hong Kong, Ireland, Macao, Singapore, Taiwan, and the US.

2006 Sales

	$ mil.	% of total
US	323.3	87
Europe	41.9	11
Asia	5.3	2
Total	**370.5**	**100**

PRODUCTS/OPERATIONS

2006 Sales

	$ mil.	% of total
Defense	117.7	32
Commercial air & space	82.6	22
Notebooks, monitors & LCD TVs	57.2	15
Medical	39.8	11
Industrial & semiconductor capital equipment	39.0	11
Mobile connectivity	34.2	9
Total	**370.5**	**100**

Selected Products

Application-specific standard products (ASSPs)
  Audio amplification integrated circuits (ICs)
  Backlight inverters
  Small computer standard interface (SCSI) terminators
Discrete components
  Automatic surge protectors
  Computer switching diodes
  Low-leakage and high-voltage diodes
  Silicon rectifiers
  Transient suppressor diodes
  Transistors
  Zener diodes
Standard linear ICs (SLICs)
  Low-dropout regulators (LDOs)
  Pulse width modulators (PWMs)

COMPETITORS

ANADIGICS
Analog Devices
Analogic Technologies
Conexant Systems
Diodes
Fairchild Semiconductor
Freescale Semiconductor
International Rectifier
IXYS
Linear Technology
Maxim Integrated Products
Micrel
Monolithic Power Systems
National Semiconductor
NXP
O2Micro
ON Semiconductor
RF Micro Devices
Sanken Electric
Semtech
Skyworks
STMicroelectronics
Texas Instruments
TriQuint
Vishay Intertechnology
Vitesse Semiconductor
Zarlink

HISTORICAL FINANCIALS

Company Type: Public

Income Statement

FYE: Sun. nearest September 30

	REVENUE ($ mil.)	NET INCOME ($ mil.)	NET PROFIT MARGIN	EMPLOYEES
9/06	370.5	35.7	9.6%	2,049
9/05	297.4	29.2	9.8%	1,443
9/04	244.8	5.6	2.3%	1,585
9/03	197.4	(11.5)	—	1,712
9/02	212.6	(4.7)	—	1,572
Annual Growth	14.9%	—		6.8%

2006 Year-End Financials

Debt ratio: —
Return on equity: 10.1%
Cash ($ mil.): 165.4
Current ratio: 6.66
Long-term debt ($ mil.): —
No. of shares (mil.): 71.6
Dividends
  Yield: —
  Payout: —
Market value ($ mil.): 1,349.1
R&D as % of sales: —
Advertising as % of sales: —

Stock History

NASDAQ (GS): MSCC

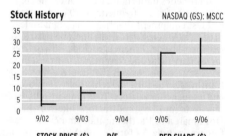

	STOCK PRICE ($) FY Close	P/E High/Low		PER SHARE ($) Earnings	Dividends	Book Value
9/06	18.85	64	38	0.50	—	6.33
9/05	25.54	57	31	0.45	—	4.01
9/04	13.72	191	82	0.09	—	3.09
9/03	8.09	—	—	(0.19)	—	5.84
9/02	2.99	—	—	(0.08)	—	6.18
Annual Growth	58.5%	—	—	—	—	0.6%

MidSouth Bancorp

For banking in the Deep South, try MidSouth. MidSouth Bancorp is the holding company for MidSouth Bank and Lamar Bank, which together operate 28 branches (22 in southern Louisiana and six in East Texas). Targeting individuals and local business customers, the banks offer such standard retail services as checking and savings accounts, savings bonds, investment accounts, and credit card services. They also provide real estate mortgages, and commercial, consumer, agricultural, and short-term business loans. MidSouth also offers lease-financing loans for business equipment.

The company expanded into Texas with its 2004 purchase of Beaumont-based Lamar Bancshares. It is changing the name of its Lamar Bank branches to MidSouth Bank to emphasize the MidSouth brand. Real estate mortgages account for the largest portion of the bank's loan portfolio, followed by business loans. MidSouth liquidated the loan portfolio of its Financial Services of the South subsidiary.

EXECUTIVES

Chairman, MidSouth Bancorp and MidSouth Bank: Will G. Charbonnet Sr., age 58
Vice Chairman: J. B. Hargroder, age 75
President, CEO, and Director, MidSouth Bancorp and MidSouth Bank: C. R. (Rusty) Cloutier, age 59, $343,183 pay
SEVP, Secretary, and Director: Karen L. Hail, age 52, $227,732 pay
EVP and CFO, MidSouth Bancorp, MidSouth Bank, and Lamar Bank: J. Eustis Corrigan Jr., age 41
SVP and Controller: Teri S. Stelly, age 46
EVP; SVP and Senior Loan Officer, MidSouth Bank: Donald R. Landry, age 49, $185,543 pay
SVP and CIO, MidSouth Bank: Jennifer S. Fontenot, age 51, $114,460 pay
SVP, Credit Administration, MidSouth Bank: Christopher J. Levanti, age 39
SVP, Retail Banking, MidSouth Bank: A. Dwight Utz, age 52, $127,532 pay
SVP, Risk Management, MidSouth Bank: Gregory E. King, age 50
Human Resources Director: Sarah Hubal
Investor Relations: Sally D. Gary
Auditors: Porter Keadle Moore, LLP

LOCATIONS

HQ: MidSouth Bancorp, Inc.
102 Versailles Blvd., Lafayette, LA 70501
Phone: 337-237-8343   **Fax:** 337-267-4434
Web: www.midsouthbank.com

MidSouth Bancorp has locations in the following Louisiana cities: Breaux Bridge, Cecilia, Houma, Jeanerette, Jennings, Lafayette, Lake Charles, Morgan City, New Iberia, Opelousas, Sulphur, and Thibodaux. The Lamar Bank division has locations in Beaumont, College Station, Conroe, and Vidor, Texas.

PRODUCTS/OPERATIONS

2005 Sales

	$ mil.	% of total
Interest		
Loans	32.3	64
Securities	5.9	12
Other	0.3	—
Noninterest		
Deposit service charges	8.3	16
Other	4.0	8
Total	**50.8**	**100**

COMPETITORS

Capital One
Hancock Holding
IBERIABANK
Regions Financial
Teche Holding
Wachovia
Whitney Holding

HISTORICAL FINANCIALS

Company Type: Public

Income Statement

FYE: December 31

	ASSETS ($ mil.)	NET INCOME ($ mil.)	INCOME AS % OF ASSETS	EMPLOYEES
12/05	698.8	7.3	1.0%	337
12/04	610.1	7.0	1.1%	300
12/03	432.7	6.3	1.5%	216
12/02	382.7	4.4	1.1%	212
12/01	363.8	2.9	0.8%	205
Annual Growth	**17.7%**	**26.0%**	**—**	**13.2%**

2005 Year-End Financials

Equity as % of assets: 7.6%
Return on assets: 1.1%
Return on equity: 14.3%
Long-term debt ($ mil.): 15.5
No. of shares (mil.): 5.0
Market value ($ mil.): 106.9
Dividends
Yield: 1.1%
Payout: 20.0%
Sales ($ mil.): 50.8
R&D as % of sales: —
Advertising as % of sales: —

Stock History

AMEX: MSL

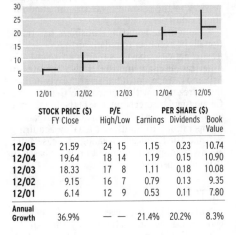

	STOCK PRICE ($) FY Close	P/E High/Low		PER SHARE ($) Earnings	Dividends	Book Value
12/05	21.59	24	15	1.15	0.23	10.74
12/04	19.64	18	14	1.19	0.15	10.90
12/03	18.33	17	8	1.11	0.18	10.08
12/02	9.15	16	7	0.79	0.13	9.35
12/01	6.14	12	9	0.53	0.11	7.80
Annual Growth	**36.9%**	**—**	**—**	**21.4%**	**20.2%**	**8.3%**

Miller Industries

If you're unfortunate enough to be involved in a car accident or to be marooned by mechanical failure, your next ride might come in a vehicle made by Miller Industries. The company makes bodies for light- and heavy-duty wreckers, along with car carriers and multi-vehicle trailers, at plants in the US and Europe. Its multi-vehicle trailers can carry as many as eight vehicles. Miller Industries' US brand names include Century, Challenger, Champion, Chevron, Eagle, Holmes, Vulcan, and Titan. The company's European brands are Jige (France) and Boniface (UK). Miller and rival Jerr-Dan dominate the US market for wrecker bodies.

In order to reduce expenses and focus on core operations, Miller Industries has exited the towing services business and is winding down the operations of its distribution business. The company's products are sold through independent distributors.

Founder, chairman, and co-CEO William Miller owns about 14% of the company.

HISTORY

Headed by William Miller, the Miller Group (which owned Challenger Wrecker and Holmes International) acquired the wrecking operations of Century Holdings in 1990 and formed the basis for Miller Industries. However, Miller Industries wasn't officially created until 1994, when the Miller Group placed all its wrecking and towing businesses under that moniker. The company went public in 1995.

With an established base in tow-truck manufacturing, Miller Industries began to expand vertically in 1996. The company created a financial services unit that year to provide loans to towing-service and distribution companies. It started acquiring towing-equipment distributors of its own at that time. Also in 1996 the company moved overseas with the acquisition of European tow-truck makers S.A. Jige Lohr Wreckers (France) and Boniface Engineering Limited (UK).

In early 1997 Miller Industries made a massive push into towing-service companies, creating RoadOne with the intention of becoming a nationwide entity. The company acquired 29 towing-service companies in fiscal 1997, 47 in 1998, and 35 in 1999. Then its pace slowed — Miller Industries acquired only a handful of towing-service businesses in 2000.

Miller proposed a 1-for-5 stock split to shareholders in 2001 in hopes of avoiding being delisted from the New York Stock Exchange. The company managed to keep its shares trading on the NYSE by trimming costs, which it accomplished by moving to exit the distribution and towing services businesses, beginning in 2002. By the end of 2004 Miller had disposed of the assets of RoadOne and nearly all of its distribution operations.

EXECUTIVES

Chairman and Co-CEO: William G. (Bill) Miller, age 59, $180,000 pay
President, Co-CEO, and Director: Jeffrey I. (Jeff) Badgley, age 54, $306,710 pay
EVP, Secretary, and General Counsel: Frank Madonia, age 57, $216,707 pay
EVP and CFO; President, Financial Services Group: J. Vincent Mish, age 55, $196,706 pay
Director, Human Resources: Bill Bakely
Auditors: Joseph Decosimo and Company, LLP

LOCATIONS

HQ: Miller Industries, Inc.
8503 Hilltop Dr., Ooltewah, TN 37363
Phone: 423-238-4171   **Fax:** 423-238-5371
Web: www.millerind.com

Miller Industries has manufacturing facilities in France, the UK, and the US (Pennsylvania and Tennessee).

2005 Sales

	$ mil.	% of total
North America	283.2	80
Other regions	68.7	20
Total	**351.9**	**100**

PRODUCTS/OPERATIONS

Selected Products

Boniface (heavy-duty wreckers for the European market)
Century (wreckers, car carriers)
Challenger (wreckers, car carriers)
Champion (car carriers)
Chevron (wreckers, car carriers, towing and recovery equipment)
Eagle (light-duty wreckers)
Holmes (mid-priced wreckers and car carriers)
Jige (light- and heavy-duty wreckers and car carriers for the European market)
Vulcan (wreckers, car carriers, towing and recovery equipment)

COMPETITORS

Jerr-Dan
Mitsubishi Fuso

HISTORICAL FINANCIALS

Company Type: Public

Income Statement

FYE: December 31

	REVENUE ($ mil.)	NET INCOME ($ mil.)	NET PROFIT MARGIN	EMPLOYEES
12/05	351.9	18.6	5.3%	900
12/04	236.3	5.5	2.3%	840
12/03	206.0	(14.1)	—	950
12/02	203.1	(45.7)	—	1,000
12/01	304.0	(21.6)	—	1,075
Annual Growth	**3.7%**	**—**	**—**	**(4.3%)**

2005 Year-End Financials

Debt ratio: 25.9%
Return on equity: 33.4%
Cash ($ mil.): 6.2
Current ratio: 1.80
Long-term debt ($ mil.): 16.8
No. of shares (mil.): 11.3

Dividends
 Yield: —
 Payout: —
Market value ($ mil.): 229.4
R&D as % of sales: —
Advertising as % of sales: —

Stock History

NYSE: MLR

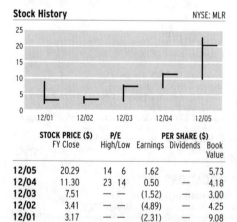

	STOCK PRICE ($) FY Close	P/E High/Low		PER SHARE ($) Earnings	Dividends	Book Value
12/05	20.29	14	6	1.62	—	5.73
12/04	11.30	23	14	0.50	—	4.18
12/03	7.51	—	—	(1.52)	—	3.00
12/02	3.41	—	—	(4.89)	—	4.25
12/01	3.17	—	—	(2.31)	—	9.08
Annual Growth	**59.1%**	**—**	**—**	**—**	**—**	**(10.9%)**

Mitcham Industries

Here's a shock. Mitcham Industries has few rivals that can match 'em when it comes to leasing and sales of seismic equipment to the global seismic industry. The company's seismic equipment offerings include channel boxes, geophones, earth vibrators, various cables, and other peripheral equipment. Through short-term leasing (three to nine months) from Mitcham Industries, oil and gas companies can improve their chances of drilling a productive well and reduce equipment costs. Most of Mitcham Industries' leases are located in North America. Its two wholly owned subsidiaries are Mitcham Canada Ltd. and Seismic Asia Pacific Pty Ltd.

Mitcham Industries' seismic surveys, used to identify and define potential reservoirs of oil and gas, involve generating an acoustic wave into the earth using compressed air, explosives, or vibrators. Geophones then capture the reflected energy, and channel boxes convert the signals from analog to digital data, which is later interpreted.

In an effort to anticipate the need for seismic surveys and create new business, Mitcham Industries formed Drilling Services Inc. (DSI) in 2002. Mitcham sold the newly formed subsidiary in 2003 to WBW Enterprises of Texas in an effort to focus on its core operating units. The company acquired Seamap International, a provider of products and services to the seismic, hydrographic, and offshore industries, in 2005.

Although the company's business has traditionally been concentrated in North America, its leasing activities have been on the rise in Latin America. Mitcham Industries also operates in Asia and Europe, and it has an exclusive marketing agreement with Compagnie Générale de Géophysique's Sercel unit, one of the top seismic equipment makers. The company has expanded its operations to Southeast Asia by acquiring Seismic Asia Pacific, an oceanographic, seismic, and hydrographic equipment provider based in Brisbane, Australia.

HISTORY

Mitcham Industries was founded in 1987 by geophysical industry veteran Billy Mitcham Jr., a former Halliburton employee. The firm's strategy included growing and diversifying its lease pool of seismic equipment, expanding its international presence, and developing alliances with major seismic equipment manufacturers. In 1994 the company entered into an agreement with leading equipment maker Input/Output (I/O): Mitcham Industries bought I/O equipment, and, in turn, I/O referred rental inquiries.

The company went public in 1995. The next year Mitcham Industries penned another agreement with Sercel (a subsidiary of France's Compagnie Générale de Géophysique, S.A.) and became the manufacturer's exclusive worldwide leasing agent. Because Sercel was a major player in Canada, the deal immediately pumped up Mitcham Industries' sales in that country.

After the oil industry downturn in 1998, the company decided it only had room for one major marketing partner: In 1999 it terminated the agreement with I/O and renewed its deal with Sercel. Mitcham Industries launched a stock buyback in 2000.

A year later, the company settled a 1998 lawsuit brought by shareholders (who claimed that Mitcham had made misleading statements about its finances) for about $2.7 million.

In 2002 Mitcham formed subsidiary Drilling Services (DSI) to provide front-end services (permitting, surveying, shot hole drilling, and other activities) for its customers. It later sold the operating assets of DSI to WBW Enterprises and returned it focus to its core operating units.

In 2003 the company moved in to the Southeast Asia market by acquiring Australian-based equipment supplier Seismic Asia Pacific. In 2004 the company decided to separate the roles of its chairman, president, and CEO positions. Billy Mitcham stepped down as chairman, retaining his role as president and CEO. Director Peter Blum replaced Mitcham as chairman.

To complement its marine rental and sales business, in 2005 Mitcham purchased Seamap International Holdings and its three subsidiaries in Texas, the UK, and Singapore for $6.5 million. The units produce proprietary products for the seismic, hydrographic, and offshore industries.

EXECUTIVES

Non-Executive Chairman: Peter H. Blum, age 49
President, CEO, and Director: Billy F. Mitcham Jr., age 58, $355,240 pay
EVP Finance, CFO, and Director: Robert P. (Rob) Capps, age 52
VP Business Development: Paul (Guy) Rogers, age 56, $163,527 pay
VP Marine Systems: Guy Malden, age 54, $160,018 pay
Manager Vibes and Drills: Tim Holden
Accounting: Cheryl Wilson
Information Technology and Web Site: Craig Middleton
Sales: Pascal Hythier
Sales: Howard White
Used Equipment Sales: Jim Croix

LOCATIONS

HQ: Mitcham Industries, Inc.
 8141 SH 75 South, Huntsville, TX 77342
Phone: 936-291-2277 **Fax:** 936-295-1922
Web: www.mitchamindustries.com

Mitcham Industries has operations in the US, Canada, Singapore, and the UK, and representatives in Argentina, Hungary, and the Netherlands.

2006 Sales

	$ mil.	% of total
North America		
US	9.4	27
Canada	8.9	26
Asia	10.5	30
South America	3.2	9
Europe	2.4	7
Other regions	0.2	1
Total	**34.6**	**100**

PRODUCTS/OPERATIONS

2006 Sales

	$ mil.	% of total
Equipment leasing	22.1	64
Equipment sales		
Lease pool equipment sales	5.2	15
Other equipment sales	7.3	21
Total	**34.6**	**100**

Selected Products

Boats	Radio systems
Buoys	Refraction systems
CDP cables	Seismographs
CDP systems	Shooting systems
Drills	Streamers
Energy sources	Tape trasports
Geophones	Telemetry systems
GPR	Telemetry cables
Heli Bags	Test equipment
Hydrophones	Vehicles
MarshPhones	Vibrators
Plotters	Vibrator electronics

COMPETITORS

Ashtead Group
Baker Hughes
CGG
Dawson Geophysical
Halliburton
Input/Output
OYO Geospace
Petroleum Geo-Services
Schlumberger
Seitel
Veritas DGC

HISTORICAL FINANCIALS
Company Type: Public

Income Statement
FYE: January 31

	REVENUE ($ mil.)	NET INCOME ($ mil.)	NET PROFIT MARGIN	EMPLOYEES
1/06	34.6	10.9	31.5%	111
1/05	26.4	2.1	8.0%	68
1/04	22.4	(6.3)	—	62
1/03	19.1	(10.1)	—	138
1/02	27.2	(8.5)	—	77
Annual Growth	6.2%	—	—	9.6%

2006 Year-End Financials

Debt ratio: 6.3%
Return on equity: 26.8%
Cash ($ mil.): 19.0
Current ratio: 4.15
Long-term debt ($ mil.): 3.0
No. of shares (mil.): 9.4
Dividends
  Yield: —
  Payout: —
Market value ($ mil.): 241.2
R&D as % of sales: —
Advertising as % of sales: —

Stock History
NASDAQ (GM): MIND

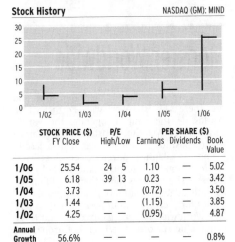

	STOCK PRICE ($) FY Close	P/E High/Low		PER SHARE ($) Earnings	Dividends	Book Value
1/06	25.54	24	5	1.10	—	5.02
1/05	6.18	39	13	0.23	—	3.42
1/04	3.73	—	—	(0.72)	—	3.50
1/03	1.44	—	—	(1.15)	—	3.85
1/02	4.25	—	—	(0.95)	—	4.87
Annual Growth	56.6%	—	—	—	—	0.8%

Mobility Electronics

Mobility Electronics wants to bridge the gap between functionality and portability. The company designs and sells universal docking stations for portable and handheld computers and other mobile devices. Its EasiDock products allow mobile computer users to connect full-size peripherals such as keyboards, mice, and monitors to their portable PCs. Mobility also designs connectivity and power products for portable computers, including products for use in cars and airplanes. It sells to computer manufacturers including Dell and Lenovo, as well as distributors and retailers. Mobility expanded its distribution channels with its 2002 acquisition of online electronics retailer iGo.

EXECUTIVES

Chairman, President, and CEO:
Charles R. (Charlie) Mollo, age 54, $368,194 pay
EVP, CFO, and Treasurer: Joan W. Brubacher, age 52, $251,503 pay
SVP, Worldwide Sales and Distribution:
Jonathan Downer
VP, Controller, and Chief Accounting Officer:
Darryl S. Baker, age 37
VP, General Counsel, and Secretary: Brian M. Roberts, age 33
Auditors: KPMG LLP

LOCATIONS

HQ: Mobility Electronics, Inc.
  17800 N. Perimeter Dr., Ste. 200,
  Scottsdale, AZ 85255
Phone: 480-596-0061   **Fax:** 480-596-0349
Web: www.mobilityelectronics.com

2005 Sales

	$ mil.	% of total
North America	73.1	86
Asia/Pacific	6.4	7
Other regions	6.0	7
Total	**85.5**	**100**

PRODUCTS/OPERATIONS

2005 Sales

	$ mil.	% of total
High-power mobile power	53.9	63
Handheld	12.2	14
Low-power mobile power	10.2	12
Expansion & docking products	6.3	7
Accessories & other	2.9	4
Total	**85.5**	**100**

2005 Sales by Channel

	% of total
OEM & private-label resellers	63
Retailers & distributors	27
Other	10
Total	**100**

Selected Products

Docking stations
Handheld cradles
Monitor stands
Peripheral component interface (PCI) and drive bay
  expanders
Power products, including in-auto and in-air chargers

COMPETITORS

ACCO Brands	Dell
Acer	Gateway
American Power	Hewlett-Packard
Conversion	Lenovo
Apple	Panasonic
Belkin	Sony
Comarco	Toshiba

HISTORICAL FINANCIALS
Company Type: Public

Income Statement
FYE: December 31

	REVENUE ($ mil.)	NET INCOME ($ mil.)	NET PROFIT MARGIN	EMPLOYEES
12/05	85.5	5.0	5.8%	156
12/04	70.2	(2.2)	—	137
12/03	51.9	(3.6)	—	123
12/02	31.3	(18.9)	—	134
12/01	28.3	(19.7)	—	126
Annual Growth	31.8%	—	—	5.5%

2005 Year-End Financials

Debt ratio: 0.0%
Return on equity: 10.0%
Cash ($ mil.): 33.9
Current ratio: 2.81
Long-term debt ($ mil.): 0.0
No. of shares (mil.): 30.8
Dividends
  Yield: —
  Payout: —
Market value ($ mil.): 298.0
R&D as % of sales: —
Advertising as % of sales: —

Stock History
NASDAQ (GM): MOBE

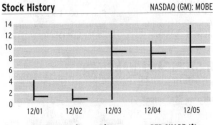

	STOCK PRICE ($) FY Close	P/E High/Low		PER SHARE ($) Earnings	Dividends	Book Value
12/05	9.66	84	38	0.16	—	1.92
12/04	8.58	—	—	(0.08)	—	1.43
12/03	8.94	—	—	(0.17)	—	1.49
12/02	0.76	—	—	(1.11)	—	0.87
12/01	1.25	—	—	(1.33)	—	1.99
Annual Growth	66.7%	—	—	—	—	(0.9%)

MOD-PAC

MOD-PAC sounds like something Austin Powers might put on, but it's just a boxmaker, baby! Yeah! Formerly a division of Astronics, MOD-PAC manufactures stock packaging for small gift and candy retailers and custom paperboard packaging products for consumer goods companies. It also prints business cards, postcards, sell sheets, party invitations, napkins, and the like, as part of its commercial and personalized printing operations. MOD-PAC serves more than 4,000 customers around the world. The company was established in 1881, acquired by Astronics in 1972, and subsequently spun off in 2003. Chairman Kevin Keane owns more than one-third of the company.

EXECUTIVES

Chairman: Kevin T. Keane, age 73
President, CEO, and Director: Daniel G. Keane, age 40, $434,000 pay
CFO: David B. Lupp
Chief Information Officer: Marie L. Smith
VP, Marketing: Charles H. (Chuck) Biddlecom
VP, Operations: Larry N. Kessler
VP, Sales: Philip C. Rechin
President, Krepe-Kraft Division: Leo T. Eckman
VP, Marketing, Krepe-Kraft Division: Diane M. Sims
VP, Krepe-Kraft Division: Donna L. Eckman
Corporate Controller: Daniel J. Geary
Auditors: Ernst & Young LLP

LOCATIONS

HQ: MOD-PAC CORP.
 1801 Elmwood Ave., Buffalo, NY 14207
Phone: 716-873-0640 **Fax:** 716-447-9201
Web: www.modpac.com

PRODUCTS/OPERATIONS

Selected Subsidiaries
MOD-PAC Air, LLC
MOD-PAC Pilot CORP.
180-1807 Elmwood Avenue, LLC

COMPETITORS

BCT International
Caraustar
Field Container
Graphic Packaging
MeadWestvaco

Modern Postcard
Schwarz
Shorewood Packaging
Smurfit-Stone Container
Taylor Corporation

HISTORICAL FINANCIALS

Company Type: Public

Income Statement

FYE: December 31

	REVENUE ($ mil.)	NET INCOME ($ mil.)	NET PROFIT MARGIN	EMPLOYEES
12/05	71.2	11.0	15.4%	435
12/04	50.3	3.7	7.4%	470
12/03	41.2	2.1	5.1%	405
12/02	32.1	2.0	6.2%	278
12/01	30.8	1.7	5.5%	160
Annual Growth	23.3%	59.5%	—	28.4%

2005 Year-End Financials

Debt ratio: 6.0%
Return on equity: 38.7%
Cash ($ mil.): 3.9
Current ratio: 2.42
Long-term debt ($ mil.): 2.0
No. of shares (mil.): 2.7

Dividends
 Yield: —
 Payout: —
Market value ($ mil.): 30.5
R&D as % of sales: —
Advertising as % of sales: 1.5%

Stock History

NASDAQ (GM): MPAC

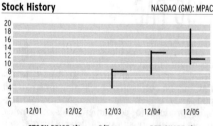

	STOCK PRICE ($) FY Close	P/E High/Low		PER SHARE ($) Earnings	Dividends	Book Value
12/05	11.24	6	3	2.97	—	12.01
12/04	12.76	14	8	0.97	—	8.93
12/03	8.00	16	7	0.54	—	7.95
Annual Growth	18.5%	—	—	134.5%	—	22.9%

Monolithic Power Systems

Monolithic Power Systems (MPS) doesn't make enormous electrical equipment, but rather tiny silicon chips. The fabless company offers analog and mixed-signal semiconductors — especially chips for lighting displays — that are used in digital cameras, PDAs, wireless LAN equipment, wireless phones, and other electronic devices. MPS outsources production of its chips to China-based foundry ASMC. The company's products are incorporated into electronic gear from tech heavyweights such as Dell, Hewlett-Packard, Motorola, Samsung Electronics, and Sony. The three largest customers for MPS' products are distributors.

Litigation with competitors such as Linear Technology, Micrel, Microsemi, and O2Micro International is a big portion of Monolithic Power's spending budget, consuming 20% of 2005 sales — more than it spent on R&D that year. The company reached settlements with Micrel and Microsemi in 2006, paying $3 million to Micrel.

InveStar Capital owns about 14% of Monolithic Power Systems. J. & W. Seligman holds around 10% of the company. BA Venture Partners, CEO Michael Hsing, and chief design engineer and director Jim Moyer each have an equity stake of about 7%. Investor Philippe Laffont and FMR (Fidelity Investments) each own more than 6% of MPS.

EXECUTIVES

President, CEO, and Director: Michael R. Hsing, age 46, $356,615 pay
CFO: Richard (Rick) Neely, age 51
VP, Finance and Controller: Daniel Benas
VP, Operations: Deming Xiao, age 43, $305,981 pay
VP and General Counsel: Saria Tseng, age 35, $216,000 pay
VP, Sales and Marketing: Maurice Sciammas, age 46, $211,346 pay
Chief Design Engineer and Director:
 James C. (Jim) Moyer, age 63, $200,716 pay
Auditors: Deloitte & Touche LLP

LOCATIONS

HQ: Monolithic Power Systems, Inc.
 983 University Ave., Bldg. A, Los Gatos, CA 95032
Phone: 408-357-6600 **Fax:** 408-357-6601
Web: www.monolithicpower.com

Monolithic Power Systems has offices in China, Japan, South Korea, Taiwan, and the US.

2005 Sales

	$ mil.	% of total
China	47.1	48
Taiwan	31.0	31
South Korea	11.9	12
Japan	4.1	4
US	2.0	2
Other countries	3.0	3
Total	**99.1**	**100**

PRODUCTS/OPERATIONS

2005 Sales

	$ mil.	% of total
DC-to-DC converters	57.8	58
LCD backlight inverters	38.1	39
Audio amplifiers	3.2	3
Total	**99.1**	**100**

COMPETITORS

Analog Devices
Fairchild Semiconductor
Intersil
Linear Technology
Maxim Integrated Products
Micrel

Microsemi
National Semiconductor
O2Micro
Semtech
STMicroelectronics
Texas Instruments

HISTORICAL FINANCIALS

Company Type: Public

Income Statement

FYE: December 31

	REVENUE ($ mil.)	NET INCOME ($ mil.)	NET PROFIT MARGIN	EMPLOYEES
12/05	99.1	5.1	5.1%	240
12/04	47.6	(3.7)	—	154
12/03	24.2	(3.0)	—	104
12/02	12.2	(3.2)	—	
Annual Growth	101.0%	—	—	51.9%

2005 Year-End Financials

Debt ratio: —
Return on equity: 7.2%
Cash ($ mil.): 63.9
Current ratio: 3.94
Long-term debt ($ mil.): —
No. of shares (mil.): 29.2

Dividends
 Yield: —
 Payout: —
Market value ($ mil.): 437.0
R&D as % of sales: 12.3%
Advertising as % of sales: —

Stock History

NASDAQ (GM): MPWR

	STOCK PRICE ($) FY Close	P/E High/Low		PER SHARE ($) Earnings	Dividends	Book Value
12/05	14.99	103	34	0.17	—	2.68
12/04	9.30	—	—	(0.54)	—	2.30
Annual Growth	61.2%	—	—	—	—	16.3%

Monster Worldwide

There are "monstrous" global companies, and then there is Monster Worldwide. Formerly TMP Worldwide, the company operates the world's #1 job search Web site, Monster. (It has retained the top position among job search sites despite losing its planned purchase of chief rival HotJobs.com to Internet giant Yahoo!.) The Monster site features more than 1 million job ads and a database of more than 34 million resumes for recruiters to browse through. Monster Worldwide has reorganized around three geographic regions: Asia/Pacific, Europe, and North America. It boasts most *FORTUNE* 500 companies as clients. Former chairman and CEO Andrew McKelvey controls about 32% of Monster Worldwide.

Monster Worldwide is reviewing its stock options grant program after it was revealed that the company often granted stock options dated before steep rises in its share price. (The US Securities and Exchange Commission is reviewing

practices at more than 30 public companies to see if options were backdated to boost top executives' compensation.) Amidst this controversy, founder Andrew McKelvey stepped down as chairman and CEO in October 2006. He resigned from the board of directors at the end of the month, refusing to answer questions about past accounting practices.

In September 2006 the company sold one of its original businesses, recruitment advertising agency TMP Worldwide Advertising & Communications, to agency managers and an investment fund managed by Veronis Suhler Stevenson for $45 million. The move caps a string of divestments — including the spinoffs of its eResourcing and Executive Search business units and the sale of its Yellow Pages advertising services segment — intended to sharpen the company's focus on the Monster business.

Along with Monster.com, Monster manages Fastweb.com and MonsterTRAK.com, job search sites for secondary school and college students, and it offers a forum for executives to search for posts (ChiefMonster).

Monster Worldwide has used more than 100 acquisitions in the past decade to stockpile its businesses, which the company hopes to converge on the Web in a network offering job seekers the ability to go from "intern-to-CEO." The company boosted its offerings in Asia with its 2005 acquisition of South Korean jobs site JobKorea for $94 million. It has also consolidated offices and cut jobs to combat the weak employment market.

In late 2006, Monster Worldwide inked a partnership deal with diversified media business Freedom Communications to provide recruitment services and branded job Web sites for Freedom's newspaper and television holdings. The deal is part of Monster's strategy to zero in on small and midsized local markets.

HISTORY

Andrew McKelvey founded TMP (which stood for Telephone Marketing Program) in 1967. It began buying up other Yellow Page ad agencies and folding them into its business, and by the end of the 1980s, the company was out in front in the Yellow Pages ad market. McKelvey began to look into other related areas of business.

In the 1990s TMP entered the recruitment classified advertising market with its 1993 purchase of Bentley, Barnes & Lynn. Over the next five years, TMP bought more than 40 recruitment ad shops, making it an international player. Its Austin Knight agency, a UK-US joint venture formed in 1997, helped TMP become the UK's largest recruitment ad firm.

The 1990s also saw the company merge onto the information superhighway at great speed. In 1993 the company launched its Online Career Center Web site, which listed some 150,000 jobs from an array of companies. In 1995 McKelvey bought Boston-based ad agency Adion and its Monster Board online job posting site for just $3 million. TMP went public in 1996. Investors eventually latched onto its Internet play and sent its stock soaring.

The next year TMP bought one Yellow Pages ad agency and four more international recruitment ad agencies. In 1998 it expanded the range of its Interactive Division with About Work, an online internship database. TMP also combined its Online Career Center and Monster Board sites to form Monster.com.

The ascent to the top spot in the industry began for TMP in 1999 with several strategic acquisitions. That year it bought LAI Worldwide, one of the top job recruitment companies in the US, which it combined with its TASA Worldwide unit, also purchased that year. In 2000 TMP bought UK-based HW Group and Toronto-based Illsley Bourbonnais, two executive headhunting firms, as part of TMP's plan to expand globally. It also bought Florida-based information technology recruiter System One Services and online relocation service VirtualRelocation.com.

Later that year the company launched relocation and real estate Web site Monstermoving.com and executive search site ChiefMonster.com. TMP also expanded its Executive Resourcing division in 2000 with the acquisitions of Stratascape and Sweden-based SCI Search Competence International. Monster.com (now just Monster) bought college job search site Jobtrak.com (now MonsterTRAK.com) in late 2000. TMP acquired Framingham, Massachusetts-based IT staffing firm ADEPT the following year. It later agreed to buy rival job site HotJobs but lost to a counterbid from Yahoo!.

In 2003 TMP spun off its eResourcing and Executive Search business units and changed its name to Monster Worldwide as it refocused its energy on its Web operations. In 2004 the company acquired Military Advantage, which offers career, educational, and other resources for military personnel and veterans, and Tickle, a provider of online career assessment testing.

The next year, Monster Worldwide acquired Emailjob.com, an online job site owned by Reed Expositions France. The company sold its Yellow Pages division in 2005 for $80 million to the Audax Group.

Focusing solely on its Monster operations, the company moved to sell off its advertising recruitment businesses in 2005 and 2006.

In October 2006, Andrew McKelvey stepped down as chairman and CEO, and William Pastore, the president and COO, was promoted to CEO.

EXECUTIVES

CEO and Director: William M. (Bill) Pastore, age 58
EVP and Head, Asia-Pacific: John McLaughlin, age 50, $1,400,000 pay
EVP Creative, Sales, and Marketing: Paul M. Camara, age 58, $1,400,000 pay
SVP and CFO: Charles (Lanny) Baker, age 39, $1,303,846 pay
SVP Customer Relationship Management: Linda Soldatos
SVP E-Business: Jeffrey Fleischman
SVP Field Sales: Brian Graham
SVP Government Relations; General Manager, Monster Government Solutions: Phillip (Phil) Bond
SVP Global Brand Manager: David Rosa
SVP Strategy and Corporate Development: Marcel Legrand
SVP Customer Service, Monster: Kurt Nipp
VP Human Resources, Monster Worldwide North America: Lori Erickson
VP Investor Relations: Robert Jones
Chief Risk Officer: Timothy P. Spillane
Global Controller and Chief Accounting Officer: Jon Trumbull, age 38
Chairman, Military.com: Christopher Michel
Group President, Europe: Peter Dolphin, age 58
Group President, International: Steve Pogorzelski, age 44
President, Asia Pacific: Tony Balfour, age 46
President, Monster North America: Douglas E. (Doug) Klinger, age 41
Auditors: BDO Seidman, LLP

LOCATIONS

HQ: Monster Worldwide, Inc.
622 3rd Ave., 39th Fl., New York, NY 10017
Phone: 212-351-7000   **Fax:** 646-658-0541
Web: www.monsterworldwide.com

Monster Worldwide has offices in approximately 25 countries around the world.

2005 Sales

	$ mil.	% of total
US	703.8	71
Europe		
UK	98.1	10
Other countries	140.1	14
Other regions	44.9	5
Total	**986.9**	**100**

PRODUCTS/OPERATIONS

2005 Sales

	$ mil.	% of total
Monster	818.3	83
Advertising & communications	168.6	17
Total	**986.9**	**100**

COMPETITORS

Bernard Hodes
CareerBuilder
HotJobs
Kforce
Russell Reynolds
Volt Information
Workstream

HISTORICAL FINANCIALS

Company Type: Public

Income Statement
FYE: December 31

	REVENUE ($ mil.)	NET INCOME ($ mil.)	NET PROFIT MARGIN	EMPLOYEES
12/05	986.9	98.2	10.0%	4,800
12/04	845.5	73.1	8.6%	5,000
12/03	679.6	(81.9)	—	4,300
12/02	1,114.6	(534.9)	—	8,500
12/01	1,448.1	69.0	4.8%	11,000
Annual Growth	**(9.1%)**	**9.2%**	**—**	**(18.7%)**

2005 Year-End Financials

Debt ratio: 1.7%	Dividends
Return on equity: 11.6%	Yield: —
Cash ($ mil.): 320.3	Payout: —
Current ratio: 1.10	Market value ($ mil.): 4,927.1
Long-term debt ($ mil.): 15.7	R&D as % of sales: —
No. of shares (mil.): 120.7	Advertising as % of sales: —

Stock History
NASDAQ (GS): MNST

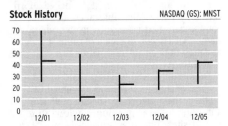

	STOCK PRICE ($) FY Close	P/E High/Low		PER SHARE ($) Earnings	Dividends	Book Value
12/05	40.82	53	28	0.79	—	7.73
12/04	33.64	56	29	0.61	—	6.53
12/03	21.96	—	—	(0.72)	—	4.32
12/02	11.31	—	—	(4.80)	—	7.63
12/01	42.90	113	41	0.61	—	11.58
Annual Growth	**(1.2%)**	**—**	**—**	**6.7%**	**—**	**(9.6%)**

Morningstar

Morningstar offers a smorgasbord of financial information to individual, professional, and institutional investors. The firm's Morningstar.com and MorningstarAdvisor.com feature content on portfolio planning, mutual funds, and stocks. Its *Morningstar Mutual Funds* is a reference publication that features one-page reports on some 1,500 mutual funds. Other publications include monthly stock newsletter *Morningstar StockInvestor*, and monthly fund newsletter *Morningstar FundInvestor*. Its software includes Morningstar Advisor Workstation, a Web-based investment planning system, and Principia, a CD-ROM-based investment research and planning application. Chairman and CEO Joe Mansueto owns 75% of Morningstar.

The company's Morningstar Style Box, which provides a visual summary of a mutual fund's underlying investment style, and Morningstar Ratings, which rates past performance based on risk- and cost-adjusted returns, have become fixtures on the investment landscape.

Morningstar's key product for institutional clients is Licensed Data, a set of investment data spanning eight core databases, available through electronic data feeds. The company also has an investment consulting practice for institutions that provides asset allocation and fund research.

Mansueto has purchased business magazines *Inc.* and *Fast Company* from Gruner + Jahr for about $35 million.

HISTORY

Joseph Mansueto founded Morningstar in 1984, using a line borrowed from Thoreau's *Walden* ("The sun is but a morning star"). Armed with an MBA and experience culled from a stint as a securities analyst for Harris Associates, Mansueto published *Mutual Fund Sourcebook,* a tome outlining performance histories and other information on 400 stock mutual funds. The boom in mutual funds during the early 1980s spurred interest in Morningstar's product and prompted the company to add a second publication, *Morningstar Mutual Funds,* two years later.

The company's 1994 acquisition of MarketBase helped the firm add stock information to its coverage. A 5% staff cut in 1996 and the cessation of some of its publications helped reverse Morningstar's sagging fortunes. It took to cyberspace the following year when it launched Morningstar.Net (now Morningstar.com). That year the company partnered with Japanese digital dynamo SOFTBANK to create Morningstar Japan and present financial information to investors in that country.

Don Phillips, who had joined Morningstar as its first analyst in 1986, was appointed CEO in 1998. The company began offering a subscription-based premium service feature for its Web site to offer users expanded financial coverage. In 1999 Morningstar extended its reach, partnering with FPG Research to offer financial information to residents of Australia and New Zealand. Later that year SOFTBANK invested $91 million in Morningstar.

In 2000 Morningstar established Web site MorningstarAdvisor.com, relaunched its flagship site with additional information and tools, and opened offices in Hong Kong, South Korea, and the UK. Founder and chairman Joe Mansueto

also assumed the role of CEO in 2000 and made Phillips a managing director of the company.

The following year the company launched its Web site in Germany, Italy, the Netherlands, Spain, and the UK. Morningstar added Australian financial publisher Aspect Huntley to its stable in 2006.

EXECUTIVES

Chairman and CEO: Joseph (Joe) Mansueto, age 49, $100,000 pay
COO: Tao Huang, age 43, $717,760 pay
CFO: Martha Dustin Boudos, age 39, $570,000 pay
Managing Director and Board Member: Don Phillips, age 44
Managing Director: Timothy K. (Tim) Armour, age 57
VP Research and New Product Development: John Rekenthaler, age 45
VP Sales: Kishore Gangwani
President and Chief Investment Officer, Morningstar Investment Services: Art Lutschaunig, age 47
President, Advisor Business: Chris Boruff, age 40
President, Data Services Business: Elizabeth (Liz) Kirscher, age 41
President, Ibbotson Associates: Mike Henkel
President, Individual Business: Catherine Gillis Odelbo, age 43, $520,000 pay
President, International Business: Bevin Desmond, age 39
President, Morningstar Associates: Patrick Reinkemeyer, age 40, $600,000 pay
Managing Director, Design: David W. Williams, age 45
Chief of Securities Research: Haywood Kelly
General Counsel and Corporate Secretary: Richard E. Robbins, age 43
Director Corporate Communications: Margaret Kirch Cohen
Director Mutual Fund Research; Editor, Morningstar FundInvestor: Russel Kinnel
Director Research: Paul D. Kaplan
Director Marketing, Morningstar.com: Maureen Dahlen
Auditors: Deloitte & Touche LLP

LOCATIONS

HQ: Morningstar, Inc.
225 W. Wacker Dr., Chicago, IL 60606
Phone: 312-696-6000   **Fax:** 312-696-6001
Web: www.morningstar.com

Morningstar has operations in 16 countries in Asia, Europe, and North America.

PRODUCTS/OPERATIONS

2005 Sales

	$ mil.	% of total
Institutional	95.9	42
Advisor	72.7	31
Individual	63.4	27
Adjustments	(4.9)	—
Total	**227.1**	**100**

Selected Products and Services

MorningstarAdvisor.com (market analysis, stock and fund information, portfolio tools, and investment research for advisors)
Morningstar Advisor Workstation (Web-based investment planning software)
Morningstar FundInvestor (monthly mutual fund newsletter)
Morningstar Licensed Data (electronic investment data feeds)
Morningstar Mutual Funds (semimonthly information on 1,700 mutual funds)
Morningstar Principia (CD-ROM-based investment planning software)
Morningstar StockInvestor (monthly stock newsletter)
Morningstar.com (market analysis, stock and fund information, portfolio tools, and investment research for individuals)

COMPETITORS

Bankrate	McGraw-Hill
Bloomberg	Motley Fool
CDA/Weisenberger	PCQuote.com
Dow Jones	Reuters
Financial Engines	TheStreet.com
HyperFeed	Thomson Corporation
Intuit	Value Line
Ipreo	WisdomTree Investments
MarketWatch	

HISTORICAL FINANCIALS

Company Type: Public

Income Statement

FYE: December 31

	REVENUE ($ mil.)	NET INCOME ($ mil.)	NET PROFIT MARGIN	EMPLOYEES
12/05	227.1	31.1	13.7%	1,130
12/04	179.7	8.8	4.9%	1,000
12/03	139.5	(11.9)	—	—
12/02	109.6	0.4	0.4%	—
12/01	91.2	(9.3)	—	800
Annual Growth	**25.6%**	**—**	**—**	**9.0%**

2005 Year-End Financials

Debt ratio: —
Return on equity: 26.1%
Cash ($ mil.): 153.2
Current ratio: 1.78
Long-term debt ($ mil.): —
No. of shares (mil.): 40.3
Dividends
  Yield: —
  Payout: —
Market value ($ mil.): 1,395.5
R&D as % of sales: 8.7%
Advertising as % of sales: 2.6%

Stock History

NASDAQ (GS): MORN

	STOCK PRICE ($) FY Close	P/E High/Low	PER SHARE ($) Earnings	Dividends	Book Value
12/05	34.64	53 26	0.70	—	4.31

Movado Group

Movado Group knows that time is of the essence. The group's more than a half dozen brands of watches — Movado, Concord, and Ebel, as well as the licensed ESQ, Coach, Tommy Hilfiger, and Hugo Boss lines — are sold worldwide and cover most watch industry categories. Prices range from $55 to more than $10,000 for exclusive watches set with diamonds and other gems. Movado sells watches to more than 10,000 major jewelry store and department store chains (mainly Macy's and Neiman Marcus), as well as to independent jewelers (primarily Helzberg and Zales). Its own retail chain consists of more than 25 boutiques and nearly 30 outlets. Founder Gerry Grinberg and his family control about 70% of Movado's voting power.

Movado makes its Movado, Concord, and Ebel watches primarily in Switzerland. Asian contractors make the ESQ and Tommy Hilfiger

lines, and Swiss suppliers provide the Coach lines. Its retail stores sell Movado designer jewelry, home décor objects, personal and desk accessories, and watches.

The company has expanded its labels by purchasing premier luxury watch brand Ebel from LVMH and signing licensing deals with Hugo Boss, Juicy Couture, and Lacoste.

HISTORY

Cuban-born Gedalio "Gerry" Grinberg arrived in Miami in 1960. He had been the exclusive distributor of Piaget and Omega watches in Cuba before Castro took over. Grinberg began distributing Piaget watches in the US in 1961, and his company took the name North American Watch in 1967 when it acquired US distribution rights to Corum, another line of gold Swiss-made watches. The firm bought the Concord brand four years later.

In 1983 North American Watch acquired Movado, a company that had begun in 1881 in the Swiss workshop of 19-year-old Achille Ditesheim. Movado ("always in motion" in Esperanto) was chosen as a brand name in 1903. The company helped usher in the era of wristwatches early in the century. In 1962 it introduced its Museum watch (a plain ebony face with a gold dot replacing the 12), the first watch chosen for the Museum of Modern Art's permanent collection.

Grinberg's son Efraim became North American Watch's president and COO in 1992. The company went public in 1993, and in 1996 it renamed itself the Movado Group. That year it launched the Vizio brand (part of its Movado line) and signed a deal to develop and distribute Coach watches.

Movado's second public offering in 1997 raised money for the opening of boutiques and other marketing efforts. The company sold its Piaget line — its original business line — to a subsidiary of Vendome Luxury Group in 1999 for about $30 million. In early 2000 Movado sold its second-oldest business, its Corum line, to the brand's Swiss owner, Corum Ries Bannwart & Co. Later that year Movado licensed its name to Lantis Eyewear for several optical and sunglass styles ranging in price from $195 to $345. Movado launched its licensed Tommy Hilfiger line of fashion watches — and its lowest-priced watches — in March 2001. Efraim was named CEO in May, with Gerry remaining as chairman.

In March 2004 Movado paid LVMH $48.9 million for premier luxury watch brand Ebel. In December of the same year Movado entered into a long-term worldwide licensing agreement with Hugo Boss to design and manufacture a collection of fashion watches under the Boss and Hugo brand names. Movado entered a similar licensing agreement with Juicy Couture in 2005.

EXECUTIVES

Chairman: Gedalio (Gerry) Grinberg, age 73, $650,000 pay
President, CEO, and Director: Efraim Grinberg, age 48, $1,391,538 pay
EVP, COO, and Director: Richard J. (Rick) Coté, age 50, $820,770 pay
SVP and CFO: Eugene J. (Gene) Karpovich, age 59, $341,953 pay
SVP, Human Resources: Vivian D'Elia
VP, Treasurer, and Assistant Secretary: Frank V. Kimick, age 39
VP, Finance and Principal Accounting Officer: Ernest R. LaPorte, age 54

President, Movado Boutiques: Ray A. Stuart, age 46
President, Ebel Worldwide: Thomas Van der Kallen, age 41
Secretary and General Counsel: Timothy F. Michno, age 49, $330,770 pay
Corporate Communications: Jill Golden
Auditors: PricewaterhouseCoopers LLP

LOCATIONS

HQ: Movado Group, Inc.
650 From Rd., Paramus, NJ 07652
Phone: 201-267-8000   **Fax:** 201-267-8070
Web: www.movadogroupinc.com

Movado Group operates internationally through wholly owned subsidiaries in Bermuda, Canada, France, Germany, Hong Kong, Japan, Singapore, Switzerland, and the UK.

PRODUCTS/OPERATIONS

2006 Sales

	$ mil.	% of total
Wholesale		
US	286.8	61
Other countries	98.6	21
Retail	85.5	18
Total	**470.9**	**100**

Selected Market Categories

Exclusive (Ebel and Concord; $10,000 and over)
Luxury (Ebel, Concord & Movado; $1,500 to $9,999)
Premium (Movado; $500 to $1,499)
Moderate (ESQ, Coach & Hugo Boss; $100 to $499)
Fashion market (Tommy Hilfiger; $55 to $99)

COMPETITORS

Armitron
Bulgari
Bulova
Cartier
CASIO COMPUTER
Citizen Watch
Fossil
Gucci
Guess
Hermès
LVMH
Patek Philippe
Richemont
Rolex
Seiko
Seiko USA
Swatch
Swiss Army Brands
Swiss Watch International
Time Products
Timex

HISTORICAL FINANCIALS

Company Type: Public

Income Statement

FYE: January 31

	REVENUE ($ mil.)	NET INCOME ($ mil.)	NET PROFIT MARGIN	EMPLOYEES
1/06	470.9	26.6	5.6%	1,300
1/05	419.0	26.3	6.3%	1,219
1/04	330.2	22.9	6.9%	943
1/03	300.1	20.1	6.7%	900
1/02	299.7	17.0	5.7%	878
Annual Growth	**12.0%**	**11.8%**	**—**	**10.3%**

2006 Year-End Financials

Debt ratio: 32.6%
Return on equity: 8.3%
Cash ($ mil.): 123.6
Current ratio: 5.02
Long-term debt ($ mil.): 105.0
No. of shares (mil.): 18.6
Dividends
 Yield: 1.1%
 Payout: 19.6%
Market value ($ mil.): 351.5
R&D as % of sales: —
Advertising as % of sales: —

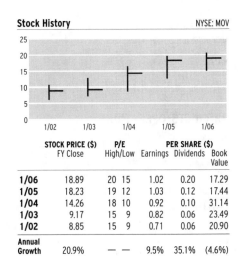

| Stock History | | | | NYSE: MOV |

	STOCK PRICE ($) FY Close	P/E High/Low	Earnings	Dividends	Book Value
1/06	18.89	20 15	1.02	0.20	17.29
1/05	18.23	19 12	1.03	0.12	17.44
1/04	14.26	18 10	0.92	0.10	31.14
1/03	9.17	15 9	0.82	0.06	23.49
1/02	8.85	15 9	0.71	0.06	20.90
Annual Growth	**20.9%**	**— —**	**9.5%**	**35.1%**	**(4.6%)**

MTC Technologies

MTC Technologies doesn't specialize in acronyms, but it can help with IT. Through its subsidiary Modern Technologies Corp., the company provides information technology (IT) services, including systems engineering and management, project management, integration, and intelligence operations support. The company also provides procurement, engineering, and project management outsourcing services for jet engine manufacturers and other commercial clients. MTC primarily serves the federal government, particularly the Department of Defense and intelligence agencies, as well as NASA and the US Air Force. Formerly privately held, MTC went public in 2002. Chairman Rajesh Soin founded MTC in 1984 and owns 36% of its stock.

In 2004 MTC acquired IT services firm Command Technologies, which serves the Department of Defense and other government entities, for $45 million. Since then, the company has also acquired Manufacturing Technology, OnBoard Software, and Eagle-D GmbH.

EXECUTIVES

Chairman and CEO: Rajesh K. (Raj) Soin, age 58
President: John E. Longhouser, age 61, $299,787 pay
COO: Mark Brown, age 54
EVP, Air Forces Group: James C. (Jim) Clark, age 63, $295,188 pay
SVP and CFO: Michael I. (Mike) Gearhardt, age 50, $312,906 pay
SVP: Michael L. Cauldwell
SVP and Director, Professional Services Solutions, Air Forces Group: Edwin C. Humphreys III
Corporate VP and CTO, Land Forces Group: Mark Holder
Corporate VP, Strategic Marketing: Bill James
VP, Finance, Controller, and Principal Accounting Officer: Stephen T. Catanzarita
VP, Legal Affairs: Bruce A. Teeters
Director, Investor Relations and Corporate Communications: Daniel (Dan) Bigelow
Auditors: Ernst & Young LLP

LOCATIONS

HQ: MTC Technologies, Inc.
4032 Linden Ave., Dayton, OH 45432
Phone: 937-252-9199   **Fax:** 937-258-3863
Web: www.modtechcorp.com

MTC Technologies has offices throughout the US.

PRODUCTS/OPERATIONS

2005 Sales

	% of total
Federal government	96
Other	4
Total	**100**

Selected Services

Acquisition management
Business process outsourcing
Command, Control, Communications, Computers, Intelligence, Surveillance, and Reconnaissance (C4ISR) services
Consulting
Database development
Enterprise application integration
Information assurance
Intelligence operations support
Maintenance
Network design and implementation
Project management
Software development
Systems engineering, development, integration, and management
Systems simulation and modeling
Testing and evaluation
Training

Selected Subsidiaries

AMCOMP Corporation
Command Technologies, Inc.
International Consultants, Inc.
Manufacturing Technology, Inc.
MTC Guam, LLC
OnBoard Software, Inc.
Vitronics Inc.

COMPETITORS

Alion
Analex
Apptis
Boeing
CACI International
Computer Sciences Corp.
EDS
General Dynamics Information Technology
Jacobs Engineering
L-3 Communications
Lockheed Martin
Northrop Grumman IT
Raytheon Technical Services
SI International

HISTORICAL FINANCIALS

Company Type: Public

Income Statement

FYE: December 31

	REVENUE ($ mil.)	NET INCOME ($ mil.)	NET PROFIT MARGIN	EMPLOYEES
12/05	373.3	21.3	5.7%	2,600
12/04	273.0	17.7	6.5%	2,100
12/03	188.7	12.5	6.6%	1,500
12/02	118.5	7.7	6.5%	1,100
12/01	92.6	7.8	8.4%	1,076
Annual Growth	**41.7%**	**28.5%**	**—**	**24.7%**

2005 Year-End Financials

Debt ratio: 29.7%	Dividends
Return on equity: 13.4%	Yield: —
Cash ($ mil.): 13.8	Payout: —
Current ratio: 1.92	Market value ($ mil.): 431.7
Long-term debt ($ mil.): 51.0	R&D as % of sales: —
No. of shares (mil.): 15.8	Advertising as % of sales: —

Stock History

NASDAQ (GS): MTCT

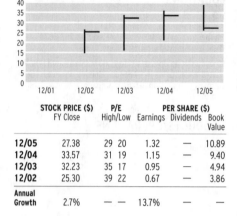

	STOCK PRICE ($) FY Close	P/E High/Low		PER SHARE ($) Earnings	Dividends	Book Value
12/05	27.38	29	20	1.32	—	10.89
12/04	33.57	31	19	1.15	—	9.40
12/03	32.23	35	17	0.95	—	4.94
12/02	25.30	39	22	0.67	—	3.86
Annual Growth	**2.7%**	**—**	**—**	**13.7%**	**—**	**—**

Multi-Color

Multi-Color wants consumers to read its labels. The company produces printed labels for goods such as fabric softeners, food products, and health and beauty aids. Heat transfer, resealable, shrink wrap, and pressure sensitive are among the label types the company prints and affixes to glass and plastic containers. Multi-Color also offers gravure printing and injection in-mold labels. The company serves about 650 clients in North and South America. Procter & Gamble accounts for one-third of sales, with Miller Lite Brewing representing 15%. In 2005 Multi-Color acquired NorthStar Print Group (label printing business) from Journal Communications.

The company plans on the NorthStar Print Group (NSPG) acquisition to significantly bolster its product portfolio; as a result, cut-and-stack label technology (the ability for labels to be pasted to containers during the labeling process) and the ability to introduce promotional products such as scratch-off coupons, shelf tags, and static clings will be offered by Multi-Color going forward.

The company's Decorating Solutions division (in-mold labels production and heat transfer labels) is by far its most lucrative, representing about 85% of the company's total sales each year. Its Packaging Services segment accounts for the remaining percentage and provides promotional packaging design services.

EXECUTIVES

Chairman: Lorrence T. Kellar, age 69
President, CEO, and Director:
Francis D. (Frank) Gerace, age 53, $801,482 pay
SVP, Finance, CFO, and Secretary: Dawn H. Bertsche, age 49, $430,797 pay

---

VP, Controller, and Chief Accounting Officer:
James H. Reynolds, age 40, $205,734 pay
VP and General Manager, Quick Pak: Johan G. Pot
VP, Human Resources: Lesha K. Spahr
VP, Sales and Marketing, Decorating Solutions Division: Mark J. Tangry
President, Decorating Solutions: Donald E. Kneir, age 42, $464,173 pay
Corporate Treasurer: Mary T. Fetch
Manager, Marketing: David E. Klotter
Auditors: Grant Thornton LLP

LOCATIONS

HQ: Multi-Color Corporation
425 Walnut St., Ste. 1300, Cincinnati, OH 45202
Phone: 513-381-1480   **Fax:** 513-381-2813
Web: www.multicolorcorp.com

Multi-Color Corporation has facilities in Indiana, Kentucky, Massachusetts, Michigan, Ohio, and Wisconsin.

PRODUCTS/OPERATIONS

2006 Sales

	$ mil.	% of total
Decorating solutions	177.0	86
Packaging services	29.1	14
Adjustments	(0.8)	—
Total	**205.3**	**100**

Selected Products and Services

Labels
  Heat transfer
  In-mold
  Neck bands
  Peel-away
  Pressure sensitive
  Resealable
  Shrink sleeve
Packaging
  Design
  Kit assembly
  Shipping
  Shrink wrapping
Pre-press

COMPETITORS

Convergent Label Technology
Fort Dearborn
Gibraltar Packaging
H. S. Crocker
Jordan Industries
Outlook Group
Schawk
YORK Label

HISTORICAL FINANCIALS

Company Type: Public

Income Statement

FYE: Sunday nearest March 31

	REVENUE ($ mil.)	NET INCOME ($ mil.)	NET PROFIT MARGIN	EMPLOYEES
3/06	205.3	9.6	4.7%	1,066
3/05	139.5	8.0	5.7%	826
3/04	127.0	6.5	5.1%	540
3/03	99.6	6.3	6.3%	490
3/02	72.6	4.7	6.5%	347
Annual Growth	**29.7%**	**19.5%**	**—**	**32.4%**

2006 Year-End Financials

Debt ratio: 41.4%	Dividends
Return on equity: 20.0%	Yield: 0.7%
Cash ($ mil.): 3.2	Payout: 14.0%
Current ratio: 1.66	Market value ($ mil.): 197.6
Long-term debt ($ mil.): 21.9	R&D as % of sales: 0.9%
No. of shares (mil.): 6.6	Advertising as % of sales: —

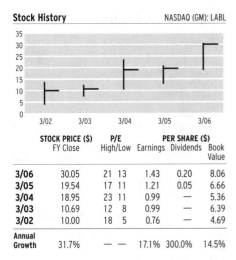

	STOCK PRICE ($) FY Close	P/E High/Low		PER SHARE ($) Earnings	Dividends	Book Value
3/06	30.05	21	13	1.43	0.20	8.06
3/05	19.54	17	11	1.21	0.05	6.66
3/04	18.95	23	11	0.99	—	5.36
3/03	10.69	12	8	0.99	—	6.39
3/02	10.00	18	5	0.76	—	4.69
Annual Growth	31.7%	—	—	17.1%	300.0%	14.5%

Multi-Fineline Electronix

Multi-Fineline Electronix tries to offer a multitude of fine electronic parts. The company, which does business as M-FLEX, makes a wide variety of flexible printed circuits and circuit assemblies. These devices are used to connect other components in various kinds of electronic gear such as laptop computers, cell phones, PDAs, and handheld bar-code scanners. Directly and through contract manufacturers, Motorola accounts for more than three-quarters of Multi-Fineline's sales. Other customers of the company include GE Healthcare, IBM, Palm, and Symbol Technologies. Holding company WBL Corporation owns about 61% of Multi-Fineline Electronix.

In early 2006 M-FLEX agreed to acquire Singapore's MFS Technology, a subsidiary of WBL, for around $500 million. When business conditions turned averse for MFS Technology later in the year, M-FLEX's special board committee withdrew its endorsement of the deal, but the company couldn't legally withdraw its offer under Singapore law, which led M-FLEX to urge shareholders to vote against the transaction.

The company later sued in Delaware Chancery Court, seeking to force WBL to vote against the MFS Technology acquisition. Meanwhile, hedge funds controlled by investors Michael A. Roth and Brian J. Stark started accumulating shares in both M-FLEX and MFS Technology. The Stark funds have acquired a stake of about 18% in M-FLEX and nearly 5% of MFS Technology. M-FLEX and the Stark funds sued each other, but then settled the cases in early 2007.

The company extended the tender offer for MFS Technology to the end of the first quarter in 2007, while continuing to recommend a "no" vote by shareholders.

Multi-Fineline gets about 70% of sales from outside the US, with more than half of sales coming from China.

In mid-2005 Multi-Fineline acquired the assets of Applied Optics, a subsidiary of Applied Image Group, for approximately $6 million in cash. Applied Optics makes optical and photonic imaging products. M-FLEX has rechristened the operation as Aurora Optical, hiring all of its employees and keeping the business in operation at its existing plant in Tucson, Arizona. The assets include patents and other intellectual property for optical components and photonic modules that can be used in cell phones, handheld scanners and data sensors, and laptop-integrated cameras, among other applications.

EXECUTIVES

Chairman and CEO: Philip A. Harding, age 74, $450,455 pay
President and COO: Reza Meshgin, age 43, $322,964 pay
CFO and Secretary: Craig Riedel, age 50, $223,473 pay
EVP, Operations: Thomas Lee, age 47, $259,373 pay
EVP and CTO: Charles Tapscott, age 64, $175,641 pay
Manager, Human Resources: Chris Farley
Auditors: PricewaterhouseCoopers LLP

LOCATIONS

HQ: Multi-Fineline Electronix, Inc.
    3140 E. Coronado St., Ste. A, Anaheim, CA 92806
Phone: 714-238-1488   **Fax:** 714-996-3834
Web: www.mflex.com

Multi-Fineline Electronix has operations in China and the US.

2006 Sales

	$ mil.	% of total
Asia/Pacific		
China	259.9	51
Hong Kong	50.4	10
Japan	4.2	1
Other countries	33.9	7
North America	144.9	29
Europe	7.3	1
Other regions	3.6	1
Total	504.2	100

PRODUCTS/OPERATIONS

2006 Sales

	% of total
Wireless telecommunications	88
Other industries	12
Total	100

COMPETITORS

Flextronics
Fujikura Ltd.
Hexion
Hon Hai
Innovex
Nitto Denko
Parlex

HISTORICAL FINANCIALS

Company Type: Public

Income Statement

FYE: September 30

	REVENUE ($ mil.)	NET INCOME ($ mil.)	NET PROFIT MARGIN	EMPLOYEES
9/06	504.2	40.4	8.0%	12,019
9/05	357.1	37.2	10.4%	10,190
9/04	253.1	25.7	10.2%	6,623
9/03	129.4	4.6	3.6%	—
9/02	110.5	5.0	4.5%	—
Annual Growth	46.2%	68.6%	—	34.7%

2006 Year-End Financials

Debt ratio: —
Return on equity: 18.9%
Cash ($ mil.): 46.0
Current ratio: 2.47
Long-term debt ($ mil.): —
No. of shares (mil.): 24.4
Dividends
  Yield: —
  Payout: —
Market value ($ mil.): 620.1
R&D as % of sales: —
Advertising as % of sales: —

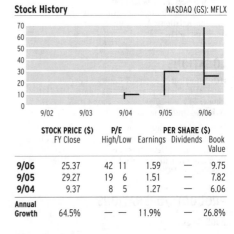

	STOCK PRICE ($) FY Close	P/E High/Low		PER SHARE ($) Earnings	Dividends	Book Value
9/06	25.37	42	11	1.59	—	9.75
9/05	29.27	19	6	1.51	—	7.82
9/04	9.37	8	5	1.27	—	6.06
Annual Growth	64.5%	—	—	11.9%	—	26.8%

Municipal Mortgage & Equity

Municipal Mortgage & Equity (MuniMae) likely has a stake in your municipality. The limited-liability company, which does business as MMA Financial (formerly MuniMae Midland), invests in tax-free municipal bonds used to build multifamily housing, including units for low-income families. The company is an active investor, reviewing budgets and rent flow, and performing regular property inspections. It also writes and services loans used to finance the construction of student housing and low-income apartment communities. Similar to a REIT, MuniMae distributes most of its income to shareholders.

In 2005 the company acquired MONY Realty Capital from AXA Financial and combined it with MuniMae's existing investment advisory business.

Later that year, MuniMae acquired Glaser Financial Group, a St. Paul, Minnesota-based commercial mortgage banker that arranges multifamily, senior housing, and commercial real estate financing predominantly in the upper Midwest.

EXECUTIVES

Chairman: Mark K. Joseph, age 67, $912,500 pay (prior to title change)
President, CEO, and Director: Michael L. Falcone, age 44, $1,023,077 pay
EVP and CFO: Melanie M. Lundquist, age 42
EVP, Affordable Housing and Construction Lending: Keith J. Gloeckl, age 54
EVP, Affordable Housing Tax Credit: Jenny Netzer, age 50, $838,573 pay
EVP, Corporate Credit and Portfolio Risk Management: Earl W. Cole III, age 53
EVP, Investment Management, MMA Realty Capital: Frank G. Creamer Jr., age 59, $767,307 pay (partial-year salary)

EVP, Market Rate Multifamily Debt Financing:
Robert W. McLewee, age 51
EVP, MMA Financial: Micheal W. Walton, age 35
EVP, Structured Finance: Charles M. Pinckney, age 48,
$446,539 pay
EVP, Tax-Exempt Bond Group: Gary A. Mentesana,
age 42, $539,231 pay
SVP and Secretary: Janet E. McHugh
General Counsel: Stephen A. Goldberg
Investor Relations: Angela Richardson
Auditors: KPMG LLP

LOCATIONS

HQ: Municipal Mortgage & Equity, LLC
621 E. Pratt St., Ste. 300, Baltimore, MD 21202
Phone: 443-263-2900 **Fax:** 410-727-5387
Web: www.munimae.com

Municipal Mortgage & Equity operates offices in
Atlanta; Baltimore; Boston; Boulder, Colorado; Chicago;
Dallas; Denver; Detroit; Irvine, California; New York
City; San Francisco; St. Paul, Minnesota; Tampa; and
Washington, DC.

PRODUCTS/OPERATIONS

2005 Sales

	$ mil.	% of total
Interest		
Bonds & interests in bond syndications	91.5	31
Loans	57.5	20
Short-term investments	5.2	2
Noninterest		
Syndication fees	43.0	15
Asset management & advisory fees	33.5	11
Net rental income	22.3	7
Guarantee fees	19.1	7
Loan servicing fees	9.3	3
Origination & brokerage fees	5.6	2
Other	6.1	2
Total	**293.1**	**100**

COMPETITORS

CharterMac
CRIIMI MAE
Fannie Mae
GMAC
IndyMac Bancorp
Thornburg Mortgage

HISTORICAL FINANCIALS

Company Type: Public

Income Statement

FYE: December 31

	ASSETS ($ mil.)	NET INCOME ($ mil.)	INCOME AS % OF ASSETS	EMPLOYEES
12/05	3,831.7	87.4	2.3%	450
12/04	3,310.3	27.0	0.8%	—
12/03	2,249.6	72.5	3.2%	—
12/02	1,552.9	29.0	1.9%	—
12/01	1,289.3	25.9	2.0%	—
Annual Growth	**31.3%**	**35.5%**	**—**	**—**

2005 Year-End Financials

Equity as % of assets: 20.1%
Return on assets: 2.4%
Return on equity: 12.1%
Long-term debt ($ mil.): 1,212.1
No. of shares (mil.): 38.1
Market value ($ mil.): 983.7
Dividends
 Yield: 7.4%
 Payout: 83.5%
Sales ($ mil.): 293.1
R&D as % of sales: —
Advertising as % of sales: —

Stock History

NYSE: MMA

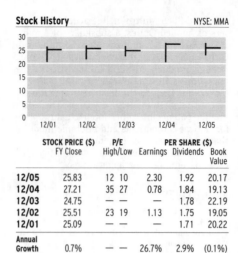

	STOCK PRICE ($) FY Close	P/E High/Low		PER SHARE ($) Earnings	Dividends	Book Value
12/05	25.83	12	10	2.30	1.92	20.17
12/04	27.21	35	27	0.78	1.84	19.13
12/03	24.75	—	—	—	1.78	22.19
12/02	25.51	23	19	1.13	1.75	19.05
12/01	25.09	—	—	—	1.71	20.22
Annual Growth	**0.7%**	**—**	**—**	**26.7%**	**2.9%**	**(0.1%)**

MVC Capital

MVC Capital has had a bit of a facelift. Formed
as meVC Draper Fisher Jurvetson Fund I in 1999
during the explosion of venture capital investing and the Internet boom, the fund's aim was
to let individual investors in on the VC action.
Unfortunately, most of its investments failed. In
2000, the firm became a closed-end investment
fund registered as a business development company (BDC). After some $120 million in losses,
shareholders voted in a new management team
and in 2003 hired former Kohlberg Kravis
Roberts general partner Michael Tokarz to turn
things around. MVC has broadened its focus beyond tech company buyouts to include investments in small to mid-market companies from
various industries.

The company's loan or equity investments
generally range from $3 million to $25 million.
Targets generally have sales of $200 million or
less and come from such industries as consumer
products, distribution, financial services, information technology, and manufacturing. MVC
Capital holds investments in companies in Asia,
Europe, and the US.

EXECUTIVES

Chairman and Portfolio Manager: Michael T. Tokarz,
age 56
Managing Director: Bruce W. Shewmaker, age 60,
$150,000 pay
CFO: Peter F. Seidenberg, age 37
VP and Secretary: Jaclyn Lauren (Jackie) Shapiro,
age 27, $175,000 pay
Chief Compliance Officer: Scott Schuenke, age 27
Auditors: Ernst & Young LLP

LOCATIONS

HQ: MVC Capital, Inc.
287 Bowman Ave., Purchase, NY 10577
Phone: 914-701-0310 **Fax:** 914-701-0315
Web: www.mvccapital.com

PRODUCTS/OPERATIONS

2006 Sales

	% of total
Interest & dividends	
Non-control/non-affiliated investments	38
Control investments	21
Affiliate investments	16
Fees	
Control investments	12
Non-control/non-affiliated investments	6
Affiliate investments	3
Other	4
Total	**100**

Selected Portfolio Companies

Amersham Corporation (machined components
 manufacturing)
Baltic Motors Corporation (auto dealerships, Latvia)
BM Auto, Ltd (auto dealerships, Latvia)
BP Clothing LLC (women's clothing line Baby Phat)
Dakota Growers Pasta Company (dry pasta
 manufacturing)
Impact Confections, Inc. (candy manufacturing and
 distribution)
JDC Lighting, LLC (commercial lighting distribution)
Marine Exhibition Corporation (owner and operator of
 Miami Seaquarium)
Octagon Credit Investors, LLC (asset management)
Ohio Medical Corporation (suction and oxygen therapy
 products)
Phoenix Coal Corporation (coal mining)
PreVisor (pre-employment assessments)
SGDA mbH (landfill remediation, Germany)
SP Industries, Inc. (laboratory equipment
 manufacturing)
Storage Canada, LLC (doing business as Dino's Storage,
 self-storage facilities)
Timberland Machines & Irrigation (landscape and
 irrigation products distribution)
Turf Products, LLC (distribution of turf-maintenance
 equipment, irrigation systems, and related products)
Vestal Manufacturing Enterprises (iron and steel
 components manufacturing)
Vitality Foodservice, Inc. (juice and dispensers for the
 foodservice industry)

COMPETITORS

Allied Capital
Gladstone Capital
Harris & Harris
MCG Capital
Warburg Pincus

HISTORICAL FINANCIALS

Company Type: Public

Income Statement

FYE: October 31

	REVENUE ($ mil.)	NET INCOME ($ mil.)	NET PROFIT MARGIN	EMPLOYEES
10/06	18.5	47.3	255.7%	13
10/05	12.2	26.3	215.6%	—
10/04	4.0	11.6	290.0%	—
10/03	2.9	(55.5)	—	—
10/02	3.7	(58.4)	—	—
Annual Growth	**49.5%**	**—**	**—**	**—**

2006 Year-End Financials

Debt ratio: 42.2%
Return on equity: 21.7%
Cash ($ mil.): 66.3
Current ratio: —
Long-term debt ($ mil.): 100.0
No. of shares (mil.): 19.1
Dividends
 Yield: 3.7%
 Payout: 19.4%
Market value ($ mil.): 249.7
R&D as % of sales: —
Advertising as % of sales: —

244

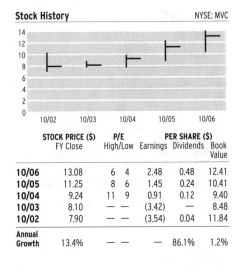

	STOCK PRICE ($) FY Close	P/E High/Low		PER SHARE ($) Earnings	Dividends	Book Value
10/06	13.08	6	4	2.48	0.48	12.41
10/05	11.25	8	6	1.45	0.24	10.41
10/04	9.24	11	9	0.91	0.12	9.40
10/03	8.10	—	—	(3.42)	—	8.48
10/02	7.90	—	—	(3.54)	0.04	11.84
Annual Growth	13.4%	—	—	—	86.1%	1.2%

Nanometrics

Makers of precision electronics who need their goods to measure up know that Nanometrics works on a nano scale. The company provides thin-film metrology and inspection systems used by makers of precision electronic gear. These stand-alone, integrated, and tabletop measurement devices gauge the thickness and consistency of film materials used in making semiconductors, magnetic recording heads, and flat-panel displays. Nanometrics has acquired Accent Optical Technologies, a supplier of semiconductor process control and metrology equipment, for about $81 million in stock and assumption of debt.

Following the merger, previous Nanometrics shareholders own approximately 73% of the combined company and Accent Optical shareholders own about 27%.

The company signed a merger agreement with August Technology, a supplier of semiconductor inspection equipment, in early 2005. Rival Rudolph Technologies prevailed with a higher bid for August Technology, however. August Technology and Nanometrics terminated their merger agreement in mid-2005. August paid Nanometrics a termination fee of $8.3 million, plus $2.6 million in reimbursed expenses, as a result.

Nanometrics is mixing it up with competitors in the courtroom, as well as in the global market for metrology systems. The company is defending itself against patent infringement lawsuits by KLA-Tencor and Nova Measuring Instruments, and has filed a countersuit against Nova.

In 2005 Nanometrics sold its flat-panel display equipment business unit to Toho Technology.

The company has acquired Soluris, a supplier of overlay and critical-dimension measurement equipment, for $7 million in cash.

Customers include Applied Materials (about 21% of sales), Dainippon Screen, Ebara Technologies (12%), Hitachi, Hynix Semiconductor, Samsung Electronics (16%), SMIC, and Tokyo Electron.

Founder and chairman Vincent Coates owns nearly 19% of Nanometrics. The TCW Group holds 8% of the company. Director and chief strategy officer Bruce Rhine, former chairman and CEO of Accent Optical Technologies, has an equity stake of more than 7%, as does Peter Joost, a private investor who was a director of Accent Optical. Dimensional Fund Advisors owns around 6%.

EXECUTIVES

Chairman and Secretary: Vincent J. Coates, age 81, $204,800 pay
President, CEO, and Director: John D. Heaton, age 46, $415,760 pay
EVP, Finance and Administration and CFO: Douglas J. (Doug) McCutcheon, age 58, $105,019 pay (partial-year salary)
SVP, Standalone Sales: Roger Ingalls Jr., age 44, $325,231 pay
VP, Engineering: Michael Weber, age 47, $106,877 pay (partial-year salary)
VP, Sales, Integrated Metrology: Jason Rollo
Chief Accounting Officer: Quentin B. Wright, $151,668 pay (partial-year salary)
Controller: Ronald Beeson, age 43
Chief Strategy Officer: Bruce C. Rhine
Auditors: BDO Seidman, LLP

LOCATIONS

HQ: Nanometrics Incorporated
    1550 Buckeye Dr., Milpitas, CA 95035
Phone: 408-435-9600   **Fax:** 408-232-5910
Web: www.nanometrics.com

Nanometrics has operations in China, France, Italy, Japan, Singapore, South Korea, Taiwan, the UK, and the US.

2005 Sales

	$ mil.	% of total
US	23.5	34
Japan	18.4	26
South Korea	17.9	25
Taiwan	7.7	11
Other countries	3.0	4
Total	**70.5**	**100**

PRODUCTS/OPERATIONS

2005 Sales

	$ mil.	% of total
Products		
Automated systems	34.3	49
Integrated systems	23.1	33
Tabletop systems	3.6	5
Service	9.5	13
Total	**70.5**	**100**

Selected Products

Noncontact thin-film metrology systems (NanoSpec)
  Automated systems
  Integrated systems
  Tabletop systems
Overlay metrology and CD measurement systems (Metra and NanoOCS)

COMPETITORS

ADE
Applied Materials
ASM International
Bio-Rad Labs
Credence Systems
Dainippon Screen
Fab Solutions
KLA-Tencor
Metara
nLine
Nova Measuring
Qcept
Rudolph Technologies
Therma-Wave
Veeco Instruments
Zygo

HISTORICAL FINANCIALS

Company Type: Public

Income Statement

			FYE: December 31

	REVENUE ($ mil.)	NET INCOME ($ mil.)	NET PROFIT MARGIN	EMPLOYEES
12/05	70.5	1.5	2.1%	305
12/04	69.9	3.7	5.3%	311
12/03	41.6	(17.5)	—	310
12/02	34.7	(8.3)	—	305
12/01	47.6	1.0	2.1%	280
Annual Growth	10.3%	10.7%	—	2.2%

2005 Year-End Financials

Debt ratio: 1.2%
Return on equity: 1.3%
Cash ($ mil.): 45.4
Current ratio: 6.27
Long-term debt ($ mil.): 1.4
No. of shares (mil.): 13.0

Dividends
  Yield: —
  Payout: —
Market value ($ mil.): 143.4
R&D as % of sales: 17.7%
Advertising as % of sales: —

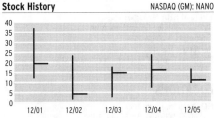

	STOCK PRICE ($) FY Close	P/E High/Low		PER SHARE ($) Earnings	Dividends	Book Value
12/05	11.00	149	89	0.11	—	9.23
12/04	16.12	84	27	0.28	—	9.30
12/03	14.71	—	—	(1.45)	—	8.91
12/02	4.19	—	—	(0.70)	—	10.34
12/01	19.40	458	155	0.08	—	11.02
Annual Growth	(13.2%)	—	—	8.3%	—	(4.3%)

Nara Bancorp

Nara Bancorp is the holding company for Nara Bank, which serves consumers and small to mid-sized minority-owned businesses through more than 15 branches and loan offices in Korean districts in and around Los Angeles and New York City. It also has locations in Seoul, as well as Northern California, Colorado, Georgia, Illinois, New Jersey, Texas, Virginia, and Washington. Real estate and construction loans make up more than 60% of the company's loan portfolio; the bank also provides commercial loans (about a third of all loans), including Small Business Administration (SBA) loans and equipment lease financing, as well as consumer loans and factoring services.

Nara Bank's international services include merchant drafts and letters of credit for its immigrant clientele.

In 2005 Nara restated its 2002 earnings after its auditor discovered it had improperly accounted for a $600,000 reimbursement to former president and CEO Benjamin Hong for country club dues and auto expenses. Since then the company's CFO was demoted and a board member was forced to resign.

Hong's successor, Ho Yang, resigned the following year for unrelated reasons. Min Kim, who replaced Yang, became the company's third CEO in two years.

Fidelity Management and director Chong-Moon Lee each own some 9% of Nara.

EXECUTIVES

Chairman, Nara Bancorp and Nara Bank:
Chong-Moon Lee, age 77
President and CEO: Min Jung Kim, age 47, $287,027 pay
EVP and CFO, Nara Bancorp and Nara Bank:
Alvin D. (Al) Kang, age 60, $157,603 pay
EVP and Chief Credit Officer: Bonita I. (Bonnie) Lee, age 42, $266,354 pay
EVP and Human Resources Manager: Elizabeth Wong
SVP, Director of Legal Affairs, and Secretary:
Michel Urich
SVP and Controller: Christine Yoon Oh, age 38, $202,188 pay
SVP and Director of Information Technology:
Mona Chui
SVP and SBA Manager: Young K. Oh
SVP and Senior Operations Administrator:
Myung Hee Hyun
Secretary: Lisa Pai
Auditors: Crowe Chizek and Company LLP

LOCATIONS

HQ: Nara Bancorp, Inc.
3731 Wilshire Blvd., Ste. 1000,
Los Angeles, CA 90010
Phone: 213-639-1700   **Fax:** 213-235-3033
Web: www.narabank.com

PRODUCTS/OPERATIONS

2005 Sales

	$ mil.	% of total
Interest		
Loans, including fees	108.2	79
Securities	6.2	4
Federal funds sold & other	2.1	2
Noninterest		
Service charges on deposit accounts	6.3	5
Net gains on sales of SBA loans	6.0	4
International service fees	2.8	2
Other income & fees	5.8	4
Total	**137.4**	**100**

COMPETITORS

Bank of America
Broadway Financial
Center Financial
East West Bancorp
Hanmi Financial
Saehan Bancorp
U.S. Bancorp
Wilshire Bancorp

HISTORICAL FINANCIALS

Company Type: Public

Income Statement
FYE: December 31

	ASSETS ($ mil.)	NET INCOME ($ mil.)	INCOME AS % OF ASSETS	EMPLOYEES
12/05	1,775.8	26.9	1.5%	376
12/04	1,507.7	19.8	1.3%	342
12/03	1,260.0	14.3	1.1%	320
12/02	979.3	15.5	1.6%	291
12/01	679.4	10.8	1.6%	264
Annual Growth	**27.2%**	**25.6%**	**—**	**9.2%**

2005 Year-End Financials

Equity as % of assets: 8.3%	Dividends
Return on assets: 1.6%	Yield: 0.6%
Return on equity: 21.7%	Payout: 10.3%
Long-term debt ($ mil.): 39.3	Sales ($ mil.): 137.4
No. of shares (mil.): 25.4	R&D as % of sales: —
Market value ($ mil.): 452.4	Advertising as % of sales: —

Stock History
NASDAQ (GS): NARA

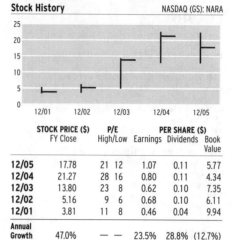

	STOCK PRICE ($) FY Close	P/E High/Low		PER SHARE ($) Earnings	Dividends	Book Value
12/05	17.78	21	12	1.07	0.11	5.77
12/04	21.27	28	16	0.80	0.11	4.34
12/03	13.80	23	8	0.62	0.10	7.35
12/02	5.16	9	6	0.68	0.10	6.11
12/01	3.81	11	8	0.46	0.04	9.94
Annual Growth	**47.0%**	**—**	**—**	**23.5%**	**28.8%**	**(12.7%)**

National Financial Partners

Not sure what to do with your millions? National Financial Partners (NFP) can help. The company is a distributor of financial services products to high-net-worth individuals and families, as well as entrepreneurial businesses. Operating as a go-between from its network of independent distributors to large financial services firms, NFP owns about 160 distributor firms and partners with more than 200 affiliates in some 40 states. The company's offerings include life insurance, estate planning, executive benefits, and financial planning and advisory services. The company has relationships with such financial services giants as AIG, The Hartford, and John Hancock. Apollo Management owns about 10% of NFP.

In April 2005 NFP bought Highland Capital Holding — its largest acquisition to date — including Highland's network of 11 divisions and 21 brokerage general agent offices. When NFP buys a firm, it requires the firm to retain its own brand and management. The former owners are contracted to stay with the acquired firm for five years, and are provided with incentives to help grow the business. CEO Jessica Bibliowicz, who took her position with the roll-up firm a few months after it began operations in 1999, is the daughter of Sandy Weill, who retired as chairman of Citigroup in 2006.

EXECUTIVES

Chairman, President, and CEO: Jessica M. Bibliowicz, age 46, $1,370,000 pay
EVP and CFO: Mark C. Biderman, age 60, $886,500 pay
EVP, General Counsel, and Secretary:
Douglas W. (Doug) Hammond, age 40, $703,750 pay
EVP and Chief Accounting Officer: Robert S. Zuccaro, age 49
EVP Marketing and Firm Operations: Elliot M. Holtz, age 42
SVP and Chief Compliance and Ethics Officer:
Stancil E. Barton
SVP and Director of Human Resources: Emily Arean
SVP Investor Relations and Strategic Marketing:
Elizabeth A. Werner
CEO, NFP Securities: Jeffrey A. Montgomery, age 39, $678,750 pay
President, NFP Insurance Services: Robert R. Carter, age 54, $872,500 pay
Auditors: PricewaterhouseCoopers LLP

LOCATIONS

HQ: National Financial Partners Corp.
787 7th Ave., 11th Fl., New York, NY 10019
Phone: 212-301-4000   **Fax:** 212-301-4001
Web: www.nfp.com

National Financial Partners has corporate offices in New York City and Austin, Texas; member firms have offices throughout the US.

2005 Sales

	% of total
Florida	19
California	10
New York	9
Other states	62
Total	**100**

PRODUCTS/OPERATIONS

Selected Products and Services

Corporate and executive benefits
Corporate benefits
401(k)/403(b) plans
COBRA administration
Disability insurance
Employee assistance programs
Flexible spending administration
Fully insured health plans
Group dental insurance
Group life insurance
Human resource consulting
Long-term care
Workers' compensation plans
Executive benefits
Bank-owned life insurance
Corporate-owned life insurance
Plan administration
Financial planning and investment advisory
Asset management
Financial planning
Funds of hedge funds
Investment consulting
Mutual funds
Traditional broker-dealer services
Life insurance and wealth transfer
Charitable giving planning
Estate planning
Financed life insurance product placement
Financial planning
Fixed and variable annuities
Individual whole, universal, and variable life insurance
Life settlements
Retirement distribution
Term life insurance
Wealth accumulation

COMPETITORS

AMVESCAP	Hilb Rogal & Hobbs
Aon	M Financial Group
Arthur Gallagher	Marsh & McLennan
Bear Stearns	Mellon Financial
Bessemer Group	Northern Trust
BISYS	Old Mutual (US)
BlackRock	Raymond James Financial
Brown & Brown	State Street
Brown Brothers Harriman	U.S. Trust
Citigroup Private Bank	USI
FMR	Willis Group
Harris Bankcorp	

HISTORICAL FINANCIALS

Company Type: Public

Income Statement

FYE: December 31

	ASSETS ($ mil.)	NET INCOME ($ mil.)	INCOME AS % OF ASSETS	EMPLOYEES
12/05	1,046.6	56.2	5.4%	2,432
12/04	826.5	40.1	4.9%	1,600
12/03	671.6	23.5	3.5%	1,450
12/02	541.3	11.6	2.1%	—
12/01	472.8	(5.7)	—	—
Annual Growth	22.0%	—	—	29.5%

2005 Year-End Financials

Equity as % of assets: 63.0%
Return on assets: 6.0%
Return on equity: 9.3%
Long-term debt ($ mil.): —
No. of shares (mil.): 36.8
Market value ($ mil.): 1,933.6

Dividends
Yield: 1.0%
Payout: 34.5%
Sales ($ mil.): 891.5
R&D as % of sales: —
Advertising as % of sales: —

Stock History

NYSE: NFP

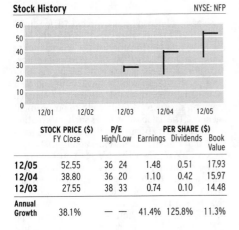

	STOCK PRICE ($) FY Close	P/E High/Low		PER SHARE ($) Earnings	Dividends	Book Value
12/05	52.55	36	24	1.48	0.51	17.93
12/04	38.80	36	20	1.10	0.42	15.97
12/03	27.55	38	33	0.74	0.10	14.48
Annual Growth	38.1%	—	—	41.4%	125.8%	11.3%

Natural Gas Services

The pressure is on to enhance oil and gas well production. Natural Gas Services Group (NGS) manufactures and leases natural gas compressors used to boost oil and gas well production levels. The company also provides flare tip burners, ignition systems, and components used to combust waste gases before entering the atmosphere. NGS leases compressors to third parties in Colorado, Kansas, Louisiana, Michigan, New Mexico, Oklahoma, Texas, and Wyoming. In early 2006 some 876 units of its fleet of 896 compressors were rented out to clients. Its main customer, XTO Energy, accounted for 36% of sales in 2005.

Founded in 1998, the company, which has grown through a number of acquisitions, purchased private compressor manufacturer Screw Compression Systems in 2005 for about $15 million in stock.

EXECUTIVES

Chairman, President, and CEO: Stephen C. Taylor, age 52
VP Accounting and Treasurer: Earl R. Wait, age 62
Director, President, SCS: Paul D. Hensley, age 53, $180,361 pay
Secretary: Scott W. Sparkman, age 43
Account Manager: Phil Nagel
Investor Relations: Jim Drewitz
Manager Business Development: Ron Braselton
Senior Account Manager: Craig Breining

LOCATIONS

HQ: Natural Gas Services Group, Inc.
2911 S. Country Rd. 1260, Midland, TX 79706
Phone: 432-563-3974 **Fax:** 432-563-4139
Web: www.ngsgi.com

Natural Gas Services operates in Michigan, New Mexico, Oklahoma, and Texas. Its manufacturing and fabrication facilities are located in Lewiston, Michigan, and Midland, Texas.

PRODUCTS/OPERATIONS

2005 Sales

	$ mil.	% of total
Sales	30.3	61
Rental	16.6	34
Service & maintenance	2.4	5
Total	**49.3**	**100**

COMPETITORS

Baker Hughes
BJ Services
CARBO Ceramics
Compressor Systems
Flotek
Hanover Compressor
Miller Petroleum
Oilgear
Universal Compression
Weatherford International

HISTORICAL FINANCIALS

Company Type: Public

Income Statement

FYE: December 31

	REVENUE ($ mil.)	NET INCOME ($ mil.)	NET PROFIT MARGIN	EMPLOYEES
12/05	49.3	4.4	8.9%	236
12/04	16.0	3.4	21.3%	111
12/03	12.8	1.3	10.2%	80
12/02	10.3	0.8	7.8%	69
12/01	8.8	0.4	4.5%	70
Annual Growth	53.8%	82.1%	—	35.5%

2005 Year-End Financials

Debt ratio: 48.6%
Return on equity: 12.8%
Cash ($ mil.): 3.3
Current ratio: 2.20
Long-term debt ($ mil.): 22.2
No. of shares (mil.): 9.0

Dividends
Yield: —
Payout: —
Market value ($ mil.): 153.0
R&D as % of sales: —
Advertising as % of sales: 0.0%

Stock History

AMEX: NGS

	STOCK PRICE ($) FY Close	P/E High/Low		PER SHARE ($) Earnings	Dividends	Book Value
12/05	16.96	77	17	0.52	—	5.06
12/04	9.43	20	10	0.52	—	3.38
12/03	5.55	32	16	0.23	—	2.87
12/02	3.88	28	20	0.16	—	2.68
Annual Growth	63.5%	—	—	47.5%	—	31.0%

Natural Resource Partners

Natural Resource Partners (NRP) makes money from coal without getting its hands dirty. Rather than mining the coal itself, NRP leases properties to coal producers. The company's properties — mainly in Appalachia but also in the Northern Powder River Basin and the Illinois Basin — contain proved and probable reserves of about 2 billion tons of coal. NRP was formed as a partnership between WPP Group (Western Pocahontas Properties, New Gauley Coal, and Great Northern Properties) and Arch Coal. Arch Coal has sold its stake in NRP but remains one of the company's top lessees, along with Alpha Natural Resources. Chairman and CEO Corbin Robertson Jr. controls about 35% of NRP, primarily through WPP Group.

In 2005 NRP acquired the mineral rights to approximately 85 million tons of coal reserves from Plum Creek Timber Company for about $21 million. In addition, NRP bought 179 million tons of coal reserves in Ohio and Pennsylvania for $29 million. It then paid $105 million for interests in 145 million tons of coal in the Illinois Basin, and continued the streak of acquisitions by buying the D.D. Shepard property in West Virginia for $110 million.

EXECUTIVES

Chairman and CEO: Corbin J. Robertson Jr., age 58
President and COO: Nick Carter, age 59, $432,200 pay
CFO and Treasurer: Dwight L. Dunlap, age 52, $235,240 pay
VP, Business Development: Kevin J. Craig, age 37
VP, Investor Relations: Kathy E. Hager, age 54
VP, General Counsel, and Secretary: Wyatt L. Hogan, age 33
VP and Chief Engineer: Kevin F. Wall, age 49, $193,500 pay
Controller: Kenneth Hudson, age 51, $166,600 pay
Auditors: Ernst & Young LLP

LOCATIONS

HQ: Natural Resource Partners L.P.
601 Jefferson St., Ste. 3600, Houston, TX 77002
Phone: 713-751-7507 **Fax:** 713-650-0606
Web: www.nrplp.com

COMPETITORS

CONSOL Energy
Foundation Coal
Kennecott Energy
Peabody Energy
Westmoreland Coal

HISTORICAL FINANCIALS

Company Type: Public

Income Statement

FYE: December 31

	REVENUE ($ mil.)	NET INCOME ($ mil.)	NET PROFIT MARGIN	EMPLOYEES
12/05	159.1	91.8	57.7%	—
12/04	121.4	59.0	48.6%	—
12/03	85.5	36.9	43.2%	—
12/02	13.9	6.4	46.0%	—
Annual Growth	125.4%	143.0%	—	—

2005 Year-End Financials

Debt ratio: 52.1%
Return on equity: 22.0%
Cash ($ mil.): 47.7
Current ratio: 4.17
Long-term debt ($ mil.): 221.9
No. of shares (mil.): 16.8

Dividends
  Yield: 5.6%
  Payout: 82.6%
Market value ($ mil.): 845.5
R&D as % of sales: —
Advertising as % of sales: —

Stock History

NYSE: NRP

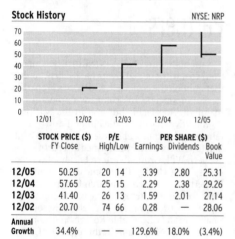

	STOCK PRICE ($) FY Close	P/E High/Low		PER SHARE ($) Earnings	Dividends	Book Value
12/05	50.25	20	14	3.39	2.80	25.31
12/04	57.65	25	15	2.29	2.38	29.26
12/03	41.40	26	13	1.59	2.01	27.14
12/02	20.70	74	66	0.28	—	28.06
Annual Growth	34.4%	—	—	129.6%	18.0%	(3.4%)

Navigant Consulting

Navigant Consulting aims to help its clients navigate troubled business waters. A significant portion of the firm's practice is devoted to issues related to business disputes, litigation, and regulatory compliance. Navigant Consulting also offers operational, strategic, and technical management consulting services. It targets customers in regulated industries such as construction, energy, financial services, health care, and insurance; in addition, the firm works with government agencies and companies involved in product liability cases. Navigant Consulting is not related to corporate travel services provider Navigant International.

Navigant Consulting has grown over the years through a series of acquisitions — 18 between 2001 and 2005 — and it has signaled that it will continue to pursue that strategy. In December 2006 the firm expanded its health care consulting practice by acquiring HP3.

Although Navigant Consulting operates primarily through its 30-plus offices in the US, the firm also maintains operations in Canada, China, the Czech Republic, and the UK.

EXECUTIVES

Chairman and CEO: William M. Goodyear, age 57
President and COO: Julie M. Howard, age 43
EVP and CFO: Ben W. Perks, age 64
VP, General Counsel, and Secretary: Richard X. Fischer
VP and Controller: David E. Wartner, age 39
VP Corporate Development: Jeffrey H. Stoecklein
VP Strategy and Organizational Development: Jeff Green
VP and Business Unit Leader, Business, Financial, and Operations: Sharon Siegel Voelzke
VP and Business Unit Leader, Dispute, Investigative, and Regulatory Advisory: J. Donald Fancher
Senior Managing Director, Government Contracting: William Keevan
Director, Marketing: Andrew J. Bosman
Investor Relations: Mary Rosinski
Auditors: KPMG LLP

LOCATIONS

HQ: Navigant Consulting, Inc.
  615 N. Wabash Ave., Chicago, IL 60611
Phone: 312-573-5600   **Fax:** 312-573-5678
Web: www.navigantconsulting.com

PRODUCTS/OPERATIONS

2005 Sales

	$ mil.	% of total
Business, financial & operational advisory services	257.8	45
Dispute, investigative & regulatory advisory services	251.6	44
Other	66.1	11
Total	**575.5**	**100**

Selected Practice Areas

Construction
Energy
Financial services
Health care
Insurance
Product liability
Public sector

COMPETITORS

Accenture
BearingPoint
CRA International
FTI Consulting
Huron Consulting
ICF International
KPMG
LECG
McKinsey & Company

HISTORICAL FINANCIALS

Company Type: Public

Income Statement

FYE: December 31

	REVENUE ($ mil.)	NET INCOME ($ mil.)	NET PROFIT MARGIN	EMPLOYEES
12/05	575.5	49.9	8.7%	2,276
12/04	482.1	40.4	8.4%	2,060
12/03	317.8	18.7	5.9%	1,367
12/02	258.0	8.9	3.4%	1,368
12/01	235.6	(5.3)	—	1,325
Annual Growth	25.0%	—	—	14.5%

2005 Year-End Financials

Debt ratio: —
Return on equity: 14.8%
Cash ($ mil.): 14.9
Current ratio: 1.25
Long-term debt ($ mil.): —
No. of shares (mil.): 50.6

Dividends
  Yield: —
  Payout: —
Market value ($ mil.): 1,112.2
R&D as % of sales: —
Advertising as % of sales: —

Stock History

NYSE: NCI

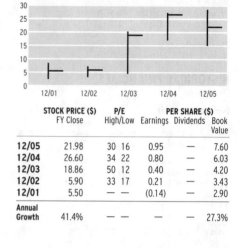

	STOCK PRICE ($) FY Close	P/E High/Low		PER SHARE ($) Earnings	Dividends	Book Value
12/05	21.98	30	16	0.95	—	7.60
12/04	26.60	34	22	0.80	—	6.03
12/03	18.86	50	12	0.40	—	4.20
12/02	5.90	33	17	0.21	—	3.43
12/01	5.50	—	—	(0.14)	—	2.90
Annual Growth	41.4%	—	—	—	—	27.3%

NAVTEQ

So what if he won't pull over and ask for directions? NAVTEQ helps people in Europe, the Middle East, and North America get where they're going. Car and navigation system manufacturers incorporate the company's NAVTEQ digital mapping database into vehicle navigation and fleet management systems, along with Web-based mapping sites. NAVTEQ also sells to government agencies. The database features such information as street names, turn restrictions, and the locations of hospitals, gas stations, and tourist destinations. BMW is NAVTEQ's biggest customer.

Two of NAVTEQ's primary competitors, Geographic Data Technology (GDT) and Tele Atlas, merged in mid-2004 to form an even stronger rival to NAVTEQ in Europe and North America. NAVTEQ acquired Picture Map International (PMI), a South Korea-based digital map company, for about $28 million the following year.

The company acquired gedas MapIT, the digital map division of gedas Mexico (a division of gedas AG), early in 2006. In late 2006 the company also announced plans to acquire The Map Network for $37.5 million. It also sold its navigation software division to longtime strategic partner NAVIGON in order to focus on its navigable map data products.

EXECUTIVES

Chairman: Christopher B. (Chris) Galvin, age 54
President, CEO, and Director: Judson C. Green, age 54, $1,568,462 pay
EVP and CFO: David B. Mullen, age 55, $680,000 pay
EVP, NAVTEQ Connected Services: John K. MacLeod, age 48

SVP, Consumer and Business Sales:
Winston V. Guillory Jr., age 49
SVP, Global Marketing and Strategy:
M. Salahuddin Khan, age 53
SVP, General Counsel, and Secretary:
Lawrence M. Kaplan, age 42
SVP, Asia/Pacific Sales: Richard E. (Rich) Shuman, age 54
SVP and CTO: Amreesh Modi
VP, Human Resources: Christine C. Moore, age 56
VP, Marketing Communications and Public Relations:
Kelly Smith
Auditors: KPMG LLP

LOCATIONS

HQ: NAVTEQ Corporation
222 Merchandise Mart, Ste. 900, Chicago, IL 60654
Phone: 312-894-7000   **Fax:** 312-894-7050
Web: www.navteq.com

2005 Sales

	$ mil.	% of total
Europe	316.2	64
North America	172.8	35
Asia/Pacific	7.5	1
Total	**496.5**	**100**

PRODUCTS/OPERATIONS

Selected Products and Services

Advanced Driver Assistance Systems (automated headlights, collision avoidance, and cruise control)
NAVTEQ DESTINATIONS+ (destinations listing)
Real-Time Map Service (digital, real-time map data)
Voice Enabled Navigation (enables verbal driving instructions)

COMPETITORS

AirIQ	OnStar
Analytical Surveys	Ordnance Survey
@Road	PlanGraphics
Autodesk	Pointer Telocation
CellPoint	QUALCOMM
DeLorme	Remote Dynamics
ESRI	Tele Atlas
Intergraph	Thales Telematics
MapInfo	Trafficmaster
Numerex	XATA
ObjectFX	

HISTORICAL FINANCIALS

Company Type: Public

Income Statement
FYE: December 31

	REVENUE ($ mil.)	NET INCOME ($ mil.)	NET PROFIT MARGIN	EMPLOYEES
12/05	496.5	170.8	34.4%	1,942
12/04	392.9	54.1	13.8%	1,541
12/03	272.6	235.8	86.5%	1,411
12/02	165.9	8.2	4.9%	1,186
12/01	110.4	(116.5)	—	
Annual Growth	**45.6%**	**—**	**—**	**17.9%**

2005 Year-End Financials

Debt ratio: —
Return on equity: 47.3%
Cash ($ mil.): 169.4
Current ratio: 2.61
Long-term debt ($ mil.): —
No. of shares (mil.): 92.1
Dividends
 Yield: —
 Payout: —
Market value ($ mil.): 4,039.8
R&D as % of sales: —
Advertising as % of sales: —

Stock History
NYSE: NVT

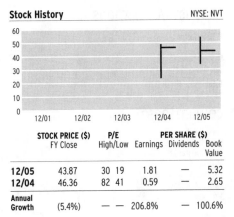

	STOCK PRICE ($) FY Close	P/E High/Low	Earnings	Dividends	Book Value
12/05	43.87	30 19	1.81	—	5.32
12/04	46.36	82 41	0.59	—	2.65
Annual Growth	**(5.4%)**	**— —**	**206.8%**	**—**	**100.6%**

Neoware

Neoware serves up an alternative to the traditional PC. The company makes Linux- and Windows-based thin-client computers. Neoware's terminals rely on centrally managed servers for computing power, eliminating the need for local storage drives and individual software installations and updates. In addition to its thin client lines, Neoware offers remote management applications and emulation software, as well as consulting and training services. The company sells directly and through resellers and systems integrators to such customers as Intel, ESPN, and Bristol-Myers Squibb.

Neoware has been active in acquisitions to expand its product line, distribution channels, and international markets. The company boosted its network appliance offerings by purchasing the Capio thin-client line from Boundless. It acquired the thin-client line of Visara International in 2004. The company has acquired TeleVideo's thin-client business for about $3 million in cash. Also, in early 2005, Neoware bought a French company, Mangrove Systems, a supplier of embedded Linux products. Neoware also acquired Maxspeed for about $24 million in cash in 2005. The Mangrove acquisition was intended to widen business in Europe, while Maxspeed will help increase Asian business.

Accounting for 17% of sales in fiscal 2006, Lenovo Group is Neoware's top customer.

Royce & Associates owns about 10% of Neoware Systems. Putnam and Discovery Equity Partners each hold around 7% of the company. FMR (Fidelity Investments) has an equity stake of 6%.

EXECUTIVES

President, CEO, and Director: Klaus P. Besier, age 55
COO: Eric N. Rubino, age 47, $323,280 pay
EVP and CFO: Keith D. Schneck, age 51, $256,824 pay
EVP, Marketing and Business Development:
Matthew D. Wrabley, age 44
EVP, EMEA Sales and Marketing: Peter Bolton, age 52, $240,132 pay
VP, Worldwide Engineering: Edward M. Parks
VP, Operations: Stephen Wickham
VP, Sales, Americas and ASPAC: James Kirby
EVP, Asia Pacific: Wei Ching, age 52
VP, Marketing Communications: C. Baker Egerton
Auditors: KPMG LLP

LOCATIONS

HQ: Neoware, Inc.
3200 Horizon Dr., King of Prussia, PA 19406
Phone: 610-277-8300   **Fax:** 610-771-4200
Web: www.neoware.com

Neoware has offices in Australia, Austria, China, France, Germany, the UK, and the US.

PRODUCTS/OPERATIONS

Selected Products

Appliance management software (ezRemote Manager, TeemTalk, ThinPC)
Thin clients (Eon, Capio)

COMPETITORS

Citrix Systems
ClearCube
Dell
Gateway
Hewlett-Packard
IGEL
IPC Corporation
Lenovo
Microsoft
MPC Computers
Sun Microsystems
Wyse Technology

HISTORICAL FINANCIALS

Company Type: Public

Income Statement
FYE: June 30

	REVENUE ($ mil.)	NET INCOME ($ mil.)	NET PROFIT MARGIN	EMPLOYEES
6/06	107.2	7.1	6.6%	179
6/05	78.8	7.4	9.4%	140
6/04	63.2	5.4	8.5%	114
6/03	57.5	6.3	11.0%	119
6/02	34.3	4.6	13.4%	101
Annual Growth	**33.0%**	**11.5%**	**—**	**15.4%**

2006 Year-End Financials

Debt ratio: —
Return on equity: 5.2%
Cash ($ mil.): 114.1
Current ratio: 8.51
Long-term debt ($ mil.): —
No. of shares (mil.): 19.8
Dividends
 Yield: —
 Payout: —
Market value ($ mil.): 243.8
R&D as % of sales: —
Advertising as % of sales: —

Stock History
NASDAQ (GS): NWRE

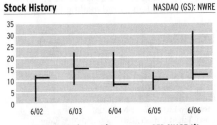

	STOCK PRICE ($) FY Close	P/E High/Low	Earnings	Dividends	Book Value
6/06	12.29	79 26	0.39	—	9.15
6/05	10.24	29 13	0.46	—	5.54
6/04	8.27	65 23	0.34	—	5.13
6/03	15.21	51 20	0.43	—	3.34
6/02	11.34	31 3	0.39	—	2.83
Annual Growth	**2.0%**	**— —**	**0.0%**	**—**	**34.1%**

Netflix

In a blend of technologies from multiple eras, Netflix steers couch potatoes away from the video store and straight to the mail box. Its Web site (Netflix.com) offers DVD rentals (over 60,000 titles) to more than 4.2 million subscribers for a monthly fee. The movies are delivered to customers the old-fashioned way: through the US Postal Service. Netflix does not charge late fees or have due dates, and the company's service employs user ratings to predict individual preferences and make movie recommendations. Netflix has more than 35 distribution centers in major US cities. Director Jay Hoag and his Technology Crossover Ventures owns about 20% of the company and CEO Reed Hastings owns about 10%.

Netflix has partnered with digital video recorder maker TiVo to develop a service that will allow both companies' customers to access DVD-quality movies via their broadband Internet connections.

In reaction to news that Amazon.com might be entering the US online DVD rental arena (Amazon has already launched its rental service in the UK) and to stay competitive with Blockbuster's online rental offering, the company cut its monthly fee and has also postponed its UK expansion plans. However, in 2006 Netflix filed suit against Blockbuster, maintaining its online rental service violates Netflix's patent on such a rental system. Blockbuster has countersued, claiming Netflix's patent is unenforceable and was questionably obtained.

In addition, Netflix had some legal problems of its own. A class-action suit was filed against the firm by customers objecting to Netflix's practice known as "throttling," which means that it delays shipments of DVDs to customers who rent the most movies and return them quickly. Users who rented fewer films each month (the company's more profitable customers since Netflix pays for shipping) typically receive their movies quicker. The firm settled the case by offering a free month to 5.5 million current and former subscribers, and paying millions in legal fees to the attorneys who originally filed the complaint.

Netflix has also begun to leverage its subscriber base by allowing companies to place ads in Netflix e-mails and on its red mailing envelopes.

EXECUTIVES

Chairman, President, and CEO: Reed Hastings, age 44
COO: William J. (Bill) Henderson, age 59
CFO and Secretary: Barry McCarthy Jr., age 51
Chief Content Officer: Ted Sarandos
Chief Marketing Officer: Leslie J. Kilgore, age 39
Chief Product Officer: Neil Hunt
Chief Talent Officer: Patricia J. (Patty) McCord
General Counsel: David Hyman
VP Advertising Sales: Peggy Fry
VP Corporate Communications: Ken Ross
Director of Investor Relations: Deborah Crawford
Auditors: KPMG LLP

LOCATIONS

HQ: Netflix, Inc.
100 Winchester Cir., Los Gatos, CA 95032
Phone: 408-540-3700
Web: www.netflix.com

Netflix has more than 35 distribution centers throughout the US.

PRODUCTS/OPERATIONS

2005 Sales

	% of total
Subscriptions	99
Sales	1
Total	**100**

COMPETITORS

Amazon.com
Best Buy
Blockbuster
Buy.com
CinemaNow
Columbia House
Comcast
Cox Communications
DIRECTV
EchoStar Communications
Hastings Entertainment
HBO
Kroger
Movie Gallery
Movielink
Showtime
Starz Entertainment
Target
Time Warner Cable
Tower Records
Wal-Mart

HISTORICAL FINANCIALS

Company Type: Public

Income Statement

FYE: December 31

	REVENUE ($ mil.)	NET INCOME ($ mil.)	NET PROFIT MARGIN	EMPLOYEES
12/05	682.2	42.0	6.2%	985
12/04	506.2	21.6	4.3%	940
12/03	272.2	6.5	2.4%	567
12/02	152.8	(22.0)	—	495
12/01	75.9	(38.6)	—	264
Annual Growth	**73.1%**	**—**	**—**	**39.0%**

2005 Year-End Financials

Debt ratio: —
Return on equity: 22.0%
Cash ($ mil.): 212.3
Current ratio: 1.77
Long-term debt ($ mil.): —
No. of shares (mil.): 54.8
Dividends
  Yield: —
  Payout: —
Market value ($ mil.): 1,481.7
R&D as % of sales: —
Advertising as % of sales: 6.8%

Stock History

NASDAQ (GS): NFLX

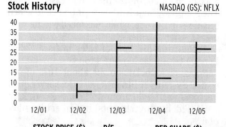

	STOCK PRICE ($) FY Close	P/E High/Low		PER SHARE ($) Earnings	Dividends	Book Value
12/05	27.06	47	14	0.64	—	4.13
12/04	12.33	121	28	0.33	—	2.96
12/03	27.34	305	53	0.10	—	2.22
12/02	5.51	—	—	(0.78)	—	3.98
Annual Growth	**70.0%**			**—**	**—**	**—**

NetLogic Microsystems

NetLogic Microsystems' chips logically address the content of the Internet. The company designs and sells packet processors and content-addressable memory (CAM) chips, which are used in routers and other devices to optimize speed and search capabilities over the Internet. NetLogic's customers include networking giants Cisco (74% of sales, including Cisco's contract manufacturers), Alcatel, and Nortel. The fabless semiconductor company has a licensing agreement with Micron Technology. NetLogic Microsystems was founded by former CEO Norman Godinho (who owns about 15% of the company) and CTO Varad Srinivasan.

NetLogic has acquired the network search engine products of Cypress Semiconductor for approximately $50 million in common stock, plus up to $20 million in cash and stock depending on revenue milestones. NetLogic will acquire the assets and intellectual property of Cypress Semi's Ayama 10000/20000 and NSE70000 network search engine device families, as well as the Sahasra 50000 algorithmic search engine family. The purchase will advance NetLogic's development of lower-cost Layer 7 applications acceleration and security processing for networking systems, among other benefits.

The company's semiconductors are principally produced by Taiwan Semiconductor Manufacturing and United Microelectronics, two of the world's biggest contract manufacturers of chips, known as silicon foundries.

NetLogic was backed by investors including Sevin Rosen Funds.

Gilder, Gagnon, Howe & Co. owns about 8% of NetLogic Microsystems.

EXECUTIVES

Chairman: Leonard C. (Len) Perham, age 63
President, CEO, and Director: Ronald (Ron) Jankov, age 47
SVP Worldwide Business Operations: Ibrahim (Abe) Korgav, age 57
VP and CFO: Donald B. (Don) Witmer, age 52
VP Product Development, CTO, and Director: Varadarajan (Varad) Srinivasan, age 55
VP Corporate Development: Niall Bartlett
VP Engineering: Dimitrios Dimitrelis, age 48
VP Sales: Marcia Zander, age 43
VP Worldwide Manufacturing: Mozafar (Mo) Maghsoudnia
Media Contact: Nancy Moore
Auditors: PricewaterhouseCoopers LLP

LOCATIONS

HQ: NetLogic Microsystems, Inc.
1875 Charleston Rd., Mountain View, CA 94043
Phone: 650-961-6676   **Fax:** 650-961-1092
Web: www.netlogicmicro.com

NetLogic Microsystems has offices in India and the US.

2005 Sales

	$ mil.	% of total
US	55.0	67
Asia/Pacific		
Malaysia	21.4	26
Other countries	4.4	6
Europe	1.0	1
Total	**81.8**	**100**

PRODUCTS/OPERATIONS

Selected Products

Classification and forwarding processors
Network search engines
Software development kits
Ternary content-addressable memory (TCAM) search
   accelerators

COMPETITORS

Agere Systems
Cavium Networks
Cypress Semiconductor
hi/fn
Integrated Device Technology
MOSAID Technologies
Mysticom
Renesas
Tarari
Teradiant Networks
TranSwitch
Vitesse Semiconductor

HISTORICAL FINANCIALS

Company Type: Public

Income Statement
FYE: December 31

	REVENUE ($ mil.)	NET INCOME ($ mil.)	NET PROFIT MARGIN	EMPLOYEES
12/05	81.8	16.4	20.0%	110
12/04	47.8	(12.0)	—	75
12/03	13.5	(32.0)	—	78
12/02	2.9	(19.9)	—	—
Annual Growth	204.4%	—	—	18.8%

2005 Year-End Financials

Debt ratio: 0.5%
Return on equity: 28.1%
Cash ($ mil.): 65.8
Current ratio: 5.01
Long-term debt ($ mil.): 0.3
No. of shares (mil.): 18.1
Dividends
   Yield: —
   Payout: —
Market value ($ mil.): 492.4
R&D as % of sales: 25.8%
Advertising as % of sales: —

Stock History
NASDAQ (GM): NETL

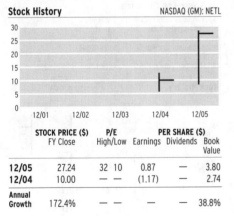

	STOCK PRICE ($) FY Close	P/E High/Low	Earnings	PER SHARE ($) Dividends	Book Value
12/05	27.24	32 10	0.87	—	3.80
12/04	10.00	— —	(1.17)	—	2.74
Annual Growth	172.4%	—	—	—	38.8%

NeuroMetrix

NeuroMetrix lets doctors keep tabs on your nerves. The company makes medical devices that are used to detect, diagnose, and monitor neurological conditions affecting the peripheral nerves and spine. The company's non-invasive NC-stat System, allows physicians to distinguish between pain caused by nerve root compression and pain caused by less serious factors. By making it usable by primary care physicians, the company hopes to reduce the need to send patients on to specialists for such diagnoses, thereby keeping care closer, and costs down. The systems are used in nearly 3,300 doctor's offices and other health care facilities. NeuroMetrix maintains an active research and development department.

The NC-stat system costs far less than the traditional needle electromyography equipment used by neurologists, and with no needles used, the NC-stat system is more comfortable for patients.

EXECUTIVES

Chairman, President, and CEO: Shai N. Gozani, age 42, $375,000 pay
COO: Gary L. Gregory, age 43, $367,367 pay
CFO and Secretary: W. Bradford (Brad) Smith, age 50, $326,534 pay
SVP, Engineering: Michael Williams, age 49, $207,054 pay
SVP, Information Technology: Guy Daniello, age 61, $199,501 pay
VP, Manufacturing: Charles Fendrock
VP, Quality Assurance and Clinical and Regulatory Affairs: Joseph F. Burke
VP, Research: Xuan Kong
Chief Medical Officer: James M. Strickland
Auditors: PricewaterhouseCoopers LLP

LOCATIONS

HQ: NeuroMetrix, Inc.
   62 4th Ave., Waltham, MA 02451
Phone: 781-890-9989   **Fax:** 781-890-1556
Web: www.neurometrix.com

PRODUCTS/OPERATIONS

2005 Sales

	$ mil.	% of total
Biosensor	30.1	88
Diagnostic devices	4.2	12
Total	**34.3**	**100**

COMPETITORS

Bio-logic
Medtronic
Oxford Instruments
VIASYS Healthcare

HISTORICAL FINANCIALS

Company Type: Public

Income Statement
FYE: December 31

	REVENUE ($ mil.)	NET INCOME ($ mil.)	NET PROFIT MARGIN	EMPLOYEES
12/05	34.3	0.9	2.6%	100
12/04	17.9	(4.3)	—	68
12/03	9.2	(3.7)	—	51
12/02	4.2	(4.8)	—	—
Annual Growth	101.4%	—	—	40.0%

2005 Year-End Financials

Debt ratio: —
Return on equity: 2.6%
Cash ($ mil.): 32.3
Current ratio: 7.16
Long-term debt ($ mil.): —
No. of shares (mil.): 12.4
Dividends
   Yield: —
   Payout: —
Market value ($ mil.): 337.6
R&D as % of sales: 11.1%
Advertising as % of sales: 0.8%

Stock History
NASDAQ (GM): NURO

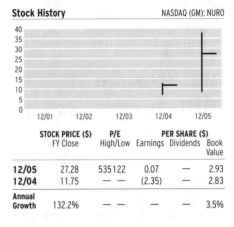

	STOCK PRICE ($) FY Close	P/E High/Low	Earnings	PER SHARE ($) Dividends	Book Value
12/05	27.28	535 122	0.07	—	2.93
12/04	11.75	— —	(2.35)	—	2.83
Annual Growth	132.2%	—	—	—	3.5%

NeuStar

NeuStar shines on the provision of third-party interoperability services used in telecommunications and Internet networks. NeuStar manages the registry of North American area codes and telephone numbers and the database used by carriers (including Verizon, Sprint, AT&T, and Cingular, now AT&T Mobility) to route phone calls. The company also operates an Internet Registry supporting domain addresses. NeuStar is a leading provider of OSS (Operations Support Systems) clearinghouse services that provides ordering, service provisioning, billing, and customer service functions for telecom carriers and other companies. Investment firm Warburg Pincus owns 10% of the company; AXA Financial owns 8%.

NeuStar is the contracted North American Numbering Plan Administrator, the National Pooling Administrator, the Administrator of local number portability for communications carriers in North America, and the lone industry registry for US Common Short Codes.

In 2006 the company agreed to acquire UltraDNS, a Reston-Virginia-based DNS and directory services firm, in a cash deal valued at $61.8 million.

EXECUTIVES

Chairman and CEO: Jeffrey E. (Jeff) Ganek, age 53, $662,500 pay
President and COO: Michael R. Lach, age 44, $557,218 pay
SVP, Operations: Steve Cory
SVP and CFO: Jeffrey A. (Jeff) Babka, age 52, $668,077 pay
SVP and CTO: Mark D. Foster, age 47, $544,327 pay
SVP, General Counsel, and Secretary: Martin Lowen, age 41
SVP and Managing Director, International: A. Reza Jafari, age 60
SVP, Corporate Development and Marketing: John Spirtos, age 40
SVP, Marketing: Steve Johnson
SVP, Sales and Business Development: John Malone, age 43, $451,288 pay

VP, Finance and Investor Relations: Paul S. Lalljie
VP, Human Resources: George Rau
Senior Director, Corporate Communications:
  Elizabeth Penniman
Auditors: Ernst & Young LLP

LOCATIONS

HQ: NeuStar, Inc.
  46000 Center Oak Plaza, Sterling, VA 20166
Phone: 571-434-5400   **Fax:** 571-434-5401
Web: www.neustar.biz

PRODUCTS/OPERATIONS

2005 Sales

	$ mil.	% of total
Addressing	75.0	31
Interoperability	52.5	22
Infrastructure & other	115.0	47
Total	**242.5**	**100**

Selected Services

Advanced services
  Convergence directory services (ENUM)
  Identity management services (Liberty Alliance)
Internet registry services
  .biz
  .cn
  .us
Telephony services
  Local number portability administration
  North American Numbering Plan Administration
    (NANPA)
  OSS (Operations Support Systems) services

COMPETITORS

Accenture
Amdocs
Billing Services Group
Boston Communications Group
BSG Clearing Solutions
CGI Group
EDS
Evolving Systems
Hewlett-Packard
IBM
ICANN
MetaSolv
NetCracker Technology
Oracle
Perot Systems
Register.com
Syniverse
Tucows
VeriSign

HISTORICAL FINANCIALS

Company Type: Public

Income Statement   FYE: December 31

	REVENUE ($ mil.)	NET INCOME ($ mil.)	NET PROFIT MARGIN	EMPLOYEES
12/05	242.5	55.4	22.8%	502
12/04	165.0	45.4	27.5%	—
12/03	111.7	24.0	21.5%	—
Annual Growth	47.3%	51.9%	—	—

2005 Year-End Financials

Debt ratio: 2.4%
Return on equity: 71.8%
Cash ($ mil.): 103.8
Current ratio: 2.66
Long-term debt ($ mil.): 4.5
No. of shares (mil.): 68.2
Dividends
  Yield: —
  Payout: —
Market value ($ mil.): 2,077.9
R&D as % of sales: 4.9%
Advertising as % of sales: 0.3%

Stock History   NYSE: NSR

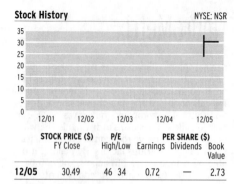

	STOCK PRICE ($) FY Close	P/E High/Low	PER SHARE ($) Earnings	Dividends	Book Value
12/05	30.49	46 34	0.72	—	2.73

New Century Bancorp

New Century Bancorp was formed in 2003 to be the holding company for the aptly named New Century Bank, which was founded in 2000, and New Century Bank South (formerly New Century Bank of Fayetteville). The banks have about five branches in central North Carolina's Cumberland, Harnett, Johnston, and Sampson counties. Targeting individuals and small to midsized businesses, they offer such services as checking and savings accounts, CDs, IRAs, and loans.

The company's loan book includes commercial mortgages, commercial loans, and residential mortgages and construction loans.

With an eye towards expanding out of the city of Fayetteville, New Century Bancorp subsidiary New Century Bank of Fayetteville changed its name to New Century Bank South in early 2006.

EXECUTIVES

Chairman: C. Lee Tart Jr., age 71
Vice Chairman: Oscar N. Harris, age 66
President, CEO, and Director; President and CEO, New Century Bank; EVP, New Century Bank South:
  John Q. Shaw Jr., age 64, $235,000 pay
President and CEO, New Century Bank South; EVP and COO, New Century Bank:
  William L. (Bill) Hedgepeth II, age 44, $130,000 pay (prior to promotion)
EVP and CFO, New Century Bancorp, New Century Bank, and New Century Bank South: Lisa F. Campbell, age 38, $138,500 pay
EVP and Chief Lending Officer, New Century Bank South: Kevin S. Bunn, age 44
EVP and Branch Administrator, New Century Bank: B. Darrell Fowler, age 40, $148,000 pay
EVP and Chief Operations Officer, New Century Bank and New Century Bank South: Joan I. Patterson, age 59
EVP and Chief Credit Officer, New Century Bank; SVP and Chief Credit Officer, New Century Bank South: Peter J. (Pete) Siemion, age 39
Auditors: Dixon Hughes PLLC

LOCATIONS

HQ: New Century Bancorp, Inc.
  700 W. Cumberland St., Dunn, NC 28334
Phone: 910-892-7080   **Fax:** 910-892-9225
Web: www.newcenturybanknc.com

PRODUCTS/OPERATIONS

2005 Sales

	$ mil.	% of total
Interest		
Loans	22.4	82
Investments	1.2	4
Federal funds sold	1.1	4
Noninterest		
Service fees & charges	1.0	4
Fees from presold mortgages	0.7	3
Other	0.8	3
Total	**27.2**	**100**

COMPETITORS

Bank of America
BB&T
First Citizens BancShares
First South Bancorp (NC)
RBC Centura Banks
Wachovia

HISTORICAL FINANCIALS

Company Type: Public

Income Statement   FYE: December 31

	ASSETS ($ mil.)	NET INCOME ($ mil.)	INCOME AS % OF ASSETS	EMPLOYEES
12/05	436.4	3.6	0.8%	92
12/04	328.3	2.1	0.6%	—
12/03	191.8	0.9	0.5%	57
12/02	126.4	0.9	0.7%	—
12/01	84.4	0.6	0.7%	—
Annual Growth	50.8%	56.5%	—	27.0%

2005 Year-End Financials

Equity as % of assets: 7.6%
Return on assets: 0.9%
Return on equity: 11.5%
Long-term debt ($ mil.): 22.4
No. of shares (mil.): 4.2
Market value ($ mil.): 105.0
Dividends
  Yield: —
  Payout: —
Sales ($ mil.): 27.2
R&D as % of sales: —
Advertising as % of sales: —

Stock History   NASDAQ (GM): NCBC

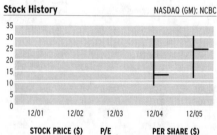

	STOCK PRICE ($) FY Close	P/E High/Low	PER SHARE ($) Earnings	Dividends	Book Value
12/05	24.75	38 16	0.79	—	7.77
12/04	13.67	64 19	0.47	—	10.47
Annual Growth	81.1%	— —	68.1%	—	(25.8%)

NewAlliance Bancshares

A new alliance has emerged on the New England banking scene. NewAlliance Bancshares (formerly New Haven Savings Bank) was formed when New Haven Savings acquired Alliance Bancorp of New England and Connecticut Bancshares in 2004.

The resulting company owns NewAlliance Bank, a community financial institution offering trust, brokerage, and insurance services through more than 70 branches in Connecticut. The bank is mainly a real estate lender, with residential mortgages accounting for approximately half of its loan portfolio; commercial mortgages add nearly 25%. In 2006 NewAlliance Bancshares added six offices to its fold with the $49 million acquisition of Cornerstone Bancorp.

In 2007 NewAlliance Bancshares acquired Massachusetts-based Westbank Corporation for $160 million in cash and stock; the deal gives NewAlliance its first toehold in Massachusetts.

The bank plans to place greater emphasis on business operating loans and home equity loans.

EXECUTIVES

Chairman, President, and CEO: Peyton R. Patterson, age 49, $1,227,596 pay
EVP and COO, NewAlliance Bancshares and NewAlliance Bank: Gail E. D. Brathwaite, age 46, $512,748 pay
EVP, CFO, and Treasurer, NewAlliance Bancshares and NewAlliance Bank: Merrill B. Blanksteen, age 52, $573,914 pay
EVP Business Banking, NewAlliance Bank: Diane L. Wishnafski, age 52
EVP and Chief Credit Officer, NewAlliance Bank: Donald T. (Don) Chaffee, age 57, $386,446 pay
EVP Corporate Communications and Investor Relations, NewAlliance Bank: Brian S. Arsenault, age 58
VP Human Resources and Benefits Manager: Barbara Bauer
Auditors: PricewaterhouseCoopers LLP

LOCATIONS

HQ: NewAlliance Bancshares, Inc.
195 Church St., New Haven, CT 06510
Phone: 203-789-2767   **Fax:** 203-789-2650
Web: www.newalliancebank.com

NewAlliance Bancshares has offices in Fairfield, Hartford, Middlesex, New Haven, Tolland, and Windham counties.

PRODUCTS/OPERATIONS

2005 Sales

	$ mil.	% of total
Interest		
Investment securities	97.4	30
Real estate mortgage loans	82.7	26
Commercial real estate loans	45.3	14
Consumer loans	29.0	9
Business loans	20.5	6
Short-term investments	1.8	1
Noninterest		
Depositor service charges	22.6	7
Investment & insurance fees	6.1	2
Trust fees	4.8	1
Rent	3.2	1
Loan & servicing income	3.0	1
Other	5.8	2
Total	**322.2**	**100**

COMPETITORS

Bank of America	People's Bank
Citibank	Sovereign Bancorp
Citizens Financial Group	TD Banknorth
JPMorgan Chase	Wachovia
Liberty Bank	Webster Financial

HISTORICAL FINANCIALS

Company Type: Public

Income Statement
FYE: December 31

	ASSETS ($ mil.)	NET INCOME ($ mil.)	INCOME AS % OF ASSETS	EMPLOYEES
12/05	6,561.4	52.6	0.8%	1,082
12/04	6,264.1	4.1	0.1%	1,032
12/03	2,536.7	12.1	0.5%	567
Annual Growth	**60.8%**	**108.5%**	**—**	**38.1%**

2005 Year-End Financials

Equity as % of assets: 20.0%
Return on assets: 0.8%
Return on equity: 3.9%
Long-term debt ($ mil.): 9.5
No. of shares (mil.): 108.8
Market value ($ mil.): 1,582.3

Dividends
Yield: 1.4%
Payout: 42.0%
Sales ($ mil.): 322.2
R&D as % of sales: —
Advertising as % of sales: —

Stock History
NYSE: NAL

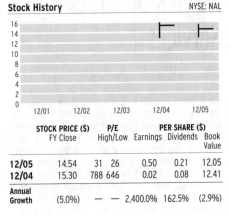

	STOCK PRICE ($) FY Close	P/E High/Low		PER SHARE ($) Earnings	Dividends	Book Value
12/05	14.54	31	26	0.50	0.21	12.05
12/04	15.30	788	646	0.02	0.08	12.41
Annual Growth	**(5.0%)**	**—**	**—**	**2,400.0%**	**162.5%**	**(2.9%)**

Newport Corporation

Newport helps all sorts of customers take a measured approach. The company makes lasers, precision components, and automated assembly, measurement, and test equipment used in the aerospace, fiber-optic communications, health care, and semiconductor manufacturing industries, and by researchers. Industrial and scientific components, including lenses and other devices for vibration and motion control, account for more than half of sales. Newport also offers automated systems used to make fiber-optic components and photonics. Customers include KLA-Tencor and Applied Materials.

Customers in the US account for about half of sales.

Newport is continuing to grow through new product introductions, primarily in the life sciences and photonics research markets. Sales to the life and health sciences market grew in 2003, while sales to the semiconductor capital equipment and other end markets continued to languish. In 2004 Newport acquired the optical technologies business of Thermo Electron (in-

cluding laser and optical gear maker Spectra-Physics) for approximately $275 million, in a deal that expands Newport's capabilities in the photonics, biophotonics, and nanotechnology market.

Newport sold off its industrial metrology systems unit in 2002. The company has also restructured — including rounds of layoffs and facility closures — in response to continued weakness in the fiber-optic communications and semiconductor equipment markets in the early years of the 21st century. Newport has announced additional restructuring plans, including the elimination of duplicate product lines and support positions, related to the integration of Spectra-Physics.

In late 2005 Newport sold its robotic systems business, which made robotic arms for semiconductor equipment and accounted for less than 5% of sales. It retained certain patents related to robotics technology. What remains of what was the company's Advanced Packaging and Automated Systems division has been folded into the Photonics and Precision Technologies division.

Private Capital Management owns nearly 13% of Newport Corp. Dimensional Fund Advisors holds about 8% of the company. Investor Joseph L. Harrosh has an equity stake of around 6%, while Michael W. Cook Asset Management owns nearly 6%.

EXECUTIVES

Chairman and CEO: Robert G. Deuster, age 55, $1,112,575 pay
President and COO: Robert J. Phillippy, age 45, $573,797 pay
SVP, CFO, and Treasurer: Charles F. Cargile, age 41, $531,748 pay
SVP, General Counsel, and Secretary: Jeffrey B. Coyne, age 39, $375,467 pay
VP, Corporate Controller, and Chief Accounting Officer: Daniel E. Della Flora
VP and General Manager, Advanced Packaging and Automation Systems Division: Kevin T. Crofton, age 45
VP and General Manager, Photonics and Precision Technologies Division: Alain Danielo, age 59, $370,264 pay
VP, Worldwide Sales and Service: Gary J. Spiegel, age 55
VP, Strategic Marketing and Business Development: Leif A. Alexandersson, age 51
Director, Marketing: David Rossi
Auditors: Ernst & Young LLP

LOCATIONS

HQ: Newport Corporation
1791 Deere Ave., Irvine, CA 92606
Phone: 949-863-3144   **Fax:** 949-253-1680
Web: www.newport.com

Newport has manufacturing facilities in France, the UK, and the US. It has sales offices in Austria, Canada, China, France, Germany, Ireland, Italy, Japan, Jordan, the Netherlands, Taiwan, the UK, and the US.

2005 Sales

	$ mil.	% of total
US	215.6	54
Europe	86.1	21
Asia/Pacific	81.6	20
Other regions	20.4	5
Total	**403.7**	**100**

PRODUCTS/OPERATIONS

2005 Sales

	$ mil.	% of total
Photonics & precision technologies	227.8	56
Lasers	175.9	44
Total	**403.7**	**100**

2005 Sales by Market

	$ mil.	% of total
Scientific research, aerospace & defense/security	155.6	38
Microelectronics	115.5	29
Life & health sciences	61.5	15
Other	71.1	18
Total	**403.7**	**100**

Selected Products and Services

Photonics and Precision Technologies
  Manual positioning components
  Optics
  Photonics
  Precision micro-positioning devices, systems, and
    subsystems
  Vibration isolation equipment
Lasers
Advanced Packaging and Automation Systems
  Assembly and packaging
  Engineering and manufacturing services (fiber-optic
    device manufacturing, packaging, process design
    and automation, and tooling)
  Final device testing and burn-in
  Instruments
  Pretest

COMPETITORS

Adept Technology
Agilent Technologies
Allied Motion Technologies
Anritsu
Bookham
Carl Zeiss
Coherent
Corning
CVI Laser
Danaher
ESEC
EXFO
II-VI
ILX Lightwave
Keithley Instruments
Kinetic Systems
Melles Griot
Nikon
Palomar Technologies
Renishaw
Roper Industries
Speedline Technologies
Thermo Fisher Scientific
Zygo

HISTORICAL FINANCIALS
Company Type: Public

Income Statement
FYE: December 31

	REVENUE ($ mil.)	NET INCOME ($ mil.)	NET PROFIT MARGIN	EMPLOYEES
12/05	403.7	11.6	2.9%	1,870
12/04	285.8	(81.4)	—	2,000
12/03	134.8	(13.2)	—	942
12/02	164.0	(100.6)	—	1,088
12/01	318.9	(6.3)	—	1,653
Annual Growth	**6.1%**	**—**	**—**	**3.1%**

2005 Year-End Financials

Debt ratio: 13.6%
Return on equity: 2.9%
Cash ($ mil.): 71.0
Current ratio: 2.73
Long-term debt ($ mil.): 51.3
No. of shares (mil.): 40.0
Dividends
  Yield: —
  Payout: —
Market value ($ mil.): 542.1
R&D as % of sales: 8.9%
Advertising as % of sales: 1.0%

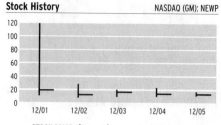

Stock History
NASDAQ (GM): NEWP

	STOCK PRICE ($) FY Close	P/E High/Low	Earnings	PER SHARE ($) Dividends	Book Value
12/05	13.54	61 45	0.27	—	9.41
12/04	14.10	— —	(1.99)	—	9.66
12/03	16.62	— —	(0.34)	—	11.23
12/02	12.56	— —	(2.65)	—	11.58
12/01	19.28	— —	(0.17)	0.01	13.33
Annual Growth	**(8.5%)**	**— —**	**—**	**—**	**(8.3%)**

Newtek Business Services

Newtek Business Services is holding company that invests in certified capital companies (CAPCOs) through its Wilshire Group subsidiary. The company has stakes in about 15 CAPCOs that issue debt and equity securities to insurance firms, then use the funds to mainly invest in financial and business services firms. Newtek's portfolio includes majority-owned companies that offer Small Business Administration (SBA) loans, electronic merchant payment processing, Web hosting, insurance, tax preparation, and back-office financial support to small and mid-sized businesses.

Chairman and CEO Barry Sloane and president and chief investment officer Jeffrey Rubin each own approximately 13% of Newtek Business Services.

EXECUTIVES

Chairman, CEO, and Secretary: Barry Sloane, age 46, $302,501 pay
President, Chief Investment Officer, and Director: Jeffrey G. Rubin, age 38, $286,668 pay
CFO: Michael J. Holden, age 54
Chief Administrative Officer: Ellen Merryman
Chief Legal Officer: Andrew E. Lewin
EVP Sales and Customer Service, Newtek Merchant Solutions: Michele Payton
EVP Newtek Information Systems: Joseph J. Carvalho
Director, Acquisitions: Sharmila Ruder-Amico
Internal Control and Credit Review Officer, Newtek Small Business Finance: Doug Keins
Chairman and Managing Partner, Newtek Strategies: Craig J. Brunet
President and COO, Universal Processing Systems: Tracy Alan (Alan) Schmidt, age 44, $84,000 pay
President and CEO, CrystalTech Web Hosting, Inc.: Tim Uzzanti, age 33, $200,000 pay
President, Newtek Small Business Finance: Peter Downs
Auditors: PricewaterhouseCoopers LLP

LOCATIONS

HQ: Newtek Business Services, Inc.
  462 7th Ave., 14th Fl., New York City, NY 10018
Phone: 212-356-9500 **Fax:** 212-643-1006
Web: www.newtekbusinessservices.com

PRODUCTS/OPERATIONS

2005 Sales

	$ mil.	% of total
Certified capital companies	37.8	37
Electronic payment processing	32.8	32
Small Business Administration lending	10.7	11
Web hosting	10.7	11
Corporate activities	5.1	5
Adjustments	(4.7)	—
Other	4.4	4
Total	**96.8**	**100**

COMPETITORS

Advantage Capital
Gateway Associates
Red Rock Ventures
Stifel Financial
Stonehenge Partners
Waveland Ventures

HISTORICAL FINANCIALS
Company Type: Public

Income Statement
FYE: December 31

	REVENUE ($ mil.)	NET INCOME ($ mil.)	NET PROFIT MARGIN	EMPLOYEES
12/05	96.8	7.7	8.0%	360
12/04	70.2	10.6	15.1%	200
12/03	60.5	9.6	15.9%	115
12/02	34.6	8.2	23.7%	160
12/01	23.8	0.9	3.8%	60
Annual Growth	**42.0%**	**71.0%**	**—**	**56.5%**

2005 Year-End Financials

Debt ratio: 155.9%
Return on equity: 9.4%
Cash ($ mil.): 32.4
Current ratio: —
Long-term debt ($ mil.): 136.4
No. of shares (mil.): 34.8
Dividends
  Yield: —
  Payout: —
Market value ($ mil.): 67.2
R&D as % of sales: —
Advertising as % of sales: —

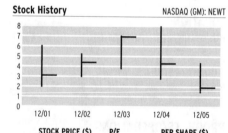

Stock History
NASDAQ (GM): NEWT

	STOCK PRICE ($) FY Close	P/E High/Low	Earnings	PER SHARE ($) Dividends	Book Value
12/05	1.93	19 6	0.23	—	2.51
12/04	4.30	23 8	0.35	—	2.27
12/03	6.94	19 10	0.37	—	1.52
12/02	4.39	15 9	0.34	—	1.07
12/01	3.10	150 50	0.04	—	0.51
Annual Growth	**(11.2%)**	**— —**	**54.9%**	**—**	**48.8%**

Nexity Financial

You'll encounter *virtually* no lines while banking with Nexity. Nexity Financial is the holding company for Nexity Bank, which provides correspondent banking services (including outsourced services and loan participations) to smaller community banks in the southeastern US. It also offers online retail banking services to more than 17,000 consumers and commercial customers throughout the US. Nexity Bank provides a variety of loans, secured primarily by real estate or bank securities; construction and mortgage loans account for some 35% and 30% of its lending portfolio, respectively. Nexity Financial has correspondent banking offices in Alabama, Georgia, North Carolina, South Carolina, and Texas.

EXECUTIVES

Chairman and CEO: Greg L. Lee, age 46, $637,000 pay
President and Director: David E. Long, age 43, $439,000 pay
EVP, CFO, and Director: John J. Moran, age 44, $439,000 pay
EVP and Senior Lending Officer, Nexity Financial and Nexity Bank: Kenneth T. Vassey, age 47, $371,598 pay
EVP Operations, Nexity Financial and Nexity Bank: Cindy W. Russo, age 48, $206,650 pay
Auditors: Mauldin & Jenkins, LLC

LOCATIONS

HQ: Nexity Financial Corporation
3500 Blue Lake Dr., Ste. 330,
Birmingham, AL 35243
Phone: 205-298-6391   **Fax:** 205-298-6395
Web: www.nexitybank.com

PRODUCTS/OPERATIONS

2005 Sales

	$ mil.	% of total
Interest income		
Loans	31.1	72
Securities	9.2	22
Federal funds sold	0.6	1
Other	0.2	—
Noninterest income		
Brokerage & investment services income	0.7	2
Gains on sales of investment securities	0.5	1
Commissions & fees	0.3	1
Other	0.4	1
Total	**43.0**	**100**

COMPETITORS

Bankers Bank	Goldleaf Financial
Bankrate	Solutions, Inc
Capital One	ING Direct USA
CUNA Mutual	NetBank
E*TRADE Bank	Online Resources
Fiserv	PrimeVest

HISTORICAL FINANCIALS

Company Type: Public

Income Statement
FYE: December 31

	ASSETS ($ mil.)	NET INCOME ($ mil.)	INCOME AS % OF ASSETS	EMPLOYEES
12/05	784.5	4.5	0.6%	88
12/04	610.8	5.4	0.9%	—
12/03	522.7	4.7	0.9%	—
Annual Growth	**22.5%**	**(2.2%)**	**—**	**—**

Stock History
NASDAQ (GM): NXTY

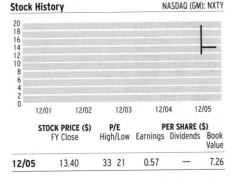

	STOCK PRICE ($) FY Close	P/E High/Low	PER SHARE ($) Earnings	Dividends	Book Value
12/05	13.40	33 21	0.57	—	7.26

Nextest Systems

Next! Nextest's systems are always ready to test another integrated circuit (IC). The company's Maverick automated testing products are used to screen application-specific integrated circuits, field programmable gate arrays and other logic devices, non-volatile (flash) memory, microcontrollers, and system-on-a-chip (SoC) semiconductors for defects. Customers include memory makers SanDisk (29% of sales), Hynix Semiconductor (18%), Samsung Electronics (15%), and Atmel (11%). Nextest, which outsources much of its manufacturing, was founded by CEO Robin Adler and VP Howard Marshall. Adler and Marshall collectively own 28% of the company.

Lower cost is the holy grail in semiconductor production testing. Chip makers are continually pushing automatic test equipment (ATE) vendors to push down the price of IC test equipment, trying to lower their production costs. Nextest Systems has responded to that perennial pressure with its Maverick testers, along with the newer Lightning and Magnum models, which reduce the capabilities of testers to specific testing requirements, such as high-volume testing of flash memories or microcontrollers.

Former company president Paul Magliocco owns around 8% of Nextest Systems.

The company has received investments from such venture capital firms as Needham Capital Partners (which owns nearly 7% of Nextest Systems) and J. & W. Seligman.

EXECUTIVES

Chairman and CEO: Robin Adler, age 58, $238,587 pay
VP, Finance, CFO, Treasurer, and Assistant Secretary: James P. (Jim) Moniz, age 49, $229,573 pay
VP, Operations and Director: Howard D. Marshall, age 57, $225,750 pay
VP, Engineering: Craig Z. Foster, age 54, $225,750 pay
VP, Sales and Marketing: Tim F. Moriarty, age 45, $206,775 pay
Secretary: Victor A. Hebert
Auditors: PricewaterhouseCoopers LLP

LOCATIONS

HQ: Nextest Systems Corporation
1901 Monterey Rd., San Jose, CA 95112
Phone: 408-817-7200   **Fax:** 408-817-7210
Web: www.nextest.com

Nextest Systems has offices in China, Italy, Japan, the Philippines, South Korea, Thailand, the UK, and the US.

2006 Sales

	$ mil.	% of total
Asia/Pacific		
South Korea	29.6	34
Taiwan	17.4	20
China	14.8	17
Thailand	4.5	5
Philippines	1.5	2
Other countries	0.6	1
North America	15.4	17
Europe, Middle East & Africa	3.9	4
Total	**87.7**	**100**

PRODUCTS/OPERATIONS

Selected Products

Lightning Series (adds analog test capability to Maverick Series testers)
Magnum Series (massively parallel testing)
Maverick Series
  64-pin for engineering and compact production (Maverick PT)
  256-pin for production (Maverick VT)
  512-pin for ASICs and 64 parallel sites for consumer chips (Maverick GT)

COMPETITORS

Advantest
Agilent Technologies
Credence Systems
Eagle Test Systems
LTX
Micro Component Technology
MOSAID Technologies
Tektronix
Teradyne
Verigy
Yokogawa Electric

HISTORICAL FINANCIALS

Company Type: Public

Income Statement
FYE: June 30

	REVENUE ($ mil.)	NET INCOME ($ mil.)	NET PROFIT MARGIN	EMPLOYEES
6/06	87.7	11.1	12.7%	199
6/05	48.5	(0.3)	—	160
6/04	44.5	6.3	14.2%	—
6/03	15.6	(6.8)	—	124
6/02	14.5	(2.8)	—	100
Annual Growth	**56.8%**	**—**	**—**	**18.8%**

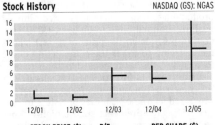

STOCK PRICE ($)	P/E	PER SHARE ($)		
FY Close	High/Low	Earnings	Dividends	Book Value
6/06 17.60	72 52	0.27	—	6.04

NGAS Resources

In gas we trust could be the new motto for NGAS Resources (formerly Daugherty Resources). The former gold and gas exploration company now primarily searches for and produces natural gas (and some oil) in the Appalachian and Illinois basins through subsidiary Daugherty Petroleum. NGAS Resources has proved reserves of 73.3 billion cu. ft. of natural gas and 328,696 barrels of oil. In 2004 the company began to operate Duke Energy's Stone Mountain natural gas gathering system. It acquired this system in 2006. The company also owns Sentra Corporation, a Kentucky public utility. NGAS Resources' inactive mining assets are in the Aleutian Islands.

The natural resources company is looking to sell or involve a third party in developing its gold and silver mining properties. It stopped active exploratory work on these properties in 1996.

EXECUTIVES

Chairman, President, and CEO: William S. Daugherty, age 51, $550,000 pay
VP Engineering and Secretary; President, DPI: D. Michael Wallen, age 51, $500,000 pay
CFO: Michael P. Windisch, age 31, $210,000 pay
VP Acquisitions and Legal Affairs; CEO, DPI: William G. (Bill) Barr III, age 56, $500,000 pay
VP Sales: Michael Hughes, age 38
Director Human Resources: Clarence Smith
Auditors: Hall, Kistler & Company LLP

LOCATIONS

HQ: NGAS Resources, Inc.
120 Prosperous Place, Ste. 201, Lexington, KY 40509
Phone: 859-263-3948 **Fax:** 859-263-4228
Web: www.ngas.com

NGAS Resources has oil and gas operations in the Appalachian and Illinois basins (primarily in Kentucky and Tennessee), and has development-stage gold and silver mining sites on the Aleutian Islands near Alaska.

PRODUCTS/OPERATIONS

2005 Sales

	$ mil.	% of total
Contract drilling	43.8	71
Oil & gas production	16.3	26
Gas transmission & compression	2.1	3
Total	**62.2**	**100**

Selected Subsidiaries

Daugherty Petroleum, Inc.
NGAS Gathering, LLC
NGAS Securities, Inc.
Sentra Corporation

COMPETITORS

Atmos Energy
Belden & Blake
Cabot Oil & Gas
Delta Natural Gas
Miller Petroleum
Penn Virginia
Petroleum Development
Range Resources
Vulcan Energy

HISTORICAL FINANCIALS

Company Type: Public

Income Statement

FYE: December 31

	REVENUE ($ mil.)	NET INCOME ($ mil.)	NET PROFIT MARGIN	EMPLOYEES
12/05	62.2	0.9	1.4%	84
12/04	48.0	1.6	3.3%	62
12/03	27.4	3.8	13.9%	31
12/02	8.4	0.6	7.1%	23
12/01	7.2	(0.3)	—	19
Annual Growth	**71.4%**	**—**	**—**	**45.0%**

2005 Year-End Financials

Debt ratio: 48.4%
Return on equity: 1.6%
Cash ($ mil.): 24.0
Current ratio: 0.98
Long-term debt ($ mil.): 35.0
No. of shares (mil.): 21.4
Dividends
  Yield: —
  Payout: —
Market value ($ mil.): 224.3
R&D as % of sales: —
Advertising as % of sales: —

Stock History

NASDAQ (GS): NGAS

STOCK PRICE ($)	P/E	PER SHARE ($)		
FY Close	High/Low	Earnings	Dividends	Book Value
12/05	10.49	317 83	0.05	—	3.38
12/04	4.57	70 37	0.10	—	2.64
12/03	5.22	20 3	0.34	—	2.45
12/02	1.02	13 5	0.11	—	1.15
12/01	0.87	— —	—	—	1.07
Annual Growth	**86.3%**	**— —**	**(23.1%)**	**—**	**33.4%**

Nicholas Financial

Nickel-less? No problem. Nicholas Financial can still get you behind the wheel of a car. The company buys subprime new and used car loans from some 1,500 car dealers in the Southeast and Midwest. It conducts its automobile finance business through more than 40 offices in 10 states. In addition to its indirect lending activities, Nicholas Financial also offers extended warranties, roadside assistance plans, and credit life, accident, and health insurance to its borrowers. The company also makes some direct consumer loans, primarily to customers whose car loans it has bought and serviced.

Subsidiary Nicholas Data Services makes accounting software for small businesses.

Chairman, president, and CEO Peter Vosotas owns approximately 15% of Nicholas Financial.

EXECUTIVES

Chairman, President, and CEO: Peter L. Vosotas, age 64, $829,659 pay
SVP Finance, CFO, Secretary, and Director: Ralph T. Finkenbrink, age 44, $233,025 pay
CIO: Michael J. Marika
VP Branch Operations: Douglas W. Marohn
VP Marketing: Matthew J. Foget
Director of Human Resources: Laura S. Botto
Director of Loss Recovery: Sotirios A. Kakalis
VP Finance and Controller: Chad W. Steinorth
Auditors: Dixon Hughes PLLC

LOCATIONS

HQ: Nicholas Financial, Inc.
2454 McMullen Booth Rd., Bldg. C, Clearwater, FL 33759
Phone: 727-726-0763 **Fax:** 727-726-2140
Web: www.nicholasfinancial.com

2006 Locations

	No.
Florida	18
North Carolina	5
Ohio	5
Georgia	4
Kentucky	3
Virginia	3
Maryland	2
South Carolina	2
Indiana	1
Michigan	1
Total	**44**

PRODUCTS/OPERATIONS

2006 Sales

	$ mil.	% of total
Interest on finance receivables	42.5	99
Sales	0.2	1
Total	**42.7**	**100**

COMPETITORS

AmeriCredit
Capital One
Consumer Portfolio
Credit Acceptance
First Investors Financial Services
iDNA
Union Acceptance Company

HISTORICAL FINANCIALS

Company Type: Public

Income Statement

FYE: March 31

	ASSETS ($ mil.)	NET INCOME ($ mil.)	INCOME AS % OF ASSETS	EMPLOYEES
3/06	149.5	10.6	7.1%	219
3/05	120.8	8.1	6.7%	189
3/04	103.2	5.2	5.0%	155
3/03	90.0	4.3	4.8%	133
3/02	77.5	3.9	5.0%	118
Annual Growth	17.9%	28.4%	—	16.7%

2006 Year-End Financials

Equity as % of assets: 39.0%
Return on assets: 7.8%
Return on equity: 20.2%
Long-term debt ($ mil.): 82.4
No. of shares (mil.): 9.9
Market value ($ mil.): 118.1
Dividends
Yield: —
Payout: —
Sales ($ mil.): 42.7
R&D as % of sales: —
Advertising as % of sales: —

Stock History

NASDAQ (GS): NICK

	STOCK PRICE ($) FY Close	P/E High	P/E Low	PER SHARE ($) Earnings	Dividends	Book Value
3/06	11.91	13	10	1.01	—	5.88
3/05	12.00	15	7	0.80	0.07	4.75
3/04	6.19	10	4	0.64	0.07	5.40
3/03	2.55	8	4	0.54	—	4.41
3/02	3.00	20	3	0.50	—	3.60
Annual Growth	41.2%	—	—	19.2%	0.0%	13.0%

Nobility Homes

Florida's prince of prefab, Nobility Homes, is a leading player in the state's competitive manufactured-home market. Nobility sells about 900 homes a year through some 20 Prestige Home Centers (about 85% of total sales) and through independent dealers. Nobility offers some 100 models that range in price from $30,000 to $100,000 and in size from about 670 sq. ft. to 2,650 sq. ft. It also operates Majestic 21, a finance company joint venture, and Mountain Financial, Inc., an insurance and mortgage subsidiary. Founder and president Terry Trexler and his son, EVP and CFO Thomas Trexler, own almost two-thirds of the company.

The company provides financing through its joint venture with 21st Century Mortgage, and it offers credit life and property and casualty insurance through its Mountain Financial subsidiary.

To keep its inventories down, Nobility generally manufactures its homes upon receipt of order. The company benefits from its ability to alter its product mix promptly to adapt to market changes.

Nobility continues to weather an industrywide inventory glut as the number of manufactured housing retail centers has outpaced consumer demand. Additionally, more stringent credit requirements are keeping formerly potential buyers from buying manufactured homes.

HISTORY

Terry Trexler, formerly a general manager at a mobile-home manufacturing plant, founded the business in 1967 and named it Nobility Homes because he felt the name symbolized quality. The company, which went public in 1971, focused solely on manufacturing while selling its homes through independent dealers. In the 1990s, however, Nobility took control of its marketing. Trexler formed TLT, Inc., to develop communities that sold homes and land as packages to retirees.

For many years, Nobility catered to the retirement market by offering small homes for empty nesters. Since 1991 Nobility has pursued entry-level buyers with families, expanding home sizes up to five bedrooms. The Trexlers invested in Prestige Home Centers, a mobile-home retailer, in 1994. To keep growing, Nobility initiated plans in 1997 to increase the number of Prestige outlets by about 25%. Also that year Nobility introduced a 30th-anniversary model, a design that proved to be popular enough to be added to its permanent line.

In 1998 the company bought six retail locations in northern Florida from Lynn Haven Homes and Emerald City Homes. It also opened a new sales center, increasing the company's retail locations to 22. As consumer demand in the industry crept downward, Nobility closed three retail outlets in 1999. An industrywide inventory glut and tighter credit standards for qualified buyers continued to affect Nobility's bottom line in 2000-01.

Reductions in both excess home inventories and repossessions at retail sales centers within the industry helped the company rebound in 2002 with increases in sales and profits, partly due to Nobility's aggressive pursuit of sales to outside park dealers.

EXECUTIVES

Chairman and President; President, TLT: Terry E. Trexler, age 66, $218,500 pay
EVP, CFO, and Director; President, Prestige Home Centers: Thomas W. Trexler, age 42, $218,500 pay
VP Engineering: Edward C. Sims, age 58
Secretary: Jean Etheredge, age 60
Treasurer: Lynn J. Cramer Jr., age 60

LOCATIONS

HQ: Nobility Homes, Inc.
3741 SW 7th St., Ocala, FL 34474
Phone: 352-732-5157   **Fax:** 352-622-6766
Web: www.nobilityhomes.com

Nobility Homes has two manufacturing plants in Florida in Belleview (for metal and concrete construction) and in Ocala (for metal construction) and 19 retail sales centers across northern and central Florida.

PRODUCTS/OPERATIONS

Selected Home Sizes

Single-wides with 14 and 16 ft. widths and 48 to 72 ft. lengths
Double-wides with 24, 26, 28, and 32 ft. widths and 32 to 76 ft. lengths
Quad-units with two sections 28 ft. long by 48 ft. and two sections 28 ft. long by 52 ft.
Triple-wides with 36, 38, and 42 ft. widths and 46 to 72 ft. lengths

Selected Brand Names

Kingswood
Regency Manor Special
Richwood
Special Edition
Springwood
Springwood Special
Tropic Isle Special

Selected Subsidiaries

Prestige Home Centers, Inc.
Majestic Homes, Inc.
  Majestic 21 (50%)
Mountain Financial, Inc.

COMPETITORS

American Homestar
Cavalier Homes
Cavco
Champion Enterprises
Clayton Homes
Fleetwood Enterprises
Four Seasons Housing
General Housing
Giles Industries
Liberty Homes
Oriole Homes
Palm Harbor Homes
Patriot Homes
Skyline
Southern Energy Homes

HISTORICAL FINANCIALS

Company Type: Public

Income Statement

FYE: Saturday nearest October 31

	REVENUE ($ mil.)	NET INCOME ($ mil.)	NET PROFIT MARGIN	EMPLOYEES
10/05	56.7	6.2	10.9%	261
10/04	50.0	4.6	9.2%	228
10/03	39.2	3.1	7.9%	218
10/02	37.9	3.1	8.2%	212
10/01	30.3	2.5	8.3%	198
Annual Growth	17.0%	25.5%	—	7.2%

2006 Year-End Financials

Debt ratio: —
Return on equity: 16.5%
Cash ($ mil.): 12.8
Current ratio: 5.05
Long-term debt ($ mil.): —
No. of shares (mil.): 4.1
Dividends
Yield: 2.2%
Payout: 37.7%
Market value ($ mil.): 111.5
R&D as % of sales: —
Advertising as % of sales: —

Stock History

NASDAQ (GM): NOBH

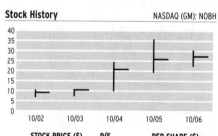

	STOCK PRICE ($) FY Close	P/E High	P/E Low	PER SHARE ($) Earnings	Dividends	Book Value
10/06	27.32	19	14	1.59	0.60	10.21
10/05	25.90	24	13	1.49	0.20	9.13
10/04	20.75	21	9	1.13	0.10	7.78
10/03	10.49	14	10	0.77	—	6.69
10/02	9.15	13	9	0.76	—	5.92
Annual Growth	31.5%	—	—	20.3%	144.9%	14.6%

Noble International

A noble undertaking it is for Noble International to help build cars and get none of the recognition. The company makes laser-welded steel blanks and tubes that are used to make automobile body components such as doors, fenders, pillars, and side panels. Customers include car manufacturers and their suppliers; DaimlerChrysler, Ford, and General Motors together account for more than 85% of Noble International's sales. The company has grown through a series of acquisitions; however, Noble International has exited its outsourced package delivery services and all-terrain fork truck operations.

Noble International operates from facilities in Australia, Canada, Mexico, and the US (Kentucky and Michigan).

In late 2006 Noble acquired Pullman Industries, a maker of shaped components and tubular products for the automotive industry. Pullman operates four manufacturing facilities in the US and two in Mexico. The acquisition lends breadth to Noble's product line while giving it access to Pullman's low labor cost facilities in Mexico. The deal was valued at $120 million.

Quick on the heels of the Pullman deal, Noble announced it would combine its laser-welded steel blank business with that of Arcelor Mittal subsidiary Arcelor S.A. The deal will increase Noble's manufacturing footprint from 12 production sites to 22. Upon completion of the deal Arcelor will become Noble's largest shareholder with about a 40% stake.

Chairman Robert Skandalaris controls about a 17% stake in the company.

EXECUTIVES

Chairman: Robert J. Skandalaris, age 53
CEO and Director: Thomas L. Saeli, age 49
President: Steve Prue, age 43
VP and CFO: David J. Fallon, age 36
VP, Administration and Secretary: Michael C. Azar, age 42
VP, Operations: Larry Garretson
VP, Sales: Craig S. Parsons
VP and General Counsel: Andrew J. Tavi
Director, Investor and Public Relations: Greg Salchow
Auditors: Deloitte & Touche LLP

LOCATIONS

HQ: Noble International, Ltd.
28213 Van Dyke Ave., Warren, MI 48093
Phone: 586-751-5600   **Fax:** 586-751-5601
Web: www.nobleintl.com

2005 Sales

	$ mil.	% of total
US	248.2	68
Canada	110.5	31
Mexico	4.4	1
Australia	0.7	—
Total	**363.8**	**100**

PRODUCTS/OPERATIONS

2005 Sales by Customer

	% of total
DaimlerChrysler	37
Ford Motor	28
General Motors	21
Other	14
Total	**100**

COMPETITORS

Bing	Olympic Steel
Delphi	Robert Bosch
Kasle Steel	Shiloh Industries
Key Safety Systems	Tower Automotive
Magna International	Visteon
Newcor	

HISTORICAL FINANCIALS
Company Type: Public

Income Statement
FYE: December 31

	REVENUE ($ mil.)	NET INCOME ($ mil.)	NET PROFIT MARGIN	EMPLOYEES
12/05	363.8	5.1	1.4%	791
12/04	332.6	15.4	4.6%	705
12/03	183.8	5.2	2.8%	578
12/02	125.2	(12.8)	—	589
12/01	138.2	5.6	4.1%	2,473
Annual Growth	**27.4%**	**(2.3%)**	**—**	**(24.8%)**

2005 Year-End Financials

Debt ratio: 49.8%
Return on equity: 6.3%
Cash ($ mil.): 22.0
Current ratio: 1.67
Long-term debt ($ mil.): 41.3
No. of shares (mil.): 14.0
Dividends
  Yield: 1.9%
  Payout: 75.0%
Market value ($ mil.): 194.7
R&D as % of sales: —
Advertising as % of sales: —

Stock History
NASDAQ (GS): NOBL

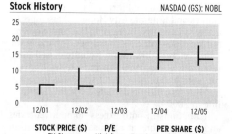

	STOCK PRICE ($) FY Close	P/E High/Low		PER SHARE ($) Earnings	Dividends	Book Value
12/05	13.89	50	34	0.36	0.27	5.91
12/04	13.59	23	11	0.96	0.27	8.56
12/03	15.26	35	8	0.44	0.21	5.64
12/02	5.20	—	—	(1.20)	0.21	4.90
12/01	5.47	10	5	0.57	0.20	6.30
Annual Growth	**26.2%**	**—**	**—**	**(10.9%)**	**7.8%**	**(1.6%)**

Northern Empire Bancshares

Grapes aren't the only things that are growing in Sonoma Valley. Northern Empire Bancshares, the holding company for Sonoma National Bank, operates about a dozen branches, plus about five loan production offices in Sonoma and Marin counties, California, and Phoenix, Arizona. The commercial bank accepts checking and savings deposits, offers money market accounts and certificates of deposit. Sonoma National Bank also makes secured and unsecured commercial, construction, other installment, and term loans, and offers other customary banking services.

About 75% of Northern Empire's loan portfolio consists of real estate mortgages. Commercial loans, including Small Business Administration (SBA) loans, account for about 20%.

EXECUTIVES

Chairman; Vice Chairman, Sonoma National Bank: Dennis R. Hunter, age 63
Vice Chairman; Chairman, Sonoma National Bank: James B. Keegan Jr., age 57
President and CEO; President, CEO, and Director, Sonoma National Bank: Deborah A. Meekins, age 53, $454,000 pay
Chief Accounting Officer; SVP and CFO, Sonoma National Bank: Jane M. Baker, age 59, $158,000 pay (prior to title change)
EVP and Senior Loan Officer, Sonoma National Bank: David F. Titus, age 53, $333,000 pay
SVP and Senior Operations Administrator, Sonoma National Bank: JoAnn Barton, age 52, $129,000 pay
Secretary; Director, Northern Empire Bancshares and Sonoma National Bank: Patrick R. Gallaher, age 60
Auditors: Moss Adams, LLP

LOCATIONS

HQ: Northern Empire Bancshares
801 4th St., Santa Rosa, CA 95404
Phone: 707-579-2265   **Fax:** 707-569-7636
Web: www.snbank.com

PRODUCTS/OPERATIONS

2005 Sales

	$ mil.	% of total
Interest		
Loans	70.6	90
Federal funds sold	2.2	3
Investments	1.5	2
Noninterest		
Sale of loans	3.0	4
Service charges	0.5	—
Other	0.9	1
Total	**78.7**	**100**

COMPETITORS

American River Bankshares
Bank of America
Bank of the West
City National
First Republic (CA)
Greater Bay
National Bank of Arizona
North Bay Bancorp
Pacific Capital Bancorp
Placer Sierra Bancshares
Sonoma Valley Bancorp
UnionBanCal
Washington Mutual
Wells Fargo
Westamerica

HISTORICAL FINANCIALS
Company Type: Public

Income Statement
FYE: December 31

	ASSETS ($ mil.)	NET INCOME ($ mil.)	INCOME AS % OF ASSETS	EMPLOYEES
12/05	1,231.7	17.3	1.4%	185
12/04	1,080.9	14.3	1.3%	—
12/03	848.2	11.3	1.3%	—
12/02	689.4	9.3	1.3%	—
12/01	561.0	8.1	1.4%	—
Annual Growth	**21.7%**	**20.9%**	**—**	**—**

2005 Year-End Financials

Equity as % of assets: 8.7%	Dividends
Return on assets: 1.5%	Yield: —
Return on equity: 17.5%	Payout: —
Long-term debt ($ mil.): —	Sales ($ mil.): 78.7
No. of shares (mil.): 10.4	R&D as % of sales: —
Market value ($ mil.): 234.3	Advertising as % of sales: 0.7%

Stock History

NASDAQ (GM): NREB

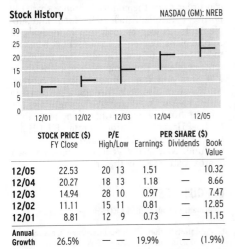

	STOCK PRICE ($) FY Close	P/E High/Low		PER SHARE ($) Earnings	Dividends	Book Value
12/05	22.53	20	13	1.51	—	10.32
12/04	20.27	18	13	1.18	—	8.66
12/03	14.94	28	10	0.97	—	7.47
12/02	11.11	15	11	0.81	—	12.85
12/01	8.81	12	9	0.73	—	11.15
Annual Growth	**26.5%**	—	—	**19.9%**	—	**(1.9%)**

Novatel Wireless

You *can* take it with you. Novatel Wireless designs wireless modems that let users access the Internet from anywhere. The company offers a series of wireless PC card modems (Merlin), embedded wireless modules for OEMs (Expedite), and desktop wireless gateway consoles (Ovation). Its MobiLink software, bundled with modems and embedded modules, connects mobile devices with wireless WANs. Novatel also offers activation, provisioning, and integration services. Customers include manufacturers, telecom service providers, and wireless service providers. The company outsources its manufacturing to LG Innotek, Celestica, and SerComm.

Artis Capital Management owns about 12% of the company. All officers and directors of Novatel Wireless as a group own about 7% of the company.

EXECUTIVES

CEO and Director: Peter V. Leparulo, age 47, $653,433 pay
COO: George B. (Brad) Weinert, age 47
CFO: Dan L. Halvorson, age 40, $312,622 pay
SVP, Engineering and CTO: Slim S. Souissi, age 40, $312,622 pay
SVP, Sales and Marketing: Robert M. Hadley, age 43, $432,133 pay
VP, Business Affairs and Secretary:
 Catherine F. Ratcliffe, age 48, $312,622 pay
VP, Operations: Christopher B. (Chris) Ross, age 52
General Manager, Europe: Peter Balchin
Investor Relations Officer: Julie Cunningham
Auditors: KPMG LLP

LOCATIONS

HQ: Novatel Wireless, Inc.
 9645 Scranton Rd., Ste. 205, San Diego, CA 92121
Phone: 858-320-8800   **Fax:** 858-812-3402
Web: www.novatelwireless.com

Novatel Wireless has offices in Canada and the US.

PRODUCTS/OPERATIONS

Selected Products

3G multimedia application consoles (Ovation)
Embedded modems (Expedite)
PC card modems (Merlin)

COMPETITORS

3Com
Huawei Technologies
Intel
Kyocera Wireless
Linksys
Motorola
Nokia
Option
Palm
RIM
Siemens Communications
Sierra Wireless
Socket Communications
Sony Ericsson Mobile
USRobotics
Wavecom

HISTORICAL FINANCIALS

Company Type: Public

Income Statement

FYE: December 31

	REVENUE ($ mil.)	NET INCOME ($ mil.)	NET PROFIT MARGIN	EMPLOYEES
12/05	161.7	11.1	6.9%	172
12/04	103.7	13.8	13.3%	112
12/03	33.8	(11.6)	—	80
12/02	28.9	(28.3)	—	92
12/01	43.6	(90.9)	—	134
Annual Growth	**38.8%**	—	—	**6.4%**

2005 Year-End Financials

Debt ratio: —	Dividends
Return on equity: 10.0%	Yield: —
Cash ($ mil.): 83.7	Payout: —
Current ratio: 2.73	Market value ($ mil.): 355.1
Long-term debt ($ mil.): —	R&D as % of sales: 12.7%
No. of shares (mil.): 29.3	Advertising as % of sales: —

Stock History

NASDAQ (GM): NVTL

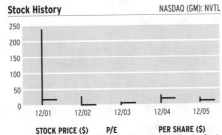

	STOCK PRICE ($) FY Close	P/E High/Low		PER SHARE ($) Earnings	Dividends	Book Value
12/05	12.11	53	23	0.37	—	4.13
12/04	19.41	60	12	0.48	—	3.45
12/03	5.99	—	—	(2.14)	—	0.71
12/02	0.97	—	—	(10.47)	—	0.93
12/01	18.30	—	—	(25.05)	—	0.44
Annual Growth	**(9.8%)**	—	—	—	—	**75.2%**

Nu Horizons Electronics

Nu Horizons Electronics sees new components on the horizon. The company distributes active components (microprocessors, memory chips, diodes, transistors) from manufacturers such as Intersil, STMicroelectronics, Vitesse Semiconductor, and Xilinx. Subsidiary NIC Components is the exclusive North American distributor of passive components (capacitors and resistors) made by Japan's Nippon Industries. Nu Horizons' other subsidiaries include components exporter Nu Horizons International and European distributors Nu Horizons Eurotech and NIC Eurotech. Nu Horizons also offers supply chain services such as warehousing, inventory control, purchasing, and transportation through its Titan Supply Chain Services subsidiary.

About 75% of the company's sales are to customers in the Americas, but Nu Horizons is expanding overseas. Its customers include a wide variety of manufacturers of consumer, medical, industrial, and military electronics.

The company has acquired a UK distributor, DT Electronics, for about $5.5 million in cash, expanding its European presence. The shareholders of DT Electronics may receive an additional £849,426 to £2.55 million (about $1.6 million to $4.8 million) over three years, depending on earnings milestones.

Dimensional Fund Advisors and Royce & Associates each own about 8% of Nu Horizons Electronics. Wasatch Advisors holds around 7% of the company. Including stock options, CEO Arthur Nadata has an equity stake of more than 6%. COO Richard Schuster owns about 6%, also including options. Babson Capital holds around 6%.

HISTORY

Industry veterans Irving Lubman, Arthur Nadata, and Richard Schuster left a small electronic components distribution company to found Nu Horizons and NIC Components in 1982. Nu Horizons went public the following year. In 1986 it formed an export subsidiary.

Initially, Nu Horizons derived most of its sales from makers of military equipment, and marketing efforts were focused on the East Coast. However, by 1993 military contractors represented just 7% of sales. In 1994 Nu Horizons bought San Jose, California-based Merit Electronics, which became its West Coast operation.

The company continued to broaden its product line. It signed a franchise agreement with Cirrus Logic in 1995, and initiated distribution of Sun Microsystems' components in 1996. Also that year Lubman stepped down as CEO and was replaced by Nadata; Lubman remained chairman. The company formed a UK subsidiary in 1998. Nu Horizons added design engineering services to its arsenal the next year.

In 2000 Nu Horizons signed a distribution agreement with Hitachi and introduced a development tool for the voice over Internet Protocol (VoIP) market. The next year, the company sold its Nu Visions Manufacturing subsidiary (contract design and assembly of circuit boards and related devices) to Golden Gate Capital for about $30 million.

In 2002 Nu Horizons continued to expand its offerings through distribution agreements with California Eastern Laboratories (itself a distributor of NEC products) and networking chip specialist Intersil.

Lubman retired as chairman and COO in June 2004; Nadata became chairman and CEO, and Schuster assumed the role of president and COO.

In 2005 Nu Horizons opened an office in Mumbai (formerly Bombay), its fourth office in India. Later that year, the company signed a global distribution agreement with IBM Microelectronics, carrying IBM's PowerPC microprocessors, digital video chips, and static random-access memories (SRAMs).

In 2006 the company formed a new division, Nu Horizons Express, specializing in sales and support for lower-volume customers.

EXECUTIVES

Chairman and CEO: Arthur Nadata, age 60, $539,000 pay
President, COO, Secretary, and Director; President, NIC Components: Richard S. (Rich) Schuster, age 57, $539,000 pay
VP, Finance, CFO, and Treasurer: Kurt Freudenberg, age 48
VP, Human Resources and Training Development: Elaine Givner
VP, Operations: Steve Mussmacher
VP, Information Technology: Burt Silverman
VP, Global Customer Business Unit: Teresa Shatsoff
VP, Marketing: Rita Megling
VP, Global Engineering: Athar Zafar
VP, OEM System Sales: Dan Romanelli
VP, Strategic Accounts: Gregg Scott
VP, Sales, Americas: Kent Smith
VP, Sales, EMS Americas: Tom Dow
VP, Strategic Accounts: Dave Nebbia
President, Distribution Division: Dave Bowers
President, Nu Horizons Electronics Asia Pte Ltd.: Wendell Boyd
Auditors: Lazar Levine & Felix LLP

LOCATIONS

HQ: Nu Horizons Electronics Corp.
70 Maxess Rd., Melville, NY 11747
Phone: 631-396-5000   **Fax:** 631-396-5050
Web: www.nuhorizons.com

Nu Horizons Electronics has offices in Australia, Canada, China, Hong Kong, India, Malaysia, Mexico, Singapore, South Korea, Taiwan, Thailand, the UK, and the US.

2006 Sales

	$ mil.	% of total
Americas	418.6	75
Asia/Pacific	125.3	22
Europe	17.4	3
Total	**561.3**	**100**

PRODUCTS/OPERATIONS

Selected Products Distributed

Capacitors
Digital and linear integrated circuits
Diodes
Fiber-optic components
Memory chips
Microprocessors
Microwave components
Networking chipsets
Optocouplers
Radio-frequency components
Relays
Resistors
Transistors

Selected Subsidiaries

NIC Components Corp. (North American outlet for passive components made by Nippon Industries)
Nu Horizons Asia Pte. Ltd.
Nu Horizons Europe Ltd.
Nu Horizons International Corp. (export distribution of electronic components)
NUHC Inc. (Canadian subsidiary)
Titan Supply Chain Services Corp. (supply chain services)

COMPETITORS

All American Semiconductor
Arrow Electronics
Avnet
Bell Microproducts
Digi-Key
Future Electronics
Jaco Electronics
N.F. Smith
Premier Farnell
Richardson Electronics
Taitron Components
TTI Inc.

HISTORICAL FINANCIALS

Company Type: Public

Income Statement

FYE: February 28

	REVENUE ($ mil.)	NET INCOME ($ mil.)	NET PROFIT MARGIN	EMPLOYEES
2/06	561.3	4.9	0.9%	659
2/05	467.9	3.1	0.7%	574
2/04	345.9	(0.9)	—	527
2/03	302.1	(2.5)	—	483
2/02	281.9	2.2	0.8%	471
Annual Growth	**18.8%**	**22.2%**	**—**	**8.8%**

2006 Year-End Financials

Debt ratio: 37.3%
Return on equity: 3.7%
Cash ($ mil.): 10.9
Current ratio: 4.34
Long-term debt ($ mil.): 50.6
No. of shares (mil.): 17.4
Dividends
　Yield: —
　Payout: —
Market value ($ mil.): 152.2
R&D as % of sales: —
Advertising as % of sales: 0.0%

Stock History

NASDAQ (GM): NUHC

	STOCK PRICE ($) FY Close	P/E High/Low	PER SHARE ($) Earnings	Dividends	Book Value
2/06	8.73	39 20	0.28	—	7.78
2/05	6.97	67 33	0.17	—	7.57
2/04	9.61	— —	(0.05)	—	7.38
2/03	5.39	— —	(0.14)	—	7.44
2/02	8.74	96 48	0.13	—	7.61
Annual Growth	**(0.0%)**	**— —**	**21.1%**	**—**	**0.5%**

NutriSystem

NutriSystem can help you trim your waistline online. Visitors to the nutrisystem.com Web site can order from the company's more than 130 portion-controlled, shelf-stable foods and supplements, as well as look into individualized calorie plans, one-on-one counseling, behavior modification, and exercise education and maintenance plans. The company also owns about 120 Slim and Tone women's fitness centers. NutriSystem also sells through a partnership with television-marketer QVC where it airs 90-minute infomercials. Chairman and CEO Michael Hagan's investment group, HJM Holdings, and director Mike DiPiano's venture capital fund, NewSpring Ventures, together own approximately 58% of the firm.

EXECUTIVES

Chairman, President, and CEO: Michael J. Hagan, age 43
EVP Administration, CFO, Secretary, and Treasurer: James D. (Jim) Brown, age 48, $508,665 pay
EVP and Chief Marketing Officer: Thomas F. (Tom) Connerty, age 43, $620,050 pay
SVP Operations and CIO: Bruce Blair, age 49, $366,923 pay
VP Program and Product Development: Jay Satz
President, Slim and Tone Division: Betsy Ludlow
Director, Advertising and Marketing: Shannon Crossin
Director, Human Resources: Carol F. Krause
Director, Operations: Chris Dominelo
Auditors: KPMG LLP

LOCATIONS

HQ: NutriSystem, Inc.
300 Welsh Rd., Bldg. 1, Ste. 100, Horsham, PA 19044
Phone: 215-706-5300   **Fax:** 215-706-5388
Web: www.nutrisystem.com

PRODUCTS/OPERATIONS

Selected Food Programs

All-Vegetarian
Men's Program
Men's Over 60 Program
Women's Program
Women's Over 60 Program
Type II Diabetic Program

COMPETITORS

Atkins Nutritionals	L A Weight Loss
Bally Total Fitness	PowerBar
Beverly Hills Weight Loss	Schiff Nutrition
eDiets.com	Slim-Fast
HMG	Weight Watchers
Jenny Craig	

HISTORICAL FINANCIALS

Company Type: Public

Income Statement

FYE: December 31

	REVENUE ($ mil.)	NET INCOME ($ mil.)	NET PROFIT MARGIN	EMPLOYEES
12/05	212.5	21.0	9.9%	589
12/04	38.0	1.0	2.6%	102
12/03	22.6	0.8	3.5%	107
12/02	27.6	2.4	8.7%	103
12/01	23.8	1.3	5.5%	137
Annual Growth	**72.9%**	**100.5%**	**—**	**44.0%**

2005 Year-End Financials

Debt ratio: 0.3%
Return on equity: 46.1%
Cash ($ mil.): 46.0
Current ratio: 3.34
Long-term debt ($ mil.): 0.3
No. of shares (mil.): 35.8

Dividends
 Yield: —
 Payout: —
Market value ($ mil.): 1,289.4
R&D as % of sales: —
Advertising as % of sales: —

Stock History

NASDAQ (GS): NTRI

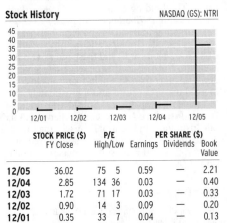

	STOCK PRICE ($) FY Close	P/E High/Low		PER SHARE ($) Earnings	Dividends	Book Value
12/05	36.02	75	5	0.59	—	2.21
12/04	2.85	134	36	0.03	—	0.40
12/03	1.72	71	17	0.03	—	0.33
12/02	0.90	14	3	0.09	—	0.20
12/01	0.35	33	7	0.04	—	0.13
Annual Growth	218.5%	—	—	96.0%	—	103.4%

NYMEX Holdings

What US exchange was formed in 1872 as the Butter and Cheese Exchange? NYMEX Holdings' subsidiary, the New York Mercantile Exchange. From meager dairy roots, it is the world's largest forum for trading energy futures, and the third largest futures exchange in the US. Trading is conducted through two divisions: NYMEX handles the crude oil, gasoline, heating oil, natural gas, platinum, and palladium markets, while COMEX serves as the marketplace for gold, silver, copper, and aluminum futures and options contracts. NYMEX ClearPort clears off-exchange trades and sells market data. The Chicago Mercantile Exchange started facilitating after-hours trading of NYMEX energy, platinum, and palladium futures in late 2006.

NYMEX Holdings went public in 2006 with funds raised to be used for capital expenditures; some $10 million will be paid to owners of COMEX division membership to satisfy the terms of its 1994 merger agreement.

In February 2006 NYMEX's board voted to offer side-by-side open outcry and electronic trading of its benchmark, physically settled energy futures contracts. Side-by-side trading launched during the second quarter of 2006.

Looking to diversify its products as well as its customer base, NYMEX has an eye on Europe. In November 2004 it established NYMEX-Europe in Dublin, Ireland (operations it later moved to London).

Then in 2005 NYMEX entered into a 50/50 venture with Dubai Holding to form the Dubai Mercantile Exchange, the Middle East's first energy futures exchange. Additionally, subsidiary NYMEX Europe Limited launched an open outcry trading floor offering Brent crude oil futures and options and Northwest Europe gas/oil futures.

In advance of the 2006 IPO, NYMEX sold a 10% stake to private equity firm General Atlantic.

EXECUTIVES

Chairman: Richard Schaeffer, age 54, $650,000 pay (prior to promotion)
Vice Chairman: Robert Halper, age 47
President, CEO, and Director: James E. Newsome, age 46, $1,400,000 pay (prior to promotion)
SVP and CFO: Kenneth D. (Ken) Shifrin, age 49
SVP and CIO: Samuel H. Gaer, age 39, $960,000 pay
SVP, Corporate Governance and Strategic Initiatives: Richard D. Kerschner, age 39
SVP, Compliance and Risk Management: Thomas F. LaSala, age 44
SVP, Marketing: Joseph Raia, age 48
Treasurer and Director: Frank Siciliano, age 58
General Counsel, Chief Administrative Officer and Secretary: Christopher K. Bowen, age 45, $714,083 pay
Auditors: KPMG LLP

LOCATIONS

HQ: NYMEX Holdings, Inc.
 1 North End Ave., World Financial Center, New York, NY 10282
Phone: 212-299-2000   **Fax:** 212-301-4623
Web: www.nymex.com

PRODUCTS/OPERATIONS

2005 Sales

	$ mil.	% of total
Clearing & transaction fees	277.6	80
Market data fees	44.5	13
Investment income	9.0	3
Interest from security lending	3.6	1
Other	11.9	3
Total	**346.6**	**100**

COMPETITORS

AMEX
CBOE
Chicago Mercantile Exchange
DTCC
LCH.Clearnet
NYSE
Options Clearing Corporation

HISTORICAL FINANCIALS

Company Type: Public

Income Statement				FYE: December 31
	REVENUE ($ mil.)	NET INCOME ($ mil.)	NET PROFIT MARGIN	EMPLOYEES
12/05	346.6	71.1	20.5%	548
12/04	241.3	27.4	11.4%	497
12/03	188.1	8.9	4.7%	481
12/02	189.2	12.3	6.5%	489
12/01	144.3	0.7	0.5%	—
Annual Growth	24.5%	217.5%	—	3.9%

2005 Year-End Financials

Debt ratio: 75.7%
Return on equity: 60.1%
Cash ($ mil.): 2,550.7

Current ratio: 1.05
Long-term debt ($ mil.): 83.1

Net Income History

NYSE: NMX

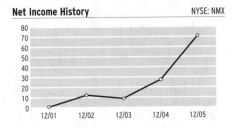

Ocwen Financial

Ocwen Financial may not write loans anymore, but it is involved in most every other aspect of the mortgage business. The company services subprime residential mortgage loans for third-parties or acquires and collects on them for its own account. It also provides real estate appraisal services, title services, and outsourced data entry, call center services, and mortgage research. The company has operations in the US, Canada, China, Germany, India, Japan, and Taiwan; much of its international business consists of servicing commercial loans. Chairman and CEO William Erbey owns about 30% of Ocwen Financial; chairman emeritus Barry Wish holds about another 13%.

To focus on its core fee-based businesses, the company "debanked" by winding down the deposit collection operations of its Ocwen Federal Bank subsidiary and divesting the unit. It began its transformation in 2000 when it exited the subprime loan origination business.

EXECUTIVES

Chairman and CEO, Ocwen Financial and Ocwen Federal Bank: William C. Erbey, age 56, $724,382 pay
President and Director; President, Ocwen Federal Bank: Ronald M. Faris, age 43, $671,650 pay
CFO: David J. Gunter, age 47
EVP, Sales and Marketing and Director: W. Michael Linn, age 57, $341,260 pay
SVP and Principal Financial Officer: Robert J. Leist Jr., age 56
SVP; President, Global Servicing Solutions: William B. Shepro, age 37, $421,050 pay
SVP and General Counsel: Paul A. Koches
SVP, Human Resources and Corporate Services: Kevin Wilcox
VP and Chief Accounting Officer: Daniel C. O'Keefe
Secretary: John R. Erbey, age 60
Auditors: PricewaterhouseCoopers LLP

LOCATIONS

HQ: Ocwen Financial Corporation
 1661 Worthington Rd., Ste. 100, West Palm Beach, FL 33409
Phone: 561-682-8000   **Fax:** 561-682-8177
Web: www.ocwen.com

PRODUCTS/OPERATIONS

2005 Sales

	$ mil.	% of total
Servicing & subservicing fees	293.6	78
Process management fees	72.0	19
Other	9.8	3
Total	**375.4**	**100**

Selected Subsidiaries

Global Financing Solutions, LLC
Ocwen Asset Investment — UK, LLC
Ocwen Capital Trust I
Ocwen Financial Solutions Private Limited (India)
Ocwen Loan Servicing, LLC
Ocwen Mortgage Asset Trust
Ocwen Partnership, L.P.
RMSI, Inc.

COMPETITORS

Accredited Home Lenders
American Home Mortgage
Countrywide Financial
Litton Loan Servicing
Wells Fargo

HISTORICAL FINANCIALS

Company Type: Public

Income Statement

FYE: December 31

	REVENUE ($ mil.)	NET INCOME ($ mil.)	NET PROFIT MARGIN	EMPLOYEES
12/05	375.4	15.1	4.0%	3,396
12/04	246.7	57.7	23.4%	3,120
12/03	209.5	4.8	2.3%	2,472
12/02	200.7	(68.8)	—	1,871
12/01	267.0	(124.8)	—	1,663
Annual Growth	8.9%	—	—	19.5%

2005 Year-End Financials

Debt ratio: 224.7%
Return on equity: 4.5%
Cash ($ mil.): 301.6
Current ratio: —
Long-term debt ($ mil.): 780.8
No. of shares (mil.): 63.1

Dividends
Yield: —
Payout: —
Market value ($ mil.): 549.3
R&D as % of sales: —
Advertising as % of sales: —

Stock History

NYSE: OCN

	STOCK PRICE ($) FY Close	P/E High/Low		PER SHARE ($) Earnings	Dividends	Book Value
12/05	8.70	40	27	0.24	—	5.50
12/04	9.56	15	9	0.82	—	5.26
12/03	8.86	129	37	0.07	—	4.70
12/02	2.80	—	—	(1.02)	—	4.61
12/01	8.48	—	—	(1.86)	—	5.63
Annual Growth	0.6%	—	—	—	—	(0.6%)

Olympic Steel

Olympic Steel has bypassed bronze, silver, and gold in favor of carbon, coated, and stainless steel. A steel service center, Olympic Steel provides flat-rolled sheet, coil, and plate steel products. Its processing services include cutting-to-length, slitting, and shearing, along with blanking, laser welding, and precision machining. Olympic Steel operates 12 processing and distribution facilities, mainly in the eastern and midwestern US. The company also participates in a Michigan-based joint ventures that supply auto manufacturers with steel products. Auto manufacturers and their suppliers account for about 12% of Olympic Steel's sales; other steel service centers account for about 10%.

Olympic Steel hopes to grow by taking advantage of the trend toward outsourcing of manufacturing processes. Toward that end, the company intends to continue to invest in processing equipment in order to add more value to its products. Olympic made a move in that direction in 2006 when it acquired PS&W, a fabricator of parts and components used by heavy equipment OEMs that is based in North Carolina. PS&W had been a part of Britain's Eliza Tinsley Group.

Ingersoll-Rand is its largest customer, accounting for more than 10% of sales. Chairman Michael Siegal, the son of the company's founder, owns about 15% of Olympic Steel.

EXECUTIVES

Chairman and CEO: Michael D. Siegal, age 52
President, COO, and Director: David A. Wolfort, age 52
CFO: Richard T. Marabito, age 41
CIO: Heber MacWilliams, age 61
VP Automotive: David K. Frink
VP Central Region, Iowa: Steve Mallory
VP New Business Development, Olympic Steel Trading: Clay Treska
VP Operations and Eastern Region: Raymond Walker
Treasurer: Richard A. Manson, age 36
Auditors: PricewaterhouseCoopers LLP

LOCATIONS

HQ: Olympic Steel, Inc.
5096 Richmond Rd., Bedford Heights, OH 44146
Phone: 216-292-3800　　**Fax:** 216-292-3974
Web: www.olysteel.com

Olympic Steel has processing plants and distribution centers in Connecticut, Georgia, Illinois, Iowa, Michigan, Minnesota, Ohio, and Pennsylvania.

COMPETITORS

Allegheny Technologies
Ferralloy
Friedman Industries
Kasle Steel
Kenwal Steel
Metals USA
Novamerican Steel
Reliance Steel
Ryerson
Shiloh Industries
Steel Technologies
Worthington Industries

HISTORICAL FINANCIALS

Company Type: Public

Income Statement

FYE: December 31

	REVENUE ($ mil.)	NET INCOME ($ mil.)	NET PROFIT MARGIN	EMPLOYEES
12/05	939.2	22.1	2.4%	850
12/04	894.2	60.1	6.7%	825
12/03	472.5	(3.3)	—	812
12/02	459.4	(5.8)	—	837
12/01	416.3	(3.7)	—	846
Annual Growth	22.6%	—	—	0.1%

2005 Year-End Financials

Debt ratio: —
Return on equity: 11.7%
Cash ($ mil.): 9.6
Current ratio: 2.41
Long-term debt ($ mil.): —
No. of shares (mil.): 10.2

Dividends
Yield: —
Payout: —
Market value ($ mil.): 252.3
R&D as % of sales: —
Advertising as % of sales: —

Stock History

NASDAQ (GM): ZEUS

	STOCK PRICE ($) FY Close	P/E High/Low		PER SHARE ($) Earnings	Dividends	Book Value
12/05	24.85	13	6	2.11	—	19.73
12/04	26.51	5	1	5.88	—	17.58
12/03	8.21	—	—	(0.34)	—	11.63
12/02	3.20	—	—	(0.60)	—	11.98
12/01	2.55	—	—	(0.38)	—	12.59
Annual Growth	76.7%	—	—	—	—	11.9%

Omega Financial

Omega Financial wants to be the be-all-and-end-all for financial services in central Pennsylvania. The holding company for Omega Bank operates almost 70 branches in nearly 15 counties, targeting individuals and local businesses; services include checking and savings accounts, CDs, IRAs, debit cards, and trust and asset management. The bank focuses on real estate lending, devoting more than 35% of its loan book to commercial real estate loans and approximately 20% to residential mortgages. Subsidiaries include Omega Insurance Agency, Central Pennsylvania Life Insurance, and Central Pennsylvania Investment Company. In 2004 Omega acquired Sun Bancorp; its Sun Bank subsidiary is now a division of Omega Bank.

EXECUTIVES

Chairman; Chairman, Omega Bank: David B. Lee, age 68, $135,000 pay
EVP and CFO, Omega Financial and Omega Bank: Daniel L. Warfel, age 58, $293,804 pay
EVP Insurance and Investments; EVP Information Technology, Omega Bank: Vincent C. Turiano
SVP Operations and Secretary; VP, Secretary, and Cashier, Omega Bank: David N. Thiel, age 61, $142,649 pay
SVP and Director; SVP and Regional President, Wilkes-Barre, Omega Bank: Maureen M. Bufalino, age 42
SVP; Regional President, Susquehanna Valley, Omega Bank: Byron Mertz III
SVP, Corporate Controller, and Director of Investor Relations: Teresa M. Ciambotti, age 44
President and CEO, Sentry Trust: Charles E. Nelson
President, Bank Capital Services: Gary P. Cook
President, Mid-Penn Insurance: Daniel R. Geise
Director Human Resources: Christina Marshall
Auditors: Ernst & Young LLP

LOCATIONS

HQ: Omega Financial Corporation
366 Walker Dr., State College, PA 16801
Phone: 814-231-7680　　**Fax:** 814-231-5797
Web: www.omegafinancial.com

Omega Financial has offices in Bedford, Blair, Centre, Clinton, Cumberland, Dauphin, Huntingdon, Juniata, Luzerne, Lycoming, Mifflin, Northumberland, Snyder, and Union counties in Pennsylvania.

PRODUCTS/OPERATIONS

2005 Sales

	$ mil.	% of total
Interest		
Interest & fees on loans	78.9	65
Interest & dividends on securities	11.2	9
Other	1.0	1
Noninterest		
Service fees on deposit accounts	9.3	8
Trust fees	6.0	5
Investment & insurance product sales	3.2	3
Other	11.8	9
Total	121.4	100

Selected Subsidiaries

Central Pennsylvania Investment Company (investment management)
　Omega Insurance Agency Inc.
Central Pennsylvania Leasing (personal property and real estate leasing)
Central Pennsylvania Life Insurance Company (credit life insurance)
Omega Bank, N.A.
　Omega Financial Company, LLC
　SunBank

COMPETITORS

Citizens Financial Group
Community Banks
First Commonwealth Financial
Fulton Financial
M&T Bank
Northwest Bancorp
Penns Woods Bancorp
PNC Financial
Sovereign Bancorp
Univest

HISTORICAL FINANCIALS

Company Type: Public

Income Statement

FYE: December 31

	ASSETS ($ mil.)	NET INCOME ($ mil.)	INCOME AS % OF ASSETS	EMPLOYEES
12/05	1,940.0	22.9	1.2%	795
12/04	2,082.6	17.0	0.8%	799
12/03	1,140.2	17.2	1.5%	531
12/02	1,154.6	18.2	1.6%	534
12/01	1,158.6	17.7	1.5%	555
Annual Growth	13.8%	6.7%	—	9.4%

2005 Year-End Financials

Equity as % of assets: 16.4%
Return on assets: 1.1%
Return on equity: 7.2%
Long-term debt ($ mil.): 94.9
No. of shares (mil.): 12.7
Market value ($ mil.): 353.6
Dividends
  Yield: 4.4%
  Payout: 68.5%
Sales ($ mil.): 121.4
R&D as % of sales: —
Advertising as % of sales: —

Stock History

NASDAQ (GS): OMEF

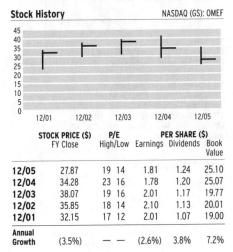

	STOCK PRICE ($) FY Close	P/E High/Low		PER SHARE ($) Earnings	Dividends	Book Value
12/05	27.87	19	14	1.81	1.24	25.10
12/04	34.28	23	16	1.78	1.20	25.07
12/03	38.07	19	16	2.01	1.17	19.77
12/02	35.85	18	14	2.10	1.13	20.01
12/01	32.15	17	12	2.01	1.07	19.00
Annual Growth	(3.5%)	—	—	(2.6%)	3.8%	7.2%

Omega Flex

Like a reed in a stream, Grasshopper, sometimes the flexible withstand pressure better than the rigid. That's certainly a concept that Omega Flex can get behind: The company makes flexible tubular and braided metal (stainless steel, bronze) hoses for liquid and gas transportation. Products include hoses specially designed to deal with high pressure, motion, extreme temperatures, harsh liquids or gases, and abrasion. Other applications include cryogenics, cargo transfer,

and propane and gas installations. Chairman John Reed and his son Stewart together own a majority of Omega Flex.

The company's typical customers include chemical and petrochemical plants, steel mills, pulp and paper mills, water and wastewater facilities, and power plants.

Omega Flex's brand names include OmegaFlex and TracPipe.

EXECUTIVES

Chairman: John E. Reed, age 90
President and CEO: Kevin R. Hoben, age 59
EVP, COO, and Director: Mark F. Albino, age 53
SVP Corporate Development and Facilities Management: Steven A. Treichel, age 55
VP Finance and CFO: E. Lynn Wilkinson, age 62
Managing Director, Omega Flex Limited:
  Bernard E. Qinlan, age 53
Auditors: Vitale, Caturano & Company, Ltd.

LOCATIONS

HQ: Omega Flex, Inc.
  451 Creamery Way, Exton, PA 19341
Phone: 610-524-7272   **Fax:** 610-524-7282
Web: www.omegaflex.com

COMPETITORS

Dixon Valve
Gates Corporation
Smiths Aerospace

HISTORICAL FINANCIALS

Company Type: Public

Income Statement

FYE: December 31

	REVENUE ($ mil.)	NET INCOME ($ mil.)	NET PROFIT MARGIN	EMPLOYEES
12/05	65.6	7.5	11.4%	105
12/04	48.2	6.0	12.4%	90
12/03	37.0	4.0	10.8%	90
12/02	35.0	3.6	10.3%	90
Annual Growth	23.3%	27.7%	—	5.3%

2005 Year-End Financials

Debt ratio: 12.4%
Return on equity: 30.0%
Cash ($ mil.): 9.9
Current ratio: 2.47
Long-term debt ($ mil.): 3.2
No. of shares (mil.): 10.2
Dividends
  Yield: —
  Payout: —
Market value ($ mil.): 176.6
R&D as % of sales: 0.8%
Advertising as % of sales: 0.6%

Stock History

NASDAQ (GM): OFLX

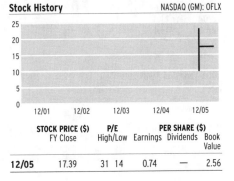

	STOCK PRICE ($) FY Close	P/E High/Low		PER SHARE ($) Earnings	Dividends	Book Value
12/05	17.39	31	14	0.74	—	2.56

OMI Corporation

Oh, my, but there's a lot of oil in that tanker. OMI provides marine transportation of crude oil and petroleum products such as gasoline. The company's fleet of some 45 double-hull vessels includes about a dozen Suezmax tankers, which are used to haul crude oil, and more than 30 product carriers. OMI's vessels have an overall capacity of about 3.5 million deadweight tons. The company charters vessels to oil companies and oil traders worldwide, both on the spot market (voyage by voyage) and on longer-term contracts. OMI markets its crude oil tankers through an alliance with Frontline. Transportation of crude oil accounts for more than 60% of OMI's sales.

EXECUTIVES

Chairman and CEO: Craig H. Stevenson Jr., age 52, $3,300,000 pay
President, COO, and Director: Robert Bugbee, age 45, $2,550,000 pay
SVP, CFO, and Treasurer: Kathleen C. Haines, age 51, $1,150,000 pay
SVP, General Counsel, and Secretary:
  Frederic S. London, age 58, $1,060,000 pay
SVP, OMI Marine Services: Henry Blaustein, age 61
SVP, OMI Marine Services: Cameron K. Mackey, age 38, $840,000 pay
VP and Economist: Stavros Skopelitis, age 59
Director, Environmental Compliance and Ombudsman:
  Ole Christian Schroder
Auditors: Deloitte & Touche LLP

LOCATIONS

HQ: OMI Corporation
  1 Station Place, Stamford, CT 06902
Phone: 203-602-6700   **Fax:** 203-602-6701
Web: www.omicorp.com

PRODUCTS/OPERATIONS

2005 Sales

	$ mil.	% of total
Crude oil fleet	410.6	63
Product carrier fleet	240.3	37
Other	1.5	—
Total	**652.4**	**100**

COMPETITORS

A.P. Møller — Mærsk
General Maritime
Knightsbridge Tankers
Mitsui O.S.K. Lines
NORDEN
Nordic American Tanker
NYK Line
Overseas Shipholding
Teekay
TORM
Tsakos Energy Navigation

HISTORICAL FINANCIALS

Company Type: Public

Income Statement

FYE: December 31

	REVENUE ($ mil.)	NET INCOME ($ mil.)	NET PROFIT MARGIN	EMPLOYEES
12/05	652.4	275.2	42.2%	1,318
12/04	564.7	245.7	43.5%	1,250
12/03	269.4	76.5	28.4%	950
12/02	199.1	15.5	7.8%	48
12/01	209.9	82.3	39.2%	47
Annual Growth	32.8%	35.2%	—	130.1%

2005 Year-End Financials

Debt ratio: 114.1%
Return on equity: 36.2%
Cash ($ mil.): 43.8
Current ratio: 1.18
Long-term debt ($ mil.): 861.4
No. of shares (mil.): 71.3

Dividends
  Yield: 1.8%
  Payout: 9.4%
Market value ($ mil.): 1,294.2
R&D as % of sales: —
Advertising as % of sales: —

Stock History

NYSE: OMM

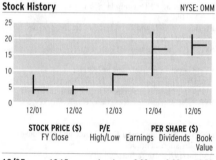

	STOCK PRICE ($) FY Close	P/E High/Low		PER SHARE ($) Earnings	Dividends	Book Value
12/05	18.15	6	4	3.39	0.32	10.59
12/04	16.85	8	3	2.86	0.22	8.96
12/03	8.93	9	4	0.98	—	6.67
12/02	4.11	24	13	0.22	—	5.70
12/01	3.98	7	2	1.21	—	5.72
Annual Growth	46.1%	—	—	29.4%	45.5%	16.6%

Omni Financial Services

Omni Financial Services doesn't try to be everything to everyone. Rather, the holding company for Omni National Bank focuses on commercial lending, such as loans for small businesses, community redevelopment, and residential construction, in addition to asset-based lending and equipment leasing. Commercial mortgages account for around three-quarters of the company's loan portfolio. Also serving local consumers, the bank has about 10 branches and loan production offices, mainly in North Carolina and Georgia, but also in Birmingham, Alabama; Chicago; and Tampa. Chairman and CEO Stephen Klein owns more than 30% of Omni Financial Services; EVP Jeffrey Levine holds some 12%.

In 2005 Omni Financial acquired the troubled Georgia Community Bank, which gave the company entry into that state. The company hopes to use some of the proceeds from its 2006 IPO to purchase other banks or financial services concerns.

EXECUTIVES

Chairman and CEO: Stephen M. Klein, age 52, $453,400 pay
President, COO, and Director: Irwin M. Berman, age 46, $275,065 pay
EVP and CFO: Constance Perrine, age 44
EVP, Community Redevelopment Lending, and Director: Jeffrey L. Levine, age 65, $353,400 pay
EVP and Chief Credit Officer: Eugene F. Lawson III, age 56
EVP and Chief Lending Officer: Charles M. Barnwell, age 46, $206,104 pay

LOCATIONS

HQ: Omni Financial Services, Inc.
6 Concourse Pkwy., Ste. 2300, Atlanta, GA 30328
Phone: 770-396-0000   **Fax:** 770-350-1300
Web: www.onb.com

Omni Financial Services has locations in Birmingham, Alabama; Atlanta and Dalton, Georgia; Tampa; Chicago; and Charlotte, Fayetteville, Highpoint, and Parkton, North Carolina.

PRODUCTS/OPERATIONS

2005 Sales

	$ mil.	% of total
Interest		
Loans, including fees	27.2	81
Investment securities & other	3.8	11
Noninterest		
Gain on sale of loans	1.3	4
Service charges on deposit accounts	0.3	1
Other	1.0	3
Total	**33.6**	**100**

COMPETITORS

Bank of America
BB&T
Fidelity Southern
First Citizens BancShares
RBC Centura Banks
Regions Financial
SunTrust
Synovus
Wachovia

HISTORICAL FINANCIALS

Company Type: Public

Income Statement

FYE: December 31

	REVENUE ($ mil.)	NET INCOME ($ mil.)	NET PROFIT MARGIN	EMPLOYEES
12/05	33.6	4.9	14.6%	131
12/04	21.8	3.6	16.5%	91
12/03	16.4	2.1	12.8%	—
Annual Growth	43.1%	52.8%		44.0%

2005 Year-End Financials

Debt ratio: —
Return on equity: 19.6%
Cash ($ mil.): —

Current ratio: —
Long-term debt ($ mil.): 20.6

Net Income History

NASDAQ (GM): OFSI

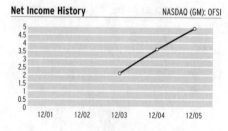

Oplink Communications

Oplink Communications puts a shine on network connections. The company makes fiber-optic components that increase the capacity of communications networks. Oplink's dense wavelength division multiplexers transmit several light signals simultaneously over a single glass fiber. Other products amplify the optical signals, monitor wavelength performance, and direct signals along the way to their destinations. Telecom equipment makers, including Nortel, ADVA, and Huawei, incorporate Oplink's components into gear used to build networks, both interoffice and international.

In addition to supplying optical components of its own design, Oplink provides photonic foundry services on a contract basis, making custom optical subsystems and full systems for customers.

Customers in North America account for around 40% of sales.

FMR (Fidelity Investments) owns about 9% of Oplink Communications. Investors Chao-Jung and Chen Hwa Chang hold nearly 7% of the company. Kopp Investment Advisors owns nearly 6%. Investors Hui Chuan and H. S. Liu have an equity stake of 5% in Oplink.

EXECUTIVES

President, CEO, and Director: Joseph Y. Liu, age 55, $150,000 pay
CFO and Treasurer: Bruce D. Horn, age 54, $225,000 pay
VP, Sales: River Gong, age 43, $135,000 pay
Chief Quality Officer: Charles Ingebretsen
General Manager, China/Macau: Chi-Min (James) Cheng, age 60, $117,500 pay
VP, Operations: Yanfeng Yang, age 42
Chairman: Leonard J. LeBlanc, age 65
Secretary: Carmen Chang
VP, Technology: Jin Hong
VP Business Development: Robert Shih
Auditors: Burr, Pilger & Mayer LLP

LOCATIONS

HQ: Oplink Communications, Inc.
46335 Landing Pkwy., Fremont, CA 94538
Phone: 510-933-7200   **Fax:** 510-933-7300
Web: www.oplink.com

Oplink Communications has manufacturing facilities in China and the US, with sales offices around the world.

2006 Sales

	$ mil.	% of total
Asia	18.6	34
US	14.8	27
Europe	14.0	25
Canada	7.4	14
Total	**54.8**	**100**

PRODUCTS/OPERATIONS

2006 Sales

	% of total
Bandwidth creation products	69
Bandwidth management products	31
Total	**100**

Selected Products

Multiplexing equipment
  Chromatic dispersion compensators
  Dense wavelength division multiplexers (DWDM)
  Dispersion Slope Compensators
  DWDM interleavers
  Noise reduction filters
  Wavelength lockers

Amplification
    Gain flattening filters
    Isolators
    Integrated hybrid components
    Polarization beam combiners
    Tap couplers
    Variable optical attenuators
    WDM pump/signal combiners
Switching equipment
    Add/drop multiplexers
    Circulators
    Optical switches

COMPETITORS

Alliance Fiber Optic Products
APA Enterprises
Avanex
Bookham
Broadwing Corporation
Ciena
DiCon Fiberoptics
Fujitsu
Furukawa Electric
Hitachi Cable
JDS Uniphase
New Focus
Santec
Sumitomo Electric
Tyco

HISTORICAL FINANCIALS

Company Type: Public

Income Statement

FYE: Sun. nearest July 30

	REVENUE ($ mil.)	NET INCOME ($ mil.)	NET PROFIT MARGIN	EMPLOYEES
6/06	54.8	1.9	3.5%	2,067
6/05	34.4	(2.7)	—	1,546
6/04	34.3	(6.4)	—	975
6/03	22.6	(36.8)	—	676
6/02	37.9	(68.4)	—	1,411
Annual Growth	9.7%	—	—	10.0%

2006 Year-End Financials

Debt ratio: —
Return on equity: 0.9%
Cash ($ mil.): 125.3
Current ratio: 13.89
Long-term debt ($ mil.): —
No. of shares (mil.): 21.5
Dividends
  Yield: —
  Payout: —
Market value ($ mil.): 394.1
R&D as % of sales: —
Advertising as % of sales: —

Stock History

NASDAQ (GM): OPLK

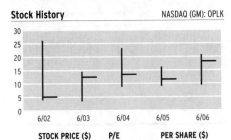

	STOCK PRICE ($) FY Close	P/E High/Low	Earnings	PER SHARE ($) Dividends	Book Value
6/06	18.31	228 107	0.09	—	10.55
6/05	11.55	— —	(0.14)	—	—
6/04	13.44	— —	(0.28)	—	—
6/03	12.46	— —	(1.61)	—	—
6/02	5.11	— —	(2.94)	—	—
Annual Growth	37.6%	— —	—	—	—

Optelecom-NKF

Optelecom-NKF (formerly Optelecom) chooses to make light of video. The company's Communications Products Division makes optical fiber-based data transmission and signal compression equipment and fiber-optic modems. Its products are used in a number of niche applications, including highway traffic monitoring, air traffic control video monitor displays, security surveillance, and manufacturing process and control applications. Optelecom-NKF's Electro-optics Technology unit makes optical fiber coils used in military rotation-sensing instruments; its customers include defense contractors such as Boeing.

In 2005 Optelecom acquired fiber optics equipment maker NKF Electronics, formerly a subsidiary of Draka Holding, for $26 million. The company subsequently changed its name to reflect the addition of NKF's product line.

EXECUTIVES

President, CEO, and Director: Edmund D. Ludwig, age 64
EVP and COO, North American Operations and Director: James (Jim) Armstrong, age 48
CFO: Steven T. Tamburo, age 37
VP, Manufacturing and Quality: Greg Hall
VP, Sales and Marketing: Leonard (Len) May
Director; EVP and COO, European Operations; Managing Director, NKF: Tom Overwijn, age 43
Director, Integrated Systems: David Nibley
Coordinator, Integrator/Rep. Support and Manager, Marketing Communications: Betsy Lanning
Manager, Human Resources: Diane Mortazavi
Investor Relations: Rick Alpert
Auditors: Grant Thornton LLP

LOCATIONS

HQ: Optelecom-NKF, Inc.
    12920 Cloverleaf Center Dr.,
    Germantown, MD 20874
Phone: 301-444-2200   **Fax:** 301-444-2299
Web: www.optelecom.com

Headquartered in Maryland, Optelecom-NKF has facilities in France, the Netherlands, Singapore, Spain, and the UK.

2005 Sales

	$ mil.	% of total
US	14.9	44
Netherlands	14.1	42
UK	2.4	7
Spain	1.8	5
Other	0.7	2
Total	33.9	100

PRODUCTS/OPERATIONS

2005 Sales

	$ mil.	% of total
Communications Products Division	32.9	97
Electro Optics Technology Unit	1.0	3
Total	33.9	100

Selected Products

Communications Products Division
    Closed circuit television and broadcast video audio and data transmission equipment
    Compressed digital video products digitization and compression equipment
    Fiber-optic modems
    High-resolution RGB transmission equipment
    Uncompressed digital video transmission equipment

Electro Optics Technology Unit
    Interferometric Fiber Optic Gyro (IFOG) coils

COMPETITORS

3Com	JDS Uniphase
ADC Telecommunications	Nortel Networks
Alcatel-Lucent	Siemens AG
ARRIS	Tellabs
Cisco Systems	TeraForce
Harmonic	

HISTORICAL FINANCIALS

Company Type: Public

Income Statement

FYE: December 31

	REVENUE ($ mil.)	NET INCOME ($ mil.)	NET PROFIT MARGIN	EMPLOYEES
12/05	33.9	2.7	8.0%	151
12/04	19.4	1.6	8.2%	78
12/03	17.1	3.5	20.5%	69
12/02	14.9	1.6	10.7%	61
12/01	13.2	(0.9)	—	55
Annual Growth	26.6%	—	—	28.7%

2005 Year-End Financials

Debt ratio: 135.4%
Return on equity: 24.9%
Cash ($ mil.): 3.0
Current ratio: 1.85
Long-term debt ($ mil.): 15.9
No. of shares (mil.): 3.3
Dividends
  Yield: —
  Payout: —
Market value ($ mil.): 44.2
R&D as % of sales: 7.2%
Advertising as % of sales: —

Stock History

NASDAQ (CM): OPTC

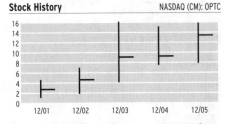

	STOCK PRICE ($) FY Close	P/E High/Low	Earnings	PER SHARE ($) Dividends	Book Value
12/05	13.40	20 10	0.80	—	3.56
12/04	9.26	31 16	0.49	—	3.12
12/03	9.09	14 4	1.11	—	2.56
12/02	4.64	12 4	0.56	—	1.28
12/01	2.74	— —	(0.33)	—	0.74
Annual Growth	48.7%	— —	—	—	48.2%

OptimumBank Holdings

OptimumBank Holdings has found a favorable position. It is the holding company for OptimumBank, which operates three branches in the communities of Plantation, Fort Lauderdale, and Deerfield Beach in South Florida. The bank is mainly a real estate lender, with residential mortgages representing the largest portion of its portfolio (nearly half), followed by commercial mortgages, developed land loans, and multifamily residential mortgages. It also offers other standard services such as checking and savings accounts, CDs, IRAs, personal loans, and business loans. OptimumBank was founded in 2000 by chairman Albert Finch and president Richard Browdy.

Executive officers and directors of Optimum-Bank collectively own nearly 45% of the bank. Director David Krinsky owns about 10%, while CEO and chairman Albert Finch and fellow board members Gordon Deckelbaum and Sam Borek each hold about 6% of OptimumBank.

EXECUTIVES

Chairman and CEO, OptimumBank Holding and OptimumBank: Albert J. Finch, age 68, $246,000 pay
Vice Chairman, OptimumBank Holding and OptimumBank: Irving P. Cohen, age 65
President, COO, CFO, and Director; President, COO, and CFO, OptimumBank: Richard L. Browdy, age 53, $210,250 pay
EVP and CTO, OptimumBank: Thomas A. Procelli, age 51, $118,300 pay
SVP, Lending, OptimumBank: Frank A. Nelson
VP and Branch Manager, OptimumBank, Plantation: Yolanda E. Jaffee
VP and Controller, OptimumBank: Gary J. Newman
VP, Bank Operations, Branch Administration, and Human Resources, OptimumBank: Leslie M. Legg
VP, Lending and Compliance, OptimumBank: Lisa Corr
Auditors: Hacker, Johnson & Smith PA

LOCATIONS

HQ: OptimumBank Holdings, Inc.
2477 E. Commercial Blvd.,
Fort Lauderdale, FL 33308
Phone: 954-776-2332 **Fax:** 954-776-2281
Web: www.optimumbank.com

PRODUCTS/OPERATIONS

2005 Sales

	$ mil.	% of total
Interest		
Loans	10.0	83
Securities & other	1.4	12
Noninterest		
Prepayment fees	0.5	4
Other	0.1	1
Total	**12.0**	**100**

COMPETITORS

BankAtlantic
BankUnited
Colonial BancGroup
SunTrust
Wachovia

HISTORICAL FINANCIALS

Company Type: Public

Income Statement

FYE: December 31

	ASSETS ($ mil.)	NET INCOME ($ mil.)	INCOME AS % OF ASSETS	EMPLOYEES
12/05	206.0	1.6	0.8%	21
12/04	164.6	1.6	1.0%	20
12/03	135.2	1.0	0.7%	—
12/02	75.3	0.5	0.7%	11
Annual Growth	**39.9%**	**47.4%**	**—**	**24.1%**

2005 Year-End Financials

Equity as % of assets: 8.9%
Return on assets: 0.9%
Return on equity: 9.1%
Long-term debt ($ mil.): 62.6
No. of shares (mil.): 2.7
Market value ($ mil.): 25.9
Dividends
 Yield: —
 Payout: —
Sales ($ mil.): 12.0
R&D as % of sales: —
Advertising as % of sales: —

Stock History NASDAQ (GM): OPHC

	STOCK PRICE ($) FY Close	P/E High/Low	PER SHARE ($) Earnings	Dividends	Book Value
12/05	9.74	23 17	0.55	—	6.91
12/04	12.52	23 14	0.55	—	6.31
12/03	7.72	30 22	0.35	—	5.70
Annual Growth	**12.3%**	**— —**	**25.4%**	**—**	**10.1%**

---

optionsXpress Holdings

In a hurry to do some options trading? optionsXpress is an online brokerage that provides a customized interface for trading options, stocks, an other products. optionsXpress also offers Xecute, an automated trading product, and StrategyScan, which helps clients identify possible trading strategies for a particular stock. optionsXpress has more than 160,000 customer accounts, with options trades representing about 75% of all trading activity. Chairman James Gray controls more than 20% of the stock of options-Xpress. Director Bruce Evans (through Summit Partners) controls 5%.

The company, which was founded in 2000 and went public in early 2005, launched subsidiary brokersXpress to extend its services to brokers and institutional investors. It also launched a futures platform in 2005. The company suffered a setback in 2006 when partner INVESTools, an educational investment firm, said it would no longer direct business to optionsXpress but was buying its own trading firm. optionsXpress is expanding geographically. It holds a minority interest in an Australian broker and plans to begin offering services in Canada and Singapore.

EXECUTIVES

Chairman: James A. Gray, age 40
CEO and Director: David S. Kalt, age 38, $408,033 pay
COO and Director; Chairman, brokersXpress: Ned W. Bennett, age 64, $403,633 pay
CFO and Director: David A. Fisher, age 35, $595,000 pay
CTO: Patrick Schuler
CEO, brokersXpress: Barry Metzger
Chief Administrative Officer: Thomas E. Stern, age 58, $246,067 pay
Chief Compliance Officer: Benjamin Morof, age 36, $275,000 pay
Auditors: Ernst & Young LLP

LOCATIONS

HQ: optionsXpress Holdings, Inc.
39 S. LaSalle St., Ste. 220, Chicago, IL 60603
Phone: 312-630-3300 **Fax:** 312-629-5256
Web: www.optionsxpress.com

optionsXpress Holdings has operations in Chicago; El Paso, Texas; and Thousand Oaks, California.

PRODUCTS/OPERATIONS

2005 Sales

	$ mil.	% of total
Commissions	91.4	71
Other brokerage-related income	24.5	19
Interest income	12.8	10
Other	0.3	—
Total	**129.0**	**100**

COMPETITORS

Alaron.com
America First Associates
Charles Schwab
Citigroup
E*TRADE Financial
FMR
Interactive Brokers
Merrill Lynch
Scottrade
TD Ameritrade
TradeStation

HISTORICAL FINANCIALS

Company Type: Public

Income Statement

FYE: December 31

	REVENUE ($ mil.)	NET INCOME ($ mil.)	NET PROFIT MARGIN	EMPLOYEES
12/05	129.0	48.7	37.8%	159
12/04	93.1	31.2	33.5%	128
12/03	48.2	16.4	34.0%	110
12/02	17.3	4.4	25.4%	—
12/01	2.1	(1.4)	—	—
Annual Growth	**180.0%**	**—**		**20.2%**

2005 Year-End Financials

Debt ratio: —
Return on equity: 64.3%
Cash ($ mil.): 106.1
Current ratio: —
Long-term debt ($ mil.): —
No. of shares (mil.): 62.1
Dividends
 Yield: 0.5%
 Payout: 15.2%
Market value ($ mil.): 1,524.6
R&D as % of sales: —
Advertising as % of sales: 4.4%

Stock History

NASDAQ (GS): OXPS

	STOCK PRICE ($) FY Close	P/E High/Low	PER SHARE ($) Earnings	Dividends	Book Value
12/05	24.55	33 16	0.79	0.12	1.91

OraSure Technologies

Diagnostic tests OraSure thing. Oral specimen kits and other diagnostic tests developed by OraSure Technologies are designed to detect HIV and drug use. The firm's OraSure products use oral specimens rather than traditional blood- or urine-based methods to test for HIV. Its Intercept line uses oral samples to test for marijuana, cocaine, opiates, PCP, and amphetamines. The firm has developed a rapid HIV blood diagnostic testing method (licensed in part from Abbott Laboratories). However, an increase in false positive results has cast doubt on the rapid test results.

OraSure sells its products in the US and internationally, primarily to the life insurance industry and public health markets.

Only about 10% of OraSure's sales come from abroad, but the company plans to expand its international sales efforts. It also wants to increase its product offerings by developing diagnostic tests for other infectious diseases (a test for hepatitis C is already in the works) and by offering some existing products, such as its oral HIV test, over-the-counter.

Prestige Brands and Quest Diagnostics account for 17% and 13% of sales, respectively. Prestige Brands distributes OraSure's wart removal product under its own Compound W brand.

Wells Fargo holds a 9% stake in OraSure. Merrill Lynch, Barclays Global Investors, and AXA Financial each own 6%.

EXECUTIVES

Chairman: Douglas G. Watson, age 62
President, CEO, and Director: Douglas A. Michels, age 49, $768,808 pay
CFO, COO, and Director: Ronald H. (Ron) Spair, age 50
EVP and Chief Science Officer: Stephen R. (Steve) Lee, age 46
EVP, Operations: P. Michael Formica, age 55, $399,546 pay
EVP, Sales and Marketing: Joseph E. Zack, age 54, $367,593 pay
SVP, Business Development: Mark Kirtland
SVP, Finance and Controller: Mark L. Kuna, age 42
SVP, General Counsel, and Secretary: Jack E. Jerrett, age 47, $326,591 pay
SVP, Human Resources: Henry B. Cohen
Auditors: KPMG LLP

LOCATIONS

HQ: OraSure Technologies, Inc.
220 E. 1st St., Bethlehem, PA 18015
Phone: 610-882-1820   **Fax:** 610-882-1830
Web: www.orasure.com

2005 Sales

	$ mil.	% of total
US	59.9	86
Europe	7.9	12
Other regions	1.6	2
Total	**69.4**	**100**

PRODUCTS/OPERATIONS

2005 Sales

	% of total
Market revenues	
Infectious disease testing	37
Cryosurgical systems	33
Substance abuse testing	19
Insurance risk assessment	10
Licensing & product development	1
Total	**100**

Selected Products

AUTO-LYTE (enzyme immunoassay tests)
Histofreezer (cryosurgical wart removal system)
Intercept (substance abuse testing)
MICRO-PLATE (plasma screening)
OraSure (saliva-based HIV test)
QED Saliva Alcohol Test

COMPETITORS

Abbott Labs	Medtox Scientific
Apogent Technologies inc.	Olympus America
Avitar	Orgenics
Bio-Rad Labs	PharmChem
Biosite	Psychemedics
Calypte Biomedical	Quest Diagnostics
Dade Behring	Quidel
eScreen	Roche Diagnostics
Johnson & Johnson	Schering-Plough Holdings
LabOne	Trinity Biotech

HISTORICAL FINANCIALS

Company Type: Public

Income Statement

FYE: December 31

	REVENUE ($ mil.)	NET INCOME ($ mil.)	NET PROFIT MARGIN	EMPLOYEES
12/05	69.4	27.5	39.6%	233
12/04	54.0	(0.6)	—	194
12/03	40.5	(1.1)	—	171
12/02	32.0	(3.3)	—	187
12/01	32.6	(3.7)	—	221
Annual Growth	**20.8%**	**—**	**—**	**1.3%**

2005 Year-End Financials

Debt ratio: 0.7%
Return on equity: 28.3%
Cash ($ mil.): 77.6
Current ratio: 9.44
Long-term debt ($ mil.): 0.9
No. of shares (mil.): 45.8
Dividends
  Yield: —
  Payout: —
Market value ($ mil.): 403.7
R&D as % of sales: 7.6%
Advertising as % of sales: 3.2%

Stock History

NASDAQ (GM): OSUR

	STOCK PRICE ($) FY Close	P/E High/Low		PER SHARE ($) Earnings	PER SHARE ($) Dividends	PER SHARE ($) Book Value
12/05	8.82	24	9	0.59	—	2.60
12/04	6.72	—	—	(0.01)	—	1.69
12/03	7.96	—	—	(0.03)	—	1.66
12/02	5.45	—	—	(0.09)	—	0.68
12/01	12.15	—	—	(0.10)	—	0.71
Annual Growth	**(7.7%)**	**—**	**—**	**—**	**—**	**38.3%**

Orleans Homebuilders

Orleans Homebuilders (OHB) prefers the City of Brotherly Love to Bourbon Street. OHB and its subsidiaries build communities of single-family homes (with average costs of about $424,000), condos, and townhomes for first-time and move-up buyers, luxury homebuyers, empty nesters, and active adult homebuyers. The company annually delivers about 2,300 homes in about 90 communities. Nowhere near the Crescent City, OHB operates mainly in the Philadelphia metro area (including several counties in New Jersey and New York), the Carolinas, and Virginia. It also builds in Arizona, Florida, and Illinois. OHB offers finance and mortgage services. Chairman and CEO Jeffrey Orleans owns more than 60% of OHB.

OHB's homes range in price from $161,000 to $298,000 in Florida; from $158,000 to $947,000 in other southern states; from $272,000 to $510,000 in the Midwest; and from $237,000 to $1,087,000 in the North. Orleans Homebuilders traditionally operated mainly in the northeastern US (suburban Philadelphia and the Delaware Valley), but has been expanding geographically. The acquisitive company moved southward into Virginia and the Carolinas by purchases in 2000 and in 2003. It expanded its operations in Philly and moved into the Chicago and Charlotte, North Carolina markets through 2005 acquisitions. A 2005 land buy in Phoenix signaled the company's entry into that market.

Jeffrey Orleans is the son of founder Marvin Orleans and grandson of A. P. Orleans (who founded the family's first construction business in 1918). Vice chairman Benjamin Goldman owns about 6% of the company.

HISTORY

In 1969 Marvin Orleans founded FPA as a public company in order to buy Florida Palm-Aire Corporation, owner of the Palm-Aire Country Club in Pompano Beach, Florida; he bought the company from Orleans Construction Corp. (OCC), his father, and other investors who had acquired it in 1965. Marvin, whose father, Alfred, was a successful developer in the Philadelphia area, enlarged Palm-Aire into a residential and resort development. But by 1985 FPA was deeply in debt and sank into more than a decade of operating losses. FPA sold Palm-Aire in 1987 (it later fell into the hands of the Resolution Trust Corporation).

The company then began working with OCC to develop real estate in the Philadelphia area, but the real estate market crashed in the Northeast. FPA and OCC lost market share, and FPA came near bankruptcy. In a 1993 recapitalization, the Orleans family sold OCC to FPA in return for stock and began a cost-cutting program. In 1994 FPA bought back Palm-Aire at fire-sale prices (it sold the resort/spa facilities but kept the country club).

In 1995 FPA started a major push to regain market share by buying more land and beefing up its marketing operations. The next year the company began expanding south and west of Philadelphia into Delaware and Chester counties, often using funds loaned by Jeffrey Orleans. In 1997 FPA opened a community in Princeton, New Jersey, and entered the adult-living market with a development in Southampton, New Jersey. The company changed its name to Orleans Homebuilders (OHB) in 1998.

OHB began operations outside Philadelphia and New Jersey in 2000 with the acquisition of Parker Lancaster, which operated in North and South Carolina and Virginia. The company ranked 33rd on *FORTUNE* magazine's "100 Fastest Growing Companies" list in 2002, 29th on the list in 2003, and 52nd in 2004. The company expanded operations into central Florida in 2003 with the purchase of Orange City-based Masterpiece Homes. The next year OHB acquired Realen Homes (Philadelphia and Chicago areas) for $60 million and Peachtree Residential Properties, Inc. (greater Atlanta area and Charlotte, North Carolina).

Big Builder magazine ranked the company as the 14th-largest public homebuilder and the 8th-largest luxury homebuilder in the US in 2005.

EXECUTIVES

Chairman and CEO: Jeffrey P. Orleans, age 60,
$4,207,270 pay
Vice Chairman: Benjamin D. Goldman, age 60
President, COO, and Director: Michael T. Vesey, age 47,
$1,913,635 pay
Controller and Interim CFO: James W. Thompson,
age 44
SEVP; President, Northern Region: Gary J. Stefanoni,
age 54
EVP, Southern Region: Thomas Vesey, age 42,
$890,065 pay
**President, Parker & Lancaster Corporation and Parker
& Orleans Homebuilders, Inc.:**
J. Russell (Russ) Parker III, age 62
Division President, Greensboro, North Carolina:
Jeffrey C. (Jeff) Guernier, age 47
Division President, Midwest: Randy Harris, age 56
Division President, Raleigh, North Carolina:
Stephen D. Leach, age 49
Director Sales and Marketing: Gary G. Schaal
Auditors: PricewaterhouseCoopers LLP

LOCATIONS

HQ: Orleans Homebuilders, Inc.
1 Greenwood Sq., 3333 Street Rd., Ste. 101,
Bensalem, PA 19020
Phone: 215-245-7500   **Fax:** 215-633-2352
Web: www.orleanshomes.com

Orleans Homebuilders builds homes in southeastern
Pennsylvania; central and southern New Jersey;
Charlotte, Greensboro, and Raleigh, North Carolina;
Chicago; Orange County, New York; Orlando, Palm Bay,
and Palm Coast, Florida; Richmond and Tidewater,
Virginia; and Phoenix.

2006 Sales

	$ mil.	% of total
Northern	393.9	40
Southern	372.9	38
Midwestern	119.0	12
Florida	93.6	9
Other	7.8	1
Total	**987.2**	**100**

2006 Residential Communities

	No.	% of total
Southern	43	48
Northern	33	37
Midwestern	9	10
Florida	4	5
Total	**89**	**100**

PRODUCTS/OPERATIONS

2006 Sales

	$ mil.	% of total
Residential sales		
Single-family homes	823.8	84
Townhouses	110.3	11
Condominiums	41.4	4
Land sales	2.0	—
Other income	9.7	1
Total	**987.2**	**100**

COMPETITORS

Beazer Homes
Calton
Centex
D.R. Horton
Hovnanian Enterprises
Lennar
M/I Homes
NVR
Pulte Homes
Ryland
Toll Brothers

HISTORICAL FINANCIALS

Company Type: Public

Income Statement

FYE: June 30

	REVENUE ($ mil.)	NET INCOME ($ mil.)	NET PROFIT MARGIN	EMPLOYEES
6/06	987.2	63.0	6.4%	988
6/05	919.2	55.6	6.0%	849
6/04	547.3	38.1	7.0%	629
6/03	388.5	27.3	7.0%	405
6/02	354.7	17.9	5.0%	367
Annual Growth	**29.2%**	**37.0%**	**—**	**28.1%**

2006 Year-End Financials

Debt ratio: 218.2%
Return on equity: 24.1%
Cash ($ mil.): 71.7
Current ratio: 0.55
Long-term debt ($ mil.): 637.1
No. of shares (mil.): 18.4

Dividends
Yield: 0.5%
Payout: 2.4%
Market value ($ mil.): 298.4
R&D as % of sales: —
Advertising as % of sales: —

Stock History

AMEX: OHB

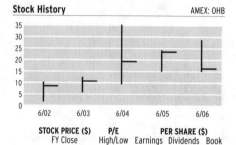

	STOCK PRICE ($) FY Close	P/E High	P/E Low	PER SHARE ($) Earnings	PER SHARE ($) Dividends	PER SHARE ($) Book Value
6/06	16.25	9	5	3.35	0.08	15.90
6/05	23.46	8	5	2.96	0.02	12.52
6/04	19.27	16	4	2.20	—	10.02
6/03	10.70	7	4	1.65	—	7.09
6/02	8.55	9	2	1.09	—	5.19
Annual Growth	**17.4%**	**—**	**—**	**32.4%**	**300.0%**	**32.3%**

Ormat Technologies

Ormat Technologies is on an environmentally
safe power trip. The company builds geothermal
as well as recovered energy power plants. Geothermal technology extracts hot water or steam
that is vaporized and used to drive turbines. The
fluid is then cooled and recycled back through
the process, making it a clean and renewable energy source. Recovered energy utilizes heat produced in other industrial processes that would
normally just disappear into the air. The company, established by Israel-based Ormat Industries, also sells power units for both types of
plants. Ormat operates geothermal plants (with
a cumulative total of 341 MW of power) in more
than 20 countries. The Bronicki family owns
30% of the company.

In 2006 Ormat Technologies acquired (from
an unrelated third party) a 51% stake in Orzunil
I de Electricidad, Limitada (Orzunil), which
owns the Zunil Geothermal Project in Guatemala, increasing its existing 21% ownership
stake in the Zunil Project to 72%.

EXECUTIVES

Chairman and CTO: Lucien Y. Bronicki, age 71,
$222,828 pay
President, CEO, and Director: Yehudit (Dita) Bronicki,
age 64, $248,828 pay
COO, North America and Director: Yoram Bronicki,
age 39
CFO: Joseph Tenne, age 50
EVP Business Development, North America:
Yeheskel (Hezy) Ram, age 56, $441,865 pay
EVP Engineering: Nadav Amir, age 55, $257,782 pay
EVP Marketing and Sales, Rest of the World:
Joseph Shiloah, age 60, $219,425 pay
EVP Project Management: Zvi Reiss, age 55
**VP Operations, Rest of the World, and Product
Support:** Aaron Choresh, age 60
VP Contract Administrator and Secretary: Etty Rosner,
age 50
VP Geothermal Engineering: Zvi Krieger, age 50
Investor Relations: Smadar Lavi
Auditors: PricewaterhouseCoopers LLP

LOCATIONS

HQ: Ormat Technologies, Inc.
980 Greg St., Sparks, NV 89431
Phone: 775-356-9029   **Fax:** 775-356-9039
Web: www.ormat.com

2005 Sales

	$ mil.	% of total
North America	170.1	72
Europe	31.8	13
Latin America	13.7	6
Pacific Rim	10.7	4
Africa	10.6	4
Asia	1.1	1
Total	**238.0**	**100**

PRODUCTS/OPERATIONS

2005 Sales

	$ mil.	% of total
Electricity	177.4	74
Products	60.6	26
Total	**238.0**	**100**

COMPETITORS

ALSTOM
Caithness Energy
Calpine
Fuji Electric
GE
Mitsubishi Electric
Siemens AG
Toshiba

HISTORICAL FINANCIALS

Company Type: Public

Income Statement

FYE: December 31

	REVENUE ($ mil.)	NET INCOME ($ mil.)	NET PROFIT MARGIN	EMPLOYEES
12/05	238.0	15.2	6.4%	733
12/04	219.2	17.8	8.1%	677
12/03	119.4	15.4	12.9%	676
12/02	85.6	(1.0)	—	—
Annual Growth	**40.6%**	**—**	**—**	**4.1%**

2005 Year-End Financials

Debt ratio: 262.3%
Return on equity: 8.7%
Cash ($ mil.): 107.3
Current ratio: 1.29
Long-term debt ($ mil.): 478.1
No. of shares (mil.): 31.6

Dividends
Yield: 0.5%
Payout: 25.0%
Market value ($ mil.): 825.0
R&D as % of sales: 1.3%
Advertising as % of sales: 0.1%

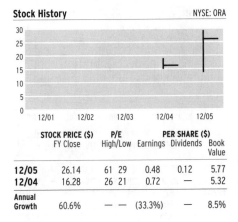

	STOCK PRICE ($) FY Close	P/E High/Low		PER SHARE ($) Earnings	Dividends	Book Value
12/05	26.14	61	29	0.48	0.12	5.77
12/04	16.28	26	21	0.72	—	5.32
Annual Growth	60.6%	—	—	(33.3%)	—	8.5%

Pacific CMA

Pacific? Atlantic? You name it — freight forwarder Pacific CMA arranges the transportation of its customers' goods by air and by sea. The company does not own transportation assets; instead, it employs a network of commercial carriers. Many of Pacific CMA's customers are in the garment industry, but the company manages the transportation of all types of cargo. Pacific CMA operates primarily from offices in New York and Hong Kong, and it maintains a network of some 230 agents in about 80 countries worldwide. Chairman and CEO Alfred Lam, through his Buller Services Corp., controls a 66% stake in Pacific CMA.

The company has built its business primarily through the purchases of freight forwarders AGI Logistics (2000) and Airgate International (2002); it has continued to expand via acquisitions. The Asia/Pacific region accounts for 60% of Pacific CMA's sales.

EXECUTIVES

Chairman, CEO, and Treasurer: Alfred Lam, age 53, $82,335 pay
President and Director: Scott Turner, age 51, $279,476 pay
CFO: Bill Stangland, age 65
EVP and Director: Kaze Chan, age 39
EVP, Strategic Development: Ling Kwok, age 35
SVP, Investor Relations: John Mazarella
CEO, Airgate International: Stanley Lee, $362,725 pay
President, Paradigm Global Logistics: Terence de Kretser, age 33
VP, Airgate International: Thomas Zambuto, $279,476 pay
Chief Accountant: Ella Choi
Secretary: Rango Lam, age 34
Auditors: BKD, LLP

LOCATIONS

HQ: Pacific CMA, Inc.
153-04 Rockaway Blvd., Jamaica, NY 11434
Phone: 718-949-9700 **Fax:** 718-949-9740
Web: www.pacificcma.com

2005 Sales

	$ mil.	% of total
Asia/Pacific region	75.4	60
Europe, Middle East & Africa	30.4	24
Americas	19.2	16
Total	**125.0**	**100**

PRODUCTS/OPERATIONS

2005 Sales

	$ mil.	% of total
Air forwarding	78.8	63
Sea forwarding	46.2	37
Total	**125.0**	**100**

Selected Subsidiaries and Affiliates

AGI Freight Singapore Pte Limited (60%, freight forwarding and logistics services)
AGI Logistics (Hong Kong) Ltd. (freight forwarding)
Airgate International Corporation (99%, freight forwarding)
Paradigm International Inc. (logistics services)
WCL Global Logistics Ltd. (51%)

COMPETITORS

DHL
EGL Eagle
Expeditors
UPS Supply Chain Solutions
UTi Worldwide

HISTORICAL FINANCIALS

Company Type: Public

Income Statement

FYE: December 31

	REVENUE ($ mil.)	NET INCOME ($ mil.)	NET PROFIT MARGIN	EMPLOYEES
12/05	125.0	0.5	0.4%	238
12/04	99.6	0.3	0.3%	193
12/03	73.1	0.0	—	115
12/02	52.9	0.7	1.3%	92
12/01	13.8	0.2	1.4%	67
Annual Growth	73.5%	25.7%	—	37.3%

2005 Year-End Financials

Debt ratio: 28.0%
Return on equity: 4.5%
Cash ($ mil.): 8.4
Current ratio: 1.54
Long-term debt ($ mil.): 3.6
No. of shares (mil.): 26.4
Dividends
  Yield: —
  Payout: —
Market value ($ mil.): 17.4
R&D as % of sales: —
Advertising as % of sales: —

Stock History

AMEX: PAM

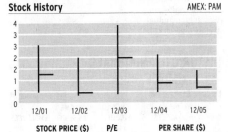

	STOCK PRICE ($) FY Close	P/E High/Low		PER SHARE ($) Earnings	Dividends	Book Value
12/05	0.66	—	—	(0.04)	—	0.48
12/04	0.86	207	49	0.01	—	0.38
12/03	1.97	—	—	—	—	0.31
12/02	0.45	65	12	0.03	—	0.26
12/01	1.25	250	50	0.01	—	0.19
Annual Growth	(14.8%)	—	—	—	—	27.0%

Pacific Premier Bancorp

Like most Southern Californians, Pacific Premier Bancorp is getting on with its second act. Formerly Life Financial, the company is the parent of Pacific Premier Bank (previously Life Bank), which has four branches and a loan office in Orange and San Bernardino counties in Southern California. The bank focuses on multifamily residential and commercial real estate loans ranging from $200,000 to $2 million (95% of its book), which the company believes is an underserved niche. It also has begun to emphasize traditional banking services such as deposit products and consumer and business loans, in part to diversify its loan portfolio. Wellington Management owns about 9% of the bank.

EXECUTIVES

Chairman, Pacific Premier Bancorp and Pacific Premier Bank: Ronald G. Skipper, age 65
President, CEO, and Director, Pacific Premier Bancorp and Pacific Premier Bank: Steven R. (Steve) Gardner, age 45, $600,000 pay
EVP, CFO, Treasurer, and Secretary, Pacific Premier Bancorp and Pacific Premier Bank: John Shindler, age 50, $200,000 pay
EVP and Chief Lending Officer, Pacific Premier Bank: Edward (Eddie) Wilcox, age 39, $225,000 pay
SVP and Chief Credit Officer, Pacific Premier Bank: Bruce Larson, $122,100 pay
SVP and Director of Operations, Pacific Premier Bank: Kathrine (Kathi) Duncan, age 48, $107,212 pay
SVP and Director of Information Technology and Security Officer, Pacific Premier Bank: James (Jim) Sanchez
SVP and Manager, SBA Loan Department, Pacific Premier Bank: Lou Malesci
VP and Manager, Commercial Lending, Pacific Premier Bank: Ronald (Ron) Meyers
Auditors: Vavrinek, Trine, Day & Co., LLP

LOCATIONS

HQ: Pacific Premier Bancorp, Inc.
1600 Sunflower Ave., 2nd Fl., Costa Mesa, CA 92626
Phone: 714-431-4000 **Fax:** 714-433-3000
Web: www.ppbi.net

2005 Sales

	$ mil.	% of total
Interest		
Loans	31.7	84
Investment securities & other	2.0	5
Noninterest		
Loan servicing fees	1.5	4
Other	2.6	7
Total	**37.8**	**100**

COMPETITORS

Bank of America
Citibank
City National
Comerica
Downey Financial
Washington Mutual
Wells Fargo
Zions Bancorporation

HISTORICAL FINANCIALS

Company Type: Public

Income Statement

FYE: December 31

	ASSETS ($ mil.)	NET INCOME ($ mil.)	INCOME AS % OF ASSETS	EMPLOYEES
12/05	702.7	7.2	1.0%	88
12/04	543.1	6.7	1.2%	83
12/03	309.4	2.1	0.7%	72
12/02	238.3	2.9	1.2%	59
12/01	243.7	(6.1)	—	74
Annual Growth	30.3%	—	—	4.4%

2005 Year-End Financials

Equity as % of assets: 7.2%
Return on assets: 1.2%
Return on equity: 15.2%
Long-term debt ($ mil.): 318.1
No. of shares (mil.): 5.2
Market value ($ mil.): 61.7

Dividends
  Yield: —
  Payout: —
Sales ($ mil.): 37.8
R&D as % of sales: —
Advertising as % of sales: —

Stock History

NASDAQ (CM): PPBI

	STOCK PRICE ($) FY Close	P/E High/Low	Earnings	PER SHARE ($) Dividends	Book Value
12/05	11.80	13 9	1.08	—	9.67
12/04	13.26	15 10	1.02	—	8.37
12/03	11.09	19 7	0.61	—	7.10
12/02	5.31	3 1	2.16	—	8.71
12/01	2.05	— —	(4.54)	—	5.74
Annual Growth	54.9%	— —	—	—	14.0%

Pacific State Bancorp

Farmers are more common than surfers in California's Long Valley, and Pacific State Bancorp is there to serve their banking needs. It's the holding company for Pacific State Bank, which offers deposit and loan products to individuals and small to midsized businesses from seven branches in Stockton and San Joaquin counties in California.

Not surprising considering the region's dependence on agriculture, the bank takes pride in being a national leader in the underwriting of USDA business and industry loans. Commercial mortgages make up about 50% of the bank's loan portfolio, followed by commercial and agricultural loans which account for more than a quarter. The bank also originates construction and installment loans.

President, CEO, and director Steven Rosso owns nearly 10% of Pacific State Bancorp; director Maxwell Freeman owns just more than 9%; chairman Harold Hand and Hot Creek Capital each own a little more than 8%.

EXECUTIVES

Chairman: Harold Hand, age 68
President, CEO, and Director, Pacific State Bancorp and Pacific State Bank: Steven A. Rosso, age 51, $243,084 pay
EVP, Chief Credit Officer, and Director, Pacific State Bancorp and Pacific State Bank: Gary A. Stewart, age 56, $159,283 pay
VP and CFO; SVP and CFO, Pacific State Bank: JoAnne C. Roberts, age 49, $89,875 pay
SVP and Regional Manager, Calaveras County, Pacific State Bank: Ron Aschwanden
SVP and Regional Manager, Stanislaus and Tuolumne Counties, Pacific State Bank: Rick Simas
SVP and Manager, Tracy, Pacific State Bank: Laura Maffei
SVP and Manager, March Lane, Pacific State Bank: Marie Verza
Secretary and Director: Steven J. Kikuchi, age 48
Auditors: Perry-Smith LLP

LOCATIONS

HQ: Pacific State Bancorp
  1899 W. March Ln., Stockton, CA 95207
Phone: 209-870-3200   **Fax:** 209-870-3250
Web: www.pacificstatebank.com

Pacific State Bank operates branches in Angels Camp, Arnold, Castro Valley, Groveland, Modesto, Stockton, and Tracy, California.

PRODUCTS/OPERATIONS

2005 Sales

	$ mil	% of total
Interest		
Loans	17.6	82
Other	1.2	6
Noninterest		
Sale of loans	0.8	4
Service charges	0.8	4
Other	0.9	4
Total	**21.3**	**100**

COMPETITORS

1867 Western Financial
Bank of America
E. J. De La Rosa
Washington Mutual
Wells Fargo

HISTORICAL FINANCIALS

Company Type: Public

Income Statement

FYE: December 31

	ASSETS ($ mil.)	NET INCOME ($ mil.)	INCOME AS % OF ASSETS	EMPLOYEES
12/05	309.6	4.3	1.4%	82
12/04	254.4	3.2	1.3%	—
12/03	200.9	2.0	1.0%	—
12/02	180.1	1.2	0.7%	—
12/01	121.3	1.0	0.8%	—
Annual Growth	26.4%	44.0%	—	—

2005 Year-End Financials

Equity as % of assets: 6.9%
Return on assets: 1.5%
Return on equity: 22.5%
Long-term debt ($ mil.): 12.8
No. of shares (mil.): 3.5
Market value ($ mil.): 65.0

Dividends
  Yield: —
  Payout: —
Sales ($ mil.): 21.3
R&D as % of sales: —
Advertising as % of sales: 0.6%

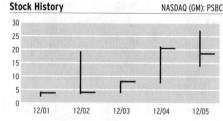

Stock History

NASDAQ (GM): PSBC

	STOCK PRICE ($) FY Close	P/E High/Low	Earnings	PER SHARE ($) Dividends	Book Value
12/05	18.50	25 13	1.10	—	6.08
12/04	20.50	25 9	0.84	—	4.88
12/03	8.07	14 7	0.59	—	7.97
12/02	4.00	55 11	0.34	—	13.71
12/01	3.75	12 8	0.33	—	12.35
Annual Growth	49.0%	— —	35.1%	—	(16.2%)

Palomar Medical Technologies

Palomar Medical Technologies' laser light show is more functional than flashy. Palomar makes lasers, delivery systems, and related disposable products that are used in medical procedures. The company's products include the EsteLux, StarLux, and MediLux systems. The company's lasers are used for a variety of medical and cosmetic applications such as tattoo and wrinkle removal, as well as leg-vein, acne, and pigmented lesion treatment. In development are laser products to perform fat reduction. Palomar Medical markets its products through distributors as well as a direct-sales force.

Palomar Medical Technologies has an agreement with Johnson & Johnson Consumer Companies to develop devices for reducing body fat and for improving appearance of the skin. The company also has a research contract for more than $3 million with the U.S. Department of the Army for the development of a self-treatment system for Pseudofolliculitis Barbae (also known as "razor bumps").

EXECUTIVES

Chairman: Louis P. (Dan) Valente, age 75, $519,000 pay
President, CEO, and Director: Joseph P. Caruso, age 47, $747,250 pay
CFO and Treasurer: Paul S. Weiner, $514,500 pay
SVP, General Counsel, and Secretary: Patricia A. Davis
SVP, Operations: Steven Armstrong
SVP, Research: Gregory Altshuler
VP and Chief Accounting Officer: Douglas Baraw
VP, Business Development: Robert Brody
VP, Clinical/Consumer Affairs: Michail Pankratov
VP, Marketing: Michael DiToro
VP, North American Sales: Jeffrey Knight
CTO: Michael H. Smotrich
Auditors: Ernst & Young LLP

LOCATIONS

HQ: Palomar Medical Technologies, Inc.
82 Cambridge St., Burlington, MA 01803
Phone: 781-993-2300   **Fax:** 781-993-2330
Web: www.palmed.com

PRODUCTS/OPERATIONS

2005 Sales

	% of total
US	71
Japan	7
Canada	7
Europe	6
Australia	3
Asia/Pacific	4
South & Central America	2
Total	**100**

COMPETITORS

Broadcast International
Candela Corporation
Cutera
Laserscope
Lumenis
Trimedyne

HISTORICAL FINANCIALS

Company Type: Public

Income Statement

FYE: December 31

	REVENUE ($ mil.)	NET INCOME ($ mil.)	NET PROFIT MARGIN	EMPLOYEES
12/05	76.2	17.5	23.0%	188
12/04	54.4	10.6	19.5%	161
12/03	34.8	3.4	9.8%	119
12/02	25.4	0.0	—	92
12/01	16.6	(5.5)	—	89
Annual Growth	**46.4%**	**—**	**—**	**20.6%**

2005 Year-End Financials

Debt ratio: —
Return on equity: 43.2%
Cash ($ mil.): 49.3
Current ratio: 4.51
Long-term debt ($ mil.): —
No. of shares (mil.): 17.1

Dividends
  Yield: —
  Payout: —
Market value ($ mil.): 600.1
R&D as % of sales: —
Advertising as % of sales: —

Stock History

NASDAQ (GS): PMTI

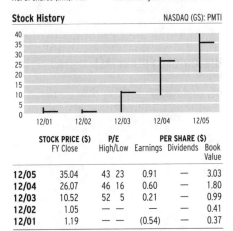

	STOCK PRICE ($) FY Close	P/E High/Low		PER SHARE ($) Earnings	Dividends	Book Value
12/05	35.04	43	23	0.91	—	3.03
12/04	26.07	46	16	0.60	—	1.80
12/03	10.52	52	5	0.21	—	0.99
12/02	1.05	—	—	—	—	0.41
12/01	1.19	—	—	(0.54)	—	0.37
Annual Growth	**132.9%**			**—**	**—**	**69.0%**

Panera Bread

Panera Bread is ready for an epochal change in American eating habits. The company is a leader in the quick-casual restaurant business with more than 870 bakery-cafes in about 35 states. Its locations, which operate under the Panera and Saint Louis Bread Company banners, offer made-to-order sandwiches built using a variety of artisan breads, including Asiago cheese bread, focaccia, and its classic sourdough bread. Its menu also features soups, salads, and gourmet coffees. In addition, Panera sells its bread, bagels, and pastries to go. About 310 of its locations are company-operated, while the rest are owned by franchisees.

Panera (which is Latin for "time for bread") has built significant brand loyalty by concentrating on the quality of its fresh-baked breads and other ingredients. It targets suburban areas where real estate is less expensive and the competition is less intense.

One of the fastest-growing and best-performing restaurant companies, Panera has been opening more than 130 new locations since 2003, mostly through franchising. It has also been acquiring a small number of locations from its franchisees to increase its company-owned store count. In 2006 Panera agreed to buy 51% of Paradise Bakery & Café, which runs a chain of more than 40 bakery-cafes in the Southwest. The $21 million deal includes the right to acquire the remaining stake in Paradise Bakery after 2008.

Chairman and CEO Ron Shaich controls more than 10% of Panera's voting stock.

HISTORY

Panera Bread traces its roots to a restaurant opened in Boston by French commercial oven manufacturer Pavailler. Au Bon Pain, opened in 1976, was intended as a showcase for Pavailler's ovens. The scent of hot croissants (and money) caught the attention of Louis Kane, who bought the business in 1978 and began expanding in Boston. Ron Shaich (pronounced "shake") joined Kane in 1981, and together they formed Au Bon Pain Co., Inc. The chain grew rapidly until the early 1990s, saturating the high-traffic areas in eastern US cities. After its IPO in 1991, Au Bon Pain began making acquisitions, including Saint Louis Bread in 1993.

Saint Louis Bread was founded in 1987 when Ken Rosenthal, spurred into the restaurant business by his brother, opened his first cafe in Kirkwood, Missouri. Based on sourdough bakeries in San Francisco, the concept eventually spread to five stores by 1990 and nearly 20 units two years later. In 1993 the company made *Inc.* magazine's list of the 500 fastest-growing companies. At the end of that year, Au Bon Pain paid $24 million for the company, franchising its new units outside of the St. Louis area as Panera Bread. Rosenthal stayed on with Au Bon Pain as chairman of its new chain before leaving to become a major franchisee.

By 1995 the company was facing new competition from coffee and bagel shops. Flat sales and sharp price increases for butter hurt the chain's bottom line. By 1997 the company had added bagels to its menu and was considering extensive renovations. It ultimately decided the chain had peaked in the US, and it limited expansion to countries with dense urban areas and emerging middle classes, such as Brazil and Indonesia.

During 1998 Au Bon Pain's Panera Bread unit perked up with new stores and growing sales. But that success was offset by the company's namesake chain, where sales continued to struggle. The company eventually sold the entire chain in 1999 to investment firm Bruckmann, Rosser, Sherrill, and Co. for $73 million. (Bruckmann, Rosser later sold the chain to UK-based Compass Group, which runs the eateries through its subsidiary ABP Corporation.) Shaich remained with the firm, which was renamed Panera Bread, as chairman and CEO. The company later moved its headquarters back to the St. Louis area.

In 2001 president and COO Rich Postle resigned to run a joint venture with Panera Bread to build and manage 40 bakery-cafes in the northern Virginia and central Pennsylvania regions.

In 2004 the company introduced its new upscale take-out program, Via Panera. With Via Panera, the company simplified the to-go ordering process while upgrading its customization, particularly for larger orders. Panera Bread also released its first cookbook that year, *The Panera Bread Cookbook: Breadmaking Essentials and Recipes from America's Favorite Bakery-Cafe.*

EXECUTIVES

Chairman and CEO: Ronald M. (Ron) Shaich, age 52, $1,083,846 pay
President: Neal J. Yanofsky, age 48, $739,591 pay (prior to title change)
SVP and CFO: Jeffrey W. (Jeff) Kip, age 38
SVP and Chief Brand Officer: Michael Markowitz, age 59
SVP and Chief Concept Officer: Scott G. Davis, age 42, $454,711 pay
SVP and Chief Development Officer: Michael J. Nolan, age 46
SVP, Chief Franchise Officer, and Assistant Secretary: Michael J. (Mike) Kupstas, age 49, $354,769 pay
SVP, Chief Legal Officer, and Secretary: Patricia A. Gray, age 51
SVP and Chief People Officer: Rebecca A. Fine, age 43
SVP and Chief Supply Chain Officer: Mark A. Borland, age 53, $441,769 pay
SVP and CIO: Thomas C. (Tom) Kish, age 40
SVP, Company and Joint Venture Operations: William H. Simpson, age 43
VP, Controller, and Chief Accounting Officer: Richard R. (Rick) Isaak
Head, Research and Development: John Taylor
Auditors: PricewaterhouseCoopers LLP

LOCATIONS

HQ: Panera Bread Company
6710 Clayton Rd., Richmond Heights, MO 63117
Phone: 314-633-7100   **Fax:** 314-633-7200
Web: www.panerabread.com

2005 Locations

	No.
Illinois	83
Ohio	75
Florida	70
Missouri	58
Pennsylvania	51
Michigan	47
New Jersey	39
Virginia	36
North Carolina	31
Maryland	30
Massachusetts	30
New York	30
Indiana	27
California	26
Minnesota	24
Georgia	22
Texas	21
Wisconsin	19
Colorado	17
Kansas	16
Oklahoma	16
Tennessee	16
Iowa	15
Connecticut	11
Alabama	10
South Carolina	10
Other states	47
Total	**877**

PRODUCTS/OPERATIONS

2005 Sales

	$ mil.	% of total
Bakery-cafe operations		
Company-owned	499.4	78
Franchising	54.3	8
Fresh dough sales	86.6	14
Total	**640.3**	**100**

2005 Locations

	No.
Franchised	566
Company-owned	311
Total	**877**

COMPETITORS

ABP Corporation
Bruegger's
California Pizza Kitchen
Caribou Coffee
Chipotle
El Pollo Loco
Fresh Enterprises
Jimmy John's
New World Restaurants
Qdoba
Quiznos
Schlotzsky's
Starbucks
Subway

HISTORICAL FINANCIALS

Company Type: Public

Income Statement				FYE: Last Tuesday in December
	REVENUE ($ mil.)	NET INCOME ($ mil.)	NET PROFIT MARGIN	EMPLOYEES
12/05	640.3	52.2	8.2%	5,100
12/04	479.1	38.6	8.1%	9,487
12/03	355.9	30.4	8.5%	8,002
12/02	277.8	21.8	7.8%	6,253
12/01	201.1	13.1	6.5%	2,478
Annual Growth	**33.6%**	**41.3%**	**—**	**19.8%**

2005 Year-End Financials

Debt ratio: —
Return on equity: 18.7%
Cash ($ mil.): 60.7
Current ratio: 1.18
Long-term debt ($ mil.): —
No. of shares (mil.): 29.8

Dividends
  Yield: —
  Payout: —
Market value ($ mil.): 1,960.4
R&D as % of sales: —
Advertising as % of sales: 1.6%

Stock History

NASDAQ (GS): PNRA

	STOCK PRICE ($) FY Close	P/E High/Low		PER SHARE ($) Earnings	Dividends	Book Value
12/05	65.68	44	24	1.65	—	10.62
12/04	40.32	36	26	1.25	—	8.32
12/03	39.52	48	25	1.00	—	6.95
12/02	34.81	52	32	0.73	—	5.62
12/01	26.02	60	16	0.46	—	9.25
Annual Growth	**26.0%**	**—**	**—**	**37.6%**	**—**	**3.5%**

Panhandle Royalty

You won't find this Panhandle on a street corner, but you will find it pocketing the oil and gas royalties from more than 4,170 producing oil or gas wells. Panhandle Royalty owns mineral interests, both working and royalty, in oil- and gas-producing properties in 10 states. The company does not operate any of its own wells but instead maintains them through partnerships with other oil and gas companies. Its major properties are located primarily in Oklahoma (44% of its net holdings), New Mexico, and Texas. Panhandle Royalty has proved reserves of 566,110 barrels of oil and 25.3 billion cu. ft. of natural gas.

Most of the company's production comes from Oklahoma's Anadarko Basin and New Mexico's Dagger Draw Field. In 2006 Chesapeake Operating was Panhandle Royalty's major customer, accounting for 14% of the company's sales.

HISTORY

In 1926, Panhandle Cooperative Royalty was formed by ranchers and farmers in Range, Oklahoma (located in that state's panhandle). At the time, Oklahoma was a homesteader state, in which hopeful landowners, after cultivating a parcel of 160 acres, would receive full title (including mineral rights) to the land. The cooperative got started by offering each prospective member one share for the undivided mineral rights to 40 acres. Royalties from any mineral production were divided, 75% to the property owner and 25% to the cooperative. Earnings remaining at year-end were split among the shareholders. Because landowners with imminent drilling prospects were uninterested in joining the cooperative, Panhandle often found itself striking deals in then-unexplored areas such as the Anadarko Basin.

In 1979, a period of rapidly rising oil prices, Panhandle realized that as a cooperative its inability to retain any earnings severely limited its

---

expansion potential. The cooperative was merged into the Panhandle Royalty Company and went public that year. In 1988 the company acquired New Mexico Osage Royalty Company, itself a cooperative. In 1995 Panhandle acquired a half interest in more than 65,000 acres from PetroCorp, Inc.

Panhandle was primarily a passive owner until 1991, when it got a new CEO, geologist H. W. Peace. The firm plans to continue expanding through acquisitions and to increase its participation in drilling projects. Peace retired in 2006.

EXECUTIVES

Chairman: E. Chris Kauffman, age 65
President and COO: Ben D. Hare, age 60
President and CFO: Michael C. Coffman, age 52
VP Land: Ben Spriestersbach, age 54
Secretary: Lonnie J. Lowry
Auditors: Ernst & Young LLP

LOCATIONS

HQ: Panhandle Royalty Company
  Grand Centre, 5400 N. Grand Blvd., Ste. 305,
  Oklahoma City, OK 73112
Phone: 405-948-1560   **Fax:** 405-948-2038
Web: www.panra.com/default.asp

Panhandle Royalty Company owns or leases mineral properties in Arkansas, Colorado, Florida, Kansas, Montana, New Mexico, North Dakota, Oklahoma, South Dakota, and Texas.

PRODUCTS/OPERATIONS

2006 Sales

	$ mil.	% of total
Oil & gas	36.0	96
Lease bonuses	0.4	1
Interest & other	1.1	3
Total	**37.5**	**100**

COMPETITORS

Anadarko Petroleum
Brigham Exploration
Cabot Oil & Gas
Cross Timbers Royalty Trust
Hugoton Royalty Trust
Range Resources
Sabine Royalty Trust

HISTORICAL FINANCIALS

Company Type: Public

Income Statement				FYE: September 30
	REVENUE ($ mil.)	NET INCOME ($ mil.)	NET PROFIT MARGIN	EMPLOYEES
9/06	37.5	10.6	28.3%	16
9/05	33.3	10.5	31.5%	18
9/04	24.6	6.7	27.2%	16
9/03	22.5	6.0	26.7%	15
9/02	13.6	0.3	2.2%	14
Annual Growth	**28.9%**	**143.8%**	**—**	**3.4%**

2006 Year-End Financials

Debt ratio: 2.4%
Return on equity: 24.2%
Cash ($ mil.): 0.4
Current ratio: 2.32
Long-term debt ($ mil.): 1.2
No. of shares (mil.): 8.4

Dividends
  Yield: 1.0%
  Payout: 15.2%
Market value ($ mil.): 151.6
R&D as % of sales: —
Advertising as % of sales: —

Stock History

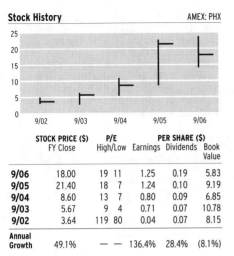

AMEX: PHX

	STOCK PRICE ($) FY Close	P/E High/Low		PER SHARE ($) Earnings	Dividends	Book Value
9/06	18.00	19	11	1.25	0.19	5.83
9/05	21.40	18	7	1.24	0.10	9.19
9/04	8.60	13	7	0.80	0.09	6.85
9/03	5.67	9	4	0.71	0.07	10.78
9/02	3.64	119	80	0.04	0.07	8.15
Annual Growth	49.1%	—	—	136.4%	28.4%	(8.1%)

Parke Bancorp

Community banking is a walk in the park for Parke Bancorp, holding company for Parke Bank, which has three bank branches in the New Jersey communities of Sewell and Northfield, as well as a loan production office in Philadelphia. The bank provides such traditional community-oriented products as checking and savings accounts, money market and individual retirement accounts, and certificates of deposit. In lending activities, Parke Bank has a strong focus on commercial real estate lending; commercial mortgages make up 60% of the bank's lending portfolio and commercial construction loans make up more than 25%. The bank also writes business and consumer loans, as well as residential construction and mortgage loans.

CEO Vito Pantilione and chairman Chuck Pennoni each own about 6% of Parke Bancorp; director Jeffrey Kripitz holds about 7%. Two limited partnerships, Banc Fund V and Banc Fund VI, together have an equity stake of more than 8%.

EXECUTIVES

Chairman, Park Bankcorp and Park Bank:
Celestino R. (Chuck) Pennoni, age 68
Vice Chairman, Park Bank: Thomas E. Hedenberg
President, CEO, and Director, Park Bancorp and Park Bank: Vito S. Pantilione, age 54, $337,500 pay
SVP; SVP, Senior Loan Officer, and Secretary, Park Bank: David O. Middlebrook, age 47, $127,500 pay
SVP and CFO, Park Bancorp and Park Bank:
Robert A. Kuehl, age 58
SVP Branch Administration and Systems:
Elizabeth Milavsky
Director of Business Development: John Campbell
Auditors: McGladrey & Pullen, LLP

LOCATIONS

HQ: Parke Bancorp, Inc.
601 Delsea Dr., Sewell, NJ 08080
Phone: 856-256-2500   **Fax:** 856-256-2590
Web: www.parkebank.com

PRODUCTS/OPERATIONS

2005 Sales

	$ mil.	% of total
Interest		
Loans	16.1	88
Securities & other	1.2	7
Service charges on deposit accounts	0.2	1
Other fee income	0.7	4
Total	**18.2**	**100**

COMPETITORS

Bank of America
Commerce Bancorp
Hudson City Bancorp
Ocean Shore

PNC Financial
Susquehanna Bancshares
Wachovia

HISTORICAL FINANCIALS

Company Type: Public

Income Statement

FYE: December 31

	ASSETS ($ mil.)	NET INCOME ($ mil.)	INCOME AS % OF ASSETS	EMPLOYEES
12/05	297.8	3.5	1.2%	40
12/04	224.3	2.7	1.2%	32
12/03	174.0	2.0	1.1%	29
Annual Growth	30.8%	32.3%	—	17.4%

2005 Year-End Financials

Equity as % of assets: 9.1%
Return on assets: 1.3%
Return on equity: 14.0%
Long-term debt ($ mil.): 15.4
No. of shares (mil.): 2.3
Market value ($ mil.): 39.0

Dividends
Yield: —
Payout: —
Sales ($ mil.): 18.2
R&D as % of sales: —
Advertising as % of sales: —

Stock History

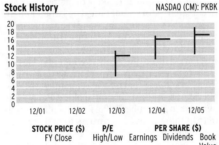

NASDAQ (CM): PKBK

	STOCK PRICE ($) FY Close	P/E High/Low		PER SHARE ($) Earnings	Dividends	Book Value
12/05	16.83	17	11	1.10	—	11.75
12/04	15.82	19	13	0.88	—	10.49
12/03	11.77	18	10	0.71	—	11.19
Annual Growth	19.6%	—	—	24.5%	—	2.4%

Parker Drilling

Parker Drilling parks its oil rigs off the beaten path. Its helicopter-transportable rigs allow the drilling contractor to work in otherwise inaccessible desert, mountain, and remote jungle locations. Its barge rigs allow the company to drill in transition zones (coastal waters such as bays and marshes). Parker Drilling owns 47 rigs, including 24 land rigs, 19 US-based barge drilling and workover rigs, and four international deep drilling barges. The company drills worldwide and has worked in 52 countries. Subsidiary Quail Tools provides rental tools for oil and gas

drilling and workover activities, with operations in the Gulf Coast, the Rocky Mountains, and West Texas regions.

During the oil industry downturn of the late 1990s, Parker Drilling turned to the US offshore market to stay afloat, and it acquired companies that operate in the shallow waters of the Gulf of Mexico. Rebounding oil prices after 2000, however, have prompted increased exploration by major oil companies and heightened demand for Parker's services.

In recent years, the company has been targeting international markets. A pioneer in arctic drilling, Parker Drilling is marketing its services to operators in the harsh environments of the Caspian Sea, Western Siberia, and Sakhalin Island. Its land drilling operations are focused primarily in the Asia/Pacific region, and the Commonwealth of Independent States (formerly the Soviet Union). Its barge drilling operations are located mainly in the Gulf of Mexico, Nigeria, and the Caspian Sea.

In late 2006 the company agreed to sell two barge-mounted workover rigs and related equipment to Basic Energy Services for $26 million.

HISTORY

Gifford Parker founded Parker Drilling in 1934, and a year later the firm pioneered the use of diesel-powered electric rigs. By the late 1940s the company was also operating five rigs in Venezuela and 12 in Canada. Robert Parker bought the firm in 1954 and committed it to new drilling techniques. By the mid-1960s it had eight deep-drilling rigs. The firm went public in 1969, and Robert Parker Jr. became president in 1977.

Parker Drilling became the first American land-drilling contractor in mainland China (1980) and in the former Soviet Union (1991). In 1995 it moved into New Zealand and began geothermal drilling in Indonesia.

The company moved into offshore drilling in 1996 by buying Mallard Drilling and doubled in size with the purchase of equipment rental company Quail Tools. The following year it acquired Bolifor (a Bolivian drilling contractor) and Houston-based Hercules Offshore and Hercules Rig. The Hercules deal added 10 Gulf of Mexico drilling rigs to Parker's inventory. In 1998 Parker announced it would merge with Superior Energy Services, an oil field tool rental company, but the deal fell through.

Meanwhile, the company was hit hard as oil prices crashed in 1998. Amid losses the next year, Parker began unloading assets. It sold all of its US land rigs to raise cash and to focus on offshore drilling in international markets. In keeping with its emphasis on offshore activities, the company moved its headquarters from Tulsa, Oklahoma, to Houston in 2001.

That year Parker and Russia's Tyumen Oil formed a joint venture to provide contract-drilling services across Russia. In 2002 Parker secured contracts to build and operate a rig to drill on Russia's Sakhalin Island.

EXECUTIVES

Chairman, President, and CEO:
Robert L. (Bobby) Parker Jr., age 57
SVP, COO, and Director: David C. Mannon, age 47
CFO: W. Kirk Brassfield, age 49
VP Operations: Michael D. Drennon
VP Engineering: Denis J. Graham, age 55
VP and General Counsel: Ronald C. Potter, age 51
Controller and Principal Accounting Officer:
Lynn Cullom

Director Business Development and Global Sales:
Frank (Joey) Husband IV
Director Human Resources: George H. Gentry III
Director Investor Relations and Treasurer:
David W. Tucker, age 49
Manager, Public Relations: Marianne Gooch
Auditors: Melton & Melton LLP

LOCATIONS

HQ: Parker Drilling Company
1401 Enclave Pkwy., Ste. 600, Houston, TX 77077
Phone: 281-406-2000　　**Fax:** 281-406-2001
Web: www.parkerdrilling.com

Parker Drilling has offices in Bolivia, Colombia, Indonesia, Kazakhstan, Kuwait, Nigeria, Papua New Guinea, Peru, Russia, Singapore, the UK, and the US.

2005 Sales

	$ mil.	% of total
US	218.1	41
Commonwealth of Independent States	153.7	29
Latin America	67.9	13
Asia/Pacific	58.6	11
Africa & Middle East	33.4	6
Total	**531.7**	**100**

PRODUCTS/OPERATIONS

2005 Sales

	$ mil.	% of total
International drilling	308.6	58
US drilling	128.3	24
Rental tools	94.8	18
Total	**531.7**	**100**

Selected Services

Helicopter-transportable rigs
Land drilling
Offshore drilling
Rental tools
Transition zone drilling

Selected Subsidiaries

Parker Drilling Company International Limited
Parker Technology, Inc. (rig design, manufacturing, modification, and servicing)
Quail Tools LLP (oil field tool rentals)

COMPETITORS

Atwood Oceanics
Baker Hughes
BJ Services
Diamond Offshore
GlobalSantaFe
Halliburton
Helmerich & Payne
Hercules Offshore
Nabors Industries
Noble
Pride International
Schlumberger
Transocean

HISTORICAL FINANCIALS

Company Type: Public

Income Statement

FYE: December 31

	REVENUE ($ mil.)	NET INCOME ($ mil.)	NET PROFIT MARGIN	EMPLOYEES
12/05	531.7	98.9	18.6%	3,040
12/04	376.5	(47.1)	—	3,014
12/03	320.8	(109.7)	—	2,920
12/02	397.0	(114.1)	—	2,898
12/01	488.0	11.1	2.3%	3,654
Annual Growth	**2.2%**	**72.8%**	**—**	**(4.5%)**

2005 Year-End Financials

Debt ratio: 146.3%
Return on equity: 48.4%
Cash ($ mil.): 78.2
Current ratio: 1.87
Long-term debt ($ mil.): 380.0
No. of shares (mil.): 97.8

Dividends
　Yield: —
　Payout: —
Market value ($ mil.): 1,059.6
R&D as % of sales: —
Advertising as % of sales: —

Stock History

NYSE: PKD

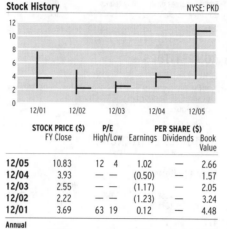

	STOCK PRICE ($) FY Close	P/E High/Low		PER SHARE ($) Earnings	Dividends	Book Value
12/05	10.83	12	4	1.02	—	2.66
12/04	3.93	—	—	(0.50)	—	1.57
12/03	2.55	—	—	(1.17)	—	2.05
12/02	2.22	—	—	(1.23)	—	3.24
12/01	3.69	63	19	0.12	—	4.48
Annual Growth	**30.9%**	—	—	**70.7%**	**—**	**(12.2%)**

Parlux Fragrances

Parlux Fragrances is likely to blame for those department store shopping trips that end in sneezing fits. The fragrance and beauty products maker is licensed to manufacture (through subcontractors) several prestigious brands, including Paris Hilton (40% of revenue) and Guess? (12% of sales). Parlux formerly made its own Animale brand but sold off the remainder of those operations in 2004. It quit making Perry Ellis perfume in December 2006. Parlux sells its products in more than 80 countries to major retailers and department stores and to specialty outlet chain Perfumania. Chairman and CEO Ilia Lekach, who owns about a quarter of Parlux Fragrances, has rescinded his bid to take the company private.

Lekach, through his company PF Acquisition of Florida, had offered $29 a share for the outstanding shares of Parlux. As part of the deal IZJD Corp. and Pacific Investments Group, both Florida-based investment firms, had agreed to contribute their Parlux shares of common stock to PF Acquisition in exchange for membership interests in Parlux. Lekach withdrew the bid in July 2006, though, when third parties offered to buy parts of the business. Soon thereafter, Glenn Nussdorf (who owns about 12% of the firm) proposed to buy Parlux but was met with resistance as Nussdorf's plan is to oust members of the Parlux board and replace them with five others and himself.

In 2004 and 2005 the company entered into worldwide licensing agreements to develop, manufacture, and distribute fragrances for Paris Hilton, Maria Sharapova, Andy Roddick, and Gund. In addition Parlux acquired worldwide licensing rights to the XOXO fragrance brand from Victory International. However, in late 2006, Parlux sold its fragrance licensing rights back to Perry Ellis for some $63 million, despite Perry Ellis having generated some 40% of its

2006 revenue. The deal, though, gives Parlux funds to fuel growth of other scents and Perry Ellis more control over the creative development of its namesake fragrance.

Hilton's first fragrance met with such great success that, in May 2005, Parlux inked additional licensing agreements with the heiress for a second fragrance, as well as Parlux's first line of watches, handbags, small leather goods, and sunglasses.

EXECUTIVES

Chairman, President, and CEO: Ilia Lekach, age 58, $560,000 pay
EVP, COO, CFO, and Director: Frank A. Buttacavoli, age 51, $399,000 pay
VP, Domestic Sales: David Schwanz
VP, Marketing: Kathleen Galvin
Director, Human Resources: Tania Espinosa
Auditors: Deloitte & Touche LLP

LOCATIONS

HQ: Parlux Fragrances, Inc.
3725 SW 30th Ave., Fort Lauderdale, FL 33312
Phone: 954-316-9008　　**Fax:** 954-316-9152
Web: www.parlux.com

PRODUCTS/OPERATIONS

Selected Brands

Andy Roddick
babyGUND
Fred Hayman Beverly Hills
Guess?
Maria Sharapova
Ocean Pacific
Paris Hilton
Royal Copenhagen
XOXO

COMPETITORS

Clarins
Coty Inc.
Dana Classic Fragrances
Elizabeth Arden Inc
Estée Lauder
Inter Parfums
LVMH
Revlon
Wella

HISTORICAL FINANCIALS

Company Type: Public

Income Statement

FYE: March 31

	REVENUE ($ mil.)	NET INCOME ($ mil.)	NET PROFIT MARGIN	EMPLOYEES
3/06	182.2	22.7	12.5%	144
3/05	100.4	10.8	10.8%	134
3/04	80.6	6.3	7.8%	120
3/03	72.3	5.5	7.6%	111
3/02	70.0	(5.7)	—	117
Annual Growth	**27.0%**	**—**	**—**	**5.3%**

2006 Year-End Financials

Debt ratio: —
Return on equity: 27.2%
Cash ($ mil.): 15.9
Current ratio: 2.17
Long-term debt ($ mil.): —
No. of shares (mil.): 17.9

Dividends
　Yield: —
　Payout: —
Market value ($ mil.): 288.7
R&D as % of sales: —
Advertising as % of sales: —

Stock History

```
20
18
16
14
12
10
 8
 6
 4
 2
 0
     3/02    3/03    3/04    3/05    3/06
```

	STOCK PRICE ($) FY Close	P/E High/Low		PER SHARE ($) Earnings	Dividends	Book Value
3/06	16.13	18	7	1.08	—	5.23
3/05	10.82	27	7	0.51	—	8.01
3/04	4.51	22	3	0.31	—	6.80
3/03	1.35	6	3	0.27	—	5.79
3/02	0.92	—	—	(0.28)	—	4.80
Annual Growth	104.6%	—	—	—	—	2.2%

Partners Trust Financial Group

Partners Trust Financial, so the bank hopes its customers will as well. The financial institution is the holding company for Partners Trust Bank (formerly SBU Bank), which operates branches in central and southern New York. With origins dating back to 1839, the bank offers traditional deposit products, trust and investment services, and loans for personal, business, and municipal customers. Residential mortgages make up about half of the company's loan portfolio, followed by consumer loans, commercial mortgages, and business loans. Partners Trust Financial more than doubled its branch network when it bought BSB Bancorp in 2004.

EXECUTIVES

Chairman: William C. Craine, age 57
President, CEO, and Director; President and CEO, Partners Trust Bank: John A. Zawadzki, age 57, $615,385 pay
SEVP and COO, Partners Trust Financial and Partners Trust Bank: Steven A. Covert, age 43, $328,885 pay
SVP, CFO, and Corporate Secretary: Amie Estrella, age 35
SVP, Retail Banking: Richard F. Callahan, age 53, $199,846 pay
SVP, Risk Management Officer, and Corporate Secretary: William M. Le Beau
SVP and Chief Credit Officer, Partners Trust Bank: Daniel J. O'Toole, age 42, $262,269 pay
Auditors: KPMG LLP

LOCATIONS

HQ: Partners Trust Financial Group, Inc.
233 Genesee St., Utica, NY 13501
Phone: 315-768-3000   **Fax:** 315-738-4978
Web: www.partnerstrust.com

PRODUCTS/OPERATIONS

2005 Sales

	$ mil.	% of total
Interest		
Loans, including fees	116.6	61
Securities	52.8	27
Other	0.3	—
Noninterest		
Service fees	15.9	8
Trust & investment services	3.2	2
Other	3.8	2
Total	**192.6**	**100**

COMPETITORS

Alliance Financial
Astoria Financial
Community Bank System
First Niagara Financial
Gouverneur Bancorp
HSBC USA
KeyCorp
M&T Bank
NBT Bancorp
Oneida Financial
Pathfinder Bancorp
Rome Bancorp
Sovereign Bancorp

HISTORICAL FINANCIALS

Company Type: Public

Income Statement

FYE: December 31

	ASSETS ($ mil.)	NET INCOME ($ mil.)	INCOME AS % OF ASSETS	EMPLOYEES
12/05	3,778.9	32.8	0.9%	831
12/04	3,651.6	12.1	0.3%	853
12/03	1,285.1	14.1	1.1%	349
12/02	1,333.5	8.4	0.6%	334
12/01	983.4	6.6	0.7%	—
Annual Growth	40.0%	49.3%	—	35.5%

2005 Year-End Financials

Equity as % of assets: 14.0%
Return on assets: 0.9%
Return on equity: 6.1%
Long-term debt ($ mil.): 897.2
No. of shares (mil.): 48.9
Market value ($ mil.): 589.7
Dividends
Yield: 2.3%
Payout: 41.2%
Sales ($ mil.): 192.6
R&D as % of sales: —
Advertising as % of sales: —

Stock History

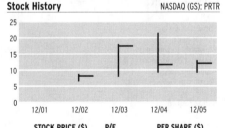

```
25
20
15
10
 5
 0
     12/01    12/02    12/03    12/04    12/05
```

	STOCK PRICE ($) FY Close	P/E High/Low		PER SHARE ($) Earnings	Dividends	Book Value
12/05	12.05	19	14	0.68	0.28	10.79
12/04	11.65	64	28	0.33	0.12	10.87
12/03	17.44	34	15	0.52	—	12.35
12/02	8.16	37	29	0.23	—	12.03
Annual Growth	13.9%	—	—	43.5%	133.3%	11.2%

PDF Solutions

PDF Solutions can solve chip design and manufacturing inefficiencies. The company's trademarked "Design-to-Silicon-Yield" program includes software and analysis services that help integrated circuit makers get more working chips out of a production batch. PDF's products are used to simulate, model, and analyze the chip design and manufacturing processes. As part of the Design-to-Silicon-Yield program, PDF also receives a portion of customers' cost savings; called "gain share."

PDF Solutions has purchased the WAMA (short for wafer map) product line from Wafer Yield, a small company based in Santa Clara, California, and hired the two co-founders of Wafer Yield. It also acquired IDS Software Systems. IDS's dataPOWER software line and the WAMA packages augment PDF's portfolio of semiconductor yield management software.

EXECUTIVES

Chairman: Lucio L. Lanza, age 62
President, CEO, and Director: John K. Kibarian, age 42, $250,000 pay
Chief Strategy Officer: David A. (Dave) Joseph, age 53, $325,000 pay
VP, Finance and CFO: Keith Jones
VP, Investor Relations and Strategic Initiatives: P. Steven (Steve) Melman, age 52, $260,000 pay
VP and General Manager, Manufacturing Process Solutions: Cornelis D. (Cees) Hartgring, age 53, $270,000 pay
VP, Marketing and Development: Kevin MacLean
VP, Human Resources: Rebecca M. (Becky) Baybrook, age 55
VP, Worldwide Sales: Zia Malik, age 53, $180,000 pay
Chief Technologist: Andrzej J. Strojwas
Investor Relations: Sonia Segovia
Auditors: Deloitte & Touche LLP

LOCATIONS

HQ: PDF Solutions, Inc.
333 W. San Carlos St., Ste. 700, San Jose, CA 95110
Phone: 408-280-7900   **Fax:** 408-280-7915
Web: www.pdf.com

PDF Solutions has offices in Germany, Italy, Japan, and the US.

PRODUCTS/OPERATIONS

2005 Sales

	$ mil.	% of total
Integrated solutions	52.7	71
Gain share	11.9	16
Software licenses	9.3	13
Total	**73.9**	**100**

Selected Products and Services

Integration assessment
Manufacturing process simulation
Yield and performance monitoring, modeling, and prediction software and services (Design-to-Silicon-Yield program)

COMPETITORS

Applied Materials	KLA-Tencor
Atrenta	Mentor Graphics
AXIOM Design	Obsidian Software
Cadence Design	Parametric Technology
Cascade Microtech	Rockwood Holdings
Electroglas	SILVACO
FEI	Synopsys
FormFactor	Teradyne
inTEST	Yield Dynamics
Intrinsix	

HISTORICAL FINANCIALS

Company Type: Public

Income Statement
FYE: December 31

	REVENUE ($ mil.)	NET INCOME ($ mil.)	NET PROFIT MARGIN	EMPLOYEES
12/05	73.9	6.5	8.8%	283
12/04	62.3	(0.6)	—	263
12/03	42.5	(4.5)	—	262
12/02	43.7	0.5	1.1%	220
12/01	35.5	(3.9)	—	197
Annual Growth	20.1%	—	—	9.5%

2005 Year-End Financials
Debt ratio: —
Return on equity: 5.6%
Cash ($ mil.): 60.5
Current ratio: 5.04
Long-term debt ($ mil.): —
No. of shares (mil.): 26.4
Dividends
  Yield: —
  Payout: —
Market value ($ mil.): 429.5
R&D as % of sales: 29.9%
Advertising as % of sales: —

Stock History
NASDAQ (GM): PDFS

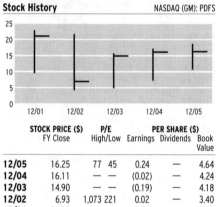

	STOCK PRICE ($) FY Close	P/E High/Low		PER SHARE ($) Earnings	Dividends	Book Value
12/05	16.25	77	45	0.24	—	4.64
12/04	16.11	—	—	(0.02)	—	4.24
12/03	14.90	—	—	(0.19)	—	4.18
12/02	6.93	1,073	221	0.02	—	3.40
12/01	21.00	—	—	(0.38)	—	3.17
Annual Growth	(6.2%)	—	—	—	—	10.0%

Penn Virginia

Incorporated in Virginia and based in Pennsylvania, Penn Virginia is an oil and gas exploration and production company operating primarily in the Appalachian area of the US. It also explores in East Texas, Mississippi, and the Gulf Coast. The company, which has proved reserves of 359 billion cu. ft. of natural gas and 2.9 million barrels of oil, and holds working interests in more than 1,500 wells, sells mostly on the spot market. It also has interests in coal (which it leases to other operators) and timber properties through 39%-owned Penn Virginia Resource Partners, which it spun off in 2001. In 2006 the

company acquired explorer Crow Creek Holding Corp. for $71.5 million.

Legendary corporate buyout artist T. Boone Pickens made an unsolicited offer to buy Penn Virginia, but abandoned the bid in 2002. The company holds some 689 million tons of proven and probable coal reserves on 241,000 acres in Kentucky, New Mexico, Virginia, and West Virginia.

EXECUTIVES

Chairman: Robert (Rob) Garrett, age 69
President, CEO, and Director: A. James (Jim) Dearlove, age 58, $352,500 pay
EVP and CFO; VP, CFO, and Director, Penn Virginia Resource GP Holdings, L.P.: Frank A. Pici, age 50, $219,000 pay (prior to title change)
EVP; President, Penn Virginia Oil and Gas: H. Baird Whitehead, age 55, $519,000 pay
EVP and Director; President and COO, Penn Virginia Resource, and Co-President, Penn Virginia Operating Co., LLC: Keith D. Horton, age 51, $450,000 pay (prior to title change)
SVP, General Counsel, and Corporate Secretary: Nancy M. Snyder, age 53, $189,000 pay
VP, Business Planning: Dana G. Wright, age 51
VP, Corporate Development: Ronald K. (Ron) Page, age 55, $360,000 pay
Auditors: KPMG LLP

LOCATIONS

HQ: Penn Virginia Corporation
  3 Radnor Corporate Center, Ste. 230, 100
  Matsonford Rd., Radnor, PA 19087
Phone: 610-687-8900   **Fax:** 610-687-3688
Web: www.pennvirginia.com

Penn Virginia has offices in Charleston, West Virginia; Houston; Kingsport, Tennessee; and Radnor, Pennsylvania.

PRODUCTS/OPERATIONS

2005 Sales

	$ mil.	% of total
Midstream	350.6	52
Oil & gas	226.8	34
Coal	95.8	14
Other	0.7	—
Total	673.9	100

COMPETITORS

Arch Coal
Cabot Oil & Gas
CONSOL Energy
Equitable Resources
Houston Exploration
Peabody Energy
Petroleum Development
PrimeEnergy
Range Resources

HISTORICAL FINANCIALS

Company Type: Public

Income Statement
FYE: December 31

	REVENUE ($ mil.)	NET INCOME ($ mil.)	NET PROFIT MARGIN	EMPLOYEES
12/05	673.9	62.1	9.2%	229
12/04	228.4	33.4	14.6%	120
12/03	181.3	28.5	15.7%	116
12/02	111.0	12.1	10.9%	104
12/01	96.6	34.3	35.5%	92
Annual Growth	62.5%	16.0%	—	25.6%

2005 Year-End Financials
Debt ratio: 105.0%
Return on equity: 22.1%
Cash ($ mil.): 25.9
Current ratio: 1.15
Long-term debt ($ mil.): 325.9
No. of shares (mil.): 18.6
Dividends
  Yield: 0.8%
  Payout: 13.6%
Market value ($ mil.): 1,070.2
R&D as % of sales: —
Advertising as % of sales: —

Stock History
NYSE: PVA

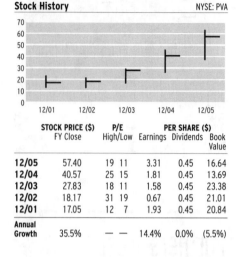

	STOCK PRICE ($) FY Close	P/E High/Low		PER SHARE ($) Earnings	Dividends	Book Value
12/05	57.40	19	11	3.31	0.45	16.64
12/04	40.57	25	15	1.81	0.45	13.69
12/03	27.83	18	11	1.58	0.45	23.38
12/02	18.17	31	19	0.67	0.45	21.01
12/01	17.05	12	7	1.93	0.45	20.84
Annual Growth	35.5%	—	—	14.4%	0.0%	(5.5%)

Penn Virginia Resource Partners

The motto for Penn Virginia Resource Partners (PVR) could be "Baby, it's *coal* outside." PVR was formed by energy company Penn Virginia Corporation to manage its coal properties. It manages coal mines in Kentucky, New Mexico, Virginia, and West Virginia; PVR leases mining rights on its properties to third-party mine operators, collecting royalties based on the amount of coal produced and the price at which it is sold. Its land contains nearly 700 million tons of proven or probable reserves (mostly low-sulfur bituminous coal). PVR also sells timber from its properties and charges fees to mine operators for use of its coal preparation and transportation facilities. Penn Virginia Corporation controls some 40% of the firm.

Expanding on its natural resource holdings, PVR bought a 50% interest in a coal storage and transportation joint venture in 2004. The following year it purchased some 3,400 miles of natural gas pipelines in Oklahoma and Texas from a division of Cantera Resources; that business now operates under the name PVR Midstream.

EXECUTIVES

Chairman and CEO: A. James (Jim) Dearlove, age 58, $183,500 pay
President and COO: Keith D. Horton, age 51, $260,000 pay
VP, CFO, and Director: Frank A. Pici, age 50, $126,500 pay
VP and Controller: Forrest W. McNair
VP, General Counsel, and Director: Nancy M. Snyder, age 53, $110,000 pay
VP Corporate Development: Ronald K. (Ron) Page, age 55, $220,000 pay
Auditors: KPMG LLP

LOCATIONS

HQ: Penn Virginia Resource Partners, L.P.
3 Radnor Corporate Center, Ste. 230,
100 Matsonford Rd., Radnor, PA 19087
Phone: 610-687-8900   **Fax:** 610-687-3688
Web: www.pvresource.com

PVR's coal properties are located in Harlan and Letcher counties, Kentucky; McKinley county, New Mexico; Buchanan, Lee, and Wise counties, Virginia; and Barbour, Boone, Fayette, Harrison, Kanawha, Lewis, Lincoln, Logan, Monongalia, Raleigh, and Upshur counties, West Virginia.

PRODUCTS/OPERATIONS

2005 Sales

	$ mil.	% of total
Natural gas	348.7	78
Coal royalties	82.7	19
Coal services	5.2	1
Other	9.8	2
Total	**446.4**	**100**

COMPETITORS

Alliance Resource
Arch Coal
Bridgeline
CONSOL Energy
Massey Energy
Peabody Energy
Westmoreland Coal

HISTORICAL FINANCIALS

Company Type: Public

Income Statement

FYE: December 31

	REVENUE ($ mil.)	NET INCOME ($ mil.)	NET PROFIT MARGIN	EMPLOYEES
12/05	446.4	51.2	11.5%	—
12/04	75.6	34.3	45.4%	—
12/03	55.6	22.7	40.8%	—
12/02	38.6	24.7	64.0%	—
12/01	37.5	16.1	42.9%	—
Annual Growth	85.7%	33.5%	—	—

2005 Year-End Financials

Debt ratio: 90.9%
Return on equity: 23.6%
Cash ($ mil.): 33.4
Current ratio: 1.10
Long-term debt ($ mil.): 258.1
No. of shares (mil.): 17.0
Dividends
  Yield: 4.5%
  Payout: 101.6%
Market value ($ mil.): 472.3
R&D as % of sales: —
Advertising as % of sales: —

Stock History

NYSE: PVR

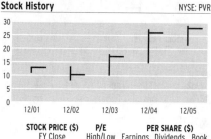

	STOCK PRICE ($) FY Close	P/E High/Low		PER SHARE ($) Earnings	Dividends	Book Value
12/05	27.78	24	18	1.22	1.24	16.71
12/04	26.05	29	16	0.93	1.06	12.16
12/03	17.14	29	17	0.62	0.77	14.83
12/02	10.31	17	11	0.79	1.17	17.72
12/01	12.90	107	92	0.12	—	14.97
Annual Growth	21.1%	—	—	78.6%	2.0%	2.8%

Pennsylvania Commerce Bancorp

Pennsylvania Commerce Bancorp brings "America's Most Convenient Bank" to Pennsylvania. A part of the Commerce Bancorp network, the company is the holding company for Commerce Bank/Harrisburg, which uses the larger company's logo and advertising in its service area. Through around 30 branches, the bank provides community banking services, including checking, savings, money market, and NOW accounts and CDs to central Pennsylvania. Commerce Bank offers commercial real estate (almost half of its loan portfolio), construction, and land development loans, as well as residential mortgage, commercial, and consumer loans. Commerce Bancorp owns about 11% of the company and supplies marketing and technical support.

Directors and executive officers collectively own about 25% of Pennsylvania Commerce Bancorp; of that, CEO Gary Nalbandian owns 9% and nearly 9% is in the hands of Wellington Management.

EXECUTIVES

Chairman, President, and CEO, Pennsylvania Commerce Bancorp and Commerce Bank:
Gary L. Nalbandian, age 63, $325,000 pay
CFO and Treasurer, Pennsylvania Commerce Bancorp and Commerce Bank: Mark A. Zody, age 42, $162,500 pay
EVP and Chief Lending Officer, Pennsylvania Commerce Bancorp and Commerce Bank:
Rory G. Ritrievi, age 42, $192,500 pay
SVP and Chief Risk Officer, Commerce Bank:
D. Scott Huggins, $120,000 pay
Public Relations Manager: Jason Kirsch
Investor Relations: Sherry Richart
Senior Credit Officer: James Ridd
SVP Operations, Commerce Bank:
Victoria G. (Vicki) Chieppa, age 57
Auditors: Beard Miller Company LLP

LOCATIONS

HQ: Pennsylvania Commerce Bancorp, Inc.
3801 Paxton St., Harrisburg, PA 17111
Phone: 717-303-3000   **Fax:** 717-412-6171
Web: www.commercepc.com

PRODUCTS/OPERATIONS

2005 Sales

	$ mil.	% of total
Interest		
Loans	48.5	52
Securities & other	31.2	33
Noninterest		
Service charges & fees	12.4	13
Other	1.7	2
Total	**93.8**	**100**

COMPETITORS

Abington Community Bancorp
Bryn Mawr Bank Corp.
Codorus Valley Bancorp
Fulton Financial
M&T Bank
Mellon Financial
PNC Financial
PSECU
Sovereign Bancorp
Stonebridge Financial
Wachovia

HISTORICAL FINANCIALS

Company Type: Public

Income Statement

FYE: December 31

	ASSETS ($ mil.)	NET INCOME ($ mil.)	INCOME AS % OF ASSETS	EMPLOYEES
12/05	1,641.1	8.8	0.5%	787
12/04	1,277.4	8.6	0.7%	710
12/03	1,052.0	6.6	0.6%	623
12/02	786.6	5.7	0.7%	382
12/01	609.9	4.4	0.7%	378
Annual Growth	28.1%	18.9%	—	20.1%

2005 Year-End Financials

Equity as % of assets: 5.6%
Return on assets: 0.6%
Return on equity: 10.0%
Long-term debt ($ mil.): 13.6
No. of shares (mil.): 6.0
Market value ($ mil.): 191.5
Dividends
  Yield: —
  Payout: —
Sales ($ mil.): 93.8
R&D as % of sales: —
Advertising as % of sales: —

Stock History

NASDAQ (GS): COBH

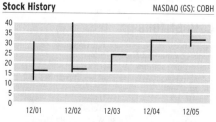

	STOCK PRICE ($) FY Close	P/E High/Low		PER SHARE ($) Earnings	Dividends	Book Value
12/05	31.85	27	21	1.38	—	15.24
12/04	31.50	19	13	1.63	—	14.49
12/03	24.29	18	12	1.34	—	21.69
12/02	16.99	34	13	1.18	—	20.22
12/01	16.11	31	12	0.97	—	17.32
Annual Growth	18.6%	—	—	9.2%	—	(3.1%)

PeopleSupport

These people are ready to support your customers via long distance. PeopleSupport is a growing provider of business process outsourcing (BPO) services with four customer care centers in the Philippines. It offers such customer relationship management services as inbound sales call handling, customer services, and technical support. It also offers call handling for direct response marketing campaigns. In addition to teleservices, PeopleSupport provides its customer care services through e-mail, online chat, and self-help Web applications. Its largest customers include Expedia and EarthLink. The company also provides accounts receivables management and collections services through its SCT Solutions subsidiary.

The company began its outsourced customer management career in Los Angeles in 1998. Like most BPO providers, however, the company soon realized that moving its operations abroad would save costs and augment its competitive edge. As a result, PeopleSupport's exodus to the Philippines began in 2000.

EXECUTIVES

Chairman, President, CEO, and Secretary:
Lance Rosenzweig, age 43
CFO: Caroline Rook, age 47
SVP and General Manager, PeopleSupport Rapidtext:
Jerome Woods, age 57
VP Global Operations; President, PeopleSupport Philippines: Rainerio (Bong) Borja, age 44
VP Global Human Resources: Rowena (Rozl) Ricafrente, age 35
VP Sales: Joseph S. (Joe) Duryea
CIO: George Hines, age 33
Director, Investor Relations and Corporate Marketing:
Peter B. Hargittay
Auditors: BDO Seidman, LLP

LOCATIONS

HQ: PeopleSupport, Inc.
1100 Glendon Ave., Ste. 1250,
Los Angeles, CA 90024
Phone: 310-824-6200   **Fax:** 310-824-6299
Web: www.peoplesupport.com

COMPETITORS

Accenture	ICT Group
Aegis Communications	Infosys
Ambergris Solutions	SITEL
APAC Customer Services	Sykes Enterprises
BearingPoint	TeleTech
ClientLogic	Unisys
Convergys	West Corporation
eTelecare Global Solutions	Wipro Technologies
IBM Global Services	

HISTORICAL FINANCIALS

Company Type: Public

Income Statement   FYE: December 31

	REVENUE ($ mil.)	NET INCOME ($ mil.)	NET PROFIT MARGIN	EMPLOYEES
12/05	62.1	22.8	36.7%	4,200
12/04	44.5	8.3	18.7%	3,602
12/03	30.0	8.0	26.7%	2,474
12/02	19.8	(2.9)	—	—
Annual Growth	**46.4%**	**—**	**—**	**30.3%**

2005 Year-End Financials

Debt ratio: —
Return on equity: 32.5%
Cash ($ mil.): 51.6
Current ratio: 6.59
Long-term debt ($ mil.): —
No. of shares (mil.): 18.5

Dividends
  Yield: —
  Payout: —
Market value ($ mil.): 156.9
R&D as % of sales: —
Advertising as % of sales: —

Stock History   NASDAQ (GM): PSPT

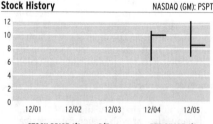

	STOCK PRICE ($) FY Close	P/E High/Low	PER SHARE ($) Earnings	Dividends	Book Value
12/05	8.49	10 6	1.21	—	4.46
12/04	9.97	19 11	0.55	—	3.22
Annual Growth	**(14.8%)**	**— —**	**120.0%**	**—**	**38.6%**

Perficient

Perficient is proficient in helping its customers use Internet-based technologies to their advantage. The information technology consulting firm's services include software development, systems integration, consulting, and support. The company specializes in developing middleware applications that are used to integrate and modernize legacy computer hardware and software. Perficient's Advanced Technology Services (ATS) group offers contracted services such as consulting, application development, and training through IBM, which is also a top customer. Other customers include Anheuser-Busch, AT&T Mobility (formerly Cingular), EMC Corporation, and Wachovia.

Perficient has expanded its offerings through the acquisitions of Genisys Consulting, Meritage Technologies, and ZettaWorks. In 2006 it acquired San Francisco-based consulting firm Bay Street Solutions in a cash and stock deal valued at more than $9 million. The company also bought the energy, government, and general business unit of Digital Consulting & Software Services, a private IT services provider that is focusing on its convenience store retail services business. The 2006 deal was valued at about $13 million.

Investor Morton Meyerson, through 2M Technology Ventures, owns about 10% of Perficient.

EXECUTIVES

Chairman and CEO: John T. (Jack) McDonald, age 42, $588,359 pay
President and COO: Jeffrey S. (Jeff) Davis, age 41, $425,301 pay
CFO: Paul E. Martin, age 47
VP, Strategic Finance: Michael D. Hill, age 36
VP, Finance and Administration and Controller:
Richard (Dick) Kalbfleish, age 50, $172,227 pay
VP, Client Development: Tim Thompson, age 45
VP, Corporate Operations: Kathy Henely
Human Resources: Tracy Robinson
Marketing and Public Relations: Bill Davis
Auditors: BDO Seidman, LLP

LOCATIONS

HQ: Perficient, Inc.
1120 S. Capital of Texas Hwy., Bldg. III, Ste. 220,
Austin, TX 78731
Phone: 512-531-6000   **Fax:** 512-531-6011
Web: www.perficient.com

2005 Sales

	$ mil.	% of total
US	95.7	99
Canada	1.3	1
Total	**97.0**	**100**

PRODUCTS/OPERATIONS

2005 Sales

	$ mil.	% of total
Services	87.2	90
Software	9.8	10
Total	**97.0**	**100**

Selected Services

Business intelligence
Custom applications development
eCommerce
Enterprise content management
Enterprise portals & collaborations
Mobile technology services
Online customer relationship management (CRM)
Service-oriented architectures and enterprise service bus
  services

COMPETITORS

Accenture
Answerthink
BearingPoint
CIBER
Cognizant Tech Solutions
EDS
Haverstick Consulting
Infosys
Quilogy
Sapient
Satyam
Software Architects
Wipro

HISTORICAL FINANCIALS

Company Type: Public

Income Statement   FYE: December 31

	REVENUE ($ mil.)	NET INCOME ($ mil.)	NET PROFIT MARGIN	EMPLOYEES
12/05	97.0	7.2	7.4%	580
12/04	58.8	3.9	6.6%	424
12/03	30.2	1.0	3.3%	147
12/02	22.5	(2.4)	—	141
12/01	20.4	(43.9)	—	97
Annual Growth	**47.7%**	**—**	**—**	**56.4%**

2005 Year-End Financials

Debt ratio: 8.1%
Return on equity: 13.0%
Cash ($ mil.): 5.1
Current ratio: 2.25
Long-term debt ($ mil.): 5.3
No. of shares (mil.): 24.2

Dividends
  Yield: —
  Payout: —
Market value ($ mil.): 215.7
R&D as % of sales: —
Advertising as % of sales: —

Stock History   NASDAQ (GS): PRFT

	STOCK PRICE ($) FY Close	P/E High/Low	PER SHARE ($) Earnings	Dividends	Book Value
12/05	8.91	37 18	0.28	—	2.72
12/04	6.56	38 11	0.19	—	2.09
12/03	2.24	56 6	0.07	—	1.06
12/02	1.00	— —	(0.53)	—	1.38
Annual Growth	**107.3%**	**— —**	**—**	**—**	**25.8%**

Pericom Semiconductor

Interface chips are hardly peripheral to Pericom Semiconductor's business. The fabless company makes high-performance digital, analog, and mixed-signal interface integrated circuits, which control the routing and transfer of data among a system's microprocessor, memory, and peripherals. Targeting the notebook computing, networking, and telecom markets, Pericom offers various chip product lines: interfaces for data transfer, switches for digital and analog signals, clock management chips, and telecommunications switches and component bridges. Pericom sells its products through distributors and a worldwide sales force to tech heavyweights such as Apple, Canon, Cisco Systems, Hewlett-Packard, IBM, and Lucent.

In 2003 the company expanded its offerings by acquiring privately held SaRonix, a maker of frequency control devices. In 2005 Pericom Semi acquired the eCERA Comtek subsidiary of AKER Technology for nearly $15 million. eCERA and its Azer Crystal Technology subsidiary make quartz crystal blanks and crystal oscillator products. Pericom was planning to make an equity investment in AKER Technology, a Taiwanese company, but was unable to reach an agreement on strategic directions with AKER's management.

Pericom has contract manufacturing relationships with Chartered Semiconductor Manufacturing, MagnaChip Semiconductor, New Japan Radio, Semiconductor Manufacturing International, and Taiwan Semiconductor.

Wasatch Advisors owns more than 10% of Pericom Semiconductor. FMR (Fidelity Investments) holds about 10% of the company, while Kennedy Capital Management has an equity stake of nearly 8%, as does Dimensional Fund Advisors. CEO Alex Chi-Ming Hui owns about 7% of Pericom. VP John Chi-Hung Hui has an equity stake of about 5%.

EXECUTIVES

Chairman, President, and CEO: Alex Chi-Ming Hui, age 49, $284,629 pay
VP, Technology and Director: John Chi-Hung Hui, age 51, $246,975 pay
VP, Finance and CFO: Angela Chen, age 47, $204,185 pay
VP, ASIC Engineering: Shau-Min (Michael) Chen
VP, Design Engineering: Tat C. Choi
VP, FCP Engineering: Craig Taylor
VP, Operations: Shujong (John) Cheng, $210,835 pay
VP, Sales: Gerald V. (Gerry) Beemiller, age 62, $193,258 pay

LOCATIONS

HQ: Pericom Semiconductor Corporation
3545 N. 1st St., San Jose, CA 95134
Phone: 408-435-0800   **Fax:** 408-435-1100
Web: www.pericom.com

Pericom Semiconductor has offices in Hong Kong, Japan, Singapore, South Korea, Taiwan, the UK, and the US.

2006 Sales

	$ mil.	% of total
Asia/Pacific		
China & Hong Kong	30.0	28
Taiwan	27.5	26
Singapore	9.4	9
US	20.5	19
Other countries	18.5	18
Total	**105.9**	**100**

PRODUCTS/OPERATIONS

2006 Sales

	$ mil.	% of total
Integrated circuits	64.5	61
Frequency control products	41.4	39
Total	**105.9**	**100**

Selected Products

Clock management devices
Frequency control devices
Interface devices
Switch devices for computer, network, and video applications
Telecommunications switch devices and bridge components

COMPETITORS

Analog Devices
Cypress Semiconductor
Dover Electronics
Epson
Fairchild Semiconductor
Freescale Semiconductor
Hitachi
Integrated Device Technology
Intel
Intersil
LGL Group
LSI Logic
Maxim Integrated Products
Murata Electronics North America
National Semiconductor
NXP
ON Semiconductor
PLX Technology
Raltron Electronics
Renesas
STMicroelectronics
Supertex
Texas Instruments
Toshiba Semiconductor
Tundra Semiconductor

HISTORICAL FINANCIALS

Company Type: Public

Income Statement

FYE: Sat. nearest June 30

	REVENUE ($ mil.)	NET INCOME ($ mil.)	NET PROFIT MARGIN	EMPLOYEES
6/06	105.9	6.0	5.7%	544
6/05	79.6	0.9	1.1%	257
6/04	66.4	(2.1)	—	274
6/03	45.0	(4.3)	—	216
6/02	47.6	(5.3)	—	241
Annual Growth	**22.1%**	**—**	**—**	**22.6%**

2006 Year-End Financials

Debt ratio: 1.9%
Return on equity: 3.3%
Cash ($ mil.): 66.3
Current ratio: 4.76
Long-term debt ($ mil.): 3.5
No. of shares (mil.): 26.1
Dividends
  Yield: —
  Payout: —
Market value ($ mil.): 216.3
R&D as % of sales: —
Advertising as % of sales: —

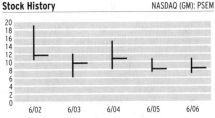

Stock History

NASDAQ (GM): PSEM

	STOCK PRICE ($) FY Close	P/E High/Low	PER SHARE ($) Earnings	Dividends	Book Value
6/06	8.30	48 33	0.22	—	7.06
6/05	8.13	353 251	0.03	—	6.87
6/04	10.71	— —	(0.08)	—	6.87
6/03	9.59	— —	(0.17)	—	7.08
6/02	11.59	— —	(0.21)	—	7.24
Annual Growth	**(8.0%)**	**— —**	**—**	**—**	**(0.6%)**

Perry Ellis International

You'll find garb made by Perry Ellis International (PEI) worn about town during the week and on the links during the weekend. It has a number of men's sportswear brands, including John Henry, Manhattan, Munsingwear, Natural Issue, and Perry Ellis. It also has licenses for the PING golf sportswear brand. PEI moved into the women's market with its acquisition of the Jantzen brand (known for swimwear, including licensed Tommy Hilfiger suits) from VF Corporation. It supplies private-label lines to Wal-Mart and Saks and is in some 15,000 stores. It bought back rights to its namesake fragrance in late 2006. The founding Feldenkreis family owns about 30% of Perry Ellis International.

PEI got into the apparel business by importing guayabera shirts (a pleated style popular in Cuba) long before the late designer Perry Ellis rose to prominence.

Formerly known as Supreme International, the company bought the Perry Ellis brand in 1999 and changed its corporate moniker accordingly. It is banking on the well-established Perry Ellis name (including the Perry Ellis America and Perry Ellis Portfolio labels) to make it a mainstay in the apparel arena. PEI licenses its once glamorous name to third parties, a strategy many fashion houses have moved away from in recent years.

PEI's apparel is made by Asian and Central American contractors and sold by retailers in the US, Canada, and Puerto Rico.

In early 2004 PEI entered a licensing agreement with SML Sport Ltd for the manufacture and distribution of two new Cuban-influenced womenswear lines: Cubavera and Havanera. PEI also entered into a separate agreement with PGA Tour to manufacture and distribute golf apparel under the PGA Tour brand.

In late 2005 the company logged three global partnerships. With LUPO International it manufactures and sells Mondo di Marco branded men's shoes for distribution in the US and Canada. Cardinal Clothing Canada makes and distributes Perry Ellis and Perry Ellis Portfolio men's top coats domestically. PEI also licensed its name to South Pacific Apparel Pty Ltd., which makes

and markets Savane and Farah branded pants and shorts for men and boys in Australia, New Zealand, and other South Pacific islands.

PEI continued to ink deals into 2006. Early in the year the company partnered with Levi Strauss & Co. to make and distribute Dockers brand outerwear (including men's jackets, fleece items, and coats) in the US and Mexico through December 2009. It entered a licensing agreement with JAG Licensing LLC, as well, to make JAG men's and women's swimwear and coverups.

In early 2005 PEI purchased ailing clothing manufacturer Tropical Sportswear International (TSI). The deal includes brands Banana Joe, Farah, and Savane. The company added Gotcha International brands Gotcha, GirlStar, MCD, and Fisherman to its portfolio in 2006. The deal expands the Perry Ellis reach into youth lifestyle brands and opens doors to surf, specialty, and department stores in 20 countries.

Having relaunched its Original Penguin brand in 2002, PEI in late 2005 announced that it plans to add to the brand's New York retail outlet by rolling out Miami and Newport Beach, California, stores.

HISTORY

George Feldenkreis, a Cuban lawyer of Ukrainian descent, came to the US in 1961 and began Carfel, a distributor of Japanese auto parts. He started Supreme International in 1967 as an importer of guayabera shirts — those pleated, four-pocket shirts favored by Hispanic men. During the next decade the company expanded into sport shirts and designing its own products. Feldenkreis' fashion-savvy son, Oscar, joined Supreme in 1980. Gradually the company began making products for more upscale retailers and in 1989 launched the Natural Issue line.

Supreme went public in 1993, paving the way for acquisitions and further expansion. The purchase that year of big-and-tall apparel maker Alexander Martin gave Supreme its first US factory. In 1995 the company licensed Isaco International, owned by Oscar's father-in-law, to make Natural Issue underwear and sleepwear. It paid $18 million the next year for rights to the Munsingwear label, related brand names, and the well-known penguin logo. The company bought sweater maker Crossings in 1997.

In April 1999 Supreme paid $75 million for Perry Ellis International, which fashion designer Perry Ellis had formed in 1978 to handle the licensing of his name. Ellis died in 1986, shortly before the peak of the Perry Ellis womenswear business.

Along with the Perry Ellis trademarks, Supreme took the Perry Ellis International name. Also in 1999 the company added labels John Henry, Manhattan, and Lady Manhattan, purchasing the trademarks from bankrupt Perry Ellis licensee Salant. That year it also obtained apparel licenses for PING-brand golf clothing, Andrew Fezza dress sportswear, and PNB Nation young men's urban apparel.

The new Perry Ellis International began working to reinvigorate the faded but well-known Perry Ellis label through dozens of new licensing arrangements, including Kellwood's early 2000 launch of a new Perry Ellis womenswear line (discontinued in mid-2001).

In February 2001 Perry Ellis International agreed to acquire certain assets of Bugle Boy Industries, a manufacturer of menswear and boy's clothing, to better compete in the young men's clothing market. The company purchased

the Jantzen brand and licensed the Tommy Hilfiger (women's swimwear only) brand in March 2002 from VF to extend into the women's and swimwear markets. In 2002 Perry Ellis also obtained the right to be the US licensee for NIKE's line of women's and girl's swimsuits, men's and boy's racing swimsuits, swim equipment, and swim accessories.

In late 2002 Perry Ellis subsidiary Jantzen, the well-known swimwear maker, entered into a licensing agreement with Trop-Tracks L.L.C. for the manufacturing and distribution of a footwear collection under the Jantzen trademark, thus starting the expansion of Jantzen beyond swimsuits and into leisurewear.

In 2003 the company bought out its largest manufacturing licensee, Salant, in order to gain tighter control of its name and greater market share in the menswear arena. It also entered into another licensing agreement with Utex for the production of women's coats, rainwear, and outerwear. Utex also distributes Perry Ellis men's tailored clothing and outerwear in Canada.

EXECUTIVES

Chairman and CEO: George Feldenkreis, age 70, $1,683,000 pay
Vice Chairman, President, and COO: Oscar Feldenkreis, age 46, $1,496,000 pay (prior to promotion)
CFO: George Pita, age 44, $330,000 pay
EVP, Operations: Joseph (Joe) Roisman
EVP, New Business Development: Anthony (Tony) Campbell
EVP, Strategic Planning and Business Development: Christopher I. (Chris) Nakatani
SVP Marketing, Perry Ellis Brands: Pablo de Echevarria
VP Denim Development: Robert J. (Bob) Arnot
VP Marketing, Non Perry Ellis Brands: Lori Medici
Group President, Perry Ellis and Premium Brands: Paul F. Rosengard, age 47, $403,385 pay (partial-year salary)
President, Licensing: Mary Gleason, age 53
President, Action Sports/Active: Seth Ellison, age 46
President, Bottoms Division: Steve Harriman, age 48
President, Perry Ellis Retail Outlet Division: Joe Shannon
SVP, Sales, Women's Swim: Gail Rhodes
President and Brand Manager, Original Penguin: Chris Kolbe
CIO: Luis Paez
Secretary and Treasurer: Fanny Hanono, age 45, $127,557 pay
Director of Corporate Sales: Michael Gann
Director of Corporate Marketing and Investor Relations: Keva Silversmith
VP, Human Resources: Lystra Nottingham
Auditors: Deloitte & Touche LLP

LOCATIONS

HQ: Perry Ellis International, Inc.
   3000 NW 107th Ave., Miami, FL 33172
Phone: 305-592-2830   **Fax:** 305-594-2307
Web: www.pery.com

Perry Ellis International's products are made in Asia and Central America and sold in Canada, Puerto Rico, and the US.

PRODUCTS/OPERATIONS

2006 Sales

	% of total
Branded product	89
Private label	11
Total	**100**

HISTORICAL FINANCIALS

Company Type: Public

Income Statement

				FYE: January 31
	REVENUE ($ mil.)	NET INCOME ($ mil.)	NET PROFIT MARGIN	EMPLOYEES
1/06	849.4	22.7	2.7%	1,958
1/05	656.6	21.0	3.2%	2,015
1/04	505.9	13.1	2.6%	1,398
1/03	305.8	10.8	3.5%	576
1/02	279.7	6.6	2.4%	471
Annual Growth	32.0%	36.2%	—	42.8%

2006 Year-End Financials

Debt ratio: 118.1%	Dividends
Return on equity: 11.0%	Yield: —
Cash ($ mil.): 9.4	Payout: —
Current ratio: 4.01	Market value ($ mil.): 130.1
Long-term debt ($ mil.): 259.0	R&D as % of sales: —
No. of shares (mil.): 9.6	Advertising as % of sales: —

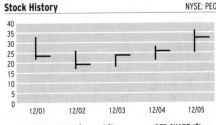

	STOCK PRICE ($) FY Close	P/E High/Low		PER SHARE ($) Earnings	Dividends	Book Value
1/06	13.54	12	8	1.51	—	22.84
1/05	14.07	14	8	1.43	—	20.57
1/04	14.83	19	11	1.06	—	17.89
1/03	11.61	11	4	1.10	—	15.47
1/02	5.00	9	5	0.67	—	13.87
Annual Growth	28.3%	—	—	22.5%	—	13.3%

Petroleum & Resources

If they're finding petroleum or resources, Petroleum & Resources Corporation wants to invest in 'em. The firm manages a closed-end fund (a fund with a limited number of shares) that invests in natural resources and basic industries stocks. Its primary holdings are in oil companies, including Exxon Mobil (its largest holding), BP, Chevron, and ConocoPhillips. It also invests in oil and gas distributors (Equitable Resources and EOG Resources) and service outfits (Schlumberger and BJ Services). To a lesser extent, Petroleum & Resources invests in paper and forest products companies, other basic materials firms, commercial paper, and US Treasury bills.

The company shares its headquarters and most of its executives with fellow closed-end fund Adams Express Company, which owns almost 10% of Petroleum & Resources.

The company has been trading on the NYSE since 1929, and boasts that it has survived both the Depression *and* disco to remain one of only a handful of closed-end funds that have operated for as long.

EXECUTIVES

Chairman and CEO: Douglas G. (Doug) Ober, age 60, $295,900 pay
VP, CFO, and Treasurer: Maureen A. Jones, age 58
VP, Chief Compliance Officer, General Counsel, and Secretary: Lawrence L. Hooper Jr., age 53
VP, Research: Robert E. Sullivan
VP, Research: Nancy J. F. Prue, $192,660 pay
Assistant Secretary: Geraldine H. (Geri) Paré
Assistant Treasurer: Christine M. Sloan
Auditors: PricewaterhouseCoopers LLP

LOCATIONS

HQ: Petroleum & Resources Corporation
7 St. Paul St., Ste. 1140, Baltimore, MD 21202
Phone: 410-752-5900 **Fax:** 410-659-0080
Web: www.peteres.com

PRODUCTS/OPERATIONS

2005 Sales

	% of total
Net realized gain on security transactions	63
Dividends	34
Interest & other	3
Total	**100**

Top 10 Holdings

Exxon Mobil Corporation
BP p.l.c. (ADR)
Chevron Corporation
ConocoPhillips
Schlumberger Limited
BJ Services Company
EOG Resources, Inc.
Devon Energy Corporation
Equitable Resources Inc.
Nabors Industries Ltd.

COMPETITORS

A.G. Edwards
Bear Stearns
BP Prudhoe Bay
Citigroup Global Markets
FMR
Hallwood Group
Janus Capital
Putnam
Resource America
San Juan Basin
T. Rowe Price
Texas Pacific Land Trust
UBS Financial Services
The Vanguard Group

HISTORICAL FINANCIALS
Company Type: Public

Income Statement
FYE: December 31

	REVENUE ($ mil.)	NET INCOME ($ mil.)	NET PROFIT MARGIN	EMPLOYEES
12/05	195.2	191.0	97.8%	—
12/04	121.4	118.3	97.4%	—
12/03	95.1	91.7	96.4%	—
12/02	25.7	(58.7)	—	—
12/01	34.5	(131.9)	—	—
Annual Growth	54.2%	—	—	—

2005 Year-End Financials

Debt ratio: 0.8%
Return on equity: 27.7%
Cash ($ mil.): 17.5
Current ratio: —
Long-term debt ($ mil.): 6.2
No. of shares (mil.): 21.6

Dividends
 Yield: 4.1%
 Payout: —
Market value ($ mil.): 699.2
R&D as % of sales: —
Advertising as % of sales: —

Stock History
NYSE: PEO

	STOCK PRICE ($) FY Close	P/E High/Low		PER SHARE ($) Earnings	Dividends	Book Value
12/05	32.34	—	—	—	1.33	35.24
12/04	25.78	—	—	—	0.49	28.16
12/03	23.74	—	—	—	0.48	24.06
12/02	19.18	—	—	—	1.11	20.98
12/01	23.46	—	—	—	1.50	24.90
Annual Growth	8.4%	—	—	—	(3.0%)	9.1%

Petroleum Development

The hills are alive with opportunity for Petroleum Development, which produces natural gas that it finds in the Rocky Mountains and the Appalachian Basin; the independent also has operations in Michigan. The company owns interests in 2,800 wells and has net proved reserves of 275 billion cu. ft. of natural gas equivalent, of which less than 10% is oil. Petroleum Development also drills and operates wells for its partners, and often sets up public limited partnerships to fund its well-drilling program. Subsidiary Riley Natural Gas markets natural gas for the company and others in Appalachia. The company has sold its Ohio-based distribution utility, Paramount Natural Gas.

Petroleum Development began in 1969 with a focus on Appalachian Basin operations in Ohio, Pennsylvania, Tennessee, and West Virginia. The company expanded its geographic scope in 1997 to include Michigan, and in 1999, the Rocky Mountains.

In 2006 it made a small move with the agreement to acquire energy company Unioil, which has operations in Colorado and Wyoming, for about $18 million.

In 2007 the company acquired assets from EXCO Resources in the Wattenberg Field area of the DJ Basin, Colorado, for $132 million.

EXECUTIVES

Chairman and CEO: Steven R. Williams, age 55, $589,597 pay
President and Director: Thomas E. Riley, age 53, $391,135 pay
CFO and Treasurer: Darwin L. Stump, age 51, $308,713 pay
EVP Exploration and Development: Eric R. Stearns, age 48, $360,374 pay
VP, Investor Relations and Communications: Celesta M. Miracle
VP, Production: Ersel E. Morgan Jr.
Director, Partnership Accounting: Janet Potter
Development Geologist: Alan H. Smith
Auditors: KPMG LLP

LOCATIONS

HQ: Petroleum Development Corporation
103 E. Main St., Bridgeport, WV 26330
Phone: 304-842-3597 **Fax:** 304-842-0913
Web: www.petd.com

Petroleum Development operates in Colorado, Kansas, Michigan, North Dakota, Pennsylvania, Tennessee, and West Virginia.

2005 Proved Reserves

	% of total
Rocky Mountains	77
Appalachian Basin	14
Michigan Basin	9
Total	**100**

PRODUCTS/OPERATIONS

2005 Sales

	$ mil.	% of total
Gas marketing	121.1	35
Oil & gas	102.5	30
Oil & gas well drilling	100.0	29
Well operations & pipelines	8.8	3
Other	10.7	3
Total	**343.1**	**100**

COMPETITORS

BP
Cabot Oil & Gas
Exxon Mobil
Penn Virginia
Quicksilver Resources
Range Resources
Royal Dutch Shell

HISTORICAL FINANCIALS

Company Type: Public

Income Statement			FYE: December 31	
	REVENUE ($ mil.)	NET INCOME ($ mil.)	NET PROFIT MARGIN	EMPLOYEES
12/05	343.1	41.5	12.1%	150
12/04	293.7	33.2	11.3%	120
12/03	202.9	22.6	11.1%	110
12/02	135.3	9.3	6.9%	94
12/01	177.1	15.0	8.5%	90
Annual Growth	18.0%	29.0%	—	13.6%

2005 Year-End Financials

Debt ratio: 12.7%
Return on equity: 24.2%
Cash ($ mil.): 102.0
Current ratio: 0.87
Long-term debt ($ mil.): 24.0
No. of shares (mil.): 16.3
Dividends
 Yield: —
 Payout: —
Market value ($ mil.): 542.8
R&D as % of sales: —
Advertising as % of sales: —

Stock History

NASDAQ (GS): PETD

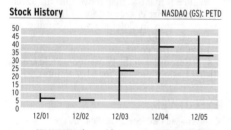

	STOCK PRICE ($) FY Close	P/E High/Low		PER SHARE ($) Earnings	Dividends	Book Value
12/05	33.34	18	9	2.52	—	11.56
12/04	38.57	25	8	2.00	—	9.28
12/03	23.70	18	4	1.39	—	7.91
12/02	5.30	11	8	0.58	—	6.43
12/01	6.17	10	5	0.90	—	5.96
Annual Growth	52.5%	—	—	29.4%	—	18.0%

P.F. Chang's China Bistro

The ancient Chinese secret behind P.F. Chang's success is upscale American service. P.F. Chang's China Bistro owns and operates about 130 full-service bistro restaurants throughout the US, offering lunch and dinner menus inspired by five culinary regions of China. The chain's restaurants offer stylish dining areas, display kitchens, and narrative murals based on ancient Chinese designs. Specialties include Chicken in Soothing Lettuce Wrap and Szechwan-style Long Beans as well as a variety of other dishes made with chicken, beef, seafood, vegetables, and noodles. The company also owns and operates almost 80 limited-service Pei Wei Asian Diners, mostly in the southwestern US.

P.F. Chang's has pursued an aggressive expansion policy, growing from seven restaurants in 1996 to more than 200 at the beginning of 2006. During 2006 the company planned to open 19 full-service bistros, 30 Pei Wei restaurants, and one new concept restaurant.

The "P.F." in P.F. Chang's stands for Paul Fleming, a former oilman and franchisee for Ruth's Chris Steak House, who opened the chain's first restaurant in Scottsdale, Arizona, in 1993. Fleming also developed Z-Tejas and Fleming's Prime Steakhouse and Wine Bar, now part of OSI Restaurant Partners. Fleming owns more than 5% of the company.

EXECUTIVES

Chairman and CEO: Richard L. (Rick) Federico, age 52, $618,000 pay
President: Robert T. (Bert) Vivian, age 47, $394,000 pay
CFO: Mark D. Mumford, age 43
EVP, Chief Administrative Officer, and Director: R. Michael Welborn, age 54
EVP; President, Pei Wei Asian Diner: Russell G. Owens, age 47, $415,000 pay
Chief Legal Officer and Secretary: Tracy M. Durchslag
Chief Development Officer: Frank W. Ziska, age 58, $226,000 pay
Chief Marketing Officer: Tim McDougall
Director Culinary Operations, P.F. Chang's China Bistro: Roberto DeAngelis
Director People Services, P.F. Chang's China Bistro: Peggy Rebenzer
Director Public Relations, P.F. Chang's China Bistro: Laura Cherry
Corporate Executive Chef, P.F. Chang's China Bistro: Bob Tam
Auditors: Ernst & Young LLP

LOCATIONS

HQ: P.F. Chang's China Bistro, Inc.
 7676 E. Pinnacle Peak Rd., Scottsdale, AZ 85255
Phone: 480-888-3000 **Fax:** 480-888-3001
Web: www.pfcb.com

2005 China Bistro Locations

	No. of restaurants
California	25
Texas	13
Florida	9
Arizona	7
Colorado	7
Ohio	6
Nevada	5
Illinois	4
Tennessee	4
Virginia	4
Georgia	3
Michigan	3
Missouri	3
New Jersey	3
New York	3
North Carolina	3
Oregon	3
Washington	3
Other states	24
Total	**132**

2005 Pei Wei Locations

	No. of restaurants
Texas	31
Arizona	16
California	9
Colorado	4
Florida	3
Minnesota	3
Nevada	3
Oklahoma	3
Other states	8
Total	**80**

PRODUCTS/OPERATIONS

2005 Sales

	$ mil.	% of total
China Bistro	675.2	83
Pei Wei	134.0	17
Total	**809.2**	**100**

COMPETITORS

BD's Mongolian Barbecue
Benihana
Brinker
BUCA
Café de Coral
California Pizza Kitchen
Carlson Restaurants
Cheesecake Factory
Darden
Doc Chey's Kitchen
Hillstone Restaurant Group
HuHot Mongolian Grill
La Madeleine
Leeann Chin
Lone Star Steakhouse
Made In Japan Japanese Restaurants
The Melting Pot
Noodles & Company
OSI Restaurant Partners
Romacorp
Ruby Tuesday
Todai
Tokyo Joe's
Typhoon!
Wild Noodles

HISTORICAL FINANCIALS

Company Type: Public

Income Statement			FYE: Sunday nearest December 31	
	REVENUE ($ mil.)	NET INCOME ($ mil.)	NET PROFIT MARGIN	EMPLOYEES
12/05	809.2	37.8	4.7%	21,800
12/04	706.9	26.0	3.7%	18,600
12/03	559.2	25.4	4.5%	16,500
12/02	422.1	20.9	5.0%	12,500
12/01	318.8	15.6	4.9%	9,500
Annual Growth	26.2%	24.8%	—	23.1%

2005 Year-End Financials

Debt ratio: 20.9%
Return on equity: 14.0%
Cash ($ mil.): 74.4
Current ratio: 1.15
Long-term debt ($ mil.): 61.3
No. of shares (mil.): 26.4
Dividends
 Yield: —
 Payout: —
Market value ($ mil.): 1,310.1
R&D as % of sales: —
Advertising as % of sales: 0.3%

Stock History

NASDAQ (GS): PFCB

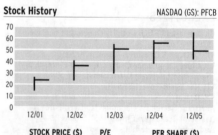

	STOCK PRICE ($) FY Close	P/E High/Low		PER SHARE ($) Earnings	Dividends	Book Value
12/05	49.63	47	31	1.40	—	11.13
12/04	56.35	59	40	0.98	—	9.38
12/03	50.88	56	31	0.97	—	8.06
12/02	36.30	50	30	0.81	—	7.01
12/01	23.65	42	24	0.62	—	11.45
Annual Growth	20.4%	—	—	22.6%	—	(0.7%)

PharmaNet Development

When searching for new drugs, drug makers cast their nets wide and PharmaNet Development Group aims to help them pull in a hit. The contract research firm (formerly SFBC International) provides both early stage (Phase I) and late stage (Phase II-IV) clinical trials and bioanalytic lab services for biotech and pharmaceutical firms. Services include recruiting test subjects, monitoring trials, managing data gathered during the trials, and assisting clients with the FDA approval process. PharmaNet specializes in studies that require such special population participants as diabetics, children, the elderly, HIV patients, and postmenopausal women. PharmaNet operates in more than 25 countries.

Founded in 1984, the company didn't become acquisitive until 2000. It has since grown through a series of purchases which expanded both its range of services and its clientele. It two largest purchases have been Anapharm (Canada, 2002, $27 million) and PharmaNet, Inc. (US, 2004, $250 million).

Building code violations, lease snarls, and a damaging article by Bloomberg Magazine about practices at its Miami, Florida facility have hampered the company's plans to expand there. It has since made sweeping management changes, and still intends to expand in southern Florida, either in the existing facility or a completely new one. In the meantime, PharmaNet is planning additional expansions to its Quebec City facilities, and intends to open a new facility in Toronto.

EXECUTIVES

Chairman: Jack Levine, age 55
President, CEO, and Director; President and CEO, PharmaNet: Jeffrey P. McMullen, age 54
EVP and CFO: John P. Hamill
EVP, Reporting and Analysis and Chief Accounting Officer: David Natan, age 53
EVP, Late Stage Development; COO, PharmaNet: Thomas J. Newman
EVP, Laboratories; President and CEO, Anapharm: Marc LeBel, age 51
EVP, Early Clinical Development; COO, Anapharm: Johanne Boucher-Champagne, age 52
EVP and COO, SFBC New Drug Services: Raymond R. Carr
EVP, SFBC New Drug Services and COO, New Drug Services Canada: Frank Naus
EVP, Late Phase Development, PharmaNet: Sean P. Larkin
EVP, Operations, Europe and Australasia, PharmaNet: Robert Reekie
EVP, U.S. Clinical Research, PharmaNet: Dalvir Gill
VP, Human Resources, PharmaNet: Robin C. Sheldrick
Executive Director, Investor Relations and Corporate Communications: Anne-Marie Hess
Auditors: Grant Thornton LLP

LOCATIONS

HQ: PharmaNet Development Group, Inc.
504 Carnegie Center, Princeton, NJ 08540
Phone: 609-951-6800 **Fax:** 609-514-0390
Web: www.pharmanet.com

PharmaNet Development Group has facilities in Florida, New Jersey, and Pennsylvania, as well as in Canada and Spain.

2005 Sales

	% of total
US	56
Canada	26
Europe	16
Other regions	2
Total	**100**

PRODUCTS/OPERATIONS

Selected Subsidiaries

Anapharm, Inc. (Canada)
Clinical Pharmacology International, Inc.
Daedel Management & Investment, Inc. (Canada)
PharmaNet, Inc.
SFBC Analytical Laboratories, Inc.
SFBC Canada, Inc.
SFBC Ft. Myers, Inc.
SFBC New Drug Services, Inc.
SFBC New Drug Services Canada, Inc.
South Florida Kinetics, Inc. (d.b.a. South Florida Bioavailability Clinic)
Synfine Research, Inc. (Canada)

COMPETITORS

Covance
ICON
Kendle
Life Sciences Research
MDS
PAREXEL
Pharmaceutical Product Development
PRA International
Quintiles Transnational

HISTORICAL FINANCIALS

Company Type: Public

Income Statement

FYE: December 31

	REVENUE ($ mil.)	NET INCOME ($ mil.)	NET PROFIT MARGIN	EMPLOYEES
12/05	429.6	4.8	1.1%	2,496
12/04	159.6	19.7	12.3%	2,100
12/03	103.8	11.6	11.2%	1,123
12/02	64.7	7.9	12.2%	874
12/01	31.5	3.8	12.1%	654
Annual Growth	**92.2%**	**6.0%**	**—**	**39.8%**

2005 Year-End Financials

Debt ratio: 53.8%
Return on equity: 2.1%
Cash ($ mil.): 38.8
Current ratio: 1.41
Long-term debt ($ mil.): 151.9
No. of shares (mil.): 18.5
Dividends
Yield: —
Payout: —
Market value ($ mil.): 296.1
R&D as % of sales: —
Advertising as % of sales: —

Stock History

NASDAQ (GS): PDGI

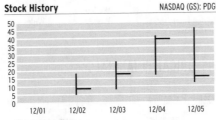

	STOCK PRICE ($) FY Close	P/E High/Low		PER SHARE ($) Earnings	Dividends	Book Value
12/05	16.01	176	48	0.26	—	15.26
12/04	39.50	33	14	1.25	—	11.45
12/03	17.71	27	9	0.93	—	15.01
12/02	8.65	25	7	0.70	—	9.25
12/01	13.67	43	0	0.54	—	8.19
Annual Growth	**4.0%**	**—**	**—**	**(16.7%)**	**—**	**16.8%**

Pharmion

Pharmion has its eye on blood and cancer treatments. The company's top-selling products are Thalidomide Pharmion, a treatment for multiple myeloma, and myelodysplastic syndrome treatment Vidaza. Thalidomide Pharmion, licensed from Celgene, is approved in Australia, New Zealand, Israel, and Turkey; the controversial drug is available on a limited basis in Europe. The firm's other marketed products are thrombosis medications Innohep and Refludan. It has also netted the rights to commercialize Satraplatin, a platinum-based compound which promises to be useful in treating a type of prostate cancer. Pharmion sells its products directly in the US and selected foreign countries.

Vidaza, which received US regulatory approval in mid-2004, was licensed from Pharmacia (now Pfizer). The drug accounted for nearly 60% of Pharmion's 2005 sales. Refludan was acquired from Schering AG and the rights to Satraplatin came from GPC Biotech AG.

Thalidomide Pharmion accounted for a third of Pharmion's 2005 sales.

New Enterprise Associates owns 9% of the company. Celgene has a 6% stake.

EXECUTIVES

President, CEO, and Director: Patrick J. Mahaffy, age 43
EVP and CFO: Erle T. Mast, age 44, $401,118 pay
EVP and Chief Medical Officer: Andrew R. Allen
EVP, Development Operations: Gillian C. Ivers-Read, age 53
EVP, International Commercial Operations: Michael Cosgrave, age 51
VP, Global Manufacturing: Joe Como
VP, Global Medical and Safety: Jay Blackstrom
VP, European Commercial: Kim Nielsen
VP, Human Resources: Pam Herriott
VP, Information Technology: Jeffrey P. Davis
VP, Strategic Planning: Barrie L. Alioth
VP and General Counsel: Steven DuPont, $334,811 pay
Auditors: Ernst & Young LLP

LOCATIONS

HQ: Pharmion Corporation
2525 28th St., Ste. 200, Boulder, CO 80301
Phone: 720-564-9100 **Fax:** 720-564-9191
Web: www.pharmion.com

Pharmion has facilities in the UK and the US.

2005 Sales

	$ mil.	% of total
US	130.9	59
Europe & other regions	90.3	41
Total	**221.2**	**100**

COMPETITORS

Abbott Labs	MGI PHARMA
Bayer Schering Pharma	Millennium
Bristol-Myers Squibb	Pharmaceuticals
Celgene	Novacea
Cytogen	Onyx Pharmaceuticals
Dendreon	OSI Pharmaceuticals
Eli Lilly	Pfizer
Genentech	Sanofi-Aventis
GlaxoSmithKline	SuperGen
Merck	

HISTORICAL FINANCIALS

Company Type: Public

Income Statement

FYE: December 31

	REVENUE ($ mil.)	NET INCOME ($ mil.)	NET PROFIT MARGIN	EMPLOYEES
12/05	221.2	2.3	1.0%	328
12/04	130.2	(17.5)	—	289
12/03	25.5	(50.1)	—	177
12/02	4.7	(34.7)	—	166
Annual Growth	261.0%	—		25.5%

2005 Year-End Financials

Debt ratio: —
Return on equity: 0.7%
Cash ($ mil.): 243.4
Current ratio: 3.75
Long-term debt ($ mil.): —
No. of shares (mil.): 31.9

Dividends
  Yield: —
  Payout: —
Market value ($ mil.): 567.1
R&D as % of sales: —
Advertising as % of sales: 3.1%

Stock History

NASDAQ (GM): PHRM

	STOCK PRICE ($) FY Close	P/E High/Low		PER SHARE ($) Earnings	Dividends	Book Value
12/05	17.77	636	236	0.07	—	10.86
12/04	42.21	—	—	(0.63)	—	11.07
12/03	15.25	—	—	(14.70)	—	4.38
Annual Growth	7.9%	—	—	—	—	57.5%

Phoenix Footwear

Rising from the ashes of its last incarnation, Phoenix Footwear is a well shod bird. Founded in 1882 as Daniel Green Company, the shoemaker changed its name 120 years later, after selling off its Daniel Green and L.B. Evans trademarks in 2001. The company now focuses on making footwear and apparel, as well as commercial combat and uniform boots. Phoenix Footwear's products are manufactured primarily in Brazil, China, and South America and are sold through about 10,000 US retailers including major department stores, mail order companies, and specialty shoe and apparel retailers. Chairman James Riedman, through insurance brokerage firm Riedman Corporation, owns more than half of Phoenix Footwear.

Riedman assumed the title of CEO on an interim basis in May 2006 when president and CEO Rick White resigned.

Phoenix Footwear has spread its wings through numerous acquisitions since 2003. In mid-2003 Phoenix Footwear acquired boot and shoe designer H.S. Trask, and later the same year, the company purchased Royal Robbins, which marked the company's debut in the outdoor and travel apparel market.

Its 2004 purchase of military boot maker Altama Delta Corporation brought Phoenix Footwear new product lines, including military-specification (mil-spec), commercial, and infantry combat boots, as well as tactical and safety and work boots. The company sells its boot lines to the US Department of Defense, as well as through footwear retailers, footwear and military catalogs, and directly to consumers via its Web site.

In June 2005 the company completed its acquisition of Chambers Belt Company, a manufacturer of men's, women's, and children's belts and accessories. In August 2005 Phoenix Footwear purchased Paradise Shoe Co., the exclusive licensee of Tommy Bahama men's and women's footwear, hosiery, and belts. The new unit is called Tommy Bahama Footwear.

EXECUTIVES

Chairman and Interim CEO: James R. (Jim) Riedman, age 47
CFO, Treasurer, and Secretary: Kenneth (Ken) Wolf, age 45, $185,926 pay
SVP, Sourcing and Development and Director: Wilhelm (Willie) Pfander, age 65, $113,750 pay
VP, Sales, and Brand Manager, Trotters: Rusty Hall
CEO, Chambers Belt: Charlie Stewart
President, Royal Robbins Division: Robert (Bob) Orlando
President, Tommy Bahama: Kelly Green
President, Institutional Group: Glen Becker
VP, Marketing and Sales, Chambers Belt: Dave Matheson
Director of Human Resources: Andrea Brueggemann
Auditors: Grant Thornton LLP

LOCATIONS

HQ: Phoenix Footwear Group, Inc.
  5759 Fleet St., Ste. 220, Carlsbad, CA 92008
Phone: 760-602-9688   **Fax:** 760-602-9684
Web: www.phoenixfootwear.com

PRODUCTS/OPERATIONS

Selected Brands

Altama (military boots)
H.S. Trask (men's and women's dress and casual footwear)
Royal Robbins (outdoor sportswear and travel apparel)
SoftWalk (women's dress and casual footwear)
Strol (men's dress and casual footwear)
Trotters (women's dress and casual footwear)

COMPETITORS

Brown Shoe	Patagonia
Cole Haan	Stride Rite
Columbia Sportswear	Tandy Brands
ECCO	Timberland
Jones Apparel	Wellco
McRae Industries	Wolverine World Wide
North Face	

HISTORICAL FINANCIALS

Company Type: Public

Income Statement

FYE: December 31

	REVENUE ($ mil.)	NET INCOME ($ mil.)	NET PROFIT MARGIN	EMPLOYEES
12/05	109.2	1.2	1.1%	558
12/04	76.4	3.0	3.9%	344
12/03	39.1	0.9	2.3%	130
12/02	36.2	1.7	4.7%	70
12/01	46.8	1.4	3.0%	70
Annual Growth	23.6%	(3.8%)	—	68.0%

2005 Year-End Financials

Debt ratio: 85.4%
Return on equity: 2.3%
Cash ($ mil.): 0.6
Current ratio: 2.22
Long-term debt ($ mil.): 46.1
No. of shares (mil.): 8.0

Dividends
  Yield: —
  Payout: —
Market value ($ mil.): 43.0
R&D as % of sales: 1.6%
Advertising as % of sales: 1.7%

Stock History

AMEX: PXG

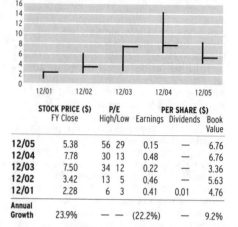

	STOCK PRICE ($) FY Close	P/E High/Low		PER SHARE ($) Earnings	Dividends	Book Value
12/05	5.38	56	29	0.15	—	6.76
12/04	7.78	30	13	0.48	—	6.76
12/03	7.50	34	12	0.22	—	3.36
12/02	3.42	13	5	0.46	—	5.63
12/01	2.28	6	3	0.41	0.01	4.76
Annual Growth	23.9%	—	—	(22.2%)	—	9.2%

Pinnacle Airlines

In an up-and-down industry, Pinnacle Airlines hopes to maintain peak performance. The holding company's main subsidiary is regional carrier Pinnacle Airlines, Inc., which flies to about 120 cities in more than 35 states and four Canadian provinces on behalf of former parent Northwest Airlines. The regional carrier, which does business as Northwest Airlink, operates a fleet of about 125 50-seat Canadair regional jets, which are made by Bombardier. The carrier shares hubs with Northwest in Detroit, Memphis, and Minneapolis/St. Paul. The Pinnacle-Northwest contract runs through 2017. Pinnacle Airlines moved to expand in 2007 by acquiring a smaller regional carrier, Colgan Air.

Pinnacle paid $20 million for Virginia-based Colgan Air, which provides regional service for three airlines — US Airways, Continental Airlines, and UAL's United Airlines — with a fleet of about 50 turboprops. Colgan Air and Pinnacle Airlines, Inc., will operate as separate subsidiaries of Pinnacle Airlines Corp.

Buying Colgan diversifies Pinnacle's revenue mix and establishes ties between the company and carriers that aren't Northwest Airlines. Northwest filed for bankruptcy protection in September 2005, and it renegotiated its contract with Pinnacle in 2006. Pinnacle settled its claim for payments from Northwest, and the regional carrier won the right to seek business from other airlines while still flying as Northwest Airlink. Pinnacle will not be able to serve other carriers from Detroit, Memphis, or Minneapolis/St. Paul, however.

Before going public in 2003, Pinnacle had been a subsidiary of Northwest since 1997. Northwest owns 11% of Pinnacle, which was founded in 1985.

EXECUTIVES

Chairman: Stephen E. Gorman, age 50
President, CEO, and Director: Philip H. Trenary, age 51, $565,161 pay
VP and COO: Douglas W. Shockey, age 47, $284,589 pay
VP and CFO: Peter D. Hunt, age 36, $281,261 pay
VP, Customer Service: Robert W. Lowe, age 58
VP, Flight Operations: Clive A. Seal, age 61
VP, Labor Relations: Nikki M. Tinker, age 35
VP, Maintenance and Engineering: Barry G. Baker, age 46, $159,543 pay
VP, Marketing and In-Flight Services: D. Philip Reed Jr., age 50
VP, Risk Management and Information Technology: Jeffrey M. (Jeff) Dato
VP, Safety and Regulatory Compliance: Edgar C. Fell, age 62, $163,504 pay
Auditors: Ernst & Young LLP

LOCATIONS

HQ: Pinnacle Airlines Corp.
1689 Nonconnah Blvd., Ste. 111,
Memphis, TN 38132
Phone: 901-348-4100   **Fax:** 901-348-4130
Web: www.nwairlink.com

COMPETITORS

Air Wisconsin Airlines	MAIR Holdings
American Eagle	Mesa Air
Champlain Enterprises	Midwest Air
Comair	Republic Airways
ExpressJet	SkyWest
Great Lakes Aviation	Trans States
Horizon Air	

HISTORICAL FINANCIALS

Company Type: Public

Income Statement

FYE: December 31

	REVENUE ($ mil.)	NET INCOME ($ mil.)	NET PROFIT MARGIN	EMPLOYEES
12/05	841.6	25.7	3.1%	3,450
12/04	635.5	40.7	6.4%	3,260
12/03	456.8	35.1	7.7%	2,250
12/02	331.6	30.8	9.3%	2,403
12/01	202.1	14.3	7.1%	—
Annual Growth	42.9%	15.8%	—	12.8%

2005 Year-End Financials

Debt ratio: 649.8%
Return on equity: 464.3%
Cash ($ mil.): 75.7
Current ratio: 1.59
Long-term debt ($ mil.): 121.0
No. of shares (mil.): 21.9
Dividends
  Yield: —
  Payout: —
Market value ($ mil.): 146.4
R&D as % of sales: —
Advertising as % of sales: —

Stock History

NASDAQ (GM): PNCL

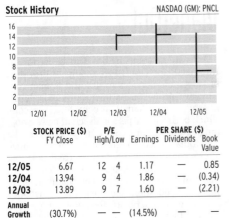

	STOCK PRICE ($) FY Close	P/E High/Low		PER SHARE ($) Earnings	Dividends	Book Value
12/05	6.67	12	4	1.17	—	0.85
12/04	13.94	9	4	1.86	—	(0.34)
12/03	13.89	9	7	1.60	—	(2.21)
Annual Growth	(30.7%)	—	—	(14.5%)	—	—

Pinnacle Data Systems

Pinnacle Data Systems lets the Sun shine in application-specific computer systems. The company builds and services made-to-order UNIX-based servers and other computer systems used in the medical, telecommunications, and process control industries, as well as in government markets. Pinnacle combines parts from Sun Microsystems, Intel, and other third-party equipment makers with its own custom parts to create its systems. The company provides its build and repair services to manufacturers that include Sun and Hewlett-Packard. Repair outsourcing and other related services account for more than 20% of sales.

In 2005 Pinnacle Data Systems acquired the assets of GNP Computers, a provider of turn-key computer systems for design, manufacturing, and lifecycle management.

EXECUTIVES

Chairman and Chief Technology and Innovation Officer: John D. Bair, age 37
President, CEO, and Director: Michael R. (Mike) Sayre, age 47
CFO, Treasurer, and Secretary: George Troutman, age 44
VP, Business Solutions Group: George K. Mehok
VP, Global Sales and Marketing; General Manager, International Business: Rob Harris
VP, Operations: Susan E. Rothberg
Controller: Thomas J. Carr
Director, Human Resources and Quality Systems: Laura A. Palko

LOCATIONS

HQ: Pinnacle Data Systems, Inc.
6600 Port Rd., Groveport, OH 43125
Phone: 614-748-1150   **Fax:** 614-409-1269
Web: www.pinnacle.com

PRODUCTS/OPERATIONS

2005 Sales

	$ mil.	% of total
Products	34.4	77
Services	10.2	23
Total	**44.6**	**100**

Selected Services

Contract manufacturing and engineering
Extended warranty support
Logistics management
Maintenance
Product modifications
Repair outsourcing

COMPETITORS

BOXX Technologies
Celestica
Dell
Flextronics
Hewlett-Packard
IBM
NEC
Plexus
Sanmina-SCI
Solectron
Sun Microsystems

HISTORICAL FINANCIALS

Company Type: Public

Income Statement

FYE: December 31

	REVENUE ($ mil.)	NET INCOME ($ mil.)	NET PROFIT MARGIN	EMPLOYEES
12/05	44.6	0.9	2.0%	162
12/04	34.4	0.9	2.6%	106
12/03	22.9	0.5	2.2%	97
12/02	15.7	0.0	—	96
12/01	22.7	(0.7)	—	99
Annual Growth	18.4%	—	—	13.1%

2005 Year-End Financials

Debt ratio: —
Return on equity: 15.3%
Cash ($ mil.): 0.5
Current ratio: 1.33
Long-term debt ($ mil.): —
No. of shares (mil.): 6.0
Dividends
  Yield: —
  Payout: —
Market value ($ mil.): 18.0
R&D as % of sales: —
Advertising as % of sales: 0.2%

Stock History

AMEX: PNS

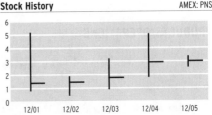

	STOCK PRICE ($) FY Close	P/E High/Low		PER SHARE ($) Earnings	Dividends	Book Value
12/05	3.00	22	17	0.15	—	1.12
12/04	2.93	36	13	0.14	—	0.90
12/03	1.78	40	12	0.08	—	0.73
12/02	1.45	—	—	—	—	0.64
12/01	1.40	—	—	(0.13)	—	0.65
Annual Growth	21.0%	—	—	—	—	14.6%

Pinnacle Financial Partners

Pinnacle Financial Partners wants to be the pinnacle of community banking in central Tennessee. It is the holding company for Pinnacle National Bank, which operates more than 15 branches. The bank's deposit products include checking, money market, and savings accounts and CDs. Business loans (including commercial real estate and construction loans) make up about 65% of its portfolio, which also includes residential mortgages and consumer loans. The company provides brokerage services through its Pinnacle Asset Management division. In 2006, Pinnacle Financial Partners acquired Cavalry Bank for about $190 million.

EXECUTIVES

Chairman and Chief Financial Services Officer: Robert A. (Rob) McCabe Jr., age 55, $293,333 pay
Vice Chairman: Ed C. Loughry Jr., age 63
Vice Chairman, President, and CEO, Pinnacle Financial and Pinnacle Bank: M. Terry Turner, age 43, $293,333 pay

EVP and Chief Administrative Officer:
Hugh M. Queener, age 50, $189,120 pay
EVP and Client Services Group Manager:
Joanne B. Jackson, age 49, $140,400 pay
EVP and Senior Lending Officer: James E. White,
age 53, $174,120 pay
EVP and Senior Credit Officer: Charles B. McMahan,
age 59, $200,636 pay
SVP and CFO: Harold R. Carpenter Jr., age 47,
$143,100 pay
SVP, Marketing and Communications Director:
Victoria Lowe
Chief People Officer: Martha B. Olsen
Auditors: KPMG LLP

LOCATIONS

HQ: Pinnacle Financial Partners, Inc.
211 Commerce St., Ste. 300, Nashville, TN 37201
Phone: 615-744-3700   **Fax:** 615-744-3861
Web: www.mypinnacle.com

Pinnacle Financial Partners has branches in Tennessee's
Bedford, Davidson, Rutherford, Sumner, and Williamson
counties.

PRODUCTS/OPERATIONS

2005 Sales

	$ mil.	% of total
Interest		
Loans, including fees	35.2	68
Securities	10.2	20
Federal funds sold & other	0.9	2
Noninterest		
Investment services	1.8	4
Gains on loans & loan participations sold	1.3	2
Service charges on deposit accounts	1.0	2
Other	1.3	2
Total	**51.7**	**100**

Selected Subsidiaries

Pinnacle Advisory Services, Inc.
Pinnacle Credit Enhancement Services, Inc.
Pinnacle National Bank
  PFP Title Company
    PNFP Holdings, Inc.
    PNFP Properties, Inc.
Pinnacle Community Development Corporation

COMPETITORS

AmSouth
Bank of America
BB&T
Capital Bancorp
First Horizon
SunTrust

HISTORICAL FINANCIALS

Company Type: Public

Income Statement

FYE: December 31

	ASSETS ($ mil.)	NET INCOME ($ mil.)	INCOME AS % OF ASSETS	EMPLOYEES
12/05	1,016.8	8.1	0.8%	159
12/04	727.1	5.3	0.7%	126
12/03	498.4	2.5	0.5%	96
12/02	305.3	0.6	0.2%	66
12/01	175.4	(1.1)	—	51
Annual Growth	**55.2%**	**—**	**—**	**32.9%**

2005 Year-End Financials

Equity as % of assets: 6.2%
Return on assets: 0.9%
Return on equity: 13.4%
Long-term debt ($ mil.): 30.9
No. of shares (mil.): 8.4
Market value ($ mil.): 210.5
Dividends
  Yield: —
  Payout: —
Sales ($ mil.): 51.7
R&D as % of sales: —
Advertising as % of sales: —

Stock History   NASDAQ (GS): PNFP

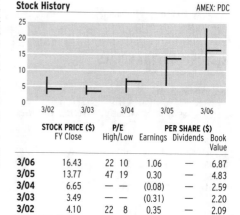

	STOCK PRICE ($) FY Close	P/E High/Low		PER SHARE ($) Earnings	Dividends	Book Value
12/05	24.98	31	24	0.85	—	7.53
12/04	22.62	41	19	0.61	—	6.90
12/03	11.75	40	20	0.32	—	9.30
12/02	6.45	63	42	0.10	—	8.78
12/01	5.13	—	—	(0.28)	—	7.91
Annual Growth	**48.5%**	**—**	**—**	**—**	**—**	**(1.2%)**

Pioneer Drilling

Pioneer Drilling digs down deep to make money
on the land where Texas pioneers used to roam.
The company, formerly South Texas Drilling &
Exploration, provides contract drilling and related
services to oil and gas companies in Texas, and to
a lesser degree in Oklahoma and the Rockies. Pioneer Drilling operates 57 land drilling rigs that
can reach depths of 8,000–18,000 feet. The company moved into East Texas by acquiring privately
owned Mustang Drilling. In 2004 the company acquired seven drilling rigs from Wolverine Drilling
and five from Allen Drilling.

Texas is the geographic focus of Pioneer
Drilling's business. In 2006 it had 18 drilling rigs
operating in East Texas, 15 in South Texas, and
seven in North Texas.

EXECUTIVES

President, CEO, and Director: William S. (Stacy) Locke,
age 50, $610,200 pay
EVP and COO: Franklin C. (Red) West, age 66,
$473,800 pay
SVP, Marketing: Donald G. Lacombe, age 52,
$244,800 pay
SVP, CFO, and Secretary: William D. Hibbetts, age 57,
$275,400 pay
VP and Chief Accounting Officer: Kurt M. Forkheim
VP and Manager, South Texas Division: Willie Walker
VP and Manager, East Texas Division: Billy King
Manager, North Texas Division: Blaine David
Auditors: KPMG LLP

LOCATIONS

HQ: Pioneer Drilling Company
1250 NE Loop 410, Ste. 1000,
San Antonio, TX 78209
Phone: 210-828-7689   **Fax:** 210-828-8228
Web: www.pioneerdrlg.com

PRODUCTS/OPERATIONS

2006 Sales

	$ mil.	% of total
Daywork contracts	252.1	89
Footage contracts	21.2	7
Turnkey contracts	10.8	4
Total	**284.1**	**100**

COMPETITORS

Grey Wolf
Helmerich & Payne
Nabors Industries
Parker Drilling
Patterson-UTI Energy
Rowan
Unit Corporation

HISTORICAL FINANCIALS

Company Type: Public

Income Statement

FYE: March 31

	REVENUE ($ mil.)	NET INCOME ($ mil.)	NET PROFIT MARGIN	EMPLOYEES
3/06	284.1	50.6	17.8%	1,540
3/05	185.3	10.8	5.8%	1,370
3/04	107.9	(1.8)	—	900
3/03	80.2	(5.1)	—	565
3/02	68.2	6.3	9.2%	410
Annual Growth	**42.9%**	**68.3%**	**—**	**39.2%**

2006 Year-End Financials

Debt ratio: —
Return on equity: 18.0%
Cash ($ mil.): 91.2
Current ratio: 4.28
Long-term debt ($ mil.): —
No. of shares (mil.): 49.6
Dividends
  Yield: —
  Payout: —
Market value ($ mil.): 814.8
R&D as % of sales: —
Advertising as % of sales: —

Stock History   AMEX: PDC

	STOCK PRICE ($) FY Close	P/E High/Low		PER SHARE ($) Earnings	Dividends	Book Value
3/06	16.43	22	10	1.06	—	6.87
3/05	13.77	47	19	0.30	—	4.83
3/04	6.65	—	—	(0.08)	—	2.59
3/03	3.49	—	—	(0.31)	—	2.20
3/02	4.10	22	8	0.35	—	2.09
Annual Growth	**41.5%**	**—**	**—**	**31.9%**	**—**	**34.6%**

PlanetOut

At least one company has a queer eye for the
Internet. PlanetOut is a Web company providing
products and services to gay and lesbian consumers worldwide. Its operations include the
flagship sites PlanetOut.com and Gay.com,
which both feature personals, chat, news, shopping guides, and community services. Its
Kleptomaniac.com e-commerce site is named
after a comment by US senator Trent Lott that
homosexuals are sick and should receive treatment like alcoholics or kleptomaniacs. More
than 150,000 subscribers pay for PlanetOut's
premium Web services. Revenue comes from
subscriptions, e-commerce, and advertising.

In 2004 the company discontinued its
OutandAbout.com site, which offered gay-
friendly travel information, and migrated all

travel-related content to Gay.com. The following year PlanetOut acquired LPI Media for $24 million in cash and about $7.1 million in debt.

PlanetOut offers specialized travel and event packages through RSVP, which the company acquired in 2006 for approximately $6.5 million. RSVP develops travel itineraries on land, at resorts, and on cruises, by contracting with third-parties who provide the basic travel services.

EXECUTIVES

Chairman: H. William (Bill) Jesse, Jr., age 54
CEO and Director: Karen Magee, age 45
President, COO, and Secretary: Jeffrey T. (Jeff) Soukup, age 40
SVP and CFO: Daniel J. (Dan) Miller, age 39
SVP and CTO: Peter Kretzman, age 49, $92,929 pay (partial-year salary)
VP Business and Legal Affairs: Todd A. Huge
VP Corporate Communications and Investor Relations: Kevin Nyland
VP Corporate Development: Portia M. Kersten
VP Finance and Controller: David M. DeFelice
VP International Marketing and Operations: Eric Wilson
Manager Public Relations: James David
Auditors: Stonefield Josephson, Inc.

LOCATIONS

HQ: PlanetOut Inc.
1355 Sansome St., San Francisco, CA 94111
Phone: 415-834-6500   **Fax:** 415-834-6502
Web: www.planetoutinc.com

PlanetOut has offices in Buenos Aires, London, Los Angeles, New York, and San Francisco.

PRODUCTS/OPERATIONS

Web sites

Gay.com (portal)
HIVPlusMag.com
Kleptomaniac.com (e-commere)
Out.com
OutTraveler.com
PlanetOut.com (portal)

2005 Sales

	$ mil.	% of total
Subscriptions	21.1	59
Advertising	11.7	33
E-commerce and other	2.8	8
Total	**35.6**	**100**

COMPETITORS

Gay Financial Network
H.I.M.
Yahoo!

HISTORICAL FINANCIALS

Company Type: Public

Income Statement

FYE: December 31

	REVENUE ($ mil.)	NET INCOME ($ mil.)	NET PROFIT MARGIN	EMPLOYEES
12/05	35.6	2.7	7.6%	305
12/04	25.0	(0.5)	—	149
12/03	19.1	(0.8)	—	128
12/02	14.0	(7.8)	—	—
12/01	7.2	(16.5)	—	100
Annual Growth	**49.1%**	**—**	**—**	**32.2%**

2005 Year-End Financials

Debt ratio: 13.7%
Return on equity: 5.3%
Cash ($ mil.): 18.5
Current ratio: 2.08
Long-term debt ($ mil.): 7.3
No. of shares (mil.): 17.2
Dividends
  Yield: —
  Payout: —
Market value ($ mil.): 149.7
R&D as % of sales: —
Advertising as % of sales: 9.2%

Stock History

NASDAQ (GM): LGBT

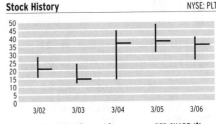

	STOCK PRICE ($) FY Close	P/E High/Low	Earnings	PER SHARE ($) Dividends	Book Value
12/05	8.68	91 41	0.15	—	3.08
12/04	13.60	— —	(0.40)	—	2.88
Annual Growth	**(36.2%)**	**— —**	**—**	**—**	**6.9%**

Plantronics

Plantronics' customers appreciate its hands-off approach. The company makes lightweight communications headsets that can be worn over the head, behind the ear, or in the ear, freeing hands for other tasks. Its other products include the Clarity brand of amplified and noise-canceling telephone handsets for hearing-impaired users, text telephones, emergency response systems, and mobile phone headsets. Plantronics sells its products worldwide through distributors and manufacturers, and through communications service providers. Plantronics acquired Altec Lansing, a maker of computer and home theater speaker systems, in 2005.

EXECUTIVES

Chairman: Marvin (Marv) Tseu, age 58
President, CEO, and Director:
  S. Kenneth (Ken) Kannappan, age 47, $651,163 pay
Managing Director, EMEA: Philip Vanhoutte, age 51, $459,201 pay
SVP, Finance and Administration, and CFO:
  Barbara V. Scherer, age 50
SVP and Chief Marketing Officer: Mark Breier, age 46, $428,541 pay
SVP, Operations: Terry Walters, age 57, $402,431 pay
SVP, Sales: Donald S. (Don) Houston, age 52
VP, and General Manager, Home and Home Office:
  Joyce Shimizu, age 51, $429,029 pay
VP, Development and CTO: Owen Brown
VP, Legal, Secretary, and General Counsel:
  Richard R. Pickard
Public Relations: Dan Race
Auditors: PricewaterhouseCoopers LLP

LOCATIONS

HQ: Plantronics, Inc.
345 Encinal St., Santa Cruz, CA 95060
Phone: 831-426-5858   **Fax:** 831-426-6098
Web: www.plantronics.com

2006 Sales

	$ mil.	% of total
US	483.5	64
Europe, Middle East & Africa	178.3	24
Asia/Pacific & Latin America	61.9	8
Other regions	26.7	4
Total	**750.4**	**100**

PRODUCTS/OPERATIONS

2006 Sales

	$ mil.	% of total
Audio Communications Group	629.7	84
Audio Entertainment Group	120.7	16
Total	**750.4**	**100**

Selected Products

Audio Communications Group (headsets for call center, computer, gaming console, mobile phone, and office use)
Audio Entertainment Group (portable and powered speaker systems for computers, gaming consoles, home theater systems, and media players)

COMPETITORS

Andrea Electronics
Apple
Bose
Creative Technology
GN Netcom
GN ReSound
Harman International
Koss
Logitech
Motorola
Nokia
Sennheiser
Telex Communications

HISTORICAL FINANCIALS

Company Type: Public

Income Statement

FYE: Saturday nearest March 31

	REVENUE ($ mil.)	NET INCOME ($ mil.)	NET PROFIT MARGIN	EMPLOYEES
3/06	750.4	81.2	10.8%	7,300
3/05	560.0	97.5	17.4%	3,900
3/04	417.0	62.3	14.9%	3,600
3/03	337.5	41.5	12.3%	2,726
3/02	311.2	36.3	11.7%	2,361
Annual Growth	**24.6%**	**22.3%**	**—**	**32.6%**

2006 Year-End Financials

Debt ratio: —
Return on equity: 19.3%
Cash ($ mil.): 76.7
Current ratio: 2.59
Long-term debt ($ mil.): —
No. of shares (mil.): 47.5
Dividends
  Yield: 0.6%
  Payout: 12.0%
Market value ($ mil.): 1,684.3
R&D as % of sales: —
Advertising as % of sales: —

Stock History

NYSE: PLT

	STOCK PRICE ($) FY Close	P/E High/Low	Earnings	PER SHARE ($) Dividends	Book Value
3/06	35.43	24 16	1.66	0.20	9.16
3/05	37.75	54 35	0.89	0.15	8.38
3/04	36.61	34 11	1.31	—	6.29
3/03	14.61	27 14	0.89	—	3.37
3/02	20.92	38 22	0.74	—	3.10
Annual Growth	**14.1%**	**— —**	**22.4%**	**33.3%**	**31.2%**

Pope Resources

More earthly than divine, Pope Resources owns some 115,000 acres of timberland and development property in Washington. The partnership annually harvests more than 60 million board ft. from its 71,000-acre Hood Canal and 44,000-acre Columbia tree farms in Washington. It sells its Douglas fir and other timber products mainly in the US and Japan: Weyerhaeuser is a major customer. Pope Resources also provides timberland management and consulting services to third-party timberland owners and managers in Washington, Oregon, and California. Its real estate unit acquires, develops, resells, and rents residential and commercial real estate. Investment advisor Private Capital Management owns 28% of Pope Resources.

Pope Resources' fee timber segment also gains revenue by selling gravel and by leasing cellular communication towers.

The partnership's Olympic Property Group real estate operations relate to its nearly 3,000-acre portfolio of higher-and-better-use properties that may be reforested, developed for sale as improved property, or sold in developed or undeveloped acreage tracts. The company's Rural Lifestyles projects allow it to resell fully logged plots that no longer have value for timber production. Its operations are focused on residential and commercial property in Port Gamble, Kingston, Bremerton, and Gig Harbor.

In 2004 the company acquired 3,300 acres of timberland in southwest Washington from Plum Creek Timber Company, Inc., for $8.5 million; it also paid about $12 million to a private party for 1,339 acres of timberland in western Washington. That year the company sold 426 acres in northern Kitsap County near Kingston, Washington, and agreed to extend to the county an option to acquire up to 360 additional acres of adjacent land; the option will expire in July 2008.

In 2006 the company sold more than 200 acres of residential land for $12 million.

Pope Resources was spun off from Pope & Talbot in 1985, and the latter retains some control of the company through managing general partner Pope MGP, Inc. Pope MGP is owned by Emily Andrews and Peter Pope (former chairman of Pope & Talbot), who own 12% and 7%, respectively, of Pope Resources.

EXECUTIVES

President, CEO, and Director: David L. (Dave) Nunes, age 44, $565,096 pay
VP and CFO: Thomas M. (Tom) Ringo, age 52, $330,058 pay
Director Business Development, Olympic Resource Management: John T. Shea
Director Real Estate and President, Olympic Property Group: Jonathon P. (Jon) Rose
Director Timberland Operations, Olympic Resource Management: Thomas (Tom) Kametz
Director Investor Outreach: Christopher Daubenmire
Auditors: KPMG LLP

LOCATIONS

HQ: Pope Resources, A Delaware Limited Partnership
19245 10th Ave. NE, Poulsbo, WA 98370
Phone: 360-697-6626   **Fax:** 360-697-1156
Web: www.poperesources.com

Pope Resources owns more than 115,000 acres of fee timberland in western Washington. It has real estate holdings in the state's Jefferson, Kitsap, and Pierce counties.

PRODUCTS/OPERATIONS

2005 Sales

	$ mil.	% of total
Fee timber	44.4	78
Timberland management & consulting	7.8	14
Real estate	4.8	8
Total	**57.0**	**100**

Species Distribution

	Mil. board ft.	% of total
Conifers		
Douglas fir	320	75
Western hemlock	50	12
Western red cedar	14	3
Other conifer	13	3
Hardwoods		
Red alder	26	6
Other hardwood	4	1
Total	**427**	**100**

Selected Subsidiaries

Olympic Property Group
Olympic Resource Management

COMPETITORS

Alcan Baltek
Hampton Affiliates
International Paper
Pacific Fiber
Plum Creek Timber
Potlatch
Simpson Investment
Weyerhaeuser

HISTORICAL FINANCIALS

Company Type: Public

Income Statement

	REVENUE ($ mil.)	NET INCOME ($ mil.)	NET PROFIT MARGIN	EMPLOYEES
			FYE: December 31	
12/05	57.0	13.7	24.0%	81
12/04	39.7	10.2	25.7%	72
12/03	27.0	3.5	13.0%	40
12/02	32.2	3.3	10.2%	37
12/01	47.8	(0.4)	—	117
Annual Growth	**4.5%**	**—**	**—**	**(8.8%)**

2005 Year-End Financials

Debt ratio: 48.6%
Return on equity: 22.7%
Cash ($ mil.): 18.4
Current ratio: 3.24
Long-term debt ($ mil.): 32.3
No. of shares (mil.): 4.6
Dividends
  Yield: 2.6%
  Payout: 27.8%
Market value ($ mil.): 144.1
R&D as % of sales: —
Advertising as % of sales: —

Stock History

NASDAQ (GM): POPEZ

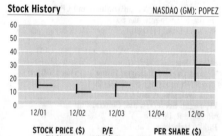

	STOCK PRICE ($) FY Close	P/E High/Low		PER SHARE ($) Earnings	Dividends	Book Value
12/05	31.02	20	7	2.88	0.80	14.29
12/04	25.00	11	7	2.22	0.44	12.01
12/03	15.43	21	9	0.78	0.24	10.19
12/02	10.11	21	13	0.74	0.10	9.65
12/01	14.75	—	—	—	—	8.98
Annual Growth	**20.4%**			**57.3%**	**100.0%**	**12.3%**

Portfolio Recovery Associates

When times get tough, some businesses find the going a little easier with Portfolio Recovery Associates. The firm makes its way in the world by collecting on defaulted consumer debt. It either collects on behalf of clients (including banks, credit unions, consumer and auto finance companies, and retail merchants) or buys charged-off debt portfolios from them and then collects the debts on its own behalf. Portfolio Recovery Associates was formed in 1996 by veterans of the consumer receivables unit of HSBC Finance's (formerly Household International) consumer receivables unit.

With Portfolio Recovery Associates' acquisition of IGS Nevada in October 2004, the company broadened its services to include skip tracing and asset location, primarily for auto finance companies. Portfolio Recovery Associates entered into the government accounts receivables management market in July 2005 when it purchased Alatax, a Birmingham, Alabama-based private company that specializes in government collections.

EXECUTIVES

Chairman, CEO, and President:
Steven D. (Steve) Fredrickson, age 47, $995,000 pay
EVP, CFO, Chief Administrative Officer, Treasurer, and Assistant Secretary: Kevin P. Stevenson, age 41, $665,000 pay
EVP, General Counsel, and Secretary: Judith S. Scott, age 60, $285,000 pay
SVP Operations: William F. O'Daire, $310,000 pay
SVP Bankruptcy Acquisitions: Michael J. Petit, $462,298 pay
VP Human Resources: JoAnn York
Auditors: PricewaterhouseCoopers LLP

LOCATIONS

HQ: Portfolio Recovery Associates, Inc.
120 Corporate Blvd., Norfolk, VA 23502
Phone: 757-519-9300   **Fax:** 757-518-0901
Web: www.portfoliorecovery.com

Portfolio Recovery Associates has operations in Birmingham and Montgomery, Alabama; Hampton and Norfolk, Virginia; Hutchinson, Kansas; and Las Vegas, Nevada.

PRODUCTS/OPERATIONS

2005 Sales

	$ mil.	% of total
Income on finance receivables	134.7	90
Commissions	13.8	10
Total	**148.5**	**100**

2005 Portfolio Composition

	No. of Accounts (thou.)	% of total
Visa/MasterCard/Discover	3,606.3	46
Consumer Finance	2,733.3	35
Private Label Credit Cards	1,298.8	16
Auto	202.9	3
Total	**7,841.3**	**100**

COMPETITORS

Asset Acceptance	NCO
Asta Funding	Outsourcing Solutions
Encore Capital Group, Inc.	Paymap
FirstCity Financial	Rampart Capital
Nationwide Recovery	

HISTORICAL FINANCIALS

Company Type: Public

Income Statement

FYE: December 31

	REVENUE ($ mil.)	NET INCOME ($ mil.)	NET PROFIT MARGIN	EMPLOYEES
12/05	148.5	36.8	24.8%	1,110
12/04	113.4	27.5	24.3%	948
12/03	84.9	20.7	24.4%	798
12/02	55.8	17.1	30.6%	581
12/01	32.3	5.6	17.3%	501
Annual Growth	46.4%	60.1%	—	22.0%

2005 Year-End Financials

Debt ratio: 8.5%
Return on equity: 21.2%
Cash ($ mil.): 16.0
Current ratio: 1.18
Long-term debt ($ mil.): 16.5
No. of shares (mil.): 15.8

Dividends
Yield: —
Payout: —
Market value ($ mil.): 732.2
R&D as % of sales: —
Advertising as % of sales: —

Stock History

NASDAQ (GS): PRAA

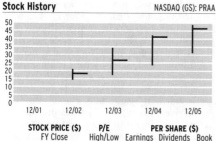

	STOCK PRICE ($) FY Close	P/E High/Low		PER SHARE ($) Earnings	Dividends	Book Value
12/05	46.44	21	14	2.28	—	12.39
12/04	41.22	24	14	1.73	—	9.77
12/03	26.55	26	13	1.32	—	7.79
12/02	18.25	—	—	—	—	5.95
Annual Growth	36.5%	—	—	31.4%	—	27.7%

Powerwave Technologies

Powerwave Technologies wants its signal to come through loud and clear. The company makes radio-frequency (RF) power amplifiers that are used in the base stations of cellular and personal communications service (PCS) networks. The amplifiers give wireless transmissions an extra kick to reduce signal interference and call disconnections. The company's single- and multi-carrier amplifiers support a variety of digital and analog transmission protocols including PCS and analog and digital cellular. Powerwave sells its products directly and through distributors to wireless equipment makers as well as wireless service carriers; its customers include Cingular (about 15% of sales), Nokia (10%+), and Nortel.

Powerwave continues to court wireless equipment makers and it has begun shipping amplifiers that support third-generation (3G) wireless transmission technology.

The company is active in acquisitions. In 2005 the company acquired certain assets of the Wireless Systems business at REMEC for around $145 million in cash and stock. Powerwave received RF conditioning products, filters, tower-mounted amplifiers, and RF power amplifiers in the transaction. REMEC holds a 7% equity interest in Powerwave, after receiving $40 million in cash and 10 million shares of Powerwave common stock.

Powerwave has acquired Filtronic's filter-based transmit/receive module and power amplifier businesses. The deal originally called for the company to pay $150 million in cash and issue 20.7 million common shares of stock, but the parties later agreed on a revision of terms, with Filtronic getting more cash ($185 million) and fewer shares of common stock (17.7 million). Filtronic now owns about 11% of Powerwave.

Powerwave sold a plant in the Philippines to Celestica, the giant provider of electronics manufacturing services. The Philippines plant came to Powerwave through its purchase of the REMEC Wireless Systems assets. Celestica paid about $19 million in cash for the plant. Celestica and Powerwave signed a long-term supply agreement as part of the deal; Celestica has been a manufacturing contractor for Powerwave since 2002.

Copper River Management holds around 5% of Powerwave Technologies.

HISTORY

While building ground-to-air base stations for the military, Alfonso Cordero discovered how expensive power amplifiers were. In response, he founded Milcom International in 1985. Through the late 1980s and early 1990s, Milcom developed new lines in two-way radio and multi-carrier amplifiers. In 1995 the company tapped into what would become its primary market — South Korea — by selling amplifiers there for digital cellular networks. Milcom changed its name to Powerwave in 1996, and went public that year.

After a promising start to 1997, the onset of the Asian economic crisis led major customers Hyundai Electronics (now Hynix Semiconductor), LGIC, and Samsung — which collectively had accounted for more than 80% of sales — to slash purchases. Sales dropped in 1998 and Powerwave scrambled for markets outside Asia.

In 1998 it signed a deal with BellSouth, followed by agreements with Ericsson, Northern Telecom (now Nortel Networks), Nokia, and QUALCOMM. That year the company acquired Hewlett-Packard's power amplifier business and its manufacturing facility. In late 1998 Cordero was succeeded as chairman by John Clendenin, who is also chairman emeritus of BellSouth.

Powerwave sold part of its land mobile radio and specialized mobile radio amplifier lines in 1999. The next year the company bought a new facility to consolidate its headquarters with some manufacturing, engineering, and sales operations. In 2001 Powerwave announced an agreement with Motorola to supply the telecom giant with high-powered multi-carrier amplifiers. Late that year Powerwave acquired UK-based telecom system designer Toracomm.

In 2004 Powerwave purchased Sweden's LGP Allgon, a supplier of wireless infrastructure equipment and software. The acquisition also

yielded a contract electronics manufacturing business called Arkivator Falkoping, which produces industrial components for the automotive and food industries, principally in the Nordic countries. Powerwave in early 2005 acquired the assets of Kaval Wireless Technologies, a supplier of RF amplifiers and repeaters for wireless communications networks.

John Clendenin stepped down as chairman in early 2005, while remaining a director of the company. He was succeeded as executive chairman by former CEO Bruce Edwards.

In 2006 Powerwave sold Arkivator Falkoping to IGC Industrial Growth Company for about $27 million in cash. It acquired most of the Wireless Infrastructure division of rival Filtronic for about $296 million in cash and stock, picking up transmit/receive filters, integrated remote radio heads, and power amplifier products.

EXECUTIVES

Chairman: Bruce C. Edwards, age 53
President, CEO, and Director: Ronald J. Buschur, age 42
SVP Finance, CFO, and Secretary: Kevin T. Michaels, age 47
SVP Global Operations: Robert J. Legendre, age 48
VP Global Sales and Marketing: Gregory K. Gaines, age 52
Auditors: Deloitte & Touche LLP

LOCATIONS

HQ: Powerwave Technologies, Inc.
1801 E. St. Andrew Pl., Santa Ana, CA 92705
Phone: 714-466-1000　**Fax:** 714-466-5800
Web: www.powerwave.com

Powerwave Technologies has facilities and offices in Australia, Brazil, Canada, China, Denmark, Estonia, Finland, Germany, Hong Kong, India, Singapore, Sweden, the UK, and the US.

2005 Sales

	$ mil.	% of total
Europe	433.8	53
US	293.1	35
Asia	76.3	9
Other regions	21.9	3
Total	825.1	100

PRODUCTS/OPERATIONS

2005 Sales

	$ mil.	% of total
Wireless communications products	784.3	95
Contract manufacturing	40.8	5
Total	825.1	100

2005 Sales of Products

	$ mil.	% of total
Base station subsystems	457.3	58
Antenna systems	246.2	32
Coverage solutions	80.8	10
Total	784.3	100

Selected Products

Cellular RF power amplifiers (MCA9000-90, PAF, G3S-800)
European RF power amplifiers
　Front end units
　Remote radio units
　900 MHz multi-carrier
　1800 MHz multi-carrier booster
PCS RF power amplifiers (G3S-1900)

COMPETITORS

ADC Telecommunications	InnerWireless
AML	KATHREIN-Werke
Andrew Corporation	Mitsubishi Electric
CalAmp	Motorola
Comtech	Nokia
Ericsson	Nortel Networks
Fujitsu	Radio Frequency Systems
Hitachi	RF Micro Devices
Huawei Technologies	Samsung Electronics

HISTORICAL FINANCIALS

Company Type: Public

Income Statement

FYE: Sunday nearest December 31

	REVENUE ($ mil.)	NET INCOME ($ mil.)	NET PROFIT MARGIN	EMPLOYEES
12/05	825.1	50.7	6.1%	4,795
12/04	473.9	(72.1)	—	1,675
12/03	239.1	(32.9)	—	448
12/02	384.9	4.1	1.1%	1,218
12/01	300.3	(20.5)	—	1,233
Annual Growth	28.7%	—	—	40.4%

2005 Year-End Financials

Debt ratio: 56.8%
Return on equity: 9.2%
Cash ($ mil.): 237.5
Current ratio: 2.79
Long-term debt ($ mil.): 330.0
No. of shares (mil.): 112.1

Dividends
Yield: —
Payout: —
Market value ($ mil.): 1,409.5
R&D as % of sales: 7.4%
Advertising as % of sales: —

Stock History

NASDAQ (GS): PWAV

	STOCK PRICE ($) FY Close	P/E High/Low		PER SHARE ($) Earnings	Dividends	Book Value
12/05	12.57	33	16	0.42	—	5.18
12/04	8.48	—	—	(0.80)	—	5.19
12/03	7.74	—	—	(0.51)	—	4.28
12/02	5.40	346	44	0.06	—	4.94
12/01	17.28	—	—	(0.33)	—	4.86
Annual Growth	(7.6%)	—	—	—	—	1.6%

POZEN

POZEN's migraine treatments are highly diversified. All of the development-stage company's primary product candidates use triptans to target migraine headaches, but use different delivery technologies. The company's lead product candidate, Trexima, is being developed in partnership with GlaxoSmithKline. The drug is based on POZEN's MT 400 technology, which treats migraines through a combination of triptans and an anti-inflammatory drug (NSAID). The company's PN line of drug candidates combines an acid inhibitor as well as NSAIDs in a single tablet. POZEN is hoping the drugs will treat pain but cause fewer gastrointestinal side effects.

Chairman and CEO John Plachetka owns about 15% of POZEN.

POZEN's previous candidate, MT 100, was designed to treat migraine sufferers less susceptible to nausea, but it was shown to have a risk of causing involuntary tongue and mouth movements. The FDA rejected the drug in 2004, and the company stopped developing the drug the next year. However, in late 2005 it was approved in the UK for the treatment of migraines.

In 2006 AstraZeneca agreed to pay up to $375 million for POZEN's collaboration on the development of a drug addressing chronic pain. The intended drug will combine POZEN's nonsteroidal anti-inflammatory drug naproxen with esomeprazole magnesium, the active ingredient in one of AstraZeneca's heartburn medications. The idea is to combine pain relief with a lowered risk of ulcers and gastro-intolerance.

EXECUTIVES

Chairman, President, and CEO: John R. Plachetka, age 52, $671,395 pay
Vice Chairman: Peter J. Wise, age 71
EVP, Product Development: Marshall E. Reese, age 60, $408,597 pay
SVP, Finance and Administration and CFO:
William L. (Bill) Hodges, age 51, $330,808 pay
SVP, Business Development: Kristina M. Adomonis, age 51, $295,215 pay
SVP and General Counsel: Gilda M. Thomas
VP, Biostatistics and Data Management: Elly Savaluny
VP, Clinical Research: Everardus Orlemans
VP, Finance and Administration: John E. Barnhardt, age 56
Director, Investor Relations: Frances (Fran) Barsky
Auditors: Ernst & Young LLP

LOCATIONS

HQ: POZEN Inc.
1414 Raleigh Rd., Ste. 400, Chapel Hill, NC 27517
Phone: 919-913-1030 **Fax:** 919-913-1039
Web: www.pozen.com

COMPETITORS

Abbott Labs
AstraZeneca
Bristol-Myers Squibb
DRAXIS
Endo Pharmaceuticals
GlaxoSmithKline
Indevus Pharmaceuticals
Johnson & Johnson
Lannett Company
Merck
Pfizer
Spectrum Pharmaceuticals

HISTORICAL FINANCIALS

Company Type: Public

Income Statement

FYE: December 31

	REVENUE ($ mil.)	NET INCOME ($ mil.)	NET PROFIT MARGIN	EMPLOYEES
12/05	28.6	2.0	7.0%	35
12/04	23.1	(5.3)	—	38
12/03	3.7	(14.9)	—	30
Annual Growth	178.0%	—	—	8.0%

2005 Year-End Financials

Debt ratio: —
Return on equity: 6.1%
Cash ($ mil.): 45.8
Current ratio: 3.94
Long-term debt ($ mil.): —
No. of shares (mil.): 29.0

Dividends
Yield: —
Payout: —
Market value ($ mil.): 278.1
R&D as % of sales: —
Advertising as % of sales: —

Stock History

NASDAQ (GM): POZN

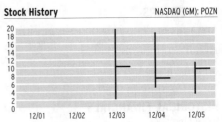

	STOCK PRICE ($) FY Close	P/E High/Low		PER SHARE ($) Earnings	Dividends	Book Value
12/05	9.59	158	50	0.07	—	1.17
12/04	7.27	—	—	(0.18)	—	1.10
12/03	10.20	—	—	(0.52)	—	1.25
Annual Growth	(3.0%)	—	—	—	—	(3.3%)

PremierWest Bancorp

PremierWest Bancorp strives to be the *principal* lending institution on the West Coast. The firm is the holding company for PremierWest Bank, which operates more than 40 branches generally located along the Interstate 5 corridor in southern Oregon and northern California. The community bank serves local businesses and consumers, using funds from deposit accounts mainly to originate loans secured by commercial and residential real estate. Bank subsidiary PremierWest Investment Services provides insurance and investment products. Consumer lender Premier Finance Company is another subsidiary of the bank; mortgage service provider PremierWest Mortgage is a division of the bank.

PremierWest Bancorp bought northern California-based Mid Valley Bank in 2004.

Chairman John Duke and his wife Marilyn own more than 5% of PremierWest Bancorp's common stock through the John A. Duke and Marilyn R. Duke Charitable Lead Annuity Trust.

EXECUTIVES

Chairman: John A. Duke, age 67
Vice Chairman: Patrick G. Huycke, age 56
CEO and Director; CEO, PremierWest Bank:
John L. Anhorn, age 63, $375,000 pay
(prior to title change)
President and Director; President, PremierWest Bank:
James M. (Jim) Ford, age 49
SEVP, COO, Secretary, and Director; EVP and COO, PremierWest Bank: Richard R. (Rich) Hieb, age 61, $265,000 pay
EVP and CFO, PremierWest Bancorp and PremierWest Bank: Tom D. Anderson, age 55, $170,000 pay
EVP and Credit Administrator, PremierWest Bank:
James V. (Jim) Earley, age 51, $160,000 pay
EVP and Branch Administration, PremierWest Bank:
Robert (Bob) DuMilieu, age 57, $127,000 pay
VP and Human Resources Director, PremierWest Bank:
Carrie Brownell
VP and Marketing Director, PremierWest Bancorp and PremierWest Bank: Jim Essany
Auditors: Moss Adams, LLP

LOCATIONS

HQ: PremierWest Bancorp
   503 Airport Rd., Medford, OR 97504
Phone: 541-618-6003   **Fax:** 541-618-6001
Web: www.premierwestbank.com

PRODUCTS/OPERATIONS

2005 Sales

	$ mil.	% of total
Interest		
Loans	56.7	88
Securities & other	0.8	1
Noninterest		
Service charges on deposits	2.7	4
Mortgage banking fees	1.4	2
Investment brokerage & annuity fees	1.3	2
Other fees	1.4	2
Other	0.6	1
Total	**64.9**	**100**

COMPETITORS

Bank of America
Community Valley Bancorp
KeyCorp
Scott Valley Bank
Umpqua Holdings
U.S. Bancorp
Washington Mutual
Wells Fargo

HISTORICAL FINANCIALS

Company Type: Public

Income Statement

FYE: December 31

	ASSETS ($ mil.)	NET INCOME ($ mil.)	INCOME AS % OF ASSETS	EMPLOYEES
12/05	913.7	13.2	1.4%	422
12/04	804.4	9.1	1.1%	398
12/03	571.3	6.0	1.1%	280
12/02	515.1	4.3	0.8%	288
12/01	488.3	2.0	0.4%	278
Annual Growth	17.0%	60.3%	—	11.0%

2005 Year-End Financials

Equity as % of assets: 10.2%
Return on assets: 1.5%
Return on equity: 15.2%
Long-term debt ($ mil.): 15.5
No. of shares (mil.): 15.4
Market value ($ mil.): 205.0
Dividends
   Yield: —
   Payout: —
Sales ($ mil.): 64.9
R&D as % of sales: —
Advertising as % of sales: 1.5%

Stock History

NASDAQ (CM): PRWT

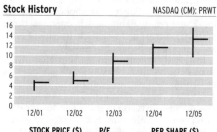

	STOCK PRICE ($) FY Close	P/E High/Low	PER SHARE ($) Earnings	Dividends	Book Value
12/05	13.33	22 14	0.71	—	6.69
12/04	11.64	22 14	0.55	—	6.20
12/03	8.85	24 11	0.42	—	5.33
12/02	4.94	22 14	0.30	—	4.25
12/01	4.54	31 19	0.16	—	4.02
Annual Growth	30.9%	— —	45.1%	—	13.5%

Presstek

Image is everything at Presstek. The company combines state-of-the-art printing-press and computer technologies in its PEARL direct imaging (DI) systems. These systems produce color printing plates and non-photosensitive films and also transfer images from computer to press. The PEARLdry process results in high-resolution plates without chemical processing or hazardous by-products. Presstek markets its products through 30 graphic arts dealers worldwide. Presstek's Lasertel subsidiary provides laser diodes crucial to the design of the company's DI systems, and supplies the optoelectronic parts to other customers. The company has more than 20,000 customers worldwide.

Printing press maker Heidelberger Druckmaschinen AG is Presstek's major customer.

Following a chemical-spill incident at a manufacturing facility in South Hadley, Massachusetts, that triggered an evacuation of nearby homes and closing of the local schools for one day since school buses could not pass by the affected plant, Presstek decided in late 2006 to discontinue manufacturing of its Precision analog newspaper plates. The business accounted for nearly 5% of sales. The company said it would help customers for the analog plate business make the transition to other vendors. Presstek continues to make digital plate products at a separate but adjacent facility in South Hadley.

The investment firm of Spear, Leeds & Kellogg owns nearly 17% of Presstek.

HISTORY

Robert and Lawrence Howard founded Presstek in 1987. Prior to launching Presstek, Robert had founded Howtek (electronic prepress equipment) and Centronics Data Computer Corporation (printers). He also invented the first impact dot matrix printer. Robert took Presstek public in 1989.

Presstek signed a licensing agreement with Heidelberger Druckmaschinen (the world's largest printing-press manufacturer) in 1991 and launched its PEARL thermal printing plate in 1993.

In 1996 Presstek acquired Catalina Coatings, a maker of digital-imaging and printing-plate equipment and systems. That year the company won a patent dispute against Agfa Gevaert. Presstek announced an agreement to cross-license certain printing technologies with rival Scitex Corporation in 1997. Presstek also agreed to collaborate with Fuji Photo in the development of printing products. Presstek, Robert Howard, and the company's president that year settled an SEC investigation into allegedly fraudulent company statements. The deal included $2.9 million in fines with no admission of wrongdoing.

Presstek acquired custom printing-press designer and manufacturer Heath Custom Press in 1998. The company recorded a loss that year in part because of acquisition costs, lower sales to Heidelberger (a primary customer for the direct-imaging systems), and increased costs for raw materials, labor, and overhead. In 1999 CEO Robert Hallman replaced Robert Varrando as president.

Presstek established subsidiary Lasertel in 2000 in order to secure a steady supply of laser diodes for manufacturing its imaging systems.

The Presstek board voted to remove Robert Hallman as CEO in 2002, and replaced him with Edward Marino, who had been on the board since 1999.

In 2004 the company acquired printing plate maker Precision Lithograining and printer A.B. Dick Company.

In 2005 Presstek announced plans to dissolve the operations of its ABD International subsidiary, which was formed when A.B. Dick was acquired. The A.B. Dick business was absorbed into the company's Presstek business segment.

EXECUTIVES

Chairman: John W. Dreyer, age 67
President, CEO, and Director: Edward J. (Ed) Marino, age 55, $504,046 pay
EVP, Finance and CFO: Moosa E. Moosa, age 48, $296,730 pay
CIO: Ronald T. (Ron) Cardone, age 50
VP, Human Resources: Cathleen V. Cavanna
VP, Manufacturing: Stephen G. Degon
VP, Marketing: Peter A. Bouchard, age 42
VP and Chief Technologist: Eugene L. Langlais III, age 61
VP, Presstek North American Service: Joesph (Joe) Musgrave, age 44
VP, Presstek North American Sales: Emile Tabassi, age 55
VP, Business Development: William T. Davison
President, Lasertel: Mark McElhinney, age 39
Managing Director, Presstek Europe: Quentin C. (Quen) Baum, age 51
Manager, Corporate Relations: Jane Miller
Chief Marketing Officer: Todd Chambers
Auditors: BDO Seidman, LLP

LOCATIONS

HQ: Presstek, Inc.
   55 Executive Dr., Hudson, NH 03051
Phone: 603-595-7000   **Fax:** 603-595-2602
Web: www.presstek.com

Presstek has facilities in Canada, the UK, and the US.

2005 Sales

	$ mil.	% of total
US	170.5	62
UK	34.8	13
Canada	15.0	5
Germany	13.2	5
Japan	8.5	3
Other countries	32.1	12
Total	**274.1**	**100**

PRODUCTS/OPERATIONS

2005 Sales

	$ mil.	% of total
Presstek	255.3	88
Precision	25.2	9
Lasertel	7.8	3
Adjustments	(14.2)	—
Total	**274.1**	**100**

Selected Subsidiaries

A.B. Dick of UK Limited
ABD Canada Holdings, Inc.
HIC, Inc.
Lasertel, Inc.
Precision Acquisition Corp.
Precision Lithograining Corporation
R/H Acquisition Corporation
SDK Realty Corp.

COMPETITORS

Agfa	Intergraph
Baldwin Technology	JDS Uniphase
Canon	Linotype-Hell
Coherent	MAN Roland
Dainippon Screen	Pitman Company
DuPont	Polaroid
Eastman Kodak	Ricoh
ECRM	Ryobi
FUJIFILM	Sony
Gerber Scientific	Toray
Heidelberg	Xerox
Hewlett-Packard	xpedx

HISTORICAL FINANCIALS

Company Type: Public

Income Statement				FYE: Saturday nearest December 31
	REVENUE ($ mil.)	NET INCOME ($ mil.)	NET PROFIT MARGIN	EMPLOYEES
12/05	274.1	6.1	2.2%	971
12/04	129.9	3.9	3.0%	1,089
12/03	87.2	8.1	9.3%	230
12/02	83.4	(8.3)	—	262
12/01	102.3	(3.8)	—	313
Annual Growth	27.9%	—	—	32.7%

2005 Year-End Financials

Debt ratio: 22.9%	Dividends
Return on equity: 6.5%	Yield: —
Cash ($ mil.): 5.6	Payout: —
Current ratio: 1.69	Market value ($ mil.): 319.7
Long-term debt ($ mil.): 22.6	R&D as % of sales: 2.7%
No. of shares (mil.): 35.4	Advertising as % of sales: —

Stock History

NASDAQ (GS): PRST

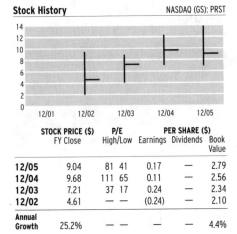

	STOCK PRICE ($) FY Close	P/E High/Low		PER SHARE ($) Earnings	Dividends	Book Value
12/05	9.04	81	41	0.17	—	2.79
12/04	9.68	111	65	0.11	—	2.56
12/03	7.21	37	17	0.24	—	2.34
12/02	4.61	—	—	(0.24)	—	2.10
Annual Growth	25.2%	—	—	—	—	4.4%

Prestige Brands

Prestige Brands is a lifesaver. Its business is resuscitating offloaded consumer products brands. The firm develops and markets over-the-counter drugs, household cleaning products, and personal care items. Prestige Brands' portfolio includes Chloraseptic, Clear Eyes, Comet, Compound W, Cutex, Denorex, Dermoplast, Murine, New-Skin, Prell, Spic and Span, and others. The company was formed in 1996 to acquire and revitalize leading but neglected consumer brands divested by major consumer companies, such as Procter & Gamble. Former shareholder MidOcean Partners sold the portfolio company to GTCR Golder

Rauner for $500 million in early 2004. GTCR controls 30% following Prestige's 2005 IPO.

Already pieced together from the parts of defunct Medtech, which offered Denorex shampoos and Cutex nail polish removers; The Spic & Span Company; and Prestige Brands International, which offered Comet cleaners and Clear Eyes eye drops, Prestige Brands has been trying to find that magic mix of products to offer. It acquired Vetco, which offered children's cold remedies Little Noses, Little Tummy's, and Little Colds, in 2004.

The next year it expanded its cleaning products line through the acquisition of Chore Boy from UK-based Reckitt Benckiser, and it acquired oral care products maker Dental Concepts from Hamilton Investment Partners.

In 2006 Prestige announced it would buy the Wartner line of wart-treatment products from Lil' Drug Store of Cedar Rapids, Iowa, for $31 million.

EXECUTIVES

Chairman and Interim President and CEO: Peter C. Mann, age 64, $442,000 pay
CFO: Peter J. Anderson, age 51, $309,000 pay
SVP, Marketing, OTC/Personal Care: Michael A. Fink, age 61
SVP, Marketing, Household: Charles Schrank, age 56
SVP, Operations: Eric M. Millar, age 62
Chief Sales Officer: Gerard F. Butler, age 57, $236,000 pay
General Counsel and Secretary: Charles N. Jolly, age 63, $215,000 pay
Auditors: PricewaterhouseCoopers LLP

LOCATIONS

HQ: Prestige Brands Holdings, Inc.
90 N. Broadway, Irvington, NY 10533
Phone: 914-524-6810   **Fax:** 914-524-6815
Web: www.prestigebrands.com

PRODUCTS/OPERATIONS

2006 Sales

	$ mil.	% of total
Over-the-counter drugs	161.0	54
Household products	107.8	36
Personal care products	27.9	10
Total	**296.7**	**100**

COMPETITORS

3M	Orange Glo
Chattem	Pfizer
Clorox	Procter & Gamble
Colgate-Palmolive	Reckitt Benckiser
Del Labs	Sally Beauty
GlaxoSmithKline	Schering-Plough
Henkel Corp.	Unilever
Johnson & Johnson	

HISTORICAL FINANCIALS

Company Type: Public

Income Statement				FYE: March 31
	REVENUE ($ mil.)	NET INCOME ($ mil.)	NET PROFIT MARGIN	EMPLOYEES
3/06	296.7	26.3	8.9%	—
3/05	303.3	13.5	4.5%	75
3/04	87.9	4.2	4.8%	73
3/03	76.4	(14.4)	—	50
3/02	46.2	0.6	1.3%	25
Annual Growth	59.2%	157.3%	—	44.2%

2006 Year-End Financials

Debt ratio: 120.9%	Dividends
Return on equity: 6.6%	Yield: —
Cash ($ mil.): 8.2	Payout: —
Current ratio: 2.41	Market value ($ mil.): 609.0
Long-term debt ($ mil.): 494.9	R&D as % of sales: —
No. of shares (mil.): 50.0	Advertising as % of sales: —

Stock History

NYSE: PBH

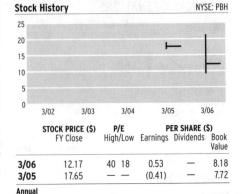

	STOCK PRICE ($) FY Close	P/E High/Low		PER SHARE ($) Earnings	Dividends	Book Value
3/06	12.17	40	18	0.53	—	8.18
3/05	17.65	—	—	(0.41)	—	7.72
Annual Growth	(31.0%)	—	—	—	—	6.0%

PrivateBancorp

It's your private banker, a banker for money, and any old teller won't do. PrivateBancorp's PrivateBank subsidiaries provide customized banking and asset management services to affluent individuals, owners of closely-held businesses, and commercial real estate investors through about a dozen offices in Chicago and its affluent suburbs, as well as in the Detroit, Milwaukee, and St. Louis metropolitan areas. It's modeled after a traditional European private bank, placing emphasis on personal service. PrivateBancorp lends mainly to businesses: Commercial mortgages account for nearly half of its loan portfolio; business operating loans add about 15%. It also writes residential, consumer, and construction loans.

PrivateBancorp expanded into the affluent Detroit communities of Bloomfield Hills, Grosse Point, and Rochester with its 2005 acquisition of Bloomfield Hills Bancorp, the holding company for The Private Bank, which operates three branches, a trust and wealth management unit, and a mortgage banking subsidiary.

In 2006 the company acquired Piedmont Bancshares, the holding company for Piedmont Bank of Georgia, whose two branches in the Atlanta area have been renamed The PrivateBank. PrivateBancorp is also opening a de novo branch in Kansas City, Missouri, and is considering expansion into selected sunbelt cities in Arizona and Florida.

EXECUTIVES

Chairman, President, and CEO, PrivateBancorp and PrivateBank: Ralph B. Mandell, age 65, $1,185,000 pay
Co-Vice Chairman and Managing Director, PrivateBank: Gary S. Collins, age 47, $495,000 pay
Co-Vice Chairman and Managing Director, PrivateBank: Hugh H. McLean, age 47, $495,000 pay
CFO and Secretary; CFO and Managing Director, PrivateBank: Dennis L. Klaeser, age 48, $495,000 pay
Director; Chairman, CEO, and Managing Director, PrivateBank (St. Louis); Managing Director, PrivateBank: Richard C. Jensen, age 60

Director; Chairman and CEO, PrivateBank
(Milwaukee): John B. (Jay) Williams, age 54
Chairman and CEO, PrivateBank (Michigan):
David T. Provost, age 52
President and COO, PrivateBank (St. Louis):
Allan D. Ivie IV, age 38
President and COO, PrivateBank (Michigan):
Patrick McQueen
General Counsel: Christopher J. Zinski, age 44
Chief Marketing Officer; Managing Director and
Director of Marketing, PrivateBank:
Thomas N. (Tom) Castronovo, age 46
Managing Director and Director; President and CEO,
Lodestar Investment Counsel: William A. Goldstein,
age 66, $665,862 pay
Auditors: Ernst & Young LLP

LOCATIONS

HQ: PrivateBancorp, Inc.
10 N. Dearborn St., 900, Chicago, IL 60602
Phone: 312-683-7100   Fax: 312-683-7111
Web: www.privatebancorp.com

PRODUCTS/OPERATIONS

2005 Sales

	$ mil.	% of total
Interest		
Loans	139.6	71
Securities & other	36.8	19
Noninterest		
Wealth management	9.9	5
Other	9.1	5
Total	**195.4**	**100**

Select Subsidiaries

Bloomfield Hills Statutory Trust I
Lodestar Investment Counsel, LLC
Private Investment Limited Partnership I
PrivateBancorp Statutory Trust II
PrivateBancorp Statutory Trust III
The PrivateBank
The PrivateBank and Trust Company
The PrivateBank Michigan
The PrivateBank Mortgage Company, LLC
TrustCo, Company

COMPETITORS

CFS Bancorp
Citizens Republic Bancorp
First Midwest Bancorp
Harris Bankcorp
MAF Bancorp
MB Financial
Northern Trust
Park Bancorp
Wintrust Financial

HISTORICAL FINANCIALS

Company Type: Public

Income Statement

FYE: December 31

	ASSETS ($ mil.)	NET INCOME ($ mil.)	INCOME AS % OF ASSETS	EMPLOYEES
12/05	3,494.2	33.4	1.0%	386
12/04	2,535.8	27.0	1.1%	261
12/03	1,984.9	19.1	1.0%	219
12/02	1,543.4	11.0	0.7%	190
12/01	1,176.8	6.2	0.5%	160
Annual Growth	**31.3%**	**52.3%**	**—**	**24.6%**

2005 Year-End Financials

Equity as % of assets: 6.7%
Return on assets: 1.1%
Return on equity: 15.5%
Long-term debt ($ mil.): 395.0
No. of shares (mil.): 21.0
Market value ($ mil.): 746.4
Dividends
  Yield: 0.5%
  Payout: 11.4%
Sales ($ mil.): 195.4
R&D as % of sales: —
Advertising as % of sales: —

Stock History

NASDAQ (GS): PVTB

	STOCK PRICE ($) FY Close	P/E High/Low		PER SHARE ($) Earnings	Dividends	Book Value
12/05	35.57	24	19	1.58	0.18	11.22
12/04	32.23	27	16	1.30	0.15	9.51
12/03	22.65	22	10	1.06	0.08	16.94
12/02	12.62	19	9	0.71	0.05	11.56
12/01	6.54	16	7	0.43	0.04	12.97
Annual Growth	**52.7%**	**—**	**—**	**38.5%**	**45.6%**	**(3.5%)**

Prosperity Bancshares

Feeling prosperous? Prosperity Bancshares wants to help you manage your riches. The company operates some 85 Prosperity Bank branches in and around major Texas cities. The bank offers traditional deposit account and cash management services. Commercial real estate loans make up the largest segment of a portfolio that also includes residential mortgage, construction, home equity, business, and agricultural loans. The acquisitive company has been buying up small banks in Texas. Its latest target is Texas United Bancshares; SNB Bancshares, located in the southern part of the state, was acquired earlier in 2006.

Prosperity Bancshares' 2005 purchases of FirstCapital Bankers and Grapeland Bancshares also expanded its presence in South Texas.

All told, the company has bought more than 15 banks since 2000.

EXECUTIVES

Chairman and CEO: David Zalman, age 49
Vice Chairman and COO: H. E. (Tim) Timanus Jr.,
age 61
Vice Chairman: D. Michael (Mike) Hunter, age 63
President, COO, and Director:
James D. (Dan) Rollins III, age 47
CFO; EVP and CFO, Prosperity Bank: David Hollaway,
age 50, $312,200 pay
Chairman, Austin Area Banking Centers:
Edward Z. (Eddie) Safady
Chairman, Houston Area: Harvey E. Zinn, age 57
Chairman, South Texas Area Banking Centers:
Steve Hipes
President, South Texas Area Banking Centers:
Bob Kuhn
President, Waugh Drive Banking Center and Chief
Credit Officer, Prosperity Bank: Chris Bagley
General Counsel; Vice Chairman and General Counsel,
Prosperity Bank: Peter E. Fisher, age 59, $255,500 pay
Auditors: Deloitte & Touche LLP

LOCATIONS

HQ: Prosperity Bancshares, Inc.
4295 San Felipe, Houston, TX 77027
Phone: 713-693-9300   Fax: 713-693-9360
Web: www.prosperitybanktx.com

PRODUCTS/OPERATIONS

2005 Sales

	$ mil.	% of total
Interest		
Loans, including fees	99.9	52
Securities	60.9	32
Other	1.4	—
Noninterest		
Service charges on deposit accounts	25.0	13
Other	5.0	3
Total	**192.2**	**100**

Selected Subsidiaries

MainCorp Leasing Co.
Prosperity Bank
Prosperity Holdings of Delaware, LLC
Prosperity Interim Corporation

COMPETITORS

Amegy Corporation
Bank of America
Compass Bancshares
Cullen/Frost Bankers
JPMorgan Chase
Sterling Bancshares
Wells Fargo

HISTORICAL FINANCIALS

Company Type: Public

Income Statement

FYE: December 31

	ASSETS ($ mil.)	NET INCOME ($ mil.)	INCOME AS % OF ASSETS	EMPLOYEES
12/05	3,586.0	47.9	1.3%	859
12/04	2,697.2	34.7	1.3%	653
12/03	2,398.7	26.5	1.1%	629
12/02	1,822.3	21.3	1.2%	457
12/01	1,262.3	13.0	1.0%	312
Annual Growth	**29.8%**	**38.5%**	**—**	**28.8%**

2005 Year-End Financials

Equity as % of assets: 13.0%
Return on assets: 1.5%
Return on equity: 12.9%
Long-term debt ($ mil.): 131.2
No. of shares (mil.): 27.8
Market value ($ mil.): 799.6
Dividends
  Yield: 1.2%
  Payout: 19.8%
Sales ($ mil.): 192.2
R&D as % of sales: —
Advertising as % of sales: —

Stock History

NASDAQ (GS): PRSP

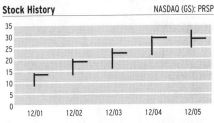

	STOCK PRICE ($) FY Close	P/E High/Low		PER SHARE ($) Earnings	Dividends	Book Value
12/05	28.74	18	14	1.77	0.35	16.70
12/04	29.21	19	14	1.59	0.31	12.32
12/03	22.64	18	12	1.36	0.25	10.49
12/02	19.00	16	11	1.22	0.22	8.19
12/01	13.49	18	11	0.79	0.19	10.95
Annual Growth	**20.8%**	**—**	**—**	**22.3%**	**16.5%**	**11.1%**

Providence Service

Providence Service Corporation contracts with state and local government agencies to manage social service programs in more than 30 states and Washington, DC. The company provides behavioral health and counseling services to individuals, families, and at-risk students. Providence Service Corporation is able to save its government clients money by providing care at the patient's home or school. The company also licenses family foster homes, recruits and trains prospective foster parents, and provides behavioral health services to foster children. In addition, Providence Service Corporation offers case management, benefit screening, and monitoring services.

Providence Service Corporation's Home and Community Based Services segment (behavioral health services) generates more than 70% of the company's revenue.

The company has been growing through expanding its services and strategically acquiring businesses in new markets. With the acquisition of Maple Star Nevada and Maple Services LLC in 2005, Providence Service expanded into Colorado, Nevada, and Oregon. In 2006 the company purchased A to Z In-Home Tutoring. It has also acquired the Correctional Services Business of MAXIMUS; the unit provides privatized probation services in five states.

EXECUTIVES

Chairman and CEO: Fletcher Jay McCusker, age 56, $210,000 pay
COO: Craig A. Norris, age 38, $195,833 pay
EVP and General Counsel: Fred D. Furman, age 57, $195,000 pay (prior to title change)
VP, CFO, Secretary, and Treasurer: Michael N. Deitch, age 49, $179,167 pay
VP, Development: Lisa Tackus
Chief Development Officer: Martin James Favis, age 46
CIO: Mike Hill
Director, Corporate Communications: Michelle Pitot
Director, Human Resources: Janet McGee
Director, Investor and Public Relations: Kate Blute
Auditors: McGladrey & Pullen, LLP

LOCATIONS

HQ: The Providence Service Corporation
5524 E. 4th St., Tucson, AZ 85711
Phone: 520-747-6600   **Fax:** 520-747-6605
Web: www.provcorp.com

Providence Service Corporation has operations throughout the US.

PRODUCTS/OPERATIONS

2005 Sales

	$ mil.	% of total
Home & community based services	115.5	79
Foster care services	15.8	11
Management fees	14.4	10
Total	**145.7**	**100**

COMPETITORS

Cornell Companies
MAXIMUS
Premier Behavioral Solutions
Psychiatric Solutions
Res-Care
Salvation Army

HISTORICAL FINANCIALS
Company Type: Public

Income Statement
FYE: December 31

	REVENUE ($ mil.)	NET INCOME ($ mil.)	NET PROFIT MARGIN	EMPLOYEES
12/05	145.7	9.4	6.5%	4,930
12/04	97.0	7.1	7.3%	3,583
12/03	59.3	2.7	4.6%	1,721
12/02*	41.8	(3.9)	—	1,158
6/02	32.8	1.3	4.0%	—
Annual Growth	**45.2%**	**64.0%**	**—**	**62.1%**

*Fiscal year change

2005 Year-End Financials

Debt ratio: 17.5%
Return on equity: 12.9%
Cash ($ mil.): 10.9
Current ratio: 2.56
Long-term debt ($ mil.): 14.2
No. of shares (mil.): 9.8
Dividends
  Yield: —
  Payout: —
Market value ($ mil.): 282.8
R&D as % of sales: —
Advertising as % of sales: —

Stock History
NASDAQ (GS): PRSC

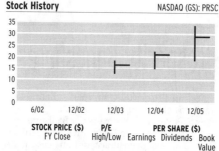

	STOCK PRICE ($) FY Close	P/E High/Low		PER SHARE ($) Earnings	Dividends	Book Value
12/05	28.79	35	20	0.95	—	8.27
12/04	20.98	29	20	0.76	—	6.81
12/03	16.33	—	—	(0.25)	—	5.24
Annual Growth	**32.8%**	**—**	**—**	**—**	**—**	**25.6%**

Provident New York Bancorp

Provident New York Bancorp is the holding company for Provident Bank, a community-based thrift operating more than 30 offices in New York's Hudson Valley region and another in New Jersey operating as Towncenter Bank. Founded in 1888, the bank attracts consumers and business clients by offering traditional deposit products such as checking and savings accounts and CDs; its Provident Municipal Bank subsidiary provides deposit services to area municipalities. The bank uses funds from deposits to originate a variety of loans. Commercial mortgages and operating loans make up slightly more than half of the bank's lending portfolio; residential mortgages represent another third.

The company also offers mutual funds and trust and investment management services; to build this business, it bought Hudson Valley Investment Advisors in 2006.

Provident Bank was mutually owned until 2004 when the company converted to stock ownership. In a simultaneous transaction, Provident New York Bancorp acquired E.N.B. Holding Company, which owned Ellenville National Bank and its nine branches. Also that year the company acquired Warwick Community Bancorp, which operated in New York and New Jersey.

Provident New York Bancorp is increasingly focused on commercial lending.

EXECUTIVES

Chairman: William F. Helmer, age 71
Vice Chairman: Dennis L. Coyle, age 69
President, CEO, and Director; President and CEO, Provident Bank: George Strayton, age 62, $520,415 pay
EVP, Chief Risk Management Officer, Regulatory Counsel, and Corporate Secretary: Daniel G. Rothstein, age 58, $250,973 pay
EVP: Stephen G. Dormer Sr., age 55, $216,085 pay
EVP, Business Services, Provident New York Bancorp and Provident Bank: Richard O. Jones, age 56
SVP and CFO: Paul A. Maisch, age 50, $1,411,546 pay
SVP and Director of Support Services: John F. Fitzpatrick, age 52
SVP and Chief Auditor: Alfred E. Friedman
SVP and Chief Credit Officer: John Carothers
SVP and Commercial Lending Manager: Carl Capuano
VP and Legal Counsel: Katherine B. Brown
VP and Human Resources Manager: Angelo Agrafiotis

LOCATIONS

HQ: Provident New York Bancorp
400 Rella Blvd., Montebello, NY 10901
Phone: 845-369-8040   **Fax:** 845-369-8255
Web: www.providentbanking.com

Provident Bank has branches in New York's Orange, Putnam, Rockland, Sullivan, and Ulster counties and New Jersey's Bergen County.

PRODUCTS/OPERATIONS

2006 Sales

	$ mil.	% of total
Interest		
Loans, including fees	95.5	63
Securities	38.6	25
Other	1.5	1
Noninterest		
Deposit fees & service charges	10.7	7
Other	6.5	4
Total	**152.8**	**63**

Selected Subsidiaries

Hardenburgh Abstract Company of Orange County, Inc.
Hudson Valley Investment Advisors, LLC
Provident Bank
  Provident Municipal Bank
Provident REIT, Inc. (real estate investment trust)

COMPETITORS

Capital One
Citibank
HSBC USA
JPMorgan Chase
M&T Bank
Pamrapo Bancorp
U.S.B.

HISTORICAL FINANCIALS
Company Type: Public

Income Statement
FYE: September 30

	ASSETS ($ mil.)	NET INCOME ($ mil.)	INCOME AS % OF ASSETS	EMPLOYEES
9/06	2,841.3	20.2	0.7%	566
9/05	2,597.4	21.2	0.8%	567
9/04	1,826.2	11.0	0.6%	452
9/03	1,174.3	11.3	1.0%	332
9/02	1,027.7	9.5	0.9%	292
Annual Growth	**28.9%**	**20.8%**	**—**	**18.0%**

2006 Year-End Financials

Equity as % of assets: 14.3%	Dividends	
Return on assets: 0.7%	Yield: 1.5%	
Return on equity: 5.0%	Payout: 40.8%	
Long-term debt ($ mil.): 4.6	Sales ($ mil.): 152.8	
No. of shares (mil.): 42.7	R&D as % of sales: —	
Market value ($ mil.): 584.1	Advertising as % of sales: —	

Stock History   NASDAQ (GS): PBNY

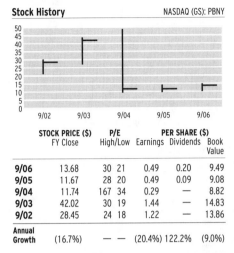

	STOCK PRICE ($) FY Close	P/E High/Low		PER SHARE ($) Earnings	Dividends	Book Value
9/06	13.68	30	21	0.49	0.20	9.49
9/05	11.67	28	20	0.49	0.09	9.08
9/04	11.74	167	34	0.29	—	8.82
9/03	42.02	30	19	1.44	—	14.83
9/02	28.45	24	18	1.22	—	13.86
Annual Growth	(16.7%)	—	—	(20.4%)	122.2%	(9.0%)

PSB Holdings

PSB Holdings thinks it offers Pretty Smart Banking for the businesses and individuals of Connecticut's Windham and New London counties. The holding company owns Putnam Savings Bank, a thrift with about a half-dozen banking locations. The bank offers standard deposit products and services, including checking and savings accounts, merchant and check cards, CDs, and IRAs. It largely uses funds from deposits to write real estate loans: Residential mortgages account for more than 70% of the company's loan portfolio; commercial mortgages account for nearly 25%. Mutual holding company Putnam Bancorp owns about 55% of PSB Holdings.

EXECUTIVES

Chairman and CEO: Thomas A. Borner, age 52, $78,368 pay

President, CFO, and Director; President, Putnam Savings Bank: Robert J. Halloran Jr., age 52, $117,945 pay

SVP, Senior Operations Manager, and Compliance Officer, Putnam Savings Bank: John T. Knierim

SVP and Senior Retail Loan Officer, Putnam Savings Bank: John F. LaFountain

SVP and Senior Commercial Loan Officer, Putnam Savings Bank: Anthony J. (Tony) Serio

SVP and Branch Administrator, Putnam Savings Bank: Lynn K. Brodeur

VP and Loan Officer, Putnam Savings Bank: LeeAnn C. Kieltyka

VP and Controller: Sandra J. (Sandy) Maciag

Assistant VP and Human Resources Officer, Putnam Savings Bank: Barbara A. Elliott

Corporate Secretary, Putnam Savings Bank: Barbara L. McGarry

Auditors: Snyder & Haller, PC

LOCATIONS

HQ: PSB Holdings, Inc.
40 Main St., Putnam, CT 06260
Phone: 860-928-6501   **Fax:** 860-928-2147
Web: www.putnamsavings.com

PRODUCTS/OPERATIONS

2006 Sales

	$ mil.	% of total
Interest		
Loans	10.9	50
Investments	8.5	39
Noninterest		
Service fees	1.7	8
Other	0.8	3
Total	**21.9**	**100**

COMPETITORS

Bank of America
Citizens Financial Group
Liberty Bank
NewAlliance Bancshares
People's Bank
SI Financial
TD Banknorth
Webster Financial

HISTORICAL FINANCIALS

Company Type: Public

Income Statement   FYE: June 30

	ASSETS ($ mil.)	NET INCOME ($ mil.)	INCOME AS % OF ASSETS	EMPLOYEES
6/06	474.4	2.1	0.4%	116
6/05	337.6	1.3	0.4%	91
6/04	279.1	1.5	0.5%	—
Annual Growth	30.4%	18.3%	—	27.5%

2006 Year-End Financials

Equity as % of assets: 10.3%	Dividends	
Return on assets: 0.5%	Yield: 2.1%	
Return on equity: 4.1%	Payout: 73.3%	
Long-term debt ($ mil.): 125.7	Sales ($ mil.): 21.9	
No. of shares (mil.): 6.8	R&D as % of sales: —	
Market value ($ mil.): 72.4	Advertising as % of sales: —	

Stock History   NASDAQ (GM): PSBH

	STOCK PRICE ($) FY Close	P/E High/Low		PER SHARE ($) Earnings	Dividends	Book Value
6/06	10.63	38	33	0.30	0.22	7.18
6/05	10.25	—	—	—	0.10	7.64
Annual Growth	3.7%	—	—	—	120.0%	(5.9%)

Psychiatric Solutions

Psychiatric Solutions has been all topsy-turvy. Traditionally an administrator of outpatient programs for people with serious mental disorders, the company changed its focus and now provides a wide range of behavioral health services to children, adolescents, and adults in an inpatient hospital environment. Psychiatric Solutions, Inc. (PSI) owns and operates some 60 psychiatric hospitals (about 6,600 beds) in 27 states. The company also manages inpatient facilities for government organizations, as well as psychiatric units within other hospitals. It has agreed to acquire Horizon Health, which operates 15 mental health hospitals and manages more than 100 mental health and rehab programs.

The Horizon acquisition fits nicely with the company's strategy to grow by acquiring additional freestanding psychiatric hospitals (91% of revenue). Pyschiatric Solutions bought 20 inpatient psychiatric facilities from Ardent Health Services in 2005 and three additional behavioral health care facilities in Florida, Indiana, and Texas in early 2006. Later that year it acquired Alternative Behavioral Services, which operates inpatient facilities, from FHC Health Systems.

HISTORY

Psychiatric Solutions may never have made it without the path laid before it by its predecessor, Psychiatric Management Resources (PMR). That company's story goes back to the 1980s, when certain trends in mental health care presented a perfect environment for its creation: the growth of outpatient services, advances in drugs to treat mental illness, and the industry's need to regain credibility. Psychiatric Management Resources was founded and went public in 1988. The next year Zaron Capital acquired the company and renamed it PMR Corporation.

PMR grew quickly in the early 1990s. In 1994 government probes of partial hospitalization programs such as those administered by PMR led to changes in how program operators could bill payors. Hit by retroactive changes, delayed or lost claims caused PMR to lose money in 1995.

In 1997 the company retooled to support its growth in existing and developing markets. In early 1998 PMR's largest customer, Scripps-Health, lost its "provider-based" status, meaning Medicare would no longer reimburse PMR for its services. A poor market ended the company's plans to acquire psychiatric hospital operator Behavioral Healthcare Corporation (BHC); the two companies did agree to operate outpatient programs jointly at 10 BHC facilities. That year PMR formed a specialty pharmacy joint venture with what is now Stadt Holdings, a subsidiary of Bergen Brunswig (now AmerisourceBergen).

The company's proposed acquisition of some American Psych Systems divisions fell through in 1998. In 1999 PMR suffered a loss after a change in accounting methods.

PMR opened 2000 by selling its stake in Stadt Solutions, and it ended its pilot managed care project with two California-based HMOs. That year the company changed its strategy again to focus on its health information operation InfoScriber after Medicare and Medicaid cutbacks caused the firm to pare its outpatient programs.

InfoScriber failed to yield anything more than losses, and PMR shifted its attention back to its management services in 2001. The company also

shut down InfoScriber and was acquired by Psychiatric Solutions in August 2002.

Psychiatric Solutions combined PMR's operations with its own and changed the name of the combined company to Psychiatric Solutions. The newly merged firm also changed its strategy to one of growth by acquisition. As such, the company acquired The Brown Schools, Ramsay Youth Services, and Alliance Health Center in 2003; and two inpatient facilities from Brentwood Behavioral Health and four inpatient behavioral health care facilities from Heartland Health in 2004.

EXECUTIVES

Chairman, President, and CEO; Chairman, Ramsay Youth Services: Joey A. Jacobs, age 52, $697,389 pay (prior to title change)
COO: William B. Rutherford, age 42
Chief Accounting Officer: Jack E. Polson, age 39, $280,069 pay
Chief Development Officer: Steven T. Davidson, age 48, $342,119 pay
EVP, Finance and Administration: Brent Turner, age 40, $280,069 pay
EVP, General Counsel, and Secretary: Christopher L. (Chris) Howard, age 39
Director, Human Resources: Cindy Dill
Auditors: Ernst & Young LLP

LOCATIONS

HQ: Psychiatric Solutions, Inc.
840 Crescent Center Dr., Ste. 460, Franklin, TN 37067
Phone: 615-312-5700   **Fax:** 615-312-5711
Web: www.psysolutions.com

Psychiatric Solutions has operations throughout the US.

PRODUCTS/OPERATIONS

2005 Sales

	$ mil.	% of total
Patient services	664.4	91
Management fees	63.4	9
Total	**727.8**	**100**

COMPETITORS

Comprehensive Care
Magellan Health
Mental Health Network
Universal Health Services

HISTORICAL FINANCIALS

Company Type: Public

Income Statement
FYE: December 31

	REVENUE ($ mil.)	NET INCOME ($ mil.)	NET PROFIT MARGIN	EMPLOYEES
12/05	727.8	27.1	3.7%	13,300
12/04	487.2	16.8	3.4%	9,100
12/03	293.7	5.2	1.8%	4,810
12/02	113.9	5.7	5.0%	1,680
Annual Growth	**85.6%**	**68.2%**	**—**	**99.3%**

2005 Year-End Financials

Debt ratio: 89.3%
Return on equity: 6.9%
Cash ($ mil.): 54.5
Current ratio: 2.38
Long-term debt ($ mil.): 482.1
No. of shares (mil.): 52.4
Dividends
  Yield: —
  Payout: —
Market value ($ mil.): 1,539.9
R&D as % of sales: —
Advertising as % of sales: —

Stock History
NASDAQ (GS): PSYS

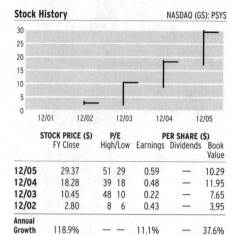

	STOCK PRICE ($) FY Close	P/E High/Low		PER SHARE ($) Earnings	Dividends	Book Value
12/05	29.37	51	29	0.59	—	10.29
12/04	18.28	39	18	0.48	—	11.95
12/03	10.45	48	10	0.22	—	7.65
12/02	2.80	8	6	0.43	—	3.95
Annual Growth	**118.9%**	**—**	**—**	**11.1%**	**—**	**37.6%**

PW Eagle

Sharp-eyed PW Eagle knows how to go with the flow. Under its own name and through its US Poly Company subsidiary, the company makes polyvinyl chloride (PVC) and polyethylene (PE) pipe for irrigation, natural gas, fiber-optic lines, plumbing, and other construction, telecommunication, and agricultural uses. The company, which does business primarily west of the Mississippi, has permanently closed one plant in Oregon. After announcing that it would review strategic options for its future, PW Eagle agreed early in 2007 to be acquired by J-M Manufacturing for about $400 million.

In 2004 the company's PWPoly Corp. unit spent $15 million to acquire Uponor Aldyl (plastic extruding) from Finland's Uponor; the resulting business was renamed US Poly Company.

PW Eagle scrapped a planned spinoff of US Poly in 2005. Also that year US Poly sold its metals parts business to R. W. Lyall.

EXECUTIVES

Chairman, President, and CEO: Jerry A. Dukes, age 58, $482,375 pay
EVP and CFO: Scott Long, age 43, $384,801 pay
EVP, Operations: John R. (Jack) Cobb, age 54, $373,112 pay
EVP, Sales and Marketing: N. Michael (Mike) Stickel, age 63, $364,815 pay
VP, Technical Director: Keith H. Steinbruck, age 56, $229,102 pay
VP, Human Resources: Neil R. Chinn, age 55
General Manager Sales: Mike Kalish
Manager Central Region Water Works Sales Department: Don Yonts
Secretary: Dobson West, age 59
Investor Relations: Linda Williams
Auditors: Grant Thornton LLP; PricewaterhouseCoopers LLP

LOCATIONS

HQ: PW Eagle, Inc.
1550 Valley River Dr., Eugene, OR 97401
Phone: 541-343-0200   **Fax:** 541-686-9248
Web: www.pweagleinc.com

PW Eagle has facilities in California, Missouri, Nebraska, Oregon, Texas, Utah, Washington, and West Virginia.

PRODUCTS/OPERATIONS

2005 Sales

	$ mil.	% of total
PVC products	612.2	88
PE products	82.0	12
Total	**694.2**	**100**

Selected Products

PVC Pipe
  American Society for Testing and Materials (ASTM) PVC Pressure Pipe (irrigation)
  American Water Works Association (AWWA) Water Main Pipe (drinking water and fire protection)
  ASTM PVC Well Casing
  Ultra-Blue Water Main Pipe (drinking water)
PE Pipe
  ASTM PE Pressure Pipe (irrigation)

COMPETITORS

Aga Foodservice
Cantex
Detrex
Diamond Plastics
Formosa Plastics
Georgia Gulf
GPJ Ventures
Habasit Holding USA
NACO Industries
NIBCO
Otter Tail
Royal Group Technologies
Westlake Chemical

HISTORICAL FINANCIALS

Company Type: Public

Income Statement
FYE: December 31

	REVENUE ($ mil.)	NET INCOME ($ mil.)	NET PROFIT MARGIN	EMPLOYEES
12/05	694.2	47.0	6.8%	1,087
12/04	475.0	(5.5)	—	1,120
12/03	331.8	(12.7)	—	924
12/02	251.3	0.6	0.2%	706
12/01	246.1	(12.9)	—	691
Annual Growth	**29.6%**	**—**	**—**	**12.0%**

2005 Year-End Financials

Debt ratio: 22.7%
Return on equity: 95.3%
Cash ($ mil.): 5.7
Current ratio: 1.31
Long-term debt ($ mil.): 19.5
No. of shares (mil.): 11.6
Dividends
  Yield: 0.4%
  Payout: 1.7%
Market value ($ mil.): 237.2
R&D as % of sales: —
Advertising as % of sales: —

Stock History
NASDAQ (GM): PWEI

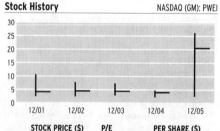

	STOCK PRICE ($) FY Close	P/E High/Low		PER SHARE ($) Earnings	Dividends	Book Value
12/05	20.50	6	1	4.65	0.08	7.43
12/04	3.98	—	—	(0.78)	—	1.68
12/03	4.40	—	—	(1.86)	—	2.11
12/02	4.50	125	44	0.06	—	3.70
12/01	4.13	—	—	(1.80)	—	3.52
Annual Growth	**49.3%**	**—**	**—**	**—**	**—**	**20.5%**

QMed, Inc.

What's your heart's Q rating? QMed makes noninvasive devices that assist doctors in diagnosing and managing coronary artery disease (CAD), stroke, congestive heart failure, and the cardiovascular complications of diabetes. Subsidiary Interactive Heart Management targets the managed care industry for sales of its ohms|cad system, which monitors heart function; the results are transmitted to an online cardiology consultancy database. Other products include the Monitor One nDx, which analyzes heart-rate variability to detect nervous system dysfunction. The disease management firm markets directly to health plans, physician groups, and government agencies. Investment firm Galen Partners owns about 23% of QMed.

In 2005 the company acquired Health e Monitoring, which provides weight management and health promotions for employers, consumers, and insurance companies. QMed's newly formed subsidiary QMedCare provides managed care services for Medicare patients.

Director and former president and CEO Michael Cox owns about 10% of QMed.

EXECUTIVES

Chairman: Bruce F. (Toby) Wesson, age 63
President, COO, and Director: Jane A. Murray, age 43
SVP, CFO, and Treasurer: William T. Schmitt Jr., age 45, $211,106 pay
SVP, Health Management Services: Teri J. Kraf, age 56, $189,024 pay
SVP, Sales and Field Services: John W. Siegel, age 49, $199,400 pay
VP, Business Development: Glenn Roth
VP, Corporate Strategy and Development: Robert Mosby, age 59
VP, Health Management Services Division: Kathleen Haley
Chief Medical Officer: Narinder Bhalla
President, Health e Monitoring: K. Randall Burt
President, QMedCare: John W. (Jack) Rohfritch, age 60
Senior Director, Technology: David Leeney
Director, Human Resources: Gayle Laing
Auditors: Amper, Politziner & Mattia, P.C.

LOCATIONS

HQ: QMed, Inc.
25 Christopher Way, Eatontown, NJ 07724
Phone: 732-544-5544 **Fax:** 732-544-5404
Web: www.qmedinc.com

QMed has facilities in New Jersey and New York.

PRODUCTS/OPERATIONS

Selected Products

Monitor One nDx (line of ischemic heart monitors and a system that analyzes heart-rate variability)
Monitor One TC Omni (ambulatory ECG monitoring technology)
ohms|cad (cardiovascular disease management system)

Selected Subsidiaries

Health e Monitoring, Inc.
HeartMasters LLC (50%)
Interactive Heart Management Corp.
QMedCare, Inc.

COMPETITORS

Advanced Biosensor	Medwave
AvMed Health Plans	Siemens Medical
BioScrip	Spacelabs Medical
GE Healthcare	Vasomedical
Healthways, Inc.	

HISTORICAL FINANCIALS

Company Type: Public

Income Statement

FYE: November 30

	REVENUE ($ mil.)	NET INCOME ($ mil.)	NET PROFIT MARGIN	EMPLOYEES
11/05	22.1	3.9	17.6%	144
11/04	15.6	(1.7)	—	140
11/03	12.9	(2.2)	—	142
11/02	12.7	0.7	5.5%	143
11/01	8.0	(1.0)	—	122
Annual Growth	28.9%	—	—	4.2%

2005 Year-End Financials

Debt ratio: 0.3%
Return on equity: 22.3%
Cash ($ mil.): 23.4
Current ratio: 8.25
Long-term debt ($ mil.): 0.1
No. of shares (mil.): 16.8
Dividends
 Yield: —
 Payout: —
Market value ($ mil.): 154.9
R&D as % of sales: 6.0%
Advertising as % of sales: —

Stock History

NASDAQ (CM): QMED

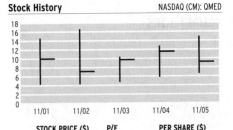

	STOCK PRICE ($) FY Close	P/E High/Low	PER SHARE ($) Earnings	Dividends	Book Value
11/05	9.23	70 32	0.21	—	1.61
11/04	11.55	— —	(0.12)	—	0.48
11/03	9.73	— —	(0.15)	—	0.48
11/02	7.15	411110	0.04	—	0.61
11/01	9.99	— —	(0.08)	—	0.47
Annual Growth	(2.0%)	— —	—	—	35.9%

Quality Systems

Quality Systems raises doctors' IQs when it comes to health care information technology. The company provides information management software for medical and dental practices, ambulatory care centers, community health centers, and medical and dental schools. Its NextGen Healthcare Information Systems division, which focuses on medical practices, makes electronic medical records and practice management systems for managing patient information, appointments, billing, referrals, and insurance claims. Through its QSI division, the company offers practice management software for dental and niche medical practices.

While Quality Systems had its start as a provider of dental practice software, the company has been growing through its NextGen medical practice software division.

Founder and chairman Sheldon Razin and his wife, Janet, together own 20% of Quality Systems. Director Ahmed Hussein owns nearly 18%.

EXECUTIVES

Chairman: Sheldon Razin, age 68
President, CEO, and Director:
Louis E. (Lou) Silverman, age 47, $656,817 pay
CFO and Secretary: Paul A. Holt, age 40, $249,154 pay
EVP; General Manager, QSI Division:
Gregory (Greg) Flynn, age 48, $230,395 pay
Director; President, NextGen Healthcare Information Systems Division: Patrick B. Cline, age 45, $665,224 pay
Auditors: Grant Thornton LLP

LOCATIONS

HQ: Quality Systems, Inc.
18191 Von Karman Ave., Ste. 450, Irvine, CA 92612
Phone: 949-255-2600 **Fax:** 949-255-2605
Web: www.qsii.com

PRODUCTS/OPERATIONS

2006 Sales

	% of total
System sales	56
Maintenance, EDI & other services	44
Total	**100**

2006 Sales

	% of total
NextGen division	87
QSI division	13
Total	**100**

Selected Products

Clinical data management software
Dental charting software
Dental practice management systems
Internet-based consumer health portal
Medical records storage software
Medical practice management systems

COMPETITORS

AMICAS
CareCentric
Cerner
CPSI
Eclipsys
Emdeon
Global Med
IDX Systems
McKesson
MEDITECH
Misys Healthcare
QCSI
QuadraMed
VantageMed

HISTORICAL FINANCIALS

Company Type: Public

Income Statement

FYE: March 31

	REVENUE ($ mil.)	NET INCOME ($ mil.)	NET PROFIT MARGIN	EMPLOYEES
3/06	119.3	23.3	19.5%	538
3/05	89.0	16.1	18.1%	418
3/04	70.9	10.4	14.7%	327
3/03	54.8	7.0	12.8%	263
3/02	44.4	5.3	11.9%	230
Annual Growth	28.0%	44.8%	—	23.7%

2006 Year-End Financials

Debt ratio: —
Return on equity: 34.5%
Cash ($ mil.): 57.2
Current ratio: 2.32
Long-term debt ($ mil.): —
No. of shares (mil.): 26.7
Dividends
 Yield: 2.6%
 Payout: 103.5%
Market value ($ mil.): 884.1
R&D as % of sales: —
Advertising as % of sales: —

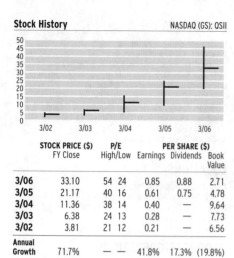

	STOCK PRICE ($)	P/E		PER SHARE ($)		
	FY Close	High/Low		Earnings	Dividends	Book Value
3/06	33.10	54	24	0.85	0.88	2.71
3/05	21.17	40	16	0.61	0.75	4.78
3/04	11.36	38	14	0.40	—	9.64
3/03	6.38	24	13	0.28	—	7.73
3/02	3.81	21	12	0.21	—	6.56
Annual Growth	71.7%	—	—	41.8%	17.3%	(19.8%)

Quicksilver Resources

With mercurial speed, Quicksilver Resources seeks to turn oil and gas finds into profits, primarily through acquiring the assets of rival oil and gas firms. The independent exploration and production company owns assets in Indiana, Kentucky, Michigan, Montana, New Mexico, Texas, and Wyoming, and Canada, as well as interests in gas gathering pipeline systems. Quicksilver Resources has proved reserves (located primarily in Michigan and Alberta) of 1.1 trillion cu. ft. of natural gas equivalent. Chairman Thomas Darden, CEO Glenn Darden, and other Darden family members control 35% of Quicksilver Resources.

The company is recognized as a leading developer and producer of unconventional natural gas reserves, including coal bed methane, shale gas, and tight sand gas.

EXECUTIVES

Chairman: Thomas F. (Toby) Darden, age 52, $594,840 pay
President, CEO, and Director: Glenn M. Darden, age 50, $594,840 pay
EVP, Operations: Jeff Cook, age 49
SVP and CFO: Philip W. Cook
SVP, General Counsel, and Secretary: John C. (Chris) Cirone, age 56
SVP and COO, MGV Energy Inc.: Dana W. Johnson, age 45
VP and Controller: D. Wayne Blair, age 48
VP, Human Resources and Director: Anne Darden Self, age 47
VP, U.S. Operations: William S. Buckler, age 44, $338,000 pay
Chairman and Adviser, Quicksilver Resources Canada: J. Michael (Mike) Gatens, age 46
Director, Investor Relations: Diane Weaver
Auditors: Deloitte & Touche LLP

LOCATIONS

HQ: Quicksilver Resources Inc.
777 W. Rosedale St., Ste. 300, Fort Worth, TX 76104
Phone: 817-665-5000   **Fax:** 817-665-5004
Web: www.qrinc.com

Quicksilver Resources has operations in Indiana, Kentucky, Michigan, Montana, New Mexico, Texas, and Wyoming, and in Alberta, Canada.

2005 Sales

	$ mil.	% of total
US	212.7	69
Canada	97.8	31
Total	**310.5**	**100**

PRODUCTS/OPERATIONS

2005 Sales

	$ mil.	% of total
Natural gas	269.6	88
Oil	28.0	9
Natural gas liquids	8.7	3
Adjustments	4.2	—
Total	**310.5**	**100**

Selected Subsidiaries and Affiliates

Beaver Creek Pipeline, L.L.C. (50%)
GTG Pipeline Corporation
Mercury Michigan, Inc.
Quicksilver Resources Canada Inc.
Terra Energy Ltd

COMPETITORS

Abraxas Petroleum
Anadarko Petroleum
BP
ConocoPhillips
Devon Energy
Exxon Mobil
Noble Energy
Royal Dutch Shell
Swift Energy

HISTORICAL FINANCIALS
Company Type: Public

Income Statement
FYE: December 31

	REVENUE ($ mil.)	NET INCOME ($ mil.)	NET PROFIT MARGIN	EMPLOYEES
12/05	310.5	87.4	28.1%	400
12/04	179.7	31.3	17.4%	342
12/03	140.9	16.2	11.5%	301
12/02	122.2	13.8	11.3%	247
12/01	143.1	19.3	13.5%	258
Annual Growth	21.4%	45.9%	—	11.6%

2005 Year-End Financials
Debt ratio: 131.9%
Return on equity: 25.4%
Cash ($ mil.): 14.9
Current ratio: 0.54
Long-term debt ($ mil.): 506.0
No. of shares (mil.): 76.1
Dividends
  Yield: —
  Payout: —
Market value ($ mil.): 3,196.1
R&D as % of sales: —
Advertising as % of sales: —

Stock History
NYSE: KWK

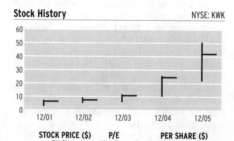

	STOCK PRICE ($)	P/E		PER SHARE ($)		
	FY Close	High/Low		Earnings	Dividends	Book Value
12/05	42.01	46	21	1.08	—	5.04
12/04	24.52	41	17	0.62	—	6.07
12/03	10.77	47	28	0.24	—	9.78
12/02	7.48	39	25	0.23	—	6.11
12/01	6.35	21	9	0.33	—	5.03
Annual Growth	60.4%	—	—	34.5%	—	0.1%

Rackable Systems

Rackable Systems provides rack-mounted computer servers designed for large-scale data center deployments. The company counts enterprises in the e-commerce (Amazon.com, 24% of sales), financial services (Deutsche Bank), government (Lawrence Livermore National Laboratory), technology (Toshiba America Electronic Components), and Internet (Yahoo!, 22% of sales) sectors among its customers. Microsoft, a good strategic customer to have, accounts for about 14% of sales. Rackable Systems relies on contract electronics manufacturers, primarily Sanmina-SCI and SYNNEX, to produce its servers. Entities affiliated with Parthenon Capital own about 42% of the company.

The company uses both AMD and Intel microprocessors in designing its servers. Rackable aims its products at IT system administrators looking to replace servers running the UNIX operating system with new equipment operating under Linux or Windows.

Rackable acquired Terrascale Technologies for $38 million in cash in 2006. Terrascale specializes in grid and cluster computing products.

Rackable Systems gets nearly all of its revenues from the US, but is looking to expand into international markets.

Co-founder and CTO Giovanni Coglitore owns about 6% of Rackable Systems. All officers and directors of the company as a group own around 27%.

EXECUTIVES

Chairman: Ronald D. Verdoorn, age 55
CEO and Director: Thomas K. (Tom) Barton, age 42
President: Todd R. Ford, age 39
CFO: Madhu Ranganathan, age 41
CTO and Director: Giovanni Coglitore, age 38, $150,010 pay
EVP, Storage Solutions: Gautham Sastri
VP, Corporate Development, General Counsel, and Secretary: William P. (Bill) Garvey, age 41
VP, Engineering: Robert (Bob) Weisickle, age 54
VP, Human Resources: Jennifer L. Pratt
VP, Information Technology: Dominic Martinelli
VP, Marketing: Colette LaForce, age 33
Auditors: Deloitte & Touche LLP

LOCATIONS

HQ: Rackable Systems, Inc.
1933 Milmont Dr., Milpitas, CA 95035
Phone: 408-240-8300   **Fax:** 408-321-0293
Web: www.rackable.com

Rackable Systems has offices in California, Georgia, Massachusetts, and Texas.

2005 Sales

	$ mil.	% of total
US	209.5	97
Other countries	5.5	3
Total	**215.0**	**100**

PRODUCTS/OPERATIONS

2005 Sales

	$ mil.	% of total
Computer servers	194.6	91
Storage systems	20.4	9
Total	**215.0**	**100**

Selected Products

Foundation Series (computer servers, data storage systems)
Scale Out Series (general-purpose computer servers)

COMPETITORS

Dell	Linux Networx
Egenera	NetApp
EMC	Sun Microsystems
Hewlett-Packard	Super Micro Computer
Hitachi Data Systems	Verari Systems
IBM	

HISTORICAL FINANCIALS

Company Type: Public

Income Statement

FYE: December 31

	REVENUE ($ mil.)	NET INCOME ($ mil.)	NET PROFIT MARGIN	EMPLOYEES
12/05	215.0	8.5	4.0%	174
12/04	109.7	(55.4)	—	119
12/03	52.9	(52.7)	—	—
12/02	27.6	(0.6)	—	31
Annual Growth	98.2%	—	—	77.7%

2005 Year-End Financials

Debt ratio: —
Return on equity: 91.9%
Cash ($ mil.): 54.2
Current ratio: 3.18
Long-term debt ($ mil.): —
No. of shares (mil.): 23.0
Dividends
  Yield: —
  Payout: —
Market value ($ mil.): 656.2
R&D as % of sales: —
Advertising as % of sales: —

Stock History

NASDAQ (GS): RACK

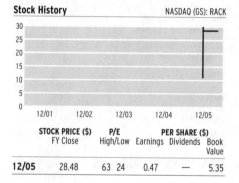

	STOCK PRICE ($) FY Close	P/E High/Low	Earnings	PER SHARE ($) Dividends	Book Value
12/05	28.48	63 24	0.47	—	5.35

Radiation Therapy Services

Radiation Therapy Services operates a network of about 75 freestanding and hospital-based radiation therapy centers in 15 states, with Florida its largest market. The company, which also does business as 21st Century Oncology, offers a wide variety of radiation therapy services, including linear accelerators for treatment of deep-seated tumors, brachytherapy for treatment directly into affected areas, seed implantation for prostate cancer, and stereotactic radiosurgery for treating brain tumors. The centers are equipped with treatment planning simulators and a computer-based system for treatment planning and verification.

Radiation Therapy Services plans to grow by building new radiation treatment centers in its existing markets, and by acquiring or developing centers in new markets. Its growth strategy for existing facilities includes increasing the number of doctor referrals and expanding its treatment options.

CEO Daniel Dosoretz owns 16% of Radiation Therapy Services. Chairman Howard Sheridan and director Michael Katin each own 10% of the company, and secretary James Rubenstein holds 12%.

EXECUTIVES

Chairman: Howard M. Sheridan, age 60, $524,937 pay
President, CEO, and Director: Daniel E. Dosoretz, age 52, $1,713,590 pay
EVP and CFO: David M. (Dave) Koeninger, age 51, $994,488 pay
Medical Director, Secretary, and Director: James H. Rubenstein, age 50, $1,369,363 pay
Treasurer: Jeffrey A. Pakrosnis
Corporate Controller and Chief Accounting Officer: Joseph Biscardi, age 36, $240,023 pay
Human Resources Director: Joyce White
Webmaster: Adrian Williams
Auditors: Ernst & Young LLP

LOCATIONS

HQ: Radiation Therapy Services, Inc.
  2234 Colonial Blvd., Fort Myers, FL 33907
Phone: 239-931-7275   **Fax:** 239-931-7380
Web: www.rtsx.com

Radiation Therapy Services operates centers in Alabama, Arizona, California, Delaware, Florida, Kentucky, Maryland, Massachusetts, Michigan, Nevada, New Jersey, New York, North Carolina, Rhode Island, and West Virginia.

PRODUCTS/OPERATIONS

2005 Sales

	% of total
Medicare & Medicaid	51
Commercial	47
Self-pay	2
Total	**100**

COMPETITORS

Aptium Oncology
OnCure Medical
US Oncology

HISTORICAL FINANCIALS

Company Type: Public

Income Statement

FYE: December 31

	REVENUE ($ mil.)	NET INCOME ($ mil.)	NET PROFIT MARGIN	EMPLOYEES
12/05	227.3	25.0	11.0%	980
12/04	171.4	9.2	5.4%	720
12/03	138.7	24.0	17.3%	690
12/02	111.1	19.3	17.4%	—
Annual Growth	26.9%	9.0%	—	19.2%

2005 Year-End Financials

Debt ratio: 122.6%
Return on equity: 30.9%
Cash ($ mil.): 14.4
Current ratio: 2.78
Long-term debt ($ mil.): 117.0
No. of shares (mil.): 22.8
Dividends
  Yield: —
  Payout: —
Market value ($ mil.): 806.2
R&D as % of sales: —
Advertising as % of sales: —

Stock History

NASDAQ (GS): RTSX

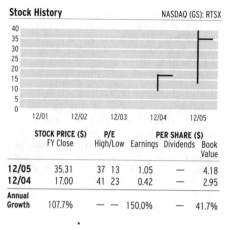

	STOCK PRICE ($) FY Close	P/E High/Low	Earnings	PER SHARE ($) Dividends	Book Value
12/05	35.31	37 13	1.05	—	4.18
12/04	17.00	41 23	0.42	—	2.95
Annual Growth	107.7%	— —	150.0%	—	41.7%

Range Resources

Range Resources is riding the range as an independent acquirer and developer of US oil and gas resources. The company's long-term strategy involves acquiring long-lived established properties and it has major development areas in the Appalachian, Gulf Coast, and Southwest (West Texas, western Oklahoma, and Texas Panhandle) regions. Natural gas accounts for about 80% of Range Resources' proved reserves of about 1.4 trillion cu. ft. of natural gas equivalent. The company holds about 2.4 million net acres of leasehold properties, and an inventory of more than 7,700 drilling locations. In 2006 Range Resources acquired Stroud Energy for $450 million.

The company has grown through some 70 property acquisitions in its core areas. However, the oil slump of the late-1990s led to heavy debts, prompting Range Resources to sell some assets and cut back on exploration, production, and acquisitions.

Range Resources formed joint venture Great Lakes Energy Partners, L.L.C., with Ohio-based utility FirstEnergy in 1999 to jointly develop their Appalachian oil and gas resources. As part of its ongoing plans to reduce debt, Range Resources sold its Sterling gas processing plant the next year for about $20 million.

In 2004 Range Resources acquired the 50% of Great Lakes Energy Partners LLC that it did not already own for $295 million.

In 2005 the company acquired Plantation Petroleum Holdings II, LLC, a company with Permian Basin oil and gas properties, for $116.5 million.

HISTORY

Lomak Petroleum was a small gas drilling company with assets in Ohio and West Virginia when Snyder Oil Company (later part of Santa Fe Snyder) bought a 75% stake in 1988. Though Snyder soon started divesting its stake, Snyder VP John Pinkerton was appointed president of Lomak in 1990 (he became CEO in 1992). Pinkerton charted a 10-year mission: Acquire a critical mass of producing properties, operate the properties to establish cash flow, and then begin exploration where it had properties and operating experience.

In 1991 Lomak acquired properties in the Permian basin of West Texas. Acquisitions continued in 1993 and 1994 as the company beefed up its Appalachian business and established positions in the midcontinent and Gulf Coast areas.

Lomak launched exploration efforts in 1996. The next year the company acquired properties in Texas and the Gulf of Mexico from American Cometra. That year Lomak purchased natural gas properties in Appalachia and oil properties in West Texas. It sold $54 million in property in 1998, including all of its San Juan Basin, New Mexico, assets. Also that year the company changed its name to Range Resources after its purchase of Domain for $217 million.

EXECUTIVES

Chairman: Charles L. Blackburn, age 78
President, CEO, and Director: John H. Pinkerton, age 52, $882,385 pay
EVP, COO, and Director: Jeffrey L. (Jeff) Ventura, age 48, $595,385 pay
SVP and CFO: Roger S. Manny, age 48, $383,269 pay
SVP Appalachia: Steven L. Grose, age 56
SVP Corporate Development: Chad L. Stephens, age 49, $342,885 pay
SVP and Manager, Gulf Coast Division:
 Steven M. Curran
SVP, Chief Compliance Officer, and Corporate Secretary: Rodney L. Waller, age 55, $394,039 pay
Human Resources Director: Carol Culpepper
Investor Relations Specialist: Karen M. Giles
Auditors: Ernst & Young LLP

LOCATIONS

HQ: Range Resources Corporation
 777 Main St., Ste. 800, Fort Worth, TX 76102
Phone: 817-870-2601   **Fax:** 817-870-2316
Web: www.rangeresources.com

2005 Proved Reserves

	% of total
Appalachia	60
Southwest	35
Gulf Coast	5
Total	**100**

PRODUCTS/OPERATIONS

2005 Sales

	$ mil.	% of total
Natural gas	380.1	72
Crude oil	117.4	22
Natural gas liquids (NGLs)	27.6	5
Transportation & gathering	2.6	1
Other	10.9	2
Adjustments	(2.6)	—
Total	**536.0**	**100**

COMPETITORS

Anadarko Petroleum
Apache
Belden & Blake
BP
Cabot Oil & Gas
Chesapeake Energy
Devon Energy
Dominion Resources
EOG
Equitable Resources
Exxon Mobil
Forest Oil
Murphy Oil
Noble Energy
Pioneer Natural Resources
Royal Dutch Shell
XTO Energy

HISTORICAL FINANCIALS

Company Type: Public

Income Statement

FYE: December 31

	REVENUE ($ mil.)	NET INCOME ($ mil.)	NET PROFIT MARGIN	EMPLOYEES
12/05	536.0	111.0	20.7%	578
12/04	320.7	42.2	13.2%	504
12/03	249.2	35.4	14.2%	151
12/02	198.2	25.8	13.0%	145
12/01	219.4	17.7	8.1%	141
Annual Growth	**25.0%**	**58.2%**	**—**	**42.3%**

2005 Year-End Financials

Debt ratio: 98.6%
Return on equity: 17.6%
Cash ($ mil.): 5.2
Current ratio: 0.65
Long-term debt ($ mil.): 687.1
No. of shares (mil.): 129.9
Dividends
 Yield: 0.2%
 Payout: 7.0%
Market value ($ mil.): 3,421.8
R&D as % of sales: —
Advertising as % of sales: —

Stock History

NYSE: RRC

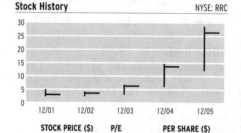

	STOCK PRICE ($) FY Close	P/E High/Low		PER SHARE ($) Earnings	Dividends	Book Value
12/05	26.34	33	14	0.86	0.06	5.36
12/04	13.64	38	16	0.38	0.03	6.97
12/03	6.30	16	8	0.41	—	4.86
12/02	3.60	13	9	0.31	—	3.75
12/01	3.03	20	11	0.24	—	4.48
Annual Growth	**71.7%**	**—**	**—**	**37.6%**	**100.0%**	**4.6%**

RC2 Corporation

RC2 makes cars that require no gas and never crash. The company makes plastic and die-cast replicas of cars and trucks, as well as infant care and play products. Popular replica items include NASCAR-licensed models, Ertl agricultural vehicles (such as tractors), and American Muscle vintage cars and trucks. It also makes video game character figurines, wheeled toys for children, and model kits, and merchandises NASCAR-related items such as apparel and trading cards. RC2's newer infant and preschool lines are marketed under the Learning Curve family of brands (The First Years, Eden, Lamaze) and include developmental toys and dolls, as well as items for feeding and safety.

RC2 grows its product line through acquisitions, including Learning Curve International, a developer of children's wooden and die-cast toys; Playing Mantis, maker of Johnny Lightning diecast car replicas and race sets; and infant and toddler products maker The First Years.

Almost all of RC2's products are manufactured in China. Certain other items (such as infant products, sports trading cards, and apparel) are sourced in the US.

Orders from specialty wholesalers and retailers (such as Learning Express and Horizon Hobby) accounted for some 26% of sales in 2005.

EXECUTIVES

Chairman: Robert E. (Bob) Dods, age 56
Vice Chairman: Boyd L. Meyer, age 63
CEO and Director; CEO, The First Years:
 Curtis W. (Curt) Stoelting, age 45, $1,104,937 pay
President: Peter J. Henseler, age 46, $425,000 pay
CFO and Secretary: Jody L. Taylor, age 36, $230,000 pay
EVP; President, Learning Curve International:
 John Walter Lee II, age 57
EVP; President, Playing Mantis:
 Thomas E. (Tom) Lowe, age 45
SVP, Marketing: Gregory R. (Greg) Miller
SVP, Motorsport Licensing: M. Kevin Camp
SVP, Planning and Corporate Development:
 Gregory J. Kilrea
EVP; Managing Director, RC2 (H.K.) Limited:
 Helena Lo, $230,000 pay
Director, Human Resources: Sharon Besler
Director, Media Relations: Diane Busman
Auditors: KPMG LLP

LOCATIONS

HQ: RC2 Corporation
 1111 W. 22nd St., Ste. 320, Oak Brook, IL 60523
Phone: 630-573-7200   **Fax:** 630-573-5500
Web: www.rc2corp.com

RC2 has operations in Kowloon, Hong Kong, and Dongguan, China.

2005 Sales

	$ mil.	% of total
North America	434.0	86
Other regions	71.7	14
Adjustments	(1.3)	—
Total	**504.4**	**100**

PRODUCTS/OPERATIONS

2005 Sales

	$ mil.	% of total
Chain retailers	314.4	62
Specialty & hobby wholesalers & retailers	128.5	26
OEM dealers	40.7	8
Corporate promotional	18.3	4
Direct to consumers	2.5	—
Total	**504.4**	**100**

2005 Sales

	$ mil.	% of total
Children's toys	220.8	44
Infant products	160.2	32
Collectible products	123.4	24
Total	**504.4**	**100**

Selected Brands

Collectible Products
 American Muscle
 Ertl Collectibles
 Johnny Lightning
 JoyRide
 Memory Lane
 Press Pass
 Racing Champions NASCAR

Children's Toys
 Bob the Builder Project: Build It
 John Deere Kids
 Learning Curve
 Take Along Bob the Builder
 Take Along Thomas
 Thomas Interactive Railway
 Thomas Wooden Railway

Infant Products
 Lamaze Infant Development System
 Learning Curve
 The First Years

COMPETITORS

Binney & Smith	Little Tikes
Corgi International	Maisto
Franklin Mint	Mattel
Hasbro	Motorsports Authentics
JAKKS Pacific	Upper Deck

HISTORICAL FINANCIALS

Company Type: Public

Income Statement				FYE: December 31
	REVENUE ($ mil.)	NET INCOME ($ mil.)	NET PROFIT MARGIN	EMPLOYEES
12/05	504.4	53.1	10.5%	842
12/04	381.4	34.0	8.9%	742
12/03	311.0	38.4	12.3%	570
12/02	213.5	24.7	11.6%	398
12/01	203.3	15.1	7.4%	418
Annual Growth	25.5%	36.9%	—	19.1%

2005 Year-End Financials

Debt ratio: 14.4%	Dividends
Return on equity: 14.2%	Yield: —
Cash ($ mil.): 25.3	Payout: —
Current ratio: 1.99	Market value ($ mil.): 735.9
Long-term debt ($ mil.): 57.4	R&D as % of sales: —
No. of shares (mil.): 20.7	Advertising as % of sales: 0.8%

Stock History

NASDAQ (GS): RCRC

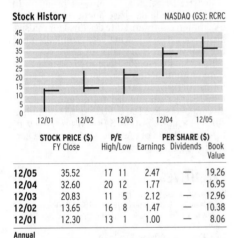

	STOCK PRICE ($) FY Close	P/E High/Low		PER SHARE ($) Earnings	Dividends	Book Value
12/05	35.52	17	11	2.47	—	19.26
12/04	32.60	20	12	1.77	—	16.95
12/03	20.83	11	5	2.12	—	12.96
12/02	13.65	16	8	1.47	—	10.38
12/01	12.30	13	1	1.00	—	8.06
Annual Growth	30.4%	—	—	25.4%	—	24.3%

RealNetworks

RealNetworks has enjoyed real success in the world of digital media — hundreds of millions of people have downloaded the company's RealPlayer product to stream audio, video, and other multimedia content. Its software and subscription services provide access to news, sports, and entertainment content (RealOne), downloadable games (RealArcade), and streaming and downloadable music (Rhapsody, RealPlayer Music Store, RadioPass). The company also serves the enterprise market with tools for creating, delivering, and licensing digital content. Founder and CEO Robert Glaser owns about 30% of the company.

RealNetworks' media player competes against Microsoft's Media Player and Apple's QuickTime, and competition with those companies has only

increased as the company has grown its music-related lines. RealNetworks' music strategy is centered on the Rhapsody subscription service gained from its 2003 acquisition of Listen.com. (The company also owned a stake in MusicNet along with Time Warner, Sony BMG, and EMI, but the former joint venture was sold to Baker Capital in 2005.)

RealNetworks closed a chapter in its long-running dispute with Microsoft late in 2005, agreeing to a settlement in an antitrust suit it filed against the software giant in 2003. Microsoft agreed to pay RealNetworks $761 million in cash and promotions.

RealNetworks' push into digital music has put it at further odds with Apple, the current leader in that market. Rhapsody and RealPlayer Music Store compete directly with Apple's iTunes products, but at the heart of the fight is the more fundamental issue of digital rights management (DRM). Apple has refused to license technology that would allow songs downloaded from competing services — including Rhapsody — to play on its popular iPod music player. Microsoft also has DRM technology used by competitors such as Napster.

In 2004 RealNetworks released Harmony, DRM translation software that allowed RealPlayer Music Store songs to play on devices using Apple's Fairplay, Microsoft's Windows Media Audio DRM, or RealNetworks' own Helix standard. A subsequent iPod release included firmware that again blocked play of RealPlayer songs, but RealNetworks continues to lobby for greater compatibility.

In addition to its Helix DRM software, the company's business software includes a suite of multimedia creation and publishing tools (Real Tools), software development kits, and broadcast servers for network service providers and enterprises. A key growth strategy for RealNetworks has been the delivery of content to wireless devices, particularly cell phones. The company has partnered with leading handset makers and service operators, including Nokia and Siemens. RealNetworks' business products accounted for about 20% of its revenues in 2004.

RealNetworks has seen growth in its game service, a business it augmented with the acquisitions of GameHouse in 2004 and Dutch game developer Zylom Media Group early in 2006. RealNetworks also generates revenue through online advertising and a range of services.

The company agreed to acquire wireless application and service provider WiderThan for about $350 million in 2006.

HISTORY

Robert Glaser, a Microsoft millionaire and VP, left to start Progressive Networks in 1994. Progressive (named for Glaser's political leanings) was formed with the idea that digital media delivery was more than an operating system or Web browser tool, but was an entity unto itself.

The company released RealAudio, for downloading audio files off the Web, in 1995. Although Progressive gave away RealAudio to consumers, it sold more complex, server-based audio programs to broadcasters and corporations. The software was soon the Web's most popular audio broadcast standard.

In 1997 the company changed its name to RealNetworks and went public. Microsoft paid $30 million for a minority stake in RealNetworks and began bundling RealPlayer with its Internet Explorer browser.

In 1998 RealNetworks boosted its presence through distribution alliances with players such as AOL (now part of Time Warner) and IBM subsidiary Lotus Development. Its relationship with Microsoft became strained when Glaser testified during the software giant's antitrust trial that Microsoft designed its own multimedia player to interfere with RealPlayer when installed on the same computer. Microsoft pulled the plug on its stake in RealNetworks.

Turning to the growing digital music market, RealNetworks in 1999 bought audio compression software developer Xing Technology and streaming media authoring specialist Vivo Software. The company realigned with Microsoft in 1999, letting Internet Explorer users connect to its RealGuide multimedia site directory. The popularity of online music downloading helped the company turn its first annual profit for 1999.

RealNetworks in 2000 acquired closely held Netzip, a specialist in software that handles downloads over the Internet, in a stock deal worth $268 million. Following its media counterparts, RealNetworks launched a paid subscription service offering certain customers access to exclusive content.

In 2001 the company established an online music subscription joint venture (MusicNet) with Time Warner, Bertelsmann, and EMI; the group sold MusicNet to Baker Capital in 2005.

EXECUTIVES

Chairman and CEO: Robert (Rob) Glaser, age 44, $786,000 pay
EVP, Worldwide Business Products and Services and International Operations: John J. Giamatteo, age 39
SVP, Finance, CFO, and Treasurer: Michael Eggers, age 34
SVP, Human Resources: Savino R. (Sid) Ferrales, age 55, $352,480 pay
SVP, Music and Video: Daniel C. (Dan) Sheeran, age 39
SVP, Legal and Business Affairs, General Counsel, and Secretary: Robert (Bob) Kimball, age 42, $1,322,375 pay
SVP, Games Division and Advertising Operations: Michael Schutzler, age 44
SVP, Media Software and Services: Harold Zeitz
SVP, North American Sales: Carla Stratfold, age 46, $373,502 pay
VP and CTO: Edmond Mesrobian
VP, Business Development: Jeffrey Schrock
VP, Carrier and System Software: Aref Matin
VP, Consumer and Web Marketing: Jackie Lang
VP, Asia: Doug Kaplan
VP, Consumer Services, EMEA and Latin America: Marco Menato
VP, Finance: Eric E. Russell
VP, Investor Relations: Caroline Hughes
Press Relations: Greg Chiemingo
Auditors: KPMG LLP

LOCATIONS

HQ: RealNetworks, Inc.
2601 Elliott Ave., Ste. 1000, Seattle, WA 98121
Phone: 206-674-2700   **Fax:** 206-674-2699
Web: www.realnetworks.com

2005 Sales

	$ mil.	% of total
US	249.9	77
Europe	44.9	14
Asia	27.9	8
Other regions	2.4	1
Total	**325.1**	**100**

PRODUCTS/OPERATIONS

2005 Sales

	$ mil.	% of total
Consumer products & services		
Music	97.5	30
Games	56.3	17
Media properties	31.2	10
Video, consumer software & other	95.0	29
Business products & services	45.1	14
Total	**325.1**	**100**

Selected Products

Consumer Media Products and Services
  RealArcade (creation and delivery of online games)
    GamePass (games subscription)
  RealJukebox (digital music management system)
  RealOne MusicPass (music subscription service)
  RealOne OpenPass (online marketplace for purchasing online content subscriptions)
  RealOne Player (integrated RealPlayer for audio and video)
  RealOne RadioPass (radio-based subscription)
  RealOne RHAPSODY (online music listening and CD burning service)
  RealOne SuperPass (media subscription service)
  RealPlayer (for listening to audio files)
  RealPresenter (integrates with Microsoft PowerPoint to broadcast presentations over the Web)
  RealSlideshow (for combining audio, video, and text into a Web-based multimedia presentation)
System Software and Services
  Helix DRM (digital rights management system)
  Helix Producer (audio/video encoding, converts to RealMedia)
  Helix Universal Gateway (media delivery and caching)
  Helix Universal Gateway (M) (streaming media proxy-cache for mobile devices)
  Helix Universal Server (media delivery platform)
  Real Broadcast Network (hosted broadcast service)

COMPETITORS

Akamai
Amazon.com
AOL
Apple
Emblaze
Google
Microsoft
MTV Games
Napster
PacketVideo
Sonic Foundry
Sony
Wal-Mart
Yahoo!

HISTORICAL FINANCIALS

Company Type: Public

Income Statement

FYE: December 31

	REVENUE ($ mil.)	NET INCOME ($ mil.)	NET PROFIT MARGIN	EMPLOYEES
12/05	325.1	312.3	96.1%	933
12/04	266.7	(23.0)	—	826
12/03	202.4	(21.5)	—	744
12/02	182.7	(38.3)	—	696
12/01	188.9	(74.8)	—	807
Annual Growth	**14.5%**	**—**	**—**	**3.7%**

2005 Year-End Financials

Debt ratio: 11.9%
Return on equity: 51.1%
Cash ($ mil.): 781.3
Current ratio: 5.63
Long-term debt ($ mil.): 100.0
No. of shares (mil.): 166.0
Dividends
  Yield: —
  Payout: —
Market value ($ mil.): 1,288.4
R&D as % of sales: 21.7%
Advertising as % of sales: —

Stock History

NASDAQ (GS): RNWK

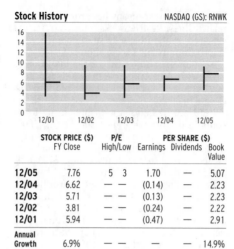

	STOCK PRICE ($) FY Close	P/E High/Low		PER SHARE ($) Earnings	Dividends	Book Value
12/05	7.76	5	3	1.70	—	5.07
12/04	6.62	—	—	(0.14)	—	2.23
12/03	5.71	—	—	(0.13)	—	2.23
12/02	3.81	—	—	(0.24)	—	2.22
12/01	5.94	—	—	(0.47)	—	2.91
Annual Growth	**6.9%**	**—**	**—**	**—**	**—**	**14.9%**

Red Hat

Red Hat hopes that businesses are ready to try open-source operating systems on for size. Red Hat dominates the market for Linux, the open-source computer operating system (OS) that is the chief rival to Microsoft's Windows operating systems. In addition to its Red Hat Enterprise Linux OS, the company's product line includes database, content, and collaboration management applications; server and embedded operating systems; and software development tools. Red Hat also provides consulting, custom software development, support, and training services. In June 2006 the company acquired JBoss for about $350 million.

Red Hat is clearly signaling that corporate use of Linux is its focus; the company notified users that it would end routine maintenance of the Red Hat Linux line in 2004 in favor of enhancing and supporting its Red Hat Enterprise Linux products. Red Hat established the Fedora Project, an open-source software effort relying on the work of volunteer programmers, for support of its original Linux distribution.

Early in 2005 the company established a government business unit; Red Hat US government customers include the Department of Energy and the Federal Aviation Administration.

HISTORY

Finnish graduate student Linus Torvalds created the Linux operating system in 1991 as a hobby. When Torvalds released its programming code free over the Internet for anyone to revise, Linux quickly attracted a core base of devoted programmers — including Marc Ewing. A programmer for IBM by day, Ewing developed improvements to Linux in his spare bedroom. Soon he began selling the improved operating system as Red Hat — named after a red and white Cornell lacrosse cap Ewing's grandfather had given him.

In 1994 Ewing was contacted by Robert Young, who after selling typewriters and running a computer leasing company had started a UNIX newsletter. But Young saw better profit margins in catalog sales. Young's ACC Corp.

---

bought the rights to Ewing's creation and the two went into business together. ACC Corp. was renamed Red Hat Software, Inc.

The company compiled Linux's most significant improvements and distributed them on a CD-ROM and through the budding Internet. Their revenues actually came from manuals and technical support sold to new users and businesses who were challenged by the software's ever-changing source code.

By 1997 Linux — and Red Hat's package — were known only among the most militant programmers who sought alternatives to Microsoft's Windows. Hundreds of developers had continually doctored Linux online to create an operating system known for its speed and reliability.

Red Hat exploded in popularity in 1998 after Intel and Netscape both made minor investments in the company. In 1999 Compaq, IBM, Novell, Oracle, and SAP invested in Red Hat. The company went public later that year.

In 2000 Red Hat used its soaring stock as currency to acquire embedded programming specialist Cygnus Solutions for $674 million and Hell's Kitchen Systems (HKS), a maker of payment processing software. President Matthew Szulik replaced Young as CEO and Ewing stepped down as CTO.

Red Hat expanded its software products in 2001 to include database applications and an e-commerce software suite designed for midsize businesses. The following year Szulik assumed the additional role of chairman.

Red Hat in late 2003 acquired Sistina Software of Minneapolis, a supplier of data storage infrastructure software for Linux operating systems. Sistina was founded in 1997 and has about 20 employees. Red Hat paid about $31 million in stock to acquire Sistina. SAP Ventures, the venture capital arm of SAP, invested in Sistina earlier in 2003.

EXECUTIVES

Chairman, President, and CEO:
  Matthew J. (Matt) Szulik, age 50, $1,040,000 pay
EVP and CFO: Charles E. (Charlie) Peters Jr., age 54, $690,833 pay
EVP, Corporate Affairs: Tom Rabon
EVP, Engineering: Paul J. Cormier, age 49, $611,667 pay
EVP, Worldwide Operations: Joanne Rohde, age 47, $635,000 pay
EVP, Worldwide Sales; President, Red Hat International: Alex Pinchev, age 56, $716,667 pay
SVP and General Manager, JBoss: Marc Fleury, age 39
Deputy General Counsel and Secretary:
  Mark H. Webbink, age 55
SVP, Worldwide Marketing and General Manager, Enterprise Products: Timothy (Tim) Yeaton
VP, Engineering and CTO: Brian Stevens
VP, Marketing: John Young
VP, Human Capital: DeLisa Alexander
Manager, Investor Relations: Gabriel Szulik
General Counsel: Michael R. Cunningham, age 46
Public Relations: Kathryn Bishop
Auditors: PricewaterhouseCoopers LLP

LOCATIONS

HQ: Red Hat, Inc.
  1801 Varsity Dr., Raleigh, NC 27606
Phone: 919-754-3700   **Fax:** 919-754-3701
Web: www.redhat.com

Red Hat has offices in Australia, Canada, Germany, Hong Kong, India, Ireland, Italy, Japan, Malaysia, South Korea, the UK, and the US.

2006 Sales

	$ mil.	% of total
Americas	187.2	67
Europe/Middle East/Africa	48.7	18
Asia/Pacific & Japan	42.4	15
Total	**278.3**	**100**

PRODUCTS/OPERATIONS

2006 Sales

	$ mil.	% of total
Subscriptions	230.4	83
Training and services	47.9	17
Total	**278.3**	**100**

Software

Red Hat Enterprise
  Red Hat Enterprise Linux AS
  Red Hat Enterprise Linux ES
  Red Hat Enterprise Linux WS
  Red Hat Desktop
  Red Hat Professional Workstation
Red Hat Network
  Update
  Management
  Provisioning
Red Hat Applications
  Red Hat Cluster Suite
  Red Hat Developer Suite
  Red Hat Content Management System
  Red Hat Portal Server

Selected Services

Consulting
Custom development
Technical support
Training

COMPETITORS

Apple
BMC Software
CA
Hewlett-Packard
IBM Global Services
IBM Software
Levanta
Linspire
LinuxForce
LynuxWorks
Mandriva
Microsoft
MontaVista Software
Novell
SCO Group
Sun Microsystems
Turbolinux
Unisys
VA Software
VaST Systems
Win4Lin

HISTORICAL FINANCIALS

Company Type: Public

Income Statement				FYE: February 28
	REVENUE ($ mil.)	NET INCOME ($ mil.)	NET PROFIT MARGIN	EMPLOYEES
2/06	278.3	79.7	28.6%	1,100
2/05	196.5	45.4	23.1%	940
2/04	124.7	13.7	11.0%	681
2/03	90.9	(6.6)	—	566
2/02	78.9	(140.2)	—	634
Annual Growth	**37.0%**	**—**	**—**	**14.8%**

2006 Year-End Financials

Debt ratio: 119.5%
Return on equity: 19.0%
Cash ($ mil.): 804.9
Current ratio: 4.39
Long-term debt ($ mil.): 570.0
No. of shares (mil.): 183.1
Dividends
  Yield: —
  Payout: —
Market value ($ mil.): 4,920.3
R&D as % of sales: 14.7%
Advertising as % of sales: —

Stock History

NYSE: RHT

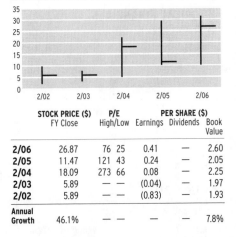

	STOCK PRICE ($) FY Close	P/E High/Low		PER SHARE ($) Earnings	Dividends	Book Value
2/06	26.87	76	25	0.41	—	2.60
2/05	11.47	121	43	0.24	—	2.05
2/04	18.09	273	66	0.08	—	2.25
2/03	5.89	—	—	(0.04)	—	1.97
2/02	5.89	—	—	(0.83)	—	1.93
Annual Growth	**46.1%**	**—**	**—**	**—**	**—**	**7.8%**

Renasant

Renasant Corporation (formerly The Peoples Holding Company) is the parent of Renasant Bank and Renasant Insurance. Through almost 60 branches in Mississippi, Tennessee, and Alabama, the bank provides a range of banking services to individuals and local businesses. Those services include checking and savings accounts, individual and business lending, and trusts. Mortgage loans account for some 65% of the bank's loan portfolio. Renasant's financial services division provides annuities and mutual funds; Renasant Insurance offers personal and business insurance. The company has been expanding beyond its home base into neighboring states through acquisitions.

After entering the Tennessee market with its purchase of Renasant Bancshares in 2004, The Peoples Holding Company in mid-2005 adopted the Renasant banner. With the Renasant deal, the company added two Memphis bank branches and loan production office. It gained a foothold in northern and central Alabama through its early 2005 acquisition of Heritage Financial Holding Corporation, the holding company for Heritage Bank.

EXECUTIVES

Chairman, President, and CEO; President and CEO, Renasant Bank: E. Robinson (Robin) McGraw, age 59, $553,578 pay
Vice Chairman: J. Larry Young, age 67
EVP and Director; President, Renasant Bank: Francis J. (Frank) Cianciola, age 55, $302,648 pay
EVP and General Counsel; SVP and General Counsel, Renasant Bank: Stephen M. Corban, age 50
EVP; President, Mississippi Division, Renasant Bank: C. Mitchell (Mitch) Waycaster, age 47
EVP; President, Alabama Division, Renasant Bank: Larry R. Mathews, age 53, $309,813 pay
EVP; SEVP and Chief Credit Officer, Renasant Bank: Harold H. Livingston, age 57

EVP; SEVP, CFO, and Cashier, Renasant Bank: Stuart R. Johnson, age 52, $292,756 pay
EVP; SEVP and Chief Credit Policy Officer, Renasant Bank: Claude H. Springfield III, age 58
Community Bank President, Amory, Renasant Bank: Larry Coggin
EVP and Director of Client and Employee Relations, Renasant Bank: H. L. Robinson
Auditors: Horne LLP

LOCATIONS

HQ: Renasant Corporation
  209 Troy St., Tupelo, MS 38802
Phone: 662-680-1001   **Fax:** 662-680-1042
Web: www.thepeopleplace.com

Renasant has offices located in Mississippi, Tennessee, and Alabama. Renasant Insurance has offices in the Mississippi communities of Corinth, Louisville, and Tupelo.

PRODUCTS/OPERATIONS

2005 Sales

	$ mil.	% of total
Interest		
Loans	109.9	65
Securities & other	18.5	11
Noninterest		
Service charges on deposit accounts	16.8	10
Fees & commissions	11.2	7
Other	12.2	7
Total	**168.6**	**100**

Selected Subsidiaries

Heritage Financial Statutory Trust I
PHC Statutory Trust I
PHC Statutory Trust II
  Renasant Bank
    Renasant Insurance, Inc.
    Primeco, Inc.

COMPETITORS

BancorpSouth
Citizens Holding
Colonial BancGroup
Compass Bancshares
Hancock Holding
Regions Financial
Trustmark
United Tennessee Bankshares

HISTORICAL FINANCIALS

Company Type: Public

Income Statement				FYE: December 31
	ASSETS ($ mil.)	NET INCOME ($ mil.)	INCOME AS % OF ASSETS	EMPLOYEES
12/05	2,397.7	24.2	1.0%	789
12/04	1,707.5	18.4	1.1%	703
12/03	1,415.2	18.2	1.3%	580
12/02	1,344.5	16.4	1.2%	587
12/01	1,254.7	14.6	1.2%	577
Annual Growth	**17.6%**	**13.5%**	**—**	**8.1%**

2005 Year-End Financials

Equity as % of assets: 9.8%
Return on assets: 1.2%
Return on equity: 11.7%
Long-term debt ($ mil.): 75.0
No. of shares (mil.): 10.4
Market value ($ mil.): 218.4
Dividends
  Yield: 3.1%
  Payout: 42.2%
Sales ($ mil.): 168.6
R&D as % of sales: —
Advertising as % of sales: 2.2%

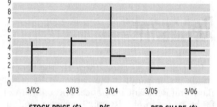

	STOCK PRICE ($) FY Close	P/E High/Low		PER SHARE ($) Earnings	Dividends	Book Value
12/05	21.09	15	12	1.54	0.65	22.74
12/04	22.07	17	13	1.43	—	19.79
12/03	22.00	16	12	1.46	—	16.79
12/02	18.11	15	11	1.30	—	23.82
12/01	16.44	15	7	1.10	—	21.66
Annual Growth	6.4%	—	—	8.8%	—	1.2%

Repligen

Repligen looks out for the kids. The firm develops drugs for neurological and autoimmune disorders, particularly for diseases that strike children. It is focusing on secretin, a gastrointestinal hormone that may treat obsessive-compulsive disorder and schizophrenia. Repligen is also working on drug candidates that may fight B-cell lymphoma, rheumatoid arthritis, and multiple sclerosis. The firm holds the rights to recombinant Protein A, which it sells to such biotechs as Amersham Biosciences, Millipore, and Applied Biosystems to mass produce therapeutic antibodies and perform R&D. Repligen also sells SecreFlo, used to assess pancreas function and diagnose gastrinoma, a gastroenterological cancer.

EXECUTIVES

Co-Chairman: Alexander Rich, age 81
Co-Chairman: Paul R. Schimmel, age 65
President, CEO, and Director: Walter C. Herlihy, age 55, $390,744 pay
CFO and Secretary: Daniel W. Muehl, age 43
SVP, Research and Development: James R. Rusche, age 52, $253,440 pay
VP, Operations: Daniel P. Witt, age 59, $214,272 pay
Auditors: Ernst & Young LLP

LOCATIONS

HQ: Repligen Corporation
41 Seyon St., Bldg. 1, Ste. 100, Waltham, MA 02453
Phone: 781-250-0111   **Fax:** 781-250-0115
Web: www.repligen.com

PRODUCTS/OPERATIONS

Selected Products

Approved
 rProtein A
 SecreFlo (synthetic porcine secretin)
In Development
 CTLA4-Ig (rheumatoid arthritis, multiple sclerosis, lupus, scleroderma)
 RG1068 (obsessive-compulsive disorder, schizophrenia)
 RG2133 (bipolar disorder, depression)

COMPETITORS

Abbott Labs
Cangene
Human Genome Sciences
Incyte
Merck
PDL

HISTORICAL FINANCIALS

Company Type: Public

Income Statement

FYE: March 31

	REVENUE ($ mil.)	NET INCOME ($ mil.)	NET PROFIT MARGIN	EMPLOYEES
3/06	12.9	0.7	5.4%	43
3/05	9.4	(3.0)	—	37
3/04	6.9	(9.6)	—	40
3/03	7.8	(4.5)	—	44
3/02	4.3	(4.5)	—	39
Annual Growth	31.6%	—	—	2.5%

2006 Year-End Financials

Debt ratio: —
Return on equity: 2.8%
Cash ($ mil.): 18.9
Current ratio: 7.32
Long-term debt ($ mil.): —
No. of shares (mil.): 30.4
Dividends
 Yield: —
 Payout: —
Market value ($ mil.): 112.4
R&D as % of sales: —
Advertising as % of sales: —

Stock History NASDAQ (GM): RGEN

	STOCK PRICE ($) FY Close	P/E High/Low		PER SHARE ($) Earnings	Dividends	Book Value
3/06	3.70	254	83	0.02	—	0.84
3/05	1.70	—	—	(0.10)	—	0.81
3/04	3.03	—	—	(0.32)	—	0.90
3/03	4.67	—	—	(0.17)	—	0.90
3/02	3.75	—	—	(0.17)	—	0.99
Annual Growth	(0.3%)	—	—	—	—	(4.2%)

Republic Airways Holdings

Four major US airlines have pledged allegiance to Republic Airways Holdings. Through subsidiaries Chautauqua Airlines, Republic Airlines, and Shuttle America, Republic Airways Holdings provides connecting flights between major airports and smaller markets under code-sharing agreements with AMR's American Airlines, Delta Air Lines, UAL's United Airlines, and US Airways. Overall, Republic Airways Holdings carriers serve some 80 cities in more than 30 states, Canada, and the Bahamas. The company maintains a fleet of about 150 Embraer regional jets that have a variety of seating capacities.

Regional jets fill a niche in the market between turbo-props and larger aircraft. The size and fuel efficiency of regional jets help keep costs in check and make it easier to serve smaller communities, making carriers like Republic Airways Holdings' operating units attractive partners for larger airlines. All three of Republic's airline subsidiaries fly under the flags of their code-sharing partners.

Investment firm Wexford Capital controls about 22% of Republic Airways Holdings.

EXECUTIVES

Chairman, President, and CEO: Bryan K. Bedford, age 44, $776,000 pay
EVP, CFO, Treasurer, and Secretary, Republic Airways and Chautauqua Airlines: Robert H. (Hal) Cooper, age 46, $537,759 pay
EVP and COO, Chautauqua Airlines: Wayne C. Heller, age 47, $533,500 pay
VP Corporate Development: Lars-Erik Arnell
VP and Controller: Beth A. Taylor
VP Customer Service: Jerry Balsano
VP Financial Planning and Analysis: Timothy P. (Tim) Dooley
VP Governmental Affairs and Communications: Warren R. Wilkinson
VP Planning: Jeffrey B. (Jeff) Jones
VP Safety: Donald D. (Don) Olvey
Director Human Resources, Republic Airways and Chautauqua Airlines: Kathy Wooldridge
Auditors: Deloitte & Touche LLP

LOCATIONS

HQ: Republic Airways Holdings Inc.
8909 Purdue Rd., Ste. 300, Indianapolis, IN 46268
Phone: 317-484-6000   **Fax:** 317-484-6040
Web: www.republicairways.com

COMPETITORS

Air Wisconsin Airlines
American Eagle
Comair
Great Lakes Aviation
Horizon Air
MAIR Holdings
Mesa Air
Midwest Air
Piedmont Airlines
SkyWest

HISTORICAL FINANCIALS

Company Type: Public

Income Statement

FYE: December 31

	REVENUE ($ mil.)	NET INCOME ($ mil.)	NET PROFIT MARGIN	EMPLOYEES
12/05	905.0	60.7	6.7%	3,060
12/04	646.3	38.8	6.0%	2,304
12/03	421.1	34.0	8.1%	—
12/02	315.5	17.0	5.4%	—
12/01	238.6	6.1	2.6%	1,118
Annual Growth	39.6%	77.6%	—	28.6%

2005 Year-End Financials

Debt ratio: 315.4%
Return on equity: 20.3%
Cash ($ mil.): 163.2
Current ratio: 1.36
Long-term debt ($ mil.): 1,339.5
No. of shares (mil.): 41.8
Dividends
 Yield: —
 Payout: —
Market value ($ mil.): 635.2
R&D as % of sales: —
Advertising as % of sales: —

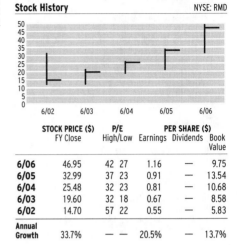

	STOCK PRICE ($) FY Close	P/E High/Low		PER SHARE ($) Earnings	Dividends	Book Value
12/05	15.20	10	6	1.66	—	10.16
12/04	13.27	9	5	1.62	—	6.83
Annual Growth	14.5%	—	—	2.5%	—	48.7%

ResMed

Breathe easy, because you won't lose any sleep while using ResMed's products. ResMed manufactures and distributes medical equipment used to diagnose, treat, and manage sleep-disordered breathing, including obstructive sleep apnea (OSA), which is characterized by restricted breathing and disrupted sleep. The company's flow generators (continuous and variable positive airway pressure — CPAP, VPAP, and AutoSet — systems) administer air through nasal masks to keep patients' airways open. ResMed also makes humidifiers, head harnesses, and other accessories.

ResMed has increased profits by remaining focused on sleep disordered breathing (SDB) while competitors diversify. The firm spends 7% of revenues on research and development, and is working on a device to treat Cheyne-Stokes Respiration (characterized by irregular breathing) in patients with congestive heart failure.

ResMed manufactures its products primarily in Australia and sells them in more than 60 countries worldwide through subsidiaries and independent distributors. The US and Germany account for nearly 70% of sales.

HISTORY

ResMed was founded as ResCare in 1989 after Peter Farrell led a management buyout of Baxter Healthcare's respiratory technology unit. ResCare initially developed the SULLIVAN nasal CPAP systems (named after inventor Colin Sullivan) in Australia. In 1991 it introduced the Bubble Mask and the APD2 portable CPAP device. Three years later ResCare began marketing its first VPAP, which applied different air pressures for inhalation and exhalation, in the US.

In 1995 the company went public, changing its name to ResMed (its former name was already taken by another medical company). Over the next two years, ResMed spent a lot of oxygen in court suing rival Respironics for patent infringements; judgments in 1997 and 1998 found in favor of Respironics, but ResMed made plans to appeal. In 1998 the firm received FDA approval to market its VPAP device as a critical-care treatment for lung diseases.

In 1999 the firm's listing was switched from the Nasdaq to the NYSE to stabilize stock prices

after court losses against Respironics; it also listed on the Australian Stock Exchange. The introduction of two new products, the AutoSet CPAP unit and the Mirage face mask, boosted sales that year. In 2001 ResMed bought MAP Medizin-Technologie, a German manufacturer of sleep-disordered breathing treatment devices. The acquisition enhanced ResMed's position in Germany, which is the company's second-biggest market for its products.

EXECUTIVES

Chairman and CEO: Peter C. Farrell, age 64, $1,123,896 pay
COO, Americas: Keith Serzen, age 53, $529,455 pay
CFO: Brett Sandercock, age 39
COO, Europe: Adrian M. Smith, age 42, $450,218 pay
COO, Sydney: Robert Douglas, age 46
SVP, Organizational Development, Global General Counsel, and Corporate Secretary: David Pendarvis, age 47, $466,068 pay
SVP, Telemedicine and Occupational Health: Dana Voien
SVP, Asia Pacific: Paul Eisen, age 47
SVP, Strategic Marketing Initiatives, Americas: Ron F. Richard
VP and Director, Marketing, Americas: Michael J. Farrell
Director, Human Resources, Americas: Lenita Maljan
President, ResMed Global: Kieran T. Gallahue, age 43, $776,965 pay
Manager, Investor Relations and Business Development: Matthew Borer
Auditors: KPMG LLP

LOCATIONS

HQ: ResMed Inc.
    14040 Danielson St., Poway, CA 92064
Phone: 858-746-2400   **Fax:** 858-746-2900
Web: www.resmed.com

ResMed has offices worldwide.

2006 Sales

	$ mil.	% of total
US	321.0	53
Germany	96.4	16
France	59.4	10
Australia	18.7	3
Other countries	111.5	18
Total	**607.0**	**100**

COMPETITORS

Allied Healthcare Products
Apria Healthcare
Cephalon
Chad Therapeutics
CNS
Mallinckrodt
Nims
Respironics
Sunrise Medical
Vital Signs

HISTORICAL FINANCIALS

Company Type: Public

Income Statement

				FYE: June 30
	REVENUE ($ mil.)	NET INCOME ($ mil.)	NET PROFIT MARGIN	EMPLOYEES
6/06	607.0	88.2	14.5%	2,500
6/05	425.5	64.8	15.2%	1,927
6/04	339.3	57.3	16.9%	1,520
6/03	273.6	45.7	16.7%	1,464
6/02	204.1	37.5	18.4%	1,250
Annual Growth	**31.3%**	**23.8%**	**—**	**18.9%**

2006 Year-End Financials

Debt ratio: 15.7%	Dividends
Return on equity: 14.6%	Yield: —
Cash ($ mil.): 219.5	Payout: —
Current ratio: 3.96	Market value ($ mil.): 3,552.7
Long-term debt ($ mil.): 116.2	R&D as % of sales: —
No. of shares (mil.): 75.7	Advertising as % of sales: —

	STOCK PRICE ($) FY Close	P/E High/Low		PER SHARE ($) Earnings	Dividends	Book Value
6/06	46.95	42	27	1.16	—	9.75
6/05	32.99	37	23	0.91	—	13.54
6/04	25.48	32	23	0.81	—	10.68
6/03	19.60	32	18	0.67	—	8.58
6/02	14.70	57	22	0.55	—	5.83
Annual Growth	33.7%	—	—	20.5%	—	13.7%

Resources Connection

Resources Connection is there when a pocket calculator just won't do. The company, which operates through its principal subsidiary Resources Global Professionals, generates the majority of its sales by providing accounting and finance professionals to clients on a project-by-project basis for services that include financial analyses, audits, and preparation of public filings. Resources Global Professionals also supplies professionals in the fields of human resources, risk management, legal services, supply chain management, and information technology. Founded in 1996, the company serves clients, including Exelon and Southwest Airlines, from more than 70 offices in the US and abroad.

Resources Connection's customers range from small start-ups to *FORTUNE* 100 companies. It has a client base of nearly 2,000 companies that includes all of the Big Four accounting firms.

The company has grown its international business, which accounts for about 20% of sales, both organically and through strategic acquisitions. In 2006 it opened eight additional offices in Europe and the Asia Pacific region. Opening the door for future expansion in India, it also acquired a regional accounting business owning offices in Mumbai and Bangalore. It expanded its European operations in 2004 with the purchase of 80% of Sweden-based Nordic Spring Management. In 2003 Resources Connection acquired Ernst & Young's Dutch subsidiary Executive Temporary Management for about $30 million.

T. Rowe Price and Wellington Management Company each own about 11% of the company.

EXECUTIVES

Chairman, President, and CEO:
Donald B. (Don) Murray, age 59, $1,145,550 pay
EVP Corporate Development, CFO, Secretary, and Director: Stephen J. Giusto, age 44, $538,940 pay
EVP Human Relations, Chief Legal Officer, and Assistant Secretary: Kate W. Duchene, age 43, $538,940 pay
EVP Operations: Anthony Cherbak, age 52, $498,455 pay
EVP, Regional Managing Director, East Coast, and Director: Karen M. Ferguson, age 42, $538,940 pay
SVP Finance: John D. Bower, age 44
Managing Director, Tokyo Office: Hiro Ueda
Controller: Erin Hartshorn
Auditors: PricewaterhouseCoopers LLP

LOCATIONS

HQ: Resources Connection, Inc.
695 Town Center Dr., Ste. 600,
Costa Mesa, CA 92626
Phone: 714-430-6400   **Fax:** 714-428-6090
Web: www.resourcesglobal.com

Resources Connection has about 50 offices across the US. It has international offices located in Australia, Canada, France, Hong Kong, Japan, the Netherlands, Sweden, Taiwan, and the UK.

2006 Sales

	$ mil.	% of total
US	499.9	79
Netherlands	62.9	10
Other countries	71.0	11
Total	**633.8**	**100**

PRODUCTS/OPERATIONS

Selected Services

Accounting and finance
  Audit preparation
  Budgeting
  Due diligence
  Financial analyses
  Payroll system design
  Public reporting
  Tax-related projects
Human capital management
  Compensation program design and implementation
  Employee training and policies
  Governmental regulation compliance
  Human resources management
Information technology
  Interim IT management
  Systems conversion, implementation, and upgrades
  Systems selection processes

COMPETITORS

Accountants
accountants on call
Acsys
Adecco
COMSYS IT Partners
Deloitte
Ernst & Young
Kelly Services
KPMG
Manpower
MPS
PricewaterhouseCoopers
Robert Half
Silicon Valley Staffing
Solomon-Page Group
Spherion
Vedior

HISTORICAL FINANCIALS

Company Type: Public

Income Statement

FYE: May 31

	REVENUE ($ mil.)	NET INCOME ($ mil.)	NET PROFIT MARGIN	EMPLOYEES
5/06	633.8	60.6	9.6%	3,607
5/05	537.6	56.1	10.4%	3,231
5/04	328.3	24.3	7.4%	2,550
5/03	202.0	12.5	6.2%	1,519
5/02	181.7	13.3	7.3%	1,372
Annual Growth	**36.7%**	**46.1%**	**—**	**27.3%**

2006 Year-End Financials

Debt ratio: —
Return on equity: 21.4%
Cash ($ mil.): 125.4
Current ratio: 3.42
Long-term debt ($ mil.): —
No. of shares (mil.): 48.3
Dividends
  Yield: —
  Payout: —
Market value ($ mil.): 1,231.1
R&D as % of sales: —
Advertising as % of sales: —

Stock History

NASDAQ (GS): RECN

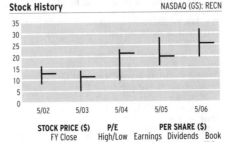

	STOCK PRICE ($) FY Close	P/E High/Low	PER SHARE ($) Earnings	PER SHARE ($) Dividends	PER SHARE ($) Book Value
5/06	25.50	27 17	1.17	—	6.58
5/05	19.92	25 15	1.11	—	5.24
5/04	21.31	46 19	0.50	—	7.77
5/03	11.19	50 19	0.28	—	6.00
5/02	12.73	54 29	0.29	—	5.24
Annual Growth	**19.0%**	**— —**	**41.7%**	**—**	**5.8%**

RightNow Technologies

RightNow Technologies can help you get answers quickly about your customers. The firm provides customer relationship management (CRM) software and services. RightNow's products (primarily delivered as hosted applications) are used to manage customer service through such channels as e-mail, live Internet chat, and telephone interactions. The company's software also includes a knowledgebase designed to ensure more accurate interactions with customers, and it handles service, call center agent desktop, sales, and marketing functions. The company also offers analytic tools and a variety of professional services. RightNow was founded by CEO Greg Gianforte, who controls about 35% of the company.

RightNow boasts a client base of more than 1,200 customers, including government agencies, educational institutions, and companies in the technology, financial services, consumer products, telecommunications, and travel and hospitality industries.

In June 2005 the company acquired Convergent Voice, a voice automation technology provider. The next year the company purchased salesforce automation software provider Salesnet for about $9 million.

EXECUTIVES

Chairman, President, and CEO: Greg R. Gianforte, age 45, $368,592 pay
President, Field Operations: Jay C. Rising
VP, Finance and Administration, CFO, Treasurer, and Assistant Secretary: Susan J. Carstensen, age 44, $247,222 pay
VP, Business Development: Scott Creighton
VP, International Operations: Didier Guibal
VP, Marketing: Jason Mittelstaedt, age 30
VP, North American Sales: Michael (Mike) Saracini
VP, Sales Engineering: Michael (Mike) Russo
VP, Worldwide Sales Operations: Jeff Davison
Media and Analyst Relations: Katie O'Connell
Auditors: KPMG LLP

LOCATIONS

HQ: RightNow Technologies, Inc.
40 Enterprise Blvd., Bozeman, MT 59718
Phone: 406-522-4200   **Fax:** 406-522-4227
Web: www.rightnow.com

2005 Sales

	% of total
US	74
Other countries	26
Total	**100**

PRODUCTS/OPERATIONS

2005 Sales

	$ mil.	% of total
Software, hosting & support	67.9	78
Professional services	19.3	22
Total	**87.2**	**100**

Selected Products and Services

Application hosting
Consulting
Implementation
Integration
RightNow Outbound (e-mail marketing management software)
RightNow Service (customer inquiry management software)
Training

COMPETITORS

Amdocs
BMC Software
eGain Communications
FrontRange Solutions
KANA
Microsoft Business Solutions
Oracle
salesforce.com
SAP

HISTORICAL FINANCIALS

Company Type: Public

Income Statement

FYE: December 31

	REVENUE ($ mil.)	NET INCOME ($ mil.)	NET PROFIT MARGIN	EMPLOYEES
12/05	87.2	7.7	8.8%	530
12/04	61.8	3.5	5.7%	403
12/03	35.9	(4.1)	—	322
12/02	26.9	(2.8)	—	—
Annual Growth	**48.0%**	**—**	**—**	**28.3%**

Debt ratio: 0.3%
Return on equity: 20.3%
Cash ($ mil.): 64.2
Current ratio: 1.76
Long-term debt ($ mil.): 0.1
No. of shares (mil.): 31.9

Dividends
 Yield: —
 Payout: —
Market value ($ mil.): 588.4
R&D as % of sales: 12.0%
Advertising as % of sales: 3.1%

Stock History

NASDAQ (GM): RNOW

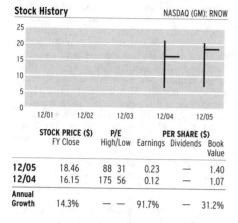

	STOCK PRICE ($) FY Close	P/E High/Low		Earnings	PER SHARE ($) Dividends	Book Value
12/05	18.46	88	31	0.23	—	1.40
12/04	16.15	175	56	0.12	—	1.07
Annual Growth	14.3%	—	—	91.7%	—	31.2%

Rimage Corporation

Rimage serves up information on a platter. The company makes CD recordable (CD-R), DVD recordable (DVD-R), and digital tape (diskette) production and duplication equipment. The majority of Rimage's sales come from its line of CD-R and DVD-R equipment, which includes systems for premastering, recording, and labeling CDs, as well as thermal printers for labeling and decorating recorded media. The company, which offers separate product lines for high-volume production (Producer) environments and smaller office applications (Desktop), also makes diskette duplication and labeling systems. The company sells directly and through distributors and resellers in the Americas, Europe, and Asia.

EXECUTIVES

Chairman: James L. Reissner, age 66
President, CEO, and Director:
 Bernard P. (Bernie) Aldrich, age 56, $463,789 pay
CFO, Secretary, and Treasurer: Robert M. (Rob) Wolf, age 37
CTO and Director: David J. Suden, age 59, $347,035 pay
EVP and COO: Manuel M. (Manny) Almeida, age 48
EVP, Sales: Kenneth J. Klinck, age 55, $242,100 pay
SVP, Engineering: William J. Farmer, age 52
VP, Business Development, Photographic Markets:
 Thomas R. Cuffari
VP, European Operations; Managing Director, Rimage Europe: Konrad E. Rotermund, age 57, $284,910 pay
VP, Marketing: Joe Stark
Auditors: KPMG LLP

LOCATIONS

HQ: Rimage Corporation
 7725 Washington Ave. South,
 Minneapolis, MN 55439
Phone: 952-944-8144   **Fax:** 952-944-7808
Web: www.rimage.com

Rimage operates facilities in Edina, Minnesota and in Dietzenbach, Germany.

2005 Sales

	$ mil.	% of total
North America	63.1	66
Europe	26.8	28
Other regions	5.5	6
Total	**95.4**	**100**

PRODUCTS/OPERATIONS

2005 Sales

	$ mil.	% of total
Equipment		
Producer	48.4	51
Desktop	10.7	11
Consumables, parts & repairs	32.7	34
Maintenance contracts	3.6	4
Total	**95.4**	**100**

COMPETITORS

Disc
Hitachi
Iomega
Matsushita
Philips Electronics
Pioneer
Plextor
Sony
STEAG HamaTech
Toshiba
Yamaha
YMI

HISTORICAL FINANCIALS

Company Type: Public

Income Statement

FYE: December 31

	REVENUE ($ mil.)	NET INCOME ($ mil.)	NET PROFIT MARGIN	EMPLOYEES
12/05	95.4	11.4	11.9%	208
12/04	70.8	9.1	12.9%	184
12/03	53.8	7.7	14.3%	157
12/02	46.6	6.5	13.9%	140
12/01	38.9	4.8	12.3%	127
Annual Growth	25.1%	24.1%	—	13.1%

2005 Year-End Financials

Debt ratio: —
Return on equity: 16.4%
Cash ($ mil.): 64.5
Current ratio: 6.93
Long-term debt ($ mil.): —
No. of shares (mil.): 9.6

Dividends
 Yield: —
 Payout: —
Market value ($ mil.): 279.1
R&D as % of sales: 5.8%
Advertising as % of sales: —

Stock History

NASDAQ (GS): RIMG

	STOCK PRICE ($) FY Close	P/E High/Low		Earnings	PER SHARE ($) Dividends	Book Value
12/05	28.98	29	14	1.10	—	7.95
12/04	16.07	19	13	0.91	—	6.70
12/03	15.84	21	10	0.79	—	5.71
12/02	8.12	16	11	0.68	—	4.84
12/01	8.12	24	11	0.51	—	4.08
Annual Growth	37.4%	—	—	21.2%	—	18.1%

Riverview Bancorp

Riverview Bancorp is the holding company for Riverview Community Bank, which has more than 15 branches in the Columbia River Gorge area of Washington State. Serving consumers and local businesses, the bank offers such standard retail banking services as checking and savings accounts, money market accounts, NOW accounts, and CDs. Commercial real estate loans account for nearly 60% of its loan portfolio. Other loans consist of one-to-four family residential mortgages, residential construction loans, and business and consumer loans. Trust and investment services are provided through 85%-owned subsidiary Riverview Asset Management. Riverview Bancorp bought Portland, Oregon-based American Pacific Bank in April 2005.

Riverview's employee stock purchase plan owns more than 7% of the company, Wellington Management owns more than 9%, and director Patrick Sheaffer owns 5%.

EXECUTIVES

Chairman and CEO; CEO, Riverview Community Bank:
 Patrick Sheaffer, age 66, $281,735 pay
President, COO, and Director; President and COO, Riverview Community Bank: Ronald A. (Ron) Wysaske, age 53, $248,815 pay
SVP and CFO: Ronald (Ron) Dobyns, age 57, $134,601 pay
EVP and Chief Credit Officer, Riverview Community Bank: David A. Dahlstrom, age 55, $209,216 pay
SVP, Riverview Community Bank; Chairman, President, and CEO, Riverview Asset Management: John A. Karas, age 57, $226,596 pay
SVP, Business and Professional Banking, Riverview Community Bank: Jeff Donaldson
SVP, Lending, Riverview Community Bank:
 Karen M. Nelson
SVP, Operations and Information Technology, Riverview Community Bank: Terry Long, age 46
SVP, Retail Banking Division, Riverview Community Bank: James D. (Jim) Baldovin, age 46, $140,324 pay
Auditors: Deloitte & Touche LLP

LOCATIONS

HQ: Riverview Bancorp, Inc.
 900 Washington St., Ste. 900, Vancouver, WA 98660
Phone: 360-693-6650   **Fax:** 360-693-6275
Web: www.riverviewbank.com

PRODUCTS/OPERATIONS

2006 Sales

	% of total
Interest	
Loans	80
Securities	4
Non-interest	
Fees & service charges	11
Asset management fees	3
Other	2
Total	**100**

COMPETITORS

Bank of America
Banner
KeyCorp
Sterling Financial (WA)
U.S. Bancorp
Washington Mutual
Wells Fargo

HISTORICAL FINANCIALS

Company Type: Public

Income Statement
FYE: March 31

	ASSETS ($ mil.)	NET INCOME ($ mil.)	INCOME AS % OF ASSETS	EMPLOYEES
3/06	763.8	9.7	1.3%	239
3/05	572.6	6.5	1.1%	197
3/04	520.5	6.6	1.3%	186
3/03	419.9	4.4	1.0%	157
3/02	392.1	4.9	1.2%	147
Annual Growth	18.1%	18.6%	—	12.9%

2006 Year-End Financials

Equity as % of assets: 12.0%
Return on assets: 1.5%
Return on equity: 12.0%
Long-term debt ($ mil.): 10.0
No. of shares (mil.): 5.8
Market value ($ mil.): 77.2

Dividends
Yield: 2.5%
Payout: 39.5%
Sales ($ mil.): 56.1
R&D as % of sales: —
Advertising as % of sales: —

Stock History
NASDAQ (GS): RVSB

	STOCK PRICE ($) FY Close	P/E High/Low		PER SHARE ($) Earnings	Dividends	Book Value
3/06	13.38	16	12	0.86	0.34	15.88
3/05	10.63	17	14	0.67	0.31	11.98
3/04	10.10	16	12	0.69	0.28	13.64
3/03	8.49	17	13	0.50	0.25	12.51
3/02	7.00	13	9	0.53	0.22	12.04
Annual Growth	17.6%			12.9%	11.5%	7.2%

Rockwell Medical Technologies

Rockwell Medical Technologies keeps on trucking with its hemodialysis products. The company makes hemodialysis concentrates, dialysis kits, and other related products for treatment of end-stage renal disease (permanent kidney failure). Subsidiary Rockwell Transportation delivers supplies to customers via a fleet of trucks.

The company markets and distributes its products directly to hemodialysis providers across the US, as well as through sales representatives and independent distributors abroad.

Rockwell Medical Technologies plans to expand its product line, as well as add manufacturing facilities and distribution centers.

CEO Robert L. Chioini owns about 18% of the company. CFO Thomas E. Klema owns about 6%.

EXECUTIVES

Chairman, President, and CEO: Robert L. Chioini, age 42, $275,000 pay
VP Finance, CFO, Treasurer, and Secretary: Thomas E. Klema, age 52, $156,600 pay
Human Resources Manager: Ed Castelmi
Auditors: Plante & Moran, PLLC

LOCATIONS

HQ: Rockwell Medical Technologies, Inc.
30142 Wixom Rd., Wixom, MI 48393
Phone: 248-960-9009 **Fax:** 248-960-9119
Web: www.rockwellmed.com

PRODUCTS/OPERATIONS

Selected Products

Acidified Dialysate Concentrate
Ancillary products (including needles, gloves, cleaning agents, and filtration salts)
Bicarbonate
Dri-Sate Dry Acid Concentrate
SteriLyte Liquid Bicarbonate (for acute care)

Subsidiaries

Rockwell Transportation, Inc.

COMPETITORS

Aksys
Baxter
Fresenius Medical Care
Gambro AB
MedaSorb Technologies
Minntech

HISTORICAL FINANCIALS

Company Type: Public

Income Statement
FYE: December 31

	REVENUE ($ mil.)	NET INCOME ($ mil.)	NET PROFIT MARGIN	EMPLOYEES
12/05	27.7	0.1	0.4%	150
12/04	17.9	0.2	1.1%	120
12/03	15.0	0.0	—	80
12/02	11.5	(1.0)	—	80
12/01	9.0	(1.6)	—	75
Annual Growth	32.5%	—	—	18.9%

2005 Year-End Financials

Debt ratio: 19.0%
Return on equity: 2.8%
Cash ($ mil.): 0.3
Current ratio: 1.15
Long-term debt ($ mil.): 0.7
No. of shares (mil.): 8.9

Dividends
Yield: —
Payout: —
Market value ($ mil.): 39.7
R&D as % of sales: —
Advertising as % of sales: —

Stock History
NASDAQ (GM): RMTI

	STOCK PRICE ($) FY Close	P/E High/Low		PER SHARE ($) Earnings	Dividends	Book Value
12/05	4.47	530	270	0.01	—	0.43
12/04	3.15	225	103	0.02	—	0.40
12/03	3.99	—	—	—	—	0.37
12/02	0.59	—	—	(0.12)	—	0.36
12/01	1.40	—	—	(0.26)	—	0.36
Annual Growth	33.7%			—	—	4.6%

Rocky Brands

Rocky is a sole survivor. Rocky Brands makes and markets premium, high-quality men's and women's footwear. Its products are organized into three categories: rugged, outdoor footwear (such as waterproof waders and hunting and hiking boots); occupational footwear (including steel toe boots for law enforcement, construction, and other industries); and casual shoes (think chukkas and oxfords) and boots (including western style). The company's products are sold primarily through sporting goods stores and catalogs in the US and Canada. Brothers William and F. M. Brooks founded Rocky in 1932; F. M.'s grandson, chairman and CEO Mike Brooks, owns about 10% of the company.

Rocky makes footwear in factories in Puerto Rico and in the Dominican Republic and also sources products from manufacturers in Asia (primarily China).

Rocky started 2005 with the acquisition of footwear maker EJ Footwear Group. The $89.5 million purchase doubled Rocky's size with licensed brands such as Lehigh Safety Shoes, Durango Boot, and Dickies Footwear. Lehigh branded shoes are sold through about 40 small warehouses and some 80 mobile stores — trucks stocked with footwear that visit corporate customer sites to outfit employees. Rocky also operates two outlet stores.

Rocky's contract to produce boots for the military was terminated in early 2006 but the company has been working to replace the revenue. Such military contracts accounted for about 9% of the company's total income in 2005. The company signed a licensing agreement in mid-2006 to produce a line of men's and women's casual footwear under the Zumfoot brand name for Sole Matters, an operator of nine shoe stores under the Zumfoot banner. A deal with Michelin Footwear, a unit of Gear Six LLC, made Rocky the private labeler for Michelin to make and market Michelin-branded footwear in North America.

Having outgrown its Rocky Shoes & Boots name, the company changed its name in May 2006 to Rocky Brands.

HISTORY

The William Brooks Shoe Company was founded in 1932 by brothers William and F.M. Brooks (Mike, the current chairman's great-uncle and grandfather, respectively) to offer shoes for the serious outdoorsman. William bought out Mike and sold the firm to the Irving Drew Shoe Co. in 1959; Mike's son John continued to work for the company. In 1974, after fighting a losing battle against imported shoes, Irving Drew sold the business to John, who was immediately joined by his son Mike.

To survive in the cutthroat shoe industry, the Brooks Company created its own niche: handmade rugged shoes. In the 1980s it began using waterproof GORE-TEX, which, along with the "Made in America" tag, made the boots an instant hit. The firm began marketing occupational shoes for police officers and mail carriers in 1983. After expanding production to the Dominican Republic and Puerto Rico in 1987, the Brooks Company was deep in debt. John, who had resisted growing the company and taking it public, retired in 1991. Two years later the firm adopted its current name, Rocky Shoes & Boots, and went public.

Since 1993 Rocky has doubled its number of styles and outsourced some of its manufacturing to China and Taiwan. The Nelsonville, Ohio, factory outlet opened in 1994 (manufacturing operations there were closed in late 2001). Order delays helped contribute to a financial loss the next year. New products in 1997 included chest and hip waders. In 1999 Rocky continued to expand its casual footwear, introducing Formz comfort sandals. In 2000 the company moved about half of its 112 manufacturing jobs overseas to take advantage of cheaper labor.

Rocky began producing military boots under government contract in 2001.

In 2003 the company acquired Gates-Mills, a producer of performance outdoor and dress gloves, which kicked off an expansion of Rocky's product line into areas beyond footwear. In January 2005 Rocky purchased EJ Footwear Group for $89.5 million plus $10 million in stock.

EXECUTIVES

Chairman and CEO: Mike Brooks, age 58, $350,000 pay
President and COO; EVP and COO, Five Star and Lifestyle: David Sharp, age 47, $285,000 pay
EVP, CFO, and Treasurer; CFO, Five Star and Lifestyle: James E. (Jim) McDonald, age 43, $230,000 pay
SVP, Sales, Wholesale Brands: Thomas R. Morrison, $200,000 pay (partial-year salary)
VP, Apparel Business Development: John Maser
VP, Women's Occupational Business Development: Scott Jenkins
Secretary and Director; Secretary, Five Star and Lifestyle: Curtis A. (Curt) Loveland, age 59
Director Human Resources: Brenda Hammond
Auditors: Deloitte & Touche LLP

LOCATIONS

HQ: Rocky Brands, Inc.
39 E. Canal St., Nelsonville, OH 45764
Phone: 740-753-1951   **Fax:** 740-753-4024
Web: www.rockyboots.com

Rocky Shoes & Boots has manufacturing plants in the Dominican Republic and Puerto Rico. The company's outlet stores are in Edgefield, South Carolina and Nelsonville, Ohio.

PRODUCTS/OPERATIONS

2005 Sales

	$ mil.	% of total
Wholesale	209.9	71
Retail	58.4	20
Military	27.7	9
Total	**296.0**	**100**

2005 Sales

	$ mil.	% of total
Work footwear	143.8	49
Western footwear	40.4	14
Outdoor footwear	38.7	13
Military footwear	27.7	9
Apparel	18.4	6
Duty footwear	16.8	6
Other	10.2	3
Total	**296.0**	**100**

COMPETITORS

Bakers Footwear	Red Wing Shoe
Brown Shoe	Reebok
Deckers Outdoor	Stride Rite
Jimlar	Timberland
LaCrosse Footwear	Wellco
NIKE	Wolverine World Wide
R. Griggs	

HISTORICAL FINANCIALS
Company Type: Public

Income Statement
FYE: December 31

	REVENUE ($ mil.)	NET INCOME ($ mil.)	NET PROFIT MARGIN	EMPLOYEES
12/05	296.0	13.0	4.4%	1,900
12/04	132.3	8.6	6.5%	1,091
12/03	106.2	6.0	5.6%	1,026
12/02	89.0	2.8	3.1%	824
12/01	103.3	1.5	1.5%	936
Annual Growth	**30.1%**	**71.6%**	**—**	**19.4%**

2005 Year-End Financials

Debt ratio: 99.9%
Return on equity: 15.3%
Cash ($ mil.): 1.6
Current ratio: 5.79
Long-term debt ($ mil.): 99.0
No. of shares (mil.): 5.4
Dividends
  Yield: —
  Payout: —
Market value ($ mil.): 130.4
R&D as % of sales: —
Advertising as % of sales: 2.7%

Stock History
NASDAQ (GS): RCKY

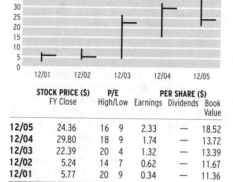

	STOCK PRICE ($) FY Close	P/E High/Low		PER SHARE ($) Earnings	Dividends	Book Value
12/05	24.36	16	9	2.33	—	18.52
12/04	29.80	18	9	1.74	—	13.72
12/03	22.39	20	4	1.32	—	13.39
12/02	5.24	14	7	0.62	—	11.67
12/01	5.77	20	9	0.34	—	11.36
Annual Growth	**43.3%**	**—**	**—**	**61.8%**	**—**	**13.0%**

RPC, Inc.

RPC helps to grease the wheels of oil and gas production. Through its Cudd Pressure Control subsidiary, the company provides oil industry consulting and technical services including snubbing, coiled tubing, nitrogen services, and well control. Another subsidiary, Patterson Services, rents specialized tools and equipment such as drill pipe, tubing, and blowout preventers. RPC also provides maintenance, emergency services, and storage and inspection services for offshore and inland vessels. The company operates in most of the world's major oil producing regions. Chairman R. Randall Rollins and his brother Gary own more than 60% of RPC.

EXECUTIVES

Chairman; Chairman and CEO, Cudd Pumping Services; CEO, Cudd Pressure Control: R. Randall Rollins, age 74, $855,000 pay
President, CEO, and Director; President and CEO, Cudd Pressure Control: Richard A. Hubbell, age 60, $905,000 pay
VP, CFO, and Treasurer; CFO, Cudd Pressure Control: Ben M. Palmer, age 44, $350,000 pay
VP, Secretary, and Director: Linda H. Graham, age 68, $180,000 pay
VP and General Manager, Cudd Pressure Control: Ray Saliba
VP and General Manager, Patterson Rental Tools: Jim Daniel
Corporate Finance: James C. (Jim) Landers
Investor Relations and Corporate Communication: Natasha Coleman
Auditors: Grant Thornton LLP

LOCATIONS

HQ: RPC, Inc.
2170 Piedmont Rd. NE, Atlanta, GA 30324
Phone: 404-321-2140   **Fax:** 404-321-5483
Web: www.rpc.net

RPC has 75 facilities, including principal operations in Houma and Morgan City, Louisiana; Houston and Kilgore, Texas; Elk City and Seminole, Oklahoma; and Rock Springs, Wyoming.

2005 Sales

	$ mil.	% of total
US	413.3	97
Other countries	14.3	3
Total	**427.6**	**100**

PRODUCTS/OPERATIONS

2005 Sales

	$ mil.	% of total
Technical services	363.1	85
Support services	64.5	15
Total	**427.6**	**100**

COMPETITORS

Baker Hughes
BJ Services
Boots & Coots
Ensign Energy Services
Grant Prideco
Halliburton Energy Services
Hanover Compressor
Precision Drilling
Schlumberger
Transocean
Weatherford International

HISTORICAL FINANCIALS
Company Type: Public

Income Statement
FYE: December 31

	REVENUE ($ mil.)	NET INCOME ($ mil.)	NET PROFIT MARGIN	EMPLOYEES
12/05	427.6	66.5	15.6%	1,600
12/04	339.8	34.8	10.2%	1,596
12/03	270.5	10.9	4.0%	1,529
12/02	209.0	(5.3)	—	1,419
12/01	264.9	27.0	10.2%	1,533
Annual Growth	**12.7%**	**25.3%**	**—**	**1.1%**

2005 Year-End Financials

Debt ratio: —
Return on equity: 32.1%
Cash ($ mil.): 12.8
Current ratio: 2.86
Long-term debt ($ mil.): —
No. of shares (mil.): 64.5
Dividends
  Yield: 0.2%
  Payout: 6.0%
Market value ($ mil.): 1,131.8
R&D as % of sales: —
Advertising as % of sales: —

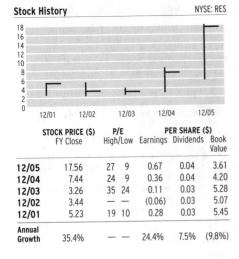

	STOCK PRICE ($) FY Close	P/E High/Low		PER SHARE ($) Earnings	Dividends	Book Value
12/05	17.56	27	9	0.67	0.04	3.61
12/04	7.44	24	9	0.36	0.04	4.20
12/03	3.26	35	24	0.11	0.03	5.28
12/02	3.44	—	—	(0.06)	0.03	5.07
12/01	5.23	19	10	0.28	0.03	5.45
Annual Growth	35.4%	—	—	24.4%	7.5%	(9.8%)

RTI International Metals

RTI International Metals hopes manufacturers that seek a lightweight yet tougher-than-nails material will have titanium on the cranium. Through its subsidiaries, the company operates in two segments: titanium products and metals fabrication and distribution. The titanium group's products include ingots, bars, plates, sheets, strips, pipes, and welded tubing that are used by the aerospace industry to make aircraft bulkheads, tail sections, engine components, and wing supports. RTI's fabrication and distribution group operates through subsidiary RTI Energy Systems and makes pipe, tubing, and offshore riser systems for the oil, gas, and geothermal energy industries.

Other titanium products include bar used in medical implants and high-performance automotive engine parts.

It may sound odd at first but rising fuel prices are actually helping RTI International. As fuel prices go up, many commercial airlines are updating their fleets with new airplanes. Aircraft manufacturers Boeing and Airbus are building new planes designed to incur lower operating costs — partly through lower fuel consumption as a result of reduced aircraft weight. Boeing and Airbus between them have a backlog of nearly 4,000 aircraft; this combined with a demand for lightweight components is great news for RTI International.

FMR Corp. owns about 15% of the company.

HISTORY

In 1964 Quantum Chemical (now a subsidiary of Millennium Chemical) and U.S. Steel (now United States Steel) formed Reactive Metals Inc. The company changed its name to RMI Titanium Company in 1971. It went public in 1990, with Quantum selling its shares and United States Steel retaining its interest.

The titanium industry is closely tied to the ups and downs of the aerospace industry, and just after RMI's IPO, the industry hit one of its cyclical slumps. RMI suffered years of losses even as it worked to cut costs and develop new markets. In 1992 it closed its titanium sponge (a porous metal used as raw material) facility and began buying lower-cost sponge from third parties. The next year it began providing seamless titanium pipe to California Energy Co. for use in that company's geothermal well. In 1995 RMI completed the world's first high-pressure titanium drilling riser for use in a Conoco North Sea oil rig.

In 1996 two events turned RMI's fortunes around. The aerospace industry took off once more, and golfers discovered titanium club heads. RMI formed a joint venture with Earthline Technologies in 1997 to offer soil-remediation services (perhaps relying on its experience as an owner of a Superfund site). In 1997 RMI bought Galt Alloys, a producer of ferrotitanium. The next year the company signed long-term supply agreements with Boeing, Northrop, and Aerospatiale. The company changed its name to RTI International Metals in 1998. USX sold off its 27% stake in 1999.

In 2000 RTI International Metals received a $6 million settlement from Boeing after the aerospace giant failed to meet the conditions of a 1999 long-term supply agreement between the two companies. Later in the year the company purchased the remaining shares of Reamet, S.A., a French-market distributor of titanium products. In 2001 RTI International Metals saw an increase in net income of about $12.1 million on sales of $285.9 million but noticed troubles ahead for its titanium group because of a weakening commercial aerospace industry.

In 2002 the company entered into agreements with Europe's largest aerospace group, European Aeronautic Defense and Space Company, to supply titanium products and parts. The following year, a work stoppage was held by the company's unionized employees at its Niles, Ohio plant. Non-union employees will operate the plant until an agreement can be hashed out between union representatives and the company's management.

EXECUTIVES

Chairman: Robert M. Hernandez, age 62
President, CEO, and Director: Timothy G. Rupert, age 60, $873,750 pay
EVP and Director: John H. Odle, age 63, $506,416 pay
SVP Administration, Chief Administrative Officer, General Counsel, and Corporate Secretary:
Dawne S. Hickton, age 48, $428,338 pay
VP and Chief Accounting Officer: William T. Hull, $158,335 pay
VP and Controller: Gordon R. Berkstresser, age 58, $149,583 pay
VP, Administration: David Z. Paull
President, Fabrication & Distribution Group:
Daniel Molina
General Manager, Fabrication & Distribution Group:
Jerome Mourain
General Manager, Galt Alloys: Bruce A. Whetzel, age 41
General Manager Sales, RTI Fabrication & Distribution: Martin J. Procko, age 48
Manager, Investor Relations: Richard E. Leone
Head of RTI Commercial Products:
Christopher P. Clancy, age 37
Auditors: PricewaterhouseCoopers LLP

LOCATIONS

HQ: RTI International Metals, Inc.
1000 Warren Ave., Niles, OH 44446
Phone: 330-652-9955   **Fax:** 330-544-7701
Web: www.rti-intl.com

RTI International Metals has titanium product manufacturing facilities in Ohio and Utah, and fabrication and distribution centers in California, Connecticut, Missouri, Pennsylvania, and Texas, in the US, and in Canada, France, and the UK.

2005 Sales

	$ mil.	% of total
US	279.7	81
Canada	19.0	6
UK	18.7	5
France	14.8	4
Germany	4.6	1
South Korea	0.5	—
Other countries	9.6	3
Total	**346.9**	**100**

PRODUCTS/OPERATIONS

2005 Sales

	$ mil.	% of total
Fabrication & Distribution Group	216.7	62
Titanium Group	130.2	38
Total	**346.9**	**100**

Selected Products

Fabricated Products
Cut shapes
Drill pipe
Engineered tubular products
Engineering services
Hot-formed parts
Offshore riser systems
Pipe
Stress joints
Titanium Mill Products
Billet
Bloom
Ingot
Plate
Sheet
Slab
Titanium powders
Welded tubes

COMPETITORS

Carpenter Technology
Hurlen Corporation
Liquidmetal
Metals USA
Titanium Metals
Wah Chang

HISTORICAL FINANCIALS

Company Type: Public

Income Statement				FYE: December 31
	REVENUE ($ mil.)	NET INCOME ($ mil.)	NET PROFIT MARGIN	EMPLOYEES
12/05	346.9	38.9	11.2%	1,225
12/04	214.6	(3.0)	—	1,185
12/03	205.5	4.7	2.3%	1,117
12/02	270.9	15.1	5.6%	1,202
12/01	285.9	12.1	4.2%	1,170
Annual Growth	5.0%	33.9%	—	1.2%

2005 Year-End Financials

Debt ratio: —
Return on equity: 11.1%
Cash ($ mil.): 55.8
Current ratio: 5.57
Long-term debt ($ mil.): —
No. of shares (mil.): 22.7

Dividends
Yield: —
Payout: —
Market value ($ mil.): 861.0
R&D as % of sales: 0.5%
Advertising as % of sales: —

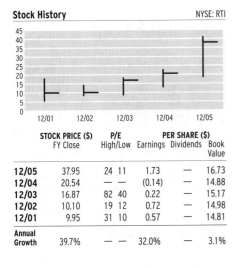

	STOCK PRICE ($) FY Close	P/E High/Low		PER SHARE ($) Earnings	Dividends	Book Value
12/05	37.95	24	11	1.73	—	16.73
12/04	20.54	—	—	(0.14)	—	14.88
12/03	16.87	82	40	0.22	—	15.17
12/02	10.10	19	12	0.72	—	14.98
12/01	9.95	31	10	0.57	—	14.81
Annual Growth	39.7%	—	—	32.0%	—	3.1%

SafeNet

SafeNet just wants the world of networks to be a safer place. The company provides network security products that employ encryption technology to secure electronic commerce transactions and communications over computer networks, with an emphasis on products for virtual private networks. Its offerings include network security systems and software, as well as hardware, chips, and software that are sold to third-parties that embed them in their own products. SafeNet's customers include financial institutions, government agencies, and large corporations.

SafeNet has expanded its roster of strategic partners and used acquisitions to grow its product lines, including the purchase of Rainbow Technologies in 2004. In June 2005 the company acquired MediaSentry, a provider of antipiracy and business management services for recording and motion picture companies. The company announced plans to purchase nCipher for about $150 million early in 2006, but the deal was later canceled.

SafeNet is targeting markets such as wireless communications and government agencies for future growth. The company's government clients include the Department of Defense, the IRS, the Department of State, and the Federal Reserve Bank; commercial customers include Citibank and Samsung.

HISTORY

Former National Security Agency engineers Douglas Kozlay and Alan Hastings founded Industrial Resource Engineering in 1983. Network security expert Anthony Caputo invested in the company in 1986 and became CEO the next year. It went public and renamed itself Information Resource Engineering (IRE) in 1989.

The company was one of the first to offer secure dial-up and packet-switched network products, and in 1994 it introduced the first portable secure modem. In 1995 IRE acquired Switzerland-based GRETACODER Data Systems, maker of encryption equipment used by European banks and government agencies. That year IRE made a $10 million product supply deal with

MCI (now WorldCom) to provide SafeNet, IRE's Internet security system that includes a firewall and a portable security modem. (The agreement was terminated in late 1996, a year in which MCI accounted for 27% of IRE's sales.)

IRE in 1996 began developing security products for Internet business communications with firewall company CyberGuard. In 1997 IRE, profitless for five years, boosted sales and marketing efforts and introduced an integrated circuit that combined encryption and modem functions. The company in 1998 provided security technology to the US Treasury Department that enabled the Treasury to issue its first electronic check (to GTE). That year IRE signed a deal with Mitsubishi to distribute IRE products in Japan. In 1999 the company joined Cisco Systems' Security Associate Program, an interoperability testing and co-marketing initiative.

In 2000, as a means of better capitalizing on its award-winning flagship product, IRE changed its name to SafeNet.

In 2002 SafeNet acquired Securealink, a European maker of chips for secure e-commerce transactions. Continuing to grow through acquisitions, the next year the company purchased Raqia Networks and Cylink.

In 2004 the company purchased Datakey and Rainbow Technologies.

Caputo resigned in 2006 after an investigation made by a special committee of independent directors found evidence of improper handling of stock options. One of the company's independent directors, Walter Straub, was appointed chairman and interim CEO.

EXECUTIVES

Chairman and Interim CEO: Walter W. Straub, age 63
President and COO: Chris S. Fedde, age 55
Chief Accounting Officer and CFO: John W. Frederick, age 40
SVP and General Manager, Embedded Security Division: David Potts, age 35, $215,009 pay
SVP, Worldwide Sales: Steve Lesem, age 52, $404,618 pay
SVP, Operations: Prakash Panjwani
SVP, Worldwide Sales: Phil Saunders
VP and General Manager, OEM/Networking Business Unit: Henk Pruim
VP, Corporate Communications: Amber Zentis
VP, Government Sales: Vince Mancuso
VP, Product Services: Steve Turner
VP, Semiconductor Development, Embedded Security Division: Peter H. Reed
VP, Human Resources: Diane Smith
Chief Marketing Officer: Ian Edward Dix
Manager, Corporate Communications: Maureen Kolb
Technology Officer, Enterprise Security Division: George L. Heron
Public Relations: Donna St. Germain
Auditors: Ernst & Young LLP

LOCATIONS

HQ: SafeNet, Inc.
4690 Millenium Dr., Belcamp, MD 21017
Phone: 410-931-7500 **Fax:** 410-931-7524
Web: www.safenet-inc.com

SafeNet has offices in Belgium, Finland, Singapore, the UK, and the US.

2005 Sales

	$ mil.	% of total
US	185.7	71
Other countries	77.4	29
Total	**263.1**	**100**

PRODUCTS/OPERATIONS

2005 Sales

	$ mil.	% of total
Enterprise security	188.0	71
Embedded security	75.1	29
Total	**263.1**	**100**

2005 Sales

	$ mil.	% of total
Products	217.1	82
Service & maintenance	28.4	11
License & royalties	17.6	7
Total	**263.1**	**100**

Selected Products

Encryption accelerator chips
Encryption and authentication client software
Frame relay encryptors
Link security systems
Secure communications chips
Secure dial-access systems
Secure modems
Security management software

Selected Services

Consulting
Network monitoring
Policy creation
Support
User enrollment
VPN deployment

COMPETITORS

Aladdin Knowledge Systems
Cavium Networks
Certicom
Check Point Software
Cisco Systems
General Dynamics
hi/fn
Juniper Networks
Level 3 Communications
Macrovision
Nortel Networks
RSA Security
Sypris Solutions
Thales

HISTORICAL FINANCIALS

Company Type: Public

Income Statement

	REVENUE ($ mil.)	NET INCOME ($ mil.)	NET PROFIT MARGIN	FYE: December 31 EMPLOYEES
12/05	263.1	3.0	1.1%	1,043
12/04	201.6	2.2	1.1%	812
12/03	66.2	(6.1)	—	238
12/02	32.2	(4.7)	—	215
12/01	18.1	(3.6)	—	139
Annual Growth	95.3%	—	—	65.5%

2005 Year-End Financials

Debt ratio: 42.9%
Return on equity: 0.5%
Cash ($ mil.): 342.7
Current ratio: 6.33
Long-term debt ($ mil.): 250.0
No. of shares (mil.): 25.5

Dividends
  Yield: —
  Payout: —
Market value ($ mil.): 823.1
R&D as % of sales: 11.9%
Advertising as % of sales: 1.1%

	STOCK PRICE ($)	P/E	PER SHARE ($)		
	FY Close	High/Low	Earnings	Dividends	Book Value
12/05	32.22	319 211	0.12	—	22.83
12/04	36.74	418 206	0.10	—	24.96
12/03	30.67	— —	(0.54)	—	13.47
12/02	25.35	— —	(0.61)	—	6.13
12/01	18.94	— —	(0.50)	—	4.99
Annual Growth	14.2%	— —	—	—	46.3%

St. Mary Land & Exploration

St. Mary Land & Exploration isn't afraid to travel. The oil and gas exploration and production company spreads its operations across the US: the midcontinent, the ArkLaTex region and Gulf Coast, the Williston Basin in North Dakota and Montana, and the Permian Basin in West Texas and New Mexico. The company has proved reserves of 794.5 billion cu. ft. of natural gas equivalent. In the late 1990s St. Mary Land & Exploration sold its Russian oil and North American copper mining investments to focus on its core US oil and gas properties. The company has expanded its activities in the Rockies through the acquisition of coalbed methane assets in Wyoming and Montana.

In addition to growing through the drill bit, St. Mary Land & Exploration makes selective acquisitions. In 2004, it acquired Goldmark Engineering, and in 2005, Agate Petroleum.

EXECUTIVES

Chairman and CEO: Mark A. Hellerstein, age 54
President; CEO-Elect: A. J. (Tony) Best, age 56
COO: Javan D. (Jay) Ottoson, age 48
VP Finance, CFO, Treasurer, and Secretary:
David W. Honeyfield, age 39, $275,671 pay
SVP and General Manager, Gulf Coast:
Jerry R. Schuyler, age 50
SVP and General Manager, Mid-Continent:
Paul M. Veatch, age 39
SVP; President and CEO, Nance Petroleum:
Robert L. Nance, age 70, $344,926 pay
VP Administration and Controller: Garry A. Wilkening, age 55
VP Land and Legal: Milam Randolph Pharo, age 53
Media: Brent A. Collins
Auditors: Deloitte & Touche LLP

LOCATIONS

HQ: St. Mary Land & Exploration Company
1776 Lincoln St., Ste. 700, Denver, CO 80203
Phone: 303-861-8140   **Fax:** 303-861-0934
Web: www.stmaryland.com

2005 Proved Reserves

	% of total
Rocky Mountains	54
Midcontinent	22
ArkLaTex	14
Permian Basin	6
Gulf Coast	4
Total	**100**

COMPETITORS

Abraxas Petroleum
Apache
BP
Devon Energy
Exxon Mobil
Pioneer Natural Resources
Range Resources
Royal Dutch Shell

HISTORICAL FINANCIALS

Company Type: Public

Income Statement

				FYE: December 31
	REVENUE ($ mil.)	NET INCOME ($ mil.)	NET PROFIT MARGIN	EMPLOYEES
12/05	739.6	151.9	20.5%	305
12/04	483.4	92.5	19.1%	256
12/03	393.9	95.6	24.3%	226
12/02	199.0	27.6	13.9%	185
12/01	207.5	40.5	19.5%	179
Annual Growth	37.4%	39.2%	—	14.3%

2005 Year-End Financials

Debt ratio: 17.5%
Return on equity: 28.8%
Cash ($ mil.): 23.2
Current ratio: 1.02
Long-term debt ($ mil.): 99.9
No. of shares (mil.): 56.8
Dividends
  Yield: 0.3%
  Payout: 4.3%
Market value ($ mil.): 2,089.4
R&D as % of sales: —
Advertising as % of sales: —

Stock History
NYSE: SM

	STOCK PRICE ($)	P/E	PER SHARE ($)		
	FY Close	High/Low	Earnings	Dividends	Book Value
12/05	36.81	18 8	2.33	0.10	10.03
12/04	20.87	15 10	1.44	0.05	17.01
12/03	14.25	11 8	1.40	0.05	13.83
12/02	12.50	28 19	0.49	0.05	10.71
12/01	10.60	25 10	0.71	0.05	9.94
Annual Growth	36.5%	— —	34.6%	18.9%	0.2%

salesforce.com

salesforce.com knows the power of good customer relations. The company offers hosted applications that manage customer information for sales, marketing, and customer support, providing clients with a rapidly deployable alternative to buying and maintaining enterprise software. salesforce.com's applications are used for generating sales leads, maintaining customer information, and tracking customer interactions. The company's services can be accessed from devices including PCs, cellular phones, and personal digital assistants. Customers include Time Warner, Wachovia, and Nokia. CEO Marc Benioff owns about 26% of the company.

The company's customers come from a variety of industries, including financial services, telecommunications, manufacturing, and entertainment. salesforce.com continues to bolster its offerings as part of a push to expand past its core market of small and midsized businesses. The company also has signed strategic partnerships with companies such as TIBCO, Informatica, and PricewaterhouseCoopers.

In April 2006 the company acquired Sendia (a provider of wireless software delivery tools) for about $15 million in cash, marking the first acquisition in salesforce.com's history.

EXECUTIVES

Chairman and CEO: Marc Benioff, age 41, $10 pay
CFO: Steven M. (Steve) Cakebread, age 54, $476,100 pay
President, Worldwide Operations: John Freeland, age 52
President, Worldwide Sales and Distribution:
Jim Steele, age 50, $647,100 pay
EVP, Americas: Dave Orrico
EVP, Global Corporate Sales: Frank R. Van Veenendaal
EVP, Law, Policy, and Corporate Strategy:
Kenneth I. (Ken) Juster, age 51, $634,800 pay
EVP, Technology: Parker Harris, age 39
SVP and General Counsel: David Schellhase, age 42
SVP, Corporate and Product Marketing: Kendall Collins
SVP, Global Integration Services: Cindy Warner
SVP, Marketing: Elizabeth Pinkham
SVP, Service Delivery and CIO: Jim Cavalieri, age 36, $419,250 pay
SVP, Worldwide Channel and Alliances:
Bobby Napiltonia
CTO: David (Dave) Moellenhoff, age 36, $369,709 pay
Auditors: Ernst & Young LLP

LOCATIONS

HQ: salesforce.com, inc.
1 Market St., Ste. 300, San Francisco, CA 94105
Phone: 415-901-7000   **Fax:** 415-901-7040
Web: www.salesforce.com

2006 Sales

	$ mil.	% of total
Americas	247.0	80
Europe	43.6	14
Asia/Pacific	19.3	6
Total	**309.9**	**100**

PRODUCTS/OPERATIONS

2006 Sales

	$ mil.	% of total
Subscription & support	280.7	91
Professional service & other	29.2	9
Total	**309.9**	**100**

Selected Services and Applications

Account management (maintaining and managing customer data)
Contact management (tracking of customer interactions)
Forecasts (forecasting revenues and customer demand)
Lead management (tracking and managing sales leads)
Reporting and enterprise integration (creation and integration of reports and other data)

COMPETITORS

Amdocs
BMC Software
Chordiant Software
Epicor Software
FrontRange Solutions
IBM
KANA
Microsoft Business Solutions
NetSuite
Onyx Software
Oracle
Pivotal
RightNow Technologies
Sage Software
Salesnet
SAP
SSA Global

HISTORICAL FINANCIALS

Company Type: Public

Income Statement

FYE: January 31

	REVENUE ($ mil.)	NET INCOME ($ mil.)	NET PROFIT MARGIN	EMPLOYEES
1/06	309.9	28.5	9.2%	1,304
1/05	176.4	7.3	4.1%	767
1/04	96.0	3.5	3.6%	—
1/03	51.0	(9.7)	—	—
1/02	22.4	(28.6)	—	—
Annual Growth	92.9%	—	—	70.0%

2006 Year-End Financials

Debt ratio: 0.1%
Return on equity: 16.7%
Cash ($ mil.): 207.6
Current ratio: 1.29
Long-term debt ($ mil.): 0.2
No. of shares (mil.): 110.5
Dividends
Yield: —
Payout: —
Market value ($ mil.): 4,536.6
R&D as % of sales: 7.5%
Advertising as % of sales: 4.2%

Stock History

NYSE: CRM

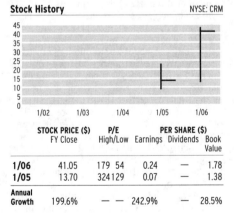

	STOCK PRICE ($) FY Close	P/E High/Low	PER SHARE ($) Earnings	Dividends	Book Value
1/06	41.05	179 54	0.24	—	1.78
1/05	13.70	324 129	0.07	—	1.38
Annual Growth	199.6%	— —	242.9%	—	28.5%

Sapient

Sapient is no sap when it comes to services. A provider of business and technology consulting services, Sapient targets information-based businesses in the financial services, communications and technology, automotive and industrial manufacturing, consumer, public services, health care, energy services, and transportation industries. Customers such as AT&T Mobility (formerly Cingular), Staples, Janus Capital, and agencies of the US government use Sapient's consulting, design, implementation, user experience research, and other services for e-commerce, customer relationship management, high-volume transaction processing, online supply chain development, learning and knowledge management, and other processes.

Sapient offers its services primarily on a fixed-price basis, targeting customers who want fast services at low costs. The company relies on its international facilities, which enable development teams to work on projects 24 hours a day, to ensure quick turnaround.

In mid-2005 the company acquired Miami-based Business Information Solutions, a provider of consulting services for companies using enterprise planning software developed by SAP.

Sapient founders Jerry Greenberg and Stuart Moore each own 17% of the company.

HISTORY

In 1991 information technology systems salesman Jerry Greenberg and software developer Stuart Moore saw a market for providing businesses with fixed-price software systems by a guaranteed delivery date. Greenberg and Moore charged more than $100,000 on their credit cards and used $60,000 of their personal savings to form Sapient.

As the company took off, Moore managed internal operations, such as creating software, and Greenberg handled sales and finance. The two worked closely together and helped establish teamwork as Sapient's most prized trait (as co-CEOs, they shared an office with only inches separating their desks, and they required the same of all senior managers).

The company began specializing in distinct areas such as telecommunications, manufacturing, and energy, and it found a third of its early clients in financial services. Specialization enabled the company to reuse software; coupling that with Sapient's proprietary team-based development process resulted in lower costs and shorter development times.

The company went public in 1996 and started expanding through acquisitions, buying systems integrators and Internet consultants. It opened offices in London in 1998, and in Italy and Australia the next year. Also in 1999 Sapient increased its staff by more than 40% and expanded its consulting services with the purchase of customer behavior specialist E.Lab.

In 2000 Sapient opened an office in India and acquired Human Code, a privately held developer of education, e-commerce, and entertainment software, for about $104 million. The next year, looking to cut costs, the company closed its Australian office, cut its workforce by about 35%,

and exited the gaming business. It also began to shift more of its project workload to its office in India in order to take advantage of lower operating costs.

Citing decreased demand for its services in the troubled economic climate, Sapient posted a loss of nearly $190 million for 2001, followed by a loss of nearly $230 million for 2002. The company continued to reduce its workforce in 2002, cutting about 600 more jobs. The following year the company began to see its service revenues pick up, and its workforce size stabilized.

EXECUTIVES

Chairman: Jeffrey M. (Jeff) Cunningham, age 53
President, CEO, and Director: Alan J. Herrick, age 40
EVP and COO: Sheeroy D. Desai, age 40, $361,572 pay
EVP and Managing Director, Indian Operations: Preston B. Bradford, age 49, $360,713 pay
SVP and CFO: Joseph S. (Joe) Tibbetts Jr., age 54
SVP and Chief Creative Officer: Gaston Legorburu
SVP, North American Operations: Alan M. Wexler
Managing Director and VP, European Operations: Christian Oversohl
SVP, General Counsel, and Secretary: Jane E. Owens, age 52
VP and CIO: Changappa Kodendera
VP and CTO: Benoit (Ben) Gaucherin
Corporate Controller and Chief Accounting Officer: Stephen P. Sarno, age 39
Director, Legal: Kyle Bettigole
Investor Relations: Noelle Faris
Media Relations: Beate Keller
Auditors: PricewaterhouseCoopers LLP

LOCATIONS

HQ: Sapient Corporation
25 1st St., Cambridge, MA 02141
Phone: 617-621-0200   **Fax:** 617-621-1300
Web: www.sapient.com

Sapient has offices in Canada, Germany, India, the UK, and the US.

2005 Sales

	% of total
US	64
Other countries	36
Total	**100**

PRODUCTS/OPERATIONS

2005 Sales

	$ mil.	% of total
Service revenues		
Financial services, automotive, consumer & energy	105.2	32
Technology, education, communications & health care	69.9	21
UK	65.7	20
Germany	28.9	8
Government	24.6	7
Canada	19.2	6
Other service revenues	6.0	2
Reimbursable expenses	13.5	4
Total	**333.0**	**100**

Selected Services

Business and operational consulting
Creative design
Internet consulting
Internet design
Software implementation
Systems design and integration
Technology development
User experience research

COMPETITORS

Accenture	EDS
Booz Allen	IBM
Boston Consulting	Inforte
Capgemini	Keane
CHC	Perot Systems
CIBER	Sapiens
Computer Sciences Corp.	Technology Solutions
Computer Task Group	Unisys
Diamond	

HISTORICAL FINANCIALS

Company Type: Public

Income Statement

FYE: December 31

	REVENUE ($ mil.)	NET INCOME ($ mil.)	NET PROFIT MARGIN	EMPLOYEES
12/05	333.0	25.7	7.7%	3,017
12/04	266.0	22.8	8.6%	2,314
12/03	194.4	(4.9)	—	1,483
12/02	182.4	(229.2)	—	1,491
12/01	329.7	(189.8)	—	2,105
Annual Growth	0.2%	—	—	9.4%

2005 Year-End Financials

Debt ratio: —
Return on equity: 13.2%
Cash ($ mil.): 156.6
Current ratio: 3.86
Long-term debt ($ mil.): —
No. of shares (mil.): 123.5

Dividends
Yield: —
Payout: —
Market value ($ mil.): 702.9
R&D as % of sales: —
Advertising as % of sales: —

Stock History

NASDAQ (GS): SAPE

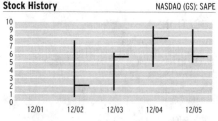

	STOCK PRICE ($) FY Close	P/E High/Low		Earnings	PER SHARE ($) Dividends	Book Value
12/05	5.69	45	25	0.20	—	1.64
12/04	7.91	52	25	0.18	—	1.50
12/03	5.64	—	—	(0.04)	—	1.25
12/02	2.05	—	—	(1.83)	—	1.28
Annual Growth	40.5%	—	—	—	—	(14.1%)

Savannah Bancorp

If money is both good and evil, than The Savannah Bancorp — holding company for The Savannah Bank and Bryan Bank & Trust — is a novel place to store it. The Savannah Bank has five branches in Garden City and Savannah, Georgia, and a loan production office on Hilton Head Island, South Carolina. Bryan Bank & Trust has a single location in Richmond Hill, Georgia. The banks offer a variety of retail services, including checking, savings, and money market accounts, and certificates of deposit. Real estate mortgage loans make up about two-thirds of the company's loan portfolio; the banks also make business, consumer, and real estate construction and development loans.

The Savannah Bancorp opened Harbourside Community Bank, a full-service extension of its mortgage operations in South Carolina, in 2006.

Directors and executives collectively control 25% of the company.

EXECUTIVES

Chairman and General Counsel, Savannah Bancorp and The Savannah Bank: J. Wiley Ellis, age 65
Vice Chairman; Chairman and CEO, Bryan Bank & Trust: E. James Burnsed, age 66, $157,823 pay
President, CEO, and Director; President and CEO, The Savannah Bank: John C. Helmken II, age 43
CFO; EVP and CFO, The Savannah Bank: Robert B. Briscoe, age 53, $155,014 pay
EVP, Lending, The Savannah Bancorp and The Savannah Bank: R. Stephen Stramm, age 55, $137,500 pay
Director; Vice Chairman, The Savannah Bank: Archie H. Davis, age 64
President, Bryan Bank & Trust: Jerry O'Dell Keith
President and CEO, Harbourside Community Bank: Thomas W. (Tom) Lennox
Secretary and Director; Secretary, The Savannah Bank: J. Curtis Lewis III, age 53
SVP, Operations: Tommy E. Wyatt
VP, Human Resources: James M. Joyce
Auditors: BDO Seidman, LLP

LOCATIONS

HQ: The Savannah Bancorp, Inc.
25 Bull St., Savannah, GA 31401
Phone: 912-629-6486   **Fax:** 912-232-3733
Web: www.savb.com

PRODUCTS/OPERATIONS

Selected Subsidiaries

Bryan Bank & Trust
The Savannah Bank, N.A.

COMPETITORS

Bank of America
BB&T
Delta Financial
SunTrust
Synovus
Wachovia

HISTORICAL FINANCIALS

Company Type: Public

Income Statement

FYE: December 31

	ASSETS ($ mil.)	NET INCOME ($ mil.)	INCOME AS % OF ASSETS	EMPLOYEES
12/05	717.9	9.0	1.3%	200
12/04	617.3	5.7	0.9%	180
12/03	476.9	4.6	1.0%	155
12/02	437.6	4.5	1.0%	139
12/01	376.2	4.4	1.2%	126
Annual Growth	17.5%	19.6%	—	12.2%

2005 Year-End Financials

Equity as % of assets: 8.2%
Return on assets: 1.3%
Return on equity: 18.3%
Long-term debt ($ mil.): 30.8
No. of shares (mil.): 4.6
Market value ($ mil.): 130.3

Dividends
Yield: 1.5%
Payout: 26.4%
Sales ($ mil.): 46.8
R&D as % of sales: —
Advertising as % of sales: 0.6%

Stock History

NASDAQ (GM): SAVB

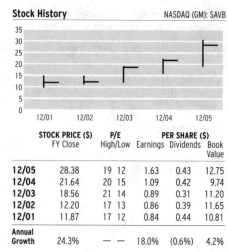

	STOCK PRICE ($) FY Close	P/E High/Low		Earnings	PER SHARE ($) Dividends	Book Value
12/05	28.38	19	12	1.63	0.43	12.75
12/04	21.64	20	15	1.09	0.42	9.74
12/03	18.56	21	14	0.89	0.31	11.20
12/02	12.20	17	13	0.86	0.39	11.65
12/01	11.87	17	12	0.84	0.44	10.81
Annual Growth	24.3%	—	—	18.0%	(0.6%)	4.2%

Schawk

Schawk has designs on others' products. The company provides digital pre-press and other graphic arts services primarily for consumer product packaging, advertising, and point-of-sale marketing. It offers expertise in digital imaging, color separations, electronic retouching, and platemaking for lithography, gravure, and flexography. Clients include more than 30 *FORTUNE* 100 companies. Schawk operates mainly in North America but also in Europe and the Asia/Pacific region. The company expanded in 2005 with the purchase of rival Seven Worldwide for $191 million. The family of founder and chairman Clarence Schawk owns a controlling stake in the company.

The addition of Seven Worldwide, along with Schawk's December 2004 acquisition of UK pre-press firm Winnetts, expanded the company's reach into the UK and other European markets and doubled the size of the company.

In 2006, Schawk sold its educational product development, catalog, publication, and New York-based advertising pre-media operations to Caps Group for about $62 million. Acquired in the Seven Worldwide transaction, the operations did not fit in Schawk's strategy of serving manufacturers, retailers, and ad firms in the consumer products sector.

Graphic services account for more than 95% of Schawk's sales. The company's Anthem unit provides brand strategy and creative design services. Schawk also offers digital asset management, workflow management, and online proofing software through its enterprise products segment.

Schawk maintained its acquisition momentum in mid-2006 when it acquired Cincinnati-based design agency WBK. Schawk subsequently folded WBK into its Anthem segment.

EXECUTIVES

Chairman: Clarence W. Schawk, age 79, $50,000 pay
President, CEO, and Director: David A. Schawk, age 49, $957,508 pay
EVP, COO, Corporate Secretary, and Director: A. Alex Sarkisian, age 53, $547,500 pay
EVP and Group Managing Director, Anthem Worldwide: Anne Marie Pagliacci
SVP and CFO: James J. Patterson, age 48, $420,500 pay
SVP Global Operations: Chuck Dale
VP Business Development, Graphic Services: Christopher Splan
VP Human Resources: Jennifer Erfurth
VP Legal Affairs, Corporate Counsel, and Assistant Secretary: Ronald J. Vittorini
CIO: Jim Hanekamp
Director Global Sales Development: Brian Weissmann
Investor Relations: Kathy M. Melvage
Auditors: Ernst & Young LLP

LOCATIONS

HQ: Schawk, Inc.
 1695 River Rd., Des Plaines, IL 60018
Phone: 847-827-9494   **Fax:** 847-827-1264
Web: www.schawk.com

2005 Sales

	$ mil.	% of total
North America		
US	473.9	77
Canada	35.9	6
Europe	82.0	13
Other regions	22.7	4
Total	**614.5**	**100**

COMPETITORS

ACG Holdings
Alcoa
CNTV Entertainment Group
Fort Dearborn
Matthews International
Multi-Color
Outlook Group
Performance Companies
Pudik Graphics
Quad/Graphics
Quebecor
ReyHan
R.R. Donnelley
Serigraph
St Ives US Division
Vertis Communications

HISTORICAL FINANCIALS

Company Type: Public

Income Statement

FYE: December 31

	REVENUE ($ mil.)	NET INCOME ($ mil.)	NET PROFIT MARGIN	EMPLOYEES
12/05	614.5	30.5	5.0%	4,300
12/04	238.3	22.7	9.5%	1,800
12/03	201.0	17.0	8.5%	1,400
12/02	186.2	13.5	7.3%	1,400
12/01	186.3	8.0	4.3%	1,400
Annual Growth	**34.8%**	**39.7%**	**—**	**32.4%**

2005 Year-End Financials

Debt ratio: 73.3%
Return on equity: 16.8%
Cash ($ mil.): 7.5
Current ratio: 1.80
Long-term debt ($ mil.): 169.6
No. of shares (mil.): 26.1
Dividends
 Yield: 0.6%
 Payout: 11.5%
Market value ($ mil.): 541.0
R&D as % of sales: —
Advertising as % of sales: —

Stock History NYSE: SGK

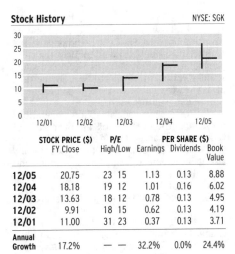

	STOCK PRICE ($) FY Close	P/E High/Low	PER SHARE ($) Earnings	Dividends	Book Value
12/05	20.75	23 15	1.13	0.13	8.88
12/04	18.18	19 12	1.01	0.16	6.02
12/03	13.63	18 12	0.78	0.13	4.95
12/02	9.91	18 15	0.62	0.13	4.19
12/01	11.00	31 23	0.37	0.13	3.71
Annual Growth	**17.2%**	**— —**	**32.2%**	**0.0%**	**24.4%**

Sciele Pharma

Sciele Pharma (formerly First Horizon Pharmaceutical) is keeping an eye on the hearts and the women of America. The company buys drugs from larger companies for cardiovascular health and women's health and sells them. Sciele Pharma's prescription drug portfolio includes more than a dozen products, such as Prenate prenatal vitamins, drugs for treating high blood pressure and menstrual pain, and a treatment for swimmer's ear. The company does not make the products it sells; instead, it has manufacturing agreements with the companies whose products it acquires, including Pfizer, Bayer, and Andrx.

Sular, an antihypertensive bought from AstraZeneca in 2002, is Sciele Pharma's best seller, accounting for nearly 40% of the company's sales. In late 2004 and early 2005, the company announced it would no longer promote peptic ulcer therapy Robinul and allergy/cold med Tanafed due to generic competition. These product lines accounted for 15% and 11%, respectively, of the company's 2004 sales.

To counter the loss of revenue from Robinul and Tanafed, Sciele Pharma in 2005 entered licensing deals with Skye Pharma and Andrx Laboratories for medications addressing diabetes, cholesterol, and prenatal care. Each of these drugs has already been introduced to the US market.

Major customers include pharmaceutical distribution firms McKesson (which accounts for 30% of 2005 sales), Cardinal Health (23%), and AmerisourceBergen (10%).

Chicago-area biotech investor and former company chairman John Kapoor owns 15% of Sciele Pharma.

EXECUTIVES

Chairman: Pierre Lapalme, age 65
President, CEO, and Director: Patrick P. Fourteau, age 58, $558,743 pay
CFO, Secretary, and Treasurer: Darrell E. Borne, age 44, $335,600 pay
EVP and Chief Commercial Officer: Edward Schutter, age 54
EVP and Chief Medical Officer: Larry M. Dillaha
EVP, Global Business Development: Michael Mavrogordato, age 54

VP, Legal Affairs: Leslie Zacks, $270,684 pay
VP, Sales: Sam F. Gibbons, $270,000 pay
VP, Scientific Affairs: Alan Roberts, $225,000 pay
Auditors: BDO Seidman, LLP

LOCATIONS

HQ: Sciele Pharma Inc.
 5 Concourse Pkwy., Ste. 1800, Atlanta, GA 30328
Phone: 678-341-1400   **Fax:** 678-341-1470
Web: www.horizonpharm.w1.com/Corp

PRODUCTS/OPERATIONS

2005 Sales

	% of total
Cardiovascular products	67
Women's health products	22
Non-promoted products	11
Total	**100**

Selected Products

Altoprev (high cholesterol)
Cognex (Alzheimer's disease)
Fortamet (type 2 diabetes)
Furadantin (urinary tract infections)
Nitrolingual Pumpspray (angina relief)
Prenate Elite (prenatal vitamins)
Sular (hypertension)
Triglide (high cholesterol)
Zebutal (headaches)
Zoto-HC (swimmer's ear)

COMPETITORS

Abbott Labs
AstraZeneca
Biovail
Bristol-Myers Squibb
Elan
Eli Lilly
Forest Labs
King Pharmaceuticals
Medicis Pharmaceutical
Merck
Pfizer
Reliant Pharmaceuticals
Shire
Teva Pharmaceuticals
Watson Pharmaceuticals

HISTORICAL FINANCIALS

Company Type: Public

Income Statement

FYE: December 31

	REVENUE ($ mil.)	NET INCOME ($ mil.)	NET PROFIT MARGIN	EMPLOYEES
12/05	216.4	39.2	18.1%	568
12/04	152.0	26.5	17.4%	477
12/03	95.3	(1.7)	—	343
12/02	115.2	6.2	5.4%	249
12/01	69.3	10.7	15.4%	195
Annual Growth	**32.9%**	**38.3%**	**—**	**30.6%**

2005 Year-End Financials

Debt ratio: 44.1%
Return on equity: 12.1%
Cash ($ mil.): 99.8
Current ratio: 6.68
Long-term debt ($ mil.): 150.0
No. of shares (mil.): 35.1
Dividends
 Yield: —
 Payout: —
Market value ($ mil.): 605.6
R&D as % of sales: 1.9%
Advertising as % of sales: 5.2%

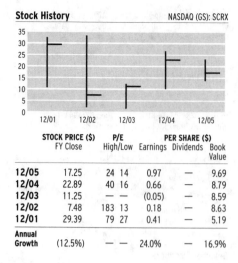

	STOCK PRICE ($) FY Close	P/E High/Low	PER SHARE ($) Earnings	Dividends	Book Value
12/05	17.25	24 14	0.97	—	9.69
12/04	22.89	40 16	0.66	—	8.79
12/03	11.25	— —	(0.05)	—	8.59
12/02	7.48	183 13	0.18	—	8.63
12/01	29.39	79 27	0.41	—	5.19
Annual Growth	(12.5%)	— —	24.0%	—	16.9%

SEACOR Holdings

Smitten by the sea, SEACOR (formerly SEACOR SMIT) operates an offshore lifeline for the oil industry. With more than 300 vessels, the marine services company delivers cargo and personnel, anchors drilling rigs, and provides construction and maintenance work to oil and gas companies operating offshore. Its fleet includes more than 100 crew boats, 52 towing and 44 supply vessels. SEACOR also provides standby safety support, logistics services, training and consulting, and environmental services such as oil spill response. It also operates helicopter services through its fleet of 108 helicopters. Its inland river barges transport grain and other bulk commodities.

In 2005 the company acquired former rival Seabulk International for $1 billion, including assumed debt. Seabulk provides offshore support to energy companies and transportation of petroleum products with a fleet of 133 vessels.

SEACOR does business primarily in the Gulf of Mexico, where more than half its vessels are stationed, but it also provides its services in oil-rich regions such as Latin America, the North Sea, and offshore Asia and West Africa. The company has invested in maritime telecommunications companies that provide data services and satellite messaging to vessels around the world. It has also expanded its air support services by acquiring the remaining 80% of Tex-Air Helicopter, which operates a fleet of 36 helicopters that provide support to offshore oil and gas rigs.

SEACOR has acquired Era Aviation, including its fleet of 128 helicopters, 16 aircraft, and 14 operating bases, from Rowan Companies for about $118 million. The company has exited its contract drilling operations through the sale of its 27% stake in Chiles Offshore to ENSCO.

HISTORY

With only two vessels, SEACOR was founded in 1989 to service offshore oil rigs in the Gulf of Mexico. It quickly expanded its fleet by buying 36 vessels from Midwest utility holding company Nicor, which had diversified into oil services in the late 1970s.

When the *Exxon Valdez* oil spill prompted a 1990 federal law requiring energy companies to have cleanup plans, SEACOR was among the first to enter the safety business. In 1991 the company joined a joint venture that operated safety standby vessels in the North Sea. By the time SEACOR went public in 1992, it had formed a similar joint venture in the US.

SEACOR expanded its Gulf operations throughout the 1990s. In 1994 it formed a joint venture with Transportacion Maritima Mexicana to operate off the coast of Mexico. The company also gained some 165 ships by acquiring John E. Graham & Sons (1995) and McCall Enterprises (1996).

Also in 1996 SEACOR bought 45 offshore support vessels from the Netherlands' SMIT Internationale. As a result of the deal, the company changed its name to SEACOR SMIT Inc. in 1997. That year the firm created another joint venture to operate offshore Argentina, and SEACOR grabbed a 55% stake in Chiles Offshore, which began building two jack-up offshore drilling rigs.

In 1998 SEACOR paid $37 million for SMIT Internationale's 5% stake in the company. It also sold 34 vessels for $144 million (11 of these were chartered back to SEACOR) and accepted delivery of 10 new vessels. Also that year SEACOR invested in Globe Wireless, a marine telecommunications company concentrating on e-mail and data transfer. In 1999 SEACOR bought Kvaerner's Marinet Systems, which provides communications services to the shipping industry, with the intent of integrating its operations into Globe Wireless.

Chiles Offshore went public in 2000; SEACOR retained a 27% stake. In 2001, SEACOR acquired UK shipping firm Stirling Shipping. The next year, SEACOR sold its stake in Chiles Offshore to ENSCO International and acquired the remaining 80% of Tex-Air Helicopters, expanding its air support operations.

In 2004 SEACOR SMIT changed its name to SEACOR Holdings.

EXECUTIVES

Chairman, President, and CEO: Charles L. Fabrikant, age 61, $2,600,000 pay
SVP and CFO: Richard Ryan, age 51
SVP; President and CEO, SEACOR Environmental Services: Randall Blank, age 55, $1,885,000 pay
SVP Corporate Development and Treasurer: Dick Fagerstal, age 45, $475,000 pay
SVP Strategy and Corporate Development: James A. F. Cowderoy, age 46
SVP and General Counsel: Alice N. Gran, age 56, $435,000 pay
SVP International Division: John Gellert, age 35, $715,000 pay
VP and Chief Accounting Officer: Lenny P. Dantin, age 52
VP and Chief Accounting Officer: Matthew Cenac, age 40
Auditors: Ernst & Young LLP

LOCATIONS

HQ: SEACOR Holdings Inc.
  2200 Eller Dr., Fort Lauderdale, FL 33316
Phone: 954-524-4200
Web: www.seacorsmit.com

SEACOR operates mainly in the Gulf of Mexico and also in the Mediterranean and the North Sea and off the coasts of countries in Asia, Latin America, and West Africa.

2005 Sales

	$ mil.	% of total
North America	703.9	72
West Africa	99.9	10
Europe	74.4	8
Latin America	34.0	4
Asia	32.4	3
Other regions	27.4	3
Total	**972.0**	**100**

PRODUCTS/OPERATIONS

2005 Sales

	$ mil.	% of total
Offshore marine services	480.0	50
Aviation services	137.6	14
Environmental services	136.6	14
Inland river services	123.2	13
Marine transportation services	72.4	7
Other	23.3	2
Adjustments	(1.1)	—
Total	**972.0**	**100**

Selected Services

Cargo delivery
Crew transportation
Environmental services
Helicopter services
Inland barge transportation
Line handling (assist tankers while loading)
Logistics services
Offshore construction support
Offshore drilling
Offshore maintenance work support
Oil spill response services
Salvage
Seismic data gathering support
Telecommunications
Towing and anchor handling (drill rigs and other equipment)
Well stimulation support

COMPETITORS

Baker Hughes
BJ Services
Bristow Group Inc
Cameron
CHC Helicopter
Crowley Maritime
ENSCO
Global Industries
GulfMark Offshore
Halliburton
Helix Energy Solutions
Horizon Offshore
Martin Resource Management
Oceaneering International
PHI, Inc.
Schlumberger
Tidewater
Trico Marine
Weatherford International

HISTORICAL FINANCIALS

Company Type: Public

Income Statement

	REVENUE ($ mil.)	NET INCOME ($ mil.)	NET PROFIT MARGIN	EMPLOYEES
12/05	972.0	170.7	17.6%	5,035
12/04	491.9	19.9	4.0%	3,900
12/03	406.2	11.9	2.9%	2,900
12/02	403.2	46.6	11.6%	3,400
12/01	434.8	70.7	16.3%	3,400
Annual Growth	22.3%	24.7%	—	10.3%

FYE: December 31

2005 Year-End Financials

Debt ratio: 71.8%
Return on equity: 15.8%
Cash ($ mil.): 538.2
Current ratio: 3.38
Long-term debt ($ mil.): 977.6
No. of shares (mil.): 24.8

Dividends
 Yield: —
 Payout: —
Market value ($ mil.): 1,690.2
R&D as % of sales: —
Advertising as % of sales: —

Stock History   NYSE: CKH

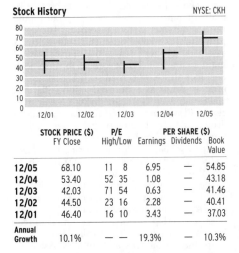

	STOCK PRICE ($) FY Close	P/E High/Low		PER SHARE ($) Earnings	Dividends	Book Value
12/05	68.10	11	8	6.95	—	54.85
12/04	53.40	52	35	1.08	—	43.18
12/03	42.03	71	54	0.63	—	41.46
12/02	44.50	23	16	2.28	—	40.41
12/01	46.40	16	10	3.43	—	37.03
Annual Growth	10.1%	—	—	19.3%	—	10.3%

Secure Computing

Secure Computing doesn't want either your employees or your network security standing idly by. The company provides a variety of network security products, including firewalls, user identification and authorization software, and Web filtering applications. Its firewall and virtual private network (VPN) gateways enable companies to securely manage and maintain network access for employees, customers, and partners. Secure Computing also provides software that enables network administrators to restrict access to specific Web sites to streamline system resources and improve employee productivity.

Secure Computing also offers security services such as network assessment, disaster recovery planning, and security policy assessment. The company's strategic partners include hardware manufacturers, software providers, and systems integrators.

CyberGuard made an unsolicited offer in July 2004 to purchase the company in a stock deal initially valued at $297 million. Secure rejected the offer shortly after receiving it. In August 2005, the roles were reversed when Secure agreed to acquire CyberGuard for $295 million; the deal closed early in 2006. Later in 2006 Secure acquired CipherTrust.

HISTORY

Secure Computing was formed in 1989 as a spinoff of Honeywell's network security operation, which at that time was developing technologies for the National Security Agency and other US government bodies. Secure Computing launched its first commercial products in 1993 and its Sidewinder firewall and virtual private network software in 1994.

In 1997 Secure Computing went on a buying spree, purchasing rival firewall company Border Network Technologies, Webster Network

Strategies (maker of software that monitors employee Internet usage), and Enigma Logic (authentication and authorization software). The company expanded abroad, opening offices in Europe and Australia.

Secure Computing decamped from its Minnesota location in 1998 and moved to Silicon Valley. In 1999 the company cut its product line in half to focus on firewalls and security authentication. In 2000 Secure Computing added public key infrastructure (PKI) capabilities to its SafeWord software. The next year the company expanded its roster of partners, signing deals with companies including Novell and Phoenix Technologies.

In 2003 the company acquired content filtering software provider N2H2 for about $20 million.

EXECUTIVES

Chairman, President, and CEO: John E. McNulty, age 59
Vice Chairman and Chief Strategy Officer: Jay Chaudhry
SVP, Marketing: Atri Chatterjee
SVP, Operations and CFO: Timothy J. (Tim) Steinkopf, age 44
SVP, Product Development: Michael J. (Mike) Gallagher, age 42
SVP, Secretary, and General Counsel: Mary K. Budge, age 50
SVP, Worldwide Sales: Vincent M. Schiavo, age 48
VP, Sales: Mike Van Bruinisse
VP, CipherTrust Products: Guru Rajan
VP, TrustedSource: Brad McArthur
CTO: Paul Judge
Investor Relations: Jane Underwood
Public Relations: David Burt
Auditors: Ernst & Young LLP

LOCATIONS

HQ: Secure Computing Corporation
 4810 Harwood Rd., San Jose, CA 95124
Phone: 408-979-6100   **Fax:** 408-979-6501
Web: www.securecomputing.com

Secure Computing has offices in Australia, China, France, Germany, Hong Kong, Singapore, the UK, and the US.

2005 Sales

	$ mil.	% of total
US	67.7	62
Other countries	41.5	38
Total	**109.2**	**100**

PRODUCTS/OPERATIONS

2005 Sales

	$ mil.	% of total
Products	79.4	73
Services	29.8	27
Total	**109.2**	**100**

Selected Products

Firewall and virtual private network gateway (Sidewinder)
User authentication software (SafeWord PremierAccess)
Web site filters (SmartFilter)

COMPETITORS

Check Point Software
Cisco Systems
Fortinet
Juniper Networks
RSA Security
SurfControl
Symantec
Websense

HISTORICAL FINANCIALS

Company Type: Public

Income Statement   FYE: December 31

	REVENUE ($ mil.)	NET INCOME ($ mil.)	NET PROFIT MARGIN	EMPLOYEES
12/05	109.2	21.4	19.6%	400
12/04	93.4	12.8	13.7%	378
12/03	76.2	8.3	10.9%	374
12/02	65.8	(6.5)	—	362
12/01	52.5	(9.0)	—	398
Annual Growth	20.1%	—	—	0.1%

2005 Year-End Financials

Debt ratio: —
Return on equity: 20.0%
Cash ($ mil.): 81.2
Current ratio: 3.08
Long-term debt ($ mil.): —
No. of shares (mil.): 37.0

Dividends
 Yield: —
 Payout: —
Market value ($ mil.): 453.9
R&D as % of sales: 15.5%
Advertising as % of sales: —

Stock History   NASDAQ (GS): SCUR

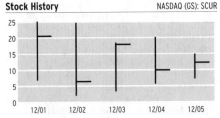

	STOCK PRICE ($) FY Close	P/E High/Low		PER SHARE ($) Earnings	Dividends	Book Value
12/05	12.26	26	13	0.57	—	3.29
12/04	9.98	59	17	0.34	—	2.57
12/03	17.91	73	14	0.25	—	2.06
12/02	6.41	—	—	(0.22)	—	1.00
12/01	20.55	—	—	(0.32)	—	1.00
Annual Growth	(12.1%)	—	—	—	—	34.9%

Semitool

Semitool provides tools that are more than just semi-useful to chip makers. The company makes semiconductor manufacturing equipment, including electrochemical deposition systems — which deposit precise layers of materials onto semiconductor wafers — and wafer surface preparation and cleaning systems. Semitool's products combine several tools into one robotically controlled unit designed to speed production, minimize chip damage, and lower manufacturing costs. Top customers include Advanced Micro Devices (about 14% of sales), Freescale Semiconductor, Intel, Qimonda, and STMicroelectronics. Founder and CEO Raymon Thompson and his wife, Ladeine, own about 31% of Semitool.

More than 60% of Semitool's sales come from customers outside the US. The company is especially targeting customers in Asia, which accounts for about 40% of sales.

During a dismal industrywide slump that lasted from 2001 to 2003, the company sold off some of its product lines so that it could focus on its core offerings.

Located off the beaten path in Montana, Semitool boasts of the longevity among its 1,200-plus

employees, with nearly 100 of them having worked 10 years or more with the company.

Royce & Associates holds 9% of Semitool, while Wells Fargo has a stake of nearly 9%.

HISTORY

Mechanical engineer Raymon Thompson formed Semitool at a machine shop in Southern California in 1978. He patented a horizontal on-axis spin rinser/dryer that removed chemicals from wafer surfaces. Thompson moved the firm to his hometown of Kalispell, Montana in 1979. The company launched its first automated tool in 1984. Thompson then formed Semitherm with a group of former Texas Instruments engineers to develop vertical furnace systems for semiconductor processing; Semitherm merged with Semitool in 1994.

Semitool went public in 1995 and bought Semy Engineering (furnace controllers and supervisor systems) the following year. Fabio Gualandris, formerly of integrated circuit maker STMicroelectronics, succeeded Thompson as CEO in 1998.

By then Semitool had teamed up with ULVAC and the Netherlands' ASM International to speed development of copper interconnect equipment. Excess capacity costs helped cause losses for fiscal 1999. Gualandris resigned in 2000, and was replaced by Thompson, who returned as president and CEO.

Early in 2001 the company sold Semy Engineering to Brooks Automation.

Larry Murphy, who joined Semitool as EVP and COO in 2004, was promoted to president in 2005, while remaining COO.

EXECUTIVES

Chairman and CEO: Raymon F. (Ray) Thompson, age 65, $457,513 pay
President and COO: Larry E. Murphy, age 47, $547,514 pay
EVP, Global Sales and Marketing, and Director: Timothy C. (Tim) Dodkin, age 57, $358,762 pay
VP, CFO, and Treasurer: Larry A. Viano, age 52, $276,305 pay
VP, Global Service: Richard P. Schuster, age 50
VP, Manufacturing: Jim Wright
VP, Marketing: Paul M. Siblerud, age 46
VP, Surface Preparation Technology: Dana R. Scranton, age 51, $193,429 pay
President, RheTech: Richard Gall
General Manager, Copper Interconnect: Klaus Pfeifer
Manager, Human Resources: Vicki Billmayer
Auditors: PricewaterhouseCoopers LLP

LOCATIONS

HQ: Semitool, Inc.
655 W. Reserve Dr., Kalispell, MT 59901
Phone: 406-752-2107   **Fax:** 406-752-5522
Web: www.semitool.com

Semitool has operations in Austria, China, France, Germany, Italy, Japan, Singapore, South Korea, the UK, and the US.

2006 Sales

	$ mil.	% of total
US	91.1	38
Asia/Pacific		
Singapore	30.2	12
Taiwan	26.7	11
Japan	16.6	7
Other countries	11.9	5
Europe		
Germany	42.0	17
Other countries	24.7	10
Total	**243.2**	**100**

PRODUCTS/OPERATIONS

Selected Products

Batch processing tools (Spectrum)
Electromechanical deposition tools (Paragon, Raider)
Single-substrate processing tools (Equinox)
Surface preparation and cleaning equipment (Millennium, Raider, Scepter)
Wafer carrier cleaning systems (Storm)

COMPETITORS

Applied Materials
ASM International
ATMI
CVD Equipment
Dainippon Screen
Ebara
FSI International
Lam Research
Novellus
SEZ Group
SUSS MicroTec
Tokyo Electron

HISTORICAL FINANCIALS

Company Type: Public

Income Statement

FYE: September 30

	REVENUE ($ mil.)	NET INCOME ($ mil.)	NET PROFIT MARGIN	EMPLOYEES
9/06	243.2	9.8	4.0%	1,312
9/05	190.4	10.1	5.3%	1,056
9/04	139.6	7.3	5.2%	958
9/03	117.1	(21.1)	—	701
9/02	123.7	(14.2)	—	1,009
Annual Growth	**18.4%**	**—**	**—**	**6.8%**

2006 Year-End Financials

Debt ratio: 2.9%
Return on equity: 7.0%
Cash ($ mil.): 17.4
Current ratio: 2.81
Long-term debt ($ mil.): 4.7
No. of shares (mil.): 31.9
Dividends
  Yield: —
  Payout: —
Market value ($ mil.): 330.1
R&D as % of sales: —
Advertising as % of sales: —

Stock History

NASDAQ (GM): SMTL

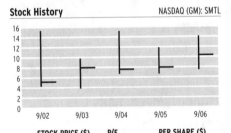

	STOCK PRICE ($) FY Close	P/E High/Low		Earnings	PER SHARE ($) Dividends	Book Value
9/06	10.34	45	24	0.31	—	5.04
9/05	7.95	34	19	0.35	—	4.19
9/04	7.59	60	27	0.25	—	3.83
9/03	7.97	—	—	(0.74)	—	3.54
9/02	5.15	—	—	(0.50)	—	4.27
Annual Growth	**19.0%**	**—**	**—**	**—**	**—**	**4.2%**

Sepracor

Helping people breathe and think properly are the core of Sepracor's business. The company focuses its drug development efforts in two main therapeutic categories: respiratory and central nervous system disorders. The company's first marketed product, Xopenex, treats asthma and other diseases that impair breathing. Its Lunesta is FDA-approved for insomnia. Sepracor also has licensed such big-name respiratory drugs as Schering-Plough's Clarinex and Sanofi-Aventis' Allegra. In 2006 the firm received FDA approval for Brovana, an inhaled drug used to treat pulmonary diseases, such as bronchitis and emphysema.

Sepracor holds a 23% stake in BioSphere Medical, which is developing technology to help treat embolism, or blocked veins.

The company sells its products to drug distributors and wholesalers. Its top customer is McKesson, which accounts for 27% of Sepracor's sales. Other big customers are Amerisource-Bergen (24%) and Cardinal Health (18%).

Xopenex accounted for about 52% of sales in 2005. Lunesta, although approved in December 2004, did not hit the US market until April 2005; by the end of the year it accounted for more than 40% of sales.

The company aims to expand its product offerings by developing treatments for such conditions as chronic obstructive pulmonary disease, depression, high blood pressure, and restless leg syndrome.

FMR Corp. owns more than 15% of Sepracor.

HISTORY

CEO Timothy Barberich founded Sepracor in 1983 to separate chemical components and purify chemicals for other drugmakers. He soon realized the same technology could separate unwanted isomers from FDA-approved drugs at a fraction of the cost of developing new ones. By the mid-1990s, six drugs were undergoing human trials and Sepracor held 10 patents.

To fund its activities, Sepracor in 1994 spun off some of its research operations, including part of BioSepra (drug and chemical purification) and HemaSure (blood purification). In 1995 it established Versicor (anti-infective drugs, now Vicuron Pharmaceuticals); in 1996 subsidiary SepraChem (chemical intermediates) joined with UK chemical maker Sterling Organics to form ChiRex.

In 1997 Sepracor patented a component of Claritin, the world's top antihistamine, and had positive results with an improved version of asthma drug Albuterol. In 1998 Sepracor partnered with Tripos to improve HIV drugs; it also licensed to Johnson & Johnson a new version of that firm's heartburn medication Propulsid.

Sepracor's improved asthma drug, Xopenex, received FDA approval in 1999, but was the subject of two FDA reprimands regarding marketing claims. The next year its Claritin ICE won approval in the European Union; in 2001 Schering-Plough won FDA approval for it (as Clarinex) in the US.

EXECUTIVES

Chairman and CEO: Timothy J. Barberich, age 59, $877,194 pay

President and COO: William James O'Shea, age 57, $829,429 pay

EVP, CFO, and Secretary: David P. Southwell, age 46, $495,341 pay

EVP, Finance and Administration and Treasurer: Robert F. Scumaci, age 47, $498,295 pay

EVP, Research and Development: Mark H.N. Corrigan, age 49, $593,803 pay

SVP, Legal Affairs and Chief Patent Counsel: Douglas E. Reedich, age 49

SVP, Commercial Technical Development: Stephen A. Wald

VP, Investor Relations and Corporate Communications: Jonae R. Barnes

SVP, Marketing and Commercial Planning: Jack W. Britts

SVP, Clinical Research: Donna R. Grogan

SVP, Regulatory Affairs and Quality Assurance: Stewart H. Mueller

SVP, Product Development: Thomas E. Rollins

SVP, Sales: Frederick H. Graff

SVP, Medical Affairs: James M. Roach

SVP, Preclinical Development Operations: Chris J. Viau

Auditors: PricewaterhouseCoopers LLP

LOCATIONS

HQ: Sepracor Inc.
84 Waterford Dr., Marlborough, MA 01752
Phone: 508-481-6700 **Fax:** 508-357-7499
Web: www.sepracor.com

Sepracor has facilities in California, Georgia, Illinois, Massachusetts, Texas, and Canada.

PRODUCTS/OPERATIONS

Selected Products

Approved
Desloratadine/Clarinex (licensed to Schering-Plough)
Fexofenadine HCl/Allegra (licensed to Sanofi-Aventis)
Levocetirizine/XUSAL (licensed to UCB Pharma)
Lunesta (insomnia)
Xopenex (asthma)

In Development
(S)-amlodipine (hypertension)
SEP-174559 (anxiety, muscle spasms)
SEP-225289 (depression)
SEP-226330 (restless leg syndrome)

COMPETITORS

Acura Pharmaceuticals
AstraZeneca
Barr Pharmaceuticals
Bayer
Bristol-Myers Squibb
Cephalon
Eli Lilly
Forest Labs
GlaxoSmithKline
Hi-Tech Pharmacal
Hoffmann-La Roche
Johnson & Johnson
King Pharmaceuticals
Merck
Mylan Labs
Neurocrine Biosciences
Novartis
Pfizer
Sanofi-Aventis
Schering-Plough
Sciele Pharma
Takeda Pharmaceutical
Watson Pharmaceuticals
Wyeth Pharmaceuticals

HISTORICAL FINANCIALS

Company Type: Public

Income Statement

FYE: December 31

	REVENUE ($ mil.)	NET INCOME ($ mil.)	NET PROFIT MARGIN	EMPLOYEES
12/05	820.9	3.9	0.5%	2,059
12/04	380.9	(295.7)	—	1,782
12/03	344.0	(135.9)	—	983
12/02	239.0	(276.5)	—	818
12/01	152.1	(224.0)	—	930
Annual Growth	52.4%	—	—	22.0%

2005 Year-End Financials

Debt ratio: —
Return on equity: —
Cash ($ mil.): 844.8
Current ratio: 3.77
Long-term debt ($ mil.): 1,162.1
No. of shares (mil.): 104.1

Dividends
Yield: —
Payout: —
Market value ($ mil.): 5,371.2
R&D as % of sales: 17.6%
Advertising as % of sales: 25.1%

Stock History

NASDAQ (GS): SEPR

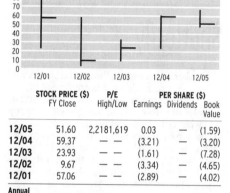

	STOCK PRICE ($) FY Close	P/E High/Low		PER SHARE ($) Earnings	Dividends	Book Value
12/05	51.60	2,218	1,619	0.03	—	(1.59)
12/04	59.37	—	—	(3.21)	—	(3.20)
12/03	23.93	—	—	(1.61)	—	(7.28)
12/02	9.67	—	—	(3.34)	—	(4.65)
12/01	57.06	—	—	(2.89)	—	(4.02)
Annual Growth	(2.5%)	—	—	—	—	—

Shuffle Master

You might be good at rearranging a deck of cards, but are you a Shuffle Master? Shuffle Master has sold or leased more than 18,000 of its single- and multi-deck automatic card shuffling devices, which in addition to the company's chip sorting devices, help increase casino security and efficiency. The company also develops table games with names like Let It Ride, Three Card Poker, Fortune Pai Gow Poker, Royal Match 21, and Casino War. About 3,600 of its table games can be found with the company's card shufflers. The private equity firm Wind Point Partners owns 66% of Shuffle Master.

Shuffle Master is working with Progressive Gaming International and International Game Technology to create a automated system for tracking table games like Roulette.

Subsidiary Shuffle Up Productions plans to take advantage of the popularity of poker on TV and produce broadcast tournaments of its games like Three Card Poker. Meanwhile, with its eye on expanding business in Asia, a second subsidiary, Shuffle Master Australasia, bought Stargames

Limited, a manufacturer of video slot machines and multiplayer games like Vegas Star. Shuffle Master already markets its own virtual card game, Table Master.

Fidelity Investments owns about 10% of Shuffle Master.

HISTORY

A former truck driver, John Breeding founded the company in 1983 to develop and market automatic card shufflers. Shuffle Master developed its first single-deck shuffling system in 1989 and installed its first automatic shuffling machine at Bally's Casino in Las Vegas in 1992, the year the company went public. Shuffle Master began licensing its Let It Ride table game the following year and became profitable by 1995. That year it introduced a multi-deck shuffler and began selling its products in addition to leasing.

To bolster its presence in the higher-margin game business, Shuffle Master formed an agreement with master game designer Mark Yoseloff in 1996 (the developer of consumer versions of Pac Man and Donkey Kong) that included access to Yoseloff's personal game library. The alliance produced Five Deck Frenzy, a video poker game that Shuffle Master debuted in 1996. The company also formed a joint marketing agreement with International Game Technology (IGT) that year to market Five Deck Frenzy and the video version of Let It Ride.

Yoseloff joined the Shuffle Master staff in 1997 as head of the New Games division. Later that year Breeding retired for health reasons (he has diabetes) and was replaced by Joseph Lahti. The company developed four new casino video games using IGT machine technology in 1998. Shuffle Master also penned an agreement with Bally Gaming that year to create a casino video version of Let's Make a Deal, based on the Monty Hall game show. The company had trouble marketing its new Three Stooges slot machine in 1999 because of concerns that the game lures children. Shuffle Master introduced its King shuffler in 2000, which shuffles cards continuously, making card counting virtually impossible.

In 2002 Yoseloff added chairman to his CEO title when Lahti retired; EVP Mark Lipparelli was named president. The following year Lipparelli resigned and was replaced by Paul Meyer. In 2004 the company began selling its slot operations to focus on its core shuffler and table game businesses. In that vein, Shuffle Master purchased BET Technology (three table games) and CARD Casinos Austria Research & Development (card shufflers and chip sorters) the same year.

EXECUTIVES

Chairman and CEO: Mark L. Yoseloff, age 59, $711,000 pay

President and COO: Paul C. Meyer, age 59, $431,000 pay

SVP and CFO: Richard L. (Rich) Baldwin, age 33, $328,000 pay

SVP: R. Brooke Dunn, age 50, $332,000 pay

SVP and General Counsel: Jerome R. (Jerry) Smith

SVP Product Management: David Lopez

VP Sales: Donald W. Bauer

President and Managing Director, Stargames: John Rouse

Managing Director, CARD: Ernest Blaha

Director Human Resources: Victoria Harper

Director Sales and Utility, Europe: Georg Fekete

Senior Sales Executive: Chris Costello

Senior Sales Executive: Steve Venuto

Sales Consultant, Canada: Maurits Vander Cruyssen

Media Relations: Kirsten Clark

Auditors: Deloitte & Touche LLP

LOCATIONS

HQ: Shuffle Master, Inc.
  1106 Palms Airport Dr., Las Vegas, NV 89119
Phone: 702-897-7150   **Fax:** 702-260-6691
Web: www.shufflemaster.com

Shuffle Master has operations in Nevada and Minnesota, as well as offices in Australia and Austria.

2006 Sales

	$ mil.	% of total
North America		
US	90.8	55
Canada	7.1	4
Other countries	2.9	2
Australia	27.2	17
Asia	24.1	15
Europe	9.9	6
Other regions	1.5	1
Total	**163.5**	**100**

PRODUCTS/OPERATIONS

2006 Sales

	$ mil.	% of total
Utility products	87.1	53
Entertainment products	76.1	47
Other	0.3	—
Total	**163.5**	**100**

Selected Products

Card shufflers
  Multi-deck batch
  Multi-deck continuous
  one2six
  Single deck
Table games
  Casino War
  Fortune Pai Gow Poker
  Let It Ride
  Let It Ride Bonus
  Let It Ride The Tournament
  Royal Match 21
  Three Card Poker

COMPETITORS

Bally Technologies
Gaming Partners International
Innovative Gaming
Progressive Gaming
VendingData

HISTORICAL FINANCIALS

Company Type: Public

Income Statement — FYE: October 31

	REVENUE ($ mil.)	NET INCOME ($ mil.)	NET PROFIT MARGIN	EMPLOYEES
10/06	163.5	6.8	4.2%	550
10/05	112.9	29.2	25.9%	320
10/04	84.8	24.1	28.4%	257
10/03	67.4	16.9	25.1%	320
10/02	56.1	14.0	25.0%	228
Annual Growth	**30.7%**	**(16.5%)**	**—**	**24.6%**

2006 Year-End Financials

Debt ratio: 464.0%
Return on equity: 28.5%
Cash ($ mil.): 19.0
Current ratio: 0.84
Long-term debt ($ mil.): 158.9
No. of shares (mil.): 34.9
Dividends
  Yield: —
  Payout: —
Market value ($ mil.): 914.2
R&D as % of sales: —
Advertising as % of sales: —

Stock History

NASDAQ (GS): SHFL

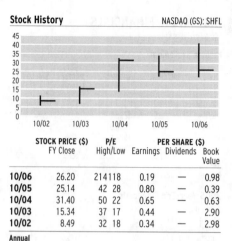

	STOCK PRICE ($) FY Close	P/E High/Low	PER SHARE ($) Earnings	Dividends	Book Value
10/06	26.20	214 118	0.19	—	0.98
10/05	25.14	42 28	0.80	—	0.39
10/04	31.40	50 22	0.65	—	0.63
10/03	15.34	37 17	0.44	—	2.90
10/02	8.49	32 18	0.34	—	2.98
Annual Growth	**32.5%**	**— —**	**(13.5%)**	**—**	**(24.2%)**

Shutterfly

Whether or not you are the consummate shutterbug, you can rely on Shutterfly for digital prints. An e-commerce company specializing in digital photo products and services (enhanced by its VividPics technology) for the consumer and professional photography markets, the company offers customers the ability to upload, share, store, and edit digital photos through its Web site. In addition to traditional 4-inch by 6-inch prints, Shutterfly offers enlargements and photo novelty items including mugs, photo books, calendars, and T-shirts. Shutterfly users are not required to become members to view shared photos. James Clark, who resigned as chairman in 2007, owns about 40% of the firm through various affiliations.

The company was founded in 1999, funded partly by Clark, a Silicon Valley investor and co-founder of Netscape Communications Corp. Shutterfly hired eBay veteran Jeff Housenbold as CEO in 2005.

Shutterfly makes about half its revenues (49%) during the fourth quarter of the year due to holiday sales.

In 2006 the company filed to go public. It intends to spend up to $35 million from funds raised to increase production capacity.

Board member Nancy Schoendorf represents investment firm Mohr, Davidow Ventures, which owns 22% of Shutterfly.

EXECUTIVES

President, CEO, and Director:
  Jeffrey T. (Jeff) Housenbold, age 36, $401,042 pay (partial-year salary)
CFO: Stephen E. (Steve) Recht, age 54, $270,250 pay
SVP Business and Corporate Development:
  Douglas J. (Doug) Galen, age 44, $194,615 pay (partial-year salary)
SVP Operations: Jeannine M. Smith, age 45, $235,200 pay
SVP Technology: Stanford S. Au, age 46
VP Consumer Marketing: Janice Gaub
VP Human Resources: Patricia (Pat) Schoof
VP Product Marketing: Peter Elarde

Chief Marketing Officer: Andrew F. (Andy) Young, age 48, $237,600 pay
Director Corporate Communications: Bridgette Thomas
Director Investor Relations: Judith H. McGarry
VP Legal: Douglas (Doug) Appleton, age 40

LOCATIONS

HQ: Shutterfly, Inc.
  2800 Bridge Pkwy., Ste. 101,
  Redwood City, CA 94065
Phone: 650-610-5200   **Fax:** 650-654-1299
Web: www.shutterfly.com

COMPETITORS

Costco Wholesale	Ritz Camera Centers
CVS	Snapfish
Kodak Imaging Network	Target
Ludicorp	Walgreen
PhotoWorks	Wal-Mart
Rite Aid	

HISTORICAL FINANCIALS

Company Type: Public

Income Statement — FYE: December 31

	REVENUE ($ mil.)	NET INCOME ($ mil.)	NET PROFIT MARGIN	EMPLOYEES
12/05	83.9	28.9	34.4%	202
12/04	54.5	3.7	6.8%	—
12/03	31.4	2.0	6.4%	—
Annual Growth	**63.5%**	**280.1%**	**—**	**—**

2005 Year-End Financials

Debt ratio: —
Return on equity: —
Cash ($ mil.): 39.2
Current ratio: 2.06
Long-term debt ($ mil.): 3.7

Net Income History

NASDAQ (GM): SFLY

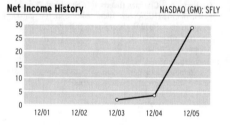

SI International

Technology services? Yes! SI International provides information technology services, including application development, network design, systems engineering and integration, and business process outsourcing. SI also offers enterprise resource planning, training, and data security services. The company serves the US government, including the Department of Defense (more than half of sales), the Air Force Space Command, and the Department of State; commercial clients include GEICO and Hewlett-Packard. Chairman Ray Oleson and former vice chairman Walter Culver founded SI International in 1998.

The company has expanded aggressively using acquisitions, including the purchases of Noblestar Federal Systems, System Technology Associates, Bridge Technology Corporation, and Zen Technology.

EXECUTIVES

Chairman: Ray J. Oleson, age 61, $839,077 pay
President, CEO, and Director: S. Bradford (Brad) Antle, age 50, $705,923 pay
EVP, CFO, and Treasurer: Thomas E. (Ted) Dunn, age 54, $573,000 pay
EVP and Chief Marketing Officer: Leslee Gault
EVP, IT Solutions Group: Marylynn Stowers, age 45
EVP, Mission Services Group: P. Michael (Mike) Becraft, age 61
EVP, Strategic Programs Group: Harry Gatanas, age 59, $195,346 pay
SVP, Human Resources: Lee Stratton
SVP, Market Development: Lou Gould
VP, Corporate Communications: Alan Hill
VP, Corporate Development: Thomas E. Lloyd, age 71, $254,423 pay
VP, General Counsel, and Secretary: James E. (Jim) Daniel
Auditors: Ernst & Young LLP

LOCATIONS

HQ: SI International, Inc.
12012 Sunset Hills Rd., Ste. 800, Reston, VA 20190
Phone: 703-234-7000 **Fax:** 703-234-7500
Web: www.si-intl.com

PRODUCTS/OPERATIONS

2005 Sales

	% of total
Federal civilian agencies	51
Department of Defense	47
Commercial entities	2
Total	**100**

2005 Sales

	% of total
Prime contract revenue	75
Subcontract revenue	25
Total	**100**

Selected Services

Application development and integration
Business process outsourcing
Consulting
Network design and implementation
Security assessment and training
Software and systems testing and validation
Systems engineering, integration, and management
Telecommunications engineering
Training and support
Transaction management
Web-based application and portal development and management

COMPETITORS

Alion
Apptis
Boeing
CACI International
Computer Sciences Corp.
EDS
IBM
ITT Defense
Lockheed Martin
MTC Technologies
Northrop Grumman IT
Raytheon
RS Information Systems
SAIC
Unisys

HISTORICAL FINANCIALS

Company Type: Public

Income Statement

FYE: Saturday nearest December 31

	REVENUE ($ mil.)	NET INCOME ($ mil.)	NET PROFIT MARGIN	EMPLOYEES
12/05	397.9	16.9	4.2%	4,000
12/04	262.3	10.9	4.2%	1,700
12/03	168.3	7.4	4.4%	1,300
12/02	149.4	2.5	1.7%	1,200
12/01	146.6	(0.7)	—	
Annual Growth	**28.4%**	**—**	**—**	**49.4%**

2005 Year-End Financials

Debt ratio: 58.5%
Return on equity: 10.8%
Cash ($ mil.): 34.0
Current ratio: 2.30
Long-term debt ($ mil.): 98.3
No. of shares (mil.): 11.3
Dividends
  Yield: —
  Payout: —
Market value ($ mil.): 346.7
R&D as % of sales: —
Advertising as % of sales: —

Stock History

NASDAQ (GS): SINT

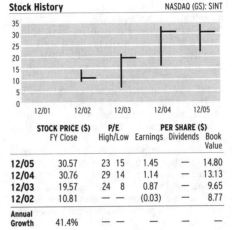

	STOCK PRICE ($) FY Close	P/E High/Low		PER SHARE ($) Earnings	Dividends	Book Value
12/05	30.57	23	15	1.45	—	14.80
12/04	30.76	29	14	1.14	—	13.13
12/03	19.57	24	8	0.87	—	9.65
12/02	10.81	—	—	(0.03)	—	8.77
Annual Growth	**41.4%**	**—**	**—**	**—**	**—**	**—**

SigmaTel

SigmaTel knows how to handle audio signals in a digital world. Long a leader in the market for PC audio encoder/decoder (codec) chips, the company has turned its expertise in designing mixed-signal integrated circuits and digital signal processors to other areas. The fabless semiconductor company now develops audio codecs and other chips used in cellular phones, CD players, and digital audio players, as well as chips used to create high-speed infrared links between PCs and other electronics devices, such as printers and digital cameras. Customers include distributor GMI Technology (about 18% of sales), Asustek Computer (15%), and Creative Technology (13%).

Additional customers include Compal, Fujitsu, Philips, Samsung Electronics, and Wistron. Customers located in Asia make up nearly all of sales, with those in China and Taiwan accounting for about three-quarters of revenues. In order to better serve its Asian customers, SigmaTel has opened an engineering and design support office in Hong Kong.

The company has sold its PC audio product line to Integrated Device Technology (IDT) for $80 million, including $72 million in cash. The line represented about 20% of SigmaTel's sales.

About 60 SigmaTel employees and associated contractors will go to work for IDT as a result.

Following the sale to IDT, SigmaTel cut some jobs. It also set plans to eliminate another 60 positions, 14% of its workforce, by the end of 2006.

SigmaTel has acquired Protocom Corp. (also known as Protocom Technology) for about $47 million in cash and stock. Protocom develops digital compression semiconductors, used in imaging applications, such as digital camcorders, personal video recorders, and personal media players. SigmaTel has also acquired the software, patents, and engineering resources of the Rio portable audio product line from D&M Holdings. D&M will retain ownership of the Rio MP3 player products, inventory, and trademarks. The Rio products contain SigmaTel chips. SigmaTel hired the Rio design team of engineers, based in Cambridge, England.

Another acquisition is Oasis Semiconductor, a fabless developer of semiconductors for printing and imaging office equipment. SigmaTel paid $57 million in cash for Oasis Semi; the shareholders of Oasis may get another $25 million in cash through a future earnout payment.

In a novel use for its technology, SigmaTel has announced that its D-Major MP3 controller will be used by Oakley in a line of eyewear that incorporates an MP3 player.

Royce & Associates owns about 6% of SigmaTel. Goldman Sachs Asset Management holds nearly 6% of the company. Citadel LP has an equity stake of more than 5%. Barclays Global Investors owns about 5%.

EXECUTIVES

Chairman: William P. Osborne, age 62
Interim CEO: Phillip E. (Phil) Pompa, age 49
SVP Operations and Engineering Services: Stephan L. (Steve) Beatty, age 39, $292,377 pay
CFO: Scott Schaefer
SVP Portable SoC Businesses: Michael R. (Mike) Wodopian, age 53, $340,627 pay
SVP Sales: Kevin Beadle, age 48
SVP Operations and Technology: Daniel P. (Danny) Mulligan
SVP Asia: Jose Lau
VP and General Counsel: Alan D. Green, age 41, $99,294 pay
VP Human Resources: Melissa C. Groff, age 40
Director, Investor Relations and Treasurer: Dave Donovan
Marketing Communications: Martha Aviles
Auditors: PricewaterhouseCoopers LLP

LOCATIONS

HQ: SigmaTel, Inc.
1601 S. MoPac Expwy., Ste. 100, Austin, TX 78746
Phone: 512-381-3700 **Fax:** 512-744-1700
Web: www.sigmatel.com

SigmaTel has offices in China, Hong Kong, Japan, Singapore, South Korea, Taiwan, the UK, and the US.

2005 Sales

	% of total
China & Hong Kong	39
Taiwan	38
Singapore	14
South Korea	3
US	2
Japan	1
Other countries	3
Total	**100**

PRODUCTS/OPERATIONS

2005 Sales

	% of total
Portable audio SoCs	91
Audio codecs	7
Other products	2
Total	**100**

Selected Products

Audio coder/decoder (codec) chips for PCs and home entertainment systems (C-Major line)
Audio decoder chips for portable audio players (D-Major line)
Digital photo frame devices (STDC7150)
Multifunction printer printer devices (STDC3000)
Wireless Universal Serial Bus (USB) infrared controllers

COMPETITORS

Actions Semiconductor	Microchip Technology
Akustica	Micronas Semiconductor
Analog Devices	NEC
Asahi Kasei	NXP
Atmel	PortalPlayer
austriamicrosystems	Samsung Electronics
Broadcom	Silicon Motion
Cirrus Logic	Sunplus
ESS Technology	Texas Instruments
Freescale Semiconductor	Yamaha
Infineon Technologies	Zoran
Macronix International	

HISTORICAL FINANCIALS

Company Type: Public

Income Statement

FYE: December 31

	REVENUE ($ mil.)	NET INCOME ($ mil.)	NET PROFIT MARGIN	EMPLOYEES
12/05	324.5	35.9	11.1%	610
12/04	194.8	52.6	27.0%	238
12/03	100.2	10.0	10.0%	135
12/02	30.9	(8.3)	—	100
12/01	24.4	(18.4)	—	—
Annual Growth	**91.0%**	**—**	**—**	**82.7%**

2005 Year-End Financials

Debt ratio: —
Return on equity: 16.3%
Cash ($ mil.): 118.9
Current ratio: 2.77
Long-term debt ($ mil.): —
No. of shares (mil.): 37.4
Dividends
 Yield: —
 Payout: —
Market value ($ mil.): 490.2
R&D as % of sales: 23.1%
Advertising as % of sales: 0.2%

Stock History

NASDAQ (GS): SGTL

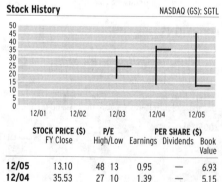

	STOCK PRICE ($) FY Close	P/E High/Low	PER SHARE ($) Earnings	PER SHARE ($) Dividends	PER SHARE ($) Book Value
12/05	13.10	48 13	0.95	—	6.93
12/04	35.53	27 10	1.39	—	5.15
12/03	24.68	773 438	0.04	—	3.69
Annual Growth	**(27.1%)**	**— —**	**387.3%**	**—**	**37.0%**

Silicon Image

It would be silly to imagine that Silicon Image's chips only produce pretty pictures. Silicon Image designs and sells a variety of integrated circuits, including digital video controllers, receivers, transmitters, and processors that are built into personal computers, set-top boxes, and DVD players. Its chips also are found in video systems such as flat-panel displays and cathode-ray tubes, as well as storage networking devices. Top customers of the fabless company include Asian distributors World Peace International (about 17% of sales) and Microtek (nearly 11%). Silicon Image primarily outsources production of its chips to Taiwan Semiconductor Manufacturing.

Customers located outside of the US account for more than 70% of Silicon Image's sales. The company has added offices in Japan, South Korea, and Taiwan to expand its customer and support operations in the Asia/Pacific region. Silicon Image sells primarily to the personal computer, storage, and consumer electronics markets.

Silicon Image is expanding its offerings in the storage components business through its acquisition of privately held TransWarp Networks (switching, CPU, and memory products for storage management). The company is also phasing out its storage subsystems products, opting to license the technology rather than develop new products.

A dispute over patent royalties due from rival Genesis Microchip was resolved in Silicon Image's favor in late 2006, with Genesis paying $4.5 million in one lump sum and a confidential amount in recalculated royalties to Silicon Image. Under a previous agreement between the competitors, reached in 2002, Genesis had already paid a total of about $11 million in royalties to Silicon Image.

Barclays Global Investors owns about 6% of Silicon Image.

EXECUTIVES

Chairman: Peter G. Hanelt, age 60
President, CEO, and Director: Steve Tirado, age 51, $653,223 pay
CFO and Chief Accounting Officer: Robert R. Freeman, age 63
VP, Worldwide Operations and Quality: Peter J. Rado
VP, Business Development and Intellectual Property Licensing: Eric C. Almgren
VP, Worldwide Marketing: Dale Zimmerman, age 46
VP, Engineering and Interim VP, Consumer Electronics: John H. J. Shin, age 50
VP, Worldwide Sales: Robert Valiton, $384,222 pay
VP, Human Resources: Doug Haslam
CTO: J. Duane Northcutt, age 46, $324,950 pay
Chief Legal Officer: Edward Lopez
Manager, Public Relations: Sheryl M. Gulizia
Investor Relations: Gloria Lee
Auditors: Deloitte & Touche LLP

LOCATIONS

HQ: Silicon Image, Inc.
 1060 E. Arques Ave., Sunnyvale, CA 94086
Phone: 408-616-4000   **Fax:** 408-830-9530
Web: www.siimage.com

Silicon Image has offices in Japan, South Korea, Taiwan, and the US.

2005 Sales

	$ mil.	% of total
US	54.6	26
Taiwan	53.6	25
Japan	46.2	22
South Korea	20.6	10
Hong Kong	6.8	3
Other countries	30.6	14
Total	**212.4**	**100**

PRODUCTS/OPERATIONS

2005 Sales

	$ mil.	% of total
Consumer electronics	108.7	51
Personal computers	49.2	23
Storage products	36.0	17
Development, licensing & royalties	18.5	9
Total	**212.4**	**100**

Selected Products

Communications integrated circuits
 Fibre Channel serializer/deserializers (SerDes)
 Receivers
 Transmitters
Controller integrated circuits for video displays
Digital video processors and processing systems
Redundant array of independent disks (RAID) storage devices
 Controller boards
 Storage subsystems

COMPETITORS

Analog Devices	National Semiconductor
ATI Technologies	NVIDIA
Avago Technologies	NXP
Broadcom	Pixelworks
Chrontel	PMC-Sierra
Conexant Systems	Promise Technology
FOCUS Enhancements	QLogic
Genesis Microchip	Silicon Integrated Systems
Intel	Silicon Optix
LSI Logic	STMicroelectronics
Macronix International	Texas Instruments
Marvell Technology	Trident Microsystems
Micronas Semiconductor	VIA Technologies
Mindspeed	Vitesse Semiconductor

HISTORICAL FINANCIALS

Company Type: Public

Income Statement

FYE: December 31

	REVENUE ($ mil.)	NET INCOME ($ mil.)	NET PROFIT MARGIN	EMPLOYEES
12/05	212.4	49.5	23.3%	384
12/04	173.2	(0.3)	—	337
12/03	103.5	(12.8)	—	250
12/02	81.5	(40.1)	—	249
12/01	52.0	(76.1)	—	266
Annual Growth	**42.2%**	**—**	**—**	**9.6%**

2005 Year-End Financials

Debt ratio: —
Return on equity: 33.2%
Cash ($ mil.): 151.6
Current ratio: 4.07
Long-term debt ($ mil.): —
No. of shares (mil.): 81.1
Dividends
 Yield: —
 Payout: —
Market value ($ mil.): 736.0
R&D as % of sales: 21.1%
Advertising as % of sales: —

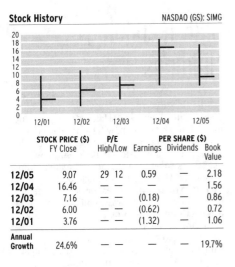

NASDAQ (GS): SIMG

	STOCK PRICE ($) FY Close	P/E High/Low		PER SHARE ($) Earnings	Dividends	Book Value
12/05	9.07	29	12	0.59	—	2.18
12/04	16.46	—	—	—	—	1.56
12/03	7.16	—	—	(0.18)	—	0.86
12/02	6.00	—	—	(0.62)	—	0.72
12/01	3.76	—	—	(1.32)	—	1.06
Annual Growth	24.6%			—	—	19.7%

Simclar

Simclar could be the name of a new superhero. Instead, the company provides contract manufacturing and services for equipment makers that serve the data processing, telecommunications, food preparation, military, and instrumentation markets. Simclar's products include printed circuit boards, custom electromechanical assemblies, cables, and wire harnesses. The company also provides product repair and refurbishment services. Simclar's customers include Illinois Tool Works (17% of sales). Contract manufacturer Simclar Group Limited (which is owned by CEO Samuel Russell and his wife, director Christina Russell) controls more than 70% of the company.

Nearly all of Simclar's sales are to customers located in the US, with a small portion in Mexico. The company is focusing on value-added services for continued growth; it acquired AG Technologies, a small contract manufacturer with facilities in Mexico and the US, in 2003. In 2005 Simclar acquired Simclar (North America) from Simclar Group, adding sheet metal fabrication and higher-level assembly capabilities.

Simclar has acquired certain US assets of Litton Interconnect Technologies, a unit of Northrop Grumman, for $16 million. At the same time, Simclar's parent company has acquired the Litton unit's assets in China and the UK for $12 million.

EXECUTIVES

Chairman and CEO: Samuel J. (Sam) Russell, age 61, $60,000 pay
President and Director: Barry Pardon, age 54, $130,000 pay
CFO, Treasurer, and Secretary: Marshall W. Griffin, age 48
VP and General Manager, Simclar Dayton Division: Edward L. McGrath, age 60, $122,411 pay
VP and General Manager, Simclar Mexico: Steven Breen
VP, Finance and Director: John I. Durie, age 49
Director of Operations, Dunfermline: Bob Waterson
Auditors: Battelle & Battelle LLP

LOCATIONS

HQ: Simclar, Inc.
2230 W. 77th St., Hialeah, FL 33016
Phone: 305-556-9210   **Fax:** 305-364-1350
Web: www.simclar.com

Simclar has operations in Florida, Massachusetts, Missouri, North Carolina, Ohio, and Texas, and in Mexico.

PRODUCTS/OPERATIONS

2005 Sales

	% of total
Printed circuit boards	51
Cable & harness assemblies	33
Refurbishing & other	16
Total	**100**

2005 Sales by Market

	% of total
Data processing	25
Food preparation equipment	18
Power equipment	17
Instrumentation	16
Telecommunications	12
Military & government	4
Other	8
Total	**100**

Products

Cable assemblies
Injection-molded and electronic assembly products
Printed circuit boards
Sheet metal
Subassemblies
Wire harnesses

Services

Contract manufacturing
Design and engineering
Reworking and refurbishing

COMPETITORS

Amphenol
Benchmark Electronics
Electronic Product Integration Corporation
Flextronics
Hon Hai
Jabil
Kimball International
Methode Electronics
Nortech Systems
Sanmina-SCI
Solectron
Sparton
Tyco Electronics
Viasystems
Volex

HISTORICAL FINANCIALS

Company Type: Public

Income Statement

FYE: December 31

	REVENUE ($ mil.)	NET INCOME ($ mil.)	NET PROFIT MARGIN	EMPLOYEES
12/05	61.0	0.9	1.5%	837
12/04	53.6	2.3	4.3%	549
12/03	36.2	1.1	3.0%	538
12/02	33.7	1.4	4.2%	284
12/01	37.0	(2.8)	—	256
Annual Growth	13.3%	—	—	34.5%

2005 Year-End Financials

Debt ratio: 19.9%
Return on equity: 6.2%
Cash ($ mil.): 0.8
Current ratio: 1.23
Long-term debt ($ mil.): 3.0
No. of shares (mil.): 6.5
Dividends
  Yield: —
  Payout: —
Market value ($ mil.): 23.1
R&D as % of sales: —
Advertising as % of sales: —

Stock History

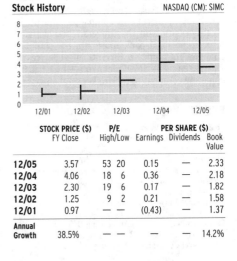

NASDAQ (CM): SIMC

	STOCK PRICE ($) FY Close	P/E High/Low		PER SHARE ($) Earnings	Dividends	Book Value
12/05	3.57	53	20	0.15	—	2.33
12/04	4.06	18	6	0.36	—	2.18
12/03	2.30	19	6	0.17	—	1.82
12/02	1.25	9	2	0.21	—	1.58
12/01	0.97	—	—	(0.43)	—	1.37
Annual Growth	38.5%			—	—	14.2%

Sirenza Microdevices

Sirenza Microdevices helps its customers transmit the siren call of the radio. Sirenza offers radio-frequency (RF) semiconductors for wireless and wireline telecom systems. The fabless firm's amplifiers, drivers, switches, and discrete devices are made from materials such as gallium arsenide and silicon germanium. Most of Sirenza's sales come through distributors; customers include Avnet (13% of sales), Ericsson, Motorola (11%), and Nokia. The company has expanded its product line through complementary acquisitions, including the purchase of Micro Linear for stock worth nearly $46 million. Founders John (chairman) and Susan (treasurer) Ocampo own around 28% of Sirenza.

Micro Linear, a supplier of wireless transceivers and other RF components, is a fabless semiconductor company, like Sirenza. The transaction closed in October 2006.

Sirenza expanded its offerings in 2003 by acquiring the assets of defunct RF component maker Vari-L. In connection with the acquisition, the company relocated its headquarters from California to Colorado.

Late in 2004 Sirenza acquired ISG Broadband, which designed RF components, from California Eastern Laboratories.

In early 2006 the company acquired Premier Devices, Inc. (PDI) for around $72 million in common stock, cash, and debt. Premier Devices makes RF components that are described as complementary to Sirenza's product line. The sole shareholders of PDI, Phillip and Yeechin Liao, own nearly 16% of Sirenza. Phillip Liao joined the Sirenza board of directors and served as president of a wholly owned subsidiary of Sirenza. He stepped down as president of the PDI subsidiary in late 2006, however, citing health and personal reasons, while remaining on the board of directors.

Sirenza was incorporated in California as Matrix Microassembly Corp. in 1985. The company began doing business as Stanford Microdevices, Inc. in 1992 and reincorporated in Delaware under that name in late 1997. It wasn't until 1999, shortly before the company filed for an IPO as Stanford Microdevices, that the chip firm heard from attorneys representing nearby Stanford University, claiming that the company's name might legally infringe on the university's trademark. After some legal back-and-forth, the company changed its name to Sirenza Microdevices in 2001, keeping its SMDI nickname, which had become the company's stock ticker symbol, as well.

EXECUTIVES

Chairman: John Ocampo, age 47, $250,000 pay
President, CEO, and Director:
Robert (Bob) Van Buskirk, age 57, $325,000 pay
CFO: Charles R. (Chuck) Bland, age 57, $252,000 pay
EVP, Business Development and Interim President, President, Premier Devices: Gerald (Jerry) Quinnell, age 48, $217,000 pay
VP, Advanced Products and CTO:
Joseph H. (Joe) Johnson, age 65
VP, Controller, and Chief Accounting Officer:
Gerald Hatley, age 36, $156,000 pay
VP, General Counsel, and Secretary: Clay B. Simpson, age 34
VP, Engineering and Product Development:
John Pelose, age 51
VP, Human Resources: Jacqueline R. (Jacquie) Maidel, age 61
VP, Human Resources: Kathryn M. Zuber
Auditors: Ernst & Young LLP

LOCATIONS

HQ: Sirenza Microdevices, Inc.
303 S. Technology Ct., Broomfield, CO 80021
Phone: 303-327-3030   **Fax:** 303-410-7088
Web: www.sirenza.com

Sirenza Microdevices has offices in China, Germany, India, Sweden, the UK, and the US.

2005 Sales

	$ mil.	% of total
US	15.9	25
Other countries	48.3	75
Total	**64.2**	**100**

PRODUCTS/OPERATIONS

2005 Sales

	$ mil.	% of total
Amplifier division	36.5	57
Signal Source division	24.5	38
Aerospace & Defense division	3.2	5
Total	**64.2**	**100**

Selected Products

Fiber-optic devices
  Limiting amplifiers
  Transimpedance amplifiers
Pre-driver, driver, and power amplifiers
Radio-frequency (RF) signal processing devices
  Down- and upconverters
  Mixers
  Modulators and demodulators
Transistors

COMPETITORS

Alps Electric
ANADIGICS
Avago Technologies
AVX
Ericsson
Freescale Semiconductor
Hittite Microwave
IBM Microelectronics
Infineon Technologies
M/A-Com
Micronetics
Microtune
Mini-Circuits
Motorola
Murata Manufacturing
NEC
Nokia
Nortel Networks
NXP
RF Micro Devices
Skyworks
Spectrum Control
STMicroelectronics
TelASIC
Teledyne Technologies
TriQuint
Wistron
WJ Communications

HISTORICAL FINANCIALS

Company Type: Public

Income Statement

FYE: December 31

	REVENUE ($ mil.)	NET INCOME ($ mil.)	NET PROFIT MARGIN	EMPLOYEES
12/05	64.2	1.4	2.2%	252
12/04	61.3	0.3	0.5%	292
12/03	38.5	(6.2)	—	256
12/02	20.7	(10.6)	—	121
12/01	19.8	(19.6)	—	95
Annual Growth	**34.2%**	**—**	**—**	**27.6%**

2005 Year-End Financials

Debt ratio: —
Return on equity: 2.9%
Cash ($ mil.): 18.2
Current ratio: 3.56
Long-term debt ($ mil.): —
No. of shares (mil.): 36.6
Dividends
  Yield: —
  Payout: —
Market value ($ mil.): 168.5
R&D as % of sales: 15.7%
Advertising as % of sales: 0.3%

Stock History

NASDAQ (GM): SMDI

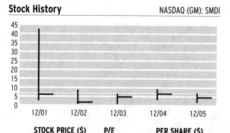

	STOCK PRICE ($) FY Close	P/E High/Low	Earnings	Dividends	Book Value
12/05	4.61	168 54	0.04	—	1.39
12/04	6.56	900 350	0.01	—	1.34
12/03	4.81	— —	(0.19)	—	1.32
12/02	1.80	— —	(0.35)	—	1.50
12/01	6.09	— —	(0.67)	—	1.82
Annual Growth	**(6.7%)**	**— —**	**—**	**—**	**(6.5%)**

SiRF Technology Holdings

Surf the seas, the highways, or the wireless Web — SiRF Technology Holdings' semiconductor designs and software will help you keep track of where you are. SiRF's products, which employ global positioning system (GPS) data, allow manufacturers to add navigation and mapping, lost person location, and fleet vehicle tracking functions into their own wireless devices. The fabless chip company, which was founded in 1995, expanded its offerings through an agreement with Conexant Systems: Conexant contributed its own GPS technology to SiRF in return for an ownership stake (now around 11%) in the company. Promate (45% of sales) and Gateway (11%) are among the company's leading customers.

In 2003 SiRF expanded its technology offerings by acquiring privately held Enuvis, a developer of specialized GPS algorithms that allow GPS devices to operate better in urban settings. In 2005 SiRF acquired Kisel Microelectronics, a Swedish design house specializing in radio-frequency integrated circuits (RFICs), for around $33 million in cash and stock. Established in late 1999 by senior IC designers from Ericsson, Kisel Micro has crafted integrated transceivers for multiple radio designs, with the chips being made through a variety of fabrication processes, from the exotic silicon germanium BiCMOS to pure bipolar and analog/RF-CMOS. Kisel's 19 employees joined a new Swedish subsidiary of SiRF.

SiRF has acquired the GPS chipset line of Motorola for $20 million in cash and will continue to provide those chipsets to the communications giant. The purchase widens SiRF's GPS portfolio. Motorola uses the chipsets in its automotive telematics equipment, cell phones, and GPS-enabled radios for public safety organizations. The deal adds about 40 Motorola employees in the UK and the US to SiRF's headcount. SiRF's chips are manufactured by IBM Microelectronics, Samsung Electronics, and STMicroelectronics.

FMR (Fidelity Investments) owns 14% of SiRF Technology. Founder and chairman Diosdado Banatao, along with his firm Tallwood Venture Capital, holds nearly 8% of the company.

EXECUTIVES

Chairman: Diosdado P. (Dado) Banatao, age 60
President, CEO, and Director: Michael L. Canning, age 65
SVP, Finance and CFO: Geoffrey G. (Geoff) Ribar
VP, Marketing and Director: Kanwar Chadha, age 47
VP, Sales: Joseph M. (Joe) LaValle, age 57
VP, Engineering: Jamshid (Jim) Basiji, age 66
VP, Operations and Quality: Atul P. Shingal, age 46
Director, Human Resources: Bill Higgins
Auditors: Ernst & Young LLP

LOCATIONS

HQ: SiRF Technology Holdings, Inc.
148 E. Brokaw Rd., San Jose, CA 95112
Phone: 408-467-0410   **Fax:** 408-467-0420
Web: www.sirf.com

SiRF Technology Holdings has offices in China, India, Japan, South Korea, Sweden, Taiwan, the UK, and the US.

2005 Sales

	$ mil.	% of total
Asia/Pacific		
Taiwan	95.5	58
Singapore	15.2	9
New Zealand	3.3	2
Japan	2.6	2
China	2.1	1
US	32.6	20
Europe		
Germany	0.4	—
Other countries	6.7	4
Other regions	6.7	4
Total	**165.1**	**100**

PRODUCTS/OPERATIONS

2005 Sales

	$ mil.	% of total
Products	153.4	93
Royalties	11.7	7
Total	**165.1**	**100**

Selected Products

SiRFDRive (software for automotive applications)
SiRFLoc and
SiRFstar semiconductors
  Embedded core software
  Enhanced digital signal processing circuit
  Internal processor and memory
  Radio-frequency integrated circuit

COMPETITORS

Analog Devices
Andrew Corporation
Cambridge Positioning Systems
CEVA
Freescale Semiconductor
Hittite Microwave
Infineon Technologies
NAVSYS
NXP
QUALCOMM
Sony
STMicroelectronics
Texas Instruments
Trimble Navigation
TruePosition

HISTORICAL FINANCIALS

Company Type: Public

Income Statement

	REVENUE ($ mil.)	NET INCOME ($ mil.)	NET PROFIT MARGIN	EMPLOYEES
12/05	165.1	30.0	18.2%	354
12/04	117.4	30.7	26.1%	202
12/03	73.2	3.6	4.9%	152
12/02	30.4	(12.5)	—	—
12/01	15.1	(23.7)	—	140
Annual Growth	**81.8%**	**—**	**—**	**26.1%**

FYE: December 31

2005 Year-End Financials

Debt ratio: 0.2%
Return on equity: 12.6%
Cash ($ mil.): 117.9
Current ratio: 7.35
Long-term debt ($ mil.): 0.4
No. of shares (mil.): 50.0
Dividends
  Yield: —
  Payout: —
Market value ($ mil.): 1,490.7
R&D as % of sales: —
Advertising as % of sales: —

Stock History

NASDAQ (GS): SIRF

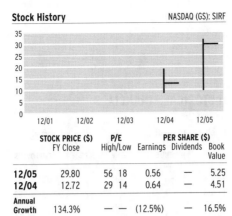

	STOCK PRICE ($) FY Close	P/E High/Low		PER SHARE ($) Earnings	Dividends	Book Value
12/05	29.80	56	18	0.56	—	5.25
12/04	12.72	29	14	0.64	—	4.51
Annual Growth	**134.3%**	**—**	**—**	**(12.5%)**	**—**	**16.5%**

Sirona Dental Systems

Smile pretty for the camera! Sirona Dental Systems makes dental digital-imaging equipment and a full line of other products and instruments for dentists. One of its leading products is a digital intraoral radiographic imaging system, an X-ray system that uses less radiation than conventional equipment, fits inside the mouth, incorporates an oral camera, and produces images on a computer instead of film. Other equipment includes film-based X-ray systems, dental treatment centers, instrument sterilizing systems, and handpieces. Sirona Dental Systems merged with Schick Technologies, a US maker of digital radiographic imaging systems and devices for the dental industry in 2006.

Sirona was founded in 1997 as a result of a private equity buyout of the former dental division of Siemens AG.

EXECUTIVES

Chairman, President, and CEO: Jost Fischer, age 52
EVP, CFO, and Director: Simone Blank, age 43
EVP and COO, US Operations; Director: Jeffrey T. Slovin, age 41
President, Schick Technologies: Michael Stone, age 52
VP, Manufacturing, Schick Technologies: Will Autz, age 51
VP, Engineering, Schick Technologies: Stan Mandelkern, age 46, $287,614 pay
VP, Management Information Systems, Schick Technologies: Ari Neugroschl, age 35
Secretary and General Counsel, Schick Technologies: Zvi N. Raskin, age 43, $212,350 pay
Director, Finance and Administration, Schick Technologies: Ronald Rosner, age 58, $179,442 pay
Manager, Human Resources, Schick Technologies: Lynn Blankenship
Auditors: Grant Thornton LLP

LOCATIONS

HQ: Sirona Dental Systems, Inc.
  30-00 47th Ave., Long Island City, NY 11101
Phone: 718-937-5765   **Fax:** 718-937-5962
Web: www.sirona.de

Schick Technologies sells its products primarily in the US, but also in Asia, Canada, Europe, and South America.

2006 Sales

	$ mil.	% of total
US	156.7	30
Germany	118.4	23
Other countries	245.5	47
Total	**520.6**	**100**

PRODUCTS/OPERATIONS

2006 Sales

	$ mil.	% of total
Dental CAD/CAM systems	183.8	35
Imaging systems	132.7	26
Treatment centers	130.1	25
Instruments	71.9	14
Other	2.1	—
Total	**520.6**	**100**

COMPETITORS

AFP Imaging
Dentrix Dental
DENTSPLY
Eastman Kodak
GE Healthcare
Henry Schein
Hologic
Philips Electronics
Siemens Medical

HISTORICAL FINANCIALS

Company Type: Public

Income Statement

FYE: September 30

	REVENUE ($ mil.)	NET INCOME ($ mil.)	NET PROFIT MARGIN	EMPLOYEES
9/06*	520.6	0.8	0.2%	1,978
3/06	70.2	15.8	22.5%	153
3/05	52.4	12.1	23.1%	139
3/04	39.4	18.1	45.9%	—
3/03	29.8	11.8	39.6%	—
Annual Growth	**104.4%**	**(49.0%)**	**—**	**277.2%**

*Fiscal year change

2006 Year-End Financials

Debt ratio: —
Return on equity: 0.3%
Cash ($ mil.): 60.8
Current ratio: 8.27
Long-term debt ($ mil.): —
No. of shares (mil.): —
Dividends
  Yield: —
  Payout: —
Market value ($ mil.): 1,798.2
R&D as % of sales: —
Advertising as % of sales: —

Stock History

NASDAQ (GS): SIRO

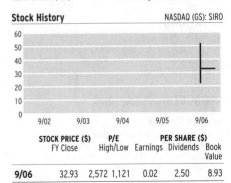

	STOCK PRICE ($) FY Close	P/E High/Low		PER SHARE ($) Earnings	Dividends	Book Value
9/06	32.93	2,572	1,121	0.02	2.50	8.93

Smith Micro Software

Smith Micro Software links you to the world. The company provides a variety of communication and utility software, including applications for sending and receiving faxes, videoconferencing, roaming between wireless wide area networks and Wi-Fi hot spots, and integrating voice, fax, and data communications. Other products include personal firewall and system utility and diagnostic software. The company also provides Web site design, hosting, and consulting services. Smith Micro sells its software directly, as well as through distributors including Apple and Verizon Wireless. Chairman William Smith and his wife, co-founder Rhonda Smith, own about 55% of the company.

Smith Micro offers wireless telephony software that enhances the performance and utilization of various operating systems.

Smith Micro also has OEM relationships in place with various wireless service providers and manufacturers, including Audiovox, Cingular Wireless, Kyocera, Samsung, and Verizon; Verizon, Kyocera, and Symantec collectively account for abut 78% of sales.

In July 2005 the company acquired Allume Systems for about $13 million.

In early 2006 the company announced plans to purchase PhoTags, a developer of technology for managing digital photos and music.

EXECUTIVES

Chairman, President, and CEO: William W. Smith Jr., age 58
CFO and Secretary: Andrew C. (Andy) Schmidt, age 44
SVP and General Manager Consumer Products: Jonathan Kahn, age 48
VP and CTO: David P. Sperling, age 37
VP Advanced Technology: Darryl Lovato
VP Business Development and Investor Relations: Bruce T. Quigley
VP Channel Sales: Jeff Costello
VP Corporate Marketing: Robert E. Elliott
VP Internet and Direct Sales: Christopher G. (Chris) Lippincott, age 34
VP Wireless and OEM Sales: William R. (Rick) Wyand, age 58
Auditors: Singer Lewak Greenbaum & Goldstein LLP

LOCATIONS

HQ: Smith Micro Software, Inc.
51 Columbia, Ste. 200, Aliso Viejo, CA 92656
Phone: 949-362-5800 **Fax:** 949-362-2300
Web: www.smithmicro.com

PRODUCTS/OPERATIONS

Selected Software

Desktop fax (FAXstfX, FAXstfX Pro, QuickLink)
Desktop file management, Internet, and systems management (CheckIt NetOptimizer, CheckIt Utilities, QuickLink Mobile Phonebook)
Integrated voice, fax, and data applications (HotFax MessageCenter,VideoLink, VideoLink Mail, VideoLink Pro)
Electronic business software (WebDNA)
Web traffic monitoring and pop-up blocking (CheckIt 86)
Wireless modem and fax (QuickLink Fax, QuickLink Mobile)

Selected Services

Consulting
Fulfillment (order fulfillment services for customer Web stores)
Web site design and hosting

COMPETITORS

CA	PCTEL
Cisco Systems	Polycom
Microsoft	Symantec
Omtool	VocalTec

HISTORICAL FINANCIALS

Company Type: Public

Income Statement
FYE: December 31

	REVENUE ($ mil.)	NET INCOME ($ mil.)	NET PROFIT MARGIN	EMPLOYEES
12/05	20.3	4.7	23.2%	91
12/04	13.3	3.4	25.6%	52
12/03	7.2	(0.9)	—	55
12/02	7.1	(0.7)	—	56
12/01	10.8	(6.1)	—	71
Annual Growth	17.1%	—	—	6.4%

2005 Year-End Financials

Debt ratio: —
Return on equity: 18.8%
Cash ($ mil.): 21.2
Current ratio: 7.74
Long-term debt ($ mil.): —
No. of shares (mil.): 22.1
Dividends
  Yield: —
  Payout: —
Market value ($ mil.): 129.6
R&D as % of sales: 19.5%
Advertising as % of sales: 1.1%

Stock History
NASDAQ (GM): SMSI

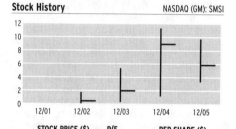

	STOCK PRICE ($) FY Close	P/E High/Low	PER SHARE ($) Earnings	Dividends	Book Value
12/05	5.85	46 16	0.21	—	1.76
12/04	8.95	59 7	0.19	—	0.62
12/03	1.99	— —	(0.06)	—	0.33
12/02	0.46	— —	(0.04)	—	0.35
Annual Growth	133.4%	— —	—	—	45.9%

Smithtown Bancorp

Smithtown Bancorp is the holding company for Bank of Smithtown, a community bank founded in 1910. The company touts its one-on-one customer service it offers through about a dozen locations on Long Island, New York. Services include checking and savings accounts, IRAs, and CDs. Through its insurance subsidiary, Seigerman Mulvey, the bank offers commercial and personal insurance products and financial services. Commercial mortgages make up more than half of Smithtown Bancorp's loan portfolio, which also includes residential mortgages, commercial and industrial loans, and real estate construction loans.

Director Augusta Kemper owns 6% of Smithtown Bancorp; directors and executive officers collectively control 12% of the company.

EXECUTIVES

Chairman, President, and CEO, Smithtown Bancorp and Bank of Smithtown: Bradley E. Rock, age 53, $692,485 pay
EVP; EVP and Chief Retail Officer, Bank of Smithtown: John A. Romano, age 48, $243,279 pay
EVP and Treasurer; EVP and CFO, Bank of Smithtown: Anita M. Florek, age 54, $250,831 pay
EVP and Chief Commercial Lending Officer, Bank of Smithtown: Thomas J. Stevens, age 46, $253,097 pay
EVP and Chief Lending Officer, Bank of Smithtown: Robert J. Anrig, age 56, $293,114 pay
SVP, Operations, Bank of Smithtown: Patricia Guidi
SVP, Consumer Lending, Bank of Smithtown: Susan Ladone
VP, Marketing and Advertising, Bank of Smithtown: John P. Schneider
Assistant VP, Human Resources, Bank of Smithtown: Deborah McElroy
Corporate Secretary; Corporate Secretary and Cashier, Bank of Smithtown: Judith Barber
General Counsel and Director: Patricia C. Delaney, age 47

LOCATIONS

HQ: Smithtown Bancorp, Inc.
100 Motor Pkwy., Ste. 160, Hauppauge, NY 11788
Phone: 631-360-9300 **Fax:** 631-360-9373
Web: www.bankofsmithtown.com

PRODUCTS/OPERATIONS

2005 Sales

	$ mil.	% of total
Interest		
Loans	44.0	78
Securities	3.4	6
Other	1.2	2
Noninterest		
Service charges on deposits	2.0	3
Trust department income	0.4	1
Other	5.8	10
Total	**56.8**	**100**

COMPETITORS

Apple Bank
Astoria Financial
Bank of America
Bank of New York
Citibank
HSBC USA
JPMorgan Chase
New York Community Bancorp
Washington Mutual

HISTORICAL FINANCIALS

Company Type: Public

Income Statement
FYE: December 31

	ASSETS ($ mil.)	NET INCOME ($ mil.)	INCOME AS % OF ASSETS	EMPLOYEES
12/05	878.3	11.1	1.3%	179
12/04	677.0	10.0	1.5%	—
12/03	565.1	9.1	1.6%	—
12/02	451.8	8.0	1.8%	—
12/01	380.2	6.1	1.6%	—
Annual Growth	23.3%	16.1%		

2005 Year-End Financials

Equity as % of assets: 6.4%
Return on assets: 1.4%
Return on equity: 21.6%
Long-term debt ($ mil.): 118.9
No. of shares (mil.): 5.9
Market value ($ mil.): 117.6
Dividends
  Yield: 0.8%
  Payout: 12.8%
Sales ($ mil.): 56.8
R&D as % of sales: —
Advertising as % of sales: —

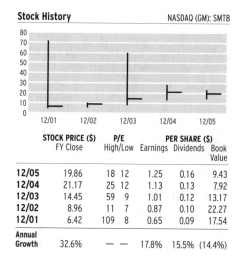

	STOCK PRICE ($) FY Close	P/E High/Low		PER SHARE ($) Earnings	Dividends	Book Value
12/05	19.86	18	12	1.25	0.16	9.43
12/04	21.17	25	12	1.13	0.13	7.92
12/03	14.45	59	9	1.01	0.12	13.17
12/02	8.96	11	7	0.87	0.10	22.27
12/01	6.42	109	8	0.65	0.09	17.54
Annual Growth	32.6%	—	—	17.8%	15.5%	(14.4%)

Somanetics

Somanetics sells the INVOS System, a non-invasive device that monitors blood-oxygen levels in the brain, primarily during surgery. Based on Somanetics' in vivo optical spectroscopy (INVOS) technology, the device's disposable SomaSensors attach to each side of the patient's forehead, and the firm's proprietary software displays oxygen levels on a computer screen. Somanetics also makes the CorRestore patch from cow's heart tissue, for use in cardiac repair and reconstruction.

Somanetics markets through a direct sales staff and distributors such as Tyco Healthcare. Customers include surgeons, anesthesiologists, and other health care providers in the US and in nearly 60 countries abroad.

Somanetics plans to continue to develop new applications for its INVOS System. The company also intends to interface its technology with other monitoring systems in hospitals.

CEO Bruce Barrett owns approximately 7% of the company.

EXECUTIVES

President, CEO, and Director: Bruce J. Barrett, age 46, $553,376 pay
VP, CFO, Controller, and Treasurer: William M. Iacona, age 35
VP, Research and Development: Richard S. Scheuing, age 50, $195,883 pay
VP, Sales and Marketing: Dominic J. Spadafore, age 46, $326,473 pay
VP, Chief Administrative Officer, and Secretary: Mary Ann Victor, age 48, $211,059 pay (prior to title change)
VP, Medical Affairs: Ronald A. Widman, age 55
VP, Operations: Pamela A. Winters, age 47, $195,883 pay
Auditors: Deloitte & Touche LLP

LOCATIONS

HQ: Somanetics Corporation
1653 E. Maple Rd., Troy, MI 48083
Phone: 248-689-3050   **Fax:** 248-689-4272
Web: www.somanetics.net

PRODUCTS/OPERATIONS

2005 Sales

	% of total
SomaSensors	78
INVOS System Monitors	18
CorRestore Systems	4
Total	**100**

Selected Products

CorRestore System (cardiac implant patch)
INVOS Cerebral Oximeters (patient monitoring system)
SomaSensors (disposable sensors used with the INVOS Cerebral Oximeters)

COMPETITORS

Aspect Medical Systems
Bio-logic
CAS
Criticare
Invivo
Nims

HISTORICAL FINANCIALS

Company Type: Public

Income Statement

FYE: November 30

	REVENUE ($ mil.)	NET INCOME ($ mil.)	NET PROFIT MARGIN	EMPLOYEES
11/05	20.5	7.8	38.0%	55
11/04	12.6	8.7	69.0%	40
11/03	9.4	0.1	1.1%	28
11/02	6.7	(1.2)	—	28
11/01	5.7	(2.3)	—	26
Annual Growth	37.7%	—	—	20.6%

2005 Year-End Financials

Debt ratio: —
Return on equity: 34.4%
Cash ($ mil.): 13.1
Current ratio: 10.60
Long-term debt ($ mil.): —
No. of shares (mil.): 10.7
Dividends
Yield: —
Payout: —
Market value ($ mil.): 331.2
R&D as % of sales: —
Advertising as % of sales: —

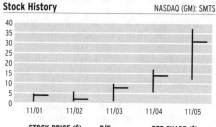

	STOCK PRICE ($) FY Close	P/E High/Low		PER SHARE ($) Earnings	Dividends	Book Value
11/05	30.91	56	19	0.66	—	2.60
11/04	13.88	22	8	0.77	—	1.73
11/03	7.82	943	148	0.01	—	0.66
11/02	2.02	—	—	(0.13)	—	0.61
11/01	3.85	—	—	(0.31)	—	0.37
Annual Growth	68.3%	—	—	—	—	62.5%

Sonic Solutions

Sonic Solutions wants to create the movie for the digital revolution. The company's products include software and hardware for creating digital audio and video titles, recording data files to CD-R and DVDs, and backing up information stored on hard drives. The company originally focused on audio products but has boosted its consumer DVD operations. Sonic Solutions also licenses its technology to third parties that incorporate it into their own products. Partners include Dell, Pioneer, Sony, IBM, and Iomega. Sonic Solutions markets to both the consumer and professional markets.

The consumer market accounts for more than 90% of Sonic's sales. Customers outside North America make up about a quarter of revenues.

In early 2004 the company acquired InterActual Technologies. With the $8.8 million purchase, Sonic Solutions further strengthened its position in the Hollywood-based DVD production market. InterActual's software lets studios add features to DVD-Video titles that are viewed on PCs.

In late 2004 Sonic Solutions acquired the consumer software division of Roxio for $80 million. The acquisition provided Sonic with a new set of consumer software brands, access to distribution channels, and relationships with retail outlets.

EXECUTIVES

Chairman: Robert J. (Bob) Doris, age 54, $218,750 pay (prior to title change)
President and CEO: David C. (Dave) Habiger, age 37, $382,901 pay
EVP, Worldwide Operations and Finance and CFO: A. Clay Leighton, age 49, $255,730 pay
EVP, Strategy: Mark Ely, age 36, $275,560 pay
SVP, Asia Pacific Rim Operations: Koki Terui
SVP, General Manager, Advanced Technology Group: Jim Taylor
SVP, General Manager, Professional Products Group: Rolf Hartley
Managing Director, European Operations, Professional Products Group: Richard Linecar
Secretary and Director: Mary C. Sauer, age 54, $158,917 pay (prior to title change)
Director, Marketing Communications: Chris Taylor
Auditors: BDO Seidman, LLP

LOCATIONS

HQ: Sonic Solutions
101 Rowland Way, Ste. 110, Novato, CA 94945
Phone: 415-893-8000   **Fax:** 415-893-8008
Web: www.sonic.com

Sonic has offices in Japan, the UK, and the US.

2006 Sales

	$ mil.	% of total
North America	114.4	77
Other regions	34.3	23
Total	**148.7**	**100**

PRODUCTS/OPERATIONS

2006 Sales

	$ mil.	% of total
Consumer	137.1	92
Professional	11.6	8
Total	**148.7**	**100**

Selected Products

Backup and copy
- BackUp MyPC
- Easy DVD Copy

CD and DVD creation and playback
- Digital Media Network
- Digital Media Studio
- DVD for Photo Story
- DVDit
- Easy Media Creator
- MyDVD
- PhotoSuite
- PrimeTime Line
- RecordNow!
- VideoWave

Mac products
- Popcorn
- The Boom Box
- Toast

Professional products
- CineVision
- DVD-Audio Creator
- DVDit Pro
- eDVD
- ReelDVD
- Scenarist

COMPETITORS

Adobe
Ahead Software
Alesis
Apple
Avid Technology
Circuit Research Labs
Dolby
Euphonix
FutureTel
Harman International
Harmonic
InterVideo
LOUD Technologies
Massive
Matsushita
Mitsubishi Corporation
Optibase
Otari
Pacific Research & Engineering Corporation
Panasonic Corporation of North America
Philips Electronics
Pioneer
Roland
Sonic Foundry
Sony
TEAC
Toshiba
Ulead
Victor Company of Japan
ZOO Digital Group

HISTORICAL FINANCIALS

Company Type: Public

Income Statement

FYE: March 31

	REVENUE ($ mil.)	NET INCOME ($ mil.)	NET PROFIT MARGIN	EMPLOYEES
3/06	148.7	19.9	13.4%	637
3/05	90.6	8.5	9.4%	212
3/04	56.8	11.1	19.5%	298
3/03	32.7	2.5	7.6%	211
3/02	19.1	(4.2)	—	100
Annual Growth	67.0%	—	—	58.9%

2006 Year-End Financials

Debt ratio: 21.6%
Return on equity: 16.7%
Cash ($ mil.): 61.1
Current ratio: 2.32
Long-term debt ($ mil.): 30.0
No. of shares (mil.): 25.9

Dividends
  Yield: —
  Payout: —
Market value ($ mil.): 468.2
R&D as % of sales: 27.3%
Advertising as % of sales: 2.5%

Stock History

NASDAQ (GS): SNIC

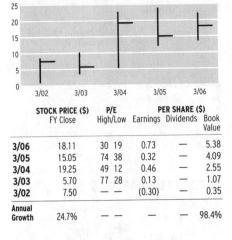

	STOCK PRICE ($) FY Close	P/E High/Low		PER SHARE ($) Earnings	Dividends	Book Value
3/06	18.11	30	19	0.73	—	5.38
3/05	15.05	74	38	0.32	—	4.09
3/04	19.25	49	12	0.46	—	2.55
3/03	5.70	77	28	0.13	—	1.07
3/02	7.50	—	—	(0.30)	—	0.35
Annual Growth	24.7%	—	—	—	—	98.4%

SonoSite

Size is everything for SonoSite. The firm makes miniaturized ultrasonic imaging devices, which have proven cheaper and more convenient than bigger machines. Its SonoSite 180PLUS provides general ultrasound imaging, and its SonoHeart ELITE performs cardiovascular imaging. The company also makes transducers for use with its devices. Obstetricians, gynecologists, radiologists, and emergency physicians can use SonoSite's technology at the point of care, rather than referring the patient to an ultrasound specialist. The company markets primarily through a direct sales force, but also via distributors and agreements with group purchasing organizations.

SonoSite has about 70 direct sales representatives in Asia, Australia, Europe, and North America. The company plans to continue to develop strategic relationships.

EXECUTIVES

Chairman: Kirby L. Cramer, age 69
President, CEO, and Director: Kevin M. Goodwin, age 48, $650,000 pay
Chief Business Development Officer, U.S. Government: Ronald S. Dickson
SVP, Marketing: Thomas J. Dugan, age 47
SVP, US Sales: Edison C. Russell, age 55, $395,000 pay
VP, Finance, CFO, and Treasurer: Michael J. Schuh, age 45, $290,000 pay
VP, Engineering: Blake Little
VP, General Counsel, and Corporate Secretary: Kathryn (Kathy) Surace-Smith, age 46
VP, Human Resources: Marla R. Koreis
VP, International: Graham D. Cox, age 47, $319,488 pay
CTO: Juin-Jet Hwang
Auditors: KPMG LLP

LOCATIONS

HQ: SonoSite, Inc.
  21919 30th Dr. SE, Bothell, WA 98021
Phone: 425-951-1200   **Fax:** 425-951-1201
Web: www.sonosite.com

2005 Sales

	$ mil.	% of total
US	79.8	54
Europe, Africa & Middle East	41.2	28
Japan	11.9	8
Canada & South & Latin America	9.6	7
Asia/Pacific	5.0	3
Total	**147.5**	**100**

COMPETITORS

Esaote
GE Healthcare
Heartlab
Hewlett-Packard
Philips North America
Siemens AG

HISTORICAL FINANCIALS

Company Type: Public

Income Statement

FYE: December 31

	REVENUE ($ mil.)	NET INCOME ($ mil.)	NET PROFIT MARGIN	EMPLOYEES
12/05	147.5	5.4	3.7%	500
12/04	115.8	23.0	19.9%	410
12/03	84.8	(1.8)	—	340
12/02	73.0	(7.7)	—	350
12/01	45.7	(16.4)	—	250
Annual Growth	34.0%	—	—	18.9%

2005 Year-End Financials

Debt ratio: —
Return on equity: 3.8%
Cash ($ mil.): 52.2
Current ratio: 6.21
Long-term debt ($ mil.): —
No. of shares (mil.): 15.9

Dividends
  Yield: —
  Payout: —
Market value ($ mil.): 555.7
R&D as % of sales: 10.3%
Advertising as % of sales: 7.6%

Stock History

NASDAQ (GM): SONO

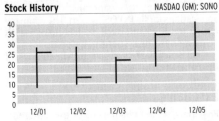

	STOCK PRICE ($) FY Close	P/E High/Low		PER SHARE ($) Earnings	Dividends	Book Value
12/05	35.01	117	69	0.34	—	9.58
12/04	33.95	24	13	1.46	—	8.74
12/03	21.49	—	—	(0.12)	—	6.54
12/02	13.07	—	—	(0.59)	—	6.52
12/01	25.69	—	—	(1.59)	—	4.90
Annual Growth	8.0%	—	—	—	—	18.2%

Sonus Networks

Sonus Networks has found a sound place in the voice infrastructure market. The company makes hardware and software that public network providers — including long-distance carriers, ISPs, and cable operators — use to provide voice and data communications services to their subscribers. Its products include switches and related network software. Sonus also provides network installation, support, and training services. The company sells its products directly and through resellers, including Nissho Electronics and Samsung, to such customers as Qwest Communications, Global Crossing, and Deutsche Telekom.

EXECUTIVES

Chairman and CEO: Hassan M. Ahmed, age 48, $454,688 pay
President, COO, and Director: Albert A. (Bert) Notini, age 49, $396,900 pay
CFO: Ellen B. Richstone, age 54, $316,761 pay
VP and Chief Marketing Officer:
  Steven (Steve) Edwards, age 46, $287,226 pay
VP Finance and Controller: Paul K. McDermott, age 43
VP, CTO, and Secretary: Michael G. Hluchyj, age 49
VP Worldwide Engineering: Chuba Udokwu
VP Worldwide Sales: James (Jim) Collier III, age 46
Chief Scientist: Vikram Saksena
Investor Relations Contact: Jocelyn Philbrook
Media Relations: Sarah McAuley
Auditors: Deloitte & Touche LLP

LOCATIONS

HQ: Sonus Networks, Inc.
  250 Apollo Dr., Chelmsford, MA 01824
Phone: 978-614-8100   **Fax:** 978-614-8101
Web: www.sonusnet.com

Sonus Networks has offices in China, the Czech Republic, France, Germany, India, Japan, Malaysia, Singapore, the UK, and the US.

PRODUCTS/OPERATIONS

2005 Sales

	$ mil.	% of total
Products	134.8	69
Services	59.8	31
Total	**194.6**	**100**

Selected Products

Call routing servers
Network management software
Signaling gateways
Switches

COMPETITORS

ADC Telecommunications
Alcatel-Lucent
Cisco Systems
Ericsson
NEC Electronics
Nortel Networks
Siemens Communications
Tellabs
Veraz
Verso Technologies

HISTORICAL FINANCIALS

Company Type: Public

Income Statement

FYE: December 31

	REVENUE ($ mil.)	NET INCOME ($ mil.)	NET PROFIT MARGIN	EMPLOYEES
12/05	194.6	8.4	4.3%	719
12/04	170.7	24.5	14.4%	537
12/03	93.2	(15.1)	—	401
12/02	62.6	(68.5)	—	361
12/01	173.2	(645.4)	—	593
Annual Growth	**3.0%**	**—**	**—**	**4.9%**

2005 Year-End Financials

Debt ratio: 0.0%
Return on equity: 3.1%
Cash ($ mil.): 296.3
Current ratio: 2.98
Long-term debt ($ mil.): 0.1
No. of shares (mil.): 249.4
Dividends
  Yield: —
  Payout: —
Market value ($ mil.): 927.9
R&D as % of sales: 23.8%
Advertising as % of sales: —

Stock History

NASDAQ (GS): SONS

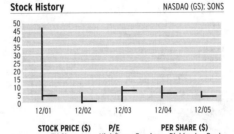

	STOCK PRICE ($) FY Close	P/E High/Low		PER SHARE ($) Earnings	Dividends	Book Value
12/05	3.72	214	105	0.03	—	1.12
12/04	5.73	100	29	0.10	—	1.07
12/03	7.54	—	—	(0.07)	—	0.96
12/02	1.00	—	—	(0.36)	—	0.28
12/01	4.62	—	—	(3.74)	—	0.50
Annual Growth	**(5.3%)**	**—**	**—**	**—**	**—**	**22.2%**

Sotheby's

Sotheby's believes that one man's trash is another man's treasure — especially when that trash happens to be someone's idea of art. The company (along with rival Christie's International) is one of the world's leading auction houses, holding hundreds of sales each year at its auction centers around the world. Sotheby's deals mainly in fine art, antiques, and collectibles; it collects commissions and fees from both the buyer and the seller on each sale. The company also provides loans (secured against works of art) to clients as part of its finance services.

Live auctions account for the bulk of Sotheby's revenues. The company has overseen the sales of such items as Picasso's *Femme Assise dans un Jardin,* Degas' *Petite Danseuse de Quatorze Ans,* and the last baseball glove used by Lou Gehrig. Sotheby's was chosen to auction off a collection of the papers of slain civil rights leader Dr. Martin Luther King Jr., but a private sale was arranged instead.

Sotheby's has leveraged its expertise and profile in art circles to offer such services as secured financing and insurance, as well as serving as a broker for private sales. Additionally, the company offers restoration and ap-

praisal services and operates two art institutes in New York City and London.

In contrast to its successes, the company is struggling to regain prestige and trust after a Justice Department investigation resulted in charges of commission fixing by both Sotheby's and Christie's. Former president and CEO Diana Brooks and former chairman Alfred Taubman were both convicted, and the company, along with Christie's, has settled a number of class action lawsuits brought against both houses, agreeing to pay $512 million (split between them) to clients in the US and $20 million to non-US clients. Taubman and family own 12% of Sotheby's after a recapitalization in 2005.

In August 2006, the auction house's legal woes continued when a Canadian antitrust entity obtained a restrictive order against Sotheby's, claiming that the company had agreed with competitors to fix the prices it charged to customers (between the years of 1993 to 2000). It is projected Sotheby's will have to pay $720,000 in investigative costs due to the price-fixing.

HISTORY

Sotheby's Holdings traces its roots to Samuel Baker, a London bookseller, who held his first auction in 1744 to dispose of an English nobleman's library. After Baker died in 1778, his nephew John Sotheby took over, placing his name over the door of the business. During the 19th century Sotheby's expanded into antiquities, paintings, jewelry, and furniture. Business boomed as newly wealthy Americans swarmed across the Atlantic seeking the status symbols of the Old World.

By the end of WWI, Sotheby's had become fully entrenched in the art market, and in 1917 the company moved to New Bond Street (where its London office still stands). Following WWII, Sotheby's expanded into the US, opening its first office in New York City in 1955. It later acquired Parke-Bernet, a leading US art auction house, in 1964. The company prospered and expanded during the 1970s as rising interest rates and inflation fueled an art market boom, and in 1977 Sotheby's went public.

A collapse of the art market left Sotheby's a target for corporate raiders in the early 1980s. The company's board asked US shopping center magnate Alfred Taubman to lead a buyout group in 1983. After weathering the storm, the company was well positioned when the art market rebounded, a turnaround driven in part by the desire of newly wealthy Japanese to confirm their status — just as Americans had done a century before. In 1988 the company went public again, with Taubman as chairman.

After the boom peaked in 1990 (Christie's International sold van Gogh's *Portrait of Dr. Gachet* that year for a record $82.5 million), Sotheby's earnings plummeted, and its share price tanked. In 1994 Diana Brooks became president and CEO. The company posted solid results in 1995, but the company slipped to the #2 auctioneer in the world for the first time in more than 20 years.

In 1997 Sotheby's acquired Chicago-based Leslie Hindman Auctioneers and Chicago wine auctioneers Davis & Co. in 1998. The next year Sotheby's created a co-branded auction Web site with Amazon.com. The site never turned a profit and was scaled back in 2000 and the partnership terminated in 2001. In 2002 Sotheby's partnered with eBay to sell high-end merchandise online within the eBay Web site.

In 2000 the US Justice Department reopened a 1997 investigation of an alleged price fixing

scheme involving Sotheby's and Christie's. After the allegations became public, Taubman and Brooks resigned, replaced by Michael Sovern (chairman) and William Ruprecht (CEO). The probe sparked additional lawsuits and investigations. Both companies agreed to pay $268 million each to settle the civil claims. Brooks pleaded guilty to violating antitrust laws but testified against Taubman in exchange for leniency; Taubman pleaded innocent and was convicted and sentenced to one year in prison after a vicious trial.

In 2001 Sotheby's laid off about 8% of its staff and raised fees in 2002 in its efforts to offset losses. Also in 2002 the company sold its Upper East Side headquarters in New York for $175 million and laid off 7% of its staff. In 2004 Sotheby's sold its International Realty operations to Cendant for about $100 million. (Cendant spun off its real estate businesses as Realogy in 2006.)

Sotheby's dropped "Holdings" from its official name in mid-2006.

EXECUTIVES

Chairman: Michael I. Sovern, age 74
Deputy Chairman: The Duke of Devonshire, age 61
President, CEO, and Director:
William F. (Bill) Ruprecht, age 50, $2,193,750 pay
EVP and CFO: William S. Sheridan, age 52, $1,755,000 pay
EVP and Chief Executive, Sotheby's Europe and Asia; Director: Robin G. Woodhead, age 54, $1,115,894 pay
EVP and Worldwide Director Press and Corporate Affairs: Diana Phillips, age 59
EVP and Worldwide Head of Human Resources: Susan Alexander, age 52
EVP and Director, Boston: William Cottingham
SVP, Controller, and Chief Accounting Officer: Michael L. Gillis
President, Sotheby's Financial Services, Inc. and Sotheby's Ventures, LLC: Mitchell Zuckerman, age 59, $1,078,750 pay
Managing Director, Global Auction Division: Daryl S. Wickstrom, age 44
Managing Director, North American Regional Division: Richard C. Buckley, age 42
Managing Director, Sotheby's Europe: George Bailey, age 52, $964,780 pay
Director, Investor Relations: Jennifer Park
Auditors: Deloitte & Touche LLP

LOCATIONS

HQ: Sotheby's
1334 York Ave., New York, NY 10021
Phone: 212-606-7000   **Fax:** 212-606-7107
Web: www.sothebys.com

Sotheby's has offices in Asia, Australia, Europe, and the US.

2005 Sales

	$ mil.	% of total
US	212.7	41
UK	194.2	38
China	32.9	6
Other countries	73.7	15
Total	**513.5**	**100**

PRODUCTS/OPERATIONS

2005 Sales

	$ mil.	% of total
Auction		
Auction commission revenues	441.3	86
Auction sales commissions	21.2	4
Auction expense recoveries	19.3	4
Other	20.2	4
Finance segment	8.3	2
License fee	1.4	—
Other	1.8	—
Total	**513.5**	**100**

Selected Operations

Acquavella Modern Art (50%, art sale brokerage)
Sotheby's (live auctions)
Sotheby's Financial Services (art financing)
Sotheby's Insurance Brokerage Services

COMPETITORS

Ableauctions.com
Christie's
DoveBid
eBay

Escala Group
Finarte-Semenzato
Phillips, de Pury
Tiffany

HISTORICAL FINANCIALS

Company Type: Public

Income Statement

FYE: December 31

	REVENUE ($ mil.)	NET INCOME ($ mil.)	NET PROFIT MARGIN	EMPLOYEES
12/05	513.5	61.6	12.0%	1,443
12/04	496.7	86.7	17.5%	1,411
12/03	319.6	(20.7)	—	1,537
12/02	345.1	(54.8)	—	1,736
12/01	336.2	(41.7)	—	1,799
Annual Growth	**11.2%**	**—**	**—**	**(5.4%)**

2005 Year-End Financials

Debt ratio: 241.4%
Return on equity: 34.0%
Cash ($ mil.): 132.6
Current ratio: 1.26
Long-term debt ($ mil.): 304.9
No. of shares (mil.): 57.8

Dividends
Yield: —
Payout: —
Market value ($ mil.): 1,062.1
R&D as % of sales: —
Advertising as % of sales: —

Stock History

NYSE: BID

	STOCK PRICE ($) FY Close	P/E High/Low		PER SHARE ($) Earnings	Dividends	Book Value
12/05	18.36	19	13	1.00	—	2.18
12/04	18.16	14	9	1.38	—	5.14
12/03	13.66	—	—	(0.34)	—	2.83
12/02	9.00	—	—	(0.89)	—	3.12
12/01	16.61	—	—	(0.69)	—	4.15
Annual Growth	**2.5%**	—	—	—	—	**(14.9%)**

South Financial

Look away from The South Financial Group for long and you may miss another growth spurt. The holding company owns Carolina First Bank, which has more than 100 branches throughout South Carolina and a portion of North Carolina. It also owns Mercantile Bank, which has more than 65 branches in South Florida and in Gainesville, Jacksonville, Ocala, Orlando, and Tampa. Catering to individuals and small businesses, the banks offer traditional deposit and loan products. Commercial mortgages account for the biggest part of the banks' combined loan portfolio (more than 35%); the portfolio also in-

cludes business, residential mortgage, construction, and consumer loans.

The company has been growing through branching and acquisitions, including its 2005 purchase of Pointe Financial in South Florida; that company's 10 offices were absorbed into Mercantile Bank. The previous year, The South Financial Group bought CNB Florida Bancshares and Florida Banks. A year earlier, the firm moved into western North Carolina with its purchase of MountainBank. The South Financial Group hopes to use its South Carolina-based agency South Group Insurance Services (formerly Gardner Associates) as a springboard to build its insurance sales segment. Other subsidiaries include institutional money manager South Financial Asset Management. Wachovia owns 5% of The South Financial Group.

EXECUTIVES

Chairman, President, and CEO: Mack I. Whittle Jr., age 57, $660,388 pay
CFO: Timothy K. Schools, age 36
EVP, General Counsel, and Secretary: William P. Crawford Jr., age 43
EVP, Human Resources: Mary A. Jeffrey, age 55
EVP, Finance: J. Stanley Ross, age 54
EVP and Chief Credit Officer: Michael W. Sperry, age 59
SVP, Investor Relations: Mary M. Gentry
Vice Chairman, Mercantile Bank: Gordon W. Campbell, age 71
President, Carolina First Bank, North Carolina and Director: J. W. Davis, age 59, $460,140 pay
President, Carolina First Bank: James W. Terry Jr., age 58, $478,740 pay
Auditors: KPMG LLP

LOCATIONS

HQ: The South Financial Group, Inc.
102 S. Main St., Poinsett Plaza, 10th Fl., Greenville, SC 29601
Phone: 864-255-7900   **Fax:** 864-239-2280
Web: www.thesouthgroup.com

PRODUCTS/OPERATIONS

2005 Sales

	$ mil.	% of total
Interest		
Loans	568.2	70
Securities & other	186.1	23
Non-interest income	55.2	7
Total	**809.5**	**100**

COMPETITORS

Bank of America
Centerstate Banks
Coastal Financial
First Citizens Bancorporation

First Financial Holdings
Regions Financial
SCBT Financial
Wachovia

HISTORICAL FINANCIALS

Company Type: Public

Income Statement

FYE: December 31

	ASSETS ($ mil.)	NET INCOME ($ mil.)	INCOME AS % OF ASSETS	EMPLOYEES
12/05	14,319.3	69.8	0.5%	2,607
12/04	13,798.2	119.5	0.9%	2,308
12/03	10,719.4	95.1	0.9%	1,918
12/02	7,941.0	59.2	0.7%	1,700
12/01	6,029.4	41.9	0.7%	1,346
Annual Growth	**24.1%**	**13.6%**	**—**	**18.0%**

2005 Year-End Financials

Equity as % of assets: 10.4%
Return on assets: 0.5%
Return on equity: 4.8%
Long-term debt ($ mil.): 1,922.2
No. of shares (mil.): 74.7
Market value ($ mil.): 2,057.8

Dividends
Yield: 2.3%
Payout: 68.1%
Sales ($ mil.): 809.5
R&D as % of sales: —
Advertising as % of sales: —

Stock History

NASDAQ (GS): TSFG

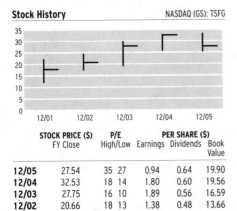

	STOCK PRICE ($) FY Close	P/E High/Low		PER SHARE ($) Earnings	Dividends	Book Value
12/05	27.54	35	27	0.94	0.64	19.90
12/04	32.53	18	14	1.80	0.60	19.56
12/03	27.75	16	10	1.89	0.56	16.59
12/02	20.66	18	13	1.38	0.48	13.66
12/01	17.75	22	12	0.98	0.44	11.11
Annual Growth	11.6%	—	—	(1.0%)	9.8%	15.7%

Southcoast Financial

Southcoast Financial Corporation pays a great deal of interest to the Palmetto State. The institution is the holding company for Southcoast Community Bank, which serves South Carolina's Berkeley, Charleston, and Dorchester counties. The bank, which targets local small businesses, offers savings, checking, NOW, IRA, and money market accounts, as well as CDs. Lending products include commercial, consumer, and real estate loans, and personal and business lines of credit. Southcoast Community Bank also offers insurance and investment products and services.

EXECUTIVES

President, CEO, and Director; President, Southcoast Community Bank: L. Wayne Pearson, age 58, $534,067 pay
EVP, COO, and Director: Paul D. Hollen III, age 57, $253,156 pay
EVP: Robert A. Daniel Jr., age 55, $189,871 pay
EVP: William B. Seabrook, age 49, $220,659 pay
SVP, Human Resources: Laura Calhoun
CFO: Clay Heslop, age 31
Chief Lending Officer: Tony Daniel
Regional President, Hilton Head, Southcoast Community Bank: William F. Steadman
Auditors: Clifton D. Bodiford

LOCATIONS

HQ: Southcoast Financial Corporation
530 Johnnie Dodds Blvd.,
Mount Pleasant, SC 29464
Phone: 843-884-0504   **Fax:** 843-884-2886
Web: www.southcoastbank.com

PRODUCTS/OPERATIONS

2005 Sales

	$ mil.	% of total
Interest		
Loans, including fees	22.2	84
Taxable securities	1.3	5
Federal funds sold	0.3	1
Noninterest		
Gain on sale of property & equipment	1.0	4
Service fees on deposit accounts	0.9	3
Gain on sale of loans	0.6	2
Other	0.3	1
Total	**26.6**	**100**

COMPETITORS

Bank of South Carolina
Regions Financial
SCBT Financial
SunTrust
Tidelands Bancshares

HISTORICAL FINANCIALS

Company Type: Public

Income Statement

FYE: December 31

	ASSETS ($ mil.)	NET INCOME ($ mil.)	INCOME AS % OF ASSETS	EMPLOYEES
12/05	476.6	4.2	0.9%	96
12/04	366.1	3.0	0.8%	80
12/03	252.9	1.7	0.7%	70
12/02	181.2	1.1	0.6%	63
12/01	124.3	0.6	0.5%	—
Annual Growth	39.9%	62.7%	—	15.1%

2005 Year-End Financials

Equity as % of assets: 15.4%
Return on assets: 1.0%
Return on equity: 7.6%
Long-term debt ($ mil.): 21.7
No. of shares (mil.): 5.0
Market value ($ mil.): 108.5

Dividends
Yield: —
Payout: —
Sales ($ mil.): 26.6
R&D as % of sales: —
Advertising as % of sales: 0.9%

Stock History

NASDAQ (GM): SQCB

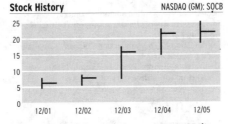

	STOCK PRICE ($) FY Close	P/E High/Low		PER SHARE ($) Earnings	Dividends	Book Value
12/05	21.91	24	18	1.06	—	14.80
12/04	21.43	28	18	0.82	—	12.31
12/03	15.78	23	10	0.74	—	12.46
12/02	7.81	16	10	0.54	—	9.61
12/01	6.21	22	14	0.35	—	9.65
Annual Growth	37.1%	—	—	31.9%	—	11.3%

Southern Community Financial

Southern Community Financial is the holding company for Southern Community Bank and Trust, which operates about 20 branches in north central North Carolina's Piedmont Triad Region. Serving individuals, small and midsized businesses, and area homebuilders; the bank offers such retail services as checking accounts, money markets, and credit cards. Southern Community Financial's loan portfolio consists mainly of commercial mortgages (about 33%), residential mortgages (nearly 30%), and commercial, industrial, and construction loans. Bank subsidiary VCS Management is the managing general partner of Salem Capital Partners, a small business investment company.

EXECUTIVES

Chairman and CEO, Southern Community Financial and Southern Community Bank and Trust: F. Scott Bauer, age 51, $315,000 pay
President, Southern Community Financial and Southern Community Bank and Trust: Jeffrey T. (Jeff) Clark, age 42, $216,000 pay
EVP and CFO: David W. Hinshaw, age 48, $114,180 pay
EVP and Chief Credit Officer, Southern Community Bank and Trust: Paul E. Neil III
EVP and Senior Operating Officer, Southern Community Bank and Trust: Merle B. Andrews
SVP and Operations Manager, Southern Community Bank and Trust: Philip M. (Phil) Doerr
SVP, Branch Administrator, Southern Community Bank and Trust: Dona W. Neal
SVP, Commercial Lending and Eastern Region Executive, Southern Community Bank and Trust: Joseph A. (Joe) DePasquale
SVP, Construction Lending, Southern Community Bank and Trust: R. Bradley (Brad) Westmoreland
SVP, Senior Commercial Lender, and Forsyth Region Executive, Southern Community Bank and Trust: William H. (Hugh) Roberts IV
VP and Human Resource Manager, Southern Community Bank and Trust: Toby A. Boles
Auditors: Dixon Hughes PLLC

LOCATIONS

HQ: Southern Community Financial Corporation
4605 Country Club Rd., Winston-Salem, NC 27104
Phone: 336-768-8500   **Fax:** 336-768-2437
Web: www.smallenoughtocare.com

PRODUCTS/OPERATIONS

2005 Sales

	% of total
Interest	
Loans	74
Investment securities available for sale	11
Investment securities held to maturity	5
Noninterest	
Service charges & fees on deposit accounts	5
Presold mortgage loan fees	1
Other	4
Total	**100**

COMPETITORS

American Community Bancshares
Bank of America
BB&T
FNB United
LSB Bancshares
Piedmont Federal
RBC Centura Banks
Wachovia
Yadkin Valley Financial Corporation

HISTORICAL FINANCIALS

Company Type: Public

Income Statement

FYE: December 31

	ASSETS ($ mil.)	NET INCOME ($ mil.)	INCOME AS % OF ASSETS	EMPLOYEES
12/05	1,287.6	7.7	0.6%	299
12/04	1,222.4	8.1	0.7%	271
12/03	798.5	3.7	0.5%	157
12/02	612.2	3.2	0.5%	141
12/01	481.2	2.1	0.4%	121
Annual Growth	27.9%	38.4%	—	25.4%

2005 Year-End Financials

Equity as % of assets: 10.5%
Return on assets: 0.6%
Return on equity: 5.7%
Long-term debt ($ mil.): 192.6
No. of shares (mil.): 17.6
Market value ($ mil.): 158.5
Dividends
Yield: 3.7%
Payout: 78.6%
Sales ($ mil.): 75.2
R&D as % of sales: —
Advertising as % of sales: 1.2%

Stock History

NASDAQ (GS): SCMF

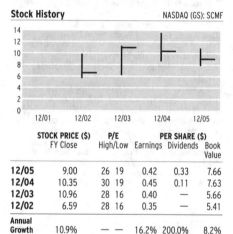

	STOCK PRICE ($) FY Close	P/E High/Low	Earnings	PER SHARE ($) Dividends	Book Value
12/05	9.00	26 19	0.42	0.33	7.66
12/04	10.35	30 19	0.45	0.11	7.63
12/03	10.96	28 16	0.40	—	5.66
12/02	6.59	28 16	0.35	—	5.41
Annual Growth	10.9%	— —	16.2%	200.0%	8.2%

Southwestern Energy

Southwestern Energy is putting a lot of energy into gas and oil exploration and production in the Southwest. The company operates in Arkansas, Louisiana, New Mexico, Oklahoma, and Texas, where it has estimated proved reserves of 826.8 billion cu. ft. of natural gas equivalent, some 93% of which is natural gas. Southwestern Energy is also engaged in natural gas transportation and marketing. The company had announced plans to sell subsidiary Arkansas Western Gas, which distributes natural gas to 148,000 customers in Arkansas, to help pay a $109 million judgment in a lawsuit brought by royalty owners. However, another court ruling in its favor allowed Southwestern Energy to take the unit off the auction block.

In 2004 Southwestern Energy formed subsidiary DeSoto Gathering Company, L.L.C., to engage in gathering activities related to its Fayetteville Shale play.

EXECUTIVES

Chairman, President, and CEO: Harold M. Korell, age 60, $500,000 pay
EVP Finance and CFO: Gregory D. (Greg) Kerley, age 49, $310,000 pay
EVP; President Southwestern Energy Production and SEECO: Richard F. Lane, age 47, $310,000 pay
EVP, Secretary, and General Counsel: Mark K. Boling, age 47, $275,000 pay
President Arkansas Western Gas: Alan N. Stewart, age 60, $222,000 pay
President Southwestern Midstream Services: Gene A. Hammons, $220,000 pay
Chief Accounting Officer and Controller: Stanley T. Wilson
Manager, Investor Relations: Brad D. Sylvester
Auditors: PricewaterhouseCoopers LLP

LOCATIONS

HQ: Southwestern Energy Company
2350 N. Sam Houston Pkwy. East, Ste. 300, Houston, TX 77032
Phone: 281-618-4700   **Fax:** 281-618-4818
Web: www.swn.com

PRODUCTS/OPERATIONS

2005 Sales

	$ mil.	% of total
Exploration & production	403.2	39
Gas distribution	178.5	17
Midstream services & other	460.8	44
Adjustments	(366.2)	—
Total	**676.3**	**100**

Selected Subsidiaries

Arkansas Western Gas Company (natural gas utility)
DeSoto Drilling, Inc. (oil and gas drilling)
DeSoto Gathering Company, L.L.C (natural gas gathering)
SEECO, Inc. (exploration and production)
Southwestern Energy Pipeline Company (natural gas pipeline)
Southwestern Energy Production Company (exploration and production)
Southwestern Energy Services Company (natural gas marketing and transportation)

COMPETITORS

Alliant Energy	National Fuel Gas
Apache	Newfield Exploration
BP	Peoples Energy
CenterPoint Energy	Pioneer Natural Resources
Chesapeake Energy	Pogo Producing
Energen	Royal Dutch Shell
Exxon Mobil	Southern Union
Hunt Consolidated	Williams Companies
Murphy Oil	

HISTORICAL FINANCIALS

Company Type: Public

Income Statement

FYE: December 31

	REVENUE ($ mil.)	NET INCOME ($ mil.)	NET PROFIT MARGIN	EMPLOYEES
12/05	676.3	147.8	21.9%	784
12/04	477.1	103.6	21.7%	595
12/03	327.4	48.9	14.9%	544
12/02	261.5	14.3	5.5%	522
12/01	344.9	35.3	10.2%	525
Annual Growth	18.3%	43.0%	—	10.5%

2005 Year-End Financials

Debt ratio: 14.5%
Return on equity: 19.0%
Cash ($ mil.): 241.2
Current ratio: 1.52
Long-term debt ($ mil.): 160.4
No. of shares (mil.): 167.2
Dividends
Yield: —
Payout: —
Market value ($ mil.): 6,010.4
R&D as % of sales: —
Advertising as % of sales: —

Stock History

NYSE: SWN

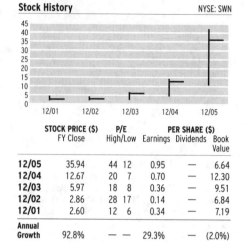

	STOCK PRICE ($) FY Close	P/E High/Low	Earnings	PER SHARE ($) Dividends	Book Value
12/05	35.94	44 12	0.95	—	6.64
12/04	12.67	20 7	0.70	—	12.30
12/03	5.97	18 8	0.36	—	9.51
12/02	2.86	28 17	0.14	—	6.84
12/01	2.60	12 6	0.34	—	7.19
Annual Growth	92.8%	— —	29.3%	—	(2.0%)

Spartan Motors

Even luxury motor homes rely on Spartan Motors products. The company's Spartan Motors Chassis unit makes heavy-duty chassis for motor homes, fire trucks, and specialty vehicles such as concrete mixers, trolleys, and utility trucks. Motor home chassis account for more than half of the company's overall sales. Spartan Motors manufactures emergency vehicles and related components through three subsidiaries that make up its EVTeam segment. Crimson Fire and Road Rescue build fire trucks and ambulances, respectively, using chassis from Spartan Motors Chassis and from third parties. Crimson Fire Aerials makes ladder units for fire trucks.

Motor home assemblers and marketers Fleetwood Enterprises and Newmar have been Spartan's top customers, but Spartan has announced that it is losing some of Fleetwood's business. Despite the loss of some business from Fleetwood, Spartan turned in record sales in 2005.

Spartan sees the greatest potential for growth among its EV Team of emergency vehicle product offerings as the US's fleet of emergency vehicles ages and homeland security measures generate increased demand. Aging baby boomers are expected to drive demand for recreational vehicles, and less happily, emergency vehicles. Founders George Sztykiel (pronounced Stee-cull) and William Foster respectively own about 8% and 3% of Spartan.

HISTORY

Spartan Motors was founded in 1975 by George Sztykiel, a former lead engineer at Chrysler's heavy truck division, along with William Foster, Jerry Geary, and John Knox. Funded with second mortgages, Spartan started by building chassis for customized fire trucks.

Spartan began producing chassis for high-end motor homes in the late 1980s. The company's

breakthrough was a chassis with a rear-mounted diesel engine that cut operating costs and gave Spartan a premium product.

George Sztykiel's son, John, took over day-to-day operations in 1992. The next year the company opened a plant in Mexico to build small, fuel-efficient buses. Spartan made a push to increase product output, but quality suffered and warranty costs jumped, hurting the company's name and its bottom line.

In 1995 a soft market for motor homes caused a drop in sales, prompting the company to begin diversifying. The next year it closed a money-losing Mexican subsidiary. Spartan's operations continued to resemble its name, with Sztykiel emphasizing limited corporate bureaucracy and frugality — he never had a secretary and regularly brown-bagged lunch.

Spartan purchased two fire truck body manufacturers (both longtime customers) in 1997. It also acquired 33% of Carpenter Industries (school bus bodies). Carpenter's poor sales caused Spartan to suffer another loss in 1997. To move into the market for ambulance chassis, the company bought Road Rescue in 1998; Spartan also recapitalized Carpenter to achieve majority ownership.

Spartan joined specialty vehicle maker Federal Signal in a purchasing alliance in 1999. It also signed agreements with RV Holdings, Damon Corporation, and Forest River to supply chassis for the three companies' motor homes. In 2000 Spartan discontinued funding its underperforming Carpenter Industries affiliate.

George Sztykiel announced plans in 2001 to step down as chairman and CEO at the end of the year; George's son, John, assumed the role of CEO in 2002.

In 2003 Spartan combined its Luverne Fire Apparatus and Quality Manufacturing units — both well-known names in the fire truck industry — to form subsidiary Crimson Fire.

EXECUTIVES

Chairman: David R. Wilson, age 69
President, CEO, and Director: John E. Sztykiel, age 48
EVP; President, Spartan Motors Chassis and Director: Richard J. Schalter, age 50
SVP; CFO, Secretary, and Treasurer: James (Jim) Knapp, age 60
VP and Director: William F. Foster, age 64
VP Engineering, Spartan Motors Chassis: James L. Logan, $246,081 pay
President, Road Rescue: Randy Knors
VP Sales, Road Rescue: Charles (Richard) Hamilton
Director, Human Resources: Janine L. Nierenberger
Auditors: Ernst & Young LLP

LOCATIONS

HQ: Spartan Motors, Inc.
1165 Reynolds Rd., Charlotte, MI 48813
Phone: 517-543-6400   **Fax:** 517-543-9269
Web: www.spartanmotors.com

Spartan Motors has manufacturing operations in Alabama, Michigan, Pennsylvania, South Carolina, and South Dakota.

PRODUCTS/OPERATIONS

2005 Sales

	$ mil.	% of total
Chassis		
Motor home	189.1	53
Fire truck	85.5	24
Other	19.5	5
EVTeam	64.8	18
Adjustments	(15.9)	—
Total	**343.0**	**100**

COMPETITORS

Collins Industries	Oshkosh Truck
DaimlerChrysler	Supreme Industries
Ford	Volvo
Mack Trucks	Workhorse Custom Chassis

HISTORICAL FINANCIALS

Company Type: Public

Income Statement

FYE: December 31

	REVENUE ($ mil.)	NET INCOME ($ mil.)	NET PROFIT MARGIN	EMPLOYEES
12/05	343.0	8.3	2.4%	920
12/04	312.3	5.9	1.9%	880
12/03	237.4	6.1	2.6%	710
12/02	259.5	11.7	4.5%	745
12/01	226.3	6.1	2.7%	730
Annual Growth	**11.0%**	**8.0%**	**—**	**6.0%**

2005 Year-End Financials

Debt ratio: 1.8%
Return on equity: 11.8%
Cash ($ mil.): 11.7
Current ratio: 2.03
Long-term debt ($ mil.): 1.3
No. of shares (mil.): 12.6

Dividends
Yield: 2.5%
Payout: 39.5%
Market value ($ mil.): 86.7
R&D as % of sales: 2.7%
Advertising as % of sales: —

Stock History

NASDAQ (GS): SPAR

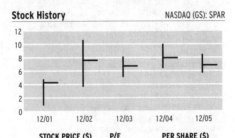

	STOCK PRICE ($) FY Close	P/E High/Low		Earnings	PER SHARE ($) Dividends	Book Value
12/05	6.86	19	13	0.43	0.17	5.75
12/04	7.95	32	21	0.31	0.15	5.38
12/03	6.73	25	16	0.33	0.13	5.01
12/02	7.59	16	6	0.65	0.11	4.69
12/01	4.27	12	3	0.39	0.05	3.44
Annual Growth	**12.6%**	**—**	**—**	**2.5%**	**35.8%**	**13.7%**

Spectrum Control

When it comes to electromagnetic interference, Spectrum Control is a control freak. The company makes control products and systems designed to protect sensitive electronics from electromagnetic, radio-frequency (RF), and microwave interference that can interrupt signals and damage equipment. Its offerings include interconnect products (filters, filtered arrays, and filtered connectors), power control products (for power distribution, management, and conditioning), and microwave products (duplexers, coaxial ceramic resonators). Spectrum Control also offers services such as product design, testing, and custom assembly.

The company's products are primarily sold to telecommunications manufacturers, such as Alcatel-Lucent and Motorola. The telecommunications market, together with military and aerospace markets — including makers of missile

defense, smart weapons and munitions, and aircraft communications systems — account for about 80% of sales. Spectrum Control also sells to the computer and office equipment, industrial control systems, and medical instrumentation markets. Nearly three-quarters of sales are from customers located in the US.

Spectrum Control has suffered from significantly lower spending by telecommunications equipment makers. The company restructured to reduce costs; it closed manufacturing plants and cut its staff by more than half. Spectrum Control has also opened a manufacturing facility in China to help control costs. The company plans to develop new products for the automotive, fiber-optic, and wireless markets.

After its ceramics plant in New Orleans was damaged by Hurricane Katrina in 2005, Spectrum Control bought a manufacturing facility and land in Pennsylvania from Murata Electronics North America, paying about $5 million. With the restoration of basic utility services delayed in the storm-stricken Big Easy, the company moved its salvageable equipment from Louisiana to Pennsylvania, and achieved nearly full production in the new facility by the end of 2006. Full production of all ceramic product lines was set for early 2007. Spectrum Control sold the New Orleans property in early 2006 for $250,000. The Pennsylvania site needs to have toxic chemicals cleaned up, which the company is doing in cooperation with the state's Department of Environmental Protection. In mid-2006 Spectrum Control paid more than $9 million to buy Advanced Thermal Products, which makes customized temperature sensors.

In early 2007 the company's Spectrum Microwave subsidiary acquired the assets of EMF Systems, a manufacturer of custom oscillator-based products, including phase-locked oscillators and synthesizers. The purchase price was about $2.3 million.

Quaker Capital Management owns about 12% of Spectrum Control. FMR (Fidelity Investments) has an equity stake of nearly 10%. Snow Capital Management holds nearly 9%, while Cannell Capital and Royce & Associates each own nearly 7% of the company. Dimensional Fund Advisors holds around 5%.

HISTORY

Spectrum Control was founded in an old hardware store in 1968 by Thomas Venable, Glenn Warnshuis, and John Lane, engineers who had worked together at Erie Technological Products. Spectrum's original products were interference filters. The company went public in 1981, and its net income had risen to $3.3 million by 1986. That year it acquired the electronic component operations of SFE Technologies, but the mishandling of the merger sent Spectrum into the red through fiscal 1991.

Declining US military spending led the company to rethink its product offerings in the early 1990s. After a financial restructuring (in which former Erie Technological executive John Johnston replaced Venable as CEO) and factory shutdowns, Spectrum returned to profitability in 1992. That year it acquired the assets of Erie Technological, which had by then been purchased by Japan's Murata Manufacturing.

Johnston died in 1996, and a year later company executive Richard Southworth was named CEO. A drop in orders in 1996 spurred Spectrum Control to streamline manufacturing in 1997. Cost reductions and expansion into power and

333

microwave products helped the company post a profit in 1997 despite lower sales.

Moving to secure its market share, in 1998 Spectrum acquired Republic Electronics (ceramic capacitors) and Potter Production (electronic filters and power products). In early 1999 Spectrum acquired the Signal Conditioning Products Division and its ceramic filter manufacturing technology and facilities from AMP, Inc. (which is now part of Tyco International).

Riding a tide of record sales, Spectrum Control moved to expand production capacity in 2000 when it began construction on a manufacturing plant in Juarez, Mexico. The company closed two US manufacturing facilities the next year amid a slow telecom equipment market. Spectrum Control also cut its workforce by half that year to lower costs.

In 2002 the company boosted its microwave filter product line with the acquisition of FSY Microwave for about $7 million. In 2004 Spectrum Control acquired privately held microwave components maker Salisbury Engineering.

Spectrum Control has expanded its offerings with its acquisition in late 2004 of the radio-frequency and microwave components product line of REMEC. In early 2005 the company acquired Amplifonix, a manufacturer of RF amplifiers, switches, detectors, integrated systems, and voltage-controlled oscillators, to strengthen its portfolio in hybrid amplifiers.

EXECUTIVES

Chairman: Gerald A. Ryan, age 70
President, CEO, and Director: Richard A. Southworth, age 63, $400,000 pay
SVP, CFO, and Director: John P. Freeman, age 51, $215,000 pay
SVP, Sales and Marketing: Brian F. Ward, age 45, $205,000 pay
SVP, Operations: Lawrence G. Howanitz, age 52, $225,000 pay
SVP, New Business and Resource Development: Robert J. (Bob) McKenna, age 51, $200,000 pay
VP, Mexican Operations: Michael Tantimonace
VP, Information Technology: Jeffrey S. Peters
Secretary and Director: James F. Toohey, age 71
Director, European Sales: Claudia Patzak-Krueger
Director, NorthEast Regional Sales: Jeff Showers
Director, Asian and Hong Kong Sales: Thomas J. Krahling
Director, SouthEast Region: Jason Russolese
Director, Western Region Sales: Jim Devere
Director, UK and Ireland Sales: Alex Tennant
Auditors: Ernst & Young LLP

LOCATIONS

HQ: Spectrum Control, Inc.
8031 Avonia Rd., Fairview, PA 16415
Phone: 814-474-2207 **Fax:** 814-474-2208
Web: www.spectrumcontrol.com

Spectrum Control has facilities in California, Delaware, Florida, Louisiana, Maryland, Mississippi, and Pennsylvania, and in China, France, Germany, Hong Kong, Mexico, and the UK.

2005 Sales

	$ mil.	% of total
US	71.9	73
Germany	4.7	5
China	3.6	4
Mexico	1.4	1
Other countries	16.7	17
Total	**98.3**	**100**

PRODUCTS/OPERATIONS

2005 Sales

	$ mil.	% of total
Signal & power integrity components	52.2	53
RF & microwave components & systems	38.4	39
Power management systems	7.1	7
Sensors & controls	0.6	1
Total	**98.3**	**100**

Selected Products

EMI Filters and Filtered Interconnects
 D-subminiature filters
 EMI shielding products
 Filter plates
 Filtered arrays
 Filtered connectors
Power Products
 Commercial custom assemblies
 Filtered terminal blocks
 Military/aerospace multisection filters
 Power entry modules
 Power entry modules fused/switched and fused
 Power line filters
 Power terminal blocks
 Single line filters
Microwave/Wireless Products
 Bandpass filters
 Cavity filters
 Coaxial ceramic resonators
 Combiners
 Duplexers
 Lumped element filters
 Patch antenna elements
 Waveguide filters
Specialty Ceramic Components
 Discoidal capacitors
 High Q capacitors
 High voltage capacitors
 Single-layer microwave capacitors
 Switch-mode capacitors
 Temperature compensating capacitors
 Tubular capacitors
Advanced Systems
 Digital radio-frequency control equipment
 Fuse and breaker interface panels
 Power distribution units
 Remote power management systems

COMPETITORS

American Technical Ceramics
Amphenol
Astec Power
AVX
Dantel
Dover
ITT Corporation
KEMET
Laird Group
M/A-Com
Maxwell Technologies
Murata Manufacturing
PECO II
Spirent
telent
Tusonix
Tyco Electronics

HISTORICAL FINANCIALS

Company Type: Public

Income Statement

	REVENUE ($ mil.)	NET INCOME ($ mil.)	NET PROFIT MARGIN	EMPLOYEES	FYE: November 30
11/05	98.3	4.6	4.7%	1,173	
11/04	80.5	4.2	5.2%	1,065	
11/03	63.0	0.9	1.4%	864	
11/02	57.2	(0.7)	—	860	
11/01	89.3	(2.9)	—	788	
Annual Growth	**2.4%**	**—**	**—**	**10.5%**	

2005 Year-End Financials

Debt ratio: 1.8%
Return on equity: 5.8%
Cash ($ mil.): 8.4
Current ratio: 4.86
Long-term debt ($ mil.): 1.4
No. of shares (mil.): 13.1
Dividends
 Yield: —
 Payout: —
Market value ($ mil.): 82.9
R&D as % of sales: —
Advertising as % of sales: —

Stock History

NASDAQ (GM): SPEC

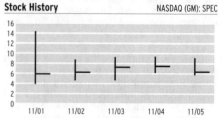

	STOCK PRICE ($) FY Close	P/E High/Low		PER SHARE ($) Earnings	Dividends	Book Value
11/05	6.35	26	17	0.35	—	6.23
11/04	7.46	29	20	0.32	—	5.90
11/03	7.25	131	68	0.07	—	5.56
11/02	6.23	—	—	(0.06)	—	5.46
11/01	5.89	—	—	(0.22)	—	5.50
Annual Growth	**1.9%**	**—**	**—**	**—**	**—**	**3.1%**

Stamps.com

Stamps.com hopes its customers keep putting letters in the mail. The company's PC Postage service lets some 349,000 registered users who have downloaded Stamps.com software buy stamps online and print the postage directly onto envelopes and labels. Customers can also order US Postal Service options such as registered mail, certified mail, and delivery confirmation, as well as printing custom stamps using virtually any image. Stamps.com charges a monthly fee for its service, which is aimed mainly at consumers, home offices, and small businesses. In addition, customers can buy mailing labels, scales, and dedicated postage printers from Stamps.com. Postage fees are sent directly to the US Postal Service.

Stamps.com was founded in 1996 as Stamp-Master and changed its name to Stamps.com in late-1998. It went public the following year.

The Internet postage firm is testing PhotoStamps, a new form of postage that allows users to turn digital photos, designs or other images into valid US postage. Rival Envelope Manager Software (aka Endicia.com) launched a custom postage service called "PictureItPostage" in 2005.

EXECUTIVES

CEO and Director: Kenneth (Ken) McBride, age 38, $436,938 pay (prior to title change)
CFO: Kyle Huebner, age 35, $304,333 pay
VP, General Counsel, and Secretary: Seth Weisberg, age 37, $282,083 pay
VP Advanced Technology: J.P. Leon, age 50, $243,691 pay
VP IT: Richard Stables
VP Postal Affairs: Mike Boswell
VP Sales and Marketing: James M. Bortnak, age 37, $291,667 pay
Investor Relations: Austin Rettig
Auditors: Ernst & Young LLP

LOCATIONS

HQ: Stamps.com Inc.
    12959 Coral Tree Place, Los Angeles, CA 90066
Phone: 310-482-5800
Web: www.stamps.com

COMPETITORS

Envelope Manager	Pitney Bowes
Software	UPS
FedEx	US Postal Service
Neopost	

HISTORICAL FINANCIALS

Company Type: Public

Income Statement

FYE: December 31

	REVENUE ($ mil.)	NET INCOME ($ mil.)	NET PROFIT MARGIN	EMPLOYEES
12/05	61.9	10.4	16.8%	155
12/04	38.1	(4.7)	—	120
12/03	21.2	(9.3)	—	108
12/02	16.3	(6.8)	—	84
12/01	19.4	(209.6)	—	65
Annual Growth	33.7%	—	—	24.3%

2005 Year-End Financials

Debt ratio: —
Return on equity: 10.2%
Cash ($ mil.): 40.8
Current ratio: 5.27
Long-term debt ($ mil.): —
No. of shares (mil.): 23.1

Dividends
  Yield: —
  Payout: —
Market value ($ mil.): 529.5
R&D as % of sales: 10.7%
Advertising as % of sales: —

Stock History

NASDAQ (GM): STMP

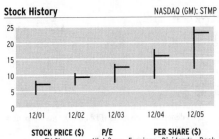

	STOCK PRICE ($) FY Close	P/E High/Low		Earnings	PER SHARE ($) Dividends	Book Value
12/05	22.96	56	27	0.44	—	4.77
12/04	15.84	—	—	(0.21)	—	4.22
12/03	12.40	—	—	(0.42)	—	3.95
12/02	9.34	—	—	(0.28)	—	4.19
12/01	7.16	—	—	(8.28)	—	4.28
Annual Growth	33.8%	—	—	—	—	2.7%

Sterling Financial

Sterling Financial has a reputation to uphold. The firm (unrelated to the Pennsylvania company of the same name) is the holding company for Sterling Savings Bank, which through about 155 branches in Washington, Oregon, Idaho, and Montana, provides such standard retail services as deposit accounts and loans. Together, residential mortgages and construction loans make up about 40% of the bank's loan portfolio, which also includes other real estate and construction loans (about 25%), as well as business and consumer loans. Action Mortgage originates residential mortgages in the bank's market states and in Utah; INTERVEST originates commercial mortgages in Washington, Oregon, Arizona, and California.

Sterling Financial is making no bones about its empire building. The company is racking up a string of acquisitions, including Montana's Empire Federal Bancorp (2003), Oregon's Klamath First Bancorp (2004), and Washington's Lynnwood Financial Group and its Golf Savings Bank (2006). The company also bought FirstBank NW, with branches in Idaho, Oregon, and Washington.

In keeping with its expanding realm, the company has agreed to buy California bank holding company Northern Empire Bancshares for $335 million in cash and stock.

EXECUTIVES

Chairman and CEO: Harold B. Gilkey, age 66, $1,000,000 pay
President, COO, and Director, Sterling Financial; Chairman and CEO, Sterling Savings Bank: William W. Zuppe, age 64, $675,000 pay
EVP Finance, CFO, and Assistant Secretary, Sterling Financial and Sterling Savings Bank: Daniel G. Byrne, age 51, $230,000 pay
SVP Human Resources: Debby J. Ogan
Associate VP Investor Relations: E. Marie Hirsch
Associate VP Compensation and Benefits Manager: Teresa Venne
Vice Chairman and COO, Sterling Savings Bank: Heidi B. Stanley, age 49, $396,000 pay
President and Chief Production Officer, Sterling Savings Bank: David P. Bobbitt, age 58, $322,000 pay
VP, Sterling Savings Bank; President, INTERVEST: John M. Harlow, age 63, $280,000 pay
Auditors: BDO Seidman, LLP

LOCATIONS

HQ: Sterling Financial Corporation
    111 N. Wall St., Spokane, WA 99201
Phone: 509-458-3711   **Fax:** 509-358-6161
Web: www.sterlingsavingsbank.com

PRODUCTS/OPERATIONS

2005 Sales

	$ mil.	% of total
Interest		
Loans	296.3	66
Securities & other	91.5	20
Fees & service charges	34.7	8
Mortgage banking operations	17.9	4
Other	7.5	2
Total	**447.9**	**100**

COMPETITORS

AmericanWest Bancorporation
BancWest
Bank of America
Banner
Columbia Banking
First Mutual Bancshares
Glacier Bancorp
U.S. Bancorp
Washington Federal
Washington Mutual
Wells Fargo

HISTORICAL FINANCIALS

Company Type: Public

Income Statement

FYE: December 31

	ASSETS ($ mil.)	NET INCOME ($ mil.)	INCOME AS % OF ASSETS	EMPLOYEES
12/05	7,558.9	61.2	0.8%	1,789
12/04	6,942.2	56.3	0.8%	1,624
12/03	4,276.9	34.9	0.8%	1,121
12/02	3,506.1	25.6	0.7%	953
12/01	3,038.6	16.2	0.5%	890
Annual Growth	25.6%	39.4%	—	19.1%

2005 Year-End Financials

Equity as % of assets: 6.7%
Return on assets: 0.8%
Return on equity: 12.5%
Long-term debt ($ mil.): 110.7
No. of shares (mil.): 34.9
Market value ($ mil.): 870.7

Dividends
  Yield: 0.4%
  Payout: 5.7%
Sales ($ mil.): 447.9
R&D as % of sales: —
Advertising as % of sales: —

Stock History

NASDAQ (GS): STSA

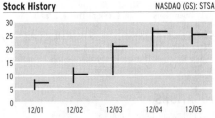

	STOCK PRICE ($) FY Close	P/E High/Low		Earnings	PER SHARE ($) Dividends	Book Value
12/05	24.98	16	12	1.75	0.10	14.54
12/04	26.17	17	12	1.62	—	20.48
12/03	20.74	14	7	1.56	—	16.84
12/02	10.37	11	6	1.15	—	17.03
12/01	7.29	10	6	0.80	—	15.71
Annual Growth	36.1%	—	—	21.6%	—	(1.9%)

Stratagene

Stratagene straddles two markets. The company's Research Supplies division makes and sells reagents, kits, and other products for gene analysis, protein analysis and cell biology, and gene discovery. This unit accounts for three-fourths of its sales. Stratagene's other division, Medical Diagnostics, makes allergy and autoimmune testing kits to help physicians diagnose and monitor the progression of these conditions. This unit also makes the KOVA urinalysis system. The company sells its products in more than 45 countries; in key markets, the firm uses its own sales force and relies on distributors for other markets. Chairman, CEO, and founder Joseph Sorge owns 60% of the company.

The company aims to expand its Medical Diagnostics sales by developing more molecular diagnostics products.

Top customers include drugmakers Amgen, Genentech, Merck, and Pfizer; the research labs of the National Institutes of Health, Harvard, and Stanford; and reference lab services providers Quest Diagnostics and LabCorp. Stratagene earns about half of its revenues through product licensing agreements; licensees include members of the Roche family and Applera.

In 2005 the company was slapped with a permanent injunction prohibiting it from selling its FullVelocity reagents. The court determined the products infringed upon the patents of Third Wave Technologies' Invader method. In addition to ceasing the sale of FullVelocity products, the court ordered Stratagene to inform potential customers its products infringe on Third Wave's patents and pay more than $5 million in fines.

Stratagene was founded in 1984 by Sorge, a former Scripps Foundation scientist. The company acquired diagnostics maker Hycor Biomedical in 2004, enabling it to become a public company.

EXECUTIVES

Chairman and CEO: Joseph A. Sorge, age 52, $607,541 pay
CFO: Steve R. Martin, age 45, $237,584 pay
EVP and General Counsel: Ronni L. Sherman, age 49, $427,398 pay
SVP, Global Sales and International Operations: John R. Pouk, age 51, $312,507 pay
SVP, Operations: Nelson F. (Skip) Thune, age 60, $316,497 pay
SVP, Marketing and Sales, Hycor Biomedical Inc.: Mary Joanne (Mary Jo) Deal, age 50
Senior Director, Human Resources: Dennis T. Ferguson
Auditors: Mayer Hoffman McCann P.C.

LOCATIONS

HQ: Stratagene Corporation
11011 N. Torrey Pines Rd., La Jolla, CA 92037
Phone: 858-535-5400   **Fax:** 858-535-0071
Web: www.stratagene.com

Stratagene has facilities in Canada, Germany, Japan, the Netherlands, the UK, and the US.

2005 Sales

	$ mil.	% of total
US	101.2	78
The Netherlands	17.8	14
Japan	5.6	4
Germany	3.9	3
UK	1.8	1
Total	**130.3**	**100**

PRODUCTS/OPERATIONS

2005 Sales

	$ mil.	% of total
Research Supplies		
Genetic analysis	46.2	36
Protein analysis & cell biology	12.7	10
Gene discovery	8.5	6
Medical Diagnostics		
Urinalysis	11.0	8
Allergy	10.3	8
Autoimmune	1.6	1
Other	40.0	31
Total	**130.3**	**100**

COMPETITORS

Agilent Technologies
Applera
Bio-Rad Labs
GE Healthcare Bio-Sciences
Invitrogen
Promega
QIAGEN
Roche
TECHNE
Third Wave Technologies

HISTORICAL FINANCIALS

Company Type: Public

Income Statement

FYE: December 31

	REVENUE ($ mil.)	NET INCOME ($ mil.)	NET PROFIT MARGIN	EMPLOYEES
12/05	130.3	7.8	6.0%	459
12/04	84.8	7.4	8.7%	467
12/03	69.7	3.3	4.7%	334
12/02	64.0	0.1	0.2%	334
12/01	60.2	0.9	1.5%	350
Annual Growth	21.3%	71.6%	—	7.0%

2005 Year-End Financials

Debt ratio: 6.5%
Return on equity: 13.7%
Cash ($ mil.): 40.7
Current ratio: 1.31
Long-term debt ($ mil.): 3.8
No. of shares (mil.): 22.3
Dividends
  Yield: 2.5%
  Payout: 71.4%
Market value ($ mil.): 224.1
R&D as % of sales: 9.6%
Advertising as % of sales: —

Stock History

NASDAQ (GM): STGN

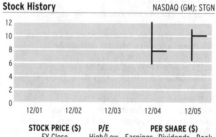

	STOCK PRICE ($) FY Close	P/E High/Low	PER SHARE ($) Earnings	Dividends	Book Value
12/05	10.04	31 18	0.35	0.25	2.62
12/04	7.75	31 15	0.39	—	2.50
Annual Growth	29.5%	— —	(10.3%)	—	4.7%

Stratasys

Stratasys doesn't make the LEGO pieces strewn across your kid's bedroom, but it does make rapid prototyping systems that designers and engineers — including the makers of LEGO toys — use to get products to market faster. The company's Insight software takes a conceptual model generated from a CAD workstation and creates a series of cross-sections to form a 3-D blueprint. Stratasys's fused deposition modeling (FDM) machines use the blueprint to create physical models by building up layers of wax and plastic polymers. Ford, Intel, NASA, and other customers use the company's products to build prototypes for cars, electronics, tools, and other products.

It's the end of Eden — for Stratasys. The company will discontinue sales of the Eden product line in 2007. Stratasys distributes and supports Eden for the product's developer, Israel-based Objet Geometries, which will take over sales of Eden in 2007. The company will continue to maintain Eden systems that it has installed through August 2007. Eden is a rapid prototyping system incorporating the PolyJet technology developed by Objet Geometries; in North America, Stratasys carries five Eden models made by Objet Geometries.

EXECUTIVES

Chairman, President, CEO, and Treasurer: S. Scott Crump, age 52, $227,624 pay
COO and Secretary: Thomas W. (Tom) Stenoien, age 55, $202,837 pay
CFO: Robert F. Gallagher, age 50, $172,596 pay (partial-year salary)
VP, FDM Sales, Marketing and Customer Service: Woodrow J. (Woody) Frost
VP, Operations: Kurt Hinrichsen
VP, Process Improvement: Paul G. Grette
VP, Research and Development: Paul Blake
Director, Human Resources: Cary Feik
Director, Investor Relations: Shane Glenn
Director, Marketing: Bob Adamzak
Manager, Public Relations: Joe Hiemenz
Auditors: Rothstein, Kass & Company, P.C.

LOCATIONS

HQ: Stratasys, Inc.
14950 Martin Dr., Eden Prairie, MN 55344
Phone: 952-937-3000   **Fax:** 952-937-0070
Web: www.stratasys.com

Stratasys has offices in California, Michigan, Minnesota, and in Germany.

2005 Sales

	% of total
North America	61
Europe	21
Asia/Pacific	17
Other regions	1
Total	**100**

PRODUCTS/OPERATIONS

2005 Sales

	$ mil.	% of total
Products	66.2	80
Services	16.6	20
Total	**82.8**	**100**

Selected Products

Modeling equipment
  3-D printer (Dimension)
  Fused deposition modelers (FDM 3000, Quantum, and Maxum)
  Prototyping system (Prodigy Plus)
  Prototying system for durable materials (Titan)
Modeling materials
  Casting wax
  Elastomer materials
  Hard polymer materials
  Medical grade polymers
  Release materials
  Water-soluble materials
Software
  3-D printer model builder (AutoGen)
  Fused deposition pre-processing (Insight)

COMPETITORS

3D Systems
Dassault
Delcam
EOS
Mitsui
Moldflow
SOGECLAIR
Solidscape
Soligen 2006
Teijin
Vero International Software
Z Corporation

HISTORICAL FINANCIALS

Company Type: Public

Income Statement

	REVENUE ($ mil.)	NET INCOME ($ mil.)	NET PROFIT MARGIN	EMPLOYEES
12/05	82.8	10.6	12.8%	325
12/04	70.3	9.1	12.9%	279
12/03	50.9	6.2	12.2%	229
12/02	39.8	3.1	7.8%	196
12/01	37.6	2.5	6.6%	190
Annual Growth	21.8%	43.5%	—	14.4%

FYE: December 31

2005 Year-End Financials

Debt ratio: —
Return on equity: 12.4%
Cash ($ mil.): 32.1
Current ratio: 3.58
Long-term debt ($ mil.): —
No. of shares (mil.): 12.3

Dividends
Yield: —
Payout: —
Market value ($ mil.): 307.3
R&D as % of sales: 7.7%
Advertising as % of sales: 4.1%

Stock History

NASDAQ (GS): SSYS

	STOCK PRICE ($) FY Close	P/E High/Low		PER SHARE ($) Earnings	Dividends	Book Value
12/05	25.01	38	20	0.99	—	7.02
12/04	33.56	43	19	0.85	—	8.13
12/03	27.05	61	9	0.64	—	7.20
12/02	6.37	18	7	0.37	—	6.14
12/01	4.41	17	5	0.31	—	5.80
Annual Growth	54.3%	—	—	33.7%	—	4.9%

Stratus Properties

Environmentalists are sometimes the cloud in Stratus' lining. Stratus Properties acquires, develops, manages, and sells commercial and residential real estate in Texas — primarily in the Austin area, where it has some 2,800 acres of developed and undeveloped land. The firm's most important developments include Austin's Barton Creek subdivision and portions of the metro area's Circle C Ranch. It is also developing a 70-acre residential project in Plano (north of Dallas) and owns a few scattered acres in San Antonio. Stratus' upscale developments have sometimes put the company at odds with Austin environmentalists over watershed protection, resulting in restrictions on some of its projects.

The company donated $2 million to the Hill Country Conservancy as a way to help smooth those ruffled feathers. Stratus Properties is joining forces with Trammell Crow to develop an urban project called Crestview Station in Austin. The project, which is being built on the site of a former Huntsman facility, will include single- and multi-family homes, offices, and retail space. Stratus Properties in 2006 sold 58 acres of its Lantana development in Austin to Advanced

Micro Devices as the site for that firm's new campus. Chairman and CEO William Armstrong owns 6% of Stratus Properties; real estate investor Carl Berg (also the CEO of Mission West Properties) owns about 20%.

EXECUTIVES

Chairman, President, and CEO:
  William H. (Beau) Armstrong III, age 41, $700,000 pay
SVP and CFO: John E. Baker, age 59, $425,000 pay
General Counsel and Secretary: Kenneth N. Jones, age 46
Engineering and Construction: Stephen A. Hay
Public Relations and Advertising: Belinda D. Wells
Auditors: PricewaterhouseCoopers LLP

LOCATIONS

HQ: Stratus Properties Inc.
  98 San Jacinto Blvd., Ste. 220, Austin, TX 78701
Phone: 512-478-5788   **Fax:** 512-482-0644
Web: www.stratusprop.com

PRODUCTS/OPERATIONS

2005 Sales

	$ mil.	% of total
Real estate	33.0	94
Rental income	1.4	4
Commissions, management fees & other	0.8	2
Total	**35.2**	**100**

2005 Sales By Segment

	$ mil.	% of total
Real estate operations	33.8	96
Commercial leasing	1.4	4
Total	**35.2**	**100**

COMPETITORS

A.G. Spanos
Choice Homes
Drees
Highland Homes
Meritage Homes
Morrison Homes
Pulte Homes
Ryland
Standard Pacific
Trammell Crow Residential

HISTORICAL FINANCIALS

Company Type: Public

Income Statement

	REVENUE ($ mil.)	NET INCOME ($ mil.)	NET PROFIT MARGIN	EMPLOYEES
12/05	35.2	8.5	24.1%	27
12/04	20.9	0.7	3.3%	23
12/03	14.4	0.0	—	20
12/02	11.6	(0.5)	—	21
12/01	14.8	3.9	26.4%	26
Annual Growth	24.2%	21.5%	—	0.9%

FYE: December 31

2005 Year-End Financials

Debt ratio: 53.2%
Return on equity: 9.3%
Cash ($ mil.): 2.8
Current ratio: 0.68
Long-term debt ($ mil.): 50.1
No. of shares (mil.): 7.2

Dividends
Yield: —
Payout: —
Market value ($ mil.): 168.4
R&D as % of sales: —
Advertising as % of sales: 0.6%

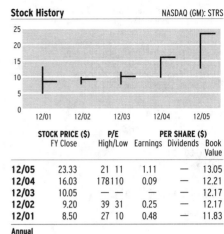

Stock History

NASDAQ (GM): STRS

	STOCK PRICE ($) FY Close	P/E High/Low		PER SHARE ($) Earnings	Dividends	Book Value
12/05	23.33	21	11	1.11	—	13.05
12/04	16.03	178	110	0.09	—	12.21
12/03	10.05	—	—	—	—	12.17
12/02	9.20	39	31	0.25	—	12.17
12/01	8.50	27	10	0.48	—	11.83
Annual Growth	28.7%	—	—	23.3%	—	2.5%

Summit Financial Group

Summit Financial Group is the holding company for Summit Community Bank and Shenandoah Valley National Bank, which includes the Loudoun National Bank, Rockingham National Bank, and People's Bank of Warrenton (opened in 2005) divisions. Summit Community Bank serves West Virginia through nearly 10 branches, while Shenandoah Valley has six locations in northwestern Virginia. Both institutions offer standard banking services and products such as deposit accounts, loans, and cash management services. Commercial real estate loans account for more than half of Summit Financial Group's loan portfolio, which also includes residential mortgages and a smaller percentage of business, construction, and consumer loans.

The company's Summit Mortgage subsidiary originates first mortgages for customers in its region and second mortgages for customers throughout the US. It sells almost all of the loans that it originates into the secondary market. Summit Financial plans to sell the struggling unit or shut it down completely if it cannot find a buyer.

The group acquired a commercial and personal insurance agency now operating as Summit Insurance Services in 2004.

EXECUTIVES

Chairman: Oscar M. Bean, age 55
Vice Chairman: George R. Ours Jr., age 74
President, CEO, and Director: H. Charles Maddy III, age 43, $494,773 pay
SVP and COO: Scott C. Jennings, age 44, $228,362 pay
SVP and CFO: Robert S. Tissue, age 42, $228,262 pay
SVP, Chief Credit Officer, and Director: Patrick N. Frye, age 47, $238,262 pay
SVP and Chief Banking Officer: Douglas T. Mitchell, age 42
VP and Chief Accounting Officer: Julie R. Cook
VP and Director of Human Resources:
  Danyl R. Freeman

Director; President and CEO, Shenandoah Valley National Bank: Ronald F. (Ron) Miller, age 61, $277,757 pay
President and CEO, Summit Community Bank: C. David Robertson, age 62, $256,294 pay
Secretary and Director: Phoebe F. Heishman, age 65
Director of Shareholder Relations: Teresa D. Sherman
Auditors: Arnett & Foster, P.L.L.C.

LOCATIONS

HQ: Summit Financial Group, Inc.
300 N. Main St., Moorefield, WV 26836
Phone: 304-530-1000   **Fax:** 304-530-7053
Web: www.summitfgi.com

PRODUCTS/OPERATIONS

2005 Sales

	% of total
Interest	
Loans, including fees	55
Securities, including dividends	11
Noninterest	
Mortgage origination revenue	31
Other	3
Total	**100**

COMPETITORS

Allegheny Bancshares	Premier Community
BB&T	Bankshares
F & M Bank	SunTrust
Fauquier Bankshares	Wachovia
Highlands Bankshares Inc.	

HISTORICAL FINANCIALS

Company Type: Public

Income Statement				FYE: December 31
	ASSETS ($ mil.)	NET INCOME ($ mil.)	INCOME AS % OF ASSETS	EMPLOYEES
12/05	1,109.5	11.2	1.0%	276
12/04	889.5	10.6	1.2%	254
12/03	791.5	8.2	1.0%	222
12/02	671.8	7.2	1.1%	162
12/01	591.8	5.3	0.9%	166
Annual Growth	**17.0%**	**20.6%**	**—**	**13.6%**

2005 Year-End Financials

Equity as % of assets: 6.7%
Return on assets: 1.1%
Return on equity: 16.2%
Long-term debt ($ mil.): 170.5
No. of shares (mil.): 7.1
Market value ($ mil.): 163.8
Dividends
  Yield: 1.3%
  Payout: 19.2%
Sales ($ mil.): 87.9
R&D as % of sales: —
Advertising as % of sales: 5.5%

Stock History

NASDAQ (CM): SMMF

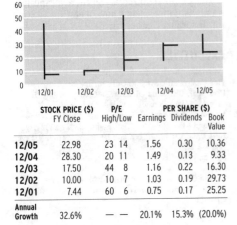

	STOCK PRICE ($) FY Close	P/E High/Low		PER SHARE ($) Earnings	Dividends	Book Value
12/05	22.98	23	14	1.56	0.30	10.36
12/04	28.30	20	11	1.49	0.13	9.33
12/03	17.50	44	8	1.16	0.22	16.30
12/02	10.00	10	7	1.03	0.19	29.73
12/01	7.44	60	6	0.75	0.17	25.25
Annual Growth	**32.6%**	**—**	**—**	**20.1%**	**15.3%**	**(20.0%)**

Sun American Bancorp

Here comes the Sun. Known as PanAmerican Bancorp until it changed its name in early 2006, Sun American Bancorp is the holding company for Sun American Bank (formerly PanAmerican Bank), which offers checking accounts, savings and money market accounts, and CDs, as well as individual retirement accounts. It has seven offices in South Florida, in and around Miami. The bank concentrates on lending to area small and midsized businesses (commercial mortgages make up the bulk of its loan portfolio), but also writes residential real estate, home equity, and other consumer loans.

The company bought the assets and branches of Gulf Bank in 2004 and is looking to open new locations or make another acquisition in the future.

Puerto Rico-based First BanCorp owns about 10% of Sun American Bancorp.

EXECUTIVES

Chairman: James F. Partridge, age 77
Vice Chairman: Nelson Famadas, age 57
President, CEO, and Director; Chairman, CEO, and Interim President, Sun American Bank: Michael E. Golden, age 62, $337,500 pay (prior to title change)
COO; EVP and COO, Sun American Bank: Alfredo Barreiro, age 39, $110,000 pay (prior to title change)
CFO, Sun American Bancorp and Sun American Bank: Robert L. Nichols, age 47, $183,958 pay
Secretary and Director: Hugo A. Castro, age 63
EVP and Chief Lending Officer, Sun American Bank: Robert K. Garrett, age 44, $113,750 pay
EVP Sales and Service, Sun American Bank: William T. Ross, age 57
President and Principal Mortgage Broker, Sun American Financial: Bernardo Reynoso

LOCATIONS

HQ: Sun American Bancorp
3400 Coral Way, Miami, FL 33145
Phone: 305-421-6800   **Fax:** 305-826-0109
Web: www.panamericanbank.com

Sun American Bancorp has branches in Boca Raton, Boynton Beach, Hollywood, and Miami, Florida.

PRODUCTS/OPERATIONS

2005 Sales

	$ mil.	% of total
Interest		
Loans, including fees	14.8	87
Other	1.2	7
Noninterest		
Service charges on deposit accounts & sale of securities	1.1	6
Total	**17.1**	**100**

COMPETITORS

Bank of America
BankUnited
Citibank
EuroBancshares
Ohio Savings Bank
Regions Financial

HISTORICAL FINANCIALS

Company Type: Public

Income Statement				FYE: December 31
	ASSETS ($ mil.)	NET INCOME ($ mil.)	INCOME AS % OF ASSETS	EMPLOYEES
12/05	277.1	2.9	1.0%	74
12/04	191.5	(0.2)	—	—
12/03	94.1	(0.4)	—	—
12/02	90.2	(0.5)	—	—
12/01	65.6	(1.1)	—	—
Annual Growth	**43.4%**	**—**	**—**	**—**

2005 Year-End Financials

Equity as % of assets: 21.5%
Return on assets: 1.2%
Return on equity: 7.2%
Long-term debt ($ mil.): —
No. of shares (mil.): 18.8
Market value ($ mil.): 82.7
Dividends
  Yield: —
  Payout: —
Sales ($ mil.): 17.1
R&D as % of sales: —
Advertising as % of sales: —

Stock History

AMEX: SBK

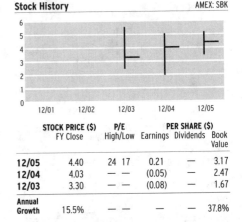

	STOCK PRICE ($) FY Close	P/E High/Low		PER SHARE ($) Earnings	Dividends	Book Value
12/05	4.40	24	17	0.21	—	3.17
12/04	4.03	—	—	(0.05)	—	2.47
12/03	3.30	—	—	(0.08)	—	1.67
Annual Growth	**15.5%**	**—**	**—**	**—**	**—**	**37.8%**

Sun Hydraulics

It's not solar power that Sun Hydraulics delivers, but fluid power. The company makes screw-in hydraulic cartridge valves and manifolds used to control force, speed, and motion in fluid power systems. About two-thirds of Sun Hydraulics' hydraulic valves and manifolds are sold for use in construction, agricultural, and utility equipment, with the remainder sold for use in machine tools and material handling equipment. The company sells its products worldwide through independent distributors, most of which are located outside the US. Former chairman Robert Koski and his family own nearly a third of the company.

Sun Hydraulics has reported a profit every year since 1972.

EXECUTIVES

Chairman: Clyde G. Nixon, age 70, $133,333 pay
President, CEO, and Director: Allen J. Carlson, age 55, $350,025 pay
CFO: Tricia L. Fulton, age 39
Director, Human Resources: Kirsten Regal
Engineering Manager: Jeffrey Cooper, age 65, $167,023 pay
General Manager, Sun Hydraulics Limited: Peter G. Robson, age 61, $143,912 pay
Investor Relations: Richard Arter
Auditors: Grant Thornton; PricewaterhouseCoopers LLP

LOCATIONS

HQ: Sun Hydraulics Corporation
    1500 W. University Pkwy., Sarasota, FL 34243
Phone: 941-362-1200   **Fax:** 941-355-4497
Web: www.sunhydraulics.com

Sun Hydraulics operates manufacturing facilities in Germany, South Korea, the UK, and the US.

2005 Sales

	$ mil.	% of total
US	74.0	63
UK	16.1	14
Germany	15.1	13
South Korea	11.6	10
Total	**116.8**	**100**

COMPETITORS

Bosch Rexroth Corp.
Koch Enterprises
Mark IV
Sauer-Danfoss
Textron

HISTORICAL FINANCIALS

Company Type: Public

Income Statement
FYE: Saturday nearest December 31

	REVENUE ($ mil.)	NET INCOME ($ mil.)	NET PROFIT MARGIN	EMPLOYEES
12/05	116.8	12.8	11.0%	597
12/04	94.5	7.8	8.3%	678
12/03	70.8	2.2	3.1%	513
12/02	64.5	1.8	2.8%	655
12/01	65.0	0.9	1.4%	678
Annual Growth	**15.8%**	**94.2%**	**—**	**(3.1%)**

2005 Year-End Financials

Debt ratio: 3.5%
Return on equity: 25.1%
Cash ($ mil.): 5.8
Current ratio: 2.61
Long-term debt ($ mil.): 2.0
No. of shares (mil.): 10.9
Dividends
  Yield: 1.3%
  Payout: 21.4%
Market value ($ mil.): 211.3
R&D as % of sales: —
Advertising as % of sales: —

Stock History
NASDAQ (GS): SNHY

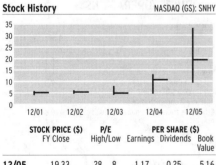

	STOCK PRICE ($) FY Close	P/E High/Low		Earnings	Dividends	Book Value
12/05	19.33	28	8	1.17	0.25	5.16
12/04	10.65	17	6	0.76	0.12	6.52
12/03	4.83	35	20	0.22	1.41	5.19
12/02	5.33	32	27	0.18	0.11	6.66
12/01	5.10	59	46	0.09	0.11	6.81
Annual Growth	**39.5%**	**—**	**—**	**89.9%**	**22.8%**	**(6.7%)**

Superior Well Services

It is superior well services, not a superior attitude, that lets Superior Well Services live up to its name. The oil service company provides technical pumping services (stimulation, nitrogen, and cementing) and down-hole surveying services (logging and perforating) that smaller rivals do not provide and at competitive prices to those offered by the big oilfield services companies such as BJ Services and Schlumberger. The bulk of Superior Well Services' customers are regional independent oil and gas companies. The technical pumping services unit owns a fleet of 345 commercial vehicles. The down-hole surveying services unit owns a fleet of 41 trucks and cranes. Directors and executives own 44.5% of the company.

Superior Well Services was founded in 1997 by three former employees of Halliburton Energy Services: David Wallace, Jacob Linaberger, and Rhys Reese.

Superior Wells Services has expanded from two service centers in the Appalachian region to 13 service centers serving customers in 37 states. Its customer base has grown from 89 in 1999 to more than 600 in 2006.

EXECUTIVES

Chairman and CEO: David E. Wallace, age 51, $415,650 pay
President: Jacob B. Linaberger, age 57, $406,600 pay
EVP, COO, and Secretary: Rhys R. Reese, age 46, $406,600 pay
VP and CFO: Thomas W. Stoelk, age 50, $50,339 pay (partial-year salary)
VP and Controller: Fred E. Kistner, age 63, $114,100 pay
Auditors: Schneider Downs & Co., Inc.

LOCATIONS

HQ: Superior Well Services, Inc.
    1380 Rt. 286 East, Ste. 121, Indiana, PA 15701
Phone: 724-465-8904   **Fax:** 724-465-8907
Web: www.superiorwells.com

Superior Well Services serves customers in several US oil and natural gas producing regions, including Appalachia and the Mid-Continent, Rocky Mountain, Southeast, and Southwest regions.

PRODUCTS/OPERATIONS

2005 Sales

	% of total
Technical pumping services	
Stimulation	55
Cementing	22
Nitrogen	13
Down-hole surveying services	10
Total	**100**

2005 Sales

	$ mil.	% of total
Technical pumping services	119.2	90
Down-hole surveying services	12.5	10
Total	**131.7**	**100**

COMPETITORS

Baker Hughes
BJ Services
Halliburton
Schlumberger
Smith International
Weatherford International

HISTORICAL FINANCIALS

Company Type: Public

Income Statement
FYE: December 31

	REVENUE ($ mil.)	NET INCOME ($ mil.)	NET PROFIT MARGIN	EMPLOYEES
12/05	131.7	9.5	7.2%	646
12/04	76.0	9.8	12.9%	—
12/03	51.5	8.2	15.9%	—
12/02	34.2	5.3	15.5%	—
Annual Growth	**56.7%**	**21.5%**	**—**	**—**

2005 Year-End Financials

Debt ratio: 1.4%
Return on equity: 15.2%
Cash ($ mil.): 10.8
Current ratio: 3.63
Long-term debt ($ mil.): 1.3
No. of shares (mil.): 19.4
Dividends
  Yield: —
  Payout: —
Market value ($ mil.): 460.4
R&D as % of sales: —
Advertising as % of sales: —

Stock History
NASDAQ (GS): SWSI

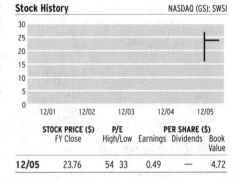

	STOCK PRICE ($) FY Close	P/E High/Low		Earnings	Dividends	Book Value
12/05	23.76	54	33	0.49	—	4.72

Swift Energy

No laggard, oil and gas exploration and production company Swift Energy has interests in 967 producing wells, primarily in Louisiana and Texas. It also has two major exploration regions in New Zealand. The company's core US production areas are the Lake Washington Field in Louisiana, and the AWP Olmos Field in Texas. Swift Energy aims to increase reserves and production by adjusting the balance between drilling and acquisition activities in response to market conditions. It is also expanding its production activities in New Zealand. The company's proved reserves consist of 761.8 billion cu. ft. of natural gas equivalent. Swift Energy Company was founded in 1979.

At the end of 2005 Swift Energy restructured as a holding company. The change separates Swift Energy's US and international operations and provides greater administrative and organizational flexibility.

In 2006 the company announced plans to explore several sites in the Cook Basin Inlet of Alaska through a participation agreement with Aurora Gas LLC.

That year it agreed to buy stakes in five onshore South Louisiana properties from BP America Production Co. for $175 million.

EXECUTIVES

Chairman and CEO; Chairman, Swift Energy International: Terry E. Swift, age 50
Vice Chairman: Raymond E. (Ray) Galvin, age 74
President and Director: Bruce H. Vincent, age 59
EVP and COO: Joseph A. (Joe) D'Amico, age 58
EVP and CFO: Alton D. Heckaman Jr., age 49
SVP Operations: James M. Kitterman, age 62
SVP Commercial Transactions and Land: James P. Mitchell, age 52
SVP and Chief Compliance Officer: Victor R. Moran, age 51
Chief General Counsel: Laurent A. (Larry) Baillargeon
General Counsel — Corporate, Chief Governance Officer, and Secretary: Karen Bryant
Director Corporate Development and Investor Relations: Scott Espenshade
President and COO, SENZ: R. Alan Cunningham
Auditors: Ernst & Young LLP

LOCATIONS

HQ: Swift Energy Company
16825 Northchase Dr., Ste. 400, Houston, TX 77060
Phone: 281-874-2700   **Fax:** 281-874-2726
Web: www.swiftenergy.com

2005 Sales

	$ mil.	% of total
US	355.9	84
New Zealand	67.9	16
Adjustments	(0.6)	—
Total	**423.2**	**100**

PRODUCTS/OPERATIONS

2005 Proved Reserves

	% of total
Crude oil	51
Natural gas	38
Natural gas liquids (NGLs)	11
Total	**100**

COMPETITORS

Adams Resources
Apache
BP
Chesapeake Energy
Devon Energy
Exxon Mobil
Forest Oil
Frontier Oil
XTO Energy

HISTORICAL FINANCIALS

Company Type: Public

Income Statement

FYE: December 31

	REVENUE ($ mil.)	NET INCOME ($ mil.)	NET PROFIT MARGIN	EMPLOYEES
12/05	423.2	115.8	27.4%	311
12/04	310.3	68.4	22.0%	272
12/03	208.9	29.9	14.3%	241
12/02	150.0	11.9	7.9%	234
12/01	183.8	(22.4)	—	209
Annual Growth	**23.2%**	**—**	**—**	**10.4%**

2005 Year-End Financials

Debt ratio: 57.7%	Dividends
Return on equity: 21.4%	Yield: —
Cash ($ mil.): 53.0	Payout: —
Current ratio: 1.17	Market value ($ mil.): 1,307.5
Long-term debt ($ mil.): 350.3	R&D as % of sales: —
No. of shares (mil.): 29.0	Advertising as % of sales: —

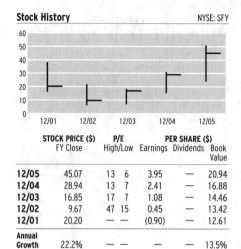

	STOCK PRICE ($) FY Close	P/E High/Low		PER SHARE ($) Earnings	Dividends	Book Value
12/05	45.07	13	6	3.95	—	20.94
12/04	28.94	13	7	2.41	—	16.88
12/03	16.85	17	7	1.08	—	14.46
12/02	9.67	47	15	0.45	—	13.42
12/01	20.20	—	—	(0.90)	—	12.61
Annual Growth	**22.2%**	**—**	**—**	**—**	**—**	**13.5%**

SWS Group

SWS Group hopes stock prices go northeast. The company offers a range of financial services to individual and institutional clients. Its primary subsidiary, Southwest Securities, provides securities clearing and brokerage services in the US, Canada, and Europe. The unit offers retail private client services through offices in Texas, Oklahoma, and New Mexico, and institutional services, including securities underwriting, through about 10 offices across the US. Another unit, Southwest Insurance Agency, sells insurance and annuities. In addition, SWS Group owns a bank, which is also called Southwest Securities.

It provides commercial and consumer loan products, as well as community banking, through five Dallas-area branches and loan production offices in Texas and Oklahoma.

HISTORY

Don Buchholz and the late Allen Cobb formed MidSouthwest Securities in 1972 ("Mid" was dropped in 1979) after the NYSE began letting members offer discounted commissions to nonmember firms. MidSouthwest Securities specialized in executing orders for nonmember brokerages, expanding after the 1975 deregulation of brokerage commissions. It added clearing services (which soon became its core business) at the request of independent brokers. The firm expanded through such buys as Pine Securities (1974) and Quinn and Company (1987). It began offering corporate financing in 1978, and in 1987 started underwriting municipal and corporate securities.

The firm formed SWS Technologies in 1996. The next year it launched discount brokerage services through Sovereign Securities. Sovereign's online trading unit, Mydiscountbroker.com, was launched in 1997. By 1999, the online business had eclipsed Sovereign, and the whole unit was renamed Mydiscountbroker.com. In 2000 SWS took advantage of deregulation in the US financial industry by acquiring ASBI Holdings, owner of First Savings Bank in Arlington, Texas. The company sold the accounts of its Mydiscountbroker.com subsidiary to Ameritrade in 2003. It also shut-

tered the information technology-related services once offered by its SWS Technologies division.

In early 2005 SWS Group agreed to pay $10 million to settle allegations of mutual fund trading abuses. Former Southwest Securities president Daniel Leland, who stepped down in 2004 amid the investigations, also was fined and suspended from the securities industry for a year.

EXECUTIVES

Chairman: Don A. Buchholz, age 77
CEO and Director: Donald W. (Don) Hultgren, age 49, $787,500 pay
President; President and CEO, Southwest Securities: William D. (Bill) Felder, age 48, $800,069 pay
EVP, CFO, and Treasurer: Kenneth R. Hanks, age 51, $630,000 pay
EVP and CIO: W. Norman Thompson, age 50
EVP; CEO, Southwest Securities Bank: Richard J. (Dick) Driscoll, age 51, $585,984 pay
EVP; CFO, Southwest Securities: Stacy M. Hodges, age 43
EVP; EVP, Public Finance Division, Southwest Securities: Richard H. Litton, age 59, $689,726 pay
EVP; CEO, SWS Financial Services; Director, Private Client Group, Southwest Securities: James H. (Jim) Ross, age 56
SVP, Public Finance, Houston: Lance G. Johnson
VP, Corporate Communications: James R. (Jim) Bowman
VP, General Counsel, and Secretary: Allen R. Tubb, age 52
President, South Arlington Banking Center, Southwest Securities: Del B. Waller
President, Southwest Insurance Agency: Michael E. (Mike) Myers
Controller: Laura Leventhal
Director, Human Resources: Jim Zimcosky
Auditors: Grant Thornton LLP

LOCATIONS

HQ: SWS Group, Inc.
1201 Elm St., Ste. 3500, Dallas, TX 75270
Phone: 214-859-1800   **Fax:** 214-859-6077
Web: www.swsgroupinc.com

PRODUCTS/OPERATIONS

2006 Sales

	$ mil.	% of total
Interest	220.6	56
Commissions	85.5	22
Investment banking fees	16.9	4
Net gains on principal transactions	16.5	4
Net revenues from clearing operations	14.7	4
Advisory & administrative fees	12.9	3
Other fees from clearing operations	10.8	3
Other	13.7	4
Total	**391.6**	**100**

COMPETITORS

A.G. Edwards	Goldman Sachs
Baird	Jefferies Group
Banc of America Securities	Legg Mason
Bear Stearns	Lehman Brothers
Charles Schwab	Merrill Lynch
CIBC World Markets	Morgan Keegan
Cowen Group	Piper Jaffray
Credit Suisse (USA)	Raymond James Financial
Deutsche Bank	RBC Dain Rauscher
E*TRADE Financial	TD Ameritrade
Edward Jones	UBS Financial Services
First Albany	

HISTORICAL FINANCIALS

Company Type: Public

Income Statement

FYE: Last Friday in June

	REVENUE ($ mil.)	NET INCOME ($ mil.)	NET PROFIT MARGIN	EMPLOYEES
6/06	391.6	41.4	10.6%	889
6/05	345.5	31.3	9.1%	1,314
6/04	273.4	2.7	1.0%	—
6/03	263.5	2.9	1.1%	941
6/02	332.1	(7.2)	—	1,004
Annual Growth	4.2%	—	—	(3.0%)

2006 Year-End Financials

Debt ratio: 1,172.2%
Return on equity: 14.9%
Cash ($ mil.): 105.3
Current ratio: —
Long-term debt ($ mil.): 3,393.3
No. of shares (mil.): 17.7

Dividends
  Yield: 5.9%
  Payout: 61.3%
Market value ($ mil.): 285.1
R&D as % of sales: —
Advertising as % of sales: —

Stock History

NYSE: SWS

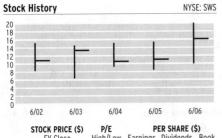

	STOCK PRICE ($) FY Close	P/E High/Low		PER SHARE ($) Earnings	Dividends	Book Value
6/06	16.08	13	7	1.55	0.95	16.33
6/05	11.03	13	7	1.20	0.27	15.34
6/04	10.57	141	88	0.11	0.33	14.47
6/03	13.33	127	58	0.11	0.27	14.73
6/02	10.83	—	—	(0.28)	0.20	14.81
Annual Growth	10.4%	—	—	—	47.6%	2.5%

Symmetry Medical

Symmetry Medical covers both sides of the orthopedic implant coin. The company makes orthopedic implants such as hips and knees and the surgical instruments that are used to implant such devices. In addition to making numerous products for the orthopedic implant market, the company markets its products to physicians that deal with spinal injuries and general trauma, dental work, cardiovascular care, and ophthalmology. Symmetry also manufactures plastic and metal cases to organize, hold, and transport medical devices. On the side it also manufactures aerofoils and aircraft engine parts for a few aerospace customers. The company uses its own sales force to promote its products worldwide.

A 2000 investment gave asset manager Olympus Partners control of Symmetry Medical, and allowed the company to expand globally through its acquisition of Mettis (UK) Limited in 2003. Olympus Partners has since reduced its holdings and now owns 14% of the company.

Symmetry Medical spent $45 million to acquire Riley Medical in 2006. Riley manufactures standard and custom cases, trays, and containers for medical devices from its operations in Switzerland and the US.

EXECUTIVES

President and CEO: Brian Moore, age 60, $630,000 pay (prior to title change)
SVP and CFO: Fred Hite, age 38, $329,000 pay
SVP and General Manager, Europe: Richard J. Senior, age 42, $326,400 pay
SVP, Marketing, Sales, and Business Development: Andrew Miclot, age 50, $379,000 pay
SVP, Quality Assurance and Regulatory Affairs and Compliance Officer: D. Darin Martin, age 54, $270,000 pay
Auditors: Ernst & Young LLP

LOCATIONS

HQ: Symmetry Medical Inc.
  220 W. Market St., Warsaw, IN 46580
Phone: 574-268-2252   **Fax:** 574-267-4551
Web: www.symmetrymedical.com

Symmetry Medical has facilities in the UK and the US.

2005 Sales

	$ mil.	% of total
US	171.6	65
UK	33.0	13
Ireland	32.5	12
Other countries	26.7	10
Total	**263.8**	**100**

PRODUCTS/OPERATIONS

2005 Sales

	$ mil.	% of total
Implants	103.5	39
Instruments	86.7	33
Cases	55.5	21
Other products & services	18.1	7
Total	**263.8**	**100**

COMPETITORS

Biomet
DePuy
Smith & Nephew
Stryker
Zimmer

HISTORICAL FINANCIALS

Company Type: Public

Income Statement

FYE: Saturday nearest December 31

	REVENUE ($ mil.)	NET INCOME ($ mil.)	NET PROFIT MARGIN	EMPLOYEES
12/05	263.8	31.8	12.1%	1,862
12/04	205.4	11.7	5.7%	1,673
12/03	122.0	5.9	4.8%	1,464
12/02	65.4	0.2	0.3%	—
Annual Growth	59.2%	441.8%	—	12.8%

2005 Year-End Financials

Debt ratio: 13.7%
Return on equity: 13.5%
Cash ($ mil.): 12.5
Current ratio: 2.66
Long-term debt ($ mil.): 34.8
No. of shares (mil.): 34.7

Dividends
  Yield: —
  Payout: —
Market value ($ mil.): 671.9
R&D as % of sales: —
Advertising as % of sales: 0.1%

Stock History

NYSE: SMA

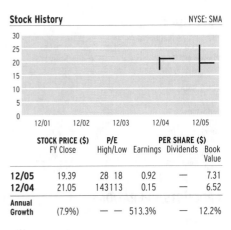

	STOCK PRICE ($) FY Close	P/E High/Low		PER SHARE ($) Earnings	Dividends	Book Value
12/05	19.39	28	18	0.92	—	7.31
12/04	21.05	143	113	0.15	—	6.52
Annual Growth	(7.9%)	—	—	513.3%	—	12.2%

Symyx Technologies

Scientific research is serious business for Symyx Technologies. The company offers outsourced materials research services to companies in the chemical and pharmaceutical industries. Symyx's research offerings (which combine automated technologies with analytical software) help discover new materials for customers such as Exxon Mobil (39% of sales), Dow Chemical (25% of sales), and Merck. Owning about 300 patents, Symyx generates revenue through research service fees, licensing of its intellectual property, and sales of its analysis equipment and software. It also typically receives royalty payments for products it helps discover.

Symyx's technology allows researchers to perform thousands of experiments at a time, reducing the time and cost to create an increasing number of new chemicals and other compounds.

In 2004 the company acquired IntelliChem, a maker of electronic lab notebooks for recording, utilizing, and managing lab research data. In 2005 it purchased Synthematix, based in Research Triangle Park, North Carolina, for $13 million in cash. Synthematix makes software that allows chemists to design, calculate, and report experiments. Keeping the acquisition momentum, Symyx announced plans to acquire Switzerland-based Autodose, a manufacturer of precision powder-dispensing equipment (which help to measure accurate doses of powdered materials), in mid-2006 for about $6.9 million.

In November of the same year, Symyx formed an independent company specializing in the research and development of applying sensor technologies and equipment to commercial uses. The new endeavor is called Visyx.

EXECUTIVES

Chairman and CEO: Steven D. Goldby, age 65, $656,250 pay
President: Isy Goldwasser, age 35, $586,250 pay
EVP and COO: Paul J. Nowak, age 50, $595,020 pay
EVP and CFO: Jeryl L. Hilleman, age 48, $542,500 pay
EVP and CTO: W. Henry Weinberg, age 60, $656,250 pay (prior to promotion)
VP Investor and Public Relations: Teresa J. Thuruthiyil
VP Marketing: Randall L. (Randy) Clark
Director Business Development and Account Management: Eric Borgstedt
Auditors: Ernst & Young LLP

LOCATIONS

HQ: Symyx Technologies, Inc.
3100 Central Expwy., Santa Clara, CA 95051
Phone: 408-764-2000   **Fax:** 408-748-0175
Web: www.symyx.com

2005 Sales

	$ mil.	% of total
North America	89.8	83
Europe		
Belgium	2.3	2
Other countries	14.2	13
Japan	1.8	2
Total	**108.1**	**100**

PRODUCTS/OPERATIONS

2005 Sales

	$ mil.	% of total
Research services	57.0	52
Research products	26.6	25
Intellectual property licensing	24.5	23
Total	**108.1**	**100**

Selected Research Areas

Automotive products
Chemicals and petrochemicals
Electronic materials
Oil and gas refining
Pharmaceutical development
Specialty polymers

COMPETITORS

Avantium
Battelle Memorial
Bayer
GE Global Research
hte
Mettler-Toledo
SRI International
Waters Corporation

HISTORICAL FINANCIALS

Company Type: Public

Income Statement

FYE: December 31

	REVENUE ($ mil.)	NET INCOME ($ mil.)	NET PROFIT MARGIN	EMPLOYEES
12/05	108.1	12.0	11.1%	350
12/04	83.2	12.9	15.5%	275
12/03	63.0	5.7	9.0%	235
12/02	64.8	5.3	8.2%	213
12/01	60.0	6.3	10.5%	204
Annual Growth	**15.9%**	**17.5%**	**—**	**14.4%**

2005 Year-End Financials

Debt ratio: —
Return on equity: 5.9%
Cash ($ mil.): 168.6
Current ratio: 8.09
Long-term debt ($ mil.): —
No. of shares (mil.): 33.2

Dividends
  Yield: —
  Payout: —
Market value ($ mil.): 905.9
R&D as % of sales: —
Advertising as % of sales: —

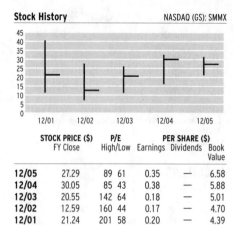

	STOCK PRICE ($) FY Close	P/E High/Low		PER SHARE ($) Earnings	Dividends	Book Value
12/05	27.29	89	61	0.35	—	6.58
12/04	30.05	85	43	0.38	—	5.88
12/03	20.55	142	64	0.18	—	5.01
12/02	12.59	160	44	0.17	—	4.70
12/01	21.24	201	58	0.20	—	4.39
Annual Growth	**6.5%**	**—**	**—**	**15.0%**	**—**	**10.6%**

Synchronoss Technologies

Synchronoss Technologies hopes to help you synch up a variety of customer service efforts. The company provides software and services that communications service providers use to manage tasks such as service activation and customer transactions including additions, subtractions, and changes to service plans. Synchronoss' customers include AT&T Mobility (formerly Cingular), Vonage, Cablevision, and Time Warner Cable. The company is targeting service providers in markets including wireless and wireline communications, as well as Voice over Internet Protocol (VoIP).

Director James McCormick controls a 20% stake in the company, while chairman, president, and CEO Stephen Waldis holds a 10% stake; other significant stakeholders include ABS Ventures (16%), Rosewood Capital (11%), and Vertek Corporation (8%).

Synchronoss was spun off from Vertek in 2000.

AT&T Mobility is responsible for about 80% of Synchronoss' sales.

EXECUTIVES

Chairman, President, and CEO: Stephen G. Waldis, age 38, $902,773 pay
CFO and Treasurer: Lawrence R. Irving, age 49, $443,283 pay
EVP, Business Development and Marketing: Joy A. Nemitz
EVP, Operations: Peter Halis, age 44, $431,709 pay
EVP, Marketing: Omar Tellez
EVP, Product Management and Service Delivery and General Manager, Western Office: Robert (Bob) Garcia, age 37, $469,633 pay
EVP, Sales: Chris Putnam, age 37
VP and CTO: David E. Berry, age 40, $427,783 pay
VP and General Counsel: Ronald Prague
Secretary: Marc F. Dupre
Auditors: Ernst & Young LLP

LOCATIONS

HQ: Synchronoss Technologies, Inc.
750 Rte. 202 South, 6th Fl., Bridgewater, NJ 08807
Phone: 908-547-1250   **Fax:** 908-547-1285
Web: www.synchronoss.com

COMPETITORS

Accenture
Motive
NeuStar
VeriSign

HISTORICAL FINANCIALS

Company Type: Public

Income Statement

FYE: December 31

	REVENUE ($ mil.)	NET INCOME ($ mil.)	NET PROFIT MARGIN	EMPLOYEES
12/05	54.2	12.4	22.9%	117
12/04	27.2	0.0	—	—
12/03	16.5	(1.0)	—	—
Annual Growth	**81.2%**	**—**	**—**	**—**

2005 Year-End Financials

Debt ratio: —
Return on equity: —
Cash ($ mil.): 12.9

Current ratio: 3.30
Long-term debt ($ mil.): 0.7

Net Income History   NASDAQ (GM): SNCR

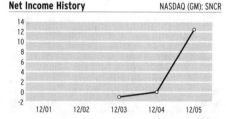

Sypris Solutions

Sypris Solutions makes products for a military family. The company's Electronics Group provides electronics design, assembly, testing, and other services to the National Security Agency and other government agencies and contractors. Sypris also makes analog data recorders, encryption devices, magnetic measurement instruments, and touch screen control software. Its Industrial Group produces forged metal parts, such as axle shafts, for medium and heavy-duty trucks. The company's top customers include Dana Corp. (39% of sales), ArvinMeritor (15%), Raytheon, Traxle Manufacturing, and Visteon. Chairman Robert Gill and his family own nearly half of Sypris Solutions.

The company's Electronics Group (31% of sales) is pursuing new contracts to provide manufacturing services for aerospace and defense customers. Sypris is also targeting the automotive, chemical, and energy markets. The company is looking to expand through value-added services and acquisitions.

Wellington Management owns about 10% of Sypris, while Dimensional Fund Advisors has an equity stake of around 8%.

HISTORY

Sypris Solutions began as a Honeywell unit that designed secure communications systems for the US military and other federal agencies. In 1988, as part of Honeywell's restructuring, the unit was spun off to Group Financial Partners as Group Technologies.

During the early 1990s Group Technologies shifted its focus from military customers to PC manufacturers and acquired the electronics contract manufacturing operations of Philips Electronics. The company went public in 1994 and expanded into Latin America. But the huge debt from the company's spinoff, plus rapid expansion and new work startups, led to losses in 1995 and 1996. That year the company cut a third of its workforce and sold its Badger line of pen-based computers. In 1997 it sold its Latin American operations to rival SCI (now Sanmina-SCI).

Thomas Lovelock, who became CEO in 1997, refocused Group Technologies on its military roots and on niche markets such as industrial controls. The company reorganized through a complicated three-way merger in 1998 and changed its name to Sypris Solutions. Robert Gill and his son Jeffrey, who had held positions at the merged companies, became Sypris' chairman and president, respectively.

In 1999 Sypris bought Lucent Technologies' calibration and repair service business. The company won contracts in 1999 and 2000 from, among others, Boeing, Honeywell, Raytheon, and the US Navy. The company consolidated some of its manufacturing operations due to a decline in demand for heavy-duty trucks and increasing electronic component costs in 2001.

Late in 2003 Sypris acquired a manufacturing plant from Dana Corp. as part of an eight-year agreement for Sypris to supply drive-train and axle components to Dana. Sypris acquired certain of the drive-train and axle components manufacturing assets of Dana as part of a long-term outsourcing agreement between the companies worth about $65 million a year.

In 2004 Sypris acquired a trailer axle beam manufacturing plant from ArvinMeritor as part of a multi-year supply agreement.

Dana, the company's largest customer, filed for Chapter 11 protection from creditors in early 2006.

EXECUTIVES

Chairman: Robert E. Gill, age 80, $284,615 pay
President, CEO, and Director: Jeffrey T. Gill, age 50, $469,615 pay
SVP: Richard L. Davis, age 52, $265,000 pay
Group VP; President, Sypris Electronics: Robert B. (Bob) Sanders, age 48
Group VP; President and CEO, Sypris Technologies: John M. Kramer, age 63, $365,000 pay
VP and CFO: T. Scott Hatton, age 39
VP, Treasurer, and Assistant Secretary: Anthony C. Allen, age 47
VP; President and CEO, Sypris Data Systems: G. Darrell Robertson, age 63
VP; President and CEO, Sypris Test & Measurement: Kathy Smith Boyd, age 52
VP: James G. Cocke, age 56
General Manager, Magnetics Division, Sypris Test & Measurement: Robert Daly
General Counsel and Secretary: John R. McGeeney, age 49, $250,000 pay
Engineering Manager, Magnetics Division, Sypris Test & Measurement: Ernesto Barrantes
Auditors: Ernst & Young LLP

LOCATIONS

HQ: Sypris Solutions, Inc.
101 Bullitt Ln., Ste. 450, Louisville, KY 40222
Phone: 502-329-2000   **Fax:** 502-329-2050
Web: www.sypris.com

Sypris Solutions has manufacturing plants in California, Florida, Kentucky, North Carolina, and Ohio, and in Mexico. It has sales offices throughout the US.

2005 Sales

	$ mil.	% of total
US	475.2	91
Other countries	47.6	9
Total	**522.8**	**100**

PRODUCTS/OPERATIONS

2005 Sales

	$ mil.	% of total
Industrial group	359.6	69
Electronics group		
Aerospace & defense	115.9	22
Test & measurement	47.3	9
Total	**522.8**	**100**

2005 Sales

	$ mil.	% of total
Outsourced services	488.4	93
Products	34.4	7
Total	**522.8**	**100**

Selected Services

Electronics and industrial manufacturing
  Assembly
  Fabrication
Technical
  Calibration
  Certification
  Component testing
  Engineering
  Test and measurement

Selected Products

Data systems
  Analog recorders
  Multiplexers
  Storage systems
  Touch screen control software
Encryption devices
Magnetics
  Current measurement probes and gaussmeters
  Current sensors
  Hall-effect generators
Specialty
  High-pressure closures
  Trailer axle beams
  Transition and insulated joints

COMPETITORS

Advanced Technology Services	Keithley Instruments
Allegro MicroSystems	LaBarge
American Axle & Manufacturing	Linamar
Ampex	Magellan Aerospace
Citation	Metaldyne
CTS	QualMark
Dana	Saturn Electronics
Davis Inotek Instruments	Sparton
Esterline	Suntron
Jabil	Teledyne Technologies
	Tower Automotive
	Transcat

HISTORICAL FINANCIALS

Company Type: Public

Income Statement

FYE: December 31

	REVENUE ($ mil.)	NET INCOME ($ mil.)	NET PROFIT MARGIN	EMPLOYEES
12/05	522.8	5.3	1.0%	2,978
12/04	425.4	7.4	1.7%	2,866
12/03	276.6	8.1	2.9%	1,730
12/02	273.5	11.4	4.2%	1,454
12/01	254.6	6.4	2.5%	1,650
Annual Growth	**19.7%**	**(4.6%)**	**—**	**15.9%**

2005 Year-End Financials

Debt ratio: 37.4%
Return on equity: 2.5%
Cash ($ mil.): 12.1
Current ratio: 2.10
Long-term debt ($ mil.): 80.0
No. of shares (mil.): 18.2
Dividends
  Yield: 1.2%
  Payout: 41.4%
Market value ($ mil.): 181.3
R&D as % of sales: 0.5%
Advertising as % of sales: —

Stock History

NASDAQ (GM): SYPR

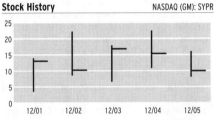

	STOCK PRICE ($) FY Close	P/E High/Low	PER SHARE ($) Earnings	Dividends	Book Value
12/05	9.98	55	28	0.29	0.12	11.77
12/04	15.31	53	26	0.42	0.12	11.54
12/03	16.81	32	12	0.56	0.12	10.10
12/02	10.21	26	10	0.84	0.06	9.66
12/01	13.02	22	6	0.63	—	7.08
Annual Growth	**(6.4%)**	**—**	**—**	**(17.6%)**	**26.0%**	**13.5%**

TALX Corporation

TALX walx the walk when it comes to employment and unemployment. The application service provider (ASP) offers unemployment cost management services and electronic employment and income verification services for mortgage lenders, pre-employment screening companies, government agencies, and corporate employers. The company's UC eXpress services help companies manage unemployment costs and process unemployment insurance claims. The Work Number automated phone service provides employment and salary verification for lenders and credit agencies. TALX also offers its ePayroll service for enabling online benefits and payroll updates, FasTime for time capture and approval, and W-2 eXpress for managing W-2 forms.

Though TALX only began offering unemployment processing and cost management services in 2002, it has rapidly grown that business, which now accounts for nearly 60% of sales. The company further expanded its unemployment operations in 2003 with its purchase of Johnson & Associates, a provider of unemployment cost management and employment tax credit administration services. In 2004 TALX bought the unemployment cost management and employment

verification businesses of the Sheakley Group for $39 million, boosting its UC eXpress and Work Number operations. The company also bought privately held tax credit consulting companies Net Profit and TBT Enterprises, expanding its service offerings. In 2005 TALX acquired the unemployment tax management division of Employers Unity for approximately $30 million in cash. The company in late 2005 acquired the assets of Management Insights (also known as Business Incentives) for about $24 million in cash. The following year it purchased Performance Assessment Network for about $75 million in cash.

In August 2004 TALX finalized a settlement with the SEC regarding the company's restatement of its 2001 and 2002 financial statements. Without admitting or denying any wrongdoing, TALX agreed to pay a fine of $2.5 million to the government under the proposed pact and promised to not violate US securities laws in the future. CEO William Canfield, who owns nearly 7% of TALX, reached a separate agreement with the SEC staff to settle a matter related to the company's financial restatements.

FMR (Fidelity Investments) owns about 13% of TALX. Other leading shareholders are Kayne Anderson Rudnick Investment Management (nearly 9%), Janus Capital (around 8%), investor Ronald J. Juvonen (about 6%), Barclays Global Investors (around 5%), and Ashford Capital (approximately 5%).

EXECUTIVES

Chairman, President, and CEO:
William W. (Bill) Canfield, age 67, $999,550 pay
SVP, CFO, and Assistant Secretary: L. Keith Graves, age 39, $476,588 pay
SVP, Marketing: Michael E. Smith, age 62, $382,775 pay
SVP, Shared Services: John Williamson
SVP, Sales: Doug Kennedy
President, TALX UC eXpress: Edward W. Chaffin, age 53, $310,400 pay
President, The Work Number: Stacey A. Simpson, age 40, $286,933 pay
Senior Director and General Counsel: Tom Werner
Senior Director, Human Resources: Ellen A. Stanko
Public Relations: Pam Stevens
Auditors: KPMG LLP

LOCATIONS

HQ: TALX Corporation
11432 Lackland Rd., St. Louis, MO 63146
Phone: 314-214-7000   **Fax:** 314-214-7588
Web: www.talx.com

PRODUCTS/OPERATIONS

2006 Sales

	$ mil.	% of total
Unemployment tax management	100.8	49
The Work Number services	91.3	44
Tax credits & incentives	13.6	6
Maintenance & support	1.7	1
Total	**207.4**	**100**

Selected Services and Products

ePayroll (personnel information and payment management)
FasTime (electronic timesheet processing)
UC eXpress (unemployment cost management)
W-2 eXpress (automation of tax statement processing)
The Work Number (verification of work and salary history)

COMPETITORS

ADP	RealLife
Ceridian	Sage Software
Gevity HR	TeamStaff
Hewitt Associates	Towers Perrin
Intuit	Ultimate Software
Paychex	Watson Wyatt

HISTORICAL FINANCIALS
Company Type: Public

Income Statement
FYE: March 31

	REVENUE ($ mil.)	NET INCOME ($ mil.)	NET PROFIT MARGIN	EMPLOYEES
3/06	207.4	30.5	14.7%	1,827
3/05	158.4	16.6	10.5%	1,383
3/04	124.4	12.7	10.2%	1,145
3/03	126.1	13.0	10.3%	1,210
3/02	44.5	3.9	8.8%	1,298
Annual Growth	**46.9%**	**67.2%**	**—**	**8.9%**

2006 Year-End Financials

Debt ratio: 59.5%
Return on equity: 18.0%
Cash ($ mil.): 11.6
Current ratio: 1.96
Long-term debt ($ mil.): 110.8
No. of shares (mil.): 32.2
Dividends
Yield: 0.5%
Payout: 14.4%
Market value ($ mil.): 917.8
R&D as % of sales: 4.3%
Advertising as % of sales: —

Stock History
NASDAQ (GS): TALX

	STOCK PRICE ($) FY Close	P/E High/Low		PER SHARE ($) Earnings	Dividends	Book Value
3/06	28.48	41	13	0.90	0.13	5.78
3/05	12.11	32	18	0.51	0.10	7.27
3/04	9.76	36	14	0.40	0.08	9.59
3/03	5.79	22	8	0.40	0.06	8.83
3/02	7.11	131	49	0.13	0.04	8.35
Annual Growth	**41.5%**	**—**	**—**	**62.2%**	**34.3%**	**(8.8%)**

Tarragon

Tarragon is spicing up its real estate activities by taking a more hands-on approach to developing projects. The firm is primarily engaged in the development and renovation of single- and multifamily residences and communities, including conversions from rentals to condominiums. Tarragon also owns and operates some office and retail space, as well as 25 complexes containing more than 6,000 apartments; it has been divesting big chunks of its investment-property portfolio in order to concentrate on its development activities. Tarragon's portfolio contains properties in Connecticut, Florida, New Jersey, Texas, and other states. CEO William Friedman and his family own more than 40% of the company.

Tarragon builds and renovates residences in dense urban locations. The company is converting several Florida apartment communities into luxury condominiums; in 2006 it announced the partial sale of a condo development in Aventura. Tarragon also has projects in New Jersey, including an affordable housing development. In partnership with other developers, the company is also developing two 37-story luxury residential towers in downtown Houston; the first tower was slated to open in 2007.

EXECUTIVES

Chairman and CEO: William S. Friedman, age 62, $950,000 pay
President, COO, and Director: Robert P. Rothenberg, age 47, $1,000,000 pay
EVP and CFO: Erin D. Pickens, age 44
EVP: Michael R. Greenberg
EVP; General Counsel, Tarragon Development: Charles Rubenstein, age 47
EVP, Secretary, and General Counsel: Kathryn Mansfield, age 45
EVP and Treasurer: Todd C. Minor, age 47
EVP Acquisitions: Saul Spitz, age 53, $450,000 pay
EVP Development: Todd M. Schefler, age 48, $635,000 pay
EVP Operations: William M. Thompson, age 45
SVP and Director, Sales and Marketing: Stephen W. Wolfson
Director; President and CEO, Tarragon Development: Robert C. Rohdie, age 65, $1,000,000 pay
President, Tarragon Management: Eileen A. Swenson, age 54
President, Tarragon South Development: James M. Cauley Jr., age 42, $615,000 pay
Auditors: Grant Thornton LLP

LOCATIONS

HQ: Tarragon Corporation
1775 Broadway, 23rd Fl., New York, NY 10019
Phone: 212-949-5000   **Fax:** 212-949-8001
Web: www.tarragoncorp.com

2005 For-Sale Communities

	No.	Home Sites
Florida	32	5,865
New Jersey	8	1,002
South Carolina	3	606
Texas	1	316
New York	1	196
Tennessee	1	21
Total	**46**	**8,006**

2005 Apartment Communities

	No.	No. of Units
Connecticut	16	3,515
Florida	8	1,882
Texas	8	1,727
Maryland	1	459
Georgia	1	360
Tennessee	1	278
Louisiana	1	200
Oklahoma	2	178
Alabama	1	178
Total	**39**	**8,777**

PRODUCTS/OPERATIONS

2005 Sales

	% of total
Homebuilding	75
Equity in income of partnerships & joint ventures	14
Rent	10
Gain on sale of real estate & other assets	1
Total	**100**

COMPETITORS

A.G. Spanos	Highwoods Properties
ARI	IORI
Berkshire Realty	J.F. Shea
Camden Property	Milestone Management
Cousins Properties	Trammell Crow Residential

HISTORICAL FINANCIALS

Company Type: Public

Income Statement

FYE: December 31

	REVENUE ($ mil.)	NET INCOME ($ mil.)	NET PROFIT MARGIN	EMPLOYEES
12/05	596.2	88.5	14.8%	622
12/04	311.0	44.7	14.4%	495
12/03	141.3	31.2	22.1%	430
12/02	114.9	5.5	4.8%	351
12/01	118.6	1.2	1.0%	320
Annual Growth	49.7%	193.0%	—	18.1%

2005 Year-End Financials

Debt ratio: 474.4%	Dividends
Return on equity: 41.2%	Yield: —
Cash ($ mil.): 67.7	Payout: —
Current ratio: —	Market value ($ mil.): 589.1
Long-term debt ($ mil.): 1,319.0	R&D as % of sales: —
No. of shares (mil.): 28.6	Advertising as % of sales: 0.2%

Stock History

NASDAQ (GS): TARR

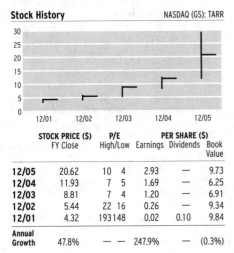

	STOCK PRICE ($) FY Close	P/E High/Low		PER SHARE ($) Earnings	Dividends	Book Value
12/05	20.62	10	4	2.93	—	9.73
12/04	11.93	7	5	1.69	—	6.25
12/03	8.81	7	4	1.20	—	6.91
12/02	5.44	22	16	0.26	—	9.34
12/01	4.32	193	148	0.02	0.10	9.84
Annual Growth	47.8%	—	—	247.9%	—	(0.3%)

Team, Inc.

Go, Team! Team tackles industrial maintenance, mainly by repairing leaks, hot tapping (adding branches to pressurized pipeline), and detecting escaping emissions in piping systems. Team repairs leaks in valves, in-use pipes, and related equipment (usually temporarily until permanent steps can be taken). It also offers field heat treatment and testing and inspection services. The firm makes custom equipment, clamps, and enclosures to augment its standard materials and sealant products. Team serves the chemical and petrochemical, pulp and paper, refining, and steel industries through more than 75 locations worldwide. It also licenses technologies through international locations.

Team was incorporated in 1973. Management controls 17% of the company; FMR and RS Investment Management each own 8%.

In 2004 Team acquired Denver-based Thermal Solutions, Inc., a provider of field heat treating services. Also that year it acquired business assets of Houston-based Cooperheat-MQS, Inc., also a provider of field heat treating services and NDE inspection services. The acquisitions more than doubled Team's revenues.

To reduce its outstanding debt, Team sold its Climax Portable Machine Tools, Inc., subsidiary to an affiliate of Horizon Partners Ltd. for $14.5 million in 2005. Climax makes portable metal-cutting machine tools used for on-site industrial maintenance and served as Team's equipment sale and rental business segment operating through six rental depots in the US and four international depots.

EXECUTIVES

Chairman and CEO: Philip J. (Phil) Hawk, age 51, $575,399 pay
President and COO: Kenneth M. Tholan, age 67, $438,477 pay
SVP Law and Administration, General Counsel, and Secretary: Gregory T. Sangalis, age 50, $296,054 pay
SVP Finance, CFO, and Treasurer: Ted W. Owen, age 54, $318,477 pay
SVP: John P. Kearns, age 50, $259,900 pay
Director Human Resources: Frank Kauffman
Auditors: KPMG LLP

LOCATIONS

HQ: Team, Inc.
    200 Hermann Dr., Alvin, TX 77511
Phone: 281-331-6154   **Fax:** 281-331-4107
Web: www.teamindustrialservices.com

Team has operations and affiliates throughout the US and in Canada, Singapore, Trinidad, and Venezuela.

2006 Sales

	$ mil.	% of total
US	223.5	86
Canada	21.3	8
Other countries	15.0	6
Total	**259.8**	**100**

PRODUCTS/OPERATIONS

Selected Industrial Services

Emissions-control services
Field machining
Field valve repair
Hot tapping
Inspections
Leak repair

COMPETITORS

APi Group
Flowserve
Halliburton
Puget Energy
T. D. Williamson
Xanser

HISTORICAL FINANCIALS

Company Type: Public

Income Statement

FYE: May 31

	REVENUE ($ mil.)	NET INCOME ($ mil.)	NET PROFIT MARGIN	EMPLOYEES
5/06	259.8	10.6	4.1%	2,700
5/05	209.0	4.8	2.3%	2,500
5/04	107.7	5.8	5.4%	988
5/03	91.9	4.4	4.8%	900
5/02	85.1	3.9	4.6%	850
Annual Growth	32.2%	28.4%		33.5%

2006 Year-End Financials

Debt ratio: 62.3%	Dividends
Return on equity: 18.8%	Yield: —
Cash ($ mil.): 2.6	Payout: —
Current ratio: 2.38	Market value ($ mil.): 271.7
Long-term debt ($ mil.): 39.8	R&D as % of sales: —
No. of shares (mil.): 8.6	Advertising as % of sales: —

Stock History

NASDAQ (GS): TISI

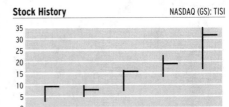

	STOCK PRICE ($) FY Close	P/E High/Low		PER SHARE ($) Earnings	Dividends	Book Value
5/06	31.45	30	15	1.16	—	7.39
5/05	19.00	42	26	0.53	—	5.94
5/04	15.70	23	11	0.69	—	5.25
5/03	7.80	18	9	0.53	—	4.17
5/02	9.25	19	6	0.48	—	3.67
Annual Growth	35.8%	—	—	24.7%	—	19.1%

Technology Research

Technology Research Corporation (TRC) doesn't think electrical devices should be shocking. The company manufactures ground fault protectors, portable leakage current interrupters, and other electrical safety products that protect people and equipment against electric shock and fires. Its products detect electrical leaks and cut off the power to equipment such as copy machines, computers, and printers. While the military (about 29% of sales) remains an important market for TRC, the company is focused on building its commercial customer base. TRC has expanded its Fire Shield product line in response to government safety regulations relating to appliance cords.

Fermont, a division of DRS Technologies (a prime contractor to the US government), is behind around 14% of sales.

Chairman Robert Wiggins owns nearly 4% of Technology Research Corp., including options.

EXECUTIVES

Chairman: Robert S. Wiggins, age 76
President and CEO: Owen Farren, age 50
SVP and Director of Government Operations and Marketing and Director: Raymond B. (Ray) Wood, age 71, $284,890 pay
SVP of Commercial Operations: Edward A. (Ned) Schiff, $188,650 pay
VP of Finance and CFO: Barry H. Black, age 59
VP of Financial Operations and Director of Investor Relations: Scott J. Loucks, age 43
VP of Engineering: Frank S. Brugner
VP of Marketing and Customer Support: Richard Checket
President and General Manager of TRC Honduras: Hamze M. Moussa, $144,400 pay
General Counsel: Bush Ross
Auditors: KPMG LLP

LOCATIONS

HQ: Technology Research Corporation
5250 140th Ave. North, Clearwater, FL 33760
Phone: 727-535-0572   **Fax:** 727-535-4828
Web: www.trci.net

Technology Research has manufacturing facilities in Honduras and the US.

2006 Sales

	$ mil.	% of total
North America	31.8	70
Asia	10.6	23
Europe	2.1	4
Other regions	1.1	3
Total	**45.6**	**100**

PRODUCTS/OPERATIONS

2006 Sales

	$ mil.	% of total
Commercial	32.2	71
Military	13.4	29
Total	**45.6**	**100**

Selected Products

Electra Shield (surge and fire protection)
Fire Shield (extension cords)
Shock Shield (ground fault protection)
Single Outlet Adaptor (portable ground fault circuit interrupter)
Surge Guard (power protection adaptors for RVs)

COMPETITORS

Active Power
American Power Conversion
Beacon Power Corp.
Elgar
Emerson Electric
Fedders
Invensys
Schneider Electric
SL Industries
Vicor Corporation

HISTORICAL FINANCIALS

Company Type: Public

Income Statement

FYE: March 31

	REVENUE ($ mil.)	NET INCOME ($ mil.)	NET PROFIT MARGIN	EMPLOYEES
3/06	45.6	2.1	4.6%	557
3/05	39.4	2.0	5.1%	1,002
3/04	24.3	2.7	11.1%	323
3/03	17.8	1.0	5.6%	306
3/02	16.7	0.2	1.2%	290
Annual Growth	**28.5%**	**80.0%**	**—**	**17.7%**

2006 Year-End Financials

Debt ratio: 10.4%
Return on equity: 11.5%
Cash ($ mil.): 3.1
Current ratio: 3.17
Long-term debt ($ mil.): 2.0
No. of shares (mil.): 5.8

Dividends
  Yield: 0.8%
  Payout: 16.7%
Market value ($ mil.): 42.4
R&D as % of sales: —
Advertising as % of sales: —

Stock History

NASDAQ (GM): TRCI

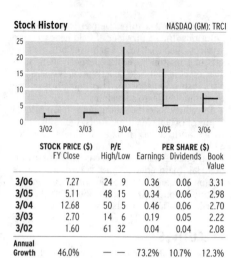

	STOCK PRICE ($) FY Close	P/E High/Low		PER SHARE ($) Earnings	Dividends	Book Value
3/06	7.27	24	9	0.36	0.06	3.31
3/05	5.11	48	15	0.34	0.06	2.98
3/04	12.68	50	5	0.46	0.06	2.70
3/03	2.70	14	6	0.19	0.05	2.22
3/02	1.60	61	32	0.04	0.04	2.08
Annual Growth	**46.0%**	**—**	**—**	**73.2%**	**10.7%**	**12.3%**

TechTeam Global

When your help desk needs a few more players, TechTeam Global is ready to get in the game. The company's business process outsourcing and information technology services include consulting, help desk support, systems integration, technical staffing, and training. Among TechTeam Global's customers are *FORTUNE* 1000 companies, government entities, and other organizations. Several US government agencies together account for about 30% of sales; Ford Motor Company accounts for more than 25%. TechTeam Global maintains help desk facilities in Belgium, Romania, and the US. About 30% of the company's sales come from Europe.

The acquisition of information technology services firm Sytel in 2005 gave a significant boost to TechTeam Global's government-related business and helped diversify the company's revenue mix. As recently as 2003, TechTeam Global reported no revenue from government contracts, and Ford accounted for more than half of the company's sales that year.

Investment firm Ramius Capital Group owns about 10% of TechTeam Global. Kern Capital Management and Costa Brava Partnership each own about 9%. TechTeam Global director Andrew Siegel works for the general partner of Costa Brava Partnership.

HISTORY

Dr. William Coyro, a dentist who kept his practice through 1994, founded National TechTeam in 1979. Coyro relied on several well-placed investors to get National TechTeam started, including a former Chrysler VP and a former director of General Motors' central purchasing. Focused on support services, National TechTeam went public in 1987. It bought Royalpar (a technical staffing firm) in 1989, and in 1993 it began providing client support for WordPerfect and Corel. The company acquired technical trainer Coup in 1996 and opened a Belgium-based call center with Paratel, a European provider of computer telephony services.

Both good and bad, 1997 was an active year for National TechTeam. The company continued to grow, purchasing Drake Technologies (interactive voice response services), WebCentric Communications (Internet telephony software), and Compuflex (an SAP software consultant). But it also battled rising costs related to that growth, an SEC investigation that led to a restatement of earnings, and shareholder suits. National TechTeam formed the GE TechTeam joint venture with General Electric that year to provide call center operations for GE's warranty programs.

To focus on its corporate help desk business, National TechTeam sold its other OEM call center contracts (including contracts with Hewlett-Packard and 3Com) to GE in 1998, which in turn contributed the business to GE TechTeam. National TechTeam also bought Capricorn Capital Group (now TechTeam Capital Group), which provides the company's leasing services. Coyro handed over the CEO title to president Harry Lewis in early 1999 and resigned the chairman post the following year.

The company sold its stake in GE TechTeam (OEM call center services and equipment leasing) to joint venture partner General Electric Warranty Management in 2000. That year the company restructured TechTeam Capital Group — terminating most of its employees, and ceasing to look for new leases.

In 2001 Coyro returned to the company as CEO. The following year National TechTeam established a subsidiary in Sweden. It also changed its name to TechTeam Global.

TechTeam Global greatly expanded its help desk support services with the 2003 purchase of Digital Support Corporation (DSC), which counts numerous US government agencies as customers, for about $6.5 million. Expansion continued with the 2004 purchase of Advanced Network Engineering (A.N.E.), a Belgium-based IT services company.

Also in 2004, TechTeam Global opened a help desk facility in Romania to take advantage of labor costs lower than those in the US and Western Europe.

Founder Coyro stepped down as president and CEO of the company in 2006. IBM veteran Chris Brown was hired to replace him.

EXECUTIVES

Chairman: Alok Mohan, age 57
President, CEO, and Director:
 William C. (Chris) Brown, age 54
COO: Larry W. Granger, age 60, $287,376 pay
SVP, Americas: Kevin P. Burke
VP, CFO, and Treasurer: Marc J. Lichtman, age 39
VP, General Counsel, and Secretary: Michael A. Sosin, age 46
VP, Human Resources: Heidi K. Hagle, age 36
VP, Operations, EMEA: Robert W. Gumber, age 57, $258,355 pay
VP, Operations, North America: Jeffery J. Ruffini, age 45
EVP, Europe, Middle East, and Africa:
 Christoph M. Neut, age 39
VP, Sales and Marketing, North America:
 James M. (Jim) Hoen, age 38, $249,892 pay
President, Digital Support: Peter S. Brigham, age 46
President and CEO, Sytel: Jeannette L. White, age 45
President, TechTeam Government Solutions:
 Dennis J. Kelly Jr.
VP, Sales and Marketing: Mark Francischetti
CTO: Steve Eydelman
Investor Relations Manager: Norma F. Robbins
Media Contact, North America: Deborah Zitny
Auditors: Ernst & Young LLP

LOCATIONS

HQ: TechTeam Global, Inc.
  27335 W. 11 Mile Rd., Southfield, MI 48034
Phone: 248-357-2866   **Fax:** 248-357-2570
Web: www.techteam.com

TechTeam Global has operations in Belgium, Sweden, Romania, and the US.

2005 Sales

	$ mil.	% of total
US	116.5	70
Europe		
Belgium	35.6	21
Other countries	14.4	9
Total	**166.5**	**100**

PRODUCTS/OPERATIONS

2005 Sales

	$ mil.	% of total
IT outsourcing services	73.8	44
Government technology services	55.6	33
IT consulting & systems integration	28.1	17
Technical staffing	8.2	5
Learning services	0.8	1
Total	**166.5**	**100**

COMPETITORS

Aquent
Bartech
Butler International
Capgemini
Capita
CHC
CIBER
COMFORCE
Computer Sciences Corp.
DecisionOne
EDS
IBM
LogicaCMG
Stream
Sykes Enterprises
Technisource

HISTORICAL FINANCIALS

Company Type: Public

Income Statement

FYE: December 31

	REVENUE ($ mil.)	NET INCOME ($ mil.)	NET PROFIT MARGIN	EMPLOYEES
12/05	166.5	5.5	3.3%	2,172
12/04	128.0	4.7	3.7%	1,738
12/03	88.1	(1.0)	—	1,593
12/02	86.6	0.3	0.3%	1,298
12/01	94.6	(3.6)	—	1,286
Annual Growth	**15.2%**	**—**	**—**	**14.0%**

2005 Year-End Financials

Debt ratio: 14.0%
Return on equity: 7.6%
Cash ($ mil.): 34.8
Current ratio: 2.65
Long-term debt ($ mil.): 10.9
No. of shares (mil.): 10.0

Dividends
  Yield: —
  Payout: —
Market value ($ mil.): 100.8
R&D as % of sales: —
Advertising as % of sales: —

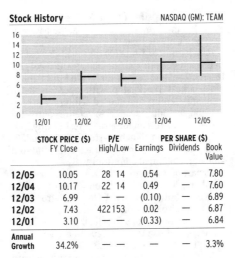

Stock History

NASDAQ (GM): TEAM

	STOCK PRICE ($) FY Close	P/E High/Low	PER SHARE ($) Earnings	Dividends	Book Value
12/05	10.05	28 14	0.54	—	7.80
12/04	10.17	22 14	0.49	—	7.60
12/03	6.99	— —	(0.10)	—	6.89
12/02	7.43	422 153	0.02	—	6.87
12/01	3.10	— —	(0.33)	—	6.84
Annual Growth	**34.2%**	**— —**	**—**	**—**	**3.3%**

Techwell

How goes tech? Well, thank you. Techwell designs decoder chips that convert analog video into digital form, and processors used to display digital video, high-definition television (HDTV), and PC data. Mixed-signal semiconductors, which blend analog and digital elements, are in high demand as popular consumer products, such as cell phones and Apple's iPod, are now capable of playing videos downloaded from the Web or from providers of wireless services. Techwell's OEM customers include Fujitsu, Samsung Electronics (12% of sales), and Toshiba. The fabless semiconductor company was founded in 1997. Technology Crossover Ventures owns about 20% of Techwell.

Techwell's chips are finding their way not only into portable consumer electronics products, such as camcorders and DVD players, but also into automotive display systems and surveillance cameras. Other applications for the company's mixed-signal integrated circuits include advanced TV sets, DVD recorders, set-top boxes, video game consoles, and VCRs. Most of Techwell's sales are to customers in Asia.

The privately held company's auditor found material weaknesses in Techwell's internal financial controls, leading the company to restate its financial results for 2002, 2003, and 2004. Techwell started turning a profit in 2005, but has an accumulated deficit of about $25 million.

As a fabless chip company, Techwell relies on contractors to produce its devices. Taiwan Semiconductor Manufacturing Co. (TSMC), the world's largest silicon foundry, makes Techwell's chips, which are then assembled, packaged, and tested by Advanced Semiconductor Engineering (ASE), one of the biggest contractors in that field.

Techwell counts Credit Suisse, Genesis Microchip, Mitsubishi, Panasonic, and Sanyo among its investors. The company has raised $43 million in private equity funding.

CEO Hiro Kozato owns nearly 7% of Techwell. Sanyo Semiconductor holds around 4% of the company.

EXECUTIVES

President, CEO, and Director: Fumihiro (Hiro) Kozato, age 46, $247,500 pay
VP, Finance and Administration and CFO: Mark Voll, age 51
VP, Sales and Marketing: Dong Wook (David) Nam, age 38, $148,500 pay
CTO: Feng Kuo, age 48, $245,000 pay
Director, Business Development: Tom Krause, age 28
Director, Manufacturing: Joe Kamei, age 49
Auditors: Deloitte & Touche LLP

LOCATIONS

HQ: Techwell, Inc.
  408 E. Plumeria Dr., San Jose, CA 95134
Phone: 408-435-3888   **Fax:** 408-435-0588
Web: www.techwellinc.com

Techwell has offices in China, South Korea, Taiwan, and the US.

2005 Sales

	% of total
South Korea	41
Taiwan	38
China & Hong Kong	16
Japan	4
US	1
Total	**100**

PRODUCTS/OPERATIONS

2005 Sales

	$ mil.	% of total
Video decoders	16.1	45
Security surveillance	13.8	38
LCD displays	5.0	14
Other	1.1	3
Total	**36.0**	**100**

COMPETITORS

ATI Technologies	NXP
Cirrus Logic	Pixelworks
Genesis Microchip	Texas Instruments
Micronas Semiconductor	Trident Microsystems
NVIDIA	Zoran

HISTORICAL FINANCIALS

Company Type: Public

Income Statement

FYE: December 31

	REVENUE ($ mil.)	NET INCOME ($ mil.)	NET PROFIT MARGIN	EMPLOYEES
12/05	36.0	4.5	12.5%	81
12/04	17.3	(1.7)	—	—
12/03	11.1	(5.2)	—	—
12/02	4.8	(6.0)	—	—
Annual Growth	**95.7%**	**—**	**—**	**—**

2005 Year-End Financials

Debt ratio: —
Return on equity: —
Cash ($ mil.): 16.8

Current ratio: 6.26
Long-term debt ($ mil.): —

Net Income History

NASDAQ (GM): TWLL

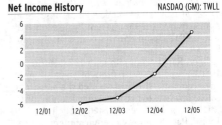

Tejon Ranch

Tejon Ranch has taken stock and is selling the herd. Historically one of the biggest cattle ranches in the US, Tejon Ranch decided its future is in real estate and sold its livestock and feedlot operations. Although livestock accounted for 75% of revenues as recently as 2000, and farming activities still account for about half of its business, the company's 270,000 acres are now considered ripe for residential and commercial development. Its property is served by three major highways, including Interstate 5, which carries 140,000 cars per day through the land. The company's directors, through equity investment firms, control 47% of Tejon Ranch.

One of California's largest privately owned contiguous chunks of land, Tejon Ranch is developing a planned community called Centennial (including a proposed 23,000 homes) and commercial real estate along a 16-mile stretch of Interstate 5 in Los Angeles County. The Tejon Industrial Complex-West is home to gas stations, restaurants, and distribution warehouses; begun with 350 acres, the park is spreading over an additional 1,100 acres. Tejon Ranch is partnering with the Rockefeller Group to develop a foreign trade zone within the complex. It also has a joint venture agreement with DMB Associates to develop Tejon Mountain Village, a 23,000-acre residential/resort community.

In addition to the Centennial residential community, the firm's development pipeline includes Tejon Mountain Village (a golf and spa resort with hundreds of luxury homes planned) and Tejon Industrial Complex-East, located across the freeway from its Complex-West counterpart.

The firm's ongoing crop operations include wine grapes, almonds, pistachios, and walnuts. It also leases land for oil, gas, and mineral production. The movie industry uses the land for filming, and portions are available for quail and wild turkey hunting. Tejon also leases 8,450 acres of land to oil companies for exploration and production of oil and gas.

The ranch plans to sell a 25-mile stretch (some 100,000 acres) of land to the Trust for Public Land that would eventually become permanently protected from development. It is also considering setting aside 37,000 acres as a preserve for the endangered California condor.

HISTORY

In 1843 the Mexican government issued grants for the three ranches and other lands that now make up Tejon Ranch. In 1854 the US government set up an Army post called Fort Tejon (abandoned, 1864). Edward Beale, a government surveyor, acquired Rancho La Liebre in 1855. By 1866 Beale owned all the Tejon Ranch property. A partnership headed by Harry Chandler of the *Los Angeles Times* (then a part of Times Mirror) and land developer Moses Sherman acquired the ranch from Beale's son Truxton in 1912. Tejon Ranch Co. was incorporated in 1936.

Tejon Ranch went public in 1973. During the 1980s, despite a severe drought and a slumping farm economy, the firm resisted the pressure to convert its land to master-planned communities.

It has not, however, resisted publicity. In 1991 Tejon Ranch allowed environmental artist Christo to unfurl 1,700 yellow umbrellas on the ranch for nearly three weeks. It also promotes

Fort Tejon as a site of Civil War reenactments. Robert Stine jumped into the saddle as president and CEO in 1996.

Ranch investor Times Mirror sold its 31% stake in the company in 1997 to focus on its media interests. The next year Tejon Ranch built California's largest truck stop with operator Petro Stopping Centers and started selling nonstrategic land, including a parcel to defense contractor Northrop Grumman for a radar test facility.

In 1999 Tejon Ranch started building a 350-acre industrial complex and agreed to build a 4,000-acre planned community.

As part of its commercial real estate development, in 2000 Tejon Ranch sold 80 acres to IKEA for a distribution facility. A 50-acre Petro Travel Plaza was also constructed. That year the company announced plans to sell all of its cattle operations, and use the proceeds to accelerate its real estate development plans.

In 2001 the company formed a joint venture with Dermody Properties to build a 650,000-square-foot distribution building next to the IKEA warehouse. That year it sold the last of its livestock and its Texas feedlot.

Tejon Ranch firmed up plans for its residential development in 2002, entering into an agreement with homebuilders Pardee Homes and Standard Pacific to develop Centennial, an 11,700 acre master planned community complete with 23,000 homes, as well as retail, office, and industrial properties.

In 2004 the company sold its interest in Pacific Almond, its Arizona almond-processing plant.

EXECUTIVES

Chairman: Kent G. Snyder, age 69
President, CEO, and Director: Robert A. (Bob) Stine, age 59, $625,000 pay
VP, CFO, Treasurer, and Assistant Secretary: Allen E. Lyda, age 48, $270,000 pay
VP and Controller: Carla Walker
VP Commercial and Industrial Marketing: Barry G. Hibbard
VP Government Affairs: Eileen Reynolds
VP Planning and Entitlements: E. Andrew Daymude
VP Corporate Communications: Barry Zoeller
VP and Secretary: Dennis F. Mullins, age 53
VP and General Counsel: Teri Bjorn
Director of Construction: Dean Brown
Human Resources: Elizabeth Grodewald
Investor Relations: Shirlene Barrington
Auditors: Ernst & Young LLP

LOCATIONS

HQ: Tejon Ranch Co.
4436 Lebec Rd., Lebec, CA 93243
Phone: 661-248-3000   **Fax:** 661-248-2318
Web: www.tejonranch.com

Tejon Ranch is located on 270,000 contiguous acres in Kern and Los Angeles counties in Southern California.

PRODUCTS/OPERATIONS

2005 Sales

	$ mil.	% of total
Farming	13.3	51
Real estate	13.1	49
Total	**26.4**	**100**

2005 Crops

	Acres
Almonds	1,686
Wine grapes	1,258
Pistachios	985
Vegetables	810
Alfalfa & forage mix	750
Wheat	600
Walnuts	295
Total	**6,384**

COMPETITORS

Blue Diamond Growers
Calcot
California Coastal Communities
C.J. Segerstrom & Sons
Corky McMillin
Dole Food
Golden West Nuts
Green Valley Pecan
Irvine Company
King Nut Company
Mauna Loa Macadamia Nut Corp.
Meridian Nut Growers
ML Macadamia Orchards
Newhall Land
Paramount Farms
Sun Growers
Sun World International
Texoma Peanut
Young Pecan

HISTORICAL FINANCIALS

Company Type: Public

Income Statement

FYE: December 31

	REVENUE ($ mil.)	NET INCOME ($ mil.)	NET PROFIT MARGIN	EMPLOYEES
12/05	26.4	1.5	5.7%	117
12/04	20.9	0.4	1.9%	104
12/03	18.7	(2.9)	—	110
12/02	21.7	0.2	0.9%	96
12/01	19.3	0.3	1.6%	102
Annual Growth	**8.1%**	**49.5%**	**—**	**3.5%**

2005 Year-End Financials

Debt ratio: 0.3%
Return on equity: 1.1%
Cash ($ mil.): 62.0
Current ratio: 16.00
Long-term debt ($ mil.): 0.4
No. of shares (mil.): 16.5

Dividends
  Yield: —
  Payout: —
Market value ($ mil.): 659.0
R&D as % of sales: —
Advertising as % of sales: —

Stock History

NYSE: TRC

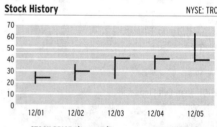

	STOCK PRICE ($) FY Close	P/E High/Low		PER SHARE ($) Earnings	Dividends	Book Value
12/05	39.92	697	431	0.09	—	8.41
12/04	40.80	1,440	1,071	0.03	—	8.06
12/03	41.01	—	—	(0.20)	—	5.13
12/02	29.70	3,513	2,200	0.01	—	5.11
12/01	23.91	1,425	950	0.02	—	5.04
Annual Growth	**13.7%**	**—**	**—**	**45.6%**	**—**	**13.7%**

Temecula Valley Bancorp

Temecula wants to protect your money from bloodsuckers. Temucula Valley Bancorp is the holding company for Temecula Valley Bank, which operates more than a dozen branches and loan and mortgage origination offices north of San Diego. A Small Business Administration (SBA) preferred lender, the company also has nearly 20 SBA loan production offices in towns throughout California and in eight other states. More than 90% of its loan portfolio is secured by real estate, mainly in the form of commercial mortgages and construction and land development loans.

As part of its business strategy, the bank is expanding its SBA lending efforts, adding offices in New Hampshire, New Jersey, and North Carolina.

Chairman, president, and CEO Stephen Wacknitz owns more than 8% of Temecula Valley Bancorp; while director Luther Mohr owns more than 5%.

EXECUTIVES

Chairman, President, and CEO, Temecula Valley Bancorp and Temecula Valley Bank:
Stephen H. Wacknitz, age 66, $1,923,000 pay
EVP, CFO, and Secretary: Donald A. Pitcher, age 56
EVP and COO, Temecula Valley Bank:
William H. (Bill) McGaughey, age 49
EVP and Chief Administrative Officer, Temecula Valley Bank: Frank Basirico Jr., age 51
EVP and Chief Credit Officer, Temecula Valley Bank:
Thomas M. Shepherd, age 51, $275,000 pay
EVP and Senior Loan Officer, Temecula Valley Bank:
Scott J. Word, age 51, $275,000 pay
EVP and Community Banking Officer, Temecula Valley Bank: Martin E. (Marty) Plourd, age 47
EVP and Coachella Valley Regional Manager, Temecula Valley Bank: Jack Brittain Jr.
EVP and East County Regional Manager, Temecula Valley Bank: Thomas P. Ivory, age 52, $282,661 pay
Auditors: Crowe Chizek and Company LLP

LOCATIONS

HQ: Temecula Valley Bancorp Inc.
27710 Jefferson Ave., Ste. A100,
Temecula, CA 92590
Phone: 951-694-9940   **Fax:** 951-694-9194
Web: www.temvalbank.com

PRODUCTS/OPERATIONS

2005 Sales

	$ mil.	% of total
Interest		
Loans	57.9	71
Securities & other	0.2	—
Noninterest		
Gain on sales of loans	13.4	16
Loan broker income	3.4	4
Servicing income	2.7	3
Other	4.4	6
Total	**82.0**	**100**

COMPETITORS

Bank of America
California Bank & Trust
Downey Financial
First PacTrust
UnionBanCal
Washington Mutual
Wells Fargo

HISTORICAL FINANCIALS
Company Type: Public

Income Statement
FYE: December 31

	ASSETS ($ mil.)	NET INCOME ($ mil.)	INCOME AS % OF ASSETS	EMPLOYEES
12/05	869.0	13.9	1.6%	281
12/04	606.8	10.6	1.7%	229
12/03	431.2	7.8	1.8%	194
12/02	310.3	4.2	1.4%	194
12/01	190.0	1.8	0.9%	156
Annual Growth	**46.2%**	**66.7%**	**—**	**15.8%**

2005 Year-End Financials

Equity as % of assets: 6.7%
Return on assets: 1.9%
Return on equity: 27.5%
Long-term debt ($ mil.): 28.9
No. of shares (mil.): 8.9
Market value ($ mil.): 202.6
Dividends
 Yield: —
 Payout: —
Sales ($ mil.): 82.0
R&D as % of sales: —
Advertising as % of sales: —

Stock History
NASDAQ (GS): TMCV

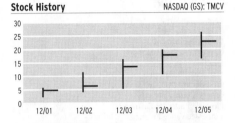

	STOCK PRICE ($) FY Close	P/E High/Low		Earnings	Dividends	Book Value
12/05	22.77	18	11	1.46	—	6.54
12/04	17.75	17	10	1.13	—	4.90
12/03	13.50	18	6	0.89	—	3.57
12/02	6.32	22	9	0.50	—	5.27
12/01	4.78	—	—	—	—	5.87
Annual Growth	**47.7%**			**42.9%**	**—**	**2.7%**

Tempur-Pedic International

Tempur-Pedic (formerly TWI Holdings) hopes you agree that its mattresses and pillows inspire sleep that is *out of this world*. Its visco-elastic foam technology was developed by NASA during the 1970s to help cushion astronauts during liftoff. The foam is used to manufacture mattresses, pillows, and related products. The company's offerings, sold under the Tempur and Tempur-Pedic brand names, are featured globally by retailers (furniture, department, specialty stores), direct response efforts and the Internet, health care channels (chiropractors, medical retailers, hospitals), and third-party distributors. About 36% of Tempur-Pedic's revenue comes from international sales.

In 2005 the company's subsidiary Tempur-Pedic Medical, Inc. formed a partnership with The ROHO Group to sell a jointly branded line of wheelchair cushions that will feature Tempur-Pedic's pressure-relieving material. The next

---

year the medical unit partnered with IES Patient Comfort System, Inc. to develop and manufacture a line of table pads, knee wedges, and positioning cushions for use with medical imaging systems, such as MRI, CT, and PET scans. As part of the agreement, which gives Tempur-Pedic an extended reach into the medical imaging niche, IES will be the line's exclusive distributor.

Together, chairman P. Andrews McLane and Jeffery S. Barber own 24% of the company's stock through their investment firm, TA Associates Fund.

EXECUTIVES

Chairman: P. Andrews McLane, age 57
President and CEO: H. Thomas (Tom) Bryant, age 58
EVP, Global Operations: Matthew D. (Matt) Clift, age 46, $324,480 pay
EVP; President, International Operations:
David Montgomery, age 44, $332,592 pay
EVP and President, North America:
Richard (Rick) Anderson, $300,000 pay
SVP, CFO, and Secretary: Dale E. Williams, age 43, $294,320 pay
SVP, Marketing: Dany Sfeir
SVP, National Accounts: David C. Fogg, age 46, $457,600 pay
VP, Strategic Planning and Chief Accounting Officer:
Bhaskar Rao, age 40
President, Retail Division: Chris Henning
Auditors: Ernst & Young LLP

LOCATIONS

HQ: Tempur-Pedic International Inc.
1713 Jaggie Fox Way, Lexington, KY 40511
Phone: 859-259-0754   **Fax:** 859-514-4422
Web: www.tempurpedic.com

Tempur Pedic manufactures products in New Mexico, Virginia, and also in Denmark.

2005 Sales

	$ mil.	% of total
US	536.3	64
Other countries	300.4	36
Total	**836.7**	**100**

PRODUCTS/OPERATIONS

2005 Sales

	$ mil.	% of total
Mattresses	566.4	68
Pillows	126.2	15
Other	144.1	17
Total	**836.7**	**100**

2005 Sales

	$ mil.	% of total
Retail	639.0	76
Direct	103.2	12
Healthcare	45.9	5
Third party	48.6	6
Total	**836.7**	**100**

COMPETITORS

Mattress Giant
Sealy
Select Comfort
Serta
Simmons Bedding
Spring Air

HISTORICAL FINANCIALS

Company Type: Public

Income Statement

FYE: December 31

	REVENUE ($ mil.)	NET INCOME ($ mil.)	NET PROFIT MARGIN	EMPLOYEES
12/05	836.7	99.3	11.9%	1,300
12/04	684.9	75.0	11.0%	1,300
12/03	479.1	37.6	7.8%	1,020
12/02	298.0	17.1	5.7%	1,000
12/01	221.5	11.9	5.4%	—
Annual Growth	39.4%	70.0%	—	9.1%

2005 Year-End Financials

Debt ratio: 138.6%
Return on equity: 45.1%
Cash ($ mil.): 17.9
Current ratio: 1.89
Long-term debt ($ mil.): 313.7
No. of shares (mil.): 92.4

Dividends
  Yield: —
  Payout: —
Market value ($ mil.): 1,063.2
R&D as % of sales: 0.3%
Advertising as % of sales: 10.9%

Stock History

NYSE: TPX

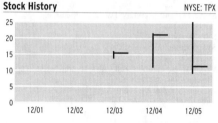

	STOCK PRICE ($) FY Close	P/E High/Low	PER SHARE ($) Earnings	Dividends	Book Value
12/05	11.50	26 10	0.97	—	2.45
12/04	21.20	29 15	0.73	—	2.18
12/03	15.50	41 36	0.39	—	1.26
Annual Growth	(13.9%)	— —	57.7%	—	39.3%

Tennessee Commerce Bancorp

You might say that Tennessee Commerce Bancorp has a genuine *interest* in Music City USA. Founded in 2000, the financial institution is the holding company for Tennessee Commerce Bank. Concentrating on the greater Nashville area, Tennessee Commerce Bank caters primarily to consumers and members of the service and manufacturing industries but avoids retail establishments as customers. Instead of creating a network of branch locations, the bank utilizes Internet options and provides free courier services for deposits.

EXECUTIVES

Chairman and CEO: Arthur F. Helf, age 68, $265,900 pay
President, Chief Lending Officer, and Director: Michael R. Sapp, age 53, $265,900 pay
Chief Administrative Officer, Secretary, and Director: H. Lamar Cox, age 63, $251,875 pay
CFO: George W. Fort, age 48, $160,233 pay
Auditors: KraftCPAs PLLC

LOCATIONS

HQ: Tennessee Commerce Bancorp, Inc.
381 Mallory Station Rd., Ste 207,
Franklin, TN 37067
Phone: 615-599-2274   **Fax:** 615-599-2275
Web: www.tncommercebank.com

PRODUCTS/OPERATIONS

2005 Sales

	$ mil.	% of total
Interest income		
Loans, including fees	22.5	90
Securities	0.9	4
Other	0.3	1
Noninterest		
Sale of loans	1.1	5
Service charges	0.1	—
Other	0.1	—
Total	**25.0**	**100**

COMPETITORS

Capital Bancorp
CFB Bancshares
Civitas BankGroup
Cornerstone Bancshares
First Horizon
First Pulaski National
First Security Group
Greene County Bancshares
Pinnacle Financial Partners
Tennessee Valley Financial Holdings

HISTORICAL FINANCIALS

Company Type: Public

Income Statement

FYE: December 31

	REVENUE ($ mil.)	NET INCOME ($ mil.)	NET PROFIT MARGIN	EMPLOYEES
12/05	25.0	3.1	12.4%	51
12/04	14.0	1.7	12.1%	—
12/03	8.6	0.9	10.5%	—
Annual Growth	70.5%	85.6%	—	—

2005 Year-End Financials

Debt ratio: —
Return on equity: 12.4%
Cash ($ mil.): —
Current ratio: —
Long-term debt ($ mil.): 8.3
No. of shares (mil.): 3.2

Dividends
  Yield: —
  Payout: —
Market value ($ mil.): 81.0
R&D as % of sales: —
Advertising as % of sales: 0.6%

Stock History

NASDAQ: TNCC

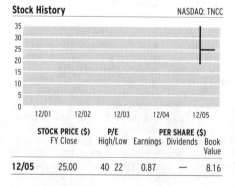

	STOCK PRICE ($) FY Close	P/E High/Low	PER SHARE ($) Earnings	Dividends	Book Value
12/05	25.00	40 22	0.87	—	8.16

Tessera Technologies

Tessera doesn't have to put nutritional labels on its packages. The company licenses a portfolio of patented semiconductor packaging technologies; these designs enable semiconductor makers to produce high-performance packages for use in mobile phones, personal digital assistants, PCs, and other electronic products. Licensees include big chip makers such as Hitachi, Intel, and Toshiba, as well as semiconductor assemblers such as ASE and Amkor. Tessera has taken on the likes of TI and Sharp in lawsuits defending its patents; TI is now among its top customers, along with Samsung Electronics (17% and 20% of sales, respectively). Tessera also offers prototype design, assembly line consulting, and related services.

Tessera has settled litigation with Infineon Technologies and its memory chip spinoff, Qimonda, with a patent licensing agreement. Infineon and Qimonda will pay a total of $50 million upfront to Tessera and will owe royalties on sales of their semiconductors for six years. Memory chip giant Micron Technology has also settled with Tessera, taking out a license on Tessera technology and paying $30 million to the company.

In mid-2006 Tessera acquired Digital Optics Corp., a supplier of micro-optical components, for nearly $60 million in cash.

Tessera has acquired certain assets of Shellcase, a supplier of wafer-level chip size packaging. The acquisition, for around $33 million in cash, takes Tessera into the new markets of wafer-level packaging for image sensors, which go into camera phones and other applications, and for microelectromechanical systems (MEMS). Tessera hired the majority of Shellcase's employees following the purchase.

Tessera sees the Digital Optics acquisition building on the wafer-level image sensor packaging technology assets acquired from Shellcase.

Flextronics, the giant multinational electronics manufacturing services provider, has licensed the Shellcase CF wafer-level assembly technology from Tessera for use in making camera modules.

In 2005 Tessera organized itself into five operating groups: the Advanced Semiconductor Packaging Group; the Emerging Markets and Technologies Group; Tessera Interconnect Materials, Inc.; the Wafer Level Technologies Division; and the Product Miniaturization Division. All but the Product Miniaturization Division are gathered under the company's intellectual property segment, while Product Miniaturization falls under services.

Goldman Sachs Asset Management owns about 14% of Tessera, while Morgan Stanley holds around 10% of the company. Fred Alger Management has an equity stake of 6%. Massachusetts Financial Services (MFS Investment Management) owns about 5%.

EXECUTIVES

Chairman, President, and CEO: Bruce M. McWilliams, age 49, $415,563 pay
EVP and CFO: Charles A. Webster, age 43
EVP, Product Division: Michael (Mike) Bereziuk, age 54
EVP, Licensing Business: Christopher M. (Chris) Pickett, age 39, $330,586 pay
EVP and Director: Al S. Joseph, age 73
SVP and CTO: David B. Tuckerman, age 48
SVP, Corporate Strategy: Nicholas J. (Nick) Colella, age 50, $278,151 pay
SVP, Business Development and Sales: Steve Chen

VP, Finance and Administration, and Corporate
  Secretary: Michael A. (Mike) Forman, age 49
VP, Marketing: Craig Mitchell
VP, Sales: John Riley
Public Relations: Joyce Smaragdis
Auditors: PricewaterhouseCoopers LLP

LOCATIONS

HQ: Tessera Technologies, Inc.
  3099 Orchard Dr., San Jose, CA 95134
Phone: 408-894-0700   Fax: 408-894-0768
Web: www.tessera.com

Tessera has facilities in Israel and the US.

2005 Sales

	$ mil.	% of total
US	40.8	43
Japan	26.9	28
South Korea	24.6	26
Taiwan	1.0	1
Singapore	0.5	1
Other countries	0.9	1
Total	**94.7**	**100**

PRODUCTS/OPERATIONS

2005 Sales

	$ mil.	% of total
Intellectual property	78.2	83
Services	16.5	17
Total	**94.7**	**100**

Services

Assembly line consulting
Prototype design
Test and failure analysis
Training

COMPETITORS

Advanced Semiconductor Engineering
Amkor
ASAT Holdings
FlipChip International
Freescale Semiconductor
Fujitsu Microelectronics
Hynix
IBIDEN
IBM Microelectronics
Infineon Technologies
Intel
Irvine Sensors
Marubeni
Micron Technology
NEC Electronics
Oki Electric
Renesas
Samsung Electronics
Sharp
STMicroelectronics
Sumitomo Electric
Texas Instruments
Toshiba Semiconductor

HISTORICAL FINANCIALS

Company Type: Public

Income Statement				FYE: December 31
	REVENUE ($ mil.)	NET INCOME ($ mil.)	NET PROFIT MARGIN	EMPLOYEES
12/05	94.7	31.5	33.3%	162
12/04	72.7	59.1	81.3%	107
12/03	37.3	9.4	25.2%	86
12/02	28.3	6.5	23.0%	81
12/01	27.0	(8.2)	—	—
Annual Growth	36.9%	—	—	26.0%

2005 Year-End Financials

Debt ratio: —
Return on equity: 20.0%
Cash ($ mil.): 127.6
Current ratio: 13.22
Long-term debt ($ mil.): —
No. of shares (mil.): 45.1

Dividends
  Yield: —
  Payout: —
Market value ($ mil.): 1,166.5
R&D as % of sales: 7.4%
Advertising as % of sales: —

Stock History

NASDAQ (GS): TSRA

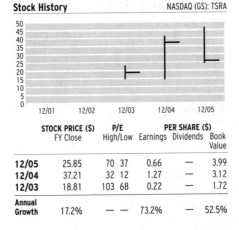

	STOCK PRICE ($) FY Close	P/E High/Low	PER SHARE ($) Earnings	Dividends	Book Value
12/05	25.85	70 37	0.66	—	3.99
12/04	37.21	32 12	1.27	—	3.12
12/03	18.81	103 68	0.22	—	1.72
Annual Growth	17.2%	— —	73.2%	—	52.5%

TETRA Technologies

TETRA Technologies is a smooth operator when it comes to discarded oil wells. The company is composed of three divisions: fluids, well abandonment services, and product enhancement. The fluids unit makes clear brine fluids as well as dry calcium chloride that aid in drilling for the oil and gas industry. Its well abandonment segment decommissions offshore platforms and pipelines. In addition to production testing services for oil and gas operations, TETRA Technologies' product enhancement division also recycles oily residuals that are a byproduct of refining and exploration. The company owns producing properties and has proved reserves of 8 million barrels of oil and 42.3 million cu. ft. of natural gas.

In 2006 TETRA Technologies acquired Beacon Resources LLC, an onshore production testing company, for $15 million coupled with a potential earn-out payment. It also acquired Epic Divers Inc. for $50 million.

EXECUTIVES

Chairman: Ralph S. Cunningham, age 65
President, CEO, and Director: Geoffrey M. Hertel,
  age 61, $770,000 pay
EVP and COO: Stuart M. Brightman, age 49,
  $393,885 pay (partial-year salary)
EVP Strategic Initiatives and Director: Paul D. Coombs,
  age 50, $600,000 pay (prior to title change)
SVP and CFO: Joseph M. (Joe) Abell III, age 51
SVP; CEO, Maritech Resources: Gary C. Hanna, age 48,
  $449,996 pay
SVP: Dennis R. Matthews, age 47
SVP: Raymond D. Symens, age 55, $298,339 pay

VP, Finance and Treasurer: Bruce A. Cobb, age 56
VP, Accounting and Controller: Ben C. Chambers,
  age 50
VP, Administration and Director, Human Resources:
  Linden Price, age 59
VP, Sales and Marketing: Ronald Foster
President, Maritech Resources: G. Matt McCarroll,
  age 46, $397,512 pay
Manager, Investor Relations: Eileen Price
General Counsel and Corporate Secretary:
  Bass C. Wallace Jr., age 46
Auditors: Ernst & Young LLP

LOCATIONS

HQ: TETRA Technologies, Inc.
  25025 I-45 North, Ste. 600,
  The Woodlands, TX 77380
Phone: 281-367-1983   Fax: 281-364-4346
Web: www.tetratec.com

TETRA Technologies has operations in Canada, Brazil, Finland, Mexico, Nigeria, the Netherlands, Norway, Saudi Arabia, Sweden, the UK, the US, Venezuela, and the Virgin Islands.

2005 Sales

	$ mil.	% of total
US	442.1	83
Europe & Africa	72.7	14
Other	16.2	3
Total	**531.0**	**100**

PRODUCTS/OPERATIONS

2005 Sales

	$ mil.	% of total
Fluids	224.6	42
Well abandonment & decommissioning	201.1	38
Product enhancement	105.6	20
Adjustments	(0.3)	—
Total	**531.0**	**100**

COMPETITORS

Baker Hughes
BJ Services
Global Industries
Halliburton
Helix Energy Solutions
Horizon Offshore
Key Energy
Schlumberger
Smith International
Superior Energy

HISTORICAL FINANCIALS

Company Type: Public

Income Statement				FYE: December 31
	REVENUE ($ mil.)	NET INCOME ($ mil.)	NET PROFIT MARGIN	EMPLOYEES
12/05	531.0	38.1	7.2%	1,668
12/04	353.2	17.7	5.0%	1,528
12/03	318.7	21.7	6.8%	1,273
12/02	242.6	8.9	3.7%	1,391
12/01	303.4	23.9	7.9%	1,452
Annual Growth	15.0%	12.4%	—	3.5%

2005 Year-End Financials

Debt ratio: 94.9%
Return on equity: 14.6%
Cash ($ mil.): 3.0
Current ratio: 1.85
Long-term debt ($ mil.): 269.7
No. of shares (mil.): 34.8

Dividends
  Yield: —
  Payout: —
Market value ($ mil.): 530.6
R&D as % of sales: 0.2%
Advertising as % of sales: 0.0%

Stock History

	STOCK PRICE ($) FY Close	P/E High/Low		PER SHARE ($) Earnings	Dividends	Book Value
12/05	15.26	31	16	0.52	—	8.17
12/04	9.43	43	28	0.25	—	10.49
12/03	8.08	28	13	0.31	—	9.53
12/02	4.75	50	28	0.13	—	12.77
12/01	4.66	18	9	0.36	—	12.05
Annual Growth	34.5%	—	—	9.6%	—	(9.3%)

Texas Capital Bancshares

Texas Capital Bancshares is the holding company for Texas Capital Bank, which has about 10 branches in Austin, Dallas, Fort Worth, Houston, Plano, and San Antonio. Targeting small and midsized businesses (with a focus on the energy industry), the bank offers personal and commercial deposit accounts and mortgages, commercial loans and leases, equipment leasing, insurance products, cash management, and trust services. It also provides private banking for wealthy individuals through subsidiary Texas Capital Bank Wealth Management. Online banking is offered through its BankDirect division.

Texas Capital Bancshares was founded in 1998 with a Texas-sized bankroll of $80 million. As a group, executive officers and directors own more than a quarter of the company.

EXECUTIVES

Chairman and CEO: Joseph M. (Jody) Grant, age 67, $422,000 pay
Director; President and CEO, Texas Capital Bank: George F. Jones Jr., age 62, $400,000 pay
CFO and Director; CFO, Texas Capital Bank: Peter B. Bartholow, age 57, $367,500 pay
Houston Regional Chairman, Texas Capital Bank: Joe M. Bailey
Austin Regional Chairman, Texas Capital Bank: Merriman Morton
San Antonio Regional President, Texas Capital Bank: Mark M. Johnson
Fort Worth Regional President, Texas Capital Bank: Michael D. Palmer
President, Texas Capital Bank, Plano: Michael (Mike) Robnett
Director of Human Resources: Lynette Rogers
Director of Investor Relations: Myrna Vance
Marketing and Communications: Tricia Linderman
Auditors: Ernst & Young LLP

LOCATIONS

HQ: Texas Capital Bancshares, Inc.
2100 McKinney Ave., Ste. 900, Dallas, TX 75201
Phone: 214-932-6600   **Fax:** 214-932-6604
Web: www.texascapitalbank.com

PRODUCTS/OPERATIONS

2005 Sales

	$ mil.	% of total
Interest		
Loans, including fees	136.2	72
Securities	30.7	16
Other	0.8	—
Noninterest		
Gain on sale of mortgage loans	8.0	4
Service charges on deposit accounts	3.2	2
Trust fees	2.7	2
Other	6.7	4
Total	**188.3**	**100**

COMPETITORS

Amegy Corporation
Bank of America
BOK Financial
Comerica
Compass Bancshares
Cullen/Frost Bankers
JPMorgan Chase
Prosperity Bancshares
State National Bancshares
Temple-Inland Financial Services
Washington Mutual
Wells Fargo

HISTORICAL FINANCIALS

Company Type: Public

Income Statement

FYE: December 31

	ASSETS ($ mil.)	NET INCOME ($ mil.)	INCOME AS % OF ASSETS	EMPLOYEES
12/05	3,042.2	27.2	0.9%	709
12/04	2,611.2	19.6	0.8%	510
12/03	2,192.9	13.8	0.6%	305
12/02	1,793.3	7.3	0.4%	215
12/01	1,164.8	5.8	0.5%	—
Annual Growth	27.1%	47.2%	—	48.8%

2005 Year-End Financials

Equity as % of assets: 7.1%
Return on assets: 1.0%
Return on equity: 13.2%
Long-term debt ($ mil.): 100.3
No. of shares (mil.): 25.7
Market value ($ mil.): 574.9
Dividends
  Yield: —
  Payout: —
Sales ($ mil.): 188.3
R&D as % of sales: —
Advertising as % of sales: —

Stock History

NASDAQ (GS): TCBI

	STOCK PRICE ($) FY Close	P/E High/Low		PER SHARE ($) Earnings	Dividends	Book Value
12/05	22.38	24	17	1.02	—	8.39
12/04	21.62	30	19	0.75	—	7.70
12/03	14.48	24	18	0.60	—	6.97
Annual Growth	24.3%	—	—	30.4%	—	9.7%

Texas Roadhouse

You might not find Patrick Swayze at this roadhouse, but you will find plenty of ribs and steaks. Texas Roadhouse operates and franchises more than 200 of its signature steak restaurants in more than 40 states. The Southwest-themed eateries serve a variety of hand-cut steaks, ribs, chicken, and seafood, as well as freshly baked bread and other sides — but only for dinner because most locations are closed on weekday afternoons. About 125 Texas Roadhouse locations are company-owned. Kent Taylor, a journeyman of the restaurant business (he has been an executive with such chains as Metromedia Restaurant Group's Bennigan's, Hooters, and KFC), controls about 55% of the voting stock.

The company has followed a vigorous expansion strategy that is heavy on building new corporate-owned locations. In 2006 Texas Roadhouse added about 30 new eateries, 25 of which were company-operated. It also acquired about a dozen locations from franchisees. It plans to open about 30 new restaurants in 2007.

EXECUTIVES

Chairman: W. Kent Taylor, age 51, $64,615 pay
President, CEO, and Director: G. J. Hart, age 49, $759,790 pay
COO: Steven L. Ortiz, age 49, $573,260 pay
CFO: Scott M. Colosi, age 42, $309,659 pay
Director Public Relations: Juli Hart
General Counsel and Corporate Secretary: Sheila C. Brown, age 54, $191,733 pay
Auditors: KPMG LLP

LOCATIONS

HQ: Texas Roadhouse, Inc.
6040 Dutchmans Ln., Ste. 400, Louisville, KY 40205
Phone: 502-426-9984   **Fax:** 502-426-3274
Web: www.texasroadhouse.com

2005 Locations

	No.
Texas	32
Indiana	18
Ohio	17
Colorado	12
Pennsylvania	12
Tennessee	11
North Carolina	10
Kentucky	9
Georgia	7
Arizona	6
Florida	6
Michigan	6
South Carolina	6
Wisconsin	6
Virginia	6
Illinois	5
Louisiana	5
Maryland	5
Massachusetts	5
Iowa	4
Oklahoma	4
Other states	29
Total	**221**

PRODUCTS/OPERATIONS

2005 Locations

	No.
Company-owned	127
Franchised & licensed	94
Total	**221**

2005 Sales

	$ mil.	% of total
Company-owned	448.3	98
Franchised	10.5	2
Total	**458.8**	**100**

COMPETITORS

Applebee's
Avado Brands
Brinker
Carlson Restaurants
CBRL Group
Cheesecake Factory
Darden
Hooters
Houlihan's
Johnny Carino's
Landry's
Lone Star Steakhouse
Metromedia Restaurant Group
O'Charley's
OSI Restaurant Partners
P.F. Chang's
RARE Hospitality
Roadhouse Grill
Romacorp
Ruby Tuesday
Specialty Restaurant Group

HISTORICAL FINANCIALS
Company Type: Public

Income Statement
FYE: Last Tuesday in December

	REVENUE ($ mil.)	NET INCOME ($ mil.)	NET PROFIT MARGIN	EMPLOYEES
12/05	458.8	30.3	6.6%	14,900
12/04	363.0	21.7	6.0%	12,500
12/03	286.5	23.1	8.1%	—
12/02	232.8	17.0	7.3%	—
12/01	159.9	8.0	5.0%	—
Annual Growth	**30.1%**	**39.5%**	**—**	**19.2%**

2005 Year-End Financials

Debt ratio: 3.0%
Return on equity: 15.0%
Cash ($ mil.): 29.0
Current ratio: 0.88
Long-term debt ($ mil.): 6.9
No. of shares (mil.): 65.3

Dividends
  Yield: —
  Payout: —
Market value ($ mil.): 1,014.9
R&D as % of sales: —
Advertising as % of sales: 0.7%

Stock History
NASDAQ (GS): TXRH

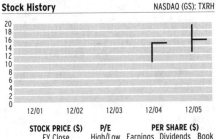

	STOCK PRICE ($) FY Close	P/E High/Low		PER SHARE ($) Earnings	Dividends	Book Value
12/05	15.55	46	30	0.42	—	3.55
12/04	14.77	60	42	0.25	—	5.60
Annual Growth	**5.3%**	**—**	**—**	**68.0%**	**—**	**(36.6%)**

TGC Industries

It might have flopped in the movie theaters, but 3-D technology works in the oil patch, and for TGC Industries. From its inception, TGC Industries has conducted seismic surveys for oil exploration companies in the US. The company principally employs land surveys using Eagle seismic systems, which obtain 3-D seismic data related to subsurface geological features. Employing radio-frequency telemetry and multichannel recorders, the system enables the exploration of rivers, swamps, and inaccessible terrain. TGC Industries also sells gravity information from its data bank to oil and gas exploration companies.

Tidelands Geophysical was founded in 1967 to conduct seismic, gravity, and magnetic surveys for oil and gas companies. It was acquired by Supreme Industries (formerly ESI Industries) in 1980. Tidelands changed its name to TGC Industries in 1986, and the company was spun off that year.

EXECUTIVES

President, CEO, and Director: Wayne A. Whitener, age 53
VP: Daniel Winn
Controller, Treasurer, and Secretary: Kenneth (Ken) Uselton, age 61
Auditors: Lane Gorman Trubitt, L.L.P.

LOCATIONS

HQ: TGC Industries, Inc.
  1304 Summit Ave., Ste. 2, Plano, TX 75074
Phone: 972-881-1099   **Fax:** 972-424-3943
Web: www.tgcseismic.com

TGC Industries operates from its facility in Plano, Texas.

COMPETITORS

Dawson Geophysical
Input/Output
Landmark Graphics
Seitel
Veritas DGC
WesternGeco

HISTORICAL FINANCIALS
Company Type: Public

Income Statement
FYE: December 31

	REVENUE ($ mil.)	NET INCOME ($ mil.)	NET PROFIT MARGIN	EMPLOYEES
12/05	30.9	6.2	20.1%	152
12/04	20.1	2.9	14.4%	—
12/03	8.5	0.6	7.1%	—
12/02	6.3	(1.7)	—	—
12/01	10.1	(1.1)	—	89
Annual Growth	**32.3%**	**—**	**—**	**14.3%**

2005 Year-End Financials

Debt ratio: 23.3%
Return on equity: 43.8%
Cash ($ mil.): 9.5
Current ratio: 2.18
Long-term debt ($ mil.): 6.2
No. of shares (mil.): 14.8

Dividends
  Yield: —
  Payout: —
Market value ($ mil.): 96.2
R&D as % of sales: —
Advertising as % of sales: —

Stock History
AMEX: TGE

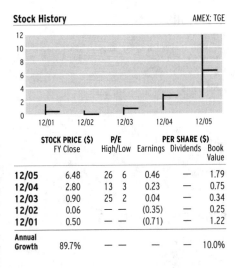

	STOCK PRICE ($) FY Close	P/E High/Low		PER SHARE ($) Earnings	Dividends	Book Value
12/05	6.48	26	6	0.46	—	1.79
12/04	2.80	13	3	0.23	—	0.75
12/03	0.90	25	2	0.04	—	0.34
12/02	0.06	—	—	(0.35)	—	0.25
12/01	0.50	—	—	(0.71)	—	1.22
Annual Growth	**89.7%**	**—**	**—**	**—**	**—**	**10.0%**

TIBCO Software

TIBCO Software can help whip your business processes into tip-top shape. The company's business integration software enables customers to integrate, manage, and monitor enterprise applications and information delivery. TIBCO's software includes applications for coordinating business processes and workflows, securely exchanging information with trading partners, creating and maintaining XML-based documents, and managing distributed systems. Customers come from industries including energy, manufacturing, financial services, and health care. The company also offers consulting and support services.

The company serves more than 2,000 customers, including Reuters, Federal Express, and Lockheed Martin. TIBCO sells and deploys its products directly, as well as through resellers and systems integrators.

The company has expanded its products to include applications for integrating and monitoring business processes. The company acquired Staffware, a provider of business process management (BPM) software, in 2004. Its acquisition of ObjectStar the following year expanded its product portfolio with software for integrating new applications with legacy mainframe databases.

EXECUTIVES

Chairman, President, and CEO: Vivek Y. Ranadivé, age 47, $1,250,000 pay
EVP, General Counsel, and Secretary: William (Bill) Hughes, $519,959 pay
EVP, Office of the CEO: Rajesh U. (Raj) Mashruwala
EVP, Global Field Operations: Christopher Larsen
EVP, Products and Technology: Thomas J. (Tom) Laffey
EVP, Strategic Markets: Murat Sonmez
EVP, Strategic Operations and CFO: Murray D. Rode
SVP and Controller: Sydney Carey
SVP, Worldwide Marketing: Ram Menon
SVP; General Manager, North American Financial Services: John N. Stopper
Auditors: PricewaterhouseCoopers LLP

LOCATIONS

HQ: TIBCO Software Inc.
3303 Hillview Ave., Palo Alto, CA 94304
Phone: 650-846-1000 **Fax:** 650-846-1005
Web: www.tibco.com

2005 Sales

	$ mil.	% of total
Americas		
US	226.0	51
Other countries	5.9	1
Europe		
UK	68.1	15
Other countries	98.9	22
Pacific Rim	47.0	11
Total	**445.9**	**100**

PRODUCTS/OPERATIONS

2005 Sales

	$ mil.	% of total
Service & maintenance	242.0	54
Licenses	203.9	46
Total	**445.9**	**100**

Selected Products Groups

Business optimization
Business process optimization (BPO)
Service-oriented architecture (SOA)

Selected Services

Maintenance and support
Professional (consulting, systems design and integration)
Training

COMPETITORS

BEA Systems
IBM
IONA Technologies
Microsoft
Oracle
Progress Software
SAP
Sun Microsystems
Vitria Technology
webMethods

HISTORICAL FINANCIALS

Company Type: Public

Income Statement

FYE: November 30

	REVENUE ($ mil.)	NET INCOME ($ mil.)	NET PROFIT MARGIN	EMPLOYEES
11/05	445.9	72.6	16.3%	1,505
11/04	387.2	44.9	11.6%	1,360
11/03	264.2	11.4	4.3%	895
11/02	273.4	(94.6)	—	1,030
11/01	319.3	(13.2)	—	1,006
Annual Growth	**8.7%**	—	—	**10.6%**

2005 Year-End Financials

Debt ratio: 5.5%
Return on equity: 8.6%
Cash ($ mil.): 477.6
Current ratio: 3.88
Long-term debt ($ mil.): 48.3
No. of shares (mil.): 210.5
Dividends
  Yield: —
  Payout: —
Market value ($ mil.): 1,762.3
R&D as % of sales: —
Advertising as % of sales: —

Stock History

NASDAQ (GS): TIBX

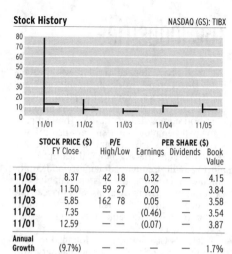

	STOCK PRICE ($) FY Close	P/E High/Low		PER SHARE ($) Earnings	Dividends	Book Value
11/05	8.37	42	18	0.32	—	4.15
11/04	11.50	59	27	0.20	—	3.84
11/03	5.85	162	78	0.05	—	3.58
11/02	7.35	—	—	(0.46)	—	3.54
11/01	12.59	—	—	(0.07)	—	3.87
Annual Growth	**(9.7%)**	—	—	—	—	**1.7%**

Titanium Metals

Titanium Metals (TIMET) is soaking up sales with its titanium sponge. Along with titanium sponge (primary titanium), the company makes melted, mill, and fabricated titanium products. Titanium is a lightweight metal used by commercial and military aerospace manufacturers and the power generation, pollution control, and auto industries. TIMET's aerospace customers, which include Boeing, Rolls-Royce, and United Technologies, use titanium for applications such as jet engine components and wing supports. TIMET operates production facilities in the US and Europe. Dallas billionaire Harold Simmons controls a majority stake in the company.

As a US-based titanium producer, TIMET has enjoyed an advantage over foreign competitors because of tariffs that have been placed on titanium products imported to the US.

EXECUTIVES

Chairman: Harold C. Simmons, age 74
Vice Chairman and CEO: Steven L. (Steve) Watson, age 55
President and COO: Charles H. (Chuck) Entrekin Jr., age 57
EVP: Robert D. Graham, age 50
VP, Finance: James W. Brown, age 49
VP, General Counsel, and Secretary: Joan H. Prusse, age 50, $379,125 pay
Auditors: PricewaterhouseCoopers LLP

LOCATIONS

HQ: Titanium Metals Corporation
5430 LBJ Fwy., Ste. 1700, Dallas, TX 75240
Phone: 972-934-5300 **Fax:** 972-934-5343
Web: www.timet.com

Titanium Metals operates manufacturing plants in France, the UK, and the US.

2005 Sales by Destination

	$ mil.	% of total
US	422.2	56
UK	136.6	18
France	87.8	12
Other countries	103.2	14
Total	**749.8**	**100**

PRODUCTS/OPERATIONS

2005 Sales

	$ mil.	% of total
Mill products	528.6	70
Melted products	112.3	15
Other products	108.9	15
Total	**749.8**	**100**

Selected Products

Fabricated titanium assemblies
Melted products (titanium ingot and slab)
Mill products (forged and rolled from ingot or slab)
  Flat products (plate, sheet, and strip)
  Long products (billet and bar)
  Pipe and pipe fittings
Titanium sponge (basic form of titanium)
Titanium tetrachloride

COMPETITORS

Allegheny Technologies
RTI International Metals
VSMPO-AVISMA

HISTORICAL FINANCIALS

Company Type: Public

Income Statement

FYE: December 31

	REVENUE ($ mil.)	NET INCOME ($ mil.)	NET PROFIT MARGIN	EMPLOYEES
12/05	749.8	155.9	20.8%	2,369
12/04	501.8	39.9	8.0%	2,227
12/03	385.3	(13.1)	—	2,055
12/02	366.5	(111.5)	—	1,956
12/01	568.7	(41.8)	—	2,410
Annual Growth	**7.2%**	—	—	**(0.4%)**

2005 Year-End Financials

Debt ratio: 13.3%
Return on equity: 49.0%
Cash ($ mil.): 17.8
Current ratio: 3.30
Long-term debt ($ mil.): 57.2
No. of shares (mil.): 71.0
Dividends
  Yield: —
  Payout: —
Market value ($ mil.): 1,122.3
R&D as % of sales: 0.4%
Advertising as % of sales: —

Stock History

NYSE: TIE

	STOCK PRICE ($) FY Close	P/E High/Low		PER SHARE ($) Earnings	Dividends	Book Value
12/05	15.81	23	3	0.86	—	7.92
12/04	3.02	12	4	0.28	—	23.85
12/03	1.31	—	—	(0.10)	—	49.73
12/02	0.48	—	—	(0.88)	—	50.03
12/01	1.00	—	—	(0.33)	—	9.36
Annual Growth	**99.4%**	—	—	—	—	**(4.1%)**

TODCO

A leading provider of contract oil and gas drilling services, TODCO provides services to exploration and production businesses operating in the shallow waters of the Gulf of Mexico, in the Gulf Coast inland marine region, as well as in Trinidad and Venezuela. TODCO, which was a part of the R&B Falcon business Transocean acquired, operates a fleet of about 70 drilling rigs consisting of jackups, barges, submersibles, a platform rig, and land rigs. The company, which held an IPO in 2004, also has a 25% stake in Delta Towing, a company that maintains a fleet of marine support vessels; Beta Marine Services LLC owns the other 75%.

The company's dayrate for rig operation ranges from a low of about $20,000 to a high of nearly $60,000. Customers include Apache, Calpine, and Swift Energy.

EXECUTIVES

Chairman: Thomas N. Amonett, age 62
President, CEO, and Director: Jan Rask, age 50, $1,737,605 pay
EVP, Finance and Administration: T. Scott O'Keefe, age 50
SVP, Operations: David J. Crowley, age 47
VP and CFO: Dale W. Wilhelm, age 43
VP, Health, Safety, and Environment: Peter V. Bridle, age 41
VP, Human Resources: Lloyd M. Pellegrin, age 58
VP, International Operations: Bryce H. Dickinson, age 48
VP, Marketing: W. Brad James
VP, Operations: Michael L. (Mike) Kelley, age 48, $347,191 pay
Auditors: Ernst & Young LLP

LOCATIONS

HQ: TODCO
  2000 W. Sam Houston Pkwy. South, Ste. 800, Houston, TX 77042
Phone: 713-278-6000   **Fax:** 713-278-6101
Web: www.theoffshoredrillingcompany.com

TODCO operates drilling rigs located in Trinidad, the US, and Venezuela.

PRODUCTS/OPERATIONS

2005 Sales

	$ mil.	% of total
US Gulf of Mexico segment	236.7	44
US inland barge segment	146.1	28
International segment	101.8	19
Delta Towing segment	49.6	9
Total	**534.2**	**100**

COMPETITORS

Atwood Oceanics
Diamond Offshore
GlobalSantaFe
Helmerich & Payne
Noble
Parker Drilling
Pride International

HISTORICAL FINANCIALS

Company Type: Public

Income Statement

FYE: December 31

	REVENUE ($ mil.)	NET INCOME ($ mil.)	NET PROFIT MARGIN	EMPLOYEES
12/05	534.2	59.4	11.1%	2,420
12/04	351.4	(28.8)	—	1,970
12/03	227.7	(286.2)	—	1,800
12/02	187.8	(5,558.2)	—	2,050
12/01	489.5	(243.4)	—	—
Annual Growth	**2.2%**	**—**	**—**	**5.7%**

2005 Year-End Financials

Debt ratio: 3.4%
Return on equity: 12.2%
Cash ($ mil.): 163.0
Current ratio: 1.87
Long-term debt ($ mil.): 16.6
No. of shares (mil.): 61.5
Dividends
  Yield: 2.6%
  Payout: 103.1%
Market value ($ mil.): 2,341.5
R&D as % of sales: —
Advertising as % of sales: —

Stock History

NYSE: THE

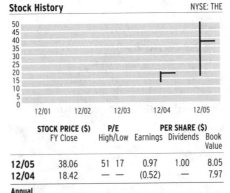

	STOCK PRICE ($) FY Close	P/E High/Low		PER SHARE ($) Earnings	Dividends	Book Value
12/05	38.06	51	17	0.97	1.00	8.05
12/04	18.42	—	—	(0.52)	—	7.97
Annual Growth	**106.6%**	**—**	**—**	**—**	**—**	**1.1%**

Toreador Resources

Toreador Resources is looking to the bull market in oil prices to lift its revenues. The oil and gas explorer, which focuses on exploration opportunities in the international arena, owns royalty and mineral interests in properties located in France, Hungary, Romania, and Turkey. In 2004 the company sold its US hydrocarbon properties, but retains stakes in more than 940 oil and gas wells in Kansas, Louisiana, New Mexico, Oklahoma, and Texas. Toreador, which has proved reserves of 15 million barrels of oil equivalent, sells its oil and gas to refiners and pipeline companies.

Toreador owns 35% of property auction Web site EnergyNet.com and has partial stakes in 3-D seismic projects. In 2005 Toreador reported a natural gas strike at its 37%-owned Akkaya-1 well in Turkey. In 2005 the company acquired Pogo Hungary from Pogo Producing for approximately $9 million.

EXECUTIVES

Chairman: John M. McLaughlin, age 74
SVP and CFO: Douglas W. Weir, age 47, $265,000 pay
SVP, Exploration and Operations: Michael J. FitzGerald, age 54, $290,000 pay

VP, Accounting and Chief Accounting Officer: Charles J. Campise, age 54, $103,125 pay (partial-year salary)
VP, Investor Relations: Stewart P. Yee
Secretary: Shirley Anderson
Director: Nigel J. B. Lovett, age 61
Auditors: Grant Thornton LLP

LOCATIONS

HQ: Toreador Resources Corporation
  4809 Cole Ave., Ste. 108, Dallas, TX 75205
Phone: 214-559-3933   **Fax:** 214-559-3945
Web: www.toreador.net

2005 Sales

	$ mil.	% of total
France	20.6	67
US	7.7	24
Turkey	2.8	9
Total	**31.1**	**100**

COMPETITORS

Avenue Group
Koç
Paladin
Regal Petroleum
Sabanci
TOTAL
Tullow Oil

HISTORICAL FINANCIALS

Company Type: Public

Income Statement

FYE: December 31

	REVENUE ($ mil.)	NET INCOME ($ mil.)	NET PROFIT MARGIN	EMPLOYEES
12/05	31.1	10.6	34.1%	67
12/04	21.0	15.4	73.3%	45
12/03	17.9	4.6	25.7%	36
12/02	23.9	(6.1)	—	40
12/01	15.7	(0.6)	—	40
Annual Growth	**18.6%**	**—**	**—**	**13.8%**

2005 Year-End Financials

Debt ratio: 69.0%
Return on equity: 10.9%
Cash ($ mil.): 93.1
Current ratio: 5.35
Long-term debt ($ mil.): 91.3
No. of shares (mil.): 15.4
Dividends
  Yield: —
  Payout: —
Market value ($ mil.): 324.9
R&D as % of sales: —
Advertising as % of sales: —

Stock History

NASDAQ (GM): TRGL

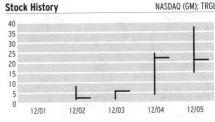

	STOCK PRICE ($) FY Close	P/E High/Low		PER SHARE ($) Earnings	Dividends	Book Value
12/05	21.07	57	23	0.65	—	8.58
12/04	22.19	12	2	1.97	—	5.75
12/03	5.73	29	10	0.20	—	4.00
12/02	2.51	—	—	(0.69)	—	3.21
Annual Growth	**103.2%**	**—**	**—**	**—**	**—**	**24.4%**

Tower Group

Tower Group is hoping to rise high in the insurance business. Through Tower Insurance Company of New York, the company sells specialty property/casualty insurance to individuals and small to midsized businesses in New York, including commercial automobile, general liability, and workers' compensation coverage. Its personal insurance lines focus on homeowners policies for moderately priced homes primarily in the New York City area. Tower Group is hoping to expand its operations into New Jersey and other eastern seaboard states; it agreed to acquire Preserver Group, which sells commercial and personal lines in eight northeastern states, for $68 million in 2006.

In addition to increasing Tower's premium volume, the Preserver acquisition expands its distribution network of retail agencies in the region.

The previous year Tower Group had bought shell insurance company North American Lumber Insurance (since renamed Tower National Insurance Company), acquiring licenses in 11 northeastern states.

Through its general agency subsidiary Tower Risk Management, Tower Group earns commissions on policies it sells for other providers. Tower Risk Management also provides underwriting, claims administration, and reinsurance intermediary services.

CEO Michael Lee owns 14% of Tower Group.

EXECUTIVES

Chairman, President, and CEO: Michael H. Lee, age 48, $875,000 pay
SVP, CFO, Treasurer, and Director:
Francis M. (Frank) Colalucci, age 61, $321,911 pay
SVP and CIO: Jerry Kaiser
SVP and Chief Underwriting Officer: Gary S. Maier, age 41
SVP, Operations: Laurie Ranegar
SVP, Claims, Secretary, and Director: Steven G. Fauth, age 45
SVP, Underwriting Operations: Christian K. Pechmann, age 56, $280,000 pay
SVP and General Counsel: Stephen L. Kibblehouse
Managing VP, Human Resources: Catherine M. Wragg
Auditors: Johnson Lambert & Co.

LOCATIONS

HQ: Tower Group, Inc.
120 Broadway, 14th Fl., New York, NY 10271
Phone: 212-655-2000   **Fax:** 212-655-2199
Web: www.twrgrp.com

PRODUCTS/OPERATIONS

2005 Sales

	% of total
Net premiums earned	75
Ceding commission revenue	11
Investment income	7
Insurance services revenue	6
Other	1
Total	**100**

Selected Subsidiaries

Tower Insurance Company of New York
Tower National Insurance Company
Tower Risk Management Corp.

COMPETITORS

ACE Limited	Nationwide
AIG	OneBeacon
Allstate	Preferred Mutual
CNA Financial	Safeco
Erie Insurance Group	Selective Insurance
GNY Insurance Companies	St. Paul Travelers
The Hartford	State Farm
Magna Carta Companies	Utica Mutual Insurance
Middlesex Mutual	

HISTORICAL FINANCIALS

Company Type: Public

Income Statement

	ASSETS ($ mil.)	NET INCOME ($ mil.)	INCOME AS % OF ASSETS	EMPLOYEES
12/05	657.5	20.8	3.2%	360
12/04	494.1	9.0	1.8%	289
12/03	286.0	6.3	2.2%	—
12/02	186.1	5.6	3.0%	—
Annual Growth	**52.3%**	**168.5%**	**—**	**24.6%**

FYE: December 31

2005 Year-End Financials

Equity as % of assets: 22.0%
Return on assets: 3.6%
Return on equity: 15.2%
Long-term debt ($ mil.): 47.4
No. of shares (mil.): 19.9
Market value ($ mil.): 436.4
Dividends
  Yield: 0.5%
  Payout: 9.7%
Sales ($ mil.): 219.8
R&D as % of sales: —
Advertising as % of sales: —

Stock History

NASDAQ (GS): TWGP

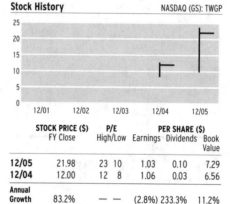

	STOCK PRICE ($) FY Close	P/E High/Low		PER SHARE ($) Earnings	Dividends	Book Value
12/05	21.98	23	10	1.03	0.10	7.29
12/04	12.00	12	8	1.06	0.03	6.56
Annual Growth	**83.2%**	**—**	**—**	**(2.8%)**	**233.3%**	**11.2%**

TradeStation Group

TradeStation is chugging along two tracks in the financial services and software markets. The company offers an electronic trading platform to provide commission-based, direct-access online brokerage services. The platform helps investors develop custom trading strategies and executes orders for equities and futures. Subsidiary TradeStation Technologies offers the TradeStation platform as either a hosted subscription-based service or a licensed software package, and it operates an online trading strategy community site. Brothers, co-founders, and co-CEOs William and Ralph Cruz collectively control just under 50% of the company.

EXECUTIVES

Co-Chairman and Co-CEO: William R. (Bill) Cruz, age 45, $365,000 pay
Co-Chairman and Co-CEO; Director, TradeStation Securities: Ralph L. Cruz, age 42, $365,000 pay
President, COO, and Director; Director, TradeStation Securities and TradeStation Technologies: Salomon Sredni, age 38, $463,000 pay
VP, Finance, CFO, and Treasurer: David H. Fleischman, age 60, $313,000 pay
VP, Corporate Development, General Counsel, and Secretary; Director, TradeStation Securities and TradeStation Technologies: Marc J. Stone, age 45, $285,000 pay
VP, Strategic Relations: Janette Perez
Controller: Mark Glassman
President, TradeStation Securities: Joseph (Joe) Nikolson, age 38, $284,208 pay
Director, Human Resources: Lenia Echemendia
Auditors: Ernst & Young LLP

LOCATIONS

HQ: TradeStation Group, Inc.
8050 SW 10th St., Ste. 4000, Plantation, FL 33324
Phone: 954-652-7000   **Fax:** 954-652-7300
Web: www.tradestation.com

COMPETITORS

Bank of America	JPMorgan Chase
Charles Schwab	Merrill Lynch
E*TRADE Financial	TD Ameritrade
FMR	Terra Nova Gold
Goldman Sachs	UBS Financial Services
Interactive Brokers	

HISTORICAL FINANCIALS

Company Type: Public

Income Statement

	REVENUE ($ mil.)	NET INCOME ($ mil.)	NET PROFIT MARGIN	EMPLOYEES
12/05	100.5	21.1	21.0%	266
12/04	71.8	14.7	20.5%	256
12/03	60.2	11.6	19.3%	238
12/02	48.4	1.8	3.7%	230
12/01	41.0	(21.9)	—	272
Annual Growth	**25.1%**	**—**	**—**	**(0.6%)**

FYE: December 31

2005 Year-End Financials

Debt ratio: —
Return on equity: 32.0%
Cash ($ mil.): 501.2
Current ratio: —
Long-term debt ($ mil.): —
No. of shares (mil.): 44.2
Dividends
  Yield: —
  Payout: —
Market value ($ mil.): 546.9
R&D as % of sales: —
Advertising as % of sales: —

Stock History

NASDAQ (GS): TRAD

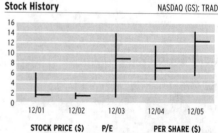

	STOCK PRICE ($) FY Close	P/E High/Low		PER SHARE ($) Earnings	Dividends	Book Value
12/05	12.38	30	12	0.48	—	1.87
12/04	7.03	35	14	0.33	—	1.18
12/03	8.86	51	5	0.27	—	0.72
12/02	1.44	48	23	0.04	—	0.31
12/01	1.56	—	—	(0.49)	—	0.39
Annual Growth	**67.8%**	**—**	**—**	**—**	**—**	**47.8%**

Traffix, Inc.

After shuffling its psychic hotlines out the door, Traffix (formerly Quintel Communications) hopes it's cruising to a better future. Traffix has recast itself as an online advertising and direct marketing firm. The company provides digital ad creation, hosting, and tracking for viewing across its network of entertainment Web sites. Traffix's various Web sites allow the company to cull new names and demographic information for its direct marketing database. The company also provides direct e-mail marketing services using its database of almost 50 million people that have opted to receive promotions in exchange for content. Traffix is also dabbling in Internet dating through its iMatchup.com Web site.

The company had experimented with other direct-to-consumer services that included an ISP (TxNet) and technical support (Click-Help). The company discontinued these operations in 2004.

About 40% of Traffix's revenues are derived from its Web site advertising operations. The remainder of its e-commerce services consist of search engine marketing, e-mail marketing, data sales and rentals, online retail of jewelry and gifts, and Internet game development. Chairman and CEO Jeffrey Schwartz owns about 16% of Traffix.

EXECUTIVES

Chairman and CEO: Jeffrey L. Schwartz, age 56, $605,000 pay
President, Secretary, and Director: Andrew Stollman, age 40, $574,500 pay
COO: Richard Wentworth, age 56, $238,539 pay
CFO: Daniel Harvey, age 48, $237,000 pay
Auditors: Goldstein Golub Kessler LLP

LOCATIONS

HQ: Traffix, Inc.
  1 Blue Hill Plaza, Pearl River, NY 10965
Phone: 845-620-1212   **Fax:** 845-620-1717
Web: www.traffixinc.com

PRODUCTS/OPERATIONS

2005 Sales

	$ mil.	% of total
E-commerce	61.9	99
LEC billed products & services	1.0	1
Total	**62.9**	**100**

Web Properties

Entertainment
  EZ-Tracks.com (music downloads)
  EZ-Greets.com (electronic greeting cards)
  GameFiesta.com
  iMatchup.com (dating)
  Lovefreegames.com
  Music of Faith
  RecipeRewards.com
  Toybox-games.com

Online Sweepstakes
  PrizeAmerica.com
  GroupLotto.com

COMPETITORS

Acxiom Digital
Alternate Marketing
  Networks
Aptimus
Claria
eAcceleration

MyPoints.com
Promotions.com
Q Interactive
Vertis Communications
yesmail

HISTORICAL FINANCIALS

Company Type: Public

Income Statement

FYE: November 30

	REVENUE ($ mil.)	NET INCOME ($ mil.)	NET PROFIT MARGIN	EMPLOYEES
11/05	62.9	2.4	3.8%	170
11/04	37.3	1.0	2.7%	131
11/03	32.4	0.4	1.2%	110
11/02	44.0	2.7	6.1%	104
11/01	32.2	0.4	1.2%	47
Annual Growth	**18.2%**	**56.5%**	**—**	**37.9%**

2005 Year-End Financials

Debt ratio: —
Return on equity: 5.5%
Cash ($ mil.): 28.2
Current ratio: 3.76
Long-term debt ($ mil.): —
No. of shares (mil.): 14.2

Dividends
  Yield: 5.9%
  Payout: 188.2%
Market value ($ mil.): 77.6
R&D as % of sales: —
Advertising as % of sales: —

Stock History

NASDAQ (GM): TRFX

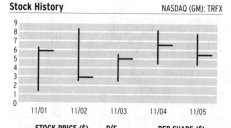

	STOCK PRICE ($) FY Close	P/E High/Low		PER SHARE ($) Earnings	Dividends	Book Value
11/05	5.46	46	26	0.17	0.32	3.13
11/04	6.55	116	64	0.07	0.32	3.22
11/03	5.00	182	84	0.03	0.16	3.36
11/02	2.91	44	13	0.19	—	3.45
11/01	5.85	207	46	0.03	—	2.97
Annual Growth	**(1.7%)**	**—**	**—**	**54.3%**	**41.4%**	**1.3%**

Travelzoo

Travelzoo displays travel deals and specials and related information on its Web sites. Travel companies, such as airlines, cruise lines, hotels, and travel agencies, pay Travelzoo to publicize fares and promotions on Travelzoo's eponymous Web site, through its *Travelzoo Top 20* newsletter, and across its *Newsflash* e-mail alert service. Travelzoo also operates *SuperSearch*, a pay-per-click search engine specializing in travel content. Clients include Budget Rent a Car, Expedia, Marriott Hotels, Royal Caribbean, and United Airlines. Travelzoo commenced its UK operations in May 2005. CEO Ralph Bartel owns 78% of the company, which was founded in 1998.

EXECUTIVES

Chairman, President, and CEO: Ralph Bartel, age 40
CFO: Wayne Lee, age 35
EVP and Director: Holger Bartel, age 39
SVP and General Manager, Travelzoo Europe: Christopher Loughlin, age 32
SVP Sales: Shirley Tafoya, age 43
VP Marketing: Kelly N. Ford, age 38
CTO: Steven M. Ledwith, age 48
Controller: Lisa Su, age 31
Auditors: KPMG LLP

LOCATIONS

HQ: Travelzoo Inc.
  590 Madison Ave., 21st Fl., New York, NY 10022
Phone: 212-521-4200   **Fax:** 212-521-4230
Web: www.travelzoo.com

Travelzoo maintains offices in Chicago, Miami, New York, and the Silicon Valley.

PRODUCTS/OPERATIONS

Selected Clients

American Airlines
Apple Vacations
ATA
Avis Rent A Car
British Airways
Budget Rent A Car
Dollar Rent A Car
Expedia
Fairmont Hotels
  and Resorts
Funjet Vacations
Hawaiian Airlines
Hilton Hotel
JetBlue Airways

Kimpton Hotels
Liberty Travel
Lufthansa
Marriott Hotels
Pleasant Holidays
Royal Caribbean
Spirit Airlines
Starwood Hotels & Resorts
Travelocity.com
United Airlines
US Airways
Virgin Atlantic

COMPETITORS

AOL
Google
Yahoo!

HISTORICAL FINANCIALS

Company Type: Public

Income Statement

FYE: December 31

	REVENUE ($ mil.)	NET INCOME ($ mil.)	NET PROFIT MARGIN	EMPLOYEES
12/05	50.8	8.0	15.7%	70
12/04	33.7	6.0	17.8%	49
12/03	18.0	2.0	11.1%	39
12/02	9.9	0.9	9.1%	27
12/01	6.2	0.4	6.5%	—
Annual Growth	**69.2%**	**111.5%**	**—**	**37.4%**

2005 Year-End Financials

Debt ratio: —
Return on equity: 18.0%
Cash ($ mil.): 44.4
Current ratio: 7.96
Long-term debt ($ mil.): —
No. of shares (mil.): 16.3

Dividends
  Yield: —
  Payout: —
Market value ($ mil.): 357.5
R&D as % of sales: —
Advertising as % of sales: 39.8%

Stock History

NASDAQ (GS): TZOO

	STOCK PRICE ($) FY Close	P/E High/Low		PER SHARE ($) Earnings	Dividends	Book Value
12/05	22.00	222	37	0.45	—	2.99
12/04	95.43	335	22	0.33	—	2.48
12/03	8.70	110	35	0.10	—	0.20
12/02	4.00	175	6	0.04	—	0.09
Annual Growth	**76.5%**	**—**	**—**	**117.8%**	**—**	**180.3%**

Trimble Navigation

Those who fear misplacing their valuables should Trimble. Trimble Navigation makes navigation systems and software based on the US government-owned global positioning system (GPS) satellite network. The company's surveying, mapping, and marine navigation equipment tracks time, longitude, latitude, and altitude. Trimble also makes devices that track ground vehicle and aircraft fleets, as well as timing devices that synchronize communications equipment. Its products are used in engineering, construction, asset management, and agricultural applications. Customers include Robert Bosch, Caterpillar (with which Trimble shares a joint venture), and Nortel Networks. Trimble also runs a joint venture with Nikon.

Trimble is expanding its reach into communications markets by integrating its technology into such wireless communications devices as mobile phones. It is also adapting optical and laser technologies acquired from Thermo Electron for machine guidance and fleet management applications.

Trimble acquired Eleven Technology, a mobile application software developer focused on the consumer packaged goods market, in 2006. The company also expanded its laser scanning business by acquiring the assets — including software for engineering and construction plant design — of BitWyse Solutions. Late in 2006 it purchased Visual Statement, a developer of crime and collision incident investigation software, and XYZ Solutions, a 3-D intelligence software provider. It also agreed to acquire Meridian Systems, a provider of enterprise project management and lifecycle software. Still later in 2006 Trimble bought Spacient Technologies, a privately held provider of field service management and mobile mapping software used by municipalities and utilities. It also agreed to acquire Road, a developer of mobile resource management systems, for about $496 million.

HISTORY

Charles Trimble founded Trimble Navigation in 1978 to design navigation products for recreational boating. In 1982 the company began developing devices using the global positioning system (GPS) satellite network; in 1984 Trimble introduced its first GPS product. The company went public in 1990, 10 days before Saddam Hussein invaded Kuwait. Trimble gained worldwide recognition when Allied troops used its GPS devices during the Persian Gulf War.

The war left Trimble expanding too quickly and overproducing. In 1992 Trimble rebounded after reorganizing to focus on nonmilitary products. Two years later it introduced a low-cost, handheld unit that helped with utilities fieldwork. In 1998 Trimble ceased manufacturing products for general aviation and allied with Siemens to develop GPS products. That year Charles Trimble was named vice chairman after he stepped down as the company's CEO. The company in 1998 also launched a cost reduction plan that cut its workforce by 8%.

The next year Trimble sold its Sunnyvale, California, manufacturing operations to contract manufacturer Solectron, which agreed to make Trimble's GPS and radio-frequency products for three years. Also in 1999 Steven Berglund, a former president of a Spectra-Physics subsidiary, was named CEO of Trimble.

In 2000 Trimble acquired the Spectra Precision businesses of Thermo Electron for about $294 million. That year the US government stopped scrambling GPS signals, opening the door for more precise devices. In 2001 the company formed a subsidiary, Trimble Information Services, to expand the company's wireless location-based services, including fleet management.

The next year Trimble and Caterpillar formed a joint venture, Caterpillar Trimble Control Technologies, to develop advanced electronic guidance and control technologies for earthmoving construction and mining machines.

EXECUTIVES

Chairman: Robert S. Cooper, age 74
President, CEO, and Director: Steven W. Berglund, age 54, $1,432,019 pay
CFO: Rajat Bahri, age 41, $558,940 pay
VP; General Manager, Component Technologies Division: Dennis L. Workman, age 61, $369,859 pay
VP; General Manager, Engineering and Construction Division: Bryn A. Fosburgh, age 43, $439,714 pay
VP; General Manager, Field Solutions Division: Alan R. Townsend, age 57
VP and General Counsel: Irwin L. Kwatek, age 66, $485,504 pay
VP Advanced Technology and Systems: Bruce E. Peetz, age 54
VP Business Transformation: Michael W. Lesyna, age 45
VP Human Resources: Debra J. (Debi) Hirshlag, age 40
VP Operations: Joseph S. Denniston Jr., age 45, $349,819 pay
VP Strategy and Business Development: Mark A. Harrington, age 50, $570,468 pay
General Manager, Survey Division: Jurgen Kliem
Treasurer: John E. Huey, age 56
Auditors: Ernst & Young LLP

LOCATIONS

HQ: Trimble Navigation Limited
935 Stewart Dr., Sunnyvale, CA 94085
Phone: 408-481-8000 **Fax:** 408-481-7781
Web: www.trimble.com

2005 Sales

	% of total
US	54
Europe	31
Asia/Pacific	8
Other regions	7
Total	**100**

PRODUCTS/OPERATIONS

2005 Sales

	$ mil.	% of total
Engineering & construction	529.0	68
Field solutions	127.8	16
Component technologies	54.0	7
Portfolio technologies	37.2	5
Mobile solutions	31.5	4
Adjustments	(4.6)	—
Total	**774.9**	**100**

Products

Engineering and Construction
Global positioning system (GPS) data collection systems (GPS Total Station)
Grade control systems (SiteVision)
Laser transmitters (Spectra)
Optical surveying equipment

Field Solutions
Agricultural information systems
Automatic tractor steering systems (AgGPS Autopilot)
Farm equipment guidance systems
Laser-based water management systems
Mapping equipment (AgGPS 132)
Geographical information systems
GPS data collection and maintenance systems (GeoExplorer)
Component Technologies
GPS chipsets for mobile communication and computing (FirstGPS)
GPS clocks (Thunderbolt)
GPS receivers for battery powered applications (Lassen LP)
Portfolio Technologies
Handheld GPS survey data collectors (Tripod Data Systems Ranger)
GPS receiver cards/modules for military applications (Force 5)
Mobile Solutions
Fleet management system hardware, software, and service (Telvisant)
GPS vehicle module (CrossCheck)

COMPETITORS

AirIQ	Motorola
@Road	Nikon
Garmin	NovAtel
Leica Geosystems	Orbital Sciences
Lowrance Electronics	Remote Dynamics
MacDonald Dettwiler	TOPCON
Magellan Navigation	XATA
Minorplanet	

HISTORICAL FINANCIALS

Company Type: Public

Income Statement

	REVENUE ($ mil.)	NET INCOME ($ mil.)	NET PROFIT MARGIN	EMPLOYEES
			FYE: Saturday nearest December 31	
12/05	774.9	84.9	11.0%	2,462
12/04	668.8	67.7	10.1%	2,160
12/03	540.9	38.5	7.1%	2,150
12/02	466.6	10.3	2.2%	2,050
12/01	475.3	(22.9)	—	2,099
Annual Growth	**13.0%**	—	—	**4.1%**

2005 Year-End Financials

Debt ratio: 0.1%
Return on equity: 16.3%
Cash ($ mil.): 73.8
Current ratio: 2.46
Long-term debt ($ mil.): 0.4
No. of shares (mil.): 53.9
Dividends
  Yield: —
  Payout: —
Market value ($ mil.): 1,913.3
R&D as % of sales: —
Advertising as % of sales: —

Stock History

NASDAQ (GS): TRMB

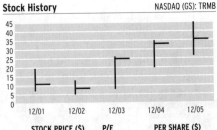

	STOCK PRICE ($) FY Close	P/E High/Low		Earnings	Dividends	Book Value
12/05	35.49	30	18	1.49	—	10.60
12/04	33.04	28	16	1.23	—	9.04
12/03	24.83	33	11	0.77	—	6.97
12/02	8.33	52	22	0.24	—	6.87
12/01	10.81	—	—	(0.62)	—	5.16
Annual Growth	**34.6%**	—	—	—	—	**19.7%**

True Religion Apparel

Who knew you could find religion just by throwing open the doors to your closet? True Religion Apparel (formerly Gusana Explorations) designs, makes, and markets high-end denimwear through its wholly owned subsidiary, Guru Denim. Its apparel offerings (jeans, skirts, denim jackets, and tops) are sold under the True Religion Brand Jeans label in 50 countries including Australia, Canada, China, Europe, Japan, the Middle East, the UK, and the US. Upscale retailers, such as Barneys New York, Bergdorf Goodman, Neiman Marcus, Nordstroms, Saks Fifth Avenue, and about 600 high-end boutiques nationwide sell True Religion's merchandise. The firm has hired Goldman Sachs to advise it on ways to boost shareholder value.

The pricey jeans maker has been considering going private to maintain its double-digit sales and earnings gains, as well as expand its store operations. It then would like to re-emerge by taking the company public again.

In the interim True Religion enlisted the expertise of InGroup Licensing to expand the brand into a lifestyle collection. A licensing deal with Pash Industries, inked in January 2007, gave True Religion its own branded outerwear and its foot in the door at many exclusive shops where Pash already sells.

The company intends to maintain its brand image by limiting distribution of its apparel to the more exclusive boutiques, specialty stores, and department stores. Its jeans retail at price points between $170 to $300 per pair. And the company creates specialty items that retail for up to $500 apiece. It opened its first retail store in California in December 2005 and its first East Coast shop in New York's Soho district in mid-2006. Expanding its retail footprint on the East Coast, the company plans to open a store in Short Hills, New Jersey, in 2007 and Oyster Bay, New York, in 2008.

To control costs and market its apparel as "Made in the USA," True Religion employs contract manufacturers, such as Atomic Denim and Pinc Fashion, in the US and a one-off supplier in Mexico.

To peddle its pricey pants in Asia, True Religion has enlisted Hong Kong-based Bright Unity International to distribute its apparel in Hong Kong, Macao, and China.

EXECUTIVES

Chairman and CEO: Jeffrey (Jeff) Lubell, age 50
President: Michael F. Buckley
COO: Daryl Rosenburg
CFO: Charles A. Lesser, age 58, $282,000 pay
VP, Women's Design; Director, Women's Products, Guru Denim: Kymberly Lubell, age 40, $350,000 pay
Design Director: Zihaad Wells, age 31
Director, Marketing and Public Relations: Emilio Fields
Auditors: Stonefield Josephson, Inc.

LOCATIONS

HQ: True Religion Apparel, Inc.
1525 Rio Vista Ave, Los Angeles, CA 90023
Phone: 323-266-3072   **Fax:** 323-266-8060
Web: www.truereligionbrandjeans.com

COMPETITORS

Abercrombie & Fitch	Levi Strauss
Armani	Phat
Calvin Klein	Polo Ralph Lauren
Diesel	Sean John
Innovo	

HISTORICAL FINANCIALS

Company Type: Public

Income Statement

FYE: December 31

	REVENUE ($ mil.)	NET INCOME ($ mil.)	NET PROFIT MARGIN	EMPLOYEES
12/05	102.6	19.5	19.0%	95
12/04	27.7	4.2	15.2%	—
12/03	2.4	0.0	—	—
12/02	9.2	0.0	—	—
Annual Growth	123.4%	—	—	—

2005 Year-End Financials

Debt ratio: —
Return on equity: 91.1%
Cash ($ mil.): 15.4
Current ratio: 4.99
Long-term debt ($ mil.): —
No. of shares (mil.): 22.2
Dividends
 Yield: —
 Payout: —
Market value ($ mil.): 342.0
R&D as % of sales: —
Advertising as % of sales: 0.1%

Stock History

NASDAQ (GM): TRLG

	STOCK PRICE ($) FY Close	P/E High/Low	PER SHARE ($) Earnings	Dividends	Book Value
12/05	15.40	22 8	0.84	—	1.59
12/04	8.10	42 3	0.20	—	0.36
12/03	1.56	— —	—	—	0.05
Annual Growth	214.2%	— —	320.0%	—	483.0%

Tufco Technologies

Solid-sounding Tufco Technologies works in paper-thin businesses. Tufco's contract manufacturing division custom-converts paper, tissue, and polyethylene film into such products as cleaning wipes and medical drapes. The company's business imaging products include specialty paper rolls (it makes Hamco-brand products for automatic teller machines and cash registers), standardized and customized guest checks (for the restaurant industry), business forms, and other precision-sheeted products. Tufco owns and operates two facilities in the US. Investment partners Robert Simon, Tufco's chairman, and Barbara Henagan jointly own about 58% of the company.

Tufco is cutting costs and looking to its contract manufacturing unit for increased profits. It has shifted manufacturing resources from its former Away from Home division (paper products for public restrooms, sold in 1999) to support new contract manufacturing agreements. In adhering to this strategy of focusing on its printing and converting services, Tufco sold its thermal laminating equipment to a customer in fiscal 2005.

HISTORY

Converting-industry veterans Samuel Bero and Patrick Garland and two colleagues founded Tufco Industries in 1974. In 1992 Robert Simon, a partner of privately held Bradford Venture Partners, teamed up with Bero and Garland and formed Tufco Technologies, which acquired Tufco Industries. The company went public in 1994. Tufco Technologies acquired Dallas firm Executive Converting in 1994 and North Carolina-based Hamco Industries in 1995.

The company moved its corporate headquarters to Dallas in 1996 and named former Scott Paper executive Louis LeCalsey as CEO. Facing a rapidly consolidating paper products industry (and a subsequent decline in outsourced converting production), Tufco began shifting its emphasis from regional contract converting to a broader portfolio of products. In 1997 the company bought Foremost Manufacturing, a St. Louis-based maker of paint sundry products. Heightened competition in 1998 forced Tufco to lower prices in its business imaging sector (its most-profitable unit) and hurt earnings.

Tufco cofounder and long-time executive Patrick Garland died in 1999. That year, to focus on contract manufacturing, Tufco sold its Away From Home business (paper products for public restrooms). In 2000 the company announced that, to cut costs, it would consolidate its paint sundries production by closing its St. Louis, Missouri, plant and expand its Manning, South Carolina, facility.

Contract manufacturing agreements with baby care and cleaning products makers helped Tufco generate a higher income in 2001. But profit margins remained low, so the company dropped inventory levels in an effort to increase profits.

The company's paint sundries unit, which makes drop cloths and latex and vinyl gloves, was sold for about $12 million in 2003 to Trimarco, LLC.

EXECUTIVES

Chairman: Robert J. Simon, age 47
President, CEO, and Director: Louis (Lou) LeCalsey III, age 67, $273,021 pay
EVP, CFO, and COO: Michael B. Wheeler, age 61
VP, Contract Manufacturing Sales and Marketing: Michele M. Corrigan, age 37
VP, Sales and Operations: Madge J. Joplin, age 58, $128,760 pay
Director, Human Resources: Terry Keehan
Senior Manager, Customer Services and Corporate Relations: Jeanne A. Stangel
Sales Manager, Green Bay: Erik Rasmussen
Manager, Flexographic Printing: Ken Kline
Auditors: Deloitte & Touche LLP

LOCATIONS

HQ: Tufco Technologies, Inc.
3161 South Ridge Rd., Green Bay, WI 54305
Phone: 920-336-0054   **Fax:** 920-336-9041
Web: www.tufco.com

Tufco Technologies owns and operates plants in North Carolina and Wisconsin.

PRODUCTS/OPERATIONS

2006 Sales

	$ mil.	% of total
Contract Manufacturing	74.1	74
Business Imaging	26.2	26
Total	**100.3**	**100**

Selected Products and Services

Contract Manufacturing
  Coating
  Custom packaging
  Cutting
  Embossed bonding
  Folding
  Hot melt adhesive laminating
  Rewinding
  Slitting
  Wet and dry wipe converting
  Wide web flexographic printing
Business Imaging
  Rolled and precision-sheeted papers (used in architectural and engineering design, high-speed data processing, point-of-sale systems, automatic teller machines, and office equipment)

COMPETITORS

Bemis
Champion Industries
International Paper
Kimberly-Clark
NCR
Outlook Group

HISTORICAL FINANCIALS

Company Type: Public

Income Statement

FYE: September 30

	REVENUE ($ mil.)	NET INCOME ($ mil.)	NET PROFIT MARGIN	EMPLOYEES
9/06	100.3	0.6	0.6%	395
9/05	79.8	0.7	0.9%	297
9/04	77.8	2.0	2.6%	348
9/03	55.2	0.8	1.4%	296
9/02	75.7	(5.4)	—	454
Annual Growth	**7.3%**	**—**	**—**	**(3.4%)**

2006 Year-End Financials

Debt ratio: 19.3%
Return on equity: 1.7%
Cash ($ mil.): 0.0
Current ratio: 2.77
Long-term debt ($ mil.): 7.1
No. of shares (mil.): 4.5
Dividends
  Yield: —
  Payout: —
Market value ($ mil.): 32.1
R&D as % of sales: —
Advertising as % of sales: —

Stock History

NASDAQ (GM): TFCO

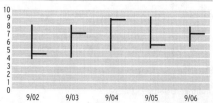

	STOCK PRICE ($) FY Close	P/E High/Low	Earnings	PER SHARE ($) Dividends	Book Value
9/06	7.07	65 46	0.12	—	8.06
9/05	5.65	61 35	0.15	—	7.90
9/04	8.76	21 12	0.43	—	7.74
9/03	7.05	47 24	0.17	—	7.31
9/02	4.47	— —	(1.17)	—	7.09
Annual Growth	**12.1%**	**— —**	**—**	**—**	**3.2%**

Ultra Petroleum

Ultra Petroleum goes to geographic extremes (Wyoming and China) in the search for petroleum products. The independent exploration and production company recovers natural gas from Cretaceous sandstone deposits in the Green River Basin of southwestern Wyoming. The oil and gas company has expanded into China though the acquisition of Pendaries Petroleum, a Houston-based oil and gas exploration company that has large oil assets in Bohai Bay. Ultra Petroleum has proved reserves of 2 trillion cu. ft. of natural gas equivalent in the US, and reserves of 30.4 billion cu. ft. of natural gas equivalent in China. The company also has assets in Pennsylvania and Texas.

EXECUTIVES

Chairman, President, and CEO: Michael D. Watford, age 51, $1,425,000 pay
CFO: Marshal D. (Mark) Smith, $330,637 pay (partial-year salary)
VP Operations: William B. (Bill) Picquet, $184,375 pay (partial-year salary)
VP Exploration, Domestic: Stephen R. Kneller, age 50, $463,333 pay
VP Exploration, International:
George M. (Mike) Patterson, age 59, $183,667 pay
Manager Financial Reporting and Principal Accounting Officer: Kristen Marron
Manager Investor Relations: David Russell
Auditors: Ernst & Young LLP

LOCATIONS

HQ: Ultra Petroleum Corp.
  363 N. Sam Houston Pkwy. East, Ste. 1200, Houston, TX 77060
Phone: 281-876-0120   **Fax:** 281-876-2831
Web: www.ultrapetroleum.com

Ultra Petroleum Corporation operates in Pennsylvania, Texas, and Wyoming in the US, and in Bohai Bay, China.

2005 Sales

	$ mil.	% of total
US	448.7	87
China	67.8	13
Total	**516.5**	**100**

PRODUCTS/OPERATIONS

2005 Sales

	$ mil.	% of total
Natural gas	422.1	82
Oil	94.4	18
Total	**516.5**	**100**

COMPETITORS

Apache
BP
Cabot Oil & Gas
ConocoPhillips
EOG
Exxon Mobil
Kestrel Energy
Royal Dutch Shell
XTO Energy

HISTORICAL FINANCIALS

Company Type: Public

Income Statement

FYE: December 31

	REVENUE ($ mil.)	NET INCOME ($ mil.)	NET PROFIT MARGIN	EMPLOYEES
12/05	516.5	228.3	44.2%	57
12/04	258.0	109.2	42.3%	41
12/03	121.6	45.3	37.3%	31
12/02	42.3	8.1	19.1%	22
12/01	41.2	17.9	43.4%	20
Annual Growth	**88.2%**	**89.0%**	**—**	**29.9%**

2005 Year-End Financials

Debt ratio: 3.6%
Return on equity: 54.4%
Cash ($ mil.): 44.6
Current ratio: 1.43
Long-term debt ($ mil.): 20.6
No. of shares (mil.): 155.2
Dividends
  Yield: —
  Payout: —
Market value ($ mil.): 8,662.2
R&D as % of sales: —
Advertising as % of sales: —

Stock History

AMEX: UPL

	STOCK PRICE ($) FY Close	P/E High/Low	Earnings	PER SHARE ($) Dividends	Book Value
12/05	55.80	43 15	1.41	—	3.68
12/04	24.07	60 13	0.68	—	3.55
12/03	15.89	58 14	0.29	—	2.00
12/02	7.78	157 56	0.05	—	1.40
12/01	4.88	48 0	0.12	—	1.30
Annual Growth	**83.9%**	**— —**	**85.1%**	**—**	**29.7%**

Umpqua Holdings

Umpqua Holdings thinks of itself not so much as a bank but as a retailer that sells financial products through its subsidiary, Umpqua Bank. Consequently, many of the company's more than 130 "stores" in Oregon, southwestern Washington, and northern California feature coffee bars and computer cafes. While customers sip Umpqua Bank-brand coffee, read the morning paper, pay bills online, or check out local bands at the bank's online music store, bank staff pitches checking and savings accounts, mortgages, business and consumer loans, and more. Mortgages make up about 60% of the bank's loan portfolio. Subsidiary Strand, Atkinson, Williams & York provides retail brokerage services through almost 20 locations.

As the largest community bank in Oregon, Umpqua Holdings has branches scattered across the state, in addition to two branches in Clark County, Washington. It entered the Northern California market with its 2004 purchase of Humboldt Bancorp and its 27 branches.

As part of its strategy to continue expanding along the Interstate 5 corridor from Seattle to Sacramento, California, Umpqua Holdings is

buying Northern California-based North Bay Bancorp for more than $150 million.

In 2006 the company acquired another Northern California bank holding company, Western Sierra Bancorp, whose principal subsidiaries, Western Sierra Bank, Central California Bank, Lake Community Bank, and Auburn Community Bank, were merged into Umpqua Bank.

EXECUTIVES

Chairman: Allyn C. Ford, age 64

Vice Chairman: Dan Giustina, age 56

President, CEO, and Director, Umpqua Holdings and Umpqua Bank: Raymond P. (Ray) Davis, age 56, $1,121,000 pay

SEVP and Chief Credit Officer, Umpqua Holdings and Umpqua Bank: Brad F. Copeland, age 57, $431,000 pay

EVP and CFO, Umpqua Holdings and Umpqua Bank: Daniel A. Sullivan, age 54, $397,500 pay

EVP and CIO: Mark J. Tarmy

EVP, Secretary, and General Counsel, Umpqua Holdings and Umpqua Bank: Steven L. Philpott, age 54

EVP, Cultural Enhancement, Umpqua Holdings and Umpqua Bank: Barbara J. Baker, age 56

EVP; President, Umpqua Bank Oregon; President, Commercial Banking, Umpqua Bank: David M. Edson, age 56, $437,500 pay

EVP; President, Umpqua Bank California: William T. (Bill) Fike, age 58, $333,076 pay

Compliance Officer and Investor Relations: Stephen M. (Steve) Bellas

Auditors: Moss Adams, LLP

LOCATIONS

HQ: Umpqua Holdings Corporation
200 SW Market St., Ste. 1900, Portland, OR 97201
Phone: 866-486-7782   **Fax:** 503-546-2498
Web: www.umpquabank.com

PRODUCTS/OPERATIONS

2005 Sales

	$ mil.	% of total
Interest		
Loans, including fees	251.7	76
Investment securities	28.8	9
Other	1.8	—
Noninterest		
Service charges on deposit accounts	21.7	7
Brokerage commissions & fees	11.3	3
Net mortgage banking revenue	6.4	2
Other	8.4	3
Total	**330.1**	**100**

COMPETITORS

Bank of America
Bank of the West
KeyCorp
U.S. Bancorp
Washington Federal
Washington Mutual
Wells Fargo
West Coast Bancorp

HISTORICAL FINANCIALS

Company Type: Public

Income Statement

FYE: December 31

	ASSETS ($ mil.)	NET INCOME ($ mil.)	INCOME AS % OF ASSETS	EMPLOYEES
12/05	5,360.6	69.7	1.3%	1,396
12/04	4,873.0	47.2	1.0%	1,328
12/03	2,963.8	34.1	1.2%	978
12/02	2,556.0	22.0	0.9%	987
12/01	1,428.7	8.6	0.6%	668
Annual Growth	39.2%	68.7%	—	20.2%

2005 Year-End Financials

Equity as % of assets: 13.8%	Dividends
Return on assets: 1.4%	Yield: 1.1%
Return on equity: 9.8%	Payout: 20.6%
Long-term debt ($ mil.): 168.9	Sales ($ mil.): 330.1
No. of shares (mil.): 44.6	R&D as % of sales: —
Market value ($ mil.): 1,271.2	Advertising as % of sales: —

Stock History

NASDAQ (GS): UMPQ

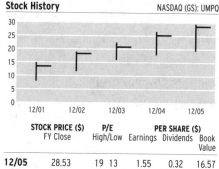

	STOCK PRICE ($) FY Close	P/E High/Low		PER SHARE ($) Earnings	Dividends	Book Value
12/05	28.53	19	13	1.55	0.32	16.57
12/04	25.21	20	14	1.30	0.22	15.55
12/03	20.79	19	14	1.19	0.16	11.23
12/02	18.25	18	12	1.03	0.16	10.30
12/01	13.50	32	18	0.45	0.16	6.78
Annual Growth	20.6%	—	—	36.2%	18.9%	25.0%

Under Armour

Under Armour has yet to show a chink. Since its 1995 foray into the sporting goods market, the maker of performance athletic undies and apparel has risen to the top of the industry pack, boasting more than 90% of the compression garment market. Under Armour is the official supplier of MLB and the NHL. Specializing in sport-specific garments, the company dresses its consumers from head (Cold Weather Hood) to toe (Team Sock). Most products are made from its moisture-wicking and heat-dispersing fabrics, able to keep athletes dry during workouts. Under Armour sells its apparel via the Internet, catalogs, and 3,000 US sporting goods stores such as Cabela's, Dick's Sporting Goods, and the Army and Air Force Exchange.

Under Armour's largest supplier, Joy Textiles in Mexico, supplied some 20% of the company's fabric in 2005. Other suppliers include McMurray Fabrics (in the Dominican Republic) and US companies Milliken & Company and United Knitting.

Nearly all of the company's products are manufactured by third parties, about 50% of which are located in Central and South America. Another 43% are headquartered in Asia, and the remaining 7% are US-based.

Thus far, Under Armour's primary consumer segment has been men (men's products represented some 67% of sales in 2005), but it is actively working to expand its apparel offerings for women and children. Under Armour sells its product lines to almost 400 women's sports teams at NCAA Division I-A colleges.

EXECUTIVES

Chairman, President, and CEO: Kevin A. Plank, age 34, $1,500,000 pay

EVP and CFO: Wayne A. Marino, age 45, $409,697 pay (prior to promotion)

SVP, Marketing: William J. Kraus, age 42, $340,870 pay (prior to promotion)

SVP, Retail: J. Scott Plank, age 40, $333,591 pay

President of UA Europe BV: Ryan S. Wood, age 33, $386,329 pay

VP and General Counsel: Kevin M. Haley, age 37

VP, North American Sales: Matthew C. Mirchin, age 46

VP, Marketing: Stephen J. (Steve) Battista, age 31

VP, Operations: Michael F. Fafaul Sr., age 48

VP, Product Creation and Merchandising: Raphael J. Peck, age 35

VP, Sourcing, Quality Assurance, and Product Development: Kip J. Fulks, age 33

VP, Human Resources: Melissa Wallace

Auditors: PricewaterhouseCoopers LLP

LOCATIONS

HQ: Under Armour, Inc.
1020 Hull St., 3rd Fl., Baltimore, MD 21230
Phone: 410-454-6428   **Fax:** 410-468-2516
Web: www.underarmour.com

2005 Sales

	$ mil.	% of total
US	266.0	95
Other countries	15.0	5
Total	**281.0**	**100**

PRODUCTS/OPERATIONS

2005 Sales

	$ mil.	% of total
Men's	189.6	67
Women's	53.5	19
Youth	18.8	7
Licensing	9.7	4
Accessories	9.4	3
Total	**281.0**	**100**

COMPETITORS

adidas
Calvin Klein
Columbia Sportswear
Fruit of the Loom
Hanesbrands
Jockey International
K2
L.L. Bean
NIKE
North Face
Patagonia
Reebok
Victoria's Secret Stores
Warnaco Swimwear

HISTORICAL FINANCIALS

Company Type: Public

Income Statement

FYE: December 31

	REVENUE ($ mil.)	NET INCOME ($ mil.)	NET PROFIT MARGIN	EMPLOYEES
12/05	281.0	19.7	7.0%	610
12/04	205.2	16.3	7.9%	—
12/03	115.4	5.8	5.0%	—
12/02	49.5	2.8	5.7%	175
Annual Growth	78.4%	91.6%	—	51.6%

2005 Year-End Financials

Debt ratio: 3.0%
Return on equity: 22.9%
Cash ($ mil.): 63.0
Current ratio: 3.81
Long-term debt ($ mil.): 4.6
No. of shares (mil.): —

Dividends
Yield: —
Payout: —
Market value ($ mil.): —
R&D as % of sales: —
Advertising as % of sales: 10.8%

Stock History

NYSE: UA

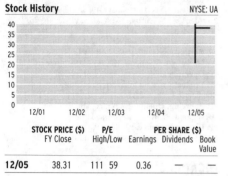

	STOCK PRICE ($) FY Close	P/E High/Low		PER SHARE ($) Earnings	Dividends	Book Value
12/05	38.31	111	59	0.36	—	—

Unica Corporation

Unica can help your company predict the behavior of even the most unique clients. The company's enterprise marketing software helps businesses identify, measure, and predict customer behaviors and preferences. Its software suite enables users to conduct large-scale, personalized marketing campaigns, incorporate enterprise data, and analyze the effectiveness of marketing efforts. Unica also offers consulting, installation, integration, and training services. Major shareholders in the company include chairman, president, and CEO Yuchun Lee (36%), Summit Partners (18%), director Bruce Evans (18%), and David Cheung (17%).

The company's customers come from a variety of fields, including financial services, health care, manufacturing, retail, and telecommunications.

In late 2005 the company acquired MarketSoft for $7.25 million.

Founded in 1992, Unica received early funding from Summit Partners and JMI Equity Fund.

EXECUTIVES

Chairman, President, and CEO: Yuchun Lee, age 41, $519,167 pay
SVP and CFO: Ralph A. Goldwasser, age 59, $214,902 pay (partial-year salary)
VP Business Development: Kevin Keane
VP Consulting Services: Richard Hale, age 56
VP Engineering: John Hogan, age 42, $226,667 pay
SVP and Chief Marketing Officer: Carol Meyers, age 45, $257,834 pay
SVP Worldwide Sales: Eric Schnadig, age 40, $376,667 pay
SVP Corporate Development, and General Manager, Internet Marketing Solutions Group: David Sweet, age 43
Senior Director, Marketing Communications: Carol Wolicki
VP, General Counsel, and Secretary: Jonathan D. (Jon) Salon, age 38
Auditors: Ernst & Young LLP

LOCATIONS

HQ: Unica Corporation
Reservoir Place North, 170 Tracer Ln.,
Waltham, MA 02451
Phone: 781-839-8000   **Fax:** 781-890-0012
Web: www.unica.com

2006 Sales

	$ mil.	% of total
North America	65.0	79
Other regions	17.4	21
Total	**82.4**	**100**

PRODUCTS/OPERATIONS

2006 Sales

	$ mil.	% of total
Maintenance & services	42.8	52
License	39.6	48
Total	**82.4**	**100**

Selected Products

Affinium Campaign (customer interaction and campaign management)
Affinium eMessage (creates, personalizes, optimizes, and tracks e-mail marketing)
Affinium Interact (online customer personalization)
Affinium Model (predictive modeling software)
Affinium Report (monitors, measures, and reports marketing status and results)

Selected Services

Consulting
Design recommendation
Implementation
Installation
Operational assessment
Training

COMPETITORS

Applix
Art Technology Group
CA
KANA
Marketswitch
Onyx Software
Oracle
Pivotal
SAP

HISTORICAL FINANCIALS

Company Type: Public

Income Statement

FYE: September 30

	REVENUE ($ mil.)	NET INCOME ($ mil.)	NET PROFIT MARGIN	EMPLOYEES
9/06	82.4	0.7	0.8%	395
9/05	63.5	4.5	7.1%	284
9/04	48.7	3.5	7.2%	—
9/03	31.3	2.5	8.0%	—
Annual Growth	**38.1%**	**(34.6%)**	**—**	**39.1%**

2006 Year-End Financials

Debt ratio: —
Return on equity: 1.4%
Cash ($ mil.): 40.3
Current ratio: 1.53
Long-term debt ($ mil.): —
No. of shares (mil.): 19.6

Dividends
Yield: —
Payout: —
Market value ($ mil.): 201.9
R&D as % of sales: —
Advertising as % of sales: —

Stock History

NASDAQ (GM): UNCA

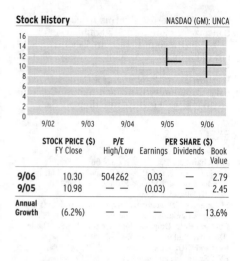

	STOCK PRICE ($) FY Close	P/E High/Low		PER SHARE ($) Earnings	Dividends	Book Value
9/06	10.30	504	262	0.03	—	2.79
9/05	10.98	—	—	(0.03)	—	2.45
Annual Growth	**(6.2%)**	**—**	**—**	**—**	**—**	**13.6%**

Union Drilling

A leading independent US drilling contractor, Union Drilling unifies hydrocarbons and pipelines via the drill bit. Operating 70 drilling rigs, the company provides contract land drilling services, primarily in the Appalachian Basin, where the majority of its rigs operate. It also has rigs operating in the Arkoma and Fort Worth basins, the Uinta Basin and the Piceance Basin in eastern Utah and western Colorado. Union Drilling's primary customers include CONSOL, Fortuna, and Great Lakes Energy. Union Drilling is controlled by a unit of Morgan Stanley.

Union Drilling was formed in 1997 to acquire the drilling equipment assets of Equitable Resources Energy. In 2005 the company acquired drilling contractors Thornton Drilling Company and SPA Drilling, LP.

EXECUTIVES

Chairman: Thomas H. O'Neill Jr., age 64
Vice Chairman: Theodore James (T. J.) Glauthier, age 62
President, CEO, and Interim EVP, Operations: Christopher D. (Chris) Strong, age 47
VP, CFO, Treasurer, and Secretary: Dan E. Steigerwald, age 64, $211,399 pay
Controller: A. J. Verdecchia
CIO: Tim Henline
Director, Environment, Health, and Safety: Rick Waltemire
Director, Human Resources: Lee Spangler
Auditors: Ernst & Young LLP

LOCATIONS

HQ: Union Drilling, Inc.
4055 International Plaza, Fort Worth, TX 76109
Phone: 817-735-8793   **Fax:** 817-735-9226
Web: www.uniondrilling.com

Union Drilling has offices and operating facilities in Buckhannon, West Virginia; Norton, Virginia; Pittsburgh and Punxsutawney, Pennsylvania; and Vernal, Utah.

2005 Sales

	$ mil.	% of total
Nonaffiliates	136.4	96
Related party	5.2	4
Total	**141.6**	**100**

COMPETITORS

Grey Wolf
Helmerich & Payne
Nabors Industries
Patterson-UTI Energy
Petroleum Development
Pride International
Resource America
Unit Corporation

HISTORICAL FINANCIALS
Company Type: Public

Income Statement
FYE: December 31

	REVENUE ($ mil.)	NET INCOME ($ mil.)	NET PROFIT MARGIN	EMPLOYEES
12/05	141.6	5.6	4.0%	1,300
12/04	67.8	3.5	5.2%	1,060
12/03	58.1	(2.6)	—	—
12/02	47.0	(3.4)	—	—
12/01	78.0	—	—	800
Annual Growth	16.1%	—	—	12.9%

2005 Year-End Financials

Debt ratio: 4.4%
Return on equity: 6.4%
Cash ($ mil.): 2.4
Current ratio: 2.21
Long-term debt ($ mil.): 5.8
No. of shares (mil.): 21.2

Dividends
　Yield: —
　Payout: —
Market value ($ mil.): 307.5
R&D as % of sales: —
Advertising as % of sales: —

Stock History
NASDAQ (GM): UDRL

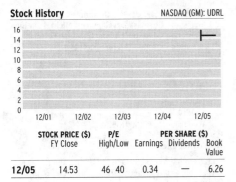

	STOCK PRICE ($) FY Close	P/E High/Low	PER SHARE ($) Earnings	Dividends	Book Value
12/05	14.53	46　40	0.34	—	6.26

Unit Corporation

It's oil for one and one for oil. With a single-minded focus on hydrocarbons, Unit conducts onshore drilling of oil and natural gas wells for customers in the Gulf Coast, Midcontinent, and Rocky Mountain regions of the US. It maintains a drilling fleet of 111 rigs having depth capacities of 5,000 feet to 40,000 feet. Unit also explores for and produces oil and gas in the Anadarko and Arkoma basins of Oklahoma and Texas. The company owns stakes in more than 6,470 wells. It has estimated proved reserves of 352.8 billion cu. ft. of natural gas and 9.9 million barrels of oil. Unit acquired Serdrilco in 2003 and PetroCorp and Sauer Drilling in 2004. In 2005 Unit bought a Strata Drilling subsidiary.

In 2005 the company's Unit Petroleum subsidiary acquired oil and natural gas properties (with proved reserves of 14 billion cu. ft. of natural gas equivalent) in Oklahoma from a private company for $23 million. That year, Unit's Unit

Drilling Company subsidiary acquired seven drilling rigs from Texas Wyoming Drilling Inc. for $32 million. In 2005 Unit also acquired oil and natural gas properties in Arkansas, Oklahoma, and Texas from a group of private entities for $82 million.

In 2006 the company also bought oil and natural gas properties in New Mexico, Oklahoma, and Texas from private owners for about $32.4 million.

EXECUTIVES

Chairman: John G. Nikkel, age 70, $187,083 pay (prior to title change)
President, CEO, and Director: Larry D. Pinkston, age 50, $353,333 pay (partial-year salary)
EVP Drilling, Unit Drilling Company: John Cromling, $224,416 pay (partial-year salary)
SVP, Secretary, and General Counsel: Mark E. Schell Sr., age 47, $278,333 pay
SVP Exploration, Unit Petroleum: Brad Guidry, $223,749 pay (partial-year salary)
CFO and Treasurer: David T. Merrill, age 44, $211,533 pay
VP and Exploration Coordinator, Unit Petroleum: Phil Livingston
Auditors: PricewaterhouseCoopers LLP

LOCATIONS

HQ: Unit Corporation
　1000 Kensington Tower, 7130 S. Lewis,
　Tulsa, OK 74136
Phone: 918-493-7700　　**Fax:** 918-493-7711
Web: www.unitcorp.com

Unit Corp. operates primarily in Louisiana, New Mexico, Oklahoma, and Texas, but also in Alabama, Arkansas, Colorado, Illinois, Michigan, Mississippi, Montana, Nebraska, North Dakota, and Wyoming. It also has some operations in Canada.

PRODUCTS/OPERATIONS

2005 Sales

	$ mil.	% of total
Contract drilling	462.1	53
Oil & natural gas	318.2	36
Gas gathering & processing	100.5	11
Adjustment	4.8	—
Total	**885.6**	**100**

Subsidiaries

Unit Drilling Company
Unit Petroleum Company

COMPETITORS

Abraxas Petroleum
Anadarko Petroleum
Apache
BP
Cabot Oil & Gas
Devon Energy
Dorchester Minerals
Exxon Mobil
Grey Wolf
Imperial Oil
Murphy Oil
Nabors Industries
Parker Drilling
Patterson-UTI Energy
Pioneer Natural Resources
Range Resources
Suncor

HISTORICAL FINANCIALS
Company Type: Public

Income Statement
FYE: December 31

	REVENUE ($ mil.)	NET INCOME ($ mil.)	NET PROFIT MARGIN	EMPLOYEES
12/05	885.6	212.4	24.0%	2,913
12/04	519.2	90.3	17.4%	2,515
12/03	302.6	50.2	16.6%	2,012
12/02	187.6	18.2	9.7%	1,291
12/01	259.2	62.8	24.2%	1,058
Annual Growth	36.0%	35.6%	—	28.8%

2005 Year-End Financials

Debt ratio: 17.3%
Return on equity: 29.4%
Cash ($ mil.): 1.2
Current ratio: 1.30
Long-term debt ($ mil.): 145.0
No. of shares (mil.): 46.2

Dividends
　Yield: —
　Payout: —
Market value ($ mil.): 2,541.2
R&D as % of sales: —
Advertising as % of sales: —

Stock History
NYSE: UNT

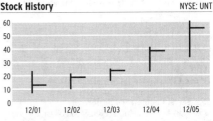

	STOCK PRICE ($) FY Close	P/E High/Low	PER SHARE ($) Earnings	Dividends	Book Value
12/05	55.03	13　7	4.60	—	18.12
12/04	38.21	21　12	1.97	—	13.30
12/03	23.55	21　14	1.15	—	11.31
12/02	18.55	45　22	0.47	—	9.73
12/01	12.90	13　4	1.73	—	7.76
Annual Growth	43.7%	—　—	27.7%	—	23.6%

United Industrial

Through subsidiary AAI, United Industrial makes automatic test equipment for avionics, electronic warfare test and training systems, training simulators for combat systems and aircraft maintenance, and unmanned aerial vehicle (UAV) systems; the US military accounts for most of AAI's sales. Subsidiary AAI Services' subsidiary McTurbine Inc. is a provider of maintenance, repair, and overhaul services for military helicopters. United Industrial exited the energy business early in 2007 when it sold Detroit Stoker (industrial stokers, gas and oil burners, alternative energy systems, and municipal solid-waste combustion systems) to DSC Services, Inc.

Director Warren G. Lichtenstein, through Steel Partners II, L.P., owns about 17% of the company.

United Industrial gets most of its sales from its defense-related operations, which have grown because of the demand for UAVs and the company's Joint Service Electronic Combat System Tester. The company has been awarded multiple government contracts to produce its RQ-7 Shadow 200 TUAV (tactical unmanned aerial vehicle), which has been deployed in Iraq.

In 2005 United Industrial completed two acquisitions that complement its defense unit. The

company acquired UK-based ESL Defence Limited. The purchase was integrated into United Industrial's test and training division. The move adds to the company's offerings of electronic warfare test products while establishing a surer footing in the European market. United Industrial also bought the unmanned aerial vehicle assets of Allied Aerospace Industries.

Late in 2006 United Industrial, through AAI, bought the McTurbine subsidiary of M International for about $31 million in cash. McTurbine is a provider of maintenance, repair, and overhaul services for military helicopter engines.

Soon after the McTurbine announcement, United Industrial said it had reached an agreement to sell its Detroit Stoker Company energy subsidiary in order to focus on its aerospace and defense business. The deal, valued at $22.4 million, will sell Detroit Stoker to a newly created company named DSC Services, Inc., which is affiliated with a private equity group. The sale of Detroit Stoker was completed early in 2007.

EXECUTIVES

Chairman: Warren G. Lichtenstein, age 40
President and CEO: Frederick M. Strader, age 52, $1,021,592 pay
VP and CFO, United Industrial and AAI: James H. Perry, age 44, $468,189 pay
VP, General Counsel, and Secretary: Jonathan A. Greenberg, age 39, $430,337 pay
Treasurer: Stuart F. Grey, age 46
EVP, Programs, AAI Corporation: Michael A. Boden
President, Detroit Stoker Company: Thomas A. Giaier
President, AAI Services: O. Paul Lavin
President, AAI/ACL Technologies, Inc.: John F. Michitsch
SVP, UAV Systems, AAI: Joseph G. Thomas
VP and Corporate Controller, AAI Corporation: Francis X. Reinhardt
Managing Director, ESL Defence Limited: John E. Parsons
Auditors: KPMG LLP

LOCATIONS

HQ: United Industrial Corporation
124 Industry Ln., Hunt Valley, MD 21030
Phone: 410-628-3500   **Fax:** 410-638-6498
Web: www.unitedindustrial.com

United Industrial operates from facilities in Alaska, Alabama, Arizona, Florida, California, Maryland, Michigan, Mississippi, Oklahoma, Ohio, South Carolina, Utah, and Virginia in the US and in the UK.

PRODUCTS/OPERATIONS

2005 Sales

	$ mil.	% of total
Defense	480.2	93
Energy	37.0	7
Total	**517.2**	**100**

Selected Subsidiaries

AAI Corporation
  AAI Services Corporation (formerly AAI Engineering Support, Inc.)
  AAI/ACL Technologies, Inc. (manufactures hydraulic, fuel, pneumatic, and electrical power-generation-component test equipment and ground support equipment)
  AAI/ACL Technologies Europe Limited (UK)
  AAI Australia Pty Ltd.
Detroit Stoker Company (manufactures stokers and related combustion equipment)

COMPETITORS

Alliant Techsystems	Israel Aircraft Industries
Berkshire Hathaway	John Zink
CAE USA	L-3 Communications
Cubic Simulation Systems	Lockheed Martin
DRS Technologies	Northrop Grumman
Eclipse	Serco Group
EDO	Thales
Elbit Systems	

HISTORICAL FINANCIALS

Company Type: Public

Income Statement				FYE: December 31
	REVENUE ($ mil.)	NET INCOME ($ mil.)	NET PROFIT MARGIN	EMPLOYEES
12/05	517.2	41.0	7.9%	2,000
12/04	385.1	26.8	7.0%	1,650
12/03	311.0	(5.8)	—	1,600
12/02	258.8	(39.1)	—	1,600
12/01	238.5	5.4	2.3%	1,500
Annual Growth	**21.4%**	**66.0%**	**—**	**7.5%**

2005 Year-End Financials

Debt ratio: 473.0%
Return on equity: 143.6%
Cash ($ mil.): 93.9
Current ratio: 2.69
Long-term debt ($ mil.): 120.7
No. of shares (mil.): 11.3

Dividends
  Yield: 1.0%
  Payout: 13.8%
Market value ($ mil.): 466.6
R&D as % of sales: 2.0%
Advertising as % of sales: —

Stock History

NYSE: UIC

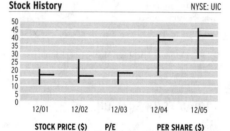

	STOCK PRICE ($) FY Close	P/E High/Low		PER SHARE ($) Earnings	Dividends	Book Value
12/05	41.37	16	10	2.89	0.40	2.26
12/04	38.74	21	9	1.99	0.40	2.57
12/03	18.05	—	—	(0.43)	0.40	3.09
12/02	16.00	—	—	(2.85)	0.30	3.64
12/01	16.75	50	27	0.40	0.40	9.28
Annual Growth	**25.4%**	**—**	**—**	**63.9%**	**0.0%**	**(29.7%)**

United Online

United Online wants to bring people together on the Web. Created in 2001 by the merger of leading US Internet service providers NetZero and Juno Online Services, United Online continues the free, advertising-supported service model of its predecessor companies; users choose either free dial-up service with hourly limits and advertising or billable service minus the ads and time restrictions. United Online also operates Internet community Classmates Online and provides free and paid Web hosting services, as well as Voice over Internet Protocol (VoIP). The company has more than 18 million users, with more than 5 million paid subscribers, mainly under the NetZero, Juno, and Classmates Online brands.

In 2006 the company acquired MyPoints.com, the subscription-based Internet direct marketing services company, from UAL in a cash deal valued at about $56 million. The previous year it added digital photo-sharing to its list of offerings with the purchase of PhotoSite from Homestead Technologies for $10 million.

When the company acquired Classmates Online in 2004, it gained more than a million paying subscribers and nearly 40 million registered users. United Online agreed to pay about $100 million in cash for the online meeting place.

EXECUTIVES

Chairman and CEO: Mark R. Goldston, age 51, $1,800,000 pay (prior to title change)
President and CFO: Charles S. Hilliard, age 42, $800,000 pay (prior to title change)
EVP and Chief Marketing Officer: Matthew (Matt) Wisk, age 46
EVP and CTO: Gerald J. Popek, age 59, $740,000 pay
EVP, General Counsel, and Secretary: Frederic A. Randall Jr., age 49, $740,000 pay
EVP Operations; General Manager, CyberTarget: Robert J. (Rusty) Taragan, age 49
EVP Sales and Chief Sales Officer: Jeremy E. Helfand, age 32
SVP Finance, Treasurer, and Chief Accounting Officer: Neil P. Edwards
SVP Media Services: David J. Dowling
SVP Sales and Business Development: Michael Mathieu
SVP Corporate Communications: Elizabeth Gengl
VP Corporate Communications: Scott Matulis
Auditors: PricewaterhouseCoopers LLP

LOCATIONS

HQ: United Online, Inc.
LNR Warner Center, 21301 Burbank Blvd., Woodland Hills, CA 91367
Phone: 818-287-3000   **Fax:** 818-287-3001
Web: www.unitedonline.net

United Online has facilities in the US in California, New York, Utah, and Washington. It also has an office in Hyderabad, India.

PRODUCTS/OPERATIONS

2005 Sales

	$ mil.	% of total
Billable services	466.0	89
Advertising & commerce	59.1	11
Total	**525.1**	**100**

Selected Services

Dial-up Internet access (BlueLight, Juno, NetZero)
E-mail (Juno MegaMail, MegaMail, NetZero)
Online community-based networking (Classmates Online, Stay Friends)
Online photo-sharing (Photo Site)
Voice over Internet Protocol (NetZero Voice)
Web hosting (50megs, Besotting, Free Servers)

COMPETITORS

AOL	PeoplePC
AT&T	Qwest
Charter Communications	Reunion.com
Comcast	Road Runner
Cox Communications	Skype
Demand Media	Time Warner Cable
EarthLink	USA.NET
Friendster	Verizon
Internet America	Vonage
Microsoft	Walmart.com
Monster	Yahoo!

HISTORICAL FINANCIALS

Company Type: Public

Income Statement

	REVENUE ($ mil.)	NET INCOME ($ mil.)	NET PROFIT MARGIN	EMPLOYEES
12/05	525.1	47.1	9.0%	900
12/04	448.6	117.5	26.2%	742
12/03*	185.7	33.3	17.9%	499
6/03	277.3	27.8	10.0%	461
6/02	167.5	(47.8)	—	420
Annual Growth	33.1%	—	—	21.0%

FYE: December 31

*Fiscal year change

2005 Year-End Financials

Debt ratio: 11.8%
Return on equity: 15.1%
Cash ($ mil.): 244.4
Current ratio: 1.90
Long-term debt ($ mil.): 38.0
No. of shares (mil.): 62.6

Dividends
  Yield: 4.2%
  Payout: 81.1%
Market value ($ mil.): 890.3
R&D as % of sales: —
Advertising as % of sales: —

Stock History

NASDAQ (GS): UNTD

	STOCK PRICE ($) FY Close	P/E High/Low		PER SHARE ($) Earnings	Dividends	Book Value
12/05	14.22	20	12	0.74	0.60	5.15
12/04	11.53	12	5	1.81	—	4.94
12/03*	11.53	51	21	0.41	—	4.99
6/03	16.79	61	18	0.48	—	3.72
6/02	10.63	—	—	(0.90)	—	4.41
Annual Growth	7.5%	—	—	—	—	4.0%

*Fiscal year change

United PanAm Financial

United PanAm Financial flies the choppy skies of subprime lending. A specialty finance firm, it originates, buys, and services auto loan contracts for high-risk customers. Through subsidiary United Auto Credit Corp. (UACC), it buys contracts from independent and franchised used car dealers. Until 2005 United PanAm also operated a bank subsidiary which served as UACC's primary funding source. Since voluntarily dissolving the bank charter, it now funds its auto finance business through securitizations and warehouse facilities. Once heavily localized in California, UACC has been expanding rapidly and now has about 110 branches in 31 states. Chairman Guillermo Bron owns two-thirds of the company.

United PanAm Financial sold the final three branches of subsidiary Pan American Bank FSB to Guaranty Bank of Austin, Texas, and Kaiser Federal Bank of Covina, California, in 2004.

Around the same time, it also discontinued its insurance premium finance business. Consequently, auto finance subsidiary United Auto Credit is now its primary business.

In August 2005 United PanAm acquired BVG West Corp., a company for which Bron served as president, director, and controlling stockholder.

The company plans to expand its auto finance business by opening additional branch offices in new and existing markets. It expects to open two dozen branches each year for the foreseeable future.

EXECUTIVES

Chairman: Guillermo Bron, age 54, $375,000 pay
President, CEO, Secretary, and Director; President and CEO, United Auto Credit: Ray C. Thousand, age 48, $685,000 pay
EVP and Chief Administrative Officer; EVP, United Auto Credit: Mario Radrigan, age 44, $250,000 pay
SVP and CFO: Arash A. Khazei, age 38
Director, Human Resources: Stacy Friederichsen
Auditors: Grobstein, Horwath & Company LLP

LOCATIONS

HQ: United PanAm Financial Corp.
  3990 Westerly Place, Ste. 200,
  Newport Beach, CA 92660
Phone: 949-224-1917   **Fax:** 949-224-1912
Web: www.upfc.com

PRODUCTS/OPERATIONS

2005 Sales

	$ mil.	% of total
Interest		
Loans	157.5	88
Securities & other	17.1	10
Noninterest		
Gain on sale of securities	3.4	2
Loan related charges & fees	0.4	—
Other	0.4	—
Total	**178.8**	**100**

COMPETITORS

AmeriCredit
Capital One
Consumer Portfolio
Credit Acceptance
First Investors Financial Services
Ford Motor Credit
GMAC
HSBC Finance
Toyota Motor Credit
Wachovia

HISTORICAL FINANCIALS

Company Type: Public

Income Statement

	ASSETS ($ mil.)	NET INCOME ($ mil.)	INCOME AS % OF ASSETS	EMPLOYEES
12/05	1,209.2	26.7	2.2%	800
12/04	1,414.9	23.7	1.7%	647
12/03	1,667.7	13.3	0.8%	545
12/02	951.3	12.5	1.3%	430
12/01	689.6	7.8	1.1%	335
Annual Growth	15.1%	36.0%	—	24.3%

FYE: December 31

2005 Year-End Financials

Equity as % of assets: 12.8%
Return on assets: 2.0%
Return on equity: 19.1%
Long-term debt ($ mil.): 585.9
No. of shares (mil.): 17.1
Market value ($ mil.): 442.9

Dividends
  Yield: —
  Payout: —
Sales ($ mil.): 178.8
R&D as % of sales: —
Advertising as % of sales: —

Stock History

NASDAQ (GS): UPFC

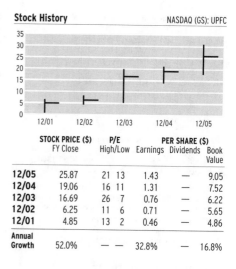

	STOCK PRICE ($) FY Close	P/E High/Low		PER SHARE ($) Earnings	Dividends	Book Value
12/05	25.87	21	13	1.43	—	9.05
12/04	19.06	16	11	1.31	—	7.52
12/03	16.69	26	7	0.76	—	6.22
12/02	6.25	11	6	0.71	—	5.65
12/01	4.85	13	2	0.46	—	4.86
Annual Growth	52.0%	—	—	32.8%	—	16.8%

United States Lime & Minerals

United States Lime & Minerals is really rockin'. The company operates limestone and lime plants in Colorado, Texas, Oklahoma, and Arkansas. It sells pulverized limestone, quicklime, and hydrated lime for use in making roof shingles, agriculture feeds, sanitation filtering systems, soil enhancers, and construction materials such as asphalt. Customers, primarily in the southwestern and south central US, include highway, street, and parking lot contractors; steel producers; roofing shingle manufacturers; municipal sanitation and water treatment facilities; paper manufacturers; chemical producers; and steel producers.

United States Lime & Minerals' Texas Lime Company subsidiary (near Cleburne) and its Arkansas Lime Company subsidiary (near Batesville) both extract limestone from open-pit quarries. Its Colorado Lime Company subsidiary owns limestone resources at Monarch Pass (near Salida), although mining activities did not take place in 2005 on the Colorado property.

United States Lime & Minerals acquired O-N Minerals (St. Clair) Company from an Oglebay Norton Company subsidiary for $14 million in cash and transaction costs at the close of 2005. St. Clair extracts limestone from an underground quarry in Oklahoma.

In 2002 United States Lime & Minerals discovered that its former CFO Larry Ohms had embezzled more than $2 million from the company over four years. Larry Ohms was sentenced to prison and ordered to repay the company.

Investor George Doumet owns nearly 60% of the company through Inberdon Enterprises. Investor Robert Beall owns 11%.

EXECUTIVES

Chairman: Antoine M. Doumet, age 46
Vice Chairman: Edward A. Odishaw, age 70
President, CEO, and Director: Timothy W. Bryne, age 48
SVP, Sales and Marketing: Billy R. Hughes, age 67, $195,667 pay

VP, CFO, Secretary, and Treasurer: M. Michael Owens, age 52, $142,208 pay
VP and and Plant Manager, Texas Lime: Richard D. Murray, age 65, $147,375 pay
VP, Manufacturing: Johnney G. Bowers, age 59, $158,025 pay
VP, Production: Russell W. Riggs, age 48
Auditors: Grant Thornton LLP

LOCATIONS

HQ: United States Lime & Minerals, Inc.
  13800 Montfort Dr., Ste. 330, Dallas, TX 75240
Phone: 972-991-8400   **Fax:** 972-385-1340
Web: www.uslm.com

United States Lime & Minerals has quarries in Batesville, Arkansas; Salida, Colorado; Marble City, Oklahoma; and Cleburne, Texas. The company sells its products primarily in Arkansas, Colorado, Indiana, Kansas, Louisiana, Mississippi, Missouri, New Mexico, Oklahoma, Pennsylvania, Tennessee, Texas, and West Virginia.

PRODUCTS/OPERATIONS

Selected Products

Limestone
  Hydrated lime (calcium hydroxide)
  Pulverized limestone (ground calcium carbonate)
  Quicklime (calcium oxide)

COMPETITORS

Cementos de Chihuahua
Chemical Lime
Edw. C. Levy
Florida Rock
Giant Cement
Hanson
Lafarge North America
Martin Marietta Materials
Meadow Valley
Monarch Cement
Oglebay Norton
Vulcan Materials

HISTORICAL FINANCIALS

Company Type: Public

Income Statement				FYE: December 31
	REVENUE ($ mil.)	NET INCOME ($ mil.)	NET PROFIT MARGIN	EMPLOYEES
12/05	81.1	7.9	9.7%	292
12/04	55.7	6.3	11.3%	211
12/03	45.3	3.9	8.6%	201
12/02	39.2	0.6	1.5%	192
12/01	39.8	1.8	4.5%	200
Annual Growth	19.5%	44.7%	—	9.9%

2005 Year-End Financials

Debt ratio: 88.7%
Return on equity: 14.8%
Cash ($ mil.): 1.3
Current ratio: 1.92
Long-term debt ($ mil.): 51.7
No. of shares (mil.): 6.0
Dividends
  Yield: —
  Payout: —
Market value ($ mil.): 159.2
R&D as % of sales: —
Advertising as % of sales: —

Stock History

NASDAQ (GM): USLM

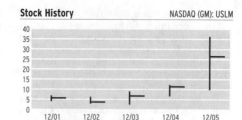

	STOCK PRICE ($) FY Close	P/E High/Low		PER SHARE ($) Earnings	Dividends	Book Value
12/05	26.47	27	8	1.31	—	9.68
12/04	11.35	11	6	1.07	—	8.25
12/03	6.75	13	4	0.67	0.05	7.22
12/02	3.70	55	29	0.11	0.10	6.61
12/01	5.66	20	14	0.32	0.10	6.64
Annual Growth	47.1%	—	—	42.2%	(29.3%)	9.9%

United Therapeutics

United Therapeutics hopes its products will be in vein. Its Remodulin treats pulmonary hypertension, which affects the blood vessels between the heart and lungs, and the company is still investigating its use for peripheral vascular disease, which affects blood vessels in the legs. Other products in the pipeline could treat other types of cardiovascular disease, various cancers, and hepatitis B and C. United Therapeutics' CardioPAL is a device sold by its Medicomp unit that monitors over the phone or Internet the hearts of patients susceptible to arrhythmia and angina.

The company completed a review by the European Union Mutual Recognition Procedure and got word that Remodulin was approved for use in more than 20 European countries in 2005.

Chairman and CEO Martine Rothblatt owns 8% of United Therapeutics.

EXECUTIVES

Chairman and CEO: Martine A. Rothblatt, age 51, $840,000 pay
President, COO, and Director: Roger Jeffs, age 44, $720,000 pay
CFO and Treasurer: John M. Ferrari, age 51
CIO: Shola Oyewole
EVP, Strategic Planning, General Counsel, and Secretary: Paul A. Mahon, age 42, $595,000 pay
President and COO, Lung Rx: Robert Roscigno
President and CEO, Unither Pharma: Yu-Lun Lin
CEO, Medicomp: Ricardo Balda, age 64
COO, Unither Pharmaceuticals: Peter C. Gonze
Chief Medical Officer, Lung Rx: Eugene Sullivan
Auditors: Ernst & Young LLP

LOCATIONS

HQ: United Therapeutics Corporation
  1110 Spring St., Silver Spring, MD 20910
Phone: 301-608-9292   **Fax:** 301-608-9291
Web: www.unither.com

PRODUCTS/OPERATIONS

2005 Sales

	$ mil.	% of total
Pharmaceuticals	110.1	95
Telemedicine	5.8	5
Total	**115.9**	**100**

Selected Products

Marketed
  CardioPAL (arrhythmia and angina monitoring system)
  Remodulin (hypertension)
In Development
  Beraprost (cardiovascular disease)
  OvaRex (ovarian cancer)

COMPETITORS

Actelion
Angiogenix
Bayer
Bayer Schering Pharma
Boehringer Ingelheim
Corautus Genetics
CoTherix
Encysive Pharmaceuticals
GlaxoSmithKline
Pfizer

HISTORICAL FINANCIALS

Company Type: Public

Income Statement				FYE: December 31
	REVENUE ($ mil.)	NET INCOME ($ mil.)	NET PROFIT MARGIN	EMPLOYEES
12/05	115.9	65.0	56.1%	210
12/04	73.6	15.4	20.9%	170
12/03	53.3	(10.0)	—	160
12/02	30.1	(23.6)	—	150
12/01	5.7	(37.3)	—	128
Annual Growth	112.3%	—	—	13.2%

2005 Year-End Financials

Debt ratio: 0.0%
Return on equity: 27.9%
Cash ($ mil.): 125.5
Current ratio: 11.48
Long-term debt ($ mil.): 0.0
No. of shares (mil.): 23.3
Dividends
  Yield: —
  Payout: —
Market value ($ mil.): 1,611.8
R&D as % of sales: —
Advertising as % of sales: —

Stock History

NASDAQ (GS): UTHR

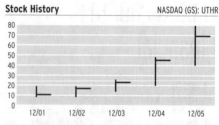

	STOCK PRICE ($) FY Close	P/E High/Low		PER SHARE ($) Earnings	Dividends	Book Value
12/05	69.12	31	16	2.58	—	11.80
12/04	45.15	72	31	0.66	—	8.54
12/03	22.95	—	—	(0.47)	—	7.87
12/02	16.70	—	—	(1.15)	—	8.20
12/01	10.41	—	—	(1.84)	—	9.71
Annual Growth	60.5%	—	—	—	—	5.0%

Universal American Financial

Universal American Financial is mining the silver-haired set for gold. The holding company owns several insurance firms, four of which target US senior citizens with such products as Medicare supplement insurance, senior life insurance, fixed annuities, and long-term care insurance. It also operates a prescription drug benefit plan in an alliance with Pharmacare Management Services. Other subsidiaries market disability insurance, hospitalization insurance, and related products to self-employed individuals in the US and Canada. Investment firm Capital Z Partners owns 35% of the company.

Subsidiary CHCS Services provides outsourced administration services for insurance and other products geared to seniors; the company serves more than 50 clients, some of which are unaffiliated with Universal American Financial, including a prescription drug plan sponsored by Arkansas Blue Cross and Blue Shield.

Universal American Financial's Senior Market Health Insurance sells Medicare and other senior health products; the segment sells through agencies and independent marketing organizations. Other segments include Senior Managed Care — Medicare Advantage, Specialty Health Insurance, Life Insurance/Annuties, and Senior Administrative Services.

Universal American Financial boosted its Medicare-related offerings with its 2004 purchase of Heritage Health Systems.

EXECUTIVES

Chairman, President, and CEO: Richard A. Barasch, age 52, $1,568,063 pay
EVP and COO; President and CEO, American Pioneer Life and American Exchange; President, Constitution Life, Marquette, Peninsular Life, and Union Bankers; Chairman, CHCS Services; Vice Chairman, American Progressive and Pennsylvania Life: Gary W. Bryant, age 56, $594,750 pay
EVP and CFO: Robert A. Waegelein, age 45, $518,500 pay
SVP Administration; COO, CHCS Services: Jason J. Israel, age 53, $457,500 pay
SVP, Corporate Development; President, CHCS Services, Ameri-Plus Preferred Care, CHCS, Inc., and WorldNet Services; SVP, American Pioneer Health Plans; SVP, Managed Care, American Pioneer Life Insurance and American Progressive: Gary Jacobs, age 55
SVP, General Counsel, and Secretary: Lisa M. Spivack, age 36
SVP and CIO: Frederick W. Rook
CEO, Heritage Health Systems: Theodore M. Carpenter Jr., age 58, $459,619 pay
Auditors: Ernst & Young LLP

LOCATIONS

HQ: Universal American Financial Corp.
6 International Dr., Ste. 190, Rye Brook, NY 10573
Phone: 914-934-5200   **Fax:** 914-934-0700
Web: www.uafc.com

Universal American Financial operates in the US and Canada.

PRODUCTS/OPERATIONS

2005 Sales

	$ mil.	% of total
Net premiums & policyholder fees		
Accident & health	773.4	83
Life	62.6	7
Net investment income	71.6	7
Realized gains on investments	5.8	1
Fees & other income	18.5	2
Total	**931.9**	**100**

2005 Sales By Segment

	$ mil.	% of total
Senior Market Health Insurance	396.3	41
Senior Managed Care — Medicare Advantage	240.7	25
Specialty Health Insurance	176.2	18
Life Insurance/Annuity	96.2	10
Senior Administrative Services	59.1	6
Corporate	1.0	—
Adjustments	(37.6)	—
Total	**931.9**	**100**

Selected Subsidiaries and Affiliates

American Exchange Life Insurance Company
American Pioneer Life Insurance Company
American Progressive Life & Health Insurance Company of New York
Ameriplus Preferred Care, Inc.
CHCS Services, Inc.
Constitution Life Insurance Company
Marquette National Life Insurance Company
Peninsular Life Insurance Company
Penncorp Life Insurance Company (Canada)
Pennsylvania Life Insurance Company
Pyramid Life Insurance Company
Union Bankers Insurance Company
Universal American Financial Corp. Statutory Trust I
Universal American Financial Services, Inc.
WorldNet Services Corp.

COMPETITORS

Aetna
AIG American General
AmerUs
CIGNA
CSO
Farmers Group
Hartford Life and Accident
MagnaCare
Phoenix Companies
Primerica
Principal Financial
Prudential
Sun Life
Torchmark
United American Insurance

HISTORICAL FINANCIALS
Company Type: Public

Income Statement
FYE: December 31

	ASSETS ($ mil.)	NET INCOME ($ mil.)	INCOME AS % OF ASSETS	EMPLOYEES
12/05	2,228.0	53.9	2.4%	1,300
12/04	2,017.1	63.9	3.2%	1,200
12/03	1,780.9	43.0	2.4%	900
12/02	1,401.7	30.1	2.1%	900
12/01	1,275.9	28.9	2.3%	860
Annual Growth	**15.0%**	**16.9%**	**—**	**10.9%**

2005 Year-End Financials

Equity as % of assets: 23.9%
Return on assets: 2.5%
Return on equity: 11.3%
Long-term debt ($ mil.): 170.8
No. of shares (mil.): 58.2
Market value ($ mil.): 877.7
Dividends
  Yield: —
  Payout: —
Sales ($ mil.): 931.9
R&D as % of sales: —
Advertising as % of sales: —

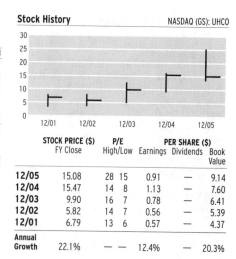

Stock History
NASDAQ (GS): UHCO

	STOCK PRICE ($) FY Close	P/E High	P/E Low	PER SHARE ($) Earnings	PER SHARE ($) Dividends	PER SHARE ($) Book Value
12/05	15.08	28	15	0.91	—	9.14
12/04	15.47	14	8	1.13	—	7.60
12/03	9.90	16	7	0.78	—	6.41
12/02	5.82	14	7	0.56	—	5.39
12/01	6.79	13	6	0.57	—	4.37
Annual Growth	**22.1%**	**—**	**—**	**12.4%**	**—**	**20.3%**

Universal Security Instruments

Where there's smoke, there's Universal Security Instruments. The company designs and markets smoke alarms and carbon monoxide alarms, as well as products such as outdoor floodlights. Most of Universal Security Instruments' products are sold through retail stores and are designed to be installed by consumers. Products that require professional installation, such as smoke alarms designed for the hearing-impaired, are marketed to electrical products distributors by subsidiary USI Electric. Universal Security Instruments owns a stake in a Hong Kong-based joint venture that manufactures many of its products at facilities in China.

EXECUTIVES

President, CEO, and Director: Harvey B. Grossblatt, age 60, $429,960 pay
CFO, Secretary, and Treasurer: James B. Huff, age 54, $129,000 pay
President, USI Electric: Ronald S. (Ron) Lazarus
Auditors: Grant Thornton LLP

LOCATIONS

HQ: Universal Security Instruments, Inc.
7-A Gwynns Mill Ct., Owings Mills, MD 21117
Phone: 410-363-3000   **Fax:** 410-363-2218
Web: www.universalsecurity.com

COMPETITORS

Bosch
Gentex
Honeywell International
Jarden
Napco Security
Tyco Fire and Security
UTC Fire & Security

HISTORICAL FINANCIALS
Company Type: Public

Income Statement
FYE: March 31

	REVENUE ($ mil.)	NET INCOME ($ mil.)	NET PROFIT MARGIN	EMPLOYEES
3/06	28.9	4.6	15.9%	15
3/05	23.5	3.4	14.5%	18
3/04	17.2	2.6	15.1%	17
3/03	15.9	2.4	15.1%	16
3/02	10.5	0.3	2.9%	17
Annual Growth	28.8%	97.9%	—	(3.1%)

2006 Year-End Financials
Debt ratio: —
Return on equity: 30.2%
Cash ($ mil.): 3.0
Current ratio: 4.60
Long-term debt ($ mil.): —
No. of shares (mil.): 1.8

Dividends
  Yield: —
  Payout: —
Market value ($ mil.): 29.6
R&D as % of sales: —
Advertising as % of sales: —

Stock History
AMEX: UUU

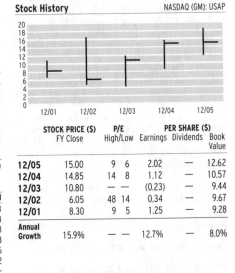

	STOCK PRICE ($) FY Close	P/E High/Low		PER SHARE ($) Earnings	Dividends	Book Value
3/06	16.35	10	5	1.89	—	9.73
3/05	11.49	10	5	1.46	—	7.80
3/04	9.62	10	4	1.12	—	5.83
3/03	4.79	5	1	1.15	—	5.78
3/02	2.08	16	3	0.16	—	3.64
Annual Growth	67.4%	—	—	85.4%	—	27.8%

EXECUTIVES
Chairman and CEO: Clarence M. (Mac) McAninch, age 70
President: Kenneth W. Matz, age 55
VP Finance, CFO, Principal Accounting Officer, Treasurer, Assistant Secretary: Richard M. Ubinger, age 45, $264,307 pay
VP Operations, Director Employee Relations, General Counsel, and Secretary: Paul A. McGrath, age 54, $278,923 pay
VP Sales and Marketing: Richard J. Hack
Director, Purchasing and Production Planning: Bruce A. Kramer
Auditors: Schneider Downs & Co., Inc.

LOCATIONS
HQ: Universal Stainless & Alloy Products, Inc.
  600 Mayer St., Bridgeville, PA 15017
Phone: 412-257-7600   **Fax:** 412-257-7640
Web: www.univstainless.com

Universal Stainless & Alloy Products operates facilities in Bridgeville and Titusville, Pennsylvania, and Dunkirk, New York.

PRODUCTS/OPERATIONS

2005 Sales by Product
	$ mil.	% of total
Steel products		
Stainless steel	135.6	80
Tool steel	20.7	12
High-strength low-alloy steel	6.6	4
High-temperature alloy steel	3.7	2
Conversion services	3.0	2
Other	0.4	—
Total	**170.0**	**100**

2005 Sales by Customer
	$ mil.	% of total
Service centers	73.2	43
Rerollers	39.2	23
Forgers	29.9	18
OEMs	14.0	8
Wire redrawers	10.3	6
Conversion services	3.0	2
Other	0.4	—
Total	**170.0**	**100**

Selected Products
Flat-rolled products (plate, slab)
Long products (bars, blooms, billets, bars, ingots)
Special shapes (precision-rolled shapes from strip or bars)

Steel Grades
High-strength low-alloy steel
High-temperature alloy steel
Stainless steel
Tool steel

COMPETITORS
Allegheny Technologies
Amsted
Carpenter Technology
Copper and Brass Sales
Liquidmetal
PAV Republic
Thomas Steel Strip
Timken

Universal Stainless & Alloy Products

At Universal Stainless & Alloy Products, even if something is just semi-finished, that's OK. The company makes both semifinished and finished specialty steels, including stainless, tool, and alloyed steels. Universal Stainless' stainless steel products are sold to customers in the automotive, aerospace, and medical industries; the company's high-temperature steel is produced mainly for the aerospace industry. Service centers, rerollers, forgers, and wire redrawers also buy the company's products. Service center Talley Metals, a unit of Carpenter Technology, accounts for about 20% of Universal Stainless' sales.

The company's finished bar, rod, and wire specialty steel products complement its semifinished products. Universal Stainless also makes specialty steel in the form of long products (ingots, blooms, billets, and bars) and flat-rolled products (slabs and plates).

Investment firm Pennant Capital Management owns about 10% of Universal Stainless.

HISTORICAL FINANCIALS
Company Type: Public

Income Statement
FYE: December 31

	REVENUE ($ mil.)	NET INCOME ($ mil.)	NET PROFIT MARGIN	EMPLOYEES
12/05	170.0	13.1	7.7%	482
12/04	120.6	7.1	5.9%	463
12/03	69.0	(1.4)	—	383
12/02	70.9	2.1	3.0%	393
12/01	90.7	7.6	8.4%	304
Annual Growth	17.0%	14.6%	—	12.2%

2005 Year-End Financials
Debt ratio: 21.4%
Return on equity: 17.7%
Cash ($ mil.): 0.6
Current ratio: 3.92
Long-term debt ($ mil.): 17.3
No. of shares (mil.): 6.4

Dividends
  Yield: —
  Payout: —
Market value ($ mil.): 96.3
R&D as % of sales: —
Advertising as % of sales: —

Stock History
NASDAQ (GM): USAP

	STOCK PRICE ($) FY Close	P/E High/Low		PER SHARE ($) Earnings	Dividends	Book Value
12/05	15.00	9	6	2.02	—	12.62
12/04	14.85	14	8	1.12	—	10.57
12/03	10.80	—	—	(0.23)	—	9.44
12/02	6.05	48	14	0.34	—	9.67
12/01	8.30	9	5	1.25	—	9.28
Annual Growth	15.9%	—	—	12.7%	—	8.0%

Universal Technical Institute

Want to make a living working on hot rods? Universal Technical Institute (UTI) offers automotive, diesel, collision repair, motorcycle, and marine technician training to some 16,000 full-time students in the US. The company provides undergraduate degree and certificate programs at 10 campuses. UTI also offers advanced manufacturer-branded training for sponsors such as Porsche, Mercedes-Benz, Harley-Davidson, and Ford at 20 additional training center locations. Undergraduate programs last 12-18 months, and tuition ranges from $18,000 to $34,000. In addition, the company provides career placement services for graduates and alumni.

UTI provides education under the banner of several different brand names, including Universal Technical Institute, Motorcycle Mechanics Institute and Marine Mechanics Institute (collectively, MMI), and NASCAR Technical Institute (NTI).

EXECUTIVES

Chairman: John C. White
President, CEO, and Director: Kimberly J. McWaters, age 42
SVP, CFO, Treasurer, and Assistant Secretary: Jennifer L. Haslip, age 41, $270,290 pay
SVP and CIO: Larry H. Wolff, age 47
SVP, General Counsel, and Secretary: Chad A. Freed, age 33
SVP, Admissions: David K. Miller, age 48, $302,065 pay
SVP, Customer Solutions: Julian E. Gorman
SVP, Custom Training Group and Support Services: Roger L. Speer, age 48
SVP, Human Resources: Thomas E. Riggs
SVP, Operations and Education: Sherrell E. Smith, age 43
VP, Marketing: Piper Jameson
Auditors: PricewaterhouseCoopers LLP

LOCATIONS

HQ: Universal Technical Institute, Inc.
20410 N. 19th Ave., Ste. 200, Phoenix, AZ 85027
Phone: 623-445-9500 **Fax:** 623-445-9501
Web: www.uticorp.com

Universal Technical Institute has campuses and training centers in Arizona, California, Florida, Illinois, Massachusetts, North Carolina, Pennsylvania, and Texas.

COMPETITORS

Corinthian Colleges
DeVry
ITT Educational

HISTORICAL FINANCIALS

Company Type: Public

Income Statement				FYE: September 30
	REVENUE ($ mil.)	NET INCOME ($ mil.)	NET PROFIT MARGIN	EMPLOYEES
9/06	347.1	27.4	7.9%	2,360
9/05	310.8	35.8	11.5%	2,300
9/04	255.1	28.8	11.3%	1,800
9/03	196.5	20.4	10.4%	1,600
9/02	144.4	9.7	6.7%	—
Annual Growth	24.5%	29.6%	—	13.8%

2006 Year-End Financials

Debt ratio: —
Return on equity: 27.6%
Cash ($ mil.): 41.4
Current ratio: 0.73
Long-term debt ($ mil.): —
No. of shares (mil.): 26.7
Dividends
  Yield: —
  Payout: —
Market value ($ mil.): 478.5
R&D as % of sales: —
Advertising as % of sales: —

Stock History

NYSE: UTI

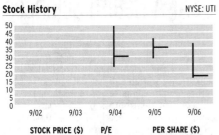

STOCK PRICE ($) FY Close	P/E High/Low		PER SHARE ($) Earnings	Dividends	Book Value
9/06	17.89	39	18	0.97	—	3.85
9/05	35.61	32	23	1.26	—	3.42
9/04	30.18	47	23	1.04	—	1.98
Annual Growth	(23.0%)	—	—	(3.4%)	—	39.4%

Universal Truckload Services

Universal Truckload Services hasn't hauled freight beyond its own galaxy yet, but the company does offer comprehensive coverage of the US and Canada. Universal Truckload Services is an "asset-light" provider of truckload freight transportation. Rather than employing drivers and investing heavily in equipment, the company operates through a network of truck owner-operators. The company can call upon a fleet of some 3,000 tractors and 4,300 trailers, including both standard dry vans and flatbeds. Universal Truckload Services generates business primarily through sales agents. Trucking magnates Matthew Moroun and his father, Manuel Moroun, control a 62% stake in Universal Truckload Services.

In addition to freight transportation, Universal Truckload Services provides freight brokerage services, matching customers' freight with carriers' capacity. The company also offers intermodal support services, which involve picking up shipping containers at ports and railheads and delivering them by truck to customers.

Universal Truckload Services expanded in 2006 by buying Alabama-based truckload carrier and freight broker Noble & Pitts. Noble & Pitts, which posted sales of about $33 million in 2005, will operate as part of Universal's Mason & Dixon Lines unit.

The Morouns also control CenTra, and Matthew Moroun owns a significant stake in truckload carrier P.A.M. Transportation Services.

EXECUTIVES

Chairman: Matthew T. Moroun, age 32
President, CEO, and Director: Donald B. Cochran, age 55, $592,762 pay
VP, CFO, Secretary, and Treasurer: Robert E. (Bob) Sigler, age 61
VP, Business Development: Leo Blumenauer, age 60, $462,125 pay
President, Universal Am-Can: Mark Limback
Auditors: KPMG LLP

LOCATIONS

HQ: Universal Truckload Services, Inc.
11355 Stephens Rd., Warren, MI 48089
Phone: 586-920-0100 **Fax:** 586-920-0258
Web: www.goutsi.com

PRODUCTS/OPERATIONS

2005 Sales

	$ mil.	% of total
Truckload	332.2	62
Brokerage	147.1	28
Intermodal support	52.0	10
Total	**531.3**	**100**

COMPETITORS

Crete Carrier
J. B. Hunt
Landstar System
Schneider National
Swift Transportation
U.S. Xpress
Werner Enterprises

HISTORICAL FINANCIALS

Company Type: Public

Income Statement				FYE: December 31
	REVENUE ($ mil.)	NET INCOME ($ mil.)	NET PROFIT MARGIN	EMPLOYEES
12/05	531.3	17.2	3.2%	494
12/04	362.0	11.1	3.1%	460
12/03	277.7	8.7	3.1%	271
12/02	252.8	7.5	3.0%	293
12/01	213.3	5.2	2.4%	286
Annual Growth	25.6%	34.9%	—	14.6%

2005 Year-End Financials

Debt ratio: —
Return on equity: 35.7%
Cash ($ mil.): 24.8
Current ratio: 2.62
Long-term debt ($ mil.): —
No. of shares (mil.): 16.1
Dividends
  Yield: —
  Payout: —
Market value ($ mil.): 370.7
R&D as % of sales: —
Advertising as % of sales: —

Stock History

NASDAQ (GM): UACL

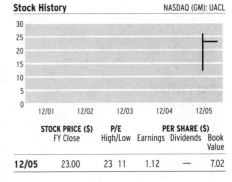

STOCK PRICE ($) FY Close	P/E High/Low		PER SHARE ($) Earnings	Dividends	Book Value
12/05	23.00	23	11	1.12	—	7.02

U.S. Global Investors

It may be a small world, but U.S. Global Investors wants to make it a little greener, after all. Along with its U.S. Global Accolade Funds, the company is an investment manager and adviser that offers no-load mutual funds generally geared toward long-term investing. Other subsidiaries of U.S. Global Investors provide transfer agent, brokerage, and mailing services. The company also engages in corporate investment, providing initial financing to start-ups and supplying capital to established businesses for expansion, acquisitions, management buyouts, or restructuring. It has more than $4.5 billion in assets under management.

EXECUTIVES

Chairman: Jerold H. (Jerry) Rubinstein, age 68
Vice Chairman: Roy D. Terracina, age 60
CEO and Chief Investment Officer: Frank E. Holmes, age 51, $2,106,152 pay
President and General Counsel: Susan B. McGee, age 47, $756,610 pay
CFO: Catherine A. Rademacher, age 46, $214,990 pay
Director, Institutional Services: Michael S. Dunn, age 44
Director, Research: John Derrick
Portfolio Manager, Charlemagne Capital: Stefan Böttcher
Portfolio Manager, U.S. Global Accolade Eastern European Fund: Andrew Wiles
Auditors: BDO Seidman, LLP

LOCATIONS

HQ: U.S. Global Investors, Inc.
7900 Callaghan Rd., San Antonio, TX 78229
Phone: 210-308-1234   **Fax:** 210-308-1223
Web: www.usfunds.com

PRODUCTS/OPERATIONS

2006 Sales

	$ mil.	% of total
Investment advisory fees	37.1	83
Transfer agent fees	5.3	12
Investment income & other	2.4	5
Total	**44.8**	**100**

Selected Mutual Funds

All American Equity Fund
China Region Opportunity Fund
Eastern European Fund
Global Resources Fund
Gold Shares Fund
Holmes Growth Fund
Megatrends Fund
Near-Term Tax Free Fund
Tax Free Fund
U.S. Government Securities Savings Fund
U.S. Treasury Securities Cash Fund
World Precious Minerals Fund

COMPETITORS

AGF Management
AIM Funds
Atalanta Sosnoff
Eaton Vance
FMR
Franklin Resources
Janus Capital
MFS
Nuveen
Oak Associates
PIMCO
Putnam
T. Rowe Price
TIAA-CREF
Van Kampen Investments
The Vanguard Group
Westwood Holdings

HISTORICAL FINANCIALS

Company Type: Public

Income Statement

FYE: June 30

	ASSETS ($ mil.)	NET INCOME ($ mil.)	INCOME AS % OF ASSETS	EMPLOYEES
6/06	29.0	10.4	35.9%	78
6/05	12.1	1.5	12.4%	67
6/04	9.5	2.2	23.2%	65
6/03	7.4	0.0	—	61
6/02	7.9	(0.2)	—	66
Annual Growth	**38.4%**	**—**	**—**	**4.3%**

2006 Year-End Financials

Equity as % of assets: 70.8%
Return on assets: 50.6%
Return on equity: 68.3%
Long-term debt ($ mil.): —
No. of shares (mil.): 6.1
Market value ($ mil.): 128.5
Dividends
  Yield: —
  Payout: —
Sales ($ mil.): 44.8
R&D as % of sales: —
Advertising as % of sales: —

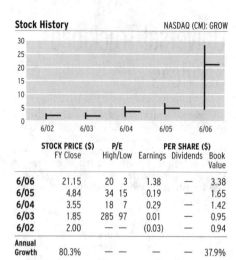

Stock History

NASDAQ (CM): GROW

	STOCK PRICE ($) FY Close	P/E High/Low		PER SHARE ($) Earnings	Dividends	Book Value
6/06	21.15	20	3	1.38	—	3.38
6/05	4.84	34	15	0.19	—	1.65
6/04	3.55	18	7	0.29	—	1.42
6/03	1.85	285	97	0.01	—	0.95
6/02	2.00	—	—	(0.03)	—	0.94
Annual Growth	**80.3%**	**—**	**—**	**—**	**—**	**37.9%**

U.S. Shipping Partners

U.S. Shipping Partners (USSP) cruises coast-wise between US ports, delivering refined and specialty petroleum and chemical products. The company operates a fleet of six integrated tug-barge units, which transport refined petroleum products; three chemical parcel tankers; and one product tanker. USSP's main customers are major oil and chemical companies. BP, Hess, and Shell together account for some 65% of the company's sales; other customers have included Dow Chemical and Exxon Mobil. An investment group led by private equity firm Sterling Investment Partners owns 46% of USSP, plus a general partner interest that gives it control of the company.

USSP has contracted with a unit of General Dynamics to acquire nine product carriers for $1 billion. Construction of the first vessel is set to begin in 2007; USSP would take delivery in 2009. Outside investors, including The Blackstone Group, are backing the deal, and at least five of the new vessels would be operated by a joint venture 60%-owned by The Blackstone Group and other investors and 40%-owned by USSP.

USSP operates under the Jones Act, a federal law that allows only vessels controlled and operated by US companies to transport cargo between US ports.

EXECUTIVES

Chairman and CEO: Paul B. Gridley, age 53, $657,000 pay
President, COO, and Director: Joseph P. Gehegan, age 60, $619,000 pay
VP and CFO: Albert E. Bergeron, age 39, $439,500 pay
VP, Operations: Alan E. Colletti, age 60, $485,500 pay
Human Resources: Tom Lord
Auditors: PricewaterhouseCoopers LLP

LOCATIONS

HQ: U.S. Shipping Partners L.P.
399 Thornall St., 8th Fl., Edison, NJ 08837
Phone: 732-635-1500   **Fax:** 732-635-1918
Web: www.usshipllc.com

COMPETITORS

Burlington Northern Santa Fe	Moran Towing
Colonial Pipeline	Norfolk Southern
Crowley Maritime	Overseas Shipholding
CSX	Plantation Pipe Line
Hornbeck Offshore	Seabulk
K-Sea Transportation	Union Pacific

HISTORICAL FINANCIALS

Company Type: Public

Income Statement

FYE: December 31

	REVENUE ($ mil.)	NET INCOME ($ mil.)	NET PROFIT MARGIN	EMPLOYEES
12/05	131.5	18.1	13.8%	435
12/04	122.4	1.5	1.2%	330
12/03	80.5	2.4	3.0%	330
12/02	64.5	4.8	7.4%	—
12/01	53.3	1.4	2.6%	—
Annual Growth	**25.3%**	**89.6%**	**—**	**14.8%**

2005 Year-End Financials

Debt ratio: 105.3%
Return on equity: 14.9%
Cash ($ mil.): 10.0
Current ratio: 1.26
Long-term debt ($ mil.): 126.2
No. of shares (mil.): 6.9
Dividends
  Yield: 7.5%
  Payout: 128.1%
Market value ($ mil.): 151.7
R&D as % of sales: —
Advertising as % of sales: —

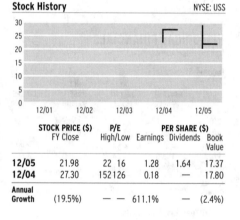

Stock History

NYSE: USS

	STOCK PRICE ($) FY Close	P/E High/Low		PER SHARE ($) Earnings	Dividends	Book Value
12/05	21.98	22	16	1.28	1.64	17.37
12/04	27.30	152	126	0.18	—	17.80
Annual Growth	**(19.5%)**	**—**	**—**	**611.1%**	**—**	**(2.4%)**

USANA Health Sciences

Health is a matter of science at USANA Health Sciences. The company makes nutritional, personal care, and weight management products and sells them through a direct-sales network marketing system composed of more than 140,000 independent distributors or "associates." The company also sells directly to some 70,000 "preferred" customers. USANA's Associates operate throughout North America and the Asia/Pacific region. The company's offerings include nutritional supplements sold under the USANA brand and a line of skin and hair care products under the Sensé brand name. Founder and CEO Myron Wentz owns 46% of the company.

USANA manufactures its nutritional and beauty products in-house, and the vast majority of its revenue comes from sales of these products. However, the company also uses its manufacturing capabilities to make personal care

products for a limited number of other companies. At one time such contract manufacturing accounted for a larger share of the company's sales, but decreased in importance once the Sensé line took off.

USANA began operations in Mexico in 2004 and plans to continue to expand into new geographic markets. It has acquired a manufacturing facility in China, and has secured permission to begin selling its products in Malaysia.

EXECUTIVES

Chairman and CEO: Myron W. Wentz, age 65
President: David A. Wentz, age 35, $172,140 pay
EVP and CFO: Gilbert A. (Gil) Fuller, age 65, $203,401 pay
EVP, Customer Relations: Mark H. Wilson, age 41, $161,207 pay
EVP, Asia Pacific: Bradford Richardson, age 41, $184,097 pay
EVP, Operations: Fred W. Cooper, age 43, $161,207 pay
EVP, Research and Development: Timothy E. Wood, age 57, $161,322 pay
EVP, Marketing: Kevin Guest, age 43
Senior Scientist: John McDonald
Auditors: Grant Thornton LLP

LOCATIONS

HQ: USANA Health Sciences, Inc.
3838 W. Parkway Blvd., Salt Lake City, UT 84120
Phone: 801-954-7100   **Fax:** 801-954-7300
Web: www.usana.com

USANA's headquarters and manufacturing facilities are located in Utah. The company has regional offices and distribution facilities in Australia, Canada, Hong Kong, Japan, Mexico, New Zealand, Singapore, South Korea, Taiwan, and the US. The company also has an office and manufacturing facility in China.

2005 Sales

	% of total
North America	
US	43
Canada	20
Mexico	4
Asia/Pacific	
Australia & New Zealand	14
Taiwan	6
Hong Kong	4
Singapore	4
Japan	3
South Korea	2
Total	**100**

PRODUCTS/OPERATIONS

2005 Sales

	$ mil.	% of total
Direct Sales	319.6	98
Contract Manufacturing	8.1	2
Total	**327.7**	**100**

COMPETITORS

Amway
Avon
Mannatech
Market America
Mary Kay
Nature's Sunshine
NBTY
Nu Skin
Schiff Nutrition International
Shaklee
Sunrider

HISTORICAL FINANCIALS
Company Type: Public

Income Statement

FYE: Saturday nearest December 31

	REVENUE ($ mil.)	NET INCOME ($ mil.)	NET PROFIT MARGIN	EMPLOYEES
12/05	327.7	39.0	11.9%	769
12/04	272.8	30.8	11.3%	672
12/03	200.0	20.8	10.4%	576
12/02	133.8	8.5	6.4%	459
12/01	114.3	2.2	1.9%	459
Annual Growth	**30.1%**	**105.2%**	**—**	**13.8%**

2005 Year-End Financials

Debt ratio: —
Return on equity: 83.4%
Cash ($ mil.): 10.6
Current ratio: 1.57
Long-term debt ($ mil.): —
No. of shares (mil.): 18.3
Dividends
  Yield: —
  Payout: —
Market value ($ mil.): 703.6
R&D as % of sales: 0.7%
Advertising as % of sales: —

Stock History

NASDAQ (GS): USNA

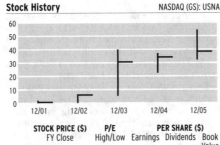

	STOCK PRICE ($) FY Close	P/E High/Low		PER SHARE ($) Earnings	Dividends	Book Value
12/05	38.36	27	16	1.98	—	2.49
12/04	34.20	24	15	1.51	—	2.52
12/03	30.60	40	6	0.98	—	2.28
12/02	6.03	15	1	0.41	—	1.98
12/01	0.61	13	5	0.12	—	1.50
Annual Growth	**181.6%**	**—**	**—**	**101.5%**	**—**	**13.5%**

UTEK Corporation

UTEK sees investing as a swap meet. The business development company (BDC) forms portfolio companies to license new technologies developed at universities and research labs. Before it makes the investment, though, UTEK finds a buyer for the technology, eventually swapping portfolio company stock for the buyer's stock. The technology-transfer firm has portfolio companies that are seeking licensing deals in such areas as biotechnology, energy, geology, manufacturing, and electronics. UTEK has also forged alliances with several universities and research centers. Founder, chairman, and CEO Clifford Gross owns 22% of UTEK.

The company has around 50 portfolio companies. Over the course of a year it may complete more than a dozen technology transfer deals and three times as many strategic alliance agreements. Deals completed in 2006 include the sale of subsidiaries Intellitouch Technologies (gaming software for people with disabilities), Advanced Glaucoma Technologies (monoclonal antibody glaucoma treatment), Natural Adhesive Technologies (wood adhesive), Advanced Fertilizer Technologies (plant-derived fertilizer), and Ultra Fine Coating Systems (powder-coating

technology). In 2005 UTEK acquired INTRA-DMS, Ltd., an Israel-based company that develops software to help universities, pharmaceutical firms, and technology companies manage their intellectual property. The company is now known as UTEKip, Ltd. UTEK in 2005 also bolstered its information services capabilities (for use both in-house and by portfolio companies) via its acquisition of Knowledge Express Data Systems, a subscription-based provider of information (such as agreements, licensing deals, and patents) related to intellectual property. The company entered into a strategic alliance with NeoStem, an adult stem cell collection, processing, and storage company, in early 2007.

EXECUTIVES

Chairman and CEO: Clifford M. Gross, age 48, $375,000 pay
COO and Chief Compliance Officer: Douglas (Doug) Schaedler, age 34, $234,273 pay
CFO, Secretary, and Treasurer: Carole R. Wright, age 44, $99,000 pay
VP: Marlin Gilbert, age 43
VP; Business Development Director, UTEK-Pax: John Allies, age 42
VP; Chairman, UTEK-Pax: John D. Emanuel, age 67
VP Business Development: Alon Bogel
VP, General Counsel, and Director: Sam Reiber, age 59, $44,000 pay
VP, Finance: Jeffrey L. Taylor
VP Technology Alliances: Joel Edelson, age 46
CTO: Jeffrey D. Bleil, age 51
Auditors: Pender Newkirk & Company

LOCATIONS

HQ: UTEK Corporation
202 S. Wheeler St., Plant City, FL 33563
Phone: 813-754-4330   **Fax:** 813-754-2383
Web: www.utekcorp.com

2005 Sales

	% of total
US	95
UK	4
Israel	1
Total	**100**

PRODUCTS/OPERATIONS

2005 Sales

	$ mil.	% of total
Sale of technology rights	18.1	80
Consulting & other services	4.2	18
Other	0.4	2
Total	**22.7**	**100**

Selected Areas of Concentration

Biotechnology and pharmaceuticals
Building and manufacturing
Electronics
Energy and conservation
Geological and soil technologies
Nutraceuticals and wellness products

COMPETITORS

Acacia Research
CMGI
CVF Technologies
ETI
IP Group
IPVALUE
Redleaf Group
Safeguard Scientifics

HISTORICAL FINANCIALS
Company Type: Public

Income Statement

	REVENUE ($ mil.)	NET INCOME ($ mil.)	NET PROFIT MARGIN	EMPLOYEES
				FYE: December 31
12/05	22.7	2.1	9.3%	50
12/04	8.7	2.3	26.4%	29
12/03	3.8	(0.5)	—	16
12/02	3.4	(2.7)	—	—
12/01	4.1	0.6	14.6%	—
Annual Growth	53.4%	36.8%	—	76.8%

2005 Year-End Financials

Debt ratio: —
Return on equity: 6.2%
Cash ($ mil.): 5.3
Current ratio: —
Long-term debt ($ mil.): —
No. of shares (mil.): 8.0

Dividends
  Yield: —
  Payout: —
Market value ($ mil.): 109.8
R&D as % of sales: —
Advertising as % of sales: —

Stock History

AMEX: UTK

	STOCK PRICE ($) FY Close	P/E High/Low	PER SHARE ($) Earnings	Dividends	Book Value
12/05	13.79	54 41	0.29	—	5.58
12/04	14.99	46 30	0.37	—	3.85
12/03	11.10	— —	(0.12)	—	2.33
12/02	6.25	— —	(0.69)	—	1.87
12/01	7.10	51 32	0.17	—	2.53
Annual Growth	18.1%	— —	14.3%	—	21.9%

VA Software

This company is fanning the flames of the open source software movement. VA Software markets software and produces Web sites aimed primarily at open source software developers and other technology enthusiasts. Its SourceForge software development suite offers a Web-based environment for collaborative programming teams to manage their work.

VA Software's online media subsidiary, OSTG (formerly Open Source Technology Group), operates a number of Web sites catering to the tech set, including SourceForge.net (an online collaborative development site), Slashdot.org (technology news), and Freshmeat.net (open source software directory). It also operates ThinkGeek, and online shop for apparel, books, and tech gadgets.

While best known for its SourceForge tool and content sites, more than 45% of VA Software's revenue comes from e-commerce. Software and online publishing account for about 23% and 30% of sales, respectively.

During 2005 the company released a new version of SourceForge with improved integration features. The application is used by more than 130 enterprises, including Hewlett-Packard and Los Alamos National Laboratory. The company's

Web sites, which generate sales mostly through advertising, boast an audience of more than 30 million people.

While a graduate student at Stanford in 1993, chairman Larry Augustin (who owns 7% of the company) chose to help start VA rather than become a co-founder of Yahoo!

HISTORY

Unable to afford a high-end Sun Microsystems workstation in 1991, Larry Augustin decided to build a Linux-based version in his living room so he could finish his dissertation at Stanford. When his experiment yielded a machine that was a third the price and twice as fast as Sun's, his fellow graduate students took notice. Instead of pursuing the business model Augustin co-wrote with friends Jerry Yang and David Filo (which eventually became Yahoo!), Augustin stuck to his engineering roots and continued to build workstations out of his house.

In 1993, still a doctoral student in electrical engineering, he started VA Research along with pal James Vera (VA comes from the initials of their surnames) with financing from their credit cards. The company incorporated in 1995. (Vera remained a researcher at Stanford.)

Because VA Research designed and built its systems from the ground up (and because Linux itself was continuously morphing into something else), it wasn't until 1997 that the company released its first high-end workstations. With funding from venture investment firm Sequoia Capital in 1998, VA Research began building its staff by hiring Linux veterans such as Leonard Zubkoff, whom Augustin lured away from Oracle to be his chief technology officer. The company also began to target the high-end server market, offering $200,000 systems to ISPs.

In 1999 VA Research changed its name to VA Linux Systems and formed alliances with Linux software vendors Red Hat and SuSE Linux to preinstall their software on its systems. The company also bought out its closest rival, Linux Hardware Solutions, as well as a Linux consulting company and a graphical user interface specialist. VA Linux went public that December — its stock price soaring a record 698 percent during its first day of trading.

The company acquired Linux information portal Andover.Net in 2000 and later launched the Open Source Development Network (OSDN). It also bought privately held TruSolutions and NetAttach in two deals with a combined value of about $230 million.

The next year — citing sluggish hardware spending and high costs — VA Linux announced that it would cut about 35% of its workforce and exit its core server and workstation business in order to focus on Linux-based development software and services. The company changed its name to VA Software late in 2001.

Company president and COO Ali Jenab was promoted to CEO the next year, while Augustin remained chairman. In 2004 the company renamed OSDN the Open Source Technology Group and redesigned many of its online publications in an effort to expand the audience for its Web sites.

In December 2005, VA Software sold its Animation Factory subsidiary to Jupitermedia Corp. for about $9.4 million.

EXECUTIVES

Chairman: Larry M. Augustin, age 44
President, CEO, and Director: Ali Jenab, age 43, $622,747 pay (prior to title change)
SVP and CFO: Patricia S. Morris, age 42, $17,308 pay (partial-year salary)
VP, Editorial Operations; Executive Editor, Slashdot: Jeff (Hemos) Bates
Group President, OSTG: Richard J. (Rich) Marino, age 57, $55,000 pay (partial-year salary)
Group President, SourceForge Enterprise Software: Darryll E. Dewan, age 55, $444,300 pay
Secretary and General Counsel; VP and General Manager, SourceForge.net: Jay Seirmarco
Corporate Controller: Jeffrey Chalmers, age 44
VP, Marketing, OSTG: Valerie Williamson
VP, Marketing, SourceForge Enterprise Edition: John Guerriere
VP, Sales, OSTG: Andrew Zeiger
VP, Sales, SourceForge Enterprise Edition: Richard Segina
General Manager, ThinkGeek, OSTG: Caroline Offutt
Auditors: Stonefield Josephson, Inc.

LOCATIONS

HQ: VA Software Corporation
46939 Bayside Pkwy., Fremont, CA 94538
Phone: 510-687-7000   **Fax:** 510-687-7155
Web: www.vasoftware.com

VA Software has operations in California and Virginia.

PRODUCTS/OPERATIONS

2006 Sales

	$ mil.	% of total
E-Commerce	20.4	47
Online media	13.2	30
Software	10.0	23
Total	**43.6**	**100**

Selected Products and Operations

E-commerce (ThinkGeek)
  Apparel
  Caffeinated products
  Electronics
  Office products
Online media
  Freshmeat.net
  Linux.com
  ITManagersJournal.com
  NewsForge.com
  Slashdot.org
  SourceForge.net
SourceForge (enterprise software development tools)

COMPETITORS

Amazon.com
AOL
Borland Software
CNET Networks
CollabNet
Fry's Electronics
Google
IBM Software
International Data Group
Microsoft
Newegg.com
Oracle
SERENA Software
Systemax
Tucows
Yahoo!
Ziff Davis Media

HISTORICAL FINANCIALS

Company Type: Public

Income Statement

FYE: July 31

	REVENUE ($ mil.)	NET INCOME ($ mil.)	NET PROFIT MARGIN	EMPLOYEES
7/06	43.6	11.0	25.2%	121
7/05	32.9	(4.7)	—	127
7/04	29.3	(7.6)	—	122
7/03	24.2	(13.8)	—	115
7/02	20.4	(91.0)	—	144
Annual Growth	20.9%	—	—	(4.3%)

2006 Year-End Financials

Debt ratio: —
Return on equity: 27.1%
Cash ($ mil.): 51.9
Current ratio: 7.30
Long-term debt ($ mil.): —
No. of shares (mil.): 64.5

Dividends
Yield: —
Payout: —
Market value ($ mil.): 256.1
R&D as % of sales: —
Advertising as % of sales: —

Stock History

NASDAQ (GM): LNUX

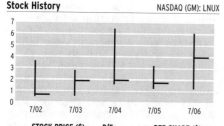

	STOCK PRICE ($) FY Close	P/E High/Low		PER SHARE ($) Earnings	Dividends	Book Value
7/06	3.97	35	8	0.17	—	0.77
7/05	1.72	—	—	(0.08)	—	0.51
7/04	1.94	—	—	(0.13)	—	0.58
7/03	1.88	—	—	(0.25)	—	0.49
7/02	0.66	—	—	(1.72)	—	0.73
Annual Growth	56.6%	—	—	—	—	1.3%

VAALCO Energy

VAALCO Energy has boldly gone where bigger players are sure to follow. The small independent, which merged with the 1818 Oil Corp. in a reverse acquisition in 1998, is engaged in the acquisition, exploration, development, and production of oil and gas. Its strategy is to balance its lower-risk domestic drilling with higher-potential international prospects. VAALCO holds offshore exploration assets in Gabon. The company sold its Philippine holdings in 2004. VAALCO has interests in the Texas Gulf Coast. It has proved reserves of 7.8 million barrels of oil and 21 million cu. ft. of gas. The 1818 fund, managed by Brown Brothers Harriman & Co. of New York., controlled 65% of VAALCO but sold this stake in 2005.

EXECUTIVES

Chairman and CEO: Robert L. Gerry III, age 68, $674,000 pay
President, CFO, and Director: W. Russell Scheirman, age 50, $456,000 pay
VP and Corporate Secretary: Gayla M. Cutrer, $221,400 pay
Auditors: Deloitte & Touche LLP

LOCATIONS

HQ: VAALCO Energy, Inc.
 4600 Post Oak Place, Ste. 309, Houston, TX 77027
Phone: 713-623-0801 **Fax:** 713-623-0982
Web: www.vaalco.com

VAALCO Energy has oil and gas exploration interests in Gabon and the US.

PRODUCTS/OPERATIONS

Selected Subsidiaries

VAALCO Energy (Gabon), Inc.
VAALCO Energy (USA), Inc.
VAALCO Garbon (Etame), Inc. (90%)
VAALCO Production (Gabon), Inc.

COMPETITORS

Exxon Mobil
Hess
Imperial Oil
Pioneer Natural Resources
Royal Dutch Shell
TOTAL

HISTORICAL FINANCIALS

Company Type: Public

Income Statement

FYE: December 31

	REVENUE ($ mil.)	NET INCOME ($ mil.)	NET PROFIT MARGIN	EMPLOYEES
12/05	84.9	29.2	34.4%	16
12/04	56.5	22.9	40.5%	12
12/03	36.0	8.9	24.7%	28
12/02	10.0	0.4	4.0%	29
12/01	1.9	(3.1)	—	24
Annual Growth	158.5%	—	—	(9.6%)

2005 Year-End Financials

Debt ratio: 1.9%
Return on equity: 46.4%
Cash ($ mil.): 45.0
Current ratio: 6.47
Long-term debt ($ mil.): 1.5
No. of shares (mil.): 57.3

Dividends
Yield: —
Payout: —
Market value ($ mil.): 242.8
R&D as % of sales: —
Advertising as % of sales: —

Stock History

NYSE: EGY

	STOCK PRICE ($) FY Close	P/E High/Low		PER SHARE ($) Earnings	Dividends	Book Value
12/05	4.24	11	6	0.50	—	1.37
12/04	3.88	15	4	0.39	—	1.46
12/03	1.40	9	6	0.16	—	1.15
12/02	1.47	150	36	0.01	—	0.73
12/01	0.55	—	—	(0.15)	—	0.49
Annual Growth	66.6%	—	—	—	—	29.4%

Valero

Performing with valor in a supporting role, Valero L.P. is part of the backbone of parent Valero Energy's refining and marketing operations in the Southwest and the Rocky Mountains. Valero L.P. expanded dramatically in 2005 by buying Kaneb Services and Kaneb Pipe Line for about $2.8 billion. Counting assets gained in the Kaneb acquisitions, Valero L.P. operates 8,389 miles of refined product pipelines, 797 miles of crude oil pipelines, 89 terminal facilities, and four crude oil storage facilities. The company has about 78 million barrels of refined product storage capacity. Valero L.P. is an indirect wholly owned subsidiary of Valero Energy. Valero GP Holdings, LLC holds the company's 2% general partner interest.

Valero L.P.'s refined product pipelines include 2,000 miles of anhydrous ammonia pipelines, and 21 associated terminals providing 4.9 million barrels of storage capacity.

In 2006 the company sold its Australia- and New Zealand-based subsidiaries and their eight terminals to ANZ Terminals Pty. Ltd. for about $65 million, plus net working capital.

That year the company agreed to buy the St. James crude oil facility in Louisiana from Koch Supply & Trading for $140 million.

EXECUTIVES

Chairman: William E. (Bill) Greehey, age 69
President, CEO, and Director: Curtis V. Anastasio, age 49, $653,500 pay
SVP and CFO: Steven A. Blank, age 51, $507,500 pay
SVP Operations: James R. Bluntzer, age 51, $358,833 pay
SVP Corporate Communications: Mary Rose Brown
VP and Controller: Clayton E. (Clay) Killinger, age 44
VP Engineering: Brad R. Ramsey, age 37, $272,800 pay (partial-year salary)
VP Business Development: James D. (Jerry) McVicker, age 50, $316,626 pay
VP Regional Operations: Rodney L. Reese, age 55, $287,123 pay
VP Investor Relations: Eric Fisher
Secretary and Disclosure and Compliance Officer: Bradley C. Barron
Auditors: Ernst & Young LLP; KPMG LLP

LOCATIONS

HQ: Valero L.P.
 1 Valero Way, San Antonio, TX 78249
Phone: 210-345-2000 **Fax:** 210-345-2103
Web: www.valerolp.com

PRODUCTS/OPERATIONS

2005 Sales

	$ mil.	% of total
Refined product terminals	411.4	62
Refined product pipelines	149.9	23
Crude oil pipelines	51.4	8
Crude oil storage tanks	46.9	7
Total	**659.6**	**100**

COMPETITORS

BP
Enbridge (U.S.)
Kinder Morgan, Inc.
Marathon Petroleum
Shell Pipeline
TransCanada

HISTORICAL FINANCIALS

Company Type: Public

Income Statement

FYE: December 31

	REVENUE ($ mil.)	NET INCOME ($ mil.)	NET PROFIT MARGIN	EMPLOYEES
12/05	659.6	111.1	16.8%	1,291
12/04	220.8	78.4	35.5%	285
12/03	181.4	69.6	38.4%	207
12/02	118.5	55.1	46.5%	200
12/01	98.8	45.9	46.5%	160
Annual Growth	60.7%	24.7%	—	68.5%

2005 Year-End Financials

Debt ratio: 61.5%
Return on equity: 9.5%
Cash ($ mil.): 36.0
Current ratio: 1.44
Long-term debt ($ mil.): 1,169.7
No. of shares (mil.): 37.2

Dividends
  Yield: 6.4%
  Payout: 115.7%
Market value ($ mil.): 1,926.0
R&D as % of sales: —
Advertising as % of sales: —

Stock History

NYSE: VLI

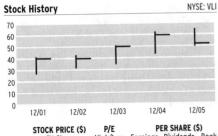

	STOCK PRICE ($) FY Close	P/E High/Low		PER SHARE ($) Earnings	Dividends	Book Value
12/05	51.76	22	18	2.86	3.31	51.08
12/04	59.43	20	14	3.15	3.15	32.61
12/03	49.77	17	12	3.02	2.90	32.60
12/02	39.70	16	12	2.72	2.65	30.44
12/01	40.05	22	15	1.82	0.60	30.37
Annual Growth	6.6%	—	—	12.0%	53.3%	13.9%

Valley Financial

Down in the valley, valley so low . . . Valley Financial has a banking business, dontcha know? The holding company for Valley Bank has about 10 locations in and around Roanoke, Virginia. Valley Bank offers traditional banking products and services to individuals and small to midsized businesses in its market area. Deposit products include checking and savings accounts, NOW accounts, and CDs. Its loan portfolio consists primarily of commercial real estate loans and business loans; it also offers residential mortgages, construction loans, and consumer loans.

Chairman George Logan owns nearly 10% of Valley Financial; as a group, executive officers and directors own more than 35%.

EXECUTIVES

Chairman, Valley Financial and Valley Bank: George W. Logan, age 61
President, CEO, and Director; President and CEO, Valley Bank: Ellis L. Gutshall, age 55, $363,200 pay
SVP and CFO: Kimberly Burch Snyder
SVP and Chief Strategic Planning Officer: Penny Y. Goodwin
SVP and Chief Credit Officer: Cathy J. Hartman
SVP and Chief Risk Officer: Mary P. Hundley, age 45

SVP and CIO: JoAnn Lloyd, age 51
SVP and Chief Lending Officer: John T. McCaleb, $110,000 pay
SVP and Chief Retail Banking Officer: Connie W. Stanley, age 53
EVP and COO, Valley Financial and Valley Bank: James Randall (Randy) Woodson, age 44, $206,580 pay
Auditors: Elliott Davis LLC

LOCATIONS

HQ: Valley Financial Corporation
  36 Church Ave. SW, Roanoke, VA 24011
Phone: 540-342-2265   **Fax:** 540-342-4514
Web: www.myvalleybank.com

PRODUCTS/OPERATIONS

2005 Sales

	$ mil.	% of total
Interest		
Loans, including fees	21.8	83
Securities & other	2.8	11
Noninterest		
Service charges on deposit accounts	0.9	3
Other	0.7	3
Total	26.2	100

COMPETITORS

Bank of America
BB&T
SunTrust
Wachovia

HISTORICAL FINANCIALS

Company Type: Public

Income Statement

FYE: December 31

	ASSETS ($ mil.)	NET INCOME ($ mil.)	INCOME AS % OF ASSETS	EMPLOYEES
12/05	499.0	3.4	0.7%	111
12/04	374.0	2.8	0.7%	—
12/03	309.0	2.6	0.8%	—
12/02	248.9	2.3	0.9%	—
12/01	193.9	1.7	0.9%	—
Annual Growth	26.7%	18.9%	—	—

2005 Year-End Financials

Equity as % of assets: 6.2%
Return on assets: 0.8%
Return on equity: 11.5%
Long-term debt ($ mil.): 48.3
No. of shares (mil.): 4.1
Market value ($ mil.): 52.4

Dividends
  Yield: 1.0%
  Payout: 16.3%
Sales ($ mil.): 26.2
R&D as % of sales: —
Advertising as % of sales: —

Stock History

NASDAQ (CM): VYFC

	STOCK PRICE ($) FY Close	P/E High/Low		PER SHARE ($) Earnings	Dividends	Book Value
12/05	12.85	18	14	0.80	0.13	7.53
12/04	14.00	39	16	0.70	0.06	6.95
12/03	11.30	17	11	0.67	—	11.76
12/02	7.55	13	9	0.60	—	10.40
12/01	5.33	13	9	0.46	—	13.44
Annual Growth	24.6%	—	—	14.8%	116.7%	(13.5%)

ValueClick

If you think that banner ad is worth a look, ValueClick will put a price on it. The company brings Web publishers together with advertisers providing the technology necessary for each side to manage online advertising. ValueClick's media services segment offers opt-in e-mail marketing, search marketing, and ad placement throughout a network of more than 10,000 Web sites. Its affiliate marketing tools and services track and analyze online marketing programs through its Commission Junction subsidiary and provide online ad serving and management tools through Mediaplex.

Founded in 1998, the company has expanded its services through the acquisitions of Web Marketing Holdings, E-Babylon, and Fastclick.

The acquisition of Web Marketing Holdings expands ValueClick's online marketing services with the addition of more than 100 promotional Web sites. ValueClick's acquisition of E-Babylon is a first step into e-commerce for ValueClick, offering ink and toner products through its 123Inkjets.com and 411inkjets.com Web sites.

In addition, ValueClick acquired Shopping.net, an operator of 27 comparison shopping Web sites, for $13 million in cash in December 2006. Shopping.net will be integrated into the company's European operations, ValueClick Europe.

EXECUTIVES

Chairman, CEO, and President: James R. Zarley, age 61
CFO: Scott H. Ray, age 41
President, ValueClick US: Thomas A. (Tom) Vadnais, age 58
VP, General Counsel, and Secretary: Scott P. Barlow, age 37
VP Marketing: Elizabeth Cholawsky
VP Corporate Strategy: John Ardis
CTO: Peter Wolfert, age 42
CEO, ValueClick Europe: Carl White, age 41
General Manager, US Media Segment: David Yovanno
Chief Administrative Officer: Samuel J. (Sam) Paisley, age 56
Director Corporate Communications: Gary J. Fuges
Auditors: PricewaterhouseCoopers LLP

LOCATIONS

HQ: ValueClick, Inc.
  30699 Russell Ranch Rd., Ste. 250,
  Westlake Village, CA 91362
Phone: 818-575-4500   **Fax:** 818-575-4501
Web: valueclick.com

ValueClick operates in France, Germany, Sweden, the UK, and the US.

2005 Sales

	$ mil.	% of total
US	263.2	84
Europe	49.1	16
Adjustments	(8.3)	—
Total	304.0	100

PRODUCTS/OPERATIONS

2005 Sales

	$ mil.	% of total
Media	210.6	67
Affiliate marketing	77.4	25
Technology	24.2	8
Adjustments	(8.2)	—
Total	304.0	100

Selected Subsidiaries and Services

ValueClick Media
  Brand marketing
  Direct marketing
  Pay Per Click Search Marketing
Commission Junction
  Affiliate marketing
  Search marketing
  Program management
Mediaplex
  Ad serving
  Publisher ad management
  E-mail management and delivery
Pricerunner
  Comparison shopping
  Consumer reviews
  Mobile services

COMPETITORS

24/7 Real Media
Acxiom Digital
Advertising.com
Agency.com
aQuantive
BURST! Media
DoubleClick
LinkShare
MIVA
Modem Media
Yahoo! Search Marketing

HISTORICAL FINANCIALS

Company Type: Public

Income Statement

FYE: December 31

	REVENUE ($ mil.)	NET INCOME ($ mil.)	NET PROFIT MARGIN	EMPLOYEES
12/05	304.0	40.6	13.4%	1,014
12/04	169.2	87.9	52.0%	620
12/03	92.5	9.8	10.6%	576
12/02	62.5	(10.6)	—	419
12/01	44.9	(7.2)	—	107
Annual Growth	61.3%	—	—	75.5%

2005 Year-End Financials

Debt ratio: 2.9%
Return on equity: 8.1%
Cash ($ mil.): 240.8
Current ratio: 4.88
Long-term debt ($ mil.): 17.7
No. of shares (mil.): 102.1

Dividends
  Yield: —
  Payout: —
Market value ($ mil.): 1,848.5
R&D as % of sales: —
Advertising as % of sales: 11.3%

Stock History

NASDAQ (GS): VCLK

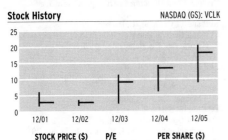

	STOCK PRICE ($) FY Close	P/E High/Low		PER SHARE ($) Earnings	Dividends	Book Value
12/05	18.11	45	20	0.45	—	6.06
12/04	13.33	13	6	1.05	—	4.69
12/03	9.07	86	20	0.13	—	3.52
12/02	2.79	—	—	(0.14)	—	3.04
12/01	2.86	—	—	(0.20)	—	3.14
Annual Growth	58.6%	—	—	—	—	17.9%

Varsity Group

Varsity Group encourages students to take a heavy course load. The company runs textbook e-tailer VarsityBooks.com, which offers thousands of discounted textbooks and school supplies to colleges and private elementary and secondary schools. Varsity Group gets its books through US wholesaler Baker & Taylor. The firm's Campus Outfitters business, acquired in 2005, sells K-12 private school uniforms through the Internet and nine retail locations, mostly in the eastern US. All told, the firm has partnerships with about 700 educational institutions representing about 240,000 students. Law school buddies Eric Kuhn and Tim Levy launched the company in 1997.

EXECUTIVES

Chairman: Eric J. Kuhn, age 35
Interim CEO and CFO: James M. Craig, age 50
SVP, Business Development and CIO: Jack M. Benson, age 37
SVP and General Manager, Branded Clothing/Uniform Business: Richard Peterson
SVP, Sales, Marketing, and Operations: Marcus May
VP, Sales: Jay Fee
Auditors: PricewaterhouseCoopers LLP

LOCATIONS

HQ: Varsity Group Inc.
  1850 M St., Ste. 1150, Washington, DC 20036
Phone: 202-667-3400   **Fax:** 202-332-5498
Web: www.varsity-group.com

PRODUCTS/OPERATIONS

2005 Sales

	$ mil.	% of total
Textbooks	40.7	81
Uniforms	5.8	12
Shipping & other	3.6	7
Total	50.1	100

COMPETITORS

Amazon.com
Barnes & Noble College Bookstores
barnesandnoble.com
Borders
Cintas
Ecampus.com
Fechheimer Brothers
Follett
MBS Textbook Exchange
Nebraska Book
Time Warner

HISTORICAL FINANCIALS

Company Type: Public

Income Statement

FYE: December 31

	REVENUE ($ mil.)	NET INCOME ($ mil.)	NET PROFIT MARGIN	EMPLOYEES
12/05	50.1	12.1	24.2%	79
12/04	37.7	6.9	18.3%	45
12/03	25.2	4.4	17.5%	30
12/02	16.6	0.7	4.2%	—
12/01	12.5	(2.2)	—	—
Annual Growth	41.5%	—	—	62.3%

2005 Year-End Financials

Debt ratio: —
Return on equity: 35.1%
Cash ($ mil.): 6.1
Current ratio: 4.92
Long-term debt ($ mil.): —
No. of shares (mil.): 17.1

Dividends
  Yield: —
  Payout: —
Market value ($ mil.): 72.8
R&D as % of sales: —
Advertising as % of sales: —

Stock History

NASDAQ (GM): VSTY

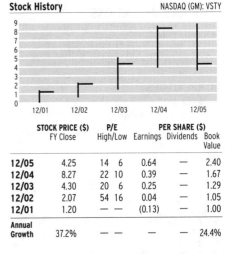

	STOCK PRICE ($) FY Close	P/E High/Low		PER SHARE ($) Earnings	Dividends	Book Value
12/05	4.25	14	6	0.64	—	2.40
12/04	8.27	22	10	0.39	—	1.67
12/03	4.30	20	6	0.25	—	1.29
12/02	2.07	54	16	0.04	—	1.05
12/01	1.20	—	—	(0.13)	—	1.00
Annual Growth	37.2%	—	—	—	—	24.4%

VASCO Data Security

VASCO Data Security International holds the key to electronic banking. Its Digipass product line features security tokens, handheld devices, and related software used for authenticating a person's identity to computer networks. The company's products incorporate authentication and digital signature security technologies, and can be used to secure intranets and extranets, as well as local area networks (LANs). In addition to banking, VASCO's products are used to provide remote workers with secure access to corporate networks; other applications include e-commerce transactions. Chairman and CEO Kendall Hunt owns about 30% of the company.

The company has more than 2,000 customers in over 100 countries. Clients have included DaimlerChrysler, Fortis Bank, and Dutch banking giant Rabobank.

VASCO acquired Able, a provider of unified threat management software, in 2006.

EXECUTIVES

Chairman and CEO: T. Kendall (Ken) Hunt, age 62, $350,000 pay
President and COO: Jan Valcke, age 51, $432,852 pay
EVP, CFO, and Secretary: Clifford K. Bown, age 54, $260,000 pay
Director, Corporate Communications: Jochem Binst
Auditors: KPMG LLP

LOCATIONS

HQ: VASCO Data Security International, Inc.
  1901 S. Meyers Rd., Ste. 210,
  Oakbrook Terrace, IL 60180
Phone: 630-932-8844   **Fax:** 630-932-8852
Web: www.vasco.com

2005 Sales

	$ mil.	% of total
Europe	39.2	72
US	3.7	7
Other regions	11.7	21
Total	**54.6**	**100**

PRODUCTS/OPERATIONS

Selected Products

Authentication devices and software (Digipass)
Authentication utilities (VACMAN)

COMPETITORS

ActivIdentity
Aladdin Knowledge Systems
BindView
CA
Check Point Software
Entrust
Litronic
McAfee
NTRU
RSA Security
SafeNet
Secure Computing
Symantec
V-ONE
WatchGuard Technologies

HISTORICAL FINANCIALS

Company Type: Public

Income Statement
FYE: December 31

	REVENUE ($ mil.)	NET INCOME ($ mil.)	NET PROFIT MARGIN	EMPLOYEES
12/05	54.6	7.7	14.1%	128
12/04	29.9	3.3	11.0%	112
12/03	22.9	2.8	12.2%	75
12/02	18.9	(4.5)	—	77
12/01	26.7	(12.0)	—	86
Annual Growth	**19.6%**	**—**	**—**	**10.5%**

2005 Year-End Financials

Debt ratio: —
Return on equity: 41.7%
Cash ($ mil.): 17.1
Current ratio: 2.03
Long-term debt ($ mil.): —
No. of shares (mil.): 36.2
Dividends
  Yield: —
  Payout: —
Market value ($ mil.): 356.7
R&D as % of sales: —
Advertising as % of sales: —

Stock History
NASDAQ (GM): VDSI

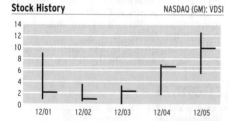

	STOCK PRICE ($) FY Close	P/E High/Low		PER SHARE ($) Earnings	Dividends	Book Value
12/05	9.86	59	26	0.21	—	0.70
12/04	6.62	77	20	0.09	—	0.39
12/03	2.34	—	—	(0.06)	—	0.29
12/02	0.97	—	—	(0.20)	—	0.10
12/01	2.10	—	—	(0.47)	—	0.25
Annual Growth	**47.2%**	**—**	**—**	**—**	**—**	**29.1%**

VCG Holding

Patrons holding dollar bills might be able to get a little extra entertainment at these establishments. VCG Holding operates about 15 nightclubs featuring live adult entertainment, primarily under the names PT's and The Penthouse Club (through a licensing agreement with publisher Penthouse Media Group).

In addition to exotic dancers, the clubs offer dining and bar services, as well as members-only VIP rooms intended for entertaining business clients. Alcohol sales account for more than 40% of business. The company's nightclubs are located mostly in Denver and in Illinois, as well as in Indianapolis; Louisville, Kentucky; and Phoenix. CEO Troy Lowrie owns nearly 60% of VCG Holding.

EXECUTIVES

Chairman and CEO: Troy H. Lowrie, age 40
President and Director: Micheal L. Ocello, age 46, $183,000 pay
Chief Financial and Accounting Officer and Treasurer: Donald W. Prosser, age 55
Secretary: Mary E. Bowles-Cook, age 52

LOCATIONS

HQ: VCG Holding Corp.
  390 Union Blvd., Ste. 540, Lakewood, CO 80228
Phone: 303-934-2424　　**Fax:** 303-922-0746
Web: www.vcgh.com

PRODUCTS/OPERATIONS

2005 Sales

	$ mil.	% of total
Alcohol	7.1	42
Services	4.0	23
Food & merchandise	1.3	8
Other	4.6	27
Total	**17.0**	**100**

Selected Nightclubs

Club Inferno (Denver)
Diamond Cabaret & Steakhouse (Denver)
The Penthouse Club (Denver; Phoenix; Sauget, Illinois)
PT's All Nude (Denver)
PT's Brooklyn (Illinois)
PT's Centreville (Illinois)
PT's Showclub (Colorado Springs, Colorado; Denver; Indianapolis; Louisville, Kentucky)
PT's Sports (Denver; Sauget, Illinois)
Roxy's (Brooklyn, Illinois)
Tabú (Denver)

HISTORICAL FINANCIALS

Company Type: Public

Income Statement
FYE: December 31

	REVENUE ($ mil.)	NET INCOME ($ mil.)	NET PROFIT MARGIN	EMPLOYEES
12/05	17.0	0.4	2.4%	335
12/04	12.2	(1.8)	—	325
12/03	9.1	0.7	7.7%	—
12/02	3.6	(0.2)	—	—
Annual Growth	**67.8%**	**—**	**—**	**3.1%**

2005 Year-End Financials

Debt ratio: 304.9%
Return on equity: 12.2%
Cash ($ mil.): 0.9
Current ratio: 0.32
Long-term debt ($ mil.): 9.3
No. of shares (mil.): 8.7
Dividends
  Yield: —
  Payout: —
Market value ($ mil.): 11.8
R&D as % of sales: —
Advertising as % of sales: —

Stock History
AMEX: PTT

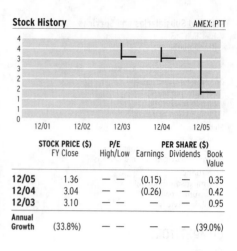

	STOCK PRICE ($) FY Close	P/E High/Low		PER SHARE ($) Earnings	Dividends	Book Value
12/05	1.36	—	—	(0.15)	—	0.35
12/04	3.04	—	—	(0.26)	—	0.42
12/03	3.10	—	—	—	—	0.95
Annual Growth	**(33.8%)**	**—**	**—**	**—**	**—**	**(39.0%)**

VeraSun Energy

VeraSun Energy hopes its profits rise with the progress of the US quest for energy independence. The company is one of the nation's leading producers of ethanol, a type of alcohol that can be blended with gasoline and used to fuel motor vehicles. In the US, ethanol is made primarily from corn, and VeraSun maintains three production facilities in the corn-growing states of Iowa and South Dakota. Two more facilities began construction in Iowa and Minnesota toward the end of 2006. The company is selling a branded fuel, VE85, at service stations in the Midwest. CEO Don Endres owns just over 50% of VeraSun Energy; South Dakota investment firm Bluestem Funds owns 33%.

VE85 is a branded version of E85, a fuel blend that can contain as much as 85% ethanol. Automakers Ford and General Motors are helping VeraSun Energy promote VE85.

EXECUTIVES

Chairman and CEO: Donald L. (Don) Endres, age 45
President and Director: Bruce A. Jamerson, age 54, $293,544 pay
SVP and CFO: Danny C. Herron, age 51
SVP and General Counsel: John M. Schweitzer, age 61
SVP Corporate Development and Director: Paul A. Schock, age 47
SVP Operations: Paul J. Caudill, age 52
SVP Sales and Marketing: William L. (Bill) Honnef, age 39, $180,173 pay
VP Finance: Ginja R. Collins, age 31
VP Ethanol Sales: Paul Kreter
VP Plant Operations: Kevin T. Biehle, age 42
VP Technology: Matthew K.R. (Matt) Janes, age 49, $208,937 pay
Director Administration and Human Resources: Ginger Scalet
Auditors: McGladrey & Pullen, LLP

LOCATIONS

HQ: VeraSun Energy Corporation
  100 22nd Ave., Brookings, SD 57006
Phone: 605-696-7200　　**Fax:** 605-696-7250
Web: www.verasun.com

COMPETITORS

Abengoa Bioenergy
ADM
Aventine
Cargill

HISTORICAL FINANCIALS

Company Type: Public

Income Statement

FYE: December 31

	REVENUE ($ mil.)	NET INCOME ($ mil.)	NET PROFIT MARGIN	EMPLOYEES
12/05	236.4	0.3	0.1%	145
12/04	193.8	14.8	7.6%	—
12/03	12.7	0.6	4.7%	—
Annual Growth	331.4%	(29.3%)	—	—

2005 Year-End Financials

Debt ratio: 144.0%
Return on equity: 0.3%
Cash ($ mil.): 29.7
Current ratio: 3.32
Long-term debt ($ mil.): 208.7

Net Income History

NYSE: VSE

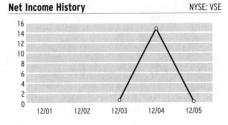

VeriFone Holdings

VeriFone's been twice swiped. The company is a leading supplier of electronic payment equipment such as point-of-sale software and terminals, smart card and check readers, receipt printers, and Internet commerce software. It also generates sales from installation, project management, training, and other services. Customers include government agencies and companies in the hospitality, retail, and health care markets. Once a division of Hewlett-Packard, Verifone has seen its ownership shift twice in recent years, acquired first by Gores Technology Group and later sold to GTCR Golder Rauner.

Verifone provides customized systems that address the specific needs of select markets, including financial services, government, health care, multi-lane retail, and petroleum. Providing pay-at-the-pump functionality to petroleum retailers is an example of such specialization. The expansion of other payment applications, including pay-at-the-table systems for restaurants, is part of the company's growth strategy.

The company racked up huge losses as a division of Hewlett-Packard. After prolonged attempts to restructure VeriFone, HP finally sold the division to Gores Technology Group in 2001. The next year, Gores sold the majority stake in VeriFone to GTCR Golder Rauner, a private equity firm with expertise in the payment industry. In 2005 Verifone went public for a second time (it was publicly traded prior to HP's acquisition in 1997).

VeriFone has cut costs significantly since leaving the HP fold. CEO Doug Bergeron's streamlining efforts have included job cuts and a renewed focus on VeriFone's core terminal market. The company has used acquisitions to bolster its terminal offerings. It acquired GO Software, a point-of-sale application developer, from Return On Investment in 2005. The following year VeriFone acquired electronic payment systems provider Lipman Electronic Engineering for about $790 million in cash and stock. It also purchased PayWare, the payment systems business of Trintech Group, for $10.9 million.

HISTORY

Scholar William Melton founded VeriFone in Hawaii in 1981 to develop electronic mail systems that would keep traveling employees in touch with their offices. By 1984 the company had diversified into transaction automation systems, introducing the first low-cost electronic credit card and check verification terminal. Former Sperry (now Unisys) executive Hatim Tyabji joined as president in 1986 and moved the company to California. He guided VeriFone away from hardware and toward software-driven systems to connect computers, printers, operating systems, and terminals.

VeriFone went public in 1990. The next year it released transaction systems that incorporated point-of-service tasks with inventory control and other functions. In 1992 VeriFone introduced an electronic cash register that verified checks and accepted credit and debit card payments. Melton devoted his energies in 1994 to founding (now defunct) Internet payment services company CyberCash.

In 1995 VeriFone made a strong push into the Internet-based transaction market, purchasing Web commerce specialist Enterprise Integration Technologies. In 1996 the company teamed with Netscape (now part of Time Warner) to develop a system to securely transfer funds over the Internet. The next year Hewlett-Packard, looking for a way to compete with IBM and others in the burgeoning Internet commerce software market, bought VeriFone for $1.3 billion. In 1998 VP Robin Abrams was named president and CEO, replacing Tyabji. She left in 1999 to lead 3Com's Palm Computing unit; HP CEO Carleton Fiorina took over the division.

In 2000 VeriFone teamed with Palm to begin developing a system that would allow Palm handheld devices to make financial transactions by accessing VeriFone point-of-sale terminals. Later in 2000 Fiorina announced that huge losses caused by restructuring efforts would result in VeriFone job cuts.

Gores Technology Group, a buyout firm specializing in technology companies, acquired VeriFone in 2001. As part of the change in control, Gores executive Douglas Bergeron took over the CEO job from Fiorina. VeriFone posted profits for its first quarter independent of HP.

In 2002 Gores recapitalized VeriFone, retaining a minority stake but selling the controlling interest to GTCR Golder Rauner, a private equity firm with expertise in the payment industry, and a minority stake to Bergeron. VeriFone launched its second IPO in 2005.

EXECUTIVES

Chairman and CEO: Douglas G. (Doug) Bergeron, age 45, $1,605,500 pay
EVP, Global Marketing and Business Development: William Atkinson, age 51, $492,050 pay
EVP, Integrated Solutions: Elmore (Bud) Waller, age 56
EVP, North America Sales: Jesse Adams, age 54, $482,955 pay
EVP, Operations: David Turnbull, age 43, $479,750 pay
SVP and CFO: Barry Zwarenstein, age 57, $500,000 pay
VP, Emerging Markets and International Marketing: William Nichols
General Manager, Integrated Retail Solutions: Jennifer Miles
Director, Business Development, Integrated Solutions: Walter Allen
Solution Engineering and Sales Support, Integrated Retail Solutions: Marty Widmann
Account Executive, Integrated Retail Solutions: Joe Biondi
Auditors: Ernst & Young LLP

LOCATIONS

HQ: VeriFone Holdings, Inc.
2099 Gateway Place, Ste. 600, San Jose, CA 95110
Phone: 408-232-7800   **Fax:** 408-232-7811
Web: www.verifone.com

2006 Sales

	$ mil.	% of total
US	315.9	54
Europe	108.9	19
Latin America	104.2	18
Asia	35.3	6
Canada	16.8	3
Total	**581.1**	**100**

PRODUCTS/OPERATIONS

2006 Sales

	$ mil.	% of total
Systems	517.2	89
Services	63.9	11
Total	**581.1**	**100**

Selected Products

Hardware
  Point-of-sale printers and peripherals
  Point-of-sale terminals
  Supplies
Software
  Payment
  Smart card
  Systems development and management
Services
  Deployment and integration
  Finance and leasing
  Project management
  Site preparation and certification
  Support and repair
  Systems design and development
  Training

COMPETITORS

Anker
CheckFree
Gemalto
Gilbarco
Hypercom
IBM
Ingenico
JDA Software
MICROS Systems
NCR
PAR Technology
Radiant
Sagem Orga
Sterling Commerce
Symbol Technologies
Thales e-Transactions
TSA

HISTORICAL FINANCIALS

Company Type: Public

Income Statement

FYE: October 31

	REVENUE ($ mil.)	NET INCOME ($ mil.)	NET PROFIT MARGIN	EMPLOYEES
10/06	581.1	59.5	10.2%	1,306
10/05	485.4	33.2	6.8%	1,050
10/04	390.1	5.6	1.4%	—
10/03	339.3	0.2	0.1%	—
10/02	295.6	(53.5)	—	—
Annual Growth	18.4%	—	—	24.4%

2006 Year-End Financials

Debt ratio: 193.3%
Return on equity: 95.0%
Cash ($ mil.): 86.6
Current ratio: 2.09
Long-term debt ($ mil.): 190.9
No. of shares (mil.): 68.1

Dividends
Yield: —
Payout: —
Market value ($ mil.): 1,990.6
R&D as % of sales: —
Advertising as % of sales: —

Stock History

NYSE: PAY

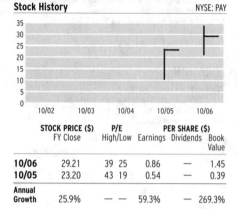

	STOCK PRICE ($) FY Close	P/E High/Low		PER SHARE ($) Earnings	Dividends	Book Value
10/06	29.21	39	25	0.86	—	1.45
10/05	23.20	43	19	0.54	—	0.39
Annual Growth	25.9%	—	—	59.3%	—	269.3%

Village Bank & Trust Financial

Does it take a village or a community? Village Bank & Trust, formerly Southern Community Financial, is the holding company for Village Bank, formerly Southern Community Bank and Trust. The bank has seven branches south of Richmond, Virginia, (primarily in the communities of Midlothian and Chester). It offers such standard services as deposit accounts, loans, and credit cards. Deposit funds are used to write loans for consumers and small businesses in the area; commercial loans account for more than a third of the bank's lending portfolio, which also includes mortgage, construction, and consumer loans. Village Bank & Trust subsidiaries provide property/casualty insurance, mortgages, and other financial services.

Village Bank & Trust focuses its business in Chesterton County and plans to explore the possibility of opening more branch offices in that market; it is also looking to expand in to nearby Henrico County, where it has already opened a loan production office.

EXECUTIVES

Chairman: Craig D. Bell, age 47
Vice Chairman: Donald J. Balzer Jr., age 49
President, CEO, and Director; President and CEO, Village Bank: Thomas W. Winfree, age 59
SVP, Lending, Village Bank: Jack M. Robeson Jr., age 56
SVP and CFO, Village Bank and Trust Financial and Village Bank: C. Harrill Whitehurst, age 53
SVP; SVP and COO, Village Bank: Raymond E. Sanders, age 51
SVP, Village Bank; President, Village Bank Mortgage: L. Anthony Bottoms III, age 54
VP and Director, Human Resources: Robert R. Staples
Auditors: BDO Seidman, LLP

LOCATIONS

HQ: Village Bank & Trust Financial Corp.
1231 Alverser Dr., Midlothian, VA 23113
Phone: 804-897-3900   **Fax:** 804-897-4750
Web: www.villagebank.com

PRODUCTS/OPERATIONS

2005 Sales

	$ mil.	% of total
Interest		
Loans	11.4	77
Securities	0.1	1
Other	0.4	3
Gain on sale of loans	2.0	13
Service charges & fees	0.4	3
Other operating income	0.5	3
Total	**14.8**	**100**

Selected Subsidiaries

Village Bank
Village Bank Mortgage Corporation
Village Financial Services Corporation
Village Insurance Agency, Inc.

COMPETITORS

Bank of America
Bank of Virginia
BB&T
C&F Financial
Central Virginia Bankshares
F & M Bank
SunTrust
Wachovia

HISTORICAL FINANCIALS

Company Type: Public

Income Statement

FYE: December 31

	ASSETS ($ mil.)	NET INCOME ($ mil.)	INCOME AS % OF ASSETS	EMPLOYEES
12/05	215.0	1.2	0.6%	101
12/04	160.3	0.9	0.6%	—
12/03	115.1	0.1	0.1%	—
12/02	80.3	(0.3)	—	—
12/01	50.7	(0.1)	—	—
Annual Growth	43.5%	—	—	—

2005 Year-End Financials

Equity as % of assets: 8.0%
Return on assets: 0.6%
Return on equity: 7.5%
Long-term debt ($ mil.): 5.6
No. of shares (mil.): 1.9
Market value ($ mil.): 23.8

Dividends
Yield: —
Payout: —
Sales ($ mil.): 14.8
R&D as % of sales: —
Advertising as % of sales: —

Stock History

NASDAQ (CM): VBFC

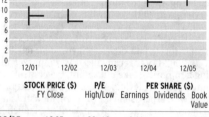

	STOCK PRICE ($) FY Close	P/E High/Low		PER SHARE ($) Earnings	Dividends	Book Value
12/05	12.85	23	18	0.61	—	9.25
12/04	11.60	31	24	0.45	—	8.51
12/03	12.40	321	190	0.04	—	7.94
12/02	7.70	—	—	(0.32)	—	7.94
12/01	8.75	—	—	(0.13)	—	8.12
Annual Growth	10.1%	—	—	—	—	3.3%

Vineyard National Bancorp

Red, white, or savings? Vineyard National Bancorp is the holding company for Vineyard Bank which operates about a dozen branches in Southern California, plus three loan production offices that specialize in Small Business Administration (SBA) loans, as well as church, income property, and private school lending. Commercial and residential real estate mortgage loans account for more than half of Vineyard National Bancorp's loan portfolio, which also includes real estate construction loans (almost 40%), and to a lesser extent commercial, industrial, and consumer loans. Deposit products offered by the bank include CDs, and checking, savings, money market, and NOW accounts.

In 2005 the company partnered with MoneyLine Lending Services to offer customers a new line of residential mortgage products. Previously it handled residential lending internally and through another outsourced provider.

EXECUTIVES

Chairman: James G. LeSieur III, age 64
President, CEO, and Director; President and CEO, Vineyard Bank: Norman A. Morales, age 45, $604,420 pay
EVP and CFO, Vineyard National Bancorp and Vineyard Bank: Gordon Fong, age 39, $222,499 pay
Secretary; EVP, COO, Chief Credit Officer, and Secretary, Vineyard Bank: Richard S. Hagan, age 54, $259,420 pay
EVP and Chief Administrative Officer: Donald H. Pelgrim Jr.
EVP and Chief Banking Officer: J. Christopher (Chris) Walsh, age 47
EVP and Chief Banking Officer, Vineyard Bank: Elizabeth (Liz) Reno, age 45
EVP and Chief Risk Officer, Vineyard Bank: Jacqueline Calhoun Schaefgen, age 36, $140,423 pay
EVP and Managing Director, Northern California Operations, Vineyard Bank: Mariano (Marty) Rubino
SVP and Chief Culture Officer, Vineyard Bank: Tina Sandoval, age 34, $137,842 pay
Auditors: KPMG LLP

LOCATIONS

HQ: Vineyard National Bancorp
9590 Foothill Blvd., Rancho Cucamonga, CA 91730
Phone: 909-581-1668   **Fax:** 909-945-2975
Web: www.vineyardbank.com

PRODUCTS/OPERATIONS

2005 Sales

	$ mil.	% of total
Interest		
Loans, including fees	98.3	85
Investment securities — taxable	12.6	11
Noninterest		
Gain on sale of SBA loans and SBA broker fee income	2.9	2
Fees & service charges	1.4	1
Other	1.0	1
Total	**116.2**	**100**

COMPETITORS

Bank of America	PFF Bancorp
Bank of the West	Provident Financial
Comerica	Holdings
CVB Financial	UnionBanCal
Downey Financial	Washington Mutual
First Community Bancorp	Wells Fargo

HISTORICAL FINANCIALS

Company Type: Public

Income Statement
FYE: December 31

	ASSETS ($ mil.)	NET INCOME ($ mil.)	INCOME AS % OF ASSETS	EMPLOYEES
12/05	1,713.6	18.9	1.1%	293
12/04	1,311.5	14.0	1.1%	244
12/03	887.8	8.0	0.9%	187
12/02	385.3	3.0	0.8%	116
12/01	191.3	1.2	0.6%	87
Annual Growth	73.0%	99.2%	—	35.5%

2005 Year-End Financials

Equity as % of assets: 5.3%	Dividends
Return on assets: 1.2%	Yield: 0.8%
Return on equity: 21.5%	Payout: 13.8%
Long-term debt ($ mil.): 101.9	Sales ($ mil.): 116.2
No. of shares (mil.): 9.4	R&D as % of sales: —
Market value ($ mil.): 290.7	Advertising as % of sales: —

Stock History
NASDAQ (GS): VNBC

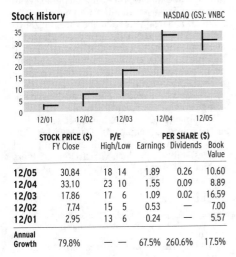

	STOCK PRICE ($) FY Close	P/E High/Low		PER SHARE ($) Earnings	Dividends	Book Value
12/05	30.84	18	14	1.89	0.26	10.60
12/04	33.10	23	10	1.55	0.09	8.89
12/03	17.86	17	6	1.09	0.02	16.59
12/02	7.74	15	5	0.53	—	7.00
12/01	2.95	13	6	0.24	—	5.57
Annual Growth	79.8%	—	—	67.5%	260.6%	17.5%

Virginia Commerce Bancorp

Virginia Commerce Bancorp is the holding company for Virginia Commerce Bank, which has about 20 offices serving metropolitan Washington, DC's northern Virginia suburbs. The bank primarily originates real estate mortgages, which account for approximately 60% of its portfolio, and real estate construction loans, which make up almost another 30%. Other offerings include checking, savings, money market, and retirement accounts; CDs; business and consumer loans; mutual funds and bonds; and asset management services. Bank subsidiary Northeast Land and Investment holds and sells foreclosed real estate.

Virginia Commerce Bancorp's customer base includes small to midsized businesses, particularly those that have contracts with the US government, and associations, retailers, industrial businesses, professionals and their firms, business executives, investors, and consumers.

Board members and executive officers collectively control about a third of Virginia Commerce Bancorp, led by vice chairman Arthur Walters' nearly 15% stake.

EXECUTIVES

Chairman: W. Douglas Fisher, age 68
Vice Chairman: David M. Guernsey, age 58
Vice Chairman: Arthur L. Walters, age 86
CEO and Director; President and CEO, Virginia Commerce Bank: Peter A. Converse, age 55, $700,000 pay
President and Director: Michael G. Anzilotti, age 56, $206,000 pay
Secretary and Director: Robert H. L'Hommedieu, age 79
Treasurer and CFO; EVP and CFO, Virginia Commerce Bank: William K. Beauchesne, age 49, $257,500 pay
EVP and Chief Lending Officer, Virginia Commerce Bank: R. B. Anderson Jr., age 51, $355,000 pay
EVP, Human Resources, Virginia Commerce Bank: Patricia M. Ostrander, age 39, $140,000 pay
EVP, Operations and Technology: John P. Perseo Jr., age 60
EVP, Retail Banking, Virginia Commerce Bank: Steven A. Reeder, age 39
Human Resources Officer, Virginia Commerce Bank: Patricia B. Smith
Auditors: Yount, Hyde & Barbour, P.C.

LOCATIONS

HQ: Virginia Commerce Bancorp, Inc.
5350 Lee Hwy., Arlington, VA 22207
Phone: 703-534-0700   **Fax:** 703-534-1782
Web: www.vcbonline.com

PRODUCTS/OPERATIONS

2005 Sales

	$ mil.	% of total
Interest		
Loans, including fees	79.6	85
Investment securities	6.2	7
Other	0.7	1
Noninterest		
Fees & net gains on loans held for sale	3.3	3
Service charges & other fees	2.6	3
Other	0.8	1
Total	**93.2**	**100**

COMPETITORS

Abigail Adams	Chevy Chase Bank
Bank of America	SunTrust
BB&T	United Bankshares
Burke & Herbert Bank	Wachovia

HISTORICAL FINANCIALS

Company Type: Public

Income Statement
FYE: December 31

	ASSETS ($ mil.)	NET INCOME ($ mil.)	INCOME AS % OF ASSETS	EMPLOYEES
12/05	1,518.4	19.7	1.3%	219
12/04	1,139.3	14.2	1.2%	189
12/03	881.1	11.6	1.3%	168
12/02	662.9	7.7	1.2%	160
12/01	489.5	4.7	1.0%	138
Annual Growth	32.7%	43.1%	—	12.2%

2005 Year-End Financials

Equity as % of assets: 7.4%	Dividends
Return on assets: 1.5%	Yield: —
Return on equity: 19.4%	Payout: —
Long-term debt ($ mil.): 44.3	Sales ($ mil.): 93.2
No. of shares (mil.): 14.0	R&D as % of sales: —
Market value ($ mil.): 272.5	Advertising as % of sales: 0.6%

Stock History
NASDAQ (GS): VCBI

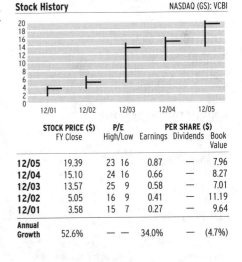

	STOCK PRICE ($) FY Close	P/E High/Low		PER SHARE ($) Earnings	Dividends	Book Value
12/05	19.39	23	16	0.87	—	7.96
12/04	15.10	24	16	0.66	—	8.27
12/03	13.57	25	9	0.58	—	7.01
12/02	5.05	16	9	0.41	—	11.19
12/01	3.58	15	7	0.27	—	9.64
Annual Growth	52.6%	—	—	34.0%	—	(4.7%)

ViroPharma

ViroPharma didn't want to wait until its drugs were approved to start making money, so it bought one that was already approved. The development-stage firm discovers drugs to combat RNA viruses, a category that includes cytomegalovirus (CMV) and hepatitis C. To finance its development, however, the company acquired the antibiotic Vancocin from Eli Lilly. The company is also developing Maribavir, which it acquired from GlaxoSmithKline, for the treatment of CMV and HCV-796 for the treatment of hepatitis C. The company ceased developing Pleconaril, an intranasal formulation that could treat the common cold, and sold the development rights to Schering-Plough.

The company is focusing on later stage opportunities and discontinuing many of its early preclinical activities. The FDA's rejection of one of its developmental drugs, Picovir, in 2002 hit the firm hard. ViroPharma ended its development and marketing agreement for Picovir with Aventis Pharmaceuticals. The company also sold its sales unit to Aventis (it had marketed Allegra and Nasacort in the US), as part of a two-thirds cut in its workforce.

EXECUTIVES

Chairman, President, and CEO: Michel de Rosen, age 55, $560,149 pay
VP, COO, CFO, and Treasurer: Vincent J. (Vinnie) Milano, age 43, $338,250 pay (prior to promotion)
VP and Chief Commercial Officer: Daniel B. (Dan) Soland, age 47
VP and Chief Scientific Officer: Colin Broom, age 49, $469,706 pay
VP, General Counsel, and Secretary: Thomas F. Doyle, age 45, $399,159 pay

VP, Business Development: Clayton Fletcher
VP, Clinical Research and Development:
Stephen (Steve) Villano
VP, Commercial Operations: Joshua M. Tarnoff, age 41,
$302,196 pay
VP, Human Resources: Carolyn Vanderweghe
**Director, Corporate Communications and Investor
Relations:** William C. (Will) Roberts
Auditors: KPMG LLP

LOCATIONS

HQ: ViroPharma Incorporated
397 Eagleview Blvd., Exton, PA 19341
Phone: 610-458-7300   **Fax:** 610-458-7380
Web: www.viropharma.com

PRODUCTS/OPERATIONS

2005 Sales

	$ mil.	% of total
License fee & milestone revenues	125.8	95
Product sales	6.6	5
Total	**132.4**	**100**

COMPETITORS

Amgen	InterMune
Antigenics	MedImmune
AstraZeneca	Oscient Pharmaceuticals
Genzyme	Roche
Gilead Sciences	Schering-Plough
GlaxoSmithKline	Valeant
Hoffmann-La Roche	Vertex Pharmaceuticals
Idenix Pharmaceuticals	

HISTORICAL FINANCIALS

Company Type: Public

Income Statement   FYE: December 31

	REVENUE ($ mil.)	NET INCOME ($ mil.)	NET PROFIT MARGIN	EMPLOYEES
12/05	132.4	113.7	85.9%	48
12/04	22.4	(19.5)	—	36
12/03	1.6	(36.9)	—	88
12/02	5.5	(15.8)	—	139
12/01	3.4	(83.0)	—	418
Annual Growth	149.8%	—	—	(41.8%)

2005 Year-End Financials

Debt ratio: —
Return on equity: 75.6%
Cash ($ mil.): 233.4
Current ratio: 2.54
Long-term debt ($ mil.): —
No. of shares (mil.): 68.6
Dividends
Yield: —
Payout: —
Market value ($ mil.): 1,268.4
R&D as % of sales: 8.0%
Advertising as % of sales: —

Stock History   NASDAQ (GS): VPHM

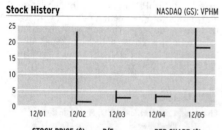

	STOCK PRICE ($) FY Close	P/E High/Low		PER SHARE ($) Earnings	Dividends	Book Value
12/05	18.50	12	1	2.02	—	4.77
12/04	3.25	—	—	(0.73)	—	(0.98)
12/03	2.77	—	—	(1.43)	—	(0.28)
12/02	1.46	—	—	(0.66)	—	1.07
Annual Growth	133.1%	—	—	—	—	28.8%

Visicu

VISICU helps keep an eye on patients in the ICU. The company offers a remote monitoring system and support services for intensive care units in hospitals across the US. Its eICU Critical Care Program consists of a center with video and audio links to patients' rooms, as well as a suite of software products. The system enables health care providers to monitor ICU patients more frequently and intervene earlier in crisis situations. Critical care staff can use multiple screens to monitor real-time data, care plans, diagnostic results, and treatment history for patients. Johns Hopkins physicians Michael Breslow and Brian Rosenfeld founded VISICU in 1998.

EXECUTIVES

Chairman, President, and CEO: Frank T. Sample, age 60, $425,481 pay
EVP, Chief Medical Officer, and Director: Brian A. Rosenfeld, age 52, $288,431 pay
EVP, Clinical Research and Development: Michael J. Breslow, age 55, $284,850 pay
SVP and CFO: Vincent E. Estrada, age 40
VP and CTO: Bill Super
VP, Clinical Operations: Martin Doerfler
VP, Engineering: Randy Holl
VP, Finance and Administration: Gary Sindler
VP, Human Resources: Kathy Herold
VP, Quality and Client Services: Nannette Spurrier
VP, Marketing: Kristin E. Yakimow
Auditors: Ernst & Young LLP

LOCATIONS

HQ: VISICU, Inc.
217 E. Redwood St., Ste. 1900,
Baltimore, MD 21202
Phone: 410-276-1960   **Fax:** 410-276-1970
Web: www.visicu.com

PRODUCTS/OPERATIONS

2005 Sales

	$ mil.	% of total
Service revenue	10.2	56
License revenue	8.2	44
Total	**18.4**	**100**

COMPETITORS

Cerner
Eclipsys
Epic
GE Healthcare
IDX Systems
McKesson
MEDITECH
Philips Medical Systems UK
Picis
Siemens Medical

HISTORICAL FINANCIALS

Company Type: Public

Income Statement   FYE: December 31

	REVENUE ($ mil.)	NET INCOME ($ mil.)	NET PROFIT MARGIN	EMPLOYEES
12/05	18.4	10.1	54.9%	94
12/04	5.5	(4.1)	—	—
12/03	2.2	(8.4)	—	—
12/02	1.4	(7.5)	—	—
Annual Growth	136.0%	—	—	—

2005 Year-End Financials

Debt ratio: —
Return on equity: —
Cash ($ mil.): 11.4
Current ratio: 1.12
Long-term debt ($ mil.): —

Net Income History   NASDAQ (GM): EICU

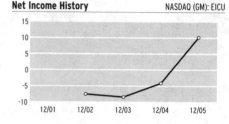

Vital Images

Vital Images knows that everything is better in 3-D. The company develops 3-D medical visualization and analysis software used primarily in clinical diagnosis, disease screening, and therapy planning. The firm's software applies computer graphics and image-processing technologies to data supplied by computed tomography (CT) scanners and magnetic resonance imaging (MRI) devices. Vital Images' flagship product Vitrea creates two-, three-, and four-dimensional views of the human body, enabling physicians and surgeons to see internal structures and recognize potential abnormalities. The company markets its products to hospitals, clinics, diagnostic imaging centers, and medical schools.

Vital Images and R2 Technology has a product distribution agreement that integrates R2's ImageChecker software application with Vital Images' software product, Vitrea. Other partners include CTI Mirada, Confirma, and Medis.

EXECUTIVES

Chairman: Douglas M. (Doug) Pihl, age 66
President, CEO, and Director: Jay D. Miller, age 46, $465,038 pay
COO, CFO, Treasurer, and Secretary: Michael H. Carrel, age 35, $389,615 pay
EVP, Corporate Development: Philip I. (Phil) Smith, age 38, $321,964 pay (prior to title change)
EVP, Global Sales: Steven P. (Steve) Canakes, age 50, $302,245 pay (prior to title change)
EVP, Marketing and Clinical Development: Susan A. Wood, age 43
VP, Quality and Customer Satisfaction: Jeremy A. Abbs, age 42, $265,752 pay
Senior Director, Human Resources: Cindy J. Edwards
Auditors: PricewaterhouseCoopers LLP

LOCATIONS

HQ: Vital Images, Inc.
5850 Opus Pkwy., Ste. 300, Minnetonka, MN 55343
Phone: 952-487-9500   **Fax:** 952-487-9510
Web: www.vitalimages.com

PRODUCTS/OPERATIONS

2005 Sales

	$ mil.	% of total
License fees	35.2	68
Maintenance & services	14.3	28
Hardware	2.2	4
Total	**51.7**	**100**

COMPETITORS

ART Advanced Research	NanoSignal
GE Healthcare	Philips Medical Systems
Medicsight	Siemens Medical
Metrx	VirtualScopics

HISTORICAL FINANCIALS

Company Type: Public

Income Statement

FYE: December 31

	REVENUE ($ mil.)	NET INCOME ($ mil.)	NET PROFIT MARGIN	EMPLOYEES
12/05	51.7	5.8	11.2%	200
12/04	36.1	0.3	0.8%	151
12/03	27.3	8.5	31.1%	134
12/02	21.1	0.8	3.8%	105
12/01	15.2	(1.0)	—	79
Annual Growth	35.8%	—	—	26.1%

2005 Year-End Financials

Debt ratio: —
Return on equity: 9.4%
Cash ($ mil.): 49.8
Current ratio: 3.23
Long-term debt ($ mil.): —
No. of shares (mil.): 12.8

Dividends
  Yield: —
  Payout: —
Market value ($ mil.): 336.0
R&D as % of sales: 15.8%
Advertising as % of sales: —

Stock History

NASDAQ (GM): VTAL

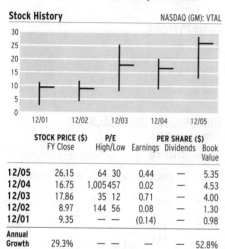

	STOCK PRICE ($) FY Close	P/E High/Low	PER SHARE ($) Earnings	Dividends	Book Value
12/05	26.15	64 30	0.44	—	5.35
12/04	16.75	1,005 457	0.02	—	4.53
12/03	17.86	35 12	0.71	—	4.00
12/02	8.97	144 56	0.08	—	1.30
12/01	9.35	— —	(0.14)	—	0.98
Annual Growth	29.3%	— —	—	—	52.8%

VNUS Medical Technologies

Whether you're suffering from painful, swollen legs or are just vain about your veins, VNUS Medical Technologies can zap your gams back to health. The company's Closure system treats venous reflux disease, a leg condition that can lead to varicose veins, swelling, and skin ulcers. The minimally invasive system uses catheters and a radio-frequency generator to close the diseased veins, usually on an outpatient basis. VNUS Medical Technologies sells and rents its Closure system generators, catheters, and accessories to interventional radiologists, general and vascular surgeons, and phlebologists in the US and certain European countries.

VNUS Medical Technologies plans to grow by expanding its market penetration of physicians who treat venous reflux.

EXECUTIVES

Chairman: W. James Fitzsimmons, age 49
President, CEO, and Director: Brian E. Farley, age 48, $361,607 pay
SVP, US Sales and Account Services: Scott H. Cramer, age 44
VP, Finance and Administration and CFO:
  Timothy A. (Tim) Marcotte, age 49, $230,673 pay
VP, General Counsel, and Secretary:
  Charlene A. Friedman, age 48
VP, Clinical Research and Education and Medical Director: Lian X. Cunningham, age 42, $158,795 pay
VP, Manufacturing and Business Development:
  Robert G. McRae, age 37, $203,949 pay
VP, Marketing and International Sales:
  Dennis Rosenberg, age 52
Director, International Sales and Marketing:
  Spencer Roeck
Auditors: PricewaterhouseCoopers LLP

LOCATIONS

HQ: VNUS Medical Technologies, Inc.
  2200 Zanker Rd., Ste. F, San Jose, CA 95131
Phone: 408-473-1100   **Fax:** 408-944-0292
Web: www.vnus.com

2005 Sales

	% of total
US	96
Europe	3
Other regions	1
Total	**100**

PRODUCTS/OPERATIONS

2005 Sales

	% of total
Catheters	76
RF Generators	18
Accessories	6
Total	**100**

COMPETITORS

AngioDynamics
BTG plc
Candela Corporation
Cutera
Diomed
Dornier
Dornier
DUSA Pharmaceuticals
Laserscope
Lumenis
Palomar Medical
Vascular Solutions

HISTORICAL FINANCIALS

Company Type: Public

Income Statement

FYE: December 31

	REVENUE ($ mil.)	NET INCOME ($ mil.)	NET PROFIT MARGIN	EMPLOYEES
12/05	49.2	5.3	10.8%	206
12/04	38.2	2.9	7.6%	163
12/03	21.8	(2.6)	—	—
12/02	10.0	(6.0)	—	—
Annual Growth	70.1%	—	—	26.4%

2005 Year-End Financials

Debt ratio: —
Return on equity: 7.0%
Cash ($ mil.): 72.5
Current ratio: 14.38
Long-term debt ($ mil.): —
No. of shares (mil.): 14.9

Dividends
  Yield: —
  Payout: —
Market value ($ mil.): 124.9
R&D as % of sales: 7.7%
Advertising as % of sales: 0.7%

Stock History

NASDAQ (GM): VNUS

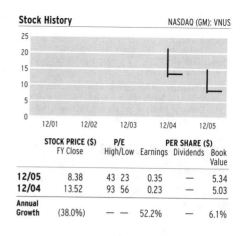

	STOCK PRICE ($) FY Close	P/E High/Low	PER SHARE ($) Earnings	Dividends	Book Value
12/05	8.38	43 23	0.35	—	5.34
12/04	13.52	93 56	0.23	—	5.03
Annual Growth	(38.0%)	— —	52.2%	—	6.1%

Volcom

Volcom says it's "youth against establishment" and this establishment comes down firmly on the side of youth — skateboarding, surfing, and snowboarding youth in Burnt Epidermis hoodies and Weirdo Chinos. Volcom designs and makes apparel and accessories for board sports and offers its wares through three stores in California and youth-focused retailers like Zumiez and Pac Sun across the US, Canada, and Puerto Rico. The company sells to distributors in Japan, South Korea, and Central America while licensing its brand in other parts of the world.

Sponsorship of various concerts, riders, and sports events, along with film and music divisions, keep Volcom's logo front and center with anti-establishment youth.

The company intends to use the proceeds of its 2005 IPO to expand the brand in Europe and develop proprietary in-store marketing displays for retailers to properly show off those trucker caps, board shorts, belts, and bags sporting the Volcom gray triangular stone logo.

Retailer Pacific Sunwear accounts for nearly 30% of sales, while the company's five largest customers account for nearly half the total.

Longtime surfer and former marketer for surfwear giant and rival Quiksilver, Richard Woolcott (president and CEO), founded the company in 1991 and owns 16% of the company shares. Chairman René Woolcott and independent investor Stephanie Kwock each own 13%.

EXECUTIVES

Chairman: René R. Woolcott, age 74
President, CEO, and Director: Richard R. Woolcott, age 40, $555,000 pay
COO: Jason W. Steris, age 36, $475,000 pay
CFO, Secretary, and Treasurer: Douglas P. Collier, age 43, $475,000 pay
VP, Marketing: Troy C. Eckert, age 33, $260,000 pay
VP, Sales: Tom D. Ruiz, age 45, $425,000 pay
Auditors: Deloitte & Touche LLP

LOCATIONS

HQ: Volcom, Inc.
  1740 Monrovia Ave., Costa Mesa, CA 92627
Phone: 949-646-2175   **Fax:** 949-646-5247
Web: www.volcom.com

Volcom has licensing agreements with companies in Australia, Brazil, South Africa, and Indonesia as well as across Europe. Licensees operate retail stores in Bali, Indonesia and Hossegor, France.

PRODUCTS/OPERATIONS

2005 Sales

	$ mil.	% of total
Products	156.7	98
Licensing	3.2	2
Total	**159.9**	**100**

Selected Sponsored Athletes

Skateboarding
  Mark Appleyard
  Lauren Perkins
  Geoff Rowley
  Ryan Sheckler

Snowboarding
  Terje Haakonsen
  Bjorn Leines
  Janna Meyen
  Shaun White

Surfing
  Claire Bevilacqua
  Bruce Irons
  Dean Morrison

Selected Subsidiaries

Veeco Productions (skateboarding, snowboarding, and surfing film production featuring sponsored athletes)
Volcom Entertainment (band representation, CD production and distribution)

COMPETITORS

Abercrombie & Fitch
Apple Computer
Billabong
Burton Snowboards
Columbia Sportswear
K2
Lost International
Mossimo
Napster
Ocean Pacific
Pacific Sunwear
Patagonia
Quiksilver
Rusty
Skechers U.S.A.
Sony BMG
Sony Corporation of America
Stüssy
Vans
Vivendi

HISTORICAL FINANCIALS

Company Type: Public

Income Statement

FYE: December 31

	REVENUE ($ mil.)	NET INCOME ($ mil.)	NET PROFIT MARGIN	EMPLOYEES
12/05	159.9	29.3	18.3%	181
12/04	113.2	24.6	21.7%	—
12/03	76.3	14.3	18.7%	—
Annual Growth	**44.8%**	**43.1%**	**—**	**—**

2005 Year-End Financials

Debt ratio: 0.2%
Return on equity: 44.3%
Cash ($ mil.): 71.7
Current ratio: 12.67
Long-term debt ($ mil.): 0.2
No. of shares (mil.): 24.2

Dividends
  Yield: —
  Payout: —
Market value ($ mil.): 823.5
R&D as % of sales: —
Advertising as % of sales: 6.2%

Stock History

NASDAQ (GS): VLCM

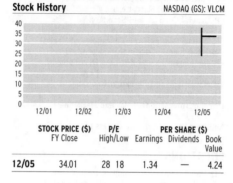

	STOCK PRICE ($) FY Close	P/E High/Low	PER SHARE ($) Earnings	Dividends	Book Value
12/05	34.01	28 18	1.34	—	4.24

VSE Corporation

VSE brings military hand-me-downs back into fashion. The company provides engineering, testing, and logistics services for the US Navy (about 70% of sales) and other government agencies on a contract basis. VSE's BAV division (formed in cooperation with management and technology consultant Booz Allen Hamilton) helps reactivate old Navy ships and transfer them to other countries. Nearly all of VSE's revenues are derived from the US government (including the Navy, the Army, and the Department of Energy) and its prime contractors. Employees own about 11% of VSE.

VSE depends heavily on just a few large contracts. Its largest, the ship transfer contract between BAV and the Navy, accounts for about half of VSE's sales. In 2004 VSE landed a share of a separate contract to provide maintenance and engineering services for the Navy that is expected to be worth as much as $1.3 billion a year for 15 years.

Investor Calvin Koonce, a member of VSE's board, controls a 22% stake in the company.

EXECUTIVES

Chairman, President, CEO, and COO:
  Donald M. Ervine, age 69, $600,000 pay
EVP, Chief Administrative Officer, and Secretary:
  Craig S. Weber, age 61, $330,000 pay
EVP and Director, International Group:
  James M. Knowlton, age 63, $400,200 pay
SVP and CFO: Thomas R. Loftus, age 50, $336,000 pay
SVP and Director, Federal Group: Thomas G. Dacus, age 60, $330,000 pay
SVP and General Manager, Fleet Maintenance Division:
  Michael E. (Mike) Hamerly, age 58
President, Energetics Incorporated: James E. Reed
Director, Business and New Product Development:
  Leonard Goldstein
Director, Human Resources: Elizabeth M. (Liz) Price
Auditors: Ernst & Young LLP

LOCATIONS

HQ: VSE Corporation
  2550 Huntington Ave., Alexandria, VA 22303
Phone: 703-960-4600   **Fax:** 703-960-2688
Web: www.vsecorp.com

PRODUCTS/OPERATIONS

2005 Sales

		$ mil.	% of total
Government			
	US Navy	196.4	70
	US Army	56.0	20
	Department of Energy	9.7	3
	US Air Firce	5.4	2
	US Coast Guard	5.0	2
	Other government	5.8	2
Commercial & other		1.8	1
Total		**280.1**	**100**

Selected Operating Units

BAV Division (ship reactivation and life cycle support services)
Coast Guard Division
Communications and Engineering Division
Engineering and Logistics Division
Fleet Maintenance Division
Management Sciences Division
Systems Engineering Division

COMPETITORS

Boeing
General Dynamics
Lockheed Martin
Northrop Grumman
Todd Shipyards

HISTORICAL FINANCIALS

Company Type: Public

Income Statement

FYE: December 31

	REVENUE ($ mil.)	NET INCOME ($ mil.)	NET PROFIT MARGIN	EMPLOYEES
12/05	280.1	6.2	2.2%	716
12/04	216.0	3.4	1.6%	625
12/03	134.5	2.0	1.5%	500
12/02	134.4	0.6	0.4%	450
12/01	111.6	0.9	0.8%	550
Annual Growth	**25.9%**	**62.0%**	**—**	**6.8%**

2005 Year-End Financials

Debt ratio: —
Return on equity: 23.3%
Cash ($ mil.): 12.7
Current ratio: 1.52
Long-term debt ($ mil.): —
No. of shares (mil.): 2.4

Dividends
  Yield: 0.5%
  Payout: 8.5%
Market value ($ mil.): 99.3
R&D as % of sales: —
Advertising as % of sales: —

Stock History

NASDAQ (GM): VSEC

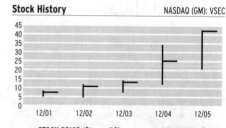

	STOCK PRICE ($) FY Close	P/E High/Low	PER SHARE ($) Earnings	Dividends	Book Value
12/05	42.10	16 8	2.58	0.22	12.78
12/04	25.17	23 8	1.49	0.18	10.11
12/03	13.25	16 9	0.90	0.16	8.61
12/02	10.76	38 17	0.30	0.16	7.80
12/01	7.40	20 13	0.40	0.16	7.66
Annual Growth	**54.4%**	**— —**	**59.4%**	**8.3%**	**13.6%**

W Holding Company

No relation to a US president, W Holding Company is the parent of Westernbank Puerto Rico, which provides consumer and business banking services through some 55 branches. Services include deposit accounts, credit cards, and trust and brokerage services. Subsidiary Westernbank Insurance sells a full range of coverage. One of the largest banks on the island, Westernbank has been expanding in San Juan (Puerto Rico's capital); some locations offer a smaller, more casual setting (espresso is served) to attract more consumer clients. The company's overall loan mix, however, leans toward business lending, including commercial mortgages and asset-based loans, which account for more than 65% of its portfolio.

Westernbank is one of the fastest-growing banks on the island, increasing its assets and loans by 25% or more for the past five years. While the bank primarily has operated in the western and southwestern regions of Puerto Rico, in 2005 it branched out into the eastern region of the island.

Honorary directors Fredeswinda Frontera and Ileana Carr own about 11% and 9% of the company, respectively; CEO Frank Stipes owns 7%.

EXECUTIVES

Chairman and CEO: Frank C. Stipes, age 50, $1,540,970 pay
President, Chief Investment Officer, and Director: Freddy Maldonado, age 55, $891,769 pay
COO: Alfredo Archilla, age 49
SEVP and Chief Strategy and Corporate Development Officer: Rafael A. Somoza, age 36
Chief Legal Officer: Aurelio J. Emanuelli, age 39
First VP, Commercial Credit; Chief Commercial Lender; and Chief Lending Officer, Southwest Puerto Rico: Ricardo Cortina
First VP and Chief Lending Officer, Northeastern Region: William Vidal, age 52
First VP, Southern Region and Director: Pedro R. Domínguez, age 61, $812,585 pay
President and CEO, Westernbank: Jose M. Biaggi, age 38, $596,500 pay
President, Expresso of Westernbank: Migdalia Rivera, age 55
President, Westernbank Business Credit: Miguel Vázquez, age 55, $1,075,641 pay
Secretary and Director: César A. Ruiz, age 71
Director, Corporate Communications and Investor Relations: Carmen T. Casellas
Auditors: Deloitte & Touche LLP

LOCATIONS

HQ: W Holding Company, Inc.
19 W. Mckinley St., Mayagüez, PR 00681
Phone: 787-834-8000   **Fax:** 787-834-0404
Web: www.wholding.com

PRODUCTS/OPERATIONS

2005 Sales

	$ mil.	% of total
Interest		
Loans, including fees	479.1	58
Investment securities	247.5	30
Money market instruments	36.4	4
Mortgage-backed securities	32.3	4
Noninterest		
Service charges on loans	11.6	1
Service charges on deposit accounts	8.7	1
Other	15.6	2
Total	**831.2**	**100**

Selected Subsidiaries

Westernbank Insurance Corp.
Westernbank Puerto Rico
 SRG Net, Inc.
 Westernbank World Plaza, Inc.

COMPETITORS

Doral Financial	Popular
First BanCorp (Puerto Rico)	R&G Financial
Oriental Financial	Santander BanCorp

HISTORICAL FINANCIALS

Company Type: Public

Income Statement

FYE: December 31

	ASSETS ($ mil.)	NET INCOME ($ mil.)	INCOME AS % OF ASSETS	EMPLOYEES
12/05	16,151.9	163.1	1.0%	1,311
12/04	14,336.7	171.9	1.2%	1,175
12/03	11,519.4	113.3	1.0%	1,092
12/02	8,205.1	86.0	1.0%	1,038
12/01	5,888.2	62.2	1.1%	823
Annual Growth	**28.7%**	**27.3%**	**—**	**12.3%**

2005 Year-End Financials

Equity as % of assets: 7.3%
Return on assets: 1.1%
Return on equity: 14.6%
Long-term debt ($ mil.): 36.4
No. of shares (mil.): 164.1
Market value ($ mil.): 1,350.5
Dividends
 Yield: 2.1%
 Payout: 23.0%
Sales ($ mil.): 831.2
R&D as % of sales: —
Advertising as % of sales: 1.1%

Stock History

NYSE: WHI

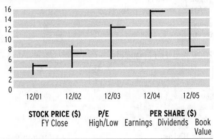

	STOCK PRICE ($) FY Close	P/E High/Low		PER SHARE ($) Earnings	Dividends	Book Value
12/05	8.23	21	10	0.74	0.17	7.27
12/04	15.29	27	18	0.56	0.13	6.60
12/03	12.16	35	16	0.36	0.10	7.79
12/02	7.01	18	9	0.47	0.09	8.56
12/01	4.61	14	8	0.36	0.01	9.35
Annual Growth	**15.6%**	**—**	**—**	**19.7%**	**103.1%**	**(6.1%)**

Waccamaw Bankshares

Waccamaw Bancshares is the holding company for, surprise, the Waccamaw Bank. The community bank, which has branches in North Carolina as well as South Carolina, provides traditional services, such as checking and savings accounts and IRAs. The bank's loan portfolio is largely made up of commercial and real estate loans, including business operating loans, commercial mortgages, residential mortgages, and construction and land development loans. The financial institution also offers investment services and insurance brokerage through Waccamaw Financial Services.

Waccamaw Bank opened its Southport and Elizabethtown offices in 2005, and acquired Lancaster County, South Carolina-based Bank of Heath Springs the following year. (South Carolina banking laws only permit out-of-state banks to operate in South Carolina through acquisitions.)

EXECUTIVES

Chairman: Alan W. Thompson, age 42
President, CEO, and Director; President and CEO, Waccamaw Bank: James G. Graham, age 55, $264,539 pay
VP and COO, Waccamaw Bank: Freda H. Gore, age 44
VP and CFO, Waccamaw Bank: David A. Godwin, age 49
VP and Senior Credit Officer, Waccamaw Bank: Richard C. Norris, age 40
VP; Human Resources and Marketing Officer: Kim T. Hutchens, age 50
Accounting Manager: Valerie Register
Operations, Security, and Compliance Officer: Gracie B. McClary
Auditors: Elliott Davis LLC

LOCATIONS

HQ: Waccamaw Bankshares, Inc.
110 N. J.K. Powell Blvd., Whiteville, NC 28472
Phone: 910-641-0044   **Fax:** 910-641-0978
Web: www.waccamawbank.com

PRODUCTS/OPERATIONS

2005 Sales

	$ mil.	% of total
Interest		
Loans, including fees	16.3	80
Securities & other	1.9	9
Noninterest		
Service charges on deposits	1.1	5
Other	1.2	6
Total	**20.5**	**100**

COMPETITORS

Bank of America
BB&T
Community Resource Bank
Cooperative Bankshares
First Bancorp (NC)
First Citizens Bancorporation
First Citizens BancShares
New Century Bancorp
RBC Centura Banks
SCBT Financial
Wachovia

HISTORICAL FINANCIALS

Company Type: Public

Income Statement

FYE: December 31

	ASSETS ($ mil.)	NET INCOME ($ mil.)	INCOME AS % OF ASSETS	EMPLOYEES
12/05	322.8	3.0	0.9%	85
12/04	258.4	2.4	0.9%	73
12/03	193.2	2.0	1.0%	60
12/02	161.3	1.6	1.0%	58
12/01	132.1	1.0	0.8%	—
Annual Growth	**25.0%**	**31.6%**	**—**	**13.6%**

2005 Year-End Financials

Equity as % of assets: 7.0%
Return on assets: 1.0%
Return on equity: 14.2%
Long-term debt ($ mil.): 14.8
No. of shares (mil.): 4.6
Market value ($ mil.): 81.0
Dividends
 Yield: —
 Payout: —
Sales ($ mil.): 20.5
R&D as % of sales: —
Advertising as % of sales: 0.9%

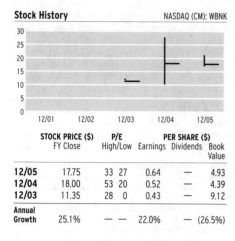

	STOCK PRICE ($) FY Close	P/E High/Low		PER SHARE ($) Earnings	Dividends	Book Value
12/05	17.75	33	27	0.64	—	4.93
12/04	18.00	53	20	0.52	—	4.39
12/03	11.35	28	0	0.43	—	9.12
Annual Growth	25.1%	—	—	22.0%	—	(26.5%)

Wayside Technology Group

Wayside is far from falling by the wayside to programmers and tech-head execs. The company, formerly Programmer's Paradise, markets technical software, hardware, and related products to technology professionals through direct sales, the Internet, and catalogs such as *Programmer's Paradise* (for software developers) and *Corporate Developer's Paradise* (for corporate information technology professionals). Its thousands of tech tools include discounted software and hardware, as well as training and reference manuals.

The company's Lifeboat Distribution subsidiary handles distribution to dealers and resellers. CDW Corporation accounts for more than 14% of sales.

The company announced in 2006 that it would change its name in an effort to pursue different market segments that operate under a variety of names. Its business segments — Programmer's Paradise and Lifeboat — continue under their current names, while the company will launch a third unit under the moniker TechXtend. TechXtend will offer corporations and organizations on-site IT services such as server consolidation, disaster recovery, and development.

EXECUTIVES

Chairman, President, and CEO: Simon F. Nynens, age 34
VP and Chief Accounting Officer: Kevin T. Scull, age 40
VP and General Manager, Canada: Steven R. McNamara, age 47
VP and General Manager, Lifeboat: Daniel T. (Dan) Jamieson, age 48, $195,025 pay
VP, Information Systems: Vito Legrottaglie, age 42, $176,637 pay
VP, Sales and Marketing: Jeffrey C. Largiader, age 49, $196,813 pay
Human Resources Manager: MaryBeth Auleta
Auditors: Amper, Politziner & Mattia, P.C.

LOCATIONS

HQ: Wayside Technology Group, Inc.
1157 Shrewsbury Ave., Shrewsbury, NJ 07702
Phone: 732-389-0932   **Fax:** 732-389-1207
Web: www.waysidetechnology.com

2005 Sales

	$ mil.	% of total
US	121.1	88
Canada	16.6	12
Total	137.7	100

COMPETITORS

Best Buy
CDW
CompUSA
Dell
Insight Enterprises
Newegg.com
PC Connection
PC Mall
Systemax
Zones

HISTORICAL FINANCIALS

Company Type: Public

Income Statement

FYE: December 31

	REVENUE ($ mil.)	NET INCOME ($ mil.)	NET PROFIT MARGIN	EMPLOYEES
12/05	137.7	2.7	2.0%	116
12/04	103.6	6.3	6.1%	117
12/03	69.6	1.0	1.4%	80
12/02	65.2	0.0	—	86
12/01	89.5	(4.5)	—	80
Annual Growth	11.4%	—	—	9.7%

2005 Year-End Financials

Debt ratio: —
Return on equity: 15.7%
Cash ($ mil.): 15.3
Current ratio: 1.56
Long-term debt ($ mil.): —
No. of shares (mil.): 4.0
Dividends
  Yield: —
  Payout: —
Market value ($ mil.): 47.7
R&D as % of sales: —
Advertising as % of sales: 1.8%

Stock History

NASDAQ (GM): WSTG

	STOCK PRICE ($) FY Close	P/E High/Low		PER SHARE ($) Earnings	Dividends	Book Value
12/05	11.93	26	13	0.61	—	4.51
12/04	14.78	10	4	1.51	—	4.27
12/03	6.89	30	8	0.25	—	2.99
12/02	1.97	295	166	0.01	—	3.05
12/01	2.70	—	—	(0.91)	—	2.79
Annual Growth	45.0%	—	—	—	—	12.8%

WCA Waste

Some might see a garbage dump, but WCA Waste sees a pile of money. WCA Waste provides collection, transfer, and disposal of nonhazardous solid waste for about 187,000 commercial, industrial, and residential customers in Alabama, Arkansas, Florida, Kansas, Missouri, North Carolina, South Carolina, Tennessee, and Texas. Through its subsidiaries, the company operates some 23 collection businesses, 21 transfer stations, and 19 landfills, including seven separate landfills that are devoted to handling municipal solid waste and 12 for construction and demolition debris. Former company director William Esping and his family own about 13% of WCA Waste.

WCA Waste has grown through a series of acquisitions. The company's plan for growth calls for more acquisitions — specifically, acquisitions of collection businesses that can use the company's existing landfills. WCA Waste also will pursue geographic expansion as opportunities arise. The company entered the Florida and North Carolina markets in 2005; it moved into Colorado and New Mexico in 2006. In 2007 it acquired Southwest Dumpster, Inc. (Fort Myers, Florida) and Sunrise Disposal (Springfield, Missouri).

A former subsidiary of Waste Corporation of America, WCA Waste began operating in 2000, when it acquired assets from industry giant Waste Management. In connection with its IPO in 2004, WCA Waste briefly became the parent of Waste Corporation of America, which was then spun off. Waste Corporation of America wound up with solid waste management operations in Colorado, Florida, and New Mexico.

EXECUTIVES

Chairman and CEO: Tom J. Fatjo Jr., age 65, $608,122 pay
President, COO, and Director: Jerome M. Kruszka, age 57, $608,122 pay
SVP and CFO: Charles A. (Chuck) Casalinova, age 48, $418,571 pay
SVP Finance and Secretary: Tom J. (Tommy) Fatjo III, age 41, $348,676 pay
Auditors: KPMG LLP

LOCATIONS

HQ: WCA Waste Corporation
1 Riverway, Ste. 1400, Houston, TX 77056
Phone: 713-292-2400   **Fax:** 713-292-2455
Web: www.wcawaste.com

WCA Waste has operations in Alabama, Arkansas, Colorado, Florida, Kansas, Missouri, New Mexico, North Carolina, South Carolina, Tennessee, and Texas.

2005 Sales

	$ mil.	% of total
Kansas & Missouri	44.5	39
Texas	25.7	22
Arkansas	12.5	11
North Carolina	8.2	7
Florida	4.1	4
Other states	19.1	17
Total	114.1	100

PRODUCTS/OPERATIONS

2005 Sales

	$ mil.	% of total
Collection	69.8	61
Disposal	30.6	27
Transfer	13.7	12
Total	**114.1**	**100**

COMPETITORS

Allied Waste	Veolia ES Solid Waste
IESI	Waste Connections
Republic Services	Waste Management

HISTORICAL FINANCIALS

Company Type: Public

Income Statement — FYE: December 31

	REVENUE ($ mil.)	NET INCOME ($ mil.)	NET PROFIT MARGIN	EMPLOYEES
12/05	114.1	3.5	3.1%	800
12/04	73.5	(4.4)	—	589
12/03	64.2	5.1	7.9%	—
12/02	62.2	1.2	1.9%	—
Annual Growth	**22.4%**	**42.9%**	**—**	**35.8%**

2005 Year-End Financials

Debt ratio: 190.9%
Return on equity: 4.2%
Cash ($ mil.): 0.9
Current ratio: 1.43
Long-term debt ($ mil.): 175.1
No. of shares (mil.): 16.8
Dividends
Yield: —
Payout: —
Market value ($ mil.): 132.8
R&D as % of sales: —
Advertising as % of sales: —

Stock History — NASDAQ (GM): WCAA

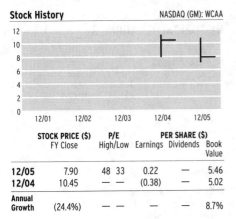

	STOCK PRICE ($) FY Close	P/E High/Low	Earnings	PER SHARE ($) Dividends	Book Value
12/05	7.90	48 33	0.22	—	5.46
12/04	10.45	— —	(0.38)	—	5.02
Annual Growth	**(24.4%)**	**— —**	**—**	**—**	**8.7%**

WebEx Communications

Getting together should never involve elaborate plans and long journeys, according to WebEx Communications. The company is a provider of Web conferencing systems that let parties conduct meetings and share information over the Internet. WebEx's hosted services enable companies to convene with employees, clients, and partners to make presentations, exchange documents, share applications, and edit documents electronically. WebEx also offers services that help businesses provide live, technical support for their customers, accessible through Web browsers.

The company's more than 23,000 customers come from a variety of industries including financial services, health care, telecommunications, and manufacturing.

In 2005 the company acquired Intranets.com, renaming it WebExOne.

EXECUTIVES

Chairman, President, and CEO: Subrah S. Iyar, age 48
CFO: Michael T. Everett, age 55, $315,809 pay
VP, General Counsel, and Secretary: David Farrington, age 48, $278,828 pay
VP, Business Development: Peter Carson, age 55
VP, Corporate Marketing: Van D. Diamandakis
VP, Europe, Middle East, and Africa: Bert van der Zwan
VP, Finance, Controller, and Chief Accounting Officer: Kelly Steckelberg
VP, Human Resources: Dean MacIntosh, age 46
VP, Product Strategy: Steven Li
VP, Products: Gary A. Griffiths, age 55
VP, Strategic Communications: Praful Shah
VP, Worldwide Sales and Services: David (Dave) Berman
Auditors: KPMG LLP

LOCATIONS

HQ: WebEx Communications, Inc.
3979 Freedom Cir., Santa Clara, CA 95054
Phone: 408-435-7000 **Fax:** 408-496-4303
Web: www.webex.com

PRODUCTS/OPERATIONS

Selected Services

WebEx Event Center (service for press briefings, product announcements, and marketing events)
WebEx Meeting Center (online meeting)
WebEx Presentation Studio (multimedia content creation)
WebEx SMARTtech (secure Web based remote access management)
WebEx Support Center (interaction with remote customer desktops)
WebEx Training Center (training and e-learning)

COMPETITORS

Cisco Systems
Citrix Systems
Genesys Telecommunications
IBM
Microsoft
West Corporation

HISTORICAL FINANCIALS

Company Type: Public

Income Statement — FYE: December 31

	REVENUE ($ mil.)	NET INCOME ($ mil.)	NET PROFIT MARGIN	EMPLOYEES
12/05	308.4	53.0	17.2%	2,091
12/04	249.1	47.9	19.2%	1,826
12/03	189.3	59.8	31.6%	1,241
12/02	139.9	16.4	11.7%	639
12/01	81.2	(27.6)	—	497
Annual Growth	**39.6%**	**—**	**—**	**43.2%**

2005 Year-End Financials

Debt ratio: —
Return on equity: 19.0%
Cash ($ mil.): 197.2
Current ratio: 5.16
Long-term debt ($ mil.): —
No. of shares (mil.): 46.1
Dividends
Yield: —
Payout: —
Market value ($ mil.): 998.1
R&D as % of sales: 14.8%
Advertising as % of sales: —

Stock History — NASDAQ (GS): WEBX

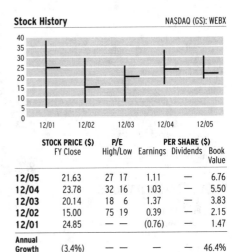

	STOCK PRICE ($) FY Close	P/E High/Low	Earnings	PER SHARE ($) Dividends	Book Value
12/05	21.63	27 17	1.11	—	6.76
12/04	23.78	32 16	1.03	—	5.50
12/03	20.14	18 6	1.37	—	3.83
12/02	15.00	75 19	0.39	—	2.15
12/01	24.85	— —	(0.76)	—	1.47
Annual Growth	**(3.4%)**	**— —**	**—**	**—**	**46.4%**

Websense

That strange feeling someone is looking over your shoulder might just be true, thanks to Websense. The company offers employee Internet management, Web filtering, and security software designed to help businesses improve (and monitor) employee productivity, control what content employees can access, and reduce network bandwidth and storage usage. Companies use the Websense Enterprise software to monitor and report employee Internet usage, block access to certain content, and set time periods for when access is available. Clients such as McDonald's and the US Army subscribe to the hosted service, which checks for compliance against a proprietary database of more than 15 million Web sites in about 90 categories.

Websense's customers range from small companies to large global corporations and government agencies. The company derives about 80% of its revenues from indirect channels such as value-added resellers in the US and overseas distributors and resellers, with the remaining 20% coming from its direct sales team. Websense is working to expand its international business, targeting clients in Europe, Latin America, and the Asia/Pacific region. Customers outside the US account for about one-third of Websense's sales.

Late in 2006 Websense agreed to acquire data protection specialist PortAuthority Technologies for $90 million in cash; the deal closed early in 2007.

EXECUTIVES

Chairman: John B. Carrington, age 62
President, CEO, and Director: Gene Hodges, age 54
SVP of Product Development: John McCormack
VP and CFO: Douglas C. Wride, age 52, $465,129 pay
VP and General Counsel: Michael A. Newman, age 36, $280,474 pay
VP of Finance and Accounting: Karen V. Goodrum, age 48
VP of Human Resources and Administration: Susan Brown
VP of Investor Relations: Kate Patterson
VP of Marketing: Leo J. Cole, age 48, $317,658 pay
VP of Sales, Americas: David Roberts
Public Relations Manager: Ronnie Manning
Auditors: Ernst & Young LLP

LOCATIONS

HQ: Websense, Inc.
10240 Sorrento Valley Rd., San Diego, CA 92121
Phone: 858-320-8000   **Fax:** 858-458-2950
Web: ww2.websense.com

2005 Sales

	$ mil.	% of total
US	99.6	67
Europe, Middle East & Africa	33.4	23
Canada & Latin America	9.5	6
Asia/Pacific	6.1	4
Total	**148.6**	**100**

PRODUCTS/OPERATIONS

Selected Customers

AmerisourceBergen
Blue Cross and Blue Shield
ConAgra Foods
Federated Department Stores
Internal Revenue Service
Kimberly-Clark
McDonald's
MetLife
Northrop Grumman
US Army

COMPETITORS

8e6 Technologies
Blue Coat
CA
Check Point Software
Cisco Systems
Internet Security Systems
McAfee
Microsoft
NetIQ
Secure Computing
SonicWALL
St. Bernard Software
SurfControl
Symantec
Trend Micro

HISTORICAL FINANCIALS

Company Type: Public

Income Statement

FYE: December 31

	REVENUE ($ mil.)	NET INCOME ($ mil.)	NET PROFIT MARGIN	EMPLOYEES
12/05	148.6	38.8	26.1%	635
12/04	111.9	26.2	23.4%	500
12/03	81.7	16.7	20.4%	400
12/02	61.0	16.7	27.4%	329
12/01	35.9	3.1	8.6%	255
Annual Growth	**42.6%**	**88.1%**	**—**	**25.6%**

2005 Year-End Financials

Debt ratio: —
Return on equity: 20.8%
Cash ($ mil.): 320.4
Current ratio: 2.86
Long-term debt ($ mil.): —
No. of shares (mil.): 24.0
Dividends
  Yield: —
  Payout: —
Market value ($ mil.): 786.7
R&D as % of sales: 11.0%
Advertising as % of sales: 3.2%

Stock History

NASDAQ (GS): WBSN

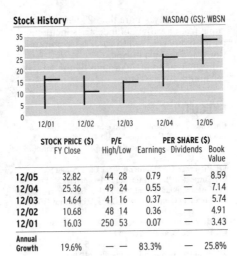

	STOCK PRICE ($) FY Close	P/E High/Low		Earnings	Dividends	Book Value
12/05	32.82	44	28	0.79	—	8.59
12/04	25.36	49	24	0.55	—	7.14
12/03	14.64	41	16	0.37	—	5.74
12/02	10.68	48	14	0.36	—	4.91
12/01	16.03	250	53	0.07	—	3.43
Annual Growth	**19.6%**	**—**	**—**	**83.3%**	**—**	**25.8%**

WebSideStory

WebSideStory reports whether your site feels oh so pretty. The company's tracking services measure and analyze Web site activity of Internet-based businesses. Its HBX sensors, which are inserted into Web pages, collect data used to improve marketing, e-commerce, and customer support. WebSideStory uses the data it gathers to produce industry white papers and reports on Internet trends. Expanding its product offerings, the company launched WebSideStory Bid in 2006, a bid management interface used by search engine marketers. Its more than 1,100 clients include Walt Disney Internet Group, Best Buy, and Federal Express. Blaise Barrelet founded WebSideStory in 1996.

Jeff Lunsford, the company's CEO since 2003, left WebSideStory to take over as CEO of content-delivery company Limelight Networks in November 2006. Jim MacIntyre, former CEO of WebSide Story's Visual Sciences unit, replaced Lunsford, who remained a board member.

Boosting its software offerings, WebSideStory acquired Avivo, a provider of on-demand digital marketing applications which is widely known as Atomz, in 2005. It picked up Visual Sciences in 2006 to further its offerings in the digital marketing area.

Competition in the sector increased in 2005 when Google announced it would provide similar Web-site tracking services for free.

EXECUTIVES

Chairman: William H. (Bill) Harris Jr., age 50
President, CEO, and Director:
 James W. (Jim) MacIntyre IV, age 38
CFO: Claire Long, age 38
SVP Administration: Sheryl Roland
SVP Development: David Rosenthal
SVP EMEA: Daniel Guilloux, age 58
SVP and General Counsel: Dru Greenhalgh, age 34
SVP Marketing: Pelin Wood
SVP Worldwide Professional Services: Warren D. Raisch
SVP Sales: Christopher (Chris) Reid, age 47
CTO: Jim Van Baalen, age 42
Corporate Communications Director: Erik Bratt
Auditors: PricewaterhouseCoopers LLP

LOCATIONS

HQ: WebSideStory, Inc.
10182 Telesis Ct., 6th Fl., San Diego, CA 92121
Phone: 858-546-0040   **Fax:** 858-546-0480
Web: www.websidestory.com

2005 Sales

	$ mil.	% of total
US	33.8	86
Europe	5.7	14
Total	**39.5**	**100**

PRODUCTS/OPERATIONS

2005 Sales

	$ mil.	% of total
Subscriptions	37.8	96
Advertising	1.7	4
Total	**39.5**	**100**

COMPETITORS

aQuantive
Coremetrics
DoubleClick
Endeca Technologies
Fireclick
Google
IBM
Interwoven
Net Perceptions
NetRatings
Omniture
SPSS
Vignette
WebTrends

HISTORICAL FINANCIALS

Company Type: Public

Income Statement

FYE: December 31

	REVENUE ($ mil.)	NET INCOME ($ mil.)	NET PROFIT MARGIN	EMPLOYEES
12/05	39.5	9.7	24.6%	214
12/04	22.6	1.8	8.0%	135
12/03	16.4	(1.9)	—	116
12/02	13.6	(2.5)	—	—
Annual Growth	**42.7%**	**—**	**—**	**35.8%**

2005 Year-End Financials

Debt ratio: 0.1%
Return on equity: 19.8%
Cash ($ mil.): 31.7
Current ratio: 2.40
Long-term debt ($ mil.): 0.1
No. of shares (mil.): 18.4
Dividends
  Yield: —
  Payout: —
Market value ($ mil.): 333.6
R&D as % of sales: 11.7%
Advertising as % of sales: 0.7%

Stock History

NASDAQ (GM): WSSI

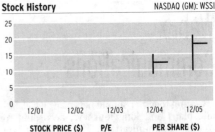

	STOCK PRICE ($) FY Close	P/E High/Low		Earnings	Dividends	Book Value
12/05	18.13	40	20	0.51	—	3.79
12/04	12.43	—	—	(0.13)	—	1.80
Annual Growth	**45.9%**	**—**	**—**	**—**	**—**	**110.7%**

Website Pros

Website Pros has everything a growing business needs to get on the Internet. The company provides Web site building software, custom design consulting, and Web hosting. Its eWorks! XL program also helps companies improve their visibility online through search engine optimization and Internet advertising. Website Pros' desktop Web design software is branded under its NetObjects Fusion label and helps customers to design their own Web site. The company sells to more than 50,000 small and midsized businesses in the US, mostly on a subscription basis. Insight Venture Partners owns about 20% of Website Pros; Norwest Venture Partners owns 15%. Website Pros was established in 1999.

Through the company's eWorks! XL program, Website Pros' goal is to have a Web site visible on the Internet for the customer within 72 hours of receiving the customer's initial information. The program includes a wide assortment of services and products including initial site design setup, the purchase and registration of the domain name, online marketing applications, Web mail, and hosting and technical support.

In 2005 the company acquired E.B.O.Z. and Leads.com, expanding its lead generation and Internet marketing offerings. The buyouts continued in 2006 when the company acquired Renovation Experts.com (Renex), an online lead generation business catering to homeowners and contractors, and 1ShoppingCart.com, a designer of online shopping cart software and services.

EXECUTIVES

President, CEO, and Director: David Brown, age 52, $387,885 pay
SVP Business Development: Darin Brannan, age 38, $160,000 pay
SVP Marketing: Roseann Duran, age 54, $160,000 pay
VP Finance and CFO: Kevin Carney, age 42, $225,577 pay
VP Acquisition Services: Lisa Anteau, age 33
VP Operations: Joel Williamson, age 57
EVP, Leads.com: Tobias Dengel, age 34
EVP, Leads.com: Todd Walrath, age 38
General Counsel: Robert C. Wiegand
Auditors: Ernst & Young LLP

LOCATIONS

HQ: Website Pros, Inc.
12735 Gran Bay Pkwy. West, Bldg. 200, Jacksonville, FL 32258
Phone: 904-680-6600   **Fax:** 904-880-0350
Web: www.websitepros.com

Website Pros has offices in California, Florida, Virginia, and Washington.

PRODUCTS/OPERATIONS

2005 Sales

	$ mil.	% of total
Subscription	32.6	86
License	3.9	10
Professional services	1.3	4
Total	**37.8**	**100**

COMPETITORS

Adobe
AOL
EarthLink
Equinix
Globix
Microsoft Business Solutions
Verio

HISTORICAL FINANCIALS
Company Type: Public

Income Statement

				FYE: December 31
	REVENUE ($ mil.)	NET INCOME ($ mil.)	NET PROFIT MARGIN	EMPLOYEES
12/05	37.8	0.8	2.1%	163
12/04	23.4	0.9	3.8%	—
12/03	17.0	(1.5)	—	—
12/02	13.7	(6.3)	—	—
Annual Growth	**40.3%**	**—**	**—**	**—**

2005 Year-End Financials

Debt ratio: 0.4%
Return on equity: 2.7%
Cash ($ mil.): 55.8
Current ratio: 7.81
Long-term debt ($ mil.): 0.2
No. of shares (mil.): 16.5
Dividends
  Yield: —
  Payout: —
Market value ($ mil.): 143.6
R&D as % of sales: —
Advertising as % of sales: —

Stock History

NASDAQ (GM): WSPI

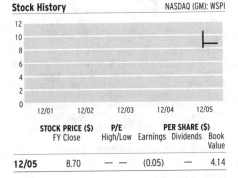

	STOCK PRICE ($) FY Close	P/E High/Low	PER SHARE ($) Earnings	Dividends	Book Value
12/05	8.70	— —	(0.05)	—	4.14

Western Alliance Bancorporation

The allies behind Western Alliance Bancorporation are Bank of Nevada (formerly BankWest of Nevada), Alliance Bank of Arizona, and Torrey Pines Bank, which together operate about 30 branches throughout Nevada, Arizona, and Southern California. The banks provide local businesses and individuals with standard deposit products, such as checking and money market accounts and CDs. Commercial real estate and construction loans dominate the banks' lending (about 40% and 25% of the company's loan portfolio, respectively). Subsidiaries Miller/Russell & Associates and Premier Trust offer financial planning and trust services. Director Marianne Boyd Johnson owns 20% of Western Alliance.

The company has been busy expanding its operations through acquisitions. In 2006 it acquired Intermountain First Bancorp (parent of Nevada First Bank) and Bank of Nevada, effectively tripling Western Alliance's size. With the latter acquisition, Western Alliance changed the name of its Nevada banking operations to Bank of Nevada. The subsidiary banks are also growing organically, with plans to add *de novo* branches for each bank. The company in 2006 moved to expand into the San Francisco Bay area under a deal to join forces with an investor group in launching start-up Alta California Bank in Oakland, California. CEO Robert Sarver owns about 15% of the company. He also is the managing partner and majority owner of the Phoenix Suns.

EXECUTIVES

Chairman, President, and CEO: Robert G. Sarver, age 44, $1,000,000 pay
EVP, Nevada Administration and Director; President and CEO, Bank of Nevada: Larry L. Woodrum, age 68, $400,000 pay
EVP, Arizona Administration; President and CEO, Alliance Bank of Arizona: James Lundy, age 56, $245,000 pay
EVP, California Administration: Gary Cady, age 52
EVP and Chief Administrative Officer: Merrill S. Wall, age 58, $342,346 pay
EVP and Chief Credit Officer: Duane Froeschle, age 53
EVP and CFO: Dale M. Gibbons, age 45, $312,000 pay
EVP and COO: Linda Mahan, age 48, $202,308 pay
Secretary: Robert E. Clark
Auditors: McGladrey & Pullen, LLP

LOCATIONS

HQ: Western Alliance Bancorporation
2700 W. Sahara Ave., Las Vegas, NV 89102
Phone: 702-248-4200   **Fax:** 702-362-2026
Web: www.westernalliancebancorp.com

Western Alliance Bancorporation's subsidiary banks have about 15 branches in Nevada, about 10 in Arizona, and about five in California.

PRODUCTS/OPERATIONS

2005 Sales

	$ mil.	% of total
Interest income		
Loans	102.5	70
Securities	29.5	20
Other	2.9	2
Noninterest income		
Trust & investment advisory services	5.7	4
Service charges	2.5	2
Income from bank-owned life insurance	1.7	1
Other	2.3	1
Total	**147.1**	**100**

COMPETITORS

Bank of America
Business Bank (NV)
Community Bancorp (NV)
Desert Schools FCU
First Banks
Nevada State Bank
Silver State Bancorp
UnionBanCal
U.S. Bancorp
Washington Mutual
Wells Fargo

HISTORICAL FINANCIALS
Company Type: Public

Income Statement

				FYE: December 31
	ASSETS ($ mil.)	NET INCOME ($ mil.)	INCOME AS % OF ASSETS	EMPLOYEES
12/05	2,857.3	28.1	1.0%	537
12/04	2,176.9	20.1	0.9%	—
12/03	1,576.8	8.7	0.6%	—
Annual Growth	**34.6%**	**79.7%**	**—**	**—**

2005 Year-End Financials

Equity as % of assets: 8.5%
Return on assets: 1.1%
Return on equity: 14.9%
Long-term debt ($ mil.): 30.9
No. of shares (mil.): 22.8
Market value ($ mil.): 681.3

Dividends
  Yield: —
  Payout: —
Sales ($ mil.): 147.1
R&D as % of sales: —
Advertising as % of sales: —

Stock History

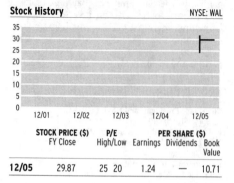

NYSE: WAL

	STOCK PRICE ($) FY Close	P/E High/Low	PER SHARE ($) Earnings	Dividends	Book Value
12/05	29.87	25 20	1.24	—	10.71

W-H Energy Services

W-h-a-t is W-H? W-H Energy Services offers diversified oil field services both onshore and off — from completion and workover related products and services to drilling related products and services. Products include specialty chemicals, drilling motors and fluids, wireline logging and perforating, and measurement-while-drilling systems. Founded in 1989, W-H Energy Services serves oil and gas firms, petrochemical companies, and other oil field service companies, primarily on the US Gulf Coast and in the Gulf of Mexico and the North Sea. The company, which has grown through acquisitions, is pursuing international expansion.

In order to focus on its core operations, in 2004 the company sold its maintenance and safety related products and services units, including Charles Holston, Inc. and Well Safe, Inc.

EXECUTIVES

Chairman, President, and CEO: Kenneth T. White Jr., age 61, $1,350,000 pay
COO: Jeffrey L. (Jeff) Tepera, age 40
VP and CFO: Ernesto Bautista III, age 34
VP: William J. (Mac) Thomas III, age 53, $680,000 pay
VP and Intellectual Property Counsel: Stuart J. Ford, age 46, $460,000 pay
President, Agri-Empresa: Stephen T. Goree
President, Charles Holston: Craig Holston
President, Drill Motor Services: Daniel M. (Dan) Spiller
President, Dyna Drill Technologies: Leif Syverson
President, Grinding and Sizing: Ronald A. Rose
President, Integrity Industries:
  William M. (Max) Duncan Jr.
President, Diamond Wireline Services and Perf-O-Log:
  Bill Bouziden
Auditors: Grant Thornton LLP

LOCATIONS

HQ: W-H Energy Services, Inc.
  10370 Richmond Ave., Ste. 990, Houston, TX 77042
Phone: 713-974-9071   **Fax:** 713-974-7029
Web: www.whes.com

W-H Energy Services has onshore operations in the US and in Brazil, Canada, Europe, the Middle East, and North Africa. It has offshore operations off the coast of Brazil and in the Gulf of Mexico, the Gulf of Suez, the Mediterranean Sea, the North Sea, and the Persian Gulf.

2005 Sales

	$ mil.	% of total
US	563.3	89
North Sea	34.3	5
Other countries & regions	36.8	6
Total	**634.4**	**100**

PRODUCTS/OPERATIONS

2005 Sales

	$ mil.	% of total
Drilling	409.2	65
Completion & workover	225.2	35
Total	**634.4**	**100**

Selected Subsidiaries

Agri-Empresa, Inc. (specialty chemicals)
Boyd's Bit Service, Inc. (drilling equipment)
Coil Tubing Services, L.L.C. (oilfield services)
Drill Motor Services, Inc.
Dyna Drill Technologies, Inc. (drilling motor services and rentals)
Grinding and Sizing Company, Inc. (drilling mud products)
Integrity Industries, Inc. (specialty chemicals)
PathFinder Energy Services AS (Norway, logging-while-drilling and measurement-while-drilling services)
PathFinder Energy Services, Inc. (logging-while-drilling and measurement-while-drilling services)
PathFinder Energy Services Limited (UK, logging-while-drilling and measurement-while-drilling services)
Perf-O-Log, Inc. (completion and workover related products and services)
Thomas Energy Services, Inc. (rental tools)

COMPETITORS

Baker Hughes
BJ Services
Dailey International Inc.
Dril-Quip
Halliburton
National Oilwell Varco
Newpark Resources
Oil States International
Schlumberger
Smith International
Weatherford International

HISTORICAL FINANCIALS

Company Type: Public

Income Statement

FYE: December 31

	REVENUE ($ mil.)	NET INCOME ($ mil.)	NET PROFIT MARGIN	EMPLOYEES
12/05	634.4	49.0	7.7%	2,333
12/04	462.4	17.9	3.9%	2,079
12/03	398.4	19.3	4.8%	2,081
12/02	313.4	16.3	5.2%	1,618
12/01	359.1	41.4	11.5%	1,386
Annual Growth	**15.3%**	**4.3%**	**—**	**13.9%**

2005 Year-End Financials

Debt ratio: 50.0%
Return on equity: 16.1%
Cash ($ mil.): 9.9
Current ratio: 3.16
Long-term debt ($ mil.): 169.5
No. of shares (mil.): 28.8

Dividends
  Yield: —
  Payout: —
Market value ($ mil.): 953.6
R&D as % of sales: 2.6%
Advertising as % of sales: —

Stock History

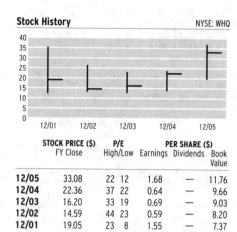

NYSE: WHQ

	STOCK PRICE ($) FY Close	P/E High/Low	PER SHARE ($) Earnings	Dividends	Book Value
12/05	33.08	22 12	1.68	—	11.76
12/04	22.36	37 22	0.64	—	9.66
12/03	16.20	33 19	0.69	—	9.03
12/02	14.59	44 23	0.59	—	8.20
12/01	19.05	23 8	1.55	—	7.37
Annual Growth	**14.8%**	**— —**	**2.0%**	**—**	**12.4%**

Whiting Petroleum

There's nothing fishy about what Whiting Petroleum is about. The company engages in oil and natural gas exploration and production activities, mainly in California, the Gulf Coast, Michigan, and the mid-continent, Permian Basin, and Rocky Mountains regions. It has estimated proved reserves of 263.6 million barrels of oil equivalent. Whiting Petroleum had 3,443 net productive wells in 2005. The company expanded in 2004 by acquiring stakes in 17 oil and gas fields in Texas and New Mexico for $345 million. It also bought Equity Oil for $76 million. In 2005 the company acquired oil and gas assets in Mississippi, Oklahoma, and Texas.

In 2005 Whiting Petroleum acquired three institutional partnerships managed by subsidiary, Whiting Programs, for about $30.5 million. The partnership properties (with reserves of 17.4 billion cu. ft.of natural gas equivalent) are located primarily in Arkansas, Louisiana, Oklahoma, Texas, and Wyoming.

EXECUTIVES

Chairman, President, and CEO: James J. Volker, age 57, $1,021,920 pay
SVP: D. Sherwin Artus, age 67, $571,493 pay
VP and CFO: Michael J. Stevens, age 39
VP Exploration and Development: Mark R. Williams, age 48, $564,188 pay
VP, General Counsel, and Secretary: Bruce R. DeBoer, age 52
VP Human Resources: Patricia J. Miller, age 67, $523,242 pay
VP Operations: James T. Brown, age 52, $533,236 pay
VP Reservoir Engineering and Acquisitions:
  J. Douglas Lang, age 55
Treasurer, Controller, and Chief Accounting Officer:
  Brent Jensen, age 35
Director Investor Relations: Mark Burford
Marketing Manager: Charles LaCouture, age 47
Auditors: Deloitte & Touche LLP

LOCATIONS

HQ: Whiting Petroleum Corporation
1700 Broadway, Ste. 2300, Denver, CO 80290
Phone: 303-837-1661 **Fax:** 303-861-4023
Web: www.whiting.com

2005 Proved Reserves

	% of total
Permian Basin	46
Rocky Mountains	22
Mid-continent	20
Gulf Coast	7
Michigan	5
Total	**100**

PRODUCTS/OPERATIONS

2005 Proved Reserves

	% of total
Oil	76
Natural gas	24
Total	**100**

COMPETITORS

Anadarko Petroleum
Black Hills
Cabot Oil & Gas
Frontier Oil
Houston Exploration
Newfield Exploration
Stone Energy

HISTORICAL FINANCIALS

Company Type: Public

Income Statement
FYE: December 31

	REVENUE ($ mil.)	NET INCOME ($ mil.)	NET PROFIT MARGIN	EMPLOYEES
12/05	540.5	121.9	22.6%	309
12/04	287.0	70.1	24.4%	171
12/03	167.4	18.3	10.9%	110
12/02	120.5	7.7	6.4%	—
12/01	139.4	41.2	29.6%	—
Annual Growth	**40.3%**	**31.2%**	**—**	**67.6%**

2005 Year-End Financials

Debt ratio: 89.9%
Return on equity: 15.1%
Cash ($ mil.): 10.4
Current ratio: 0.80
Long-term debt ($ mil.): 896.9
No. of shares (mil.): 36.8

Dividends
　Yield: —
　Payout: —
Market value ($ mil.): 1,473.7
R&D as % of sales: —
Advertising as % of sales: —

Stock History
NYSE: WLL

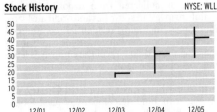

	STOCK PRICE ($) FY Close	P/E High/Low		PER SHARE ($) Earnings	Dividends	Book Value
12/05	40.00	12	7	3.88	—	27.08
12/04	30.25	10	5	3.38	—	20.61
12/03	18.40	19	16	0.98	—	13.84
Annual Growth	**47.4%**	**—**	**—**	**99.0%**	**—**	**39.9%**

Whittier Energy

A clever company, no doubt, Whittier Energy (formerly Olympic Resources) knows how to make money. The natural gas exploration and production independent has primary operations in Louisiana, New Mexico, Oklahoma, and Texas. The company has estimated proved reserves of 6.7 million barrels of oil equivalent. In 2005 Whittier Energy acquired Rimco Production for $56 million. Rimco had proved reserves of 32.8 billion cu. ft. of natural gas equivalent. The deal also gives Whittier Energy an additional 116 active wells in 18 producing fields in Alabama, Louisiana, and Texas. In 2007 the company agreed to be acquired by UK-based oil and gas explorer Sterling Energy.

Founded in Canada in 1986, as Global Data Systems Corp., the company was renamed Comtron Enterprises in 1989, and then became Olympic Resources Ltd. in 1993. In 2000 Olympic Resources sold most of its Canadian assets and began focusing on natural gas exploration and production in the US. It became Whittier Energy in 2003 in a reverse stock split.

EXECUTIVES

President, CEO, and Director: Bryce W. Rhodes, age 53
COO: Daniel Silverman
VP, Finance and Chief Accounting Officer:
　Geoffrey M. Stone
Auditors: Grant Thornton LLP

LOCATIONS

HQ: Whittier Energy Corporation
333 Clay St., Ste. 700, Houston, TX 77002
Phone: 713-850-1880 **Fax:** 713-850-1879
Web: www.whittierenergy.com

Whittier Energy has assets in Alabama, California, Colorado, Louisiana, New Mexico, Oklahoma, Pennsylvania, Texas, Utah, and Wyoming.

PRODUCTS/OPERATIONS

Selected Subsidiaries

Whittier Energy Company
　Olympic Resources (Arizona) Ltd.

Whittier Operating, Inc.

COMPETITORS

Apex Resources Group
Aurora Oil & Gas
Tristream Energy

HISTORICAL FINANCIALS

Company Type: Public

Income Statement
FYE: December 31

	REVENUE ($ mil.)	NET INCOME ($ mil.)	NET PROFIT MARGIN	EMPLOYEES
12/05	26.9	5.3	19.7%	20
12/04	10.1	1.4	13.9%	6
12/03*	6.2	(0.2)	—	4
2/03	0.7	(0.2)	—	—
2/02	0.1	(1.3)	—	—
Annual Growth	**305.0%**	**—**	**—**	**123.6%**

*Fiscal year change

2005 Year-End Financials

Debt ratio: 26.9%
Return on equity: 14.6%
Cash ($ mil.): 5.1
Current ratio: 1.22
Long-term debt ($ mil.): 16.3
No. of shares (mil.): 12.5

Dividends
　Yield: —
　Payout: —
Market value ($ mil.): 131.4
R&D as % of sales: —
Advertising as % of sales: —

Stock History
NASDAQ (GM): WHIT

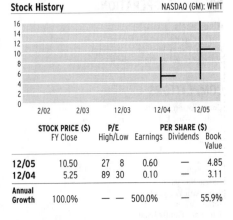

	STOCK PRICE ($) FY Close	P/E High/Low		PER SHARE ($) Earnings	Dividends	Book Value
12/05	10.50	27	8	0.60	—	4.85
12/04	5.25	89	30	0.10	—	3.11
Annual Growth	**100.0%**	**—**	**—**	**500.0%**	**—**	**55.9%**

Willamette Valley Vineyards

In the heart of Oregon's Willamette Valley, apart from California's wine country, you'll find Willamette Valley Vineyards. The company makes premium varietal wines, including pinot noir (its flagship varietal), chardonnay, dry Riesling, and pinot gris under the Willamette Valley Vineyards, Tualatin Estates, and Griffin Creek labels. Its wines are sold to visitors at its winery, in restaurants and at retail, and through wine distributors across the US. Retail prices for the company's wines range from $7 to $50 a bottle. Willamette Valley Vineyards controls about 280 acres, which supplies about 50% of the grapes needed for production. Founder Jim Bernau owns 21% of the company.

Willamette Valley Vineyards plans to produce as many as 124,000 cases of wine per year, making it one of the largest in the state. Like many small and midsized wineries, Willamette Valley Vineyards is capitalizing on a 2005 Supreme Court decision that opened up interstate sales of wine in those states that allow wine to ship directly to consumers without first passing through a wholesaler.

EXECUTIVES

Chairman and President: James W. (Jim) Bernau, age 52, $196,158 pay
VP Corporate, Secretary, Director HR, and Board Member: James L. Ellis, age 61
Controller: Sean M. Cary, age 33
National Sales Manager: Cara Pepper
Communications Coordinator: Shelby Zadow
Auditors: Moss Adams, LLP

LOCATIONS

HQ: Willamette Valley Vineyards, Inc.
8800 Enchanted Way, SE, Turner, OR 97392
Phone: 503-588-9463   **Fax:** 503-588-8894
Web: www.wvv.com

PRODUCTS/OPERATIONS

Wine Labels

Griffin Creek
Tualatin Estate Vineyards
Willamette Valley Vineyards

COMPETITORS

Constellation Brands
Foster's Wine Estates Americas
Gallo
Kendall-Jackson
Newton Vineyard
Ravenswood Winery
R.H. Phillips
Scheid Vineyards
Sebastiani Vineyards
Terlato Wine
Trinchero Family Estates
Yamhill Valley Vineyards

HISTORICAL FINANCIALS

Company Type: Public

Income Statement

FYE: December 31

	REVENUE ($ mil.)	NET INCOME ($ mil.)	NET PROFIT MARGIN	EMPLOYEES
12/05	13.7	1.2	8.8%	86
12/04	9.4	0.5	5.3%	76
12/03	7.4	0.2	2.7%	80
12/02	6.0	0.1	1.7%	60
12/01	7.0	0.1	1.4%	67
Annual Growth	18.3%	86.1%	—	6.4%

2005 Year-End Financials

Debt ratio: 20.5%
Return on equity: 13.4%
Cash ($ mil.): 0.4
Current ratio: 4.00
Long-term debt ($ mil.): 2.0
No. of shares (mil.): 4.7

Dividends
  Yield: —
  Payout: —
Market value ($ mil.): 22.8
R&D as % of sales: —
Advertising as % of sales: —

Stock History

NASDAQ (CM): WVVI

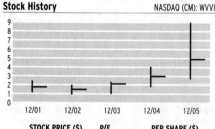

	STOCK PRICE ($) FY Close	P/E High/Low	Earnings	Dividends	Book Value
12/05	4.90	36 11	0.25	—	2.09
12/04	2.99	40 19	0.10	—	1.81
12/03	2.12	58 27	0.04	—	1.71
12/02	1.50	65 33	0.03	—	1.68
12/01	1.75	240 119	0.01	—	1.65
Annual Growth	29.4%	— —	123.6%	—	6.0%

Williams Partners

Fractionating natural gas liquids is a big fraction of what Williams Partners does. The company is engaged in gathering, transporting, and processing natural gas and the fractionating and storing of natural gas liquids (such as ethane, propane, and butane). Its assets include 40%-owned Discovery Producer Services, which owns a gas gathering and transportation pipeline system running from the Gulf of Mexico to a processing facility in Louisiana; the Carbonate Trend gas gathering pipeline off the coast of Alabama; and three integrated NGL storage facilities and a 50%-owned fractionator in Kansas. The Williams Companies spun off Williams Partners in 2005, and retains a 59% stake in the company.

NGLs, the result of natural gas processing and crude oil refining, are used in a number of industry applications, including gasoline additives, heating fuels, and petrochemical feedstocks.

Williams Partners intends to pursue a growth strategy that includes acquisitions. In 2006 the company spent $360 million for a 25% interest in the Williams Companies' Four Corners natural gas gathering subsidiary, and agreed to by the remainder for $1.2 billion.

EXECUTIVES

Chairman and CEO: Steven J. (Steve) Malcolm, age 57
COO and Director: Alan S. Armstrong, age 43
CFO and Director: Donald R. (Don) Chappel, age 54
General Counsel: James J. Bender, age 48
Auditors: Ernst & Young LLP

LOCATIONS

HQ: Williams Partners L.P.
1 Williams Ctr., Tulsa, OK 74172
Phone: 918-573-2000

PRODUCTS/OPERATIONS

2005 Sales

	$ mil.	% of total
NGL services	48.3	93
Gathering & processing	3.5	7
Total	**51.8**	**100**

2005 Sales

	% of total
Williams Power Company	26
SemStream L.P.	17
Enterprise Products Partners	14
BP Products North America	14
Other customers	29
Total	**100**

COMPETITORS

Dynegy
Enterprise Products
TEPPCO Partners

HISTORICAL FINANCIALS

Company Type: Public

Income Statement

FYE: December 31

	REVENUE ($ mil.)	NET INCOME ($ mil.)	NET PROFIT MARGIN	EMPLOYEES
12/05	51.8	4.8	9.3%	66
12/04	41.0	(13.4)	—	120
12/03	28.3	5.2	18.4%	—
12/02	25.7	7.8	30.4%	—
Annual Growth	26.3%	(14.9%)	—	(45.0%)

2005 Year-End Financials

Debt ratio: —
Return on equity: 4.0%
Cash ($ mil.): 6.8
Current ratio: 1.24
Long-term debt ($ mil.): —
No. of shares (mil.): 7.0

Dividends
  Yield: 0.5%
  Payout: 34.1%
Market value ($ mil.): 218.2
R&D as % of sales: —
Advertising as % of sales: —

Stock History

NYSE: WPZ

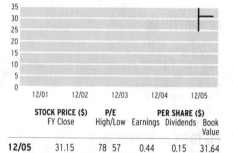

	STOCK PRICE ($) FY Close	P/E High/Low	Earnings	Dividends	Book Value
12/05	31.15	78 57	0.44	0.15	31.64

Willow Financial Bancorp

Willow Financial Bancorp (formerly Willow Grove Bancorp) is the holding company for Willow Financial Bank (previously Willow Grove Bank), which operates about 30 branches in suburban Philadelphia. Founded in 1909, the bank uses funds collected from deposit accounts mainly to invest in securities and originate loans. Mortgages, including residential, commercial real estate, construction, and home equity loans make up more than 90% of the company's lending portfolio. The bank also writes business and consumer loans.

In 2005 the company acquired Chester Valley Bancorp, holding company of First Financial Bank, which kept its name and operates as a division of Willow Financial Bank. Former Chester Valley CEO Donna Coughey took the helm of the combined company.

Willow Financial Bancorp also picked up investment advisory and broker-dealer subsidiary Philadelphia Corporation for Investment Services (PCIS) as part of its purchase of Chester Valley Bancorp. In 2007 the company announced it will buy Philadelphia-area employee benefits consulting firm BeneServ to expand its offerings for small businesses.

EXECUTIVES

Chairman: Rosemary C. Loring, age 55
President, CEO, and Director, Willow Grove Bancorp and Willow Grove Bank: Donna M. Coughey, age 56, $453,310 pay
COO: Christopher E. Bell, age 47, $171,713 pay
CFO and Treasurer, Willow Grove Bancorp and Willow Grove Bank; Secretary: Joseph T. Crowley, age 44, $242,797 pay
Regional President, First Financial Division, Willow Grove Bank: Colin N. Maropis, age 54
Regional President, Bucks and Montgomery Counties: John T. Powers, age 56
SVP and Chief Retail Officer: Richard Hymanson
Chief Accounting Officer: Neelesh (Neil) Kalani, age 31
Chief Lending and Sales Officer, Willow Grove Bank: G. Richard (Dick) Bertolet, age 59, $196,629 pay
Chief Wealth Management Officer, Willow Grove Bank: Matthew D. Kelly, age 42, $170,500 pay
Chief Credit Officer: Ammon J. Baus, age 57, $203,115 pay
Treasurer: Jerome P. Arrison, age 53, $151,381 pay
Auditors: KPMG LLP

LOCATIONS

HQ: Willow Financial Bancorp, Inc.
170 S. Warner Rd., Wayne, PA 19087
Phone: 610-995-1700
Web: www.willowgrovebank.com

PRODUCTS/OPERATIONS

2006 Sales

	$ mil.	% of total
Interest		
Loans	65.5	73
Securities	16.1	18
Noninterest		
Service charges & fees	5.0	5
Investment services	2.6	3
Other	0.9	1
Total	**90.1**	**100**

COMPETITORS

Citizens Financial Group
Harleysville National
M&T Bank
National Penn Bancshares
PNC Financial
Sovereign Bancorp
Wachovia

HISTORICAL FINANCIALS

Company Type: Public

Income Statement

FYE: June 30

	ASSETS ($ mil.)	NET INCOME ($ mil.)	INCOME AS % OF ASSETS	EMPLOYEES
6/06	1,576.7	11.1	0.7%	372
6/05	959.3	6.7	0.7%	220
6/04	921.6	6.1	0.7%	246
6/03	845.1	7.5	0.9%	245
6/02	759.7	5.5	0.7%	238
Annual Growth	**20.0%**	**19.2%**	**—**	**11.8%**

2006 Year-End Financials

Equity as % of assets: 12.9%
Return on assets: 0.9%
Return on equity: 7.2%
Long-term debt ($ mil.): 36.2
No. of shares (mil.): 14.8
Market value ($ mil.): 236.2
Dividends
 Yield: 3.0%
 Payout: 59.3%
Sales ($ mil.): 90.1
R&D as % of sales: —
Advertising as % of sales: —

Stock History

NASDAQ (GS): WFBC

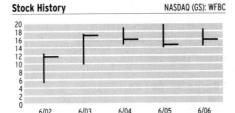

	STOCK PRICE ($) FY Close	P/E High/Low		PER SHARE ($) Earnings	Dividends	Book Value
6/06	15.91	23	18	0.81	0.48	13.68
6/05	14.66	28	20	0.71	0.46	—
6/04	15.99	30	24	0.62	0.38	—
6/03	17.00	24	14	0.71	0.30	—
6/02	11.73	24	11	0.51	0.19	—
Annual Growth	**7.9%**	**—**	**—**	**12.3%**	**26.1%**	**—**

Wilshire Bancorp

Wilshire Bancorp is the holding company for Wilshire State Bank, where ethnic minorities are the banking majority. Based in the Koreatown section of Los Angeles, the bank has some 15 branches mainly in Southern California but also in Texas and New York. It has about 10 loan production offices in those states and four others. Wilshire State Bank targets small to midsized minority-owned businesses and ethnic groups underserved by most national banking institutions. In addition to offering standard deposit services (including checking, savings, and money market accounts, and IRAs), the bank specializes in Small Business Administration loans.

Wilshire Bancorp has expanded into Hispanic and Vietnamese markets from its Korean-American base. In 2006 the company acquired Liberty Bank of New York and its two locations in the New York metropolitan area, and arranged to buy a branch in Fort Lee, New Jersey. The acquisitions help broaden Wilshire's nationwide presence as it expands on the East Coast.

Chairman Steven Koh owns almost 20% of the company. As a group, board members and executive officers of Wilshire Bancorp control nearly half of the company.

EXECUTIVES

Chairman: Steven Koh, age 60
President, CEO, and Director: Soo Bong Min, age 68, $532,000 pay
EVP and CFO: Eung-Rae (Brian) Cho, age 45, $235,515 pay
EVP and Chief Lending Officer: Joanne Kim, age 51, $281,353 pay
SVP and Chief Compliance Officer: Jean Lim
SVP and Chief Credit Administrator: Haekyong (Jane) Kim
SVP and Chief Information Officer: Jake Seo
EVP and Manager, SBA Department: Sung Soo Han, age 49, $312,612 pay
Auditors: Deloitte & Touche LLP

LOCATIONS

HQ: Wilshire Bancorp, Inc.
3200 Wilshire Blvd., Los Angeles, CA 90010
Phone: 213-387-3200 **Fax:** 213-427-6562
Web: www.wilshirebank.com

PRODUCTS/OPERATIONS

2005 Sales

	$ mil.	% of total
Interest		
Loans, including fees	89.6	76
Investment securities & deposits in other financial institutions	4.9	4
Federal funds sold & other cash equivalents	2.8	2
Noninterest		
Gain on sale of loans	8.3	7
Service charges on deposit accounts	7.6	7
Loan-related servicing income	2.0	2
Other	2.6	2
Total	**117.8**	**100**

COMPETITORS

Bank of America
Bank of the West
Broadway Financial
California Bank & Trust
California National Bank
Cathay General Bancorp
Center Financial
Citibank
Citigroup
City National
Comerica
East West Bancorp
FirstFed Financial
Hanmi Financial
Nara Bancorp
UnionBanCal
U.S. Bancorp
Washington Mutual
Wells Fargo

HISTORICAL FINANCIALS

Company Type: Public

Income Statement

FYE: December 31

	ASSETS ($ mil.)	NET INCOME ($ mil.)	INCOME AS % OF ASSETS	EMPLOYEES
12/05	1,666.3	27.8	1.7%	278
12/04	1,265.6	19.5	1.5%	245
12/03	983.3	12.8	1.3%	212
12/02	692.8	8.6	1.2%	173
12/01	490.0	6.2	1.3%	145
Annual Growth	**35.8%**	**45.5%**	**—**	**17.7%**

2005 Year-End Financials

Equity as % of assets: 6.8%
Return on assets: 1.9%
Return on equity: 27.6%
Long-term debt ($ mil.): 61.5
No. of shares (mil.): 28.6
Market value ($ mil.): 492.2
Dividends
 Yield: 0.9%
 Payout: 16.7%
Sales ($ mil.): 117.8
R&D as % of sales: —
Advertising as % of sales: —

Stock History

NASDAQ (GS): WIBC

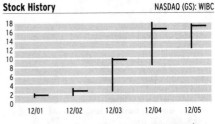

	STOCK PRICE ($) FY Close	P/E High/Low		PER SHARE ($) Earnings	Dividends	Book Value
12/05	17.19	18	13	0.96	0.16	3.95
12/04	16.54	26	13	0.68	—	3.14
12/03	9.71	22	6	0.44	—	4.54
12/02	2.70	10	5	0.32	—	7.80
12/01	1.79	9	6	0.23	—	12.70
Annual Growth	**76.0%**	**—**	**—**	**42.9%**	**—**	**(25.3%)**

Wintrust Financial

Put yer hands up . . . we're buying you out! That seems to be the battle cry for ever-acquisitive Wintrust Financial, a multibank holding company engaged in banking and specialty financial services in several affluent Chicago suburbs. Through 13 community banks and a total of nearly 60 branches, Wintrust Financial emphasizes business and commercial real estate loans (nearly 60% of the portfolio) and provides receivables financing (20%), indirect auto loans, and residential mortgages. Milwaukee-based subsidiary Tricom provides financing and administrative services to the temporary staffing industry. Wintrust Financial continues to grow like gangbusters.

In fact, Wintrust Financial bought Advantage National Bancorp in October 2003 and closed its purchase of Village Bancorp in December of that year. In 2004 the company acquired SGB Corporation (dba WestAmerica Mortgage) and its affiliate Guardian Real Estate Services. Soon thereafter it bought Northview Financial and its subsidiaries Northview Bank and Trust (which it renamed Wheaton Bank) and Northview Mortgage. Then it snagged Wisconsin-based Town Bankshares.

In early 2005 it completed the acquisition of Antioch Holding Company, parent of State Bank of The Lakes, and First Northwest Bancorp, and the next year it purchased Hinsbrook Bancshares.

The company's banking subsidiaries now include Advantage Bank, Barrington Bank, Beverly Bank, Crystal Lake Bank, First Northwest Bank, Hinsdale Bank, Lake Forest Bank, Libertyville Bank, North Shore Bank, Northbrook Bank, State Bank of The Lakes, Town Bank, Village Bank, and Wheaton Bank.

Wintrust also operates several nonbank subsidiaries. First Insurance Funding serves commercial loan customers throughout the country. Tricom offers administrative services that range from payroll processing to temporary staffing. Other subsidiaries provide real estate loan support, including WestAmerica Mortgage, Guardian Real Estate Services, and Northview Mortgage. Wayne Hummer Investments offers a full range of private client and brokerage services; Wayne Hummer Asset Management provides wealth management advice.

The company established another community bank, Old Plank Trail Community Bank, in the Chicago area, in 2006.

EXECUTIVES

Chairman: John S. Lillard, age 74
President, CEO, and Director: Edward J. Wehmer, age 51
SEVP, COO, Secretary, and Treasurer; Director, Libertyville Bank & Trust: David A. Dykstra, age 44
EVP and CFO; Director, Beverly Bank & Trust: David L. Stoehr, $213,307 pay
EVP and Chief Credit Officer; President, COO, and Director, Hinsdale Bank & Trust: Richard B. Murphy, age 45, $241,375 pay
EVP, Marketing: Robert F. Key, age 50, $227,583 pay
EVP, Risk Management: John S. Fleshood, age 43
EVP, Technology; President, CEO, and Director, Wintrust Information Technology Services: Lloyd M. Bowden, age 51
EVP, Wealth Management; President, CEO, and Director, Wayne Hummer Trust Company, Wayne Hummer Asset Management, and Wayne Hummer Investments: James F. Duca II, age 47
VP, Human Resources: Michael A. Cherwin
Auditors: Ernst & Young LLP

LOCATIONS

HQ: Wintrust Financial Corporation
727 N. Bank Ln., Lake Forest, IL 60045
Phone: 847-615-4096   **Fax:** 847-615-4076
Web: www.wintrust.com

PRODUCTS/OPERATIONS

2005 Sales

	$ mil.	% of total
Interest income		
Loans	335.4	67
Securities & other	71.6	14
Noninterest income		
Wealth management fees	30.0	6
Mortgage banking	25.9	5
Other	37.7	8
Total	**500.6**	**100**

COMPETITORS

Citigroup
Citizens Financial Group
Citizens Republic Bancorp
Corus Bankshares
Cummins-American
First Midwest Bancorp
Harris Bankcorp
MAF Bancorp
Midwest Banc Holdings
National City
Northern States Financial
Northern Trust
Princeton National Bancorp
PrivateBancorp
Sky Financial
U.S. Bancorp

HISTORICAL FINANCIALS

Company Type: Public

Income Statement

FYE: December 31

	ASSETS ($ mil.)	NET INCOME ($ mil.)	INCOME AS % OF ASSETS	EMPLOYEES
12/05	8,177.0	67.0	0.8%	1,678
12/04	6,419.0	51.3	0.8%	1,414
12/03	4,747.4	38.1	0.8%	929
12/02	3,721.6	27.9	0.7%	822
12/01	2,705.4	18.4	0.7%	566
Annual Growth	**31.9%**	**38.1%**	**—**	**31.2%**

2005 Year-End Financials

Equity as % of assets: 7.7%
Return on assets: 0.9%
Return on equity: 12.2%
Long-term debt ($ mil.): 377.3
No. of shares (mil.): 23.9
Market value ($ mil.): 1,314.3

Dividends
Yield: 0.4%
Payout: 8.7%
Sales ($ mil.): 500.6
R&D as % of sales: —
Advertising as % of sales: —

Stock History

NASDAQ (GS): WTFC

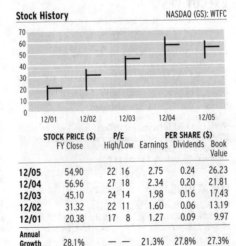

	STOCK PRICE ($) FY Close	P/E High/Low		PER SHARE ($) Earnings	Dividends	Book Value
12/05	54.90	22	16	2.75	0.24	26.23
12/04	56.96	27	18	2.34	0.20	21.81
12/03	45.10	24	14	1.98	0.16	17.43
12/02	31.32	22	11	1.60	0.06	13.19
12/01	20.38	17	8	1.27	0.09	9.97
Annual Growth	**28.1%**		**—**	**21.3%**	**27.8%**	**27.3%**

Wireless Telecom

In an industry that abhors noise, Wireless Telecom Group sure makes a lot of it. The company, which markets its products under the brand name Noise Com, makes electronic noise generators for wireless telecommunications systems. Its products are used to test whether such systems can receive transmitted information. Its noise emulator products also operate in radar and satellite systems to continually monitor and test receivers or to jam signals. Wireless Telecom's Boonton Electronics subsidiary makes radio-frequency (RF) and microwave test equipment. Its Microlab/FXR subsidiary makes high-power, passive microwave components. Investcorp Technology Ventures owns one-quarter of Wireless Telecom.

Wireless Telecom Group markets its products through in-house representatives and manufacturer representatives primarily to commercial customers (about three-quarters of sales); the remaining revenue comes from government and military clients. The company has expanded its line of products in an effort to reach a wider range of customers.

In 2005 Wireless Telecom acquired Willtek Communications GmbH in exchange for 8 million shares of its common stock. Willtek's shareholders now own approximately 31% of Wireless Telecom. Willtek makes test and measurement instruments, specializing in RF applications. The acquisition more than doubled Wireless Telecom's headcount.

FMR owns nearly 6% of Wireless Telecom Group, as does Damany Holding.

HISTORY

Founded in Paramus, New Jersey, in 1985 by Gary Simonyan, Noise Com began providing noise sources and systems testing for the military. Its products determined whether sophisticated communications devices were receiving and understanding the information being transmitted. Until 1992, the majority of sales continued to come from government and military contracts.

In the wake of defense cutbacks, in 1993 the company expanded its commercial product lines to include signal testing devices for the commercial telecommunications market, which by 1997 accounted for 95% of sales. In 1994 the company changed its name to Wireless Telecom; it continued to market its noise source products under the name of Noise Com, and distributed test systems under its new name. Simonyan stepped away from day-to-day responsibilities in 1996, and was replaced by president Dale Sydnor.

In 1997 the company began providing test systems for ICO Global Communications' satellite network. Lowered sales in its wireless and satellite test emulator line caused a drop in profits for 1998. In 1999 longtime Wireless Telecom employee Edward Garcia replaced Sydnor as chairman and CEO. As part of a reorganization around noise generators, the company that year sold its wireless and satellite communications test equipment business to Telecom Analysis Systems (TAS), a subsidiary of electronics company Bowthorpe. As part of the deal, Wireless Telecom gained TAS's noise generation product line.

In 2000 the company acquired test equipment maker Boonton Electronics to expand its line of products for measuring wireless signal power. The next year Wireless Telecom added passive

components to its catalog in 2002 with the purchase of Microlab/FXR.

Later in 2002 Wireless Telecom relocated its corporate headquarters and other offices in the former HQ of Boonton Electronics in Parsippany, New Jersey. Boonton Electronics took its name from the New Jersey town just north of Parsippany, where it was located for many years. Boonton Electronics was established in nearby Morris Plains in 1947.

Wireless Telecom greatly grew in size with its 2005 acquisition of Willtek Communications, a German test and measurement firm. Sales increased in all geographic regions of the world, especially in Europe, as a result of the acquisition.

EXECUTIVES

Chairman: Savio W. Tung, age 56
Vice Chairman and CEO: James M. (Monty) Johnson Jr., age 51
President and CFO: Paul Genova, age 50, $249,000 pay
EVP, Marketing: Bent Hessen-Schmidt, age 42, $151,463 pay
Controller: Reed E. DuBow
Auditors: Lazar Levine & Felix LLP; Ernst & Young AG

LOCATIONS

HQ: Wireless Telecom Group, Inc.
25 Eastmans Rd., Parsippany, NJ 07054
Phone: 907-386-9696   **Fax:** 907-386-9191
Web: www.wtt.bz

Wireless Telecom Group has facilities in Germany and the US.

2005 Sales

	$ mil.	% of total
Americas	21.2	54
Europe	10.7	28
Asia	5.8	15
Other regions	1.1	3
Total	**38.8**	**100**

PRODUCTS/OPERATIONS

2005 Sales

	% of total
Commercial	87
Government & military contractors	13
Total	**100**

Selected Products

Broadband test equipment
Electronic testing and measuring instruments
Noise figure measurement devices
Noise generators
Passive components
   Directional couplers
   Filters
   Power splitters
Wireless communications network test equipment
   Air interface testing
   Terminal testing

COMPETITORS

Aeroflex
Agilent Technologies
Anaren
Anritsu
COM DEV
KATHREIN-Werke
M/A-Com
Merrimac Industries
Micronetics

Murata Manufacturing
ORBIT/FR
Rohde & Schwarz
STC Microwave Systems
Tektronix
telent
Tyco Electronics
Vishay Intertechnology
Wavelink

HISTORICAL FINANCIALS

Company Type: Public

Income Statement

FYE: December 31

	REVENUE ($ mil.)	NET INCOME ($ mil.)	NET PROFIT MARGIN	EMPLOYEES
12/05	38.8	3.5	9.0%	229
12/04	22.1	2.3	10.4%	106
12/03	19.7	1.8	9.1%	106
12/02	20.8	1.8	8.7%	110
12/01	19.0	1.2	6.3%	127
Annual Growth	**19.5%**	**30.7%**	**—**	**15.9%**

2005 Year-End Financials

Debt ratio: 8.6%
Return on equity: 8.5%
Cash ($ mil.): 13.9
Current ratio: 2.35
Long-term debt ($ mil.): 4.5
No. of shares (mil.): 25.6
Dividends
  Yield: 4.5%
  Payout: 75.0%
Market value ($ mil.): 67.8
R&D as % of sales: 11.3%
Advertising as % of sales: 1.2%

Stock History

AMEX: WTT

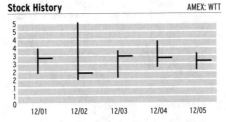

	STOCK PRICE ($) FY Close	P/E High/Low		PER SHARE ($) Earnings	Dividends	Book Value
12/05	2.65	19	13	0.16	0.12	2.06
12/04	2.84	30	18	0.13	0.15	1.69
12/03	2.95	32	16	0.10	0.09	1.67
12/02	1.89	50	15	0.10	0.06	1.65
12/01	2.83	49	27	0.07	0.06	1.63
Annual Growth	**(1.6%)**	**—**	**—**	**23.0%**	**18.9%**	**5.9%**

Wireless Xcessories

Wireless Xcessories Group dresses up cellular phones. The company markets and distributes about 4,000 accessory products for wireless phones, pagers, and two-way radios primarily in North America. Decorative faceplates, carrying cases, hands-free kits, rechargeable batteries, antennae, and like items are sold mainly through third-party retailers or from retail Web sites that the company develops for vendors. The company's Taiwan office oversees product development and selection; more than 70% of its products are manufactured outside of the US. CEO Stephen Rade owns 16% of Wireless Xcessories Group.

Rade founded Advanced Fox Antenna in 1985. That company designed the first 3-watt transportable phone in a briefcase, a "mobile" phone with a lead acid battery that weighed more than 25 pounds and sold for nearly $3,000.

Advanced Fox Antenna was acquired in 1996 by Batteries Batteries, Inc., and has evolved into Wireless Xcessories Group.

EXECUTIVES

Chairman, President, and CEO: Stephen Rade, age 68, $298,000 pay
CFO and Secretary: Ronald E. (Ron) Badke, age 60, $126,000 pay
VP and Sales Account Manager: Susan Rade, $183,942 pay
VP, New Business Development Manager, and Purchasing Director: Dawn Kenderdine, age 36, $119,756 pay
Director, Information Services: Edward Sides Jr.
Customer Service Manager: Susan Hershock
Quality Control Manager: Bill Earnest
Auditors: Bagell, Josephs & Company, LLC

LOCATIONS

HQ: Wireless Xcessories Group, Inc.
1840 County Line Rd., Huntingdon Valley, PA 19006
Phone: 215-322-4600   **Fax:** 888-233-0220
Web: www.wirexgroup.com

COMPETITORS

Brightpoint Inc.
CellStar
LG Electronics
Uniden

HISTORICAL FINANCIALS

Company Type: Public

Income Statement

FYE: December 31

	REVENUE ($ mil.)	NET INCOME ($ mil.)	NET PROFIT MARGIN	EMPLOYEES
12/05	22.1	2.0	9.0%	83
12/04	15.3	1.0	6.5%	80
12/03	11.5	(0.2)	—	71
12/02	14.1	(0.5)	—	70
12/01	20.9	(2.9)	—	108
Annual Growth	**1.4%**	**—**	**—**	**(6.4%)**

2005 Year-End Financials

Debt ratio: —
Return on equity: 39.1%
Cash ($ mil.): 2.7
Current ratio: 6.05
Long-term debt ($ mil.): —
No. of shares (mil.): 4.5
Dividends
  Yield: —
  Payout: —
Market value ($ mil.): 22.6
R&D as % of sales: —
Advertising as % of sales: —

Stock History

AMEX: XWG

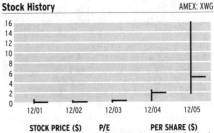

	STOCK PRICE ($) FY Close	P/E High/Low		PER SHARE ($) Earnings	Dividends	Book Value
12/05	5.04	36	4	0.44	—	1.38
12/04	1.92	11	2	0.21	—	0.91
12/03	0.40	—	—	(0.03)	—	0.70
12/02	0.15	—	—	(0.11)	—	0.73
12/01	0.13	—	—	(0.56)	—	0.80
Annual Growth	**149.5%**	**—**	**—**	**—**	**—**	**14.4%**

WMS Industries

WMS Industries used to be the pinball wizard, but now spins its reels in the casinos. The company was the world's #1 maker of pinball machines, featuring such brands as Williams and Bally. However, WMS has shut down all pinball operations to focus on its lottery terminal and slot machine business. The firm's products include standard and progressive slot machines, and video lottery terminals. In addition to its internally branded machines such as *Cow Tippin* and *Pyramid*, WMS also makes machines based on licensed brands including the *Monopoly* board game, *Hollywood Squares*, and several Clint Eastwood films. Viacom and CBS Corp. chairman Sumner Redstone owns about 11% of the firm.

WMS Industries gains most of its revenues (nearly 70%) from the sale of its machines. The rest comes from leasing participation games, such as progressive slot machines, and licensing fees from other gaming machine makers that incorporate WMS content. The *Monopoly*-branded machines have proved to be the company's most popular, and it has an agreement with Hasbro (the game's maker) to continue using the brand until 2011. New games for 2006 included machines based on the World Series of Poker professional gambling circuit, and the popular *Powerball* multi-state lottery game.

The company has also significantly expanded its international presence, and now has machines installed in almost 90 legal gaming jurisdictions worldwide.

In 2006 WMS Industries acquired privately held Orion Gaming, a Netherlands-based company that designs, manufactures, and distributes gaming machines, for approximately $30 million.

HISTORY

WMS traces its roots to the Automatic Amusement Company, founded by Harry Williams in the 1930s. Williams produced his first game, called *Advance*, and soon followed it with industry innovations such as the tilt mechanism, and in 1933, electricity. In 1964 his company, Williams Electronics, was bought by jukebox maker Seeburg, which in turn was bought in the 1970s by Xcor, led by Chicago wheeler-dealer Louis Nicastro. Williams went public in 1974. After Seeburg went bankrupt in 1980, it spun off Williams, and Nicastro became CEO.

Williams changed its name to WMS in 1987, and the next year it bought the amusement-game lines of rival Bally/Midway, enhancing its position as a world leader in arcade gaming. In 1990 WMS moved its headquarters from New York City to Chicago and diversified into hotel and casino management.

In 1994 WMS created a joint venture (Williams/Nintendo) to market games for Nintendo platforms and moved into the home video game market with the acquisition of Tradewest Inc. The following year it announced plans to divide into three publicly traded businesses — hotels and casinos (WHG Resorts & Casinos), arcade and video operations (Midway Games),

and casino gambling devices, pinball games, and lottery terminals (WMS Industries). In 1998 it spun off its 87% stake in Midway Games, which caused profits to take a hit. WMS's fiscal pain was eased somewhat by the successful debut of its *Monopoly*-themed slot machines in 1998. However, slumping pinball sales prompted the company to cease making pinball machines the following year.

In 2000 the company announced the release of a series of machines based on popular board and word games such as *Scrabble, Pictionary*, and *Jumble*. Also that year its coin-operated video machines went the way of pinball machines when WMS discontinued their production. In 2001 president and COO Brian Gamache was named CEO. Nicastro stepped back to non-executive chairman. Also that year WMS began expanding outside North America, installing its Jackpot Party video slot machines in Australia. In 2002 the company overhauled its technology in order to rectify defects in it gaming systems. That year it also launched three new game series (*Hollywood Squares, Survivor*, and *Pac-Man*) and opened an office in Johannesburg, South Africa.

In 2004 WMS launched new mechanical reel-spinning game devices along with a new operating system and gaming platform, CPU-NXT.

EXECUTIVES

Chairman: Louis J. Nicastro, age 78
President, CEO, and Director: Brian R. Gamache, age 47, $662,500 pay
EVP and COO: Orrin J. Edidin, age 45, $718,749 pay
EVP, CFO, and Treasurer: Scott D. Schweinfurth, age 52, $658,443 pay
VP, General Counsel, and Secretary: Kathleen J. McJohn, age 47, $332,500 pay
VP Investor Relations: William H. (Bill) Pfund
VP North American Sales: Brian R. Pierce
VP Sales Operations: Mark N. Jason
SVP Supply Chain and Business Processes, WMS Gaming: Patricia C. Barten, age 53
VP, Controller, and Chief Accounting Officer: John McNicholas Jr., age 52
Auditors: Ernst & Young LLP

LOCATIONS

HQ: WMS Industries Inc.
800 S. Northpoint Blvd., Waukegan, IL 60085
Phone: 847-785-3000   **Fax:** 847-785-3058
Web: www.wms.com

WMS Industries has operations in Australia, the Netherlands, South Africa, Spain, the UK, and the US.

PRODUCTS/OPERATIONS

Selected Gaming Machines

Monopoly-themed machines
All in the Cards
Cash Flow
Grand Hotel
Once Around Deluxe
Reel Riches
Shake Rattle and Roll
Multi-coin, multi-line video machines
The Jade Monkey
Life of Luxury
Milk Money
Quackers
Rakin' It In
Robin Hood's Sherwood Treasure
Reel-spinning slot machines
Aftershock
Beat the Clock
Reel 'em In
Royal Family
Yin & Yang

COMPETITORS

Aristocrat Leisure
Atronic Casino Technology
Bally Technologies
Danoptra
GTECH Holdings
International Game Technology
Konami Gaming
Progressive Gaming
Scientific Games
Sigma Game

HISTORICAL FINANCIALS

Company Type: Public

Income Statement

FYE: June 30

	REVENUE ($ mil.)	NET INCOME ($ mil.)	NET PROFIT MARGIN	EMPLOYEES
6/06	451.2	33.3	7.4%	1,320
6/05	388.4	21.2	5.5%	1,221
6/04	230.2	(0.9)	—	1,165
6/03	178.7	(8.3)	—	1,015
6/02	174.7	9.9	5.7%	838
Annual Growth	26.8%	35.4%	—	12.0%

2006 Year-End Financials

Debt ratio: 35.3%
Return on equity: 10.9%
Cash ($ mil.): 52.7
Current ratio: 4.16
Long-term debt ($ mil.): 115.0
No. of shares (mil.): 31.6
Dividends
  Yield: —
  Payout: —
Market value ($ mil.): 865.5
R&D as % of sales: —
Advertising as % of sales: —

Stock History

NYSE: WMS

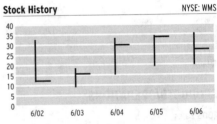

	STOCK PRICE ($) FY Close	P/E High/Low		PER SHARE ($) Earnings	Dividends	Book Value
6/06	27.39	37	21	0.94	—	10.30
6/05	33.75	55	31	0.62	—	9.01
6/04	29.80	—	—	(0.03)	—	7.89
6/03	15.59	—	—	(0.27)	—	7.50
6/02	12.25	108	40	0.30	—	8.12
Annual Growth	22.3%	—	—	33.0%	—	6.1%

WSB Financial Group

WSB Financial aims to be the real estate lender of choice in the west Puget Sound area. WSB is the holding company for Westsound Bank (in business since 1999). Deposits and loans command the bulk of the group's annual income. WSB's lending centers on short- and long-term financing for real estate development, small to medium-sized businesses, and residential mortgages. Retail and office loans comprise the bulk of WSB's commercial real estate portfolio; construction loans make up some 34% of total approved loans. The company plans to continue opening about three branches a year throughout the area.

EXECUTIVES

Chairman, WSB Financial Group and Westsound Bank:
Louis J. Weir, age 65
President, CEO, and Director, WSB Financial Group and Westsound Bank: David K. Johnson, age 41, $375,000 pay
EVP, Finance and Operations and CFO, WSB Financial Group and Westsound Bank: Mark D. Freeman, age 53, $116,859 pay (partial-year salary)
SVP, Chief Risk Officer, and Secretary, WSB Financial Group and Westsound Bank: Veronica R. Colburn, age 43, $123,000 pay
EVP, Sales and Lending, Westsound Bank:
Brett T. Green, age 44, $650,485 pay
SVP and Chief Lending Officer, Westsound Bank:
Brent A. Stenman, age 41, $110,236 pay
Auditors: Moss Adams, LLP

LOCATIONS

HQ: WSB Financial Group, Inc.
607 Pacific Ave., Bremerton, WA 98337
Phone: 360-405-1200   **Fax:** 360-405-1206
Web: www.westsoundbank.com

COMPETITORS

BECU
Columbia Banking
Horizon Financial

HISTORICAL FINANCIALS

Company Type: Public

Income Statement

	REVENUE ($ mil.)	NET INCOME ($ mil.)	NET PROFIT MARGIN	EMPLOYEES
12/05	20.9	2.4	11.5%	108
12/04	10.8	1.3	12.0%	—
12/03	4.7	0.6	12.8%	—
Annual Growth	110.9%	100.0%	—	—

FYE: December 31

2005 Year-End Financials

Debt ratio: 51.5%
Return on equity: 16.6%
Cash ($ mil.): 26.6
Current ratio: —
Long-term debt ($ mil.): 8.3

Net Income History

NASDAQ (GM): WSFG

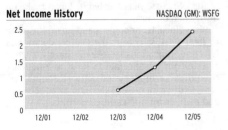

Youbet.com

Youbet.com lets its customers watch and play the ponies nationwide. Its You Bet Network facilitates online wagering on horse races in most US states, as well as in Australia, Canada, Hong Kong, Japan, and South Africa. Charging a portion of each wager, Youbet.com lets customers place bets via Youbet Express, a Web-based betting system. Subscribers can enjoy the network's features, including up-to-the-minute odds and live audio and video feeds from more than 150 tracks, 24 hours a day. The company has a deal with Gemstar-TV Guide that enables Youbet.com users to place wagers on races broadcast on TVG Network's horse racing channel.

Youbet.com is reaching out to a younger generation of gamblers through the Internet. One prong to this strategy is providing horse racing audio and video to major Web outlets like CBS Sportsline.com. Youbet.com, which also does business under the name of its subsidiary, International Racing Group, also looks to grow worldwide by adding races from tracks in the UK and Canada and launching a Web site that brings US horseracing to China.

EXECUTIVES

Chairman, President, and CEO:
Charles F. (Chuck) Champion, age 51, $714,884 pay
Vice Chairman: David M. Marshall, age 42
CFO: Gary Sproule, age 55, $455,000 pay
VP Advertising and Strategic Media Alliances:
David B. (Dave) Bonfield
VP Client Services: Todd Galbate
VP Human Resources and Administration and Head of Member Services: Archi Padilla
VP Sales and Marketing: Thomas L. (Tom) Levenick
VP Strategic Marketing: Christa S. Myers
Chief Accounting Officer and Controller:
Michael Nelson, age 52
President, Youbet Online Services: Jeff Franklin, age 53
General Counsel: Scott Solomon
Auditors: Piercy Bowler Taylor & Kern

LOCATIONS

HQ: Youbet.com, Inc.
5901 De Soto Ave., Woodland Hills, CA 91367
Phone: 818-668-2100   **Fax:** 818-668-2101
Web: www.youbet.com

PRODUCTS/OPERATIONS

Selected Services

Direct wagering in horse track pools
Handicapping and performance data
Immediate access to results, payout, and account status
Live audio and video feeds
Simultaneous wagering
Up-to-the-minute odds

COMPETITORS

Gemstar-TV Guide
Intertops.com
Magna Entertainment
World Gaming

HISTORICAL FINANCIALS

Company Type: Public

Income Statement

	REVENUE ($ mil.)	NET INCOME ($ mil.)	NET PROFIT MARGIN	EMPLOYEES
12/05	88.8	5.7	6.4%	106
12/04	65.3	4.6	7.0%	81
12/03	53.1	(4.0)	—	80
12/02	25.9	(9.0)	—	67
12/01	6.3	(14.8)	—	76
Annual Growth	93.8%	—	—	8.7%

FYE: December 31

2005 Year-End Financials

Debt ratio: 0.8%
Return on equity: 30.8%
Cash ($ mil.): 21.9
Current ratio: 1.68
Long-term debt ($ mil.): 0.2
No. of shares (mil.): 33.5
Dividends
  Yield: —
  Payout: —
Market value ($ mil.): 158.2
R&D as % of sales: 1.8%
Advertising as % of sales: 2.3%

Stock History

NASDAQ (CM): UBET

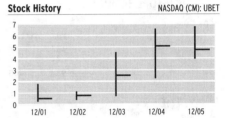

	STOCK PRICE ($) FY Close	P/E High/Low	PER SHARE ($) Earnings	PER SHARE ($) Dividends	PER SHARE ($) Book Value
12/05	4.73	42 25	0.16	—	0.68
12/04	5.06	46 16	0.14	—	0.46
12/03	2.51	— —	(0.15)	—	0.27
12/02	0.77	— —	(0.41)	—	0.34
12/01	0.51	— —	(0.76)	—	0.83
Annual Growth	74.5%	— —	—	—	(4.8%)

ZipRealty

ZipRealty would like to move you to a new ZIP code with the speed of the Internet. The residential real estate brokerage firm maintains an online, searchable database of homes for sale in more than 15 metropolitan markets. Buyers are able to streamline their house hunt, narrowing searches by location, price range, and size; online tours of homes are also available (at no charge to the sellers). The firm offers financing pre-approval, provided by E-LOAN, through its online mortgage center. ZipRealty officers and directors collectively own 65% of the company.

ZipRealty, founded in 1999 by former EVP Scott Kucirek and director Juan Mini, has some 1,350 sales agents (ZipAgents) in about a dozen states and Washington, DC. That the company employs its own cadre of realtors is unique in an industry dominated by independent contractors.

EXECUTIVES

Chairman: Donald F. (Don) Wood, age 51
CEO: Richard F. Sommer
President: Joseph P. (Patrick) Lashinsky, age 38, $189,250 pay (prior to promotion)
Interim CFO: David A. Rector, age 59

EVP Operations and Business Development:
William C. (Bill) Sinclair, age 56, $178,125 pay
SVP Sales: Jeffrey G. (Jeff) Wagoner, $231,610 pay
VP, General Counsel, and Secretary: Karen B. Seto, age 40
VP Human Resources: Alain J. Ané, age 47
Auditors: PricewaterhouseCoopers LLP

LOCATIONS

HQ: ZipRealty, Inc.
    2000 Powell St., Ste. 300, Emeryville, CA 94608
Phone: 510-735-2600   **Fax:** 510-735-2850
Web: www.ziprealty.com

ZipRealty has operations in the metropolitan areas of Atlanta; Austin, Texas; Baltimore/Washington, DC/Northern Virginia; Boston; Chicago; Dallas; Houston; Las Vegas; Los Angeles; Minneapolis/St. Paul; Orange County, California; Miami/Fort Lauderdale, Florida; Phoenix/Scottsdale, Arizona; Sacramento, California; San Diego; San Francisco; Seattle; and Tampa.

PRODUCTS/OPERATIONS

2005 Sales

	$ mil.	% of total
Net transaction revenues	91.1	98
Referral & other revenues	2.3	2
Total	**93.4**	**100**

COMPETITORS

Baird & Warner
Century 21
Coldwell Banker
HouseValues
LendingTree
Move
NRT Inc.
The Prudential Real Estate Affiliates
RE/MAX

HISTORICAL FINANCIALS
Company Type: Public

Income Statement				FYE: December 31
	REVENUE ($ mil.)	NET INCOME ($ mil.)	NET PROFIT MARGIN	EMPLOYEES
12/05	93.4	20.5	21.9%	1,556
12/04	62.3	3.2	5.1%	1,059
12/03	33.8	(4.6)	—	708
12/02	17.2	(14.8)	—	—
Annual Growth	**75.8%**	**—**	**—**	**48.2%**

2005 Year-End Financials

Debt ratio: —
Return on equity: 22.0%
Cash ($ mil.): 88.9
Current ratio: 9.30
Long-term debt ($ mil.): —
No. of shares (mil.): 20.3
Dividends
    Yield: —
    Payout: —
Market value ($ mil.): 170.7
R&D as % of sales: —
Advertising as % of sales: 0.8%

Stock History   NASDAQ (GM): ZIPR

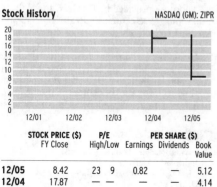

	STOCK PRICE ($) FY Close	P/E High/Low		PER SHARE ($) Earnings	Dividends	Book Value
12/05	8.42	23	9	0.82	—	5.12
12/04	17.87	—	—	—	—	4.14
Annual Growth	**(52.9%)**	**—**	**—**	**—**	**—**	**23.7%**

Zumiez

Zumiez's customers like to zoom. The online and mall-based retailer offers swank swag-like clothing, shoes, accessories, and gear to 12-to-24-year-olds who enjoy such action sports as snowboarding, BMX, skateboarding, and surfing. From about 190 stores in 19 states, Zumiez sells popular youth brands like Billabong, Burton, Hurley, Quiksilver, Vans, and Spy Optic, as well as private-label goods. Besides the usual hoodies, T-shirts, puffy skater shoes, and snowboarding goggles, stores also sport couches, video games, and sales clerks who really use the gear — all designed to encourage the kids to hang out. Zumiez was founded in 1978 by its chairman Thomas Campion, who owns 25% of the company's stock.

The sporting goods retailer planned to open about 40 stores in 2006. To this end Zumiez acquired the Fast Forward sporting goods chain. Fast Forward operates 19 stores, mostly in Texas. The company plans to convert all of its Fast Forward stores to the Zumiez nameplate by 2008.

President and CEO Richard Brooks owns some 15% of the company. Director William Barnam Jr. owns about 6% through Brentwood-Zumiez Investors LLC, which is controlled by Brentwood Associates.

EXECUTIVES

Chairman: Thomas D. Campion, age 57, $394,250 pay
President, CEO and Director: Richard M. Brooks, age 46, $394,250 pay
CFO: Brenda I. Morris, age 41, $376,000 pay
General Merchandising Manager: Lynn K. Kilbourne, age 43, $388,469 pay
Auditors: Moss Adams, LLP

LOCATIONS

HQ: Zumiez Inc.
    6300 Merrill Creek Pkwy., Ste. B, Everett, WA 98203
Phone: 425-551-1500   **Fax:** 425-551-1555
Web: www.zumiez.com

2006 Stores

	No.
California	36
New York	22
Washington	22
Colorado	13
Oregon	11
Utah	11
Arizona	10
Minnesota	10
Illinois	9
Idaho	5
Montana	4
Nevada	4
New Jersey	4
New Mexico	4
Texas	3
Other states	6
Total	**174**

COMPETITORS

Abercrombie & Fitch
Aéropostale
American Eagle Outfitters
Big 5
Buckle
Charlotte Russe Holding
Claire's Stores
Dick's Sporting Goods
Forever 21
Hot Topic
Old Navy
Pacific Sunwear
Sport Chalet
Sports Authority
Urban Outfitters
Wet Seal

HISTORICAL FINANCIALS
Company Type: Public

Income Statement			FYE: Saturday nearest January 31	
	REVENUE ($ mil.)	NET INCOME ($ mil.)	NET PROFIT MARGIN	EMPLOYEES
1/06	205.6	12.9	6.3%	2,273
1/05	153.6	7.3	4.8%	—
1/04	117.9	4.5	3.8%	—
Annual Growth	**32.1%**	**69.3%**	**—**	**—**

2006 Year-End Financials

Debt ratio: —
Return on equity: 25.9%
Cash ($ mil.): 43.0
Current ratio: 2.50
Long-term debt ($ mil.): —
No. of shares (mil.): 13.6
Dividends
    Yield: —
    Payout: —
Market value ($ mil.): 337.1
R&D as % of sales: —
Advertising as % of sales: 0.1%

Stock History   NASDAQ (GS): ZUMZ

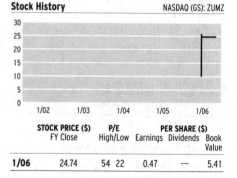

	STOCK PRICE ($) FY Close	P/E High/Low		PER SHARE ($) Earnings	Dividends	Book Value
1/06	24.74	54	22	0.47	—	5.41

Zygo Corporation

Zygo knows how to measure precisely what its customers need. The company makes high-precision electro-optical inspection and measurement equipment, automation systems, and optical components. One of Zygo's main products is the interferometer, which measures surface shape, roughness, and other characteristics by means of two light beams ("zygo" is Greek for "pair") used to produce 3-D surface profiles for comparing test objects with control samples. Zygo also offers optical design, testing, certification, and assembly services. Customers include Canon (36% of sales), AU Optronics, KLA-Tencor, Nikon, Lockheed Martin, and Samsung.

Zygo's products are used primarily for quality control in semiconductor (more than half of sales) and industrial manufacturing markets. Sales to the industrial equipment market have continued to grow despite tough market conditions, comprising about 45% of the company's sales. About two-thirds of its sales are to clients based outside of the US; customers located in Japan make up nearly half of sales.

With global technology spending on the wane in 2000-2001, sales from the semiconductor and telecommunications sectors fell sharply. Zygo is banking on advancements in semiconductor equipment technology and optical assembly services to drive increased sales, and has discontinued its telecommunications business.

Dimensional Fund Advisors owns 7% of Zygo. Canon holds nearly 7% of the company. Royce & Associates has an equity stake of nearly 6%. Gruber & McBaine Capital Management owns around 5%.

HISTORY

Carl Zanoni, Paul Forman, and Sol Laufer founded Zygo in 1970 with funding from Canon. (Zanoni still serves as an SVP and director, although Forman and Laufer have both retired.) The company intended to provide cutting-edge optical fabrication manufacturing services. Unsatisfied with the interferometers available, they decided to build and sell their own.

Zygo introduced the modular GH-1 Interferometer in 1972 and in 1978 unveiled an improved version that worked in conjunction with a data reduction system to extract more usable information from the measurements. Zygo went public in 1983. In 1985 it introduced a user-programmable version of its interferometer. In 1995 Zygo introduced the industry's first tester able to measure the flying height of magnetic read/write heads.

During the next two years Zygo acquired makers of manufacturing quality control equipment. These included NexStar Automation (automation and parts handling equipment) and Sight Systems (data storage yield improvement). In 1998 Zygo became a global distributor of IBM's Atomic Force Microscope for measuring submicron features. In 1999 process control industry veteran Bruce Robinson replaced Gary Willis as president and CEO.

In 2000 the company purchased Firefly Technologies, which became subsidiary Zygo TeraOptix, and entered the optical communications market. Zygo sold its Automation Systems Group, which made handlers, sorters, and inspection systems for wafer reticles, to Brooks Automation the next year.

The company put Zygo TeraOptix up for sale in 2002 (there were no takers in the telecom bust of the time) and left the optical communications business. In 2003 Zygo formed the Zygo Applied Optics group to focus on business opportunities in the aerospace and military electro-optic systems market.

The following year the company sold the vacant facility that once housed Zygo TeraOptix. Later in 2004, Zygo opened a sales and support office in Shanghai, China.

In early 2006 the company restated financial results for six consecutive quarters, from July 1, 2004, through December 31, 2005, due to inadvertent accounting errors for intercompany revenues from foreign operations, its Singapore and Taiwan subsidiaries in particular. The restatement knocked about $800,000 out of fiscal 2005 sales, and $500,000 from sales in the first half of fiscal 2006. Zygo also restated results from the four previous fiscal years.

EXECUTIVES

Chairman Emeritus: Paul F. Forman, age 73
Chairman, President, and CEO: J. Bruce Robinson, age 64, $735,244 pay
SVP, Technology and Director: Carl A. Zanoni, age 65, $381,608 pay
VP, Finance, CFO, and Treasurer: Walter A. Shephard, age 52, $326,409 pay
VP, Corporate Quality and Support Services: William H. Bacon, age 56
VP, Human Resources: David J. Person, age 58
VP, Worldwide Sales and Marketing: Brian J. Monti, age 50, $346,333 pay
VP, Metrology: Robert J. Stoner, age 43
President, Metrology: James R. Northup, age 45
Staff Assistant to the President: Lawrence C. Martin
Secretary: Paul Jacobs
Auditors: Deloitte & Touche LLP

LOCATIONS

HQ: Zygo Corporation
Laurel Brook Rd., Middlefield, CT 06455
Phone: 860-347-8506   **Fax:** 860-347-8372
Web: www.zygo.com

Zygo has operations in China, Germany, Japan, Singapore, South Korea, Taiwan, and the US.

2006 Sales

	$ mil.	% of total
Asia/Pacific		
Japan	76.6	45
Other countries	18.2	11
Americas	58.4	35
Europe	14.9	9
Total	**168.1**	**100**

PRODUCTS/OPERATIONS

2006 Sales

	$ mil.	% of total
Semiconductor	93.0	55
Industrial	75.1	45
Total	**168.1**	**100**

2006 Sales by Category

	$ mil.	% of total
Metrology	83.8	50
Optical Systems Solutions	42.3	25
Precision Positioning Systems	42.0	25
Total	**168.1**	**100**

Selected Products

Automation
   Flat-panel display inspection system (FPD series)
   Wafer-level surface measuring systems (APEX series)
Macro-optics and assemblies
   Laser optics
   Lenses and lens systems
   Optical coatings
   Prisms, rhomboids, and beamsplitters
   Reference flat mirrors
   Stage mirrors
Metrology
   Digital video disk interferometer
   Geometrically desensitized interferometer
   Interferometers
   Interferometric microscopes
   Large-aperture wavefront interferometer
   Photomask critical dimension metrology systems
   Small-aperture wavefront interferometer

COMPETITORS

ADE
Adept Technology
Agilent Technologies
AMETEK
Applied Materials
Carl Zeiss
CyberOptics
Electro Scientific Industries
Electroglas
II-VI
Jenoptik
KLA-Tencor
Leica Camera
Nanometrics
Newport
Nova Measuring
Renishaw
Spectris
Therma-Wave
Veeco Instruments
Yokogawa Electric

HISTORICAL FINANCIALS

Company Type: Public

Income Statement

FYE: June 30

	REVENUE ($ mil.)	NET INCOME ($ mil.)	NET PROFIT MARGIN	EMPLOYEES
6/06	168.1	14.5	8.6%	533
6/05	141.4	9.0	6.4%	526
6/04	116.6	(3.4)	—	476
6/03	102.6	(10.6)	—	477
6/02	84.4	(11.7)	—	537
Annual Growth	**18.8%**	**—**	**—**	**(0.2%)**

2006 Year-End Financials

Debt ratio: —
Return on equity: 9.7%
Cash ($ mil.): 41.7
Current ratio: 2.79
Long-term debt ($ mil.): —
No. of shares (mil.): 18.1

Dividends
   Yield: —
   Payout: —
Market value ($ mil.): 296.7
R&D as % of sales: —
Advertising as % of sales: —

Stock History

NASDAQ (GS): ZIGO

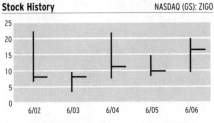

	STOCK PRICE ($) FY Close	P/E High/Low	PER SHARE ($) Earnings	Dividends	Book Value
6/06	16.39	25 12	0.79	—	8.78
6/05	9.80	29 17	0.50	—	7.85
6/04	11.19	— —	(0.19)	—	7.30
6/03	8.07	— —	(0.60)	—	7.38
6/02	8.05	— —	(0.67)	—	8.03
Annual Growth	**19.5%**	**— —**	**—**	**—**	**2.3%**

Hoover's Handbook of

Emerging Companies

Master Index for all
2007 Hoover's Handbooks

Index by Industry

Messaging, Conferencing & Communications Software
PAR3 Communications P376
Smith Micro Software E326
WebEx Communications E385

Multimedia, Graphics & Publishing Software
Adobe Systems A39
Avid Technology E45
Bitstream E57
DivX E118
RealNetworks E301
Sonic Solutions E327

Networking & Connectivity Software
ACE*COMM E18
Continuous Computing P147
F5 Networks E140
Novell, Inc. A617
Telcordia Technologies P473

Retail, Point-Of-Sale & Inventory Management Software
PROS Revenue Management P400

Security Software
SafeNet E311
Secure Computing E317
Symantec Corporation A793
VASCO Data Security E375

Storage & Systems Management Software
CA, Inc. A171
CommVault Systems E97
FalconStor Software E141

Supply Chain Management & Logistics Software
Infor Global Solutions P254
Logility E221

CONSTRUCTION

Construction & Design Services
A. G. Spanos Companies P32
Adams Homes of Northwest Florida P22
AECOM Technology P28
American Homestar P44
Anthony & Sylvan Pools P54
Austin Industries P67
Barton Malow P74
BE&K, Inc. P77
Beazer Homes USA A130
Bechtel Group A131, P78
Black & Veatch P87
Bouygues W71
Brasfield & Gorrie P101
Callison Architecture P107
Cavco Industries E74
Centex Corporation A194
CH2M HILL Companies P124
Champion Enterprises A199
Choice Homes P129
Clark Enterprises P133
Comstock Homebuilding E99
Day & Zimmermann P162
D.R. Horton A289
Drees Co. P177
Dunn Industries P180
EMCOR Group A317
ENGlobal E132
Fluor Corporation A349
Foster Wheeler A357
Gilbane, Inc. P209
Halliburton A397
Hensel Phelps Construction P240
Home Solutions of America E180
Hopewell Holdings W154
Hovnanian Enterprises A437

InfraSource Services E190
Jacobs Engineering Group A465
J.F. Shea Co. P267
John Wieland Homes P269
KB Home A481
Kimball Hill P280
Kitchell Corporation P283
Layne Christensen E214
Lennar Corporation A510
Levitt Corporation E217
Louis Berger Group P300
McCarthy Building P316
McDermott International A554
McGrath RentCorp E228
Nobility Homes E257
NVR, Inc. A621
Orleans Homebuilders E267
Parsons Brinckerhoff P377
Parsons Corporation P377
Patriot Homes P379
PBSJ Corporation P379
Peter Kiewit Sons' A657, P385
Pulte Homes A691
Rooney Holdings P422
Ryland Group A722
Shaw Group A753
SmithGroup, Inc. P446
Structure Tone P462
Swinerton Incorporated P467
Tata Group W323
Team, Inc. E345
Technical Olympic USA A800
Toll Brothers A825
Turner Industries P492
URS Corporation A861
VINCI W354
Walsh Group P523
Washington Group A888
Weitz Group P527
Whiting-Turner Contracting P531
WL Homes P536
WorleyParsons Corp. P537
Yates Companies P538
Zachry Construction P540

Construction Materials
Advanced Environmental Recycling E21
American Standard A81
Andersen Corporation P52
Associated Materials P63
Atrium Companies P66
Drew Industries E120
Eagle Materials E122
G-I Holdings P207
Hampton Affiliates P229
Hanson W145
JELD-WEN, inc. P266
Kohler Co. P285
Lafarge W194
Lennox International A511
Louisiana-Pacific A528
Martin Marietta Materials A546
Masco Corporation A547
McFarland Cascade P316
Omega Flex E263
Owens Corning A637
Pella Corporation P380
Pope Resources E288
Saint-Gobain (Compagnie de Saint-Gobain) W290
Sierra Pacific Industries P443
Simpson Investment P443
Texas Industries A812
United States Lime & Minerals E365
USG Corporation A865
Vulcan Materials A878
Weyerhaeuser A902

CONSUMER PRODUCTS MANUFACTURERS

Apparel
adidas W25
Anvil Holdings P55
Broder Bros. P101
Crocs E107
Deckers Outdoor E115
Guess? E165
Hartmarx Corporation A408
Jones Apparel Group A476
Levi Strauss & Co. A514, P293
Liz Claiborne A522
LVMH W206
New Balance Athletic Shoe P354
NIKE, Inc. A606
Perry Ellis International E279
Phillips-Van Heusen A663
Phoenix Footwear E284
Polo Ralph Lauren A674
Rocky Brands E308
Sara Lee A734
Timberland A820
True Religion Apparel E359
Under Armour E361
VF Corporation A873
Warnaco Group A886

Appliances
Alliance Laundry Holdings P37
BISSELL Homecare P86
Conair Corporation P141
Electrolux W118
iRobot E199
Minuteman International P335
Whirlpool A904

Cleaning Products
Church & Dwight Co. A209
Clorox A221
Henkel W149
Reckitt Benckiser W270
S.C. Johnson & Son A735, P431

Consumer Electronics
Bose Corporation P97
CASIO COMPUTER W91
Creative Technology W97
Harman International A403
Matsushita W211
Nintendo W230
Philips Electronics (Royal Philips Electronics N.V.) W254
Pioneer W256
SANYO Electric W296
Sony W314
Telex Communications P474

Hand Tools, Power Tools, Lawn & Garden Equipment
Black & Decker A147
MTD Products P339
Snap-on Incorporated A764
Stanley Works A778
Toro A828
Werner Co. P527

Home Furniture
Ashley Furniture Industries P62
Berkline/BenchCraft P82
Furniture Brands A366
La-Z-Boy A504
Leggett & Platt A508
Sauder Woodworking P429

Housewares
AAC Group Holding P17
Amscan Holdings P49
Home Products International P244
Lifetime Brands E219
Newell Rubbermaid A601

Tupperware Brands A838
Waterford Wedgwood W363

Jewelry & Watch Manufacturing
Lazare Kaplan International E215
Movado Group E240
Swatch W321
Tiffany & Co. A819

Linens
Springs Global US P455

Mattress & Bed Manufacturers
Tempur-Pedic International E349

Musical Equipment
Gibson Guitar P208
Taylor-Listug, Inc. P470
Yamaha W370

Office & Business Furniture, Fixtures & Equipment
Haworth, Inc. P232
Herman Miller A420
HNI Corporation A431
Steelcase Inc. A785

Office, School & Art Supplies
Deluxe Corporation A272
Ennis E133
Esselte Corporation P189

Personal Care Products
Alberto-Culver A55
Alticor Inc. P38
Avon Products A117
Colgate-Palmolive A228
Estée Lauder A325
Forever Living Products P202
Inter Parfums E193
John Paul Mitchell Systems P269
Kao W178
Kimberly-Clark A487
L'Oréal W202
MacAndrews & Forbes A534, P303
Mary Kay Inc. P311
Parlux Fragrances E274
Procter & Gamble A684
Revlon A708
Shiseido W305
Unilever W352

Pet Products
PetSmart A658
Professional Veterinary Products P399

Photographic & Optical Equipment/Supplies Manufacturers
Eastman Kodak A302
FUJIFILM W135
Nikon W229

Sporting Goods & Equipment
Aldila E23
Colt's Manufacturing P138
ICON Health & Fitness P250
Quiksilver, Inc. A696
Remington Arms P415
True Temper Sports P487
Volcom E381

Tobacco
Alliance One International A62
Altria Group A67
British American Tobacco W76
Gallaher Group W138
Imperial Tobacco W163
Japan Tobacco W176
Reynolds American A709
Universal Corporation A858
UST Inc. A867

Toys & Games
Hasbro, Inc. A410
JAKKS Pacific E203

FOUNDATIONS

GOVERNMENT

HEALTH CARE

INDUSTRIAL MANUFACTURING

MEDIA

Film & Video

Information Collection & Delivery

Internet Content Providers

Internet Search & Navigation Services

Music

Publishing

Radio Broadcasting & Programming

Television

MEMBERSHIP ORGANIZATIONS

METALS & MINING

Aluminum Production

Coal Mining & Processing

Copper Mining & Processing

Industrial Metals & Minerals

Metals Distribution

Precious Metals Mining & Processing

Specialty & Exotic Materials

Steel Production

Steel Service Centers

PHARMACEUTICALS

Biotechnology

Pharmaceuticals Distribution & Wholesale

Pharmaceuticals Manufacturers

REAL ESTATE

Commercial Property Investment

Commercial Real Estate Brokerage

Commercial Real Estate Development

Real Estate Investment Trusts (REITs)

Residential Property Investment

Residential Real Estate Brokerage

Residential Real Estate Development

Index by Headquarters

ARGENTINA

Buenos Aires
YPF W371

AUSTRALIA

Bella Vista
Woolworths W368

Mascot
Qantas Airways W266

Melbourne
BHP Billiton W66
National Australia Bank W225
Rio Tinto W277
Telstra W335

Southbank
Foster's Group W132

Sydney
AMP Limited W40

Tooronga
Coles Group W95

AUSTRIA

Vienna
OMV W246

BELGIUM

Brussels
Dexia W113
Fortis W131

Leuven
InBev W164

BERMUDA

Pembroke
Bacardi & Company W51

BRAZIL

Rio de Janeiro
PETROBRAS (PETRÓLEO
BRASILEIRO S.A. -
PETROBRAS) W250

CANADA

Aurora
Magna International W207

Brampton
Loblaw W200

Calgary
Agrium W27
Imperial Oil W162

Montreal
Alcan W32
BCE W62
Bombardier W70
Quebecor W267

Toronto
Bank of Montreal W56
Canadian Imperial Bank of
Commerce W83
George Weston W142
Hollinger W152
Inco (CVRD Inco Limited) W166
Nortel Networks W238
Rogers Communications W281
Royal Bank of Canada W285
Thomson W339
Toronto-Dominion Bank W345

CHILE

Santiago
Telefonica Chile (Compañía de
Telecomunicaciones de Chile
S.A.) W331

CHINA

Beijing
Bank of China W55

Shanghai
Sinopec Shanghai
Petrochemical W309

DENMARK

Bagsværd
Novo Nordisk W241

Billund
LEGO W197

Copenhagen
A.P. Møller — Mærsk W42

Valby
Carlsberg W87

FINLAND

Espoo
Nokia W235

Helsinki
Stora Enso Oyj W318

FRANCE

Blagnac
Airbus W29

Boulogne-Billancourt
Renault W272

Clermont-Ferrand
Michelin (Compagnie Générale des
Établissements Michelin) W215

Clichy
L'Oréal W202

Courbevoie
Saint-Gobain W290
TOTAL W347

Évry
Accor W22

Montigny-le-Bretonneux
Sodexho Alliance W311

Paris
Alcatel-Lucent W33
Atos Origin W45
AXA W49
BNP Paribas W68
Capgemini W86
Carrefour W88
Club Méditerranée W93
CNP Assurances W94
Crédit Agricole W98
Danone W104
Electricité de France W117
France Telecom W134
Gaz de France W139
Lafarge W194
Lagardère W195
LVMH W206
Pernod Ricard W249
Peugeot (PSA Peugeot Citroën
S.A.) W253
PPR W261
Publicis W265
Rallye W268
Sanofi-Aventis W294
SNCF (Société Nationale des Chemins
de Fer Français) W310
Veolia Environnement W353
Vivendi W356

Roissy
Air France W28

Rueil-Malmaison
Schneider Electric W299
VINCI W354

Saint-Etienne
Casino Guichard-Perrachon W89

Saint-Quentin-en-Yvelines
Bouygues W71

Villeneuve d'Ascq
Auchan W46

GERMANY

Berlin
Axel Springer W50
Deutsche Bahn W109

Bonn
Deutsche Post W111
Deutsche Telekom W112

Cologne
Lufthansa (Deutsche Lufthansa
AG) W204

Düsseldorf
E.ON W124
Henkel W149
METRO W214
ThyssenKrupp W340

Essen
ALDI W35
Karstadt Quelle W179
RWE W288

Frankfurt am Main
Deutsche Bank W110

Gütersloh
Bertelsmann W65

Hamburg
Otto GmbH & Co W247

Hanover
TUI W349

Herzogenaurach
adidas W25

Leverkusen
Bayer W60

Ludwigshafen
BASF W58

Mülheim an der Ruhr
Tengelmann W337

Munich
Allianz W38
BMW (Bayerische Motoren Werke
AG) W67
MAN W209

ViewSonic Corporation P516

Walnut Creek
Longs Drug Stores A527

West Sacramento
Raley's Inc. P409

Westlake Village
Consolidated Electrical
Distributors P144
Dole Food A280, P174
Guitar Center A396
ValueClick E374

Woodland Hills
Health Net A415
Panavision Inc. P375
United Online E364
Youbet.com E395

Yuba City
Sunsweet Growers P465

COLORADO

Boulder
Dynamic Materials E121
Noodles & Company P362
Pharmion E283

Broomfield
Ball Corporation A120
Level 3 Communications A513
Sirenza Microdevices E323

Centennial
Vistar Corporation P518

Denver
Bill Barrett E55
Catholic Health Initiatives P118
Chipotle Mexican Grill E83
Colorado Avalanche P138
CREDO Petroleum E105
DCP Midstream Partners E113
Denver Nuggets P168
Leprino Foods P292
MediaNews Group P319
Newmont Mining A602
Quiznos P407
Qwest Communications A697
St. Mary Land & Exploration E312
VICORP Restaurants P515
Whiting Petroleum E388

Englewood
Allied Motion Technologies E25
CH2M HILL Companies P124
EchoStar Communications A306
Liberty Media Holding A516
MarkWest Energy Partners E226

Golden
Health Grades E171
Jacobs Entertainment P264
Molson Coors Brewing A577

Greeley
Hensel Phelps Construction P240
Swift & Company P466

Greenwood Village
First Data A344

Lakewood
VCG Holding E376

Littleton
ADA-ES E18

Louisville
Rock Bottom Restaurants P420

Niwot
Crocs E107

CONNECTICUT

Avon
Magellan Health Services A535

Berlin
Northeast Utilities A611

Branford
CAS Medical Systems E72

Bristol
ESPN, Inc. P189

Danbury
ATMI E44
Praxair, Inc. A678

Darien
Jupitermedia E204

Dayville
United Natural Foods A848

Enfield
Retail Brand Alliance P417

Fairfield
General Electric A378
IMS Health A447

Farmington
Darwin Professional
Underwriters E111

Greenwich
Interactive Brokers P258
LGL Group, Inc. E217
United Rentals A850
UST Inc. A867

Hartford
Aetna Inc. A44
Hartford Financial Services
Group A407
United Technologies A856

Mashantucket
Mashantucket Pequot Tribal
Nation P312

Middlefield
Zygo Corporation E396

Milford
Doctor's Associates P173

New Britain
Connecticut Lottery P143
Stanley Works A778

New Haven
NewAlliance Bancshares E253
Yale University P538

Norwalk
Bolt Technology E60
EMCOR Group A317
FactSet Research Systems E140
webloyalty.com P526

Norwich
Gunther International P227

Putnam
PSB Holdings E295

Shelton
Clayton Holdings E85

Stamford
Citizens Communications A219
Crane A253
Esselte Corporation P189
MeadWestvaco Corporation A560
OMI Corporation E263
Pitney Bowes A669
Purdue Pharma P403
Towers Perrin P482

Xerox Corporation A917

Uncasville
Mohegan Tribal Gaming
Authority P336

West Hartford
Colt's Manufacturing P138

Westport
Terex Corporation A809

DELAWARE

Newark
W. L. Gore & Associates P535

Wilmington
DuPont (E. I. du Pont de Nemours
and Company) A296
Hercules Incorporated A418

DISTRICT OF COLUMBIA

Washington
AARP P18
AFL-CIO P30
American Red Cross P45
Amtrak (National Railroad Passenger
Corporation) P50
Bureau of National Affairs P103
Carlyle Group P114
Corporate Executive Board E102
Corporation for Public
Broadcasting P149
Danaher Corporation A260
Fannie Mae A335
Federal Prison Industries P193
Federal Reserve System P194
Harman International A403
Lincoln Hockey P297
NASD A586, P343
National Geographic Society P346
Smithsonian Institution P447
Teamsters (International Brotherhood
of Teamsters) P471
United States Postal Service A852,
P498
Varsity Group E375
Washington Post A891

FLORIDA

Altamonte Springs
International Assets Holding
Corporation E194

Boca Raton
American Media P44
Purity Wholesale Grocers P403

Clearwater
Nicholas Financial E256
Tech Data A799
Technology Research E345

Coral Gables
Avatar Holdings E44

Davie
Bristol West Holdings E63

Daytona Beach
NASCAR (National Association for
Stock Car Auto Racing, Inc.) P342

Deerfield Beach
JM Family Enterprises P267

Delray Beach
Office Depot A624

Fort Lauderdale
AutoNation A111
Citrix Systems E85
Levitt Corporation E217
OptimumBank Holdings E265
Parlux Fragrances E274
Republic Services A707
SEACOR Holdings E316
Spherion Corporation A775

Fort Myers
Radiation Therapy Services E299
SmartDisk Corporation P446

Gulf Breeze
Adams Homes of Northwest
Florida P22

Hialeah
Simclar E323

Hollywood
HEICO E174
Technical Olympic USA A800

Jacksonville
Armor Holdings A103
CSX Corporation A255
Fidelity National Financial A340
Jacksonville Bancorp E202
Main Street America P305
Vurv Technology P520
VyStar Credit Union P521
Website Pros E387
Winn-Dixie Stores A908

Juno Beach
FPL Group A360

Lake Mary
FARO Technologies E142

Lakeland
Publix Super Markets A690, P401

Largo
GeoPharma E157

Maitland
Tandem Health Care P468

Melbourne
Harris Corporation A406

Miami
Burger King Holdings A169
Carnival Corporation A185
Heat Group P237
Lennar Corporation A510
PBSJ Corporation P379
Perry Ellis International E279
Related Group P414
Royal Caribbean Cruises A717
Ryder System A720
Southern Wine & Spirits P451
Sun American Bancorp E338
World Fuel Services A910

Naples
Bank of Florida E48
Health Management Associates A414
Rooney Holdings P422

North Miami
AESP, Inc. P29

Ocala
Nobility Homes E257

Orlando
Attorneys' Title Insurance Fund P67
Darden Restaurants A261
Orlando Magic P371
Tupperware Brands A838

Pinellas Park
First Community Bank
Corporation E145

Inland Retail Real Estate Trust P257
McDonald's A556
Norcross Safety Products P363
RC2 Corporation E300

Oakbrook Terrace
VASCO Data Security E375

Pekin
Pekin Life Insurance P380

Peoria
Advanced Technology Services P24
Caterpillar Inc. A187

River Grove
Follett Corporation P200

Rolling Meadows
Kimball Hill P280

Rosemont
Reyes Holdings P417

Schaumburg
Motorola, Inc. A581
Pliant Corporation P392

Skokie
Forsythe Technology P203
Rand McNally P409
Topco Associates P481

Springfield
Illinois Lottery P252

Urbana
Flex-N-Gate Corporation P198
University of Illinois P503

Vernon Hills
CDW Corporation A192

Warrenville
Navistar International A593

Waukegan
Coleman Cable P137
WMS Industries E394

Westmont
Ty Inc. P493

INDIANA

Anderson
Remy International P415

Batesville
Hillenbrand Industries A427

Bloomington
Indiana University P253

Carmel
Conseco, Inc. A236

Columbus
Cummins, Inc. A256

Elkhart
Patriot Homes P379

Evansville
BPC Holding P100

Fort Wayne
Kelley Automotive P278

Indianapolis
Aearo Technologies P28
American United Mutual
  Insurance P47
Eli Lilly A314
Hurco Companies E182
Indiana Pacers (Pacers Sports &
  Entertainment) P253
National Wine & Spirits P350
Obsidian Enterprises P366

Republic Airways Holdings E304
Simon Property Group A758
WellPoint, Inc. A894

Kokomo
Haynes International P233

Merrillville
NiSource Inc. A607

Plainfield
Brightpoint, Inc. A159

Shelbyville
Blue River Bancshares E58

Warsaw
Biomet, Inc. A144
Symmetry Medical E341

IOWA

Ankeny
Casey's General Stores A186

Boone
Fareway Stores P192

Des Moines
MidAmerican Energy Holdings P330
Principal Financial A683
Weitz Group P527

Hills
Hills Bancorporation P242

Iowa City
University of Iowa Hospitals and
  Clinics P503

Muscatine
HNI Corporation A431

Pella
Pella Corporation P380

Sioux City
Terra Industries A810

West Des Moines
Hy-Vee, Inc. P249

KANSAS

Kansas City
Associated Wholesale Grocers P65
EPIQ Systems E134

Leawood
Euronet Worldwide E137
Houlihan's Restaurants P247

Mission
Concorde Career Colleges P142

Mission Woods
Layne Christensen E214

Overland Park
Brooke E63
Ferrellgas Partners A339
Scoular P436
YRC Worldwide A920

Shawnee
Perceptive Software P384

Shawnee Mission
Seaboard Corporation A743
VT, Inc. P519

Topeka
Payless ShoeSource A647
Westar Energy A900

Wichita
Airxcel Holdings P32
Koch Industries A493, P283

KENTUCKY

Bowling Green
Houchens Industries P246

Covington
Ashland Inc. A107
Omnicare, Inc. A629

Fort Mitchell
Drees Co. P177

Hazard
Kentucky First Federal Bancorp E206

Highland Heights
General Cable A375

Lexington
Lexmark International A515
NGAS Resources E256
Tempur-Pedic International E349

Louisville
Brown-Forman A166
Humana Inc. A439
Kentucky Lottery P278
Kindred Healthcare A488
Sypris Solutions E342
Texas Roadhouse E352
University of Louisville P504
YUM! Brands A921

Owensboro
Boardwalk Pipeline Partners E59

LOUISIANA

Baton Rouge
Amedisys E28
Shaw Group A753
Turner Industries P492

Covington
Hornbeck Offshore Services E181

Lafayette
LHC Group E218
MidSouth Bancorp E235

LaPlace
Bayou Steel P77

Monroe
CenturyTel, Inc. A196

New Orleans
Energy Partners E132
Entergy Corporation A319
Freeport-McMoRan Copper &
  Gold A364
New Orleans Hornets P355

MAINE

Damariscotta
First National Lincoln E147

Freeport
L.L. Bean P298

MARYLAND

Baltimore
Chimes, Inc. P129
Laureate Education E213
Legg Mason A506
Maryland Lottery P312
Municipal Mortgage & Equity E243
NAACP P341
Petroleum & Resources E281
Under Armour E361
Vertis Communications P515
Visicu E380

Whiting-Turner Contracting P531

Belcamp
SafeNet E311

Beltsville
Ritz Camera Centers P419

Bethesda
American Capital Strategies E29
Clark Enterprises P133
Eagle Bancorp E121
FLAVORx, Inc. P197
Lockheed Martin A524
Marriott International A541

Chevy Chase
CapitalSource E69

Columbia
Martek Biosciences E226
W. R. Grace A911

Gaithersburg
ACE*COMM E18
Digene E117

Germantown
Optelecom-NKF E265

Hagerstown
Phoenix Color P388

Hanover
Allegis Group P35

Hunt Valley
United Industrial E363

Lutherville
Bay National E51

Owings Mills
Universal Security Instruments E367

Rockville
Emergent BioSolutions E127
Goodwill Industries P214
HealthExtras E171

Salisbury
Perdue Farms P384

Silver Spring
Discovery Communications P171
United Therapeutics E366

Sparks
McCormick & Company A553

Towson
Black & Decker A147

MASSACHUSETTS

Bedford
Hologic E178

Billerica
American Science and
  Engineering E31

Boston
ABP Corporation P19
Blue Cross and Blue Shield of
  Massachusetts P90
Boston Consulting P98
Boston Private Financial
  Holdings E61
Boston Red Sox P98
Cabot Corporation A173
Color Kinetics E94
CRA International E104
Eastern Bank P182
Eaton Vance E123
First Marblehead Corporation E146
FMR Corp. A352, P199
Houghton Mifflin P246

Richfield
Best Buy A141

Rochester
Mayo Foundation P314

St. Paul
3M Company A26
APi Group P55
Ecolab Inc. A308
Minnesota Wild (Minnesota Sports & Entertainment) P334
Patterson Companies A646
Securian Financial Group P437
Sportsman's Guide P454
St. Jude Medical A728
St. Paul Travelers A729

Shoreview
Deluxe Corporation A272

Wayzata
Cargill, Incorporated A181, P111

MISSISSIPPI

Greenwood
Staple Cotton Cooperative P458

Jackson
Ergon, Inc. P187

Natchez
Callon Petroleum E68

Philadelphia
Yates Companies P538

Tupelo
Renasant E303

MISSOURI

Carthage
Leggett & Platt A508

Chesterfield
Outsourcing Solutions P372
Sisters of Mercy Health System P444

Clayton
First Banks P196
Olin Corporation A627

Columbia
University of Missouri P505

Des Peres
Jones Financial P272

Earth City
CCA Global Partners P122

Fenton
Maritz Inc. P307
UniGroup, Inc. P496

Kansas City
AMC Entertainment P39
Barkley Evergreen P73
Bartlett and Company P74
Black & Veatch P87
Dairy Farmers of America P155
DeBruce Grain P164
Dickinson Financial P170
DST Systems A292
Dunn Industries P180
H&R Block A400
Hallmark Cards A399, P228
Midwest Research Institute P332
Russell Stover Candies P425

Maryland Heights
Express Scripts A331

Richmond Heights
Panera Bread E271

St. Charles
American Railcar Industries E30

St. Louis
A.G. Edwards A47
Ameren Corporation A71
Anheuser-Busch A90
Arch Coal A102
Ascension Health P60
BJC HealthCare P87
Brown Shoe Company A165
Build-A-Bear Workshop E66
Center Oil P123
Charter Communications A202
Emerson Electric A318
Enterprise Rent-A-Car P186
Furniture Brands A366
Graybar Electric P219
International Wire P260
LaBarge E212
McCarthy Building P316
Monsanto A579
St. Louis Blues P426
Schnuck Markets P433
Scottrade, Inc. P436
TALX Corporation E343
World Wide Technology P537

Springfield
Bass Pro Shops P75
Guaranty Federal Bancshares E165

MONTANA

Billings
First Interstate BancSystem P197

Bozeman
RightNow Technologies E306

Great Falls
Davidson Companies P162

Kalispell
Semitool E317

Missoula
Washington Companies P524

NEBRASKA

Lincoln
Nebraska Book Company P353
University of Nebraska P505

Omaha
Ag Processing P31
Ballantyne of Omaha E46
Berkshire Hathaway A139
ConAgra Foods A234
GiftCertificates.com P209
Great Western Bancorporation P220
Mutual of Omaha P339
Peter Kiewit Sons' A657, P385
Professional Veterinary Products P399
Tenaska, Inc. P474
Union Pacific A845
Werner Enterprises A898

NEVADA

Las Vegas
Allegiant Travel E25
Boyd Gaming A157
Community Bancorp E96
Gaming Partners International E155
Hard Rock Hotel P230
Harrah's Entertainment A405
MGM MIRAGE A570

Shuffle Master E319
Tang Industries P468
Western Alliance Bancorporation E387

Reno
AMERCO A70
Bank Holdings E47
Circus and Eldorado P132
International Game Technology A456

Sparks
Ormat Technologies E268

NEW HAMPSHIRE

Concord
Aavid Thermal Technologies P19

Hudson
Micronetics E233
Presstek E291

Keene
C&S Wholesale Grocers P109

Merrimack
Brookstone, Inc. P102

Stratham
Timberland A820

NEW JERSEY

Avenel
Bradco Supply P101

Basking Ridge
Barnes & Noble College Bookstores P73

Bayonne
BCB Bancorp E51

Bedminster
Cellco Partnership P123

Berkeley Heights
Connell Company P143

Branchburg
LifeCell Corporation E218

Bridgewater
Synchronoss Technologies E342

Camden
Campbell Soup A176

Carteret
Di Giorgio Corporation P170
Pathmark Stores A645

Cedar Knolls
Newton Group P361

Cherry Hill
Pinnacle Foods P389

Chester
Adams Respiratory Therapeutics E19

Clinton
Foster Wheeler A357

Cranford
Metalico E232
Newark Group P361

Delanco
Jevic Transportation P266

East Brunswick
K-Sea Transportation Partners E211

East Orange
Louis Berger Group P300

East Rutherford
Metromedia Company P326
New Jersey Devils P354
New Jersey Nets (Nets Sports & Entertainment, LLC) P355
New York Giants (New York Football Giants) P357

East Windsor
Conair Corporation P141

Eatontown
QMed, Inc. E297

Edison
J.M. Huber Corporation P268
U.S. Shipping Partners E370

Elizabeth
Wakefern Food A881, P522

Elmwood Park
Bio-Reference Laboratories E56
Kreisler Manufacturing E210

Englewood Cliffs
Asta Funding E39

Fairfield
Bradley Pharmaceuticals E61
Covanta E103

Florham Park
Global Crossing A386

Forked River
Allstates WorldCargo P37

Fort Lee
American Banknote P40
Empire Resources E129

Franklin Lakes
Becton, Dickinson A134
Medco Health Solutions A561

Hackensack
I.D. Systems E185

Hillside
Integrated BioPharma E192

Kenilworth
Schering-Plough A737

Leonia
Infocrossing E188

Liberty Corner
Reliant Pharmaceuticals P414

Linden
Turtle & Hughes P493

Long Branch
Central Jersey Bancorp E78

Lyndhurst
Quest Diagnostics A695

Madison
Wyeth A915

Monmouth Junction
Dow Jones Reuters P176

Montvale
A & P (The Great Atlantic & Pacific Tea Company, Inc.) A28
Ingersoll-Rand A448

Morristown
Honeywell International A434

Murray Hill
C. R. Bard A252

New Brunswick
Johnson & Johnson A473

A = AMERICAN BUSINESS
E = EMERGING COMPANIES
P = PRIVATE COMPANIES
W = WORLD BUSINESS

Medina
RPM International A718

Middletown
AK Steel Holding A53

Nelsonville
Rocky Brands E308

New Albany
Abercrombie & Fitch A32
Commercial Vehicle Group E95

New Bremen
Crown Equipment P153

Niles
RTI International Metals E310

North Canton
Belden & Blake P79
Diebold, Incorporated A276

Orrville
J. M. Smucker A470

Solon
Advanced Lighting Technologies P24

Toledo
Block Communications P88
Manor Care A537
Owens Corning A637
Owens-Illinois, Inc. A638

Valley City
MTD Products P339

Warren
First Place Financial E149

Westlake
TravelCenters of America P486

Wickliffe
Lubrizol A532

Youngstown
DeBartolo P163

OKLAHOMA

Oklahoma City
Chesapeake Energy A203
Devon Energy A275
Feed The Children P195
GMX Resources E161
Gulfport Energy E167
Hobby Lobby Stores P243
Love's Travel Stops P301
Midland Financial P331
Panhandle Royalty E272

Tulsa
Arena Resources E36
ONEOK, Inc. A631
QuikTrip Corporation P405
SemGroup, L.P. P439
Unit Corporation E363
Williams Companies A906
Williams Partners E390

OREGON

Beaverton
NIKE, Inc. A606

Bend
Cascade Bancorp E73

Corvallis
Citizens Bancorp P132

Eugene
PW Eagle E296

Forest Grove
Merix Corporation E231

Klamath Falls
JELD-WEN, inc. P266

Medford
PremierWest Bancorp E290

Portland
Bonneville Power P94
Hampton Affiliates P229
North Pacific Group P363
Portland Trail Blazers (Trail Blazers, Inc.) P394
Precision Castparts A679
Regence Group P413
Umpqua Holdings E360

Prineville
Les Schwab Tire Centers P292

Tigard
Western Family Foods P529

Tillamook
Tillamook County Creamery Association P479

Turner
Willamette Valley Vineyards E389

Wilsonville
FLIR Systems E151

PENNSYLVANIA

Allentown
Air Products and Chemicals A51
PPL Corporation A676

Altoona
Sheetz, Inc. P441

Bala Cynwyd
Central European Distribution E77
Primavera Systems P397

Bensalem
Charming Shoppes A201
Orleans Homebuilders E267

Bethlehem
KNBT Bancorp E207
OraSure Technologies E266

Blue Bell
Unisys Corporation A847

Bridgeville
Universal Stainless & Alloy Products E368

Bristol
Jones Apparel Group A476

Camp Hill
Rite Aid A710

Chesterbrook
AmerisourceBergen A83

Devon
DecisionOne P164

Eighty Four
84 Lumber P16

Exton
Bentley Systems P81
Omega Flex E263
ViroPharma E379

Fairview
Spectrum Control E333

Gap
Auntie Anne's P67

Greensburg
Allegheny Energy A58

Greenville
Werner Co. P527

Hanover
Hanover Foods P229

Harrisburg
D&H Distributing P158
Pennsylvania Commerce Bancorp E277

Hatboro
Refinery, Inc. P413

Hershey
Hershey A421

Horsham
Astea International E40
NutriSystem E260
Penn Mutual Life Insurance P381
Toll Brothers A825

Huntingdon Valley
Wireless Xcessories E393

Indiana
Superior Well Services E339

King of Prussia
AmeriGas Partners A82
GSI Commerce E164
Neoware E249
UGI Corporation A844

Lancaster
Herley Industries E177

Latrobe
Kennametal Inc. A485

Malvern
IKON Office Solutions A445
Vanguard Group A870, P513
Vishay Intertechnology A876

McConnellsburg
JLG Industries A469

Mechanicsburg
Select Medical P438

Media
InfraSource Services E190

Middletown
Pennsylvania Lottery P382

Moon Township
Atlas America E43
Atlas Pipeline Partners E43

Newtown Square
Catholic Health East P117

Philadelphia
ARAMARK Corporation A101
Berwind Group P83
CIGNA Corporation A210
Comcast Corporation A229
Crown Holdings A254
Day & Zimmermann P162
FMC CORPORATION A351
Lincoln National A520
The Pep Boys A649
Rohm and Haas A714
Sunoco, Inc. A788
University of Pennsylvania P506

Pittsburgh
Allegheny Technologies A59

CONSOL Energy A237
GENCO Distribution System P206
Giant Eagle P207
H. J. Heinz A430
Highmark Inc. A427, P241
Mellon Financial A564
Pittsburgh Penguins P390
Pittsburgh Steelers P390
PNC Financial Services Group A671
PPG Industries A675
United States Steel A853
WESCO International A899

Radnor
Airgas, Inc. A52
Penn Virginia E276
Penn Virginia Resource Partners E276
Radnor Holdings P408

Reading
Boscov's Department Store P97

Saxonburg
II-VI Incorporated E16

State College
Omega Financial E262

Trevose
Broder Bros. P101

Warrendale
American Eagle Outfitters A72

Wawa
Wawa, Inc. P524

Wayne
Kenexa E205
MEDecision E229
Safeguard Scientifics A726
SunGard Data Systems P463
Willow Financial Bancorp E390

West Chester
VWR International P521

West Conshohocken
Keystone Foods P279

Willow Grove
Asplundh Tree P63

York
Graham Packaging P217

PUERTO RICO

Mayagüez
W Holding Company E383

San Juan
EuroBancshares E136

RHODE ISLAND

Johnston
Factory Mutual Insurance P191

Pawtucket
Hasbro, Inc. A410
Teknor Apex P473

Providence
Gilbane, Inc. P209
Textron Inc. A814
Warren Equities P524

West Kingston
American Power Conversion A80

West Warwick
AMTROL Inc. P51

Woonsocket
CVS Corporation A257

SOUTH CAROLINA

Columbia
SCANA Corporation A736

Fort Mill
Muzak Holdings P341
Springs Global US P455

Greenville
Bowater Incorporated A156
Greenville First Bancshares E163
Greenville Hospital System P222
South Financial E330
Springhill Lake Investors P455

Hartsville
Sonoco Products A767

Laurens
Palmetto Bancshares P375

Lexington
First Community Corporation E145
Southeastern Freight Lines P450

Mount Pleasant
Southcoast Financial E331

Myrtle Beach
Beach First National Bancshares E52

Spartanburg
Denny's Corporation A274
First National Bancshares E147
Milliken & Company P332

SOUTH DAKOTA

Brookings
Daktronics E110
VeraSun Energy E376

Volga
South Dakota Soybean
Processors P450

Wentworth
Lake Area Corn Processors P289

TENNESSEE

Brentwood
ACG Holdings P21

Chattanooga
First Security Group E150
Krystal P288
UnumProvident A860

Cleveland
Life Care Centers P296

Collegedale
McKee Foods P317

Franklin
IASIS Healthcare P250
Psychiatric Solutions E295
Tennessee Commerce Bancorp E350

Goodlettsville
Dollar General A281

Kingsport
Eastman Chemical A301

Knoxville
Anderson News P53
Goody's Family Clothing P214
H.T. Hackney Company P248
Team Health P470
Tennessee Valley Authority A808,
P475

La Vergne
Ingram Entertainment P255

Lebanon
CBRL Group A190

Memphis
AutoZone A112
Baker, Donelson P72
Dunavant Enterprises P179
FedEx Corporation A338
International Paper A457
Memphis Grizzlies P322
Pinnacle Airlines E284
Sedgwick Claims Management
Services P438
True Temper Sports P487

Milan
Milan Express Co. P332

Morristown
Berkline/BenchCraft P82

Nashville
Ardent Health Services P57
Captain D's P110
Caremark Rx A180
ClientLogic Corporation P134
Direct General E118
First Acceptance E142
Gibson Guitar P208
HCA Inc. A412
HealthSpring E172
Healthways E173
Ingram Industries P255
Louisiana-Pacific A528
Pinnacle Financial Partners E285
Vanderbilt University P513
Vanguard Health Systems P514

Ooltewah
Miller Industries E235

TEXAS

Addison
Affirmative Insurance E22
Concentra Inc. P141
Dresser, Inc. P177
Mary Kay Inc. P311

Alvin
Team, Inc. E345

Angleton
Benchmark Electronics A138

Arlington
Choice Homes P129
First Cash Financial Services E144

Austin
AAC Group Holding P17
Activant Solutions Holdings P22
ArthroCare E38
Brigham Exploration E62
DMX, Inc. P172
Freescale Semiconductor A365
HealthTronics E172
Lower Colorado River Authority P301
Merkel McDonald P324
Perficient E278
SigmaTel E321
Stratus Properties E337
Temple-Inland Inc. A804
Texas Lottery P477
University of Texas P507
Wayport, Inc. P525
Whole Foods Market A905

Carrollton
Home Interiors & Gifts P244

College Station
Texas A&M University P476

Coppell
Container Store P145
Mannatech E224

Corpus Christi
Whataburger, Inc. P529

Dallas
7-Eleven, Inc. A27
Affiliated Computer Services A45
Army and Air Force Exchange
Service P59
Atrium Companies P66
Austin Industries P67
Blockbuster A148
Brinker International A160
Capital Southwest E69
Centex Corporation A194
Children's Medical Center of
Dallas P129
ClubCorp, Inc. P135
Collegiate Pacific E94
Dallas Mavericks P157
Dave & Buster's P160
Dean Foods A263
Dorchester Minerals E119
Eagle Materials E122
GAINSCO E154
Glazer's Wholesale Drug
Company P210
Holly Corporation A432
Home Solutions of America E180
Hunt Consolidated P249
Interstate Battery P260
la Madeleine de Corps P288
Methodist Hospitals of Dallas P325
Monitronics International P336
Neiman Marcus P353
Richards Group P419
Sammons Enterprises P427
Southwest Airlines A771
SWS Group E340
Tenet Healthcare A806
Texas Capital Bancshares E352
Texas Industries A812
Texas Instruments A813
Titanium Metals E354
Toreador Resources E355
Trinity Industries A835
TXU Corp. A839
United States Lime & Minerals E365
Vought Aircraft P518

El Paso
Petro Stopping Centers P386

Fort Worth
AMR Corporation A87
Ben E. Keith Company P81
Burlington Northern Santa Fe A170
D.R. Horton A289
Encore Acquisition E130
Pier 1 Imports A665
Quicksilver Resources E298
RadioShack A698
Range Resources E299
TTI, Inc. P490
Union Drilling E362

Grapevine
GameStop Corp. A367

Houston
Adams Resources & Energy A37
Allis-Chalmers Energy E26
Apache Corporation A95
Baker Botts P72
Baker Hughes A119
BJ Services A145
Carrizo Oil & Gas E72
CenterPoint Energy A193

Complete Production Services E98
ConocoPhillips A235
Continental Airlines A242
Cooper Industries A244
Copano Energy E101
Dynegy Inc. A298
Edge Petroleum E125
El Paso A310
ENGlobal E132
EOG Resources A321
EV Energy Partners E137
Franklin Bank Corp. E153
Grey Wolf E163
Grocers Supply Co. P223
Gulf States Toyota P226
Gundle/SLT Environmental P226
Halliburton A397
Harvest Natural Resources E169
Helix Energy Solutions E175
Houston Rockets P247
Hydril E185
IWL Communications P263
King Ranch A489
KMG Chemicals E207
Lyondell Chemical A533
Marathon Oil A539
McDermott International A554
Men's Wearhouse A565
Motiva Enterprises P337
Natural Resource Partners E247
Parker Drilling E273
Philip Services P387
Plains All American Pipeline A670
PROS Revenue Management P400
Prosperity Bancshares E293
Quanex Corporation A694
Service Corporation A750
Shell Oil A754
Southern Union A770
Southwestern Energy E332
Swift Energy E339
SYSCO Corporation A796
TODCO E355
Transocean Inc. A831
Ultra Petroleum E360
US Oncology P510
VAALCO Energy E373
Waste Management A892
WCA Waste E384
Weatherford International A893
W-H Energy Services E388
Whittier Energy E389
WorleyParsons Corp. P537

Huntsville
Mitcham Industries E236

Irving
BancTec, Inc. P73
Boy Scouts P99
Commercial Metals A231
Dallas Cowboys P157
EFJ E127
Exxon Mobil A333
Fluor Corporation A349
Kimberly-Clark A487
Michaels Stores A571
NCH Corporation P352
Pioneer Natural Resources A668
Zale Corporation A923

Katy
Academy Sports & Outdoors P20

Kilgore
Martin Midstream Partners E227

League City
American Homestar P44

Lubbock
United Supermarkets P499

Index of Executives

A = AMERICAN BUSINESS
E = EMERGING COMPANIES
P = PRIVATE COMPANIES
W = WORLD BUSINESS

Beilinson, Nan E39
Beilman, Bart A905
Beissner, Sheree P154
Beisswanger, Mark L. A723
Beitcher, Robert L. P376
Bekkedahl, Carolyn P44
Bekkers, John A389
Bekman, Kenneth A239
Bekolay, Michael P115
Belasco, Michelle P324
Belcher, Donald D. P99
Belcher, Eric D. E191
Belda, Alain J. P. A57
Belda, Ricardo E. A57
Belden, Christopher P. A100
Belek, Marilynn P167
Belford, Christopher M. E128
Belger, Gale E129
Belgya, Mark R. A471
Belitz, Gary R. A907
Belk, H. W. McKay P80
Belk, Jeffrey K. A693
Belk, John R. P80
Belk, Larry R. E150
Belk, Robert L. A754
Belk, Thomas M. Jr. P80
Bell, Bradley J. A586
Bell, Charles P145
Bell, Chris (Apple Computer) A98
Bell, Christopher (Ladbrokes) W193
Bell, Christopher E. (Willow Financial
 Bancorp) E391
Bell, Christy W. (Horizon Healthcare
 Services) P245
Bell, Craig D. E378
Bell, David (Schnuck Markets) P433
Bell, David A. (Interpublic Group) A459
Bell, David C. M. (Pearson) W248
Bell, Don Carlos III P262
Bell, Ernie A881, P523
Bell, G. Russell A133
Bell, Gary C. A414
Bell, Graeme A567
Bell, Greg E105
Bell, James (Tyson Foods) A843
Bell, James A. (Boeing) A151
Bell, James R. III (National City) A589
Bell, Jana Ahlfinger E127
Bell, Jane A. A174
Bell, John (j2 Global) E202
Bell, John M. (Verizon) A872
Bell, Katherine Button A319
Bell, Keith A643
Bell, Lawrence T. A308
Bell, Mary A149
Bell, Michael W. A211
Bell, Paul D. A268
Bell, Richard W344
Bell, Sally P136
Bell, Stanley R. P94
Bell, Stephen M. (FMR) A352, P199
Bell, Steven F. (Globalstar) E160
Bell, Tim W369
Bell, W. Donald A137
Bellamy, Adrian D. P. W271
Bellando, John A41
Bellas, Stephen M. E361
Bellas, Tony P187
Bellavance, Peter P469
Bellezza, Anthony J. A711
Bellhouse, Rob C. W202
Bellinger, Delaney A922
Bellingham, Olivia A172
Bellini, Karen P230
Bellino, George A. E84
Bellis, Arnold M. P395
Bellmann, Matthias W180
Bello, Stephane W340

Bellon, Nolan X. A924
Bellon, Pierre W312
Belloni, Antonio W206
Belman, Harris W53
Belote, Brandon R. A614
Belser, Alan P520
Belsham, Martin W270
Belsheim, Edmund O. Jr. E190
Belsito, Jack W82
Belsito, Louis J. A291
Belsky, Joel A. A337
Belton, Howard W352
Belton, Y. Marc A380
Benac, William P. E31
Benacin, Philippe E193
Bénaich, Pierre W266
Benas, Daniel E238
Benaszeski, Gary P534
Bench, Sherice P. P17
Bencomo, Jim A866
Bender, A. Thomas E101
Bender, Brian W. P442
Bender, David E. A253
Bender, James (AutoNation) A111
Bender, James J. (Williams Companies,
 Williams Partners) A907, E390
Bender, Jeffrey M. A95
Bender, John R. A833
Bender, Kevin B. E31
Bendheim, Daniel M. P387
Bendheim, Jack C. P387
Bené, Stephen G. A312
Benedetti, Joseph C. P354
Benedict, Greg P43
Benet, Jay S. A730
Benetton, Alessandro W64
Benetton, Carlo W64
Benetton, Gilberto W329
Benetton, Luciano W64
Bénézit, Michel W347
Beng Hock, Gerard Yeap W309
Bengali, Abdul P315
Bengtsson, Lars W319
Bengü, Hasan W184
Benham, Bret L. P479
Benhamou, Eric A. A642
Benhase, Daniel B. A440
Beniac, Phillip P429
Benioff, Marc E312
Benitez, Daniel E46
Benito, Javier A783
Benjamin, Deborah E. P491
Benjamin, Gerald A. A418
Benjamin, James P72
Benjamin, Lawrence S. W284
Benjumea, Ignacio W54
Benkovich, Carl A839
Bennack, Frank A. Jr. A417, P237
Benner, David P253
Benner, Kathy P209
Bennet, Carl W335
Bennett, Alan M. A44
Bennett, Connie A558
Bennett, Dori P102
Bennett, Ed (NASCAR) P342
Bennett, Edgar (Green Bay
 Packers) A395, P221
Bennett, Fiona W96
Bennett, Glenn W26
Bennett, Jana W78
Bennett, Joel M. E203
Bennett, Lerone Jr. P270
Bennett, Marc P172
Bennett, Martin A. A527
Bennett, Michael L. A811
Bennett, Ned W. E266
Bennett, Patrick W. A60
Bennett, Paul B. A623
Bennett, R. E. T. W156
Bennett, Rich (Best Western) P84
Bennett, Richard H. Jr. (United
 Technologies) A856
Bennett, Ruth B. P95

Bennett, Scott L. A558
Bennett, Stephen M. (Intuit) A460
Bennett, Steven A. (USAA) A865, P511
Bennett, Tim P231
Bennett, Walter L. A818
Bennewitz, Dallas P75
Benning, Kathleen M. E65
Bennitt, Brent M. P537
Benoist, Gilles W94
Benoliel, Joel A248
Benoski, James E. A212
Benqué, Jean-Pierre W117
Bensel, Norbert W109
Bensinger, Roger Jr. A753
Bensinger, Steven J. A79
Benson, Anne W301
Benson, Gregory V. E99
Benson, Jack M. (Varsity Group) E375
Benson, James B. A110
Benson, Jared P. P217
Benson, John A. (Hills
 Bancorporation) P242
Benson, Keith W. III A779
Benson, Kevin E. A502
Benson, Michael J. (Apache) A95
Benson, Michael R. (DIRECTV) A279
Benson, Mike (Colorado
 Avalanche) P138
Benson, Randall C. W153
Benson, Richard A. E41
Benson, Robert L. A584
Benson-Armer, Richard W340
Bensten, William P. E99
Bent, Ritchie W178
Bent, S. David A855
Bentegeat, Renaud W355
Benten, R. Anthony A600
Benthall, Timothy P255
Bentham, Jeremy B. W287
Bentivegna, Joseph E45
Bentley, Fred A412
Bentley, Gregory S. P82
Bentley, John E. E70
Bentley, Julia A. A731
Bentley, Phillip K. W92
Bentley, Ray P82
Benton, Mike P352
Benz, Brad E35
Benzel, Craig A395, P221
Benzing, William A444, P252
Benzon, Jessica A119, P71
Beran, Dennis K. A469
Beran, John R. A231
Berardi, Roberto A488
Berchtold, Walter W100
Bercow, Mark S. A642
Bercu, Nanette P269
Berdan, Robert J. A617, P364
Berdick, Edward P465
Berengolts, Michael J. E60
Berenson, Marvin P93
Beresford-Wylie, Simon W235
Bereziuk, Michael E350
Berg, David A. P42
Berg, Eric A. A597
Berg, Gunilla W299
Berg, Jason A. A71
Berg, Joel W64
Berg, Mark S. A668
Berg, Ronald C. A855
Berg, Thomas C. P50
Bergant, Paul R. A467
Bergen, Christopher E84
Bergen, David G. A515, P294
Berger, Darryl D. P513
Berger, Dennis G. A193
Berger, Eric A263
Berger, Hanno P169
Berger, Jeff H. (Bechtel) A132
Berger, Jeffrey P. (Heinz) A430
Berger, Ken A816
Berger, Laurence J. P362
Berger, Morris A443

Berger, Norbert L. J. W284
Berger-Gross, Victoria A820
Bergeron, Albert E. E370
Bergeron, Douglas G. E377
Bergeron, Kayla P393
Berggren, Marie N. P501
Berglund, Steven W. E358
Berglund, Thomas W302
Bergly, Kris A705
Bergman, Alan A885
Bergman, J. David A260
Bergman, Lawrence G. E196
Bergman, Michelle D. P178
Bergman, Miro I. E137
Bergman, Stanley M. A418
Bergmann, Burckhard W125
Bergmann, Thomas E. A403
Bergqvist, Paul W88
Bergreen, Zack B. E40
Bergren, Scott A922
Bergseth, Stig W317
Bergstrom, Christopher W. E71
Bergsund, Rich P533
Berigan, Karen E. A255
Berisford, John L. A651
Berit, Debra A93
Berk, Alexander L. A240
Berk, Jeffrey L. A353
Berke, Kent R. P518
Berke, Richard C. A110
Berkeley, Linda P347
Berkery, Rosemary T. A568
Berkett, Neil W200
Berkley, William R. P360
Berkowitz, Amy A192
Berkstresser, Gordon R. E310
Berlien, Olaf W341
Berlik, Leonard J. W162
Berlin, Andy W61
Berlin, John E. A183
Berman, Ann E. P232
Berman, David E385
Berman, Irwin M. E264
Berman, Laurence W93
Berman, Richard K. A134
Berman, Robert L. A303
Berman, Stephen G. E203
Bermingham, Robert P. P540
Bern, Dorrit J. A202
Bernacki, E.J. P294
Bernal, Javier W61
Bernandes, Ricardo P107
Bernanke, Ben S. P194
Bernard, Daniel W181
Bernard, Peter A398
Bernard, Richard P. A623
Bernardin, Thomas W265
Bernat, Rodney A96
Bernau, James W. E389
Bernauer, David W. A882
Bernd, David L. P439
Berndt, Gary P53
Berneke, Lutz P474
Berner, G. Gary E148
Berney, Arnold A508
Berney, Rand C. A235
Bernhard, James M. Jr. A754
Bernhardt, James H. P28
Bernheim, Antoine W142, W206
Bernick, Alan P53
Bernick, Carol Lavin A56
Bernick, Craig A56
Bernick, Howard B. A56, A705
Berning, Klaus W259
Bernotat, Wulf H. W125
Bernsmeier, Jack W. A157
Bernstein, Alison R. P202
Bernstein, Dale B. A235
Bernstein, David (Carnival) A186
Bernstein, David C. (CNET
 Networks) E87
Bernstein, Harvey N. A233
Bernstein, Michael E203

Butler, Lisa M. P270
Butler, Liz P512
Butler, Lolanda E218
Butler, Michael P400
Butler, Robert C. E76
Butler, Steve N. W338
Butler, William T. A534
Butt, Charles C. P234
Butt, Howard III P234
Butt, Stephen P234
Buttacavoli, Frank A. E274
Butterfield, Gregory S. E27
Butterworth, Charles W358
Buttigieg, Joseph J. III A231
Butts, James E. A198
Butz, Theodore H. A351
Butzer, Bart A798
Buxton, Richard M. E154
Buzas, Jill P172
Buzby, Paul E40
Buzy, Peter L. E226
Buzzard, James A. A561
Byal, Jeff P209
Bye, Mark L. A52
Bye, Scott P404
Byerlein, Anne P. A922
Byers, Cameron W73
Byers, Fritz P88
Byers, Mark P218
Byers, Walter (Mercantile Bank) E229
Byers, Walter G. (Dearborn Bancorp) E114
Byford, David A299
Byford, Mark W78
Bygge, Claes Johan W119
Bynum, Joseph R. A809, P475
Byone, Steve A686
Byots, Bruce J. A751
Byrd, Arthur J. P236
Byrd, Chadwick J. E27
Byrd, Teresa A747
Byrd, Vincent C. A471
Byrne, Brian A. P19
Byrne, Daniel G. E335
Byrne, Gerry W39
Byrne, Joseph E. P361
Byrne, Patrick J. A50
Byrne, Raymond F. E31
Byrne, Robert J. A91
Byrne, Stephen A. A737
Byrne, Thomas E222
Byrnes, Brian P437
Byrnes, Bruce L. A685
Byrnes, Jim P254
Byrnes, John P453
Byrnes, Scott P391
Byron, Deborah P532
Byrum, D. Michael A909
Bywater, Willis M. P242

C

Cabe, Charla R. P424
Cabiallavetta, Mathis A544
Cabot, Jennifer P184
Cabrera, Angel P520
Cabrera, Carlos A. A435
Cacace, Gary P526
Cacioppo, Gary P421
Caddell, Douglas D. P200
Caddell, Lynn M. A893
Cadieux, Chester P405
Cadieux, Chester III P405
Cadsby, Ted R. W84
Cady, Gary E387
Cadzow, Leslie W146
Caffarella, Joseph P40
Caffe, Steven A127
Cagni, Pascal A98
Cahan, Paul L. P415
Cahill, Dennis P177
Cahill, Gerald R. A186

Cahill, John T. A651
Cahill, Kurt E192
Cahill, Tim P299
Cahill, William J. III A338
Cahillane, Steve W165
Cahuzac, Jean P. A832
Caiazzo, Joseph E153
Caillère, Yann W23
Cain, Delmar P476
Cain Krauter, Lana A469
Caine, Brett M. E85
Cairns, Ann W22
Cairns, Thomas A595
Cakebread, Steven M. E312
Calabrese, Gary S. A714
Calabrese, Jeannie L. P67
Calabrese, Margaret M. A845
Calado, Miguel M. A264
Calagna, John A569
Calamari, Mathew F. A838, P490
Calamos, John P. E67
Calamos, Nick P. E67
Calandra, Susan P458
Calantzopoulos, André A68
Calavia, Philippe W29
Caldarella, Joseph A163
Caldarelli, O. Joe E104
Caldarello, Becky P183
Calderaro, Michael E223
Calderini, Pablo W111
Calderon, Alberto W67
Caldon, Daniel T. P86
Caldwell, Alan P111
Caldwell, Barry H. A893
Caldwell, Bret P471
Caldwell, Ethan A. E225
Caldwell, Trevor E225
Calello, Paul W100
Calestini, Gregg P48
Caley, Carolyn A648
Calhoun, David L. A379
Calhoun, Edwin L. P240
Calhoun, Ford W145
Calhoun, Jay S. A599, P359
Calhoun, Laura E331
Calhoun Schaefgen, Jacqueline E378
Caliari, Roberto W291
Calio, Nicholas E. A218
Calkins, Dan P159
Calkins, John C. A548
Call, John G. A716
Callagee, Cathy A850
Callaghan, Brian P55
Callahan, Dennis S. P225
Callahan, Jack F. Jr. A264
Callahan, Kevin R. E22
Callahan, Larry P462
Callahan, Michael (Yahoo!) A919
Callahan, Michael J. (Bed Bath & Beyond) A136
Callahan, Richard F. (Partners Trust Financial) E275
Callahan, Richard P. (Oxbow) P372
Callahan, Robert F. (Ziff Davis Media) P541
Callahan, Robert T. (Illinois Tool Works) A446
Callahan, Timothy M. P83
Callas, George S. E78
Callaway, James W. A109
Callerame, Joseph E32
Callery, T. Grant A587, P343
Callicutt, Richard D. II E59
Callihan, William H. A672
Callon, Fred L. E68
Calvert, Jerry L. E147
Calvert, Karen P311
Calvert, Stanton C. P476
Calvert, Valerie A694
Calvillo Armendáriz, Juan F. W333
Calvin, John C. P152
Calwell, Ken C. A284
Camacho, Francisco W105

Camara, Paul M. E239
Cámara Peón, Victor Manuel W253
Camardo, Michael F. A525
Camarena, Ruben W362
Cambria, Christopher C. A501
Camden, Carl T. A484
Camera, Nicholas J. A459
Camerlo, James P. P156
Cameron, Johnny A. N. W286
Cameron, Keith W211
Cameron, Luzius W351
Cameron, Patricia A196
Cameron, Peter B. W364
Cameron, Scott W308
Camilleri, Louis C. A68
Camiolo, Karen M. A590
Cammack, Randy P471
Cammaker, Sheldon I. A317
Cammarata, Bernard A825
Camp, Alistair W58
Camp, David C. P458
Camp, Kenneth A. A428
Camp, M. Kevin E300
Camp, Rob P530
Camp, William H. A38
Campagna, Peter A460
Campana, Claudio W142
Campbell, Alan (Freescale Semiconductor) A365
Campbell, Allen J. (Cooper-Standard Automotive) P147
Campbell, Anthony E280
Campbell, Bernard W. A767
Campbell, Brett P273
Campbell, Brian L. A112
Campbell, Carolyn M. A299
Campbell, Christian L. A922
Campbell, Colin P348
Campbell, Cynthia A625
Campbell, David A. A840
Campbell, Don H. (Remington Arms) P415
Campbell, Donald G. (TJX Companies) A825
Campbell, Donald H. (Heritage Oaks Bancorp) E176
Campbell, Eileen M. A540
Campbell, Gordon W. E330
Campbell, H. Ed E59
Campbell, Hew W286
Campbell, Jack R. (Illinois Tool Works) A446
Campbell, James P. A379
Campbell, Jeffrey C. (McKesson) A559
Campbell, Jeffrey J. (Burlington Northern Santa Fe) A170
Campbell, John (Anderson News) P53
Campbell, John (Atos Origin) W46
Campbell, John (Parke Bancorp) E273
Campbell, John (Scottish Power) W301
Campbell, John W. (Horizon Healthcare Services) P245
Campbell, Judith E. A599, P359
Campbell, Keith M. P437
Campbell, Kevin P. A249
Campbell, Kirk P259
Campbell, Lewis B. A815
Campbell, Lisa F. E252
Campbell, Michael H. (Delta Air) A272
Campbell, Michael L. (Fareway Stores) P192
Campbell, Patrick D. A26
Campbell, Robert (Holman Enterprises) P244
Campbell, Robert D. (NiSource) A608
Campbell, Russell T. E54
Campbell, Steven T. A852
Campbell, Travis A907
Campbell, Victor L. A413
Campbell, William I. (JPMorgan Chase, Visa) A479, A875, P517
Campbell, William V. (Intuit, Columbia University) A460, P140

Campellone, John A878
Campi, John P. A434
Campion, Patrick W111
Campion, Thomas D. E396
Campione, Richard W298
Campise, Charles J. E355
Campo, Javier W89
Campos, Denise P270
Campos, Dya P234
Campos-Neto, Antonio A228
Camus, Daniel W117
Camus, Philippe W195
Canaday, Shawn M. E53
Canakes, Steven P. E380
Canavan, Alex E193
Canavan, Beth O. A820
Canavan, Patrick J. A582
Cancio, Luis A. A774
Cancro, Lawrence C. P99
Candee, William J. III A356
Candelas, Enrique García W54
Candito, Tony P482
Canestrari, Ken A825
Canetty-Clarke, Neil W173
Canfield, Charles F. P521
Canfield, William W. E344
Cannatelli, Vincenzo W121
Canning, Michael L. E324
Canning, Rick P121
Cannizzaro, Michael N. P257
Cannon, David C. Jr. A58
Cannon, Fred P93
Cannon, James W. Jr. P72
Cannon, John III A211
Cannon, Marc A111
Cannon, Michael R. A766
Cano, Néstor A799
Cano Fernández, Ángel W61
Canright, David P419
Cantagallo, Simone W36
Cantamessa, Joseph J. A288
Cantarell, Luis W228
Cantelli, Irene P115
Canter, Charles W. Jr. A530
Canter, Stephen E. A564
Canterna, Don L. A778
Cantone, Jeanette A519
Cantrell, Gary A815
Cantwell, Guy A. A832
Cantwell, William J. A52
Canty, Stephen D. P305
Cao, Robert W93
Cao, Stefano W123
Capaldi, Elizabeth D. P460
Capasso, John A778
Capatides, Michael G. W84
Cape, Olwen B. A636
Capelli, Paul A780
Capes, M. W. W370
Capewell, Dale E199
Capilla, Anne-Marie W46
Caplan, David L. A49
Caplan, Mitchell H. A326
Capobianco, John H. E229
Caponi, Catherine A430
Caponi, Julie A. A57
Caponi, Marianne P127
Capozzi, Louis W265
Capp, Brian P292
Cappeline, Gary A. A107
Capps, Robert P. E236
Capps, Thomas E. A283
Cappucci, Lou P473
Cappuccio, Aldo W329
Cappuccio, Paul T. A822
Capt, Edmond W321
Capuano, Carl E294
Capuano, Chris A496
Capuano, Linda A766
Capus, Steve A595
Caputo, Anne S. P177
Caputo, Louise P124
Carabias Príncipe, Rafael W333

A = AMERICAN BUSINESS
E = EMERGING COMPANIES
P = PRIVATE COMPANIES
W = WORLD BUSINESS

de Magalhães Villas-Boas,
   Manuel W128
de Man, Thom W148
De Marco, Pasquale A565
de Margerie, Chrisophe W347
de Margerie, Gilles W99
de Martini, Maria A34
De Mattia, Giada W64
de Maynadier, Patrick D. A428
De Menten, Eric W347
de Metz, Robert W357
De Mey, Jozef W132
de Mézerac, Xavier W47
de Molina, Alvaro G. A122
de Oliveira Estrella, Guilherme W251
de Palo, Armand M. P225
de Pesquidoux, Hubert W34
de Raismes, Ann M. A408
De Respino, Laurence J. A71
de Rivaz, Vincent W117
de Roquemaurel, Gérald W195
de Rosen, Michel E379
de Saint Edmond, Luiz Fernando
   Zeigler W165
De Salvio, Robert P312
De Santa, Richard P. A29
de Segundo, Karen W287
de Seze, Amaury W69
de Silguy, Yves-Thibault W355
De Simone, Lawrence E. A612
de Souza, Teresa W128
de Souza Duque, Renato W251
de Stasio, Vittorio W58
De Stigter, Glenn H. P527
de Vaucleroy, Jacques W169
de Vauplane, Hugues W94
de Virville, Michel W273
de Vos, Harry W118
De Vries, James P238
de Waal, Ronald A731
de Walque, Xavier W114
de Weck, Pierre W111
de Win, Thomas W60
De Young, Kathryn S. E102
Deacon, Jennifer L. E71
Deal, Mary Joanne E336
Dealy, Richard P. A668
Deam, William P406
Dean, H. Ed E71
Dean, Jerry P279
Dean, John S. (Steelcase) A786
Dean, John S. Sr. (Crescent
   Banking) E106
Dean, Lloyd H. P121
Dean, Roy D. A638
Dean, Shawn A849
Dean, Thompson P165
Dean, Warren M. A466
Deane, Alastair R. A824
Deane, Frank M. A315
Deane, Nancy A796
DeAngelis, Peter L. Jr. P118
DeAngelis, Roberto E282
DeAngelo, Joseph J. A434
Dearden, Thomas L. E125
Dearen, Gates P66
Dearing, Michael E. A542
Dearlove, A. James E276
Deas, Thomas C. Jr. A351
Deason, Darwin A45
Deason, David (Colonial Group) P138
Deason, David S. (Barnes &
   Noble) A125
Deason, Robert A. A555
Deasy, Dana S. A841
Deaton, Brady J. P505
Deaton, Chad C. A120
Deavens, Gregory P313

Deaver, Michael K. P184
DeBarr, Alexander S. A25
DeBarr, Robert E. A592
DeBartolo, Peggy R. E149
DeBartolo York, Marie Denise P164
Debertin, Jay D. A207
DeBiasi, Glenn P34
DeBlandre, Alain P454
Deboeck, Michel W132
DeBoer, Bruce R. E388
deBoer Henderson, Deborah A106
DeBois, Lisa A670
Debold, Patrick J. P142
Debon, Pascal A239
Debrosse, Didier W148
Debrowski, Thomas A. A552
DeBruce, Paul P164
DeBrunner, David J. A342
Debry, Eric W350
Debs, Duane G. P528
Debs, Michael E. A484
DeBuck, Donald G. A233
DeCamp, Cary P384
DeCamp, Donald D. P127
DeCandia, Leonardo A84
DeCarlo, M. Steven P48
DeCaro, Thomas C. A572
DeCarolis, Donna L. A590
DeCenzo, Georgiann P25
DeCerchio, John P525
DeCesaris, Geaton A. Jr. A438
Dechant, Timothy L. P535
DeCherney, G. Stephen P406
Deck, Richard C. E92
Deckelman, William L. Jr. A45
Decker, Bill P349
Decker, Mark P143
Decker, Susan L. A919
Decornoy, Jean-Luc A497
DeCorte, Tom P60
DeCosmo, James M. A805
Decyk, Roxanne J. A755
Dederan, Susan A289
Dedman, Robert H. Jr. P135
Dedo, Jacqueline A. A824
Dedrick, Gregg R. A922
Dee, Mike P99
Deegan, Donald J. A837, P489
Deel, Jeffrey A. A763
Deely, Brendan J. A866
Deeney, William J. A397
Deenihan, Ed A598
Deer, R. Alan A704
Deese, Brian P355
Deese, George E. A349
Deese, Willie A. A567
DeFalco, Robert A. P49
Defebaugh, James E. IV A492
DeFehr, Kenneth J. E105
DeFelice, David M. E287
DeFeo, Ronald M. A810
DeFranco, James A307
Deft, Christopher W164
DeFurio, Anthony P503
Degen, Sean J. A692
Degenfelder, D. Steven E119
DeGenova, Paul P86
Degg, Stuart W199
DeGiorgio, Kenneth D. A343
Degler, Sandra C. P104
Degn, Douglas J. A884
Degnan, John J. A208
Degnan, Martin J. P54
Degois-Sainz, Maria A155
Degon, Stephen G. E291
DeGroot, Greg A199
DeHart, Don A199
Dehart, Monnie E161
DeHaven, Michael A. P87
Dehecq, Jean-François W295
Dehen, Wolfgang W307
Dehler, Joseph P113
Deibel, Stefan Robert W59

Deitch, Michael N. E294
Deitchle, Gerald W. E58
Deith, Harry E145
Deitz, Scott A. A638, W319
DeIuliis, Nicholas J. A238
Dejanovic, Darko A834
DeJoria, John Paul P269
DeJuncker, Ron P198
DeKam, Kathleen A. P21
DeKaser, Richard J. A589
DeKay, Donald F. P260
Dekkers, Marijn E. A816
Del Moral-Niles, Christopher A343
Del Pino, Eulogio W252
del Río, Xavier W362
Del Río Jiménez, José M. E136
Del Sindaco, Joseph M. P395
Del Vecchio, Claudio P417
Delabrière, Yann W254
Delafon, Blandine W72
Delalande, Philippe W47
Deland, Rick P53
Delane, Alton E62
Delaney, Dennis P256
Delaney, Douglas J. E109
Delaney, Gregory M. A680
Delaney, James (D&B) A296
Delaney, James M. (Ryerson) A722
Delaney, John K. E69
Delaney, Keenan A46
Delaney, Kevin P. A694
Delaney, Michael V. A867
Delaney, Patricia C. E326
Delaney, Terence P. A789
Delangle, Nina W170
Delanoue, Philippe P40
DelBianco, David J. E232
Delcommune, Michel-Marc W224
Delehanty, Martha P123
deLeon, Rudy F. A151
Delfassy, Gilles A814
Delgado, Alice E35
Delgado, Natalia E183
DelGrosso, Douglas G. A506
D'Elia, Robyn A136
D'Elia, Vivian E241
Deliberto, Robert A184
DeLiema, Robert E58
Deline, Donald A. A398
Delk, Mary R. P80
Delker, Wayne L. A222
Dell, Donna M. A34
Dell, Michael S. A268
Della Flora, Daniel E. E253
della Sala, Umberto A358
Dellaquila, Frank J. A319
Dellinger, Robert J. A271
Delly, Gayla J. A139
Delman, Michael A574
Delmar, Steven R. E18
DeLoach, Harris E. Jr. A767
DeLong, Bob P292
Delong, Kimberly M. E202
DeLozier, Phil C. A321
Delpon de Vaux, Jean-Marc W290
DelSignore, Arthur Jr. P359
DeLuca, Frederick A. P173
Deluca, Vincent E188
Delvin, Michael J. E73
Delvy, Linda P411
DeMane, Michael F. A563
Demarais, Patricia P173
DeMarco, Frederick L. P149
Demaré, Michel W20
Demaree, George Jr. P278
Demarest, David P458
DeMarino, Theodore A706
DeMars, Jerry V. A620
DeMattei, David M. A908
DeMatteo, Daniel A. A367
DeMayo, Carole M. A418
Dembner, Perry E108
Demchak, William S. A672

Deméré, Robert H. Jr. P138
Demerling, Donna J. A824
Demeter, Dan E210
Demilio, Mark S. A535
Demme, James A. A649
Demmer, John E. E114
Demmert, William J. P50
DeMoss, Lisa S. P91
Dempsey, Anneke A757
Dempsey, Dennis A90
Dempsey, Kelly P129
Dempsey, Patrick W365
Dempsey, William G. A30
Demsey, John A325
DeMuro, Gerard J. A377
DeMuth, David P525
den Hartog, Grace R. A636
DeNale, Carol A258
Denault, Leo P. A320
DenBoer, Vicki K. E223
Dénes, Ferenc W224
Dengel, Tobias E387
Denham, Benny W. P368
Denham, Robert A. A129
Denhert, Robert G. P374
DeNicola, T. Kevin A534
Denius, Franklin W. A771
Denk, Gregory P. P283
Denka, Andrew G. A712
Denman, John W. A471
Denman-Jones, Darlene A585
Denner, Volkmar W279
Denney, William C. A214
Dennis, Dana A. A644
Dennis, David E. E105
Dennis, Kimberly K. A428
Dennis, Steven P. P353
Dennis, William C. Jr. E214
Denniston, Brackett B. III A379
Denniston, Joseph S. Jr. E358
Denny, Diane S. P118
Denny, James (QuikTrip) P405
Denny, James M. (Gilead
   Sciences) A385
Denny, Ron A129
Densing, Kristina P129
Denson, Charles D. A607
Denson, William F. III A879
Dent, Gerald J. A924
Dentato, Patrick P281
Denver, Andrew A641
DePalma, Vincent A670
DePaola, Ken A834
DePasquale, Joseph A. E331
Dépatie, Robert W268
DePaul, Phillip P. A627
DePaula, Joseph L. P51
DePeau, Jamie A819, P478
DePeters, Jack P526
DePew, Barry A. A826
DePhillips, Henry A. III E229
Depies, John R. P56
DePinto, Joseph M. A28
Deppe, Hans A42
Depperman, Chris P519
DePrey, Mark P433
Derbesse, Michel W71
Derderian, John T. A646
Dere, Willard A85
Derechin, Adam M. E90
Deremo, John B. A688
Derenzo, Mitchell A. E31
Derhaag, Gregory J. A138
Derheimer, Mark J. P496
Derhofer, George N. A873
Derickson, Mike A207
Derickson, Sandra L. W156
DeRiggi, Mario P374
Derins, Mike P413
Derkach, John W365
Dermody, William P106
DeRodes, Robert P. A434
Deroo, Paul A. E74

A = AMERICAN BUSINESS
E = EMERGING COMPANIES
P = PRIVATE COMPANIES
W = WORLD BUSINESS

Ferraioli, Brian K. A358
Ferrales, Savino R. E301
Ferramosca, Frank P55
Ferrando, Jonathan P. A111
Ferrante, Barbara W64
Ferrara, Albert E. Jr. A54
Ferrara, John C. E217
Ferrarell, Timothy M. A914
Ferrari, John M. E366
Ferrari Bigares Careto, José M. W122
Ferrario, Giovanni W329
Ferraro, John W127
Ferraz Flores, Luís Pedro W122
Ferree, Thomas J. P56
Ferreira, Steven J. A643
Ferrell, James E. A339
Ferren, John P. W84
Ferrero, David J. P85
Ferret, Jean-Francois A539
Ferrie, John C. P98
Ferrier, Gérald W23
Ferriola, John J. A620
Ferro, Carlo W318
Ferro, Jason E166
Ferron, Martin R. E175
Ferroni, Cameron E225
Ferry, Danny P122
Ferst, Leigh W352
Fertman, Don P173
Feshbach, Andrew D. E54
Fessard, Jérôme W291
Festa, Alfred E. A912
Fetch, Mary T. E242
Fetherston, Richard A. P43
Fetig, James A701
Fetter, Lee F. P87
Fetter, Trevor A806
Fettig, Jeff M. A904
Fetting, Mark R. A507
Fetzer, John M. A37
Feucht, Kenneth H. E157
Feuerhake, Rainer W350
Feuerstein, Stefan W215
Feuss, Linda U. A198
Fevelo-Hoad, Barbara A93
Fewer, Donald P. E158
Fhaner, Eileen P69
Fialkowski, Kathryn L. A419
Fiasca, Christina H. P364
Fichtel, Michael D. P129
Fick, Daniel S. P503
Fickel, Todd A389
Ficken, Ann P272
Fickett, Robert A. E104
Fiebrink, Mark A518, P296
Fiedler, Frank W360
Fiedler, Richard G. E184
Field, James M. A265
Field, Thomas W. Jr. P461
Fielder, Allan W58
Fielder, John R. A309
Fielding, Patti K. P455
Fielding, Robert J. P49
Fielding, Ronald W. A437
Fields, Arthur W. A295
Fields, Emilio E359
Fields, Felicia J. A355
Fields, Lee C. E188
Fields, Mark A354
Fields, Sara A. A844
Fields, Stephen G. E96
Fielke, Neville W133
Fieramosca, Charles E. A923
Fife, James D. A503, P290
Fife, Jerry P513
Figueroa, John A559
Fike, Carin A500
Fike, Randy K. E172
Fike, William T. E361
Fikre, Ted P300
Filer, Jim A53
Fili-Krushel, Patricia A822
Filios, George P32

Filipe, Carla E160
Filippi, Charles-Henri W156
Filipps, Frank P. E86
Filkouski, Craig P220
Filliat, Jean-Paul W47
Filliater, Jeff E. A206
Filmer, Anthony O. W166
Filo, David A919
Filoni, Dave P303
Filusch, Edward J. A228
Fimbianti, Joseph P. A449
Finan, Irial A225
Finan, Kevin P. A55
Finard, Jeri B. A498
Finazzo, Kathy P461
Finch, Albert J. E266
Findlay, D. Cameron A94
Fine, Michael J. A648
Fine, Molly M. P165
Fine, Randall A. A405
Fine, Rebecca A. E271
Fine, Todd J. P395
Finer, Dustin K. A373
Finger, Stephen N. A857
Fingerman, Jeremy J. P407
Finglass, Joel P157
Fink, Franz A365
Fink, Laurence D. P360
Fink, Michael A. E292
Fink, Rich A493, P284
Fink, Scott P366
Fink, Thomas A. E69
Finkbeiner, Gerd W209
Finkelstein, Paul D. A705
Finkenbrink, Ralph T. E256
Finlayson, Chris W287
Finlayson, Eric W. E232
Finley, Bruce C. Jr. E47
Finley, Sara J. A180
Finley, Teresa A850
Finn, Brian D. W100
Finn, Dennis F. A718
Finn, Edwin A. Jr. A417, P237
Finn, Richard E234
Finn, Tracy A629
Finnegan, John D. A208
Finnegan, Wilfred A. P114
Finneran, John G. Jr. A178
Finnerty, William J. A812
Finney, Jared P147
Finnigan, Daniel J. A919
Finnin, Farrell P122
Fino, Arthur F. A264
Finocchi, Richard A. P203
Finucane, Anne M. A123
Fiola, Janet S. A563
Fiore, Christopher A73
Fiore, Peter P109
Fiorentino, Edward J. A30
Fiori, Giovanni A475
Fiorilli, Matthew A136
Firestone, James A. A918
Firestone, Marc S. A498
Firrell, Paul A. P226
Firstenberg, David J. A401
Firth, Robert R. E43
Fisch, Joseph J. Jr. P350
Fischbach, Gerald D. P140
Fischer, Addison M. P446
Fischer, Andrew M. P160
Fischer, Béatrice W100
Fischer, Bruce G. A788
Fischer, David (Google) A394
Fischer, David B. (Greif) A396
Fischer, Donald R. A427, P241
Fischer, Harry A. III P160
Fischer, Harry A. Jr. P160
Fischer, John E. A628
Fischer, Jost E325
Fischer, Leonhard H. W100
Fischer, Marcelo A443
Fischer, Mark D. A664
Fischer, Paul F. P50

Fischer, Peter D. P160
Fischer, Ralph P322
Fischer, Rich (Medtronic) A563
Fischer, Richard X. (Navigant
  Consulting) E248
Fischer, Robert H. P28
Fischer, Susan A753
Fischer, Thomas B. (Great Western
  Bancorporation) P220
Fischer, Thomas R. (RWE) W288
Fischer-Colbrie, Mark D. E20
Fischl, Kenneth P309
Fish, Alan F. A771
Fish, Jason M. E69
Fish, John W145
Fish, Lawrence K. W286
Fishbein, Robert A655
Fishel, Stuart E193
Fisher, Andrew S. A251
Fisher, Catherine A709
Fisher, Christine P407
Fisher, David (HBOS) W147
Fisher, David A. (optionsXpress) E266
Fisher, David I. (Capital Group) P110
Fisher, Dawn P472
Fisher, Delbert A. A695
Fisher, Edward D. A371
Fisher, Eric A868, E373
Fisher, Franklin M. E104
Fisher, G. Robert P273
Fisher, J. Bradley E72
Fisher, J. Daniel E156
Fisher, James R. (Bristol West) E63
Fisher, Jeanne B. A84
Fisher, Jeff (Heinz) A430
Fisher, Jeffrey A. (Chesapeake
  Energy) A204
Fisher, Jeffrey D. (NVIDIA) A620
Fisher, Jeffrey T. (Charter
  Communications) A203
Fisher, Jim (ABP Corporation) P19
Fisher, John W. A121
Fisher, Joseph (Affirmative
  Insurance) E22
Fisher, Joseph V. (Topco
  Associates) P481
Fisher, Lawrence N. A350
Fisher, Mark W286
Fisher, Michael A. P399
Fisher, Paul S. P124
Fisher, Peter E. E293
Fisher, R. Bruce A82
Fisher, Richard W. P194
Fisher, Robert J. A370
Fisher, Ronald D. W313
Fisher, Shana A442
Fisher, W. Douglas E379
Fisher, Wayne W373
Fisher, William C. A673
Fishkin, Cory E56
Fishkin, Lee P47
Fishman, Jay S. A730
Fishman, Jerald G. A89
Fishman, Mark C. W240
Fishman, Steven S. A143
Fisk, Hayward D. A233
Fitch, Bob W53
Fitch, Rodney W369
Fitchett, John P407
Fite, Charles D. E31
Fitschen, Jürgen W111
Fitts, Clive A696
Fitts, John R. P183
Fitz, Stefan W138
Fitzgerald, Barbara A. A659
Fitzgerald, David E176
Fitzgerald, Douglas W. A719
Fitzgerald, Gabriella P. A76
Fitzgerald, Hiram E. P329
Fitzgerald, James A. Jr. A413
Fitzgerald, Jan P111
Fitzgerald, Joseph M. (Boston
  Scientific) A155

Fitzgerald, Joseph M. (MGM) P326
Fitzgerald, Kevin J. A633
Fitzgerald, Matt P157
Fitzgerald, Megan L. E160
Fitzgerald, Michael
  (DecisionOne) P164
FitzGerald, Michael J. (Toreador
  Resources) E355
FitzGerald, Niall W275
Fitzgerald, Pat P122
Fitzgerald, Sean P105
Fitzgerald, Thomas P. P533
Fitzgerald, Walter L. A194
Fitzgibbon, Patrick W193
Fitzhenry, James A. E152
Fitzhugh, Michael D. E47
Fitzmaurice, Lisa P359
FitzPatrick, Dennis P410
Fitzpatrick, Jayne P180
Fitzpatrick, Jim A460
Fitzpatrick, John (Burger King) A169
Fitzpatrick, John F. (Provident New
  York Bancorp) E294
Fitzpatrick, Thomas J. A761
Fitzpatrick, Tim A516
Fitzsimmons, Ellen M. A256
Fitzsimmons, Joseph J. A884
Fitzsimmons, W. James E381
FitzSimons, Dennis J. A834
Fitzsimons, Ian W250
Fiumefreddo, John J. P527
Five, Kaci Kullmann W316
Fivel, Steven E. A159
Fjeldheim, Norm A693
Flack, Robert J. P31
Flack, Steven E143
Flacke, Robert J. P433
Flagg, Claude A. A812
Flaharty, Gary R. A120
Flahaux, José A732
Flaherty, Greg P299
Flaherty, James P. A596
Flaherty, Kathy P372
Flaherty, Lauren P. W239
Flaim, John A119
Flaim, Theresa A. A809, P475
Flaissier, Yves W250
Flamholz, Sam P97
Flanagan, Carey A792
Flanagan, Jack P208
Flanagan, James E164
Flanagan, Lawrence A550
Flanagan, Robert J. P133
Flanagan Chamberlain, Glenda A905
Flanders, Brent P384
Flanders, Michael J. A119
Flanders, Paul R. P117
Flanigan, Matthew C. A508
Flann, Jeremy P222
Flannery, Matthew W69
Flater, Marybeth A329
Flatt, Dean M. A435
Flatt, James E226
Flaum, James P136
Flaum, Russell M. A446
Flaws, James B. A247
Flax, Samuel A. E29
Flaxman, Jon E. A426
Flaxman, Michael W23
Fleet, Samuel H. P48
Fleig, Günther W104
Fleischauer, John I. Jr. A704
Fleischer, Gene A732
Fleischhacker, James E. A577
Fleischman, David H. E356
Fleischman, Jeffrey E239
Fleisher, Michael D. A888
Fleisher, Beverly J. A613
Fleming, Bruce F. A210
Fleming, David D. A384
Fleming, Gregory J. A568
Fleming, John (Ford) A354
Fleming, John E. (Wal-Mart) A883

A = AMERICAN BUSINESS
E = EMERGING COMPANIES
P = PRIVATE COMPANIES
W = WORLD BUSINESS

Ivory, Thomas P. E349
Ivy, Conway G. A756
Iwabu, Hideki W190
Iwabuchi, Junichi W223
Iwai, Mutsuo W177
Iwano, Hideaki W303
Iwasa, Yoshio W296
Iwasaki, Jiro W327
Iwasaki, Jun W230
Iwashita, Tomochika W217
Iwashita, Tomonori W85
Iwata, Jon C. A454
Iwata, Satoru W231
Iwatsuki, Shinro W107
Iyar, Subrah S. E385
Iyobe, Tsuneo W218
Izard, Pierre W311
Izawa, Nobuo W190
Izganics, Joe C. A434
Izumisawa, Tomoyuki W74

J

Jaacks, James R. P444
Jaaskelainen, Markku E89
Jaber, Mohamad P446
Jablonski, Brian J. E178
Jablonski, Zygmunt P497
Jaccoud, Pierre W280
Jack, Clifford J. W264
Jack, D. Michael A803
Jack, Michael A595
Jackowski, Julie L. A187
Jacks, Ethan E. E45
Jackson, Alan P98
Jackson, Darren R. A142
Jackson, David (American Media) P44
Jackson, David A. (Knight
    Transportation) E208
Jackson, David J. (BP) W73
Jackson, Deanna A696
Jackson, Don P203
Jackson, Edward L. P393
Jackson, Eric H. P436
Jackson, Greg (Taylor
    Corporation) P470
Jackson, Gregory A. (University of
    Chicago) P502
Jackson, Jackie A264
Jackson, James (Harman
    Management) P230
Jackson, Jeff (Sun Microsystems) A787
Jackson, Jeffery M. (Sabre) A724
Jackson, Jim (Bechtel) P79
Jackson, Joanne B. E286
Jackson, Joy P64
Jackson, Kathe R. (The PBSJ
    Corporation) P380
Jackson, Kathryn J. (TVA) A809, P475
Jackson, Margaret A. W267
Jackson, Marianne P92
Jackson, Mark W. A307
Jackson, Martin F. P438
Jackson, M.C. A764
Jackson, Michael A.
    (Weyerhaeuser) A903
Jackson, Michael J. (AutoNation) A111
Jackson, Michael L.
    (SUPERVALU) A791
Jackson, Michael L. (USC) P507
Jackson, Peter (Foster's) W133
Jackson, Peter J. (Kingfisher) W181
Jackson, Phil P300
Jackson, R. Wayne A681, W263
Jackson, Roger A. (Lear) A506
Jackson, Roger C. (KMG
    Chemicals) E207
Jackson, Ronald C. A704
Jackson, Russell M. A662
Jackson, Stephen P. Jr. P415
Jackson, Stu P344
Jackson, Timothy E. A807

Jackson, Wes P499
Jacob, Edward S. III E164
Jacob, John E. A91
Jacob, Ken P98
Jacob, Leonard S. E62
Jacob, Philippe Loïc W105
Jacobellis, Luke P269
Jacobs, Andrew W. A421
Jacobs, Bradley S. A851
Jacobs, Charlie P165
Jacobs, Eric D. E114
Jacobs, Gary (Universal American
    Financial) E367
Jacobs, Gary N. (MGM MIRAGE) A571
Jacobs, Irwin L. (Genmar
    Holdings) P206
Jacobs, Irwin Mark (QUALCOMM) A693
Jacobs, Jay R. A665
Jacobs, Jeffrey P. P264
Jacobs, Jeremy M. Jr. P165
Jacobs, Jeremy M. Sr. P165
Jacobs, Joanne P295
Jacobs, Joey A. E296
Jacobs, Klaus J. W25
Jacobs, Lawrence A. (News Corp.) A604
Jacobs, Lawrence R. (VyStar Credit
    Union) P521
Jacobs, Louis M. P165
Jacobs, Michael C. P483
Jacobs, Paul (Zygo) E397
Jacobs, Paul E. (QUALCOMM) A693
Jacobs, Robert S. E130
Jacobs, Ron L. E134
Jacobs, Seth A. P92
Jacobs, Tami P308
Jacobs, Terryl P350
Jacobs, Walker W275
Jacobsen, Barry A753
Jacobsen, Jon A. W316
Jacobson, Benjamin R. P83
Jacobson, Bill P70
Jacobson, Douglas J. A204
Jacobson, Harry R. P513
Jacobson, Joni P303
Jacobson, Larry E46
Jacobson, Matthew A696
Jacobson, Michael R. A306
Jacobson, Paul A. A272
Jacobson, Richard J. A251, P150
Jacobson, Tim P321
Jacobus, Mary A600
Jacoub, Maryann E23
Jacques, Alison A546
Jacques, Michel W33
Jacquesson, Olivier W295
Jacquet, Richard J. A137
Jaeger, Steve P404
Jafari, A. Reza E251
Jaffe, Jeffrey M. A618
Jaffe, Jonathan M. A511
Jaffe, Kineret S. P502
Jaffe, Seth R. A908
Jaffee, Yolanda E. E266
Jaffer, Azeezaly S. A853, P498
Jaffy, Stanley A. A138
Jagadeesh, B. V. E85
Jaggers, Joseph N. E55
Jagid, Jeffrey M. E186
Jagodzinski, Jeff A395, P221
Jagtiani, Anil A399, P228
Jahn, Michael P451
Jahner, Floyd P157
Jain, Anshu W111
Jain, Terri P323
Jain, Vivek W255
Jainsinghani, Haresh A43
Jakobsen, Thomas K. W88
Jaksich, Daniel J. A140
Jakubowicz, Donna P74
Jalbert, Michael E. E127
Jalink, G.H. W31
Jamerson, Bruce A. E376
James, Alison E130

James, Bill E241
James, Brian P333
James, Catherine W115
James, Charles A. A205
James, Courtland W. A700
James, David P518
James, Donald M. A879
James, Donna A. A593, P351
James, Elizabeth R. A795
James, John B. E48
James, Julian W199
James, Kim P373
James, Laura A. P29
James, Michael R. A896
James, Phyllis A. A571
James, Robert A29
James, Thomas A. (Raymond James
    Financial) A700
James, Tom (San Antonio Spurs) P428
James, Ulla W235
James, W. Brad E355
Jamesley, Karen C. A581
Jameson, Mark P122
Jameson, Piper E369
Jamet, Marc-Antoine W207
Jamieson, Daniel T. E384
Jamieson, James M. A151
Jamieson, Mark T. A721
Jamieson, Scott A246
Jamison, Douglas W. E169
Jamison, Edward M. E96
Jamison, Greg P428
Jamison, John R. A461
Jancola, Mark E181
Jancsurák, Zoltán W224
Jandegian, Gary V. A861
Janes, Matthew K.R. E376
Janeway, Dean A881, P523
Jangbahadur, KS A479
Janik, Douglas J. A549
Janiszewski, Charles A. P31
Jank, Michael J. A274
Janke, Dean H. P417
Janke, Kenneth S. Jr. A47
Janker, Franz A100
Janki, Daniel C. A379
Jankov, Ronald E250
Jankus, Tom P403
Jannausch, Julia P. A243
Jannini, Michael E. A542
Janowski, Seffi A779
Jansanti, Kristen P17
Jansen, Kathrin U. A916
Jansen, Peter W204
Jansen, Philip W312
Jansen, William P84
Janssen, Vincent H. A. M. A735
Jansson, Dwain P62
Jansson, Mats W299
Janulis, Theodore P. A509
Janz, Greta P203
Janzen, Peter A503, P290
Japy, Nicholas W312
Jaquinto, Roberto W123
Jarchow, Edward R. P74
Jardeleza, Francis H. W293
Jardin, Alexander Gordon E153
Jardin, Joao Louis S. A444, P252
Jarrett, Charles E. A687
Jarrett, David A46
Jarrett, Thomas K. A265
Jarry, Philippe W89
Jarvis, Mark W202
Jarvis, Paul A199
Jasiek, Jerry P426
Jasinkiewicz, Ken A881, P523
Jasinski, James E88
Jasmer, Amy A515, P294
Jason, Mark N. E394
Jaspan, Stanley S. P200
Jaspar, Benoit W142
Jasper, Daniel W. P197
Jasper, Deborah P377

Jastrow, Kenneth M. II A805
Javosky, Rudolph V. A337
Jay, Martin W170
Jean, Raymond A. A694
Jean, Roger L. A518, P296
Jedlicka, Joseph F. III A91
Jefferies, Graham E129
Jefferies, Robert A. Jr. A508
Jeffers, Paul C. P463
Jefferson, Barbara P75
Jefferson, John A755, P337
Jefferson, Linda P104
Jeffery, Jeff W138
Jeffery, Michael J. E216
Jeffrey, Bob W370
Jeffrey, Mary A. A330
Jeffries, Douglas A306
Jeffries, Mark A. E156
Jeffries, Mary L. P387
Jeffries, Michael S. A32
Jeffries, Nicola W193
Jeffries, Telvin A496
Jeffs, David R. W201
Jeffs, Roger E366
Jeffs, Rohan K. S. W368
Jelinek, W. Craig A248
Jellig, Donald V. P439
Jellison, Gary A753
Jenab, Ali E372
Jendrzejewski, George P94
Jenkins, Benjamin P. III A880
Jenkins, Bob A28
Jenkins, Carlton J. P540
Jenkins, Charles H. Jr. A691, P402
Jenkins, Claire W138
Jenkins, Derek L. A798
Jenkins, George P159
Jenkins, Howard M. A691, P402
Jenkins, Huw W351
Jenkins, James R. (Deere) A265
Jenkins, James R. (U.S. Cellular) A852
Jenkins, Margaret L. A274
Jenkins, Scott E309
Jenkins, Sharon K. A737
Jenkins, Sheila P270
Jenne, Jason A. P487
Jenne-Lindenberg, Ursula W225
Jenner, Barry W138
Jenner, Paul A448
Jenness, James M. A483
Jennifer, Jackie R. P245
Jennings, Allan L. P245
Jennings, Andrew A731
Jennings, Brian J. A275
Jennings, Don D. E206
Jennings, Gary P65
Jennings, Gayle S. A343
Jennings, John S. A627
Jennings, Karen E. A109
Jennings, Paul P297
Jennings, Reynold J. A806
Jennings, Scott C. E337
Jens, Reinier W255
Jensen, Brent E388
Jensen, Carol P525
Jensen, Dick (Morris Murdock) P336
Jensen, James B. A760
Jensen, Jørn P. W88
Jensen, Julia A552
Jensen, Keith A. A77
Jensen, Kenneth R. A346
Jensen, Kris P527
Jensen, Larry P292
Jensen, Linda A. A611
Jensen, Morten A763
Jensen, Paul W367
Jensen, Peder K. A738
Jensen, Richard C.
    (PrivateBancorp) E292
Jensen, Robert P111
Jensen, Rodney L. P242
Jensen, Roy P411
Jenson, Warren C. A312

A = AMERICAN BUSINESS
E = EMERGING COMPANIES
P = PRIVATE COMPANIES
W = WORLD BUSINESS

Kanasugi, Akinobu W227
Kanda, Hiroshi W179
Kanda, Masaki W213
Kandarian, Steven A. A569
Kanders, Warren B. A104
Kandes, Carrie A. A277
Kane, Archie G. W200
Kane, Jacqueline P. A222
Kane, Kevin P173
Kane, Linda S. P402
Kane, Lynette P105
Kane, Rebecca P208
Kane, Tom A192
Kaneb, Gary R. P248
Kaneb, Jeffrey J. P248
Kaneb, John A. P248
Kanematsu, Hiroshi W314
Kanenari, Hideyuki W175
Kang, Alvin D. E246
Kang, Chang-Oh W261
Kang, Ho-Moon W292
Kang, Matthew S. A538
Kang, P. Kacy E128
Kangas, Edward A. A806
Kangas, Paul A825
Kangdry, Stephanie E196
Kankkunen, Antti A804
Kann, Peter R. A288
Kannappan, S. Kenneth E287
Kanter, Harvey S. A572
Kanter, Troy A. E205
Kantor, Jonathan D. A224
Kanzler, Michael W. P494
Kao, Andy P376
Kapelus, Jerome V. E100
Kaplan, Alard A540
Kaplan, Anne C. P364
Kaplan, Doug E301
Kaplan, Elliot S. A142
Kaplan, Herbert P524
Kaplan, Lawrence M. E249
Kaplan, Lee R. P187
Kaplan, Paul D. E240
Kaplan, Ralph A733
Kaplan, Richard J. P165
Kapnick, Scott B. A390
Kapoor, Rakesh W271
Kapoor, Rohit E139
Kappelman, Peter A503, P290
Kapples, John W. A701
Kapral, Mike P115
Kapur, Deepak T. A594
Kapur, Rahul P28
Kapusansky, David W35
Kaput, Jim L. A751
Kar, Pratip W324
Karaev, Isaak W275
Karafa, Jeffrey L. E114
Karam, George A874
Karas, John A. E307
Karatsu, Osamu P456
Karatz, Bruce E. A481
Karch, Paul J. P56
Kardos, John A. E54
Karecki, Jöel W255
Karel, Steven A712
Karenko, Larry A412
Karet, Laura P208
Karges, Thomas R. E41
Kargula, Michael R. P211
Kari, Ross J. A725
Karim, Nozad A86
Kariya, Michio W229
Karl, George P168
Karlberg, Kenneth W335
Karlsen, Lars Guldbæk W242
Karlsson, Håkan W361
Karlsten, Peter W361

Karmanos, Jason P115
Karmanos, Peter Jr. P115
Karpovich, Eugene J. E241
Karro, Bradley S. A180
Karrol, Peter E94
Karsan, Nooruddin S. E205
Karsbergen, Frank W325
Karsian, Andrea P482
Karskens, Paulus A456
Karst, Darren W. P424
Karst, William B. P107
Kartarik, Mark A705
Karvinen, Jouko W319
Kasai, Shinjiro W151
Kasbar, Michael J. A910
Kasberger, John L. A530
Kasdin, Robert A. P140
Kase, Yutaka W314
Kashima, Ikusaburo W212
Kashimer, William A228
Kashio, Akira W91
Kashio, Kazuo W91
Kashio, Toshio W91
Kashio, Yukio W91
Kashiwagi, Shigesuke W237
Kashkoush, Marwan A644
Kashner, Heather W198
Kashnow, Richard A. E209
Kashuda, Mark J. A771
Kaskie, James R. P276
Kasper, M. Katharine E124
Kasputys, Joseph E. P211
Kasriel, Bernard L.M. W194
Kassel, Theodore M. P518
Kassing, Suzanne P175
Kassovic, Vratko W224
Kastan, Jay P28
Kastelic, David A207
Katayama, Masanori W171
Katayama, Michinori W327
Katayama, Mikio W304
Katayama, Morimitsu W190
Katen-Bahensky, Donna M. P503
Kato, Hirokazu W371
Kato, Hisatoyo W136
Kato, Kazuyasu W182
Kato, Makoto W172
Kato, Mitsuharu W107
Kato, Sadao W232
Katovsich, Dennis F. P316
Katsaros, Arthur T. A52
Katsaros, Penny E26
Katsumata, Tsunehisa W342
Katsumura, Hajime W218
Katt, Heather A61
Katten, Melvin L. P277
Katz, Aaron I. A797
Katz, Ariel E40
Katz, Bruce E203
Katz, Francine I. A91
Katz, Howard P346
Katz, Joshua P303
Katz, Karen W. P353
Katz, Leslye G. A448
Katz, Marc D. (Foot Locker) A353
Katz, Marcia A641
Katz, Mark (Esselte) P189
Katz, Matthew D. A707
Katz, Nancy J. A136
Katz, Samuel L. A535, P304
Katz, William D. (AmeriGas Partners) A83
Katz, William D. (UGI) A845
Katz, Yona A443
Katz Armoza, Marcela P133
Katzenmeyer, Thomas A519
Katzman, David B. P122
Kauffman, Charles E211
Kauffman, E. Chris E272
Kauffman, Emma Jo A282
Kauffman, Frank E345
Kauffman, James B. A58
Kauffman, Mike A476

Kaufman, Alison A856
Kaufman, Bob P151
Kaufman, Carol R. E101
Kaufman, David S. A102
Kaufman, Frank J. A558
Kaufman, Harold P355
Kaufman, Mark A438
Kaufman, Victor A. A442
Kaufmann, Michael P167
Kaufmann, Paul K. A764
Kaul, Pradman P. A279
Kauser, Nicolas P134
Kavanagh, K. C. A783
Kavanaugh, Bridget M. P151
Kavanaugh, James P. P537
Kavarana, Farrokh K. W324
Kavitsky, Charles W38
Kavner, Robert M. A301
Kawabata, Masao W256
Kawaguchi, Hitoshi W234
Kawahara, Kazuo W231
Kawai, Yoshimichi W229
Kawakami, Junzo W151
Kawakami, Tetsuya W212
Kawamura, Makoto W192
Kawamura, Toshiro W227
Kawasaki, Hideichi W245
Kay, Bruce A541
Kay, Christina M. E192
Kay, E. Gerald E192
Kay, Kenneth J. A189
Kay, Robert B. E192
Kay, Stephen H. A373
Kay, Walter A. P512
Kayata, Taizo W185
Kaye, Alan A552
Kaye, Diane A271
Kayne, Fred E54
Kazerounian, Reza W318
Keairns, Jim A811
Kealy, Thomas P. E64
Kean, Thomas H. P420
Keane, Daniel G. E238
Keane, Dayton E35
Keane, James P. A786
Keane, John B. A74
Keane, Kevin (Unica) E362
Keane, Kevin T. (Astronics, MOD-PAC) E41, E238
Keane, Michael E. A233
Keane, Terrence P. E26
Kearney, Christopher J. A778
Kearney, Kathryn A. E61
Kearney, Pam A400
Kearney, Sandra W. A389
Kearns, John P. E345
Kearns, Kim A173
Kearns, Richard P. W373
Keast, Brodie A744
Keating, Mary Ellen (Barnes & Noble) A125
Keating, Mary Jo (Northeast Utilities) A611
Keating, Ronald C. A485
Keating, Timothy J. A435
Keches, George A. P495
Keck, Kim A. A44
Keck, Ray III P476
Keddy, Patrick A670
Keebaugh, Michael D. A701
Keefe, Michael D. A403
Keefe, Patrick E. A629
Keefer, Elizabeth J. P140
Keefer, Jeffrey L. A297
Keegan, James B. Jr. E258
Keegan, Peter W. A526
Keegan, Robert A392
Keegan, Tracy L. E48
Keegel, C. Thomas P471
Keehan, Terry E359
Keel, Clarence A129
Keel, Michael C. P319

Keeler, Jim P525
Keeley, Rupert G. A876
Keen, Graham P. A38
Keen, Paul R. P58
Keenan, Lisa W133
Keenan, Terence W. E103
Keenan, Vince A116
Keene, Linda B. A741
Keeney, Frank D. P55
Kees, Robert L. P370
Keese, Kyle W. E128
Keesee, Gloria P521
Keeshan, Lawrence W. A681, P397, W263
Keevan, William E248
Keevil, Tom W138
Kefer, Volker W109
Kehl, Kurt P297
Kehoe, Michael E. W240
Keifer, Alan J. A120
Keilly, Chris P208
Keins, Doug E254
Keiser, Kenneth E. A652
Keisling, James D. E126
Keisling, Jeffrey E. A916
Keister, John E225
Keitch, Cindy L. A440
Keitel, William E. A693
Keith, Claudia P106
Keith, Jerry O'Dell E314
Keith, Robert E. Jr. A726
Keitt, John R. Jr. P64
Kelch, Robert P. P504
Kelderhouse, Robert J. A719
Keleghan, Kevin T. P372
Kelfer, Gerald D. E44
Kella, Rob W267
Kellar, Lorrence T. E242
Kelleher, Brian M. A620
Kelleher, Herbert D. A772
Kelleher, Kevin P449
Kelleher, Warren J. P435
Keller, Beate E313
Keller, Bryan J. P165
Keller, David L. A555
Keller, Gottlieb A. W280
Keller, James P. (Cooper Tire & Rubber) A246
Keller, James R. (Weyerhaeuser) A903
Keller, Mark A. A48
Keller, Michael C. A593, P351
Keller, Richard G. A428
Kellert, Bob P203
Kelley, Barbara M. A126
Kelley, Byron R. A194
Kelley, David P251
Kelley, Edward B. A865, P511
Kelley, James P. P143
Kelley, Janet G. A335
Kelley, John (White Castle) P530
Kelley, John E. III (IBM) A454
Kelley, John M. (Herley Industries) E177
Kelley, Karen P264
Kelley, Mark A. P240
Kelley, Mary Lou P299
Kelley, Michael L. E355
Kelley, R. David E132
Kelley, Rick P278
Kelley, Scott C. (University of Texas System) P508
Kelley, Scott D. (Aspect Medical Systems) E39
Kelley, Thomas W. (Kelley Automotive) P278
Kelley, Tom (IDEO) P251
Kelley, Vincent J. A788
Kellick, Patrick W. P21
Kellie, Gillian A888
Kelliher, Matthew E. E173
Kellner, Lawrence W. A242
Kellogg, Fernanda M. A820
Kellum, Danny L. A668

A = AMERICAN BUSINESS
E = EMERGING COMPANIES
P = PRIVATE COMPANIES
W = WORLD BUSINESS

Kim, Jason A726
Kim, Jeong H. W34
Kim, Jing-Wan W292
Kim, Joanne E391
Kim, JooHo A86
Kim, Min Jung E246
Kim, Miung E168
Kim, Neil Y. A164
Kim, Paul E88
Kim, Peter S. (Merck) A567
Kim, Peter Y. S. (Center Financial) E77
Kim, Sang-Ho (POSCO) W261
Kim, Sang-Young (POSCO) W261
Kim, Sookeun W292
Kimata, Masatoshi W190
Kimball, Jim P472
Kimball, Kevin M. A542
Kimball, Lee A159
Kimball, Robert E301
Kimber, Michael N. (George Weston) W143
Kimber, Michael N. (Loblaw) W201
Kimble, Donald R. A440
Kimbro, Kenneth J. A843
Kimbrough, Mark A413
Kime, Jeffery L. A818
Kimick, Frank V. E241
Kimishima, Tatsumi W231
Kimmel, Kenneth P180
Kimmel, Sidney A476
Kimmins, Jon W. P483
Kimmins, William J. Jr. A91
Kimmitt, Joseph H. A634
Kimura, Hiroshi W176
Kimura, Keiji W315
Kimura, Makoto W229
Kimura, Nobuo A584
Kimura, Shigeru W342
Kimura, Toshio W303
Kimura, Tsuyoshi W346
Kincaid, Lawrence H. P500
Kincaid, Steven M. A504
Kinder, Lawrence E. A115
Kindig, Karl W. A237
Kindle, Fred W20
Kindler, Jeffrey B. A660
Kindorf, William A. E146
Kindts, Rudi W76
King, Allen B. A859
King, Andrew W. A827
King, Anne M. E53
King, Bernadette W145
King, Billy (Pioneer Drilling) E286
King, Carolyn A688
King, Catherine J. A484
King, David E. (ACA Capital Holdings) E17
King, David R. H. (SmithGroup) P446
King, Deryk I. W92
King, Diana A643
King, Francis P247
King, Fraser W202
King, Gregory C. (Valero Energy) A868
King, Gregory E. (MidSouth Bancorp) E235
King, Ian W53
King, James D. (Scotts Miracle-Gro) A742
King, Jeff (Barkley Evergreen & Partners) P73
King, Jeffrey J. (Expeditors) A331
King, Jim (Brightpoint Inc.) A159
King, John E. (Perot Systems) A656
King, John R. (Weatherford International) A894
King, Jon J. (Benchmark Electronics) A139
King, Jon M. (Tiffany) A820

King, Joshua A. A408
King, Justin W174
King, Kelly S. A128
King, Kimberly N. A481
King, Mark (adidas) W26
King, Mark A. (Affiliated Computer Services) A45
King, Michael H. E173
King, Pamela A498
King, Robert C. A651
King, Roger M. A192
King, Ronald (Apollo Group) A96
King, Ronald S. (Western Family) P529
King, Russell W41
King, Shauna R. P538
King, Stephen Dale (Hewitt Associates) A425
King, Stephen M. (Dave & Buster's) P160
King, Steven (Hitachi) W151
King, Thomas A. (Progressive Corporation) A687
King, Thomas B. (PG&E) A662
King, Thomas S. (American Family Insurance) P43
King, Tim (Brookshire Grocery) P102
King, Timothy J. (KeyCorp) A486
King, Vivian P424
King, W. Russell A364
King, William H. (Danaher) A260
King, William K. (State Farm) A784, P459
Kinghorn, Dwain A. E27
King-Lavinder, Joyce A227
Kingo, Lise W242
Kingsbury, Thomas A. A496
Kingsdale, Jon M. P491
Kingsley, James D. A238
Kingsley, Robert T. E230
Kingsley, Stuart A. E110
Kingston, John III E21
Kini, M. Narendra P487
Kinkela, David P216
Kinley, Colin B. E215
Kinloch, Jim W174
Kinnel, Russel E240
Kinnen, Michael R. P515
Kinney, Catherine R. A623
Kinney, Mike A528
Kinney, Valerie P67
Kinohara, Mikio W102
Kinoshita, Kenji W185
Kinoshita, Mitsuo W349
Kinsch, Joseph W222
Kinscherff, R. Paul A151
Kinschner, William H. A538
Kinsella, Mike P169
Kinsella, W. M. W39
Kinser, Dennis P65
Kinsey, Keith P363
Kinsey, R. Steve A349
Kintzinger, Douglas P. P266
Kinzey, Cara A699
Kinzie, Jack L. P72
Kinzler, Alexander C. E49
Kinzler, Morton H. E49
Kip, Jeffrey W. E271
Kipkie, William B. W166
Kiplin, Kimberly P477
Kiplinger, Austin H. P148
Kira, Yasuhiro W371
Kiraç, Suna W184
Kiraly, Thomas E. P141
Kirby, C. Eugene A790
Kirby, J. Scott A863
Kirby, James E249
Kirby, Suz Ann P499
Kirchner, Bruce P312
Kirchoffner, Donald P. A329
Kirincic, Paul E. A559
Kiriyama, Takahira W320
Kirk, Adelle A523
Kirk, David B. A621

Kirk, Matthew W358
Kirk, Stephen F. A532
Kirk Kristiansen, Kjeld W198
Kirkby, Robert W. W66
Kirkham, Brian L. E154
Kirkland, George L. A205
Kirkland, Ronald E. A47
Kirkpatrick, Keith P386
Kirley, Tim P273
Kirpalani, Rohit H. E98
Kirsch, Jason E277
Kirsch, Nancy P263
Kirscher, Elizabeth E240
Kirshner, Alan I. A540
Kirst, Fred L. A837, P489
Kirsten, A. Stefan W341
Kirsten, Reiner W120
Kirtland, Mark E267
Kirtley, Melvyn A820
Kirven, Cathy Y. A737
Kirwan, Karen S. A852
Kiser, Glenn P303
Kiser, Jason A307
Kish, Thomas C. E271
Kishi, Eiji W315
Kishida, Katsuhiko W371
Kishimoto, Isao W192
Kislak, Lisa H. P135
Kispert, John H. A491
Kissel, W. Craig A82
Kissinger, James G. A776
Kistenbroker, David H. P277
Kistner, Fred E. E339
Kistner-L'Hour, Estelle W262
Kita, Satoru W102
Kitabayashi, Hironori W245
Kitabayashi, Katsuhiko W37
Kitagawa, Mitsuo W233
Kitajima, Yoshinari W101
Kitajima, Yoshitoshi W101
Kitamura, Masaji W185
Kitamura, Yoshihiko W182
Kitaoka, Masayoshi W190
Kitchell, Samuel F. P283
Kitchen, Denise P469
Kitchen, Donna C. E156
Kitchen, Mike P426
Kitchin, Kraig A221
Kitei, Lisa P268
Kitson, John D. P197
Kitsos, Costas E57
Kittelberger, Larry E. A435
Kittenbrink, Douglas A. A60
Kitterman, James M. E340
Kittoe, Larry P164
Kitz, Edward G. P424
Kitzmiller, James W146
Kivisto, Thomas L. P439
Kiyama, Hiroshi W223
Kiyono, Shinji W102
Kizilbash, Imran A740
Kjellman, Jan W160
Klaben, Matthew J. E81
Klaeser, Dennis L. E292
Klaey, Hans-Peter W298
Klaidman, Daniel A891
Klane, Larry A. A178
Klann, Jason W300
Klapatch, Tom P454
Klarik, Wendy E166
Klarr, James P. A504
Klass, Stephen P. P502
Klatsky, Bruce J. A664
Klatt, David A. Jr. A602
Klatzkin, Terri D. P133
Klaus, L. George E134
Klaus, Lauri E134
Klausner, Jeffrey E189
Klausner, Steven A876
Klawitter, Susan A409
Klebe, Terry A. A244
Klehm, Henry W111
Kleiber, Bob E117

Kleidermacher, David P222
Kleifges, James W. P257
Kleiman, Steve A598
Klein, Barbara A. A193
Klein, Christopher J. A357
Klein, Danny E40
Klein, Dean A. A573
Klein, Harvey S. P209
Klein, James F. P197
Klein, John (Young's Market) P539
Klein, John E. (Cognizant Tech Solutions) E90
Klein, Paul P418
Klein, Peter P29
Klein, Philippe W273
Klein, Pierre W347
Klein, Ronald H. A264
Klein, Russell B. A169
Klein, Stephen M. E264
Klein, Thomas A724
Kleinbaum, Linda P328
Kleiner, Madeleine A. A429
Kleiner, Rolf E. A484
Kleinert, Robert W. Jr. A133
Kleinfeld, Klaus W307
Kleinke, J.D. E171
Kleinman, Harold F. P325
Kleinschmidt, Robert P113
Kleisner, Theodore J. A256
Kleisterlee, Gerard W255
Klema, Thomas E. E308
Kleman, Lee P164
Klemann, Gilbert L. II A117
Klemens, Bryon L. A421
Klemm, Erich W103
Klemp, Jeff A583
Kleopfer, Stuart G. A144
Klepchick, Andrew R. A795
Klepper, Kenneth O. A562
Klesse, William R. A868
Kletjian, Richard J. P495
Kletjian, Robert P. P495
Kletjian, Steven C. P495
Klett, John M. E103
Klettner, Janice A463
Kletz, Patti Ann P327
Kleva, Jim P64
Klevan, Leonard A99
Kliem, Jurgen E358
Klier, Helmut W180
Klim, Olivia M. E51
Klima, Viktor W360
Klimas, Steve A217
Klimes, Elizabeth H. A315
Klinck, John L. A564
Klinck, Kenneth J. E307
Kline, Doug A748
Kline, Howard P278
Kline, James E. A246
Kline, John R. A236
Kline, Ken E359
Kline, Lowry F. A227
Kline, Thomas A127
Klinefelter, Christopher W. A234
Kling, Robert A665
Klingensmith, James A427, P241
Klingensmith, Rick L. A677
Klinger, Douglas E. E239
Klinges, Vincent C. E221
Klink, David C. P47
Klinker, Charles P446
Kliphuis, Tom W169
Klippel, Charles H. A44
Klipper, Kenneth E146
Klipper, Mitchell S. A125
Klocke, Tina E66
Kloeters, Michael W35
Klomparens, Karen L. P329
Kloosterboer, Jay A43
Kloosterman, Lex W22, W132
Kloppers, Marius W67
Klotter, David E. E242
Kluempke, Patrick A207

A = AMERICAN BUSINESS
E = EMERGING COMPANIES
P = PRIVATE COMPANIES
W = WORLD BUSINESS

Kozlowski, Mark P404
Kozouz, Rana P196
Kozuback, Richard E159
Kozy, William A. A134
Kraeger, Rob P123
Kraemer, Harry M. J. Jr. P142
Kraemer, Jan P316
Kraemer, Robert B. P396
Kraeutler, John A. E231
Kraf, Teri J. E297
Krafft, Kay W65
Kraft, Alan H. P331
Kraft, Michael A. (Ceradyne) E79
Kraft, Michael J. (CenterPoint Properties) P124
Kraft, Ron A175, P108
Kraftsik, Leo Günther W180
Krahling, Thomas J. E334
Krajewski, Steven J. P483
Krakaur, Kenneth M. P439
Krakora, Kevin J. A276
Krakowsky, Philippe A459
Kral, Robert M. A882
Krall, David A. E45
Kramer, Bruce A. E368
Kramer, Francis J. E16
Kramer, Gary L. P70
Kramer, J. Matthew A232
Kramer, Jack (CVS) A258
Kramer, James S. E41
Kramer, Jeffrey A52
Kramer, John M. (Sypris Solutions) E343
Kramer, Larry D. P458
Kramer, Marc C. A646
Kramer, Michael W. A32
Kramer, Phillip D. A671
Kramer, Randy S. A678
Kramer, Richard J. A392
Kramer, Robert G. Sr. E128
Kramer, Stephen S. P129
Kramm, Kenneth P198
Krammer, Michael W189
Kranc, Lisa R. A112
Krane, Harold P66
Krane, Hilary K. A515, P294
Kranzley, Arthur D. A550
Krasik, Carl A564
Krasnoff, Eric A641
Krasnostein, David M. W226
Kratcoski, Leslie H. A131
Kratochvil, James M. P100
Kratovil, Edward D. A867
Krattebol, David M. A205
Kratter, Leslie M. A362
Kratz, Owen E. E175
Kraupp, Michael J. A760
Kraus, Peter S. A390
Kraus, Timothy J. A536
Kraus, Walter H. W143
Kraus, William (CIGNA) A211
Kraus, William J. (Under Armour) E361
Krause, Carol F. E260
Krause, Daryl A772
Krause, David E. P129
Krause, Douglas P. E123
Krause, Roy G. A775
Krause, Stefan W68
Krause, Tom E347
Krauss, Clifford H. E124
Krautter, Jochen W150
Kravas, Connie P508
Kravis, Henry R. A494, P285
Krawcheck, Sallie L. A218
Krawitz, Natalie R. P505
Kraynick, John A. A801
Krch, Cindy P534

Kreager, Heather P427
Krebs, Sean A370
Kredi, Saul P44
Kreditor, Alan P507
Kreeger, Craig S. A87
Kreh, Susan M. A676
Krehbiel, Frederick A. (Molex) A577
Krehbiel, Frederick L. (Molex) A577
Krehbiel, John H. Jr. A577
Kreider, Torsten A255
Kreidler, Robert C. A922
Kreimeyer, Andreas W59
Kreinberg, Romeo A287
Kreindler, Peter M. A435
Krekeler, Hans-Dirk W111
Krekeler, Richard W247
Kremer, Andrew F. A466
Kremer, Don F. P126
Kremin, Alan P256
Krenek, Alan E50
Krenicki, John Jr. A379
Krentz, Lenore L. P200
Kreplin, Klaus W298
Kreps, Steven M. A206
Kresa, Kent A113, P114
Kreter, Paul E376
Kretzman, Peter E287
Kretzman, Robert K. III A708
Kreuser, Paul G. P302
Krevans, Sarah P465
Kreykes, William P487
Krick, Robert W. A83, A845
Krieger, Burton C. P97
Krieger, Zvi E268
Krier, Cindy T. P508
Krier, Mary A349
Krigbaum, Stephen A68
Kripalani, Ranjit A250
Krishnamurthy, Nirup N. A613
Krishnan, Sabu P24
Krishnan, Sekhar W308
Krishock, David A. A703
Krislov, Marvin P504
Kristal, Sam P279
Kristensen, Orla W88
Kristiansen, Sue A648
Kristoff, John D. A277
Kristoffersen, Helle W34
Krivsky, William A. E89
Kroeger, John F. P389
Kroenke, E. Stanley P138, P168
Krogsgaard-Larsen, Povl W88
Krois, Rod P53
Krol, Joseph A. A643
Kroll, Carolyn E102
Kroll, Nicholas W78
Kroll, Robert P525
Kroll, Teresa E66
Kromer, Mary Lou A361
Kromidas, Larry A. A628
Kroner, Norbert P. P163
Kronick, Susan D. A337
Kronschnabl, Peter W68
Krop, Pamela S. A729
Kropp, Ronald D. A446
Krott, Joseph P. A789
Krow, Gary A. A197
Krubasik, Edward G. W307
Krueger, David G. A165
Krueger, Dorrie E66
Krueger, Michael P440
Kruger, Logan W. W166
Kruger, Paula A698
Kruger, Roland W68
Krugle, Mike P208
Kruglov, Andrei Vyacheslavovich W140
Kruhly, Leslie Laird P506
Kruk, Bernadette M. P435
Krull, Stephen K. A638
Krumnow, Jürgen W350
Krump, Paul J. A208
Krüper, Manfred W125
Krupinski, Steve A203

Kruse, D. Patrick P494
Kruse, Stein A186
Kruszka, Jerome M. E384
Krutick, Jill S. A888
Krutter, Forrest N. A140
Kryder, Mark A744
Krzeminski, James A. P86
Krzesinski, George P371
Krzywosz, Vincent P143
Kuba, Tetsuo W192
Kubasik, Christopher E. A525
Kubek, Anne A153
Kubera, Daniel A168
Kubo, Koshichiro W37
Kubodera, Masao W343
Kubota, Akira W315
Kubota, Kenji W303
Kucheman, William H. A155
Küchler, Gunter W204
Kuck, Timothy W. P500
Kuechle, Scott E. A391
Kueck, Mark P75
Kuehl, Robert A. E273
Kuehn, Kurt P. A850
Kuehn, Ronald L. Jr. A311
Kuehne, Carl W. P43
Kuffner, Charles P. P467
Kugler, Joe A312
Kuhbach, Robert G. A285
Kuhl, Edward J. P305
Kuhlman, Erin M. P378
Kuhn, Bob E293
Kuhn, Edwin P. P486
Kuhn, Eric J. E375
Kühn, Klaus W60
Kuhn, Ron J. A131
Kuhn, Stephen L. P313
Kuhns, Cleo R. A187
Kuiper, Joost Ch. L. W22
Kukowski, Dale P290
Kukura, Sergei P. W205
Kulhanek, Timothy A. A839
Kulikowski, Thomas J. P474
Kulka, Jeffrey S. P28
Kullman, Ellen J. A297
Kullman, Timothy E. A659
Kulovaara, Harri A717
Kulthol, May A782
Kumagai, Akihiko W304
Kumagai, Bunya W244
Kumakura, Ichiro W176
Kumano, Yoshimaru W305
Kumar, Biren A299
Kumar, Madhu W64
Kumar, Niranjan P112
Kumar, Pratik W366
Kumar, R. K. Krishna W324
Kumar, Ravi P112
Kumar, Sanjay P358
Kumar, Satyendra W168
Kumar, Shiv E139
Kumar, Sunil P259
Kumar, Surinder A913
Kumar, TLV A99
Kumazawa, Masami W230
Kummant, Alexander P51
Kümmel, Gerhard W279
Kumpf, Sue P160
Kuna, Mark L. E267
Kunberger, George A. Jr. A466
Kuncic, Ana-Barbara W246
Kundert, David J. A479
Kundert, Glen A770
Kundrun, Bernd W65
Kuner, Christopher P249
Kunes, Richard W. A325
Kuniansky, Max A59
Kunii, Hideko W276
Kunimura, Robert E67
Kunin, David B. A705
Kunin, Myron A705
Kunis, Suzanne A535
Kunk, James E. A440

Kunkel, Joseph S. A184
Kunkel, Thomas A730
Kuntz, Edward L. A489
Kuntz, Kevin P316
Kuntz, Richard A563
Kunz, Detlev J. A592
Kunz, Heidi P92
Kunz, John E. A807
Kunz, Thomas W105
Kuo, Feng E347
Kuo, Yuyun Tristan E107
Kupchak, Mitch P300
Kupper, William P. Jr. A558
Küppers, Rainer W225
Kuppinger, Mike P281
Kuprionis, M. Denise A328
Kupstas, Michael J. E271
Kurer, Peter W351
Kurian, Thomas A633
Kurihara, Seiichiro W256
Kurikawa, Katsutoshi W233
Kuritzkes, Michael S. A788
Kurkowski, Richard M. P457
Kurland, David P127
Kurland, Larry A449
Kurland, Stanford L. A250
Kurnick, Robert H. Jr. P383
Kuroda, Hiroshi W154
Kuroe, Tsuneo W371
Kurokawa, Hiroaki W137
Kuropatwa, Hans W358
Kurowski, Mike P138
Kuroyanagi, Nobuo W219
Kurtenbach, Aelred J. E111
Kurtenbach, Frank J. E111
Kurtenbach, Reece A. E111
Kurth, Wolfgang P. P339
Kurtin, Ronnie A755
Kurtz, Larry A559
Kurtz, Mark P227
Kurtzhals, Peter W242
Kurtzman, Gary J. A726
Kurushima, Masakazu P107
Kurvers, Tom P151
Kurz, Karl F. A88
Kurzius, Lawrence A554
Kusaka Fraser, Kathy A806
Kusama, Saburo W303
Küsel, Ottmar C. W364
Kushar, Kent A300, P181
Kushner, Jurij Z. A126
Kushner, Terry A649
Kusmierski, Jeanine E41
Kussell, Will P180
Kuster, Andrew A28
Kutaragi, Ken W315
Kutka, J. James Jr. A854
Kutscher, Lawrence M. A296
Kutsovsky, Yakov A174
Kuwabara, Akito W232
Kux, Barbara W255
Kuykendall, William P206
Kuzman, John J. A54
Kvitko, Mike A335
Kwakkel, Rinus W367
Kwan, Mary A696
Kwasny, David P191
Kwatek, Irwin L. E358
Kwederis, Joseph J. P392
Kwock, Danny A696
Kwok, Josiah C. L. W155
Kwok, Ling E269
Kwon, Hyung-Suk W247
Kwon, Oh-Joon W261
Kwon, Young-Tae W261
Kydland, Torgeir W238
Kyle, David L. A632
Kyle, John F. W163
Kyllo, Brenda W93
Kypreos, Nick M. P490
Kyriakou, Linda G. A749
Kyser, Kevin A46

A = AMERICAN BUSINESS
E = EMERGING COMPANIES
P = PRIVATE COMPANIES
W = WORLD BUSINESS

Larson, David R. (Anadarko Petroleum) A88
Larson, Eric P95
Larson, Gary (Lennox) A512
Larson, Gary L. (Hillenbrand) A428
Larson, Gregg M. A26
Larson, Jeffery E. E62
Larson, John E. P354
Larson, Kent T. A917
Larson, Linda P404
Larson, Paula W170
Larson, Robert J. A219
Larson, Stephen R. (Esterline) E135
Larson, Steven G. (LaserCard) E213
Larson, Thomas D. A207
Larson, William B. A232
Larsson, Kent A.W. A143
Larsson, William D. A680
Lartigue, Jean-Bernard W348
LaRussa, Benny P264
LaRusso, Frank A543
LaSala, Joseph A. Jr. A618
LaSala, Thomas F. E261
LaSalle, Gar P471
Lasater, Edward B. A199
Lasater, Roger D. A199
Laschober, Glen C. A629
Lashinsky, Joseph P. E395
Lasky, William M. A470
LaSorda, Thomas W. W103
LaSorsa, Louis P388
Laspa, Jude A132, P79
Laspisa, Esther K. A425
Lassa, Judith M. P94
Lassen, Lars Christian W242
Lassonde, Pierre A603
Lassus, Bruno E88
Lassus, Don P537
Lastrina, Stacy A476
Lataille, Ron A872
Latham, L. Paul E86
Lathe, Timothy J. A589
Latimer, Chad S. E27
Latimer, David P386
Latimer, Matthew D. P46
Lato, Giovanni P251
Latta, G. Michael A874
Lattmann, Susan E. A136
Latzer, Julie P227
Lau, James K. A598
Lau, Jose E321
Laub, John W351
Laube, Richard T. W228
Laubies, Pierre A543, P310
Lauda, Thomas C. A738
Laudati, Thomas E188
Laudato, Andy A665
Lauder, Evelyn H. A325
Lauder, Leonard A. A325
Lauder, William P. A325
Lauderbach, John P363
Lauderdale, Katherine P401
Laudicino, Stephan P302
Lauer, Elizabeth E107
Lauer, John N. A276
Lauer, Stefan (Lufthansa) W204
Lauer, Steven K. (Topco Associates) P481
Laufer, Robert C. P462
Laughery, Tom W145
Lauman, Laura A99
Launer, Leland C. Jr. A569
Laurain, Steve P60
Laurell, Marianne W335
Laurello, David J. P462
Lauren, David A674
Lauren, Jerome A674
Lauren, Ralph A674

Laurence, Guy W358
Laurent-Ottomane, Charlotte W34
Laurino, Carl J. A536
Laursen, Thomas E. A924
Laus, Christopher A. P51
Lauterbach, Tom P226
Lautzenheiser, Dennis P38
Lauve, Davis J. P492
Lauxen, Bob P279
Lavalette, Gordon P354, P355
LaValle, Joseph M. E324
Lavallee, Robert H. E179
LaValley, Dan P434
LaValley, James D. A893
Lavandier, Bruno A586
LaVanway, D. Keith P63
Lavayssière, Bertrand W86
LaVecchia, Jean M. A612
Lavelle, Kate P180
Lavely, Jerry A649
Lavender, Kevin P. A342
Lavenir, Frédéric W69
Laverty Elsenhans, Lynn A755
Lavet, Robert S. A761
Lavey, Richard W. A401
Lavi, Smadar E268
Lavin, Leonard H. A56
Lavin, O. Paul E364
Lavin, Richard P. A188
Lavin, Sheldon P371
Lavine, Gilbert S. P104
LaViolette, Paul A. A155
Laviolette, Peter P115
Lavizzo-Mourey, Risa J. P420
Lavoie, Luc W268
Lavrack, Wayne P206
Lawhorn, Caron A. A632
Lawing, Douglas L. E102
Lawler, James G. W284
Lawler, John A296
Lawler, Julia M. A683
Lawler, Michael F. P474
Lawler, Paul J. P535
Lawless, Anette W277
Lawless, Robert J. A554
Lawlor, James E. P495
Lawrence, James A. A380
Lawrence, Jeffrey D. A284
Lawrence, Josh P489
Lawrence, Mary Beth A448
Lawrence, Robert A. (FMR) P199
Lawrence, Robert H. Jr. (UST) A867
Lawrence, Rodney D. P442
Lawrence, Stephanie W198
Lawrence, Stewart A88
Lawrence, Taylor W. A701
Lawrence, William A850
Lawrence, Zach P198
Lawrence-Lightfoot, Sara P304
Laws, Stuart G. P158
Laws, Theodore H. Jr. A351
Lawson, A. Peter A582
Lawson, David G. (Universal Hospital) P500
Lawson, David R. (Capital One) A178
Lawson, Eugene F. III E264
Lawson, Peter M. A414
Lawson, Rodger A. A689
Lawson, Thomas A. P191
Lawther Krill, Katherine A93
Lawton, Jennifer W301
Lawton, Michael T. A284
Laxton, Stephen D. A620
Lay, Daniel M. E148
Laybourne, Stanley A451
Layman, David A. A504
Laymon, Joe W. A355
Layzell, Stacey P532
Lazar, Eliot J. P362
Lazar, Jack R. E42
Lazarewicz, Garry E188
Lazaridis, Elaine P40
Lazarus, Barry L. P256, P257

Lazarus, Rob P381
Lazarus, Ronald S. E367
Lazo, Philip A794
Lazor, Linda P391
Le Beau, William M. E275
Le Bouc, Hervé W72
Le Brouster, Jean-Yves W355
Le Corre, Eric W216
Le Corvec, Alain W255
Le Fur, Gérard W295
Le Goff, Alain W271
Le Grignou, Philippe W47
Le Jeune, Martin W79
Le Lay, Patrick W72
Le Mener, Georges W23
Le Poidevin, Andrew W92
Leach, Bobby W358
Leach, Stephen D. E268
Leach, Thomas D. A834
Leaf, Craig P49
Leahey, Patrick E197
Leahy, Christine A. A193
Leahy, John J. W30
Leahy, Martha P83
Leahy, Peter G. A785
Leahy, Terry P. W338
Leak, Kevin P521
Leaman, Stephen J. W373
Leamer, Marybeth H. A251, P150
Leaming, Paul W40
Leamon, Jerry P. W106
Leape, James P161
Learish, John A711
Learmouth, Duncan W145
Leary, John P. A856
Leatherby, Dennis A843
Leathers, Derek J. A898
Leavitt, Oliver P57
Leavy, Bob P218
Leavy, David P172
Lebda, Douglas R. A442
Lebel, Jean-Jacques W203
LeBel, Marc E283
LeBel, Timothy A543, P310
Lebens, Michael C. P474
Leblanc, Bernard W139
LeBlanc, Floyd J. A194
LeBlanc, Joseph H. Jr. E132
LeBlanc, Leonard J. E264
Lebolt, David M. E45
Lebow, Jodi P205
Lebrat, Didier W79
LeBrun, Patrick W355
Lebson, Evan M. A384
LeCalsey, Louis III E359
Lechleiter, John C. A315
Lechleiter, Richard A. A489
Lechner, Alfred J. Jr. A841
Lechner, David E. P505
Leckman, Linda C. P258
Leclair, Donat R. A354
Leclaire, Bruno W194
Lecuona, Miguel P217
Ledbetter, Bureon E. Jr. P128
Ledbetter, Cheryl P264
Lederer, Ann E. E151
Ledford, Nancy A302
Ledford, Randall D. A319
Lednicky, Lynn A299
Ledwith, Lon F. E58
Ledwith, Steven M. E357
Lee, Billie (First Advantage) E143
Lee, Bonita I. E246
Lee, Brett Daniel P129
Lee, Bruce K. A342
Lee, Bryan R. P152
Lee, Catherine C. (Sempra Energy) A748
Lee, Chih-Tsun W130
Lee, Chong-Moon E246
Lee, Chung-Shing A814
Lee, Dakota E42
Lee, David B. E262

Lee, Dennis E225
Lee, Dong-Hee W261
Lee, Douglas A. P326
Lee, Gloria E322
Lee, Greg A. (Coca-Cola Enterprises) A227
Lee, Greg L. (Nexity) E255
Lee, Greg W. (Tyson Foods) A843
Lee, Hak-Soo W292
Lee, James B. Jr. (JPMorgan Chase) A479
Lee, James W. (Stater Bros.) P461
Lee, Jerry S. A391
Lee, John (New Orleans Hornets) P355
Lee, John C. Jr. (Old Dominion Electric) P370
Lee, John M. (Trinity Industries) A835
Lee, John Walter II (RC2) E300
Lee, Katherine Spencer (Robert Half) A712
Lee, Kun-Hee W292
Lee, Ku-Taek W261
Lee, Mario P103
Lee, Michael H. (ENGlobal) E132
Lee, Michael H. (Tower Group) E356
Lee, Nigel A344
Lee, Peter Y. W. W155
Lee, Raymond W. H. W55
Lee, Rebecca F. A33
Lee, Regina A110
Lee, Robert E. Jr. E139
Lee, Soo-Chang W292
Lee, Spencer S. E83
Lee, Stanley E269
Lee, Stephen Ching Yen (Singapore Airlines) W309
Lee, Stephen R. (OraSure) E267
Lee, Steven C. (TravelCenters of America) P486
Lee, Steven U. (Vance Publishing) P512
Lee, Terry A573
Lee, Thai P448
Lee, Theresa K. A302
Lee, Thomas (Multi-Fineline Electronix) E243
Lee, Tommy (NVIDIA) A621
Lee, V. Paul A312
Lee, Wayne E357
Lee, William A. (Gilead Sciences) A385
Lee, Yong-Soon W292
Lee, Youn W261
Lee, Yuchun E362
Lee, Yun-Woo W292
Leech, Paul P180
Lee-Chung, Sonya A93
Leedle, Ben R. Jr. E173
Leeds, Candace A526
Leeds, Eric M. A682
Leedy, Brian E91
Leedy, Shelly D. E132
Leehealey, Tim E167
Leekley, John R. A548
Leemputte, Peter G. A168
Leenaars, Eli P. W169
Leeney, David E297
Leer, Steven F. A103
Lees, David W325
Leets, Karen L. A866
Leever, Karen A492
Lefar, Marc P131
LeFave, Richard T. C. A776
Lefebvre, Françoise W114
Lefebvre, Laurel A780
LeFever, Jeff A673
Lefevre, Gordon W226
Lefèvre, Jacques W194
Leff, Daniel V. E169
Leffel, Keith E161
Lefkowitz, Bruce A359
Lefler, Vern R. P25
Lefort, Neil A577
LeFrak, Harrison P292
LeFrak, James P292

A = AMERICAN BUSINESS
E = EMERGING COMPANIES
P = PRIVATE COMPANIES
W = WORLD BUSINESS

Lichtenstein, Morris A443
Lichtenstein, Susan R. A127
Lichtenstein, Warren G. E364
Lichtman, Marc J. E346
Lico, James A. A260
Liddell, Christopher P. A574
Liddell, Kim C. E71
Liddell, Mike E167
Liddle, Lynn M. A284
Liddy, Brian P434
Liddy, Edward M. A66
Lidiard, Mark W67
Lidvall, Ned R. P420
Lieb, Gregory P. A532
Lieb, Jeanne R. P191
Lieb, Peter A597
Liebel, Hartmut A464
Liebentritt, Donald J. A323
Lieberman, Edward P388
Lieberman, Evelyn S. P447
Lieberman, Gerald M. P36, W50
Lieberman, Stephen A844
Liebert, Carl C. III A434
Liebman, Jeannette A100
Liebmann, Kathy A504
Liedel, Christopher A. P347
Liedtke, Donald G. A45
Liedtke, Eric W26
Lienenbrugger, Herbert G. P381
Lienhard, Jerome T. II A790
Lienhart, Ross M. A680
Liepmann, Holger A30
Liesen, Klaus W125
Liewald, Robert W. E164
Liftin, John M. A124
Ligan, Warren J. A766
Light, Brian T. A780
Light, Geoff A850
Light, Lawrence A556
Ligocki, Kathleen A. A829
Ligon, Duke R. A275
Liguori, Peter A359
Liguori, Robert A549
Like, Steve P379
Liles, Kevin A888
Liles, T. Allen E71
Lilien, R. Jarrett A326
Lilienthal, Stephen W. A224
Liljegren, Paul F. A921
Lillard, John S. E392
Lillard, Richard S. A706
Lilley, David A259
Lilley, Robert McG. E117
Lillie, Charisse R. A230
Lillis, James J. A193
Lilly, Kevin (AGCO) A49
Lilly, Kevin L. (SPX) A778
Lilly, Peter B. A238
Lilly, Steven L. P350
Lim, Eunice U. E168
Lim, Helen A321
Lim, Jean E391
Limbacher, Randy L. A235
Limback, Mark E369
Liming, Dave P50
Limongelli, Victor E167
Lin, C. T. W326
Lin, H. H. W326
Lin, Han-Fu W130
Lin, James W168
Lin, Jason W130
Lin, Sandra Beach A113
Lin, Tingsheng W326
Lin, W. T. W326
Lin, Weishan W326
Lin, Yu-Lun E366
Linaberger, Jacob B. E339
Linardakis, Connie A924

Linares López, Julio W330
Linari, Giovanni W46
Linaugh, Mark W369
Linch, Robert O. P239
Lind, Philip B. W281
Lind, Tacy P363
Lindahl, Richard S. A776
Lindbæk, Jannik W316
Lindberg, Randle E. A849
Lindberg, Steven C. A870
Lindbloom, Chad M. A198
Lindemann, Ellen N. A770
Lindemann, George L. A771
Lindemann, James J. A319
Linden, Derek W. A587, P343
Lindenmeyer, Peter A825
Linder, Alois W150
Linder, Greg W. (Abbott Labs) A30
Linder, Gregg (Scarborough Research) P432
Linder, James M. E110
Linder, Mary Carroll A616
Linder, Wolfgang W247
Linderman, Tricia E352
Lindgren, Lars W299
Lindgren, Timothy P465
Lindholm, Wayne S. P240
Lindler, Patricia T. A413
Lindner, Carl H. (American Financial) A77
Lindner, Carl H. III (American Financial) A77
Lindner, Janet E. P538
Lindner, Richard G. A109
Lindner, S. Craig A77
Lindpaintner, Klaus W280
Lindsay, Judith A. E96
Lindsay, Mark A858
Lindsay, Richard J. P467
Lindsay, Robert T. A156
Lindsay, Roger W. A824
Lindsay, Ronald C. A302
Lindseth, Alfred A. A671
Lindsey, Dennis P247
Lindsey, Frank P141
Lindsey, John E114
Lindsey, Richard O. E78
Lindskog, Åse W126
Linebarger, Dale P59
Linebarger, N. Thomas A257
Linecar, Richard E327
Linehan, D. Patrick A598
Linehan, Steve A178
Lines, Phil P262
Ling, Dennis A117
Ling, Robert M. Jr. P496
Lingen, Charles B. P454
Lingo, Michael P60
Linhardt, Karlin A. P103
Linhart, Michael J. A246
Link, Doug E190
Link, Loree A796
Link, Mark A. A316
Linklater, William J. A119, P71
Linn, W. Michael E261
Linnebank, Geert W275
Linnen, Joseph C. P273
Linnert, Terrence G. A391
Linney, Reid A42
Linse, Kees W287
Linsert, Henry Jr. E226
Linsky, Barry R. A459
Linsky, Melissa L. P227
Linsky, Michele A. E207
Linstrom, Steve P435
Lintner, Alexander M. A460
Lintner, Nancy T. A856
Linton, Michael A. A142
Linton, Thomas K. P105
Linton, William A. (Promega) P399
Linton, William W. (Rogers Communications) W281
Linville, Randal L. P436

Linzner, Charles A163
Linzner, Joel A312
Liolios, Tom J. E108
Liollio, Constantine S. A194
Lione, Gail A. A403
Lipe, Perry L. A106
Liphart, Will P158
Lipke, Brian J. P276
Lipman, Gustave K. P225
Lipman, Ira A. P225
Lipman, Joshua S. P225
Lipman, M. Benjamin P225
Lipp, Marie P144
Lippens, Maurice W132
Lippert, Jason D. E120
Lippert, Karl W290
Lippert, L. Douglas E120
Lippert, Martin J. W285
Lippert, Philip A. A915
Lippincott, Christopher G. E326
Lipsanen, Juho W335
Lipscomb, James L. A569
Lipscomb, Jeffrey W. P130
Lipscomb, Michael S. P58
Lipsett, Robert F. W163
Lipski, Wayne E183
Lipsky, Charles I. P395
Lipsky, John A479
Lipstein, Steven H. P87
Lipton, Martin P360
Lis, Daniel T. A484
Lischer, Charles D. A227
Lisenby, Terry S. A620
Liske, Stefan W360
Lisman, Eric I. P25
Liss, Anne P126
Liss, Walter C. Jr. A31
Lissowski, Antoine W94
List, John J. P350
Lister, David W275
Listi, Frank P212
Liston, Thomas J. A439
Listug, Kurt P470
L'Italien, Carroll W70
Litman, Peter E34
Litrell, Kathee A375
Little, Blake E328
Little, Caroline H. A891
Little, Daniel F. A609
Little, Gavin D. A710, W76
Little, Mark A. (Remington Arms) P415
Little, Mark M. (GE) A379
Little, Mike (Feld Entertainment) P196
Little, Mike (J.F. Shea) P267
Little, Rita A136
Little, Robert P278
Littlefield, Ralph L. Jr. A649
Littlejohn, Stephen E. A332
Littlepage, Melton E. III P205
Littleton, John W. E56
Littman, Joel A. E104
Litton, Richard H. A340
Littrell, Barry A183
Littrell, Terry J. A588
Litwak, James A. A831
Litwin, Jim P515
Litzsinger, R. Mark P201
Liu, C.S. A592
Liu, Don H. A826
Liu, John D. E162
Liu, Joseph Y. E264
Liu, Lillian E107
Liu, Nina A778
Liu, Stanley P376
Liutkus, Tom P486
Liveris, Andrew N. A287
Livermore, Ann M. A426
Livingston, Brian W. W163
Livingston, Harold H. E303
Livingston, Ian P. W80
Livingston, John T. P480
Livingston, Phil E363

Livingston, Randall S. P458
Livingston, Rob (Topa Equities) P480
Livingston, Robert A. (Dover) A285
Livingstone, Michelle P109
Lizak, Steven E219
Llewellyn, W. Joseph P314
Lloyd, Anne H. A547
Lloyd, David G. P83
Lloyd, Emily P140
Lloyd, Geoff W30
Lloyd, JoAnn E374
Lloyd, Mike W283
Lloyd, Monty C. E192
Lloyd, Rjay P202
Lloyd, Robert (Cisco Systems) A216
Lloyd, Robert A. (GameStop) A367
Lloyd, Thomas E. E321
Llurba, Matteo W372
Lo, Helena E300
Lo, Sophia A397
Loader, Adrian W287
Lobacki, Joseph M. A384
Löbbe, Klaus Peter W59
Loberti, Joe A81
LoCascio, Robert P. E220
Löchelt, Dieter W68
Lock, Andrew J. A420
Lock, Chris A280, P174
Lockard, John A. P352
Lockard, Richard A366
Locke, Deborah S. P111
Locke, William S. E286
Lockhart, Bruce R. E79
Lockhart, Gary C. A28
Lockie, Anne W285
Lockman, David P299
Lockridge, B. Russell A168
Lockwood, Kenneth H. A350
Locutura, Enrique W372
Locutura Rupérez, Enrique W274
Lodis, Steve P148
Lodovic, Joseph J. IV P320
Loebbaka, Charles R. P365
Loebl, Margaret M. A38
Loeffler, Robert D. P234
Loehr, Kathleen E. P45
Loepp, Daniel J. P91
Loesch, George A177
Loesch, Mary Beth P22
Loescher, Peter A567
Loffreda, Brigid P136
Loffredo, Kenneth P141
Loffredo, Nicholas L. A765
Lofgren, Anders A172
Lofgren, Christina A825
Lofgren, Christopher B. P433
Löf-Jennische, Lennart W299
Loflin, Brian P250
Loftin, Nancy C. A667
Loftis, Harry E. P418
Lofton, Deborah C. E190
Lofton, Kevin E. P119
Lofts, Philip J. W351
Loftus, Brian P280
Loftus, John A. Jr. A726
Loftus, Thomas R. E382
Logan, George W. E374
Logan, James L. E333
Logan, Mark P73
Logan, Stanley N. E183
Loggia, Joseph P25
Lograsso, John P496
Logue, Ronald E. A785
Loh, Meng See W309
Lohman, John H. Jr. A120
Lohnes, George R. P495
Lohr, David H. A854
Lohr, William J. P440
Lohrman, Richard D. P394
Lohse, Albert R. A750
Loiacono, John P. A39
Loiseau, Gaelle E193

Malave, Ernesto P133
Malbrán, Mauricio W331
Malchine, John L. P70
Malchione, Robert M. A113
Malchodi, William B. A408
Malchow, Wolfgang W279
Malcolm, Christine A480, P275
Malcolm, Lynn A853, P498
Malcolm, Robert M. W115
Malcolm, Steven J. A907, E390
Malcolm, Thomas W. P377
Malcolm, Waynewright A511
Malden, Guy E236
Maldonado, Freddy E383
Maldonado Ramos, José W61
Malear, Cathy P496
Maleh, Paul E104
Malek, Catherine W262
Malenfant, Matt P521
Malerba, Marilynn R. P336
Malesci, Lou E269
Maley, J. Patrick III A805
Malfitano, Ricardo S. A678
Malhotra, Pradeep P147
Malhotra, Surin M. E174
Malia, Stephen P. A639
Malik, Zia E275
Malin, Herbert P473
Malinconico, Nancy L. E78
Malkiel, Nancy Weiss P398
Mallak, James A829
Mallery, Gilbert O. P51
Mallet, Rosalyn P289
Mallett, Christopher P. A181, P112
Mallett, Robert L. A660
Mallette, Jacques W268
Malliate, Paul P71
Malliet, Dan P494
Mallitz, M. Rand P28
Mallo, Bob P201
Malloch, Richard P. A417, P237
Mallonee, Marty P456
Mallory, Bill P74
Mallory, Bruce P229
Mallory, R. Mark A834
Mallory, Steve E262
Malmskog, David L. P42
Malnak, Brian P. A755
Malo, Norman R. P199
Malone, Brenda Richardson P133
Malone, Chris A102
Malone, John (NeuStar) E251
Malone, John C. (Liberty Media
   Holding) A517
Malone, Michael W. A673
Malone, Richie L. P272
Malone, Robert A. W73
Malone, Thomas J. P333
Malone, William K. P317
Maloney, Bill P74
Maloney, Cathleen M. A146
Maloney, Daniel J. A629
Maloney, Karen A. A741
Maloney, Lynn P370
Maloney, Sean M. A452
Maloof, Gavin P425
Maloof, Joe G. P425
Malouf, Joan P340
Malovany, Howard A913
Malpocher, Raymond V. P474
Maltarich, Robert P392
Maltz, Allen P. P90
Malugen, Joe Thomas A583
Malutinok, Paul M. A165
Malveaux, Floyd J. A567
Malzacher, H. Michael A377
Malzahn, Dan A621
Mammen, Jens P446
Manabe, Kenshi W315
Mañas Antón, Luis W274
Manberg, Paul J. E39
Mancini, Louis P102
Mancuso, Vince E311

Mandel, Irwin P127
Mandel, Larry P106
Mandelbaum, Josef A. A78
Mandelkern, Stan E325
Mandell, Andrew J. P512
Mandell, Lawrence P279
Mandell, Ralph B. E292
Mandell, Richard A. E130
Manders, Mark P411
Mandeville, Jean F. H. P. A386
Mandil, Daniel M. P449
Maneki, Freya A280
Manen, Martin G. W308
Maneri, K. Peter A233
Maness, Joel H. A788
Maney, Brian E29
Manfred, Robert D. Jr. P306
Mangan, Michael D. A148
Manganello, Timothy M. A154
Mangano, Ross J. P154
Mangano, Vito W36
Mange, Patrick W69
Mangiagalli, Marco W123
Mangum, David E. E82
Manheimer, Heidi W306
Manian, Vahid A164
Manion, Jane M. P518
Manion, Mark D. A610
Manitakos, Daniel L. E152
Manitz, R. Mark E48
Mankarios, Mourad W255
Manlapit, Alberto A. W293
Manley, Michael W104
Manley, Robin P420
Manly, Marc E. A295
Mann, Bruce M. W281
Mann, Cathy G. A398
Mann, Neil P35
Mann, Peter C. E292
Manna, John R. Jr. A530
Manne, Kenneth W. A501
Manning, Clark P. Jr. W264
Manning, Dennis J. P225
Manning, Gordon P339
Manning, Katie E75
Manning, Keith D. P540
Manning, Richard W146
Manning, Ronnie E385
Manning, Sylvia P503
Manning, Timothy R. A618
Mannion, John A694
Mannix, Kevin A881, P523
Mannon, David C. E273
Manny, Roger S. E300
Mano Pinto Simões, Maria J. W122
Manoogian, Richard A. A548
Manos, George A. A854
Manos, Kristen L. A420
Mansbart, Johannes A372
Mansell, Kevin B. A496
Mansfield, Christopher C. A518, P296
Mansfield, Kathryn E344
Mansfield, Rick E143
Mansfield, Stephen L. P325
Mansfield, William L. A869
Manske, Susan E. P304
Manson, Craig A197
Manson, Eric E198
Manson, Richard A. E262
Mansoor, Leah P186
Mansour, James M. P217
Mansueto, Joseph E240
Mansur, Bernadette P348
Manupella, Mary T. A586
Manville, Brook P500
Manwani, Harish W352
Manze, Vince A595
Manzi, Jim P. A816
Manzolillo, Barbara A. P320
Manzoni, John A. W73
Mao, Robert Y. L. W239
Mapes, Harold C. E33
Maquet, Alain A450

Mara, John K. P357
Marabeti, Dean P215
Marabito, Richard T. E262
Maranell, Michael L. P31
Marano, Jim P383
Marantette, Thomas M. Jr. P151
Marantz, Leon P300
Marasco, Alexander R. E82
Marathe, Ajay A42
Maraver Sánchez-Valdepeñas,
   Óscar W330
Marbach, Paula J. A136
March, Kevin P. A814
March, Stanley W318
Marchal, Laurent E166
Marchand, Jean-Louis W355
Marchand-Arpoumé, Jean-Pierre W355
Marchese, Larry E146
Marchetti, Michael A312
Marchetto, Carl A. A303
Marchio, Michael J. A208
Marchioli, Nelson J. A274
Marchionne, Sergio W129
Marchman, Robert A. A623
Marcial, Edwin E194
Marciano, Maurice E166
Marciano, Paul E166
Marcinelli, Ronald P. A231
Marciniak, Jere D. P176
Marcinowski, Stefan W59
Marcogliese, Richard J. A868
Marcos, Ann Takiguchi E79
Marcotte, Gary A111
Marcotte, Timothy A. E381
Marcovich, Toby E. P509
Marcucci, Mark A. A694
Marcum, R. Alan A275
Marcus, Annora C. A532
Marcus, Bruce D. A558
Marcus, Lawrence P168
Marcus, Richard C. A923
Marczak, Kathryn A403
Mardrus, Christian W273
Marek, Scott A. E154
Marek, Tracy P122
Marengi, Joseph A. A268
Maresca, Robert A. P327
Maresh, Richard E133
Marfatia, Noshirwan P480
Marfilius, Peggy P388
Margetts, Rob J. W196
Margolis, Bruce A825
Margolis, Jay M. A519
Margolis, John D. P365
Margolis, Julius B. P129
Margolis, Lawrence A. E37
Margolis, Michael C. E107
Margulis, Heidi S. A439
Maria Ranero Diaz, Jose W372
Mariani, Frank P300
Mariani, Kenneth P79
Mariani, Pierre W69
Mariano, Robert A. P424
Mariette, Bernard A696
Marika, Michael J. E256
Marilley, Leanne D. A610
Marin, Lori P. P271
Marinangeli, Daniel A. W345
Marineau, Philip A. A515, P294
Mariner, Jonathan D. P306
Marini, James A. E227
Marino, Anthony S. A511
Marino, Edward J. E291
Marino, Michael P524
Marino, Richard J. E372
Marino, Robert A. P245
Marino, Robin A546
Marino, V. James A56
Marino, Wayne A. E361
Marino, William J. P245
Marino D'Arienzo, Annette P92
Marinos, E. P. E37
Mario, Ernest P414

Marion, Fred L. A291
Marion, Pat P316
Maritz, W. Stephen P307
Mark, Reuben A228
Mark, William P456
Markeborn, Bengt Göran W238
Markee, Richard L. P483
Markel, Anthony F. A540
Markel, Steven A. A540
Marker, Andy P477
Markfield, Roger S. A73
Markham, Jackie P518
Markham, Rudy W352
Markl, Barry L. A882
Markley, Grant S. P67
Markley, H. J. A265
Markley, William C. III A466
Markmann, Melanie W337
Markoe, Bruce P326
Markoff, Steven C. P38
Markovich, Paul P92
Markow, Jonathan P140
Markowicz, John R. E103
Markowitz, Michael E271
Markowski, Stephen A793
Marks, Ann A288
Marks, David P154
Marks, Gordon W. P467
Marks, Gretchen J. E92
Marks, John J. P321
Marks, Peter W279
Marks, Rebecca A595
Marks, Ronald D. A342
Marks, Terrance M. A227
Marle, Kim E226
MarLett, Charles D. A87
Marlett, Wendy A481
Marley, Brian T. P80
Marlin, Kevin A706
Marlow, Carol A186
Marlowe, Martin A476
Marmer, Lynn A500
Marmion, Bridget P246
Marney, Mark S. P454
Marney, R. Michael P454
Marohn, Douglas W. E256
Marohn, William D. A602
Marone, Emil J. E176
Maroney, James F. III E98
Maroni, Alice Collier P447
Maronna, Graciela A119
Maroone, Michael E. A111
Maropis, Colin N. E391
Marosits, Joseph E. A259
Marotta, Daniel A. A164
Marotta, Dean L. A924
Marovich, Jim P107
Marple, Harris A608
Marquet, Jean-Claude W318
Marquez, Theresa P152
Marquie, Serge W111
Marr, Ann W. P537
Marra, Thomas M. A408
Marrett, Cora B. P509
Marrett, Phillip E. P47
Marrie, Mike P20
Marrinan, Susan F. A765
Marriott, Daniel C. A442
Marriott, J. W. Jr. A542
Marriott, John W. III A542
Marron, Kristen E360
Marrone, Virgilio W159
Mars, Dale W. E180
Mars, Jacqueline Badger A543, P310
Mars, John Franklyn A543, P310
Mars, Thomas A. A884
Marsden, John O. A663
Marseillan, Ignacio P457
Marsh, Brenda A125
Marsh, Carol W. E70
Marsh, George T. A525
Marsh, Jim W81
Marsh, Kevin B. A737

Miller, Patricia J. E388
Miller, Peter D. (Regions
  Financial) A704
Miller, Peter M. (A.G. Edwards) A48
Miller, Philip P451
Miller, Richard (Barton Malow) P74
Miller, Richard C. (Astronics) E41
Miller, Richard L. (ADA-ES) E18
Miller, Rick (Tastefully Simple) P469
Miller, Robert (Albertsons) P34
Miller, Robert A. Jr. (Paul,
  Hastings) P379
Miller, Robert D. (Globalstar) E160
Miller, Robert G. (Iron Mountain) A461
Miller, Robert G. (Rite Aid) A711
Miller, Robert J. Jr. (D&H
  Distributing) P158
Miller, Robert S. Jr. (Delphi) A271
Miller, Ronald F. E338
Miller, Sarah W. A588
Miller, Scott P306
Miller, Sidney A. E116
Miller, Stacy P270
Miller, Stephen W. (Chesapeake
  Energy) A204
Miller, Steven O. (Penn Mutual) P381
Miller, Stuart A. A511
Miller, Susan E. P359
Miller, Ted A. P466
Miller, Teri A775
Miller, Thomas B. E201
Miller, Toni P75
Miller, William G. (Miller
  Industries) E235
Miller, William H. Jr. (Harris
  Corp.) A407
Miller Paules, Gretchen P420
Millian, Stephanie P45
Milligan, Cynthia H. P535
Milligan, John F. (Gilead
  Sciences) A385
Milligan, John W. (Cintas) A213
Milligan, Nick W79
Milligan, Peter J. A463
Milligan, Stephen D. A902
Milliken, James B. P505
Milliken, John D. A471
Milliken, Roger P333
Millington, Roy W33
Millner, Thomas L. P415
Millot, Caroline W203
Mills, Andy P321
Mills, Bradford A. W202
Mills, Charles S. P321
Mills, Cheryl P360
Mills, David D. A445
Mills, Gerald T. P415
Mills, Michael P365
Mills, Richard (Holiday
  Companies) P243
Mills, Richard E. (Anthony & Sylvan
  Pools) P54
Mills, Rick J. (Cummins) A257
Mills, Steve (Cablevision
  Systems) A173
Mills, Steven A. (IBM) A454
Mills, Steven R. (ADM) A38
Millsaps, Carole A339
Milman, Harvey F. E120
Milne, Doug A543
Milne, Garth L. A582
Milne, Gordon A. A723
Milne, Justin W336
Milne, Matthew P516
Milone, Libero A269, P166, W106
Milone, Michael D. A430
Milovich, Lori A367
Milroy, Doug A308
Milstein, Howard P. P185
Miltin, Philippe A757
Mimeault, Victor J. P49
Mims, Joyce E. A722
Mimura, Akio W233

Min, Soo Bong E391
Minagawa, Takashi W232
Minami, Akira W102
Minamitani, Yosuke W172
Mindiak, Donald E51
Minehan, Cathy E. P194
Minella, Lynn C. A52
Miner, Jerome T. E41
Ming, Jenny J. A370
Mingasson, Paul W311
Mingle, Robyn T. A438
Minick, Russell S. A432
Minicucci, Robert A. P73
Minikes, Michael A130
Minnaugh, Mark P208
Minnich, George E. A462
Minnick, Mary E. A225
Minor, G. Gilmer III A636
Minor, Todd C. E344
Minster, Joel P410
Minter, Gordon P246
Minto, Anne W92
Minto, Rebecca E47
Minton, Dwight C. A210
Minton, Jennifer L. A633
Minton Beddoes, Andrea A560, P319
Minturn, Frederick K. P339
Mintz, Jordan H. A195
Mintz, Joshua J. P304
Mintz, Louis N. P452
Mintzer, Damon E164
Minucci, Aldo W142
Miquelon, Wade D. A843
Miracle, Celesta M. E281
Miraglia, Salvatore J. Jr. A824
Miranda, Isidoro W194
Miraton, Didier W216
Mirchandani, Sanjay A316
Mirchin, Matthew C. E361
Mirdamadi, Susan L. A274
Mirman, Richard E. A405
Mirzayantz, Nicolas A455
Mischell, Thomas E. A77
Mischke, Werner W360
Misener, Paul A69
Misenhimer, Holly P105
Mish, J. Vincent E235
Mishkin, Sandy P122
Miskewitz, Regina E227
Miskimins, Lisa J. P302
Misner, Jeffrey J. A242
Misra, Alka E139
Missano, Anthony J. P431
Missett, Judi Sheppard P265
Missett, Kathy P265
Mita, Shinichi W179
Mita, Yoshifumi W137
Mitarai, Akira W304
Mitarai, Fujio W85
Mitau, Lee R. A864
Mitcham, Billy F. Jr. E236
Mitchell, Andrew W301
Mitchell, Cheryl P322
Mitchell, Christopher D. A733
Mitchell, Clarence D. P368
Mitchell, Craig E351
Mitchell, Dan P446
Mitchell, Demetrai P76
Mitchell, Douglas T. E337
Mitchell, George J. A885
Mitchell, Gladys A46
Mitchell, Gregg P210
Mitchell, H. Thomas P103
Mitchell, Hugh W287
Mitchell, J. Barry A329
Mitchell, James G. (Steelcase) A786
Mitchell, James P. (Swift Energy) E340
Mitchell, Jim (Corbis) P148
Mitchell, Joann (University of
  Pennsylvania) P506
Mitchell, Joanne (JELD-WEN) P266
Mitchell, John R. P376
Mitchell, Lee Roy P130

Mitchell, Mark A726
Mitchell, Max H. A253
Mitchell, Michael A206
Mitchell, Patrick A913
Mitchell, Richard K. A275
Mitchell, Robert D.
  (AngioDynamics) E33
Mitchell, Robert W. Jr. (Cintas) A213
Mitchell, Rodney L. E58
Mitchell, Samuel J. Jr. A107
Mitchell, Susan A834
Mitchell, Tandy P130
Mitchell, Thomas H. (Dollar
  General) A282
Mitchell, Thomas H. (KMG
  Chemicals) E207
Mitchell, Thomas L. (Apache) A95
Mitchell, Timothy W373
Mitchell, Tony P27
Mitchell, William E. (Arrow
  Electronics) A105
Mitchell, William G. (Jacobs
  Engineering) A466
Mitsch, George P496
Mitscherlich, Matthias W209
Mitsuda, Minoru W213
Mitsuhashi, Yasuo W85
Mitsui, Akio W136
Mittag, Andrew K. W28
Mittal, Aditya W222
Mittal, Lakshmi N. W222
Mittal, Vinay E139
Mittelstadt, Alison A326
Mittelstaedt, Jason E306
Mittler, Gilbert W132
Miura, Satoru W221
Miura, Satoshi W243
Miura, Zenji W276
Miwa, Sal E21
Mixon, James P. A492
Mixon, Peter H. A175, P108
Mixon, William C. P510
Miyajima, Hiroshi W217
Miyakawa, Giichi W74
Miyamoto, Masao W218
Miyamoto, Shigeru W231
Miyaoka, Yasushi W136
Miyashita, Masao W245
Miyata, Kazuo W137
Miyatake, Kiyoharu W245
Miyauchi, Ken W313
Miyauchi, Norio W229
Miyauchi, Yoshihiko W314
Miyoshi, Takashi W151
Mizell, Steven C. A579
Mizell, Will P522
Mizerany, Charles P264
Mizokuchi, Makoto W343
Mizuno, Ichiro W218
Mizuno, Toshihide W219
Mizuochi, Shoji W74
Mizutani, Katsumi W342
Mladenovic, Rudy A180
Mlotek, Mark E. A418
Moake, James P250
Moar, Nathalie A325
Moayeri, Ali A248
Moberg, Anders C. W284
Moberg, Lars-Göran W361
Mobili, Sergio W121
Mobius, Painer W35
Mobley, Jeffrey L. A204
Mobley, Stacey J. A297
Mockler, Ed P19
Moden, Ralph A853, P498
Modi, Pradeep P391
Modjtabai, Avid A896
Modory, Kim P469
Modrzynski, Chris P354
Mody, Apurva S. A267
Moe, Donald M. A547
Moe, Doug P168
Moehle, Mary Jo A203

Moehn, Kevin F. A761
Moellenhoff, David E312
Moeller, Jeff P300
Moeller, Joseph W. P284
Moeller, Kate W93
Moeller, Pam A137
Moeller, Tom A913
Moen, Dan E93
Moen, Timothy P. A613
Moerdyk, Carol B. A627
Moerk, Hallstein W235
Moffat, Brian W156
Moffat, Robert W. Jr. A454
Moffatt, David W336
Moffatt, Donald E. W281
Moffett, David M. A864
Moffett, James R. A364
Mog, Steve P53
Mogavero, Sally E219
Mogford, Steven L. W53
Mogg, Jim W. A295, E113
Moggio, Paula P396
Moghadam, Farhad A100
Moghadam, Hossein M. A902
Mogren, Håkan W45
Mogulescu, John P133
Mohamed, Nadir H. W281
Mohamed, YBhg Datuk Syed Tamin
  Syed W308
Mohan, Alok E346
Mohan, Pat W325
Mohapatra, Surya N. A695
Mohl, Andrew W40
Mohler, Hugh W. E51
Mohler, Lucy E51
Mohler, Max P534
Mohn, Jarl E87
Mohn, Johannes W65
Mohn, Reinhard W65
Mohr, James G. P328
Mohr, Larry P527
Mohr, Marshall L. E197
Mohr, Michael P38
Mohr, Ronnie A503, P290
Moine, Véronique W300
Moir, Sammy A397
Moisset, Jacques E129
Mok, Barry C. T. W155
Molay, Hilary A923
Molendorp, Dayton H. P47
Moler, Elizabeth Ann A329
Moler, Spencer C. A538
Moles Valenzuela, José W331
Molfetas, Jason P528
Molina, Daniel E310
Molina, Michael P499
Molinari, Marco A432
Molinaro, Samuel L. Jr. A130
Molinaro, Vincent J. W34
Molinaroli, Alex A. A475
Molinini, Michael L. A53
Molkhou, Brigitte W94
Moll, Curtis E. P339
Moll, Magdalena W59
Moll, Theodore S. P339
Moll, William G. A221
Mollen, John T. A316
Mollenkopf, John C. E226
Möller, Peter W299
Mollien, Jerry W. A548
Mollo, Charles R. E237
Molnar, Attila W60
Molnár, József W224
Molod, Jon P413
Moloney, Chris X. P436
Moloney, Daniel M. A582
Molson, Eric H. A578
Moltner, Bill A512
Momeyer, Alan A526
Momii, Katsuo W221
Mon, Antonio B. A801
Mon, Hector A157
Monaco, Carmen P214

Parks, Scott A149
Parks, Wendy P270
Parlier, Harry E29
Parmenter, Robert E. A304
Parmley, John R. E212
Parnell, Michael A. A392
Paro, Jeffrey N. A682
Parodi, Ben P77
Parodi, Dennis R. A73
Paroski, Margaret P276
Parr, George P297
Parr, Richard A. II P141
Parr, Steven A682
Parra, Rosendo G. A268
Parrett, William G. A269, P166, P500, W106
Parrish, Al P400
Parrish, Charles S. A812
Parrish, D. Michael A620
Parrish, H. Harrison A583
Parrish, Steven C. A68
Parrot, Graham W173
Parrott, Stephen J. E64
Parrs, Marianne Miller A458
Parry, Bill P208
Parry, Dave A757
Parry, Edward J. III A401
Parry, Michael A317
Parry, Richard D. A889
Parry, Timothy R. A414
Parry-Jones, Richard A355
Parsky, Barbara J. A309
Parson, Alex W164
Parsons, Craig S. E258
Parsons, Graham T. W56
Parsons, John E. E364
Parsons, Richard D. (Time Warner) A822
Parsons, Rick (Bank of America) A122
Parsons, Robert R. P212
Partilla, John A822
Partridge, James F. E338
Partridge, John M. (Visa) A876, P517
Partridge, John W. Jr. (NiSource) A608
Parulekar, Suneil V. A592
Pascal, Philippe W207
Pasche, Stephanie L. P302
Pasek, Gary P331
Pash, Jeff P346
Pasin, Mario P408
Pasin, Paul P408
Pasin, Robert P408
Pasinski, Janess A96
Pasqualini, Thomas P449
Passa, Lester M. A256
Passell, Brian J. A687
Passero, Davide W142
Passig, Theodore O. A648
Passov, Richard A. A660
Paster, Howard G. W369
Pasterick, Robert J. A151
Pastor, Daniel P208
Pastore, William M. E239
Pastorelli, Adolfo W64
Paszkiewicz, Ladislas W348
Patch, Art P430
Pate, Thomas R. A190
Pate, William C. A323
Patel, Ashvinkumar A919
Patel, Bharatan R. P19
Patel, Elaine P192
Patel, Homi B. A409
Patel, Kal P20
Patel, Kalendu A142
Patel, Kiran A460
Patel, Prabhuling P29
Patel, Sunit S. A513
Patel, Zarin W78
Paternot, Thierry A779
Paterson, Brian P62
Paterson, David J. A156
Paterson, John A454
Pathmarajah, Allen J. A233

Patil, Sadanand A592
Patineau, Paula J. A63
Patinkin, Matthew M. P530
Patkotak, Crawford P57
Patmore, Kimberly S. A344
Patracuolla, James D. A867
Patrick, Belinda O. E117
Patrick, Donna A664
Patrick, Doug A388, P211
Patrick, Jason J. P317
Patrick, Richard M. P297
Patrick, Stephen C. A228
Patrikis, Ernest T. A80
Patrnchak, Joseph P90
Patron, Luigi W123
Patrone, Anthony P336
Patsalos-Fox, Michael A560, P318
Patsley, Pamela H. A344
Patstone, Cheryl E42
Pattee, Russell A528
Patten, Rose M. W56
Patten, Sue P413
Patterson, Andrew W. A544
Patterson, Barry P318
Patterson, Dennis M. A790
Patterson, Douglas E. A658, P385
Patterson, George M. E360
Patterson, Ian P436
Patterson, James F. (Nationwide) A593, P351
Patterson, James J. (Schawk) E315
Patterson, Joan I. E252
Patterson, John W45
Patterson, Kate E385
Patterson, Kimberly S. P78
Patterson, L. Leon P375
Patterson, Lincoln P173
Patterson, Michael E. P140
Patterson, Penny P399
Patterson, Peyton R. E253
Patterson, Samuel R. A672
Patterson, Steve (JR Simplot) P274
Patterson, Steve (Portland Trail Blazers) P394
Patterson, Wayne S. A826
Patti, Tony A233
Pattison, Doug P231
Patton, Charles R. (AEP) A74
Patton, Charles R. (Ryder) A721
Patton, Gregory N. E31
Patton, Jo Allen P520
Patton, Jock A792
Patton, Michael C. (Greif) A396
Patton, Michael M. (ENGlobal) E132
Patton, Michele A93
Pattullo, John W112
Pattullo, Scott P204
Patzakis, John M. E167
Patzak-Krueger, Claudia E334
Pauget, Georges W99
Paugh, Laura E. A542
Paukovits, Timothy J. A677
Paul, Amy S. A252
Paul, Donald L. A205
Paul, Gerald A876
Paul, Joseph R. P161
Paul, Les W45
Paul, Ronald D. E122
Paul, Steven M. A315
Paul, William P. P407
Paulenich, Fred D. A515, P294
Pauley, Stanley F. P115
Paulik, Diana P524
Paulk, Tommy P33
Paull, David Z. E310
Paull, Matthew H. A556
Paulley, Betsy P278
Paulsen, Larry A668
Paulsen, Marcia E146
Paulsen, Robert J. P380
Paulsen, Teresa A234
Paulson, Duane P209
Paulson, Erika P540

Paulson, Gerry P266
Paulson, Kenneth A. A369
Paulson, Sidney C. P258
Paulus, Connie M. E60
Pauly, Lothar W113
Pautler, Paul F. A48
Pauze, Philippe W89
Pavelka, Darrel J. A648
Paver, Howard A424
Paver, Robert L. A464
Pavey, Nancy P77
Pavlis, Alex E176
Pavloff, John M. P497
Pavlova, Olga Petrovna W140
Paxson, John P127
Paylor, Craig E. A470
Payment, Philip H. Jr. A909
Payne, Dennis M. A109
Payne, Kitty B. E147
Payne, Lawrence P428
Payne, Michael P111
Payne, Mitchell H. P504
Payne, Park P339
Payne, Penelope P447
Payne, Richard B. Jr. A589, A864
Payne, Robert L. A531
Payne, Tommy J. A710
Payne, William R. P38
Payson, Norman C. P141
Payton, Michele E254
Paz, David W187
Paz, George A332
Pazaras, Matt P355
Pazzani, John A821
Peabody, Mark E41
Peace, David P404
Peace, N. Brian A530
Peach, Susan E. P119
Peacock, Kerry A. W345
Peacock, Lynne M. W226
Pearce, Harry J. W239
Pearce, Mike P111
Pearce, Randy L. A705
Pearce-Smith, Louisa W194
Pearl, Suzanne J. A874
Pearlman, Michelle A93
Pearlson, Paul A. P300
Pearman-Gillman, Kim E200
Pearson, Harriet A454
Pearson, Ian W80
Pearson, L. Wayne E331
Pearson, Robert L. P492
Pearson, Stephen L. E166
Pearson, Thomas M. A723
Pearson, Tracy P191
Pease, Andrew J. A164
Pease, Bob A592
Pease, Jo A755
Pease, Kendell M. A377
Pease, Mark L. A88
Pease, Martha P297
Pease, Richard G. A685
Pébereau, Michel W69
Pecchini, Daniele W129
Pechmann, Christian K. E356
Pecht, Carrie J. A427
Peck, Art A370
Peck, Darcie A448
Peck, Diane P458
Peck, Patricia A. A353
Peck, Raphael J. E361
Peck, Tom A571
Pecker, David J. P44
Peconi, Maurice V. A676
Peddicord, Kenneth L. P476
Peden, John R. P352
Peden, Keith J. A701
Pedersen, John B. A155
Pedersen, Robert J. A853
Pederson, Molly P57
Pederson, Robin P254
Pedini, Claire W34
Pedowitz, Mark A31

Pedrick, Colin W165
Pedtke, Richard F. A449
Pedulla, Thomas V. P19
Peebler, Robert P. E192
Peebles, Douglas J. P36
Peebles, Robert M. A859
Peek, David G. P214
Peek, Jeffrey M. A217
Peel, Michael A. A380
Peeler, Mark P485
Peers, Gil P340
Peers, James A. E158
Peeters, Paul W255
Peetz, Bruce E. E358
Pefanis, Harry N. A671
Peffer, Keri P492
Pehrson, H. Gary P258
Peigh, Terry D. A459
Peiros, Lawrence S. A222
Peixotto, Bob P299
Pekarek, Nancy W145
Pekarski, Erik R. A692
Pekarsky, John E179
Pekor, Allan J. A511
Péladeau, Érik W268
Péladeau, Pierre Karl W268
Pélata, Patrick W273
Peleo-Lazar, Marlena A556
Pelfrey, Gwen R. E176
Pelgrim, Donald H. Jr. E378
Pelini, Richard A. A516
Pélisson, Gilles W23
Pelka, Herbert W362
Pell, Gordon W286
Pelland, Daniel A578
Pellegrin, Lloyd M. E355
Pellegrino, Phillip F. A774
Pellegrino Puhl, Frances P65
Pellerito, Thomas J. A438
Pelligreen, Chris P123
Pellissier, Gervais W134
Pellizzer, Steven D. E108
Pellizzon, Jerrold J. E79
Pelose, John E324
Peltier, Ronald J. P330
Peltz, Nelson A833
Peluso, John P225
Peluso, Michelle A. A724
Pemán, Manuel Guerrero W274
Pemberton, Robin P342
Pena, Arturo P414
Penalver, Georges W134
Pence, Dennis C. E93
Pence, Robin A43
Pendarvis, David E305
Pendleton, Mark J. P283
Pendleton, Patrick C. P212
Pendley, James T. A244
Pénisson, René W357
Penland, Maria P493
Penman, Patricia A736, P432
Penman, Steven E. P438
Penn, Andrew W49
Penn, Loretta A. A775
Penn, Mark J. W370
Penn, Richard J. E184
Penn, Tom P322
Penna, Giovanni W329
Penna da Silva, Alexandre M. W334
Pennella, William A. P152
Penner, Elliott W271
Pennie, Debbie P39
Penniman, Elizabeth E252
Pennings, Harry W367
Pennington, Kevin P. W281
Pennington, Richard A456
Pennington, Skip P101
Pennington, William Lane P260
Pennoni, Celestino R. E273
Pensa, Marc A106
Pensabene, Gregory M. A88
Penshorn, John S. A858
Penske, Roger S. P383

A = AMERICAN BUSINESS
E = EMERGING COMPANIES
P = PRIVATE COMPANIES
W = WORLD BUSINESS

Pentecost, William R. E143
Pentikäinen, Markku W319
Penuela, Ozzie P396
Penzig, Gina A901
Pepe, Alex A365
Pepe, Michael A296
Peper, John H. E132
Pepicello, William A96
Peplow, Michael D. P73
Peponis, Stephanie Klein A708
Pepper, Cara E389
Peppiatt-Combes, James P487
Pepy, Guillaume W311
Percenti, Donald A. P17
Percival, Matthew W40
Perdue, David A. Jr. A282
Perdue, James A. P384
Perdue, Kenny P30
Perdue, Richard T. E70
Perel, David P44
Perello, Joseph P310
Perelman, Ronald O. A535, A708, P304, P376
Perez, Antonio M. A303
Perez, Arnaldo A186
Perez, Brenda P411
Perez, Derek A621
Perez, Janette E356
Perez, Jorge M. P414
Perez, Joseph P216
Perez, Linda P198
Perez, Paul G. E222
Perez, Peter M. A234
Perez, Roberto A641
Perez, Victor M. E26
Perez de Alonso, Marcela A426
Pérez Gómez, Jaime W332
Pérez Simón, Juan Antonio W332
Perham, Leonard C. E250
Perier, Francis I. Jr. A355
Periquito, Paulo F. M. O. A904
Perissich, Riccardo W329
Perissinotto, Giovanni W142
Perkins, Bruce A439
Perkins, Charlotte A655
Perkins, Cheryl A. A488
Perkins, David (Freescale Semiconductor) A365
Perkins, David (Molson Coors) A578
Perkins, Jim C. P239
Perkins, Larry P115
Perkins, Marc I. P227
Perkins, Robert W45
Perkins, Scott W. A636
Perkins, Tom P406
Perkovic, Olga A861
Perks, Ben W. E248
Perl, Martha Loveman P129
Perl, Terry Allan P129
Perlet, Helmut W38
Perlick, Mark A. A154
Perlin, Gary L. A178
Perlin, Jonathan B. A413
Perlitz, Thomas J. A253
Perlman, Doug P348
Perlmutter, David A452
Perlmutter, Roger M. A85
Perna, Robert J. A594
Pernotto, Stephen J. P80
Perot, Ross Jr. A656
Perot, Ross Sr. A656
Perraud, Jean-Marc A739
Perrault, Victoria L. A804
Perrin, Charles R. A886
Perrin, Sallye P378
Perrine, Constance E264
Perrine, Robert E. A288
Perron, David N. A780

Perron, Kirk J. P264
Perrone, Frank A490
Perrott, Pam A541
Perruzza, Albert L. A703
Perry, Amber P452
Perry, Anthony C. A54
Perry, Denise P367
Perry, Don (Chick-fil-A) P128
Perry, Donald D. (Clear Channel) A221
Perry, Frank A. P290
Perry, Harvey P. A196
Perry, James E. (Trinity Industries) A835
Perry, James H. (United Industrial) E364
Perry, Larry W. A167
Perry, M. Marnette A500
Perry, Marie L. A161
Perry, Mark L. A385
Perry, Pat A796
Perry, Ralph D. P432
Perry, Russell P446
Perry, Tony P122
Perry, Victor A. III A251
Perry, Wayne P99
Perryman, Brett S. E21
Perryman, Vicki A179
Perseo, John P. Jr. E379
Persichilli, Judith M. P118
Persing, David A. P327
Persinger, Terry L. E224
Person, Chuck P253
Person, David J. E397
Person, Derek P366
Persson, Eva W361
Persson, Olaf W361
Pertsch, J. Michael A547
Peru, Ramiro G. A663
Pesaturo, John F. E35
Pesavento, Robert J. P240
Pesce, Peter A342
Pesci, Robert A. A745
Pesesky, Larry P300
Peskens, Kathleen A749
Petach, Ann Marie A355
Peterffy, Thomas P258
Peterfy, Charles G. P468
Peterman, George M. E32
Peterman, Tim A. A327
Peters, Andrew D. P378
Peters, Brian W70
Peters, Carter M. E165
Peters, Charles E. Jr. E302
Peters, Greg P113
Peters, Ian W92
Peters, Jeffrey S. E334
Peters, John G. (Northern Illinois University) P364
Peters, Jon D. (Phillips-Van Heusen) A664
Peters, Jürgen W360
Peters, Kevin A. A915
Peters, Lauren B. A353
Peters, Leonard K. P76
Peters, Lisa B. A564
Peters, Richard J. P383
Peters, Robert E. A695
Peters, William E. A464
Petersen, Greg B. P22
Petersen, James E. E73
Petersen, Patricia M. A801
Petersen, Roger L. A677
Petersen, Sheldon C. P350
Petersen, Soren W235
Peterson, Brian F. A38
Peterson, Bruce D. A293
Peterson, Denny P489
Peterson, Eric P269
Peterson, James J. A234
Peterson, Jeffery P. P495
Peterson, Jori A31
Peterson, Karin P381
Peterson, Keith A197

Peterson, Mark S. E225
Peterson, Per A. A474
Peterson, Ralph R. P125
Peterson, Randall B. A748
Peterson, Raymond E. P256
Peterson, Rebecca E24
Peterson, Richard (Varsity Group) E375
Peterson, Richard D. (Flying J) P198
Peterson, Robert A. (Norcross Safety Products) P363
Peterson, Robert J. (Sedgwick Claims Management Services) P438
Peterson, Robert T. (AMERCO) A71
Peterson, Terry D. A273
Peterson, Tom P238
Peterson, William B. A327
Petit, Gilles W89
Petit, Jim A277
Petit, Michael J. E288
Petitt, Anthony B. E206
Petkanics, Donna M. P532
Petralia, Michael A. P393
Petram, Hans-Dieter W112
Petratis, David D. W300
Petrell, Sharon P305
Petrella, Russell C. A535
Petren, Carol Ann A211
Petrichevich, Renee P390
Petrides, Yiannis A651
Petrie, Geoff P425
Petrillo, John C. A443
Petrini, Kenneth R. A52
Petro, Francis J. P233
Petronella, Sandy A494, P285
Petrou, David R. P271
Petrovich, Dushan A913
Petrovich, Steven C. P57
Petrowski, Joe P226
Petrozzi, Mark P95
Petrucci, Laurie J. A353
Petrullo, Dennis P426
Petrullo, Michael A. A544
Petruska, Steven C. A692
Petry, Jacques W312
Petrylak, Paul G. A217
Petters, C. Michael A614
Petters, Thomas J. P387
Petterson, David S. A248
Petterson, John S. A820
Pettus, Don K. P225
Petty, Carloyne E171
Petty, Wendy E141
Petz, Carl P87
Peugeot, Robert W254
Peugeot, Thierry W254
Peugh, David B. A448
Pew, Robert C. III A786
Peyre, Philippe W295
Pfander, Wilhelm E284
Pfanner, Jennifer P91
Pfaus, Chris A765
Pfeffer, Gerald S. P386
Pfeifer, Klaus E318
Pfeifer, Mary A296
Pfeiffer, Gary M. A297
Pfeiffer, Peter W104
Pfeil, Larry J. A437
Pferdehirt, Doug A739
Pflugfelder, Jennifer A659
Pforzheimer, Harry A460
Pfund, Randy P237
Pfund, William H. A765, E394
Pfutzenreuter, Richard H. P505
Phalen, Michael P. A155
Phaneuf, Daniel D. P154
Phanstiel, Howard G. A858
Pharo, Milam Randolph E312
Phelan, Daniel W145
Phelan, John P. W225
Phelizon, Jean-François W291
Phelps, Charles E. P506
Phelps, R. Michael A658, P386
Phelps, Robert T. A144

Phelps, Steve P342
Philbrook, Jocelyn E329
Philip, Craig E. P256
Philip, Fran P299
Philip, Jim P520
Philipp, Michael G. W100
Philips, Bryan P529
Philips, Jeremy A604
Phillippy, Robert J. E253
Phillips, Barnet IV A759, P445
Phillips, Brandon W226
Phillips, Brett A. P463
Phillips, Charles E. Jr. A633
Phillips, Chris P367
Phillips, Cindy L E28
Phillips, Craig E219
Phillips, Daniel M P25
Phillips, David P. A691, P402
Phillips, Diana A768, E330
Phillips, Don E240
Phillips, Douglas W. P506
Phillips, Ed P353
Phillips, Gary A. (Associated Wholesale Grocers) P65
Phillips, Gary M. (Bausch & Lomb) A126
Phillips, Hank A111
Phillips, Jack (American Tire) P47
Phillips, James M. (Aearo) P28
Phillips, James M. (NACCO Industries) A584
Phillips, Jon (Phoenix Suns) P388
Phillips, Mark W365
Phillips, Matthew W164
Phillips, Michael (Hampton Affiliates) P229
Phillips, Michael D. (Health Grades) E171
Phillips, Richard B. A458
Phillips, Ronald P279
Phillips, Sherri A515
Phillips, Stephen (IPC Acquisition) P262
Phillips, Sterling E. Jr. E32
Phillips, Steve (Avnet) A116
Phillips, Steven L. (Werner Enterprises) A898
Phillips, W. Norman Jr. A534
Phillipson, Brian W53
Philpott, Steven L. E361
Phippen, Peter S. W78
Phipps, P. Cody A855
Phipps, Robin W196
Phlegar, Jeffrey S. P36
Phoenix, Angela A874
Phua, Stephen A448
Piacentini, Diego A69
Piacquad, David A. A738
Piaget, Eric E129
Pianalto, Sandra P194
Pianalto Cameron, Rose P194
Pianin, Randy A625
Piano, Phyllis J. A85
Piasecki, Matthew A875, P517
Pibollo, Colleen P307
Picard, Jean-Paul P166
Picard, Lynn P297
Picard, Olivier W34
Piccinini, Robert M. P430
Piccoli, Kevin C. A124
Piccolo, C. A. A180
Picek, John S. A63
Pichot, Jacques W29
Pichotta, Nicholas J. E101
Pici, Frank A. E276
Pick, Robert S. A229
Pickard, Frank C. III A873
Pickard, John G. A338
Pickard, Richard R. E287
Pickart, George A223
Pickelny, Michael A409
Pickens, David T. A262
Pickens, Erin D. E344

A = AMERICAN BUSINESS
E = EMERGING COMPANIES
P = PRIVATE COMPANIES
W = WORLD BUSINESS

Rumbough, Roy A. Jr. A512
Rumery, Doris P342
Rummelt, Andreas W240
Rumpke, Jeffrey E. P424
Rumpke, Mark J. P424
Rumpke, Matthew J. P424
Rumpke, Todd P424
Rumpke, William J. Jr. P424
Rumpke, William J. Sr. P424
Rumsby, Mike W203
Runau, Jan W26
Runion, Lorie Y. E52
Runkel, John (Heinz) A430
Runkel, John F. (Intuitive Surgical) E197
Runnels, Jim P187
Running, Mark D. A635
Runowicz, Carolyn D. P41
Runyon, Dee P77
Runyon, Robert B. E129
Rupe, Robert A. P353
Rupert, Catherine M. A889
Rupert, Timothy G. E310
Rupkus, Shanon P491
Rupp, Joseph D. A628
Rupp, Lindsey A. E215
Ruppel, James A. A772
Rupprecht, Gerhard W38
Rupprecht, Rudolf W209
Ruprecht, William F. A768, E330
Rusakova, Vlada Vilorikovna W140
Rusche, James R. E304
Rusckowski, Stephen H. W255
Rusert, Beth P307
Rushing, Coretha M. A322
Rusk, Richard A. E172
Ruskowski, Gary P278
Russ, Chandler A809, P475
Russak, Donald A. P395
Russell, Allan P429
Russell, Andrew L. P149
Russell, Anthony P. A104
Russell, Barbara P227
Russell, Cecil P430
Russell, Chris E119
Russell, Dana C. (Novell) A618
Russell, Daniel (InfoSpace) E190
Russell, David E360
Russell, Douglas K. A730
Russell, Edison C. E328
Russell, Eric E. E301
Russell, Gary A235
Russell, George W173
Russell, John G. (CMS Energy) A223
Russell, John K. (Harley-Davidson) A403
Russell, John S. (Quintiles Transnational) P406
Russell, Joyce W25
Russell, Keith B. W319
Russell, Kent P428
Russell, M. Frank E139
Russell, Mark E234
Russell, Neil G. E185
Russell, Ron P490
Russell, Samuel J. E323
Russell, Terry P269
Russo, Carmine E203
Russo, Christopher J. P346
Russo, Cindy W. E255
Russo, Glenn A513
Russo, Jeffrey M. E85
Russo, Mario W36
Russo, Michael E306
Russo, Patricia F. W34
Russo, Robert A291
Russo, Roberto W129
Russo, Sam P355

Russo, Thomas A. A509
Russo, Vincent (Bellco Health) P81
Russo, Vincent A. (Phillips-Van Heusen) A664
Russolese, Jason E334
Rust, Edward B. Jr. A784, P459
Rust, John H. Jr. E71
Ruth, Deborah E. P150
Rutherford, Alan W. A255
Rutherford, Clive W325
Rutherford, Clyde E. P156
Rutherford, David W301
Rutherford, Jim P115
Rutherford, Kimberly P510
Rutherford, Linda P177
Rutherford, Travis P326
Rutherford, William B. E296
Ruthizer, Jeffrey A31
Ruthven, John A172
Rutkowski, Joseph A. A620
Rutkowski, Lawrence R. A886
Rutledge, A. Bradley Sr. E106
Rutledge, Richard E. A902
Rutledge, Thomas M. A173
Rutledge, William P. A413
Rutner, Alan P403
Rutrough, James E. A784, P459
Rutt, Sheila M. A276
Ruttenstorfer, Wolfgang W246
Ruud, Morten W238
Ruzzini, Paolo W121
Ryan, Arthur F. A689
Ryan, Courtney J. A464
Ryan, Daniel W. A735
Ryan, Diarmuid P. P271
Ryan, Frederick J. Jr. P35
Ryan, Gerald A. E334
Ryan, Greg E164
Ryan, James R. (Lockheed Martin) A525
Ryan, James T. (W.W. Grainger) A914
Ryan, John (Hewitt Associates) A425
Ryan, John J. (Parsons Brinckerhoff) P377
Ryan, John O. (Macrovision) E224
Ryan, John P. (Dresser) P177
Ryan, John R. (SUNY) P460
Ryan, Joseph (Marriott) A542
Ryan, Joseph B. Jr. (Tishman) P480
Ryan, Marsha P. A74
Ryan, Martin A420
Ryan, Michael J. A449
Ryan, Patrick (Royal Caribbean Cruises) A717
Ryan, Patrick G. (Aon) A94
Ryan, Paul A46
Ryan, Ray P441
Ryan, Richard E316
Ryan, Thomas C. (Quiznos) P407
Ryan, Thomas L. (Service Corporation International) A750
Ryan, Thomas M. (CVS) A258
Ryan, Tim P54
Ryan, William J. W345
Ryazanov, Alexander Nikolaevich W140
Ryder, Thomas O. A703
Rydzik, Pat P404
Rykhoek, Phil E116
Ryman, Christopher P. P95
Ryman, Steve A747
Ryoo, Kyeong-Ryul W261
Ryöppönen, Hannu W319
Rystedt, Fredrik W118
Ryu, James E77

S

Saad, Suhail W138
Saarinen, Seppo O. A584
Sabalete, Juan Pedro Maza W274
Sabatino, Thomas J. Jr. A738
Sabean, Bill P452

Sabelhaus, Robert G. A507
Sabella, John P388
Saber, Rommel C. A331
Sabia, Jim A578
Sabia, Michael J. W63
Sabin, Thomas W. Jr. E67
Sabino, Steve A292
Sabiston, Jim P315
Sabló, Thomas A. P347
Sabo, Tony A837, P489
Sabol, Cynthia A. E96
Sabol, Stephen J. E162
Sabourin, Denis W268
Sacco, Marian E. E20
Sachdev, Rakesh A106
Sachs, Harold L. A465
Sack, Diethelm W109
Sack, James M. A621
Sacks, Dana A652
Sacks, Gary P299
Sacks, Lee B. P27
Sacks, Leon J. P71
Sacks, Rodney C. E168
Sadana, Sumit A345
Sadler, Andres W367
Sadler, Edward F. A572
Sadler, Michael W. A573
Sadler, Robert D. E63
Sadler, Sue W211
Sadler, Tom E159
Sadoff, Laurence R. A466
Sadove, Stephen I. A731
Sadowski, Frank A69
Sadowski, Peter T. A340
Sadowski, Raymond A116
Saeger, Rebecca A200
Saeki, Tatsuyuki A448
Saeli, Thomas L. E258
Saenger, Eleonore A559
Sáenz, Alfredo W54
Sætre, Eldar W316
Saetre, Jorunn A398
Safady, Edward Z. E293
Safady, Randa S. P508
Safavi, Massoud E127
Safety, Joe P299
Saffari, Ali A456
Saffer, Adam P416
Safier, Steven P173
Safon, Teresa P149
Safra, Jacob E. P186
Safran, Jon A244
Sagaert, Sabine W165
Sagan, Paul L. E22
Sagara, Kevin C. A748
Sage-Gavin, Eva A370
Sagehorn, David M. A634
Sager, Mike P281
Sahadevan, Robert A844
Sahler, Darin E142
Sahney, Vinod K. P240
Saidel, Barbara G. P424
Saikawa, Hiroto W234
Sailer, Rita R. E173
Saimpert, Philippe W139
Saint-Arnaud, Louis W268
Saint-Geours, Frédéric W254
Sáinz, Francisco Fernández W116
Saito, Akihiko W107
Saito, Hiroshi W223
Saito, Masayuki W223
Saito, Shozo W151
Saito, Shunichi W175
Saito, Tadakatsu W305
Saito, Toshihide W179
Sajedi, Allen S. E142
Sajeva, Angelo W129
Saji, Hiroshi W304
Sakai, Kiyoshi W276
Sakamaki, Tadatoshi W276
Sakamoto, Akihiro W320
Sakamoto, Satoru W190
Sakamoto, Takashi W244

Sakamoto, Toshihiro W212
Sakane, Masahiro W185
Sakata, Gary P449
Sakkab, Nabil Y. A685
Saksen, Louis P129
Saksena, Vikram E329
Sakumi, Hisashi W192
Sakura, Sumiyoshi P98
Sakurai, Atsuo W237
Sakurai, Masamitsu W276
Sakuru, Raghuveer E205
Salama, Eric W370
Salamon, François W93
Salamon, Miklos W66
Salas, Nicole A851
Salce, Lou P141
Salchow, Greg E258
Saleem, Amer E52
Saleh, Paul N. A776
Salem, Enrique T. A793
Salem, Karen E. A450
Salemme, R. Gerard P134
Salerno, Charles A910
Sales, William J. P480
Saletta, Jill A483
Salhus, Victoria D. A173
Saliba, Ray E309
Saligram, Ravi K. A102, A210
Salins, Peter D. P460
Salisbury, Lois P161
Salk, Barbara P414
Salky, Molly R. E66
Sall, John P. P429
Saller, Richard P. P502
Salley, Joe P333
Sallorenzo, Gaetano A886
Salmini, Jörg W25
Salmirs, Scott A34
Salmon, Dave P229
Salmon, Rob A598
Salnoske, Karl D. A738
Salon, Jonathan D. E362
Salpeas, P. Takis P378
Salsman, Monte P534
Saltalamacchia, Francis A438
Salter, Sue A96
Salter, Theodore L. E156
Saltiel, Rob A832
Saltik, Tahsin W184
Saltonstall, G. West E124
Salts, Rick E46
Saltzberg, Gregory M. A821
Saltzman, Bettylou K. P338
Saltzman, Michael P395
Salva, Lawrence J. A229
Salvador, Luc-François W86
Salvatore, Louis R. A506
Salvette, John A. A412
Salyers, Gregory E. A585
Salz, Anthony W78
Salzberg, Mike A177
Salzwedel, Jack C. P43
Sämann, Karl-Heinz W307
Samargya, Bradley J. A172
Samath, Jamie E. A592
Sambol, David A250
Sambrook, Richard W78
Samila, Tatiana W153
Sammaritano, John A476
Sammon, Maureen E. P330
Sammons, Chris D. A754
Sammons, Elaine D. P427
Sammons, Mary F. A711
Samolczyk, Mark J. A824
Sampl, Scott A50
Sample, Anne D. A652
Sample, Frank T. E380
Sample, Michael M. (Indiana University) P253
Sample, Mike (EDS) A313
Sample, Steven B. P507
Sampson, Thomas H. A498
Samra, Bal W78

Samson, David A205
Samuel, Bill P30
Samueli, Henry A164, P54
Samueli, Susan P54
Samuelian, Michael R. E27
Samuels, Brian M. A757
Samuels, Gary A695
Samuels, John M. A610
Samuels, Marty A696
Samuels, Sandor E. A250
Samuelson, Kevin P254
Samuelson, Kirk R. A658, P385
Samuelson, Larry R. A383
Samuelsson, Håkan W209
San Juan, Christine P83
Sanchez, Alexander M. P500
Sanchez, Annette L. P438
Sanchez, James E269
Sanchez, Jose R. P357
Sanchez, Mario W362
Sanchez, Rafael A186
Sanchez, Robert E. A721
Sanchez, Sergio E138
Sanchez, Virginia W115
Sánchez de León, Luis W25
Sánchez-Asiaín Sanz, Ignacio W61
Sandberg, Daniel M. A412
Sandberg, Sheryl A394
Sandefur, Jennifer A250
Sandel, David P255
Sandell, Robert P470
Sander, Craig A42
Sander, Weldon P164
Sandercock, Brett E305
Sanderlin, James L. A283
Sanders, Barry A742
Sanders, Dan P499
Sanders, Emil Lee E65
Sanders, Jeffrey W. A502
Sanders, Lewis A. P36
Sanders, M. Jack A767
Sanders, Mike (GATX) A372
Sanders, Mike (Milwaukee Bucks) P333
Sanders, Norman R. E38
Sanders, Raymond E. E378
Sanders, Richard M. (Reynolds American) A710
Sanders, Richard S. Jr. (Terra Industries) A811
Sanders, Robert B. E343
Sanders, Steve (Interactive Brokers) P258
Sanders, Steven D. (Inland Retail Real Estate Trust) P257
Sanders, W. David A656
Sanders, William L. E206
Sanderson, Bill P213
Sandford, Paul G. P211
Sandfort, Gregory A. A572
Sandison, George F. A424
Sandker, Timothy J. A285
Sandler, Robert M. A79
Sandler, Vicki G. A667
Sandman, Dan D. A854
Sandman, Paul W. A155
Sandner, John F. A326
Sandor, Douglas P133
Sandoval, Tina E378
Sands, Dawn M. P323
Sands, Leo E. P510
Sands, Richard (Constellation Brands) A240
Sands, Rick (MGM) P326
Sands, Robert A240
Sanfilippo, Fred P369
Sanford, James L. A614
Sanford, Linda S. A454
Sanford, W. Scott A564
Sangalis, Gregory T. E345
Sanger, Stephen W. A380
Sanger, William A. A502
Sani, Shawn T. A571
Sank, Michael P485

Sankey, Laura A698
Sannino, Louis J. A555
Sano, Jeannine P169
Sano, Mitsuo W313
Sano, Shigehisa W74
Sano, Takami W212
Sansom, Paul A159
Sansom, William B. (H.T. Hackney) P248
Sansom, William B. (TVA) A809, P475
Sansone, Daniel F. A879
Sansone, Frank J. E167
Sansone, Thomas A. A464
Sansot, Karen A312
Sansweet, Steve P303
Santa, Richard A. E121
Santaroni, Luciana W123
Santee, M. Catherine P125
Santi, E. Scott A446
Santi, Philippe E193
Santillan, Victor P192
Santilli, Ronald J. E108
Santini, Gino A315
Santisteban, Miguel P40
Santo, Anthony F. A405
Santomero, Camillo M. III E154
Santona, Gloria A556
Santone, Roger P66
Santoro, Barbara A. A449
Santoro, Jeffrey G. A157
Santos, David S. W293
Santos, Eduardo A833
Santos, Gerald A386
Santucci, Amedeo W123
Santulli, William P. P27
Sapan, Joshua W. A173
Saper, Jeffrey D. P532
Sapp, G. David P47
Sapp, Michael R. P350
Saracini, Michael E306
Saraçoglu, Rüsdü W184
Sarandos, Ted E250
Sardellitti, Rolando W143
Sardina, Eduardo M. W52
Sardo, Salvatore W121
Sareeram, Ray R. A146
Saretsky, Gregg A. A55
Sargent, David P154
Sargent, Kelly E159
Sargent, Ronald L. A780
Sari, Robert B. A711
Sarikas, Bridgette A912
Sarin, Arun W358
Sarkisian, A. Alex E315
Sarno, John N. P84
Sarno, Stephen P. E313
Sarnoff, Richard W65
Sarsynski, Elaine A549, P313
Sartain, Elizabeth P. A919
Sarti, Marco W36
Sartor, Annmarie A196
Sartor, Federico W64
Sartor, Richard A. E139
Sartorelli, Claudio W121
Sartori, Giuliano E166
Saruwatari, Satoshi W101
Sarvary, Mark A. A176
Sarver, Reed A641
Sarver, Robert G. E387
Sarwal, Andy P217
Sasaki, Hajime W227
Sasaki, Leo P276
Sasaki, Mikio W218
Sasaki, Noboru W136
Sasaki, Shinichi W349
Sasaki, Tadashi W136
Sasaki, Takeo K. E54
Sasaki, Tsutomu W371
Sasazu, Kyoji W349
Sase, Masataka W245
Sasfy, Cliff A773
Sasina, David J. A195
Sass, Harvey P. A756

Sasse, Art P394
Sasso, Greg W. A144
Sasso, Vincent D. Jr. P327
Sasson, Gideon A200
Sastre, Olivier W93
Sastri, Gautham E298
Satake, Kazutoshi W306
Sateja, John J. P145
Satinet, Claude W254
Sato, Kazuhiro W182
Sato, Kiyoshi W343
Sato, Kozo W136
Sato, Kyoichiro W305
Sato, Masanori A497
Sato, Naoki W245
Sato, Seiki W177
Sato, Yoji W314
Sato, Yoshiaki W346
Satoh, Masakazu W102
Satoh, Naomitsu W91
Satoh, Osamu W102
Satomi, Shunichi W171
Satrazemis, Asterios A851
Satterlee, Perry S. P134
Satterthwaite, Dan A149
Sattler, Brian R. P435
Sattler, Theodore A664
Satz, Jay E260
Sauder, Kevin P430
Sauder, Maynard P430
Sauder, Myrl P430
Sauder, R. Barry E190
Saudo, Phillipe W47
Sauer, Brad T. A26
Sauer, Ildo L. W251
Sauer, Jon W. A95
Sauer, Mary C. E327
Sauer, Matthew A. A450
Sauerhoff, David C. A91
Sauerland, John P. A687
Sauers, Bruce E26
Saufley, Church P278
Saugstad, Bruce P435
Saunders, Anne A782
Saunders, Barry L. A767
Saunders, Jill E66
Saunders, Joseph W. A890
Saunders, Sioux E193
Saunier, Patrick A532
Sauter, George U. A871, P514
Savacool, Kristi A. A425
Savage, Dave P28
Savage, Glenn R. A222
Savage, Kelly P38
Savage, Luke W199
Savage, Thomas J. (MTA) P328
Savage, Thomas R. (Briggs & Stratton) A158
Savaluny, Elly E290
Savander, Niklas W235
Savant, Matt P54
Saville, Dale W. P135
Saville, Paul C. A621
Savinel, Philippe W250
Savitt, Katherine J. A73
Savner, David A. A377
Savoff, Mark T. A320
Savoia, Sally A. A678
Sawabe, Hajime W327
Sawada, Shozo W182
Sawall, Mary M. E183
Sawallich, Keith A243
Sawdye, Carol A. A759, P445
Sawicki, Richard J. P524
Sawyer, David T. E156
Sawyer, George A. P452
Sawyer, James S. A678
Sawyer, John T. P381
Sawyer, Joseph G. E145
Sawyer, Kathleen P. E53
Sawyer, Ken P390
Sawyer, Otis S. A504
Sawyer, Steve D. A246

Sayavedra, Leo P476
Sayed-Friel, Hoda P320
Sayer, Dave P401
Sayers, Michael W275
Sayler, Linda C. A728
Sayles, Helen E. R. A518, P296
Sayles, Thomas S. A748
Saylor, Patti E82
Sayre, Michael R. E285
Sayre, Peter A689
Sayre, Scott E. A874
Sbarro, Anthony P431
Sbarro, Joseph P431
Sbarro, Mario P431
Sbertoli, Chris P392
Sbiti, Chakib A739
Scaduto, James A. A288
Scaggs, Neal W. E151
Scagliotti, Dario W258
Scala, Lou W364
Scalamandre, Jill A117
Scales, Reginald P374
Scalet, Ginger E376
Scalet, J. Chris A567
Scallorn, Doug P519
Scancarella, Neil A708
Scanlon, Edward J. A148
Scanlon, George P. E217
Scanlon, John J. A335
Scanlon, M. Colleen P119
Scannell, Bill A316
Scapillato, Cary B. P538
Scarborough, Dean A. A113
Scarborough, Todd E133
Scarcella, Barbara E. W340
Scardina, Richard P. A180
Scardino, Janet W275
Scardino, Marjorie M. W248
Scarfone, Anthony C. A273
Scaroni, Paolo W123
Scarpa, Michael A523
Scaturro, Peter K. A200
Scavo, Anthony P292
Scavuzzo, Ronald J. P361
Scelfo, J. J. A424
Sceppaguercio, Maria A. A709
Schaal, Gary G. E268
Schaal, John Eric A866
Schabert, Hans M. W307
Schacht, David A758
Schachter, Rozalie E177
Schaden, Richard E. (Quiznos) P407
Schaden, Richard F. (Quiznos) P407
Schaedler, Douglas E371
Schaefer, Barbara W. A846
Schaefer, Fred H. A833
Schaefer, George A. Jr. A342
Schaefer, Michael J. P325
Schaefer, R. Scott E184
Schaefer, Rick P226
Schaefer, Scott E321
Schaeffer, Richard E261
Schaefgen, Brian R. E28
Schafer, Agnes P156
Schafer, Charles J. A501
Schafer, James A. P347
Schäfer, Rolf W247
Schaffer, Daniel W. P191
Schaffer, Frederick P. P133
Schaffler, Bill P289
Schaffner, Tom P496
Schaible, Dexter E. A49
Schalk, Janet M. A798
Schaller, Stephan W360
Schalter, Richard J. E333
Schanefelt, Robert W325
Schanwald, Steve P127
Schanzer, Kenneth A595
Schaper, C. James P254
Schapiro, Ian A. E190
Schapiro, Mary L. A587, P343
Schar, Dwight C. A621
Schar, Mark A460

A = AMERICAN BUSINESS
E = EMERGING COMPANIES
P = PRIVATE COMPANIES
W = WORLD BUSINESS

Spek, Hanspeter W295
Spellacy, Suzanne P470
Spellmeyer, Arthur W. A758
Speltz, Christopher P22
Spence, David P218
Spence, Jean E. A498
Spence, Kenneth F. III A730
Spence, Paul W86
Spence, William H. A677
Spencer, Aaron D. P509
Spencer, Christopher S. P43
Spencer, David B. E59
Spencer, Jameel P70
Spencer, James A. A271
Spencer, Richard V. E194
Spencer, Robert S. A119, P71
Spencer, Steven D. A538
Spendlove, G. Scott A812
Spendlove, Justin P204
Spenst, Brett P26
Speranza, Ernest V. P277
Speranza, Paul S. Jr. P526
Speranzo, Anthony J. P61
Sperber, Burton S. P512
Sperber, Richard A. P512
Sperber, Stuart J. P512
Sperl, Andreas W30
Sperlich, Harold K. P415
Sperling, David P. E326
Sperling, Jac (Minnesota Wild) P335
Sperling, John G. (Apollo Group) A96
Sperling, Peter V. A96
Spero, Tim P355
Speroni, Stefano P169
Speros, James D. A544
Sperry, Dwight A81
Sperry, Michael W. E330
Spetner, Don E210
Speyer, Ann P447
Spiegel, Gary J. E253
Spiegel, Merle P403
Spiegel, Robert J. A738
Spiegel, Steven A544
Spiegelberg, Laurie A. A889
Spielman, Joseph D. A381
Spielmann, Rodolfo A267
Spier, William E129
Spierkel, Gregory M.E. A450
Spiers-Lopez, Pernille W160
Spiesshofer, Ulrich W20
Spigarelli, James L. P332
Spigelmyer, Toni R. A797
Spigner, David L. E123
Spilka, Adam P36
Spillane, Timothy P. E239
Spille, Kent W. P153
Spiller, Daniel M. E388
Spiller, Scott L. P37
Spinell, Gary M. E225
Spinelli, Francesca M. A659
Spinetta, Jean-Cyril W29
Spinner, Steven L. A655
Spinnickie, Benjamin P216
Spire, Mark P73
Spirer, Lee A. A296
Spires, William J. A876
Spirtos, John E251
Spitler, Kenneth F. A797
Spitz, Richard E210
Spitz, Saul E344
Spitz, William T. P513
Spitzer, Shane P526
Spivack, Lisa M. E367
Spivak, Kenin M. P269
Spizzo, Allen A. A419
Splaine, David A. P165
Splan, Christopher E315
Splinter, Michael R. A100

Spoerl, Lawrence A. P398
Spofford, John A50
Spohr, Carsten W204
Sponaugle, Charles J. P233
Spooner, John P. A308
Spottiswood, John P405
Spradlin, Dale E99
Sprague, Carol Lee H. A759, P445
Sprague, Charles W. A346
Sprague, Joseph A. A55
Sprague, William D. A84
Spraley, David A. A156
Spratlen, Susan A. A668
Spratt, Randall N. A559
Spratt, Tim W271
Spreafico, Germanio W329
Sprecher, Jeffrey C. E194
Spreen, Paul P406
Sprenger, Gina A798
Spriestersbach, Ben E272
Springer, Colby H. P135
Springer, Drew A835
Springer, M. B. A222
Springer, Rango P164
Springer, Richard C. E51
Springer, William F. A188
Springfield, Claude H. III E303
Springman, Paul J. (Equifax) A322
Springman, Paul W. (Markel) A540
Springs, Julien E. E52
Sprinkle, Steve A300, P181
Sproger, Phil A52
Sproule, Gary E395
Sproule, Michael E. A599, P359
Sprout, Debra P154
Spurgeon, William W. A285
Spurrier, Nannette E380
Spyres, Ana P465
Squeri, Stephen A76
Squier, David L. P114
Squires, James A. A610
Squyres, Tyri E25
Sredni, Salomon E356
Srigley, Kevin P208
Srinivasan, Krishnakumar E98
Srinivasan, Varadarajan E250
Srnecz, Jean P72
St. Clair, David E229
St. Dennis, Thomas A100
St. Germain, Donna E311
St. John, Julie A336
Stabingas, Mark A69
Stabinski, Diane P193
Stables, Richard E334
Stack, James P334
Stack, John P. A611
Stack, Robert J. W82
Stackhouse, Frank P433
Stacom, Darcy A. A189
Stacy, Joe P101
Stacy, Kelly P305
Stadler, Gerald P. P496
Stadler, Matthew S. E90
Stadnikia, Paul A. A223
Staed, Michael B. P372
Stafeil, Jeffrey M. P325
Staff, Marc L. E64
Stafford, Darius P168
Stafford, David B. A558
Stafford, Ewen W226
Stafford, Ingrid S. P365
Stafford, Julie L. P533
Stafford, Paula P107
Stafford, Raymond A355
Stager, Nancy Huntington P182
Staggs, Thomas O. A885
Stahl, Jack L. A708
Stair, Frederick J. P79
Stake, James B. A26
Stakem, Alan P68
Staker, Douglas L. E200
Staky, Richard P536
Stalder, F. Bernard W100

Staley, Greg P277
Staley, James D. (YRC Worldwide) A921
Staley, James E. (JPMorgan Chase) A479
Staley, John H. P503
Staley, Tom P440
Staley, Warren R. A181, P112
Stalker, Robin W26
Stall, John A. A361
Stallings, Alex P439
Stallings, Robert W. E154
Stallings, Thomas J. E195
Stam, Cornelius P265
Stam, Heidi A871, P514
Stamatakos, Michael P367
Stambaugh, Cris P382
Stambaugh, Dana A523
Stambuk, Danko A280, P174
Stamerjohn, Scott P175
Stamminger, Erich W26
Stammler, Gebhard W180
Stan, Ron W52
Stanbrook, Steven P. A736, P432
Stancil, Anthony N. E106
Stanczak, William J. A83
Standefer, Marc C. A855
Standing, Larry D. E31
Standish, Clive W351
Standish, Jeffrey P. A678
Standish, Thomas R. A194
Standish, Walter E. III E52
Standke, Thomas A438
Standley, John T. A646
Stanek, Robert V. P118
Stanford, Jim P102
Stanford, Linda O. P329
Stang, John Q. A485
Stangeby, Allison P357
Stangel, Jeanne A. P359
Stangl, Gustav R. A62
Stangl, Peter E. A502
Stangland, Bill E269
Stanhagen, William D. A238
Stanhaus, John A481
Stanhope, John W336
Stanich, Lauren Podlach A546
Stanion, John W355
Stanislav, Martin T. A525
Stankey, John T. A109
Stanko, Ellen A. E344
Stanley, Aurelia P41
Stanley, Connie W. E374
Stanley, Deirdre W340
Stanley, Heidi B. E335
Stanley, James W301
Stanley, Richard H. A432
Stanley, Steven C. A635
Stanley, Timothy S. A405
Stanley, Travis P213
Stanos, Peter P250
Stansel, Eugene A. Jr. P458
Stansfield, David A. P34
Stansik, James G. A284
Stanton, Amy A546
Stanton, Bill P480
Stanton, Harold N. A528
Stanton, Kathryn A. P201
Stanton, Nancy P213
Stanton, Ronald P. P485
Stanutz, Nicholas G. A440
Stanzione, Robert J. E37
Staples, David M. A773
Staples, Robert R. E378
Stapleton, T. Dale P353
Stapley, David W. A291
Stara, Friedrich W150
Stark, Andrew R. A652
Stark, Arthur A136
Stark, Christoph W68
Stark, David A579
Stark, Jim E127
Stark, Joe E307
Stark, P. Mark E139

Stark, Sandra M. E146
Starkenburg, Michael A373
Starks, Daniel J. A729
Starnes, Thomas M. A274
Starr, Jackie E122
Starr, James E. P45
Starr, Jeremy P225
Starr, Rogers F. A466
Starr, William J. A194
Stasch, Julia M. P304
Stasik, Robert W. A564
Staskiel, James A. P316
Stassi, Philip J. A466
Stata, Ray A89
Staten, Reesa M. A712
Stater, Edward A. P461
Statton, Tim A132, P79
Staub, Julie A111
Stauback, Lawrence P469
Stauffer, Jerry P72
Stausboll, Anne A175, P108
Stautberg, Timothy E. A328
Stavro, William A552
Stavros, Christopher G. A624
Stead, Tatiana A178
Steadman, William F. E331
Steager, Eric A726
Steakley, Joseph N. A413
Stearns, Eric R. E281
Stebbins, Paul H. A910
Steber, John H. P236
Stecher, Esta Eiger A390
Stecher, Kenneth W. A212
Steckelberg, Kelly E385
Stecklein, Leonard F. A617, P364
Steckley, Warren D. E49
Stecko, Paul T. A807
Stedman, Scott P540
Steed, J. David A530
Steel, Gary W20
Steelberg, Cheryl P512
Steele, Andrew P111
Steele, Bill P99
Steele, C. David A103
Steele, Jim E312
Steele, John J. (Werner Enterprises) A898
Steele, John M. (HCA) A413
Steele, Ken P121
Steele, Kevin D. P16
Steele, Milton A351
Steele, Patrick S. P167
Steele, Susan M. P78
Steele, Tammy S. P141
Steele, Tom P352
Steen, Donald E. P49
Steeneck, Craig D. P389
Steenland, Douglas M. A616
Steer, Robert L. A743
Steers, Robert H. E90
Stefanoni, Gary J. E268
Stefanski, Michael T. P123
Steffenhagen, Julian L. A133
Steffey, Ken E142
Stegeman, Mark A. A504
Stegemiller, James L. A412
Stegmayer, Joseph H. E74
Stegner, Bob A450
Steidl, Eric D. P165
Steier, Larry J. P31
Steiger, Paul E. A289
Steigerwald, Dan E. E362
Steigman, Don S. A806
Steilberg, Robert Christopher A721
Stein, Andrew A704
Stein, Bradley A717
Stein, Charles W. Jr. A638
Stein, Darrell W211
Stein, Gary M. A623
Stein, J. C. A424
Stein, Jay A. E179
Stein, Jonathan J. P256
Stein, Keith J. W208

A = AMERICAN BUSINESS
E = EMERGING COMPANIES
P = PRIVATE COMPANIES
W = WORLD BUSINESS

Weinstein, Herschel S. A356
Weinstein, Martin A749
Weinstein, Paul E204
Weir, Douglas W. E355
Weir, Helen A. W200
Weir, Jeff A592
Weir, Louis J. E395
Weir, Tom A863
Weis, Charles P338
Weis, Frank R. E73
Weisberg, Seth E334
Weisberger, James E56
Weisenburger, Randall J. A630
Weiser, Irving W285
Weisfeld, Brian E. P528
Weisgarber, Robert L. E98
Weishan, Jim P440
Weishar, Gregory S. A258
Weisickle, Robert E298
Weisman, Harlan A474
Weiss, Albert L. P203
Weiss, Andrew A838, P490
Weiss, David A. (BJC HealthCare) P87
Weiss, David I. (Interpublic
  Group) A459
Weiss, Erwin A78
Weiss, Jeffrey M. A78
Weiss, Kevin A670
Weiss, Morry A78
Weiss, Peter W. P483
Weiss, Robert S. E101
Weiss, Scott A. W133
Weiss, Stephen H. (Cornell
  University) P148
Weiss, Steven H. (McGraw-Hill) A558
Weiss, Zev A78
Weisselberg, Allen A838, P490
Weissenborn, Stephen L. A910
Weissmann, Brian E315
Weitman, Gary A834
Weitz, Bruce P281
Welborn, R. Michael E282
Welch, Daniel A. P387
Welch, Dennis E. A74
Welch, Derek W31
Welch, Ed P64
Welch, James L. (YRC Worldwide) A921
Welch, James M. (Cooper
  Companies) E101
Welch, James S. Jr. (Brown-
  Forman) A167
Welch, James W. (Swift
  Transportation) A792
Welch, Jim (Hallmark) A399, P228
Welch, John P168
Welch, Martin E. III A851
Welch, Patricia A560, P319
Welch, Patrick J. E113
Welcomme, Justine W72
Weldon, Dave A461
Weldon, Julie W365
Weldon, William C. A474
Welker, Jeffrey P414
Wellborn, W. Christopher A576
Wellen, Jeffrey L. A572
Weller, Charles D. A455
Weller, Gary L. P372
Weller, Rick L. E137
Wellford, Hill B. Jr. P249
Welling, Josie A267
Wellman, Larry E117
Wells, Belinda D. E337
Wells, Ben K. A169
Wells, Betty E36
Wells, Bret A145
Wells, Darren R. A392
Wells, Donna A460
Wells, Greg A772
Wells, J. Alan E150
Wells, James M. III A790
Wells, John P486
Wells, Mike W264
Wells, Robert J. A756

Wells, Steve W. P487
Wells, Stuart A787
Wells, W. Michael A237
Wells, Zihaad E359
Welsch, Jerome K. A372
Welsh, Cathy E22
Welsh, John E. III A376
Welsh, Kelly R. A613
Welsh, Thomas M. A345
Welsh, William F. II E46
Welsman, Alan E190
Welte, William B. P337
Welters, Anthony (NYU) P360
Welters, Anthony (UnitedHealth
  Group) A858
Weltman, Jeff P168
Welton, Mike W. W146
Welts, Rick P388
Welyki, Robert J. A193
Welzenbach, Mark A401
Wemmer, Dieter W373
Wenaas, Jeffrey P240
Wendel, Jon P250
Wendell, Beth P220
Wendlandt, Gary E. A599, P359
Wendler, Walter V. P450
Wendt, Edward A415
Wendt, Richard L. P266
Wendt, Roderick C. P266
Wenes, Louis-Pierre W134
Wenger, Brian D. A652
Wenig, Devin N. W275
Wenk, Donna B. P374
Wenmoth, R. Bruce E149
Wennemer, Robert G. A57
Wenning, Werner W60
Wentjärvi, Stefan W299
Wentworth, Carol A837, P489
Wentworth, Gerry P338
Wentworth, Peter D. E19
Wentworth, Richard E357
Wentworth, Robert J. P392
Wentworth, Timothy C. A562
Wentz, Billy P264
Wentz, David A. E371
Wentz, Myron W. E371
Wenzel, Irene E635
Wenzell, Marty P73
Wenzl, Sharon A829
Werdann, Suzanne P355
Werlen, Thomas W240
Werner, Anthony G. A517
Werner, Christopher T. A392
Werner, Clarence L. A898
Werner, Donald M. P527
Werner, Elizabeth A. E246
Werner, Eric J. P527
Werner, Frederick W. P28
Werner, Gary L. A898
Werner, Gregory L. A898
Werner, Jordan P162
Werner, Mark B. A123
Werner, Mary Ann A891
Werner, Thomas C. (Boston Red
  Sox) P99
Werner, Thomas L. (Adventist Health
  System) P27
Werner, Tom (TALX) E344
Wernet, Stephanie K. A392
Wernig, Ruth P507
Werpy, David G. A26
Wertanzl, Dietmar A717
Wertheim, Ram D. A553
Werthman, Sandy P283
Wertman, Howard P. P54
Wertz, Byron A. A803
Wesley, James P297
Wesley, Norman H. A357
Wesley, Rosalyn A357
Wesner, Patricia A. A864
Wessel, Rick L. E144
Wessendorf, Charles K. A851
Wessner, Michael P. A485

Wesson, Bruce F. E297
West, Barry J. A776
West, David (CommVault) E97
West, David (Jazzercise) P265
West, David E. (Rent-A-Center) A706
West, David J. (Hershey) A421
West, Dobson E296
West, Edward A. A895
West, Elena A712
West, Franklin C. E286
West, Henry J. P309
West, Jeffrey N. A535
West, Jerry P322
West, Jim E142
West, John L. A256
West, Linda B. A297
West, Marc A400
West, Mary Jo P75
West, Matt P115
West, Neal A371
West, Richard P. P106
West, Stephen O. (Gold Kist) A389
West, Stephen R. (NACCO
  Industries) A584
West, Teresa L. (Texas
  Instruments) A814
West, Terry R. (VyStar Credit
  Union) P521
Westbrock, Leon E. A207
Westbrook, Terri A175, P108
Westburg, Al P99
Westcott, Grant C. W84
Westcott, Jeffrey B. P225
Westen, B. Curtis A415
Westenborg, Jack P210
Wester, David A. E83
Westerdahl, Joyce A633
Westerlaken, Arie W255
Westerlund, David A. A121
Western, James R. Jr. A641
Westfall, Kevin P. A111
Westfall, Lynn D. A812
Westh, Joakim W126
Westlake, W. James W285
Westman, Dean J. E186
Westmoreland, R. Bradley E331
Weston, Charles M. A909
Weston, Chris W92
Weston, Galen G. W201
Weston, Leah W198
Weston, W. Galen W143
Weston-Webb, Andy A543, P310
Westphal, Mark (Army and Air Force
  Exchange) P59
Westphal, Mark (Michael Foods,
  Inc.) P328
Wetekam, Don P59
Wethered, Tom A497, P287, W188
Wetmore, Douglas J. A455
Wetmore, Stephen G. W63
Wetterau, Mark S. P212
Wettstein, Jonathan C. E162
Wexler, Alan M. E313
Wexner, Leslie H. A519
Weyerhaeuser, George H. Jr. A903
Weyl, Brenda S. A852
Weyman, Amy A388, P211
Weymuller, Bruno W347
Wezdenko, David E. E138
Whalen, Ann M. P56
Whalen, Edward J. E154
Whalen, Jerry A853
Whalen, Kevin R. E232
Whalen, T. J. E162
Whaley, Bobby P214
Whaley, Chris P384
Whaley, Ruth M. A553
Whalley, Tom A888
Whatley, Earl P101
Whatley, Tom P311
Whealy, Michael T. A344
Wheat, Bill W. A290
Wheatcroft, Allen W272

Wheatley, Arthur E. A162
Wheatley, Richard A311
Wheeler, Arnie P74
Wheeler, Colin A344
Wheeler, Daniel J. P509
Wheeler, Douglas E141
Wheeler, Frank I. E73
Wheeler, Jennifer A609
Wheeler, Jonathan R. A195
Wheeler, Michael B. E359
Wheeler, Robert A818
Wheeler, Steven M. A667
Wheeler, William J. A569
Wheeler, Wilson A. E22
Wheelock, Pamela P335
Whelan, Daniel E134
Whelan, John M. A858
Whelan, Karen M. L. A859
Whelan, Michael A. A722
Whelan, Pat P377
Whelan, Robert J. E61
Whelan, Thomas M. E48
Whelan, Timothy P262
Whelley, Eileen G. A595
Whent, Peter W138
Whetsell, M. Heyward Jr. P509
Whetstone, Steven P195
Whetten, John P105
Whetzel, Bruce A. E310
Whigham, Terri P128
Whipple, David R. P276
Whirty, Ed P116, P206
Whisenhunt, David P407
Whisler, J. Steven A663
Whiston, John W173
Whitacre, Bill P274
Whitacre, Edward E. Jr. A109
Whitaker, Mark A891
Whitaker, Richard W48
Whitaker, Tony D. E206
Whitaker, Wharton P. E124
Whitby, Phil W200
Whitcomb, Gail P184
Whitcup, Scott M. A61
White, Albert G. E101
White, B. Joseph P503
White, Barbara P256
White, Bill (Amkor) A86
White, Bill (Darden) A262
White, Bill (Sprint Nextel) A776
White, C. Douglas E117
White, Carl E374
White, Charles J. A706
White, Cheryl L. A127
White, Colleen A135
White, Darin L. E75
White, David (Swinerton) P467
White, David L. (Sanmina-SCI) A733
White, David J. (Campbell Soup) A176
White, David R. (Isais Healthcare) P250
White, Edward C. (Owens-
  Illinois) A639
White, Edward W. (Alaska Air) A55
White, Eileen B. A246
White, George A888
White, Gerald J. P87
White, Gregory W. P370
White, H. Katherine A745
White, Hollis J. P312
White, Howard E236
White, J. Randall A735
White, J. Terrell E102
White, James E. E286
White, Jeannette L. E346
White, Jeffrey P140
White, Joey A292
White, John (Atos Origin) W46
White, John D. (Texas A&M) P476
White, John T. (Structure Tone) P463
White, John V. Jr. (Regions
  Financial) A704
White, Joyce E299
White, Kenneth T. Jr. E388

Willis, Roger P414
Willis, Thurman L. Jr. P317
Willisch, Ludwig W68
Willkie, Wendell L. II A561
Willmott, Nicholas J. P282
Wills, Kevin G. A731
Willumstad, Robert B. A550
Wilmers, John P. E46
Wilmoski, Scott P65
Wilmot, Patricia A. A284
Wilmott, Timothy J. A405
Wilms, Anne M. A715
Wilner, Robert D. E84
Wilson, Alan D. A554
Wilson, Barry W. A563
Wilson, Bill (Activant Solutions) P22
Wilson, Bob P122
Wilson, Bret G. A400
Wilson, C. Leon III A128
Wilson, Carl A542
Wilson, Cheryl E236
Wilson, Colin A584
Wilson, D. Ellen A352, P199
Wilson, D. Michael A351
Wilson, David E. (Clear Channel) A220
Wilson, David R. (Spartan Motors) E333
Wilson, Diana M. A565
Wilson, Doug P428
Wilson, Dwight T. A53
Wilson, Ed A359
Wilson, Eric (PlanetOut) E287
Wilson, Eric F. G. (Raley's) P409
Wilson, Eric L. (Hensel Phelps Construction) P240
Wilson, Fred S. A184
Wilson, Gary L. A616
Wilson, Geoffrey H. W143, W201
Wilson, Harold A. A143
Wilson, James (California Steel) P107
Wilson, James (SABMiller) W290
Wilson, Jay R. A424
Wilson, Jerry P279
Wilson, Jim (Spectrum Health) P453
Wilson, John (Hunton & Williams) P249
Wilson, John (New Balance) P354
Wilson, John F. (PBS) P401
Wilson, John J. (Dairy Farmers of America) P156
Wilson, John M. (Alcoa) A57
Wilson, Jon M. (Foley & Lardner) P200
Wilson, Judy (Adeza Biomedical) E20
Wilson, Judy (Protective Life) A688
Wilson, Karol O. A859
Wilson, Kathryn J. P380
Wilson, Keith M. P374
Wilson, L. Michelle A69
Wilson, Larry P276
Wilson, Lowell D. P31
Wilson, Marcus (Pall) A641
Wilson, Mark (Reckitt Benckiser) W271
Wilson, Mark H. (USANA Health Sciences) E371
Wilson, Maryruth P481
Wilson, Michael L. (Ross Stores) A716
Wilson, Michael M. (Agrium) W28
Wilson, Michael S. (General Dynamics) A377
Wilson, Mitsy A359
Wilson, Nick A847
Wilson, Peter W. A224
Wilson, R. Todd P342
Wilson, Richard E. A146
Wilson, Roger G. A150, P90
Wilson, Ron (San Jose Sharks) P428
Wilson, Ronald F. (Direct General) E118
Wilson, Roy J. A61
Wilson, Stanley T. E332
Wilson, Steve W373
Wilson, Thomas J. II (Allstate) A66

Wilson, Thomas R. (Alliant Techsystems) A63
Wilson, W. Keith A240
Wilson, William L. (Belk) P80
Wilson, William R. (Herley Industries) E177
Wilson-Thompson, Kathleen A483
Wilton, Scott P257
Wiltz, James W. A647
Wilver, Peter M. A816
Wimes, Ed P505
Wimmer, Kurt A368
Wimmer, Peter D. P197
Winant, Don P223
Winarsky, Norman D. P456
Winberg, Håkan W302
Winder, Catherine P303
Windisch, Michael P. E256
Windmeier, Jane P. A798
Wineberg, Danette A821
Wineinger, Matthew P466
Winemiller, Bert P400
Winestock, James F. A850
Winfree, Thomas W. E378
Winfrey, Oprah P231
Wing, David M. A844
Wingert, Lee P373
Winhoffer, Orsi P198
Winiarski, Michael J. E168
Winiecki, Alexander M. P102
Winkelmann, Ginny P160
Winkelried, Jon A390
Winkleblack, Arthur B. A430
Winkleman, Dennis R. A478
Winkler, Joseph C. E98
Winkler, Matthew P89
Winland, Virgil L. A911
Winn, Daniel E353
Winn, Greg W336
Winn, J. Michael A292
Winn, John A737
Winn, Penny W368
Winn Settino, Mary A651
Winner, Timothy A. A583
Winning, Patricia U. P129
Winograd, Charles M. W285
Winslow, Paula P428
Winslow, Stephen P154
Winslow, Terry A650
Winstanly, Derek M. P406
Winston, Bruce E165
Winston, Mary A. A741
Winston, Sue W48
Winter, Donald C. A614
Winter, Katie P324
Winter, Richard P309
Winterhalter, Gary G. A56
Winterkorn, Martin W360
Winters, Pamela A. E327
Winters, Phil P429
Winters, William T. A479
Winthrop, Ronald W. E132
Winton, Jeffrey A. A738
Winton, Steven K. A522
Winton, Thomas L. A204
Winton, Wayne R. P452
Wintrob, Jay S. A79
Wiper, Anne A821
Wirt, Ken A642
Wirta, Raymond E. A189
Wirth, Michael K. A205
Wirth, Paul C. A581
Wirth, Peter A384
Wirtz, Eli J. A187
Wirtz, William Rockwell (Wirtz) P534
Wirtz, William W. (Wirtz) P534
Wisdom, Jennifer A706
Wise, Charles W. A676
Wise, Joan S. P18
Wise, John G. P214
Wise, Monique A206
Wise, Peter J. E290
Wise, Phyllis P508

Wise, Seth M. E217
Wise, Stephen D. A433
Wise, Suzanne W138
Wiseman, Donald F. P466
Wiseman, Eric C. A873
Wiseman, Paul A29
Wisener, Ruth Ann A843
Wiser, Brian A450
Wishart, Ben W365
Wishnafski, Diane L. E253
Wishner, Steven R. A202
Wisinger, John E. A208
Wisk, Matthew E364
Wisner, Frank G. A79
Wisniewski, Janusz W258
Wisnom, Marge P129
Wisor, Russell C. A57
Wissle, Andrew P338
Wistreich, Carl G. P109
Wiszniak, Richard P143
Witcosky, Irvin F. E176
Withee, John P354
Withey, Howard G. P87
Withington, David P395
Withington, Neil W76
Witkins, James P. A363
Witkowski, Dariusz W258
Witmer, Deborah A603
Witmer, Donald B. E250
Witmer, Mark D. P328
Witt, Daniel P. E304
Witt, Darrell R. P319
Witt, Robert E. P500
Witt, Steve A50
Witte, Lisa P399
Witte, Lucy P145
Witteck, Lars W150
Witten, Peer W247
Wittenberg, C. William Jr. P82
Wittenberg, Margaret A905
Wittenbraker, Richard L. A893
Witterschein, Judith A. A568
Wittig, John P350
Wittman, Paige A673
Wittmann, Karl W225
Witty, Tim E. P31
Witzgall, David J. A77
Wixted, John J. Jr. A672
Wodatch, Elizabeth P297
Wodopian, Michael R. E321
Woeller, Michael D. W84
Woellfer, Gale P215
Woertz, Patricia A. A38
Woeste, Albrecht W150
Woestemeyer, Ron P400
Woetzel, Johnathan A560, P318
Wofford, Jeff P144
Wohlschlaeger, Jeff P127
Wohlwender, Edward R. A801
Wojcik, Charles A. P480
Wojcik, Paul N. P104
Wojczynski, Jim P68
Wolber, Jeffrey J. E114
Wolbert, Frank P72
Wold, Andrew J. A640
Wold, Mary Katherine A916
Woldt, Brian D. P289
Wolf, Abe P239
Wolf, Charles R. P419
Wolf, Denise P520
Wolf, Henry C. A610
Wolf, Howard P458
Wolf, Jacquelyn H. A231
Wolf, Joe E129
Wolf, John P122
Wolf, Karen S. P283
Wolf, Kenneth E284
Wolf, Penny P254
Wolf, Richard J. (Cendant) A115
Wolf, Richard W. (Clear Channel) A220
Wolf, Robert (UBS) W351
Wolf, Robert M. (Rimage) E307
Wolf, Siegfried W208

Wolf, Timothy V. A578
Wolf, Yvonne A274
Wolfcale, Amy L. A288
Wolfe, Abbott A240
Wolfe, Colin R. A156
Wolfe, Daniel B. E169
Wolfe, Frederick P411
Wolfe, Jason E117
Wolfe, Monica E171
Wolfe, Peggy P329
Wolfe, Russel P481
Wolfe, Stephen P. A828
Wolfe, Thomas F. P29
Wolfert, Frederick E. A217
Wolfert, Marc S. P236
Wolfert, Peter E374
Wolff, Alan Wm. P169
Wolff, Benjamin G. P134
Wolff, Derish M. P300
Wolff, Larry H. E369
Wolff, Richard W211
Wolfish, Barry A503, P290
Wolford, Richard G. A267
Wolford, Sonya A760
Wolfort, David A. E262
Wolfovski, Michel W93
Wolfson, Stephen W. E344
Wolfzorn, E. John A328
Wolgemuth, Richard L. A163
Wolicki, Carol E362
Wolin, Neal S. A408
Wolinsky, Kenneth A. A113
Wolkoff, Neal L. P47
Wollen, Foster A132, P79
Wolley, Charles S. A120
Wollman, Thomas P406
Woloszko, Jean A. E38
Woloszyk, Jim P333
Wolowski, Rich P215
Wolpert, Stephen M. A168
Wolski, John E46
Wolski, Lawrence G. P238
Wolters, Dennis R. P163
Wolters, Ulrich W35
Woltil, Robert D. P177
Wolynetz, Vlad P39
Womack, C. Suzanne A521
Womack, Michael A. A213
Womble, Mathew C. A851
Wong, Elizabeth E246
Wong, Irwin E73
Wong, John P98
Wong, Martin A218
Wong, Peter P388
Wong, Stova P379
Wood, Alison W53
Wood, Barbara S. A832
Wood, Bill (Baker & McKenzie) P71
Wood, Brian P147
Wood, Daniel S. E100
Wood, Donald F. E395
Wood, Elizabeth A886
Wood, Elwyn D. A686
Wood, Fred G. III A283
Wood, Gerard P38
Wood, Graham R. A351
Wood, Jeff P160
Wood, John (Derive Technologies) P168
Wood, John (John Wieland Homes) P269
Wood, Joseph W. A165
Wood, Karen J. W67
Wood, Paul W352
Wood, Pelin E386
Wood, Phoebe A. A167
Wood, Raymond B. E345
Wood, Richard (Esterline) E135
Wood, Richard D. Jr. (Wawa, Inc.) P525
Wood, Richard F. (BNC Bancorp) E59
Wood, Richard R. (University of Nebraska) P505
Wood, Robert (NIKE) A607

A = AMERICAN BUSINESS
E = EMERGING COMPANIES
P = PRIVATE COMPANIES
W = WORLD BUSINESS

Wood, Robert L. (NASD) A587, P343
Wood, Roger J. A154
Wood, Ronald R. P87
Wood, Ryan S. E361
Wood, Stephen (EchoStar
  Communications) A307
Wood, Susan A. E380
Wood, Thomas L. (Valspar) A870
Wood, Timothy E. E371
Wood, Tom (Activant Solutions) P22
Wood, William C. Jr. (CarMax) A184
Woodall, Timothy E132
Woodard, Edward J. Jr. E96
Woodard, John R. P143
Woodard, M. Rufus Jr. P102
Woodberry, Paul P84
Woodbridge, Ron P151
Woodcock, Jim P426
Woodcock, Stephen F. E68
Woodhams, Norbert E. Sr. P389
Woodhead, Robin G. A768, E330
Woodhouse, Loraine W181
Woodhouse, Michael A. A190
Woodlock, Ed P99
Woodruff, Bob A607
Woodrum, Larry L. E387
Woods, Betty A133
Woods, Duane C. A893
Woods, E. Anthony E216
Woods, Jerome E278
Woods, John F. A890
Woods, Laura E232
Woods, Robert F. A445
Woods, Sandra J. P402
Woods, Timothy A779
Woods, Tom D. W84
Woodson, Eric E25
Woodward, James H. Jr. (JLG
  Industries) A470
Woodward, Jimmy M. (Flowers
  Foods) A349
Woodward, Joyce A149
Woodward, Ralph P75
Woodworth, John K. A26
Woodyard, David B. P135
Wookey, John A633
Woolbright, John A796
Woolcott, René R. E381
Woolcott, Richard R. E381
Wooldridge, Coleman R. P392
Wooldridge, Kathy E304
Woolworth, Eric P237
Wooten, James H. Jr. A446
Wooten, Ronald J. P406
Wootton, Charles A. E148
Wootton, Michael J. P465
Woram, Brian J. A195
Worcester, Robert P. P487
Word, Scott J. E349
Worden, Jeffrey A. A676
Wordsworth, Jerry L. P315
Wordsworth-Daughtridge, Debbie P315
Wories, John Jr. P50
Workman, Dennis L. E358
Workman, Gary P356
Worley, Peter E115
Wormington, Stephen L. A812
Worroll, David P173
Worthington, Bruce R. A662
Worthington, John M. A496
Worthington, Michael K. E151
Worthington, Paul W181
Wortsmann, Judy P292
Wotring, Randall A. A861
Wouters, Caroline W367
Wozniak, Thomas P. A259
Wrabley, Matthew D. E249

Wragg, Catherine M. E356
Wranesh, Tracy P26
Wrathall, Andrew W53
Wray, John P121
Wray, Susan P233
Wren, Erica P73
Wren, J. Robert Jr. P395
Wren, John D. A630
Wrench, H. Blain A366
Wride, Douglas C. E385
Wright, Alan P288
Wright, Albert B. III P347
Wright, Barbara P. P161
Wright, Belinda A643
Wright, Bryan L. A571
Wright, Carole R. E371
Wright, Craig W285
Wright, Damon S. E134
Wright, Dana G. E276
Wright, Dennis P252
Wright, Doreen A. A176
Wright, Elease E. A44
Wright, Felix E. A508
Wright, George C. P476
Wright, Gregory A. A812
Wright, James T. (Bowater) A156
Wright, Jason H. A568
Wright, Jim (Semitool) E318
Wright, John E215
Wright, Joseph C. A158
Wright, Laura H. A772
Wright, Mark H. A865
Wright, Marvin E. P505
Wright, Pandit F. P172
Wright, Phillip D. A907
Wright, Quentin B. E245
Wright, Richard K. A60
Wright, Robert A. (Pilgrim's
  Pride) A666
Wright, Robert C. (GE) A379
Wright, Robert D. (Wendy's) A898
Wright, Ronald P109
Wright, Samuel A115
Wright, Stephen J. P95
Wright, Tanya P238
Wright, Tom A399, P228
Wright, Usha A462
Wright, Vicente P107
Wright, Walter L. P27
Wright, Wesley P451
Wright, William S. A717
Wrigley, William Jr. A913
Wrobleski, Ann A458
Wrubel, Harvey E129
Wrubel, Robert W. E35
Wu, Bernard E141
Wu, Gordon Y. S. W155
Wu, Haijun W310
Wu, James M. H. (Hopewell
  Holdings) W155
Wu, Jimmy (FalconStor) E141
Wu, Peter E73
Wu, Thomas J. W155
Wu, Zhensheng W239
Wucherer, Klaus W307
Wuertz, Bill A531
Wuest, Michael J. A634
Wuesthoff, Robert E164
Wuffli, Peter A. W351
Wuhrl, Klaus W119
Wulf, Jane P436
Wulf, Lee P363
Wulf, Vikki P363
Wulff, Kevin W26
Wulfsohn, William A. A676
Wunderlich, Sharon P482
Wunning, Steven H. A188
Wurfbain, Henk W284
Wurl, Douglas N. P442
Wurth, Michel W222
Wurtz, Alex E182
Wurtz, Thomas J. A880
Wurtzel, Alan A595

Wurzbacher, Bonnie P. A225
Wurzburg, Stephen M. E213
Wusman, Harman W35
Wuthich, Gordon P286
Wuycheck, John P136
Wyand, William R. E326
Wyatt, Bob P74
Wyatt, Christopher J. A149
Wyatt, Tommy E. E314
Wyckoff, Mark D. A608
Wycks, Charles W147
Wykes, Simon W270
Wyland, Dwight P206
Wyly, Charles J. Jr. A572
Wyly, Sam A572
Wyman, Kenneth R. E25
Wyman, Malcolm I. W290
Wynaendts, Alexander R. W27
Wynn, Margaret B. A39
Wynne, Brian E. A227
Wynne, Diana S. A190
Wyrsch, Martha B. A295
Wysaske, Ronald A. E307
Wyse, Kenneth L. A664
Wysham, Lark E. P132
Wyszawski, Tom P180
Wyszomierski, Jack L. P521
Wytkind, Ed P30
Wyzga, Michael S. A384

X

Xenos, Jim P301
Xiao, Deming E238
Xiao, Gang W55
Xie, Jian E88
Xu, Jane E232
Xu, Yanger A60

Y

Yabuki, Jeffery W. A346
Yageel, Michal W187
Yaggi, W. Timothy A904
Yagi, Ken W243
Yagi, Toshiro W217
Yahata, Yasushi W371
Yahes, Jarrod E139
Yahia, Laurance H. S. A518, P296
Yajima, Torao W303
Yakich, Wayne J. A678
Yakimow, Kristin E. E380
Yamada, Koji W185
Yamada, Masayoshi W101
Yamada, Osamu W256
Yamada, Ryoichi W176
Yamada, Ryuji W243
Yamada, Tadataka P85
Yamada, Tsutomu W171
Yamada, Yoshihiko W212
Yamada, Yoshinobu W91
Yamaguchi, Dave P243
Yamaguchi, Hiroshi W74
Yamaguchi, Koji W171
Yamaguchi, Michihiro W305
Yamaguchi, Tadahiro W256
Yamaki, Masaharu W213
Yamamoto, Hironori W85
Yamamoto, Kazunori W256
Yamamoto, Kenjuro W102
Yamamoto, Masahiko W227
Yamamoto, Michihisa W192
Yamamoto, Mineo W37
Yamamoto, Shigeru W245
Yamamura, Yuzo W192
Yamanouchi, Takashi W213
Yamasaki, Steven T. A921
Yamashita, Mitsuhiko W234
Yamashita, Tsutomu T. E209
Yamazaki, Hiromasa W237
Yamazaki, Keijiro W85

Yamazumi, Ken W182
Yamonouchi, Toyohiko W108
Yamori, Tsutomu W192
Yanagiya, Takashi W237
Yanan, Frank J. A425
Yanay, Elisha A582
Yancey, Carol B. A383
Yancey, Gary L. E34
Yancy, Larry F. P440
Yang, Jerry A919
Yang, Patrick Y. A375
Yang, Taiyin A385
Yang, Uen-Long W130
Yang, Vivian A822
Yang, Yanfeng E264
Yankowski, Daniel H. A678
Yannotta, Pat P141
Yannucci, Thomas D. P282
Yano, Eiji W305
Yano, James A. A33
Yano, Kaoru W227
Yanofsky, Neal J. E271
Yanos, Neal A807
Yanowitz, Harry F. A650
Yao, Jonathan P436
Yap, Kim Wah W309
Yap, Rosemary A149
Yarber, Jeff P81
Yarbrough, Joe W. Jr. A576
Yarbrough, Will P319
Yardis, Robert P463
Yardley, James C. A311
Yarrington, Patricia E. A205
Yassa, Arlette E48
Yasuda, Shinji W256
Yasukawa, Takuji W179
Yasunaga, Sumio W175
Yates, David A344
Yates, Gary R. P439
Yates, Philip R. P217
Yates, Richard L. A815
Yates, Stephen E. A486
Yates, Timothy T. A794
Yates, William G. III P538
Yates, William G. Jr. P538
Yavuz, Oya W367
Yazawa, Atsushi W91
Yazdi, Mahvash A309
Ybarra, Stacy E190
Yeager, Frederick C. A822
Yeager, J. Michael W67
Yearley, Douglas C. Jr. A826
Yearwood, Carlton A893
Yeatman, Perry A498
Yeaton, Timothy E302
Yecies, Michael S. E43
Yee, Stewart P. E22, E355
Yefsky, Alan P410
Yegnashankaran, Mohan A592
Yellen, Janet L. P194
Yellin, Gary S. E216
Yellin, Jonathan D. E105
Yelverton-Zamarripa, Karen P106
Yen, David W. A787
Yentob, Alan W78
Yeoh, Nancy P. Y. W308
Yeomans, Janet L. A26
Yerman, Robert N. E216
Yetman, G. Gary P137
Yetman, Gary A568
Yeung, Albert K. Y. W155
Yeung, Jason C. W. W55
Yi, John E199
Yiakas, Constantinos D. P537
Yin, Jihai W310
Ying, Charles W. E57
Yiu, Joe A365
Yngen, Magnus W118
Yoder, David P430
Yoder, John P430
Yoder, Suzi P84
Yoh, Harold L. III P162
Yohe, D. Scott A272

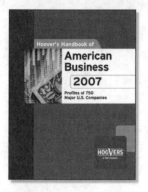

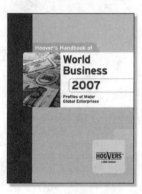